sociology
a brief introduction

14th edition

High School Edition

Richard T. Schaefer
DePaul University

SOCIOLOGY: A BRIEF INTRODUCTION, FOURTEENTH EDITION

1 2 3 4 5 6 7 8 9 LWI 25 24 23 22

ISBN 978-1-26-590173-8
MHID 1-26-590173-2

Portfolio Manager: *Erika Lo*
Senior Product Developer: *Lauren A. Finn*
Product Development Manager: *Dawn Groundwater*
Marketing Manager: *Kim Schroeder-Freund*
Content Project Managers: *Sandy Wille; Katie Reuter*
Senior Buyer: *Laura Fuller*
Designer: *Beth Blech*
Content Licensing Specialists: *Sarah Flynn*
Front Cover Image: *real444/Getty Images, kali9/Getty Images, Wavebreakmedia/Getty Images, G-Stock Studio/Shutterstock, Phonix_a Pk.sarote/Shutterstock, gilaxia/E+/Getty Images, Jacob Lund/Shutterstock, as-artmedia/Shutterstock*
Back Cover: *McGraw Hill*
Compositor: *Straive*

Library of Congress Cataloging-in-Publication Data

Names: Schaefer, Richard T., author.
Title: Sociology : a brief introduction / Richard T. Schaefer, DePaul
    University.
Description: 14th edition. | Dubuque : McGraw Hill Education, 2022. |
    Revised edition of the author's Sociology, [2019]
Identifiers: LCCN 2020026597 (print) | LCCN 2020026598 (ebook) | ISBN
    9781265901738 (hardcover)
Subjects: LCSH: Sociology.
Classification: LCC HM585 .S324 2022 (print) | LCC HM585 (ebook) | DDC
    301—dc23
LC record available at https://lccn.loc.gov/2020026597
LC ebook record available at https://lccn.loc.gov/2020026598

mheducation.com/prek-12

dedication

To my grandchildren, Matilda and Reuben. May they enjoy exploring life's possibilities.

about the author

Courtesy of Richard T. Schaefer

Richard T. Schaefer: Professor Emeritus, DePaul University BA, Northwestern University, MA, PhD, University of Chicago

Growing up in Chicago at a time when neighborhoods were going through transitions in ethnic and racial composition, Richard T. Schaefer found himself increasingly intrigued by what was happening, how people were reacting, and how these changes were affecting neighborhoods and people's jobs. His interest in social issues caused him to gravitate to sociology courses at Northwestern University, where he eventually received a BA in sociology.

"Originally as an undergraduate I thought I would go on to law school and become a lawyer. But after taking a few sociology courses, I found myself wanting to learn more about what sociologists studied, and fascinated by the kinds of questions they raised." This fascination led him to obtain his MA and PhD in sociology from the University of Chicago. Dr. Schaefer's continuing interest in race relations led him to write his master's thesis on the membership of the Ku Klux Klan and his doctoral thesis on racial prejudice and race relations in Great Britain.

Dr. Schaefer went on to become a professor of sociology at DePaul University in Chicago. In 2004 he was named to the Vincent DePaul professorship in recognition of his undergraduate teaching and scholarship. He has taught introductory sociology for over 35 years to students in colleges, adult education programs, nursing programs, and even a maximum-security prison. Dr. Schaefer's love of teaching is apparent in his interaction with his students. "I find myself constantly learning from the students who are in my classes and from reading what they write. Their insights into the material we read or current events that we discuss often become part of future course material and sometimes even find their way into my writing."

Dr. Schaefer is the author of *Sociology in Modules,* fifth edition (McGraw Hill, 2020), the seventh edition of *Sociology Matters* (McGraw Hill, 2019), and, with Robert Feldman, *Sociology and Your Life with P.O.W.E.R. Learning* (2016). He is also the author of *Racial and Ethnic Groups,* now in its fifteenth edition update (2021) and *Race and Ethnicity in the United States* (ninth edition, 2019), both published by Pearson. Together with William Zellner, he coauthored the ninth edition of *Extraordinary Groups,* published by Waveland Press in 2015. Dr. Schaefer served as the general editor of the three-volume *Encyclopedia of Race, Ethnicity, and Society,* published by Sage in 2008. These books have been translated into Chinese (long and short forms), Sinhalese. Indonesian, Turkish, Japanese, Portuguese, and Spanish, as well as adapted for use in Canadian colleges.

Dr. Schaefer's articles and book reviews have appeared in many journals, including *American Journal of Sociology; Phylon: A Review of Race and Culture; Contemporary Sociology; Sociology and Social Research; Sociological Quarterly; Patterns of Prejudice;* and *Teaching Sociology.* He served as president of the Midwest Sociological Society in 1994–1995.

Dr. Schaefer's advice to students is to "look at the material and make connections to your own life and experiences. Sociology will make you a more attentive observer of how people in groups interact and function. It will also make you more aware of people's different needs and interests—and perhaps more ready to work for the common good, while still recognizing the individuality of each person."

brief contents

contents

South_agency/Getty Images

Mario Tama/Getty Images

Agencja Fotograficzna Caro/Alamy Stock Photo

FamVeld/Shutterstock.

Pal2iyawit/Shutterstock

YinYang/E+/Getty Images

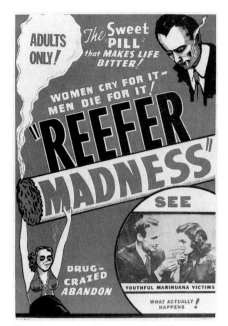

Contraband Collection/Alamy Stock Photo

FREDERIC J. BROWN/AFP/Getty Images

Paralaxis/iStock/Getty Images

Diego G Diaz/Shutterstock

Jupiterimages/Getty Images

Ariel Skelley/Getty Images

Andrew Cribb/Alamy Stock Photo

Paul M. Driftmier/Shutterstock

Hiroshi Watanabe/Getty Images

NurPhoto/Getty Images

16   Social Change in the Global Community 406

chapter opening excerpts

Chapter 1
Outcasts United by Warren T. St. John 2

Chapter 2
"'Anytime, Anywhere': Vaping as Social Practice" by Helen Keane, Megan Weier, Doug Fraser, and Coral Gartner 29

Chapter 3
"Body Ritual among the Nacirema" by Horace Miner 54

Chapter 4
"'Forging Selfhood: Social Categorisation and Identity in Arizona's Prison Wildfire Programme" by Lindsey Raisa Feldman 78

Chapter 5
"The Psychology of Imprisonment" by Philip Zimbardo 101

Chapter 6
Reclaiming Conversation: The Power of Talk in a Digital Age by Sherry Turkle 131

boxed features

RESEARCH TODAY

Ingram Publishing

SOCIOLOGY IN THE GLOBAL COMMUNITY

Don Hammond/Design Pics

OUR WIRED WORLD

Eric Audras/ONOKY/Superstock

SOCIOLOGY IN EDUCATION

Andersen Ross/Blend Images

TAKING SOCIOLOGY TO WORK

Ingram Publishing

social policy sections

Last Resort/PhotoDisc/Getty Images

Designed for Student Success

What do a police officer, a nurse, and a local business owner need to know about the community that they serve? It turns out quite a lot. And *Sociology: A Brief Introduction* is poised to give students the tools they need to take sociology with them as they pursue their studies and their careers, and as they get involved in their communities and the world at large.

The 14th edition of *Sociology: A Brief Introduction* is aligned to the American Sociological Association's National Standards for High School Sociology and delivers full coverage of the

domains, competencies, and concepts students need to master in their Sociology course. Concrete examples, contextualized in real-world scenarios, bring relevance to the learning experience and engage students by making clear connections between sociological concepts and their everyday lives.

In-chapter features frame concepts and theories within specific areas of focus to guide students in exploring sociology using specific situations and experiences as seen through a variety of perspectives.

Features include:

- **Chapter Opening Excerpts** – Every chapter begins with a thought-provoking, real-life story that applies sociological inquiry to the chapter topic and introduces readers to concepts they will learn about.

- **Research Today** – Data and information gathered from sociological research are used to examine topics of interest such as sports, social media, and discrimination. Prompts at the end of each feature foster lively class discussion.

- **Sociology in the Global Community** – Students build cross-cultural awareness as they are asked to compare and contrast societies and cultures around the world through a sociological lens focusing on a variety of topics including cultural diffusion, tourism, and women's social movements.

- **Our Wired World** – Students explore how technology is integrated into so many aspects of contemporary societies and its effects on social relationships and behaviors in our daily lives.

- **Sociology in Education** – Issues in education are examined through sociological perspectives prompting students to consider how they may affected by these issues.

- **Taking Sociology to Work** – Individuals with jobs in which the ability to think sociologically is a critical skill are profiled, helping students connect course knowledge to career possibilities.

- **Social Policy** – These features delve into the interconnected nature of sociological issues and social policy and ask students to explore how looking at issues through a sociological perspective affects policy.

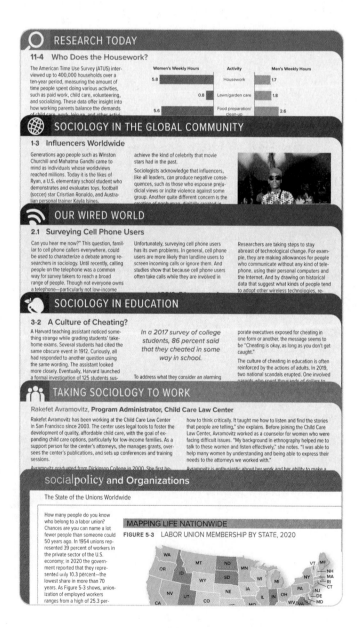

Tracking Sociological Perspectives tables highlight the major sociological perspectives and the fundamental differences between them to provide students with a solid understanding of key topics in the chapter, such as development of self; race and ethnicity; and health and illness, from these various points of view.

Thinking Critically and **Use Your Sociology Imagination** activities encourage students to use higher-order thinking skills to analyze an issue and to put themselves in the shoes of others as they consider behavioral responses in a variety of scenarios.

Figures and **Tables** are provided throughout the book to illustrate topics and concepts through data and visual representation.

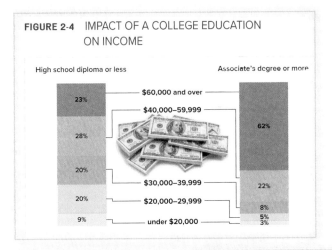

FIGURE 2-4   IMPACT OF A COLLEGE EDUCATION ON INCOME

High school diploma or less — Associate's degree or more

	High school diploma or less	Associate's degree or more
$60,000 and over	23%	62%
$40,000–59,999	28%	
$30,000–39,999	20%	22%
$20,000–29,999	20%	8%
under $20,000	9%	5% / 3%

MAPPING LIFE WORLDWIDE
FIGURE 14-5   GLOBAL PEACE INDEX

State Of Peace
More peaceful
not included

Less peaceful

Source: International Institute for Democracy and Electoral Assistance 2020. *Flags:* admin_design/Shutterstock

Mastering This Chapter revisits and reinforces learning at the chapter-level by including:

- A **summary** of the chapter content.
- A review of **key terms** with definitions and page references to where the term is introduced.
- **Taking Sociology with You** which delivers engaging activities specifically developed for high school students to connect what they've learned to their daily lives. This section includes **Writing Sociology** to hone students' writing skills using the topics they have learned about in the chapter. These writing activities also provide students with practice in effectively using appropriate terminology.
- A **self-quiz** enables students to check their understanding before moving on.

MASTERING THIS CHAPTER

Summary

Sociology is the scientific study of social behavior and human groups. This chapter examines the nature of sociological theory, the founders of the discipline, theoretical perspectives in contemporary sociology, practical applications for sociological theory and research, and ways to exercise the *sociological imagination*.

TAKING SOCIOLOGY with you

1. Watch a movie about a natural disaster. Make note of the government's response. What sociological factors were or should have been considered in the response? What plans do you think a government

Best in Class
Digital Resources

Sociology: A Brief Introduction **is enriched with multimedia content including videos with assessments, interactivities, real-life scenarios, and adaptive tools that enhance the teaching and learning experience both inside and outside of the classroom.**

Authored by one of the world's leading subject matter experts, the resources provide students with multiple opportunities to contextualize and apply their understanding. Teachers can save time, customize lessons, monitor student progress, and make data-driven decisions in the classroom with the flexible, easy-to-navigate instructional tools.

Intuitive Design

Resources are organized at the chapter level. To enhance the core content, teachers can add assignments, activities, and instructional aides to any lesson.

The chapter landing page gives students access to:

- assigned activities,

- resources and assessments,

- an interactive eBook,

- adaptive **SmartBook**® assignments,

- interactivities in which students view issues through a sociological lens.

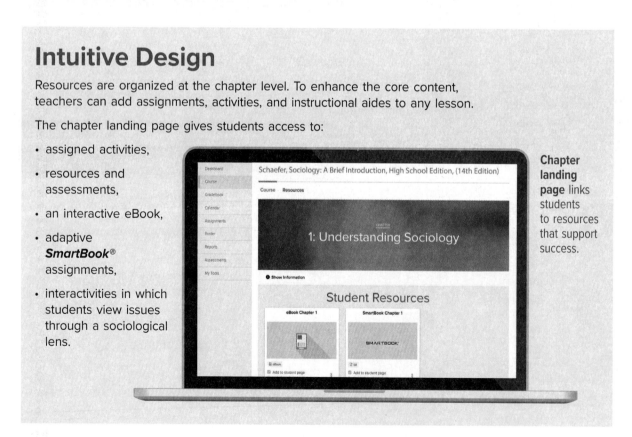

Chapter landing page links students to resources that support success.

 Mobile Ready   Access to course content on-the-go is easier and more efficient than ever before with the *ReadAnywhere* mobile app.

Adaptive Study Tools

SMARTBOOK® is the assignable, adaptive study tool. The interactive features personalize learning with self-guided tools that:

- assess proficiency and knowledge,
- track which topics have been mastered,
- identify areas that need more study,
- deliver meaningful practice with guidance and instant feedback,
- recharge learning with previously completed assignments and personalized recommendations,
- allow teachers to assign material at the subtopic level.

Highlighted content continuously adapts as students work through exercises.

Practice sets measure depth of understanding and present a personalized learning path based on student responses.

Teacher Resources

Teachers have access to the interactive student eBook, adaptive *SmartBook®*, plus a wealth of customizable chapter resources and powerful gradebook tools.

Resources include:

- an online Teacher Manual with chapter overviews, instructional support, essay prompts, and critical thinking questions,
- student performance reports to help teachers identify gaps, make data-driven decisions, and adjust instruction,
- customizable PowerPoint presentations.

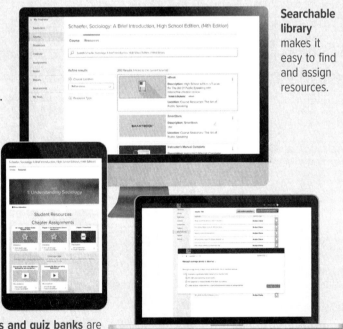

Searchable library makes it easy to find and assign resources.

Customizable assignments and quiz banks are automatically graded and populate easy-to-read reports.

Harness technology, unlock success with the digital resources *for Sociology: A Brief Introduction*
Visit My.MHEducation.com

McGraw Hill

maps

tracking sociological perspectives tables

summing up tables

Chapter Changes

Changes to the Fourteenth Edition reflect new research findings, updated statistics, and hot topics and issues. In addition, a new feature added to every chapter is the "Writing Sociology" question included in the Mastering This Chapter summary-and-review section.

Chapter 1: Understanding Sociology

- chapter-opening photo illustrating environmental cleanup
- extensive discussion of how different social sciences would address the issue of climate change
- cartoon illustrating why different people have different attitudes to climate change
- "Thinking Critically" question about Marx's influence on current thinking
- photo illustrating an interactionist study of new patterns of facial coverings and social distancing during the coronavirus pandemic
- Research Today box, "The Third Place," including impact of coronavirus on behavior in public places
- example highlighting male vs. female acceptable behavior on the tennis court
- example and photo highlighting how conflict theory focuses on issues of long-term social and racial inequality
- Sociology in the Global Community box, "Influencers Worldwide"

Chapter 2: Sociological Research

- chapter-opening vignette drawn from a sociological study of why teenagers use vaping products
- photo and text example to illustrate how sociologists control for various biases in study subjects
- Figure 2-2, "Educational Level and Household Income in the United States," extensively updated
- explanation of new Census relationship questions and how they relate to sociological research
- coverage of research on parental involvement in children's education during the coronavirus pandemic
- extensive example of how content analysis reveals how men are portrayed in country music
- discussion of how the study of effects of education on income can be broadened to include race and gender factors
- discussion of how being gay influences racial attitudes

Chapter 3: Culture

- chapter-opening photo emphasizing the effects of technology on culture
- discussion of the #MeToo movement in the context of changing norms
- enhanced and updated discussion of the culture of cheating in college admissions
- Figure 3-3, "Values: Acceptance of Government Efforts to Reduce Income Inequality"
- photo of neo-Nazi group to illustrate culture shock
- discussion of use of sanctions for failure to comply with orders to social distance and wear face coverings during the coronavirus pandemic
- Sociology in the Global Community box: "Culture Encapsulated on an Island"
- discussion of the culture of vaping as an emerging subculture
- Figure 3-4, "Most Commonly Spoken Language, Other than English or Spanish, by State"
- update of Figure 3-5, "Percentage of People Who Speak a Language Other than English at Home, by State"
- coverage of the impact of COVID-19 on globalization
- discussion of the need for bilingual health care workers during the coronavirus pandemic

Chapter 4: Socialization and the Life Course

- chapter-opening photo illustrating the role of family in socialization
- chapter-opening vignette focusing on how people navigate between different cultures
- updated discussion of the importance and findings of twin studies
- photo illustrating role taking in childhood
- enhanced discussion of face-work, with example drawn from *American Idol*
- discussion of ZOOM and impression management
- extended discussion of young children and media use
- Wired World box, "Teens Controlling Access to Their Social Media," including figure
- enhanced discussion of employment by older workers
- coverage of childcare during the coronavirus pandemic
- Figure 4-1, "Support for Increased Government Spending on Retirement"

Chapter 5: Social Interaction, Groups, and Social Structure

- chapter-opening photo featuring female athletes
- updated discussion of the Zimbardo Prison Experiment featuring recent criticisms
- enhanced discussion of ascribed and achieved statuses focusing on the elderly in China
- Research Today box, "Decision Making in the Jury Room"
- discussion of the impact on social reality caused by the wearing of face coverings, with focus on Black men
- coverage of the impact of the coronavirus pandemic on union organizing
- likening of Gemeinschaft to contemporary sharing economy

- discussion of privacy concerns during the pandemic
- updated and expanded Our Wired World box, "Twitter Networks: From Wildfires to Hurricanes," with new figure

Chapter 6: Mass Media and Social Media

- chapter-opening photo highlighting the international reach of U.S. media
- updated chapter-opening excerpt from new edition of *Alone Together: Why We Expect More from Technology and Less from Each Other*
- discussion of sociological study of media usage by young Muslims in Australia
- photo of a Donald Trump tweet, with discussion of his use of Twitter for presidential communications
- discussion of dissemination of false reports by political parties and governments
- coverage of the use of telecom data and apps to trace the spread of the coronavirus pandemic
- enhanced discussion of online stereotyping
- discussion of facial recognition software and its interactionist implications
- major revisions to Figure 6-2, "Who Uses Social Media?"
- expanded discussion of audience targeting in elections campaigns
- enhanced discussion of influencers, with Key Term treatment
- revision of Social Policy feature, "Censorship," to focus on misinformation in social media

Chapter 7: Deviance, Crime, and Social Control

- chapter-opening image: movie poster for the 1939 film *Reefer Madness*
- discussion of attitudes toward policing and race
- subsection, "Obedience and Virtual reality," updating coverage of Milgram's classic experiment, with photo
- image of crowded beaches during the COVID-19 pandemic as an example of deviance
- enhanced and updated coverage of the effects of child abuse
- Research Today box, "Gun Control"
- updated discussion of the bail system in the Research Today box, "Debtors' Jails in the Twenty-First Century"
- image of Bansky's "The Flower Thrower in Jerusalem" to illustrate labeling theory
- enhanced discussion of the feminist perspective to include coverage of domestic violence during the coronavirus pandemic
- updated discussion of disadvantages experienced by Blacks in the justice system
- Figure 7-3, "State Hate-Crime Laws: The Fifty States Vary in What They Categorize as Hate Crimes," with expended discussion of hate crime
- Key Term treatment for "racial profiling"

Chapter 8: Stratification and Social Mobility in the United States

- chapter-opening image showing a celebrity serving in a soup kitchen
- chapter-opening vignette based on a speech about inequality by Jerome Powell, chair of the Federal Reserve board of governors
- revised material on the shrinking middle class, with Research Today box, "Precarious Work"
- complete revision of section on class warfare, focusing on recent tax changes that benefit the rich
- coverage of the differential impact of the coronavirus pandemic on different classes and on racial and ethnic minorities
- enhanced coverage on women's unpaid labor and efforts to measure its economic value
- updated coverage of differences in wealth between racial and ethnic groups
- expanded treatment of intergenerational mobility, focusing on the Millennials
- discussion of the impact of the coronavirus pandemic on unemployment rates
- enhanced discussion of poverty, including new focus on geographic distribution of both poverty and affluence
- discussion of aspects of COVID-19 related to stratification and mobility: impact on life chances, on occupational prestige, and CEO salaries
- Key Term treatment for "precarious work," with discussion of the impact of the coronavirus pandemic

Chapter 9: Global Inequality

- chapter-opening photo showing a squatter settlement in the developing world
- discussion of the coronavirus pandemic's likely effects on recent progress in reducing poverty
- chapter-opening vignette excerpted from the updated United Nations Millennium Development Goals
- Sociology on Campus box, "International Students," with figure showing countries of origin for international students in the United States
- Sociology in the Global Community box, "Social Stratification in Japan," with photo
- major revisions to Social Policy section, "Rethinking Welfare in Europe and North American," focusing on current research into effectiveness of various programs and the impact of the pandemic
- Taking Sociology with You question on the impact of the pandemic
- Key Term treatment for "conspicuous consumption"

Chapter 10: Racial and Ethnic Inequality

- discussion of inclusion of triracial categories in recent census questions
- Research Today box on prejudice and discrimination, "Avoiding Interracial Relationships Online," with photos

- coverage of 2020 racial justice protests, white privilege, and the role of institutional discrimination
- discussion of voting requirements as an example of institutional discrimination
- enhanced and expanded section on racial profiling, with photo
- Sociology in the Global Community box, "The Maori of New Zealand," with photo
- updated discussion of Asian Americans as a "model minority," with Research Today box, "Is There a Model Minority?" including anti-Asian sentiment during the coronavirus pandemic
- updated and enhanced discussion of Chinese Americans, Indian Americans, effects of Hurricane Maria and COVID-19 on Puerto Rican Americans, and recent antisemitic incidents
- updated and expanded discussion of recent attempts to limit immigration and their social effects
- Key Term treatment for "double consciousness" and "model minority"

Chapter 11: Stratification by Gender and Sexuality
- updated and expanded coverage of gender roles, with photo
- revised and updated Sociology in the Global Community box, "No Gender, Please, It's Preschool"
- enhanced coverage of gender fluidity in text and in Research Today box, "Measuring Discrimination Based on Gender Identity"
- coverage of the 2020 Supreme Court ruling that the Civil Rights Act protects gays and transgender people in the workplace
- discussion of interactionist perspective on increased domestic violence during the coronavirus pandemic
- Table 11-3, "The Global Gender Gap," with Think About It question
- Sociology in the Global Community box, "The Gender Gap in Japan," with photo
- Figure 11-3, "Women's Participation in the Labor Force, 1975–2018"
- Research Today box, "Who Does the Housework?" with figure
- updated coverage of women's activism, including recent efforts to revive the ERA
- updated Social Policy section, "Workplace Sexual Harassment," with cartoon

Chapter 12: The Family and Household Diversity
- chapter-opening photo showing large family reunion
- enhanced coverage of interactionist perspective on step-parenting and online dating, with updates to Our Wired World box, "Love in in the Air and on the Web"
- coverage of increased online messaging and dating during the coronavirus pandemic
- expanded discussion of couples in which the female partner earns more than the male
- discussion of tendency to marry later in life

- Sociology in the Global Community box, "Arranged and Hybrid Marriage," with figure
- Figure 12-4, "Grandparents Who Support Grandchildren, 2018"
- expanded discussion of married people living apart and dual-income couples
- Research Today box, "Challenges to LGBTQ Adoptions"
- updated and expanded discussion of cohabitation
- expanded discussion of remaining single and childlessness, including 2020 statistics showing all-time low marriage rate
- Key Term treatment of "arranged marriage" and "hybrid marriage"

Chapter 13: Education and Religion
- Figure 13-2, "Annual Earnings by Degree Level, 2018"
- updated discussion of racial isolation in public schools
- updated discussion of credentialism
- updated Box 13-1, "The Debate Over Title IX," to include research on negative effects of sports and the #MeToo movement
- updated discussion of the teaching profession
- updated and expanded coverage of homeschooling
- Research Today box, "The Growth of None of the Above"
- discussion of religion and social support and religious ritual updated to include effects of coronavirus pandemic
- Figure 13-7, "Religion Is Very Important in My Life"
- Research Today box, "Wicca: Religion or Quasi-Religion?" with photo
- Social Policy section: "Religion in the Schools," with cartoon
- Key Term treatment of "creationism" and "intelligent design"

Chapter 14: Government and the Economy
- chapter-opening photo focusing on coronavirus pandemic
- capitalism coverage updated to include government measures passed during the coronavirus pandemic
- updated and expanded discussion of political influence, with Key Term treatment of "influencers"
- photos to illustrate Arab Americans in Congress and the influence of the power elite
- updated and expanded coverage of the global power elite
- Our Wired World box, "Politicking Online," updated to include recent developments in use of social media in elections
- discussion of online misinformation about COVID-19 during the pandemic
- discussion of recent classification of white supremacist groups as terrorists
- Social Policy section, "The Response to the Coronavirus Pandemic," with photo and cartoon
- Key Term treatment for "influencer," "obedience," and "precarious work"

Chapter 15: Health, Population, and the Environment

- chapter-opening photo showing the effects of the coronavirus lockdown on pollution
- chapter-opening vignette featuring Greta Thunberg's 2019 address to the UN
- updated Figure 15-1, "Infant Mortality Rates in Selected Countries," and Figure 15-2, "AIDS by the Numbers Worldwide"
- updated discussion of health insurance coverage, including impact of the pandemic
- enhanced discussion of the medical profession as an agent of social control
- revised and updated discussion of differences in mortality among racial and ethnic groups
- expanded discussion of *curanderismo*
- Research Today box, "The Color of COVID-19"
- discussion of racial and ethnic differences in access to mental health care
- photo illustrating reliance of people with mental health issues on telemedicine during the pandemic
- updated Figure 15-4, "Total Health Care Expenditures in the United States, 1960-2028 (Projected)"
- expanded discussion of air pollution in the United States and worldwide; updated discussion of water pollution
- cartoon highlighting insufficient efforts to curb carbon emissions
- Key Term treatment for "comorbidity"
- Thinking Critically questions about the U.S. government's role in health care and why societies find it difficult to address climate change

Chapter 16: Social Change in the Global Community

- chapter-opening photo illustrating pro-democracy demonstrations in Hong Kong
- updated Figure 16-1, "Declining Drive-Ins, 1954–2019," and Figure 16-2, "Walking to Work, 1980–2019"
- discussion of implications of coronavirus pandemic, social change in Dubai, artificial intelligence
- photo of recent teacher protest to illustrate section on Social Movements
- refocused discussion of feminist perspective on social movement

- updated and expanded coverage of communication and social movements
- Figure 16-3, "The Changing U.S. Economy, 2018-2028 (Projected)"
- updated and expanded discussions of resistance to technology and artificial intelligence
- updated Figure 16-4, "Estimated Annual Global Sale of Industrial Robots, 2010-2022," and Figure 16-5, "Impact of Artificial Intelligence on Select Occupations"
- Figure 16-6, "Origin and Destination of Transnationals, 2019," with Think About It question
- Thinking Critically question about social change resulting from the coronavirus pandemic
- discussion of misreporting of health data with reference to coronavirus pandemic

Teaching Resources

Instructor's Manual. The Instructor's Manual includes detailed chapter outlines and chapter summaries; learning objectives; a chapter-by-chapter bulleted list of new content; key terms; essay questions; and critical thinking questions.

Acknowledgments

Author Acknowledgments

The Fourteenth Edition of *Sociology: A Brief Introduction* reflects the input of many talented individuals. Since 2010, Elaine Silverstein has played a most significant role in the development of my introductory sociology books. Fortunately for me, in this Fourteenth Edition, Elaine has once again been responsible for the smooth integration of all changes and updates.

This edition continues to reflect the many insightful suggestions made by reviewers of the 13 previous brief editions.

As is evident from these acknowledgments, the preparation of a textbook is truly a team effort. The most valuable member of this effort continues to be my wife, Sandy. She provides the support so necessary in my creative and scholarly activities.

I have had the good fortune to introduce students to sociology for many years. These students have been enormously helpful in spurring on my sociological imagination. In ways I can fully appreciate but cannot fully acknowledge, their questions in class and queries in the hallway have found their way into this textbook.

Richard T. Schaefer
schaeferrt@aol.com

Academic Reviewers

This current edition has benefited from constructive and thorough evaluations provided by sociologists from both two-year and four-year institutions.

Adriana Bohm, *Delaware County Community College*

Matthew Cazessus, *Greenville Technical College*

Marlese Durr, *Wright State University*

Tammie Foltz, *Des Moines Area Community College*

Mike Fonge, *Houston Community College*

Claire Giesen, *Delgado Community College*

Happy Gingras, *Pitt Community College*

Mehdi Haghshenas, *University of Texas*

Lucy Hurston, *Manchester Community College*

Margaret Jendrek, *Miami University–Oxford*

Laurie J. Linhart, *Des Moines Area Community College*

David Liu, *Harrisburg Area Community College*

Becky Marth, *Milwaukee Area Technical College*

Carla Mercy, *Louisiana Delta Community College*

Joseph Oaster, *Harcum College*

Tiffany Parsons, *University of West Georgia*

LiErin Probasco, *Oklahoma City Community College*

Deborah Robinson, *Louisiana Delta Community College*

Andrew Rochus, *Western Virginia University at Parkersburg*

Amy Ruedisueli, *Tidewater Community College, Virginia Beach*

Luis Salinas, *University of Houston*

Rhianan Smith, *Waukesha County Technical College*

Jolene Sundlie, *Saint Paul College*

Okori Uneke, *Winston-Salem State University*

Amanda Vandivier, *Frostburg State University*

Tina Villareal, *Texas State University*

Gregory Zachrison, *Massosoit Community College*

Understanding Sociology

South_agency/Getty Images

One of the things sociologists study is how people organize themselves into groups to perform tasks necessary to society. Volunteers pick up garbage in a local woodlands park for eventual recycling.

▶ INSIDE

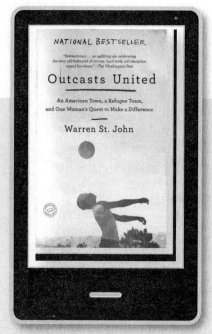

Ira C. Roberts

Have you ever reacted totally differently from the people around you because of different life experiences?

Journalist Warren St. John shows how people with varied backgrounds struggle to adjust to their new environment and to each other.

❝ On a cool spring afternoon at a soccer field in northern Georgia, two teams of teenage boys were going through their pregame warm-ups when the heavens began to shake. The field had been quiet save the sounds of soccer balls thumping against forefeet and the rustling of the balls against the nylon nets that hung from the goals. But as the rumble grew louder, all motion stopped as boys from both teams looked quizzically skyward. Soon a cluster of darts appeared in the gap of sky between the pine trees on the horizon and the cottony clumps of cloud vapor overhead. It was a precision flying squadron of fighter jets, performing at an air show miles away in Atlanta. The aircraft banked in close formation in the direction of the field and came closer, so that the boys could now make out the markings on the wings and the white helmets of the pilots in the cockpits. Then with an earthshaking roar deep enough to rattle the change in your pocket, the jets split in different directions like an exploding firework, their contrails carving the sky into giant wedges.

On the field below, the two groups of boys watched the spectacle with craned necks, and from different perspectives. The players of the home team—a group of thirteen- and fourteen-year-old boys from the nearby Atlanta suburbs playing with the North Atlanta Soccer Association—gestured to the sky and wore expressions of awe.

The boys at the other end of the field were members of an all-refugee soccer team called the Fugees [as in "reFugees"]. Many had actually seen the machinery of war in action, and all had felt its awful consequences firsthand. There were Sudanese players on the team whose villages had been bombed by old Russian-made Antonov bombers flown by the Sudanese Air Force, and Liberians who'd lived through barrages of mortar fire that pierced the roofs of their neighbors' homes, taking out whole families. As the jets flew by the field, several members of the Fugees flinched.

This was the first time I'd ever seen the Fugees play. I'd shown up knowing little about the team other than that the players were refugees and the coach a woman, and that the team was based in a town called Clarkston. In a little more than a decade, the process of refugee resettlement had transformed Clarkston from a simple southern town into one of the most diverse communities in America. And yet few in Atlanta, let alone in the world beyond, had taken notice. ❞

Source: St. John 2009, pp. 1–2, 6.

On the field below, the two groups of boys watched the spectacle with craned necks, and from different perspectives.

In *Outcasts United,* journalist Warren St. John takes us into the social world of a soccer team, a world composed of refugees who find themselves in a suburban Georgia town of 13,000, located about ten miles from Atlanta, that annually receives 1,500 refugees. Many of the "Fugees" have escaped violence in their home countries. Now they are making the United States their home, with all the adjustments that radical change entails. While they adapt to their new environment, their neighbors must adapt to having the refugees among them. And their competitors on the soccer field must learn what it means to live in a diverse, changing society.

We cannot assume that everyone we meet or communicate with, even when we are young, will be just like ourselves. Today, we learn to work together with people who are very different, and we sometimes struggle to create a sense of community despite our differences. In Clarkston, one-third of the population is foreign born, and residents represent over 40 nationalities. While the town's diversity may be greater than that in many other communities, learning to work in new and changing social environments is critical to an individual's and the entire society's success (Carnes 2019).

As a field of study, sociology is extremely broad in scope. You will see throughout this book the range of topics sociologists investigate—from immigration to suicide, from Amish society to global economic patterns, from peer pressure to genetic engineering. Sociology looks at how others influence our behavior; how major social institutions like the government, religion, and the economy affect us; and how we ourselves affect other individuals, groups, and even organizations.

How did sociology develop? In what ways does it differ from other social sciences? This chapter will explore the nature of sociology as both a field of inquiry and an exercise of the "sociological imagination." We'll look at the discipline as a science and consider its relationship to other social sciences. We'll meet four pioneering thinkers—Émile Durkheim, Max Weber, Karl Marx, and W. E. B. DuBois—and examine the theoretical perspectives that grew out of their work. We'll note some of the practical applications for sociological theory and research. Finally, we'll see how sociology helps us to develop a sociological imagination. For those students interested in exploring career opportunities in sociology, the chapter closes with a special appendix.

What Is Sociology?

"What has sociology got to do with me or with my life?" As a student, you might well have asked this question when you signed up for your introductory sociology course. To answer it, consider these points: Are you influenced by what you see on television? Do you use the Internet? Are you part of a clique? These are just a few of the everyday life situations described in this book that sociology can shed light on. But as the opening excerpt indicates, sociology also looks at large social issues. We use sociology to investigate why thousands of jobs have moved from the United States to developing nations, what social forces promote prejudice, what leads someone to join a social movement and work for social change, how access to computer technology can reduce social inequality, and why relationships between men and women in Seattle differ from those in Singapore.

Sociology is, simply, the scientific study of social behavior and human groups. It focuses on social relationships; how those relationships influence people's behavior; and how societies, the sum total of those relationships, develop and change.

The Sociological Imagination

In attempting to understand social behavior, sociologists rely on a particular type of critical thinking. A leading sociologist, C. Wright Mills, described such thinking as the **sociological imagination**—an awareness of the relationship between an individual and the wider society, both today and in the past (Mills [1959] 2000a). This awareness allows all of us (not just sociologists) to comprehend the links between our immediate, personal social settings and the remote, impersonal social world that surrounds and helps to shape us.

A key element in the sociological imagination is the ability to view one's own society as an outsider would, rather than only from the perspective of personal experiences and cultural biases. Consider something as simple as sporting events. On college campuses in the United States, thousands of students cheer well-trained football players. In parts of South America and the Caribbean, spectators gather around two cages, each holding a finch. The covers are lifted, and the owner of the first bird to sing 50 songs wins a trophy, a cash prize, and great prestige. In speed singing as in football, eager spectators debate the merits of their favorites and bet on the outcome of the events. Yet what is considered a normal sporting event in one part of the world is considered unusual in another part (Rueb 2015).

The sociological imagination allows us to go beyond personal experiences and observations to understand broader public issues. Divorce, for example, is unquestionably a personal hardship for a husband and wife who split apart. However, C. Wright Mills advocated using the sociological imagination to view divorce not as simply an individual's personal problem but rather as a societal concern. Using this perspective, we can see that an increase in the divorce rate actually redefines a major social institution—the family. Today's households frequently include stepparents and half-siblings whose parents have divorced and remarried. Through the complexities of the blended family, this private concern becomes a public issue that affects schools, government agencies, businesses, and religious institutions.

The sociological imagination is an empowering tool. It allows us to look beyond a limited understanding of human behavior to see the world and its people in a new way and through a broader lens than we might otherwise use. It may be as simple as understanding why a roommate prefers country music to hip-hop, or it may open up a whole different way of understanding other populations in the world. For example, in the aftermath of the terrorist attacks on the United States on September 11, 2001, many citizens wanted to understand how Muslims throughout the world perceived their country, and why. From time to time this textbook will offer you the chance to exercise your sociological imagination in a variety of situations.

USE YOUR SOCIOLOGICAL IMAGINATION

You are walking down the street in your city or hometown. In looking around you, you can't help noticing that half or more of the people you see are overweight. How do you explain your observation? If you were C. Wright Mills, how do you think you would explain it?

Sociology and the Social Sciences

Is sociology a science? The term **science** refers to the body of knowledge obtained by methods based on systematic observation. Just like other scientific disciplines, sociology involves the organized, systematic study of phenomena (in this case, human behavior) in order to enhance understanding. All scientists, whether studying mushrooms or murderers, attempt to collect precise information through methods of study that are as objective as possible. They rely on careful recording of observations and accumulation of data.

Of course, there is a great difference between sociology and physics, between psychology and astronomy. For this reason, the sciences are commonly divided into natural and social sciences. **Natural science** is the study of the physical features of nature and the ways in which they interact and change. Astronomy, biology, chemistry, geology, and physics are all natural sciences. **Social science** is the study of the social features of humans and the ways in which they interact and change. The social sciences include sociology, anthropology, economics, history, psychology, and political science.

These social science disciplines have a common focus on the social behavior of people, yet each has a particular orientation.

Rawpixel.com/Shutterstock

Sociology is the scientific study of social behavior and human groups.

Anthropologists usually study past cultures and preindustrial societies that continue today, as well as the origins of humans. Economists explore the ways in which people produce and exchange goods and services, along with money and other resources. Historians are concerned with the peoples and events of the past and their significance for us today. Political scientists study international relations, the workings of government, and the exercise of power and authority. Psychologists investigate personality and individual behavior. So what do *sociologists* focus on? They study the influence that society has on people's attitudes and behavior and the ways in which people interact and shape society. Because humans are social animals, sociologists examine our social relationships scientifically. The range of the relationships they investigate is vast, as the current list of sections in the American Sociological Association suggests (Table 1-1).

Let's consider how different social scientists might study the issue of climate change. Psychologists would look at the impact on the well-being of individuals who live and work in the areas most vulnerable to the impact of climate change, such as flood-prone areas along the coasts. Political scientists would consider the differences between countries, states, and cities that take steps to combat climate change. They would also consider how increasingly politicians are unable to avoid being questioned about their own position on climate change at election time. And economists would consider how, through climate change, the unintended effects of human activity affect long-term economic growth and well-being.

What approach would sociologists take? They would be interested in why a relatively large number of Americans deny that climate change is occurring or feel human activities are not responsible. In 2019, nearly 20 percent of the U.S. public held those views, compared to less than 5 percent in Germany, Great Britain, or China. Sociology moves us past viewing individuals as the primary agents producing carbon emissions and instead sees that individual actions are embedded in the workings of society as a whole. How individuals

Fran/Cartoon Stock

As the world considers issues related to climate change, sociologists use a variety of insights, including why people differ in their willingness to accept that human activity affects the global environment.

TABLE 1-1 SECTIONS OF THE AMERICAN SOCIOLOGICAL ASSOCIATION

Aging and the Life Course	Inequality, Poverty, and Mobility	Sociology of Body and Embodiment
Altruism, Morality, and Social Solidarity	International Migration	Sociology of Consumers and Consumption
Animals and Society	Labor and Labor Movements	Sociology of Culture
Asia and Asian America	Latina/o Sociology	Sociology of Development
Children and Youth	Marxist Sociology	Sociology of Education
Collective Behavior and Social Movements	Mathematical Sociology	Sociology of Emotions
Communication, Information Technologies, and Media	Medical Sociology	Sociology of Human Rights
Community and Urban Sociology	Methodology	Sociology of Law
Comparative-Historical Sociology	Organizations, Occupations, and Work	Sociology of Mental Health
Crime, Law, and Deviance	Peace, War, and Social Conflict	Sociology of Population
Disability in Society	Political Economy of the World-System	Sociology of Religion
Economic Sociology	Political Sociology	Sociology of Sex and Gender
Environmental Sociology	Race, Gender, and Class	Sociology of Sexualities
Ethnomethodology and Conversation Analysis	Racial and Ethnic Minorities	Teaching and Learning
Evolution, Biology, and Society	Rationality and Society	Theory
Family	Science, Knowledge, and Technology	
Global and Transnational Sociology	Social Psychology	
History of Sociology and Social Thought	Sociological Practice and Public Sociology	

Think about It   Which of these topics do you think would interest you the most? Why?

Source: American Sociological Association. 2022. Current Sections.

The range of sociological issues is very broad. For example, sociologists who belong to the Animals and Society section of the ASA may study the animal rights movement; those who belong to the Sociology of Sexualities section may study global sex workers or the gay, bisexual, and transgender movements. Economic sociologists may investigate globalization or consumerism, among many other topics.

confront climate change is constrained by social, economic, and political dynamics.

Similarly, sociology considers how the impact of climate change is not evenly felt and demonstrates that the poor are among the most vulnerable, both in the United States and around the world. Poor people often live in low-lying areas most vulnerable to floods and storms, and poor nations lack the means to build protective infrastructure. Social protests and movements to try to mobilize people to confront the human contribution to climate change would also be a prime focus of sociological analysis (Dunlap and Brulle 2019; Milman and Harvey 2019).

Sociologists would take a similar approach to studying episodes of extreme violence and hatred. In 2017, the nation was shocked by the open display of pro-Nazi and pro–Ku Klux Klan sympathy by marchers in Charlottesville, Virginia, at a "Unite the Right" rally protesting the removal of a statue of Confederate General Robert E. Lee. Months earlier, a lone gunman with leftist leanings opened fire at a Republican congressional baseball practice, shooting four members of Congress. Observers struggled to explain these individual and collective events by placing them in a larger social context. For sociologists in particular, these events raised numerous issues and topics for study, including the role of social media as a platform for extremist thought, growing anger against government and people in authority, the gun control debate, and the inadequacy of the nation's mental health system.

Besides doing research, sociologists have a long history of advising government agencies on how to respond to disasters.

Certainly the poverty of the Gulf Coast region complicated the challenge of evacuating New Orleans in 2005. With Hurricane Katrina bearing down on the Gulf Coast, thousands of poor inner-city residents had no automobiles or other means of escaping the storm. Added to that difficulty was the high incidence of disability in the area. New Orleans ranked second among the nation's 70 largest cities in the proportion of people over age 65 who were disabled—56 percent. Moving wheelchair-bound residents to safety requires specially equipped vehicles, to say nothing of handicap-accessible accommodations in public shelters. Clearly, officials must consider these factors in developing evacuation plans (Bureau of the Census 2005b).

Sociological analysis of the disaster did not end when the floodwaters receded. Indeed, several steps were taken that improved the response to hurricanes Harvey and Irma, which hit Texas and Florida in 2017. These included:

- Requiring communities to develop workable disaster response plans in advance.

- Delivering emergency supplies to secure holding areas before the storms struck.

- Permitting prior approval for taking action rather than requiring plan submission after the disaster.

- Identifying emergency shelters that take pets to avoid people remaining at home to safeguard their pets.

- Ending federal prohibition against accepting volunteer responders, especially when the scope of the disaster increases.

Tragically, many Katrina victims had relocated to Houston, where they then had to be sheltered again after Harvey struck in 2017, but they often expressed the realization that disaster response had improved. However, just a month later the slow response in the aftermath of Hurricane Maria on Puerto Rico, with most of the island left without clean water, power, or cell phone service for weeks, left many scholars looking for still further ways to improve both disaster preparedness and response (Carey 2017; Philips 2017).

Throughout this textbook, you will see how sociologists develop theories and conduct research to study and better understand societies. And you will be encouraged to use your sociological imagination to examine the United States (and other societies) from the viewpoint of a respectful but questioning outsider.

Sociology and Common Sense

Sociology focuses on the study of human behavior. Yet we all have experience with human behavior and at least some knowledge of it. All of us might well have theories about why people become homeless, for example. Our theories and opinions typically come from common sense—that is, from our experiences and conversations, from what we read, from what we see on television, and so forth.

In our daily lives, we rely on common sense to get us through many unfamiliar situations. However, this commonsense knowledge, while sometimes accurate, is not always reliable because it rests on commonly held beliefs rather than on systematic analysis of facts. It was once considered common sense to accept that the earth was flat—a view rightly questioned by Pythagoras and Aristotle. But incorrect commonsense notions are not just a part of the distant past; they remain with us today.

Contrary to the common notion that women tend to be chatty compared to men, for instance, researchers have found little difference between the sexes in terms of their talkativeness. Over a five-year period they placed unobtrusive microphones on 396 college students in various fields, at campuses in Mexico as well as the United States. They found that both men and women spoke about 16,000 words per day (Mehl et al. 2007).

Similarly, common sense tells us that today, violent crime holds communities on the border between the United States and Mexico in a kind of death grip, creating an atmosphere of lawlessness reminiscent of the old Wild West. Based on televised news stories and on concerns expressed by elected officials, this assertion may sound reasonable; however, it is not true. Although some communities in Mexico have fallen under the control of drug cartels, the story is different on the U.S. side of the border. All available crime data—documented by the FBI—show that all the counties along the U.S.–Mexico border have crime rates at least 2 percent lower than that in the rest of the United States. Furthermore, the crime rate has been dropping

faster near the border than in other similar-size U.S. communities for at least the last 15 years (Nowrasteh 2019).

Like other social scientists, sociologists do not accept something as a fact because "everyone knows it." Instead, each piece of information must be tested and recorded, then analyzed in relation to other data. Sociologists rely on scientific studies to describe and understand a social environment. At times, the findings of sociologists may seem like common sense because they deal with familiar facets of everyday life. The difference is that such findings have been *tested* by researchers. Common sense now tells us that the earth is round, but this particular commonsense notion is based on centuries of scientific work that began with the breakthroughs made by Pythagoras and Aristotle.

THINKING CRITICALLY

What aspects of the social and work environment in a fast-food restaurant would be of particular interest to a sociologist? How would the sociological imagination help in analyzing the topic?

What Is Sociological Theory?

Why do people die by suicide? One traditional commonsense answer is that people inherit the desire to kill themselves. Another view is that sunspots drive people to take their lives. These explanations may not seem especially convincing to contemporary researchers, but they represent beliefs widely held as recently as 1900.

Sociologists are not particularly interested in why any one individual dies by suicide; they are more concerned with identifying the social forces that systematically cause some people to take their own lives. To undertake this research, sociologists develop a theory that offers a general explanation of suicidal behavior.

We can think of theories as attempts to explain events, forces, materials, ideas, or behavior in a comprehensive manner. In sociology, a **theory** is a set of statements that seeks to explain problems, actions, or behavior. An effective theory may have both explanatory and predictive power. That is, it can help us to see the relationships among seemingly isolated phenomena,

USE YOUR SOCIOLOGICAL IMAGINATION

If you were Durkheim's successor in his research on suicide, how would you investigate the factors that may explain the increase in suicide rates among people age 55 and older in the United States today?

as well as to understand how one type of change in an environment leads to other changes.

The World Health Organization (2018a) estimates that 800,000 people die from suicide every year. More than a hundred years ago, a sociologist tried to look at suicide data scientifically. Émile Durkheim ([1897] 1951) developed a highly original theory about the relationship between suicide and social factors. Durkheim was primarily concerned not with the personalities of individual suicide victims, but rather with suicide rates and how they varied from country to

Digital Vision/Getty Images

country. As a result, when he looked at the number of reported suicides in France, England, and Denmark in 1869, he also noted the total population of each country in order to determine the rate of suicide in each nation. He found that whereas England had only 67 reported suicides per million inhabitants, France had 135 per million and Denmark had 277 per million. The question then became "Why did Denmark have a comparatively high rate of reported suicide?"

Durkheim went much deeper into his investigation of suicide rates. The result was his landmark work *Suicide*, published in 1897. Durkheim refused to accept unproved explanations regarding suicide, including the beliefs that inherited tendencies or cosmic forces caused such deaths. Instead, he focused on social factors, such as the cohesiveness or lack of cohesiveness of religious, social, and occupational groups.

Durkheim's research suggested that suicide, although it is a solitary act, is related to group life. He found that people without religious affiliations had a higher suicide rate than those who were affiliated; the unmarried had much higher rates than married people; and soldiers had a higher rate than civilians. In addition, there seemed to be higher rates of suicide in times of peace than in times of war and revolution, and in times of economic instability and recession rather than in times of prosperity. Durkheim concluded that the suicide rates of a society reflected the extent to which people were or were not integrated into the group life of the society.

Émile Durkheim, like many other social scientists, developed a theory to explain how individual behavior can be understood within a social context. He pointed out the influence of groups and societal forces on what had always been viewed as a highly personal act. Clearly, Durkheim offered a more *scientific* explanation for the causes of suicide than that of inherited tendencies or sunspots. His theory has predictive power, since it suggests that suicide rates will rise or fall in conjunction with certain social and economic changes.

Of course, a theory—even the best of theories—is not a final statement about human behavior. Durkheim's theory of suicide is no exception. Sociologists continue to examine factors that contribute to differences in suicide rates around the world and to a particular society's rate of suicide. In Las Vegas, and Nevada as a whole, for example, sociologists have observed that the chances of dying by suicide are strikingly high—about 45 percent higher than those in the United States as a whole. Noting Durkheim's emphasis on the relationship between suicide and social isolation, researchers have suggested that Las Vegas's rapid growth and constant influx of tourists have undermined the community's sense of permanence, even among longtime residents. Although gambling—or more accurately, losing while gambling—may seem a likely precipitating factor in suicides there, careful study of the data has allowed researchers to dismiss that explanation. What happens in Vegas may stay in Vegas, but the sense of community cohesiveness that the rest of the country enjoys may be lacking (Bekker 2019).

THINKING CRITICALLY

Can you think of any other explanation for the high suicide rate in Las Vegas? Does that explanation agree with Durkheim's theory?

The Development of Sociology

People have always been curious about sociological matters—how we get along with others, what we do for a living, whom we select as our leaders. Philosophers and religious authorities of ancient and medieval societies made countless observations about human behavior. They did not test or verify those observations scientifically; nevertheless, their observations often became the foundation for moral codes. Several of these early social philosophers correctly predicted that a systematic study of human behavior would emerge one day. Beginning in the 19th century, European theorists made pioneering contributions to the development of a science of human behavior.

Early Thinkers

Auguste Comte The 19th century was an unsettling time in France. The French monarchy had been deposed in the revolution of 1789, and Napoleon had suffered defeat in his effort to conquer Europe. Amid this chaos, philosophers considered how society might be improved. Auguste Comte (1798–1857), credited with being the most influential of the philosophers of the early 1800s, believed that a theoretical science of society and a systematic investigation of behavior were needed to improve society. He coined the term *sociology* to apply to the science of human behavior.

Alonzo Chappel/Georgios Kollidas/Alamy Stock Photo

Harriet Martineau, a pioneer of sociology who studied social behavior both in her native England and in the United States. Martineau proposed some of the methods still used by sociologists, including systematic observation.

Martineau's writings emphasized the impact that the economy, law, trade, health, and population could have on social problems. She spoke out in favor of the rights of women, the emancipation of slaves, and religious tolerance. Later in life, deafness did not keep her from being an activist. In Martineau's ([1837] 1962) view, intellectuals and scholars should not simply offer observations of social conditions; they should *act* on their convictions in a manner that will benefit society. That is why Martineau conducted research on the nature of female employment and pointed to the need for further investigation of the issue (Deegan 2003; Hill and Hoecker-Drysdale 2001).

Herbert Spencer   Another important early contributor to the discipline of sociology was Herbert Spencer (1820–1903). A relatively prosperous Victorian Englishman, Spencer (unlike Martineau) did not feel compelled to correct or improve society; instead, he merely hoped to understand it better. Drawing on Charles Darwin's study *On the Origin of Species,* Spencer applied the concept of evolution of the species to societies in order to explain how they change, or evolve, over time. Similarly, he adapted Darwin's evolutionary view of the "survival of the fittest" by arguing that it is "natural" that some people are rich while others are poor.

Spencer's approach to societal change was extremely popular in his lifetime. Unlike Comte, Spencer suggested that since societies are bound to change eventually, one need not be highly critical of present social arrangements or work actively for social change. This viewpoint appealed to many influential people in England and the United States who had a vested interest in the status quo and were suspicious of social thinkers who endorsed change.

Émile Durkheim

Émile Durkheim made many pioneering contributions to sociology, including his important theoretical work on suicide. The son of a rabbi, Durkheim (1858–1917) was educated in both France and Germany. He established an impressive academic reputation and was appointed one of the first professors of sociology in France. Above all, Durkheim will be remembered for his insistence that behavior must be understood within a larger social context, not just in individualistic terms.

To give one example of this emphasis, Durkheim ([1912] 2001) developed a fundamental thesis to help explain all forms of society. Through intensive study of the Arunta, an Australian tribe, he focused on the functions that religion performed and underscored the role of group life in defining what we consider to be religion. Durkheim concluded that like other forms of group behavior, religion reinforces a group's solidarity.

Another of Durkheim's main interests was the consequences of work in modern societies. In his view, the growing division of labor in industrial societies, as workers' tasks became more

Writing in the 1800s, Comte feared that the excesses of the French Revolution had permanently impaired France's stability. Yet he hoped that the systematic study of social behavior would eventually lead to more rational human interactions. In Comte's hierarchy of the sciences, sociology was at the top. He called it the "queen," and its practitioners "scientist-priests." This French theorist did not simply give sociology its name; he presented a rather ambitious challenge to the fledgling discipline.

Harriet Martineau   Scholars learned of Comte's works largely through translations by the English sociologist Harriet Martineau (1802–1876). But Martineau was a pathbreaker in her own right: she offered insightful observations of the customs and social practices of both her native Britain and the United States.

Martineau's book *Society in America* ([1837] 1962) examined religion, politics, child rearing, and immigration in the young nation. It gave special attention to social class distinctions and to such factors as gender and race. Martineau ([1838] 1989) also wrote the first book on sociological methods.

and more specialized, led to what he called "anomie." **Anomie** refers to the loss of direction felt in a society when social control of individual behavior has become ineffective. Often, the state of anomie occurs during a time of profound social change, when people have lost their sense of purpose or direction. In a period of anomie, people are so confused and unable to cope with the new social environment that they may resort to death by suicide.

Durkheim was concerned about the dangers that alienation, loneliness, and isolation might pose for modern industrial societies. He shared Comte's belief that sociology should provide direction for social change. As a result, he advocated the creation of new social groups—mediators between the individual's family and the state—that would provide a sense of belonging for members of huge, impersonal societies. Unions would be an example of such groups.

Like many other sociologists, Durkheim did not limit his interests to one aspect of social behavior. Later in this book we will consider his thinking on crime and punishment, religion, and the workplace. Few sociologists have had such a dramatic impact on so many different areas within the discipline.

Max Weber

Another important early theorist was Max Weber (pronounced vay-ber). Born in Germany, Weber (1864–1920) studied legal and economic history, but gradually developed an interest in sociology. Eventually, he became a professor at various German universities. Weber taught his students that they should employ **verstehen** (pronounced fair-shtay-en), the German word for "understanding" or "insight," in their intellectual work. He pointed out that we cannot analyze our social behavior by the same type of objective criteria we use to measure weight or temperature. To fully comprehend behavior, we must learn the subjective meanings people attach to their actions—how they themselves view and explain their behavior.

For example, suppose that a sociologist was studying the social ranking of individuals in a fraternity. Weber would expect the researcher to employ *verstehen* to determine the significance of the fraternity's social hierarchy for its members. The researcher might examine the effects of athleticism or grades or social skills or seniority on standing within the fraternity. He or she would seek to learn how the fraternity members relate to other members of higher or lower status. While investigating these questions, the researcher would take into account people's emotions, thoughts, beliefs, and attitudes (L. Coser 1977).

We also owe credit to Weber for a key conceptual tool: the ideal type. An **ideal type** is a construct or model for evaluating specific cases. In his works, Weber identified various characteristics of bureaucracy as an ideal type (discussed in detail in Chapter 5). In presenting this model of bureaucracy, Weber was not describing any particular organization, nor was he using the term *ideal* in a way that suggested a positive evaluation. Instead, his purpose was to provide a useful standard for measuring how bureaucratic an actual organization is (Gerth and Mills 1958). Later in this book, we will use the concept of *ideal type* to study the family, religion, authority, and economic systems, as well as to analyze bureaucracy.

Although their professional careers coincided, Émile Durkheim and Max Weber never met and probably were unaware of each other's ideas. Such was not true of the work of Karl Marx. Durkheim's thinking about the impact of the division of labor in industrial societies was related to Marx's writings, while Weber's concern for a value-free, objective sociology was a direct response to Marx's deeply held convictions. Thus, it is not surprising that Karl Marx is viewed as a major figure in the

Gary Conner/Getty Images

FIGURE 1-1   CONTRIBUTORS TO SOCIOLOGY

	The Art Gallery Collection/Alamy Stock Photo	Keystone Pictures USA/Alamy Stock Photo	Everett Historical/Shutterstock	Library of Congress Prints and Photographs Division [LC-DIG-ppmsca-38818]
	Émile Durkheim 1858–1917	**Max Weber 1864–1920**	**Karl Marx 1818–1883**	**W. E. B. DuBois 1868–1963**
Academic training	Philosophy	Law, economics, history, philosophy	Philosophy, law	Sociology
Key works	1893—*The Division of Labor in Society* 1897—*Suicide: A Study in Sociology* 1912—*Elementary Forms of Religious Life*	1904–1905—*The Protestant Ethic and the Spirit of Capitalism* 1921—*Economy and Society*	1848—*The Communist Manifesto* 1867—*Das Kapital*	1899—*The Philadelphia Negro* 1903—*The Negro Church* 1903—*Souls of Black Folk*

development of sociology, as well as several other social sciences (Figure 1-1).

Karl Marx

Karl Marx (1818–1883) shared with Durkheim and Weber a dual interest in abstract philosophical issues and the concrete reality of everyday life. Unlike them, however, Marx was so critical of existing institutions that a conventional academic career was impossible. He spent most of his life in exile from his native Germany.

Marx's personal life was a difficult struggle. When a paper he had written was suppressed, he fled to France. In Paris, he met Friedrich Engels (1820–1895), with whom he formed a lifelong friendship. The two lived at a time when European and North American economic life was increasingly dominated by the factory rather than the farm.

While in London in 1847, Marx and Engels attended secret meetings of an illegal coalition of labor unions known as the Communist League. The following year they prepared a platform called *The Communist Manifesto,* in which they argued that the masses of people with no resources other than their labor (whom they referred to as the *proletariat*) should unite to fight for the overthrow of capitalist societies. In the words of Marx and Engels:

> The history of all hitherto existing society is the history of class struggles. . . .
> The proletarians have nothing to lose but their chains. They have a world to win.
> WORKING MEN OF ALL COUNTRIES, UNITE! (Tucker 1978:473, 500)

After completing *The Communist Manifesto,* Marx returned to Germany, only to be expelled. He then moved to England, where he continued to write books and essays. Marx lived

there in extreme poverty; he pawned most of his possessions, and several of his children died of malnutrition and disease. Marx clearly was an outsider in British society, a fact that may well have influenced his view of Western cultures.

In Marx's analysis, society was fundamentally divided between two classes that clashed in pursuit of their own interests. When he examined the industrial societies of his time, such as Germany, England, and the United States, he saw the factory as the center of conflict between the exploiters (the owners of the means of production) and the exploited (the workers). Marx viewed these relationships in systematic terms; that is, he believed that a system of economic, social, and political relationships maintained the power and dominance of the owners over the workers. Consequently, Marx and Engels argued that the working class should overthrow the existing class system. Marx's writings inspired those who would later lead communist revolutions in Russia, China, Cuba, Vietnam, and elsewhere.

Even apart from the political revolutions that his work fostered, Marx's significance is profound. Marx emphasized the *group* identifications and associations that influence an *individual's* place in society. This area of study is the major focus of contemporary sociology. Throughout this textbook, we will consider how membership in a particular gender classification, age group, racial group, or economic class affects a person's attitudes and behavior. In an important sense, we can trace this way of understanding society back to the pioneering work of Karl Marx.

THINKING CRITICALLY

What influences do Marx's ideas have on current social and political issues?

W. E. B. DuBois

Marx's work encouraged sociologists to view society through the eyes of those segments of the population that rarely influence decision making. In the United States, some early Black sociologists, including W. E. B. DuBois (1868–1963), conducted research that they hoped would assist in the struggle for a racially egalitarian society. DuBois (pronounced doo-boyss) believed that knowledge was essential in combating prejudice and achieving tolerance and justice. Sociologists, he contended, needed to draw on scientific principles to study social problems such as those experienced by Blacks in the United States. To separate opinion from fact, he advocated research on the lives of Blacks. Through his in-depth studies of urban life, both white and Black, in cities such as Philadelphia and Atlanta, DuBois ([1899] 1995) made a major contribution to sociology.

Like Durkheim and Weber, DuBois saw the importance of religion to society. However, he tended to focus on religion at the community level and on the role of the church in the lives of its members (DuBois [1903] 2003). DuBois had little patience with theorists such as Herbert Spencer, who seemed content with the status quo. He believed that the granting of full political rights to Blacks was essential to their social and economic progress.

Through what became known as the Atlanta Sociological Laboratory, DuBois also promoted groundbreaking research by other scholars. While investigating religion, crime, and race relations, these colleagues trained their students in sociological research. The extensive interviews conducted by students in Atlanta still enrich our understanding of human behavior (Earl Wright II 2012).

Because many of his ideas challenged the status quo, DuBois did not always find a receptive audience within either the government or the academic world. As a result, he became increasingly involved with organizations whose members questioned the established social order. In 1909 he helped to found the National Association for the Advancement of Colored People, known today as the NAACP (Morris 2015, Wortham 2008).

DuBois's insights have been lasting. In 1897 he coined the term **double consciousness** to refer to the division of an individual's identity into two or more social realities. He used the term to describe the experience of being Black in white America. African Americans have held the highest offices in the land, including President of the United States. Yet for millions of African Americans, the reality of being Black in the United States typically is not one of power (DuBois [1903] 1961).

Twentieth-Century Developments

Sociology today builds on the firm foundation developed by Émile Durkheim, Max Weber, Karl Marx, and W. E. B. DuBois. However, the field certainly has not remained stagnant over the past hundred years. While Europeans have continued to make contributions to the discipline, sociologists from throughout the world and especially the United States have advanced sociological theory and research. Their new insights have helped us to better understand the workings of society.

Charles Horton Cooley Charles Horton Cooley (1864–1929) was typical of the sociologists who came to prominence in the early 1900s. Born in Ann Arbor, Michigan, Cooley received his graduate training in economics but later became a sociology professor at the University of Michigan. Like other early sociologists, he had become interested in this new discipline while pursuing a related area of study.

Cooley shared the desire of Durkheim, Weber, and Marx to learn more about society. But to do so effectively, he preferred to use the sociological perspective to look first at smaller units—intimate, face-to-face groups such as families, gangs, and friendship networks. He saw these groups as the seedbeds of society, in the sense that they shape people's ideals, beliefs, values, and social nature. Cooley's work increased our understanding of groups of relatively small size.

Jane Addams In the early 1900s, many leading sociologists in the United States saw themselves as social reformers dedicated to systematically studying and then improving a corrupt society. They were genuinely concerned about the lives of immigrants in the nation's growing cities, whether those immigrants came

Library of Congress Prints and Photographs Division [LC-H25-71336-BF]

Jane Addams was a pioneer both in sociology and in the settlement house movement. She was also an activist for many causes, including the worldwide campaign for peace.

from Europe or from the rural American South. Early female sociologists, in particular, often took active roles in poor urban areas as leaders of community centers known as *settlement houses.* For example, Jane Addams (1860–1935), a member of the American Sociological Society, co-founded the famous Chicago settlement house called Hull House.

Addams and other pioneering female sociologists commonly combined intellectual inquiry, social service work, and political activism—all with the goal of assisting the underprivileged and creating a more egalitarian society. For example, working with the Black journalist and educator Ida Wells-Barnett, Addams successfully prevented racial segregation in the Chicago public schools. Addams's efforts to establish a juvenile court system and a women's trade union reveal the practical focus of her work (Addams 1910, 1930; Deegan 1991; Lengermann and Niebrugge-Brantley 1998).

By the middle of the 20th century, however, the focus of the discipline had shifted. Sociologists for the most part restricted themselves to theorizing and gathering information; the aim of transforming society was left to social workers and activists. This shift away from social reform was accompanied by a growing commitment to scientific methods of research and to value-free interpretation of data. Not all sociologists were happy with this emphasis. A new organization, the Society for the Study of Social Problems, was created in 1950 to deal more directly with social inequality and other social problems.

Robert Merton   Sociologist Robert Merton (1910–2003) made an important contribution to the discipline by successfully combining theory and research. Born to Slavic immigrant parents in Philadelphia, Merton won a scholarship to Temple University. He continued his studies at Harvard, where he acquired his lifelong interest in sociology. Merton's teaching career was based at Columbia University.

Merton (1968) produced a theory that is one of the most frequently cited explanations of deviant behavior. He noted different ways in which people attempt to achieve success in life. In his view, some may deviate from the socially approved goal of accumulating material goods or the socially accepted means of achieving that goal. For example, in Merton's classification scheme, *innovators* are people who accept the goal of pursuing material wealth but use illegal means to do so, including robbery, burglary, and extortion. Although Merton based his explanation of crime on individual behavior that has been influenced by society's approved goals and means, it has wider applications. His theory helps to account for the high crime rates among the nation's poor, who may see no hope of advancing themselves through traditional roads to success. Chapter 7 discusses Merton's theory in greater detail.

Merton also emphasized that sociology should strive to bring together the *macro-level* and *micro-level* approaches to the study of society. **Macrosociology** concentrates on large-scale phenomena or entire civilizations. Harriet Martineau's study of religion and politics in the United States is an example of macro-level research. More recently, macrosociologists have examined international crime rates (see Chapter 7) and the stereotype of Asian Americans as a "model minority" (see Chapter 10). In contrast, **microsociology** stresses the study of small groups, often through experimental means. Sociological research on the micro level has included studies of how divorced men and women disengage from significant social roles (see Chapter 5) and of how a teacher's expectations can affect a student's academic performance (see Chapter 13).

While Merton intended to be inclusive of all research, over the past 50 years sociologists have identified two additional levels of research: *mesosociology* and *global sociology.* **Mesosociology** is an intermediate level of analysis embracing study of formal organizations and social movements. Max Weber's analysis of bureaucracies (see Chapter 5) and the study of environmentalism (see Chapter 15) illustrate mesosociology. **Global sociology** makes comparisons among nations, typically using entire societies as the units of analysis. Émile Durkheim's cross-cultural study of suicide is an example of global sociology, as is the study of international crime rates (Smelser 1997).

Pierre Bourdieu   Increasingly, scholars in the United States have been drawing on the insights of sociologists in other countries. The ideas of the French sociologist Pierre Bourdieu (1930–2002) have found a broad following in North America and elsewhere. As a young man, Bourdieu did fieldwork in Algeria during its struggle for independence from France. Today, scholars study Bourdieu's research techniques as well as his conclusions.

Bourdieu wrote about how capital in its many forms sustains individuals and families from one generation to the next. To Bourdieu, *capital* included not just material goods, but cultural and social assets. **Cultural capital** refers to noneconomic goods, such as family background and education, which are reflected in a knowledge of language and the arts. Not necessarily book knowledge, cultural capital refers to the kind of education that is valued by the socially elite. Though a knowledge of Chinese cuisine is culture, for example, it is not the prestigious kind of culture that is valued by the elite. In the United States, immigrants—especially those who arrived in large numbers and settled in ethnic enclaves—have generally taken two or three generations to develop the same level of cultural capital enjoyed by more established groups.

In comparison, **social capital** refers to the collective benefit of social networks, which are built on reciprocal trust. Much has been written about the importance of family and friendship networks in providing people with an opportunity to advance. Social bonds and capital have great value in health, happiness, educational achievement, and economic success. In his emphasis on cultural and social capital, Bourdieu's work extends the insights of early social thinkers such as Marx and

Weber (Bourdieu and Passerson 1990; Poder 2011; Putnam 2015:207).

Today sociology reflects the diverse contributions of earlier theorists. As sociologists approach such topics as divorce, drug addiction, and religious cults, they can draw on the theoretical insights of the discipline's pioneers. A careful reader can hear Comte, Durkheim, Weber, Marx, DuBois, Cooley, Addams, and many others speaking through the pages of current research. Sociology has also broadened beyond the intellectual confines of North America and Europe. Contributions to the discipline now come from sociologists studying and researching human behavior in other parts of the world. In describing the work of these sociologists, it is helpful to examine a number of influential *theoretical perspectives,* also known as *approaches* or *views.*

©John M Lund Photography Inc/GettyImages

Functionalists would see the family, as shown here in Panama City, Panama, as important to contributing to the stability of the society.

THINKING CRITICALLY

What kinds of social and cultural capital do you possess? How did you acquire them? What keeps you from acquiring more?

Major Theoretical Perspectives

Sociologists view society in different ways. Some see the world basically as a stable and ongoing entity. They are impressed with the endurance of the family, organized religion, and other social institutions. Other sociologists see society as composed of many groups in conflict, competing for scarce resources. To still other sociologists, the most fascinating aspects of the social world are the everyday, routine interactions among individuals that we sometimes take for granted. These three views, the ones most widely used by sociologists, are the functionalist, conflict, and interactionist perspectives. Together, these approaches will provide an introductory look at the discipline.

Functionalist Perspective

Think of society as a living organism in which each part of the organism contributes to its survival. This view is the **functionalist perspective**, which emphasizes the way in which the parts of a society are structured to maintain its stability. In examining any aspect of society, then, functionalists emphasize the contribution that it makes to overall social stability.

Talcott Parsons (1902–1979), a Harvard University sociologist, was a key figure in the development of functionalist theory. Parsons was greatly influenced by the work of Émile Durkheim, Max Weber, and other European sociologists. For more than four decades, he dominated sociology in the United States with his advocacy of functionalism. Parsons saw any society as a vast network of connected parts, each of which helps to maintain the

system as a whole. His approach, carried forward by German sociologist Niklas Luhmann (1927–1998), holds that if an aspect of social life does not contribute to a society's stability or survival—if it does not serve some identifiably useful function or promote value consensus among members of society—it will not be passed on from one generation to the next (Joas and Knöbl 2009; Knudsen 2010).

Let's examine an example of the functionalist perspective. Many Americans have difficulty understanding the Hindu prohibition against slaughtering cows (specifically, zebu). Cattle browse unhindered through Indian street markets, helping themselves to oranges and mangoes while people bargain for the little food they can afford. What explains this devotion to the cow in the face of human deprivation—a devotion that appears to be dysfunctional?

The simple explanation is that cow worship is highly functional in Indian society, according to economists, agronomists, and social scientists who have studied the matter. Cows perform two essential tasks: plowing the fields and producing milk. If eating beef were permitted, hungry families might be tempted to slaughter their cows for immediate consumption, leaving themselves without a means of cultivation. Cows also produce dung, which doubles as a fertilizer and a fuel for cooking. Finally, cow meat sustains the neediest group in society, the *Dalit,* or untouchables, who sometimes resort to eating beef in secrecy. If eating beef were socially acceptable, higher-status Indians would no doubt bid up its price, placing it beyond the reach of the hungriest.

Manifest and Latent Functions A college catalog typically states various functions of the institution. It may inform you, for example, that the university intends to "offer each student a broad education in classical and contemporary thought, in the humanities, in the sciences, and in the arts." However, it would be quite a surprise to find a catalog that declared, "This university was founded in 1895 to assist people in finding a marriage partner." No college catalog will declare this as the purpose of the university. Yet societal institutions serve many functions, some of them quite subtle. The university, in fact, *does* facilitate mate selection.

Robert Merton (1968) made an important distinction between manifest and latent functions. **Manifest functions** of institutions are open, stated, and conscious functions. They involve the intended, recognized consequences of an aspect of society, such as the university's role in certifying academic competence and excellence. In contrast, **latent functions** are unconscious or unintended functions that may reflect hidden purposes of an institution. One latent function of universities is to hold down unemployment. Another is to serve as a meeting ground for people seeking marital partners.

Dysfunctions Functionalists acknowledge that not all parts of a society contribute to its stability all the time. A **dysfunction** refers to an element or process of a society that may actually disrupt the social system or reduce its stability.

We view many dysfunctional behavior patterns, such as homicide, as undesirable. Yet we should not automatically interpret them in this way. The evaluation of a dysfunction depends on one's own values, or as the saying goes, on "where you sit." For example, the official view in prisons in the United States is that inmate gangs should be eradicated because they are dysfunctional to smooth operations. Yet some guards have come to view prison gangs as a functional part of their jobs. The danger posed by gangs creates a "threat to security," requiring increased surveillance and more overtime work for guards, as well as requests for special staffing to address gang problems (G. Scott 2001).

Conflict Perspective

Where functionalists see stability and consensus, conflict sociologists see a social world in continual struggle. The **conflict perspective** assumes that social behavior is best understood in terms of tension between groups over power or the allocation of resources, including housing, money, access to services, and political representation. The tension between competing groups need not be violent; it can take the form of labor negotiations, party politics, competition between religious groups for new members, or disputes over the federal budget.

Throughout most of the 1900s, the functionalist perspective had the upper hand in sociology in the United States. However, the conflict approach has become increasingly persuasive since the late 1960s. The widespread social unrest resulting from battles over civil rights, bitter divisions over the war in Vietnam, the rise of the feminist and gay liberation movements, the Watergate political scandal, urban riots, confrontations at abortion clinics, and shrinking economic prospects for the middle class have offered support for the conflict approach—the view that our social world is characterized by continual struggle between competing groups. Currently, the discipline of sociology accepts conflict theory as one valid way to gain insight into a society.

The Marxist View As we saw earlier, Karl Marx viewed struggle between social classes as inevitable, given the exploitation of workers that he perceived under capitalism. Expanding on Marx's work, sociologists and other social scientists have come to see conflict not merely as a class phenomenon but as a part of everyday life in all societies. In studying any culture, organization, or social group, sociologists want to know who benefits, who suffers, and who dominates at the expense of others. They are concerned with the conflicts between women and men, parents and children, cities and suburbs, whites and Blacks, to name only a few. Conflict theorists are interested in how society's institutions—including the family, government, religion, education, and the media—may help to maintain the privileges of some groups and keep others in a subservient position. Their emphasis on social change and the redistribution of resources makes conflict theorists more radical and activist than functionalists (Dahrendorf 1959).

Building upon the work of the conflict perspective, sociologists today have drawn greater attention to social inequality as it dramatically impacts people of color. Eduardo Bonilla-Silva grew up in Puerto Rico, where his mother was a sociologist who authored a book focusing on domestic abuse. Proud of his family and ethnic background, Bonilla-Silva's scholarship asks us to rethink racism as it occurs subtly by outwardly tolerant people as well as violently in everyday life. Significant change is required to overcome this centuries old, long-standing pattern of inequality (Bonilla-Silva 2019; Silva-Bonilla 1985).

Photo permission, Duke University

Eduardo Bonilla-Silva, president of the American Sociological Association in 2018, has drawn upon conflict theory to focus on issues of long-term social and racial inequality.

The Feminist Perspective Sociologists began embracing the feminist perspective only in the 1970s, although it has a long tradition in many other disciplines. The **feminist perspective** sees inequity in gender as central to all behavior and organization. Because it focuses clearly on one aspect of inequality, it is often allied with the conflict perspective. Proponents of the feminist view tend to focus on the macro level, just as conflict theorists do. Drawing on the work of Marx and Engels, contemporary feminist theorists often view women's subordination as inherent in capitalist societies. Some radical feminist theorists, however, view the oppression of women as inevitable in *all* male-dominated societies, whether capitalist, socialist, or communist (Ferguson 2017).

Smithsonian Libraries/Science Source

Ida Wells-Barnett explored what it meant to be female and Black in the United States. Her work established her as one of the earliest feminist theorists.

An early example of this perspective (long before the label came into use by sociologists) can be seen in the life and writings of Ida Wells-Barnett (1862–1931). Following her groundbreaking publications in the 1890s on the practice of lynching Black Americans, she became an advocate in the women's rights campaign, especially the struggle to win the vote for women. Like feminist theorists who succeeded her, Wells-Barnett used her analysis of society as a means of resisting oppression. In her case, she researched what it meant to be Black, a woman in the United States, and a Black woman in the United States (Giddings 2008; Wells-Barnett 1970).

A more recent contribution that continues to spark discussion is the notion of the *intersectionalities,* or the interlocking matrix of domination. In all societies, privilege or lack of privilege is determined by multiple social factors, such as gender, age, race, sexual orientation, and religion. Patricia Hill Collins (2000), among other feminist theorists, drew attention to these interlocking factors, demonstrating that it is not just wealth that influences how we navigate our daily lives in any society.

Queer Theory Traditionally, sociologists and other researchers have assumed that men and women are heterosexual. They either ignored other sexual identifications or treated them as abnormal. Yet as French social theorist Michel Foucault (1978) has pointed out, what is regarded as normal or even acceptable human sexuality varies dramatically from one culture to another, as well as from one time period to another. Today, in *queer theory,* sociologists have moved beyond narrow assumptions to study sexuality in all its forms.

Historically, the word *queer* was used in a derogatory manner, to stigmatize a person or behavior. Beginning in the early 1970s, however, gay and lesbian activists began to use the word as a term of empowerment. They dismissed the notion of heterosexuality as the only normal form of sexuality, along with the belief that people must be either heterosexual or homosexual. Instead, they recognized multiple sexual identities, including bisexuality. **Queer theory** is the study of society from the perspective of a broad spectrum of sexual identities, including heterosexuality, homosexuality, and bisexuality.

Queer theorist Eve Sedgwick (1990) argues that any analysis of society is incomplete if it does not include the spectrum of sexual identities that people embrace. Consider, for example, the reelection of President Obama in 2012. Political scientists have often noted the overwhelming support the president received from African Americans, Latinos, and women voters. Yet most have ignored the huge support—76 percent—that the president enjoyed among gay, lesbian, and bisexual voters. In comparison, heterosexual voters split evenly (49 percent to 49 percent nationwide) between Obama and his opponent, Mitt Romney. In the three battleground states of Florida, Ohio, and Virginia, support from gay, lesbian, and bisexual voters alone was enough to put Obama over the top. If Romney had carried just 51 percent of the gay, lesbian, and bisexual vote nationwide, he would have become the next president of the United States (Gates 2012).

USE YOUR SOCIOLOGICAL IMAGINATION

You are a sociologist who takes the conflict perspective. How would you interpret the practice of prostitution? How would your view of prostitution differ if you took the functionalist perspective? The feminist perspective? The perspective of queer theory?

Interactionist Perspective

Workers interacting on the job, encounters in public places like bus stops and parks, behavior in small groups—all these aspects of microsociology catch the attention of interactionists. Whereas functionalist and conflict theorists both analyze large-scale, society-wide patterns of behavior, theorists who take the **interactionist perspective** generalize about everyday forms of social interaction in order to explain society as a whole.

Today, given concern over traffic congestion and commuting costs, interactionists have begun to study a form of commuter behavior called "slugging." To avoid driving to work, commuters

MikeDotta/Shutterstock

Interactionists studied the new patterns of everyday behavior during the coronavirus pandemic as people wore gloves and facial coverings and maintained distances between themselves and others.

gather at certain preappointed places to seek rides from complete strangers. When a driver pulls into the parking area or vacant lot and announces his destination, the first slug in line who is headed for that destination jumps in. Rules of etiquette have emerged to smooth the social interaction between driver and passenger: neither the driver nor the passenger may eat or smoke; the slug may not adjust the windows or radio or talk on a cell phone. The presence of the slugs, who get a free ride, may allow the driver to use special lanes reserved for high-occupancy vehicles (Slug-Lines.com 2020).

Interactionism (also referred to as *symbolic interactionism*) is a sociological framework in which human beings are viewed as living in a world of meaningful objects. Those "objects" may include material things, actions, other people, relationships, and even symbols. Interactionists see symbols as an especially important part of human communication (thus the term *symbolic* interactionism). Symbols have a shared social meaning that is understood by all members of a society. In the United States, for example, a salute symbolizes respect, while a clenched fist signifies defiance. Another culture might use different gestures to convey a feeling of respect or defiance. These types of symbolic interaction are classified as forms of **nonverbal communication**, which can include many other gestures, facial expressions, and postures (Hall et al. 2019).

Manipulation of symbols can be seen in dress codes. Schools frown on students who wear clothes displaying messages that appear to endorse violence or drug and alcohol consumption. Businesses stipulate the attire employees are allowed to wear

on the job in order to impress their customers or clients. In 2018, U.S. Tennis Open officials gave a violation to a tennis player who briefly removed her shirt and revealed her sports bra on the court, after realizing the shirt was on backwards. Yet male tennis players frequently change shirts without incident. After an outcry about the differential treatment, professional tennis organizations revised their policies to be more equitable.

While the functionalist and conflict approaches were initiated in Europe, interactionism developed first in the United States. George Herbert Mead (1863–1931) is widely regarded as the founder of the interactionist perspective. Mead taught at the University of Chicago from 1893 until his death. As his teachings have become better known, sociologists have expressed greater interest in the interactionist perspective. Many have moved away from what may have been an excessive preoccupation with the macro (large-scale) level of social behavior and have redirected their attention toward behavior that occurs on the micro (small-scale) level.

Erving Goffman (1922–1982) popularized a particular type of interactionist method known as the **dramaturgical approach**, in which people are seen as theatrical performers. The dramaturgist compares everyday life to the setting of the theater and stage. Just as actors project certain images, all of us seek to present particular features of our personalities while we hide other features. Thus, in a class, we may feel the need to project a serious image; at a party, we may want to look relaxed and friendly.

Interactionists give special attention to everyday behavior that occurs in what has come to be called "the third place," as described in Box 1-1.

The Sociological Approach

Which perspective should a sociologist use in studying human behavior? Functionalist? Conflict? Interactionist? Feminist? Queer theorist? We simply cannot squeeze all sociological thinking into 4 or 5 theoretical categories—or even 10, if we include several other productive approaches. However, by studying the three major frameworks, we can better grasp how sociologists seek to explore social behavior. Table 1-2 summarizes these three broad approaches to sociological study.

Although no one approach is correct by itself, and sociologists draw on all of them for various purposes, many sociologists tend to favor one particular perspective over others. A sociologist's theoretical orientation influences his or her approach to a research problem in important ways—including the choice of what to study, how to study it, and what questions to pose (or not to pose). Box 1-2 shows how researchers would study sports from different sociological perspectives.

RESEARCH TODAY

1-1 The Third Place

For a generation, sociologists have spoken of the "**third place**," a social setting in addition to the "first place" of home and the "second place" of work. People gather routinely in the third place, typically restaurants or recreation centers or health clubs, to see familiar faces or make new friends. Will this social pattern persist? Sociologists have identified forces that both encourage and discourage it.

Free wi-fi encourages people to seek out such establishments, but do laptops truly enhance social interactions? And though talking among friends may be easy in the living-room settings that coffeehouses provide, proprietors don't always welcome these social gatherings. Some enforce anti-littering regulations or require patrons to make purchases at regular time intervals.

Still, as the second place (the workplace) becomes less relevant to growing numbers of telecommuters, the third place appears to have been growing in social significance.

Yet the coronavirus pandemic may cause some people to think twice about socializing in crowded indoor places.

In 2018, the third place dramatically came to the forefront of discussions of racism as the behavior of people who gathered there was called into question. At Yale University, a white graduate student called campus police when she found a Black female graduate student napping in her dormitory's common room. In Philadelphia, two Black men were arrested at a Starbucks when they asked to use the bathroom while

> *As the second place (the workplace) becomes less relevant to growing numbers of telecommuters, the third place may continue to grow in social significance.*

waiting for a third person to arrive for a meeting. Observers of these instances question whether police would have been summoned if the napping student or waiting men had been white. This differential behavior seemed to hearken back seventy years to a time when overt discrimination in public spaces was the norm. Because of these and other instances, organizations have sought to teach students and employees how to navigate the third place without engaging in discriminatory behavior.

LET'S DISCUSS

1. Think about acceptable third-place behavior. In what types of situations do people tend to separate by race, class, or gender in third places?
2. What third places do you visit regularly? Are some more public places than really third places?

Sources: Butler and Diaz 2016; Finlay 2020; Oldenburg 1999, 2000; Pomrenze and Simon 2018; Putnam 1995.

TABLE 1-2 MAJOR SOCIOLOGICAL PERSPECTIVES

Tracking Sociological Perspectives

	Functionalist	Conflict	Interactionist
View of Society	Stable, well integrated	Characterized by tension and struggle between groups	Active in influencing and affecting everyday social interaction
Level of Analysis Emphasized	Macro Meso Global	Macro Meso Global	Micro, as a way of understanding the larger social phenomena
Key Concepts	Manifest functions Latent functions Dysfunctions	Inequality Capitalism Stratification	Symbols Nonverbal communication Face-to-face interaction
View of the Individual	People are socialized to perform societal functions	People are shaped by power, coercion, and authority	People manipulate symbols and create their social worlds through interaction
View of the Social Order	Maintained through cooperation and consensus	Maintained through force and coercion	Maintained by shared understanding of everyday behavior
View of Social Change	Predictable, reinforcing	Change takes place all the time and may have positive consequences	Reflected in people's social positions and their communications with others
Example	Public punishments reinforce the social order	Laws reinforce the positions of those in power	People respect laws or disobey them based on their own past experience
Proponents	Émile Durkheim Talcott Parsons Robert Merton	Karl Marx W. E. B. DuBois Ida Wells-Barnett	George Herbert Mead Charles Horton Cooley Erving Goffman

RESEARCH TODAY

1-2   Looking at Sports from Five Sociological Perspectives

We watch sports. Talk sports. Spend money on sports. Some of us live and breathe sports. Because sports occupy much of our time and directly or indirectly consume and generate a great deal of money, it should not be surprising that sports have sociological components that can be analyzed from various theoretical perspectives. In this section we will look at sports from five major sociological perspectives.

FUNCTIONALIST VIEW

In examining any aspect of society, functionalists emphasize the contribution it makes to overall social stability. Functionalists regard sports as an almost religious institution that uses ritual and ceremony to reinforce the common values of a society. For example:

- Sports socialize young people into such values as competition and patriotism.
- Sports help to maintain people's physical well-being.
- Sports serve as a safety valve for both participants and spectators, who are allowed to shed tension and aggressive energy in a socially acceptable way.

- Sports bring together members of a community (who support local athletes and teams) or even a nation (during World Cup matches and the Olympics) and promote an overall feeling of unity and social solidarity.

CONFLICT VIEW

Conflict theorists argue that the social order is based on coercion and exploitation. They emphasize that sports reflect and even exacerbate many of the divisions of society:

- Sports are a form of big business in which profits are more important than the health and safety of the workers (athletes).
- Sports perpetuate the false idea that success can be achieved simply through hard work, while failure should be blamed on the individual alone (rather than on injustices in the larger social system).
- Professional athletes' behavior can promote violence and the use of performance-enhancing drugs.
- Communities divert scarce resources to subsidize the construction of professional sports facilities.

- Sports maintain the subordinate role of Blacks and Latinos, who toil as athletes but are less visible in supervisory positions as coaches, managers, and owners.
- Team logos and mascots (like the Washington Redskins) disparage American Indians.

FEMINIST VIEW

Feminist theorists consider how watching or participating in sports reinforces the roles that men and women play in the larger society:

- Although sports generally promote fitness and health, they may also have an adverse effect on participants' health. Men are more likely to resort to illegal steroid use (among bodybuilders and baseball players, for example); women, to excessive dieting (among gymnasts and figure skaters, for example).
- Gender expectations encourage female athletes to be passive and gentle, qualities that do not support the emphasis on competitiveness in sports. As a result, women find it difficult to enter sports traditionally dominated by men, such as Indy or NASCAR.
- Although professional women athletes' earnings are increasing, they typically trail those of male athletes.

Despite their differences, functionalists, conflict theorists, feminists, queer theorists, and interactionists would all agree that there is much more to sports than exercise or recreation.

QUEER THEORY

Proponents of queer theory emphasize the ways in which sports promote heterosexuality as the only acceptable sexual identity for athletes:

- Coaches and players routinely use slurs based on negative stereotypes of homosexuals to stigmatize athletes whose performance is inadequate.
- As a group, professional athletes are highly reluctant to display any sexual identity other than heterosexuality in public, for fear of damaging their careers and losing their fans and commercial sponsors.

Sergei Bachlakov/Shutterstock

Professional golfer Brooke Henderson of Canada won $1.7 million in 2019, making her the fourth most successful woman on the pro golf circuit that year. Among men, her winnings would have put her in 64th place.

- Parents who are not heterosexual encounter hostility when they try to register their children for sports or scouting programs, and are often rejected from coaching and other support roles.

INTERACTIONIST VIEW

In studying the social order, interactionists are especially interested in shared understandings of everyday behavior. Interactionists examine sports on the micro level by focusing on how day-to-day social behavior is shaped by the distinctive norms, values, and demands of the world of sports:

- Sports often heighten parent–child involvement; they may lead to parental expectations for participation, and sometimes unrealistically, for success.

- Participation in sports builds the friendship networks that permeate everyday life.
- Despite class, racial, and religious differences, teammates may work together harmoniously and may even abandon common stereotypes and prejudices.
- Relationships in the sports world are defined by people's social positions as players, coaches, and referees—as well as by the high or low status that individuals hold as a result of their performances and reputations.

Despite their differences, functionalists, conflict theorists, feminists, queer theorists, and interactionists would all agree that there is much more to sports than exercise or recreation. They would also agree that sports and other popular forms of culture are worthy subjects of serious study by sociologists.

LET'S DISCUSS

1. Have you experienced or witnessed discrimination in sports based on gender, race, or sexual identity? If so, how did you react? Has the representation of Blacks, women, or gays on teams been controversial at your school? In what ways?

2. Which of the five sociological perspectives seems most useful to you in analyzing sports? Why?

Sources: Acosta and Carpenter 2001; Eitzen 2009; Fine 1987; Sefiha 2012; Sharp et al. 2013; Young 2004; Zirin 2008.

Whatever the purpose of sociologists' work, their research will always be guided by their theoretical viewpoints. For example, sociologist Elijah Anderson (1990) embraces both the interactionist perspective and the groundbreaking work of W. E. B. DuBois. For 14 years Anderson conducted fieldwork in Philadelphia, where he studied the interactions of Black and white residents who lived in adjoining neighborhoods. In particular, he was interested in their public behavior, including their eye contact—or lack of it—as they passed one another on the street. Anderson's research tells us much about the everyday social interactions of Blacks and whites in the United States, but it does not explain the larger issues behind those interactions. Like theories, research results illuminate one part of the stage, leaving other parts in relative darkness.

THINKING CRITICALLY

Relate the toys on display in your local store to issues of race, class, and gender.

Taking Sociology with You

You've seen how sociologists employ the major sociological perspectives in their research. How does sociology relate to *you,* your own studies, and your own career? In this section you'll learn about *applied* and *clinical sociology,* two growing fields that allow sociology majors and those with advanced degrees in sociology to apply what they have learned to real-world settings. You'll also see how to develop your sociological imagination, one of the keys to thinking like a sociologist. See the appendix at the end of this chapter for more information on careers in sociology.

Applied and Clinical Sociology

Many early sociologists—notably, Jane Addams, W. E. B. DuBois, and George Herbert Mead—were strong advocates for social reform. They wanted their theories and findings to be relevant to policymakers and to people's lives in general. For instance, Mead was the treasurer of Hull House, where he applied his theory to improving the lives of those who were powerless (especially immigrants). He also served on committees dealing with Chicago's labor problems and public education. DuBois led the Atlanta Sociological Laboratory from 1895 to 1924, supporting scholars in their applied research on business, criminal justice, health care, and philanthropy (Earl Wright II 2012).

Today, **applied sociology** is the use of the discipline of sociology with the specific intent of yielding practical applications for human behavior and organizations. By extension, Michael Burawoy (2005), in his presidential address to the American Sociological Association, endorsed what he called *public sociology,* encouraging scholars to engage a broader audience in bringing about positive outcomes. In effect, the applied sociologist reaches out to others and joins them in their efforts to better society.

Often, the goal of applied or public sociology is to assist in resolving a social problem. For example, in the past 50 years, eight presidents of the United States have established commissions to delve into major societal concerns facing our nation. Sociologists are often asked to apply their expertise to studying such issues as violence, pornography, crime, immigration, and population. In Europe, both academic and government research departments are offering increasing financial support for applied studies.

One example of applied sociology is the growing interest in learning more about local communities. Since its founding in 1994, the Northeast Florida Center for Community Initiatives

Ian Hooton/SPL/Alamy Stock Photo

The Center for Community Initiatives's Magnolia Project, an example of applied sociology, aims to decrease high rates of infant mortality.

(CCI), based at the University of North Florida in Jacksonville, has conducted several community studies, including a homeless census and survey, an analysis of the economic impact of the arts in Jacksonville, and a long-term survey of the effects of Hurricane Katrina. Typical of applied sociology, these outreach efforts are collaborative, involving faculty, undergraduate and graduate students, volunteers, and community residents (Center for Community Initiatives 2014).

Another of CCI's applications of sociology, the Magnolia Project, is based in a storefront clinic in an underprivileged area of Jacksonville. Part of the federal Healthy Start initiative, which aims to decrease high infant mortality rates, the project serves women of childbearing age who have little or no regular access to health care. CCI's responsibilities include (1) interviewing and surveying key community participants, (2) coordinating data collection by the project's staff, (3) analyzing data, and (4) preparing progress reports for funding agencies and community partners. Through June 2014, not a single infant death had occurred among the 662 participants in the program (Center for Community Initiatives 2014).

Growing interest in applied sociology has led to such specializations as *medical sociology* and *environmental sociology.* The former includes research on how health care professionals and patients deal with disease. To give one example, medical sociologists have studied the social impact of the AIDS crisis and the coronavirus pandemic on families, friends, and communities (see Chapter 15). Environmental sociologists examine the relationship between human societies and the physical environment. One focus of their work is the issue of "environmental justice" (see Chapter 15), raised when researchers and community activists found that hazardous waste dumps are especially likely to be situated in poor and minority neighborhoods (M. Martin 1996).

The growing popularity of applied sociology has led to the rise of the specialty of clinical sociology. Louis Wirth (1931) wrote about clinical sociology almost 90 years ago, but the term itself has become popular only in recent years. While applied sociology may simply evaluate social issues, **clinical sociology** is dedicated to facilitating change by altering social relationships (as in family therapy) or restructuring social institutions (as in the reorganization of a medical center).

Applied sociologists generally leave it to policymakers to act on their evaluations. In contrast, clinical sociologists take direct responsibility for implementation and view those with whom they work as their clients. This specialty has become increasingly attractive to graduate students in sociology because it offers an opportunity to apply intellectual learning in a practical way. A shrinking job market in the academic world has made such alternative career routes appealing.

Applied and clinical sociology can be contrasted with **basic sociology** (also called *pure sociology*), which seeks a more profound knowledge of the fundamental aspects of social phenomena. This type of research is not necessarily meant to generate specific applications, although such ideas may result once findings are analyzed. When Durkheim studied suicide rates, he was not primarily interested in discovering a way to eliminate suicide. In this sense, his research was an example of basic rather than applied sociology.

Developing a Sociological Imagination

In this book, we will be illustrating the sociological imagination in several different ways—by showing theory in practice and in current research; by noting the ways in which electronic devices and apps are changing our social behavior; by thinking globally; by exploring the significance of social inequality; by speaking across race, gender, and religious boundaries; and by highlighting social policy throughout the world.

Theory in Practice We will illustrate how the major sociological perspectives can be helpful in understanding today's issues, from capital punishment to abortion. Sociologists do not necessarily declare, "Here I am using functionalism," but their research

Source: ©Milt Priggee, Puget Sound Business Journal, June 27, 2005.

The interconnectedness across the world makes globalization increasingly important to many aspects of daily life.

and approaches do tend to draw on one or more theoretical frameworks, as will become clear in the pages to follow.

Research Today Sociologists actively investigate a variety of issues and social behavior. We have already seen that research can shed light on the social factors that affect suicide rates. Sociological research often plays a direct role in improving people's lives, as in the case of increasing the participation of African Americans in diabetes testing. Throughout the rest of the book, the research performed by sociologists and other social scientists will shed light on group behavior of all types.

Our Wired World "What is the news today?" For many people, "the news" means the latest comments, pictures, and videos posted online by friends and acquaintances. For some, such up-to-the-minute connectivity has become addictive. Sociologists see the "third place" as reflecting both face-to-face social interaction *and* as a place where people gather together, each with his or her face buried in a smartphone or laptop.

Thinking Globally Whatever their theoretical perspective or research techniques, sociologists recognize that social behavior must be viewed in a global context. **Globalization** is the worldwide integration of government policies, cultures, social movements, and financial markets through trade and the exchange of ideas. Although public discussion of globalization is relatively recent, intellectuals have been pondering both its negative and positive social consequences for a long time. Karl Marx and Friedrich Engels warned in *The Communist Manifesto* (written in 1848) of a world market that would lead to production in distant lands, sweeping away existing working relationships.

In the chapter-opening excerpt from *Outcasts United,* Warren St. John might have been focusing on a small Georgia town, but the key players on the team he described were from Liberia, Iraq, Sudan, Burundi, Congo, and Jordan. Such diversity is increasingly common throughout the United States. Locally, this diversity serves to globalize local communities; it also reflects major societal events and movements throughout the world (Fiss and Hirsch 2005).

Another aspect of the world landscape is the growing role of influencers, as described in Box 1-3.

The Significance of Social Inequality

Who holds power? Who doesn't? Who has prestige? Who lacks it? Perhaps the major theme of analysis in sociology today is **social inequality**, a condition in which members of society have differing amounts of wealth, prestige, or power. The impact of Hurricane Katrina on residents of the Gulf Coast drew attention to social inequality in the United States. Predictably, the people who were hit the hardest by the massive storm were the poor, who had the greatest difficulty evacuating before the storm and have had the most difficulty recovering from it.

Some sociologists, in seeking to understand the effects of inequality, have made the case for social justice. W. E. B. DuBois ([1940] 1968:418) noted that the greatest power in the land is not "thought or ethics, but wealth." As we have seen, the contributions of Karl Marx, Jane Addams, and Ida Wells-Barnett also stressed this belief in the overarching significance of social inequality, and by extension, social justice. In this book, social inequality will be the central focus of Chapters 8 and 9, and sociologists' work on inequality will be highlighted throughout.

Speaking across Race, Gender, and Religious Boundaries

Sociologists include both men and women, who come from a variety of ethnic, national, and religious origins. In their work, sociologists seek to draw conclusions that speak to all people—not just the affluent or powerful. Doing so is not always easy. Insights into how a corporation can increase its profits tend to attract more attention and financial support than do, say, the merits of a needle exchange program for low-income inner-city residents. Yet today more than ever, sociology seeks to better understand the experiences of all people.

Sociologists have noted, for example, that the huge tsunami that hit South Asia in 2004 affected men and women differently. When the waves hit, mothers and grandmothers

SOCIOLOGY IN THE GLOBAL COMMUNITY

1-3   Influencers Worldwide

Generations ago people such as Winston Churchill and Mahatma Gandhi came to mind as individuals whose worldviews reached millions. Today it is the likes of Ryan, a U.S. elementary school student who demonstrates and evaluates toys, football (soccer) star Crisrtian Ronaldo, and Australian personal trainer Kayla Isines.

An **influencer** is a social media user who has established credibility in a specific industry, has access to a huge audience, and can persuade others to act based on his or her recommendations. Unlike most world leaders, influencers churn out content 24/7 on such platforms as YouTube, TikTok, or Instagram.

Influencers achieve their world mark by different means. Some are brilliant thinkers who offer insights into a broad range of issues or use their celebrity status to bring attention to selected social causes. Others are conventionally attractive, good at video games, excel at sports, or set fashion trends.

Typically they begin by posting content and trying to create a group following; for some online users, they become significant influencers in their own niche, whether cooking Greek dishes or attempting to scale climbing walls. As their numbers of followers grow, they become entrepreneurs, hiring staff and managing budgets. This does not go unnoticed by corporations: soon consumer brands sponsor them to highlight products. In some respects, these social media stars

achieve the kind of celebrity that movie stars had in the past.

Sociologists acknowledge that influencers, like all leaders, can produce negative consequences, such as those who espouse prejudicial views or incite violence against some group. Another quite different concern is the creation of nonhuman, digitally created influencers. Sometimes it is good fun, as viewers typically are aware they are interacting with a digital creation, but some nonhuman influencers are made to mislead and misinform the online community. After two years of concealing "her" nonhuman origins, Lil Miquela, a Brazilian American, became such an online celebrity that Prada and Nike sponsored.

LET'S DISCUSS

1. Who do you consider to be important influencers? In what fields do they exercise influence?
2. What are the potential consequences if an influencer sponsors a company's products? Can this happen without followers' being aware of the sponsorship?

Sources: Grygiel 2016; Guttman 2019; Roose 2019.

Oupa Bopape/Gallo Images via Getty Images

Influencers, including South African designer Paledi Segapo, are now integral to global social media.

Today global influencers reach across societies and are increasingly being monetized by commercial enterprises, at the same time they are becoming more and more entrenched in our daily interactions.

---

were at home with the children; men were outside working, where they were more likely to become aware of the impending disaster. Moreover, most of the men knew how to swim, a survival skill that women in these traditional societies usually do not learn. As a result, many more men than women survived the catastrophe—about 10 men for every 1 woman. In one Indonesian village typical of the disaster area, 97 of 1,300 people survived; only 4 were women. The impact of this gender imbalance will be felt for some time, given women's primary role as caregivers for children and the elderly within Indonesian culture (BBC News 2005).

Social Policy throughout the World   One important way we can use a sociological imagination is to enhance our understanding of current social issues throughout the world. Beginning with Chapter 2, each chapter will conclude with a discussion of a contemporary social policy issue. In some cases we will examine a specific issue facing national governments.

For example, government funding of child care centers will be discussed in Chapter 4, Socialization and the Life Course; global immigration in Chapter 10, Racial and Ethnic Inequality; and religion in the schools in Chapter 13, Education and Religion. These Social Policy sections will demonstrate how fundamental sociological concepts can enhance our critical thinking skills and help us to better understand current public policy debates taking place around the world.

In addition, sociology has been used to evaluate the success of programs or the impact of changes brought about by policymakers and political activists. For example, Chapter 9, Global Inequality, includes a discussion of research on the effectiveness of welfare programs. Such discussions underscore the many practical applications of sociological theory and research.

Sociologists expect the next quarter century to be perhaps the most exciting and critical period in the history of the discipline. That is because of a growing recognition—both in the

United States and around the world—that current social problems must be addressed before their magnitude overwhelms human societies. We can expect sociologists to play an increasing role in government by researching and developing public policy alternatives. It seems only natural for this textbook to focus on the connection between the work of sociologists and the difficult questions confronting policymakers and people in the United States and around the world.

THINKING CRITICALLY

What issues facing your local community would you like to address with applied sociological research? Do you see any global connections to these local issues?

APPENDIX Careers in Sociology

For the past two decades, more than 25,000 college students have graduated annually with a bachelor's degree in sociology. In this appendix we'll consider some of the options these students have after completing their education.

How do students first learn about the sociological perspective on society? Some may take a sociology course in high school. Others may study sociology at community college, where 40 percent of all college students in the United States are enrolled. Indeed, many future sociology majors first develop their sociological imaginations at a community college.

An undergraduate degree in sociology doesn't just serve as excellent preparation for future graduate work in sociology. It also provides a strong liberal arts background for entry-level positions in business, social services, foundations, community organizations, not-for-profit groups, law enforcement, and many government jobs. A number of fields—among them marketing, public relations, and broadcasting—now require investigative skills and an understanding of the diverse groups found in today's multiethnic and multinational environment. Moreover, a sociology degree requires accomplishment in oral and written communication, interpersonal skills, problem solving, ability to work in a team, organizational skills, data analysis, and critical thinking—all job-related skills that may give sociology graduates an advantage over those who pursue more technical degrees (Hecht 2016).

Consequently, while few occupations specifically require an undergraduate degree in sociology, such academic training can be an important asset in entering a wide range of occupations. To emphasize this point, a number of chapters in this book highlight a real-life professional who describes how the study of sociology has helped in his or her career. For example, in Chapter 6 a Taking Sociology to Work box explains how a college graduate uses her training in sociology as a social media manager for nonprofit organizations. And in Chapter 14, another Taking Sociology to Work box shows how a recent graduate uses the skill set he acquired as a sociology major in his role as a government analyst.

Figure 1-2 summarizes the sources of employment for those with BA or BS degrees in sociology. It shows that fields including nonprofit organizations, education, business, and government offer major career opportunities for sociology graduates. Undergraduates who know where their career interests lie are well advised to enroll in sociology courses and specialties best suited to those interests. For example, students hoping to become health planners would take a class in medical sociology; students seeking employment as social science research assistants would focus on courses in statistics and methods. Internships, such as placements at city planning agencies and survey research organizations, afford another way for sociology students to prepare for careers. Studies show that students who choose an internship placement have less trouble finding jobs, obtain better jobs, and

FIGURE 1-2 OCCUPATIONS OF GRADUATING SOCIOLOGY MAJORS

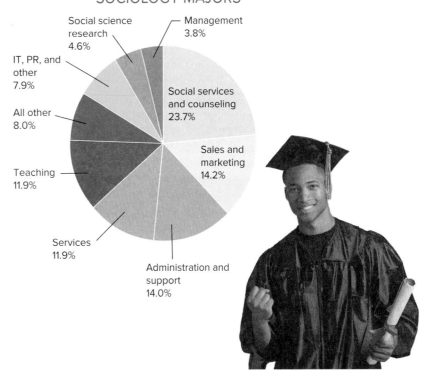

Social science research 4.6%

Management 3.8%

IT, PR, and other 7.9%

Social services and counseling 23.7%

All other 8.0%

Sales and marketing 14.2%

Teaching 11.9%

Services 11.9%

Administration and support 14.0%

Note: Based on a national survey of current occupation in 2013 of 759 graduates with a sociology major in the Class of 2012.

Source: Spalter-Roth et al. 2013. *Photo:* Flashon Studio/Shutterstock

Aleksei Ivanov/123RF

One year after graduation, one out of four sociology majors was employed in the social services as a counselor, child advocate, forensic interviewer, program director, or caseworker.

enjoy greater job satisfaction than students without internship placements. Finally, students should expect to change fields during their first five years of employment after graduation—for example, from sales and marketing to management (American Sociological Association 2013; Salem and Grabarek 1986).

Many college students view social work as the field most closely associated with sociology. Traditionally, social workers received their undergraduate training in sociology and allied fields such as psychology and counseling. After some practical experience, social workers would generally seek a master's degree in social work (MSW) to be considered for supervisory or administrative positions. Today, however, some students choose (where it is available) to pursue a bachelor's degree in social work (BSW). This degree prepares graduates for direct service positions, such as caseworker or group worker.

Many students continue their sociological training beyond the bachelor's degree. More than 190 universities in the United States have graduate programs in sociology that offer PhD and/or master's degrees. These programs differ greatly in their areas of specialization, course requirements, costs, and the research and teaching opportunities available to graduate students. About 61 percent of doctoral graduates are women (American Sociological Association 2020b).

Higher education is an important source of employment for sociologists with graduate degrees. Recently, 85 percent of recent PhD recipients in sociology have sought employment in colleges and universities. These sociologists teach not only majors who are committed to the discipline but also students hoping to become doctors, nurses, lawyers, police officers, and so forth (National Science Foundation 2019).

Sociologists who teach in colleges and universities may use their knowledge and training to influence public policy. For example, sociologist Andrew Cherlin (2003) commented on the debate over whether to provide federal funding to promote marriage among welfare recipients. Citing the results of two of his studies, Cherlin questioned the potential effectiveness of such a policy in strengthening

low-income families. Because many single mothers choose to marry someone other than the father of their children—sometimes for good reason—their children often grow up in stepfamilies. Cherlin's research shows that children who are raised in stepfamilies are no better off than those in single-parent families. He sees government efforts to promote marriage as a politically motivated attempt to foster traditional social values in a society that has become increasingly diverse.

For sociology graduates who are interested in academic careers, the road to a PhD (or doctorate) can be long and difficult. This degree symbolizes competence in original research; each candidate must prepare a book-length study known as a dissertation. Typically, a doctoral student in sociology will engage in four to seven years of intensive work, including the time required to complete the dissertation. Yet even this effort is no guarantee of a job as a sociology professor.

The demand for college instructors is projected to grow 15 percent from 2016 to 2026, faster than the average for all occupations, but the majority of this employment growth is likely to be part-time positions. Anyone who launches an academic career must be prepared for considerable uncertainty and competition in the college job market (Bureau of Labor Statistics 2019a).

Of course, not all people who work as sociologists teach or hold doctoral degrees. Take government, for example. The Census Bureau relies on people with sociological training to interpret data for other government agencies and the general public. Virtually every agency depends on survey research—a field in which sociology students can specialize—in order to assess everything from community needs to the morale of the agency's workers. In addition, people with sociological training can put their academic knowledge to effective use in probation and parole, health sciences, community development, and recreational services. Some people working in government or private industry have a master's degree (MA or MS) in sociology; others have a bachelor's degree (BA or BS).

Currently, about 15 percent of the members of the American Sociological Association use their sociological skills outside the academic world, whether in social service agencies or in marketing positions for business firms. Increasing numbers of sociologists with graduate degrees are employed by businesses, industry, hospitals, and nonprofit organizations. Studies show that many sociology graduates are making career changes from social service areas to business and commerce. For an undergraduate major, sociology is excellent preparation for employment in many parts of the business world (Spalter-Roth et al. 2013).

Whether you take a few courses in sociology or complete a degree, you will benefit from the critical thinking skills developed in this discipline. Sociologists emphasize the value of being able to analyze, interpret, and function within a variety of working situations—an asset in virtually any career. Moreover, given rapid technological change and the expanding global economy, all of us will need to adapt to substantial social change, even in our own careers. Sociology provides a rich conceptual framework that can serve as a foundation for flexible career development and assist you in taking advantage of new employment opportunities.

MASTERING THIS CHAPTER

Summary

Sociology is the scientific study of social behavior and human groups. This chapter examines the nature of sociological theory, the founders of the discipline, theoretical perspectives in contemporary sociology, practical applications for sociological theory and research, and ways to exercise the *sociological imagination*.

1. The **sociological imagination** is an awareness of the relationship between an individual and the wider society. It is based on the ability to view our own society as an outsider might, rather than from the perspective of our limited experiences and cultural biases.

2. In contrast to other **social sciences**, sociology emphasizes the influence that groups can have on people's behavior and attitudes and the ways in which people shape society.

3. Knowledge that relies on common sense is not always reliable. Sociologists must test and analyze each piece of information they use.

4. Sociologists employ **theories** to examine relationships between observations or data that may seem completely unrelated.

5. Nineteenth-century thinkers who contributed sociological insights included Auguste Comte, a French philosopher; Harriet Martineau, an English sociologist; and Herbert Spencer, an English scholar.

6. Other important figures in the development of sociology were Émile Durkheim, who pioneered work on suicide; Max Weber, who taught the need for insight in intellectual work; Karl Marx, who emphasized the importance of the economy and social conflict; and W. E. B. DuBois, who advocated the usefulness of both basic and applied research in combating prejudice and fostering racial tolerance and justice.

7. In the 20th century, the discipline of sociology was indebted to the U.S. sociologists Charles Horton Cooley and Robert Merton, as well as to the French sociologist Pierre Bourdieu.

8. **Macrosociology** concentrates on large-scale phenomena or entire civilizations; **microsociology** stresses the study of small groups. **Mesosociology** is an intermediate level of analysis that focuses on formal organizations and social movements. **Global sociology** compares nations or entire societies.

9. The **functionalist perspective** emphasizes the way in which the parts of a society are structured to maintain its stability.

10. The **conflict perspective** assumes that social behavior is best understood in terms of conflict or tension between competing groups.

11. The **feminist perspective**, which is often allied with the conflict perspective, sees inequity in gender as central to all behavior and organization.

12. **Queer theory** stresses that to fully understand society, scholars must study it from the perspective of a range of sexual identities, rather than exclusively from a "normal" heterosexual point of view.

13. The **interactionist perspective** is concerned primarily with fundamental or everyday forms of interaction, including symbols and other types of **nonverbal communication**.

14. Sociologists make use of all five perspectives, since each offers unique insights into the same issue.

15. **Applied** and **clinical sociology** apply the discipline of sociology to the solution of practical problems in human behavior and organizations. In contrast, **basic sociology** is sociological inquiry that seeks only a deeper knowledge of the fundamental aspects of social phenomena.

16. This textbook makes use of the sociological imagination by showing theory in practice and in current research; by noting the ways in which electronic devices and apps are changing our social behavior; by thinking globally; by focusing on the significance of social inequality; by speaking across race, gender, and religious boundaries; and by highlighting social policy around the world.

Key Terms

Anomie Durkheim's term for the loss of direction felt in a society when social control of individual behavior has become ineffective. (page 9)

Applied sociology The use of the discipline of sociology with the specific intent of yielding practical applications for human behavior and organizations. (19)

Basic sociology Sociological inquiry conducted with the objective of gaining a more profound knowledge of the fundamental aspects of social phenomena. Also known as *pure sociology*. (20)

Clinical sociology The use of the discipline of sociology with the specific intent of altering social relationships or restructuring social institutions. (20)

Conflict perspective A sociological approach that assumes that social behavior is best understood in terms of tension between groups over power or the allocation of resources, including housing, money, access to services, and political representation. (14)

Cultural capital Noneconomic goods, such as family background and education, which are reflected in a knowledge of language and the arts. (12)

Double consciousness The division of an individual's identity into two or more social realities. (11)

Dramaturgical approach A view of social interaction, popularized by Erving Goffman, in which people are seen as theatrical performers. (16)

Dysfunction An element or process of a society that may disrupt the social system or reduce its stability. (14)

Feminist perspective A sociological approach that views inequity in gender as central to all behavior and organization. (15)

Functionalist perspective A sociological approach that emphasizes the way in which the parts of a society are structured to maintain its stability. (13)

Global sociology A level of sociological analysis that makes comparisons between entire nations, using entire societies as units of analysis. (12)

Globalization The worldwide integration of government policies, cultures, social movements, and financial markets through trade and the exchange of ideas. (21)

Ideal type A construct or model for evaluating specific cases. (9)

Influencer A social media user who has established credibility in a specific industry, such as fashion or electronics or toys. (22)

Interactionist perspective A sociological approach that generalizes about everyday forms of social interaction in order to explain society as a whole. (16)

Latent function An unconscious or unintended function that may reflect hidden purposes. (14)

Macrosociology Sociological investigation that concentrates on large-scale phenomena or entire civilizations. (12)

Manifest function An open, stated, and conscious function. (14)

Mesosociology An intermediate level of sociological analysis that focuses on formal organizations and social movements. (12)

Microsociology Sociological investigation that stresses the study of small groups, often through experimental means. (12)

Natural science The study of the physical features of nature and the ways in which they interact and change. (3)

Nonverbal communication The sending of messages through the use of gestures, facial expressions, and postures. (16)

Queer theory The study of society from the perspective of a broad spectrum of sexual identities, including heterosexuality, homosexuality, and bisexuality. (15)

Science The body of knowledge obtained by methods based on systematic observation. (3)

Social capital The collective benefit of social networks, which are built on reciprocal trust. (12)

Social inequality A condition in which members of society have differing amounts of wealth, prestige, or power. (21)

Social science The study of the social features of humans and the ways in which they interact and change. (3)

Sociological imagination An awareness of the relationship between an individual and the wider society, both today and in the past. (3)

Sociology The scientific study of social behavior and human groups. (3)

Theory In sociology, a set of statements that seeks to explain problems, actions, or behavior. (6)

Third place A social setting in addition to the "first place" of home and the "second place" of work where people routinely gather. (17)

Verstehen The German word for "understanding" or "insight"; used by Max Weber to stress the need for sociologists to take into account the subjective meanings people attach to their actions. (9)

TAKING SOCIOLOGY with you

1. Watch a movie about a natural disaster. Make note of the government's response. What sociological factors were or should have been considered in the response? What plans do you think a government should put into place if the same or a similar disaster occurs in real life? Why? Share your ideas with the class.

2. Over the next week, look for consumer brands that are being promoted by influencers on social media and video streaming sites that you frequent. What products are being promoted in association with each influencer? Are the products promoted through ads or are they getting mentioned by the influencer? Which promotional approach do you find most convincing? Why? Discuss your findings with the class.

3. Over the next week or so, take notice of different family members' "second and third places." (See page 17.) What everyday behaviors do they exhibit within each of these settings? In what ways do these behaviors differ from setting to setting? How can the differences be explained? Share your findings with the class.

4. **Writing Sociology** Choose a topic of interest to you from Table 1-1: Sections of the American Sociological Association on page 5 to research. Write a report about the topic and share it with the class.

Self-Quiz

Read each question carefully and then select the best answer.

1. Sociology is
   a. very narrow in scope.
   b. concerned with what one individual does or does not do.
   c. the systematic study of social behavior and human groups.
   d. the study of interactions between two individuals at a time.

2. Which of the following thinkers introduced the concept of the sociological imagination?
   a. Émile Durkheim
   b. Max Weber
   c. Karl Marx
   d. C. Wright Mills

3. Émile Durkheim's research on suicide suggested that
   a. people with religious affiliations had a higher suicide rate than those who were unaffiliated.
   b. suicide rates seemed to be higher in times of peace than in times of war and revolution.
   c. civilians were more likely to take their lives than soldiers.
   d. suicide is a solitary act, unrelated to group life.

4. Max Weber taught his students that they should employ which of the following in their intellectual work?
   a. anomie
   b. *verstehen*
   c. the sociological imagination
   d. microsociology

5. Robert Merton's contributions to sociology include
   a. successfully combining theory and research.
   b. producing a theory that is one of the most frequently cited explanations of deviant behavior.
   c. an attempt to bring macro-level and micro-level analyses together.
   d. all of the above

6. Which sociologist made a major contribution to society through his in-depth studies of urban life, including both Blacks and whites?
   a. W. E. B. DuBois
   b. Robert Merton
   c. Auguste Comte
   d. Charles Horton Cooley

7. In the late 19th century, before the term "feminist view" was even coined, the ideas behind this major theoretical approach appeared in the writings of
   a. Karl Marx.
   b. Ida Wells-Barnett.
   c. Charles Horton Cooley.
   d. Pierre Bourdieu.

8. Thinking of society as a living organism in which each part of the organism contributes to its survival is a reflection of which theoretical perspective?
   a. the functionalist perspective
   b. the conflict perspective
   c. the feminist perspective
   d. the interactionist perspective

9. Karl Marx's view of the struggle between social classes inspired the contemporary
   a. functionalist perspective.
   b. conflict perspective.
   c. interactionist perspective.
   d. dramaturgical approach.

10. Erving Goffman's dramaturgical approach, which postulates that people present certain aspects of their personalities while obscuring other aspects, is a derivative of which major theoretical perspective?
    a. the functionalist perspective
    b. the conflict perspective
    c. the feminist perspective
    d. the interactionist perspective

11. Within sociology, a(n) _____ is a set of statements that seeks to explain problems, actions, or behavior.

12. In _____ _____'s hierarchy of the sciences, sociology was the "queen," and its practitioners were "scientist-priests."

13. In *Society in America*, originally published in 1837, English scholar _____ _____ examined religion, politics, child rearing, and immigration in the young nation.

14. _____ _____ adapted Charles Darwin's evolutionary view of the "survival of the fittest" by arguing that it is "natural" that some people are rich while others are poor.

15. Sociologist Max Weber coined the term _____ _____ in referring to a construct or model that serves as a measuring rod against which actual cases can be evaluated.

16. In *The Communist Manifesto*, _____ _____ and _____ _____ argued that the masses of people who have no resources other than their labor (the proletariat) should unite to fight for the overthrow of capitalist societies.

17. _____ _____ , an early female sociologist, cofounded the famous Chicago settlement house called Hull House and also tried to establish a juvenile court system.

18. The university's role in certifying academic competence and excellence is an example of a(n) _____ function.

19. The _____ _____ draws on the work of Karl Marx and Friedrich Engels in that it often views women's subordination as inherent in capitalist societies.

20. Looking at society from the broad spectrum of sexual identity, including heterosexuality, homosexuality, and bisexuality, is called _____ theory.

Answers

1 (c); 2 (d); 3 (b); 4 (b); 5 (d); 6 (a); 7 (b); 8 (a); 9 (b); 10 (d) 11 theory; 12 Auguste Comte; 13 Harriet Martineau; 14 Herbert Spencer; 15 ideal type; 16 Karl Marx, Friedrich Engels; 17 Jane Addams; 18 manifest; 19 feminist perspective; 20 queer

2 Sociological Research

Mario Tama/Getty Images

A volunteer interviews a man who is homeless on a New York City subway in the early morning hours. Surveys are just one of the methods sociologists use to collect data.

▶ INSIDE

What Is the Scientific Method?

Major Research Designs

Ethics of Research

Feminist Methodology

Queer Theory and Methodology

The Data-Rich Future

Social Policy and Sociological Research: Studying Human Sexuality

Appendix I: Using Statistics and Graphs

Appendix II: Writing a Research Report

How do sociologists provide useful information about public health concerns?

Sociologist Helen Keane and her colleagues explore the reasons why people engage in the use of e-cigarettes or vaping. Read on to see what they learned.

AleksandrYu/iStockphoto/Getty Images

66 The use of e-cigarettes has increased dramatically over the past decade. . . .

Two opposing discourses characterise this debate. The currently dominant view is that e-cigarettes present a threat to health both through their ability to produce and/or maintain addiction in users and their potential to undermine the denormalisation of smoking tobacco. Their appeal to children is frequently invoked, and the fact that tobacco companies are buying into the e-cigarette market exacerbates these concerns. On the other hand, e-cigarettes have also been incorporated into a discourse of tobacco harm reduction, including discussions of 'endgame' strategies for smoking. From this perspective, e-cigarettes represent an opportunity to improve health by providing a less harmful way of consuming nicotine, which is appealing to smokers who have failed to quit using conventional methods.

The researchers monitored an online vaper forum and then asked vapers to 'tell us anything you would like to about personal vaporisers' (PVs). There were 705 responses used in their final analysis, and 97 percent of respondents reported that they had been daily smokers before using e-cigarettes.

The survey provided insights into the transmission of vaping as a social practice. The survey responses suggested that vaping is being spread efficiently through word of mouth or personal contact. Many respondents mentioned being introduced to vaping by a friend or family member. Several respondents received a gift of a PV starter kit as a form of intervention by a concerned non-vaping friend or family member.

Others mentioned curiosity, piqued by seeing people vaping or hearing about the new technology, as the precursor to vaping.

Other people were talking about it so I thought I would give it a try. Wasn't really thinking about giving up smoking as such.

From the dominant public health perspective this kind of spread through social contacts is readily interpreted as the spectre of contagion and proof of vaping's capacity to renormalise nicotine consumption. But to these vapers it is understood as a positive process in which useful knowledge is shared, friendship and care communicated, and the social elements of the practice reinforced. . . .

Vapers expressed a sense of liberation which was not just about escape from an unwanted habit but from a depressing pattern of repeated experiences of failure.

Since using these devices and quitting smoking, I don't get out of bed and cough till I wretch. I am no longer short of breath with a feeling of doom that lung cancer will destroy my life . . . I can now enjoy the pleasant effects of nicotine without the fear that it is killing me. I can still have the punctuation marks of the day but without the stink, ill health, burns in the carpet, dirty ashtrays etc. . . .

For some, the devices had an almost magical quality in that they transformed the sick, guilty and unhappy smoker into the healthy happy vaper without the suffering and struggle associated with previous quit attempts. 99

Source: Keane et al. 2017.

For some, the devices had an almost magical quality in that they transformed the sick, guilty and unhappy smoker into the healthy happy vaper without the suffering and struggle associated with previous quit attempts.

By engaging users of e-cigarettes, the researchers were able to inform public health discussions by showing that many vapers see their practice as healthy or at least as healthier than reliance on tobacco products. The researchers found that users see vaping as somehow more socially acceptable and "cleaner." As public health concerns about vaping grow, and efforts increase to discourage the practice, public health officials will need research such as this from sociologists to better understand what motivates vaping.

Among the insights that such sociological research has revealed is that young people, especially teens, do not recognize that using e-cigarette products from Juul Labs is vaping. When asked whether they use nicotine products or vape, many use the term "Juuling" to describe what they are

doing, and may not even recognize that they are vaping (Edney 2019).

Effective sociological research can be quite thought-provoking. It may suggest many new questions that require further study, such as why we make assumptions about people who engage in atypical behaviors like self-injury. In some cases, rather than raising additional questions, a study will simply confirm previous beliefs and findings. Sociological research can also have practical applications. For instance, research results that disconfirm accepted beliefs about marriage and the family may lead to changes in public policy.

This chapter will examine the research process used in conducting sociological studies. How do sociologists go about setting up a research project? How do they ensure that the results of the research are reliable and accurate? Can they carry out their research without violating the rights of those they study?

We will look first at the steps that make up the scientific method used in research. Then we will look at various techniques commonly used in sociological research, such as experiments, observations, and surveys. We will pay particular attention to the ethical challenges sociologists face in studying human behavior, and to the debate raised by Max Weber's call for "value neutrality" in social science research. We will also examine feminists' and queer theorists' methodologies and the role technology plays in research today.

Though sociological researchers can study almost any subject, in this chapter we will concentrate on two in particular. The first is the relationship of education to income, which we will use as an example in the section on the scientific method. The second is the controversial subject of human sexual behavior. Like self-injury, sexual behavior is private and personal, and therefore hard to study. The Social Policy section that closes this chapter describes the difficulties and challenges of researching closely guarded sexual behaviors.

Whatever the area of sociological inquiry and whatever the perspective of the sociologist—whether functionalist, conflict, feminist, queer theorist, interactionist, or any other—there is one crucial requirement: imaginative, responsible research that meets the highest scientific and ethical standards.

What Is the Scientific Method?

Like all of us, sociologists are interested in the central questions of our time: Is the family falling apart? Why is there so much crime in the United States? Can the world feed a growing population? Such issues concern most people, whether or not they have academic training. However, unlike the typical citizen, the sociologist has a commitment to use the **scientific method** in studying society. The scientific method is a systematic, organized series of steps that ensures maximum objectivity and consistency in researching a problem.

Many of us will never actually conduct scientific research. Why, then, is it important that we understand the scientific method? The answer is that it plays a major role in the workings of our society. Residents of the United States are constantly bombarded with "facts" or "data." A television news report informs us that "one in every two marriages in this country now ends in divorce," yet as Chapter 12 will show, that assertion is based on misleading statistics. Almost daily, advertisers cite supposedly scientific studies to prove that their products are superior. Such claims may be accurate or exaggerated. We can better evaluate such information—and will not be fooled so easily—if we are familiar with the standards of scientific research.

These standards are quite stringent, and they demand as strict adherence as possible. The scientific method requires precise preparation in developing research. Otherwise, the research data collected may not prove accurate. Sociologists and other researchers follow five basic steps in the scientific method: (1) defining the problem, (2) reviewing the literature, (3) formulating the hypothesis, (4) selecting the research design and then collecting and analyzing data, and (5) developing the conclusion (Figure 2-1). After reaching the conclusion, researchers write a report on their study. Often the report will begin with an *executive summary* of the method they followed and their conclusion. In the sections that follow, we'll use an actual example to illustrate the scientific method.

FIGURE 2-1   THE SCIENTIFIC METHOD

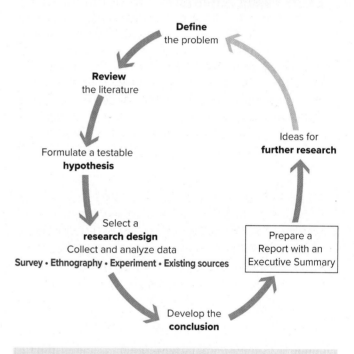

The scientific method allows sociologists to objectively and logically evaluate the data they collect. Their findings can suggest ideas for further sociological research.

Defining the Problem

Does it "pay" to go to college? Some people make great sacrifices and work hard to get a college education. Parents borrow money for their children's tuition. Students work part-time jobs or even take full-time positions while attending evening or weekend classes. Does it pay off? Are there monetary returns for getting that degree?

The first step in any research project is to state as clearly as possible what you hope to investigate—that is, *define the problem*. In this instance, we are interested in knowing how schooling relates to income. We want to find out the earnings of people with different levels of formal schooling.

Early on, any social science researcher must develop an operational definition of each concept being studied. An **operational definition** is an explanation of an abstract concept that is specific enough to allow a researcher to assess the concept. For example, a sociologist interested in status might use membership in exclusive social clubs as an operational definition of status. Someone studying prejudice might consider a person's unwillingness to hire or work with members of minority groups as an operational definition of prejudice. In our example, we need to develop two operational definitions—education and earnings—in order to study whether it pays to get an advanced educational degree. We'll define *education* as the number of years of schooling a person has achieved and *earnings* as the income a person reports having received in the past year.

Jason Lindsey/Alamy Stock Photo

It seems reasonable that these graduates of Fort Bethold Community College on the Fort Bethold Reservation, North Dakota, will earn more income than high school graduates. How would you go about testing that hypothesis?

Reviewing the Literature

By conducting a *review of the literature*—examining relevant scholarly studies and information—researchers refine the problem under study, clarify possible techniques to be used in collecting data, and eliminate or reduce avoidable mistakes. In our example, we would examine information about the salaries for different occupations. We would see if jobs that require more academic training are better rewarded. It would also be appropriate to review other studies on the relationship between education and income.

The review of the literature would soon tell us that many factors besides years of schooling influence earning potential. For example, we would learn that the children of rich parents are more likely to go to college than those of poor parents, so we might consider the possibility that rich parents may later help their children to secure better-paying jobs.

We might also look at macro-level data, such as state-by-state comparisons of income and educational levels. In one macro-level study based on census data, researchers found that in states whose residents have a relatively high level of education, household income levels are high as well (Figure 2-2). This finding suggests that schooling may well be related to income, though it does not speak to the micro-level relationship we are interested in. That is, we want to know whether *individuals* who are well educated are also well paid.

Formulating the Hypothesis

After reviewing earlier research and drawing on the contributions of sociological theorists, the researchers may then *formulate the hypothesis*. A **hypothesis** is a speculative statement about the relationship between two or more factors known as variables. Income, religion, occupation, and gender

can all serve as variables in a study. We can define a **variable** as a measurable trait or characteristic that is subject to change under different conditions.

Researchers who formulate a hypothesis generally must suggest how one aspect of human behavior influences or affects another. The variable hypothesized to cause or influence another is called the **independent variable.** The other variable is termed the **dependent variable** because its action *depends* on the influence of the independent variable. In other words, the researcher believes that the independent variable predicts or causes change in the dependent variable. For example, a researcher in sociology might anticipate that the availability of affordable housing (the independent variable, *x*) affects the level of homelessness in a community (the dependent variable, *y*).

Our hypothesis is that the higher one's educational degree, the more money one will earn. The independent variable that is to be measured is the level of education. The variable that is thought to depend on it—income—must also be measured.

Identifying independent and dependent variables is a critical step in clarifying cause-and-effect relationships. As shown in Figure 2-3, **causal logic** involves the relationship between a condition or variable and a particular consequence, with one leading to the other. For instance, being less integrated into society may be directly related to, or produce a greater likelihood of, suicide. Similarly, the time students spend reviewing material for a quiz may be directly related to, or produce a greater likelihood of, getting a high score on the quiz.

A **correlation** exists when a change in one variable coincides with a change in the other. Correlations are an indication that causality *may* be present; they do not necessarily indicate causation. For example, data indicate that people who prefer to watch televised news programs are less knowledgeable than

MAPPING LIFE NATIONWIDE

FIGURE 2-2   EDUCATIONAL LEVEL AND HOUSEHOLD INCOME IN THE UNITED STATES

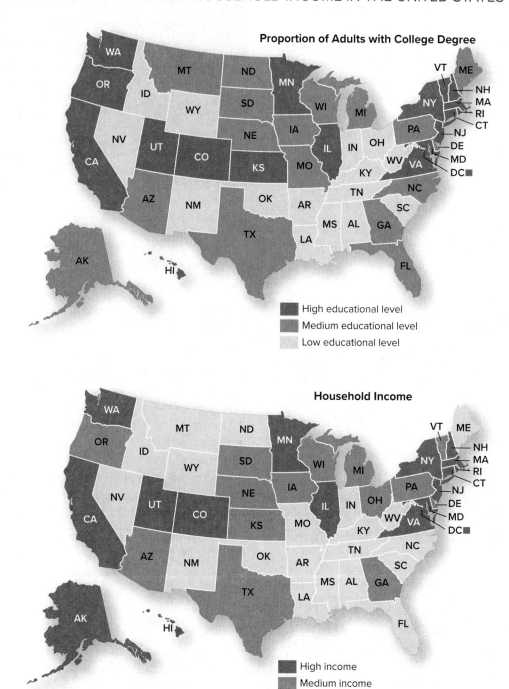

Proportion of Adults with College Degree

- High educational level
- Medium educational level
- Low educational level

Household Income

- High income
- Medium income
- Low income

Note: Incomes declined following the coronavirus pandemic affecting data such as these. However the relative relationship between states has not changed. Median percentage for the entire nation of those 25 years of age and over completing college was 32.6 percent in 2018 and the national household median income was $61,927. *Source:* American Community Survey. 2019a.

those who read newspapers and news magazines. This correlation between people's relative knowledge and their choice of news media seems to make sense, because it agrees with the common belief that television dumbs down information. But the correlation between the two variables is actually caused by a third variable, people's relative ability to comprehend large amounts of information. People with poor reading skills are much more likely than others to get their news from television, while those who are more educated or skilled turn more often to the print media. Though television viewing is *correlated* with lower news comprehension, then, it does not *cause* it. Sociologists seek to identify the *causal* link between variables; the suspected causal link is generally described in the hypothesis (Neuman 2009).

FIGURE 2-3   CAUSAL LOGIC

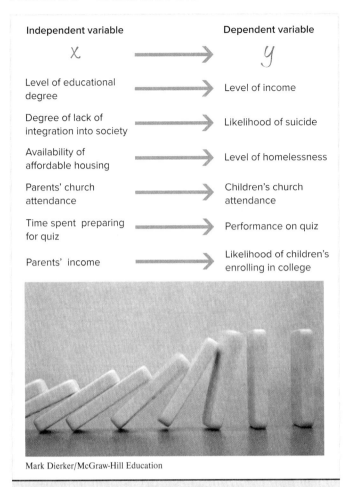

Independent variable	Dependent variable
x	y
Level of educational degree	Level of income
Degree of lack of integration into society	Likelihood of suicide
Availability of affordable housing	Level of homelessness
Parents' church attendance	Children's church attendance
Time spent preparing for quiz	Performance on quiz
Parents' income	Likelihood of children's enrolling in college

Mark Dierker/McGraw-Hill Education

Think about It Identify two or three dependent variables that might be influenced by this independent variable: use of e-cigarettes.

In *causal logic*, an independent variable (often designated by the symbol x) influences a dependent variable (often designated as y); thus, x leads to y. For example, parents who attend church regularly (x) are more likely to have children who are churchgoers (y). Notice that the first two pairs of variables are taken from studies already described in this textbook.

Collecting and Analyzing Data

How do you test a hypothesis to determine if it is supported or refuted? You need to collect information, using one of the research designs described later in the chapter. The research design guides the researcher in collecting research designs described later in the chapter. The research design guides the researcher in collecting and analyzing data.

Selecting the Sample   In most studies, social scientists must carefully select what is known as a sample. A **sample** is a selection from a larger population that is statistically representative of that population. There are many kinds of samples, but the one social scientists use most frequently is the random sample. In a **random sample,** every member of an entire population being studied has the same chance of being selected. Thus, if researchers want to examine opinions of people from a complete listing of neighborhood residences, they might use a

computer to randomly select addresses from the listing. The results would constitute a random sample. The advantage of using specialized sampling techniques is that sociologists do not need to question everyone in a population (Igo 2007).

In some cases, the subjects researchers want to study are hard to identify, either because their activities are clandestine or because lists of such people are not readily available. How do researchers create a sample of illegal drug users, for instance, or of women whose husbands are at least 10 years younger than they are? In such cases, researchers employ what are called *snowball* or *convenience samples*—that is, they recruit participants through word of mouth or by posting notices on the Internet. With the help of special statistical techniques, researchers can draw conclusions from such nonrandom samples.

It is all too easy to confuse the careful scientific techniques used in representative sampling with the many *nonscientific* polls that receive much more media attention. For example, website viewers are often encouraged to register their views on headline news or political contests. Such polls reflect nothing more than the views of those who happened to visit the website and took the time, perhaps at some cost, to register their opinions. These data do not necessarily reflect (and indeed may distort) the views of the broader population. Not everyone has access to a computer on a regular basis, or the means and/or inclination to register their opinions. Even when these techniques include answers from tens of thousands of people, they will be far less accurate than a carefully selected representative sample of 1,500 respondents.

For the purposes of our research example, we will use information collected in the American Community Survey conducted by the Bureau of the Census. Each year, the Census Bureau surveys approximately 3.5 million households across the United States. Technicians at the bureau then use the data to estimate the nation's entire population.

Ensuring Validity and Reliability   The scientific method requires that research results be both valid and reliable. **Validity** refers to the degree to which a measure or scale truly reflects the phenomenon under study. A valid measure of income depends on the gathering of accurate data. Various studies show that people are reasonably accurate in reporting how much money they earned in the most recent year. If a question is written unclearly, however, the resulting data might not be accurate. For example, respondents to an unclear question about income might report their parents' or spouse's income instead of their own.

Reliability refers to the extent to which a measure produces consistent results. Some people may not disclose accurate information, but most do. In the American Community Survey, about 98 percent of the households that researchers approach participate in the survey. The Census Bureau checks their responses against those of similar households, to ensure that the data do not differ significantly from other known responses. The bureau also checks their responses for reliability, since more and more data are being collected online (Population Reference Bureau 2019).

Developing the Conclusion

Scientific studies, including those conducted by sociologists, do not aim to answer all the questions that can be raised about a particular subject. Therefore, the conclusion of a research study represents both an end and a beginning. Although it terminates a specific phase of the investigation, it should also generate ideas for future study.

Supporting Hypotheses In our example, we find that the data support our hypothesis: people with more formal schooling *do* earn more money than others. Those with a high school diploma earn more than those who failed to complete high school, but those with an associate's degree earn more than high school graduates. The relationship continues through more advanced levels of schooling, so that those with graduate degrees earn the most.

The relationship is not perfect, however. Some people who drop out of high school end up with high incomes, and some with advanced degrees earn modest incomes, as shown in Figure 2-4. A successful entrepreneur, for example, might not have much formal schooling, while the holder of a doctorate may choose to work for a low-paying nonprofit institution. Sociologists are interested in both the general pattern that emerges from their data and exceptions to the pattern.

Sociological studies do not always generate data that support the original hypothesis. Many times, a hypothesis is refuted, and researchers must reformulate their conclusions. Unexpected results may also lead sociologists to reexamine their methodology and make changes in the research design.

Controlling for Other Factors A **control variable** is a factor that is held constant to test the relative impact of an independent variable. For example, if researchers wanted to know how adults feel about immigration, they probably would attempt to learn if they are immigrants themselves or the children of immigrants. They would also seek to learn if

FIGURE 2-4 IMPACT OF A COLLEGE EDUCATION ON INCOME

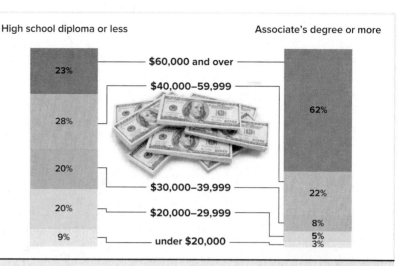

Think about It What kinds of knowledge and skills do people with an associate's degree or higher possess, compared to those with a high school education or less? Why would employers value those kinds of knowledge and skills?

Source: Author's analysis of Census data in Semega et al. 2019:PINC-03. Photo: Rob Bartee/Alamy Stock Photo

Eighteen percent of people with a high school diploma or less (left) earn under $25,000 per year, while only 25 percent earn $60,000 or more. In contrast, only 5 percent of those with an associate's degree or higher (right) earn less than $25,000, while 58 percent earn $60,000 or more.

the respondents considered immigrants to be among their close friends or relatives. This information would allow researchers to learn how contact with immigrants affects whether one favors lenient or strict immigration policies.

Immigration policy is a major social issue that is the subject of national surveys. Here we see immigrants crossing from Juare, Mexico to El Paso, Texas.

Our study of the influence of education on income suggests that not everyone enjoys equal educational opportunities, a disparity that is one of the causes of social inequality. Since education affects a person's income, we may wish to call on the conflict perspective to explore this topic further. What impact does a person's race or gender have? Is a woman with a college degree likely to earn as much as a man with similar schooling? Later in this textbook we will consider these other factors and variables. That is, we will examine the impact that education has on income while controlling for variables such as gender and race.

During the coronavirus pandemic, millions of parents were assisting their children with their school lessons. Researchers had puzzled for years over findings that showed that help with homework was associated with lower educational outcomes. Then sociologists at the University of Oklahoma decided to introduce a control variable—performance of schoolchildren prior to any parental help. They suspected that poor performing students were more likely to receive regular parental or adult help outside the classroom. Once this control was added, they found that parental involvement improved outcomes for both good and more modestly performing children. Such research reassured parents helping their children during the pandemic (Hill 2020; Li and Hamlin 2019).

In Summary: The Scientific Method

Let us briefly summarize the process of the scientific method through a review of the example. We *defined a problem* (the question of whether it pays to get a higher educational degree). We *reviewed the literature* (other studies of the relationship between education and income) and *formulated a hypothesis* (the higher one's educational degree, the more money one will earn). We *collected and analyzed the data,* making sure the sample was representative and the data were valid and reliable. Finally, we *developed the conclusion:* the data do support our hypothesis about the influence of education on income.

THINKING CRITICALLY

Suppose that two researchers used different operational definitions for the same term. Could both researchers' results be reliable and valid? Explain your answer.

Major Research Designs

An important aspect of sociological research is deciding *how* to collect the data. A **research design** is a detailed plan or method for obtaining data scientifically. Selection of a research design is often based on the theories and hypotheses the researcher starts with (Merton 1948). The choice requires creativity and ingenuity, because it directly influences both the cost of the project and the amount of time needed to collect the data. Research designs that sociologists regularly use to generate data include surveys, ethnography, experiments, and existing sources.

Surveys

Almost all of us have responded to surveys of one kind or another. We may have been asked what kind of detergent we use, which presidential candidate we intend to vote for, or what our favorite television program is. A **survey** is a study, generally in the form of an interview or questionnaire, that provides researchers with information about how people think and act. As anyone who watches the news during presidential campaigns knows, surveys have become a staple of political life.

When you think of surveys, you may recall seeing online polls that offer instant results. Although such polls can be highly interesting, they reflect only the opinions of those who visit the website and choose to respond online. As we have seen, a survey must be based on precise, representative sampling if it is to genuinely reflect a broad range of the population. In our wired world, more and more people can be reached only through their cell phones. Box 2-1 describes the challenges of conducting a public opinion survey on a cell phone.

Web-based surveys are becoming attractive options because the costs are so low once the questionnaire is developed. But are these anonymous Internet responses accurate? They can be quite valid. One such example is a study that used an audience of more than 1 million residents in the United States that had opted in through Internet advertising and direct-mail contacts. Using this database, researchers carefully developed a sample representative of the general population and asked sensitive questions about racial stereotypes. The responses closely match the results obtained when similar questions were asked in face-to-face interviews conducted in different national samples at about the same time. Comparisons like these are encouraging for the future of web-based surveys (Simmons and Bobo 2015).

In preparing to conduct a survey, sociologists must not only develop representative samples; they must also exercise great care in the wording of questions. An effective survey question must be simple and clear enough for people to understand. It must also be specific enough so that there are no problems in interpreting the results. Open-ended questions ("What do you think of changes in the earth's climate?") must be carefully phrased to solicit the type of information desired. Surveys

OUR WIRED WORLD

2.1 Surveying Cell Phone Users

Can you hear me now?" This question, familiar to cell phone callers everywhere, could be used to characterize a debate among researchers in sociology. Until recently, calling people on the telephone was a common way for survey takers to reach a broad range of people. Though not everyone owns a telephone—particularly not low-income people—researchers managed to account for that relatively small portion of the population in other ways.

However, the fact that many people now have a cell phone but no landline presents a serious methodological problem to scholars who depend on surveys and public opinion polling. As of 2018, 54 percent of households in the United States could be reached only by cell phone, and the proportion was rising. Among those under 18–29, the abandonment of landlines is even greater, with 72 percent accessible only by cell phone.

Scholars are reluctant to rely only on landline-based surveys. They are concerned about the potential for misleading results, such as underestimates of the prevalence of health problems. For example, 38 percent of cell phone–only households have a binge drinker, compared to only 17 percent of landline households. And 28 percent of cell phone–only households do not have health insurance, compared to 14 percent of landline households.

Unfortunately, surveying cell phone users has its own problems. In general, cell phone users are more likely than landline users to screen incoming calls or ignore them. And studies show that because cell phone users often take calls while they are involved in

As of 2018, 54 percent of households in the United States could be reached only by cell phone, and the proportion was rising.

other activities, they are much more likely to break off a call midsurvey than someone who is speaking on a landline. It takes an average of nine calls to a working cell phone number to complete one survey, compared to five calls to a working landline number. Furthermore, federal law requires that calls to cell phones be hand-dialed; the use of automatic dialers, a standard tool of survey firms, is illegal. Survey takers have also found that calling cell phone numbers means they will reach a higher proportion of nonadults than when calling landline numbers. Finally, there are some ethical issues involved in randomly dialing cell phone users, who may be driving a motor vehicle or operating dangerous machinery when they answer.

Researchers are taking steps to stay abreast of technological change. For example, they are making allowances for people who communicate without any kind of telephone, using their personal computers and the Internet. And by drawing on historical data that suggest what kinds of people tend to adopt other wireless technologies, researchers are projecting which people are likely to abandon their landlines in the near future.

LET'S DISCUSS

1. Are you a cell phone–only user? If so, do you generally accept calls from unknown numbers? Aside from underestimating certain health problems and distorting the degree of support for certain politicians, what other problems might result from excluding cell phone–only users from survey research?

2. Apply what you have just learned to the task of surveying Internet users. Which of the problems that arise during telephone surveys might also arise during Internet surveys? Might Internet surveys involve some unique problems?

Sources: Blumberg and Luke 2007; Blumberg and Luke 2018; David Brown 2009; Burger 2015; Lavrakas et al. 2007; McGeeney 2016.

---

can be indispensable sources of information, but only if the sampling is done properly and the questions are worded accurately and without bias.

In wording questions, researchers must also pay careful attention to changes in society. Beginning in 2019, Census relationship questions no longer included just two categories:

- husband or wife
- unmarried partner

Instead, these questions split the category into four possibilities:

- Opposite–sex husband/wife/spouse
- Opposite–sex unmarried partner
- Same-sex husband/wife/spouse
- Same-sex unmarried partner

The Census Bureau will closely review responses to determine if they offer an accurate portrayal of the social reality (Population Reference Bureau 2019).

There are two main forms of the survey: the **interview,** in which a researcher obtains information through face-to-face, phone, or online questioning, and the **questionnaire,** in which the researcher uses a printed or written form to obtain information from a respondent. Each of these has its own advantages. An interviewer can obtain a higher response rate, because people find it more difficult to turn down a personal request for an interview than to throw away a written questionnaire. In addition, a skillful interviewer can go beyond written questions and probe for a subject's underlying feelings and reasons. On the other hand, questionnaires have the advantage of being cheaper, especially in large samples.

Why do people have sex? A straightforward question, but until recently it was rarely investigated scientifically, despite its

Source: ©Gatis Sluka, Latvijas Avize, Latvia, June 9, 2017.
Interviewers must carefully record all responses and not appear judgmental of any answer they receive.

significance to public health, marital counseling, and criminology. To find the answer, researchers interviewed nearly 2,000 undergraduates at the University of Texas at Austin. In developing the question for the interview, they first asked a random sample of 400 students to list all the reasons why they had ever had sex. The explanations were highly diverse. The team then asked another sample of 1,500 students to rate the importance of each of the 287 reasons given by the first group. Nearly every reason was rated most important by at least some respondents. Though there were some gender differences in the replies, there was significant consensus between men and women on the top 10 reasons (Meston and Buss 2007).

Studies have shown that the characteristics of the interviewer have an impact on survey data. For example, female interviewers tend to receive more feminist responses from female subjects than do male interviewers, and Black interviewers tend to receive more detailed responses about race-related issues from Black subjects than do white interviewers. The possible impact of gender and race indicates again how much care social research requires (Hibben, Pennell, and Scott 2017).

The survey is an example of **quantitative research,** which collects and reports data primarily in numerical form. Most of

the survey research discussed so far in this book has been quantitative. While this type of research can make use of large samples, it can't offer great depth and detail on a topic. That is why researchers also make use of **qualitative research,** which relies on what is seen in field and naturalistic settings, and often focuses on small groups and communities rather than on large groups or whole nations. The most common form of qualitative research is ethnography, or observation, which we consider next. Throughout this book you will find examples of both quantitative and qualitative research, since both are used widely. Some sociologists prefer one type of research to the other, but we learn most when we draw on many different research designs and do not limit ourselves to a particular type of research.

Ethnography

Investigators often collect information or test hypotheses through firsthand studies. **Ethnography** is the study of an entire social setting through extended systematic fieldwork. **Observation,** or direct participation in closely watching a group or organization, is the basic technique of ethnography. However, ethnographic research also includes the collection of historical information and the conduct of in-person interviews. Although ethnography may seem a relatively informal method compared to surveys or experiments, ethnographic researchers are careful to take detailed notes while observing their subjects.

In some cases, the sociologist actually joins a group for a period, to get an accurate sense of how it operates. This approach is called *participant observation.* In Barbara Ehrenreich's widely read book *Nickel and Dimed: On (Not) Getting By in America,* the author was a participant observer. Disguising herself as a divorced, middle-aged housewife without a college degree, Ehrenreich set out to see what life was like for low-wage workers. Her book chronicles her own and others' experiences trying to make ends meet on a minimum wage (Ehrenreich 2001).

During the late 1930s, in a classic example of participant-observation research, William F. Whyte moved into a low-income Italian neighborhood in Boston. For nearly four years he was a member of the social circle of "corner boys" that he describes in *Street Corner Society.* Whyte revealed his identity to these men and joined in their conversations, bowling, and other leisure-time activities. His goal was to gain greater insight into the community that these men had established. As Whyte ([1943] 1993:303) listened to Doc, the leader of the group, he "learned the answers to questions I would not even have had the sense to ask if I had been getting my information solely on an interviewing basis." Whyte's work was especially valuable, since at the time the academic world had little direct knowledge of the poor, and tended to rely for information on the records of social service agencies, hospitals, and courts (P. Adler et al. 1992).

The initial challenge that Whyte faced—and that every participant observer encounters—was to gain acceptance into an unfamiliar group. It is no simple matter for a college-trained sociologist to win the trust of a religious cult, a youth gang, a poor Appalachian community, or a circle of skid row residents. It requires a great deal of patience and an accepting, nonthreatening type of personality on the part of the observer.

Ethnographic research poses other complex challenges for the investigator. Sociologists must be able to fully understand what they are observing. In a sense, then, researchers must learn to see the world as the group sees it in order to fully comprehend the events taking place around them. This raises a delicate issue. If the research is to be successful, the observer cannot allow the close associations or even friendships that inevitably develop to influence the subjects' behavior or the conclusions of the study. Even while working hard to gain acceptance from the group being studied, the participant observer *must* maintain some degree of detachment.

An exciting tool for many ethnographers is visual sociology, described in Box 2-2.

Pat Tuson/Alamy Stock Photo

Ethnography is the study of an entire social setting through extended systematic research. Research on pizza deliverers has identified social splits between those who do it as a full-time job and those who do it temporarily. Regardless, of these differences, all deliverers share stories of customers' peculiarities as well as how to navigate delivery areas perceived as dangerous.

Experiments

When sociologists want to study a possible cause-and-effect relationship, they may conduct experiments. An **experiment** is an artificially created situation that allows a researcher to manipulate variables.

In the classic method of conducting an experiment, two groups of people are selected and matched for similar characteristics, such as age or education. The researchers then assign the subjects to one of two groups: the experimental or the control group. The **experimental group** is exposed to an independent variable; the **control group** is not. Thus, if scientists were testing a new type of antibiotic, they would administer the drug to an experimental group but not to a control group.

In some experiments, just as in observation research, the presence of a social scientist or other observer may affect the behavior of the people being studied. Sociologists have used the term **Hawthorne effect** to refer to the unintended influence that observers of experiments can have on their subjects. The term originated as the result of an experiment conducted at the Hawthorne plant of the Western Electric Company during the 1920s and 1930s. Researchers found that *every* change they made in working conditions—even reduced lighting—seemed to have a positive effect on workers' productivity. They concluded that workers had made a special effort to impress their observers. Though the carefully constructed study did identify some causes for changes in the workers' behavior that did not have to do with their being observed, the term *Hawthorne effect* has become synonymous with a placebo or guinea pig effect (Franke and Kaul 1978).

THINKING CRITICALLY

How would you go about setting up an experiment to measure the effect of screen time on school children's grades?

Use of Existing Sources

Sociologists do not necessarily need to collect new data in order to conduct research and test hypotheses. The term **secondary analysis** refers to a variety of research techniques that make use of previously collected and publicly accessible information and data. Generally, in conducting secondary analysis, researchers use data in ways that were unintended by the initial collectors of information. For example, census data are compiled for specific uses by the federal government but are also valuable to marketing specialists in locating everything from bicycle stores to nursing homes.

Sociologists consider secondary analysis to be *nonreactive*—that is, it does not influence people's behavior. For example, Émile Durkheim's statistical analysis of suicide neither increased nor decreased human self-destruction. Researchers, then, can avoid the Hawthorne effect by using secondary analysis.

There is one inherent problem, however: the researcher who relies on data collected by someone else may not find exactly

RESEARCH TODAY

2-2 Visual Sociology

As a discipline, sociology relies on the scientific observation of human behavior, whether directly or through data gathered in surveys, experiments, and existing sources. Increasingly, however, sociologists also recognize visual documents as a significant research tool. **Visual sociology** is the use of photographs, film, and video to study society. Sociologist Howard Becker drew attention to the importance of images in his influential essay "Photography and Sociology." For over three decades the International Visual Sociology Association has encouraged scholarship in visual sociology, not only by sociologists but also by anthropologists, communications scholars, and psychologists.

> *"Photography and sociology have approximately the same birth date," in the 1830s.*

Although the term *visual sociology* is relatively new, the roots of visual research methods go deep. As Becker (1974:3) reminds us, "Photography and sociology have approximately the same birth date," in the 1830s. Early sociological works made use of photographs and other visuals, such as maps, not merely as illustrations but as the basis of research. The hardships of the American Civil War, conflicts between Native Americans and U.S. Cavalry, and the Crimean War were all analyzed using early photographs. In the 20th century, scholars assessed the toll of the Great Depression in the United States by looking at photographs assembled by the Farm Security Administration. At the time, however, such studies did not receive much acceptance by sociologists. Until recently, only numerical data were deemed appropriate for study.

Inti St. Clair/Spaces Images/Blend Images LLC

Asking residents to describe photographs helps to call attention to details that are often overlooked, such as an emphasis on security.

Visual sociology includes the conscious creation of a visual record through documentary films or photography. Sociologist Charles Suchar studied gentrification by photographing commercial and residential areas over time and then analyzing the record to note how neighborhoods had changed. The photographs became the basis for interviews with residents and merchants about the details they revealed and the concerns they suggested, such as the desire for privacy and the need for security.

Photographic records can also be useful in comparative studies. Imagine what sociologists might learn by contrasting images of a suburban barbecue and an Amish community raising a barn. In both cases, images would be treated as data, not merely as instructional aids.

Today, visual sociology is proving useful in **applied sociology,** the use of the discipline of sociology to yield practical applications for human behavior and organizations. In England, public health researchers photographed neighborhoods where illegal drug use was common. The images, which showed drug users injecting themselves in parks and public toilets, helped to identify unsafe areas where discarded needles and syringes littered the ground. Although the visuals were not necessary to the research, they proved invaluable in the researchers' effort to convince social services and law enforcement agencies that intervention was needed.

In short, the uses of visual sociology are as wide as the discipline of sociology itself. Technological innovations such as the Internet, smartphones equipped with high-quality cameras, social media, media, camera-equipped drones, and 3D copiers will only continue to expand the field.

LET'S DISCUSS

1. Choose an image or series of images from reality TV or social media and discuss it from a sociological perspective. What can you learn from it? What sociological concepts can you relate to it?
2. Might some images be misinterpreted by researchers? Give an example. How might scholars guard against such misinterpretation?

Sources: Becker 1974; Goffman 1979; Harper 1988; International Visual Sociology Association 2020; Parkin and Coomber 2009; Stryker and Wood [1935–1943] 1973; Suchar 1997; Van den Scott 2018.

Library of Congress Prints and Photographs Division [LC-B8184-7964-A]

Photographs and other visual images improve our understanding of events that affect social behavior. This scene from a Civil War battlefield suggests the utter devastation visited on society by that war.

what is needed. Social scientists who are studying family violence can use statistics from police and social service agencies on *reported* cases of spouse abuse and child abuse, but how many cases are not reported? Government bodies have no precise data on *all* cases of abuse.

USE YOUR SOCIOLOGICAL IMAGINATION

Imagine you are a legislator or government policymaker working on a complex social problem. What might happen if you were to base your decision on faulty research?

Many social scientists find it useful to study cultural, economic, and political documents, including newspapers, periodicals, radio and television tapes, the Internet, scripts, diaries, songs, folklore, and legal papers (Table 2-1). In examining these sources, researchers employ a technique known as **content analysis,** which is the systematic coding and objective recording of data, guided by some rationale. Content analysis can be revealing. Following a recent concern about depiction of masculinity in mass media, a sociologist undertook an analysis of how men are portrayed in the lyrics of mainstream country music. Considering *Billboard* music charts from the 1980s to the present, the researcher found a notable shift from men portrayed as the traditional family breadwinner and undertaking working-class employment to men portrayed as providing women with alcohol, transportation, and places to hook up. Furthermore, in 21st-century lyrics, men are less likely to be engaged in housework and women are less likely to be engaged in paid labor than they were two decades earlier.

Content analysis can also document what we suspect is happening as well as reveal surprising trends. Women play sports, but you might not see that easily from watching TV coverage. It was not until 1992 that women's sports coverage exceeded that of televised dog and horse competition. A 2015 study analyzed coverage of women's sports on the Los Angeles local television market as well as on ESPN over 25 years. Despite

TABLE 2-1   EXISTING SOURCES USED IN SOCIOLOGICAL RESEARCH

Most Frequently Used Sources
Census data
Crime statistics
Birth, death, marriage, divorce, and health statistics

Other Sources
Newspapers and periodicals
Personal journals, diaries, e-mail, and letters
Records and archival material of religious organizations, corporations, and other organizations
Transcripts of radio programs
Motion pictures and television programs
Web pages, blogs, and social media
Song lyrics
Scientific records (such as patent applications)
Speeches of public figures (such as politicians)
Votes cast in elections or by elected officials on specific legislative proposals
Attendance records for public events
Videos of social protests and rallies
Literature, including folklore

Summing Up

Think about It Which of these sources do you access to collect information?

the tremendous increase in women's participation in sports over the last quarter century, content analysis revealed that only 3.2 percent of airtime was devoted to women's sports; further, this represented a decline from the levels back in 1989. ESPN's heavily watched SportCenter consistently devotes 2 percent of airtime to women; of this, 82 percent represents coverage of basketball (Cooky et al. 2015; Scheadler and Wagstaff 2018).

Table 2-2 summarizes the major research designs, along with their advantages and limitations.

TABLE 2-2   MAJOR RESEARCH DESIGNS

Summing Up

Method	Examples	Advantages	Limitations
Survey	Questionnaires; Interviews	Yields information about specific issues	Can be expensive and time-consuming
Ethnography	Observation	Yields detailed information about specific groups or organizations	Involves months if not years of labor-intensive data
Experiment	Deliberate manipulation of people's social behavior	Yields direct measures of people's behavior	Ethical limitations on the degree to which subjects' behavior can be manipulated
Existing sources/Secondary analysis	Analysis of census or health data	Cost-efficiency	Limited to data collected for some other purpose

Ethics of Research

A biochemist cannot inject a drug into a human being unless it has been thoroughly tested and the subject agrees to the shot. To do otherwise would be both unethical and illegal. Sociologists, too, must abide by certain specific standards in conducting research, called a **code of ethics.** The professional society of the discipline, the American Sociological Association (ASA), first published the society's *Code of Ethics* in 1971 and reviewed it most recently in 2018. It puts forth the following basic principles:

1. Maintain objectivity and integrity in research.
2. Respect the people's rights, dignity, and diversity.
3. Protect subjects from personal harm.
4. Preserve confidentiality.
5. Seek informed consent when data are collected from research participants or when behavior occurs in a private context.
6. Acknowledge research collaboration and assistance.
7. Disclose all sources of financial support.
    (American Sociological Association 2018)

These basic principles probably seem clear-cut. How could they lead to any disagreement or controversy? Yet many delicate ethical questions cannot be resolved simply by reading these seven principles. For example, should a sociologist who is engaged in participant-observation research always protect the confidentiality of subjects? What if the subjects are members of a religious cult allegedly involved in unethical and possibly illegal activities? What if the sociologist is interviewing political activists and is questioned by government authorities about the research?

Because most sociological research uses *people* as sources of information—as respondents to survey questions, subjects of ethnography, or participants in experiments—these sorts of questions are important. In all cases, sociologists need to be certain they are not invading their subjects' privacy. Generally, they do so by assuring subjects of anonymity and by guaranteeing the confidentiality of personal information. In addition, research proposals that involve human subjects must now be overseen by a review board, whose members seek to ensure that subjects are not placed at an unreasonable level of risk. If necessary, the board may ask researchers to revise their research designs to conform to the code of ethics.

We can appreciate the seriousness of the ethical problems researchers confront by considering the experience of sociologist Rik Scarce, described in the next section. Scarce's vow to protect his subjects' confidentiality got him into considerable trouble with the law.

Confidentiality

Like journalists, sociologists occasionally find themselves subject to questions from law enforcement authorities because of knowledge they have gained in the course of their work. This uncomfortable situation raises profound ethical questions.

In May 1993, Rik Scarce, a doctoral candidate in sociology at Washington State University, was jailed for contempt of court. Scarce had declined to tell a federal grand jury what he knew—or even whether he knew anything—about a 1991 raid on a university research laboratory by animal rights activists. At the time, Scarce was conducting research for a book about environmental protesters and knew at least one suspect in the break-in. Curiously, although he was chastised by a federal judge, Scarce won respect from fellow prison inmates, who regarded him as a man who "wouldn't snitch" (Monaghan 1993:A8).

The American Sociological Association supported Scarce's position when he appealed his sentence. Scarce maintained his silence. Ultimately the judge ruled that nothing would be gained by further incarceration, and Scarce was released after serving 159 days in jail. In January 1994, the U.S. Supreme Court declined to hear Scarce's case on appeal. The Court's failure to consider his case led Scarce (2005) to argue that federal legislation is needed to clarify the right of scholars and members of the press to preserve the confidentiality of those they interview.

Conflict of Interest

Sometimes disclosing all the sources of funding for a study, as required in principle 7 of the ASA's *Code of Ethics,* is not a sufficient guarantee of ethical conduct. Especially in the case of both corporate and government funding, money given ostensibly for the support of basic research may come with strings attached. Accepting funds from a private organization or even a government agency that stands to benefit from a study's results can call into question a researcher's objectivity and integrity (principle 1).

Another example is the Exxon Corporation's support for research on jury verdicts. In 1989, the Exxon oil tanker *Valdez* hit a reef off the coast of Alaska, spilling more than 11 million gallons of oil into Prince William Sound. Five years later a federal court ordered Exxon to pay $5.3 billion in damages for the accident. Exxon appealed the verdict and began approaching legal scholars, sociologists, and psychologists who might be willing to study jury deliberations. The corporation's objective was to develop academic support for its lawyers' contention that the punitive judgments in such cases result from faulty deliberations and do not have a deterrent effect.

Some scholars have questioned the propriety of accepting funds under these circumstances, even if the source is

TAKING SOCIOLOGY TO WORK

Dave Eberbach, **Associate Director, Iowa Institute for Community Alliances**

Dave Eberbach is a people person who has been working with computers most of his career. In 1994 he was hired as a research coordinator by the United Way of Central Iowa. In that position he helped to create and implement Iowa's Homeless Management Information System (HMIS), which coordinates data on housing and homeless service providers. Eberbach also collaborated with the Human Service Planning Alliance to create and maintain a "data warehouse" of social statistics from diverse sources. As a research coordinator, he found that the data helped him to identify small pockets of poverty that were generally hidden in state and county statistics.

Courtesy of Dave Eberbach

Today, Eberbach works at the Iowa Institute for Community Alliances, a small nonprofit organization that offers computerized client management and on-site program monitoring to homeless and housing service providers. As Associate Director, Eberbach oversees a staff of seven and meets with clients who are working to improve service delivery to vulnerable people. "As fewer resources are being spent on social programs, it has been imperative to make sure that the focus of programs is on client success, not maintaining systems," he explains.

Eberbach went to Grinnell College, where he took a variety of social science courses before settling on sociology as a major. While there,

he benefited from the presence of several visiting professors, who exposed him to a variety of racial and cultural perspectives. He found that his personal acquaintance with them complemented the concepts he was learning in his sociology classes. Today, Eberbach draws on his college experiences in his work, which brings him into contact with a diverse group of people.

As a student, Eberbach recalls, he never thought he would use statistics in his career, and didn't work very hard in the course. "As it turned out," he says, "I use it nearly every day. Understanding data and statistics and being able to explain numbers to others has been very important in my job." The reverse has also been true, however: having a background in sociology has been helpful to him in systems design. "Understanding that systems need to work for a variety of groups of people, not just folks that grew up like I did," he explains, has been very helpful. "The world is not a computer problem or a math problem to be solved," he continues, "but rather a complex environment where groups of people continually bump into one another."

LET'S DISCUSS

1. Do you know what you want to be doing 10 years from now? If so, how might a knowledge of statistics help you in your future occupation?
2. What kinds of statistics, specifically, might you find in the Human Service Planning Alliance's data warehouse? Where would they come from?

John Gaps III/AP Images

A floating containment barrier (or boom) encircles the Exxon oil tanker *Valdez* after it was grounded on a reef off the coast of Alaska. Exxon was found negligent in the environmental disaster and was ordered to pay $5.3 billion to local residents and fisheries for the cleanup. On appeal, the company managed to reduce the damages to $500 million based on academic research that it had funded—research that some scholars believe involved a conflict of interest.

disclosed. In at least one case, an Exxon employee explicitly told a sociologist that the corporation offers financial support to scholars who have shown the tendency to express views similar to its own. An argument can also be made that Exxon was attempting to set scholars' research agendas with its huge war chest. Rather than funding studies on the improvement of cleanup technologies or the assignment of long-term environmental costs, Exxon chose to shift scientists' attention to the validity of the legal awards in environmental cases.

The scholars who accepted Exxon's support deny that it influenced their work or changed their conclusions. Some received support from other sources as well, such as the National Science Foundation and Harvard University's Olin Center for Law, Economics, and Business. Many of their findings were published in respected academic journals after review by a jury of peers. Still, at least one researcher who participated in the studies refused monetary support from Exxon to avoid even the suggestion of a conflict of interest.

Exxon spent roughly $1 million on the research, and at least one compilation of studies congenial to the corporation's point of view has been published. As ethical considerations require, the academics who conducted the studies disclosed Exxon's role in funding them. Nevertheless, the investment appears to have paid off. In 2006, drawing on these studies, Exxon's lawyers succeeded in persuading an appeals court to reduce the corporation's legal damages from $5.3 to $2.5 billion. In 2008 Exxon appealed that judgment to the Supreme Court, which further reduced the damages to $500 million. The final award, shared by about 32,000 plaintiffs, resulted in payments of about $15,000 to each person (Freudenburg 2005; Liptak 2008).

Value Neutrality

The ethical considerations of sociologists lie not only in the methods they use and the funding they accept, but also in the way they interpret their results. Max Weber ([1904] 1949) recognized that personal values would influence the questions that sociologists select for research. In his view, that was perfectly acceptable, but under no conditions could a researcher allow his or her personal feelings to influence the *interpretation* of data. In Weber's phrase, sociologists must practice **value neutrality** in their research.

As part of this neutrality, investigators have an ethical obligation to accept research findings even when the data run counter to their personal views, to theoretically based explanations, or to widely accepted beliefs. For example, Émile Durkheim challenged popular conceptions when he reported that social (rather than supernatural) forces were an important factor in suicide.

Although some sociologists believe that neutrality is impossible, ignoring the issue would be irresponsible. Let's consider what might happen if researchers brought their own biases to the investigation. A person investigating the impact of intercollegiate sports on alumni contributions, for example, might focus only on the highly visible revenue-generating sports of football and basketball and neglect the so-called minor sports, such as tennis or soccer, which are more likely to involve women athletes. Despite the early work of W. E. B. DuBois and Jane Addams, sociologists still need to be reminded that the discipline often fails to adequately consider all people's social behavior.

In her book *The Death of White Sociology* (1973), Joyce Ladner called attention to the tendency of mainstream sociology to treat the lives of African Americans as a social problem. More recently, sociologist Earl Wright II (2020) has argued that sociological research should not only be inclusive but should also be open to bringing about globally oriented social change and to drawing on relevant research by nonsociologists. For example, one might want to broaden the study of the impact of education on income to consider how it may operate differently for women and for racial and ethnic minorities. Or one

might ask whether this pattern operates differently in other nations' education systems. The issue of value neutrality does not mean that sociologists can't have opinions, but it does mean that they must work to overcome any biases, however unintentional, that they may bring to their analysis of research.

Sociologist Peter Rossi (1987) admits to having liberal inclinations that direct him to certain fields of study. Yet in line with Weber's view of value neutrality, Rossi's commitment to rigorous research methods and objective interpretation of data has sometimes led him to controversial findings that are not necessarily supportive of his liberal values. For example, his measure of the extent of homelessness in Chicago in the mid-1980s fell far below the estimates of the Chicago Coalition for the Homeless. Coalition members bitterly attacked Rossi for hampering their social reform efforts by minimizing the extent of homelessness. Rossi (1987:79) concluded that "in the short term, good social research will often be greeted as a betrayal of one or another side to a particular controversy."

THINKING CRITICALLY

Why did Max Weber specify the need for neutrality in the interpretation of data? Is complete value neutrality possible in research? To what extent should researchers try to overcome their own biases?

Feminist Methodology

The feminist perspective has had a great impact on the current generation of social researchers. How might this perspective influence research? Although researchers must be objective, their theoretical orientation may influence the questions they ask—or just as important, the questions they fail to ask. Until recently, for example, researchers frequently studied work and the family separately. Yet feminist theorists see the two spheres of activity as being closely integrated. Similarly, work and leisure, paid and unpaid domestic work may be seen not as two separate spheres, but as two sides of the same coin.

Recently, feminist scholars have become interested in self-injury. Research shows that 85 percent of self-injurers are female; feminist researchers seek to explain why women predominate in this population. Rather than treat the behavior as a medical disorder, they note that society encourages women much more than men to attend to their bodies through hair removal, skin treatments, and depigmentation. Given this heightened attention to the female body, feminists suggest that specific instances of victimization can lead women to self-injure. They also seek to better understand male self-injurers, and are testing the hypothesis that among men, self-injury is a manifestation of hypermasculinity in the tolerance of pain (P. Adler and Adler 2011:25–27, 35–36).

Winston George/Alamy Stock Photo

Feminist theorists see the global trafficking of sex workers as a sign of the close relationship between the supposedly separate worlds of industrial nations and dependent developing nations.

The feminist perspective has also had an impact on global research. To feminist theorists, the traditional distinction between industrial nations and developing nations overlooks the close relationship between these two supposedly separate worlds. Feminist theorists have called for more research on the special role that immigrant women play in maintaining their households; on the use of domestic workers from less developed nations by households in industrial nations; and on the global trafficking of sex workers (Cheng 2003; Cooper et al. 2007; Sprague 2005).

Feminist researchers tend to involve and consult their subjects more than other researchers, and they are more oriented toward seeking change, raising the public consciousness, and influencing policy. They are particularly open to a multidisciplinary approach, such as making use of historical evidence or legal studies (T. Baker 1999; Lofland 1975; Reinharz 1992).

THINKING CRITICALLY

Even if women are represented in a study, could the researcher's gender influence the data that are collected? If so, how, and how might the problem be prevented?

Queer Theory and Methodology

If researchers wish to generalize about society, their findings must be representative of all people. Over the last generation, feminist theorists have insisted that women deserve as much attention from researchers as men. Similarly, exponents of queer theory ask whether researchers consider gays and lesbians in their studies, or simply assume that the generalizations they make apply to everyone, whether heterosexual, gay, or transgender (Ghaziani and Brim 2019).

How might being gay influence a person's behavior, beyond their sexual activity? Sociologist Eric Anthony Grollman looked at racial attitudes among a national sample of adults for whom there was also information as to whether they identified as lesbian, gay, or bisexual. The results show that white LGBTQ respondents differed significantly from white heterosexuals in the expression of racial attitudes. For example, one might assume that gay people, who are sometimes victimized, would show sympathy to other groups that experience discrimination. While that explains part of the difference, Grollman found that even those LGBTQ respondents who had not experienced discrimination were significantly less prejudiced than straight adults. Such research shows how the social outlook of people with non-straight sexual orientations might affect how they see the larger social environment (Grollman 2018).

According to the National Bureau of Economic Research, most research significantly underreports the proportion of gays and lesbians in the population; it also underestimates the percentage of people who hold anti-gay views. The bureau suggests using a "veiled reporting" technique, in which respondents are asked whether they consider themselves to be heterosexual in the context of other much less sensitive questions, such as "Did you spend a lot of time playing video games as a child?" In one study, when respondents were asked about their sexual orientation within a group of such questions, 19 percent of them reported that they were nonheterosexual; when the question was asked more directly, the proportion was 11 percent (Coffman et al. 2013).

This study suggests that if researchers want to generalize about *both* heterosexuals and homosexuals, they should be extremely careful in wording questions about respondents' sexual orientation—compared even to other sensitive topics, such as political and religious affiliations.

THINKING CRITICALLY

How might recent advances in LGBTQ rights affect queer studies research?

The Data-Rich Future

Advances in technology have affected all aspects of our lives, and sociological research is no exception. Massive increases in available data have allowed sociologists to undertake research that was virtually impossible just a decade ago. In the recent past, only people with grants or major institutional support could work easily with large amounts of data. Now anyone with a computer can access huge amounts of data and learn more about social behavior.

When it comes to big data, the nation's prison population offers many avenues of research—the United States has about 5 percent of the world's population but nearly 25 percent of its prisoners. While precise numbers are difficult to obtain because of the changing prison population and the myriad of correctional departments in operation in the nation, there are nearly 7 million adults in correctional systems. Further, it is estimated that somewhere in excess of 1.7 million children under age 18 have a parent in prison or jail. These children, often in low-income households and in poor health, need help to cope with such a life-changing circumstance. For example, Sesame Street has mounted a program called "Little Children Big Challenges: Incarceration" aimed to provide comfort for children as young as three years old (Lynch 2012; Sesame Street 2018).

So do these programs help children? Further, how can they be strengthened? Sociologists delve into mounds of data to evaluate program offerings and discover ways to improve them. Weber State University sociologist R. C. Morris (2017) considered two programs: a Big Brothers Big Sisters (BBBS) mentoring program in metropolitan Indianapolis, and the national Fractured Family (FF) survey that followed 5,000 children over a period of nine years.

Morris's hypothesis was that social intervention would reduce the likelihood that children with parents in jail would have problems such as causing property damage, stealing, and cheating in school. This research shows the importance of having data before assuming that a hypothesis is correct. Unexpectedly, the participants in the mentoring program had more problems than a similar group in the FF survey who were not in the program.

Why would children who received mentoring experience more problems than children who did not? The data did not reveal a simple casual effect. The analysis came to a similar conclusion described earlier in this chapter about parental involvement in children's homework. Children in the BBBS had more reports of problems before the mentoring began compared to the control sample, so the challenges they faced were greater. Second, the mentoring program was intended to focus on school success and therefore may have had the unintended effect of leading some participants to commit academic dishonesty while trying to "succeed." Third, the BBBS program focused on older children than did many similar interventions, which meant the analysis was measuring the impact of the continuing incarceration of a parent more than a few more months of mentoring. In other words, the older children had to overcome the effects of longer parental incarcerations or even multiple parental absences. Morris suggests that to be effective, mentoring might need to last longer than a year and perhaps go beyond focusing on improving school grades, such as including skills that help children cope in a very stressful social environment.

We have seen that researchers rely on a number of tools, from time-tested observational research and use of existing sources to the latest in computer technology. The Social Policy section that follows will describe researchers' efforts to survey the general population about a controversial aspect of human behavior: human sexuality. This investigation was complicated by its potential social policy implications. Because in the real world, sociological research can have far-reaching consequences for public policy and public welfare, each of the following chapters in this book will close with a Social Policy section.

THINKING CRITICALLY

Explain how the evaluation of the mentoring program for children with incarcerated parents reflected the different steps of the scientific method.

In Pictures Ltd./Corbis/Getty Images

Incarceration has a major impact on an inmate's children. Shown here, a father and his sons during an all-too-infrequent family visit session.

socialpolicy and Sociological Research

Studying Human Sexuality

How can researchers study human sexual behavior? Neuroscientists Ogi Ogas and Sai Gaddam (2011) studied millions of web searches, websites, and videos related to sex. They found that women and men differ decidedly in their preferences, but very little (if any) distinction between heterosexuals and homosexuals, other than their sexual orientation. This type of research has significant limitations, however. Ogas and Gaddam could not distinguish between online fantasies and rational desires, or between a single search and one of many repeated searches by the same person. Nevertheless, this cyber study is a step forward in the effort to understand human sexual behavior (Bartlett 2011).

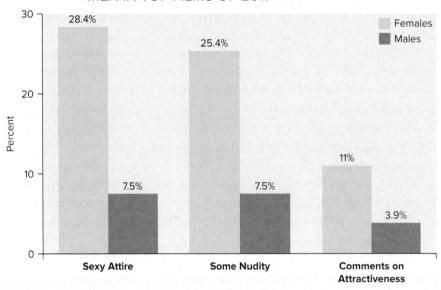

FIGURE 2-5   WOMEN MORE SEXUALIZED THAN MEN IN TOP FILMS OF 2017

Note: Based on analysis of 100 top-grossing movies of 2017.
Source: Smith, Stacy L. et al. 2018.

Looking at the Issue

In this age of devastating sexually transmitted diseases, there is no time more important to increase our scientific understanding of human sexuality. As we will see, however, this is a difficult topic to research, not only because of privacy concerns but because of all the preconceptions, myths, and beliefs people bring to the subject of sexuality. Many people actively oppose research on human sexuality. How does one carry out scientific research on such a controversial and personal topic?

There is little question that we live in a highly sexualized society. The mass media continually bombard us with sexual ideas and images. However, as a study released in 2018 reveals, it is women rather than men who are disproportionately sexualized, particularly in motion pictures. A content analysis of the characters in top box-office films of 2017 showed that women are much more likely than men to be shown in sexy attire, with some degree of nudity, or specifically referred to as "attractive" (see Figure 2-5).

Applying Sociology

Sociologists have little reliable national data on patterns of sexual behavior in the United States. Until the 1990s, the only comprehensive study of sexual behavior was the famous two-volume *Kinsey Report,* prepared in the 1940s (Kinsey et al. 1948, 1953; see also Igo 2007). Although the *Kinsey Report* is still widely quoted, the volunteers interviewed for the report were not representative of the nation's adult population.

In part, we lack reliable data on patterns of sexual behavior because it is difficult for researchers to obtain accurate information about this sensitive subject. Moreover, until AIDS emerged in the 1980s, there was little scientific demand for data on sexual behavior, except for specific concerns such as contraception. And even though the AIDS crisis has reached dramatic proportions, government funding for studies of sexual behavior is still controversial and therefore difficult to obtain.

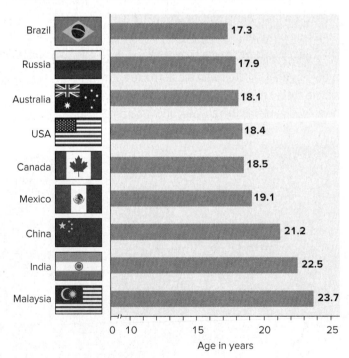

FIGURE 2-6   MEDIAN AGE OF FIRST SEX

Source: Durex 2013. *Flags:* admin_design/Shutterstock

The controversy surrounding research on human sexual behavior raises the issue of value neutrality, which becomes especially delicate when one considers the relationship of sociology to the government. The federal government has become the major source of funding for sociological research. Yet Max Weber urged that sociology remain an autonomous discipline and not become unduly influenced by any one segment of society. According to Weber's ideal of value neutrality, sociologists must remain free to reveal information that is embarrassing to the government, or for that matter, supportive of government institutions.

Initiating Policy

In 1987 the National Institute of Child Health and Human Development sought proposals for a national survey of sexual behavior. Sociologists responded with various plans that a review panel of scientists approved for funding. However, in 1991, the U.S. Senate voted to forbid funding any survey of adult sexual practices. Despite the vote, sociologists developed the National Health and Social Life Survey (NHSLS) to better understand the sexual practices of adults in the United States. The researchers raised $1.6 million of *private* funding to make their study possible (Laumann et al. 1994a, 1994b).

The authors of the NHSLS believe that their research is important. They argue that data from their survey allow interest groups to more easily address public policy issues such as AIDS, sexual harassment, welfare reform, sex discrimination, abortion, teenage pregnancy, and family planning. Moreover, the research findings help to counter

some commonsense notions. For instance, contrary to the popular beliefs that women regularly use abortion for birth control and that poor teens are the most likely socioeconomic group to have abortions, researchers found that three-fourths of all abortions are the first for the woman, and that well-educated and affluent women are more likely to have abortions than poor teens (Sweet 2001).

The usefulness of the NHSLS in addressing public policy issues has proved influential. As Figure 2-6 shows, scholars around the world are now studying human sexual behavior, in an effort to reduce the occurrence of HIV/AIDS.

Take the Issue with You

1. Do you see any merit in the position of those who oppose government funding for research on sexual behavior? Explain your reasoning.

2. Exactly how could the results of research on human sexual behavior be used to control sexually transmitted diseases?

3. Compare the issue of value neutrality in government-funded research to the same issue in corporate-funded research. Are concerns about conflict of interest more or less serious in regard to government funding?

APPENDIX I Using Statistics and Graphs

In their effort to better understand social behavior, sociologists rely heavily on numbers and statistics. For example, how have attitudes toward the legalization of marijuana changed over the past 50 years? A quick look at the results of 20 national surveys shows that support for legalization of the drug has increased (Figure 2-7), to the point that the most recent survey shows almost majority support for legalization.

Recent legislation on the state level has complicated the task of assessing public opinion on this issue. Some states have passed initiatives legalizing the possession of small amounts of marijuana, even though possession remains illegal under the federal Controlled Substances Act. Researchers now must track how public opinion differs from the national trend in states where marijuana use is both tolerated and legal.

FIGURE 2-7   CHANGING ATTITUDES TOWARD THE LEGALIZATION OF MARIJUANA

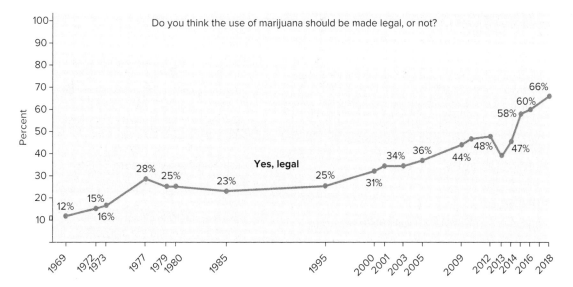

Source: McCarthy, Justin. "Two in Three Americans Now Support Legalizing Marijuana." Gallup, October 22, 2018. https://news.gallup.com/poll/243908/two-three-americans-support-legalizing-marijuana.aspx.

Using Statistics

The most common summary measures used by sociologists are percentages, means, modes, and medians. A **percentage** is a portion of 100. Use of percentages allows us to compare groups of different sizes. For example, if we were comparing financial contributors to a town's Baptist and Roman Catholic churches, the absolute numbers of contributors in each group could be misleading if there were many more Baptists than Catholics in the town. By using percentages, we could obtain a more meaningful comparison, showing the proportion of persons in each group who contribute to churches.

The **mean,** or *average,* is a number calculated by adding a series of values and then dividing by the number of values. For example, to find the mean of the numbers 5, 19, and 27, we would add them together (for a total of 51), divide by the number of values (3), and discover that the mean is 17.

The **mode** is the single most common value in a series of scores. Suppose we were looking at the following scores on a 10-point quiz:

10 10 9 9 8 8 7 7 7 6 5

The mode—the most frequent score on the quiz—is 7. While the mode is easier to identify than other summary measures, it tells sociologists little about all the other values. Hence, you will find much less use of the mode in this book than of the mean and the median.

The **median** is the midpoint or number that divides a series of values into two groups of equal numbers of values. For the quiz just discussed, the median, or central value, is 8. The mean, or average, would be 86 (the sum of all scores) divided by 11 (the total number of scores), or 7.8.

Some of these statistics may seem confusing at first. But think how difficult it is to comb through an endless list of numbers to identify a pattern or central tendency. Percentages, means, modes, and medians are essential time-savers in sociological research and analysis.

Reading Graphs

Tables and figures (that is, graphs) allow social scientists to display data and develop their conclusions more easily. In October 2018, the Gallup poll interviewed 1,019 people in the United States age 18 and over, by both cell phone and landlines. Each respondent was asked, "Do you think the use of marijuana should be made legal, or not?" Without some type of summary, there is no way that analysts could examine the hundreds of individual responses to this question and reach firm conclusions. One type of summary sociologists use, a **cross-tabulation**, shows the relationship between two or more variables. Through the cross-tabulations presented graphically in Figure 2-8, we can quickly see that older people are less likely to favor the legalization of marijuana than younger people, and that Republicans are less supportive of legalization than Democrats.

Graphs, like tables, can be quite useful to sociologists. And illustrations are often easier for the general public to understand, whether in newspapers or in PowerPoint presentations. Still, as with all data, we need to be careful how they are presented.

FIGURE 2-8   PEOPLE WHO FAVOR LEGALIZATION OF MARIJUANA BY POLITICAL AFFILIATION AND AGE

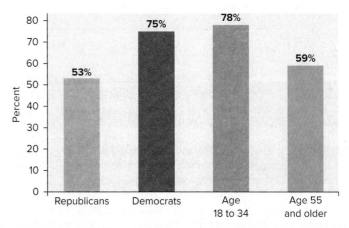

Source: McCarthy 2018.

APPENDIX II   Writing a Research Report

Let's say you have decided to write a report on cohabitation (unmarried couples living together). How do you go about doing the necessary library research? Students must follow procedures similar to those used by sociologists in conducting original research. For your first step you must define the problem that you wish to study—perhaps in this case, how much cohabitation occurs and what its impact is on later marital happiness. The next step is to review the literature, which generally requires library research.

Finding Information

The following steps will be helpful in finding information:

1. Don't forget to begin with the materials closest at hand. Check this textbook and other textbooks that you own.

2. Use the library's online catalog. Computerized library systems now access not only the library's collection but also books and magazines from other libraries, available through interlibrary loans. These systems allow you to search for books by author or title. You can use title searches to locate books by subject as well. For example, if you search the title base for the keyword *cohabitation,* you will learn where books with that word in the title are located in the library's stacks. Near those books will be other works on cohabitation, which may not happen to have that word in the title. You may also want to search other, related keywords, such as *unmarried couples.*

3. Investigate using computerized periodical indexes, if they are available in your library. *Sociological Abstracts* online covers most sociological writing since 1952. In 2020, a search of just this one database found exactly 3,314 documents having either *cohabitation* or *unmarried couples* as words in the abstract or summary. Some dealt with laws about cohabitation, while others focused on trends in other countries. If you limited your topic to same-sex couples, you would find 169 citations. Other electronic databases cover general-interest periodicals (*Time, Ms., National*

Review, The Atlantic, and so forth), reference materials, or newspapers. These electronic systems may be connected to a printer, allowing you to produce a printout complete with bibliographic information, and sometimes even complete copies of articles.

4. Examine government documents. The U.S. government, states and cities, and the United Nations publish information on virtually every subject of interest to social science researchers. Publications of the Census Bureau, for example, include tables showing the number of unmarried couples living together and some social characteristics of those households.

5. Ask people, organizations, and agencies concerned with the topic for information and assistance. Be as specific as possible in making requests. You might receive very different information on the issue of cohabitation from talking with marriage counselors and with clergy from different religions.

6. If you run into difficulties, consult the instructor or the reference librarian at your school library.

A word of caution: be extremely careful in using the Internet to do research. Much of the information on the Internet is simply incorrect—even if it looks authoritative, is accompanied by impressive graphics, or has been widely circulated. Unlike the information in a library, which must be screened by a highly qualified librarian, "information" on the Internet can be created and posted by anyone with a computer. Check the sources for the information and note the web page sponsor. Is the author qualified to write on the subject? Is the author even identified? Is the web page sponsor likely to be biased? Whenever possible, try to confirm what you have read on the Internet through a well-known, reputable source or organization. If the accuracy of the information could be affected by how old it is, check

the date on which the page or article was created or updated. Used intelligently, the Internet is a wonderful tool that offers students access to many of the reliable print sources noted earlier, including government documents and newspaper archives extending back over a century.

Writing the Report

Once you have completed all your research, you can begin writing the report. Here are a few tips:

- Be sure the topic you have chosen is not too broad. You must be able to cover it adequately in a reasonable amount of time and a reasonable number of pages.

- Develop an outline for your report. You should have an introduction and a conclusion that relate to each other, and the discussion should proceed logically throughout the paper. Use headings within the paper if they will improve clarity and organization.

- Do not leave all the writing until the last minute. It is best to write a rough draft, let it sit for a few days, and then take a fresh look before beginning revisions.

- If possible, read your paper aloud. Doing so may be helpful in locating sections or phrases that don't make sense.

Remember that you *must* cite all information you have obtained from other sources, including the Internet. Plagiarism is a serious academic offense, for which the penalties are severe. If you use an author's exact words, it is essential that you place them in quotation marks. Even if you reworked someone else's ideas, you must indicate the source of those ideas.

MASTERING THIS CHAPTER

Summary

Sociologists are committed to the use of the **scientific method** in their research efforts. In this chapter we examined the basic principles of the scientific method and studied various techniques used by sociologists in conducting research.

1. There are five basic steps in the **scientific method:** defining the problem, reviewing the literature, formulating the hypothesis, collecting and analyzing the data, and developing the conclusion.

2. Whenever researchers wish to study abstract concepts, such as intelligence or prejudice, they must develop workable **operational definitions.**

3. A **hypothesis** states a possible relationship between two or more variables.

4. By using a **sample,** sociologists avoid having to test everyone in a population.

5. According to the scientific method, research results must possess both **validity** and **reliability.**

6. An important part of scientific research is devising a plan for collecting data, called a **research design.**

7. The two principal forms of survey research are the **interview** and the **questionnaire.**

8. **Ethnography** allows sociologists to study certain behaviors and communities that cannot be investigated through other research methods.

9. When sociologists wish to study a cause-and-effect relationship, they may conduct an **experiment.**

10. Sociologists also make use of existing sources in **secondary analysis** and **content analysis.**

11. The *Code of Ethics* of the American Sociological Association calls for objectivity and integrity in research, confidentiality, and disclosure of all sources of financial support.

12. Max Weber urged sociologists to practice **value neutrality** in their research by ensuring that their personal feelings do not influence their interpretation of data.

13. Technology plays an important role in sociological research, whether through a computer database or information obtained from the Internet.

14. Despite failure to obtain government funding, researchers developed the National Health and Social Life Survey (NHSLS) to better understand the sexual practices of adults in the United States.

Key Terms

Applied sociology The use of the discipline of sociology with the specific intent of yielding practical applications for human behavior and organizations. (page 39)

Causal logic The relationship between a condition or variable and a particular consequence, with one leading to the other. (31)

Code of ethics The standards of acceptable behavior developed by and for members of a profession. (41)

Content analysis The systematic coding and objective recording of data, guided by some rationale. (40)

Control group The subjects in an experiment who are not introduced to the independent variable by the researcher. (38)

Control variable A factor that is held constant to test the relative impact of an independent variable. (34)

Correlation A relationship between two variables in which a change in one coincides with a change in the other. (31)

Cross-tabulation A table or matrix that shows the relationship between two or more variables. (48)

Dependent variable The variable in a causal relationship that is subject to the influence of another variable. (31)

Ethnography The study of an entire social setting through extended systematic fieldwork. (37)

Experiment An artificially created situation that allows a researcher to manipulate variables. (38)

Experimental group The subjects in an experiment who are exposed to an independent variable introduced by a researcher. (38)

Hawthorne effect The unintended influence that observers of experiments can have on their subjects. (38)

Hypothesis A speculative statement about the relationship between two or more variables. (31)

Independent variable The variable in a causal relationship that causes or influences a change in another variable. (31)

Interview A face-to-face, phone, or online questioning of a respondent to obtain desired information. (36)

Mean A number calculated by adding a series of values and then dividing by the number of values. (48)

Median The midpoint or number that divides a series of values into two groups of equal numbers of values. (48)

Mode The single most common value in a series of scores. (48)

Observation A research technique in which an investigator collects information through direct participation, by closely watching a group or community. (37)

Operational definition An explanation of an abstract concept that is specific enough to allow a researcher to assess the concept. (31)

Percentage A portion of 100. (48)

Qualitative research Research that relies on what is seen in field or naturalistic settings more than on statistical data. (37)

Quantitative research Research that collects and reports data primarily in numerical form. (37)

Questionnaire A printed or written form used to obtain information from a respondent. (36)

Random sample A sample for which every member of an entire population has the same chance of being selected. (33)

Reliability The extent to which a measure produces consistent results. (33)

Research design A detailed plan or method for obtaining data scientifically. (35)

Sample A selection from a larger population that is statistically representative of that population. (33)

Scientific method A systematic, organized series of steps that ensures maximum objectivity and consistency in researching a problem. (30)

Secondary analysis A variety of research techniques that make use of previously collected and publicly accessible information and data. (38)

Survey A study, generally in the form of an interview or questionnaire, that provides researchers with information about how people think and act. (35)

Validity The degree to which a measure or scale truly reflects the phenomenon under study. (33)

Value neutrality Max Weber's term for objectivity of sociologists in the interpretation of data. (43)

Variable A measurable trait or characteristic that is subject to change under different conditions. (31)

Visual sociology The use of photographs, film, and video to study society. (39)

TAKING SOCIOLOGY with you

1. Find photos of a sporting or music event. Then ask five different people (different ages, genders) who were not at the event to describe what they see. Do you get different responses? Share your findings with the class.

2. Pick a current issue in your community. How would you go about studying that issue using the scientific method? Begin by defining your terms and stating a working hypothesis. Then consider the most appropriate research methods to use.

3. Choose an aspect of your day-to-day environment that could be studied using the techniques of visual sociology. How would you design a research study using these techniques?

4. **Writing Sociology.** Go to the Census Bureau's website (https://www.census.gov/) and browse the topics on the site. Choose a topic of interest to you and read one or more news stories or publications on the topic. Write a summary of how data was used and what the data supported and share it with the class.

Self-Quiz

Read each question carefully and then select the best answer.

1. The first step in any sociological research project is to
   a. collect data.
   b. define the problem.
   c. review previous research.
   d. formulate a hypothesis.

2. An explanation of an abstract concept that is specific enough to allow a researcher to measure the concept is a(n)
   a. hypothesis.
   b. correlation.
   c. operational definition.
   d. variable.

3. The variable hypothesized to cause or influence another is called the
   a. dependent variable.
   b. hypothetical variable.
   c. correlation variable.
   d. independent variable.

4. A correlation exists when
   a. one variable causes something to occur in another variable.
   b. two or more variables are causally related.
   c. a change in one variable coincides with a change in another variable.
   d. a negative relationship exists between two variables.

5. Through which type of research technique does a sociologist ensure that data are statistically representative of the population being studied?
   a. sampling
   b. experiments
   c. ethnography
   d. control variables

6. In order to obtain a random sample, a researcher might
   a. administer a questionnaire to every fifth woman who enters a business office.
   b. examine the attitudes of undergraduates at a college by interviewing every 100th name in the official list of currently enrolled students.
   c. study the attitudes of registered Democratic voters by choosing every 10th name found on a city's list of registered Democrats.
   d. do all of the above.

7. A researcher can obtain a higher response rate by using which type of survey?
   a. an interview
   b. a questionnaire
   c. representative samples
   d. ethnographic techniques

8. In the 1930s, William F. Whyte moved into a low-income Italian neighborhood in Boston. For nearly four years, he was a member of the social circle of "corner boys" that he describes in *Street Corner Society*. His goal was to gain greater insight into the community established by these men. What type of research technique did Whyte use?
   a. experiment
   b. survey
   c. secondary analysis
   d. participant observation

9. When sociologists want to study a possible cause-and-effect relationship, they may engage in what kind of research technique?
   a. ethnography
   b. survey research
   c. secondary analysis
   d. experiment

10. Émile Durkheim's statistical analysis of suicide was an example of what kind of research technique?
    a. ethnography
    b. observation research
    c. secondary analysis
    d. experimental research

11. Unlike the typical citizen, the sociologist has a commitment to use the _____ method in studying society.

12. A(n) _____ is a speculative statement about the relationship between two or more factors known as variables.

13. _____ refers to the degree to which a measure or scale truly reflects the phenomenon under study.

14. In order to obtain data scientifically, researchers need to select a research _____ .

15. If scientists were testing a new type of toothpaste in an experimental setting, they would administer the toothpaste to a(n) _____ _____ group, but not to a(n) _____ group.

16. The term _____ refers to the unintended influence that observers of experiments can have on their subjects.

17. Using census data in a way unintended by its initial collectors would be an example of _____ .

18. Using _____ , researchers conducted a study of gender-stereotyped behavior in children's coloring books.

19. The American Sociological Association's *Code of* _____ requires sociologists to maintain objectivity and integrity and to preserve the confidentiality of their subjects.

20. As part of their commitment to _____ neutrality, investigators have an ethical obligation to accept research findings even when the data run counter to their personal views or to widely accepted beliefs.

_____

Culture

Agencja Fotograficzna Caro/Alamy Stock Photo

Culture is a part of every society, but that does not mean it remains static over time. In Thailand, novice Buddhist monks amuse themselves by playing computer games. Computers and the Internet here also promote the Dharma—the Buddha's teachings—in ways unimaginable just a generation ago.

▶ INSIDE

NASA

What do you think of the society described here by anthropologist Horace Miner?

Could you live in such a culture?

"Nacirema culture is characterized by a highly developed market economy which has evolved in a rich natural habitat. While much of the people's time is devoted to economic pursuits, a large part of the fruits of these labors and a considerable portion of the day are spent in ritual activity. The focus of this activity is the human body, the appearance and health of which loom as a dominant concern in the ethos of the people.

The fundamental belief underlying the whole system appears to be that the human body is ugly and that its natural tendency is to debility and disease. (The) only hope is to avert these characteristics through the use of the powerful influences of ritual and ceremony. The more powerful individuals in the society have several shrines in their houses and, in fact, the opulence of a house is often referred to in terms of the number of such ritual centers it possesses.

While each family has at least one such shrine, the rituals associated with it are not family ceremonies but are private and secret. The rites are normally only discussed with children, and then only during the period when they are being initiated into these mysteries.

The focal point of the shrine is a box or chest which is built into the wall. In this chest are kept the many charms and magical potions without which no native believes he could live. These preparations are secured from a variety of specialized practitioners. The most powerful of these are the medicine men, whose assistance must be rewarded with substantial gifts. However, the medicine men do not provide the curative potions for their clients, but decide what the ingredients should be and then write them down in an ancient and secret language."

Source: Miner 1956.

The focal point of the shrine is a box or chest which is built into the wall. In this chest are kept the many charms and magical potions without which no native believes he could live.

In this excerpt from his journal article "Body Ritual among the Nacirema," Horace Miner casts an anthropologist's observant eye on the intriguing rituals of an exotic culture. If some aspects of this culture seem familiar to you, you are right, for what Miner is describing is actually the culture of the United States ("Nacirema" is "American" spelled backward). The "shrine" Miner writes of is the bathroom; he correctly informs us that in this culture, one measure of wealth is how many bathrooms one's home has. In their bathroom rituals, he goes on, the Nacirema use charms and magical potions (beauty products and prescription drugs) obtained from specialized practitioners (such as hair stylists), herbalists (pharmacists), and medicine men (physicians). Using our sociological imaginations, we could update Miner's description of the Nacirema's charms, written in 1956, by adding tooth whiteners, contact lens cases, electronic toothbrushes, and hair gel.

When we step back and examine a culture thoughtfully and objectively, whether it is our own culture in disguise or another less familiar to us, we learn something new about society. Take Fiji, an island in the Pacific where a robust, nicely rounded body has always been the ideal for both men and women. This is a society in which traditionally "You've gained weight" has been

considered a compliment, and "Your legs are skinny" an insult. Yet a recent study shows that for the first time, eating disorders have been showing up among young people in Fiji.

What has happened to change their body image? Since the introduction of cable television in 1995, many Fiji islanders, especially young women, have begun to emulate not their mothers and aunts, but the small-waisted stars of television programs still airing there, like *The Bachelor*, *Criminal Minds*, and *Black-ish*. Studying culture in places like Fiji, then, sheds light on our society as well (A. Becker 2007; Fiji TV 2020).

In this chapter we will see just how basic the study of culture is to sociology. Our discussion will focus both on general cultural practices found in all societies and on the wide variations that can distinguish one society from another. We will define and explore the major aspects of culture, including language, norms, sanctions, and values. We will see how cultures develop a dominant ideology, and how functionalist and conflict theorists view culture. And we'll study the development of culture around the world, including the cultural effects of globalization. Finally, in the Social Policy section, we will look at the conflicts in cultural values that underlie current debates over bilingualism.

What Is Culture?

Culture is the totality of learned, socially transmitted customs, knowledge, material objects, and behavior. It includes the ideas, values, and artifacts (for example, DVDs, comic books, and birth control devices) of groups of people. Patriotic attachment to the flag of the United States is an aspect of U.S. culture, as is a national passion for the tango in Argentina's culture.

Sometimes people refer to a particular person as "very cultured" or to a city as having "lots of culture." That use of the term *culture* is different from our use in this textbook. In sociological terms, culture does not refer solely to the fine arts and refined intellectual taste. It consists of *all* objects and ideas within a society, including slang words, ice-cream cones, and rock music. Sociologists consider both a portrait by Rembrandt and the work of graffiti spray painters to be aspects of culture. A tribe that cultivates soil by hand has just as much culture as a people that relies on computer-operated machinery. Each people has a distinctive culture with its own characteristic ways of gathering and preparing food, constructing homes, structuring the family, and promoting standards of right and wrong.

The fact that you share a similar culture with others helps to define the group or society to which you belong. A fairly large number of people are said to constitute a **society** when they live in the same territory, are relatively independent of people outside their area, and participate in a common culture.

Rob Watkins/Alamy Stock Photo

Play ball! Baseball in Finland is not the same game we know in North America. The pitcher stands next to the batter and throws the ball up to be hit. If successful, the batter runs to first base (where we would expect third base to be). Surveys show that baseball is the second most popular sport (after ice hockey) among men and the most popular among women. Introduced in 1907, baseball evolved very differently in Finland than in the United States, but in both countries it is a vital part of the culture.

Metropolitan Los Angeles is more populous than at least 130 nations, yet sociologists do not consider it a society in its own right. Rather, they see it as part of—and dependent on—the larger society of the United States.

A society is the largest form of human group. It consists of people who share a common heritage and culture. Members of the society learn this culture and transmit it from one generation to the next. They even preserve their distinctive culture through literature, art, video recordings, and other means of expression.

Sociologists have long recognized the many ways in which culture influences human behavior. Through what has been termed a tool kit of habits, skills, and styles, people of a common culture construct their acquisition of knowledge, their interactions with kinfolk, their entrance into the job market—in short, the way in which they live. If it were not for the social transmission of culture, each generation would have to reinvent communication, not to mention the wheel.

Having a common culture also simplifies many day-to-day interactions. For example, when you buy an airline ticket, you know you don't have to bring along hundreds of dollars in cash. You can pay with a credit card. When you are part of a society, you take for granted many small (as well as more important) cultural patterns. You assume that theaters will provide seats for the audience, that physicians will not disclose confidential information, and that parents will be careful when crossing the street with young children. All these assumptions reflect basic values, beliefs, and customs of the culture of the United States.

Today, when text, sound, and video can be transmitted around the world instantaneously, some aspects of culture transcend national borders. The German philosopher Theodor Adorno and others have spoken of the worldwide "culture industry" that standardizes the goods and services demanded by consumers. Adorno contends that globally, the primary effect of popular culture is to limit people's choices. Yet others have shown that the culture industry's influence does not always permeate international borders. Sometimes the culture industry is embraced; at other times, soundly rejected (Adorno [1971] 1991:98–106; Horkheimer and Adorno [1944] 2002).

Cultural Universals

All societies have developed certain common practices and beliefs, known as **cultural universals.** Many cultural universals are, in fact, adaptations to meet essential human needs, such as the need for food, shelter, and clothing. Polish-born anthropologist George Murdock (1945:124) compiled a list of cultural universals, including athletic sports, cooking, dancing, visiting, personal names, marriage, medicine, religious ritual, funeral ceremonies, sexual restrictions, and trade.

The cultural practices Murdock listed may be universal, but the manner in which they are expressed varies from culture to culture. For example, one society may let its members choose their marriage partners; another may encourage marriages arranged by the parents.

Not only does the expression of cultural universals vary from one society to another; within a society, it may also change dramatically over time. Each generation, and each year for that matter, most human cultures change and expand.

Ethnocentrism

Many everyday statements reflect our attitude that our culture is best. We use terms such as *underdeveloped, backward,* and *primitive* to refer to other societies. What "we" believe is a religion; what "they" believe is superstition and mythology.

It is tempting to evaluate the practices of other cultures on the basis of our perspectives. Sociologist William Graham Sumner (1906) coined the term **ethnocentrism** to refer to the tendency to assume that one's own culture and way of life represent the norm or are superior to all others. The ethnocentric person sees his or her group as the center or defining point of culture and views all other cultures as deviations from what is "normal." Westerners who think cattle are to be used for food might look down on India's Hindu religion and culture, which view the cow as sacred. Or people in one culture may dismiss as unthinkable the mate selection or child-rearing practices of another culture. In sum, our view of the world is dramatically influenced by the society in which we were raised.

Ethnocentrism is hardly limited to citizens of the United States. Visitors from many African cultures are surprised at the disrespect that children in the United States show their parents. People from India may be repelled by our practice of living in the same household with dogs and cats. Many Islamic fundamentalists in the Arab world and Asia view the United States as corrupt, decadent, and doomed to destruction. All these people may feel comforted by membership in cultures that in their view are superior to ours.

Cultural Relativism

While ethnocentrism means evaluating foreign cultures using the familiar culture of the observer as a standard of correct behavior, **cultural relativism** means viewing people's behavior from the perspective of their own culture. It places a priority on understanding other cultures, rather than dismissing them as "strange" or "exotic." Unlike ethnocentrists, cultural relativists employ the kind of value neutrality in scientific study that Max Weber saw as so important.

Cultural relativism stresses that different social contexts give rise to different norms and values. Thus, we must examine practices such as polygamy, bullfighting, and monarchy within the particular contexts of the cultures in which they are found. Although cultural relativism does not suggest that we must unquestionably accept every cultural variation, it does require a serious and unbiased effort to evaluate norms, values, and customs in light of their distinctive culture.

Consider the practice of children marrying adults. Most people in North America cannot fathom the idea of a 12-year-old girl marrying. The U.S. government has spent millions to discourage the practice in many of the countries with the highest child marriage rates (Figure 3-1).

From the perspective of cultural relativism, we might ask whether one society should spend its resources to dictate the norms of another. However, federal officials have defended the government's actions. They contend that child marriage deprives girls of education, threatens their health, and weakens public health efforts to combat HIV/AIDS (UNICEF 2018).

Sociobiology and Culture

While sociology emphasizes diversity and change in the expression of culture, another school of thought, sociobiology, stresses the universal aspects of culture. **Sociobiology** is the systematic study of how biology affects human social behavior. Sociobiologists assert that many of the cultural traits humans display, such as the almost universal expectation that women will be nurturers and men will be providers, are not learned but are rooted in our genetic makeup.

Sociobiology is founded on the naturalist Charles Darwin's (1859) theory of evolution. In traveling the world, Darwin had noted small variations in species—in the shape of a bird's beak, for example—from one location to another. He theorized that over hundreds of generations, random variations in genetic makeup had helped certain members of a species to survive in a particular environment. A bird with a differently shaped beak might have been better at gathering seeds than other birds, for instance. In reproducing, these lucky individuals had passed on their advantageous genes to succeeding generations. Eventually, given their advantage in survival, individuals with the variation began to outnumber other members of the species. The species was slowly adapting to its environment. Darwin called this process of adaptation to the environment through random genetic variation *natural selection*.

Sociobiologists apply Darwin's principle of natural selection to the study of social behavior. They assume that particular forms of behavior become genetically linked to a species if they contribute to its fitness to survive (van den Berghe 1978). In its extreme form, sociobiology suggests that *all* behavior is the result of genetic or biological factors, and that social interactions play no role in shaping people's conduct.

Sociobiologists do not seek to describe individual behavior on the level of "Why is Fred more aggressive than Jim?" Rather,

MAPPING LIFE WORLDWIDE

FIGURE 3-1   COUNTRIES WITH HIGH CHILD MARRIAGE RATES

In 16 countries, 40 percent or more of women under age 18 are married.

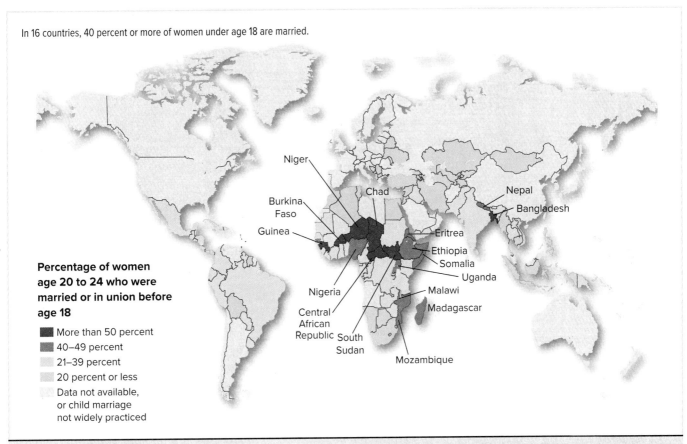

Percentage of women age 20 to 24 who were married or in union before age 18

- More than 50 percent
- 40–49 percent
- 21–39 percent
- 20 percent or less
- Data not available, or child marriage not widely practiced

Niger, Burkina Faso, Guinea, Nigeria, Central African Republic, South Sudan, Chad, Eritrea, Ethiopia, Somalia, Uganda, Malawi, Madagascar, Mozambique, Nepal, Bangladesh

Think about It What does tolerance of child marriage imply about a culture's attitude toward women? Toward children?

Note: Data are the most recent available, ranging from 2003 to 2017.

Source: UNICEF 2018.

they focus on how human nature is affected by the genetic composition of a *group* of people who share certain characteristics (such as men or women, or members of isolated tribal bands). In general, sociobiologists have stressed the basic genetic heritage that *all* humans share and have shown little interest in speculating about alleged differences between racial groups or nationalities. A few researchers have tried to trace specific behaviors, like criminal activity, to certain genetic markers, but those markers are not deterministic. Family cohesiveness, peer group behavior, and other social factors can override genetic influences on behavior (Guo et al. 2008; E. O. Wilson 1975, 1978).

THINKING CRITICALLY

Select three cultural universals from George Murdock's list and analyze them from a functionalist perspective. Why are these practices found in every culture? What functions do they serve?

Certainly most social scientists agree that there is a biological basis for social behavior. However, regardless of their theoretical position, most sociologists would likewise agree that people's behavior, not their genetic structure, defines social reality. Conflict theorists fear that the sociobiological approach could be used as an argument against efforts to assist disadvantaged people, such as schoolchildren who are not competing successfully (Freese 2008; Machalek and Martin 2010; E. O. Wilson 2000).

Role of Language

Language is one of the major elements of culture. It is also an important component of cultural capital. Recall from Chapter 1 that Pierre Bourdieu used the term **cultural capital** to describe noneconomic assets, such as family background and past educational investments, which are reflected in a person's knowledge of language and the arts.

Members of a society generally share a common language, which facilitates day-to-day exchanges with others. When you ask a hardware store clerk for a flashlight, you don't need to draw a picture of the instrument. You share the same cultural term for a small, portable, battery-operated light. However, if you were in England and needed this item, you would have to ask for an electric torch. Of course, even within the same society, a term can have a number of different meanings. In the United States, *pot* signifies both a container that is used for cooking and an intoxicating drug. In this section we will examine the cultural influence of language, which includes both the written and spoken word and nonverbal communication.

Language: Written and Spoken

Seven thousand languages are spoken in the world today—many more than the number of countries. For the speakers of each one, whether they number 2,000 or 200 million, language is fundamental to their shared culture.

The English language, for example, makes extensive use of words dealing with war. We speak of "conquering" space,

Courtesy of the Oneida Indian Nation

A native speaker trains instructors from the Oneida Nation of New York in the Berlitz method of language teaching. As of 2019, there were only around 34 fully fluent speakers of the Oneida language. Many Native American tribes are taking similar steps to recover their seldom used languages, realizing that language is the essential foundation of any culture.

"fighting" the "battle" of the budget, "waging war" on drugs, making a "killing" on the stock market, and "bombing" an examination; something monumental or great is "the bomb." An observer from an entirely different culture could gauge the importance that war and the military have had in our lives simply by recognizing the prominence that militaristic terms have in our language. Similarly, the Sami people of northern Norway and Sweden have a rich diversity of terms for snow, ice, and reindeer (Haviland et al. 2015; Magga 2006).

Language is the foundation of every culture. **Language** is an abstract system of word meanings and symbols for all aspects of culture. It includes speech, written characters, numerals, symbols, and nonverbal gestures and expressions. Because language is the foundation of every culture, the ability to speak other languages is crucial to intercultural relations. Throughout the Cold War era, beginning in the 1950s and continuing well into the 1970s, the U.S. government encouraged the study of Russian by developing special language schools for diplomats and military advisers who dealt with the Soviet Union.

Language does more than simply describe reality; it also serves to *shape* the reality of a culture. For example, most people in the United States cannot easily make the verbal distinctions concerning snow and ice that are possible in the Sami culture. As a result, they are less likely to notice such differences.

For decades, the Navajo have referred to cancer as *lood doo na'dziihii.* Now, through a project funded by the National Cancer Institute, the tribal college is seeking to change the phrase. Why? Literally, the phrase means "the sore that does not heal," and health educators are concerned that tribal members who have been diagnosed with cancer view it as a death sentence. Their effort to change the Navajo language, not easy in itself, is complicated by the Navajo belief that to talk about the disease is to bring it on one's people (Fonseca 2008).

Similarly, feminist theorists have noted that gender-related language can reflect—although in itself it does not determine—the traditional acceptance of men and women in certain occupations. Each time we use a term such as *mailman, policeman,* or *fireman,* we are implying (especially to young children) that these occupations can be filled only by males. Yet many women work as *mail carriers, police officers,* and *firefighters*—a fact that is being increasingly recognized and legitimized through the use of such nonsexist language.

Language can shape how we see, taste, smell, feel, and hear. It also influences the way we think about the people, ideas, and objects around us. Language communicates a culture's most important norms, values, and sanctions. That's why the decline of an old language or the introduction of a new one is such a sensitive issue in many parts of the world (see the Social Policy section at the end of this chapter).

Interaction increasingly takes place via mobile devices rather than face to face. Social scientists are beginning to investigate how language used in texting varies in different societies and cultures. For example, in much of Africa, small farmers use texting for the vital task of checking commodity prices. You probably use texting to perform a wide range of communication tasks.

Nonverbal Communication

If you don't like the way a meeting is going, you might suddenly sit back, fold your arms, and turn down the corners of your mouth. When you see a friend in tears, you may give a quick hug. After winning a big game, you probably high-five your teammates. These are all examples of **nonverbal communication,** the use of gestures, facial expressions, and other visual images to communicate.

Think about It What meaning do Confederate symbols have for you? Do you think they should be removed or replaced?

LM Otero/AP Images

Symbols can be powerful, yet different people may understand them in different ways. In recent years there has been a call to remove or place in a different context statues and other monuments honoring the Confederate States of America because of the inherent meaning they represent. Others feel that such symbols represent important values of the past. Here we see a statue of Confederate General Robert E. Lee being removed by Dallas city workers in 2017.

We are not born with these expressions. We learn them, just as we learn other forms of language, from people who share our same culture. This statement is as true for the basic expressions of happiness and sadness as it is for more complex emotions, such as shame or distress (Hall et al. 2019).

Like other forms of language, nonverbal communication is not the same in all cultures. For example, sociological research done at the micro-level documents that people from various cultures differ in the degree to which they touch others during the course of normal social interactions. Even experienced travelers are sometimes caught off guard by these differences. In Saudi Arabia, a middle-aged man may want to hold hands with a partner after closing a business deal. In Egypt, heterosexual men walk hand in hand in the street; in cafés, they fall asleep while lounging in each other's arms. These gestures, which would shock an American businessman, are considered compliments in those cultures. The meaning of hand signals is another form of nonverbal communication that can differ from one culture to the next. In Australia, the thumbs-up sign is considered rude (Passero 2002; Vaughan 2007).

A related form of communication is the use of symbols to convey meaning to others. **Symbols** are the gestures, objects, and words that form the basis of human communication. The thumbs-up gesture, a gold star sticker, and the smiley face in an e-mail are all symbols. Often deceptively simple, many symbols are rich in meaning and may not convey the same meaning in all social contexts. Around someone's neck, for example, a cross can symbolize religious reverence; over a grave site, a belief in everlasting life; or set in flames, racial hatred. Box 3-1 describes the delicate task of designing an appropriate symbol for the 9/11 memorial at New York's former World Trade Center—one that would have meaning for everyone who lost loved ones there, regardless of nationality or religious faith.

THINKING CRITICALLY

Explain how the way you communicate verbally and nonverbally can be a form of cultural capital.

Norms and Values

"Wash your hands before dinner." "Thou shalt not kill." "Respect your elders." All societies have ways of encouraging and enforcing what they view as appropriate behavior while discouraging and punishing what they consider to be inappropriate behavior. They also have a collective idea of what is good and desirable in life—or not. In this section we will learn to distinguish between the closely related concepts of norms and values.

SOCIOLOGY IN THE GLOBAL COMMUNITY

3-1 Symbolizing 9/11

On September 11, 2001, the World Trade Center's Twin Towers took only minutes to collapse. Nearly a decade later, the creator of the memorial to those lost that day was still perfecting the site plan. Thirty-four-year-old architect Michael Arad, the man who submitted the winning design, had drawn two sunken squares, measuring an acre each, in the footprints left by the collapsed towers. His design, "Reflecting Absence," places each empty square in a reflecting pool surrounded by cascading water. Today, as visitors to the massive memorial stand at the edge of the site, they are struck by both the sound of the thundering water and the absence of life.

The memorial does not encompass the entire area destroyed in the attack, as some had wanted. In one of the great commercial capitals of the world, economic forces demanded that some part of the property produce income. Others had argued against constructing a memorial of any kind on what they regarded as hallowed ground. "Don't build on my sister's grave," one of them pleaded. They too had to compromise. On all sides of the eight-acre memorial site, new high-rises have been and continue to be built. When construction is finished, the site will also accommodate a new underground transit hub.

Originally, the architect's plans called for the 2,982 victims of the attack to be listed elsewhere on the site. Today, in a revised plan, the names are displayed prominently along the sides of the reflecting pool. Arad had suggested that they be placed randomly, to symbolize the "haphazard brutality of life." Survivors objected, perhaps because they worried about locating their loved ones' names. In a compromise, the names were chiseled into the bronze walls of the memorial in groups that Arad calls "meaningful adjacencies": friends and co-workers; fellow passengers on the two downed aircraft, arranged by seat number; and first responders, grouped by their agencies or fire companies.

Erica Simone Leeds/McGraw-Hill Education

Numerous small monuments and simple plaques grace intersections throughout metropolitan New York, particularly those that had a direct line of sight to the Twin Towers.

Suggestions that would give first responders special recognition were set aside. The list includes victims of the simultaneous attack on the Pentagon in Washington, D.C., and passengers on the flight headed for the White House, who were attempting to thwart the attack when the plane crashed in a field in Pennsylvania. The six people who perished in the 1993 truck bombing at the World Trade Center are also memorialized.

Also at Ground Zero is the National September 11 Memorial Museum, which opened with great anticipation as well as criticism.

Some objected to showing pictures of the 19 hijackers, on the grounds that this would symbolically honor them. Others objected to images that would seem to objectify the victims. Unusual for a museum, recording studios were installed to allow visitors to record where they were on 9/11, remember the victims, or respond to the exhibits.

Memorials are not unchanging symbols. In 2019 a series of stone monoliths pointing skyward were added at the site. Their purpose was to recognize the first responders and relief workers who have died or who are currently suffering from illnesses caused by toxins they were exposed to following the September 11 attacks.

Away from Ground Zero, symbols of 9/11 abound. Numerous small monuments and simple plaques grace intersections throughout metropolitan New York, particularly those that had a direct line of sight to the Twin Towers. In hundreds of cities worldwide, scraps of steel from the twisted buildings and remnants of destroyed emergency vehicles have been incorporated into memorials. And the USS *New York,* whose bow was forged from seven and a half tons of steel debris salvaged from the towers, has served as a working symbol of 9/11 since its commissioning in 2009.

LET'S DISCUSS

1. What does the 9/11 memorial symbolize to you? Explain the meaning of the cascading water, the reflecting pools, and the empty footprints. What does the placement of the victims' names suggest?

2. If you were designing a 9/11 memorial, what symbol or symbols would you incorporate? Use your sociological imagination to predict how various groups would respond to your design.

Sources: Blais and Rasic 2011; Cohen 2012; Gannon 2019; Kennicott 2011; Needham 2011.

Norms

Norms are the established standards of behavior maintained by a society. For a norm to become significant, it must be widely shared and understood. For example, in movie theaters in the United States, we typically expect that people will be quiet while the film is shown. Of course, the application of this norm can vary, depending on the particular film and type of audience. People who are viewing a serious artistic film will be more likely to insist on the norm of silence than those who are watching a slapstick comedy or horror movie.

One persistent social norm in contemporary society is that of heterosexuality. As sociologists, and queer theorists especially, note, children are socialized to accept this norm from a very young age. Overwhelmingly, parents describe adult romantic relationships to their children exclusively as heterosexual relationships. That is not necessarily because they consider same-sex relationships unacceptable, but more likely because they see heterosexuality as the norm in marital partnerships. According to a national survey, about one-fifth of those under 35 years of age still find homosexually abnormal. Most parents assume their children will be heterosexual, but according to another study, only one in four mothers of three- to six-year-olds teaches her young children that homosexuality is wrong. The same survey showed that parenting reflects the dominant ideology, in which homosexuality is treated as a rare exception. Most parents assume that their children are heterosexual; only one in four has even considered whether his or her child might grow up to be gay or lesbian (K. Martin 2009; Saad 2012).

Types of Norms Sociologists distinguish between norms in two ways. First, norms are classified as either formal or informal. **Formal norms** generally have been written down and specify strict punishments for violators. In the United States, we often formalize norms into laws, which are very precise in defining proper and improper behavior. Sociologist Donald Black (1995) has termed **law** "governmental social control," meaning that laws are formal norms enforced by the state. Laws are just one example of formal norms. Parking restrictions and the rules of a football or basketball game are also considered formal norms.

In contrast, **informal norms** are generally understood but not precisely recorded. Standards of proper dress are a common example of informal norms. Our society has no specific punishment, or *sanction,* for a person who shows up at school or work wearing inappropriate clothing. Laughter is usually the most likely response.

Norms are also classified by their relative importance to society. When classified in this way, they are known as *mores* and *folkways.* **Mores** (pronounced "*mor*-ays") are norms deemed highly necessary to the welfare of a society, often because they embody the most cherished principles of a people. Each society demands obedience to its mores; violation can lead to severe penalties. Thus, the United States has strong mores against murder, treason, and child abuse, which have been institutionalized into formal norms.

Folkways are norms governing everyday behavior. Folkways play an important role in shaping the daily behavior of members of a culture. Society is less likely to formalize folkways than mores, and their violation raises comparatively little concern. For example, walking up a down escalator in a department store challenges our standards of appropriate behavior, but it will not result in a fine or a jail sentence.

Norms and Sanctions Suppose a football coach sends a 12th player onto the field. Imagine a college graduate showing up in shorts for a job interview at a large bank. Or consider a driver who neglects to put money in a parking meter. These people have violated widely shared and understood norms. So what happens? In each of these situations, the person will receive sanctions if his or her behavior is detected.

Sanctions are penalties and rewards for conduct concerning a social norm. Note that the concept of *reward* is included in this definition. Conformity to a norm can lead to *positive sanctions* such as a pay raise, a medal, a word of gratitude, or a pat on the back. Failure to conform can lead to *negative sanctions* such as fines, threats, imprisonment, and stares of contempt.

Table 3-1 summarizes the relationship between norms and sanctions. As you can see, the sanctions that are associated with formal norms (which are written down and codified) tend to be formal as well. If a college football coach sends too many players onto the field, the team will be penalized

TABLE 3-1 NORMS AND SANCTIONS

Norms	Sanctions	
	Positive	Negative
Formal	Salary bonus	Demotion
	Testimonial dinner	Firing from a job
	Medal	Jail sentence
	Diploma	Expulsion
Informal	Smile	Frown
	Compliment	Humiliation
	Cheers	Bullying

15 yards. The driver who fails to put money in the parking meter will receive a ticket and have to pay a fine. But sanctions for violations of informal norms can vary. The college graduate who goes to the bank interview in shorts will probably lose any chance of getting the job; on the other hand, he or she might be so brilliant that bank officials will overlook the unconventional attire.

The entire fabric of norms and sanctions in a culture reflects that culture's values and priorities. During the coronavirus pandemic, people debated restrictions on social distancing and the use of face coverings and whether governments should sanction the failure to comply with orders to assist public health officials. The most cherished values will be most heavily sanctioned; matters regarded as less critical will carry light and informal sanctions.

Acceptance of Norms   People do not follow norms, whether formal or informal, in all situations. In some cases, they can evade a norm because they know it is weakly enforced. It is illegal for U.S. teenagers to drink alcoholic beverages, yet drinking by minors is common throughout the nation. In fact, teenage alcoholism is a serious social problem.

In some instances, behavior that appears to violate society's norms may actually represent adherence to the norms of a particular group. Teenage drinkers are conforming to the standards of their peer group when they violate norms that condemn underage drinking. Similarly, business executives who use shady accounting techniques may be responding to a corporate culture that demands the maximization of profits at any cost, including the deception of investors and government regulatory agencies.

Norms are violated in some instances because one norm conflicts with another. For example, suppose that you live in an apartment building and one night hear the screams of the woman next door, who is being beaten by her husband. If you decide to intervene by ringing their doorbell or calling the police, you are violating the norm of minding your own business, while following the norm of assisting a victim of violence.

Acceptance of norms is subject to change as the political, economic, and social conditions of a culture are transformed. Until the 1960s, for example, formal norms throughout much of the United States prohibited the marriage of people from different racial groups. Over the past half century, however, such legal prohibitions were cast aside. The process of change can be seen today in the increasing acceptance of single parents and even more in the legalization of same-sex marriage. Further, the #MeToo movement has focused attention on sexual harassment and abuse in major social institutions such as college campuses and the workplace.

When circumstances require the sudden violation of long-standing cultural norms, the change can upset an entire population.

In Iraq, where Muslim custom strictly forbids touching by strangers for men and especially for women, the 2003–2009 war brought numerous daily violations of the norm. Outside important mosques, government offices, and other facilities likely to be targeted by terrorists, visitors had to be patted down and have their bags searched by Iraqi security guards. To reduce the discomfort caused by the procedure, women were searched by female guards and men by male guards. Despite that concession, and the fact that many Iraqis admitted or even insisted on the need for such measures, people still winced at the invasion of their personal privacy. In reaction to the searches, Iraqi women began to limit the contents of the bags they carried or simply to leave them at home (Rubin 2003).

THINKING CRITICALLY

In the United States, is the norm of heterosexuality a formal norm or an informal norm? Would you categorize it with mores or folkways? Explain your reasoning.

Values

Though we each have a personal set of values—which may include caring or fitness or success in business—we also share a general set of values as members of a society. Cultural **values** are these collective conceptions of what is considered good, desirable, and proper—or bad, undesirable, and improper—in a culture. They indicate what people in a given culture prefer as well as what they find important and morally right (or wrong). Values may be specific, such as honoring one's parents and owning a home, or they may be more general, such as health, love, and democracy. Of course, the members of a society do not uniformly share its values. Angry political debates and billboards promoting conflicting causes tell us that much.

Values influence people's behavior and serve as criteria for evaluating the actions of others. The values, norms, and sanctions of a culture are often directly related. For example, if a culture places a high value on the institution of marriage, it may have norms (and strict sanctions) that prohibit the act of adultery or make divorce difficult. If a culture views private property as a basic value, it will probably have stiff laws against theft and vandalism.

The values of a culture may change, but most remain relatively stable during any one person's lifetime. Socially shared, intensely felt values are a fundamental part of our lives in the United States. Sociologist Robin Williams (1970) has offered a list of basic values. It includes achievement, efficiency, material comfort, nationalism, equality, and the supremacy of science and reason over faith. Obviously, not all 333 million people in this country agree on all these values, but such a list serves as a starting point in defining the national character.

Each year nearly 127,000 full-time, newly entering students at 178 of the nation's four-year colleges fill out a questionnaire about their values. Because this survey focuses on an array of issues, beliefs, and life goals, it is commonly cited as a barometer of the nation's values. The respondents are asked what values are personally important to them. Over the past half century, the value of "being very well-off financially" has shown the strongest gain in popularity; the proportion of first-year college students who endorse this value as "essential" or "very important" doubled from 42 percent in 1966 to 84 percent in 2019 (Figure 3-2).

Beginning in the 1980s, support for values having to do with money, power, and status grew. But so too did concern about racial tolerance. The proportion of students concerned with helping to promote racial tolerance reached 49 percent in 2017. Like other aspects of culture, such as language and norms, a nation's values are not necessarily fixed.

Whether the slogan is "Think Green" or "Reduce Your Carbon Footprint," students have been exposed to values associated with environmentalism. How many of them accept those values? Poll results over the past 50 years show fluctuations, in the percentage of students indicating a desire to clean up the environment. By the 1980s, however, student support for embracing this objective had dropped to around 20 percent or even lower (see Figure 3-2). Even with recent attention to climate change, the proportion reached only 45 percent of first-year students in 2016 (Stolzenberg et al. 2019).

Recently, cheating has become a hot issue on college campuses. Professors who take advantage of computerized services that can identify plagiarism have been shocked to learn that many of the papers their students hand in are plagiarized in whole or in part. Box 3-2 examines the shift in values that underlies this decline in academic integrity.

Values can also differ in subtle ways not just among individuals and groups, but from one culture to another. For example, in Japan, young children spend long hours working with *hagwoons*, or private tutors, preparing for entrance exams required for admission to selective schools. No stigma is attached to these services; in fact, they are highly valued. Yet in South Korea, people have begun to complain that so-called "cram schools" give affluent students an unfair advantage. Since 2008, the South Korean government has regulated the after-school tutoring industry, limiting its hours and imposing fees on the schools. Some think this policy has lowered their society's expectations of students, describing it as an attempt to make South Koreans "more American" (Mani 2018; Ramstad 2011; Ripley 2011).

Another example of cultural differences in values is public opinion regarding government efforts to reduce income inequality. As Figure 3-3 shows, opinion varies dramatically from one country to another.

Global Culture War

For almost a generation, public attention in the United States has focused on what has been referred to as the "culture war," or the polarization of society over controversial cultural elements. Originally, in the 1990s, the term referred to political debates over heated issues such as abortion, religious expression, gun control, and sexual orientation. Soon, however, it took on a global meaning—especially after 9/11, as Americans wondered, "Why do they hate us?" Through 2000, global studies of public opinion had reported favorable views of the United States in countries as diverse as Morocco and Germany. But after the United States established a military presence in Iraq and Afghanistan and then took an anti-immigrant and anti-refugee position beginning in 2016, foreign opinion of the United States became quite negative (Gramlich 2019).

FIGURE 3-2 LIFE GOALS OF FIRST-YEAR COLLEGE STUDENTS IN THE UNITED STATES, 1966–2018

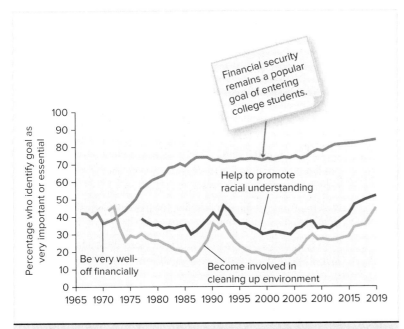

Think about It Why do you think values have shifted among college students in the past few decades? Which of these values is important to you?

Sources: Stolzenberg et al. 2019:40; Pryor et al. 2007

SOCIOLOGY IN EDUCATION

3-2   A Culture of Cheating?

A Harvard teaching assistant noticed something strange while grading students' take-home exams. Several students had cited the same obscure event in 1912. Curiously, all had responded to another question using the same wording. The assistant looked more closely. Eventually, Harvard launched a formal investigation of 125 students suspected of plagiarism and illicit collaboration. At the same time, in New York City more than 70 students at a high school for high achievers were caught sharing test information using their cell phones.

Now that students do their research online, the temptation to cut and paste passages from website postings and pass them off as one's own is apparently irresistible to many. In 2017, a survey of college students was released that showed the following values relating to cheating:

- 86% claimed they cheated in some way in school.

- 54% felt cheating is "OK." Some went so far as to say it is necessary to stay competitive.

- 97% of the admitted cheaters said that they have never been identified as cheating.

- 76% copied word for word someone else's assignments

- 79% of the students surveyed admitted to plagiarizing their assignments from the Internet.

In a 2017 survey of college students, 86 percent said that they cheated in some way in school.

To address what they consider an alarming trend, many colleges are rewriting or adopting new academic honor codes. Observers contend that the increase in student cheating reflects widely publicized instances of cheating in public life, which have served to create an alternative set of values in which the end justifies the means. When young people see sports heroes, authors, entertainers, and cor-

Eric Audras/PhotoAlto/Getty Images

porate executives exposed for cheating in one form or another, the message seems to be "Cheating is okay, as long as you don't get caught."

The culture of cheating in education is often reinforced by the actions of adults. In 2019, two national scandals erupted. One involved parents who spent thousands of dollars to have their children's test scores altered or their athletic abilities grossly exaggerated to ensure acceptance at elite universities. The second involved parents who transferred guardianship of their children so that they were declared wards of the states. As a result, the parents' household income would not be considered in the determination of financial aid.

LET'S DISCUSS

1. Do you know anyone who has engaged in Internet plagiarism? What about cheating on tests or falsifying laboratory results? If so, how did the person justify these forms of dishonesty?

2. Even if cheaters aren't caught, what negative effects does their academic dishonesty have on them? What effects does it have on students who are honest? Could an entire college or university suffer from students' dishonesty?

Sources: Argetsinger and Krim 2002; Bartlett 2009; Kessler Institute 2017; R. Thomas 2003; Toppo 2011; Zernike 2002.

In the past 30 years, extensive efforts have been made to compare values in different nations, recognizing the challenges in interpreting value concepts in a similar manner across cultures. Psychologist Shalom Schwartz has measured values in more than 60 countries. Around the world, certain values are widely shared, including benevolence, which is defined as "forgiveness and loyalty." In contrast, power, defined as "control or dominance over people and resources," is a value that is endorsed much less often (Hitlin and Piliavin 2004; S. Schwartz and Bardi 2001).

Despite this evidence of shared values, some scholars have interpreted the terrorism, genocide, wars, and military occupations of the early 21st century as a "clash of civilizations." According to this thesis, cultural and religious identities, rather than national or political loyalties, are becoming the prime

source of international conflict. Critics of this thesis point out that conflict over values is nothing new; only our ability to create havoc and violence has grown. Furthermore, speaking of a clash of "civilizations" disguises the sharp divisions that exist within large groups. Christianity, for example, runs the gamut from Quaker-style pacifism to certain elements of the Ku Klux Klan's ideology (Brooks 2011; Huntington 1993; Said 2001; Schrad 2014).

THINKING CRITICALLY

Do you believe that the world is experiencing a clash of civilizations rather than of nations, as some scholars assert? Why or why not?

FIGURE 3-3 VALUES: ACCEPTANCE OF GOVERNMENT EFFORTS TO
REDUCE INCOME INEQUALITY

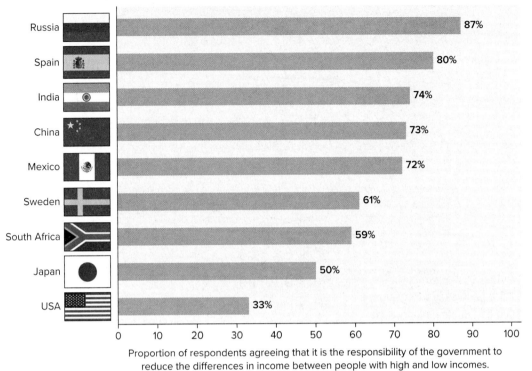

Proportion of respondents agreeing that it is the responsibility of the government to
reduce the differences in income between people with high and low incomes.

Source: International Survey Study Programme 2019: 34–35. *Flags:* admin_design/Shutterstock

Sociological Perspectives on Culture

Functionalist and conflict theorists agree that culture and society are mutually supportive, but for different reasons. Functionalists maintain that social stability requires a consensus and the support of society's members; strong central values and common norms provide that support. This view of culture became popular in sociology beginning in the 1950s. It was borrowed from British anthropologists who saw cultural traits as a stabilizing element in a culture. From a functionalist perspective, a cultural trait or practice will persist if it performs functions that society seems to need or contributes to overall social stability and consensus.

Conflict theorists agree that a common culture may exist, but they argue that it serves to maintain the privileges of certain groups. Moreover, while protecting their self-interest, powerful groups may keep others in a subservient position. The term **dominant ideology** describes the set of cultural beliefs and practices that helps to maintain powerful social, economic, and political interests. This concept was first used by Hungarian Marxist Georg Lukacs (1923) and Italian Marxist Antonio Gramsci (1929), but it did not gain an audience in the United States until the early 1970s. In Karl Marx's view, a capitalist society has a dominant ideology that serves the interests of the ruling class.

From a conflict perspective, the dominant ideology has major social significance. Not only do a society's most powerful groups and institutions control wealth and property; even more important, they control the means of producing beliefs about reality through religion, education, and the media. Feminists would also argue that if all a society's most important institutions tell women they should be subservient to men, that dominant ideology will help to control women and keep them in a subordinate position.

A growing number of social scientists believe that it is not easy to identify a core culture in the United States. For support, they point to the lack of consensus on national values, the diffusion of cultural traits, the diversity within our culture, and the changing views of young people (look again at Figure 3-2). Instead, they suggest that the core culture provides the tools that people of all persuasions need to develop strategies for social change. Still, there is no denying that certain expressions of values have greater influence than others, even in as complex a society as the United States (Swidler 1986).

Table 3-2 summarizes the major sociological perspectives on culture.

THINKING CRITICALLY

Look around your school. Do the people you see suggest that the United States has a core culture with a dominant ideology, or a diverse culture with differing values and ideologies? What about the city or town where your school is located—does it suggest the same conclusion?

Cultural Variation

Despite the presence of cultural universals such as courtship and religion, great diversity exists among the world's many cultures. Inuit tribes in northern Canada, dressed in fur for the

TABLE 3-2   SOCIOLOGICAL PERSPECTIVES
ON CULTURE

Tracking Sociological Perspectives

	Functionalist Perspective	Conflict Perspective	Feminist Perspective	Interactionist Perspective
Norms	Reinforce societal standards	Reinforce patterns of dominance	Reinforce roles of men and women	Are maintained through face-to-face interaction
Values	Are collective conceptions of what is good	May perpetuate social inequality	May perpetuate men's dominance	Are defined and redefined through social interaction
Culture and Society	Culture reflects a society's strong central values	Culture reflects a society's dominant ideology	Culture reflects society's view of men and women	A society's core culture is perpetuated through daily social interactions
Cultural Variation	Subcultures serve the interests of subgroups	Countercultures question the dominant social order; ethnocentrism devalues groups	Cultural relativism respects variations in the way men and women are viewed in different societies	Customs and traditions are transmitted through intergroup contact and through the media

hunt, share little with farmers in southeast Asia, who dress lightly for work in their hot, humid rice paddies. Cultures adapt to meet specific circumstances, such as climate, level of technology, population, and geography.

Even *within* a single nation, certain segments of the populace develop cultural patterns that differ from the patterns of the dominant society—thus the difficulty of identifying a core culture in the United States, where regional differences fuel culture wars between conservatives and liberals. Moreover, in every region, specific communities tend to band together to form their own culture within a culture, called a *subculture.*

Chuck Savage/Corbis/Getty Images

Hip-hop is an example of a subculture. Disc-jockeying is a big part of the hip-hop subculture.

Subcultures

Rodeo riders, residents of a retirement community, workers on an offshore oil rig—all are examples of what sociologists refer to as *subcultures*. A **subculture** is a segment of society that shares a distinctive pattern of customs, rules, and traditions that differs from the pattern of the larger society. The existence of many subcultures is characteristic of complex societies such as the United States.

Members of a subculture participate in the dominant culture while engaging in unique and distinctive forms of behavior. Frequently, a subculture will develop an **argot,** or specialized language that distinguishes it from the wider society. Athletes who play *parkour,* an extreme sport that combines forward running with fence leaping and the vaulting of walls, water barriers, and even moving cars, speak an argot they devised especially to describe their feats. Parkour runners talk about doing *King Kong vaults*—diving arms first over a wall or grocery cart and landing in a standing position. They may follow this maneuver with a *tic tac*—kicking off a wall to overcome some kind of obstacle (Kidder 2012).

The practice of vaping has also created its own subculture, especially among younger users who engage in the practice secretly. They learn from vapers how to acquire the supplies and with what type of chemicals and substances to create liquids for vaping. They also distinguish between *substitutes,* who have taken to vaping instead of smoking cigarettes, and *cloud chasers,* who are deeply involved in the subculture of using vaping devices (Tokle and Pedersen 2020).

RESEARCH TODAY

3-3   How Millennials View The Nation: Racial and Ethnic Vantage Points

We read about continuing progress since the days of the civil rights movements and hear about the "postracial America" heralded by the election of Barack Obama. However, the reality is that members of different racial and ethnic groups see America very differently. In May 2017, a national survey asked millennials (young adults age 18 to 34) to name the most important issues facing the nation. Respondents could select among several dozen areas, including economic growth, military strength, crime, and social security. Here are the results for white non-Hispanics:

- **White non-Hispanics:** #1 health care, #2 terrorism and home security, #3 national debt.

These all seem reasonable choices. But consider how differently millennials who were members of racial and ethnic minorities saw the nation at the same time:

- **African Americans:** #1 racism, #2 heath care, #3 poverty and education (tied).

- **Asian Americans:** #1 health care, #2 education, #3 immigration.
- **Latinos:** #1 immigration, #2 racism, #3 terrorism and home security.

> *While there are some common concerns, we can identify important differences across race and ethnicity that likely reflect the millennials' lived experiences.*

While there are some common concerns about health care, we can identify important differences across race and ethnicity that likely reflect the millennials' lived experiences. Both African Americans and Latinos emphasized racism; both Asian Americans and Latinos, immigration. Neither made the top three for whites.

In a survey conducted just a few months earlier, at the time of the polarizing presidential race between Donald Trump and Hillary Clinton, all three minority groups noted racism as one of the top three issues, and African Americans listed "police brutality" as the number two issue facing the nation. Neither racism nor police brutality made it on the top 10 list of white non-Hispanics.

LET'S DISCUSS

1. How would you rank the issues discussed in order of importance? Do you think your ranking reflects your racial or ethnic affiliation?
2. Why do you think the different groups' views are so divergent? Do you think this would be the case for people of other age groups?

Sources: Cohen, Luttig, and Rogowski 2017; GenForward 2016.

Such argot allows insiders—the members of the subculture—to understand words with special meanings. It also establishes patterns of communication that outsiders can't understand. Sociologists associated with the interactionist perspective emphasize that language and symbols offer a powerful way for a subculture to feel cohesive and maintain its identity.

In India, a new subculture has developed among employees at the international call centers established by multinational corporations. To serve customers in the United States and Europe, the young men and women who work there must be fluent speakers of English. But the corporations that employ them demand more than proficiency in a foreign language; they expect their Indian employees to adopt Western values and work habits, including the grueling pace U.S. workers take for granted.

In effect, workers at these call centers live in a state of virtual migration—not quite in India, but not in the United States, either. Significantly, call centers allow employees to take the day off only on U.S. holidays, like Labor Day and Thanksgiving—not on Indian holidays like Diwali, the Hindu festival of lights. While most Indian families are home celebrating, call center employees see only each other; when they have the day off, no one else is free to socialize with them. As a result, these employees have formed a tight-knit subculture based on hard work and a taste for Western luxury goods and leisure-time pursuits.

Another shared characteristic among some employees at Indian call centers is their contempt for the callers they serve. In performing their monotonous, repetitive job day after day, hundreds of thousands of these workers have come to see the faceless Americans they deal with as slow, often rude customers. Such shared understandings underpin this emerging subculture (Krishnamurthy 2018).

However, we do not need to make cross-national comparisons to identify different ways of viewing society. The racial and ethnic diversity of the United States underscores how divergently different groups can view what is really important to society (Box 3-3).

Countercultures

By the end of the 1960s, an extensive subculture had emerged in the United States, composed of young people turned off by a society they believed was too materialistic and technological. The group included primarily political radicals and hippies who had dropped out of mainstream social institutions. These young men and women rejected the pressure to accumulate cars, homes, and an endless array of material goods. Instead, they expressed a desire to live in a culture based on more humanistic values, such as sharing, love, and coexistence with the environment. As a political force, this subculture opposed the United States' involvement in the war in Vietnam and encouraged draft resistance (Flacks 1971; Roszak 1969).

When a subculture conspicuously and deliberately opposes certain aspects of the larger culture, it is known as a **counter-culture.** Countercultures typically thrive among the young, who have the least investment in the existing culture. In most cases, a 20-year-old can adjust to new cultural standards more easily than someone who has spent 60 years following the patterns of the dominant culture (Zellner 1995).

In the last decade, counterterrorism experts have become concerned about the growth of ultraconservative militia groups in the United States. Secretive and well-armed, members of these countercultural groups tend to be antigovernment, and they often tolerate racism in their midst. Watchdogs estimate that 940 hate groups operate in the United States with an increase of 55 percent of white Nationalist hate groups between 2017 and 2020 (Southern Poverty Law Center 2020).

Culture Shock

Ever stepped out the door on your first day in a foreign country and felt weak in the knees? Anyone who feels disoriented, uncertain, out of place, or even fearful when immersed in an unfamiliar culture may be experiencing **culture shock.** This unsettling experience may even be mutual—the visitor's cultural habits may shock members of the host culture. Imagine, for example, that you are traveling in Japan. You know that you should remove your shoes and leave them at the door when you visit someone's home. However, there are many more customs that you are unfamiliar with. During a visit with one family, as you enter the bathroom, you see several pairs of identical slippers. Thinking they are for guests, you put on a pair and rejoin your host, who reacts with horror. Unwittingly, you have worn a pair of toilet slippers into the living room (McLane 2013).

rawpixel/123RF

Employees of an international call center in India socialize after their shift has ended. Call center employees, whose odd working hours isolate them from others, tend to form tight-knit subcultures.

All of us, to some extent, take for granted the cultural practices of our society. As a result, it can be surprising and even disturbing to realize that other cultures do not follow our way of life. The fact is, customs that seem strange to us may be considered normal and proper in other cultures, which may see our social practices as odd.

USE YOUR SOCIOLOGICAL IMAGINATION

You arrive in a developing African country as a Peace Corps volunteer. What aspects of a very different culture do you think would be the hardest to adjust to? Explain. What might the citizens of that country find shocking about your culture?

Development of Culture around the World

Today, despite the preference most of us have for our own way of life, powerful forces link us to others around the world. Thus, students in the United States may study the novels of Leo Tolstoy, the art of Pablo Picasso, or the films of Bong Joon-ho. They may listen to pop music from Nigeria or India, or follow the progress of social movements in Iran, Egypt, or Hong Kong via satellite TV and social media. In this section we will examine two of the social processes that make these global links possible: innovation and the diffusion of culture through globalization and technology.

Innovation

The process of introducing a new idea or object to a culture is known as **innovation.** Innovation interests sociologists because of the social consequences of introducing something new. There are two forms of innovation: discovery and invention. **Discovery** involves making known or sharing the existence of an aspect of reality. The finding of the structure of the DNA molecule and the identification of a new moon of Saturn are both acts of discovery. A significant factor in the process of discovery is the sharing of newfound knowledge with others. In contrast, an **invention** results when existing cultural items are combined into a form that did not exist before. The bow and arrow, the automobile, and the television are all examples of inventions, as are Protestantism and democracy.

Globalization, Diffusion, and Technology

While people in Asia are beginning to enjoy coffee, people in North America have discovered sushi, which has evolved from a once-exotic dish in the United States to a mainstream food commonly found in supermarket refrigerators. Yet its move across the Pacific has changed the delicacy. Americans tend to treat sushi as a take-out or menu item. The authentic way to eat sushi is to sit at a bar and engage the chef in conversation about the day's catch.

More and more cultural expressions and practices are crossing national borders and affecting the traditions and customs of the societies exposed to them. Sociologists use the term **diffusion** to refer to the process by which a cultural item spreads from group to group or society to society. Diffusion can occur through a variety of means, among them exploration, military conquest, missionary work, and the influence of the mass media, tourism, the Internet (Box 3-4), and the fast-food restaurant.

Sociologist George Ritzer coined the term **McDonaldization** of society to describe how the principles of fast-food restaurants, developed in the United States, have come to dominate more and more sectors of societies throughout the world. For example, hair salons and medical clinics now take walk-ins. In Hong Kong, sex selection clinics offer a menu of items, from fertility enhancement to methods of increasing the likelihood of having a child of the desired sex. And religious groups—from evangelical preachers on local stations or websites to priests at the Vatican Television Center—use marketing techniques similar to those that are used to sell Happy Meals.

McDonaldization is associated with the melding of cultures, through which we see more and more similarities in cultural expression. In Japan, for example, African entrepreneurs have found a thriving market for hip-hop fashions popularized by teens in the United States. Similarly, the familiar Golden Arches of McDonald's can be seen around the world. Yet corporations

Frank Zeller/AFP/Getty Images

Members of Big Toe Crew, a Vietnamese hip-hop group, rehearse for a performance. Through tourism and the mass media, music and dance spread from one culture to another in a process called diffusion.

like McDonald's have had to make some adjustments of their own. Until 2001, McDonald's ran its *overseas* operations from corporate headquarters in suburban Chicago.

After a few false starts, executives at McDonald's recognized the need to develop the restaurant's menus and marketing strategies overseas, relying on advice from local people. Now, at over 3,700 restaurants in Japan, customers can enjoy the Mega Tamago Burger—beef, bacon, and fried egg with special sauces. In India, patrons who don't eat beef can order a vegetarian McAloo Tikki potato burger. Because some strict vegetarians in India refuse to eat among nonvegetarians, in 2013 McDonald's began opening vegetarian-only restaurants there (Gasparro and Jargon 2012; Ritzer 2018).

McDonaldization affects the tourist industry and has given travelers new ways to experience new cultures without actually leaving their own (Box 3-5). While people may wish to explore new cultures, often tour industry organizations strive to make the experience as limited as possible.

Technology in its many forms has increased the speed of cultural diffusion and broadened the distribution of cultural elements. Sociologist Gerhard Lenski has defined **technology** as "cultural information about the ways in which the material resources of the environment may be used to satisfy human needs and desires" (Nolan and Lenski 2015:357). Today's technological developments no longer await publication in journals with limited circulation. Press conferences, often carried simultaneously on the Internet, trumpet the new developments.

Technology not only accelerates the diffusion of scientific innovations but also transmits culture. The English language and North American culture dominate the Internet and World Wide Web. Such control, or at least dominance, of technology influences the direction of cultural diffusion. For example, websites cover even the most superficial aspects of U.S. culture but offer little information about the pressing issues faced by citizens of other nations. People all over the world find it easier to visit electronic chat rooms about the latest reality TV shows than to learn about their own governments' policies on day care or infant nutrition.

Sociologist William F. Ogburn (1922) made a useful distinction between the elements of *material* and *nonmaterial culture*. **Material culture** refers to the physical or technological aspects of our daily lives, including food, houses, factories, and raw materials. **Nonmaterial culture** refers to ways of using material objects, as well as to customs, beliefs, philosophies, governments, and patterns of communication. Generally, the nonmaterial culture is more resistant to change than the material culture. Consequently, Ogburn introduced the term **culture lag** to refer to the period of maladjustment when the nonmaterial culture is still struggling to adapt to new material conditions. For example,

SOCIOLOGY IN THE GLOBAL COMMUNITY

3-4 Life in the Global Village

Imagine a "borderless world" in which culture, trade, commerce, money, and even people move freely from one place to another. Popular culture is widely shared, whether it be Japanese sushi or American running shoes, and the English speaker who answers questions over the telephone about your credit card account is as likely to be in India or Ireland as in the United States. In this world, even the sovereignty of nations is at risk, challenged by political movements and ideologies that span nations.

What caused this great wave of cultural diffusion? First, sociologists take note of advances in communication technology. Satellite TV, streaming video, cellphones, and the Internet allow information to flow freely across the world, linking global markets. Consumers can view videos and surf the Internet on their phones, shopping online from cars, airports, and cafeterias. Second, corporations in industrial nations have become multinational, with both factories and markets in developing countries. Third, these multinational firms have cooperated with global financial institutions,

> *Superhero moves and Lady Gaga may be seen as threats to native cultures.*

organizations, and governments to promote free trade—unrestricted or lightly regulated commerce across national borders.

Globalization is not universally welcome. Many critics see the dominance of businesses without borders as benefiting the rich, particularly the very wealthy in industrial countries, at the expense of the poor in less developed nations. They consider globalization to be a successor to the imperialism and colonialism that oppressed Third World nations for centuries.

Another criticism of globalization comes from people who feel overwhelmed by global culture. Superhero movies and Lady Gaga may be seen as threats to native cultures, if they dominate the media at the expense of local art forms.

The response to the coronavirus pandemic by closing border crossings and suspending international air travel could be viewed as reversing the trend toward globalization. Instead, new patterns emerged with greater medical scrutiny of travels just as after 9/11 new security measures were introduced. Supply chain routes changed between countries but did not end altogether.

Globalization continues to have its positive side. Many developing nations are taking their place in the world of commerce and bringing in much needed income. The communications revolution helps people stay connected and gives them access to knowledge that can improve living standards and save lives.

LET'S DISCUSS

1. How are you affected by globalization? What aspects of globalization do you find advantageous, and which objectionable?
2. How would you feel if the customs and traditions you grew up with were replaced by the culture or values of another country? How might you try to protect your culture?

Sources: Dodds 2000; Hirst and Thompson 1996; Karabell 2020; D. Martin et al. 2006; Ritzer and Dean 2019; Sernau 2001.

David Pearson/Alamy Stock Photo

McDonald's menu board in India.

in 2010, manufacturers introduced electronic cigarettes, battery-powered tubes that turn nicotine-laced liquid into a vapor mist. The innovation soon had officials at airlines (which ban smoking) and the Food and Drug Administration scrambling to respond to the latest technology (Kesmodel and Yadron 2010; Swidler 1986).

USE YOUR SOCIOLOGICAL IMAGINATION

If you grew up in your grandparents' generation—without computers, e-mail, and smartphones—how would your daily life differ from the one you lead today?

SOCIOLOGY IN THE GLOBAL COMMUNITY

3-5 Culture Encapsulated on an Island

You are visiting the Dominican Republic, Haiti, Belize, or the Bahamas. But are you really experiencing that country and its people?

Since the 1990s, major cruise lines have purchased entire islands and peninsulas to create ports for a single disembarkation of thousands of passengers who wish to visit a foreign country. The travelers' access to the country and exposure to its culture are very limited. Most visits consist of beach excursions, water sports, zip lines, shops, and barbecues, all operated by the cruise line. Tourists cannot wander around and talk to villagers, visit places of worship, or go to museums.

Even the devastating Haitian earthquake of 2010 and Hurricane Dorian, which struck the Bahamas in 2019, did not interrupt cruise passengers' visits to their private ports.

From the travelers' perspective, this is an easy way to visit a foreign country. They do not have to deal with a foreign currency or passport control. The country they "visit" typically receives a stipend of about $15 per disembarking passenger, as well as seasonal part-time employment for a couple of hundred workers at each of these cruise-owned ports of call.

The cruise line often promotes the safety of such visits, implying that actually visiting the country might be dangerous. Even the devastating Haitian earthquake of 2010 and Hurricane Dorian, which struck the Bahamas in 2019, did not interrupt cruise passengers' visits to their private ports; the rest of the country slowly rebuilt outside of the tourists' view. One exception was a 2016 blockade of small boats, which prevented a Royal Caribbean Cruise ship from docking at its private port of Labadee as the Haitians protested government policies. But that only lasted one week: the government, working with the cruise line, quickly stemmed protests.

Admittedly most tourists only begin to dip their toes into a nation's culture, as their movements are usually limited to popular sites and highly publicized shopping districts. Yet the advent of tourist industry-owned property has taken this limitation to a new level.

LET'S DISCUSS

1. Is this kind of tourism an example of cultural diffusion? of globalization? Explain your answer.
2. Why is the kind of tourism described here increasingly popular? What does this suggest about how people react to cultural differences?

Sources: Deerwester 2019; Ellwood 2019; Golden 2016.

Solarisys/Shutterstock

Royal Caribbean, Oasis of the Seas docked at its private port Labadee, Haiti.

Robert Laberge/Getty Images

When a society's nonmaterial culture (its values and laws) does not keep pace with rapid changes in its material culture, people experience an awkward period of maladjustment called culture lag. The transition to nuclear power generation that began in the second half of the 20th century brought widespread protests against the new technology, as well as serious accidents that government officials were poorly prepared to deal with. Tensions over the controversial technology have not run as high in some countries as in others, however. France, where this nuclear power plant is situated, generates 72 percent of all its electricity through nuclear power. The technology is not as controversial there as in the United States and Canada, which generate less than 20 percent of their electricity through nuclear reaction.

THINKING CRITICALLY

Name one culturally significant discovery and one culturally significant invention that have occurred in your lifetime. Explain how these innovations have affected the culture to which you belong.

socialpolicy and Culture

Bilingualism

Looking at the Issue

The staff in the emergency room is unprepared. Although the issue is not a medical one, the doctors and nurses do not understand the patient's complaints, nor can they communicate effectively with her companion. This type of incident, which occurs frequently, can have serious consequences. According to a study of two large pediatric emergency departments in Massachusetts, even when the second language is a common one like Spanish, interpreting errors can lead to clinically significant mistakes in 22 percent of such cases. In other words, language errors put patients at risk (Flores et al. 2012).

How can we learn to work and live effectively when Americans speak so many different languages? As Figure 3-4 shows, American households speak many languages in addition to English and Spanish. Throughout the world, not just emergency rooms but schools and other institutions must deal with people who speak many languages. **Bilingualism** refers to the use of two languages in a particular setting, such as the workplace or schoolroom, treating each language as equally legitimate. Thus, a teacher of bilingual education may instruct children in their native language while gradually introducing them to the language of the host society. If the curriculum is also bicultural, children will learn about the mores and folkways of both the dominant culture and the subculture.

To what degree should schools in the United States present the curriculum in a language other than English? This issue has prompted a great deal of debate among educators and policymakers. According to the Bureau of the Census, 66 million U.S. residents over age five—that's about 22 percent of the population—spoke a language other than English as their primary language at home in 2018 (Figure 3-5). Indeed, 29 other languages are each spoken by at least 200,000 U.S. residents (American Community Survey 2018b; C. Ryan 2013).

Do bilingual programs help the children of these families to learn English? It is difficult to reach firm conclusions, because bilingual programs in general vary so widely in their quality and approach. They differ in the length of the transition to English and in how long they allow students to remain in bilingual classrooms. Moreover, results have been mixed. As of mid-2020, in the years since California effectively dismantled its bilingual education program, reading and math scores of students with limited English proficiency have risen dramatically, especially in the lower grades. Yet a major overview of 17 studies, done at Johns Hopkins University, found that students who are offered lessons in both English and their home languages make better progress than similar students who are taught only in English (Bialystok 2018; Goldenberg and Wagner 2015).

Applying Sociology

For a long time, people in the United States demanded conformity to a single language. This demand coincided with the functionalist view that language serves to unify members of a society.

Little respect was granted to immigrants' cultural traditions; a young person would often be teased about his or her "funny" name, accent, or style of dress.

Recent decades have seen challenges to this pattern of forced obedience to the dominant ideology. Beginning in the 1960s, active movements for Black pride and ethnic pride insisted that people regard the traditions of all racial and ethnic subcultures as legitimate and important. Conflict theorists explain this development as a case of subordinated language minorities seeking opportunities for self-expression. Partly as a result of these challenges, people began to view bilingualism as an asset. It seemed to provide a sensitive way of assisting millions of non-English-speaking people in

FIGURE 3-4   MOST COMMONLY SPOKEN LANGUAGE, OTHER THAN ENGLISH OR SPANISH, BY STATE

U.S. households speak many languages in addition to English and Spanish. Some, such as German, Italian, and Portuguese, reflect older waves or immigrants, while others, such as Chinese, Vietnamese, Tagalog, and Russian, reflect more recent immigrant waves. And in four states the roots of Native American languages, Dakota, Navajo, and Yupik, remain strong.

Source: American Community Survey 2020a.

MAPPING LIFE NATIONWIDE

FIGURE 3-5 PERCENTAGE OF PEOPLE WHO SPEAK A LANGUAGE OTHER THAN ENGLISH AT HOME, BY STATE

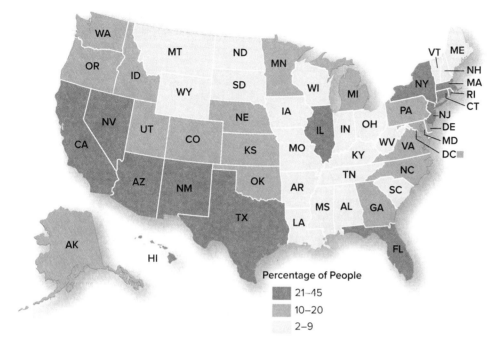

Percentage of People
- 21–45
- 10–20
- 2–9

Note: Data for 2018 for people 5 years of age or older. National average was 22 percent.
Source: American Community Survey 2019a.

learned English elsewhere in Canada. While special laws like this one have advanced French in the province, dissatisfied Québécois have tried to form their own separate country. In 1995, the people of Québec indicated their preference of remaining united with Canada by only the narrowest of margins (50.5 percent). Language and language-related cultural areas both unify and divide this nation of 37 million people (*The Economist* 2005b; R. Schaefer 2021).

Policymakers in the United States have been somewhat ambivalent in dealing with the issue of bilingualism. In 1965, the Elementary and Secondary Education Act (ESEA) provided for bilingual, bicultural education. In the 1970s, the federal government took an active role in establishing the proper form for bilingual programs. However, more recently, federal policy has been less supportive of bilingualism, and local school districts have been forced to provide an increased share of funding for their bilingual programs. Yet bilingual programs are an expense that

the United States to *learn* English in order to function more effectively within the society.

The perspective of conflict theory also helps us to understand some of the attacks on bilingual programs. Many of them stem from an ethnocentric point of view, which holds that any deviation from the majority is bad. This attitude tends to be expressed by those who wish to stamp out foreign influence wherever it occurs, especially in our schools. It does not take into account that success in bilingual education may actually have beneficial results, such as decreasing the number of high school dropouts and increasing the number of Hispanics in colleges and universities.

Initiating Policy

Bilingualism has policy implications largely in two areas: efforts to maintain language purity and programs to enhance bilingual education. Nations vary dramatically in their tolerance for a variety of languages. China continues to tighten its cultural control over Tibet by extending instruction of Mandarin, a Chinese dialect, from high school into the elementary schools there, which will now be bilingual along with Tibetan. In contrast, nearby Singapore establishes English as the medium of instruction but allows students to take their mother tongue as a second language, be it Chinese, Malay, or Tamil.

One bilingual hot spot is Québec, the French-speaking province of Canada. The Québécois, as they are known, represent 83 percent of the province's population, but only 25 percent of Canada's total population. A law implemented in 1978 mandated education in French for all Québec's children except those whose parents or siblings had

many communities and states are unwilling to pay for and are quick to cut back. In 1998, voters in California approved a proposition that all but eliminated bilingual education only to reinstate it in 2017. It requires instruction in English for 1.4 million children who are not fluent in the language.

In the United States, repeated efforts have been made to introduce a constitutional amendment declaring English as the nation's official language. As of 2020, 32 states had declared English their official language—an action that is now more symbolic than legislative in its significance. However, in 2018, the lobbying group ProEnglish met twice with White House officials seeking their support in repealing a 2000 government action that mandates foreign language translations of certain government documents and forms.

Public concern over a potential decline in the use of English appears to be overblown. In reality, most immigrants and their offspring quickly become fluent in English and abandon their mother tongue. This pattern of language lost coupled with the relatively little interest in learning foreign languages by the adult population has left the nation fairly monolingual compared to many industrial nations. There is need for more facility in languages other than English and well beyond those displayed in the map in Figure 3-4. During the coronavirus pandemic, it was apparent that both health delivery systems and public health offices were in dire need of people who could effectively communicate with different language communities. Hospitals, testing centers, and medical clinics had unmet need for translation services at point of care. Significant clusters of COVID-19 existed in communities not fluent in English that were in special need of intervention. The health of these limited English households were shown to suffer more from the effects of the pandemic (Goldberg 2020; U.S. English 2020).

In the end, the immigrant's experience is not only about learning a new language. It is about learning a whole new culture—a new totality of socially transmitted customs, knowledge, material objects, and behavior.

Take the Issue with You

1. Have you attended a school with students for whom English is a second language? If so, can you identify the presence of different cultures or subcultures?

2. The ultimate goal of both English-only and bilingual programs is for foreign-born students to become proficient in English. In what ways is this goal functional? Analyze the goal of such programs from the conflict and interactionist perspectives.

3. Besides bilingualism, can you think of another issue that has become controversial recently because of a clash of cultures? If so, analyze the issue from a sociological point of view.

MASTERING THIS CHAPTER

Summary

Culture is the totality of learned, socially transmitted customs, knowledge, material objects, and behavior. This chapter examines social practices common to all cultures, the basic elements that make up a culture, and variations that distinguish one culture from another.

1. A shared **culture** helps to define the group or **society** to which we belong.

2. Anthropologist George Murdock compiled a list of **cultural universals,** or common practices found in every culture, including marriage, sports, cooking, medicine, and sexual restrictions.

3. People who assume that their culture is superior to others engage in **ethnocentrism.** In contrast, **cultural relativism** is the practice of viewing other people's behavior from the perspective of their own culture.

4. **Language,** an important element of culture, includes speech, written characters, numerals, and **symbols,** as well as gestures and other forms of nonverbal communication. Language both describes culture and shapes it.

5. Sociologists distinguish between **norms** in two ways, classifying them as **formal** or **informal** and as **mores** or **folkways.**

6. The formal norms of a culture will carry the heaviest **sanctions;** informal norms will carry light sanctions.

7. The **dominant ideology** of a culture is the set of cultural beliefs and practices that helps to maintain powerful social, economic, and political interests.

8. In a sense, a **subculture** can be thought of as a small culture that exists within a larger, dominant culture. **Countercultures** are subcultures that deliberately oppose aspects of the larger culture.

9. Culture is constantly expanding through the process of **innovation,** which includes both **discovery** and **invention.**

10. **Diffusion**—the spread of cultural items such as **McDonaldization,** from one place to another—has fostered globalization. Still, people resist ideas that seem too foreign, as well as those they perceive as threatening to their values and beliefs.

11. The social policy of **bilingualism** calls for the use of two languages, treating each as equally legitimate. It is supported by those who want to ease the transition of non-native-language speakers into a host society, but opposed by those who adhere to a single cultural tradition and language.

Key Terms

Argot Specialized language used by members of a group or subculture. (page 66)

Bilingualism The use of two languages in a particular setting, such as the workplace or schoolroom, treating each language as equally legitimate. (71)

Counterculture A subculture that deliberately opposes certain aspects of the larger culture. (68)

Cultural capital Noneconomic goods, such as family background and education, which are reflected in a knowledge of language and the arts. (57)

Cultural relativism The viewing of people's behavior from the perspective of their own culture. (56)

Cultural universal A common practice or belief found in every culture. (55)

Culture The totality of learned, socially transmitted customs, knowledge, material objects, and behavior. (55)

Culture lag A period of maladjustment when the nonmaterial culture is still struggling to adapt to new material conditions. (69)

Culture shock The feeling of surprise and disorientation that people experience when they encounter cultural practices that are different from their own. (68)

Diffusion The process by which a cultural item spreads from group to group or society to society. (69)

Discovery The process of making known or sharing the existence of an aspect of reality. (68)

Dominant ideology A set of cultural beliefs and practices that helps to maintain powerful social, economic, and political interests. (65)

Ethnocentrism The tendency to assume that one's own culture and way of life represent the norm or are superior to all others. (56)

Folkway A norm governing everyday behavior whose violation raises comparatively little concern. (61)

Formal norm A norm that has been written down and that specifies strict punishments for violators. (61)

Informal norm A norm that is generally understood but not precisely recorded. (61)

Innovation The process of introducing a new idea or object to a culture through discovery or invention. (68)

Invention The combination of existing cultural items into a form that did not exist before. (68)

Language An abstract system of word meanings and symbols for all aspects of culture; includes gestures and other nonverbal communication. (58)

Law Governmental social control. (61)

McDonaldization The process by which the principles of bureaucratization have increasingly shaped organizations worldwide. (69)

Material culture The physical or technological aspects of our daily lives. (69)

Mores Norms deemed highly necessary to the welfare of a society. (61)

Nonmaterial culture Ways of using material objects, as well as customs, beliefs, philosophies, governments, and patterns of communication. (69)

Nonverbal communication The sending of messages through the use of gestures, facial expressions, and postures. (59)

Norm An established standard of behavior maintained by a society. (56)

Sanction A penalty or reward for conduct concerning a social norm. (61)

Society A fairly large number of people who live in the same territory, are relatively independent of people outside their area, and participate in a common culture. (55)

Sociobiology The systematic study of how biology affects human social behavior. (56)

Subculture A segment of society that shares a distinctive pattern of customs, rules, and traditions that differs from the pattern of the larger society. (66)

Symbol A gesture, object, or word that forms the basis of human communication. (59)

Technology Cultural information about the ways in which the material resources of the environment may be used to satisfy human needs and desires. (69)

Value A collective conception of what is considered good, desirable, and proper—or bad, undesirable, and improper—in a culture. (62)

TAKING SOCIOLOGY with you

1. Locate ethnocentrism. For two days, bearing in mind what sociologists mean by *ethnocentrism,* systematically record the places where you see or hear evidence of it.

2. Study popular culture. For two days, record whatever evidence of the dominant culture you see on the Internet or in literature, music, movies, theater, television programs, and sporting events.

3. Document a subculture. For two days, record the norms, values, sanctions, and argot evident in a subculture you are familiar with.

4. **Writing Sociology.** For a 24-hour period, note 20 different aspects of the material culture around you. Then research each item online to determine in what country or culture it originated. What do the results tell you about diffusion? What do they reveal about your own assumptions about what is American and what is foreign?

Self-Quiz

Read each question carefully and then select the best answer.

1. Which of the following is an aspect of culture?
   a. a comic book
   b. patriotic attachment to the flag of the United States
   c. slang words
   d. all of the above

2. People's adaptations to meet the needs for food, shelter, and clothing are examples of what George Murdock referred to as
   a. norms.
   b. folkways.
   c. cultural universals.
   d. sanctions.

3. What term do sociologists use to refer to the process by which a cultural item spreads from group to group or society to society?
   a. diffusion
   b. globalization
   c. innovation
   d. cultural relativism

4. The appearance of Starbucks coffeehouses in China is a sign of what aspect of culture?
   a. innovation
   b. globalization
   c. diffusion
   d. cultural relativism

5. Which statement about language is correct?
   a. Language is a major element of culture.
   b. A common language facilitates everyday interaction.
   c. Thousands of languages are spoken around the world.
   d. All of the above.

6. Which of the following statements about norms is correct?
   a. People do not follow norms in all situations. In some cases, they evade a norm because they know it is weakly enforced.
   b. In some instances, behavior that appears to violate society's norms may actually represent adherence to the norms of a particular group.
   c. Norms are violated in some instances because one norm conflicts with another.
   d. all of the above

7. Which of the following statements about values is correct?
   a. Values never change.
   b. The values of a culture may change, but most remain relatively stable during any one person's lifetime.
   c. Values are constantly changing; sociologists view them as being very unstable.
   d. all of the above

8. Which of the following terms describes the set of cultural beliefs and practices that help to maintain powerful social, economic, and political interests?
   a. mores
   b. dominant ideology
   c. consensus
   d. values

9. Terrorist groups are examples of
   a. cultural universals.
   b. subcultures.
   c. countercultures.
   d. dominant ideologies.

10. What is the term used when one places a priority on understanding other cultures, rather than dismissing them as "strange" or "exotic"?
   a. ethnocentrism
   b. culture shock
   c. cultural relativism
   d. cultural value

11. _____ are gestures, objects, and/or words that form the basis of human communication.

12. _____ is the process of introducing a new idea or object to a culture.

13. The bow and arrow, the automobile, and the television are all examples of _____.

14. Sociologists associated with the _____ perspective emphasize that language and symbols offer a powerful way for a subculture to maintain its identity.

15. "Put on some clean clothes for dinner" and "Thou shalt not kill" are both examples of _____ found in U.S. culture.

16. The United States has strong _____ against murder, treason, and other forms of abuse that have been institutionalized into formal norms.

17. From a(n) _____ perspective, the dominant ideology has major social significance. Not only do a society's most powerful groups and institutions control wealth and property; more important, they control the means of production.

18. Countercultures (for example, hippies) are typically popular among the _____, who have the least investment in the existing culture.

19. A person experiences _____ _____ when he or she feels disoriented, uncertain, out of place, even fearful when immersed in an unfamiliar culture.

20. From the _____ perspective, subcultures are evidence that differences can exist within a common culture.

Socialization and the Life Course

FamVeld/Shutterstock

A father teaches his daughter to paddle a kayak. Around the world, the family is the most important agent of socialization.

▶ Inside

Akhararat Wathanasing/123RF

What does it mean to be socialized into a culture different from the one in which you were born and brought up? What would it be like to straddle two cultures: to behave in totally different ways depending on the social environment in which you find yourself at any given time?

Sociologist Lindsay Feldman spent 15 months observing crews of prison inmates who battle wildfires in the West. She studied the wide variation between the social roles of the crew members as inmates and their social roles as heroic firefighters. She became a certified wildland firefighter herself and battled fires alongside the inmate firefighters, considering how they became socialized to their two widely varying roles and how they navigated between them.

66 *Fieldnotes, 10 June 2016:* Twenty-five wildland firefighters walked through the doors of a local restaurant. They cut a formidable figure. Wearing matching shirts and fire boots, their faces were sooty and burnt from a three-day battle in the mountains of Arizona. As the doors closed behind them, the restaurant-goers stood up and applauded. In rural communities of the western U.S., wildland firefighters are not heroes abstractly, but in a directly personal way—landscapes bear the charcoal scars of fires past, and residents remember which crews saved their properties and open spaces. This day, a young admirer broke free from his parents' table and ambushed one of the crewmembers, hugging his leg and precociously exclaiming: 'I want to be like you when I grow up!' The crew laughed, and so especially did Sammy, whose leg had a beaming boy attached. The crew's laughter held multiple meanings; it was a genuine response to the boy's sweet nature, but it was also an ironic, inside joke: Sammy was currently serving nine years in prison for possession of methamphetamines. In fact, the fire crew was made up of 22 prisoners and three correctional officers. After ruffling the little boy's hair and sending him back to his parents, Sammy and the crew graciously accepted the rest of the applause and made their way to the tables to eat. I sat down beside Sammy intending to ask him about this encounter, but he pre-empted my question by looking at me with tears in his eyes, and saying simply: 'That just healed me.'

This set of fieldnotes describes one of many public interactions that participants had in the Inmate Wildfire Program (IWP), a skilled labour programme offered by the Arizona Department of Corrections (ADC) in which incarcerated people travel throughout this southwestern U.S. state to fight wildfires. Their interactions ranged from the exceptional, like in the excerpt above, to the more mundane, like the simple act of driving through the desert landscape with the ease of a wildland firefighter. Every day the crew left the prison, a space where criminality is defined and maintained, and moved into a more fluid space, somewhere between the social categories 'criminal' and 'hero,' and somewhere in between the identities that arise from these categorisations. 99

Source: Feldman 2018:1–2.

> *I sat down beside Sammy intending to ask him about this encounter, but he pre-empted my question by looking at me with tears in his eyes, and saying simply: 'That just healed me.'*

Lindsey Feldman followed a group of prisoners assigned to the skilled labor task of fighting wildfires, working alongside the crews and interviewing crew members, their supervisors, and community members. Prisoners are categorized and treated as criminals; every aspect of their lives, including work, food, and clothing, is driven by this negative categorization, and over time, an incarcerated individual may take on and internalize this negative identity.

Feldman found that wildland firefighters, in contrast, form a highly positive, almost heroic, identity. Prisoners who serve as firefighters fill a highly valued role in the community, as the excerpt above shows. Feldman found that prisoners who became firefighters had to function differently from those who remained within the prison environment: they needed to use critical-thinking skills and to interact with the non-prison population, and they enjoyed freedoms not available to most prisoners. As a result, they were able to construct more positive identities that resulted in more positive life outcomes, both within prison and after their release. In many cases, these positive outcomes radically changed the firefighter-prisoners' life courses.

Sociologists, in general, are interested in the patterns of behavior and attitudes that emerge throughout the life course, from infancy to old age. These patterns are part of the lifelong process of **socialization,** in which people learn the attitudes, values, and behaviors appropriate for members of a particular culture. Socialization occurs through human interactions that begin in infancy and continue through retirement. We learn a great deal from those people most important in our lives—family members, friends, and teachers. But we also learn from people we see on the street, on television, through social media, and in films and magazines.

Socialization also shapes our self-images. For example, in the United States, people who do not conform to ideal cultural standards of physical attractiveness are disadvantaged not only in social situations but also in hiring practices. This kind of unfavorable evaluation can significantly influence a person's self-esteem. In everyday speech, the term **personality** is used to refer to a person's typical patterns of attitudes, needs, characteristics, and behavior.

How much of a person's personality is shaped by culture? In what ways does socialization continue into adulthood? Who are the most powerful agents of socialization? In this chapter we will examine the role of socialization in human development. We will begin by analyzing the interaction of heredity with environmental factors. Then we will explore how people develop perceptions, feelings, and beliefs about themselves. We will pay particular attention to important agents of socialization, including the family, schools, peers, the media and technology, the workplace, and religion. As we will see, socialization is a process that spans the entire life course. In the Social Policy section that closes the chapter, we will focus on the socialization experience of group child care for young children.

The Role of Socialization

What makes us who we are? Is it the genes we are born with, or the environment in which we grow up? Researchers have traditionally clashed over the relative importance of biological inheritance and environmental factors in human development—a conflict called the *nature versus nurture* (or *heredity versus environment*) debate. Today, most social scientists have moved beyond this debate, acknowledging instead the *interaction* of these variables in shaping human development. However, we can better appreciate how heredity and environmental factors interact and influence the socialization process if we first examine situations in which one factor operates almost entirely without the other (Homans 1979).

Social Environment: The Impact of Isolation

The chapter-opening example of wildland firefighters who learn to function in two very different social worlds shows the enormous effects that socialization has even on adults. The effects of early social experiences on children are at least as important. The two cases that follow describe the documented effects of extreme social isolation and neglect in childhood.

Extreme Isolation: Isabelle   The dramatic story of a child called Isabelle was all too real. For the first six years of her life, Isabelle lived in almost total seclusion in a darkened room. She had little contact with other people, with the exception of her mother, who could neither speak nor hear. Isabelle's mother's parents had been so deeply ashamed of Isabelle's illegitimate birth that they kept her hidden away from the world. Ohio authorities finally discovered the child in 1938, when Isabelle's mother escaped from her parents' home, taking her daughter with her.

When she was discovered at age six, Isabelle could not speak; she could merely make various croaking sounds. Her only communications with her mother were simple gestures. Isabelle had been largely deprived of the typical interactions and socialization experiences of childhood. Since she had seen few people, she showed a strong fear of strangers and reacted almost like a wild animal when confronted with an unfamiliar person. As she became accustomed to seeing certain individuals, her reaction changed to one of extreme apathy. At first, observers believed that Isabelle was deaf, but she soon began to react to nearby sounds. On tests of maturity, she scored at the level of an infant rather than a six-year-old.

Specialists developed a systematic training program to help Isabelle adapt to human relationships and socialization. After a few days of training, she made her first attempt to verbalize. Although she started slowly, Isabelle quickly passed through six years of development. In a little over two months she was speaking in complete sentences. Nine months later she could identify both words and sentences. Before Isabelle reached age 9, she was ready to attend school with other children. By age 14 she was in sixth grade, doing well in school, and emotionally well adjusted.

Yet without an opportunity to experience socialization in her first six years, Isabelle had been hardly human in the social sense when she was first discovered. Her inability to communicate at the time of her discovery—despite her physical and cognitive potential to learn—and her remarkable progress over the next few years underscore the impact of socialization on human development (K. Davis 1947:435–437).

The scientists involved with Isabelle's case concluded that all children need socialization in the form of love, care, and affection. Absent that kind of attention, humans cannot learn to speak and interact with others as expected. This need for positive social interaction does not end with childhood; it continues throughout the life span.

Unfortunately, other children who have been locked away or severely neglected have not fared so well as Isabelle. In many instances, the consequences of their social isolation have proved much more damaging.

Extreme Neglect: Romanian Orphans   Isabelle's experience is important to researchers because there are only a few cases of children who were reared in total isolation. However, there are many cases of children raised in extremely neglectful social circumstances. In the 1990s, public attention focused on infants and young children who grew up in orphanages in the formerly communist countries of eastern Europe. In Romanian orphanages, babies once lay in their cribs for 18 to 20 hours a day, curled against their feeding bottles, receiving little care from adults. This minimal attention continued for the first five years of their lives. Many of them grew up fearful of human contact, and prone to unpredictable antisocial behavior. As recently as 2004, some 32,000 Romanian children were institutionalized in this manner.

This situation came to light as families in North America and Europe began to adopt thousands of the orphans. For about 20 percent of those adopted, adjustment problems were so dramatic that the adopting families suffered guilty fears of being ill-fit parents. Many of them asked for assistance in dealing with the children. Slowly, efforts are being made to introduce the deprived youngsters to feelings of attachment and socialization that they have never experienced before.

In 2001, Romania bowed to pressure and placed a moratorium on international adoptions. The state took steps to reunite orphans with their birth families, place them with adoptive families in Romania, or settle them in small group homes. With supervision from attentive caregivers and specialists, the once-abandoned children have made remarkable progress. UNICEF is now using the program as a model for other nations that are dealing with such children. Worldwide, an estimated 2.7 million children are living in institutional care (Petrowski, Cappa, and Gross 2017).

As with Isabelle, the Romanian orphans underscored the significance of the social environment in a child's development. Increasingly, researchers are emphasizing the importance of the earliest socialization experiences for all children, including those who grow up in more normal environments. We know

Thomas Coex/AFP/Getty Images

In Romania, special programs emphasizing social interaction have helped orphans to overcome years of social isolation.

now that it is not enough to care for an infant's physical needs; parents must also concern themselves with their children's social development. If, for example, children are discouraged from having friends even as toddlers, they will miss out on experiences with peers that are critical to their socialization and emotional growth.

Primate Studies   Studies of animals raised in isolation also support the importance of socialization in development. Harry Harlow (1971), a researcher at the primate laboratory of the University of Wisconsin, conducted tests with rhesus monkeys that had been raised away from their mothers and away from contact with other monkeys. As was the case with Isabelle, the rhesus monkeys raised in isolation were fearful and easily frightened. They did not mate, and the females who were artificially inseminated became abusive mothers. Apparently, isolation had had a damaging effect on the monkeys.

A creative aspect of Harlow's experimentation was his use of "artificial mothers." In one such experiment, Harlow presented monkeys raised in isolation with two substitute mothers—one cloth-covered replica and one covered with wire that had the ability to offer milk. Monkey after monkey went to the wire mother for the life-giving milk, yet spent much more time clinging to the more motherlike cloth model. It appears that the infant monkeys developed greater social attachments from their need for warmth, comfort, and intimacy than from their need for milk.

While these studies may seem to suggest that heredity can be dismissed as a factor in the social development of humans and animals, studies of twins reveal a fascinating interplay between heredity and environment.

USE YOUR SOCIOLOGICAL IMAGINATION

What events in your life have had a strong influence on who you are?

The Influence of Heredity

Identical twins Oskar Stohr and Jack Yufe were separated soon after their birth and raised on different continents, in very different cultural settings. Oskar was reared as a strict Catholic by his maternal grandmother in the Sudetenland of Czechoslovakia. As a member of the Hitler Youth movement in Nazi Germany, he learned to hate Jews. In contrast, his brother Jack was reared in Trinidad by the twins' Jewish father. Jack joined an Israeli kibbutz (a collective settlement) at age 17 and later served in the Israeli army. When the twins were reunited in middle age, however, some startling similarities emerged: They both wore wire-rimmed glasses and mustaches. They both liked spicy foods and sweet liqueurs, were

Alamy Stock Photo

Despite the striking physical resemblance between these pairs of identical twins at the Twins Convention at Twinsburg, Ohio, there are undoubtedly many differences between them. Research points to some behavioral similarities between twins, but little beyond the likenesses found among nontwin siblings.

absentminded, flushed the toilet before using it, stored rubber bands on their wrists, and dipped buttered toast in their coffee (Holden 1980).

The twins also differed in many important respects: Jack was a workaholic; Oskar enjoyed leisure-time activities. Oskar was a traditionalist who was domineering toward women; Jack was a political liberal who was much more accepting of feminism. Finally, Jack was extremely proud of being Jewish, whereas Oskar never mentioned his Jewish heritage (Holden 1987).

Oskar and Jack are prime examples of the interplay of heredity and environment. For a number of years, the Minnesota Twin Family Study has been following 137 sets of identical twins reared apart to determine what similarities, if any, they show in personality traits, behavior, and intelligence. Results from the available twin studies indicate that *both* genetic factors *and* socialization experiences are influential in human development. Certain characteristics, such as temperaments, voice patterns, and nervous habits, appear to be strikingly similar even in twins reared apart, suggesting that these qualities may be linked to hereditary causes. However, identical twins reared apart differ far more in their attitudes, values, chosen mates, and even drinking habits; these qualities, it would seem, are influenced by environmental factors.

Researchers have also been impressed with the similar scores on intelligence tests of twins reared apart in *roughly similar* social settings. Most of the identical twins register scores even closer than those that would be expected if the same person took a test twice. At the same time, however,

identical twins brought up in *dramatically different* social environments score quite differently on intelligence tests—a finding that supports the impact of socialization on human development (Segal 2012).

Internationally, there have now been well over 2,700 twin studies involving a staggering number of twins—14.5 million. While virtually all these twins were reared from birth in the same home by the same parents, newer and more sophisticated statistical techniques have supplemented the Minnesota Twin research to assess the relative impact of heredity and social environment. The conclusion has been that it is not nature *vs.* nurture but nature *and* nurture. Some traits, such as bipolar disorder (in the past referred to as manic depressive), have significant genetic components, while others, such as eating disorders, have a much more significant social environment component (Lakhani et al. 2019; Polderman et al. 2015).

THINKING CRITICALLY

What are some social policy implications of research on the effects of early socialization experiences?

The Self and Socialization

We all have various perceptions, feelings, and beliefs about who we are and what we are like. How do we come to develop them? Do they change as we age?

We were not born with these understandings. Building on the work of George Herbert Mead (1964b), sociologists recognize that our concept of who we are, the *self*, emerges as we interact with others. The **self** is a distinct identity that sets us apart from others. It is not a static phenomenon but continues to develop and change throughout our lives.

Sociologists and psychologists alike have expressed interest in how the individual develops and modifies the sense of self as a result of social interaction. The work of sociologists Charles Horton Cooley and George Herbert Mead, pioneers of the interactionist approach, has been especially useful in furthering our understanding of these important issues.

Sociological Approaches to the Self

Cooley: Looking-Glass Self In the early 1900s, Charles Horton Cooley advanced the belief that we learn who we are by interacting with others. Our view of ourselves, then, comes not only from direct contemplation of our personal qualities but also from our impressions of how others perceive us. Cooley used the phrase **looking-glass self** to emphasize that the self is the product of our social interactions.

The process of developing a self-identity or self-concept has three phases. First, we imagine how we present ourselves to others—to relatives, friends, even strangers on the street. Then we imagine how others evaluate us (attractive, intelligent, shy, or strange). Finally, we develop some sort of feeling about ourselves, such as respect or shame, as a result of these impressions (Cooley 1956).

The looking glass self is a broader view of what W. E. B. DuBois ([1903] 1961) termed **double consciousness,** as we learned in Chapter 1. Being Black in America means having one identity in social interaction with people who are not African American and another in interactions with other Black Americans.

A subtle but critical aspect of Cooley's looking-glass self is that the self results from an individual's "imagination" of how others view him or her. As a result, we can develop self-identities based on *incorrect* perceptions of how others see us. A student may react strongly to a teacher's criticism and decide (wrongly) that the instructor views the student as stupid. This misperception may be converted into a negative self-identity through the following process: (1) the teacher criticized me, (2) the teacher must think that I'm stupid, (3) I *am* stupid. Yet self-identities are also subject to change. If the student receives an A at the end of the course, he or she will probably no longer feel stupid.

Mead: Stages of the Self George Herbert Mead continued Cooley's exploration of interactionist theory. Mead (1964a, [1934] 2015) developed a useful model of the process by which

Saleh Al-Obeidi/AFP/Getty Images

Socialization can be negative as well as positive. When the very young come to view harmful behaviors like smoking or illegal drug use as "normal," socialization is negative. In Yemen, these child soldiers have learned to use an automatic weapon.

the self emerges, defined by three distinct stages: the preparatory stage, the play stage, and the game stage (Table 4-1).

The Preparatory Stage During the *preparatory stage,* children merely imitate the people around them, especially family members with whom they continually interact. Thus, a small child will bang on a piece of wood while a parent is engaged in carpentry work, or will try to throw a ball if an older sibling is doing so nearby.

As they grow older, children become more adept at using symbols, including the gestures and words that form the basis of human communication. By interacting with relatives and friends, as well as by watching cartoons on television and looking at picture books, children in the preparatory stage begin to understand symbols. They will continue to use this form of communication throughout their lives.

The Play Stage Mead was among the first to analyze the relationship of symbols to socialization. As children develop skill in communicating through symbols, they gradually become more aware of social relationships. As a result, during

TABLE 4-1   MEAD'S STAGES OF THE SELF

Summing Up

Stage	Self Present?	Definition	Example
Preparatory	No	Child imitates the actions of others.	When adults laugh and smile, child laughs and smiles.
Play	Developing	Child takes the role of a single other, as if he or she were the other.	Child first takes the role of doctor, then the role of patient.
Game	Yes	Child considers the roles of two or more others simultaneously.	In game of hide-and-seek, child takes into account the roles of both hider and seeker.

the *play stage,* they begin to pretend to be other people. Just as an actor "becomes" a character, a child becomes a doctor, parent, superhero, or ship captain.

Mead, in fact, noted that an important aspect of the play stage is role-playing. **Role taking** is the process of mentally assuming the perspective of another and responding from that imagined viewpoint. For example, through this process a young child will gradually learn when it is best to ask a parent for favors. If the parent usually comes home from work in a bad mood, the child will wait until after dinner, when the parent is more relaxed and approachable.

The Game Stage

In Mead's third stage, the *game stage,* the child of about age eight or nine no longer just plays roles but begins to consider several tasks and relationships simultaneously. At this point in development, children grasp not only their own social positions but also those of others around them—just as in a football game the players must understand their own and everyone else's positions. Consider a girl or boy who is part of a Scout troop out on a weekend hike in the mountains. The child must understand what he or she is expected to do but must also recognize the responsibilities of other Scouts as well as the leaders. This is the final stage of development under Mead's model: the child can now respond to numerous members of the social environment.

Mead uses the term **generalized other** to refer to the attitudes, viewpoints, and expectations of society as a whole that a child takes into account in his or her behavior. Simply put, this concept suggests that when an individual acts, he or she takes into account an entire group of people. For example, a child will not act courteously merely to please a particular parent. Rather, the child comes to understand that courtesy is a widespread social value endorsed by parents, teachers, and religious leaders.

Table 4-1 summarizes the three stages of the self outlined by George Herbert Mead.

Mead: Theory of the Self Mead is best known for his theory of the self. According to Mead (1964b), the self begins at a privileged, central position in a person's world. Young children picture themselves as the focus of everything around them and find it difficult to consider the perspectives of others. For example, when shown a mountain scene and asked to describe what an observer on the opposite side of the mountain might see (such as a lake or hikers), young children describe only objects visible from their vantage point. This childhood tendency to place ourselves at the center of events never entirely disappears. Many people with a fear of flying automatically assume that if any plane goes down, it will be the one they are on. And who reads the horoscope section in the paper without looking at their own horoscope first? Why

Ariel Skelley/DigitalVision/Getty Images

Role taking is the process of mentally assuming the perspective of another, even an astronaut, and taking on that imagined viewpoint.

else do we buy lottery tickets, if we do not imagine ourselves winning?

Nonetheless, as people mature, the self changes and begins to reflect greater concern about the reactions of others. Parents, friends, co-workers, coaches, and teachers are often among those who play a major role in shaping a person's self. The term **significant others** is used to refer to those individuals who are most important in the development of the self. Many young people, for example, find themselves drawn to the same kind of work their parents engage in.

USE YOUR SOCIOLOGICAL IMAGINATION

How do you view yourself as you interact with others around you? How do you think you formed this view of yourself?

Goffman: Presentation of the Self How do we manage our "self"? How do we display to others who we are? Erving Goffman, a sociologist associated with the interactionist perspective, suggested that many of our daily activities involve attempts to convey impressions of who we are. We learn to slant our presentation of the self in order to create distinctive appearances and satisfy particular audiences. Goffman (1959) referred to this altering of the presentation of the self as **impression management.** Box 4-1 describes an everyday example of this concept—the way students behave after receiving their exam grades.

During the coronavirus pandemic, sociologists observed how we engaged in impression management during the Zoom meetings that became common during the self-quarantine. While the point of a video call is to see friends, fellow workers,

SOCIOLOGY IN EDUCATION

4-1   Impression Management by Students

When you and fellow classmates get an exam back, you probably react differently depending on the grades each of you earned. This distinction is part of *impression management*. Researchers have found that students' reactions differ depending on the grades that others received, compared to their own. These encounters can be divided into three categories: those in which all students earned high grades (Ace–Ace encounters); those between Aces and students who received low or failing grades (Ace–Bomber encounters); and those between students who all got low grades (Bomber–Bomber encounters).

Ace–Ace encounters occur in a rather open atmosphere, because there is comfort in sharing a high mark with another high achiever. It is even acceptable to violate the norm of modesty and brag when among other Aces, since as one student admitted, "It's much easier to admit a high mark to someone who has done better than you, or at least as well."

Ace–Bomber encounters are often sensitive. Bombers generally attempt to avoid such ex-

changes, because "you . . . emerge looking like the dumb one" or "feel like you are lazy or unreliable." When forced into interactions with Aces, Bombers work to appear gracious and congratulatory. For their part, Aces offer sympathy and support to the dissatisfied Bombers and even rationalize their own "lucky" high scores. To help Bombers save face, Aces may emphasize the difficulty and unfairness of the examination.

Bomber–Bomber encounters tend to be closed, reflecting the group effort to wall off the feared disdain of others. Yet within the safety of these encounters, Bombers openly share their disappointment and engage in expressions of mutual self-pity that they themselves call "pity parties." They devise face-saving excuses for their poor perfor-

When forced into interactions with Aces, Bombers work to appear gracious and congratulatory.

mance, such as "I wasn't feeling well all week" or "I had four exams and two papers due that week."

Of course, grade comparisons are not the only occasion when students engage in impression management. Another study has shown that students' perceptions of how often fellow students work out can also influence their social encounters. In athletic terms, a bomber would be someone who doesn't work out; an ace would be someone who works hard at physical fitness.

LET'S DISCUSS

1. How do you react to those who have received higher or lower grades than you? Do you engage in impression management? How would you like others to react to your grade?
2. What social norms govern students' impression management strategies?

Sources: Albas and Albas 1988, 1996; Austin 2009; M. Mack 2003; Scott 2016.

and family, most people constantly stare at themselves in their front-view cameras to double-check the impression they are conveying. Some even insert an exotic background as if messaging what type of person they are (Thomson 2020).

In analyzing such everyday social interactions, Goffman makes so many explicit parallels to the theater that his view has been termed the **dramaturgical approach.** According to this perspective, people resemble performers in action. For example, a clerk may try to appear busier than he or she actually is if a supervisor happens to be watching. Similarly, the prison inmate wildfire fighters described in the opening excerpt allow the general public to mistake them for full-time firefighters.

Goffman (1959) also drew attention to another aspect of the self, **face-work.** How often do you initiate some kind of face-saving behavior when you feel embarrassed or rejected? In response to a rejection at the singles' bar, a person may engage in face-work by saying, "There really isn't an interesting person in this entire crowd." We feel the need to maintain a proper image of the self if we are to continue social interaction.

Face-work is clearly evident when a person must deliver bad news. Goffman (1952) referred to the strategy as *cooling out:* for example, during a college or job interview, the interviewer

might give the candidate a chance but ultimately deliver the bad news. Sociologist Junhow Wei (2016) studied how contestants on *American Idol* are let down. Rejected performers are allowed to vent and encouraged to minimize the significance of their failure by being reassured they do "have the talent."

Goffman's work on the self represents a logical progression of sociological studies begun by Cooley and Mead on how personality is acquired through socialization and how we manage the presentation of the self to others. Cooley stressed the process by which we create a self; Mead focused on how the self develops as we learn to interact with others; Goffman emphasized the ways in which we consciously create images of ourselves for others.

FOX Image Collection/Getty images

Face-work: When contestants are let down on the popular TV program *American Idol*, they are given a "cooling out" period when they are allowed to vent and reassured that they do not lack talent.

Psychological Approaches to the Self

Psychologists have shared the interest of Cooley, Mead, and other sociologists in the development of the self. Early work in psychology, such as that of Sigmund Freud (1856–1939), stressed the role of inborn drives—among them the drive for sexual gratification—in channeling human behavior. More recently, psychologists such as Jean Piaget have emphasized the stages through which human development progresses.

Like Charles Horton Cooley and George Herbert Mead, Freud believed that the self is a social product, and that aspects of one's personality are influenced by other people (especially one's parents). However, unlike Cooley and Mead, he suggested that the self has components that work in opposition to each other. According to Freud, our natural impulsive instincts are in constant conflict with societal constraints. Part of us seeks limitless pleasure, while another part favors rational behavior. By interacting with others, we learn the expectations of society and then select behavior most appropriate to our culture. (Of course, as Freud was well aware, we sometimes distort reality and behave irrationally.)

Research on newborn babies by the Swiss child psychologist Jean Piaget (1896–1980) has underscored the importance of social interactions in developing a sense of self. Piaget found that newborns have no self in the sense of a looking-glass image. Ironically, though, they are quite self-centered; they demand that all attention be directed toward them. Newborns have not yet separated themselves from the universe of which they are a part. For these babies, the phrase "you and me" has no meaning; they understand only "me." However, as they mature, children are gradually socialized into social relationships, even within their rather self-centered world.

In his well-known **cognitive theory of development,** Piaget (1954) identified four stages in the development of children's thought processes. In the first, or *sensorimotor,* stage, young children use their senses to make discoveries. For example, through touching they discover that their hands are actually a part of themselves. During the second, or *preoperational,* stage, children begin to use words and symbols to distinguish objects and ideas. The milestone in the third, or *concrete operational,* stage is that children engage in more logical thinking. They learn that even when a formless lump of clay is shaped into a snake, it is still the same clay. In the fourth, or *formal operational,* stage, adolescents become capable of sophisticated abstract thought and can deal logically with ideas and values.

According to Piaget, social interaction is the key to development. As children grow older, they pay increasing attention to how other people think and why they act in particular ways. In order to develop a distinct personality, each of us needs opportunities to interact with others. As we saw earlier, Isabelle was deprived of the chance for normal social interactions, and the consequences were severe (Kitchener 1991).

We have seen that a number of thinkers considered social interaction the key to the development of an individual's sense of self. As is generally true, we can best understand this topic by drawing on a variety of theory and research. Table 4-2 summarizes the rich literature, both sociological and psychological, on the development of the self.

THINKING CRITICALLY

What are some similarities between Mead's stages of the self and Piaget's cognitive development stages? What are some differences?

Agents of Socialization

As we have seen, the culture of the United States is defined by rather gradual movements from one stage of socialization to the next. The continuing and lifelong socialization process involves many different social forces that influence our lives and alter our self-images.

TABLE 4-2 THEORETICAL APPROACHES TO DEVELOPMENT OF THE SELF

Tracking Sociological Perspectives

Scholar	Key Concepts and Contributions	Major Points of Theory
Charles Horton Cooley 1864–1929 sociologist (USA)	Looking-glass self	Stages of development not distinct; feelings toward ourselves developed through interaction with others
George Herbert Mead 1863–1931 sociologist (USA)	The self Generalized other	Three distinct stages of development; self develops as children grasp the roles of others in their lives
Erving Goffman 1922–1982 sociologist (USA)	Impression management Dramaturgical approach Face-work	Self developed through the impressions we convey to others and to groups
Sigmund Freud 1856–1939 psychotherapist (Austria)	Psychoanalysis	Self influenced by parents and by inborn drives, such as the drive for sexual gratification
Jean Piaget 1896–1980 child psychologist (Switzerland)	Cognitive theory of development	Four stages of cognitive development

The family is the most important agent of socialization in the United States, especially for children. In this chapter, we'll also discuss six other agents of socialization: the school, the peer group, the mass media and technology, the workplace, religion, and the state.

Family

The lifelong process of learning begins shortly after birth. Since newborns can hear, see, smell, taste, and feel heat, cold, and pain, they are constantly orienting themselves to the surrounding world. Human beings, especially family members, constitute an important part of their social environment. People minister to the baby's needs by feeding, cleaning, carrying, and comforting the baby.

All families engage in socialization, but the way that Amish families encourage their children to accept their community's subculture is particularly striking. Box 4-2 describes their tolerance for the period of rebellion known as *rumspringa*, during

which Amish children flirt with the adolescent subculture of mainstream American society.

In the United States, social development also includes exposure to cultural assumptions regarding gender and race. Black parents, for example, have learned that children as young as age two can absorb negative messages about Blacks in children's books, toys, and television shows—all of which are designed primarily for white consumers. At the same time, Black children are exposed more often than others to the inner-city youth gang culture. Because most Blacks, even those who are middle class, live near very poor neighborhoods, their children are susceptible to these influences, despite their parents' strong family values (Linn and Poussaint 1999; Umaña-Taylor and Hill 2020).

The term **gender role** refers to expectations regarding the proper behavior, attitudes, and activities of males and females. For example, we traditionally think of "toughness" as masculine—and desirable only in men—while we view "tenderness" as feminine. Other cultures do not necessarily assign these qualities to each gender in the way that our culture

RESEARCH TODAY

4-2   *Rumspringa:* Raising Children Amish Style

All families face challenges raising their children, but what if your parents expected you not to dance, listen to music, watch television, or access the Internet? This is the challenge faced by Amish teens and their parents, who embrace a lifestyle of the mid-1800s. Amish youths—boys in particular—often rebel against their parents' strict morals by getting drunk, behaving disrespectfully, and indulging in "worldly" activities, such as buying a car. At times even the girls may become involved, to their families' dismay. As one scholar puts it, "The rowdiness of Amish youth is an embarrassment to church leaders and a stigma in the larger community" (Kraybill 2019).

> *All families face challenges raising their children, but what if your parents expected you not to dance, listen to music, watch television, or access the Internet?*

Yet the strong pull of mainstream American culture has led Amish parents to routinize, almost to accept, some of their children's worldly activities. They expect adolescents to test their subculture's boundaries during

©Lee Snider Photo Images/Shutterstock

a period of discovery called *rumspringa,* a German term meaning "running around." A common occurrence during which young people attend barn dances and break social norms that forbid drinking, smoking, and driving cars, *rumspringa* is definitely not supported by the Amish religion.

Parents often react to these escapades by looking the other way, sometimes literally. If they hear radio music coming from the barn, or a motorcycle driving on to their property in the middle of the night, they don't punish their offspring. Instead, they pretend not to notice, secure in the knowledge that Amish children almost always return to the community's traditional values. Indeed, despite the flirtation with popular culture and modern technology that is common during the *rumspringa,* the vast majority of Amish youths

do return to the Amish community and become baptized. Scholars report that 85 to 90 percent of Amish children accept the faith as young adults.

To mainstream Americans, this little known and understood subculture has become a source of entertainment, as several reality series have appeared on cable TV, including *Breaking Amish, Return to Amish, Amish in the City, Amish Mafia,* and *Amish: Out of Order.* All feature the exploits of Amish youth during *rumspringa.* On behalf of the Amish community, some critics called the series exploitative, a sign of how vulnerable the Amish are. No similar series would be developed on the rebellion of Muslim or Orthodox Jewish youths, they charged.

LET'S DISCUSS

1. Do you or anyone you know come from a subculture that rejects mainstream American culture? If so, describe the community's norms and values. How do they resemble and how do they differ from Amish norms and values?
2. Why do you think so many Amish youths return to their families' way of life after rebelling against it?

Sources: Amish America 2019; Kraybill 2019; R. Schaefer and Zellner 2015; Shachtman 2006; Stevick 2007.

does. The existence of gender roles does not imply that inevitably, males and females will assume certain roles, nor does it imply that those roles are quite distinct from one another. Rather, gender roles emphasize the fact that males and females are not genetically predetermined to occupy certain roles.

Experiments can help illuminate this aspect of social behavior. Sociologist Nelta Edwards at the University of Alaska, Anchorage, would ask her students to polish the fingernails of a friend of the opposite sex with supplies she provided. Men were very reluctant to have their nails polished and typically chose clear or black as the color. When they then went out in public, they encountered taunts and name-calling, even from strangers. The male students reported that they either avoided going out in public, quickly removed the polish, or engaged in some impression management: "I had to do it for my Soc 101 class."

A daughter learns how to weave fabric from her mother in Guatemala. The family is the most important agent of socialization.

The women whose nails were polished by men often expressed concern with the sloppiness with which their fingernails were done. When men did the job well, the female students admitted feeling surprised. Such an experiment easily showed how gender roles can be defined. But since experiments with people need to be carried out carefully, Edwards (2010) acknowledges that the experimenter must be mindful that a student could be physically abused or that the experiment might intensify anti-gay feelings.

As the primary agents of childhood socialization, parents play a critical role in guiding children into those gender roles deemed

A college experiment asking students to polish the fingernails of someone of the opposite sex reveals both how we view gender expectations as well as the care that needs to be shown in conducting experiments with human subjects.

appropriate in a society. Other adults, older siblings, the mass media, and religious and educational institutions also have a noticeable impact on a child's socialization into feminine and masculine norms. A culture or subculture may require that one sex or the other take primary responsibility for the socialization of children, economic support of the family, or religious or intellectual leadership. In some societies, girls are socialized mainly by their mothers and boys by their fathers—an arrangement that may prevent girls from learning critical survival skills. In South Asia, fathers teach their sons to swim to prepare them for a life as fishermen; girls typically do not learn to swim. When a deadly tsunami hit the coast of South Asia in 2004, many more men survived than women.

School

Like the family, schools have an explicit mandate to socialize people in the United States—especially children—into the norms and values of our culture.

As conflict theorists Samuel Bowles and Herbert Gintis ([1976] 2011) have observed, schools in this country foster competition through built-in systems of reward and punishment, such as grades and evaluations by teachers. Consequently, a child who is experiencing difficulty trying to learn a new skill can sometimes come to feel stupid and unsuccessful. However, as the self matures, children become capable of increasingly realistic assessments of their intellectual, physical, and social abilities.

Functionalists point out that schools, as agents of socialization, fulfill the function of teaching children the values and customs of the larger society. Conflict theorists agree, but add that schools can reinforce the divisive aspects of society, especially those of social class. For example, higher education in the United States is costly, despite the existence of financial aid programs. Students from affluent backgrounds therefore have an advantage in gaining access to universities and professional training. At the same time, less affluent young people may never receive the preparation that would qualify them for the best-paying and most prestigious jobs.

Peer Group

As a child grows older, the family becomes somewhat less important in social development. Instead, peer groups increasingly assume the role of Mead's significant others. Within the peer group, young people associate with others who are approximately their age, and who often enjoy a similar social status (Giordano 2003).

We can see how important peer groups are to young people when their social lives are strained by war or disaster. In Syria, social groupings have been torn apart by civil war, invasion, and bombings. In 2012, Fatmeh described her life as that of a typical teenager whose daily routine was all about school, classes, friends, and homework. Three years later, at age 15, she was living in a makeshift shelter in Lebanon. When she left Syria, she still hoped to continue her studies in Lebanon and become a language teacher, but that is unlikely to happen, because her whole family must do farm work seven days a week to maintain their meager life. Her only connection beyond her immediate family is her cell phone, which allows her to keep up with news about Syria and to hear songs about her homeland. Fatmeh says she still has "very small hope" that someday she will be able to return to school and eventually go to college. "Very small, small hope," she says (Beaubien and Davis 2015).

The importance of peers or friends cannot be overstated. Imagine you arrive in a different country, a very different culture where you will live for some time. You are both alone and lonely. In Japan, new arrivals can literally rent a friend. Tokyo-based women-only Client Partners recognizes that "people cannot survive alone, because essentially, happiness is born from relationships between people." For a price they provide a friend or even an entire family to help migrants navigate Japan with instant companions (Client Partners 2020; Colin 2016).

Gender differences are noteworthy among adolescents. Boys and girls are socialized by their parents, peers, and the media to identify many of the same paths to popularity, but to different degrees. Table 4-3 compares male and female college students' reports of how girls and boys they knew became popular in high school. The two groups named many of the same paths to popularity but gave them a different order of importance. While neither men nor women named sexual activity, drug use, or alcohol use as one of the top five paths, college men were much more likely than women to mention those behaviors as a means to becoming popular, for both boys and girls.

TAKING SOCIOLOGY TO WORK

Rakefet Avramovitz, **Program Administrator, Child Care Law Center**

Rakefet Avramovitz has been working at the Child Care Law Center in San Francisco since 2003. The center uses legal tools to foster the development of quality, affordable child care, with the goal of expanding child care options, particularly for low-income families. As a support person for the center's attorneys, she manages grants, oversees the center's publications, and sets up conferences and training sessions.

Avramovitz graduated from Dickinson College in 2000. She first became interested in sociology when she took a social analysis course. Though she enjoyed her qualitative courses most, she found her quantitative courses fun, "in that we got to do surveys of people on campus. I've always enjoyed fieldwork," she notes. Avramovitz's most memorable course was one that gave her the opportunity to interact with migrant farmworkers for an entire semester. "I learned ethnography and how to work with people of different cultures. It changed my life," she says.

Avramovitz finds that the skills she learned in her sociology courses are a great help to her on the job. "Sociology taught me how to work with people . . . and

Courtesy of Rakefet Avriamovitz

how to think critically. It taught me how to listen and find the stories that people are telling," she explains. Before joining the Child Care Law Center, Avramovitz worked as a counselor for women who were facing difficult issues. "My background in ethnography helped me to talk to these women and listen effectively," she notes. "I was able to help many women by understanding and being able to express their needs to the attorneys we worked with."

Avramovitz is enthusiastic about her work and her ability to make a difference in other people's lives. Maybe that is why she looks forward to summer at the center, when the staff welcomes several law students as interns. "It is really neat to see people learn and get jazzed about child care issues," she says.

LET'S DISCUSS

1. What might be some of the broad, long-term effects of the center's work to expand child care options? Explain.

2. Besides the law, what other professions might benefit from the skills a sociology major has to offer?

TABLE 4-3   HIGH SCHOOL POPULARITY

What makes high school girls popular?		What makes high school boys popular?	
According to college men:	According to college women:	According to college men:	According to college women:
1. Physical attractiveness	1. Grades/intelligence	1. Participation in sports	1. Participation in sports
2. Grades/intelligence	2. Participation in sports	2. Grades/intelligence	2. Grades/intelligence
3. Participation in sports	3. General sociability	3. Popularity with girls	3. General sociability
4. General sociability	4. Physical attractiveness	4. General sociability	4. Physical attractiveness
5. Popularity with boys	5. Clothes	5. Car	5. School clubs/government

Think about It This is what college students thought about high school popularity in 1998. Do you think ideas have changed since then?

Note: Students at the following universities were asked in which ways adolescents in their high schools had gained prestige with their peers: Cornell University, Louisiana State University, Southeastern Louisiana University, State University of New York at Albany, State University of New York at Stony Brook, University of Georgia, and University of New Hampshire.

Source: Suitor et al. 2001.

Mass Media and Technology

In the past century, media innovations—radio, motion pictures, recorded music, television, and the Internet—have become important agents of socialization. The question is no longer whether young people are plugged in, but how they use these resources.

Increasingly, then, socialization occurs online. The age at which young people go online has also been dropping, prompting concern about the potential for media abuse at an earlier and earlier age. Over the last decade, the American Academy of Pediatrics began publishing concerns about teen use of the Internet. Infants, toddlers, and preschoolers are now growing up in environments saturated with new technolo-gies, which they are adopting at increasing rates. Although the Academy sees much hope for the educational potential of interactive media for young children, they are concerned about their overuse during this crucial period of rapid brain development. Research in this area remains limited, but based on research done so far, experts contend that digital media use should be avoided (except video-chatting) in children younger than 18 to 24 months. If parents want to introduce digital media for children ages 18 to 24 months of age, they should choose high-quality programming and always use media together with their child. Avoid solo media use in this age group (American Academy of Pediatrics 2016).

As young people become more sophisticated with social media they begin to control how others may access their activity, as shown in Box 4-3.

Not just in industrial nations, but in Africa and other developing areas, people have been socialized into relying on new communications technologies. Not long ago, if Zadhe Iyombe wanted to talk to his mother, he had to make an eight-day trip from the capital city of Kinshasa up the Congo River by boat to the rural town where he was born. Now both he and his mother have access to a cell phone, and they send text messages to each other daily. Iyombe and his mother are not atypical. Cell phones, especially those with broadband service, are not cheap: fewer than 1 in 100 people in low-income nations have them, compared to 22 out of 100 in middle-income, that is, wealthier nations (World Bank 2019).

Jake Lyell/Alamy Stock Photo

In Soroti, Uganda, a woman makes a quick telephone call. Cell phones play a critical role in communications and commerce in developing countries, where other ways of connecting are less available or more expensive.

Workplace

Learning to behave appropriately in an occupation is a fundamental aspect of human socialization. It used to be that going to work began with the end of our formal schooling, but that is

OUR WIRED WORLD

4-3   Teens Controlling Access to Their Social Media

Almost every day, we see stories about outside groups obtaining access to our social media or parents seeking to control what their children see or post. But what about young people themselves controlling access to their own content?

A U.S. study found that 95 percent of teens ages 13 to 17 have a smartphone and 45 percent say they are online "almost constantly." This finding is not unique to the United States. Other surveys have found that 68 percent of British teens and 48 percent of Japanese teens report being online every hour.

Teens find ways to navigate social norms around who can access their postings, what can be accessed, and how often material is available. The need to do this follows from the burgeoning of what some of have termed the *me-economy,* the tendency of individuals to (over)share their feelings, photos, and comments. Not only do youth play an active role in controlling the content they see in their social media feeds; they also prevent figures of authority from viewing what they post there. Perhaps surprisingly, about half of teens surveyed in the United States say they never or rarely post selfies online. However, about half of teens say that they rarely edit their online presence in any way.

Even fewer teens delete or restrict access to their posts because their parents might see them or because posts might have negative impacts in the future. As shown in the accompanying figure, just one-third of teens

PERCENT OF U.S. TEENS WHO SAY THEY EVER DO THE FOLLOWING ON SOCIAL MEDIA

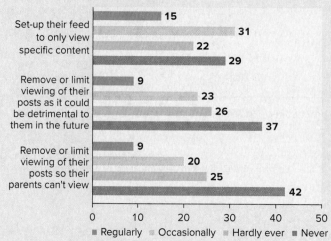

Source: Anderson and Jiang. 2018b.
Note: Respondents who did not give an answer are not included.

Not only do youth play an active role in controlling the content they see in their social media feeds; they also prevent figures of authority from viewing what they post there.

say they often or sometimes delete or restrict access to things they share on social media because of potential future negative impacts. Similarly, only about one-third delete or restrict posts because they don't want their parents to view them.

LET'S DISCUSS

1. Were you surprised at how many teens restrict their social media posts, or how few? Explain your answer.
2. Have you ever restricted access to your social media posts by your parents or anyone else? Why or why not?

Sources: Anderson and Jiang 2018a, 2018b; *The Economist* 2019c; Robb et al. 2017, 2018.

---

no longer the case, at least not in the United States. More and more young people work today, and not just for a parent or relative. Adolescents generally seek jobs in order to make spending money; 80 percent of high school seniors say that little or none of what they earn goes to family expenses. These teens rarely look on their employment as a means of exploring vocational interests or getting on-the-job training.

Some observers feel that the increasing number of teenagers who are working earlier in life and for longer hours are finding the workplace almost as important an agent of socialization as school. In fact, a number of educators complain that student time at work is adversely affecting schoolwork. The level of teenage employment in the United States is the highest among industrial countries, which may provide one explanation for why U.S. high school students lag behind those in other countries on international achievement tests.

Socialization in the workplace changes when it involves a more permanent shift from an after-school job to full-time employment. Occupational socialization can be most intense during the transition from school to job, but it continues throughout one's work history. Technological advances may alter the requirements of the position and necessitate some degree of resocialization. Today, men and women change occupations, employers, or places of work many times during their adult years. For example, the typical worker spends about four years with an employer. Occupational socialization continues, then, throughout a person's years in the labor market (Bialik 2010).

College students today recognize that occupational socialization is not socialization into one lifetime occupation. They anticipate going through a number of jobs. The Bureau of Labor Statistics (2019i) has found that from ages 18 to 52, the typical person has held 12 jobs, but nearly half of these jobs are held between ages 18 and 24. This high rate of turnover in employment applies to both men and women, and to those with a college degree as well as those with a high school diploma.

Religion and the State

Increasingly, social scientists are recognizing the importance of both religion and government ("the state") as agents of socialization, because of their impact on the life course. Traditionally, family members have served as the primary caregivers in our culture, but in the 20th century, the family's protective function was steadily transferred to outside agencies such as hospitals, mental health clinics, and child care centers. Many of these agencies are run by groups affiliated with certain religions or by the state.

Both organized religion and government have impacted the life course by reinstituting some of the rites of passage once observed in agricultural communities and early industrial societies. For example, religious organizations stipulate certain traditional rites that may bring together all the members of an extended family, even if they never meet for any other reason. And government regulations stipulate the ages at which a person may drive a car, drink alcohol, vote in elections, marry without parental permission, work overtime, and retire. These regulations do not constitute strict rites of passage: most 18-year-olds choose not to vote, and most people choose their age of retirement without reference to government dictates.

In the Social Policy section at the end of this chapter, we will see that government is under pressure to become a provider of child care, which would give it a new and direct role in the socialization of infants and young children.

THINKING CRITICALLY

How would functionalist and conflict theorists differ in their analysis of socialization by the mass media?

Socialization throughout the Life Course

The Life Course

Among the Kota people of the Congo in Africa, adolescents paint themselves blue. Mexican American girls go on a day-long religious retreat before dancing the night away. Egyptian mothers step over their newborn infants seven times, and graduating students at the Naval Academy throw their hats in

Paul Chesley/The Image Bank/Getty Images

A young Apache woman undergoes a mudding ceremony traditionally used in rites of passage, such as puberty and in some cases weddings.

the air. These are all ways of celebrating **rites of passage,** or rituals that mark a symbolic transition from one social position to another. Rites of passage are ways of validating and/or dramatizing changes in a person's status. They may mark a separation, as in a graduation ceremony, or an incorporation, as in an initiation into an organization (Van Gennep [1909] 1960).

Rites of passage are a worldwide social phenomenon. The Kota rite marks the passage to adulthood. The color blue, viewed as the color of death, symbolizes the death of childhood. Hispanic girls celebrate reaching womanhood with a *quinceañera* ceremony at age 15. In the Cuban American community of Miami, the popularity of the *quinceañera* supports a network of party planners, caterers, dress designers, and the Miss Quinceañera Latina pageant. For thousands of years, Egyptian mothers have welcomed their newborns to the world in the Soboa ceremony by stepping over the seven-day-old infant seven times.

These specific ceremonies mark stages of development in the life course. They indicate that the process of socialization continues through all stages of the life cycle. In fact, some researchers have chosen to concentrate on socialization as a lifelong process. Sociologists and other social scientists who take such a **life course approach** look closely at the social factors that influence people throughout their lives, from birth to death, including gender and income. They recognize that biological changes mold but do not dictate human behavior.

Several life events mark the passage to adulthood, including marriage and the birth of a first child. Of course, these turning points vary from one society or even one generation to the next. In the United States, the key event seems to be the completion of formal schooling. However, educational completion is not as clearly defined today as it was a generation or two ago.

More and more people are taking full-time jobs while finishing their schooling, or returning to school to obtain a professional certificate or advanced degree. Similarly, the milestones associated with leaving home, finding a stable job, and establishing a long-term personal relationship do not now occur at specific ages (Silva 2012; T. Smith 2003).

One result of these overlapping steps to independence is that in the United States, unlike some other societies, there is no clear dividing line between adolescence and adulthood. Nowadays, few young people finish school, get married, and leave home at about the same age, clearly establishing their transition to adulthood. The terms *youthhood, emerging adulthood, pre-adult* and *not quite adult* have been coined to describe the prolonged ambiguous status that young people in their 20s experience (Gilmore 2019).

Source: Cpl. Benjamin E. Woodle, United States Marine Corp

Marine recruits undergoing grueling basic training at Parris Island, South Carolina. The military is an example of what sociologists call a total institution.

USE YOUR SOCIOLOGICAL IMAGINATION

Why do you think the end of formal schooling is the most important milestone of adulthood today? What about marriage, full-time employment, or financial independence from parents or guardians? Which milestone do you think is the most important?

Anticipatory Socialization and Resocialization

The development of a social self is literally a lifelong transformation that begins in the crib and continues as one prepares for death. Two types of socialization occur at many points throughout the life course: anticipatory socialization and resocialization.

Anticipatory socialization refers to processes of socialization in which a person rehearses for future positions, occupations, and social relationships. A culture can function more efficiently and smoothly if members become acquainted with the norms, values, and behavior associated with a social position before actually assuming that status. Preparation for many aspects of adult life begins with anticipatory socialization during childhood and adolescence, and continues throughout our lives as we prepare for new responsibilities.

You can see the process of anticipatory socialization take place when high school students start to consider what colleges they may attend. Traditionally, this task meant looking at publications received in the mail or making campus visits. However, with new technology, students use the web to begin their college experience. Colleges invest in developing attractive websites through which students can take virtual campus tours and hear audio clips of everything from the college anthem to a sample zoology lecture.

Occasionally, assuming a new social or occupational position requires us to *unlearn* an established orientation. **Resocialization** refers to the process of discarding former behavior patterns and accepting new ones as part of a transition in one's life. Often resocialization occurs during an explicit effort to transform an individual, as happens in reform schools, therapy groups, prisons, religious conversion settings, and political indoctrination camps. We saw this in the chapter-opening example about prisoners who became firefighters. The process of resocialization typically involves considerable stress for the individual—much more so than socialization in general, or even anticipatory socialization (Gecas 2004).

Resocialization is particularly effective when it occurs within a total institution. Erving Goffman (1961) coined the term **total institution** to refer to an institution that regulates all aspects of a person's life under a single authority, such as a prison, the military, a mental hospital, or a convent. Because the total institution is generally cut off from the rest of society, it provides for all the needs of its members. Quite literally, the crew of a merchant vessel at sea becomes part of a total institution. So elaborate are its requirements, so all-encompassing its activities, a total institution often represents a miniature society.

Goffman (1961) identified four common traits of total institutions:

- All aspects of life are conducted in the same place under the control of a single authority.

- Any activities within the institution are conducted in the company of others in the same circumstances—for example, army recruits or novices in a convent.

- The authorities devise rules and schedule activities without consulting the participants.
- All aspects of life within a total institution are designed to fulfill the purpose of the organization. Thus, all activities in a monastery might be centered on prayer and communion with God (Davies 1989; P. Rose et al. 1979).

People often lose their individuality within total institutions. For example, a person entering prison may experience the humiliation of a **degradation ceremony** as he or she is stripped of clothing, jewelry, and other personal possessions. From this point on, scheduled daily routines allow for little or no personal initiative. The individual becomes secondary and rather invisible in the overbearing social environment (Garfinkel 1956).

THINKING CRITICALLY

What examples of anticipatory socialization did you experience as a child? What examples are you currently experiencing?

Role Transitions throughout the Life Course

We have seen that socialization is a lifelong process. We simply do not experience things the same way at different points in the life course. For example, one study found that even falling in love differs according to where we are in the life course. Young unmarried adults tend to treat love as a noncommittal game or an obsession characterized by possessiveness and dependency. People over age 50 are much more likely to see love as involving commitment, and they tend to take a practical approach to finding a partner who meets a set of rational criteria. That does not mean that romance is dead among the older generation, however. Among those age 65 and over, 39 percent are "head over heels in love," compared to only 25 percent of those ages 18 to 34. The life course, then, affects the manner in which we relate to one another (G. Anderson 2009; Montgomery and Sorell 1997).

How we move through the life course varies dramatically, depending on our personal preferences and circumstances. Some of us marry early, others late; some have children and some don't. These individual patterns are influenced by social factors such as class, race, and gender. Only in the most general terms, then, can we speak of stages or periods in the life course.

One transitional stage, identified by psychologist Daniel Levinson, begins at the time at which an individual gradually enters the adult world, perhaps by moving out of the parental home, beginning a career, or entering a marriage. The next transitional period, the midlife transition, typically begins at about age 40. Men and women often experience a stressful period of self-evaluation, commonly known as the **midlife crisis,** in which they realize that they have not achieved basic goals and ambitions and have little time left to do so. Thus, Levinson (1978, 1996) found that most adults surveyed experienced tumultuous midlife conflicts within the self and with the external world.

Not all the challenges at this time of life come from career or one's partner. In the next section we will examine a special challenge faced by a growing number of middle-aged adults: caring for two generations at once.

The Sandwich Generation

During the late 1990s social scientists began to focus on the **sandwich generation**—adults who simultaneously try to meet the competing needs of their parents and their children. That is, caregiving goes in two directions: (1) to children, who even as young adults may still require significant direction, and (2) to aging parents, whose health and economic problems may demand intervention by their adult children. By 2018, 12 percent of parents with children under 18 at home were also caring for an adult, typically a relative (Livingston 2018).

Like the role of caring for children, the role of caring for aging parents falls disproportionately on women. Overall, women provide 60 percent of the care their parents receive, and even more as the demands of the role grow more intense and time-consuming. Increasingly, middle-aged women and younger are finding themselves on the "daughter track," as their time and attention are diverted by the needs of their aging mothers and fathers (National Alliance for Caregiving 2015).

The last major transition identified by Levinson occurs after age 60—sometimes well after that age, given advances in health care, greater longevity, and gradual acceptance within society of older people. Nonetheless, there is a point at which people transition to a different lifestyle. As we will see, this is a time of dramatic changes in people's everyday lives.

Adjusting to Retirement

You enter the labor force, you work until a certain age, and you retire. Retirement is a rite of passage that marks a critical transition from one phase of life to another. Increasingly people either delay retirement or move into a different type of job. More and more people are working into their later years, a trend that is expected to continue. Recently, about 40 percent of people age 55 and older were working or actively looking for work. That number, known as a *labor force participation rate,* is expected to increase fastest for the oldest segments of the population—most notably, people ages 65 to 74 and even

75 and older—through 2024. Although they make up a small number of workers overall, the older age groups are projected to have faster rates of labor force growth annually.

Workers age 55 and older are employed across many types of occupations. More than 42 percent of these workers were in management, professional, and related occupations, a somewhat higher proportion than that for all workers. Workers in older age groups also have higher rates of self-employment than do workers in younger groups. Knowledge and resources gained through years of experience may put older workers in a good position to work for themselves (Toossi and Torpey 2017).

A variety of factors explains this reversal in the trend toward earlier retirement. Changes in Social Security benefits, the recent economic uncertainty, and workers' concern about maintaining their health insurance and pension benefits have all contributed. At the same time, life expectancy has increased and the quality of people's health has improved (Toossi 2012).

Phases of Retirement   Gerontologist Robert Atchley (1976) has identified several phases of the retirement experience:

- *Preretirement,* a period of anticipatory socialization as the person prepares for retirement

- *The near phase,* when the person establishes a specific departure date from his or her job

- *The honeymoon phase,* an often euphoric period in which the person pursues activities that he or she never had time for before

- *The disenchantment phase,* in which retirees feel a sense of letdown or even depression as they cope with their new lives, which may include illness or poverty

- *The reorientation phase,* which involves the development of a more realistic view of retirement alternatives

- *The stability phase,* a period in which the person has learned to deal with life after retirement in a reasonable and comfortable fashion

- *The termination phase,* which begins when the person can no longer engage in basic, day-to-day activities such as self-care and housework

Retirement is not a single transition, then, but rather a series of adjustments that varies from one person to another. The length and timing of each phase will differ for each individual, depending on such factors as financial status and health. A particular person will not necessarily go through all the phases identified by Atchley (Reitzes and Mutran 2006).

Some factors, such as being forced into retirement or being burdened with financial difficulties, can further complicate the retirement process. People who enter retirement involuntarily or without the necessary means may never experience the honeymoon phase. In the United States, many retirees continue in the paid labor force, often taking part-time jobs to supplement their pensions.

What should public policy be toward people who have moved out of the labor force at an older age? Should the government do more for its senior citizens? In a national survey, adults were asked whether they would like to see more or less government spending on retirement benefits (see Figure 4-1). There was broad support for more spending but of course, respondents were not necessarily thinking how increased revenue would be found (NORC 2019).

Like other aspects of life in the United States, the experience of retirement varies according to gender, race, and ethnicity. White males are most likely to benefit from retirement wages, as well as to have participated in a formal retirement preparation program. As a result, anticipatory socialization for retirement is most complete for white men. In contrast, members of racial and ethnic minority groups—especially African Americans—are more

Big Cheese Photo LLC/Alamy Stock Photo

This sandwich-generation mom cares for both her aging parent and her children. Increasingly, members of the baby boom generation find themselves caring for two generations at once.

FIGURE 4-1 SUPPORT FOR INCREASED GOVERNMENT SPENDING ON RETIREMENT

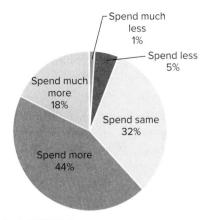

Source: 2016 survey data in NORC 2019.

"I prefer 'Baby Boomer' rather than 'Senior Citizen'."

Dave Carpenter/Cartoon Stock

likely to exit the paid labor force through disability than through retirement. Because of their comparatively lower incomes and smaller savings, men and women from racial and ethnic minority groups work intermittently after retirement more often than older whites (National Institute on Aging 1999; Quadagno 2018).

Naturally Occurring Retirement Communities (NORCs)

With recent improvements in health care, older Americans have gained new choices in where to live. Today, rather than residing in nursing homes or planned retirement communities, many of them congregate in areas that have gradually become informal centers for senior citizens. Social scientists have dubbed such areas **naturally occurring retirement communities (NORCs).** These develop when people who lived in proximity with other middle-aged people remain in the same area, effectively aging in place rather than relocating (Office for the Aging 2020).

Using observation research, census data, and interviews, sociologists have developed some interesting conclusions about NORCs in the United States, which account for an estimated 17 to 25 percent of people age 65 or older. These communities can be as small as a single apartment building or as large as a neighborhood in a big city. Often, they emerge as singles and young couples move out and older people move in. Sometimes couples simply remain where they are; as they grow older, the community becomes noticeably grayer. Such has been the case in the Fort Hamilton neighborhood in Brooklyn, New York, where a third of residents are now over 55. In time, business establishments that cater to the elderly—pharmacies, medical supply outlets, small restaurants, senior citizen centers—relocate to NORCs, making them even more attractive to older citizens.

Unfortunately, residents of some of these communities are threatened by gentrification, or the takeover of low-income

neighborhoods by higher-income residents. In Chicago, a high-rise building known as Ontario Place is converting to a condominium, at prices that current residents cannot afford. About half the building's occupants are Russian immigrants; most of the others are people who are elderly or disabled living on fixed incomes. These people are distressed not just because they will need to move, but because their community is being destroyed (Gregor 2013; Piturro 2012; Sheehan 2005).

THINKING CRITICALLY

Today, many young adults continue to live with their parents after finishing their schooling. Contrast their situation with that of the elderly who live with their children. Does society treat dependent adult children in the same way as dependent parents? Why or why not?

USE YOUR SOCIOLOGICAL IMAGINATION

How have people close to you, such as relatives, personally handled their retirement from the labor force?

socialpolicy and Sociological Research

Child Care around the World

Child care programs are not just babysitting services; they have an enormous influence on the development of young children—an influence that has grown with the movement of more and more women into the paid labor force. The rise in single-parent families, increased job opportunities for women, and the need for additional family income have all propelled mothers of young children into the working world. Who should care for the children of working mothers during working hours?

Looking at the Issue

Preschoolers typically are not cared for by their parents. Eighty-eight percent of employed mothers depend on others to care for their children, and 30 percent of mothers who aren't employed have regular care arrangements. In fact, children age 3–5 are more likely to be cared for on a daily basis by other relatives than by their parents. Over a third of them are cared for by nonrelatives in nursery schools, Head Start programs, day care centers, family day care, and other arrangements (Bureau of the Census 2015b; National Center for Educational Statistics 2019f).

Researchers have found that high-quality child care centers do not adversely affect the socialization of children; in fact, good day care benefits children. The value of preschool programs was documented in a series of studies conducted in the United States. Researchers found no significant differences in infants who had received extensive nonmaternal care compared with those who had been cared for solely by their mothers. They also reported that more and more infants in the United States are being placed in child care outside the home, and that overall, the quality of those arrangements is better than has been found in previous studies. It is difficult, however, to generalize about child care, since there is so much variability among day care providers, and even among government policies from one state to another (Campbell et al. 2014; NICHD 2007).

The coronavirus pandemic brought new attention to the need for childcare. While this was true in many nations, the United Sates is alone among industrial nations in not proving subsidized childcare options. Many locales in the United States hit hard by COVID-19 had to revisit how childcare was provided when schools were closed and essential workers, such as those in health care, food supply, and transportation, needed to care for their children. Suddenly childcare workers were viewed as essential. Their importance was acknowledged, although they rarely received the hazard pay that was awarded to other essential workers. In the post-pandemic world, cash-strapped childcare centers were faced with absorbing the high costs of new hygiene proce-

dures as well as convincing returning parents that they could care for their children safely (Goldstein and Bosman 2020).

Applying Sociology

Studies that assess the quality of child care outside the home reflect the micro level of analysis and the interest of interactionists in the impact of face-to-face interaction. These studies also explore macro-level implications for the functioning of social institutions like the family. Some of the issues surrounding day care have also been of interest to those who take the conflict perspective.

From a functionalist perspective, countries such as those in Scandinavia that provide government-subsidized day care or preschool programs find that such services help introduce children from immigrant families into the values and culture of their new country. In fact, Denmark recently considered imposing a mandate that children in poor neighborhoods, mostly immigrants, attend daycare for a minimum of 25 hours a week (*The Economist* 2019b).

In the United States, high-quality day care is not equally available to all families. Parents in affluent communities have an easier time finding day care than those in poor or working-class communities. Finding *affordable* child care is also a problem. Viewed from a conflict perspective, child care costs are an especially serious burden for lower-class families. The poorest families spend 25 percent of their income for preschool child care, whereas families who are *not* poor pay only 6 percent or less of their income. Despite these problems, subsidized child care has steadily declined over the last decade.

Courtesy of Communicare, Perth, Australia

Children play at the Communicare day care center in Perth, Australia. The Australian government subsidizes children's attendance at day care and afterschool programs from birth to age 12.

Feminist theorists echo the concern of conflict theorists that high-quality child care receives little government support because it is regarded as "merely a way to let women work." Nearly all child care workers (97 percent) are women; many find themselves in low-status, minimum-wage jobs. Typically, food servers, messengers, and gas station attendants make more money than the 564,000 million child care workers in the United States, whose average annual salary of $23,20, or about $11 per hour, puts them below the poverty level for a family of four (Bureau of Labor Statistics 2019c; Semega et al. 2019:49).

Initiating Policy

Policies regarding child care outside the home vary throughout the world. Most developing nations do not have the economic base to provide subsidized child care. Thus, working mothers rely largely on relatives or take their children to work. In the comparatively wealthy industrialized countries of western Europe, government provides child care as a basic service, at little or no expense to parents. But even those countries with tax-subsidized programs occasionally fall short of the need for high-quality child care.

When policymakers decide that child care is desirable, they must determine the degree to which taxpayers should subsidize it. In Sweden and Denmark, one-half to two-thirds of preschoolers are in government-subsidized child care full-time. In the United States, average 2019 annual fees for full-time child care of an infant range from $5,760 in Mississippi to $20,880 in Massachusetts (Child Care Aware 2020; Morath 2016).

Japan is facing a special dilemma. Traditionally, married women and certainly married mothers did not remain in the labor force. Although this social pattern is slowly changing, the availability of day care has not kept pace. Many Japanese policymakers have difficulty recognizing the need for day care. "Is your work so important that you must put your baby in childcare?" they ask. "Why are you being so self-centered?" Little wonder that a single private day care center in Japan recently had a waiting list of 25,000 children (Tabuchi 2013:A9).

We have a long way to go in making high-quality child care more affordable and accessible, not just in the United States but throughout the world as well. In an attempt to reduce government spending, many European countries have reduced subsidies. Indeed, 53 percent of women report that they either do not work or are forced to work part-time because child care is too expensive. Another 25 percent are unable to locate child care services. Increasingly European parents, like those in the United States, are forced to cobble together child care out of after-school programs and informal care with friends and relatives (Janta 2014).

Take the Issue with You

1. Were you ever in a day care program? If so, do you recall the experience as good or bad? In general, do you think it is desirable to expose young children to the socializing influence of day care?

2. In the view of conflict theorists, child care receives little government support because it is "merely a way to let women work." Can you think of other explanations?

3. Should the costs of day care programs be paid by government, by the private sector, or entirely by parents?

MASTERING THIS CHAPTER

Summary

Socialization is the process through which people learn the attitudes, values, and actions appropriate for members of a particular culture. This chapter examines the role of socialization in human development; the way in which people develop perceptions, feelings, and beliefs about themselves; important agents of socialization; and the lifelong nature of the socialization process.

1. **Socialization** affects the overall cultural practices of a society; it also shapes the images that we hold of ourselves.

2. Heredity and environmental factors interact in influencing the socialization process.

3. In the early 1900s, Charles Horton Cooley advanced the belief that we learn who we are by interacting with others, a phenomenon he called the **looking-glass self.**

4. George Herbert Mead, best known for his theory of the **self,** proposed that as people mature, their selves begin to reflect their concern about reactions from others—both **generalized others** and **significant others.**

5. Erving Goffman has shown that in many of our daily activities, we try to convey distinct impressions of who we are, a process he called **impression management.**

6. As the primary agents of socialization, parents play a critical role in guiding children into those **gender roles** deemed appropriate in a society.

7. Like the family, schools in the United States have an explicit mandate to socialize people—especially children—into the norms and values of our culture.

8. Peer groups and the mass media, especially television and the Internet, are important agents of socialization for adolescents.

9. Socialization in the workplace begins with part-time employment while we are in school and continues as we work full-time and change jobs throughout our lives.

10. Religion and the state shape the socialization process by regulating the life course and influencing our views of appropriate behavior at particular ages.

11. Socialization proceeds throughout the life course. Some societies mark stages of development with formal **rites of passage.** In the culture of the United States, significant events such as the end of formal schooling serve to change a person's status.

12. As more and more mothers of young children have entered the labor market, the demand for child care has increased dramatically, posing policy questions for many nations around the world.

Key Terms

Anticipatory socialization Processes of socialization in which a person rehearses for future positions, occupations, and social relationships. (page 92)

Cognitive theory of development Jean Piaget's theory that children's thought progresses through four stages of development. (85)

Degradation ceremony An aspect of the socialization process within some total institutions, in which people are subjected to humiliating rituals. (93)

Double consciousness The division of an individual's identity into two or more social realities. (82)

Dramaturgical approach A view of social interaction, popularized by Erving Goffman, in which people are seen as theatrical performers. (84)

Face-work A term used by Erving Goffman to refer to the efforts people make to maintain the proper image and avoid public embarrassment. (84)

Gender role Expectations regarding the proper behavior, attitudes, and activities of males and females. (86)

Generalized other A term used by George Herbert Mead to refer to the attitudes, viewpoints, and expectations of society as a whole that a child takes into account in his or her behavior. (83)

Impression management A term used by Erving Goffman to refer to the altering of the presentation of the self in order to create distinctive appearances and satisfy particular audiences. (83)

Life course approach A research orientation in which sociologists and other social scientists look closely at the social factors that influence people throughout their lives, from birth to death. (91)

Looking-glass self A concept used by Charles Horton Cooley that emphasizes the self as the product of our social interactions. (82)

Midlife crisis A stressful period of self-evaluation that begins at about age 40. (93)

Naturally occurring retirement community (NORC) An area that has gradually become an informal center for senior citizens. (95)

Personality A person's typical patterns of attitudes, needs, characteristics, and behavior. (79)

Resocialization The process of discarding former behavior patterns and accepting new ones as part of a transition in one's life. (92)

Rite of passage A ritual marking the symbolic transition from one social position to another. (91)

Role taking The process of mentally assuming the perspective of another and responding from that imagined viewpoint. (83)

Sandwich generation The generation of adults who simultaneously try to meet the competing needs of their parents and their children. (93)

Self According to George Herbert Mead, a distinct identity that sets us apart from others. (81)

Significant other A term used by George Herbert Mead to refer to an individual who is most important in the development of the self, such as a parent, friend, or teacher. (83)

Socialization The lifelong process in which people learn the attitudes, values, and behaviors appropriate for members of a particular culture. (78)

Total institution A term coined by Erving Goffman to refer to an institution that regulates all aspects of a person's life under a single authority, such as a prison, the military, a mental hospital, or a convent. (92)

TAKING SOCIOLOGY with you

1. On social media, look for examples of "face-work," or face-saving behavior, as a means to manage the presentation of self to others. What is the behavior? Take notes over the next several days and discuss your findings with the class.

2. In TV shows or streaming series that you're currently watching or in a movie that you've recently seen, are any of the characters in a transitional life stage, such as getting married or moving out of the home where they grew up; experiencing a mid-life crisis; caring for two generations at once; or adjusting to retirement? What are the characters experiencing during their transitional life stage? Take notes and discuss your findings with the class.

3. Make a list of the age at which members of your immediate and extended family finished schooling, left home, got married, and had children or note if they have not experienced these transitions. Discuss your findings with the class. Is there a pattern? If so, why do you think this may be? How might inconsistencies be explained?

4. **Writing Sociology.** Go to the Minnesota Center for Twin and Family Research website (https://mctfr.psych.umn.edu/index.html) or another reputable site focusing on socialization research. Choose a topic related to socialization that you learned about in this chapter to research and summarize it. Share your summary with the class.

Self-Quiz

Read each question carefully and then select the best answer.

1. Which of the following social scientists used the phrase *looking-glass self* to emphasize that the self is the product of our social interactions with other people?
   a. George Herbert Mead
   b. Charles Horton Cooley
   c. Erving Goffman
   d. Jean Piaget

2. In what he called the *play stage* of socialization, George Herbert Mead asserted that people mentally assume the perspectives of others, thereby enabling them to respond from that imagined viewpoint. This process is referred to as
   a. role taking.
   b. the peer group.
   c. the significant other.
   d. impression management.

3. George Herbert Mead is best known for his theory of what?
   a. rites of passage
   b. cognitive development
   c. the self
   d. impression management

4. Suppose a clerk tries to appear busier than he or she actually is when a supervisor happens to be watching. Erving Goffman would study this behavior from what approach?
   a. functionalist
   b. conflict
   c. psychological
   d. interactionist

5. According to child psychologist Jean Piaget's cognitive theory of development, children begin to use words and symbols to distinguish objects and ideas during which stage in the development of the thought process?
   a. the sensorimotor stage
   b. the preoperational stage
   c. the concrete operational stage
   d. the formal operational stage

6. On the first day of basic training in the army, a recruit has his civilian clothes replaced by army "greens," has his hair shaved off, loses his privacy, and finds that he must use a communal bathroom. All these humiliating activities are part of
   a. becoming a significant other.
   b. impression management.
   c. a degradation ceremony.
   d. face-work.

7. Which social institution is considered to be the most important agent of socialization in the United States, especially for children?
   a. the family
   b. the school
   c. the peer group
   d. the mass media

8. The term *gender role* refers to
   a. the biological fact that we are male or female.
   b. a role that is given to us by a teacher.
   c. a role that is given to us in a play.
   d. expectations regarding the proper behavior, attitudes, and activities of males and females.

9. Which sociological perspective emphasizes that schools in the United States foster competition through built-in systems of reward and punishment?
   a. the functionalist perspective
   b. the conflict perspective
   c. the interactionist perspective
   d. the psychological perspective

10. A University of Alaska sociologist asked her male and female students to apply fingernail polish to people of the opposite sex. This experiment demonstrated
    a. a rite of passage.
    b. a total institution.
    c. gender roles.
    d. generalized other.

11. _____ is the term used by sociologists in referring to the lifelong process whereby people learn the attitudes, values, and behaviors appropriate for members of a particular culture.

12. In everyday speech, the term _____ is used to refer to a person's typical patterns of attitudes, needs, characteristics, and behavior.

13. Studies of twins raised apart suggest that both _____ and _____ influence human development.

14. A(n) _____ _____ is an individual such as a parent, friend, or teacher who is most important in the development of the self.

15. Early work in _____ , such as that by Sigmund Freud, stressed the role of inborn drives—among them the drive for sexual gratification—in channeling human behavior.

16. The Swiss psychologist Jean Piaget developed the _____ theory of development.

17. Preparation for many aspects of adult life begins with _____ socialization during childhood and adolescence and continues throughout our lives as we prepare for new responsibilities.

18. Resocialization is particularly effective when it occurs within a(n) _____ institution.

19. The _____ perspective emphasizes the role of schools in teaching the values and customs of the larger society.

20. As children grow older, the family becomes less important in social development, while _____ groups become more important.

5

Social Interaction, Groups, and Social Structure

Pal2iyawit/Shutterstock

Groups of different sizes help individuals to navigate through the larger social world, including both informal interactions and complex social organizations. Here players from Thailand and South Korea compete in a martial arts game.

▶ INSIDE

Social Interaction and Reality

Elements of Social Structure

Understanding Organizations

Social Structure in Global Perspective

Social Policy and Organizations: The State of the Unions Worldwide

Courtesy of Phil Zimbardo, Stanford University

If you were a prison guard, would you mistreat the inmates?

To find the answer to this question, social psychologist Philip Zimbardo created a mock prison and enlisted college students to serve as the inmates and guards.

66 The quiet of a summer Sunday morning in Palo Alto, California, was shattered by a screeching squad car siren as police swept through the city picking up college students in a surprise mass arrest. Each suspect was charged with a felony; warned of his constitutional rights; spread-eagled against the car; searched, handcuffed, and carted off in the back seat of the squad car to the police station for booking.

After being fingerprinted and having identification forms prepared for his 'jacket' (central information file), each prisoner was left isolated in a detention cell to wonder what he had done to get himself into this mess. After a while, he was blindfolded and transported to the 'Stanford County Prison.' Here he began the induction process of becoming a prisoner—stripped naked, skin searched, deloused, and issued a uniform, bedding, soap, and towel. By late afternoon when nine such arrests had been completed, these youthful 'first offenders' sat in dazed silence on the cots in their barren cells. These men were part of a very unusual kind of prison, an experimental or mock prison, created by social psychologists for the purpose of intensively studying the effects of imprisonment upon volunteer research subjects.

When we planned our two-week-long simulation of prison life, we were primarily concerned about understanding the process by which people adapt to the novel and alien environment in which those called 'prisoners' lose their liberty, civil rights, independence, and privacy, while those called 'guards' gain social power by accepting the responsibility for controlling and managing the lives of their dependent charges.

Our final sample of participants (10 prisoners and 11 guards) were selected from over 75 volunteers recruited through ads in the city and campus newspapers. . . . Half were randomly assigned to role-play being guards, the others to be prisoners. Thus, there were no measurable differences between the guards and the prisoners at the start of this experiment.

At the end of only six days we had to close down our mock prison because what we saw was frightening. It was no longer apparent to most of the subjects (or to us) where reality ended and their roles began. The majority had indeed become prisoners or guards, no longer able to clearly differentiate between role-playing and self. There were dramatic changes in virtually every aspect of their behavior, thinking, and feeling. In less than a week the experience of imprisonment undid (temporarily) a lifetime of learning: human values were suspended; self-concepts were challenged; and the ugliest, most base, pathological side of human nature surfaced. We were horrified because we saw some boys (guards) treat others as if they were despicable animals, taking pleasure in cruelty, while other boys (prisoners) became servile, dehumanized robots who thought only of escape, of their own individual survival, and of their mounting hatred for the guards. 99

Source: Zimbardo et al. 1974: 61–73.

> *The quiet of a summer Sunday morning in Palo Alto, California, was shattered by a screeching squad car siren as police swept through the city picking up college students in a surprise mass arrest.*

In this study, directed and described by author Philip Zimbardo, college students adopted the patterns of social interaction expected of guards and prisoners when they were placed in a mock prison. Sociologists use the term **social interaction** to refer to the ways in which people respond to one another, whether face-to-face or over the telephone or on the computer. In the mock prison, social interactions between guards and prisoners were highly impersonal. The guards addressed the prisoners by number rather than name, and they wore reflective sunglasses that made eye contact impossible.

As in many real-life prisons, the simulated prison at Stanford University had a social structure in which guards held virtually total control over prisoners. The term **social structure** refers to the way in which a society is organized into predictable relationships. The social structure of Zimbardo's mock prison influenced how the guards and prisoners interacted. Zimbardo and his colleagues (2009:516) note that it was a real prison "in the minds of the jailers and their captives."* His simulated prison experiment, first conducted almost 50 years ago, has subsequently been repeated (with similar findings) both in the United States and in other countries.

Zimbardo's prison experiment has consistently received enormous attention since its results were first published in 1971. Some of the attention has been critical of his use of students as experimental subjects. The most relevant criticism is the suggestion that he coached the student "guards" to torment the student "prisoners." While Zimbardo admits he did not interfere to limit the guards' cruelty, available documentation from the study shows he did not encourage or even suggest it (Zimbardo 2018).

Zimbardo's experiment took on new relevance in 2004, in the wake of shocking revelations of prisoner abuse at the U.S.-run Abu Ghraib military facility in Iraq. Graphic "trophy photos" showed U.S. soldiers humiliating naked Iraqi prisoners and threatening to attack them with police dogs. The structure of the wartime prison, coupled with intense pressure on military intelligence officers to secure information regarding terrorist plots, contributed to the breakdown in the guards' behavior. But Zimbardo himself noted that the guards' depraved conduct could have been predicted simply on the basis of his research (Ratnesar 2011; Zimbardo 2015).

Understandably the Zimbardo experiment is typically brought up in discussions of conditions in correctional facilities. Yet there are implications for other contexts as well. The researcher reported, in the first phase of the experiment, how confused, disoriented, and dehumanized the participants felt upon being confronted by the police.

Today there is little cause for wonder how police–civilian encounters can become unpredictable and turn violent, as demonstrated by the rise of #BlackLivesMatter and the 2020 racial justice protests across the nation. The Zimbardo experiment of over fifty years ago illuminates contemporary day-to-day interactions between law enforcement and members of the public.

The two concepts of *social interaction* and *social structure* are central to sociological study. They are closely related to *socialization,* the process through which people learn the attitudes, values, and behaviors appropriate to their culture. When the students in Zimbardo's experiment entered the mock prison, they began a process of resocialization. In that process, they adjusted to a new social structure and learned new rules for social interaction.

In this chapter we will study social structure and its effect on our social interactions. What determines a person's status in society? How do our social roles affect our social interactions? What is the place of social institutions such as the family, religion, and government in our social structure? How can we better understand and manage large organizations such as multinational corporations? We'll begin by considering how social interactions shape the way we view the world around us. Next, we'll focus on the five basic elements of social structure: statuses, social roles, groups, social networks, and social institutions such as the family, religion, government, and the mass media. We'll see that functionalists, conflict theorists, and interactionists approach social institutions quite differently. Finally, we'll compare our modern social structure with simpler forms, using typologies developed by Émile Durkheim, Ferdinand Tönnies, and Gerhard Lenski. The Social Policy section at the end of the chapter focuses on the changing role of labor unions.

Social Interaction and Reality

When someone in a crowd shoves you, do you automatically push back? Or do you consider the circumstances of the incident and the attitude of the instigator before you react? Chances are you do the latter. According to sociologist Herbert Blumer (1969:79), the distinctive characteristic of social interaction among people is that "human beings interpret or 'define' each other's actions instead of merely reacting to each other's actions." In other words, our response to someone's behavior is based on the *meaning* we attach to his or her actions. Reality is shaped by our perceptions, evaluations, and definitions.

These meanings typically reflect the norms and values of the dominant culture and our socialization experiences within that culture. As interactionists emphasize, the meanings that we attach to people's behavior are shaped by our interactions with them and with the larger society. Social reality is literally constructed from our social interactions (Berger and Luckmann 1966).

How do we define our social reality? People wearing medical masks in public until recently was very unusual except in some Asian nations.

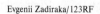
Evgenii Zadiraka/123RF

With the coronavirus pandemic, it was common and even recommended or required by governments and by shopkeepers. People would sometimes color silly expressions on homemade masks or display logos to show loyalty to a sports team. Such actions perhaps make them less frightening at a time when many felt uncomfortable to be in public engaged in social interaction. It had special significance for racial and ethnic minorities, especially Black men, using masks in public, even when expected. Frequently it caused them to be viewed suspiciously and even denied entry to stores where face coverings were recommended (Taylor 2020).

The nature of social interaction and what constitutes reality varies across cultures. In Western societies, with their emphasis on romantic love, couples see marriage as a relationship as well as a social status. From Valentine's Day flowers to more informal, everyday gestures, professions of love are an expected part of marriage.

In Japan, however, marriage is considered more a social status than a relationship. Although many or most Japanese couples undoubtedly do love each other, saying "I love you" does not come easily to them, especially not to husbands. Nor do most husbands call their wives by name (they prefer "Mother") or look them in the eyes. In 2006, in an effort to change these restrictive customs, some Japanese men formed the Devoted Husband Organization, which has been sponsoring a new holiday, Beloved Wives Day. In 2008, this group organized an event called Shout Your Love from the Middle of a Cabbage Patch Day. Dozens of men stood in a cabbage patch north of Tokyo and shouted, "I love you!" to their wives, some of whom had never heard their husbands say those words. In another rare gesture, husbands pledged to be home by 8 p.m. that day (Japan Aisaika Organization 2020; Kambayashi 2008).

THINKING CRITICALLY

Think back over the events of the past few days. Identify two occasions on which different people defined the same social reality differently.

The ability to define social reality reflects a group's power within a society. In fact, one of the most crucial aspects of the relationship between dominant and subordinate groups is the ability of the dominant or majority group to define a society's values. Sociologist William I. Thomas (1923), an early critic of theories of racial and gender differences, recognized that the "definition of the situation" could mold the thinking and personality of the individual. Writing from an interactionist perspective, Thomas observed that people respond not only to the objective features of a person or situation but also to the *meaning* that person or situation has for them. For example, in Philip Zimbardo's mock prison experiment, student "guards" and "prisoners" accepted the definition of the situation (including the traditional roles and behavior associated with being a guard or prisoner) and acted accordingly.

As we have seen throughout the past 70 years—first in the civil rights movement of the 1950s and 1960s and since then among such groups as women, the elderly, gays and lesbians, and people with disabilities—an important aspect of the process of social change involves redefining or reconstructing social reality. Members of subordinate groups challenge traditional definitions and begin to perceive and experience reality in a new way.

Elements of Social Structure

All social interaction takes place within a social structure, including those interactions that redefine social reality. For purposes of study, we can break down any social structure into five elements: statuses, social roles, groups, social networks, and social institutions. These elements make up social structure just as a foundation, walls, and ceilings make up a building's structure.

Statuses

We normally think of a person's *status* as having to do with influence, wealth, and fame. However, sociologists use the term **status** to refer to any of the full range of socially defined positions within a large group or society, from the lowest to the highest. Within our society, a person can occupy the status of president of the United States, fruit picker, son or daughter, violinist, teenager, resident of Minneapolis, dental technician, or neighbor. A person can hold a number of statuses at the same time.

Ascribed and Achieved Status Sociologists view some statuses as *ascribed* and others as *achieved* (Figure 5-1). An **ascribed status** is assigned to a person by society without regard for the person's unique talents or characteristics.

FIGURE 5-1   SOCIAL STATUSES

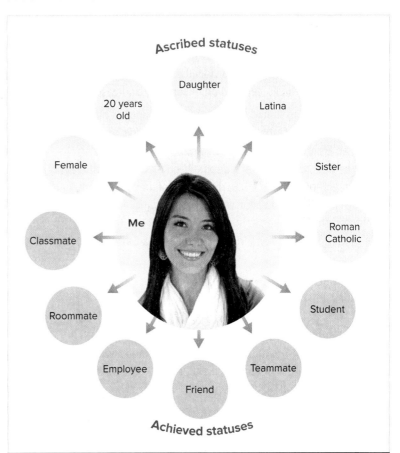

Think about It The young woman in this figure—"me"—occupies many positions in society, each of which involves distinct statuses. How would you define your statuses? Which have the most influence in your life?

(photo): ESB Professional/Shutterstock

Generally, the assignment takes place at birth; thus, a person's racial background, gender, and age are all considered ascribed statuses. Though these characteristics are biological in origin, they are significant mainly because of the *social* meanings they have in our culture. Conflict theorists are especially interested in ascribed statuses, since they often confer privileges or reflect a person's membership in a subordinate group (Linton 1936).

In most cases, we can do little to change an ascribed status, but we can attempt to change the traditional constraints associated with it. For example, the Gray Panthers—an activist political group founded in 1971 to work for the rights of older people—have tried to modify society's negative and confining stereotypes of the elderly. As a result of their work and that of other groups supporting older citizens, the ascribed status of "senior citizen" is no longer as difficult for millions of older people.

An ascribed status does not necessarily have the same social meaning in every society. In a cross-cultural study, sociologist Gary Huang (1988) confirmed the long-held view that respect for the elderly is an important cultural norm in China. In many cases, the prefix "old" is used respectfully: calling someone "old teacher" or "old person" is like calling a judge in the United States "your honor." Huang points out that positive age-seniority language distinctions are uncommon in the United States; consequently, we view the term *old man* as more of an insult than a celebration of seniority and wisdom.

These observations should not suggest that younger Chinese people never neglect the elderly. In 2013, China felt compelled to pass an Elderly Rights Law that warns adult children to "never neglect or snub elderly people" and mandates that they visit their elderly parents often, regardless of how far away they live. The law includes enforcement mechanisms: for example, offspring who fail to make such trips face potential punishment ranging from fines to jail time (Martinez-Carter 2013).

Unlike ascribed statuses, an **achieved status** comes to us largely through our own efforts. Both "computer programmer" and "prison guard" are achieved statuses, as are "lawyer," "pianist," "sorority member," "convict," and "social worker." We must do something to acquire an achieved status—go to school, learn a skill, establish a friendship, invent a new product. But as we will see in the next section, our ascribed status heavily influences our achieved status.

Before we continue, consider the complexity of a status. *First,* ascribed status heavily influences achieved status. Being male, for example, would decrease the likelihood that a person would be encouraged to consider a career in child care. *Second,* a given status may or may not be desirable. Your family background, an ascribed status, can place you in a positive or negative position. An achieved status—criminal or hero—can also be desirable or not. *Third,* some statuses can be either

achieved or ascribed, depending upon the individual's circumstances. Consider religion—it is an ascribed status if a person carries on the family's faith, but it is an achieved status if he or she settles on a religion after exploring a variety of belief systems. For the purposes of the illustration in Figure 5-1, we have listed the person's religion as an ascribed status, implying that she continued the faith of her parents (Foladare 1969).

Master Status   Each person holds many different and sometimes conflicting statuses; some may connote higher social position and some, lower position. How, then, do others view one's overall social position? According to sociologist Everett Hughes (1945), societies deal with inconsistencies by agreeing that certain statuses are more important than others. A **master status** is a status that dominates other statuses and thereby determines a person's general position in society. Throughout the world, many people with disabilities find that their status as having a disability receives undue weight, overshadowing their actual ability to perform successfully in meaningful employment (Box 5-1).

Our society gives such importance to race and gender that they often dominate our lives. These ascribed statuses frequently influence our achieved status. James Blake was born into a middle-class family and overcame severe scoliosis (ascribed statuses) while playing sports as a teenager. He decided to pursue tennis; eventually he ranked #1 among U.S. male players and #4 in the world (achieved status). Even after retiring from competition, he remained active in promoting the sport. In 2015, he was awaiting a ride outside a fancy New York hotel to go the U.S. Open. Suddenly a white man in shorts and T-shirt lunged at him and wrestled him to the pavement. Instinctively as an African American (ascribed status), Blake considered the possibility that this was an armed undercover police officer, which the attacker indeed turned out to be. Therefore Blake did not resist, but he did seek to find out what the man was doing. The police officer had mistaken Blake for a wanted Black man. Blake, the grandson of a New York City police officer, for whom he was named, sued the department, not for money but for an apology, which was eventually granted.

In the United States, the ascribed statuses of race and gender can function as master statuses that have an important impact on one's potential to achieve a desired professional and social status (Rourke 2019).

THINKING CRITICALLY

Describe a specific master status and explain how it is established. Is it a negative status? If so, how would a person overcome it?

RESEARCH TODAY

5-1 Disability as a Master Status

Throughout history and around the world, people with disabilities have been subjected to cruel and inhuman treatment. For example, in the 20th century, people with disabilities were frequently viewed as subhuman creatures who were a menace to society. In Japan more than 16,000 women with disabilities were involuntarily sterilized, with government approval, from 1945 to 1995. Sweden apologized for the same action taken against 62,000 of its citizens in the 1970s.

Such blatantly hostile treatment of people with disabilities has given way to a *medical model,* in which people with disabilities are viewed as chronic patients. Increasingly, however, people concerned with the rights of people with disabilities have criticized this model as well. In their view, it is the unnecessary and discriminatory barriers present in the environment—both physical and attitudinal—that stand in the way of people with disabilities, more than any biological limitations. Applying a *civil rights model,* activists emphasize that those with disabilities face widespread prejudice, discrimination, and segregation. For example, most voting places are inaccessible to wheelchair users and fail to provide ballots that can be used by those unable to read print.

Drawing on the earlier work of Erving Goffman, contemporary sociologists have suggested that society attaches a stigma to many forms of disability, a stigma that leads to prejudicial treatment. People with disabilities frequently observe that the people without disabilities see them only as blind, wheelchair users, and so forth, rather than as complex human beings with individual strengths and weaknesses, whose blindness or use of a wheelchair is merely one aspect of their lives.

> *In Japan more than 16,000 women with disabilities were involuntarily sterilized with government approval from 1945 to 1995.*

People with disabilities face challenges that are not readily apparent. Federal law prevents employers with more than 15 workers from discriminating against people with disabilities, but workers must decide when and how to disclose their disability if they need accommodations. This can be a difficult discussion, but it is the worker with the disability who is forced to initiate it. Disability is a master status.

Image Source/Getty Images

LET'S DISCUSS

1. Does your school present barriers to students with disabilities? If so, what kinds of barriers—physical, attitudinal, or both? Describe some of them.
2. Why do you think people without disabilities see disability as the most important characteristic of a person with a disability? What can be done to help people see beyond the wheelchair and the Seeing Eye dog?

Sources: Albrecht 2004; Goffman 1963; Murphy 1997; Newsday 1997; R. Schaefer 2021; J. Shapiro 1993.

Social Roles

What Are Social Roles? Throughout our lives, we acquire what sociologists call social roles. A **social role** is a set of expectations for people who occupy a given social position or status. Thus, in the United States, we expect that cab and Uber drivers will know how to get around a city and that police officers will take action if they see a citizen being threatened. With each distinctive social status—whether ascribed or achieved—come particular role expectations. However, actual performance varies from individual to individual. One secretary may assume extensive administrative responsibilities, while another may focus on clerical duties. Similarly, in Philip Zimbardo's mock prison experiment, some students were brutal and sadistic guards; others were not.

Roles are a significant component of social structure. Viewed from a functionalist perspective, roles contribute to a society's stability by enabling members to anticipate the behavior of others and to pattern their actions accordingly. Yet social roles can also be dysfunctional if they restrict people's interactions and relationships.

If we view a person *only* as a "police officer" or "supervisor," it will be difficult to relate to him or her as a friend or neighbor.

Role Conflict Imagine the delicate situation of a woman who has worked for a decade on an assembly line in an electrical plant, and has recently been named supervisor of her unit. How is this woman expected to relate to her longtime friends and co-workers? Should she still go out to lunch with them, as she has done almost daily for years? Is it her responsibility to recommend the firing of an old friend who cannot keep up with the demands of the assembly line?

USE YOUR SOCIOLOGICAL IMAGINATION

If you were a male nurse, what aspects of role conflict might you experience? Now imagine you are a female professional boxer. What conflicting role expectations might that involve? In both cases, how well do you think you would handle role conflict?

J. Luke/PhotoLink/Getty Images

In 2015, President Barack Obama issued an order to change the name of the nation's tallest peak, Mount McKinley, back to Denali, its original Athabascan name. Alaska's elected officials had been asking for this change for over 40 years. Republicans protested the decision as yet another example of the president sidestepping Congress. Senator Lisa Murkowski (R-Alaska) praised the decision, thus resolving her role conflict by siding with her state rather than her party.

Role conflict occurs when incompatible expectations arise from two or more social positions held by the same person. Fulfillment of the roles associated with one status may directly violate the roles linked to a second status. In the example just given, the newly promoted supervisor will most likely experience a sharp conflict between her social and occupational roles. Such role conflicts call for important ethical choices. The new supervisor will have to make a difficult decision about how much allegiance she owes her friend and how much she owes her employers, who have given her supervisory responsibilities.

Another type of role conflict occurs when individuals move into occupations that are not common among people with their ascribed status. Male preschool teachers and female police officers experience this type of role conflict. In the latter case, female officers must strive to reconcile their workplace role in law enforcement with the societal view of a woman's role, which does not embrace many skills needed in police work. And while female police officers encounter sexual harassment, as women do throughout the labor force, they must also deal with the "code of silence," an informal norm that precludes their implicating fellow officers in wrongdoing (Fletcher 1995; S. Martin 1994).

Role Strain Role conflict describes the situation of a person dealing with the challenge of occupying two social positions simultaneously. However, even a single position can cause problems. Sociologists use the term **role strain** to describe the difficulty that arises when the same social position imposes conflicting demands and expectations.

People who belong to minority cultures may experience role strain while working in the mainstream culture. Criminologist

Larry Gould (2002) interviewed officers of the Navajo Nation Police Department about their relations with conventional law enforcement officials, such as sheriffs and FBI agents. Besides enforcing the law, Navajo Nation officers practice an alternative form of justice known as Peacemaking, in which they seek reconciliation between the parties to a crime. The officers expressed great confidence in Peacemaking, but worried that if they did not make arrests, other law enforcement officials would think they were too soft, or "just taking care of their own." Regardless of the strength of their ties to traditional Navajo ways, all felt the strain of being considered "too Navajo" or "not Navajo enough."

Role Exit Often, when we think of assuming a social role, we focus on the preparation and anticipatory socialization a person undergoes for that role. Such is true if a person is about to become an attorney, a chef, a spouse, or a parent. Yet until recently, social scientists have given little attention to the adjustments involved in *leaving* social roles.

Sociologist Helen Rose Fuchs Ebaugh (1988) developed the term **role exit** to describe the process of disengagement from a role that is central to one's self-identity in order to establish a new role and identity. Drawing on interviews with 185 people—among them ex-convicts, divorced men and women, recovering alcoholics, ex-nuns, former doctors, retirees, and transexuals—Ebaugh (herself an ex-nun) studied the process of voluntarily exiting from significant social roles.

Ebaugh has offered a four-stage model of role exit. The first stage begins with *doubt*. The person experiences frustration, burnout, or simply unhappiness with an accustomed status and the roles associated with the social position. The second stage involves a *search for alternatives*. A person who is unhappy with his or her career may take a leave of absence; an unhappily married couple may begin what they see as a temporary separation.

The third stage of role exit is the *action stage* or *departure*. Ebaugh found that the vast majority of her respondents could identify a clear turning point that made them feel it was essential to take final action and leave their jobs, end their marriages, or engage in another type of role exit. Twenty percent of respondents saw their role exit as a gradual, evolutionary process that had no single turning point.

The fourth stage of role exit involves the *creation of a new identity*. Many of you participated in a role exit when you made the transition from middle school to high school. You left behind your younger years and took on the role of a somewhat independent student, perhaps getting a driving permit, and so forth. Sociologist Ira Silver (1996) studied the central role that material objects play when students go off to college. The objects students choose to leave at home (like stuffed animals and dolls) are associated with their prior identities. They may remain deeply attached to those objects, but do not want them to be seen as part of their new identities at college. The objects they bring with them symbolize how they now see themselves and how they wish to be perceived. iPhones and wall posters, for example, are calculated to say, "This is me."

Groups

In sociological terms, a **group** is any number of people with similar norms, values, and expectations who interact with one another on a regular basis. The members of a women's basketball team, a hospital's business office, a synagogue, or a symphony orchestra constitute a group. However, the residents of a suburb would not be considered a group, since they rarely interact with one another at one time.

Groups play a vital part in a society's social structure. Much of our social interaction takes place within groups and is influenced by their norms and sanctions. Being a teenager or a retired person takes on special meanings when we interact within groups designed for people with that particular status. The expectations associated with many social roles, including those accompanying the statuses of brother, sister, and student, become more clearly defined in the context of a group.

Sociologists and other social scientists have conducted a significant amount of research on groups given their importance in society. After the family, juries have been the focus of the most research (Box 5-2).

The groups we interact with also play an important role in our daily lives, sometimes in unexpected ways. Émile Durkheim ([1893] 1933) noted how a heinous crime can shock us, eliciting a communal response that serves to protect us in the future. In April 2007, a senior at Virginia Tech fired nearly 300 rounds of ammunition at two locations on campus, killing 32 people and wounding 17 others. Sociologists James Hawdon and John Ryan (2011) of Virginia Tech conducted three web-based surveys of the students and faculty, the first of them nine days after the shooting and the last of them 10 months later. They found that people who joined in with group activities that were specific to the tragedy did not necessarily find relief or a sense of solidarity with other members of the community. More critical to people's recovery was continued participation in clubs and friendship groups in the weeks following the tragedy. Group solidarity does make a difference.

Primary and Secondary Groups Charles Horton Cooley (1956) coined the term **primary group** to refer to a small group characterized by intimate, face-to-face association and cooperation

Think about It According to sociologist Helen Rose Fuchs Ebaugh, role exit is a four-stage process. Is this transgender person in the first or the fourth stage of role exit?

Valentino Photography/Shutterstock

(Table 5-1). The members of a street gang constitute a primary group; so do members of a family living in the same household, as do a group of "sisters" in a college sorority.

Primary groups play a pivotal role in the socialization process. The importance of primary groups was underscored during the coronavirus pandemic as we sought to maintain face-to-face interaction through video chat apps like Zoom, FaceTime, Houseparty, and Skype. When we find ourselves identifying with a group, whether in person or online, it is probably a primary group.

TABLE 5-1 COMPARISON OF PRIMARY AND SECONDARY GROUPS

Summing Up

Primary Group	Secondary Group
Generally small	Usually large
Relatively long period of interaction	Relatively short duration, often temporary
Intimate, face-to-face association	Little social intimacy or mutual understanding
Some emotional depth to relationships	Relationships generally superficial
Cooperative, friendly	More formal and impersonal

RESEARCH TODAY

5-2   Decision Making in the Jury Room

Scholars have used several research methods to investigate juries' decision-making processes. Four types of research have been employed: interviews with jury members after they reach a verdict; observation of jurors as they sit through and react to courtroom events; observation of actual jury deliberations, which has been permitted by presiding judges in a few instances; and experiments that use volunteers to create mock juries.

In the 1957 motion picture *Twelve Angry Men,* famed actor Henry Fonda played a juror who begins as the lone voice favoring acquittal of a criminal defendant; in the end, he convinces the entire jury of the defendant's innocence. While *Twelve Angry Men* made for great drama, recent research suggests that jurors generally do not change their minds after the first ballot. For example, a study of 225 cases indicated that if a majority of jurors vote to convict a defendant on the first ballot, there is only a 5 percent chance that the defendant will later be acquitted.

Interestingly, a jury's decision making may even occur *before* the first ballot. Despite judges' instructions to the contrary, many jurors form tentative verdict preferences early in a trial. Studies suggest that jurors with initial feelings of "guilty" or "not guilty" give disproportionate weight to supporting testimony that reinforces their initial verdict preferences, while discounting testimony that undermines this preference.

> *If a majority of jurors vote to convict a defendant on the first ballot, there is only a 5 percent chance that the defendant will later be acquitted.*

moodboard/Brand X Pictures/Getty Images

Most research on jury decision making in criminal trials has focused on how juries decide if a defendant is guilty or not guilty. However, in a significant number of criminal cases, a defendant is tried on several counts, or he or she may be found to be not guilty by reason of insanity. A number of studies have shown that a jury is more likely to convict a defendant on some charge if they are given several alternatives to an absolute verdict of "not guilty."

Jury decision-making scholarship has confirmed that judgment is harsher on defendants whose race or ethnicity is different from the jurors' or in cases where the victim's race or ethnicity is the same as that of the jurors. Racial bias is not automatic and can be tempered in cases where character evidence makes the defendant appear to be more or less sympathetic.

Research is always expanding to deal with changes in the experience of being a juror.

Some jurors arrive at court expecting the sophisticated DNA and other crime scene analysis they see on *CSI* or read in "true crime" blogs. Jurors' decision making appears to be influenced when the real prosecutor and defense attorney do not live up to their media counterparts. For example, jurors might wonder why extraordinary investigative tests were not used to confirm identity or locate alternative suspects.

LET'S DISCUSS

1. Think of a character from a book, show, or film who served on a jury. What influenced their decision making?
2. Is a jury a typical group? Why or why not?

Sources: Diamond and Rose 2018; Hunt 2015; MacCoun 1989; Sunwolf and Seibold 1998.

We also participate in many groups that are not characterized by close bonds of friendship, such as large college classes and business associations. The term **secondary group** refers to a formal, impersonal group in which there is little social intimacy or mutual understanding (Table 5-1). Secondary groups often emerge in the workplace among those who share special understandings about their occupation.

In-Groups and Out-Groups   A group can hold special meaning for members because of its relationship to other groups. For example, people in one group sometimes feel antagonistic toward or threatened by another group, especially if that group is perceived as being different, either culturally or racially. To identify these "we" and "they" feelings, sociologists use two terms first employed by William Graham Sumner (1906): *in-group* and *out-group*.

Conflict between in-groups and out-groups can turn violent on a personal as well as a political level. In 1999 two disaffected students at Columbine High School in Littleton, Colorado, launched an attack on the school that left 15 students and teachers dead, including themselves. The gunmen, members of an out-group that other students referred to as the Trench-coat Mafia, apparently resented taunting by an in-group referred to as the Jocks. Similar episodes have occurred in schools across the nation, where rejected adolescents, overwhelmed by personal and family problems, peer group pressure, academic responsibilities, or media images of violence, have struck out against more popular classmates.

fizkes/Shutterstock

Sociologists distinguish between primary and secondary groups. Without knowing more information, this group in conversation could be a primary group but is more likely a secondary group.

An **in-group** can be defined as any group or category to which people feel they belong. Simply put, it comprises everyone who is regarded as "we" or "us." The in-group may be as narrow as a teenage clique or as broad as an entire society. The very existence of an in-group implies that there is an out-group that is viewed as "they" or "them." An **out-group** is a group or category to which people feel they do *not* belong.

In-group members typically feel distinct and superior, seeing themselves as better than people in the out-group. Proper behavior for the in-group is simultaneously viewed as unacceptable behavior for the out-group. This double standard enhances the sense of superiority. Sociologist Robert Merton (1968) described this process as the conversion of "in-group virtues" into "out-group vices." We can see this differential standard operating in worldwide discussions of terrorism. When a group or a nation takes aggressive actions, it usually justifies them as necessary, even if civilians are hurt or killed. Opponents are quick to label such actions with the emotion-laden term of *terrorist* and appeal to the world community for condemnation. Yet these same people may themselves retaliate with actions that hurt civilians, which the first group will then condemn.

USE YOUR SOCIOLOGICAL IMAGINATION

Try putting yourself in the shoes of an out-group member. What does your in-group look like from that perspective?

Stan Honda/Getty Images

At a powwow, a drum circle breathes spirit into an ancient tribal tradition. These accomplished ceremonial musicians may serve as a reference group for onlookers who want to know more about drumming.

Reference Groups Both primary groups and in-groups can dramatically influence the way an individual thinks and behaves. Sociologists call any group that individuals use as a standard for evaluating themselves and their own behavior a **reference group.** For example, a high school student who aspires to join a social circle of hip-hop music devotees will pattern his or her behavior after that of the group. The student will begin dressing like these peers, listening to the same downloads and DVDs, and hanging out at the same stores and clubs.

Reference groups have two basic purposes. They serve a normative function by setting and enforcing standards of conduct and belief. The high school student who wants the approval of the hip-hop crowd will have to follow the group's dictates, at least to some extent. Reference groups also perform a comparison function by serving as a standard against which

TAKING SOCIOLOGY TO WORK

Sarah Levy, **Owner, S. Levy Foods**

Sarah Levy didn't know anything about sociology when she entered Northwestern University, but she knew that someday she wanted to start a bakery. After graduating from Northwestern with a major in sociology, she enrolled in Chicago's French Pastry School and spent some time interning at local bakeries and restaurants. A year later she started her own bakery in her mother's kitchen. Today Sarah owns and manages S. Levy Foods, which operates food concessions at airports in New York, Sacramento, Phoenix, and San Diego.

Like many small-business owners, Sarah does anything and everything in a typical workweek, from consulting to blogging ("Simply Sweet") and serving as brand ambassador for Callebut chocolate, Karo, and Fleischmann's yeast. She is also the dining editor for *Today's Chicago Woman* magazine. A gifted publicist, Sarah once participated in a Food Network challenge that involved baking a three-foot animated dinosaur cake. Through Sarah's Pastries & Candies, a bricks-and-mortar store she once owned in downtown Chicago, she contributed to several charities, including

Courtesy of Sarah Levy

Meals on Wheels, Common Threads, and For the Love of Chocolate Foundation.

Sarah saw the connection between business and sociology in her introductory sociology course, in which she used this textbook. Learning about how people interact, she says, has broadened her horizons and taught her how to step back and analyze a situation from a sociological perspective. "In my job, I am constantly interacting with people—employees, customers, vendors," she explains. "I think one of my greatest strengths is my ability to get along with people from all sorts of backgrounds, and make everyone get along with each other and work together towards the same goal."

LET'S DISCUSS

1. Have you ever thought of starting your own business? If so, what do you think the key to your success might be?
2. Would business have been a more practical major for Sarah? Why or why not?

people can measure themselves and others. An actor will evaluate himself or herself against a reference group composed of others in the acting profession (Merton and Kitt 1950).

Reference groups may help the process of anticipatory socialization. For example, a college student majoring in finance may read the *Wall Street Journal,* study the annual reports of corporations, and monitor stock market news on a smartphone. Such a student is using financial experts as a reference group to which he or she aspires.

Often, two or more reference groups influence us at the same time. Our family members, neighbors, and co-workers all shape different aspects of our self-evaluation. In addition, reference group attachments change during the life cycle. A corporate executive who quits the rat race at age 45 to become a social worker will find new reference groups to use as standards for evaluation. We shift reference groups as we take on different statuses during our lives.

Coalitions As groups grow larger, coalitions begin to develop. A **coalition** is a temporary or permanent alliance geared toward a common goal. Coalitions can be broad-based or narrow and can take on many different objectives. Sociologist William Julius Wilson (1999) described community-based organizations in Texas that include whites and Latinos, working class and affluent, who have banded together to work for improved sidewalks, better drainage systems, and comprehensive street paving. Out of this type of coalition building, Wilson hopes, will emerge better interracial understanding.

Some coalitions are intentionally short-lived. For example, short-term coalition building is a key to success in popular TV programs like *Survivor.* Often we question the ability of Congress to "work across the aisle" and form a coalition, but it does occur. Congress avoided a total government deadlock over several controversial issues by approving a budget for 2020 and 2021 that removed the federal debt ceiling for two years, funded the 2020 Census, allowed spending on a border wall, and increased defense spending. In effect, members of

Robert Voets/TNS/Newscom

Can you outwit, outplay, and outlast your competition? Maybe a coalition can help. In *Survivor: Island of the Idols,* coalition building continued to be a key to success in the long-running television series, now in its 39th season.

Congress agreed to limit expressions of anger to their own constituencies rather than express their feelings openly on the floor of Congress. This allowed them to vote, reluctantly, to keep the government running.

USE YOUR SOCIOLOGICAL IMAGINATION

Describe an experience you have had with coalition building, or one that you have read about—perhaps in politics. Was the coalition effective? What problems did the members need to overcome?

Social Networks

Groups do not merely serve to define other elements of the social structure, such as roles and statuses; they also link the individual with the larger society. We all belong to a number of different groups, and through our acquaintances make connections with people in different social circles. These connections are known as a **social network**—a series of social relationships that link a person directly to others, and through them indirectly to still more people. Social networks are one of the five basic elements of social structure.

Broadly speaking, social networks encompass all the routine social interaction we have with other individuals. Traditionally, researchers have limited their network studies to face-to-face contacts and phone conversations, although recently they have begun to study interaction through all types of new media. We should be careful, however, not to equate social media like Instagram with social networks, which include a much broader spectrum of social interaction.

Social networks can center on virtually any activity, from sharing job information to exchanging news and gossip, or even sharing sex. In the mid-1990s, sociologists studied romantic relationships at a high school with about 1,000 students. They found that about 61 percent of the girls had been sexually active over the past 18 months. Among the sexually active respondents, the researchers counted only 63 steady couples, or pairs with no other partners. A much larger group of 288 students—almost a third of the sample—was involved in a free-flowing network of relationships (Bearman et al. 2004).

Involvement in social networks—commonly known as *networking*—is especially valuable in finding employment. Albert Einstein was successful in finding a job only when a classmate's father put him in touch with his future employer. These kinds of contacts—even those that are weak and distant—can be crucial in establishing social networks and facilitating the transmission of information.

Research indicates, however, that both in person and online, not everyone participates equally in social networks. Networks, like in-groups, can become elitist or exclusionary. Women and racial and ethnic minorities are at a disadvantage when seeking new and better job opportunities or social contacts (Erikson and Occhiuto 2017; Trimble and Kmec 2011).

Another drawback of networking online is the way it distorts social reality. For example, the frequency of highly social activities such as drinking and partying is likely to be exaggerated online due to their visual impact, while images of more solitary activities as reading, doing homework, or praying are rarely posted online. Also, the phenomenon called the *friendship paradox* means that 98 percent of people have many fewer real-life friends than they do online "friends." This difference has been found to foster a sense of isolation, especially among adolescents (Jackson 2019).

A generation ago, research into networking focused on face-to-face encounters, phone calls, and even letter writing. More and more network research builds on these early findings and focuses on social media, as shown in Box 5-3.

Social Institutions

The mass media, the government, the economy, the family, and the health care system are all examples of social institutions found in our society. **Social institutions** are organized patterns of beliefs and behavior centered on basic social needs, such as replacing personnel (the family) and preserving order (the government). Figure 5-2 summarizes the various elements of social structure, including social institutions.

A close look at social institutions gives sociologists insight into the structure of a society. Consider religion, for example. The

FIGURE 5-2 THE ELEMENTS OF SOCIAL STRUCTURE: AN OVERVIEW

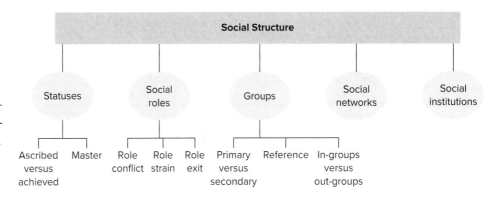

OUR WIRED WORLD

5-3 Twitter Networks: From Wildfires to Hurricanes

Scholars of communication research, social media, and disaster response planning have increasingly considered how Twitter functions as an important social networking tool. With an estimated 126 million active daily users in 2019, Twitter has a significant audience.

University of Vermont researchers looking at the five costliest disasters of the 2010s found that individuals with relatively small followings (200 to 300 people) had the greatest impact in offering information about issues of food security and emergency supplies and hands-on details of dealing with the disaster. As shown in the accompanying figure, individuals' impact can be considered at three stages: before, during, and after the disaster. At each key moment local Twitter accounts with small followings were critical in spreading information to a large audience. Close analysis showed that the type of information shared differed depending upon the time period. At the time of the event, the information most often shared concerned locations of available generators. However, if the disaster was well anticipated, such as flooding from swollen rivers, this same information is most critical in the preparatory stage. This research suggested to relief agencies the importance of disseminating information widely so that local-oriented online users can share the information in a timely way.

A group of researchers receiving grant support from the Army Research Office and the National Science Foundation studied how Twitter functions when the public is faced with an imminent threat. Would Twitter supplement the long-time reliance on warnings through mass media channels or even sirens? Twitter

> *The study found that particular elements within a message increased the likelihood that information would be passed on, regardless of the type of threat.*

affords a way to reach individual users; then it allows those users to reach out through their own social network via retweets.

By using available data and a software program that allowed them to monitor thousands of Twitter feeds without identifying specific users, researchers saw how the online network responds to disaster threats. Specifically, they considered how often users would re-transmit three specific kinds of messages: general informational messages, messages about closure or opening of facilities, and messages about evacuation and shelter. They found that the frequency with which people retransmitted the different types of messages varied.

For *informational messages* about a threat (official messages that provided phone numbers or websites), they found the following rank order in frequency of transmission of messages:

1. Flood (most retweets)
2. Hurricane
3. Terrorist attack
4. Blizzard
5. Wildfire (fewest retweets)

Messages about *closure or opening* of facilities or roads had a somewhat different pattern of retransmission:

1. Terrorist attack (most retweets)
2. Flood
3. Blizzard
4. Hurricane
5. Wildfire (fewest retweets)

And the pattern differed yet again for tweets about *evacuation and shelter*:

1. Wildfire (most retweets)
2. Flood
3. Terrorist attack
4. Blizzard
5. Hurricane (fewest retweets)

The study found that particular elements within a message increased the likelihood

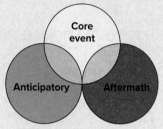

Adapted from Meredith T. Niles, Benjamin F. Emery, Andrew J. Reagan, Peter Sheridan Dodds, and Christopher M. Danforth. Social media usage patterns during natural hazards. California: PLUS ONE. February 13, 2019.

Assessing Tweets During Natural Disasters: When a natural disaster occurs, social media use, and tweets in particular, can be tracked in real time. Tweets seem to build before an event, peak during the event itself, and taper off afterwards.

that information would be passed on, regardless of the type of threat. Tweets that provided means to access more information (such as URLs) or that included emotive phrases such as "stand strong" were especially salient to online users.

In an Australian study using a similar research method, the scholars found that during an event, Twitter can provide real-time information about the severity and location of damage. Probably the most remarkable aspect of such social research is that it can be done at virtually no cost and without interfering in any way with preparation for or response to a threat. As social media penetration increases among the general public, we can assume emergency planners and first responders will increasingly use such research.

LET'S DISCUSS

1. Why did the number of retweets vary by type of disaster and type of message? Would you have studied any other variables?

2. What are the most important practical implications of this research?

Sources: Niles et al. 2019; Shaban 2019; Sutton et al. 2015.

institution of religion adapts to the segment of society that it serves. Church work has very different meanings for ministers who serve a skid row area and those who serve a suburban middle-class community. Religious leaders assigned to a skid

row mission will focus on tending to the ill and providing food and shelter. In contrast, clergy in affluent suburbs will be occupied with counseling those considering marriage and divorce, arranging youth activities, and overseeing cultural events.

Functionalist Perspective One way to understand social institutions is to see how they fulfill essential functions. Anthropologists and sociologists have identified five major tasks, or functional prerequisites, that a society or relatively permanent group must accomplish if it is to survive:

1. *Replacing personnel.* Any group or society must replace personnel when they die, leave, or become incapacitated. This task is accomplished through such means as immigration, annexation of neighboring groups, acquisition of slaves, or sexual reproduction. The Shakers, a religious sect that came to the United States in 1774, are a conspicuous example of a group that has *failed* to replace personnel. Their religious beliefs commit the Shakers to celibacy; to survive, the group must recruit new members. At first, the Shakers proved quite successful in attracting members, reaching a peak of about 6,000 members in the United States during the 1840s. As of 2020, however, the only Shaker community left in this country was a farm in Maine with two members—one man and one woman.

2. *Teaching new recruits.* No group or society can survive if many of its members reject the group's established behavior and responsibilities. Thus, finding or producing new members is not sufficient; the group or society must also encourage recruits to learn and accept its values and customs. Such learning can take place formally, within schools (where learning is a manifest function), or informally, through interaction in peer groups (where learning is a latent function).

3. *Producing and distributing goods and services.* Any relatively permanent group or society must provide and distribute desired goods and services to its members. Each society establishes a set of rules for the allocation of financial and other resources. The group must satisfy the needs of most members to some extent, or it will risk the possibility of discontent and ultimately disorder.

4. *Preserving order.* Throughout the world, indigenous and aboriginal peoples have struggled to protect themselves from outside invaders, with varying degrees of success. Failure to preserve order and defend against conquest leads to the death not only of a people, but of a culture as well.

5. *Providing and maintaining a sense of purpose.* In order to fulfill the first four requirements, people must feel motivated to continue as members of a group or society. Patriotism, tribal identities, religious values, or personal moral codes can help people to develop and maintain such a sense of purpose. Whatever the motivator, in any society there remains one common and critical reality: if an individual does not have a sense of purpose, he or she has little reason to contribute to a society's survival.

This list of functional prerequisites does not specify *how* a society and its corresponding social institutions will perform each task. For example, one society may protect itself from external attack by amassing a frightening arsenal of weaponry, while another may make determined efforts to remain neutral in world politics and to promote cooperative relationships with its neighbors. No matter what its particular strategy, any society or relatively permanent group must attempt to satisfy all these functional prerequisites for survival. If it fails on even one condition, the society runs the risk of extinction (Aberle et al. 1950; R. Mack and Bradford 1979).

Conflict Perspective Conflict theorists do not agree with the functionalist approach to social institutions. Although proponents of both perspectives agree that social institutions are organized to meet basic social needs, conflict theorists object to the idea that the outcome is necessarily efficient and desirable.

From a conflict perspective, the present organization of social institutions is no accident. Major institutions, such as education, help to maintain the privileges of the most powerful individuals and groups within a society, while contributing to the powerlessness of others. To give one example, public schools in the United States are financed largely through property taxes. This arrangement allows more affluent areas to provide their children with better-equipped schools and better-paid teachers than low-income areas can afford. As a result, children from prosperous communities are better prepared to compete academically than children from impoverished communities. The structure of the nation's educational system permits and even promotes such unequal treatment of schoolchildren.

Conflict theorists argue that social institutions such as education have an inherently conservative nature. Without question, it has been difficult to implement educational reforms that promote equal opportunity—whether bilingual education, school desegregation, or mainstreaming of students with disabilities. From a functionalist perspective, social change can be dysfunctional, since it often leads to instability. However, from a conflict view, why should we preserve the existing social structure if it is unfair and discriminatory?

Social institutions also operate in gendered and racist environments, as conflict theorists, as well as feminists and interactionists, have pointed out. In schools, offices, and government institutions, assumptions about what people can do reflect the sexism and racism of the larger society. For instance, many people assume that women cannot make tough decisions—even those in the top echelons of corporate management. Others assume that all Black students at elite colleges represent affirmative action admissions. Inequality based on gender, economic status, race, and ethnicity thrives in such an environment—to which we might add discrimination based on age, physical disability, and sexual orientation. The truth of this assertion can be seen in routine decisions by employers on how to advertise jobs, as well as whether to provide fringe benefits such as child care and parental leave.

TABLE 5-2 SOCIOLOGICAL PERSPECTIVES ON
SOCIAL INSTITUTIONS

Tracking **Sociological Perspectives**

Perspective	Role of Social Institutions	Focus
Functionalist	Meeting basic social needs	Essential functions
Conflict	Meeting basic social needs	Maintenance of privileges and inequality
Interactionist	Fostering everyday behavior	Influence of the roles and statuses we accept

Interactionist Perspective Social institutions affect our everyday behavior, whether we are driving down the street or waiting in a long shopping line. For example, a significant amount of scholarly research has been done about the positive impact that humor shared in the workplace can have in promoting efficiency. It has been shown that employees who laugh together are more creative and more collaborative, resulting in higher productivity and profitability.

Yet the role of humor in social interaction is complex. Joke telling cannot be at the expense of some person, especially if the joke is told by a supervisor about a subordinate. Also it is important that jokes not be in bad taste. If they are, they may encourage employees to behave badly. However, done properly, humor can not only make people laugh but also motivate people to act for the good of the organization (Yam 2017).

Interactionist theorists emphasize that our social behavior is conditioned by the roles and statuses we accept, the groups to which we belong, and the institutions within which we function. For example, the social roles associated with being a judge occur within the larger context of the criminal justice system. The status of judge stands in relation to other statuses, such as attorney, plaintiff, defendant, and witness, as well as to the social institution of government. Although courts and jails have great symbolic importance, the judicial system derives its continued significance from the roles people carry out in social interactions (Berger and Luckmann 1966).

Table 5-2 summarizes the three major sociological perspectives on social institutions.

THINKING CRITICALLY

Describe an institution you are part of from a functionalist, conflict, and interactionist perspective.

Understanding Organizations
Formal Organizations and Bureaucracies

As contemporary societies have shifted to more advanced forms of technology and their social structures have become more complex, our lives have become increasingly dominated by large secondary groups referred to as *formal organizations*. A **formal organization** is a group designed for a special purpose and structured for maximum efficiency. The U.S. Postal Service, McDonald's, and the Boston Pops orchestra are examples of formal organizations. Though organizations vary in their size, specificity of goals, and degree of efficiency, they are all structured to facilitate the management of large-scale operations. They also have a bureaucratic form of organization, described in the next section.

In our society, formal organizations fulfill an enormous variety of personal and societal needs, shaping the lives of everyone of us. In fact, formal organizations have become such a dominant force that we must create organizations to supervise other organizations, such as the Securities and Exchange Commission (SEC) to regulate brokerage companies. Although it sounds more exciting to say that we live in the "computer age" than to say that we live in the "age of formal organization," the latter is probably a more accurate description (Azumi and Hage 1972; Etzioni 1964).

While few people initially aspire to work in a huge formal organization, most of us will. Over half of all retail employees work for organizations with over 2,500 employees; the same is true for one-third of those in the service and financial sectors. Despite all the attention given to entrepreneurs and start-ups, large organizations rule the economy. Typical is the experience of Bonnie Chih, who graduated from pharmacy school at Washington State University in 2017 and declared, "I don't think I could ever work at a chain." Well, she and eight of her classmates did manage to work for independent, hospital, or clinic pharmacies, but 52 found employment at chain stores (Francis 2017).

Ascribed statuses such as gender, race, and ethnicity can influence how we see ourselves within formal organizations. For example, a study followed the careers of nearly 4,000 women and men who entered the bar in 2000 and found that among full-time lawyers, women earned an average of $6,000 less per year than men who were at the same stage of the profession. The discrepancy held even after considering type of firm, specialization within law, and work history (whether the lawyer had taken family leave, for example).

This consistent gender wage inequality appeared to stem from a devaluation of women and their work within legal organizations.

Regrettably, women lawyers operating in this work culture may come to perceive themselves as worth less and entitled to less, which in turn creates further gendered compensatory practices. For example, over time, women and men record billable hours differently: men bill for every snippet of conversation, while women bill more selectively. This pattern of organizational culture, which perpetuates salary differences and ultimately discourages women from being as tough as men at salary negotiation, has been documented in a variety of occupations (Dinovitzer et al. 2009; Sandberg 2015).

Characteristics of a Bureaucracy

A **bureaucracy** is a component of formal organization that uses rules and hierarchical ranking to achieve efficiency. Rows of desks staffed by seemingly faceless people, endless lines and forms, impossibly complex language, and frustrating encounters with red tape—all these unpleasant images have combined to make *bureaucracy* a dirty word and an easy target in political campaigns. As a result, few people want to identify their occupation as "bureaucrat," despite the fact that all of us perform various bureaucratic tasks. In an industrial society, elements of bureaucracy enter into almost every occupation.

Max Weber ([1913–1922] 1947) first directed researchers to the significance of bureaucratic structure. In an important sociological advance, Weber emphasized the basic similarity of structure and process found in the otherwise dissimilar enterprises of religion, government, education, and business. Weber saw bureaucracy as a form of organization quite different from the family-run business. For analytical purposes, he developed an ideal type of bureaucracy that would reflect the most characteristic aspects of all human organizations. By **ideal type** Weber meant a construct or model for evaluating specific cases. In actuality, perfect bureaucracies do not exist; no real-world organization corresponds exactly to Weber's ideal type.

Weber proposed that whether the purpose is to run a church, a corporation, or an army, the ideal bureaucracy displays five basic characteristics. A discussion of those characteristics, as well as the dysfunctions of a bureaucracy, follows.

1. **Division of labor.** Specialized experts perform specific tasks. In a college bureaucracy, the admissions officer does not do the job of registrar; the guidance counselor does not see to the maintenance of buildings. By working at a specific task, people are more likely to become highly skilled and carry out a job with maximum efficiency. This emphasis on specialization is so basic a part of our lives that we may not realize it is a fairly recent development in Western culture.

Brand X Pictures/Punchstock

The downside of division of labor is that the fragmentation of work into smaller and smaller tasks can divide workers and remove any connection they might feel to the overall objective of the bureaucracy. In *The Communist Manifesto* (written in 1848), Karl Marx and Friedrich Engels charged that the capitalist system reduces workers to a mere "appendage of the machine" (Tucker 1978).

Having such sharp divisions of labor and narrow areas of expertise, they wrote, produces extreme **alienation**—a condition of estrangement or dissociation from the surrounding society. According to both Marx and conflict theorists, restricting workers to very small tasks also weakens their job security, since new employees can easily be trained to replace them.

Although division of labor has certainly enhanced the performance of many complex bureaucracies, in some cases it can lead to **trained incapacity**; that is, workers become so specialized that they develop blind spots and fail to notice obvious problems. Even worse, they may not care about what is happening in the next department. This failure to communicate within a corporation across divisions has been termed the "silo effect." Some observers believe that such developments have caused workers in the United States to become less productive on the job (Tett 2015; Veblen 1914).

In some cases, the bureaucratic division of labor can have tragic results. In the wake of the coordinated attacks on the World Trade Center and the Pentagon on September 11, 2001, Americans wondered aloud how the FBI and CIA could have failed to detect the terrorists' elaborately planned operation. The problem, in part, turned out to be the division of labor between the FBI, which focuses on domestic matters, and the CIA, which operates overseas. Officials at these intelligence-gathering organizations, both of which are huge bureaucracies, are well known for jealously guarding information from one another. They were unwilling or unable to see and communicate beyond their own "silo."

Subsequent investigations revealed that they knew about Osama bin Laden and his Al-Qaeda terrorist network in the early 1990s. Unfortunately, five federal agencies—the CIA, FBI, National Security Agency, Defense Intelligence Agency, and National Reconnaissance Office—failed to share their leads on the network. Although the hijacking of the four commercial airliners used in the massive attacks might not have been preventable, the bureaucratic division of labor definitely hindered efforts to defend against terrorism, undermining U.S. national security.

2. **Hierarchy of authority.** Bureaucracies follow the principle of hierarchy; that is, each position is under the supervision of a higher authority. A president heads a college bureaucracy; he or she selects

Dinodia Photo/Photos of India/Alamy Stock Photo

Being an accountant in a large corporation may be a relatively high-paying occupation. In Marxist terms, however, accountants are vulnerable to alienation, since they are far removed from the product or service that the corporation creates.

members of the administration, who in turn hire their own staff. In the Roman Catholic Church, the pope is the supreme authority; under him are cardinals, bishops, and so forth.

3. Written rules and regulations.
What if your sociology professor gave your classmate an A for having such a friendly smile? You might think that wasn't fair, that it was against the rules. Through written rules and regulations, bureaucracies generally offer employees clear standards for an adequate (or exceptional) performance. In addition, procedures provide a valuable sense of continuity in a bureaucracy. Individual workers will come and go, but the structure and past records of the organization give it a life of its own that outlives the services of any one bureaucrat.

Of course, rules and regulations can overshadow the larger goals of an organization to the point that they become dysfunctional. What if a domestic abuse counselor failed to

BUREAUCRACY

Gatis Sluka, Latvijas Avize, Latvia

Bureaucracies are characterized by hierarchy, or layers of authority.

listen to an injured woman because she had no valid proof of U.S. citizenship? If blindly applied, rules no longer serve as a means to achieving an objective, but instead become important (and perhaps too important) in their own right. Robert Merton (1968) used the term **goal displacement** to refer to overzealous conformity to official regulations.

4. Impersonality.
Max Weber wrote that in a bureaucracy, work is carried out *sine ira et studio,* "without hatred or passion." Bureaucratic norms dictate that officials perform their duties without giving personal consideration to people as individuals. Although this norm is intended to guarantee equal treatment for each person, it also contributes to the often cold and uncaring feeling associated with modern organizations. We typically think of big government and big business when we think of impersonal bureaucracies. In some cases, the impersonality that is associated with a bureaucracy can have tragic results. More frequently, bureaucratic impersonality produces frustration and disaffection. Today, even small firms filter callers with electronic menus.

5. Employment based on technical qualifications.
Within the ideal bureaucracy, hiring is based on technical qualifications rather than on favoritism, and performance is measured against specific standards. Written personnel policies dictate who gets promoted, and people often have a right to appeal if they believe that particular rules have been violated. Such procedures protect bureaucrats against arbitrary dismissal, provide a measure of security, and encourage loyalty to the organization.

Although, ideally, any bureaucracy will value technical and professional competence, personnel decisions do not always follow that ideal pattern. Dysfunctions within bureaucracy have become well publicized, particularly because of the work of Laurence J. Peter. According to the **Peter principle,** every employee within a hierarchy tends to rise to his or her level of incompetence (Peter and Hull 1969). This hypothesis, which has not been directly or systematically tested, reflects a possible dysfunctional outcome of advancement on the basis of merit. Talented people receive promotion after promotion, until sadly, some of them finally achieve positions that they cannot handle with their usual competence.

Table 5-3 summarizes the five characteristics of bureaucracy. These characteristics,

TABLE 5-3   CHARACTERISTICS OF A BUREAUCRACY

	Positive Consequence	Negative Consequence	
		For the Individual	For the Organization
Division of labor	Produces efficiency in a large-scale corporation	Produces trained incapacity	Produces a narrow perspective
Hierarchy of authority	Clarifies who is in command	Deprives employees of a voice in decision making	Permits concealment of mistakes
Written rules and regulations	Let workers know what is expected of them	Stifle initiative and imagination	Lead to goal displacement
Impersonality	Reduces bias	Contributes to feelings of alienation	Discourages loyalty to company
Employment based on technical qualifications	Discourages favoritism and reduces petty rivalries	Discourages ambition to improve oneself elsewhere	Fosters Peter principle

developed by Max Weber a century ago, describe an ideal type rather than an actual bureaucracy. Not every formal organization will possess all five of Weber's characteristics. In fact, wide variation exists among actual bureaucratic organizations.

Bureaucracy pervades modern life; through McDonaldization, it has reached new heights. As Box 5-4 shows, the McDonald's organization provides an excellent illustration of Weber's concept of bureaucracy (Ritzer 2018).

Bureaucratization as a Process Have you ever had to speak to 10 or 12 individuals in a corporation or government agency just to find out which official has jurisdiction over a particular problem? Ever been transferred from one department to another until you finally hung up in disgust? Sociologists have used the term **bureaucratization** to refer to the process by which a group, organization, or social movement becomes increasingly bureaucratic.

Normally, we think of bureaucratization in terms of large organizations. But bureaucratization also takes place within small-group settings. Sociologist Jennifer Bickman Mendez (1998) studied domestic houseworkers employed in central California by a nationwide franchise. She found that housekeeping tasks were minutely defined, to the point that employees had to follow 22 written steps for cleaning a bathroom. Complaints and special requests went not to the workers, but to an office-based manager.

Andre J. Jackson/MCT/Newscom

Menlo Innovations of Ann Arbor, Michigan, a software design and development company, operates without managers: employees basically supervise themselves. Menlo is relatively small, but such "flat" hierarchies are attracting interest from researchers in organizational development.

Bureaucratization is not limited to Western industrial societies. In 2012, Xi Jinping became general secretary of China's Communist Party, the nation's highest office. In his first public address, Xi pledged to end the party's "undue emphasis on formalities and bureaucracy" in order to deliver a "better life" for the Chinese people (I. Johnson 2012:A19; Malcolm Moore 2012).

Oligarchy: Rule by a Few Conflict theorists have examined the bureaucratization of social movements. The German sociologist Robert Michels (1915) studied socialist parties and labor unions in Europe before World War I and found that such organizations were becoming increasingly bureaucratic. The emerging leaders of the organizations—even some of the most radical—had a vested interest in clinging to power. If they lost their leadership posts, they would have to return to full-time work as manual laborers.

SOCIOLOGY IN THE GLOBAL COMMUNITY

5-4 McDonald's and the Worldwide Bureaucratization of Society

In his book *The McDonaldization of Society*, sociologist George Ritzer notes the enormous influence of a well-known fast-food organization on modern-day culture and social life.

Not surprisingly, Max Weber's five characteristics of bureaucracy are apparent in McDonald's restaurants, as well as in the global corporation behind them. Food preparation and order-taking reflect a painstaking *division of labor*, implemented by a *hierarchy of authority* that stretches from the food workers up to the store operator, and ultimately to the corporate board of directors. Store operators learn McDonald's *written rules and regulations*, which govern even the amount of ketchup or mustard placed on a hamburger, at McDonald's Hamburger University.

Little bonding occurs between servers and customers, creating a pervasive sense of *impersonality*. The emphasis on efficiency is partly to blame for this characteristic. Because McDonald's French fry machines lift the fries out of the hot oil automatically, for example, employees cannot meet a customer request for "crispy" fries. Finally, employees are expected to have specific *technical qualifications*, although most of the skills they need to perform routine tasks can be learned in a brief training period.

McDonaldization is the process by which the principles of bureaucratization have increasingly shaped organizations worldwide. Its real significance is that it is not confined to the food-service industry or to coffee shops like Starbucks. Worldwide, McDonald's brand of predictability, efficiency, and dependence on nonhuman technology has become customary in a number of services, ranging from medical care to wedding planning to education.

Even sporting events reflect the influence of bureaucratization. Around the world, stadiums are becoming increasingly similar, both physically and in the way they present the sport to spectators. All seats offer spectators an unrestricted view, and a big screen

Mikhail Markovskiy/Shutterstock

Believe it or not, you are aboard a cruise ship! Giving consumers no surprises and highly predictable experiences are hallmarks of McDonaldization. Ironically, many people today spend large amounts of money to travel to distant ports on cruise ships only to have minimal, if any, exposure to foreign culture or people.

> *Worldwide, McDonald's brand of predictability, efficiency, and dependence on nonhuman technology has become customary in a number of services, ranging from medical care to wedding planning to education.*

guarantees them access to instant replays, which fans have become accustomed to seeing at home and in sports bars. Scores, player statistics, and attendance figures are updated automatically by computer and displayed on an automated scoreboard or fed to people's smartphones. Spectator enthusiasm is manufactured through digital displays urging applause or rhythmic chanting. And of course, the merchandising of teams'

and even players' names and images is highly controlled.

McDonald's reliance on the five characteristics of bureaucracy is not revolutionary. What is new is the bureaucratization of services and life events that once were highly individualized, at times even spontaneous. More and more, society itself is undergoing McDonaldization.

LET'S DISCUSS

1. What features of fast-food restaurants do you appreciate? Do you have any complaints about them?
2. Analyze life at your school using Weber's model of bureaucracy. What elements of McDonaldization do you see? Do you wish life were less McDonaldized?

Sources: Ormond 2005; Ritzer 2018.

USE YOUR SOCIOLOGICAL IMAGINATION

Your school or workplace suddenly ceases to exhibit one of the five characteristics of bureaucracy. Which characteristic is it, and what are the consequences?

Through his research, Michels originated the idea of the **iron law of oligarchy,** which describes how even a democratic organization will eventually develop into a bureaucracy ruled by a few, called an oligarchy. Why do oligarchies emerge? People who achieve leadership roles usually have the skills, knowledge, or charismatic appeal (as Weber noted) to direct, if not control, others. Michels argued that the rank and file of a movement or organization look to leaders for direction and thereby reinforce the process of rule by a few. In addition, members of an oligarchy are strongly motivated to maintain their leadership roles, privileges, and power.

Bureaucracy and Organizational Culture

How does bureaucratization affect the average individual who works in an organization? The early theorists of formal organizations tended to neglect this question. Max Weber, for example, focused on the management personnel in bureaucracies, but had little to say about workers in industry or clerks in government agencies.

According to the **classical theory** of formal organizations, or **scientific management approach,** workers are motivated almost entirely by economic rewards. This theory stresses that only the physical constraints on workers limit their productivity. Therefore, workers may be treated as a resource, much like the machines that began to replace them in the 20th century. Under the scientific management approach, management attempts to achieve maximum work efficiency through scientific planning, established performance standards, and careful supervision of workers and production. Planning involves efficiency studies but not studies of workers' attitudes or job satisfaction.

Not until workers organized unions—and forced management to recognize that they were not objects—did theorists of formal organizations begin to revise the classical approach. Social scientists became aware that along with management and administrators, informal groups of workers have an important impact on organizations. An alternative way of considering bureaucratic dynamics, the **human relations approach,** emphasizes the role of people, communication, and participation in a bureaucracy. This type of analysis reflects the interest of interactionist theorists in small-group behavior. Unlike planning under the scientific management approach, planning based on the human relations approach focuses on workers' feelings, frustrations, and emotional need for job satisfaction.

The gradual move away from a sole focus on the physical aspects of getting the job done—and toward the concerns and needs of workers—led advocates of the human relations approach to stress the less formal aspects of bureaucratic structure. Informal groups and social networks within organizations develop partly as a result of people's ability to create more direct forms of communication than under the formal structure. Charles Page (1946) used the term *bureaucracy's other face* to refer to the unofficial activities and interactions that are such a basic part of daily organizational life.

Today, research on formal organizations is following new avenues. Among them are:

- The recent arrival of a small number of women and minority group members in high-level management.
- In large corporations, the decision-making role of groups that lie outside the top ranks of leadership.
- The presence or lack of diversity in terms of gender, race, ethnicity, ability status, and sexual orientation within large organizations.
- The development of bossless offices with flat or horizontal hierarchies, where middle managers are eliminated and employees increasingly supervise themselves.
- The loss of fixed boundaries in organizations that have outsourced key functions.
- The role of the Internet in influencing business and consumer preferences.

Though research on organizations still embraces Max Weber's insights, it has gone well beyond them (Edgell et al. 2017; Hutson 2014).

Researchers and organizations themselves have begun to use the electronic footprints that workers leave behind when they use social media, e-mail, and certain apps. For example, analysis of e-mail content can inform employers how rapidly new employees are adopting the language and knowledge they are expected to employ to be functioning parts of the organization. The results of such studies can inform bureaucracies of how well workers are fitting in as well as identify innovative ideas that can be adopted at large (Coritore, Goldberg, and Srivasta 2020).

THINKING CRITICALLY

Recall a job that you once held or think of a job you'd like to have. First, analyze the workplace using classical theory (the scientific management approach). Then analyze it using the human relations approach. Which approach do you find more useful in understanding that workplace?

Social Structure in Global Perspective

Modern societies are complex, especially compared to earlier social arrangements. Sociologists Émile Durkheim, Ferdinand Tönnies, and Gerhard Lenski developed ways to contrast modern societies with simpler forms of social structure.

Durkheim's Mechanical and Organic Solidarity

In his *Division of Labor* ([1893] 1933), Durkheim argued that social structure depends on the division of labor in a society—in other words, on the manner in which tasks are performed. Thus, a task such as providing food can be carried out almost totally by one individual, or it can be divided among many people. The latter pattern is typical of modern societies, in which the cultivation, processing, distribution, and retailing of a single food item are performed by literally hundreds of people.

In societies in which there is minimal division of labor, a collective consciousness develops that emphasizes group solidarity. Durkheim termed this collective frame of mind **mechanical solidarity,** implying that all individuals perform the same tasks. In this type of society, no one needs to ask, "What do your parents do?" since all are engaged in similar work. Each person prepares food, hunts, makes clothing, builds homes, and so forth. Because people have few options regarding what to do with their lives, there is little concern for individual needs. Instead, the group is the dominating force in society. Both social interaction and negotiation are based on close, intimate, face-to-face social contacts. Since there is little specialization, there are few social roles.

As societies become more advanced technologically, they rely on greater division of labor, so that no individual can go it alone. Dependence on others becomes essential for group survival. In Durkheim's terms, mechanical solidarity is replaced by **organic solidarity,** a collective consciousness resting on the need a society's members have for one another. Durkheim chose the term *organic solidarity* because in his view, individuals become interdependent in much the same way as organs of the human body.

Tönnies's *Gemeinschaft* and *Gesellschaft*

Ferdinand Tönnies (1855–1936) was appalled by the rise of an industrial city in his native Germany during the late 1800s. In his view, the city marked a dramatic change from the ideal of a close-knit community, which Tönnies termed a *Gemeinschaft,* to that of an impersonal mass society, known as a *Gesellschaft* (Beckwith 2019; Tönnies [1887] 1988).

The **Gemeinschaft** (pronounced GUH-mine-shoft) is typical of rural life. It is a small community in which people have similar backgrounds and life experiences. Virtually everyone knows one another, and social interactions are intimate and familiar, almost as among kinfolk. In this community there is a commitment to the larger social group and a sense of togetherness among members. People relate to others in a personal way, not just as "clerk" or "manager." With this personal interaction comes little privacy, however: we know too much about everyone.

Social control in the *Gemeinschaft* is maintained through informal means such as moral persuasion, gossip, and even gestures. These techniques work effectively because people genuinely care how others feel about them. Social change is relatively limited in the *Gemeinschaft;* the lives of members of one generation may be quite similar to those of their grandparents.

Some have likened new apps where you share your name and location with Uber drivers, buyers on Craigs List, Airbnb hosts, and repair people as a return to village life of Gemeinschaft. Everyone knows your name and people trust each other (Ravenelle 2017).

In contrast, the **Gesellschaft** (pronounced GUH-zell-shoft) is an ideal community that is characteristic of modern urban life. In this community most people are strangers who feel little in common with other residents. Relationships are governed by social roles that grow out of immediate tasks, such as purchasing a product or arranging a business meeting. Self-interest dominates, and there is little consensus concerning values or commitment to the group. As a result, social control must rest on more formal techniques, such as laws and legally defined punishments. Social change is an important aspect of life in the *Gesellschaft;* it can be strikingly evident even within a single generation.

Table 5-4 summarizes the differences between the *Gemeinschaft* and the *Gesellschaft.* Sociologists have used these terms to compare social structures that stress close relationships with those that emphasize less personal ties. It is easy to view the *Gemeinschaft* with nostalgia, as a far better way of life than the rat race of contemporary existence. However, the more intimate relationships of the *Gemeinschaft* come at a price. The prejudice and discrimination found there can be quite confining; ascribed statuses such as family background often outweigh a person's unique talents and achievements. In addition, the *Gemeinschaft* tends to distrust individuals who seek to be creative or just to be different.

Lenski's Sociocultural Evolution Approach

Sociologist Gerhard Lenski (1924–2015) took a very different view of society and social structure. Rather than distinguishing between two opposite types of society, as Tönnies did, Lenski saw human societies as undergoing a process of change characterized by a dominant pattern known as **sociocultural**

TABLE 5-4   COMPARISON OF THE *GEMEINSCHAFT* AND *GESELLSCHAFT*

Gemeinschaft	Gesellschaft
Rural life typifies this form.	Urban life typifies this form.
People share a feeling of community that results from their similar backgrounds and life experiences.	People have little sense of commonality. Their differences appear more striking than their similarities.
Social interactions are intimate and familiar.	Social interactions are likely to be impersonal and task-specific.
People maintain a spirit of cooperation and unity of will.	Self-interest dominates.
Tasks and personal relationships cannot be separated.	The task being performed is paramount; relationships are subordinate.
People place little emphasis on individual privacy.	Privacy is valued.
Informal social control predominates.	Formal social control is evident.
People are not very tolerant of deviance.	People are more tolerant of deviance.
Emphasis is on ascribed statuses.	Emphasis is on achieved statuses.
Social change is relatively limited.	Social change is very evident, even within a generation.

Think about It How would you classify the communities with which you are familiar? Are they more *Gemeinschaft* or *Gesellschaft*?

evolution. This term refers to long-term social trends resulting from the interplay of continuity, innovation, and selection (Nolan and Lenski 2015:415).

In Lenski's view, a society's level of technology is critical to the way it is organized. Lenski defined **technology** as "cultural information about the ways in which the material resources of the environment may be used to satisfy human needs and desires" (Nolan and Lenski 2015:415). The available technology does not completely define the form that a particular society and its social structure take. Nevertheless, a low level of technology may limit the degree to which a society can depend on such things as irrigation or complex machinery. As technology advances, Lenski wrote, a community evolves from a preindustrial to an industrial and finally a postindustrial society.

Preindustrial Societies How does a preindustrial society organize its economy? If we know that, we can categorize the society. The first type of preindustrial society to emerge in human history was the **hunting-and-gathering society,** in which people simply rely on whatever foods and fibers are readily available. Technology in such societies is minimal. Organized into groups, people move constantly in search of food. There is little division of labor into specialized tasks.

Hunting-and-gathering societies are composed of small, widely dispersed groups. Each group consists almost entirely of people who are related to one another. As a result, kinship ties are the source of authority and influence, and the social institution of the family takes on a particularly important role. Tönnies would certainly view such societies as examples of the *Gemeinschaft*.

Social differentiation within the hunting-and-gathering society is based on ascribed statuses such as gender, age, and family

Mike Goldwater/Alamy Stock Photo

Preindustrial societies still exist in some remote areas. These indigenous people are from the Envira region of the Amazon rain forest, in Brazil.

background. Since resources are scarce, there is relatively little inequality in terms of material goods. By the close of the 20th century, hunting-and-gathering societies had virtually disappeared (Nolan and Lenski 2015).

Horticultural societies, in which people plant seeds and crops rather than merely subsist on available foods, emerged about 12,000 years ago. Members of horticultural societies are much less nomadic than hunters and gatherers. They place greater emphasis on the production of tools and household objects. Yet technology remains rather limited in these societies, whose members cultivate crops with the aid of digging sticks or hoes (Wilford 1997).

The last stage of preindustrial development is the **agrarian society,** which emerged about 5,000 years ago. As in horticultural societies, members of agrarian societies engage primarily in the production of food. However, technological innovations such as the plow allow farmers to dramatically increase their crop yields. They can cultivate the same fields over generations, allowing the emergence of larger settlements.

The agrarian society continues to rely on the physical power of humans and animals (as opposed to mechanical power). Nevertheless, its social structure has more carefully defined roles than that of horticultural societies. Individuals focus on specialized tasks, such as the repair of fishing nets or blacksmithing. As human settlements become more established and stable, social institutions become more elaborate and property rights more important. The comparative permanence and greater surpluses of an agrarian society allow members to create artifacts such as statues, public monuments, and art objects and to pass them on from one generation to the next.

Table 5-5 summarizes Lenski's three stages of sociocultural evolution, as well as the stages that follow, described next.

Industrial Societies Although the Industrial Revolution did not topple monarchs, it produced changes every bit as significant as those resulting from political revolutions. The Industrial Revolution, which took place largely in England during the period 1760 to 1830, was a scientific revolution focused on the application of nonanimal (mechanical) sources of power to labor tasks. An **industrial society** is a society that depends on mechanization to produce its goods and services. Industrial societies rely on new inventions that facilitate agricultural and industrial production, and on new sources of energy, such as steam.

As the Industrial Revolution proceeded, a new form of social structure emerged. Many societies underwent an irrevocable shift from an agrarian-oriented economy to an industrial base. No longer did an individual or a family typically make an entire product. Instead, specialization of tasks and manufacturing of goods became increasingly common. Workers, generally men but also women and even children, left their family homesteads to work in central locations such as factories.

Postindustrial and Postmodern Societies When Lenski first proposed the sociocultural evolutionary approach in the 1960s, he paid relatively little attention to how maturing industrialized societies may change with the emergence of even more advanced forms of technology. More recently, he and other sociologists have studied the significant changes in the occupational structure of industrial societies as they shift from manufacturing to service economies. In the 1970s, sociologist Daniel Bell wrote about the technologically advanced **postindustrial society,** whose economic system is engaged primarily in the processing and control of information. The main output of a postindustrial society is services rather than manufactured goods. Large numbers of people become involved in occupations devoted to the teaching, generation, and dissemination of ideas. Jobs in fields such as advertising, public relations, human resources, and computer information systems would be typical of a postindustrial society (D. Bell [1973] 1999).

Bell views the transition from industrial to postindustrial society as a positive development. He sees a general decline in organized working-class groups and a rise in interest groups concerned with national issues such as health, education, and the environment. Bell's outlook is functionalist, because he portrays the postindustrial society as basically consensual. As organizations and interest groups engage in an open and competitive process of decision making, Bell believes, the level of conflict between diverse groups will diminish, strengthening social stability.

Conflict theorists take issue with Bell's functionalist analysis of the postindustrial society. For example, Michael Harrington (1980), who alerted the nation to the problems of the poor in his book *The Other America,* questioned the significance that

TABLE 5-5 STAGES OF SOCIOCULTURAL EVOLUTION   Summing Up

Societal Type	First Appearance	Characteristics
Hunting-and-gathering	Beginning of human life	Nomadic; reliance on readily available food and fibers
Horticultural	About 12,000 years ago	More settled; development of agriculture and limited technology
Agrarian	About 5,000 years ago	Larger, more stable settlements; improved technology and increased crop yields
Industrial	1760–1850	Reliance on mechanical power and new sources of energy; centralized workplaces; economic interdependence; formal education
Postindustrial	1960s	Reliance on services, especially the processing and control of information; expanded middle class
Postmodern	Latter 1970s	High technology; mass consumption of consumer goods and media images; cross-cultural integration

Bell attached to the growing class of white-collar workers. Harrington conceded that scientists, engineers, and economists are involved in important political and economic decisions, but he disagreed with Bell's claim that they have a free hand in decision making, independent of the interests of the rich. Harrington followed in the tradition of Marx by arguing that conflict between social classes will continue in the postindustrial society.

Sociologists have gone beyond discussion of the postindustrial society to the idea of the postmodern society. A **postmodern**

society is a technologically sophisticated society that is preoccupied with consumer goods and media images (Lemert 2013). Such societies consume goods and information on a mass scale. Postmodern theorists take a global perspective, noting the ways that culture crosses national boundaries. For example, residents of the United States may listen to reggae music from Jamaica, eat sushi and other Japanese foods, and wear clogs from Sweden. And online social networks know no national boundaries. Box 5-5 describes one of the fixtures of the postmodern society, the theme park.

🌐 SOCIOLOGY IN THE GLOBAL COMMUNITY

5-5   Disney World: A Postmodern Theme Park

In the late 1970s, scholars began writing about the postmodern society and its preoccupation with consumer goods and media images. Walt Disney World is a living example of this type of society. Globally, over 157 million people visit a Disney theme park each year. In fact, Disney operates the eight most visited amusement parks in the world. On three different continents, the Magic Kingdom funnels newly arrived visitors through a quaint-looking Main Street, where Cinderella's Castle beckons to children of all ages.

Behind the Main Street façade, one finds endless opportunities to shop. In heavily air-conditioned stores, visitors can indulge in buying sprees that typify the postmodern preoccupation with consumer goods. Later, at the exits from popular attractions, visitors encounter more shopping opportunities, tailored to what they have just seen. This practice of piggy-backing shops on exhibits is now duplicated in prestigious museums throughout the world, where shops are located just outside special exhibitions of real art and authentic treasures.

The French sociologist Jean Baudrillard (1929–2007) coined the term **hyperconsumerism** to refer to the practice of buying more than we need or want, and often more than we can afford, under such circumstances. Of course, one need not walk down Main Street in Orlando to engage in hyperconsumerism. Advertising permeates the modern world, whether we are on foot or online, tempting us to engage in unnecessary purchases out of a desire that approaches greed. Consumption is so important in the postmodern world that it

Peter Schaefer

In the postmodern world, time–space is often compressed. Clutching a toy version of a fictional bear from the 1920s (Winnie-the-Pooh), a young visitor to Disney World reserves a ticket for a trip to New Orleans in the 1850s (the Pirates of the Caribbean attraction). In the meantime, she will travel through the 1930s in one continuous boat ride on the Congo, Zambezi, Amazon, and Irrawaddy Rivers (the Jungle Cruise attraction).

has become a means of self-identification. Today, conversations are more likely to start with "Where did you get that stroller?" or "Who are you wearing?" than with any reference to the social issues that plague the postmodern world.

> *Behind the Main Street façade, one finds endless opportunities to shop.*

Another essential element of postmodernism, *globalism,* is on display at Disney World, where cultural elements have been stripped of any foreign trappings. Here, Cinderella and

Snow White are not figures taken from German folklore, but "Disney characters." Similarly, Belle from *Beauty and the Beast* has largely lost her 18th-century French roots, and Pinocchio is no longer recognizable as an Italian.

Nearby, Epcot's World Showcase takes the opposite approach, offering museum-like re-creations of specific cultures. Here one finds no evidence of cultural diffusion or globalization—no Starbucks in Epcot's China, no Dunkin' Donuts in Great Britain, no hip-hop in Japan. Instead, a representation of a Mayan temple is flanked by a replica of a medieval Norwegian wooden-stave church and a re-creation of the Temple of Heaven in Beijing. Visitors stroll through a managed reality that is both an ideal and a simplified rendering of 10 different cultures, compressed in time-space.

Postmodernism is on display everywhere, not just in the theme park. It can be seen in the information-driven, consumer-oriented global society we all inhabit. Whether we like it or not, new technologies and the digital transmission of culture are constantly disengaging us from a particular time or place, facilitating our hyperconsumerism.

LET'S DISCUSS

1. In just the last 24 hours, what evidence of hyperconsumerism have you witnessed?
2. How often do you find yourself moving seamlessly across time or space, in one way or another?

Sources: Baudrillard [1970] 1998; Boje 1995; Brannigan 1992; Bryman 1995; Fjellman 1992; L. Klein 1994; Kratz and Karp 1993; Scoville 2010; Themed Entertainment Association 2019.

Durkheim, Tönnies, and Lenski present three visions of society's social structure. While they differ, each is useful, and this textbook will draw on all three. The sociocultural evolutionary approach emphasizes a historical perspective. It does not picture different types of social structure coexisting within the same society. Consequently, one would not expect a single society to include hunters and gatherers along with a postmodern culture. In contrast, Durkheim's and Tönnies's theories allow for the existence of different types of community—such as a *Gemeinschaft* and a *Gesellschaft*—in the same society. Thus, a rural New Hampshire community located 100 miles from Boston can be linked to the city by modern information technology. The main difference between these two theories is a matter of emphasis. While Tönnies emphasized the overriding concern in each type of community—one's own self-interest or the well-being of the larger society—Durkheim emphasized the division (or lack of division) of labor.

The work of these three thinkers reminds us that a major focus of sociology has been to identify changes in social structure and the consequences for human behavior. At the macro level, we see society shifting to more advanced forms of technology. The social structure becomes increasingly complex, and new social institutions emerge to assume some functions that once were performed by the family. On the micro level, these changes affect the nature of social interactions. Each individual takes on multiple social roles, and people come to rely more on social networks and less on kinship ties. As the social structure becomes more complex, people's relationships become more impersonal, transient, and fragmented.

THINKING CRITICALLY

Describe any personal experiences you have had with a nonindustrial, or developing, society. If you have not had that kind of experience, how do you think you would prepare for it?

social policy and Organizations

The State of the Unions Worldwide

How many people do you know who belong to a labor union? Chances are you can name a lot fewer people than someone could 50 years ago. In 1954 unions represented 39 percent of workers in the private sector of the U.S. economy; in 2020 the government reported that they represented only 10.3 percent—the lowest share in more than 70 years. As Figure 5-3 shows, unionization of employed workers ranges from a high of 25.3 percent in New York to a low of 3.9 percent in South Carolina. What has happened to diminish the importance of organized labor? Can workers be represented adequately without strong unions?

Looking at the Issue

Labor unions consist of organized workers who share either the same skill (as in electronics) or the same employer (as in the case of postal employees). Unions began to emerge during the Industrial Revolution in England, in the

MAPPING LIFE NATIONWIDE

FIGURE 5-3   LABOR UNION MEMBERSHIP BY STATE, 2020

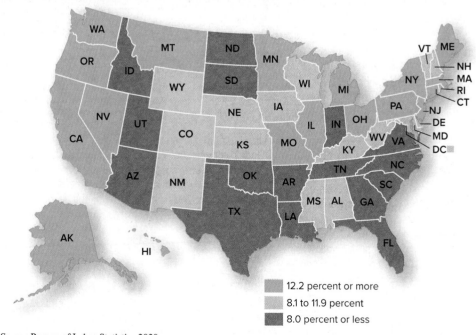

- 12.2 percent or more
- 8.1 to 11.9 percent
- 8.0 percent or less

Source: Bureau of Labor Statistics 2020a.

1700s. Groups of workers banded together to extract concessions from employers (for example, safer working conditions, a shorter workweek) and to protect their positions.

Historically, labor unions have engaged in restrictive practices that are regarded today as discriminatory. They frequently tried to protect their jobs by limiting entry to their occupation based on gender, race, ethnicity, citizenship, age, and sometimes rather arbitrary measures of skill levels. Today we see less of this protection of special interests. In selected industries, unions now play a vital role in keeping Blacks' wages competitive with those of whites (Rosenfeld and Klegkamp 2012).

The power of labor unions varies widely from country to country, but the decline in union membership has occurred worldwide (see Figure 5-4).

Among the reasons for the decline are the following:

1. **Changes in the type of industry.** Manufacturing jobs, the traditional heart of the labor union, have declined, giving way to postindustrial service jobs.

2. **Growth in part-time jobs.** In 1968, fewer than 14 percent of U.S. employees were part-timers. By 2019 it was more than 17 percent.

3. **The legal system.** The United States has not made it particularly easy for unions to organize and bargain, and some government actions have made it more difficult. Significant legal challenges in 2018 limit the long-standing right of unions that represent a company's workforce to collect dues from nonmembers.

4. **Globalization.** The threat of jobs leaving the country has undercut the ability of union leaders to organize workers at home. Some say that labor union demands for wage increases and additional benefits have themselves spurred the exodus of jobs to developing nations, where wages are significantly lower and unions are virtually nonexistent.

5. **Employer offensives.** Increasingly hostile employers have taken court action to block unions' efforts to represent their members.

6. **Automation.** The advent of driverless trucks and cars and drones directly reduces jobs formerly held by loyal union members.

Around the world, tougher negotiations between large corporations and representatives of their workers have rolled back the bargaining ability of many unions.

Applying Sociology

Both Marxists and functionalists would view unions as a logical response to the emergence of impersonal, large-scale, formal, and often alienating organizations. This view certainly characterized the growth of unions in major manufacturing industries with a sharp division of labor. However, as manufacturing has declined, unions have had to look elsewhere for growth.

Worldwide, today's labor unions bear little resemblance to those early unions organized spontaneously by exploited workers. In line with Robert Michels's iron law of oligarchy, unions have become increasingly bureaucratized under a sometimes self-serving leadership. Conflict theorists would point out that the longer union leaders are in office, the less responsive they are to the needs and demands of the rank and file, and the more concerned with maintaining their own positions and power. Yet research shows that under certain circumstances, union leadership can change significantly. Smaller unions are vulnerable to changes in leadership, as are unions whose membership shifts in composition from predominantly white to African American or Latino.

Interactionists have pointed to the growing reliance of unions on communicating through social media. This serves to advantage women, who are just as likely as men, if not more so, to engage with social media. Historically women were less welcomed in the traditional face-to-face meetings that unions relied on for all their activities (Thornthwaite et al. 2018).

Sociologists have linked the recent decline in private-sector union membership to a widening gap between hourly workers' wages and managerial and executive compensation. As union membership declined—and with it the unions' bargaining power—employers began to offer union workers less attractive pay packages. Eventually, the trend spread to nonunionized companies in the same industries, which typically strive to match union compensation in order to be competitive. In these businesses, employers no longer feel a need to raise wages to attract employees (Rosenfeld 2014).

Initiating Policy

U.S. law grants workers the right to self-organize via unions. However, the United States is unique among industrial democracies in allowing employers to actively oppose their employees' decision to organize. The economic recession that began in 2009 compounded employers' opposition to unions and threatened workers' rights in established unions as state and local governments across the United States faced significant budget deficits. In an effort to cut costs,

FIGURE 5-4 LABOR UNION MEMBERSHIP WORLDWIDE

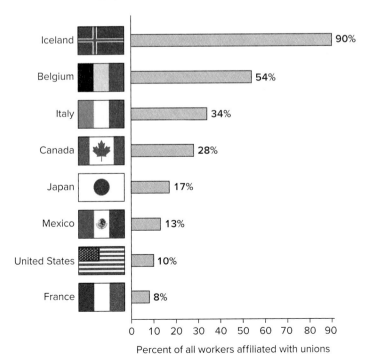

Country	Percent
Iceland	90%
Belgium	54%
Italy	34%
Canada	28%
Japan	17%
Mexico	13%
United States	10%
France	8%

Percent of all workers affiliated with unions

Note: U.S. data for 2019; other countries' data are for 2016.
Sources: Bureau of Labor Statistics 2020a; International Labour Organization 2019.
Flags: admin_design/Shutterstock

many elected officials moved to shrink the pensions that government workers gained through collective bargaining. In some states, officials want not only to reduce retirees' benefits, but also to curtail union workers' collective bargaining rights.

A far-reaching 2018 Supreme Court decision allows government workers to opt out of paying union dues or fees even if they are represented in collective bargaining and receive union services. While renewed organizing efforts have increased the rate of unionization of public employees, especially schoolteachers, the change does not equal the number of government workers in jobs covered by union contracts who are discontinuing their dues (Maher 2019).

In an unusual pro-union trend, beginning in 2015 the National Labor Relations Board made it easier for fast-food workers to organize. The ruling stipulated that employees may negotiate with a corporate headquarters even if a franchise owner operates the individual outlet where they work. Challenges to the ruling are likely, and even if the change is permanent, collective bargaining will not be easy (Schreiber and Strom 2015).

During the coronavirus pandemic as layoffs mounted, uncertainty grew: future job security, limited health and leave benefits, and workplace safety were all called into question. As a result, unions in the United States and other industrial nations perceived renewed interest in joining and organizing. Whether this will materialize remains to be seen, as the union organizations themselves took

significant economic hits during the pandemic (Roosevelt 2020; Wallender 2020).

In Europe, labor unions tend to play a major role in elections. One of the major parties in Great Britain, in fact, is called the Labour Party. Unions play a lesser role in U.S. politics, although they have recently been attacked for their large financial contributions to political campaigns. In addition to the role of unions in national politics, international trade unions sometimes speak out on common issues. They have condemned "corporate grand theft"—a reference to corporate executives who spend lavishly on themselves while laying off workers. Despite efforts dating back to Karl Marx and Friedrich Engels's call for the workers of all countries to unite, no global union has emerged (International Trade Union Confederation 2009).

Take the Issue with You

1. What unions are represented in your community? Have you been aware of union activity? Has there been any opposition to the unions on the part of local government?

2. Why should employees who provide essential public services, such as nurses, teachers, and police officers, be allowed to organize into a union? What impact does union membership have on their representation if they cannot strike?

3. Should state and local officials be allowed to reduce government workers' retirement benefits and take away their right to collective bargaining?

MASTERING THIS CHAPTER

Summary

Social interaction refers to the ways in which people respond to one another. **Social structure** refers to the way in which a society is organized into predictable relationships. This chapter examines the five basic elements of social structure: **statuses, social roles, groups, social networks,** and **social institutions.**

1. People shape their social reality based on what they learn through their **social interactions.** Social change comes from redefining or reconstructing social reality.

2. An **ascribed status** is generally assigned to a person at birth, whereas an **achieved status** is attained largely through one's own effort. Some ascribed statuses, such as race and gender, can function as **master statuses** that affect a person's potential to achieve a certain professional or social status.

3. With each distinctive status—whether ascribed or achieved—come particular **social roles,** the set of expectations for people who occupy that status.

4. Much of our social behavior takes place in **groups.** When we find ourselves identifying closely with a group, it is probably a **primary group.** A **secondary group** is more formal and impersonal.

5. People tend to see the world in terms of **in-groups** and **out-groups,** a perception often fostered by the very groups to which they belong.

6. **Reference groups** set and enforce standards of conduct and serve as a source of comparison for people's evaluations of themselves and others.

7. Interactionist researchers have noted that groups allow **coalitions** to form and serve as links to **social networks** and their vast resources.

8. **Social institutions** fulfill essential functions, such as replacing personnel, training new recruits, and preserving order. The mass media, the government, the economy, the family, and the health care system are all examples of social institutions.

9. Conflict theorists charge that social institutions help to maintain the privileges of the powerful while contributing to the powerlessness of others.

10. Interactionist theorists stress that our social behavior is conditioned by the roles and statuses we accept, the groups to which we belong, and the institutions within which we function.

11. As societies have become more complex, large **formal organizations** have become more powerful and pervasive.

12. Max Weber argued that in its ideal form, every **bureaucracy** has five basic characteristics: division of labor, hierarchical authority, written rules

and regulations, impersonality, and employment based on technical qualifications. Carefully constructed bureaucratic policies can be undermined or redefined by an organization's informal structure, however.

13. Émile Durkheim thought that social structure depends on the division of labor in a society. According to Durkheim, societies with minimal division of labor have a collective consciousness called **mechanical solidarity**; those with greater division of labor show an interdependence called **organic solidarity.**

14. Ferdinand Tönnies distinguished the close-knit community of *Gemeinschaft* from the impersonal mass society of *Gesellschaft*.

15. Gerhard Lenski thinks that a society's social structure changes as its culture and technology become more sophisticated, a process he calls **sociocultural evolution.**

16. Over the past half century, major shifts in the economy have caused **labor union** membership to decline.

Key Terms

Achieved status A social position that a person attains largely through his or her own efforts. (page 104)

Agrarian society The most technologically advanced form of preindustrial society. Members engage primarily in the production of food, but increase their crop yields through technological innovations such as the plow. (122)

Alienation A condition of estrangement or dissociation from the surrounding society. (115)

Ascribed status A social position assigned to a person by society without regard for the person's unique talents or characteristics. (103)

Bureaucracy A component of formal organization that uses rules and hierarchical ranking to achieve efficiency. (115)

Bureaucratization The process by which a group, organization, or social movement becomes increasingly bureaucratic. (117)

Classical theory An approach to the study of formal organizations that views workers as being motivated almost entirely by economic rewards. (119)

Coalition A temporary or permanent alliance geared toward a common goal. (110)

Formal organization A group designed for a special purpose and structured for maximum efficiency. (114)

Gemeinschaft A term used by Ferdinand Tönnies to describe a close-knit community, often found in rural areas, in which strong personal bonds unite members. (120)

Gesellschaft A term used by Ferdinand Tönnies to describe a community, often urban, that is large and impersonal, with little commitment to the group or consensus on values. (120)

Goal displacement Overzealous conformity to official regulations of a bureaucracy. (116)

Group Any number of people with similar norms, values, and expectations who interact with one another on a regular basis. (107)

Horticultural society A preindustrial society in which people plant seeds and crops rather than merely subsist on available foods. (122)

Human relations approach An approach to the study of formal organizations that emphasizes the role of people, communication, and participation in a bureaucracy and tends to focus on the informal structure of the organization. (119)

Hunting-and-gathering society A preindustrial society in which people rely on whatever foods and fibers are readily available in order to survive. (121)

Hyperconsumerism The practice of buying more than we need or want, and often more than we can afford; a preoccupation of postmodern consumers. (123)

Ideal type A construct or model for evaluating specific cases. (115)

Industrial society A society that depends on mechanization to produce its goods and services. (122)

In-group Any group or category to which people feel they belong. (109)

Iron law of oligarchy A principle of organizational life developed by Robert Michels, under which even a democratic organization will eventually develop into a bureaucracy ruled by a few individuals. (119)

Labor union Organized workers who share either the same skill or the same employer. (124)

Master status A status that dominates others and thereby determines a person's general position in society. (104)

McDonaldization The process by which the principles of bureaucratization have increasingly shaped organizations worldwide. (118)

Mechanical solidarity A collective consciousness that emphasizes group solidarity, characteristic of societies with minimal division of labor. (120)

Organic solidarity A collective consciousness that rests on mutual interdependence, characteristic of societies with a complex division of labor. (120)

Out-group A group or category to which people feel they do not belong. (109)

Peter principle A principle of organizational life, originated by Laurence J. Peter, according to which every employee within a hierarchy tends to rise to his or her level of incompetence. (116)

Postindustrial society A society whose economic system is engaged primarily in the processing and control of information. (122)

Postmodern society A technologically sophisticated society that is preoccupied with consumer goods and media images. (123)

Primary group A small group characterized by intimate, face-to-face association and cooperation. (107)

Reference group Any group that individuals use as a standard for evaluating themselves and their own behavior. (109)

Role conflict The situation that occurs when incompatible expectations arise from two or more social positions held by the same person. (106)

Role exit The process of disengagement from a role that is central to one's self-identity in order to establish a new role and identity. (106)

Role strain The difficulty that arises when the same social position imposes conflicting demands and expectations. (106)

Scientific management approach Another name for the classical theory of formal organizations. (119)

Secondary group A formal, impersonal group in which there is little social intimacy or mutual understanding. (108)

Social institution An organized pattern of beliefs and behavior centered on basic social needs. (111)

Social interaction The ways in which people respond to one another. (101)

Social network A series of social relationships that link a person directly to others, and through them indirectly to still more people. (111)

Social role A set of expectations for people who occupy a given social position or status. (105)

Social structure The way in which a society is organized into predictable relationships. (101)

Sociocultural evolution Long-term social trends resulting from the interplay of continuity, innovation, and selection. (120)

Status A term used by sociologists to refer to any of the full range of socially defined positions within a large group or society. (103)

Technology Cultural information about the ways in which the material resources of the environment may be used to satisfy human needs and desires. (121)

Trained incapacity The tendency of workers in a bureaucracy to become so specialized that they develop blind spots and fail to notice obvious problems. (115)

TAKING SOCIOLOGY with you

1. List both ascribed and achieved statuses of various characters in a show you're watching or a book you're reading. Note which seem to have the most influence on their lives and why. Are there certain circumstances when one status appears to have more influence than the others? Are any of them conflicting, with some connoting higher social position and some lower? Is one of them a master status (one that society deems as counting more than the others)? Does the fact that the one that is a master status seem fair? Share your findings with the class.

2. On social media, look for examples of affiliations with both primary and secondary groups. Which do you find the most of? Why do you suppose this is? Share your findings with the class.

3. Listen to a podcast or TED Talk on the influence of social networks. Share a summary of the podcast with the class.

4. **Writing Sociology.** Research an institutional community. Find out how it fulfills one or more of the five major functions of survival—replacing personnel, teaching new recruits, producing and distributing goods and services, preserving order, providing and maintaining a sense of purpose. Write a summary of your findings and share it with the class.

Self-Quiz

Read each question carefully and then select the best answer.

1. In the United States, we expect that cab drivers will know how to get around a city. This expectation is an example of which of the following?
   a. role conflict
   b. role strain
   c. social role
   d. master status

2. What occurs when incompatible expectations arise from two or more social positions held by the same person?
   a. role conflict
   b. role strain
   c. role exit
   d. both a and b

3. In sociological terms, what do we call any number of people with similar norms, values, and expectations who interact with one another on a regular basis?
   a. a category
   b. a group
   c. an aggregate
   d. a society

4. The Shakers, a religious sect that came to the United States in 1774, has seen their group's membership diminish significantly due to their inability to
   a. teach new recruits.
   b. preserve order.
   c. replace personnel.
   d. provide and maintain a sense of purpose.

5. Which sociological perspective argues that the present organization of social institutions is no accident?
   a. the functionalist perspective
   b. the conflict perspective
   c. the interactionist perspective
   d. the global perspective

6. The U.S. Postal Service, the Boston Pops orchestra, and the school you attend are all examples of
   a. primary groups.
   b. reference groups.
   c. formal organizations.
   d. triads.

7. One positive consequence of bureaucracy is that it reduces bias. Reduction of bias results from which characteristic of a bureaucracy?
   a. impersonality
   b. hierarchy of authority
   c. written rules and regulations
   d. employment based on technical qualifications

8. According to the Peter principle,
   a. all bureaucracies are notoriously inefficient.
   b. if something *can* go wrong, it *will*.
   c. every employee within a hierarchy tends to rise to his or her level of incompetence.
   d. all line workers get burned in the end.

9. Social control in what Ferdinand Tönnies termed a *Gemeinschaft* community is maintained through all but which of the following means?
   a. moral persuasion
   b. gossip
   c. legally defined punishment
   d. gestures

10. Sociologist Daniel Bell uses which of the following terms to refer to a society whose economic system is engaged primarily in the processing and control of information?
   a. gathering
   b. horticultural
   c. industrial
   d. postindustrial

11. The term _____ _____ refers to the way in which a society is organized into predictable relationships.

12. The African American activist Malcolm X wrote in his autobiography that his position as a Black man, a(n) _____ status, was an obstacle to his dream of becoming a lawyer, a(n) _____ status.

13. Sociologist Helen Rose Fuchs Ebaugh developed the term _____ _____ to describe the process of disengagement from a role that is central to one's self-identity in order to establish a new role and identity.

14. _____ groups often emerge in the workplace among those who share special understandings about their occupation.

15. In many cases, people model their behavior after groups to which they may not belong. These groups are called _____ groups.

16. Any permanent group or society must provide and distribute desired goods and services to its members. This idea is an example of the _____ perspective.

17. Max Weber developed a(n) _____ _____ of bureaucracy, which reflects the most characteristic aspects of all human organizations.

18. According to Émile Durkheim, societies with a minimal division of labor are characterized by _____ solidarity, while societies with a complex division of labor are characterized by _____ solidarity.

19. In Gerhard Lenski's theory of sociocultural evolution, a society's level of _____ is critical to the way it is organized.

20. A(n) _____ society is a technologically sophisticated society that is preoccupied with consumer goods and media images.

_____

6

Mass Media and Social Media

YinYang/E+/Getty Images

Media cross boundaries and cultures. Increased use of streaming allows people to access all types of media at home and on the go.

▶ INSIDE

Sociological Perspectives on the Media

The Audience

The Media's Global Reach

Social Policy and the Media: Censorship

130

Yellow Dog Productions/The Image Bank/
Getty Images

Think about the social media you use today. How do they affect the way you interact with your social world?

Sociologist and psychologist Sherry Turkle feels that our continual use of social media has radically transformed the way we present ourselves to one another.

66 Over and over I hear, 'I would rather text than talk.' And what I'm seeing is that people get so used to being short-changed out of real conversation, so used to getting by with less, that they've become almost willing to dispense with people altogether.

People will readily say that in face-to-face conversation they learn how to get on with other people and gather important understandings about their children, spouses, parents and partners. And yet they will also say they are happy to use technology to flee these conversations. Why? Because face-to-face conversations are difficult. Awkward. Spontaneous. Unscripted. Messy. One young man tells me he will do anything to avoid a conversation. 'Conversation? I'll tell you what's wrong with conversation. It takes place in real time, and you can't control what you are going to say.'

Among family and friends, among colleagues and lovers, we turn to our phones instead of each other. We readily admit we would rather send an electronic message or mail than commit to a face-to-face meeting or a telephone call.

We hide from each other even when we're constantly connected to each other. For on our screens, we are tempted to present ourselves as we would like to be. Of course, performance is part of any meeting, anywhere, but online and at our leisure, it is easy to compose, edit, and improve as we revise.

We say we turn to our phones when we're 'bored.' And we often find ourselves bored because we have become accustomed to a constant feed of connection, information, and entertainment. We are forever elsewhere. At class or at church or business meetings, we pay attention to what interests us and then when it doesn't, we look to our devices to find something that does. There is now a word in the dictionary called 'phubbing.' It means maintaining eye contact while texting. My students tell me they do it all the time and that it's not that hard.

We begin to think of ourselves as a tribe of one, loyal to our own party. We check our messages during a quiet moment or when the pull of the online world simply feels irresistible.

These days, our online practices put us in a world where the real question is 'What do you have to give today?' We exist alongside digital representations of ourselves—digital doubles—that are useful to different parties at different times, or for some, at a time to be determined. The digital self is archived forever.

Gradually, we have come to learn all of this. . . . We have learned more—that the calls, locations, and online searches of ordinary Americans are monitored. But almost everything about this process remains as secret as possible, shrouded under the mantle of national security or the claim of proprietary interest. Exactly what is taken? In what form? How long is it kept? What is it used for? What most people have come to understand is that this is out of their hands.

What happens to conversation in these circumstances? One thing is that people tend to forget their circumstances. This is one of the great paradoxes of digital conversation: It feels private despite the fact that you are onstage. If you are on Gmail, your email is searched for clues for how to best sell to you, but for the individual, the experience of being on email remains intimate. You face a glowing screen and you feel alone. The experience of digital communication is out of sync with its reality. Online you are under a kind of surveillance. 99

Source: Turkle 2017: xxii.

This is one of the great paradoxes of digital conversation: It feels private despite the fact that you are onstage.

In this excerpt from her book *Alone Together: Why We Expect More from Technology and Less from Each Other* as well as her other work, Turkle points out how social media invades our everyday social interaction and how our reliance on it potentially subjects us to continual surveillance. In particular, social media changes the way we relate to others: although digital communications pervade our lives, they cannot substitute for face-to-face communications. And their very pervasiveness threatens to rob us of our privacy.

Media is a broad area that fundamentally affects our participation in society and society itself. Media can be divided into mass media and social media, although the line between them is not finely drawn. **Mass media** embrace print and electronic means of communication that carry messages to widespread audiences. Advertising is also a form of mass media. **Social media** refers to the websites and online applications that enable people to create and share content or to participate in social networking.

The social impact of the media is obvious. Consider a few examples. Today, you can watch or listen to any content whenever and wherever you want, and screen time has gone well beyond television viewing to include time spent on smartphones. Candidates for political office use social media to get their message out to voters and rely on media consultants to project a winning image. World leaders use all forms of media for political advantage, whether to gain territory or to bid on hosting the Olympics. And in parts of Africa and Asia, coronavirus pandemic public health projects owe much of their success to media campaigns.

Few aspects of society are as central as the media. Through the media we expand our understanding of people and events beyond what we experience in person. The media inform us about different cultures and lifestyles and about the latest forms of technology. For sociologists, the key questions about media are how they affect our social institutions and how they influence our social behavior.

Why are the media so influential? Who benefits from media influence, and why? How do we maintain cultural and ethical standards in the face of negative media images? In this chapter we will consider the ways sociology helps us to answer these questions. First we will look at how proponents of the various sociological perspectives view the media. Then we will examine who makes up the media's audience, not just at home but around the world. The chapter closes with a Social Policy section on censorship on the Internet.

Sociological Perspectives on the Media

Over the past decade, new technologies have made new forms of media available to U.S. households. These new technologies have changed people's viewing and listening habits. People spend a lot of time with the media, more and more of it on the Internet. Media consumers have moved away from television and toward digital images downloaded to their computers and portable devices. Podcasts and music streaming compete with radio. Increasingly, consumers of media learn not just about the famous but about ordinary people by viewing their Facebook pages or by keeping in touch with their friends via Instagram or Twitter.

How do people's viewing and listening habits affect their social behavior? In the following sections we'll use the four major sociological perspectives to examine the impact of the media and changes in their usage patterns.

Functionalist Perspective

One obvious function of the media is to entertain. Except for clearly identified news or educational programming, we often think the explicit purpose of the media is to occupy our leisure time—from newspaper comics and online gaming to streaming music on the Internet. While that is true, the media have other important functions. They also socialize us, enforce social norms, confer status, and promote consumption. An important dysfunction of the media is that they may act as a narcotic, desensitizing us to distressing events (Lazarsfeld and Merton 1948; C. Wright 1986).

Agent of Socialization The media increase social cohesion by presenting a common, more or less standardized view of culture through mass communication. Early in the 20th century, sociologist Robert Park (1922) studied how newspapers helped immigrants to the United States adjust to their environment by

Kaspars Grinvalds/123RF

President Donald Trump transformed White House communications with his practice of tweeting directly to the public everything from announcements of staff changes, diplomatic overtures, and personal views. He tweeted about seven times a day during his first year in office (2017); by 2020, he averaged 35 times a day.

changing their customary habits and teaching them the opinions of people in their new home country. Unquestionably, the media play a significant role in providing a collective experience for members of society. Think about how the media bring together members of a community or even a nation by broadcasting important events and ceremonies (such as inaugurations, press conferences, parades, state funerals, and the Olympics) and by covering disasters.

Which media outlets did people turn to in the aftermath of the September 11, 2001, tragedy? Television, radio, and the telephone were the primary means by which people in the United States bonded. But the Internet also played a prominent role. About half of all Internet users—more than 5 million people—received some kind of news about the attacks online (D. Miller and Darlington 2002).

Today, the news media have moved further online. Afghans of all political persuasions now connect with the Muslim commu-

TABLE 6-1 CELEBRITY STATUS, AS MEASURED BY NUMBER OF GLOBAL GOOGLE SEARCHES

2010	2013	2019
Broadimage/Shutterstock	Oscar Max/Alamy Stock Photo	Joe Sargent/Sport/Getty Images
1. Justin Bieber	1. Nelson Mandela	1. Antonio Brown
2. Katy Perry	2. Paul Walker	2. Neymar
3. Selena Gomez	3. Malala Yousafzai	3. James Charles
4. Kim Kardashian	4. James Gandolfini	4. Jussie Smollett
5. Eminem	5. Miley Cyrus	5. Kevin Hart
6. Lady Gaga	6. Oscar Pistorius	6. Billie Eilish
7. Miley Cyrus	7. Jennifer Lawrence	7. Greta Thunberg
8. Taylor Lautner	8. Aaron Hernandez	8. R. Kelly
9. Megan Fox	9. Charlie Hunnam	9. Joaquin Phoenix
10. Robert Pattinson	10. Adrian Peterson	10. Jordyn Woods

Think about It In what way do Google searches reflect the status people enjoy in the media?

Source: Google ranks based on Google Trends 2010, Trending 2013, Trends 2019.

nity overseas to gain both social and financial support. In the realm of popular culture, a spontaneous sharing crashed Twitter in 2014 as Oscar host Ellen DeGeneres herded Meryl Streep, Jennifer Lawrence, Bradley Cooper, Angelina Jolie, Lupita Nyongia and others into a selfie. The sheer number of A-listers packed into the shot apparently caused the social media platform to crash, leaving thousands of Twitter users temporarily locked out (Altia News 2017).

Some are concerned about the media's socialization function, however. For instance, many people worry about the effect of using television as a babysitter and the impact of violent video games on children's behavior. Some people adopt a blame-the-media mentality, holding the media accountable for anything that goes wrong, especially with young people. Yet the media also have positive effects on young people. For young and even not-so-young adults, for example, a new sort of tribalism is emerging online, in which communities develop around common interests or shared identities (Tyrene Adams and Smith 2008; American Academy of Pediatrics 2020).

Enforcer of Social Norms The media often reaffirm proper behavior by showing what happens to people who act in a way that violates societal expectations. These messages are conveyed when the bad guy gets clobbered in cartoons or is thrown in jail on *CSI*. Yet the media also sometimes glorify disapproved behavior, whether it is physical violence, disrespect to a teacher, or drug use.

The media also play a critical role in human sexuality. For example, programs have been created to persuade teens not to send nude images of themselves to selected friends. Such images often go viral (that is, spread across the Internet) and may be used to harass teens and their parents. To define normative behavior regarding these images, one organization has launched a "That's not cool" campaign, complete with stalker messages that can be e-mailed to those who misuse such images. The widespread dissemination of compromising images that were meant to be shared only among close friends is just one aspect of the social phenomenon called *cyberbullying* (Hinduja and Patchin 2015).

Another way the media confer celebrity status on individuals is by publishing information about the frequency of Internet searches. Some newspapers and websites carry regularly updated lists of the most heavily researched individuals and topics of the week. This changes dramatically over time: none of the Google top 10 people searches were in the top 10 the year before (see Table 6-1).

USE YOUR SOCIOLOGICAL IMAGINATION

You are browsing through media outlets. Are you more likely than not to go to an outlet based on the person being featured? What kind of image would attract you?

Daniel Hurlimann/Shutterstock

Product placement ("brand casting") is an increasingly important source of revenue for media and entertainment outlets. Here racecar driver Danica Patrick displays a number of brand logos, some of which have little to do with her sport.

USE YOUR SOCIOLOGICAL IMAGINATION

You are a news junkie. Where do you gather your facts or information—from newspapers, tabloids, magazines, TV newscasts, blogs, or social media? Why did you choose that medium?

With innovations in media, conferral of status can come in many ways, including through social media outlets. For example, Kim Kardashian West has over 30 million "likes" on Facebook and about 175 million followers on Instagram. Her celebrity appearances online take place 24/7: they do not await the publication of a weekly magazine. And on social media, unlike traditional media, celebrities can respond with their own "likes," comments, and retweets to keep their status alive and interactive.

Promotion of Consumption Postmodern societies are characterized by **hyperconsumerism,** a term coined by the French sociologist Jean Baudrillard (1929–2007) to refer to the practice of buying more than we need or want, and often more than we can afford. The media certainly promote this behavior pattern. Twenty thousand commercials a year—that is the number the average child in the United States watches on television alone, not to mention other media platforms.

Young people cannot escape commercial messages. They show up on high school scoreboards, at rock concerts, and as banners on web pages. They also surface in the form of *product placement*. Product placement is nothing new. In 1951 *The African Queen* prominently displayed Gordon's Gin aboard the boat carrying Katharine Hepburn and Humphrey Bogart. However, commercial promotion has become far more common today: from Reese's Pieces in *E.T. The Extraterrestrial* to AOC, a Taiwanese electronics company, in *The Martian*.

Using advertising to develop a brand name with global appeal is an especially powerful way to encourage consumption. U.S.

corporations have been particularly successful in creating global brands. An analysis of the 100 most successful brands worldwide, each of which derives at least 30 percent of its earnings outside the home country, shows that 48 of them originated in the United States; 52 others come from 14 different countries (Figure 6-1).

Media advertising has several clear functions: it supports the economy, provides information about products, and underwrites the cost of media. In some cases, advertising becomes part of the entertainment. A national survey showed that 24 percent of viewers watch the Super Bowl primarily for the commercials. Yet advertising's functions are related to dysfunctions. Media advertising contributes to a consumer culture that creates needs and raises unrealistic expectations of what is required to be happy or satisfied. Moreover, because the media depend heavily on advertising revenue, advertisers can influence media content (Marketing Charts 2018).

Dysfunction: The Narcotizing Effect In addition to the functions just noted, the media perform a *dysfunction*. Sociologists Paul Lazarsfeld and Robert Merton (1948) created the term **narcotizing dysfunction** to refer to the phenomenon in which the media provide such massive amounts of coverage that the audience becomes numb and fails to act on the information, regardless of how compelling the issue. Interested citizens may take in the information but make no decision or take no action.

Consider how often the media initiate a great outpouring of philanthropic support in response to natural disasters or family crises. But then what happens? Research shows that as time passes, viewer fatigue sets in. The media audience becomes numb, desensitized to the suffering, and may even conclude that a solution to the crisis has been found (Baran and Davis 2015).

The media's narcotizing dysfunction was identified 70 years ago, when just a few homes had television—well before the advent of electronic media. At that time, the dysfunction went largely unnoticed, but today commentators often point out the ill effects of addiction to screen time, especially among young people. Street crime, explicit sex, war, and HIV/AIDS apparently are such overwhelming topics that some in the audience may feel they have acted—or at the very least learned all they need to know—simply through social media.

MAPPING LIFE WORLDWIDE

FIGURE 6-1   BRANDING THE GLOBE

Based on revenue and name recognition, these are the brands that dominate the global marketplace. Just 15 nations account for all the top 100 brands.

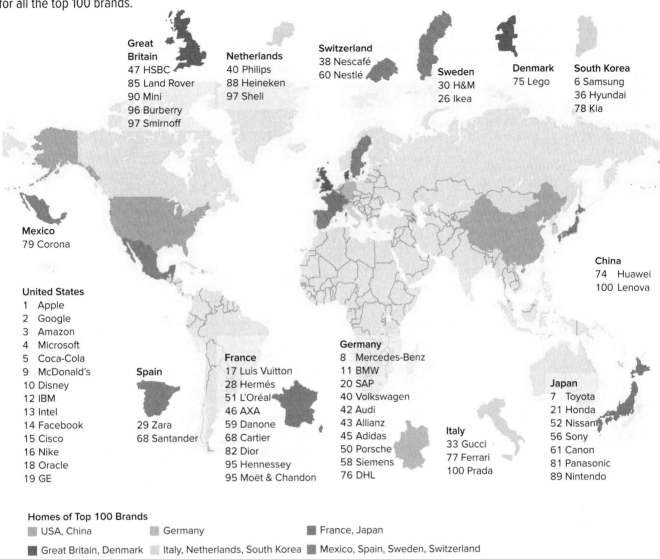

Great Britain
47 HSBC
85 Land Rover
90 Mini
96 Burberry
97 Smirnoff

Netherlands
40 Philips
88 Heineken
97 Shell

Switzerland
38 Nescafé
60 Nestlé

Sweden
30 H&M
26 Ikea

Denmark
75 Lego

South Korea
6 Samsung
36 Hyundai
78 Kia

Mexico
79 Corona

United States
1   Apple
2   Google
3   Amazon
4   Microsoft
5   Coca-Cola
9   McDonald's
10 Disney
12 IBM
13 Intel
14 Facebook
15 Cisco
16 Nike
18 Oracle
19 GE

Spain
29 Zara
68 Santander

France
17 Luis Vuitton
28 Hermés
51 L'Oréal
46 AXA
59 Danone
68 Cartier
82 Dior
95 Hennessey
95 Moët & Chandon

Germany
8   Mercedes-Benz
11 BMW
20 SAP
40 Volkswagen
42 Audi
43 Allianz
45 Adidas
50 Porsche
58 Siemens
76 DHL

Italy
33 Gucci
77 Ferrari
100 Prada

China
74   Huawei
100 Lenova

Japan
7   Toyota
21 Honda
52 Nissan
56 Sony
61 Canon
81 Panasonic
89 Nintendo

Homes of Top 100 Brands
- USA, China
- Germany
- France, Japan
- Great Britain, Denmark
- Italy, Netherlands, South Korea
- Mexico, Spain, Sweden, Switzerland

Think about It How many of these brands do you recognize? Did any of the countries of ownership surprise you?

Note: Map shows the top 100 brands in the world in 2019 by country of ownership, except for the United States, for which only brands in the top 20 are shown. The United States has a total of 48 of the 100 leading brands, down from 54 in 2017. Just 14 nations account for the top 100 brands.

Source: Interbrand 2019.

Conflict Perspective

Conflict theorists emphasize that the media reflect and even exacerbate many of the divisions in our society and world, including those based on gender, race, ethnicity, and social class. They point in particular to the media's ability to decide what is transmitted, through a process called *gatekeeping*. Conflict theorists also stress the way powerful groups transmit society's dominant ideology through the media and the technological gap between the haves and have-nots, which limits people's access to the Internet.

Gatekeeping What story pops up when you turn on your phone? What motion picture plays on three screens rather than one at the local cineplex? What picture isn't released at all? Behind these decisions are powerful figures—publishers, editors, and other media moguls.

The media constitute a form of big business in which profits are generally more important than the quality of the programming. Within the media, a relatively small number of people control what eventually reaches the audience through **gatekeeping.**

OUR WIRED WORLD

6-1   Inside the Bubble: Internet Search Filters

Through Facebook, Classmates, and LinkedIn, the Internet allows us to reach out to those who are different from ourselves—or does it? Today, the search engines we use to navigate the Internet are personalized. Google, for example, uses as many as 57 sources of information, including location and past searches, to make calculated guesses about the sites a person might like to visit. Its searches have been personalized in this way since 2009. In 2012 Google carried the process one step further by collecting information from the websites that people "friend" through social media, and then using that information to direct their web searches. Google sees this personalization of its searches as a service, one that helps people to cut through irrelevant information and quickly find what they are looking for.

A 2019 analysis showed some troubling results when different search engines are used. For example, Google will likely autocorrect the query of "Abortion is" with "legal" but Bing is just as likely to say "immoral" or "bad." In another case, search engines might complete "Immigrants are" with "law abiding" or "increasing taxes" or even "animals." When these results were made public search, engines immediately corrected the most troubling findings, but this correction still leaves out tens of thousands of filters that are problematic.

Although Google's approach may at first sound convenient, critics charge that it can trap users in their own worlds, by routing them ever more narrowly in the same direction. In his book *The Filter Bubble*, online political activist Eli Pariser complains that when a search engine filters our searches, it encloses us in a kind of invisible bubble that limits what we see to what we are already familiar with. Thus, we are not likely to

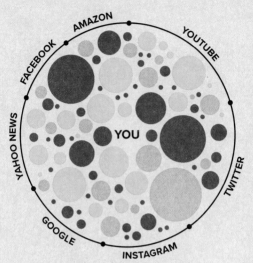

When a search engine filters our searches, it encloses us in a kind of invisible bubble that limits what we see to what we are already familiar with.

discover people, places, and ideas that are outside our comfort zone. Secure in our online bubble, which we may not even realize is there, we visit only safe, predictable sites.

What is wrong with that result? Given a choice, most of us go only to restaurants whose food we enjoy, read and listen to only those books and radio programs we know we like. Yet because of the way the online world is filtered, many if not most people filter out truly important events. Stories or in-depth research about Afghanistan, world poverty, and the continuing refugee crisis do not get viewed, much less read. Syria and policies about new policing methods must

compete in the same search pool with cat pictures and Candy Crush and everything else people search for online. The solution—according to Pariser—is to figure out how to make the truly important issues more engaging and compelling.

Until recently the personalization of social media has been viewed as either directed by the user or carried out for commercial purposes. The 2016 presidential election changed this understanding, as it emerged that Russia covertly placed thousands of political advertisements on the Facebook or Twitter accounts of individuals who were thought to be susceptible to the inaccurate messages in the ads. These "advertisements" mostly either attacked Hillary Clinton or praised Donald Trump. In this instance the filter bubble was infiltrated for devious political purposes.

One possibility, according to researchers at MIT and Yahoo Labs, is to include contrasting or opposing views in online searches. Although their work is just beginning, the hope is that someday, despite the technological challenges, the Internet will become less isolating and more open to different perspectives.

LET'S DISCUSS

1. How could you craft an Internet search to obtain a wider range of facts and opinions about a topic?
2. Choose a topic of interest to you and do an Internet search on it; ask several friends or classmates to do the same. Do your results differ? In what way?

Sources: Bakshy et al. 2016; Bruni 2016; *Economist* 2019d; Graells-Garrido et al. 2016; Grind et al. 2019; Hess 2017; Pariser 2011a, 2011b; Shane and Isaac 2017.

This term describes how material must travel through a series of gates (or checkpoints) before reaching the public. Thus, a select few decide what images to bring to a broad audience. In many countries the government plays a gatekeeping role. Even the champions of Internet freedom, who pride themselves on allowing people to pass freely through the gate, may quickly channel them in certain directions (see Box 6-1).

Gatekeeping, which prevails in all kinds of media, is not a new concept. The term was coined by a journalism scholar in the

1940s to refer to the way that small-town newspaper editors control which events receive public attention. As sociologist C. Wright Mills ([1956] 2000b) observed, the real power of the media is that they can control what is being presented. In the recording industry, gatekeepers may reject a popular local band because it competes with a group already on their label. Even if the band is recorded, radio programmers may reject the music because it does not fit the station's sound. Television programmers may keep a pilot for a new TV series off the

Traveler1116/Getty Images

In 2015 a shooter killed nine people in an African American church in South Carolina's capitol of Charleston. The gunman's online presence displayed racist language and the Confederate battle flag. In 2020, protesters across the nation called for removal of all symbols of the Confederacy, including tributes to its leaders.

air because they believe it does not appeal to the target audience (which is sometimes determined by advertising sponsors). Similar decisions are made by gatekeepers in the publishing industry.

Gatekeeping is not as dominant in at least one form of media, the Internet. You can send virtually any message, podcast, or video to social media, and create a web page or blog to advance any argument, including one that insists the earth is flat. The Internet is a means of quickly disseminating information (or misinformation) without going through any significant gatekeeping process.

Nevertheless, the Internet is not totally without restrictions. In many nations, laws regulate content on issues such as gambling, pornography, and even politics. And popular Internet service providers will terminate accounts for offensive behavior. After the terrorist attacks in 2001, eBay did not allow people to sell parts of the World Trade Center via its online auction. In 2015, nine people were killed inside an African Methodist Church in South Carolina. The shooter had posted an online racist manifesto illustrated with the Confederate flag. In the wake of the tragedy, eBay, along with other retail outlets, banned the sale of Confederate flags and their images. Despite, or maybe because of, such gatekeeping, growing numbers of people are involved in online communities.

Today, many countries try to control political dissent by restricting citizens' access to online comments unfavorable to the government. In recent years, authoritarian regimes throughout the world have temporarily or permanently suspended access to the Internet to thwart those they felt were attempting to undermine the central government. In addition, political parties or even national militaries may dispense false reports. In 2019 Facebook tried to reign in fabricated content posing as "news" of Indian and Pakistani atrocities toward each other. The reports were eventually linked to various Indian and Pakistani organizations (Goel and Frenkel 2019).

Dominant Ideology: Constructing Reality

Conflict theorists argue that the mass media maintain the privileges of certain groups. Moreover, powerful groups may limit the media's representation of others to protect their own interests. The term **dominant ideology** describes a set of cultural beliefs and practices that helps to maintain powerful social, economic, and political interests. The media transmit messages that essentially define what we regard as the real world, even though those images frequently vary from the ones that the larger society experiences.

Media decision makers are overwhelmingly white, male, and wealthy. It may come as no surprise, then, that the media tend to ignore the lives and ambitions of subordinate groups, among them working-class people, African Americans, Hispanics, gays and lesbians, people with disabilities, overweight people, and older people. Worse yet, media content may create false images or stereotypes of these groups that then become accepted as accurate portrayals of reality. **Stereotypes** are unreliable generalizations about all members of a group that do not recognize individual differences within the group. Some broadcasters use stereotypes deliberately in a desperate bid for attention, with the winking approval of media executives.

This issue of stereotyping has emerged online with apps that force people to make choices about their racial or gender identity. Based on these choices, some programs move people in certain directions in their online selections, much as the filter bubble in search engines described earlier (Wachter-Boettcher 2017).

Queer theorists have long studied the way the media present homosexuality. They have analyzed the frequent invisibility of homosexual characters, as well as the problematic ways in which they are made visible. From the perspective of queer theorists, significant strides have been made in the portrayal of nonheterosexuality as a normal and possible alternative to heterosexuality. Still, stigmatization of gays and lesbians persists, in the media as well as in society. A study of the 1,100 most popular films from 2007 to 2017 showed that of 4,403 characters, only 31, or less than 1 percent of the total, were lesbian, gay, or bisexual (Smith et al. 2018).

TAKING SOCIOLOGY TO WORK

Lindsey Wallem, **Social Media Consultant**

Lindsey Wallem graduated from DePaul University with a major in sociology. She chose sociology because she wanted to help people, perhaps as a social worker for a nonprofit organization. Then, in her junior year, when her political science professor offered extra credit for work on a political campaign, Wallem's life took an unexpected turn. "I showed up at the Obama headquarters just as they were moving into their downtown Chicago office," Wallem remembers. "I was assigned to the New Media department, using Facebook and MySpace to reach out to voters." At the time, the use of social media tools in a political campaign was groundbreaking. "It was an exciting place to be," she recalls. "I stayed on as a volunteer in New Media through the end of the campaign. When I graduated in 2008, I used that experience to pitch my social media services to nonprofits."

Today, Wallem is a social media manager for several nonprofit organizations in the Chicago area. She enjoys using her expertise in online organizing to help these worthy organizations grow. Wallem's work with a nonprofit that fights homelessness has been particularly satisfying to her. In 2010–11, her clients joined a coalition of organizations dedicated to creating more affordable housing in the city. "My role was to attend city council meetings and 'live-tweet' the proceedings for supporters who couldn't be in the room," she explains. "On the day when a version of our legislation was passed, it was an exciting task indeed!"

Wallem also teaches an online course in social media to high school students, through the Gifted LearningLinks program at Northwestern University. In the first few weeks of the course, she draws from her

Courtesy of Lindsey Wallem

old textbooks to give students a brief lesson in sociological theory. Then she asks them to apply the theory to Facebook and Twitter. "For the next generation, the Internet is the new frontier," she muses. "It's pretty amazing to see the perspectives of these 'digital natives' at work."

Wallem finds that her background in sociology is quite relevant to her career. "I spend much of my workweek interacting with communities on Facebook and Twitter, building a content schedule, and looking for content to share with my audience," she explains. To measure and track the success of her social media campaigns—a necessity in online organizing—Wallem relies on her training in statistics. "Metrics in social media is more than just counting the number of 'Likes' you have," she notes. "You need to look at the data and determine what kind of story it is telling you, what your audience is like and what they need from you." Wallem also applies what she learned in her senior capstone course, Visual Sociology, which taught her to use photography or video to tell a story about a sociological trend. "I use this tactic every day on Facebook and YouTube—visuals are what grab attention and add weight to the message you are trying to convey," she says.

LET'S DISCUSS

1. Have you ever used social media to participate in an online campaign? If so, how did you participate—by donating money, for example, or attending a fundraising event?
2. How might you use social media in your own career?

Television also offers many examples of this tendency to ignore reality. How many overweight TV characters can you name? Even though in real life 1 out of every 4 women is obese (30 or more pounds over a healthy body weight), only 3 out of 100 TV characters are portrayed as obese. Heavyset television characters have fewer romances, talk less about sex, eat more often, and are more often the object of ridicule than their thin counterparts (Hellmich 2001; J. Whyte 2010).

On the other hand, television news and other media outlets do alert people to the health implications of obesity. As with constructions of reality, whether some of this coverage is truly educational is debatable. Increasingly, the media have framed the problem not merely as an individual or personal one, but as a broad structural problem involving, for example, the manner in which food is processed and sold (Saguy and Almeling 2008).

Dominant Ideology: Whose Culture? *The Walking Dead* and *Grey's Anatomy* are big hits in France, despite that nation's pride in its "exception culturelle," which protects French film,

television, and music producers from foreign competition. In Japan, *Glee* is must-watch TV, and *Columbo* reruns still garner viewers. Those are only the legally viewed hit shows. In Latin America, where illicit downloading of TV programs is common, the most popular shows include *The X-Factor, Breaking Bad, Homeland,* and *Modern Family.* In North Korea, *Desperate Housewives* is a cult hit. Although government officials and cultural purists may decry these shows' popularity, U.S. media are still widely watched and imitated. As sociologist Todd Gitlin puts it, American popular culture is something that "people love, and love to hate" (2002:177; Statista 2018).

USE YOUR SOCIOLOGICAL IMAGINATION

How do your favorite media reflect U.S. culture as a whole? How do they reflect the culture of your local community? How do they reflect the cultures of the rest of the world?

We risk being ethnocentric if we overstress U.S. dominance, however. For example, *Survivor, Who Wants to Be a Millionaire, Big Brother,* and *Iron Chef*—immensely popular TV programs in the United States—came from Sweden, Britain, the Netherlands, and Japan, respectively. Even *American Idol* originated in Britain as *Pop Idol,* featuring Simon Cowell. And the steamy telenovelas of Mexico and other Spanish-speaking countries owe very little of their origin to the soap operas on U.S. television. Television is gradually moving away from U.S. domination and is now more likely to be locally produced (Bielby and Harrington 2008; Colucci 2008).

A related trend, the most novel one to date in this century, is the growth of **hyper-local media,** which refers to reporting that is highly local. What has been going on in that vacant lot down the street? Which Chinese takeout food is popular in your neighborhood? Why did all those police cars converge on Main Street the night before last? Hyper-local media answer these questions. The term was coined in 1991 to refer to the inclusion of local news on 24-hour cable news channels, but now more often refers to social networks such as Nextdoor and Social Street.

Today, with the development of websites and blogs such as patch.com, hyper-local media have become even more localized. In the summer of 2020 many Americans discovered the importance of hyper-local media outlets. First the coronavirus pandemic sent self-isolating individuals to local news websites to learn where people were practicing social distancing or what businesses were providing curbside pickup. Then the spontaneous protest marches in favor of racial justice that sprang up in thousands of small towns led people to hyper-local media to learn more about marches in their areas.

Nations that feel a loss of identity may try to defend against the cultural invasion from foreign countries, especially the economically dominant United States. Yet as sociologists know, audiences are not necessarily passive recipients of foreign cultural messages, either in developing nations or in industrial nations. Thus, research on consumers of cultural products like television, music, and film must be placed in social context. Although people may watch and even enjoy media content, that does not mean that they will accept values that are alien to their own (Bielby and Harrington 2008).

Many developing nations have long argued for a greatly improved two-way flow of news and information between industrial nations and developing nations. They complain that news from the Third World is scant, and what news there is reflects unfavorably on the developing nations. For example, what do you know about South America? Most people in the United States will mention the two topics that dominate the news from countries south of the border: revolution and drugs. Most know little else about the continent.

To remedy this imbalance, a resolution to monitor the news and content that cross the borders of developing nations was passed by the United Nations Educational, Scientific, and Cultural Organization (UNESCO) in the 1980s. The United States has continued to oppose UNESCO plans, even though they were globally regarded as an important step toward protecting threatened cultures and media markets in developing nations. The Trump administration withdrew from UNESCO in 2019.

The continuing opposition to media products from the United States is not limited to UNESCO or developing nations. South Korea places limits on how many days movie houses can show foreign motion pictures (primarily those from the United States). As programming is increasingly streamed, the European Union has sought to limit U.S.-based Netflix's "cultural dumping," which it regards as a threat to national cultural identity as well as to the European media industry (Baran 2015:397–398; Barbière 2014).

The Digital Divide Finally, as numerous studies have shown, advances in communications technology are not evenly distributed. Worldwide, low-income groups, racial and ethnic minorities, rural residents, and the citizens of developing countries have far less access than others to the latest technologies—a gap that is called the **digital divide.**

While many people embrace the Internet, access is not evenly distributed throughout the population. Figure 6-2 breaks down Internet usage by gender, age, race, income, education, and community type. Note the disparities in usage between those with high and low incomes, and between those with more and less education. Though educators and politicians have touted the potential benefits to the disadvantaged, Internet usage may be reinforcing existing social-class and educational differences.

People in low-income households, rural areas, and developing countries, for example, are less likely than others to have Internet access. When marginalized people do gain Internet access, they are still likely to trail the privileged. They may have dial-up service instead of broadband, or broadband instead of wireless Internet. The issue is not merely access to the Internet, but the cost and availability of high-capacity broadband service. The importance of high-speed Internet access became especially apparent when millions of students tried to attend virtual classes and complete their schoolwork online during the coronavirus pandemic. Box 6-2 examines the global disconnect between the haves and have-nots of the information age (Ingram 2019).

The digital divide is pervasive. For example, the popular Pokémon GO smartphone game released in 2016 allows players to create their own avatar and then search worldwide in real time to "catch" Pokémons appearing in an augmented reality, such as next to a mailbox or in a park. Players try to acquire as

FIGURE 6-2   WHO USES SOCIAL MEDIA?

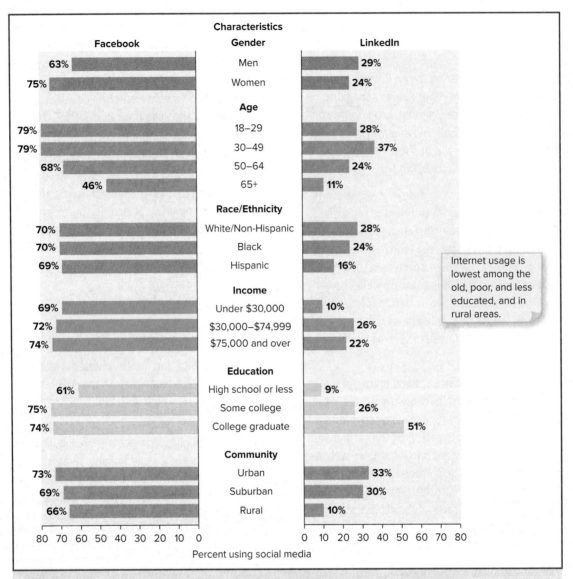

Internet usage is lowest among the old, poor, and less educated, and in rural areas.

Think about It What are the most likely reasons for the disparities? Are they likely to increase or to lessen over time?

Source: Based on national survey data from January/February 2019 in Perrin and Anderson 2019.

many of the more than 250 Pokémons as possible. However, research shows that in the United States, African American and Latino neighborhoods are much less likely to be the site of PokéStops where the characters can be apprehended than are white neighborhoods (Juhász and Hochmair 2017).

THINKING CRITICALLY

Have you ever experienced the digital divide? What other effects might lack of Internet access cause besides those mentioned in the text?

Feminist Perspective

Feminists share the view of conflict theorists that the mass media stereotype and misrepresent social reality. According to this view, the media powerfully influence how we look at men and women, communicating unrealistic, stereotypical, and limiting images of the sexes.

Educators and social scientists have long noted the stereotypical portrayal of women and men in the mass media. Women are often shown as being shallow and obsessed with beauty. They are more likely than men to be presented unclothed, in danger, or even physically victimized. When women achieve newsworthy feats in fields traditionally dominated by men,

SOCIOLOGY IN THE GLOBAL COMMUNITY

6-2 The Network Readiness Index

Bogdan Ghirda, a Romanian, is paid 50 cents an hour to participate in multiplayer games like City of Heroes and Star Wars. He is sitting in for someone in an industrialized country who does not want to spend days ascending to the highest levels of competition in order to compete with players who are already "well armed." This arrangement is not unusual. U.S.-based services can earn hundreds of dollars for recruiting someone in a less developed country, like Ghirda, to represent a single player in an affluent industrial country.

Meanwhile, in Africa, the resource-poor nation of Rwanda is developing its economy by encouraging investments in information and communications technologies. In 2011, through a combination of public investment and private competition among telecommunications companies, mobile phone and data transmission service in the country reached 96 percent. The challenges Rwanda faces remain immense: energy needs that are expensive to meet, a shortage of skilled computer specialists, and weak finances, to name a few. However, this nation of 12 million, with an annual per capita gross national income of just $780 may be able to create a stable economy based on new telecommunications technologies.

These two situations illustrate the technological disconnect between the developing and industrial nations. Around the world, developing nations lag far behind industrial nations in their access to and use of new technologies. The Network Readiness Index

(NRI), created by the World Economic Forum and now tabulated annually by the Portulans Institute, is a ranking of 121 nations that shows the relative preparedness of individuals, businesses, and governments to benefit from information technologies. As the accompanying table shows, the haves of the world—countries like Singapore, Switzerland, and the United States—are network ready; the have-nots—countries like Yemen,

For developing nations, the consequences of the global disconnect are far more serious than an inability to surf the Net.

Ethiopia, and Madagascar—are not.

For developing nations, the consequences of the global disconnect are far more serious than an inability to surf the Internet. Thanks to the Internet, multinational organizations can now function as a single global unit, responding instantly in real time, 24 hours a day. This new capability has fostered the emergence of what sociologist Manuel Castells calls a "global economy." But if large numbers of people—indeed, entire nations—are disconnected from the new global economy, their economic growth will remain slow and the well-being of their peo-

NETWORK READINESS INDEX

Top 10 Countries	Bottom 10 Countries
1. Sweden	112. Zambia
2. Singapore	113. Cameroon
3. Netherlands	114. Eswatini (Swaziland)
4. Norway	115. Mali
5. Switzerland	116. Ethiopia
6. Denmark	117. Malawi
7. Finland	118. Madagascar
8. United States	119. Zimbabwe
9. Germany	120. Mozambique
10. United Kingdom	121. Yemen

Source: Portulans Institute 2019.

ple will remain retarded. Those citizens who are educated and skilled will emigrate to other labor markets, deepening the impoverishment of nations on the periphery.

LET'S DISCUSS

1. For nations on the periphery, what might be some specific social and economic consequences of the global disconnect?
2. What factors might complicate efforts to remedy the global disconnect in developing nations?

Sources: Anatale et al. 2013; Castells 2010a; Thompson 2005; World Bank 2020.

such as professional sports, the media are often slow to recognize their accomplishments.

A continuing, troubling issue for feminists and society as a whole is pornography. Feminists tend to be very supportive of freedom of expression and self-determination, rights that are denied to women more often than to men. Yet pornography presents women as sex objects and seems to make viewing women that way acceptable. Nor are concerns about pornography limited to this type of objectification and imagery in itself; pornography can project an implicit endorsement of violence against women. The industry that creates risqué adult images for video and the Internet is largely unregulated, even putting its performers at risk.

Feminist scholars are concerned about the digital divide that persists in some countries in access to media. In the United States and many other industrial countries, women are slightly more likely than men to use electronic media. However, in rural areas of India, China, Indonesia, Mexico, Egypt, and Niger women fall behind their male counterparts, largely because ownership of or access to cell phones is discouraged or even locally prohibited. Media access is viewed as giving women too much freedom. It is estimated that globally 200 million women are denied access to cell phones (Bellman and Malhotra 2017; Concave Brand Tracking 2017).

Richard Schaefer

It's Trick or Treat time for Pokémon GO players! Ardent followers of the smartphone game Pokémon GO like these, costumed as Pikachu (right) and Pokémon Catcher (left), may be able to go anywhere, but the digital divide is manifested even in this world of altered reality: African American and Latino communities are less likely to be used as places to catch the imaginary creatures.

Interactionist Perspective

Social Capital Interactionists are especially interested in shared understandings of everyday behavior. As we saw in the opening excerpt in this chapter, sociologists are concerned about how social media shape day-to-day social behavior. Researchers have focused recently on both social capital and the introduction of facial recognition software.

Increasingly, researchers talk about mass media in the context of *social capital,* as described by sociologist Pierre Bourdieu. **Social capital** is the collective benefit of social networks, which are built on reciprocal trust. The Internet generally, and social media in particular, offers us almost constant connectivity with others. These media increase our contact with family members, friends, and acquaintances, both those who live nearby and those who are far away. They also facilitate the development of new ties and new social networks (Bourdieu and Passerson 1990; Neves 2013).

Social Networks Social networks have become a new way of promoting consumption. As Figure 6-3 shows, advertisers have traditionally marketed products and services through one-way spot ads, mass mailings, or billboards, whether they are promoting flat-screen televisions or public service messages like "Don't drink and drive." Now, using social media, they can find consumers online and attempt to develop a two-way relationship with them there. Through Facebook, for example, Burger King awarded a free Whopper to anyone who would delete 10 friends. Facebook's staff was not happy with Burger King's promotion, which notified 239,906 Facebook users that they had been dropped for a burger—an action that violated the network's policy.

Nevertheless, Burger King created a vast network of consumers who enjoy Whoppers. Similarly, Kraft Foods encouraged people to post images of the Wiener-mobile on the photo site Flickr (Bacon Lovers' Talk 2009; Burger King 2009; Gaudin 2009).

Relationship marketing is not the only new use for online social networks. As Box 6-3 shows, monitoring cell phones became a potential way to track human migration during the refugee crisis that has recently swept across Europe.

Interactionists note, too, that friendship networks can emerge from shared viewing habits or from recollection of a cherished television series from the past.

FIGURE 6-3   MARKETING ONLINE THROUGH SOCIAL NETWORKS

Traditional forms of advertising (left) allow only one-way communication, from the advertiser to the consumer. Online social networks (right) offer two-way communication, allowing advertisers to develop a relationship with consumers.

Traditional Marketing

Online Marketing

Advertiser

Advertiser

Think about It From an advertiser's point of view, how does marketing through social networks differ from traditional marketing? How do they differ from the consumer's point of view?

OUR WIRED WORLD

6-3 Apps for Global Refugees

The world continues to be gripped by images of vast numbers of migrants, both economic and political refugees, making their way across seas and deserts. Ongoing violence, natural disasters, and grinding poverty have led millions to flee their homeland—over 65 million people in 2017 alone. The conflict in Syria was by far the biggest driver of the migration, but the ongoing violence in Afghanistan; abuses of forced labor in Eritrea; as well as grinding poverty in Iraq, Nigeria, Kosovo, Pakistan, Somalia, and Sudan also led individuals, families, and entire villages to seek new lives elsewhere.

Surprisingly, cell phones may offer a solution to some of the challenges of such massive and unexpected migrations. For governments and aid groups to be able to assist migrants effectively, they need accurate and timely statistics about who the migrants are and how many are arriving. Such statistics can also counter common misperceptions that only serve to postpone urgently needed political and humanitarian response. Without migration statistics, a country can't meaningfully plan how to allocate resources—for instance, to assist asylum-seekers or migrants in need.

So how do cell phones figure into this? There are now more than 7 billion mobile phone subscriptions globally, at least 5 billion of which are in developing countries. Mobile phone penetration is growing fast, particularly across Asia and Africa, as is the number of Internet users worldwide. This means that an unprecedentedly large and complex amount of data is being generated in real time, every time a call or an online payment is made, or every time people interact on social media.

Indeed, as the refugee crises continue, more and more apps that specifically benefit

Iakovos Hatzistavrou/AFP/Getty Images

Surprisingly, cell phones may offer a solution to some of the challenges of such massive and unexpected migrations.

asylum seekers have been developed. These include the following:

- Instant intelligence on available services and shelter.
- Health advice through an app that links to local governments and offers medical guidance until refugees can receive personal attention.
- Help in finding family and letting others know where the user is in the chaotic world of refugee camps.
- Identity protection, which is important for people moving about with little if any personal possessions. A management system is available online in 25 nations that collects fingerprints, iris scans, and photographs to create a biometric identity.

Significantly these apps are usually available in many different languages, since the language barrier is another challenge that is difficult to overcome in a strange environment.

However, the world of social media is not universally helpful. The use of cell phones was observed during the refugee crisis but not always in a positive way. When images appeared of refugees huddled together using their smartphones, online comments quickly became hostile: people scoffed about how needy "these people" could be if all they were doing was updating their Facebook accounts. Further, there have been isolated accounts of governments locating and restricting the movements of refugees by tracking their mobile phone use.

As refugees move about the globe and reliance on social media increases, new apps are being developed to assist those fortunate enough to find permanent resettlement. For example, the free app FindHello was built with support from UNHCR and community organizations across the United States. FindHello has information about thousands of services available to immigrants, asylum seekers, and refugees in the United States.

LET'S DISCUSS

1. Have you ever used a smartphone for your own or someone else's safety during an emergency or natural disaster? What are the effects of having (or not having) this technology in such circumstances?
2. Are smartphones and other new technologies frills or vital services during emergencies? If you worked for an aid agency, how would smartphone technology help you do your job during a refugee crisis?

Sources: Mancini et al. 2019; UNHCR 2018; USAHello. 2020; Weiss-Meyer 2017; Williams 2015.

Family members and friends often gather for parties centered on the broadcasting of popular events such as the Super Bowl or the Academy Awards. And as we've seen, television often serves as a babysitter or playmate for children and even infants.

The Internet has also facilitated new forms of communication and social interaction. Grandparents can now keep up with their grandchildren via e-mail, or chat with them via Skype. As the pandemic led to self-quarantining, FaceTime and Zooming and other forms of video conferencing allowed a new form of face-to-face interaction to flourish. LGBTQ teens have online resources for support and information. Many people find their lifetime partners through computer dating services.

Some troubling issues have been raised about day-to-day life on the Internet, however. What, if anything, should be done about terrorists and other extremist groups who use the Internet to exchange messages of hatred and even bomb-making recipes? What, if anything, should be done about the issue of sexual expression on the Internet? How can children be protected from it? Should "hot chat" and X-rated film clips be censored? Or should expression be completely free?

Though the Internet has created a new platform for extremists, hate groups, and pornographers, it has also given people greater control over what they see and hear. That is, the Internet allows people to manage their media exposure so as to avoid sounds, images, and ideas they do not enjoy or approve of. The legal scholar Cass Sunstein (2002) has referred to this

personalized approach to news information gathering as *egocasting.* One social consequence of this trend may be a less tolerant society. If we read, see, and hear only what we know and agree with, we may be much less prepared to meet people from different backgrounds or converse with those who express new viewpoints.

Facial Recognition Software *Facial recognition software,* which links a person's image to their name, is often heralded as a great step forward. It helps you unlock your phone, speeds up passport control lines, and even lets parents identify online their children amidst many images taken by staff at summer camps.

Facial recognition and other AI technologies learn their skills by analyzing vast amounts of digital image data, typically without people being aware and often without consent. Drawn from old websites, cyberdating platforms, and even academic projects, these images often contain subtle biases and other flaws. For example, at some point in the past, a person may have tagged an image, correctly or not, as "cheerleader," "welder," or "college student," or in less neutral terms such as "not hired," "depressed," or "loser." Such tags can accompany images online and then reemerge when that image is selected through facial recognition software, So a person seeking to find someone may do so but also see they are "unsuccessful" or a "non-starter."

Tracking Sociological Perspectives

TABLE 6-2 SOCIOLOGICAL PERSPECTIVES ON THE MEDIA

Theoretical Perspective	Emphasis
Functionalist	Socialization
	Enforcement of social norms
	Conferral of status
	Promotion of consumption
	Narcotizing effect (dysfunction)
Conflict	Gatekeeping
	Media monitoring
	Construction of reality
	Digital divide
Feminist	Misrepresentation of women
	Differential impact on women
Interactionist	Impact on social behavior
	Source of friendship networks
	Social capital

THINKING CRITICALLY

What do you think is the most important function of the media in our society? Why? Which of the problems associated with the media troubles you most, and why?

This software and the social interaction it leads to can be beneficial, such as when it helps to locate a missing person. But it also can reinforce layers of bias, racism, or sexism. In 2019, it was revealed that at least three states, among them Utah and Vermont, that offer driver's licenses to undocumented immigrants had granted access to the license photos to federal immigration officials, thus allowing the government to identify unauthorized immigrants. Currently there are no federal regulations on the use of facial recognition software for commercial or government use. The majority of Americans trust law enforcement to use facial recognition responsibly, but the public is less trusting of advertisers and technology companies (Collins 2019; Edmonson 2019a, 2019b).

Table 6-2 summarizes the various sociological perspectives on the media.

The Audience

Ever feel like texting everyone you know, to encourage them to vote for your favorite performer on a certain reality program? Ever looked over someone's shoulder as he watched last week's episode of *Game of Thrones* on his iPhone—and been tempted to reveal the ending to him? Ever come across an old CD and tried to remember the last time you or a friend listened to one, or heard the songs in the order in which they were recorded? In this and many other ways, we are reminded that we are all part of a larger audience.

Who Is in the Audience?

The media are distinguished from other social institutions by the necessary presence of an audience. It can be an identifiable, finite group, such as an audience at a jazz club or a Broadway musical, or a much larger and undefined group, such as *Black Panther* viewers or readers of the same issue of *USA Today.* The audience may be a secondary group gathered in a large auditorium or a primary group, such as a family watching the latest Disney video at home.

We can look at the audience from the level of both *microsociology* and *macrosociology.* At the micro level, we might consider how audience members, interacting among themselves, respond to the media, or in the case of live performances, actually influence the performers. At the macro level, we might examine broader societal consequences of the media, such as the early childhood education delivered through programming like *Sesame Street.*

Even if an audience is spread out over a wide geographic area and members don't know one another, it is still distinctive in terms of age, gender, income, political party, formal schooling, race, and ethnicity. The audience for a ballet, for example, would likely differ substantially from the audience for alternative music.

The Segmented Audience

Increasingly, the media market themselves to a *particular* audience. Once a media outlet, such as a radio station or a website, has identified its audience, it targets that group. To some degree, this specialization is driven by advertising. Media specialists have sharpened their ability, through survey research, to identify particular target audiences. For the 2016 races, political media specialists built upon this pattern by targeting specific social media audiences. Facebook allows advertisers to target users based on their education, field of study, income, net worth, gender, marital status, age, work history, political affiliation, and whether one is Hispanic or not. Depending on whom you want to get a specific message, you can define the pool of recipients (Herrman 2018).

The specialized targeting of audiences has led some scholars to question the "mass" in "mass media." For example, the British social psychologist Sonia Livingstone (2004) has written that the media have become so segmented, they have taken on the appearance almost of individualization. Are viewing audiences so segmented that large collective audiences are a thing of the past? That is not yet clear. Even though we seem to be living in an age of *personal* computers, large formal organizations still do transmit public messages that reach a sizable, heterogeneous, and scattered audience.

Media specialists have sharpened their ability, through survey research, to target particular audiences. During election campaigns, candidates and political action groups place advertisements in markets where surveys indicate they will find support. In the past this meant selecting television and radio programs. Now digital strategists rely on micro-targeting, using accumulated voter files to send out messages and solicit campaign contributions, Campaigns identify ad recipients by the hashtags they use on Twitter or the videos and photos they post on Snapchat. Using Facebook and Instagram, campaigns target voters by congressional district, interest, gender and age, or any combination of these factors.

USE YOUR SOCIOLOGICAL IMAGINATION

Think about the last time you were part of an audience. Describe the performance. How similar to or different from yourself were the other audience members? What might account for whatever similarities or differences you noticed?

The impact of online political messaging, including outright false charges about candidates, became particularly intense in the 2016 and 2018 elections. Recognizing that it was unable to secure the content of hyperpartisan political messages, Twitter took the extraordinary move in 2019 of no longer accepting any paid political advertisements (Weintraub 2019).

Audience Behavior

Sociologists have long researched how audiences interact with one another and how they share information after a media event. The role of audience members as opinion leaders particularly intrigues social researchers. An **opinion leader** is someone who influences the opinions and decisions of others through day-to-day personal contact and communication. For example, a movie or theater critic functions as an opinion leader. Sociologist Paul Lazarsfeld and his colleagues (1948)

FIGURE 6-4   INTERNET AND SOCIAL MEDIA PENETRATION IN SELECTED COUNTRIES

Cell phone ownership and active use of social media reach high levels of the population around much of the world.

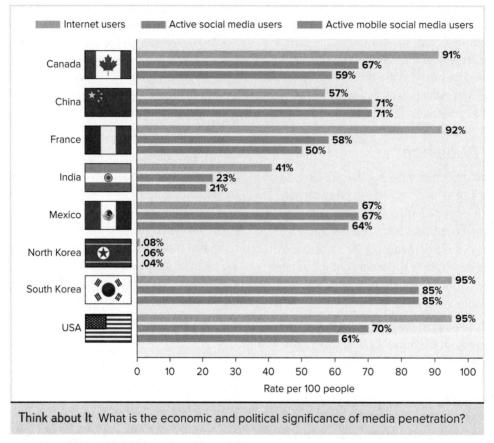

Think about It What is the economic and political significance of media penetration?

Source: Hootsuite & We Are Social 2019.
Flags: admin_design/Shutterstock

pioneered the study of opinion leaders in their research on voting behavior in the 1940s.

In addition to the types of opinion leaders that Lazarsfeld spoke about, the online world has given rise to influencers (see Chapter 1). An **influencer** is a social media user who has established credibility in a specific industry, such as fashion or electronics or toys. Unlike opinion leaders, who we occasionally meet face-to-face, or who have developed their reputation over many years, these influencers are relatively new to the

scene and churn out content 24/7 on such platforms as YouTube, TikTok, or Instagram (Tiffany 2019).

The term "audience" may connote a passive group, but this is often not the case. Protesters at political rallies or attendees who boo performers, athletes, or speakers are anything but passive. Opinion leaders may play a role here as well, by encouraging such tactics, which in turn may lead to collective action on the part of audience members (see Chapter 16). The activist role of the audience specifically and media in general becomes apparent in the next section, as we consider the global reach of the media (Croteau et al. 2012).

In recent years, the manipulation of the audience by the mass media has taken on new meaning with the advent of false news stories or fictitious events targeted to certain audiences online. While online audiences are increasingly wary of content, they often overlook falsehoods that are created to appeal specifically to users' preferences or biases.

THINKING CRITICALLY

What kind of audience is targeted by the producers of televised professional wrestling? By the creators of an animated film? By a rap group? What factors determine who makes up a particular audience?

Creators of fake news identify their audience's biases and efficiently target them by accessing their online viewing history (Carey 2017).

The Media's Global Reach

Has the rise of the electronic media created a *global village*? Canadian media theorist Marshall McLuhan predicted it would nearly 60 years ago. Today, physical distance is no longer a barrier, and instant messaging is possible across the world. The media have indeed created a global village. Not all countries are equally connected, as Figure 6-4 shows, but the progress has been staggering, considering that voice transmission was just beginning 120 years ago (McLuhan 1964, 1967).

Sociologist Todd Gitlin considers *global torrent* a more apt metaphor for the media's reach than *global village*. The media permeate all aspects of everyday life. Take advertising, for example. Consumer goods are marketed vigorously worldwide, from advertisements on airport baggage carriers to imprints on sandy beaches. Little wonder that people around the world develop loyalty to a brand and are as likely to sport a Nike, Coca-Cola, or Harley-Davidson logo as they are their favorite soccer or baseball insignia (Gitlin 2002; Klein 1999).

Noah Flanigan 2009

New technologies can create new social norms. In Gurupá, Brazil, television watching became a community social activity when three new TV owners agreed to share their sets with the community of 3,000.

THINKING CRITICALLY

Use the functionalist, conflict, and interactionist perspectives to assess the effects of global TV programming on developing countries.

In some developing countries, people manage to watch television even though they don't own one. Consider the town of Gurupá, in the remote Amazon area of Brazil. In 1982, the wealthiest three households in this community bought televisions. To please the rest of the town, they agreed to place their TVs near the window so that their neighbors could watch them as well. As the TV owners proudly displayed their new status symbol, TV watching became a community social activity. The introduction of a new technology had created a new social norm (Kenny 2009; Pace 1993, 1998).

Media use can take on added importance in combating infectious diseases. During a malaria outbreak in Kenya, public health researchers monitored the text messages Kenyans sent on their 15 million cell phones and used the content to map the spread of the dreaded disease. Surprisingly, they found that travelers were carrying the disease along less-traveled regional routes rather than the heavily traveled roads to and from the capital city, Nairobi. During the coronavirus pandemic, several countries used telecom data and dowloaded apps to track the spread of COVID-19 once people infected with the disease were identified. Information such as at this proved vital in concentrating malaria and coronavirus pandemic control efforts (Lin and Martin 2020; Wesolowski et al. 2012).

Whatever the broadband limitations in developing nations, people can still typically text messages. Inexpensive cell phones equipped with icons, emojis, and voice recognition software allow people who cannot read to communicate with others, even to those who do not speak the same language (Jennings 2014).

Around the world, people rely increasingly on digital media, from cell phones to the Internet. This trend has raised new concerns about the right to privacy. Should government officials have the right to monitor people's text messages, even if they are protecting the public's health? The Social Policy section that follows examines the social implications of digital media, from censorship to criminal activity.

socialpolicy and the Media

Censorship

"Thousands, perhaps as many as 100,000 Black men served as soldiers in the Confederacy during the Civil War. This undercuts the often-stated notion that the main issue of the Civil War was slavery rather than the effort of the Southern states to maintain a measure of autonomy."

The above statement is false. No African Americans served in the Confederate Army; indeed, they were barred from serving. Yes, enslaved men and women built fortifications and served their masters by washing, sewing, and preparing food, but they were neither willing to support the cause nor soldiers in uniform. However, in the late 20th century, in response to realistic representations of the brutality of slavery in the United States, such as Alex Haley's best seller *Roots* and Ken Burns's PBS documentary *The Civil War,* the myth emerged in print and then on the Internet that Black Confederate soldiers had valiantly fought to preserve the southern plantation way of life. Convincing images appeared. Contemporary photos of the gravesites of enslaved men with decorative Confederate soldier markers could be viewed online (Jackson 2019:179–187; Levin 2019; Stern 2019).

So how is social media to manage such misinformation? Ban it? Place some sort of banner warning viewers about false content, or redirect readers to authoritative cites? Who is to judge what is a myth and what are facts about life in the past, much less the present?

So is censorship appropriate when falsehoods are placed online as if they were facts? President Obama decried "the wild west" of the media and called for some means of filtering for "truthiness." President Trump regularly lambasted the spread of "fake news." So how have governments responded? British officials have unsuccessfully pressured Facebook and Google to take down sites or social media that spread false information about vaccines causing autism. In 2019 Singapore passed the Protection from Online Falsehoods and Manipulation Act. The government presented this law as an anti–fake news measure, but it remains to be seen if it will stifle online dissent (*The Economist* 2019d; Roose 2017).

Looking at the Issue

Censoring the Internet and social media, even when there is a consensus that such censorship is desirable, is vastly challenging given the sheer amount of material. Back in the 1930s, when Hollywood created a code that all motion pictures had to meet, a few hundred

MAPPING LIFE WORLDWIDE

FIGURE 6-5   FREEDOM ON THE INTERNET

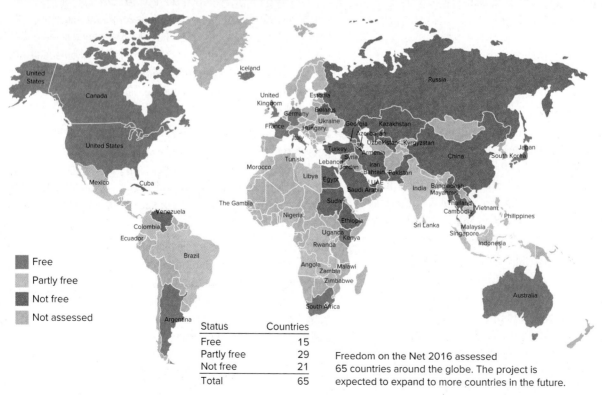

Status	Countries
Free	15
Partly free	29
Not free	21
Total	65

Freedom on the Net 2016 assessed 65 countries around the globe. The project is expected to expand to more countries in the future.

Source: Freedom House 2019.

movies needed to be monitored annually. Contrast that to a contemporary situation. A few years ago, the United States government tried to overcome Iranian government censorship without offending the conservative values of the Iranian people. The State Department removed offending words, such as "ass," from domain names, only to realize that this blocked the Iranian people's access to usembassy. state.gov—the State Department's online portal for overseas missions (Zittrain 2008).

Ironically the spread of mass media and social media, both of which make the sharing of information easier and faster, has been accompanied by increased censorship. The well-regarded nonprofit organization Freedom House has monitored freedom on the Internet since 2009. As shown in Figure 6-5, this assessment considers obstacles to online access, such as infrastructure and ownership control over Internet service providers, legal or technical limits on content, and violations of user rights through surveillance, privacy, and imprisonment. As of 2019, two-thirds of all Internet users lived in countries where criticism of the government, military, or the ruling family was subject to censorship.

The 2019 survey concluded that governments were increasingly using sophisticated technology to monitor their citizens' behavior on social media. This form of mass surveillance was limited to the world's foremost intelligence agencies and has now made its way to a range of countries, from major authoritarian powers to smaller or poorer states that nevertheless hope to track dissidents and persecute minorities. Coupled with an alarming rise in the number of countries where social media users have been arrested for their legitimate online activities, the growing employment of social media surveillance threatens to squeeze the space for privacy and civic activism on most digital platforms (Shahbaz and Funk 2019).

Applying Sociology

From a sociological point of view, the complex issues of censorship can be considered to be an illustration of **culture lag,** a period of maladjustment when the nonmaterial culture is still struggling to adapt to new material conditions. As usual, the material culture (technology) is changing faster than the nonmaterial culture (norms for controlling the use of technology). Too often, the result is an anything-goes approach to the use of new technologies.

Sociologists' views on the use and abuse of new technologies, such as facial recognition software, differ depending on their theoretical perspective. Functionalists take a generally positive view of the Internet, pointing to its manifest function of facilitating communication. From their perspective, the Internet performs the latent function of empowering people with few resources—from hate groups to special-interest organizations—to communicate with the masses. In contrast, conflict theorists express concern about those with power, whether media companies or governments, exercising control over what people can read.

Interactionists would see the debate over media content as an extension of everyday life. Many of us may have wondered at one time or another how we could intervene to prevent people close to us from engaging in antisocial behavior. Similarly, interactionists consider how mass media and social media serve to influence everyday behavior, whether positively or negatively.

Initiating Policy

So how might censorship either function or be curtailed online? In general, support for censorship is weak, as we can see even with public attitudes toward pornography: Even though pornography has long been decried, increasingly few people are concerned about censoring pornography, except for depictions of children. As of 2018, 43 percent of people surveyed see pornography as morally acceptable, the highest percentage on record (Dugan 2018).

One possible use of censorship that does often receive attention relates to cyberbullying. This online harassment with the intent to do harm can take many forms, ranging from posting disparaging rumors, to spreading sexual innuendos, and making confidential information public online. In a 2018 survey, nearly 40 percent of middle-schoolers and 27 percent of high-schoolers said that they had been bullied. However, restricting social media or other online forums to curtail bullying is a challenge. No federal law specifically applies to bullying except if it is based on race, color, national origin, gender, disability, or religion (McClellan 2019).

Private companies have more latitude, however. PayPal, the popular online payment platform, announced in 2017 that it would bar users from accepting donations to promote hate, violence, and intolerance. This was in response to revelations that the company played a key role in raising money for a white supremacist rally that turned deadly. The company, in a lengthy blog post, outlined its long-standing policy of not allowing its services to be used to accept payments or donations to organizations that advocate racist views.

PayPal singled out the Ku Klux Klan, white supremacist groups, and neo-Nazi groups—all of which were involved in the Charlottesville white supremacist rally. "Intolerance can take on a range of on-line and off-line forms, across a wide array of content and language," the company wrote. "It is with this backdrop that PayPal strives to navigate the balance between freedom of expression and open dialogue—and the limiting and closing of sites that accept payments or raise funds to promote hate, violence and intolerance" (Passache 2017).

On the Internet, it is often users, rather than content providers, that must censor content. For example, sites like YouTube and Wikipedia provide protocols for drawing attention to inappropriate or inaccurate content on their websites. Facebook allows people to ban certain words from their feed, and Twitter allows users to remove individual tweets or to block an account altogether.

Yet another challenge is online terrorist threats or advocacy of harmful acts or ideas associated with terrorists. For example, in 2019 a mass shooting at an El Paso Walmart took 20 lives and left 27 people wounded. The shooter told authorities he feared a "Hispanic Invasion of Texas" and had taken inspiration from the words and actions of a white nationalist attack at a New Zealand mosque that left 51 people dead. Online sites offer hints about how to maximize bodily injury in mass shootings.

Existing laws do not make such online material illegal. YouTube does accompany some terrorist **propaganda** with a label stating that the videos "may be inappropriate or offensive to some audiences." Nonetheless, potential viewers can indicate they understand the warning and watch as well as receive recommendations of similar online material. Many who find the presence of such material

Andriy Popov/123RF

Does the use of facial recognition software by government agencies represent a threat to everyday social interaction? Reflecting such a concern and abuse by law enforcement agencies, San Francisco became the first major city to ban facial recognition surveillance (Conger et al. 2019).

offensive still argue that society should not prohibit or censor dissenting viewpoints (Counter Extremism Project 2017; Eckholm 2015; *New York Times* 2019; Shane 2015).

It is an understatement to say that in the United States censorship, especially government censorship, is strongly opposed. A basic democratic principle is that society is governed best when citizens have full access to information. In part that is why so much attention is given to the digital divide: because most people believe that everyone should have equal access to everything. However, as more and more nations issue their own restrictions on what can be made available online, the Internet becomes further splintered, and the idea of

a single global network that looks the same wherever you are begins to vanish (Baran 2017; *The Economist* 2019d).

Take the Issue with You

1. How would you react if you discovered that the government was monitoring your use of media?

2. If your safety were in jeopardy, would you be willing to accept censorship?

3. Do some research to learn more about the methods of propaganda used to influence social behavior. Discuss your findings with the class.

MASTERING THIS CHAPTER

Summary

The media are print and electronic instruments of communication that carry messages to often widespread audiences. They pervade all social institutions, from entertainment to education to politics. This chapter examines how the **mass media** and **social media** affect those institutions and influence our social behavior.

1. From the functionalist perspective, the media entertain, socialize, enforce social norms, confer status, and promote consumption. They can be dysfunctional to the extent that they desensitize us to serious events and issues, a phenomenon called the **narcotizing dysfunction.**

2. Conflict theorists think the media reflect and even deepen the divisions in society through **gatekeeping,** or control over which material reaches the public; and support of the **dominant ideology,** which defines reality, overwhelming local cultures.

3. Feminist theorists point out that media images of the sexes communicate unrealistic, stereotypical, limiting, and sometimes violent perceptions of women.

4. Interactionists examine the media on the micro level to see how they shape day-to-day social behavior. Interactionists have studied shared TV viewing and intergenerational e-mail.

5. The media require the presence of an audience, whether it is small and well defined or large and amorphous. With increasing numbers of media outlets has come more and more targeting of segmented (or specialized) audiences.

6. Social researchers have studied the role of **opinion leaders** and **influencers** in influencing audiences.

7. The media have a global reach thanks to new communications technologies, especially the Internet.

8. In the postmodern digital age, new technologies that facilitate the collection and sharing of personal information are threatening people's right to privacy.

Key Terms

Culture lag A period of maladjustment when the nonmaterial culture is still struggling to adapt to new material conditions. (page 149)

Digital divide The relative lack of access to the latest technologies among low-income groups, racial and ethnic minorities, rural residents, and the citizens of developing countries. (139)

Dominant ideology A set of cultural beliefs and practices that helps to maintain powerful social, economic, and political interests. (137)

Gatekeeping The process by which a relatively small number of people in the media industry control what material eventually reaches the audience. (135)

Hyper-local media Reporting that is highly local and typically Internet-based. (139)

Hyperconsumerism The practice of buying more than we need or want, and often more than we can afford; a preoccupation of postmodern consumers. (134)

Influencer A social media user who has established credibility in a specific industry, such as fashion or electronics or toys. (146)

Mass media Print and electronic means of communication that carry messages to widespread audiences. (131)

Narcotizing dysfunction The phenomenon in which the media provide such massive amounts of coverage that the audience becomes numb and fails to act on the information, regardless of how compelling the issue. (134)

Opinion leader Someone who influences the opinions and decisions of others through day-to-day personal contact and communication. (145)

Propaganda Biased or misleading information that is used to convince people of the validity of a certain cause or viewpoint. (149)

Social capital The collective benefit of social networks, which are built on reciprocal trust. (142)

Social media Websites and online applications that enable people to create and share content or to participate in social networking. (131)

Stereotype An unreliable generalization about all members of a group that does not recognize individual differences within the group. (137)

TAKING SOCIOLOGY with you

1. For one day, categorize every media message you receive in terms of its function: Does it socialize, enforce a social norm, confer status, or promote consumption? Keep a record and tally the results. Which function was the most common? What can you conclude from the results?

2. Pick a specific audience—students in your classes for example—and track their media preferences over the next day or two. Which media are they watching, reading, or listening to? Which media are the most popular and which the least popular? How segmented is this particular media audience?

3. In a TV show you are watching, a book you are reading, or on social media, look for examples of how incorrect communications, such as rumors or gossip, influence group behavior. Share your findings with the class.

4. **Writing Sociology.** Pick a foreign film, television program, or Internet site and study it from the point of view of a sociologist. Describe what it tells you about the culture that produced it.

Self-Quiz

Read each question carefully and then select the best answer.

1. From the functionalist perspective, the media can be dysfunctional in what way?
   a. They enforce social norms.
   b. They confer status.
   c. They desensitize us to events.
   d. They are agents of socialization.

2. Sociologist Robert Park studied how newspapers helped immigrants to the United States adjust to their environment by changing their customary habits and by teaching them the opinions held by people in their new home country. His study was conducted from which sociological perspective?
   a. the functionalist perspective
   b. the conflict perspective
   c. the modernist perspective
   d. the dramaturgical perspective

3. There are problems inherent in the socialization function of the media. For example, many people worry about
   a. the effect of using the television as a babysitter.
   b. the impact of violent programming on viewer behavior.
   c. the unequal ability of all individuals to purchase televisions.
   d. both a and b.

4. Media advertising has several clear functions, but it also has dysfunctions. Sociologists are concerned that
   a. it creates unrealistic expectations of what is required to be happy.
   b. it creates new consumer needs.
   c. advertisers are able to influence media content.
   d. all of the above

5. Gatekeeping, the process by which a relatively small number of people control what material reaches an audience, is *least* dominant in which of the following media?
   a. television
   b. the Internet
   c. publishing
   d. music

6. Which sociological perspective is especially concerned with the media's ability to decide what gets transmitted through gatekeeping?
   a. the functionalist perspective
   b. the conflict perspective
   c. the interactionist perspective
   d. the dramaturgical perspective

7. Which of the following is *not* a problem feminist theorists see with media coverage?
   a. Women are underrepresented, suggesting that men are the cultural standard and that women are insignificant.
   b. Men and women are portrayed in ways that reflect and perpetuate stereotypical views of gender.
   c. Female athletes are treated differently from male athletes in television commentary.
   d. The increasing frequency of single moms in the media is providing a negative role model for women.

8. Which of the following is *not* true concerning how men and women use the Internet?
   a. Men are more likely to use the Internet daily.
   b. Women are more likely to use e-mail to maintain friendships.
   c. Men account for 100 percent of players in online sports fantasy leagues.
   d. Men are slightly more likely to have ever used the Internet than women are.

9. Sociologist Paul Lazarsfeld and his colleagues pioneered the study of
   a. the audience.
   b. opinion leaders.
   c. the media's global reach.
   d. media violence.

10. Which term refers to the relative lack of access to technology among low-income groups, racial and ethnic minorities, rural residents, and citizens of developing countries?
    a. digital divide
    b. culture lag
    c. cultural convergence
    d. narcotizing dysfunction

11. The media increase social cohesion by presenting a more or less standardized, common view of culture through mass communication. This statement reflects the _____ perspective.

12. Paul Lazarsfeld and Robert Merton created the term _____ to refer to the phenomenon in which the media provide such massive amounts of information that the audience becomes numb and generally fails to act on the information, regardless of how compelling the issue.

13. _____ is the term used to describe the set of cultural beliefs and practices that helps to maintain powerful social, economic, and political interests.

14. Sociologists blame the media for the creation and perpetuation of _____ , or generalizations about all members of a group that do not recognize individual differences within the group.

15. The _____ perspective contends that television distorts the political process.

16. We risk being _____ if we overstress U.S. dominance and assume that other nations do not play a role in media cultural exports.

17. Both _____ and _____ theorists are troubled that the victims depicted in violent imagery are often those who are given less respect in real life: women, children, the poor, racial minorities, citizens of foreign countries, and even those who are physically disabled.

18. The _____ perspective examines the media on the micro level to see how they shape day-to-day social behavior.

19. From a sociological point of view, the current controversy over censorship illustrates the concept of _____ _____ .

20. Nearly 50 years ago, Canadian media theorist _____ _____ predicted that the rise of the electronic media would create a "global village."

Deviance, Crime, and Social Control

Contraband Collection/Alamy Stock Photo

Initially intended to educate parents that smoking marijuana cigarettes was the true "public enemy no. 1," the 1936 motion picture *Reefer Madness* eventually became a midnight cult classic. In the 1980s, it was shown on college campuses to raise money for legalizing marijuana initiatives. What is considered to be deviant is different from one culture to another, may become the subject of policy debates that continue for generations, and may change dramatically over time. (E. Schaefer 1999)

▶ INSIDE

Ira C. Roberts/Chad Enterprises Corporation

What do you think (or know) life is like in a high-crime area?

To learn about crime firsthand, sociologist Peter Moskos became a Baltimore police officer

"Living in Baltimore City, I was required to carry my gun both on and off duty. I never fired a shot outside of training. Only rarely was my service weapon—a charged semi-automatic nine-millimeter Glock-17 with no safety and a seventeen-round clip—pointed at somebody. But in my police duties, my gun was very routinely removed from its holster, probably every other shift. I did occasionally chase people down alleys and wrestled a few suspects. I maced one person, but did not hit anybody. As a police officer, I tried to speak softly and carry a big stick. The department issued a twenty-nine-inch straight wooden baton just for this purpose. I brought it along to all my calls.

In any account of police work, inevitably the noncriminal public, the routine, and the working folks all get short shrift. Police don't deal with a random cross-section of society, even within the areas they work. And this book reflects that."

Moskos emphasizes that the people his fellow police officers interact with are not representative of Baltimore's population. Rather, the ghetto residents sometimes transcend stereotypes and sometimes fulfill them. Families in the ghetto continually strive to make it against crushing odds. Residents rise well before dawn to go to work. Ladies and their families go to church wearing beautiful hats and listen intently to their preachers.

The stereotypes can be found as well, according to Moskos: vacant and abandoned buildings, too many liquor stores and fast food operations, Korean American–operated corner stores, and the occasional Jewish pawnshop. Living conditions are worse than those in Third World squatter enclaves. There are filthy apartments with no plumbing or electricity, families thrown out on the street on eviction day, drug addicts neglecting their children, and everywhere signs of violence and despair.

As a middle-class white man policing the ghetto, Moskos pleads no contest to the charge of "exoticism": using the poor residents for his own advantage. If you're not from the ghetto, the ghetto *is* exotic, even though it may not be politically correct to say so. One field-training officer accused Moskos of being "*fascinated* by the ghetto," and he was. Moskos was genuinely fascinated by Baltimore in general and life in inner-city neighborhoods in particular, but his central focus was on police.

He continues, "Twenty months in Baltimore wasn't very long, but it was long enough to see five police officers killed in the line of duty. And there were other cops, friends of mine, who were hurt, shot, and lucky to live. A year after I quit the force, my friend and academy classmate became the first Baltimore policewoman killed in the line of duty, dying in a car crash on the way to back up another police officer."

Source: Moskos 2008.

> *Twenty months in Baltimore wasn't very long, but it was long enough to see five police officers killed in the line of duty.*

Peter Moskos's route to becoming a sworn police officer was a bit unusual, considering that becoming one was never his goal. None of his friends were on the force, nor did he come from a family of police officers: his father was a well-known and respected sociologist. During his graduate studies, however, Moskos decided that he wanted to learn more about law enforcement. So he persuaded Baltimore's police commissioner to let him attend the police academy, as both a student and a sociologist.

On the second day of class, the commissioner was suddenly and unexpectedly ousted from office, to be replaced by a new commissioner who questioned Moskos's motives. "Why don't you want to be a cop for real?" he challenged Moskos. That was the beginning of Moskos's 20-month tour of duty with the Baltimore Police Department, during which he responded to crimes that included disorderly conduct, domestic abuse, and a 12-person shooting.

In this excerpt from his book *Cop in the Hood: My Year Policing Baltimore's Eastern District,* Moskos describes his beat as seen through the eyes of a sociologist doing an ethnographic study. Looking beyond the stereotypes, he found a diverse and vibrant community, one he would get to know by mingling with its residents. Moskos took the same approach in his study of police work, taking sociology with him to the academy, the station house, and the street.

The policing Moskos sought to understand has taken on renewed national attention in light of widely viewed police-civilians encounters in which some police appear to take extraordinarily brutal means to subdue unarmed individuals. Particularly attention grabbing are police interactions with African Americans, which gave rise to the #BlackLivesMatter movement. By the summer of 2020 a national survey showed that 91 percent of Blacks would not agree with the statement "the vast majority of police officers treat everyone fairly regardless of race." In the same survey, 57 percent of whites also could not agree with that declaration (Shannon 2020).

Another example of a behavior that can be seen as either socially acceptable or socially unacceptable depending on your reference group is binge drinking. On the one hand, we can view binge drinking as *deviant,* as violating a college campus' standards of conduct and endangering a person's health. On the other hand, we can see it as *conforming,* or complying with peer culture. In the United States, people are socialized to have mixed feelings about both conforming and nonconforming behavior. The term *conformity* can conjure up images of mindless imitation of a peer group—whether a circle of teenagers wearing "phat pants" or a group of business executives all dressed in gray suits. Yet the same term can also suggest that an individual is cooperative, or a "team player." What about police who use excessive force with civilians? They may be respected by some fellow officers as someone "who has their back" in dangerous situations but considered by others as only making it more difficult to maintain public safety.

This chapter examines the relationships among deviance and conformity, crime and social control. What is deviance, and what are its consequences? What causes crime? How does society control people's behavior, convincing us to conform to both unwritten rules and formal laws? We will begin by defining deviance and describing the stigma that is associated with it. Then we will distinguish between conformity and obedience, and examine a surprising experiment on obedience to authority. We will study the mechanisms societies use, both formal and informal, to encourage conformity and discourage deviance, paying particular attention to the law and how it reflects our social values.

Next, we will focus on theoretical explanations for deviance, including the functionalist approach employed by Émile Durkheim and Robert Merton; interactionist-based theories; labeling theory, which draws on both the interactionist and the conflict perspectives; and conflict theory. In the last part of the chapter we will focus on crime, a specific type of deviant behavior. As a form of deviance that is subject to official, written norms, crime has been a special concern of both policymakers and the public in general. We will look at various types of crime found in the United States, the ways crime is measured, and international crime rates. Finally, the Social Policy section considers the controversial topic of the death penalty.

What Is Deviance?

For sociologists, the term *deviance* does not mean perversion or depravity. **Deviance** is behavior that violates the standards of conduct or expectations of a group or society. In the United States, alcoholics, compulsive gamblers, and people with mental illness would all be classified as deviants. Being late for class is categorized as a deviant act; the same is true of wearing jeans to a formal wedding. On the basis of the sociological definition, we are all deviant from time to time. Each of us violates common social norms in certain situations (Best 2004).

Is being overweight an example of deviance? In the United States and many other cultures, unrealistic standards of appearance and body image place a huge strain on people—especially women and girls—based on how they look. Journalist Naomi Wolf (1992) has used the term *beauty myth* to refer to an exaggerated ideal of beauty, beyond the reach of all but a few females, which has unfortunate consequences. In order to shed their "deviant" image and conform to unrealistic societal norms, many women and girls become consumed with adjusting their appearances. Yet what is deviant in one culture may be celebrated in another.

Deviance involves the violation of group norms, which may or may not be formalized into law. It is a comprehensive concept that includes not only criminal behavior but also many actions that are not subject to prosecution. The public official who takes a bribe has defied social norms, but so has the high school student who refuses to sit in an assigned seat or cuts class. Of course, deviation from norms is not always negative, let alone criminal. A member of an exclusive social club who speaks out against a traditional policy of not admitting women, Blacks, and Jews is deviating from the club's norms. So is a police officer who blows the whistle on corruption or brutality within the department.

Think about It If your friends or teammates violate a social norm, is their behavior deviant? At what point does deviance begin?

Focus On Sport/Getty Images

Singer and actor Demi Lovato has become as well known for her drug abuse, alcoholism, and repeated stints in rehab as her many talents. As shown here, she once again took to the stage to sing the National Anthem at the 2020 Super Bowl.

From a sociological perspective, deviance is hardly objective or set in stone. Rather, it is subject to social definition within a particular society and at a particular time. For that reason, what is considered deviant can shift from one social era to another. In most instances, those individuals and groups with the greatest status and power define what is acceptable and what is deviant.

For example, despite serious medical warnings against the dangers of tobacco, made since 1964, cigarette smoking continued to be accepted for decades—in good part because of the power of tobacco farmers and cigarette manufacturers. Only after a long campaign led by public health and anticancer activists did cigarette smoking become more of a deviant activity. Today, many state and local laws limit where people can smoke.

The definition of acceptable behavior changes over time. Tattoos were long considered inappropriate for U.S. military recruits. Although the Navy lifted the ban in 2012 and the Army in 2015, tattoos must still be invisible when a soldier is uniformed and may not be racist, extremist, or vulgar.

Deviance and Social Stigma

A person can acquire a deviant identity in many ways. Because of physical or behavioral characteristics, some people are unwillingly cast in negative social roles. Once assigned a deviant role, they have trouble presenting a positive image to others and may even experience lowered self-esteem. Whole groups of people—for instance, "short people" or "redheads"—may be labeled in this way. The interactionist Erving Goffman coined the term **stigma** to describe the labels society uses to devalue members of certain social groups (Goffman 1963; Heckert and Best 1997).

In the aftermath of the 2012 shooting at Sandy Hook Elementary School in Newtown, Connecticut, the issue of mental illness surfaced almost immediately, amid rumors that the shooter suffered from an untreated mental disorder. In many people's eyes, such assumptions stigmatize all people with mental illness, whatever the definition of the term, as potentially violent criminals. Overwhelming evidence shows that the opposite is true, however: the vast majority of people with psychiatric disorders do *not* commit violent acts and relatively few violent acts are the result of actions by people with mental illnesses (Lu and Temple 2019). Only 4 percent of violent crimes in the United States can be attributed to people with mental illness (R. Friedman 2012; Nocera 2012).

Stigmatization also affects people who look different from others in the eyes of their peers. Prevailing expectations about beauty and body shape may prevent people who are regarded as ugly or obese from advancing as rapidly as their abilities permit. Both overweight and anorexic people are assumed to be weak in character, slaves to their appetites or to media images. Because they do not conform to the beauty myth, they may be viewed as "disfigured" or "strange" in appearance, bearers of what Goffman calls a "spoiled identity." However, what constitutes disfigurement is a matter of interpretation. Of the 18 million cosmetic procedures done every year in the United States alone, many are performed on women who would be defined objectively as having a normal appearance. And while feminist sociologists have accurately noted that the beauty myth makes many women feel uncomfortable with themselves, men too lack confidence in their appearance. The number of males who choose to undergo cosmetic procedures has risen sharply in recent years (American Society of Plastic Surgeons 2019).

Often people are stigmatized for deviant behaviors they may no longer engage in. The labels "compulsive gambler," "ex-convict," "recovering alcoholic," and "ex–mental patient" can stick to a person for life. Goffman draws a useful distinction between a prestige symbol that draws attention to a positive aspect of one's identity, such as a wedding band, and a stigma symbol that discredits or debases one's identity, such as a conviction for child molestation. While stigma symbols may not always be obvious, they can become a matter of public knowledge. Starting in 1994, many states required convicted sex offenders to register with local police departments. Some communities publish the names and addresses, and in some instances even the pictures, of convicted sex offenders on the web.

While some types of deviance will stigmatize a person, other types do not carry a significant penalty. Examples of socially tolerated forms of deviance can be found in the world of high technology.

Deviance and Technology

Technological innovations such as smartphones can redefine social interactions and the standards of behavior related to them. When the Internet was first made available to the general public, no norms or regulations governed its use. Because online communication offers a high degree of anonymity, uncivil behavior—speaking harshly of others or monopolizing chat room space—quickly became common. Online bulletin boards designed to carry items of community interest became littered with commercial advertisements. Such deviant acts are beginning to provoke calls for the establishment of formal rules for online behavior. For example, policymakers have debated whether to regulate the content of websites featuring hate speech and pornography (see Chapter 6).

Some deviant uses of technology are criminal, though not all participants see it that way. On the street, the for-profit pirating of software, motion pictures, and music has become a big business. On the Internet, the downloading of music by individual listeners, which is typically forbidden by copyright, is widely accepted. The music and motion picture industries have waged much-publicized campaigns to stop these illegal uses of their products, yet among many people, no social stigma attaches to them. Deviance, then, is a complex concept. Sometimes it is trivial, sometimes profoundly harmful. Sometimes it is accepted by society and sometimes soundly rejected.

THINKING CRITICALLY

In the United States, breastfeeding a child in public is typically protected by state and federal law. Using the concept of deviance, explain why some people consider breastfeeding in public to be wrong, while some mothers are comfortable with the practice.

Social Control

As we saw in Chapter 3, each culture, subculture, and group has distinctive norms governing appropriate behavior. Laws, dress codes, organizational bylaws, course requirements, and the rules of sports and games all express social norms.

How does a society bring about acceptance of basic norms? The term **social control** refers to the techniques and strategies for preventing deviant human behavior in any society. Social control occurs on all levels of society. In the family, we are socialized to obey our parents simply because they are our parents. Peer groups introduce us to informal norms, such as dress codes, that govern the behavior of their members. Colleges establish standards they expect of students. In bureaucratic organizations, workers encounter a formal system of rules and regulations. Finally, the government of every society legislates and enforces social norms.

Most of us respect and accept basic social norms and assume that others will do the same. Even without thinking, we obey the instructions of police officers, follow the day-to-day rules at our jobs, and move to the rear of elevators when people enter. Such behavior reflects an effective process of socialization to the dominant standards of a culture. At the same time, we are well aware that individuals, groups, and institutions *expect* us to act "properly." This expectation carries with it **sanctions,** or penalties and rewards for conduct concerning a social norm. If we fail to live up to the norm, we may face punishment through informal sanctions such as fear and ridicule or formal sanctions such as jail sentences or fines.

The challenge to effective social control is that people often receive competing messages about how to behave. While the state or government may clearly define acceptable behavior, friends or fellow employees may encourage quite different behavior patterns. Historically, legal measures aimed at blocking discrimination based on race, religion, gender, age, and sexual orientation have been difficult to implement, because many people tacitly encourage the violation of such measures.

Functionalists maintain that people must respect social norms if any group or society is to survive. In their view, societies literally could not function if massive numbers of people defied standards of appropriate conduct. In contrast, conflict theorists contend that the successful functioning of a society will consistently benefit the powerful and work to the disadvantage of other groups. They point out that in the United States, widespread resistance to social norms was necessary to win our independence from Great Britain, to overturn the institution of slavery, to allow women to vote, to secure civil rights, and to force an end to the war in Vietnam.

Conformity and Obedience

Techniques for social control operate on both the group level and the

bartuchna@yahoo.pl/Shutterstock

Is crowding on a public beach on a sunny day deviant? During the pandemic, governments cautioned against such activity and even when legal, many regarded it as inappropriate.

societal level. People we think of as peers or equals influence us to act in particular ways; the same is true of people who hold authority over us or occupy awe-inspiring positions. Social psychologist Stanley Milgram (1975) made a useful distinction between these two levels of social control.

The Milgram Experiment   Milgram used the term **conformity** to mean going along with peers—individuals of our own status who have no special right to direct our behavior. In contrast, **obedience** is compliance with higher authorities in a hierarchical structure. Thus, a recruit entering military service will typically *conform* to the habits and language of other recruits and *obey* the orders of superior officers. College students will *conform* to social behaviors, like the drinking behavior of their peers and *obey* the requests of campus security officers.

If ordered to do so, would you comply with an experimenter's instruction to administer increasingly painful electric shocks to a subject? Most people would say no; yet Milgram's research (1963, 1975) suggests that most of us *would* obey such orders. In his words (1975: xi), "Behavior that is unthinkable in an individual . . . acting on his own may be executed without hesitation when carried out under orders."

Milgram placed advertisements in New Haven, Connecticut, newspapers to recruit subjects for a learning experiment at Yale University. Participants included postal clerks, engineers, high school teachers, and laborers. They were told that the purpose of the research was to investigate the effects of punishment on learning. The experimenter, dressed in a gray technician's coat, explained that in each test, one subject would be randomly selected as the "learner," while another would function as the "teacher." However, the experiment was rigged so that the real subject would always be the teacher, while an associate of Milgram's served as the learner.

At this point, the learner's hand was strapped to an electric apparatus. The teacher was taken to an electronic "shock generator" with 30 levered switches labeled from 15 to 450 volts. Before beginning the experiment, all subjects received sample shocks of 45 volts, to convince them of the authenticity of the experiment. The experimenter then instructed the teacher to apply shocks of increasing voltage each time the learner gave an incorrect answer on a memory test. Teachers were told that "although the shocks can be extremely painful, they cause no permanent tissue damage." In reality, the learner did not receive any shocks.

In a prearranged script, the learner deliberately gave incorrect answers and expressed pain when "shocked." For example, at 150 volts, the learner would cry out, "Get me out of here!" At 270 volts, the learner would scream in agony. When the shock reached 350 volts, the learner would fall silent. If the teacher wanted to stop the experiment, the experimenter would insist that the teacher continue, using such statements as "The experiment requires that you continue" and "You have no other choice; you *must* go on" (Milgram 1975:19–23).

Reflecting on the Milgram Experiment   The results of this unusual experiment stunned and dismayed Milgram and other social scientists. A sample of psychiatrists had predicted that virtually all subjects would refuse to shock innocent victims. In their view, only a "pathological fringe" of less than 2 percent would continue administering shocks up to the maximum level. Yet almost *two-thirds* of participants fell into the category of "obedient subjects."

Why did these subjects obey? Why were they willing to inflict seemingly painful shocks on innocent victims who had never done them any harm? There is no evidence that these subjects were unusually sadistic; few seemed to enjoy administering the shocks. Instead, in Milgram's view, the key to obedience was the experimenter's social role as a "scientist" and "seeker of knowledge."

Milgram pointed out that in the modern industrial world, we are accustomed to submitting to impersonal authority figures whose status is indicated by a title (professor, lieutenant, doctor) or by a uniform (the technician's coat). Because we view the

From the film Obedience ©1968 by Stanley Milgram. ©Renewed 1993 by Alexandra Milgram. Distributed by Alexander Street Press.

In one of Stanley Milgram's experiments, the learner supposedly received an electric shock from a shock plate when he answered a question incorrectly. At the 150-volt level, the learner would demand to be released and would refuse to place his hand on the shock plate. The experimenter would then order the actual subject, the teacher, to force the hand onto the plate, as shown in the photo. Though 40 percent of the true subjects stopped complying with Milgram at this point, 30 percent did force the learner's hand onto the shock plate, despite his pretended agony.

authority as larger and more important than the individual, we shift responsibility for our behavior to the authority figure. Milgram's subjects frequently stated, "If it were up to me, I would not have administered shocks." They saw themselves as merely doing their duty (Milgram 1975).

From an interactionist perspective, one important aspect of Milgram's findings is the fact that subjects in follow-up studies were less likely to inflict the supposed shocks as they were moved physically closer to their victims. Moreover, interactionists emphasize the effect of *incrementally* administering additional dosages of 15 volts. In effect, the experimenter negotiated with the teacher and convinced the teacher to continue inflicting higher levels of punishment. It is doubtful that anywhere near the two-thirds rate of obedience would have been reached had the experimenter told the teachers to administer 450 volts immediately (Allen 1978; Katovich 1987).

Milgram launched his experimental study of obedience to better understand the involvement of Germans in the annihilation of 6 million Jews and millions of other people during World War II. In an interview conducted long after the publication of his study, he suggested that "if a system of death camps were set up in the United States of the sort we had seen in Nazi Germany, one would be able to find sufficient personnel for those camps in any medium-sized American town." Though many people questioned his remark, the revealing photos taken at Iraq's Abu Ghraib prison in 2004, showing U.S. military guards humiliating if not torturing Iraqi prisoners, recalled the

experiment Milgram had done two generations earlier. Under conducive circumstances, otherwise normal people can and often do treat one another inhumanely (CBS News 1979:7–8; Hayden 2004; Zimbardo 2007a).

Although many people may be skeptical of the high levels of conformity Milgram found, recent replications of his experiment confirm his findings. In 2006, using additional safeguards to protect participants' welfare, psychologist Jerry Burger (2009, 2014) repeated part of Milgram's experiment with college undergraduates. To avoid biasing the participants, Burger was careful to screen out students who had heard of Milgram's study. The results of the replication were startlingly similar to Milgram's: participants showed a high level of willingness to shock the learner, just as the participants in Milgram's experiment had almost half a century earlier. At the most comparable point in the two studies, Burger measured a rate of 70 percent full obedience—lower, but not significantly so, than the rate of 82.5 percent measured two generations earlier.

Obedience and Virtual Reality How willing would people be today to shock learners? While many people may be skeptical of Milgram's findings, virtual reality (VR) has allowed researchers to re-create the experiment. In these instances the learners, wearing 3D stereo glasses, were told that they were applying "electric shocks" to a "virtual trainee" when that trainee made errors. In some variations they only heard the learner respond to the shock; in others they actually saw the VR learner's response.

Mark Nazh/Shutterstock

Virtual reality (VR) has now allowed researchers to re-create the Milgram experiment. These replications using the latest technology confirm people's willingness to obey and conform.

Remarkably, these VR replications of this almost 60-year-old study have found that the teachers felt levels of stress similar to what Milgram found. Teachers still largely obeyed the instructions. They continued to carry out a task that they clearly regarded as unpleasant, at the very least. These creations of a realistic immersive social environment have been significant for not only confirming Milgram's findings but for suggesting that VR can be used in other studies of social behavior. In other words, VR can be utilized to re-create real-life situations in a much more dramatic fashion than pencil-and-paper questionnaires describing hypothetical social situations (Cornet and Van Gelder 2020; Slater et al. 2006).

RESEARCH TODAY

7-1   Gun Control

Guns and ammunition are big business in the United States, where the Second Amendment to the Constitution guarantees the "right of the people to keep and bear arms." Currently, about 40 percent of U.S. households have some type of firearm on the premises. Informal gun clubs of both a primary- and secondary-group nature flourish across the country. On a national basis, powerful formal organizations promote gun ownership. Clearly, owning a gun is not a deviant act in our society.

Over the last two decades, the demand for stricter gun controls has declined rather than grown.

At its highest point of support in 2000, about 67 percent of Americans felt that controlling gun ownership was more important than protecting the right to own a gun. Support had dropped to 53 percent by 2019. During this time, the National Rifle Association (NRA) used its impressive power to block or dilute gun control efforts. In 2013, the year after the Sandy Hook elementary school shooting in Newtown, Connecticut, state legislatures enacted 109 new gun laws. Seventy of them loosened firearms restrictions, and 39 tightened them. Anti–gun control forces were so powerful that sociologists and other researchers had great difficulty securing federal funding for research on firearms ownership. Federal funds were not provided for such research from 1996 until 2020.

Conflict theorists contend that powerful groups like the NRA can dominate the legislative process to block research because of their ability to mobilize resources in opposition to the will of the majority. Founded in 1871, the NRA has over 4 million members; state rifle associations, with 4 to 5 million members, support many of the NRA's goals. In contrast, the Brady Campaign to Prevent Gun Violence, a key organization in the gun control battle, has only 50,000 members. Compared to the NRA's formidable war chest, the resources of gun control groups are limited.

Taylor McKnight/Shutterstock

In early 2018 a shooting at the Marjory Stoneman Douglas High School in Parkland, Florida, left 17 dead. In the absence of government action, high school students nationwide began to lobby legislators, take to social media, and organize school walkouts as part of the #MarchForOurLives Movement.

Interactionists have studied how gun rights organizations like the National Rifle Association present their argument to their own members. These organizations frame the issue not so much as one of safety or crime, but of civil rights. Gun rights advocates see the Constitution as the basis for their campaign to facilitate gun ownership.

Public health advocates have also weighed in on the issue, noting the 40,000 people in the United States who die every year through gun violence, whether by suicide, homicide, or accidental discharge. These researchers advocate making guns safer—for example, by adding an indicator that the gun is loaded or a latch that prevents a magazine from being removed with a bullet still in the firing chamber. A more sophisticated approach to increasing safety would be to require the gun owner or user to activate a code before the gun can be used.

Many observers note the great disparity between the number of gun deaths in the United States and in other developed nations. Yet every mass shooting, such as the Sandy Hook tragedy, seems only to weaken existing controls. Legislatures often react by loosening restrictions rather than tightening existing laws on who can own guns and which types of guns are legal. The future social impact of the NRA, the Brady Campaign, and the student-led movement remains to be seen.

LET'S DISCUSS

1. Do you see guns more as weapons that could jeopardize your safety or as a protection against those who could harm you?
2. What kinds of research do you think sociologists or other social scientists should carry out related to gun ownership? What questions should they pose?

Sources: Centers for Disease Control and Prevention 2020b; Gramlich and Schaeffer 2019; Holmes 2019; K. Schaeffer 2019; Vasilogambros 2018; Yourish and Buchanan 2013.

USE YOUR SOCIOLOGICAL IMAGINATION

If you were a participant in Milgram's research on conformity, how far do you think you would go in carrying out orders? Do you see any ethical problem with the experimenter's manipulation of the subjects? Explain your answer.

Informal and Formal Social Control

The sanctions that are used to encourage conformity and obedience—and to discourage violation of social norms—are carried out through both informal and formal social control. As the term implies, people use **informal social control** casually to enforce norms. Examples include smiles, laughter, a raised eyebrow, and ridicule.

In the United States and many other cultures, adults often view spanking, slapping, or kicking children as a proper and necessary means of informal social control. Child development specialists counter that such corporal punishment is inappropriate because it teaches children to solve problems through violence. They warn that slapping and spanking can escalate into more serious forms of abuse. Research shows that this kind of negative interaction, even when previously accompanied by warm parenting practices, is linked to adolescent social conduct disorder. Not surprisingly, only 6 percent of pediatricians surveyed hold positive views of spanking, and less than 3 percent said that spanking resulted in positive outcomes. Yet many in our culture still accept this form of informal social control (Chung et al. 2009; Sege and Siegel 2018).

Formal social control is carried out by authorized agents, such as police officers, judges, school administrators, employers, military officers, and managers of movie theaters. It can serve as a last resort when socialization and informal sanctions do not bring about desired behavior. Sometimes, informal social control can actually undermine formal social control, encouraging people to violate social norms.

Historically, the death penalty has served as a significant form of social control. The threat of execution was meant as much to discourage others from committing capital crimes as it was to punish those who did. However, researchers have been unable to establish what if any deterrence effect executions may have, leading many people to question the effectiveness of the death penalty.

In the aftermath of September 11, 2001, new measures of social control became the norm in the United States. Some of them, such as stepped-up security and surveillance at airports and high-rise buildings, were highly visible to the public. The federal government has also publicly urged citizens to engage in informal social control by watching for and reporting people whose actions seem suspicious (Monahan 2011).

Many people think this kind of social control goes too far. Civil rights advocates worry that the government's request for information on suspicious activities may encourage negative stereotyping of Muslims and Arab Americans and lead to violent encounters. Clearly, there is a trade-off between the benefits of surveillance and the right to privacy.

Other aspects of government social control have also undergone criticism. Solitary confinement—defined as at least 22 hours per day removed from the general prison population for at least 30 days—has become increasingly common in the United States. In 2016, at least 100,000 inmates were in solitary confinement or isolated housing in state and federal prisons on any given day. Prison officials defend the practice as necessary to managing the inmate population, while critics point to the absence of research evaluating its effectiveness or impact on the prisoners themselves. In 2016, President Obama ordered the end of solitary confinement for youths and for low-level offenders. This policy would end solitary confinement for about 10 percent of those experiencing this type of social control (Shear 2016; The Liman Program 2015).

Controlling society involves both informal and formal social control. One policy issue that sociologists have considered is gun control. While many hobbyists and hunters collect and use firearms, others view them primarily as a form of protection, while still others think that private citizens should not be allowed to own guns. In Box 7-1 we consider sociological insights into regulating firearms.

THINKING CRITICALLY

Should youths who have been convicted of violent crimes be subject to the death penalty? Why or why not?

Law and Society

Some norms are so important to a society that they are formalized into laws regarding people's behavior. **Law** may be defined as governmental social control (Black 1995). Some laws, such as the prohibition against murder, are directed at all members of society. Others, such as fishing and hunting regulations, affect particular categories of people. Still others govern the behavior of social institutions (for instance, corporate law and laws regarding the taxing of nonprofit enterprises).

Sociologists see the creation of laws as a social process. Because governments make laws in response to a perceived need for formal social control, sociologists have sought to explain how and why such a perception arises. In their view, law is not merely a static body of rules handed down from generation to generation. Rather, it reflects continually changing standards of what is right and wrong, of how violations are to be determined, and of what sanctions are to be applied (Schur 1968).

Sociologists representing varying theoretical perspectives agree that the legal order reflects the values of those in authority. Therefore, the creation of civil and criminal law can be highly controversial. Should it be against the law to employ unauthorized immigrants, to have an abortion, to allow prayer in public schools, or to smoke on an airplane? Such issues have been bitterly debated, because they require a choice among competing values. Not surprisingly, laws that are unpopular—such as the one-time prohibition of alcohol under the Eighteenth Amendment and the widespread establishment of a 55-mile-per-hour speed limit on highways—become difficult to enforce when there is no consensus supporting the norms.

One current and controversial debate over laws governing behavior is whether people should be allowed to use marijuana legally, for medical purposes. Although the majority of adults polled in national surveys support such a use, the federal government continues to regard all uses of marijuana as illegal. In 2005 the Supreme Court upheld the federal government's position. Nevertheless, as of 2020, 11 states and the District of Columbia had legalized the recreational use of marijuana and

THINKING CRITICALLY

Should some illegal drugs be decriminalized? Why or why not?

22 states had granted citizens the right to use marijuana for medical purposes—even if that privilege rests on dubious legal grounds (Figure 7-1).

Socialization is the primary source of conforming and obedient behavior, including obedience to law. Generally, it is not external pressure from a peer group or authority figure that makes us go along with social norms. Rather, we have internalized such norms as valid and desirable and are committed to observing them. In a profound sense, we want to see ourselves (and to be seen) as loyal, cooperative, responsible, and respectful of others. In the United States and other societies around the world, people are socialized both to want to belong and to fear being viewed as different or deviant.

Control theory suggests that our connection to members of society leads us to systematically conform to society's norms. According to sociologist Travis Hirschi and other control theorists, our bonds to family members, friends, and peers induce us to follow the mores and folkways of our society. We give little conscious thought to whether we will be sanctioned if we fail to conform. Socialization develops our self-control so well that we don't need further pressure to obey social norms.

Although control theory does not effectively explain the rationale for every conforming act, it nevertheless reminds us that while the media may focus on crime and disorder, most members of most societies conform to and obey basic norms (Schmalleger 2020:127–131; Hirschi 1969).

Control theory focuses on societally recognized deviance and crime, which typically does not include lacking money. As we see in Box 7-2, an increasing proportion of people are in jail for their inability to pay money while they await trial.

MAPPING LIFE NATIONWIDE

FIGURE 7-1 THE STATUS OF STATE LEGALIZATION OF MARIJUANA

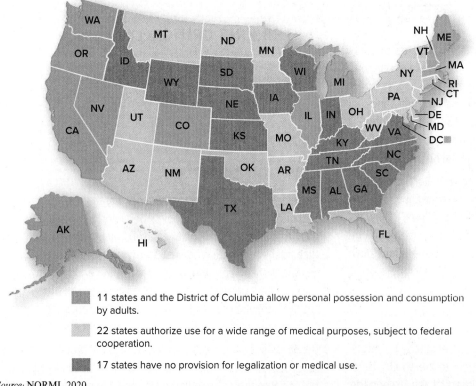

■ 11 states and the District of Columbia allow personal possession and consumption by adults.

■ 22 states authorize use for a wide range of medical purposes, subject to federal cooperation.

■ 17 states have no provision for legalization or medical use.

Source: NORML 2020.

RESEARCH TODAY

7-2   Debtors' Jails in the Twenty-First Century

Being in jail means you have committed a crime, right? Most likely, not correct. About two-thirds of people in jails have not been convicted of a crime. They just cannot pay the bail to allow themselves to be free during the long wait to stand trial. Lack of money and jail time have a long history.

Charles Dickens is well known for writing about people living on the margins of society, whether it is Oliver Twist, a street beggar, or Bob Cratchit, the miserably paid clerk of Ebenezer Scrooge. It is easy to understand his sympathy for the downtrodden. When he was 12, his father was forced by his creditors into a debtors' prison. As was the custom, his wife, Charles, and four younger children joined him there. At age 12, Charles was regarded as old enough to support himself. His father was finally able to leave prison upon the death of a relative, whose modest estate provided enough money to cover the debts.

We can understand, then, why the Eighth Amendment to the Constitution asserts that "Excessive bail shall not be required." However, over two hundred years later, an increasing number of people are concerned about the impact of bail on the accused who happen to be poor.

Nationwide, in 1990 three out of every five defendants in felony cases who were released pending trial were let go on their own recognizance or on some other condition that did not involve bail. By 2015, three out of five were required to post bail.

Defendants who can't make bail, regardless of their accused crime, are four times more likely to be sentenced to time in prison.

Besides the obvious disruptions to one's life and family, being incarcerated awaiting trial makes it more difficult to mount a defense. Defendants who can't make bail, regardless of their accused crime, are four times more likely to be sentenced to time in prison. In addition, individuals held in jail plead guilty 92 percent of the time, compared to 40 percent for those awaiting trial at home.

Legally, before demanding bail the government must show that a person is a flight risk (someone who is likely to flee the county or state to avoid prosecution). In practice the assumption of flight risk trumps the presumption of innocence. Increasingly courts also consider whether the indicted person is also likely to pose a danger to the community independent of the crime for which he or she was arrested. Research shows that from 1995 to 2010, the proportion of people out on bail who committed any misconduct gradually dropped to about 17 percent—and the vast majority of these were typically technical violations

regarding court appearances. Fewer than 2 percent fail to appear for trial.

Some people feel that the only sensible reform is to remove money from the bail system. New York State did just that in 2020, eliminating cash bail for many nonviolent criminal defendants. Within days, several high-profile assaults occurred, causing much of the public to question the reform. Data from New Jersey, which changed its bail system in 2017, indicates that eliminating cash bail does not lead to a surge in crime and that defendants show up in court at the same rates as before. However, New York did not give judges the discretion to consider whether a person posed a threat to public safety in deciding whether to hold them. So many commentators embrace the reform yet feel that some further changes are needed.

LET'S DISCUSS

1. Do you agree with the statement "Lack of money and jail time have a long history"? Why do the two seem to go together?
2. What are some possible solutions to the problem of poverty and jail time?

Sources: American Civil Liberties Union 2020; Ewing 2015; Lewis 2020; McKinley and Mays 2020; Minton and Golinelli 2014; Subramanian et al. 2015.

THINKING CRITICALLY

The text states that law reflects changing standards of right and wrong. Recent changes in laws regarding marijuana use and same-sex marriage support this statement. What other laws do you think are likely to change in the near future because of changing societal standards?

Sociological Perspectives on Deviance

Why do people violate social norms? We have seen that deviant acts are subject to both informal and formal social control. The

nonconforming or disobedient person may face disapproval, loss of friends, fines, or even imprisonment. Why, then, does deviance occur?

Early explanations for behavior that deviated from societal expectations blamed supernatural causes or genetic factors (such as "bad blood" or evolutionary throwbacks to primitive ancestors). By the 1800s, substantial research efforts were being made to identify biological factors that lead to deviance, and especially to criminal activity. Though such research was discredited in the 20th century, contemporary studies, primarily by biochemists, have sought to isolate genetic factors that suggest a likelihood of certain personality traits. Although criminality (much less deviance) is hardly a personality characteristic, researchers have focused on traits that might lead to crime, such as aggression. Of course, aggression can also lead to success in the corporate world, in professional sports, or in other walks of life.

The contemporary study of the possible biological roots of criminality is but one aspect of the larger debate over sociobiology. In general, sociologists have been critical of any emphasis on the genetic roots of crime and deviance. The limitations of current knowledge about the link between genetics and antisocial behavior have led them to draw largely on other approaches to explain deviance (Cohen 2011).

Functionalist Perspective

According to functionalists, deviance is a common part of human existence, with positive as well as negative consequences for social stability. Deviance helps to define the limits of proper behavior. Children who see one parent scold the other for belching at the dinner table learn about approved conduct. The same is true of the driver who receives a speeding ticket, the department store cashier who is fired for yelling at a customer, and the student who is penalized for handing in papers weeks overdue.

Durkheim's Legacy Émile Durkheim ([1895] 1964) focused his sociological investigations mainly on criminal acts, yet his conclusions have implications for all types of deviant behavior. In Durkheim's view, the punishments established within a culture (including both formal and informal mechanisms of social control) help to define acceptable behavior and thus contribute to stability. If improper acts were not sanctioned, people might stretch their standards of what constitutes appropriate conduct.

Sociologist Kai Erikson (1966) illustrated the boundary-maintenance function of deviance in his study of the Puritans of 17th-century New England. By today's standards, the Puritans placed tremendous emphasis on conventional morals. Their persecution and execution of women as witches represented a continuing attempt to define and redefine the boundaries of their community. In effect, their changing social norms created crime waves, as people whose behavior was previously acceptable suddenly faced punishment for being deviant (R. Schaefer and Zellner 2015).

Durkheim ([1897] 1951) introduced the term **anomie** into sociological literature to describe the loss of direction felt in a society when social control of individual behavior has become ineffective. Anomie is a state of normlessness that typically occurs during a period of profound social change and disorder, such as a time of economic collapse. People become more aggressive or depressed, which results in higher rates of violent crime and suicide. Since there is much less agreement on what constitutes proper behavior during times of revolution, sudden prosperity, or economic depression, conformity and obedience become less significant as social forces. It also becomes much more difficult to state exactly what constitutes deviance.

Merton's Theory of Deviance What do a mugger and a teacher have in common? Each is "working" to obtain money that can then be exchanged for desired goods. As this example illustrates, behavior that violates accepted norms (such as mugging) may be based on the same basic objectives as the behavior of people who pursue more conventional lifestyles.

TABLE 7-1   MERTON'S DEVIANCE THEORY

Summing Up

Does the individual accept:	Type of Behavior				
	Nondeviant	Deviant			
	Conformity	Retreatism	Innovation	Ritualism	Rebellion
the goals of society, such as acquisition of wealth?	👍	👎	👍	👎	👎👍
the use of acceptable means, such as hard work?	👍	👎	👎	👍	👎👍

Sources: Adapted by author, Richard Schaefer, from Chapter VI, "Social Structure and Anomie," in Merton 1968. Photos: Moneybag: Givaga/Shutterstock; *Time clock:* Alamy Stock Photo

On the basis of this kind of analysis, sociologist Robert Merton (1968) adapted Durkheim's notion of anomie to explain why people accept or reject the goals of a society, the socially approved means of fulfilling their aspirations, or both. Merton maintained that one important cultural goal in the United States is success, measured largely in terms of money. In addition to providing this goal for people, our society offers specific instructions on how to pursue success—go to school, work hard, do not quit, take advantage of opportunities, and so forth.

What happens to individuals in a society with a heavy emphasis on wealth as a basic symbol of success? Merton reasoned that people adapt in certain ways, either by conforming to or by deviating from such cultural expectations. His **anomie theory of deviance** posits five types of behavior or basic forms of adaptation (Table 7-1).

The other four types of behavior represented in Table 7-1 all involve some departure from conformity. The *retreatist* has basically retreated (or withdrawn) from both the goals and the means of society. In the United States, drug addicts and vagrants are typically portrayed as retreatists. Concern has been growing that adolescents who are addicted to alcohol will become retreatists at an early age.

In Merton's typology, the *innovator* accepts the goals of society but pursues them with means that are regarded as improper. For instance, a safecracker may steal money to buy consumer goods and expensive vacations.

The *ritualist* has abandoned the goal of material success and become compulsively committed to the institutional means. Work becomes simply a way of life rather than a means to the goal of success. An example would be the bureaucratic official who blindly applies rules and regulations without remembering the larger goals of the organization. Certainly that would be true of a welfare caseworker who refuses to assist a homeless family because their last apartment was in another district.

The final type of behavior or adaptation identified by Merton reflects people's attempts to create a *new* social structure. The *rebel* feels alienated from the dominant means and goals and may seek a dramatically different social order. Members of a revolutionary political organization, such as a militia group, can be categorized as rebels according to Merton's model.

Merton made a key contribution to the sociological understanding of deviance by pointing out that deviants such as innovators and ritualists share a great deal with conforming people. The convicted felon may hold many of the same aspirations as people with no criminal background. The theory helps us to understand deviance as a socially created behavior rather than as the result of momentary pathological impulses. However, this theory of deviance has not been applied systematically to real-world crime. Box 7-3 examines scholars' efforts to confirm the theory's validity.

Interactionist Perspective

The functionalist approach to deviance explains why rule violations continue to happen despite pressure to conform and obey. However, functionalists do not indicate how a given person comes to commit a deviant act or why on some occasions crimes do or do not occur. The emphasis on everyday behavior that is the focus of the interactionist perspective offers such an explanation: cultural transmission theory.

Cultural Transmission   In the course of studying graffiti writing by gangs in Los Angeles, sociologist Susan A. Phillips (1999) discovered that the writers learned from one another. In fact, Phillips was surprised by how stable their focus was over time. She also noted how other ethnic groups built on the models of the African American and Chicano gangs, superimposing Cambodian, Chinese, or Vietnamese symbols.

Humans *learn* how to behave in social situations, whether properly or improperly. There is no natural, innate manner in which people interact with one another. These simple ideas are not disputed today, but such was not the case when sociologist Edwin Sutherland (1883–1950) first advanced the idea that an individual undergoes the same basic socialization process in learning conforming and deviant acts.

Sutherland's ideas have been the dominating force in criminology. He drew on the **cultural transmission** school, which emphasizes that one learns criminal behavior by interacting with others. Such learning includes not only the techniques of lawbreaking (for example, how to break into a car quickly and quietly) but also the motives, drives, and rationalizations of the criminal. The cultural transmission approach can also be used to explain the behavior of those who habitually abuse alcohol or drugs.

Sutherland maintained that through interactions with a primary group and significant others, people acquire definitions of proper and improper behavior. He used the term **differential association** to describe the process through which exposure to attitudes *favorable* to criminal acts leads to the violation of rules. Research suggests that this view of differential association also applies to noncriminal deviant acts, such as smoking, truancy, and early sexual behavior.

Sutherland offers the example of a boy who is sociable, outgoing, and athletic and who lives in an area with a high rate of delinquency. The youth is very likely to come into contact with

RESEARCH TODAY

7-3 Does Crime Pay?

A driver violates the speed limit to get to a job interview on time. A financially strapped parent shoplifts goods that her family needs. These people may feel justified in violating the law because they do so to meet a reasonable objective. In Robert Merton's terms, they are innovators—people who violate social norms to achieve a commonly shared societal goal. Although their actions are criminal and potentially hurtful to others, from their own short-term perspective, their actions are functional.

Stockbyte/Getty Images

Less than 5 percent of even the gang leaders earned $100,000 per year. The rest of the leaders and virtually all the rank and file earned less than the minimum wage.

Carried to its logical conclusion, innovation can and does become a career for some people. Yet from a purely economic point of view, even considering the fact that crime may pay is controversial, because doing so may seem to tolerate or encourage rule violation. Nothing is more controversial than the suggestion that gang-run drug deals are profitable and produce "good jobs." Although some people may see drug dealers as a cross between MBA-educated professionals and streetwise entrepreneurs, society in general does not admire these innovators.

Sociologist Sudhir Venkatesh collected detailed data on the illegal drug trade during his observation research on a Chicago street gang. Working with economist Steven Levitt, coauthor of the best seller Freakonomics, to analyze the business of selling crack cocaine, he found that less than 5 percent of even the gang leaders earned $100,000 per year. The rest of the leaders and virtually all the rank and file earned less than the minimum wage. In fact, most were unpaid workers seeking to move up in the gang hierarchy (thus the title of a chapter in Levitt's book, "Why Do Drug Dealers Still Live with Their Moms?"). As Levitt notes, the drug gang is like most corporations: the top 2 percent of workers take home most of the money.

Why, from a sociological and an economic perspective, do these nonprofitable practices persist, especially considering that one in every four members of drug-oriented street gangs is eventually killed? One reason, of course, is the public's almost insatiable demand for illegal drugs. And from the drug peddler's perspective, few legitimate jobs are available to young adults in poverty-stricken areas, urban or rural. Functionally, these youths are contributing to their household incomes by dealing drugs.

Scholars see a need for further research on Merton's concept of innovation. Why, for example, do some disadvantaged groups have lower rates of reported crime than others? Why do many people who are caught in adverse circumstances reject criminal activity as a viable alternative? Merton's theory of deviance does not easily answer such questions.

There does appear to be a significant exception to the adage that crime does not pay. In certain high-end professional criminal endeavors, people may make money, a lot of it, even after being caught. Many perpetrators of antitrust and insider trading crimes still profit even after paying penalties, since jail time is rarely assigned. We will talk about what is termed *white collar crime* later in this chapter.

LET'S DISCUSS

1. Do you know anyone who has stolen out of need? If so, did the person feel justified in stealing, or did he or she feel guilty? How long did the theft continue?
2. Economically, profit is the difference between revenues and costs. What are the costs of the illegal drug trade, both economic and social? Is this economic activity profitable for society?

Sources: Connor and Lande 2019; S. Levitt and Dubner 2006; S. Levitt and Venkatesh 2000; Rosen and Venkatesh 2008; Venkatesh 2008.

---

peers who commit acts of vandalism, fail to attend school, and so forth, and may come to adopt such behavior. However, an introverted boy who lives in the same neighborhood may stay away from his peers and avoid delinquency. In another community, an outgoing and athletic boy may join a soccer team or participate in a Big Brothers Big Sisters program. Thus, Sutherland views improper behavior as the result of the types of groups to which one belongs and the kinds of friendships one has.

According to critics, the cultural transmission approach may explain the deviant behavior of juvenile delinquents or graffiti artists, but it fails to explain the conduct of the first-time impulsive shoplifter or the impoverished person who steals out of necessity. While it is not a precise statement of the process through which one becomes a criminal, differential association theory does direct our attention to the paramount role of social interaction in increasing a person's motivation to engage in deviant behavior (Schmalleger 2020: 125–126; Sutherland et al. 1992).

Social Disorganization Theory The social relationships that exist in a community or neighborhood affect people's behavior. Philip Zimbardo (2007a), author of the mock prison experiment described in Chapter 5, once did an experiment that demonstrated the power of communal relationships. He abandoned a car in each of two different neighborhoods,

Frank and Helena/Cultura/Getty Images

According to social disorganization theory, strong communal bonds can enhance neighborhood ties, reducing the likelihood of criminal behavior.

leaving its hood up and removing its hubcaps. In one neighborhood, people started to strip the car for parts before Zimbardo had finished setting up a remote video camera to record their behavior. In the other neighborhood, weeks passed without the car being touched, except for a pedestrian who stopped to close the hood during a rainstorm.

What accounts for the strikingly different outcomes of Zimbardo's experiment in the two communities? According to **social disorganization theory,** increases in crime and deviance can be attributed to the absence or breakdown of communal relationships and social institutions, such as the family, school, church, and local government. This theory was developed at the University of Chicago in the early 1900s to describe the apparent disorganization that occurred as cities expanded with rapid immigration and migration from rural areas. Using the latest survey techniques, Clifford Shaw and Henry McKay literally mapped the distribution of social problems in Chicago. They found high rates of social problems in neighborhoods where buildings had deteriorated and the population had declined. Interestingly, the patterns persisted over time, despite changes in the neighborhoods' ethnic and racial composition.

This theory is not without its critics. To some, social disorganization theory seems to "blame the victim," leaving larger societal forces, such as the lack of jobs or high-quality schools, unaccountable. Critics also argue that even troubled neighborhoods have viable, healthy organizations, which persist despite the problems that surround them.

More recently, social disorganization theorists have taken to emphasizing the effect of social networks on communal bonds. These researchers acknowledge that communities are not isolated islands. Residents' bonds may be enhanced or weakened by their ties to groups outside the immediate community (Bellair 2017; Sampson and Graves 1989; Shaw and McKay 1942).

Labeling Perspective

The Saints and the Roughnecks were groups of high school males who were continually engaged in excessive drinking, reckless driving, truancy, petty theft, and vandalism. There the similarity ended. None of the Saints was ever arrested, but every Roughneck was frequently in trouble with police and townspeople. Why the disparity in their treatment? On the basis of observation research in their high school, sociologist William Chambliss (1973; Chambliss and Haas 2012) concluded that social class played an important role in the varying fortunes of the two groups.

The Saints hid behind a facade of respectability. They came from "good families," were active in school organizations, planned on attending college, and received good grades. People generally viewed their delinquent acts as a few isolated cases of sowing wild oats. The Roughnecks had no such aura of respectability. They drove around town in beat-up cars, were generally unsuccessful in school, and aroused suspicion no matter what they did.

We can understand such discrepancies by using an approach to deviance known as **labeling theory.** Unlike Sutherland's work, labeling theory does not focus on why some individuals come to commit deviant acts. Instead, it attempts to explain why certain people (such as the Roughnecks) are *viewed* as deviants, delinquents, bad kids, losers, and criminals, whereas others whose behavior is similar (such as the Saints) are not seen in such harsh terms. Reflecting the contribution of interactionist theorists, labeling theory emphasizes how a person comes to be labeled as deviant or to accept that label. Sociologist Howard Becker ([1953] 2015; 1963:9; 1964), who popularized this approach, summed it up with this statement: "Deviant behavior is behavior that people so label."

Labeling theory is also called the **societal-reaction approach,** reminding us that it is the *response* to an act, not the behavior itself, that determines deviance. For example, studies have shown that some school personnel and therapists expand educational programs designed for learning-disabled students

to include those with behavioral problems. Consequently, a "troublemaker" can be improperly labeled as "learning-disabled," and vice versa (Grattet 2011).

Labeling and Agents of Social Control   Traditionally, research on deviance has focused on people who violate social norms. In contrast, labeling theory focuses on police, probation officers, psychiatrists, judges, teachers, employers, school officials, and other regulators of social control. These agents, it is argued, play a significant role in creating the deviant identity by designating certain people (and not others) as deviant. An important aspect of labeling theory is the recognition that some individuals or groups have the power to *define* labels and *apply* them to others. This view ties into the conflict perspective's emphasis on the social significance of power.

In recent years the practice of racial profiling has come under public scrutiny. **Racial profiling** is any arbitrary action initiated by an authority based on race, ethnicity, or national origin rather than on a person's behavior. Studies confirm the public's suspicions that in some jurisdictions, police are much more likely to stop Black males than white males for routine traffic violations. The protest marches of the summer of 2020 in the wake of the death of an unarmed Black man, George Floyd, by Minneapolis police, highlighted concerns that law enforcement routinely treats Black males more harshly. Others responded that there was need for more law and order, making it a major issue in the 2020 presidential campaign. (Racial profiling will be examined in more detail in Chapter 10.)

The popularity of labeling theory is reflected in the emergence of a related perspective, called social constructionism. According to the **social constructionist perspective,** deviance is the product of the culture we live in. Social constructionists focus specifically on the decision-making process that creates the deviant identity. They point out that "child abductors," "deadbeat dads," "spree killers," and "date rapists" have always been with us, but at times have become *the* major social concern of policymakers because of intensive media coverage (Liska and Messner 1999; E. R. Wright et al. 2000).

How do certain behaviors come to be viewed as a problem? Cigarette smoking, which was once regarded as a polite, gentlemanly activity, is now considered a serious health hazard, not only to the smoker but also to others nearby who don't smoke. Recently, people have become concerned about the danger, especially to children, posed by *thirdhand smoke*—smoke-related chemicals that cling to clothes and linger in rooms, cars, even elevators (Winickoff et al. 2009).

USE YOUR SOCIOLOGICAL IMAGINATION

You are a teacher. What labels, freely used in education, might you attach to your students?

Conflict Perspective

Conflict theorists point out that people with power protect their interests and define deviance to suit their needs. Sociologist Richard Quinney (1974, 1979, 1980) was a leading exponent of the view that the criminal justice system serves the interests of the powerful. Crime, according to Quinney (1970), is a definition of conduct created by authorized agents of social control—such as legislators and law enforcement officers—in a politically organized society. He and other conflict theorists argue that lawmaking is often an attempt by the powerful to coerce others into their morality.

This theory helps to explain why our society has laws against gambling, drug use, and prostitution, many of which are violated on a massive scale. (We will examine these "victimless crimes" later in the chapter.) According to conflict theorists, criminal law does not represent a consistent application of societal values, but instead reflects competing values and interests. Thus, the U.S. criminal code outlaws marijuana because of its alleged harm to users, yet cigarettes and alcohol—both of which can be harmful to users—are sold legally almost everywhere.

In fact, conflict theorists contend that the entire criminal justice system in the United States treats suspects differently based on their racial, ethnic, or social-class background. In many cases, officials in the system use their own discretion to make biased decisions about whether to press charges or drop them, whether to set bail and how much, whether to offer parole or deny it. Researchers have found that this kind of **differential justice**—differences in the way social control is exercised over different groups—puts African Americans at a disadvantage. The policies and practices of criminal justice agencies, coupled with the conditions in which many Black Americans live, have contributed to an overrepresentation of African Americans within police interactions and arrests, in courts and sentencing, corrections, and juvenile justice (Yusef et al. 2019).

The perspective advanced by conflict and labeling theorists forms quite a contrast to the functionalist approach to deviance. Functionalists see standards of deviant behavior as merely reflecting cultural norms; conflict and labeling theorists point out that the most powerful groups in a society can shape laws and standards and determine who is (or is not) prosecuted as a criminal. These groups would be unlikely to apply the label "deviant" to the corporate executive whose decisions lead to large-scale environmental pollution. In the opinion of conflict theorists, agents of social control and other powerful groups can impose their own self-serving definitions of deviance on the general public.

Feminist Perspective

Feminist criminologists such as Freda Adler (1996) and Meda Chesney-Lind (2017) have suggested that many of the existing

Guy Corbishley/Alamy Stock Photo

How do we label people's behavior? Is this vandalism? Artwork? Political protest? The English street artist Banksy executed this work, often given the title "Rage, The Flower Thrower," in Jerusalem in 2003. It was painted on the West Bank barrier wall separating Israel from its occupied territories. The image depicts a protester in the act of hurling a bouquet of colorful flowers, not a Molotov cocktail. This was one of many controversial artworks that Banksy executed to support Palestinian rights.

It took repeated protests by feminist organizations to get changes in the criminal law defining rape (Pauly 2019).

Feminist analysis shows that about 80 to 95 percent of campus sexual assault against women students is not reported to college officials. This may change due to the nationwide #MeToo movement, which encourages women to speak out about sexual assault, but colleges must redefine the expectations of campus culture. Traditionally that culture has normalized a certain level of male sexual aggression (Spencer et al. 2017).

In the future, feminist scholarship can be expected to grow dramatically. Research will explore to what degree family violence escalates during prolonged confinement such as during the pandemic. In addition, feminist researchers will delve into such topics as white-collar crime, drinking behavior, drug abuse, and differential sentencing rates between the genders.

approaches to deviance and crime were developed with only men in mind. For example, in the United States, for many years any husband who forced his wife to have sexual intercourse—without her consent and against her will—was not legally considered to have committed rape. The law defined rape as pertaining only to sexual relations between people who were not married to each other, reflecting the overwhelmingly male composition of state legislatures at the time.

We have seen that over the past century, sociologists have taken many different approaches in studying deviance, arousing some controversy in the process. Table 7-2 summarizes the various theoretical approaches to this topic.

TABLE 7-2 SOCIOLOGICAL PERSPECTIVES ON DEVIANCE Tracking Sociological Perspectives

Approach	Theoretical Perspective	Proponents	Emphasis
Anomie	Functionalist	Émile Durkheim Robert Merton	Adaptation to societal norms
Cultural transmission/ Differential association	Interactionist	Edwin Sutherland	Patterns learned through others
Social disorganization	Interactionist	Clifford Shaw Henry McKay	Communal relationships
Labeling/Social constructionist	Interactionist	Howard Becker William Chambliss	Societal response to acts
Conflict	Conflict	Richard Quinney	Dominance by authorized agents Discretionary justice
Feminist	Conflict/Feminist	Freda Adler Meda Chesney-Lind	Role of gender Women as victims and perpetrators

Think about It Which sociological perspective is most useful in analyzing white-collar crime? Vandalism? Cocaine use?

Crime: A Sociological Approach

Crime is on everyone's mind. Until recently, college campuses were viewed as havens from crime. But as Box 7-4 shows, at today's colleges and universities, there have been increased calls to allow members of the campus community to carry firearms.

Crime is a violation of criminal law for which some governmental authority applies formal penalties. It represents a deviation from formal social norms administered by the state. Laws divide crimes into various categories, depending on the severity of the offense, the age of the offender, the potential punishment, and the court that holds jurisdiction over the case. Rather than relying solely on legal categories, however, sociologists classify crimes in terms of how they are committed and how society views the offenses. In this section we will examine six types of crime differentiated by sociologists: victimless crime, professional crime, organized crime, white-collar and technology-based crime, hate crimes, and transnational crime.

Victimless Crime

When we think of crime, we tend to think of acts that endanger people's economic or personal well-being against their will (or without their direct knowledge). In contrast, sociologists use the term **victimless crime** to describe the willing exchange among adults of widely desired but illegal goods and services, such as prostitution (Schur 1965, 1985).

Some activists are working to decriminalize many of these illegal practices. Supporters of decriminalization are troubled by the attempt to legislate a moral code for adults. In their view, prostitution, drug abuse, gambling, and other victimless crimes are impossible to prevent. The already overburdened criminal justice system should instead devote its resources to street crimes and other offenses with obvious victims.

Despite widespread use of the term *victimless crime,* however, many people object to the notion that there is no victim other than the offender in such crimes. Excessive drinking, compulsive gambling, and illegal drug use contribute to an enormous amount of personal and property damage. A person with a drinking problem may become abusive to a spouse or children; a compulsive gambler or drug user may steal to pursue his or her obsession. And feminist sociologists contend that prostitution, as well as the more disturbing aspects of pornography, reinforce the misconception that women are "toys" who can be treated as objects rather than people. According to critics of decriminalization, society must not give tacit approval to conduct that has such harmful consequences (Melissa Farley and Malarek 2008).

Ingram Publishing/SuperStock

The controversy over decriminalization reminds us of the important insights of labeling that conflict theorists presented earlier. Underlying this debate are two questions: Who has the power to label gambling, prostitution, and public drunkenness as "crimes"? and Who has the power to label such behaviors as "victimless"? The answer is generally the state legislatures, and in some cases, the police and the courts.

Professional Crime

Although the adage "Crime doesn't pay" is familiar, many people do make a career of illegal activities. A **professional criminal,** or *career criminal,* is a person who pursues crime as a day-to-day occupation, developing skilled techniques and enjoying a certain degree of status among other criminals. Some professional criminals specialize in burglary, safecracking, hijacking of cargo, pickpocketing, and shoplifting. Such people have acquired skills that reduce the likelihood of arrest, conviction, and imprisonment. As a result, they may have long careers in their chosen professions.

Edwin Sutherland (1937) offered pioneering insights into the behavior of professional criminals by publishing an annotated account written by a professional thief. Unlike the person who engages in crime only once or twice, professional thieves make a business of stealing. They devote their entire working time to planning and executing crimes, and sometimes travel across the nation to pursue their "professional duties." Like people in regular occupations, professional thieves consult with their colleagues concerning the demands of work, becoming part of a subculture of similarly occupied individuals. They exchange information on places to burglarize, on outlets for unloading stolen goods, and on ways of securing bail bonds if arrested.

Organized Crime

A 1976 government report devotes three pages to defining the term *organized crime.* For our purposes, we will consider **organized crime** to be the work of a group that regulates relations among criminal enterprises involved in illegal activities, including prostitution, gambling, and the smuggling and sale of illegal drugs. Organized crime dominates the world of illegal business just as large corporations dominate the conventional business world. It allocates territory, sets prices for goods and services, and acts as an arbitrator in internal disputes. A secret, conspiratorial activity, it generally evades law enforcement. It takes over legitimate businesses, gains influence over labor unions, corrupts public officials, intimidates witnesses in criminal trials, and even "taxes"

SOCIOLOGY IN EDUCATION

7-4 Packing Firearms on Campus

The average college student's backpack probably contains notebooks, textbooks, and a laptop. What if it were legal for it to hold a gun as well? While college campuses are generally very safe, high-profile campus shootings have led to a number of changes in laws about concealed firearms on campus.

In 2007, in the wake of the mass shooting at Virginia Tech, many college officials reviewed security measures on their campuses. Administrators were reluctant to end or even limit the relative freedom of movement students enjoyed. Instead, they concentrated on improving emergency communications between campus police and students, faculty, and staff. Relying on technology to maintain social control, college leaders called for replacement of the "old" technology of e-mail with instant alerts that could be sent to cell phones via instant messaging.

Among the calls for change was the much more controversial one of allowing people to carry concealed weapons on campus. All states allow concealed weapons permits, but such provisions are strictly regulated and, until recently, have always banned weapons in schools at any level.

As of 2018, campus carry laws were enacted in 11 states, whereas 16 states ban concealed weapons. In 23 states the decision to ban or allow guns at higher education

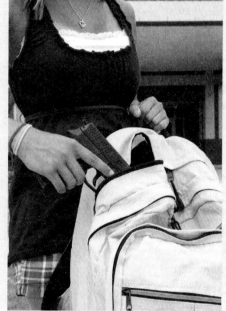

jabejon/Getty Images

In the last few years, a dozen or more state legislatures introduced bills to allow guns on campus.

institutions is left to university systems or individual schools.

Research has shown that factors unrelated to crime on school grounds led to the intro-

duction and enactment of these bills. Campus carry legislation has not been driven by actual active shooter incidents in educational contexts, but rather is associated with shootings anywhere in a state. Recent shootings have encouraged legislators to strengthen existing firearm regulations. In several states, legislation was introduced to prohibit concealed carry weapons on campus. None of these bills passed.

In the debates thus far, whether in legislatures or on campuses, the same arguments keep coming up. Supporters of the right to carry concealed weapons on campus argue that it's a constitutional right, an argument with which courts frequently agree, and will make campuses safe from shooters and other criminals. Opponents—who usually include administrators, faculty members, and campus law enforcement officers—claim that more firearms will increase the risk of dangerous situations.

LET'S DISCUSS

1. Are concealed weapons allowed on college campuses where you live? Find out what the policies are. Do you support them?
2. Is allowing guns on campus an example of social control? Why or why not?

Sources: Armed Campuses 2015; Horner 2015; Johnson and Zhang 2020; Mulhere 2015.

merchants in exchange for "protection" (National Advisory Commission on Criminal Justice 1976).

Organized crime serves as a means of upward mobility for groups of people struggling to escape poverty. Sociologist Daniel Bell (1953) used the term *ethnic succession* to describe the sequential passage of leadership from Irish Americans in the early part of the 20th century to Jewish Americans in the 1920s and then to Italian Americans in the early 1930s. Ethnic succession has become more complex, reflecting the diversity of the nation's latest immigrants. Colombian, Mexican, Russian, Chinese, Pakistani, and Nigerian immigrants are among those who have begun to play a significant role in organized crime activities (Herman 2005).

White-Collar and Technology-Based Crime

Income tax evasion, stock manipulation, consumer fraud, bribery and extraction of kickbacks, embezzlement, and misrepresentation in advertising—these are all examples of

white-collar crime, illegal acts committed in the course of business activities, often by affluent, "respectable" people. In his 1939 presidential address to the American Sociological Association, Edwin Sutherland (1949, 1983) likened these crimes to organized crime because they are often perpetrated through occupational roles. Sutherland was building on earlier observations by sociologist W. E. B. DuBois ([1899] 1995) that the courts had always favored the rich. For example, embezzlement tends to be treated more leniently than petty thievery.

A new type of white-collar crime has emerged in recent decades: cybercrime. **Cybercrime** is illegal activity primarily conducted through the use of computer hardware or software. Encompassed within cybercrime is cyberespionage and cyberterrorism. Cybercrime is a global problem, but the United States is victim to 80 percent of the data breaches. Because of the high value of U.S. targets, it is estimated that this country accounts for over 90 percent of the global cost of these breaches. By 2021, the global cost of cybercrime will run to $6 trillion, up from $3 trillion in 2015 (Juniper Research 2015; Morgan 2017).

When Charles Horton Cooley spoke of the self and Erving Goffman of impression management, surely neither scholar could have envisioned the insidious crime of identity theft. Each year about 7 percent of all adults find that their personal information has been misused for criminal purposes. Unfortunately, with our society's growing reliance on electronic financial transactions, assuming someone else's identity has become increasingly easy (Harrel 2015).

Identity theft does not necessarily require technology. A criminal can obtain someone's personal information by pickpocketing or by intercepting mail. However, the widespread exchange of information online has allowed criminals to access large amounts of personal information. Public awareness of the potential harm from identity theft took a giant leap in the aftermath of September 11, 2001, when investigations revealed that several hijackers had used fraudulent IDs to open bank accounts, rent apartments, and board planes. A law enacted in 2004 makes identity theft punishable by a mandatory prison sentence if it is linked to other crimes. Still, unauthorized disclosures of information, even if accidental, persist.

Sutherland (1940) coined the term *white-collar crime* in 1939 to refer to acts by individuals, but the term has been broadened more recently to include offenses by businesses and corporations as well. *Corporate crime,* or any act by a corporation that is punishable by the government, takes many forms and includes individuals, organizations, and institutions among its victims. Corporations may engage in anticompetitive behavior, environmental pollution, medical fraud, tax fraud, stock fraud and manipulation, accounting fraud, the production of unsafe goods, bribery and corruption, and health and safety violations (Simpson 2019).

For many years, corporate wrongdoers got off lightly in court by documenting their long history of charitable contributions and agreeing to help law enforcement officials find other white-collar criminals. Unfortunately, that is still the case. The highly visible jailing of multimedia personality Martha Stewart in 2004, as well as recent disclosures of "Wall Street greed," may lead the casual observer to think that government is cracking down on white-collar crime. An analysis of Department of Justice data shows that criminal prosecution of corporate violators fell to a historic 20-year low through February 2016 (Transactional Records Access Clearinghouse 2016).

Even when a person is convicted of corporate crime, the verdict generally

"KICKBACKS, EMBEZZLEMENT, PRICE FIXING, BRIBERY... THIS IS AN EXTREMELY HIGH-CRIME AREA."

does not harm his or her reputation and career aspirations nearly so much as conviction for street crime would. Apparently, the label "white-collar criminal" does not carry the stigma of the label "felon convicted of a violent crime." Conflict theorists don't find such differential treatment surprising. They argue that the criminal justice system largely disregards the crimes of the affluent, focusing on crimes committed by the poor. Generally, if an offender holds a position of status and influence, his or her crime is treated as less serious, and the sanction is much more lenient (Simpson 2013).

Hate Crimes

In contrast to other crimes, hate crimes are defined not only by the perpetrators' actions, but by the purpose of their conduct. The government considers an ordinary crime to be a **hate crime** when the offender is motivated to choose a victim based on race, religion, ethnic group, national origin, or sexual orientation, and when evidence shows that hatred prompted the offender to commit the crime. Hate crimes are sometimes referred to as *bias crimes* (Department of Justice 2008).

In 1990, Congress passed the Hate Crimes Statistics Act, which created a national mandate to identify crimes based on race, religion, ethnic group, and national origin. (Before that time, only 12 states had monitored such crimes.) Since then the act has been broadened to include disabilities, both physical and mental, and sexual orientation. In addition, some jurisdictions impose harsher sanctions (jail time or fines) for hate crimes than for other crimes. For example, if the penalty for assault is a year in jail, the penalty for an assault identified as a hate crime might be two years.

In 2020, law enforcement agencies submitted data on hate crimes to the federal government. The statistics included official reports of 8,263 hate crimes and bias-motivated offenses. As Figure 7-2 shows, race ethnicity, and ancestry was the apparent motivation in approximately 58 percent of the reports. Although vandalism and intimidation were the most common crimes, 35 percent of the incidents involved assault, rape, or murder.

States differ on what is legally categorized as a hate crime. Only three states—Arkansas, South Carolina, and Wyoming—do not have hate crime laws, while the others have different categories, as shown in Figure 7-3.

FIGURE 7-2 CATEGORIZATION OF REPORTED HATE CRIMES

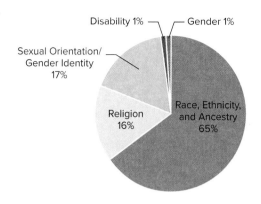

Source: Federal Bureau of Investigation. 2021. *Hate Crime Statistics, 2020.*
Note: Multiple incidents involve more than one category of hate crime.

Frequently, one hears the concept of hate crime being questioned or disputed. After all, the skeptics ask, is not hate involved in every assault or act of vandalism? While many non–hate crimes may be motivated by hatred toward an individual or organization, a hate or bias crime directed toward a member of a minority group is intended to carry a message well beyond the individual victim. When a person is assaulted because he or she is LGBTQ, the act is meant to terrorize all members of the LGBTQ community. Vandalizing a mosque or synagogue is meant to warn all Muslims or Jews that they are not wanted and that their religious faith is considered inferior. In many respects, today's hate crimes are like the terrorist efforts of the Ku Klux Klan generations ago. Targets may be randomly selected, but the group being terrorized is carefully chosen.

In many jurisdictions, having a crime officially classified as a hate crime can increase the punishment. For example, a misdemeanor such as vandalism may become a felony if categorized as a hate crime and thus would carry a longer prison sentence. The imposition of more stringent sanctions for hate crimes was upheld by the U.S. Supreme Court in the 1993 decision *Mitchell v. Wisconsin,* which recognized that greater harm might be done by hate-motivated crimes.

Regardless of what is classified as a hate crime, the vast majority of hate crimes, although not all of them, are committed by members of the dominant group against those who are relatively powerless. One in every five racially based hate crimes is an anti-white incident. Except for the most horrific hate crimes, these offenses receive little media attention; anti-white incidents probably receive even less. Clearly, hostility based on race knows no boundaries.

Transnational Crime

More and more, scholars and police officials are turning their attention to **transnational crime,** or crime that occurs across multiple national borders. In the past, international crime was often limited to the clandestine shipment of goods across the border between two countries. But increasingly, crime is no more restricted by such borders than is legal commerce. Rather than concentrating on specific countries, international crime now spans the globe.

Historically, probably the most dreadful example of transnational crime has been slavery. At first, governments did not regard slavery as a crime, but merely regulated it as they would the trade in goods. In the 20th century, transnational crime grew to embrace trafficking in people, endangered species, drugs, and stolen art and antiquities.

Public concern over cyberattacks from overseas has greatly increased. Studies of public opinion in 26 countries conducted in 2019 found cyberattacks were of great international concern, exceeded only by climate change and terrorism. Among people in the United States and Japan, cyberattacks were the most pressing issue (Poushter and Huang 2019).

FIGURE 7-3 STATE HATE-CRIME LAWS
Fifty states vary on what they categorize as hate crimes.

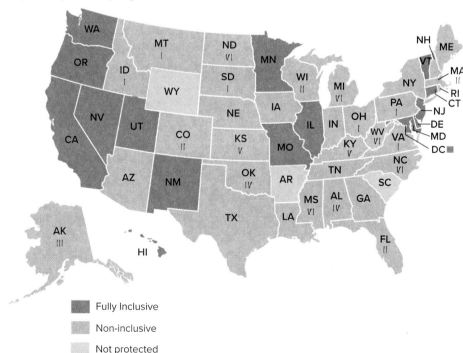

Note: "Fully inclusive" means hate crimes include all types of bias. "Non-inclusive" means: I- Only race, ethnicity, and religion covered; II- No coverage of gender; III- No coverage of sexual orientation; IV- No coverage of gender or sexual orientation; V- No coverage of gender or disability; VI- No coverage of sexual orientation or disability
Source: Anti-Defamation League 2020.

Transnational crime is not exclusive of some of the other types of crime we have discussed. For example, organized criminal networks are increasingly global. Technology definitely facilitates their illegal activities, such as trafficking in child pornography. Beginning in the 1990s, the United Nations began to categorize transnational crimes; Table 7-3 lists some of the more common types.

Bilateral cooperation in the pursuit of border criminals such as smugglers has been common for many years. The first global effort to control international crime was the International Criminal Police Organization (Interpol), a cooperative network of European police forces founded to stem the movement of political revolutionaries across borders. While such efforts to fight transnational crime may seem lofty—an activity with which any government should cooperate—they are complicated by sensitive legal and security issues.

Most nations that have signed protocols issued by the United Nations, including the United States, have expressed concern over potential encroachments on their national judicial systems, as well as concern over their national security. Thus, they have been reluctant to share certain types of intelligence data. Similarly, the investigation into Russian involvement in disrupting the 2016 U.S. presidential campaigns and election precipitated renewed interest in safeguarding online information.

TABLE 7-3   TYPES OF TRANSNATIONAL CRIME

Bankruptcy and insurance fraud

Computer crime (treating computers as both a tool and a target of crime

Corruption and bribery of public officials

Counterfeiting

Environmental crime

Hijacking of airplanes (skyjacking)

Illegal drug trade

Illegal money transfers (money laundering)

Illegal sales of firearms and ammunition

Infiltration of legal businesses

Intellectual property crime

Migrant smuggling

Networking of criminal organizations

Sea piracy

Terrorism

Theft of art and cultural objects

Trafficking in body parts (includes illegal organ transplants)

Trafficking in human beings (includes sex trade)

Think about It Which of these crimes do you read or hear about the least? Why do you think that is?

USE YOUR SOCIOLOGICAL IMAGINATION

As the editor of an online news service, how might you treat stories on corporate or white-collar crime differently from those on violent crime?

Crime Statistics

Crime statistics are not as accurate as social scientists would like, especially since they deal with an issue of grave concern to the people of the United States. Unfortunately, they are frequently cited as if they were completely reliable. Such data do serve as an indicator of police activity, as well as an approximate indication of the level of certain crimes. Yet it would be a mistake to interpret these data as an exact representation of the incidence of crime.

Index Crimes and Victimization Surveys

Typically, the crime data reported in the United States are based on **index crimes**, or the eight types of crime tabulated each year by the Federal Bureau of Investigation (FBI). This category of criminal behavior generally consists of those serious offenses that people think of when they express concern about the nation's crime problem. Index crimes include murder, rape, robbery, and assault—all of which are violent crimes committed against people—as well as the property crimes of burglary, larceny-theft, motor vehicle theft, and arson (Table 7-4).

Obviously, many serious offenses, such as white-collar crimes, are not included in this index (although they are recorded elsewhere). In addition, the crime index is disproportionately devoted to property crimes, whereas most citizens are more worried about violent crimes. Thus, a significant decrease in the number of rapes and robberies could be overshadowed by a slightly larger increase in the number of automobiles stolen, leading to the mistaken impression that *personal* safety is more at risk than before.

The most serious limitation of official crime statistics is that they include only those crimes actually *reported* to law enforcement agencies. Because members of racial and ethnic minority groups often distrust law enforcement agencies, they may not contact the police. Feminist sociologists and others have noted that many women do not report rape or spousal abuse out of fear they will be blamed for the crime.

Partly because of these deficiencies in official statistics, the National Crime Victimization Survey was initiated in 1972. The Bureau of Justice Statistics, in compiling this annual report, not only seeks information from law enforcement agencies, but

TABLE 7-4   NATIONAL CRIME RATES AND PERCENTAGE CHANGE

Crime Index Offenses in 2018	Number Reported	Rate per 100,000 Inhabitants	Percentage Change 2007–2019
Violent crime			
Murder	15,020	5	+1
Rape	129,958	44	+8
Robbery	248,681	85	−20
Aggravated assault	744,434	253	+5
Total	1,135,093	387	−2
Property crime			
Burglary	1,104,712	337	−31
Larceny-theft	4,659,007	1,569	−13
Motor vehicle theft	667,300	228	−1
Total	6,358,176	2,130	−6

Think about It Which kinds of crime have increased in incidence over the past 15 years? Which have decreased? Do these data match your perceptions?

Source: Federal Bureau of Investigation. 2020a: Tables 1a, 12, 16.

also interviews households across the nation and asks if they were victims of a specific set of crimes during the preceding year. In general, those who administer **victimization surveys** question ordinary people, not police officers, to determine whether they have been victims of crime.

Unfortunately, like other crime data, victimization surveys have particular limitations. They require that victims understand what has happened to them and are willing to disclose such information to interviewers. Fraud, income tax evasion, and blackmail are examples of crimes that are unlikely to be reported in victimization studies.

Crime Trends

The coronavirus pandemic showed some atypical crime patterns. With everyone staying at home, street robberies and home burglaries plummeted but retail burglaries escalated. Researchers are trying to assess how the significant reduction in police-civilian encounters during the pandemic affected official reported crime. Also, attention was given to new types of crime, such as attacks on health personnel and breaches of infection-control laws being enforced by store and park personnel (Sawyer 2020).

Independent of short-term changes during the pandemic, there has been a significant decline in violent crime in the United States in recent years, after many years of increases.

How much has crime declined? Consider this: the rate of crime being reported in 2020 was comparable to what it was back when gasoline cost 29 cents a gallon and the average person earned less than $6,000 a year. That was 1963.

Dramatic declines have occurred within the last decade. As Table 7-4 shows, both violent crime and property crime dropped about 20 percent in the last 10 years. Although a tragic 15,498 people were murdered in 2018, in 1991 that number was a staggering 24,700. Declines have also been registered in victimization surveys (Figure 7-4).

What explains these declines in both index crimes and victimization rates? Possible explanations include the following:

- Community-oriented policing and crime prevention programs

- A massive increase in the prison population, which at least prevents inmates from committing crimes outside prison

- New surveillance technologies

FIGURE 7-4   VICTIMIZATION RATES, 1993–2018

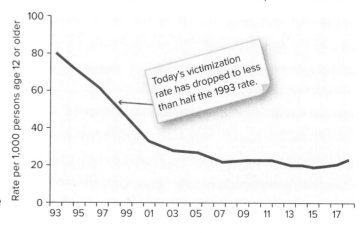

Today's victimization rate has dropped to less than half the 1993 rate.

Note: Data shown for violent crime.
Source: Morgan and Oudekerk 2019: Figure Five.

TAKING SOCIOLOGY TO WORK

Stephanie Vezzani, **Special Agent, U.S. Secret Service**

Stephanie Vezzani wasn't sure what she wanted to major in when she entered the University of Akron, but she did know what she wanted to do with her life: she wanted a career as a crime fighter. Vezzani began as an accounting major, but switched to sociology when she discovered the department offered a special concentration in law enforcement.

Vezzani is now an agent with the U.S. Secret Service, whose twofold mission is to protect high-ranking officials and their families and to investigate financial crimes, including counterfeiting, identity theft, and computer-based attacks on the financial, banking, and telecommunications industries. She has tackled both aspects of the job. For her, a typical week would include working on a criminal investigation in a field office or traveling around the country with a government official in need of protection.

Vezzani finds that travel is one of the most exciting aspects of her job. Over the past six years she has visited Russia, Turkey, Jordan, Vietnam, and South Korea. She also attended the 2002 Winter Olympics in Salt Lake City, where she provided protection for the athletes

Stephen Mulcahey/Alamy Stock Photo

living in the Olympic Village. Vezzani relishes meeting people from different cultures, and of course she loves the sights she gets to see. "The architecture in St. Petersburg, Russia, was amazing," she says.

Vezzani uses her training in sociology on a daily basis, as she interviews suspects, witnesses, and victims of crime. "It is critical in the field of law enforcement to have an understanding of people's relationships and the beliefs and value systems that contribute to their decision making," she explains. "Sociology has provided me the knowledge to speak to and listen to people with different values and cultures in order to complete my job at the highest level possible."

LET'S DISCUSS

1. Besides an awareness of different beliefs, values, and cultures, what else might sociology offer to those who serve in law enforcement?
2. Law enforcement is a relatively new career option for women. What special strengths do you think a woman might bring to police work?

- Better residential and business security
- The decline of the crack cocaine epidemic, which soared in the late 1980s
- The aging of the population, as the number of people in their 50s increased and the number in their 20s decreased

No single explanation could account for such a marked change in crime rates. Taken together, however, these changes in public policy, public health, technology, and demographics may well explain it (Tonry 2014).

Despite the declines in crime, the general public still perceives crime to be a growing threat: Most people surveyed in each of the last 50 years have believed that there is more crime than there was the year before. How do we explain this perception, which is so different from reality? News media emphasize violent crimes in the local area and, nationally, we are bombarded by coverage of highly publicized shootings at schools, workplaces, concerts, and places of worship (Gallup 2020b).

Feminist scholars draw our attention to one significant countertrend: the proportion of major crimes committed by women has increased. However, violent crimes committed by women, which have never been common, have declined. Despite the "mean girls" references in popular culture, every reliable measure shows that among women, fights, weapons possession, assaults, and violent injuries have plunged over the last decade (Federal Bureau of Investigation 2020; Males and Chesney-Lind 2010).

International Crime Rates

If developing reliable crime data is difficult in the United States, making useful cross-national comparisons is even more difficult. Nevertheless, with some care, we can offer preliminary conclusions about how crime rates differ around the world.

Beginning in the 1980s, and continuing into the 21st century, violent crimes have been much more common in the United States than in western Europe. Murders, rapes, and robberies are reported to the police at much higher rates in the United States. Yet the incidence of certain other types of crime appears to be higher elsewhere. For example, England, Ireland, Denmark, and New Zealand all have higher rates of car theft than the United States. Developing nations have significant rates of reported homicide due to civil unrest and political conflict among civilians (United Nations Office on Drugs and Crime 2015b).

A cross-national comparison finds that Venezuela has the highest crime rate, attributed to the country's poor political and economic environment. At the low end of the spectrum are countries such as Switzerland, Denmark, Norway, Japan, and New Zealand (World Population Review 2020).

A particularly worrisome development has been the rapid escalation in homicide rates in developing countries that supply drugs to industrialized countries, especially the United States. The huge profits generated by cocaine exports to North America and Europe have allowed drug gangs to arm themselves to the point of becoming illegal armies. Homicide rates in Mexico are now about twice as high as those in the United

States. Honduras, Guatemala, Venezuela, and El Salvador's homicide rates are three to five times those of Mexico (Luhnow 2014).

Why are rates of violent crime generally so much higher in the United States than in western Europe? Sociologist Elliot Currie (1985, 1998) has suggested that our society places greater emphasis on individual economic achievement than other societies do. At the same time, many observers have noted that the culture of the United States has long tolerated, if not condoned, many forms of violence. Coupled with sharp disparities between poor and affluent citizens, significant unemployment, and substantial alcohol and drug abuse, these factors combine to produce a climate conducive to crime.

Another difference between the United States and other democracies is in use of the death penalty. The United States is alone among advanced democratic societies in using this extreme form of punishment (Amnesty International 2015). In the Social Policy section that follows, we'll consider the issues involved in administration of the death penalty in the United States.

THINKING CRITICALLY

Why is it useful to sociologists to have victimization surveys in addition to reported crime data?

social|policy and Social Control

The Death Penalty in the United States and Worldwide

On June 11, 2001, Timothy McVeigh—the man who killed hundreds of innocent people when he bombed the federal building in Oklahoma City in 1995—was executed by the U.S. government. McVeigh was the first federal prisoner to be put to death in nearly four decades. His execution, and that of others who received the death penalty for their crimes, has raised many questions, both from supporters and from critics of capital punishment. How can the government prevent the execution of innocent men and women? Is it right to resort to a punishment that imitates the crime it seeks to condemn? Is life in prison enough of a punishment for a truly heinous crime?

Looking at the Issue

Historically, execution has been a significant form of punishment, both for deviance from social norms and for criminal behavior. In North America, the death penalty has been used for centuries to punish murder, alleged witchcraft, and a few other crimes. Yet for most of that time, little thought was given to its justification; capital punishment was simply assumed to be morally and religiously right. Today, the death penalty is still on the books in most states, where it is used to a greater or lesser extent, depending on the state (Figure 7-5).

FIGURE 7-5 EXECUTIONS BY STATE SINCE 1976

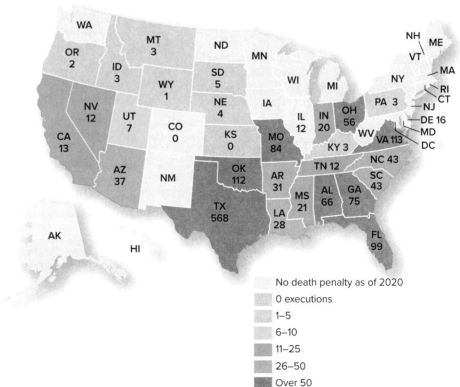

No death penalty as of 2020
0 executions
1–5
6–10
11–25
26–50
Over 50

Note: Number of executions carried out from January 17, 1977, to January 16, 2020, not including three federal executions. The U.S. government has 61 people on death row; the military has 4. Connecticut, Maryland, and New Mexico, which still have people on death row, have abolished the death penalty for future cases. The death penalty still exists in California, Oregon, and Pennsylvania, but those states' governors have imposed moratoriums on its use. *Source:* Death Penalty Information Center 2020a.

In other parts of the world, serious thought has been given to the ethical implications of the ultimate penalty. Each year a few countries abolish the death penalty; about 20 nations still carry out

left: Serpico/Alamy Stock Photo; right: YuriAbas/Shutterstock

Attitudes toward the death penalty and how to execute are constantly changing. In the late 19th century, many people were horrified by botched hangings. The idea of using high-voltage electricity was suggested soon after electricity became available commercially. Famed inventor Thomas Edison advocated the use of alternating current, which he championed for such purposes. Today, the question of whether capital punishment is justified is a commonly debated issue with passionate supporters and critics.

executions. The United States ranks seventh, behind China, Iran, Saudi Arabia, Vietnam, Iraq, and Egypt (Amnesty International 2019).

Applying Sociology

Traditionally, the debate over the death penalty has focused on its appropriateness as a form of punishment and its value in deterring crime. Viewed from Émile Durkheim's functionalist perspective, sanctions against deviant acts help to reinforce society's standards of proper behavior. Supporters of capital punishment insist that fear of execution will prevent at least some criminals from committing serious offenses. Moreover, even if it does not serve as a deterrent, they still see the death penalty as justified, because they believe the worst criminals deserve to die for their crimes.

The death penalty also creates some dysfunctions, however. Although many citizens are concerned that the alternative to execution, life in prison, is unnecessarily expensive, sentencing a person to death is not cheap. According to a recent analysis, in Oklahoma, prosecuting death penalty cases costs 3.2 times more than prosecuting cases involving life without parole. Housing, health care, and legal representation also cost more for convicts on death row than for other inmates (Death Penalty Information Center 2020a).

Conflict theorists counter that the persistence of social inequality in today's society puts poor people at a disadvantage in the criminal justice system. Simply put, the poor cannot afford to hire the best lawyers, but must rely instead on court-appointed attorneys, who typically are overworked and underpaid. This unequal access to legal resources may mean the difference between life and death for poor defendants. Indeed, the American Bar Association (1997) has repeatedly expressed concern about the limited defense most defendants who face the death penalty receive. As of 2020, 166 death row inmates have been exonerated (Death Penalty Information Center 2020b).

Another issue of crucial concern to conflict theorists and researchers is the possibility of racial discrimination. Numerous studies show that defendants are more likely to be sentenced to death if their victims were white rather than Black. About 76 percent of the victims in

death penalty cases are white, even though only 50 percent of all murder victims are white. And there is some evidence that Black defendants, who constituted 42 percent of all death row inmates in 2020, are more likely to face execution than whites in the same legal circumstance. Evidence exists that capital defendants receive poor legal services because of the racist attitudes of their own defense counsel. While racism is never acceptable, it is particularly devastating in the criminal justice system, where the legal process can result in an execution (Death Penalty Information Center 2016; Petrie and Coverdill 2010).

Initiating Policy

Many people hesitate to endorse the death penalty, yet when confronted with a horrendous crime, they feel the death penalty should be available, at least in some cases. In most people's minds, for example, Timothy McVeigh's sentence would be an appropriate use of the death penalty, although opinion on this point has fluctuated. In 2019, support for the death penalty was 56 percent—about the same level as when the question was first posed in 1937, in a national survey (Gallup 2020a).

Recently, policy initiatives have moved in two different directions. In several death penalty states, legislators are considering broadening the range of offenses for which convicted criminals may be sentenced to execution. In these states, child molesters who did not murder their victims could become eligible for the death penalty, along with certain repeat offenders. The countertrend, a movement away from the death penalty, is based on doubts about whether an execution can be carried out humanely.

Legal action has been taken on behalf of those convicted to die, especially by lethal injection, which is used in virtually all death penalty jurisdictions. Concerns about lethal injection range from medical ethics (the injection must be administered by a medical technician) to the effectiveness of the technique, which sometimes takes a long time to cause death. Opponents contend that death can be excruciating. In 2008 and again in 2015, the Supreme Court ruled that lethal injections procedures were constitutional, but specified protocols for the use of chemicals, personnel training, medical supervision, and error risk that apply in all 30 states that use lethal injection (Death Penalty Information Center 2018).

Surprisingly, only about 20 to 40 death sentences are handed out for the more than 14,000 reported murders that occur every year. Courts continue to address the question of how this ultimate penalty can be administered in a judicially fair manner. Policymakers, however, do not seem concerned with such questions. In recent years, federal and state legislatures have declared additional crimes to be punishable by death, curtailed appeals by death row inmates, and reimbursed far fewer lawyers for their defense of condemned criminals.

Internationally, attention has focused on those nations where executions are relatively common, such as China and Iraq. Foes of the

death penalty see these nations as violators of human rights. In the United States, which usually regards itself as a champion of human rights, pressure to abolish capital punishment both at home and abroad has grown.

Take the Issue with You

1. Does the death penalty deter crime? If so, why are crime rates in the United States high compared to those in other nations?

2. What is your position on the death penalty—should it be legal or should it be abolished? Explain your reasoning.

3. Should youths who have been convicted of violent crimes be subject to the death penalty? Why or why not?

MASTERING THIS CHAPTER

Summary

Conformity and **deviance** are two ways in which people respond to real or imagined pressure from others. In this chapter we examined the relationships among deviance and conformity, **crime** and **social control**. We studied the mechanisms societies use, both formal and informal, to encourage conformity and discourage deviance, paying particular attention to the **law** and how it reflects our social values**.**

1. Deviant behavior violates social norms. Some forms of **deviance** carry a negative social **stigma,** while other forms are more or less accepted.

2. A society uses **social control** to encourage the acceptance of basic norms.

3. Stanley Milgram defined **conformity** as going along with one's peers; **obedience** is defined as compliance with higher authorities in a hierarchical structure.

4. Some norms are so important to a society, they are formalized into laws. Socialization is a primary source of conforming and obedient behavior, including obedience to **law.**

5. From a functionalist point of view, deviance and its consequences help to define the limits of proper behavior.

6. Some interactionists maintain that people learn criminal behavior by interacting with others (**cultural transmission**). To them, deviance results from exposure to attitudes that are favorable to criminal acts (**differential association**).

7. Other interactionists attribute increases in crime and deviance to the absence or breakdown of communal relationships and social institutions, such as the family, school, church, and local government (**social disorganization theory**).

8. An important aspect of **labeling theory** is the recognition that some people are viewed as deviant, while others who engage in the same behavior are not.

9. From the conflict perspective, laws and punishments are a reflection of the interests of the powerful.

10. The feminist perspective emphasizes that cultural attitudes and differential economic relationships help to explain gender differences in deviance and crime.

11. **Crime** represents a deviation from formal social norms administered by the state.

12. Sociologists differentiate among **victimless crime** (such as drug use and prostitution), *professional crime,* **organized crime, white-collar crime, hate crimes,** and **transnational crime.**

13. Crime statistics are among the least reliable social data, partly because so many crimes are not reported to law enforcement agencies. Rates of violent crime are higher in the United States than in other Western societies, although they have been dropping.

14. Gun violence is a major problem in the United States. Yet gun control legislation is extremely controversial, opposed by powerful interest groups whose members see it as an abridgment of their constitutional right to bear arms.

Key Terms

Anomie Durkheim's term for the loss of direction felt in a society when social control of individual behavior has become ineffective. (page 164)

Anomie theory of deviance Robert Merton's theory of deviance as an adaptation of socially prescribed goals or of the means governing their attainment, or both. (165)

Conformity Going along with peers—individuals of our own status who have no special right to direct our behavior. (158)

Control theory A view of conformity and deviance that suggests that our connection to members of society leads us to systematically conform to society's norms. (162)

Crime A violation of criminal law for which some governmental authority applies formal penalties. (170)

Cultural transmission A school of criminology that argues that criminal behavior is learned through social interactions. (165)

Cybercrime Illegal activity primarily conducted through the use of computer hardware or software. (171)

Deviance Behavior that violates the standards of conduct or expectations of a group or society. (155)

Differential association A theory of deviance proposed by Edwin Sutherland that holds that violation of rules results from exposure to attitudes favorable to criminal acts. (165)

Differential justice Differences in the way social control is exercised over different groups. (168)

Formal social control Social control that is carried out by authorized agents, such as police officers, judges, school administrators, and employers. (161)

Hate crime A criminal offense committed because of the offender's bias against a race, religion, ethnic group, national origin, or sexual orientation. Also referred to as bias crime. (172)

Index crimes The eight types of crime tabulated each year by the FBI in the Uniform Crime Reports: murder, rape, robbery, assault, burglary, theft, motor vehicle theft, and arson. (174)

Informal social control Social control that is carried out casually by ordinary people through such means as laughter, smiles, and ridicule. (161)

Labeling theory An approach to deviance that attempts to explain why certain people are viewed as deviants while others engaged in the same behavior are not. (167)

Law Governmental social control. (161)

Obedience Compliance with higher authorities in a hierarchical structure. (158)

Organized crime The work of a group that regulates relations between criminal enterprises involved in illegal activities, including prostitution, gambling, and the smuggling and sale of illegal drugs. (170)

Professional criminal A person who pursues crime as a day-to-day occupation, developing skilled techniques and enjoying a certain degree of status among other criminals. (170)

Racial profiling Any arbitrary action initiated by an authority based on race, ethnicity, or national origin rather than on a person's behavior. (168)

Sanction A penalty or reward for conduct concerning a social norm. (157)

Social constructionist perspective An approach to deviance that emphasizes the role of culture in the creation of the deviant identity. (168)

Social control The techniques and strategies for preventing deviant human behavior in any society. (157)

Social disorganization theory The theory that crime and deviance are caused by the absence or breakdown of communal relationships and social institutions. (166)

Societal-reaction approach Another name for labeling theory. (167)

Stigma A label used to devalue members of certain social groups. (156)

Transnational crime Crime that occurs across multiple national borders. (173)

Victimless crime A term used by sociologists to describe the willing exchange among adults of widely desired but illegal goods and services. (170)

Victimization survey A questionnaire or interview given to a sample of the population to determine whether people have been victims of crime. A questionnaire or interview given to a sample of the population to determine whether people have been victims of crime. (175)

White-collar crime Illegal acts committed by affluent, "respectable" individuals in the course of business activities. (171)

TAKING SOCIOLOGY with you

1. Look for instances of social control in one or more shows that you're currently watching or in a book that you're reading. What are the different social controls among peers, in families, in the workplace, or imposed by the government? What are some different ways that the characters react to the exercise of social control? Share your findings with the class.

2. Listen to a podcast on the website for the Brady Campaign to Prevent Gun Violence (https://www.bradyunited.org/podcast). Take notes keeping in mind one theoretical perspective used by sociologists. Share your findings with the class.

3. Watch a movie about a professional criminal or organized or white-collar crime. How are the criminals portrayed? Are they labeled differently by different members of society and government bodies? What motivated their criminal activities? Share your findings with the class.

4. **Writing Sociology.** Go to Amnesty International's website and click on What We Do (https://www.amnesty.org). Choose a topic related to the content of this chapter to read about. Write a report and share it with the class.

Self-Quiz

Read each question carefully and then select the best answer.

1. Society brings about acceptance of basic norms through techniques and strategies for preventing deviant human behavior. This process is termed
   a. stigmatization.
   b. labeling.
   c. law.
   d. social control.

2. Which sociological perspective argues that people must respect social norms if any group or society is to survive?
   a. the conflict perspective
   b. the interactionist perspective
   c. the functionalist perspective
   d. the feminist perspective

3. Stanley Milgram used the word conformity to mean
   a. going along with peers.
   b. compliance with higher authorities in a hierarchical structure.
   c. techniques and strategies for preventing deviant human behavior in any society.
   d. penalties and rewards for conduct concerning a social norm.

4. Which sociological theory suggests that our connection to members of society leads us to conform systematically to society's norms?
   a. feminist theory
   b. control theory
   c. differential theory
   d. functionalist theory

5. Which of the following statements is true of deviance?
   a. Deviance is always criminal behavior.
   b. Deviance is behavior that violates the standards of conduct or expectations of a group or society.
   c. Deviance is perverse behavior.
   d. Deviance is inappropriate behavior that cuts across all cultures and social orders.

6. Which sociologist illustrated the boundary-maintenance function of deviance in his study of Puritans in 17th-century New England?
   a. Kai Erikson
   b. Émile Durkheim
   c. Robert Merton
   d. Edwin Sutherland

7. Which of the following is an example of innovation as defined in Robert Merton's anomie theory of deviance?
   a. An advocate for a new form of government initiates a blog.
   b. A bureaucrat demands higher wages.
   c. A prison guard agitates for a labor union.
   d. Rather than writing an original essay, a student copies his submission from the Internet.

8. Which sociologist first advanced the idea that an individual undergoes the same basic socialization process whether learning conforming or deviant acts?
   a. Robert Merton
   b. Edwin Sutherland
   c. Travis Hirschi
   d. William Chambliss

9. Which of the following theories contends that criminal victimization increases when communal relationships and social institutions break down?
   a. labeling theory
   b. conflict theory
   c. social disorganization theory
   d. differential association theory

10. Which of the following conducted observation research on two groups of high school males (the Saints and the Roughnecks) and concluded that social class played an important role in the varying fortunes of the two groups?
   a. Richard Quinney
   b. Edwin Sutherland
   c. Émile Durkheim
   d. William Chambliss

11. If we fail to respect and obey social norms, we may face punishment through informal or formal _____.

12. Police officers, judges, administrators, employers, military officers, and managers of movie theaters are all instruments of _____ _____ social control.

13. Some norms are considered so important by a society that they are formalized into _____ controlling people's behavior.

14. It is important to underscore the fact that _____ is the primary source of conformity and obedience, including obedience to law.

15. _____ is a state of normlessness that typically occurs during a period of profound social change and disorder, such as a time of economic collapse.

16. Labeling theory was developed by _____ _____.

17. _____ theorists view standards of deviant behavior as merely reflecting cultural norms, whereas ___ _____ and _____ theorists point out that the most powerful groups in a society can shape laws and standards and determine who is (or is not) prosecuted as a criminal.

18. Feminists contend that prostitution and some forms of pornography are not _____ crimes.

19. Daniel Bell used the term _____ _____ to describe the process during which leadership of organized crime was transferred from Irish Americans to Jewish Americans and later to Italian Americans and others.

20. Consumer fraud, bribery, and income tax evasion are considered _____ _____ _____ crimes.

FREDERIC J. BROWN/AFP/Getty Images

Significant inequality exists in the United States, where many people have insufficient means to meet their social and economic needs. Even with the public efforts of wealthy people, needs remain unmet. Here Kim Kardashian, who has a net worth of several hundred million dollars, serves the poor and homeless at a Los Angeles soup kitchen.

▶ INSIDE

What are the causes of income inequality in society? Can inequality be eliminated or at least controlled?

Elected leaders such as the president and members of Congress and leaders such as Jerome Powell, chair of the Board of Governors of the Federal Reserve Bank, have turned their attention to inequality and stratification in the United States. Powell addressed this pressing problem in a 2019 speech.

Glow Images

❝While there are many definitions of 'middle class,' I think we can agree that achieving a basic level of economic security is fundamental. Surveys suggest that many Americans believe being middle class means having a secure job and the ability to save. In recent decades, income growth for middle-income households has lagged behind that for high-income households. In addition, economic resources differ markedly by race, education, occupation, geography, and other factors. Those circumstances underscore a two-fold challenge for our country: fostering the conditions that will help lower-income families reach the middle class, while ensuring that middle-class status still provides the basic economic security that it has traditionally offered. . . .

[There are] three key observations that are fundamental to addressing the challenges related to the middle class.

The first observation is to note the long-term decline in relative income growth and upward economic mobility for those in the middle. According to a number of measures, income has grown more slowly for middle-class households since the 1970s than for those with higher incomes, resulting in wider income inequality. The kind of generational improvements in living standards that were long the hallmark of the American middle class have steadily diminished. In the 1950s, better than 80 percent of children born in middle-class households grew up to out-earn their parents, but more recently only around half do. One factor in this decline is the increase in income inequality I just noted, and another is slower productivity growth. This conference will touch on other possible reasons for this decline in upward mobility and relative income, such as changes in the prospects for career advancement that vary by occupation and location.

The second observation is the widening gap in economic status and prospects between those with a college degree and those without

one. In the 1960s, well over 90 percent of working-age men held a job, and there was very little difference in employment between those with or without a college degree. While the share of college-educated working-age men with a job has fallen from more than 95 percent in 1967 to around 90 percent in 2017, it has plunged for others. Ninety-five percent of male high school graduates were working in 1967, but only about 80 percent of them were working as of 2017. Among working-age men without a high school diploma, about 90 percent had a job in 1967 versus a bit more than 70 percent in 2017. For women of working age, the trends are less clear, but those without a college degree are also less likely to work today. Research presented this morning will discuss some possible explanations for the divergence in employment, income, and other economic prospects between college grads and others.

The third observation is that the prospect of moving up the economic ladder depends on factors beyond effort and talent, including your family, the neighborhood you grow up in, and the quality of the primary and secondary schools you attend. Your chances for attending college are much better if you are raised in a higher-income household, and that advantage has increased substantially since the 1980s. Another factor is geography. Some research indicates that economic prospects are better for those who grow up in neighborhoods with less income inequality, less concentrated poverty, and better performing schools. Finally, across so many dimensions, we continue to see disparities in economic outcomes by race and ethnicity.

These issues are crucial. Sound public policies can support families and businesses and help more Americans reach and remain in the middle class. ❞

Source: Powell 2019.

The kind of generational improvements in living standards that were long the hallmark of the American middle class have steadily diminished. In the 1950s, better than 80 percent of children born in middle-class households grew up to out-earn their parents, but more recently only around half do.

Jerome Powell's remarks in May 2019 at the Chicago Federal Reserve System Community Development Research Conference attracted the attention of the gathering of researchers, policymakers, and practitioners. Here was the head of the national banking system drawing attention to what he saw as a grave issue of social inequality and stratification—what was the future of the middle class?

Ever since people began to speculate about the nature of human society, their attention has been drawn to the difference between individuals and groups within society. The term **social inequality,** which has been much in the headlines recently, describes a condition in which members of society have differing amounts of wealth, prestige, or power. All societies demonstrate some degree of social inequality.

When a system of social inequality is based on a hierarchy of groups, sociologists refer to it as **stratification:** a structured ranking of entire groups of people that perpetuates unequal economic rewards and power in a society. These unequal rewards are evident not only in the distribution of wealth and income, but even in the distressing mortality rates of impoverished communities. Stratification involves the ways in which one generation passes on social inequalities to the next, producing groups of people arranged in rank order, from low to high.

Stratification is a crucial subject of sociological investigation because of its pervasive influence on human interactions and institutions. It results inevitably in social inequality, because certain groups of people stand higher in social rankings, control scarce resources, wield power, and receive special treatment. As we will see in this chapter, the consequences of stratification are evident in the unequal distribution of both income and wealth in industrial societies. The term **income** refers to salaries and wages, interest on savings, stock dividends, and rental income. In contrast, **wealth** is an inclusive term encompassing all a person's material assets, including land, stocks, and other types of property.

ANDREW CABALLERO-REYNOLDS/AFP/Getty Images

Jerome H. Powell was appointed on February 5, 2018, to a four-year term as Chair of the Board of Governors of the Federal Reserve System. The Federal Reserve's tasks, regulating the banking system and helping to keep the economy on track, greatly affect access to economic opportunity for people at all levels of the social hierarchy in the United States.

Is social inequality an inescapable part of society? How does government policy affect the life chances of the working poor? Is this country still a place where a hardworking person can move up the social ladder? This chapter focuses on the unequal distribution of socially valued rewards and its consequences. We will begin by examining four general systems of stratification, including the one most familiar to us, the social class system. We will examine three sociological perspectives on stratification, paying particular attention to the theories of Karl Marx and Max Weber. We'll also ask whether stratification is universal and see what sociologists, including functionalist and conflict theorists, have to say about that question.

We will see too how sociologists define social class, and examine the consequences of stratification for people's wealth and income, safety, and educational opportunities. Then we will take a close look at poverty, particularly the question of who belongs to the underclass and why. And we will confront the question of social mobility, both upward and downward. Finally, in the Social Policy section, we will examine the issue of corporate compensation—the huge salaries and bonuses that corporate executives earn even when their companies are losing money and employees are losing their jobs.

Systems of Stratification

Sociologists consider stratification on many levels, ranging from its impact on the individual to worldwide patterns of inequality. No matter where we look, however, disparities in wealth and income are substantial. Take income and poverty patterns in the United States, for example. As the top part of Figure 8-1 shows, in some states the median household income is 75 percent higher than that in other states. And as the bottom part of the figure shows, the poverty rate in many states is twice that of other states. Later in this chapter we will address the meaning of such statistics. We'll begin our discussion here with an overview of the four basic systems of stratification. Then we'll see what sociologists have had to say on the subject of social inequality.

Look at the four general systems of stratification examined here—slavery, castes, estates, and social classes—as ideal types useful for purposes of analysis. Any stratification system may include elements of more than one type. For example, prior to the Civil War, you could find in the southern states of

the United States both social classes dividing whites from whites and the institutionalized enslavement of Blacks.

To understand these systems better, it may be helpful to review the distinction between *achieved status* and *ascribed status,* explained in Chapter 5. **Ascribed status** is a social position assigned to a person by society without regard for the person's unique talents or characteristics. In contrast, **achieved status** is a social position that a person attains largely through his or her own efforts. The two are closely linked. The nation's most affluent families generally inherit wealth and status, while many members of racial and ethnic minorities inherit disadvantaged status. Age and gender, as well, are ascribed statuses that influence a person's wealth and social position.

Slavery

The most extreme form of legalized social inequality for both individuals and groups is **slavery.** What distinguishes this oppressive system of stratification is that enslaved individuals are *owned* by other people, who treat these human beings as property, just as if they were household pets or appliances.

MAPPING LIFE NATIONWIDE

FIGURE 8-1 THE 50 STATES: CONTRASTS IN INCOME AND POVERTY LEVELS, 2018

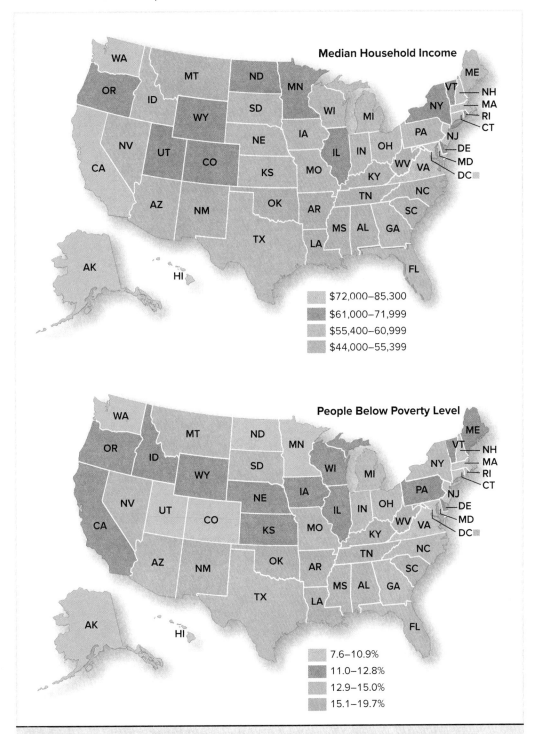

Median Household Income

$72,000–85,300
$61,000–71,999
$55,400–60,999
$44,000–55,399

People Below Poverty Level

7.6–10.9%
11.0–12.8%
12.9–15.0%
15.1–19.7%

Think about It Explain the correlation between income and poverty levels. What other socioeconomic factors might be related?

Note: National median household income was $61,937; national poverty rate, 13.1 percent. Incomes declined and poverty rates increased following the coronavirus pandemic affecting data such as these. However the relative relationship between states has not changed.
Source: American Community Survey. 2019a. "2018 American Community Survey 1-Year Estimates." Accessible at www.census.gov.

TABLE 8-1   HUMAN TRAFFICKING REPORT

Tier 1 Full Compliance	Tier 2 Significant Effort	Tier 2 Watch List Some Effort, But Trafficking Remains a Concern	Tier 3 Noncompliant, No Effort
Canada	Brazil	Belize	Algeria
Chile	Costa Rica	Columbia	China
Colombia	Denmark	Ireland	Iran
France	Germany	Pakistan	North Korea
Great Britain	India	Romania	Russia
Namibia	Lebanon	South Africa	Saudi Arabia
Philippines	Mexico	Tanzania	Syria
Taiwan	Ukraine	Vietnam	Venezuela

Note: Each tier lists only a sample of all nations classified. The *Human Trafficking Report* is created by the State Department. In the report the level of compliance by the United States is considered to be "full compliance."
Source: Department of State 2021.

Slavery has varied in the way it has been practiced. In ancient Greece, the main source of enslaved persons was piracy and captives of war. Although succeeding generations could inherit slave status, it was not necessarily permanent. A person's status might change, depending on which city-state happened to triumph in a military conflict. In effect, all citizens had the potential to become enslaved or free, depending on the circumstances of history. In contrast, in the United States and Latin America, where slavery was an ascribed status, racial and legal barriers prevented the freeing of enslaved persons. In both Europe and the New World, the rise of slavery was essential to the growth and development of **capitalism**—an economic system described in detail in Chapter 14—in the nineteenth century (Desmond 2019).

Today, the Universal Declaration of Human Rights, which is binding on all members of the United Nations, prohibits slavery in all its forms. Yet more people are enslaved today than at any point in world history. In many developing countries, bonded laborers are imprisoned in virtual lifetime employment; in some countries, human beings are owned outright. But a form of slavery also exists in Europe and the United States, where guest workers and undocumented workers have been forced to labor for years under terrible conditions, either to pay off debts or to avoid being turned over to immigration authorities.

Both these situations are likely to involve the transnational crime of trafficking in humans. Data on human trafficking and slavery are difficult to assess since no government will voluntarily and publicly disclose such numbers. According to the Walk Free Foundation (2019), over 40 million people are enslaved worldwide at any given time. Clearly slavery as a form of stratification has not vanished. Indeed, for several years faith-based groups have organized under the banner of "Abolition Now" to fight trafficking.

In 2000, the U.S. Congress passed the Trafficking Victims Protection Act, which established minimum standards for the elimination of human trafficking. The act requires the State Department to monitor other countries' efforts to vigorously investigate, prosecute, and convict individuals who participate in trafficking—including government officials. Each year, the department reports its findings, some of which are shown in Table 8-1. Tier 1 and Tier 2 countries are thought to be largely in compliance with the act. Tier 2 Watch countries are making efforts to comply, though trafficking remains a significant concern. Tier 3 countries are not compliant and are not making significant efforts to comply.

Castes

Castes are hereditary ranks that are usually religiously dictated and that tend to be fixed and immobile. Caste membership is an ascribed status (at birth, children automatically assume the same position as their parents). Each caste is quite sharply defined, and members are expected to marry within that caste.

The caste system is generally associated with Hinduism in India and other countries. In India there are four major castes, called *varnas*. A fifth category of outcastes, referred to as the *untouchables,* represents 16 percent of the population; its members are considered so lowly and unclean as to have no place within this stratification system. In an effort to avoid perpetuating the historical stigma these people bear, the government now refers to the untouchables as *scheduled castes*. The untouchables themselves prefer *Dalit* ("the repressed"), a term that communicates their desire to overcome their disadvantaged status.

In 1950, after gaining independence from Great Britain, India adopted a new constitution that formally outlawed the caste system. Over the past decade or two, however, urbanization and technological advances have brought more change to India's caste system than the government or politics has in more than half a century. The anonymity of city life tends to blur caste boundaries, allowing the *Dalit* to pass unrecognized in temples, schools, and places of employment. And the globalization of high technology has opened up India's social order, bringing new opportunities to those who possess the skills and ability to capitalize on them.

The term *caste* can also be applied in recent historical contexts outside India. For example, the system of stratification that characterized the southern United States from the end of the Civil War through the 1960s resembled a caste system. So did the rigid system of segregation that prevailed in the Republic of South Africa under apartheid, from 1948 through the 1990s. In both cases, race was the defining factor that placed a person in the social hierarchy (Wilkerson 2020).

Estates

A third type of stratification system, called *estates,* was associated with feudal societies during the Middle Ages. The **estate system,** or *feudalism,* required peasants to work land leased to them by nobles in exchange for military protection and other services. The basis for the system was the nobles' ownership of land, which was critical to their superior and privileged status. As in systems based on slavery and caste, inheritance of one's position largely defined the estate system. The nobles inherited their titles and property; the peasants were born into a subservient position within an agrarian society.

As the estate system developed, it became more differentiated. Nobles began to achieve varying degrees of authority. By the 12th century, a priesthood had emerged in most of Europe, along with classes of merchants and artisans. For the first time there were groups of people whose wealth did not depend on land ownership or agriculture. This economic change had profound social consequences as the estate system ended and a class system of stratification came into existence.

THINKING CRITICALLY

What are the differences between slavery and caste systems? What are the similarities?

Social Classes

A **class system** is a social ranking based primarily on economic position in which achieved characteristics can influence social mobility. In contrast to slavery and caste systems, the boundaries between classes are imprecisely defined, and one can move from one stratum, or level, of society to another. Even so, class systems maintain stable stratification hierarchies and patterns of class division, and they, too, are marked by unequal distribution of wealth and power. Class standing, although it is achieved, is heavily dependent on family and ascribed factors, such as race and ethnicity.

Sociologist Daniel Rossides (1997) uses a five-class model to describe the class system of the United States: the upper class, the upper-middle class, the lower-middle class, the working class, and the lower class. Although the lines separating social classes in his model are not so sharp as the divisions between castes, members of the five classes differ significantly in ways other than just income level.

Upper and Lower Classes Rossides characterizes about 1 to 2 percent of the people of the United States as *upper class.* They typically accumulate wealth, which is then passed on to the next generation. In contrast, the *lower class,* consisting of approximately 20 to 25 percent of the population, disproportionately consists of Blacks, Hispanics, single mothers with dependent children, and people who cannot find regular work or must make do with low-paying work. This class lacks both wealth and income and is too weak politically to exercise significant power (Killewald et al. 2017).

Both these classes, at opposite ends of the nation's social hierarchy, reflect the importance of ascribed status and achieved status. Ascribed statuses such as race and disability clearly influence a person's wealth and social position. People with disabilities are particularly vulnerable to unemployment, are often poorly paid, and tend to occupy the lower rungs of the occupational ladder. Regardless of their actual performance on the job, disabled people are stigmatized as not earning their keep. Such are the effects of ascribed status. We will look again at the plight of the lower class when we consider poverty and welfare policies.

John Tlumacki/The Boston Globe/Getty Images

Inherited wealth leads to all sorts of excesses, some illegal. Pictured here is Michelle Janavs, whose family's company developed the microwavable snack Hot Pockets. Janavs is shown leaving the federal courthouse after being sentenced to $300,000 bribes on behalf of her daughters in connection with a nationwide college admissions cheating scheme in 2020.

The economist John Kenneth Galbraith (1977:44) observed that "of all classes the rich are the most noticed and the least studied." The poor receive a good deal of attention from reporters, social activists, and policymakers seeking to alleviate their poverty, but the very affluent, who live apart from the rest of the population, are largely a mystery. Since Galbraith's comment, moreover, the residential separation of the rich has grown. The newspaper's society page may give us a peek at members of this class, but we know very little about their everyday lives. As of the end of 2019, over 173,000 households in the United States were worth more than $25 million each. Fewer than 25 percent of these people inherited even a tenth of their money, and very few of them are celebrities. Contrary to conventional wisdom, the nation's richest families are not living off inherited wealth. Today's truly rich have largely gained their money in the fields of finance, insurance, and health care. Just 17 percent of their wealth is inherited (Bothwell 2017; Spectrum Group 2019; Wolff 2017).

Middle Class Sandwiched between the upper and lower classes in this model are the upper-middle class, the lower-middle class, and the working class. The *upper-middle class,* about 10 to 15 percent of the population, includes professionals such as doctors, lawyers, and architects. They participate extensively in politics and take leadership roles in voluntary associations. The *lower-middle class,* about 30 to 35 percent of the population, includes less affluent professionals, such as elementary school teachers, and nurses, owners of small businesses, and a sizable number of clerical workers.

While not all members of the middle class hold degrees from a college, they share the goal of sending their children there. Yet as noted by Federal Reserve Board Chair Jerome Powell at the beginning of the chapter, concerns have grown about this social class's ability to keep up. Using a widely accepted definition of a middle-class household as one whose income falls between two-thirds and twice the nation's median household income (that is, between $42,000 and $126,000), only about 40 percent of American households would have been classified as middle class in 2018, compared to 57 percent in 1967 (Semega et al. 2019: Table A-2).

Contributing to the challenges of the middle class has been the growth of what is termed precarious work, as described in Box 8-1.

Working Class Rossides describes the *working class*—about 40 to 45 percent of the population—as people who hold regular manual or blue-collar jobs. Certain members of this class, such as electricians, may have higher incomes than people in the lower-middle class. Yet even if they have achieved some degree of economic security, they tend to identify with manual workers and their long history of involvement in the labor movement of the United States.

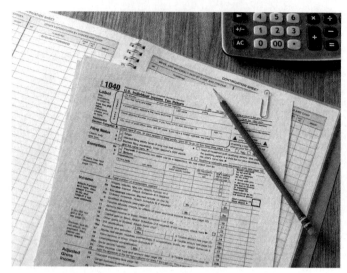

Jeffrey Hamilton/Digital Vision/Getty Images

Of the five classes, the working class is declining noticeably in size. In the economy of the United States, service and technical jobs are replacing those involved in the actual manufacturing or transportation of goods.

Class Warfare No one likes taxes, but policymakers and seekers of elected office differ dramatically on how they feel citizens in vastly different levels of the stratification system should be taxed.

Consider this difference between President Donald Trump's tax overhaul in 2017 and a Democrat challenger's proposal made during the 2020 campaign.

- The maximum income tax rate for the richest Americans was about 40 percent. Trump dropped the top rate to 37 percent, while Senator Bernie Sanders proposed raising it to 52 percent.

- Trump doubled the size of estates exempt from federal estate or inheritance tax from $5.5 million to $11 million, while Sanders proposed lowering the exemption to $3.5 million.

The general public is evenly divided between those who feel the federal taxes they pay are about right or unfair. Interestingly, only 9 percent of the richest feel they pay too much, and this remained unchanged after Trump's tax changes.

However, regardless of how they feel about their own taxes, most people in the United States (61 percent) think there is too much economic inequality in the country these days, and about half say addressing inequality requires significant changes to the economic system. Even so, even among those who see too much inequality, most say some amount of inequality is acceptable.

About four in ten Americans say that reducing inequality should be a top priority for the federal government. Among this group, large majorities say the influence inequality gives to the wealthy and the limits it places on people's opportunities are major reasons why reducing it should be given priority.

RESEARCH TODAY

8-1 Precarious Work

On-call workers. Consultants who have never been employed full-time. Shared economy entrepreneurs. Gig workers. Independent contractors.

Whatever you call them, there are millions of Americans who have been reduced to doing **precarious work**—employment that is poorly paid, and from the worker's perspective, insecure and unprotected. People who engage in precarious work often cannot support a household, and they are vulnerable to falling into poverty.

Even before economists recognized the economic downturn in 2009, there was ample statistical evidence that precarious work was increasing, despite the fact that the unemployment rate remained steady. In his presidential address to the ASA, Arne L. Kalleberg offered the following five social indicators:

1. A decline in the average length of time workers remain with an employer. This trend has been especially noticeable among older white men, who in the past were protected by employers.
2. An increase in long-term unemployment. The proportion of workers who remained unemployed after six months rose in the 2000s, when the number of manufacturing jobs shrank and fewer new jobs were created.
3. A decrease in job security. Given the increase in long-term unemployment and the decrease in average time spent with an employer, workers became increasingly insecure about their ability to replace a lost job.
4. An increase in outsourcing and temporary work. To meet cyclical fluctuations in supply and demand, employers have turned more and more to nontraditional

Comstock Images/Alamy Stock Photo

labor sources. Today, virtually any job can be outsourced, including accounting, legal, and military services.
5. A shift in risk from employers to employees. Few companies offer traditional pensions anymore. Employees are being asked to shoulder at least part of the cost and risk not only of their retirement investments, but of their health insurance plans as well.

> *To meet cyclical fluctuations in supply and demand, employers have turned more and more to nontraditional labor sources. Today, virtually any job can be outsourced, including accounting, legal, and military services.*

Although precarious work is becoming more common, people differ in their vulnerability to it. Members of racial and ethnic minorities are more likely than others to be engaged in precarious work. Immigrants, including those who are in the United States legally, are also more likely than others to be pre-

cariously employed. Around the world—in the United States, other industrial countries, and developing nations—women are much more likely than men to do precarious work.

The coronavirus pandemic underscored the fragile status of precarious workers. Typically they were the first to lose their jobs but also have had the greatest difficulty finding new employment.

What can be done to revitalize labor markets so that fewer workers end up doing substandard work—or at least, so that those who do will suffer less from it? Denmark is one country that has tried to deal with the problem. Although the government there cannot make jobs more secure, it does provide significant assistance to the unemployed. Help finding a job, significant income compensation (90 percent of a worker's previous wage for one year, without conditions), and subsidized education and training are all available to Danish workers who have lost their jobs.

LET'S DISCUSS

1. Has the trend toward increasing reliance on precarious work touched your family or friends? Has anyone you know been unemployed longer than six months? If so, did that person or persons belong to one or more of the groups that are particularly vulnerable to precarious work?
2. Looking forward to your own career, can you think of a strategy for avoiding precarious work, frequent job loss, and long-term unemployment?

Sources: Ahmed 2020; Bureau of Labor Statistics 2018b; Kalleberg 2009, 2012; Kalleberg and Vallas 2018; Westergaard-Nielsen 2008.

Yet relative to other social policy issues, though, the public does not rank inequality among the country's biggest problems (Gallup 2019; Horowitz et al. 2020).

THINKING CRITICALLY

What is the relationship between social class structure and power? Does widening inequality have an effect on politics?

Sociological Perspectives on Stratification

Sociologists have hotly debated stratification and social inequality and have reached varying conclusions. No theorist stressed the significance of class for society—and for social change—more strongly than Karl Marx. Marx viewed class differentiation as the crucial determinant of social, economic, and political inequality. In contrast, Max Weber questioned Marx's emphasis on the overriding importance of the economic sector, arguing that stratification should be viewed as having many dimensions.

Karl Marx's View of Class Differentiation

Karl Marx was concerned with stratification in all types of human society, beginning with primitive agricultural tribes and continuing into feudalism. However, his main focus was on the effects of economic inequality on all aspects of 19th-century Europe. The plight of the working class made him feel that it was imperative to strive for changes in the class structure of society.

In Marx's view, social relations during any period of history depend on who controls the primary mode of economic production, such as land or factories. Differential access to scarce resources shapes the relationship between groups. Thus, under the feudal estate system, most production was agricultural, and the land was owned by the nobility. Peasants had little choice but to work according to terms dictated by those who owned the land.

Using this type of analysis, Marx examined social relations within **capitalism**—an economic system in which the means of production are held largely in private hands and the main incentive for economic activity is the accumulation of profits. Marx focused on the two classes that began to emerge as the feudal estate system declined, the bourgeoisie and the proletariat. The **bourgeoisie,** or capitalist class, owns the means of production, such as factories and machinery; the **proletariat** is the working class. In capitalist societies, the members of the bourgeoisie maximize profit in competition with other firms. In the process, they exploit workers, who must exchange their labor for subsistence wages. In Marx's view, members of each class share a distinctive culture. Marx was most interested in the culture of the proletariat, but he also examined the ideology of the bourgeoisie, through which that class justifies its dominance over workers.

According to Marx, exploitation of the proletariat will inevitably lead to the destruction of the capitalist system, because the workers will revolt. But first, the working class must develop **class consciousness**—a subjective awareness of common vested interests and the need for collective political action to bring about social change. Often, workers must overcome what Marx termed **false consciousness,** or an attitude held by members of a class that does not accurately reflect their objective position. A worker with false consciousness may adopt an individualistic viewpoint toward capitalist

exploitation ("*I* am being exploited by *my* boss"). In contrast, the class-conscious worker realizes that all workers are being exploited by the bourgeoisie and have a common stake in revolution.

For Marx, class consciousness was part of a collective process in which the proletariat comes to identify the bourgeoisie as the source of its oppression. Revolutionary leaders will guide the working class in its struggle. Ultimately, the proletariat will overthrow the rule of both the bourgeoisie and the government (which Marx saw as representing the interests of capitalists) and will eliminate private ownership of the means of production. In Marx's rather utopian view, classes and oppression will cease to exist in the postrevolutionary workers' state.

How accurate were Marx's predictions? He failed to anticipate the emergence of labor unions, whose power in collective bargaining weakens the stranglehold that capitalists maintain over workers. Moreover, as contemporary conflict theorists note, he did not foresee the extent to which political liberties and relative prosperity could contribute to false consciousness. Many workers came to view themselves as individuals striving for improvement within free societies that offer substantial mobility, rather than as downtrodden members of a social class who face a collective fate. Even today, "class warfare" seems to refer more to diminished individual expectations than to a collective identity. Finally, Marx did not predict that Communist Party rule would be established and later overthrown in the former Soviet Union and throughout Eastern Europe. Still, the Marxist approach to the study of class is useful in stressing the importance of stratification as a

Aaron Black/Exactostock-1672/Superstock

An operator stands on sand on a fracking site. Karl Marx would identify such workers, who extract oil or gas from deep underground, as members of the proletariat, or working class. Even today, fracking operators must cover their own expenses and work in desolate locations with considerable dangers from exposure to chemicals. Such exploitation of the working class is a core principle of Marxist theory.

determinant of social behavior and the fundamental separation in many societies between two distinct groups, the rich and the poor.

Max Weber's View of Stratification

Unlike Karl Marx, Max Weber ([1913–1922] 1947) insisted that no single characteristic (such as class) totally defines a person's position within the stratification system. Instead, writing in 1916, he identified three distinct components of stratification: class, status, and power.

Weber used the term **class** to refer to a group of people who have a similar level of wealth and income. For example, certain workers in the United States try to support their families through minimum-wage jobs. According to Weber's definition, these wage earners constitute a class because they share the same economic position and fate. Although Weber agreed with Marx on the importance of this economic dimension of stratification, he argued that the actions of individuals and groups cannot be understood *solely* in economic terms.

Weber used the term **status group** to refer to people who have the same prestige or lifestyle. An individual gains status through membership in a desirable group, such as the medical profession. But status is not the same as economic class standing. In our culture, a successful pickpocket may belong to the same income class as a college professor. Yet the thief is widely regarded as holding low status, whereas the professor holds high status.

For Weber, the third major component of stratification has a political dimension. **Power** is the ability to exercise one's will over others. In the United States, power stems from membership in particularly influential groups, such as corporate boards of directors, government bodies, and interest groups. Conflict theorists generally agree that two major sources of power—big business and government—are closely interrelated. For instance, heads of major corporations have gone on to hold powerful positions in government, and former government and military leaders now play key roles in corporations.

To summarize, in Weber's view, each of us has not one rank in society but three. Our position in a stratification system reflects some combination of class, status, and power. Each factor influences the other two, and in fact the rankings on these three dimensions often tend to coincide. John F. Kennedy came from an extremely wealthy family, attended exclusive preparatory schools, graduated from Harvard University, and went on to become president of the United States. Like Kennedy, many people from affluent backgrounds achieve impressive status and power.

Interactionist Perspective

Both Karl Marx and Max Weber looked at inequality primarily from a macrosociological perspective, considering the entire society or even the global economy. Marx did suggest the importance of a more microsociological analysis, however, when he stressed the ways in which individuals develop a true class consciousness.

Interactionists, as well as economists, have long been interested in the importance of social class in shaping a person's lifestyle. The theorist Thorstein Veblen (1857–1929) noted that those at the top of the social hierarchy typically convert part of their wealth into **conspicuous consumption**—that is, they purchase goods not to survive but to flaunt their superior wealth and social standing. For example, they may purchase more automobiles than they can reasonably use, or build homes with more rooms than they can possibly occupy. In an element of conspicuous consumption called *conspicuous leisure,* they may jet to a remote destination, staying just long enough to have dinner or view a sunset over some historic locale (Veblen [1899] 1964).

Today, conspicuous consumption has found a new outlet in the cyberworld. Users of social media can now see their friends'

Kevin Scanlon for The New York Times/Redux

Do you think this would qualify as conspicuous consumption? How about this location for a play date? The rich now spend $275,00 to $400,000 on their children's playhouses and tree houses.

vacations and snazzy new cars online—an experience that can provoke what researchers call *Facebook envy.* Studies done in the United States and Germany show that even otherwise happy people can suffer envy and distress over this kind of digitally shared conspicuous consumption (Taylor and Strutton 2016).

At the other end of the spectrum, behavior that is judged to be typical of the lower class is subject not only to ridicule but even to legal action. Communities have, from time to time, banned trailers from people's front yards and sofas from their front porches. In some communities, it is illegal to leave a pickup truck in front of the house overnight. In others, street vendors who sell fruit, flowers, and water face restrictions meant not to serve the general public, but to protect their storefront competitors.

During the coronavirus pandemic, interactionists observed how the poor were especially vulnerable by their inability to social distance at the type of jobs they held and by their residence whether it be in the high density public housing in urban United States or in the tightly packed slums of Rio de Janeiro (Bassett 2020).

> ### THINKING CRITICALLY
>
> Give some examples of conspicuous consumption among students at your school. Which are obvious and which more subtle?

Is Stratification Universal?

Must some members of society receive greater rewards than others? Do people need to feel socially and economically superior to others? Can social life be organized without structured inequality? These questions have been debated for centuries, especially among political activists. Utopian socialists, religious minorities, and members of recent countercultures have all attempted to establish communities that to some extent would abolish inequality in social relationships.

Social scientists have found that inequality exists in all societies—even the simplest. For example, when anthropologist Gunnar Landtman ([1938] 1968) studied the Kiwai Papuans of New Guinea, at first he noticed little differentiation among them. Every man in the village did the same work and lived in similar housing. However, on closer inspection, Landtman observed that certain Papuans—men who were warriors, harpooners, and sorcerers—were described as "a little more high" than others. In contrast, villagers who were female, unemployed, or unmarried were considered "down a little bit" and were barred from owning land.

Stratification is universal in that all societies maintain some form of social inequality among members. Depending on its values, a society may assign people to distinctive ranks based on their religious knowledge, skill in hunting, physical attractiveness, trading expertise, or ability to provide health care. But why has such inequality developed in human societies? And how much differentiation among people, if any, is essential?

Functionalist and conflict theorists offer contrasting explanations for the existence and necessity of social stratification. Functionalists maintain that a differential system of rewards and punishments is necessary for the efficient operation of society. Conflict theorists argue that competition for scarce resources results in significant political, economic, and social inequality.

Functionalist Perspective

Would people go to school for many years to become physicians if they could make as much money and gain as much respect working as street cleaners? Functionalists say no, which is partly why they believe that stratification is universal.

In the view of Kingsley Davis and Wilbert Moore (1945), society must distribute its members among a variety of social positions. It must make sure not only that these positions are filled but also that they are filled by people with the appropriate talents and abilities. Rewards, including money and prestige, are based on the importance of a position and the relative scarcity of qualified personnel. Yet this assessment often devalues work performed by certain segments of society, such as women's work in the home or in occupations traditionally filled by women, or low-status work in fast-food outlets.

Davis and Moore argue that stratification is universal and that social inequality is necessary so that people will be motivated to fill functionally important positions. But critics say that unequal rewards are not the only means of encouraging people

Matthew Eisman/WireImage/Getty Images

The reality television series *Ice Road Truckers* ran for 11 seasons until 2017. The series suggests that long-haul truck drivers take pride in their low-prestige job. According to the conflict perspective, the cultural beliefs that form a society's dominant ideology, such as the popular image of the truck driver as hero, help the wealthy to maintain their power and control at the expense of the lower classes.

to fill critical positions and occupations. Personal pleasure, intrinsic satisfaction, and value orientations also motivate people to enter particular careers. Functionalists agree, but they note that society must use some type of reward to motivate people to enter unpleasant or dangerous jobs and professions that require long training periods. This response does not address stratification systems in which status is largely inherited, such as slave or caste societies. Moreover, even if stratification is inevitable, the functionalist explanation for differential rewards does not explain the wide disparity between the rich and the poor (R. Collins 1975; Kerbo 2012).

Conflict Perspective

The writings of Karl Marx lie at the heart of conflict theory. Marx viewed history as a continuous struggle between the oppressors and the oppressed, which ultimately would culminate in an egalitarian, classless society. In terms of stratification, he argued that under capitalism, the dominant class—the bourgeoisie—manipulates the economic and political systems in order to maintain control over the exploited proletariat. Marx did not believe that stratification was inevitable, but he did see inequality and oppression as inherent in capitalism (E. O. Wright 2015).

Like Marx, contemporary conflict theorists believe that human beings are prone to conflict over scarce resources such as wealth, status, and power. However, Marx focused primarily on class conflict; more recent theorists have extended the analysis to include conflicts based on gender, race, age, and other dimensions. British sociologist Ralf Dahrendorf (1929–2009) is one of the most influential contributors to the conflict approach.

Dahrendorf (1959) modified Marx's analysis of capitalist society to apply to modern capitalist societies. For Dahrendorf, social classes are groups of people who share common interests resulting from their authority relationships. In identifying the most powerful groups in society, he includes not only the bourgeoisie—the owners of the means of production—but also the managers of industry, legislators, the judiciary, heads of the government bureaucracy, and others. In that respect,

Dahrendorf merged Marx's emphasis on class conflict with Weber's recognition that power is an important element of stratification (Cuff et al. 1990).

Conflict theorists, including Dahrendorf, contend that the powerful of today, like the bourgeoisie of Marx's time, want society to run smoothly so that they can enjoy their privileged positions. Because the status quo suits those with wealth, status, and power, they have a clear interest in preventing, minimizing, or controlling societal conflict.

One way for the powerful to maintain the status quo is to define and disseminate the society's dominant ideology. The term **dominant ideology** describes a set of cultural beliefs and practices that helps to maintain powerful social, economic, and political interests. For Marx, the dominant ideology in a capitalist society served the interests of the ruling class. From a conflict perspective, the social significance of the dominant ideology is that not only do a society's most powerful groups and institutions control wealth and property; even more important, they control the means of producing beliefs about reality through religion, education, and the media (Knowles and Castro 2019).

The powerful, such as leaders of government, also use limited social reforms to buy off the oppressed and reduce the danger of challenges to their dominance. For example, minimum-wage laws and unemployment compensation unquestionably give some valuable assistance to men and women in need. Yet these reforms also serve to pacify those who might otherwise rebel. Of course, in the view of conflict theorists, such maneuvers can never entirely eliminate conflict, since workers will continue to demand equality, and the powerful will not give up their control of society.

Conflict theorists see stratification as a major source of societal tension and conflict. They do not agree with Davis and Moore that stratification is functional for a society or that it serves as a source of stability. Rather, conflict sociologists argue that stratification will inevitably lead to instability and social change (R. Collins 1975; L. Coser 1977).

Table 8-2 summarizes and compares the three major perspectives on social stratification.

TABLE 8-2 SOCIOLOGICAL PERSPECTIVES ON SOCIAL STRATIFICATION

Tracking Sociological Perspectives

	Functionalist	Conflict	Interactionist
Purpose of social stratification	Facilitates filling of social positions	Facilitates exploitation	Influences people's lifestyles
Attitude toward social inequality	Necessary to some extent	Excessive and growing	Influences intergroup relations
Analysis of the wealthy	Talented and skilled, creating opportunities for others	Use the dominant ideology to further their own interests	Exhibit conspicuous consumption and conspicuous leisure

Think about It Which perspective seems to best account for the stratification you see in society? Explain your choice.

Lenski's Viewpoint

Let's return to the question posed earlier—Is stratification universal?—and consider the sociological response. Some form of differentiation is found in every culture, from the most primitive to the most advanced industrial societies of our time. Sociologist Gerhard Lenski, in his sociocultural evolution approach, described how economic systems change as their level of technology becomes more complex, beginning with hunting and gathering and culminating eventually with industrial society.

In subsistence-based hunting-and-gathering societies, people focus on survival. While some inequality and differentiation are evident, a stratification system based on social class does not emerge because there is no real wealth to be claimed. As a society advances technologically, it becomes capable of producing a considerable surplus of goods. The emergence of surplus resources greatly expands the possibilities for inequality in status, influence, and power, allowing a well-defined, rigid social class system to develop. To minimize strikes, slowdowns, and industrial sabotage, the elites may share a portion of the economic surplus with the lower classes, but not enough to reduce their own power and privilege.

As Lenski argued, the allocation of surplus goods and services controlled by those with wealth, status, and power reinforces the social inequality that accompanies stratification systems. While this reward system may once have served the overall purposes of society, as functionalists contend, the same cannot be said for the large disparities separating the haves from the have-nots in current societies. In contemporary industrial society, the degree of social and economic inequality far exceeds what is needed to provide for goods and services (Lenski 1966; Nolan 2004; Nolan and Lenski 2015).

Lenski and others have debated whether stratification is inevitable and how it developed. One possible way to redistribute income is by means of the tax structure, as discussed in Box 8-2.

THINKING CRITICALLY

In your view, is the extent of social inequality in the United States helpful or harmful to society as a whole? Explain.

RESEARCH TODAY

8-2 Taxes as Opportunity

"Nothing can be said to be certain, except death and taxes." This famous aphorism is usually attributed to Ben Franklin. Even before his time and ever since, people have complained about taxes. However, taxes used to raise public funds can be constructed to rearrange a stratification system.

The first federal income tax was levied in the United States in 1861 to help pay the government's costs of the Civil War. By 1895, the Supreme Court had decided that some aspects of the income tax were unconstitutional. This led to the passage of the Sixteenth Amendment in 1916, which gave Congress the authority to impose an income tax. At that time most people paid 1 percent of their income; top earners paid up to 7 percent.

For a generation, the majority of the population has agreed that the income tax they pay is fair. And 52 percent agree with the idea that "heavy taxes on the rich" are a good way to redistribute wealth. So increasing the tax rate that very rich people pay, or removing some exemptions that benefit the very rich, would be acceptable to many people and could also reduce inequality, especially between the middle and upper class.

However, as with everything dealing with taxes, nothing is simple. Affluent people typically have considerable freedom to adjust when and how they receive income. Changes in tax rates can be negated if individuals come up with legal ways to be compensated that are immune from new taxes or higher rates.

For a generation, the majority of the population has agreed that the income tax they pay is fair.

At the other end of the stratification system, tax policy has been viewed as an instrument for alleviating poverty. Low-income households receive payments, rather than paying taxes, through an Earned Income Tax Credit (EITC). On the positive side, this tax credit avoids much of the social stigma associated with applying for traditional welfare checks. Typically families receive the EITC as a lump-sum payment, and they can use it to enhance economic advancement, such as by purchasing a car or making a security deposit on an apartment. Over 28 million

working families receive the EITC, and 39 percent of them are lofted above the poverty line because of it.

Fiscal sociology, or the study of tax policy and its relationship to the stratification system, is relatively new. The redistributive effects of changing tax policy seem obvious, but wealthy individuals and their advisers can often counter changes in tax law with measures that allow them to legally escape paying more. Tax law changes also tend to have unintended consequences that may maintain inequalities or even exacerbate income differences among households.

LET'S DISCUSS

1. Do you think that high tax rates and fewer tax loopholes for the rich are a good way to alleviate inequality? Why or why not?
2. In what ways do you think that people's perceptions of the fairness of the tax system are affected by their income level?

Sources: Center on Budget and Policy Priorities 2019; Martin and Prasad 2014; Newport 2017a, 2017b, 2019.

Stratification by Social Class

We continually assess how wealthy people are by looking at the cars they drive, the houses they live in, the clothes they wear, and so on. Yet it is not so easy to locate an individual within our social hierarchies as it would be in slavery or caste systems of stratification. To determine someone's class position, sociologists generally rely on the objective method.

Objective Method of Measuring Social Class

In the **objective method** of measuring social class, class is viewed largely as a statistical category. Researchers assign individuals to social classes on the basis of criteria such as occupation, education, income, and place of residence. The key to the objective method is that the *researcher,* rather than the person being classified, identifies an individual's class position.

The first step in using this method is to decide what indicators or causal factors will be measured objectively, whether wealth, income, education, or occupation. The prestige ranking of

occupations has proved to be a useful indicator of a person's class position. For one thing, it is much easier to determine accurately than income or wealth. The term **prestige** refers to the respect and admiration that an occupation holds in a society. "My daughter, the physicist" connotes something very different from "my daughter, the waitress." Prestige is independent of the particular individual who occupies a job, a characteristic that distinguishes it from esteem. **Esteem** refers to the reputation that a specific person has earned within an occupation. Therefore, one can say that the position of president of the United States has high prestige, even though it has been occupied by people with varying degrees of esteem. A hair stylist may have the esteem of his clients, but he lacks the prestige of a corporate executive.

Table 8-3 ranks the prestige of a number of well-known occupations. In a series of national surveys, sociologists assigned prestige rankings to about 500 occupations, ranging from surgeon to panhandler. The highest possible prestige score was 100; the lowest was 0. Physician, college professor, lawyer, dentist, and banker were the most highly regarded occupations. Sociologists have used such data to assign prestige rankings to virtually all jobs and have found a stability in

TABLE 8-3 PRESTIGE RANKINGS OF OCCUPATIONS

Occupation	Score	Occupation	Score
Physician	86	Bank teller	50
College professor	78	Electrician	49
Lawyer	76	Farm manager	48
Dentist	74	Insurance agent	47
Banker	72	Mail carrier	42
Architect	71	Farmer	41
Airline pilot	70	Correctional officer	40
Clergy	69	Carpenter	40
Registered nurse	66	Barber	38
High school teacher	63	Child care worker	36
Pharmacist	61	Hotel clerk	32
Elementary school teacher	60	Bus driver	32
Veterinarian	60	Truck driver	30
Police officer or detective	60	Salesworker (shoes)	28
Prekindergarten teacher	60	Waiter and waitress	28
Accountant	57	Cook (short-order)	28
Librarian	55	Bartender	25
Firefighter	53	Garbage collector	17
Funeral director	52	Janitor	16
Social worker	52	Newspaper vendor	15

Think about It Can you name what you think are two more high-prestige occupations? Two more low-prestige occupations? Explain why you consider those jobs to be of high or low prestige.

Note: 100 is the highest and 0 the lowest possible prestige score.
Source: T. Smith et al. 2019:3260–3266.

rankings from 1925 to the present. Similar studies in other countries have also developed useful prestige rankings of occupations (Connelly et al. 2017).

During the pandemic many occupations regarded as front-line workers who faced the risks of infection with COVID-19 received renewed respect. One could easily observe how occupations of both moderate prestige, such as nursing and EMTs, and even others with modest prestige, such as grocery store clerk and delivery people, received greater admiration and were even termed "heroes."

Gender and Occupational Prestige

For many years, studies of social class neglected the occupations and incomes of *women* as determinants of social rank. With more than half of all married women working outside the home, this approach seems outmoded. How should we judge class or status in dual-career families—by the occupation regarded as having greater prestige, the average, or some other combination of the two? Sociologists—in particular, feminist sociologists in Great Britain—have drawn on new approaches to assess women's social class standing. One approach is to focus on the individual (rather than the family or household) as the basis for categorizing a woman's class position. Thus, a woman would be classified according to her own occupational status rather than that of her spouse (Mandel 2016; McCall 2008).

Another feminist effort to measure the contribution of women to the economy reflects a more clearly political agenda. Organizations, including those affiliated with the United Nations, have sought to give a monetary value to women's unpaid work. On average, women globally spend 4.5 hours of each day on unpaid work, while men spend about half that time. In richer countries, the gap is smaller, but nowhere in the world do men do as much unpaid work as women. In Norway, a country often regarded as a society where the genders are equal, women spend about an hour more on unpaid work daily than men. But in India, women spend almost six hours on unpaid labor each day, while men spend less than an hour (Oxfam 2020).

Multiple Measures

Another complication in measuring social class is that advances in statistical methods and computer technology have multiplied the factors used to define class under the objective method. No longer are sociologists limited to annual income and education in evaluating a person's class position. Today, studies use as criteria the value of homes, sources of income, assets, years in present occupations, neighborhoods, and considerations regarding dual careers. Adding these variables will not necessarily paint a different picture of class differentiation in the United States, but it does allow sociologists to measure class in a more complex and multidimensional way. When researchers use multiple measures, they typically speak of **socioeconomic status (SES)**, a measure of social class that is based on income, education, and occupation. To determine the socioeconomic status of a young person, such as a college student under age 25, they use *parental* income, education, and occupation.

Whatever the technique used to measure class, the sociologist is interested in real and often dramatic differences in power, privilege, and opportunity in a society. The study of stratification is a study of inequality. Nowhere is the truth of that statement more evident than in the distribution of income and wealth.

THINKING CRITICALLY

How are students motivated by prestige in choosing their future occupations? What are the advantages and disadvantages of including prestige in career decisions? Explain.

Income and Wealth

By all measures, income in the United States is distributed unevenly. Nobel Prize–winning economist Paul Samuelson has described the situation in the following words: "If we made an income pyramid out of building blocks, with each layer portraying $500 of income, the peak would be far higher than Mount Everest, but most people would be within a few feet of the ground" (Samuelson and Nordhaus 2010:324).

Recent data support Samuelson's analogy. In 2020, the median household income in the United States was $67,512. In other words, half of all households had higher incomes that year and half had lower incomes. However, this fact does not fully convey the income disparities in our society.

We can gain some insight into income inequality in the United States by looking at the relative placement of households within the income distribution. One of the most common ways of doing so is to line up all income-earning households from low to high and then break them into quintiles, or fifths. Because there are approximately 129 million households in the United States, each quintile includes an equal number of about 25 million households. This method gives us a sense of the average income within each quintile, along with the percentage of the nation's total income earned in each quintile.

As Figure 8-2 shows, looking at the population in this way reveals a significant degree of income inequality. The mean income for households in the lowest quintile is $14,589; in the top quintile, it is $253,484. If we were to move up to the highest end of the income distribution, we would find that the top 5 percent of taxpayers—about 6,500 households—have mean incomes of $446,030 a year (Semega et al. 2019).

FIGURE 8-2 MEAN HOUSEHOLD INCOME BY QUINTILE, 2018

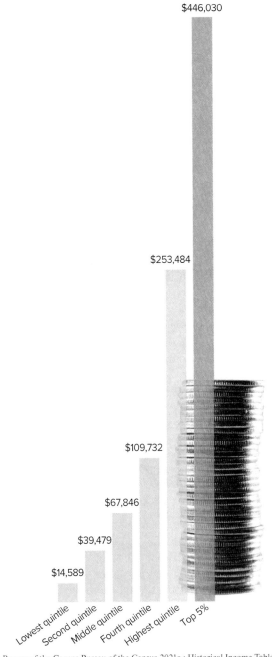

$446,030

$253,484

$109,732

$67,846

$39,479

$14,589

Lowest quintile | Second quintile | Middle quintile | Fourth quintile | Highest quintile | Top 5%

Source: Bureau of the Census Bureau of the Census 2021a.: Historical Income Tables: Households. Table H-3. November 8. Accessible at www.census.gov. (Stockbyte/Getty Images)

There has been a modest redistribution of income in the United States from 1929 through 1970, primarily the result of the government's economic and tax policies, which shifted some income to the poor. However, in the past four decades, federal tax policies have favored the affluent. Moreover, while the salaries of highly skilled workers and professionals have continued to rise, the wages of less skilled workers have *decreased* when controlled for inflation. Since 1979, wages for the top 1% increased 160 percent, while the share of

wages for the bottom 90 percent actually decreased. Little wonder that the middle class is shrinking (Billitteri 2009).

Globalization is often blamed for this growing inequality, because it has forced less skilled workers to compete with lower-paid foreign-born workers. While that is true, research suggests that the number of displaced workers who are reemployed at similarly paid or even higher-paid jobs roughly equals the number of workers whose earnings drop.

The growing inequality in income is mirrored in increasing inequality in wealth. Consider the years between 1970 and 2015. The incomes of both the upper and lower classes increased, while the middle class's share of income declined. Gains in net worth, even with the Great Recession, have been decidedly in favor of the most wealthy. The pattern is clear: the biggest winners have been the affluent (Pew Research Center 2015d).

Indeed, wealth is distributed much more unevenly than income in the United States. A 2020 Federal Reserve Bank study showed that 1 percent of the nation's families control about 31 percent of the nation's wealth (Figure 8-3).

Researchers have also found a dramatic disparity in the wealth of Blacks and Hispanics compared to that of whites. Among these three groups, the nation's wealth is shared as follows:

- White non-Hispanic families, 91.3%
- African-American families, 4.6%
- Hispanic families, 3.5%

FIGURE 8-3 DISTRIBUTION OF FAMILY WEALTH IN THE UNITED STATES

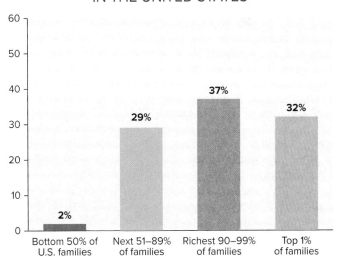

Bottom 50% of U.S. families: 2%
Next 51–89% of families: 29%
Richest 90–99% of families: 37%
Top 1% of families: 32%

Note: Wealth levels declined for some following the coronavirus pandemic, affecting data such as these. However the relative relationship between groups has not changed.
Source: Board of Governers of the Federal Reserve Bank. Distributional Financial Accounts: Overview of Third Quarter 2019. December 23, 2020. Accessible at www.federalreserve.gov.

Although most families do have some wealth, the number with zero or negative net worth is significant and varies widely by race/ethnicity. As of 2019, the 100 wealthiest white families owned as much wealth as all Blacks combined. Nearly 20 percent of Black households have zero or negative net worth. The share of white households without any wealth is considerably lower at 9 percent. Hispanic and other households fall somewhere in between white and Black families on this measure. This large racial wealth gap has persisted over decades. The coronavirus pandemic greatly affected household income and wealth, but the patterns of inequality may be increasing (Thomas et al, 2020; Wu 2020).

THINKING CRITICALLY

What does the pattern of income distribution in the United States tell you about your future income? How much can you expect it to grow over the years?

Poverty

About 13 percent of the people in the United States live below the poverty line established by the federal government. In 2019, more than 40 million people were living in poverty. Despite very low unemployment rates, the economy passed these people by. A Bureau of the Census report shows that one in six

RESEARCH TODAY

8-3   Calculating Your Risk of Poverty

We know from existing research that certain people are more likely to experience poverty—that is, for a single individual, an income less than $12,780 in 2020. Among the factors affecting whether a person becomes poor are age, gender, race and ethnicity, marital status, region of the country, urban or rural, and disability status.

Most people think of poverty as something that happens to someone else, someone who belongs to the distant-from-us underclass. As a result, the poor have been thought of as falling outside the mainstream and therefore been marginalized. The divide between "us" (the nonpoor) and "them" (the poor) is wide.

However, research shows that between the ages of 20 and 75, nearly 60 percent of the American population will experience at least one year in poverty (below the official poverty line). Social work professor Mark Rank and sociologist Thomas A. Hirschi developed the poverty risk calculator, which allows anyone to determine the probability he or she will experience poverty in the next 5, 10, or 15 years.

So, let's assume a white person is single and between the ages 20 and 24. The likelihood this person will fall below the poverty line in the next 5 years is:

- 20.4 percent for a man or a woman with a high school diploma who is continuing his or her education
- 24.5 percent for a man with no schooling beyond high school

- 38.8 percent for a woman with no schooling beyond high school

For non-white males, the odds of falling into poverty are higher:

- 53.9 percent for a man with no schooling beyond high school
- 45.3 percent for a man with more than a high school diploma

For non-white females, the risk is highest of all:

- 69.9 percent for a woman with no schooling beyond high school
- 43.8 percent for a woman with more than a high school diploma

> *Most people think of poverty as something that happens to someone else, someone who belongs to the distant-from-us underclass.*

Clearly a large proportion of the population is likely to experience poverty at some point in their lives, especially those who are not white.

How are these probabilities calculated? One tool researchers used in the government survey, the Panel Study of Income Dynamics (or PSID), is the longest-running longitudinal data set in the world. Begun in 1968 by drawing a representative sample of U.S. households, the study has followed them ever since and now includes several hundred thousand cases. By following the same individuals over time, researchers can see what happens to them in response to a variety of economic and social changes.

The estimates given above are for just the next 5 years. As one projects out across longer time periods, the likelihood of an event occurring increases. For example, as we extend out to 15 years, there is a greater chance that a detrimental event, such as losing a job, experiencing a health emergency, or getting divorced, will throw you into poverty. Indeed, over a 55-year period, a majority of Americans will experience poverty. Because most people do not think about such long time periods, we tend to underestimate the probability that an adverse event will happen. This partially explains why so many people believe that poverty will never happen to them.

LET'S DISCUSS

1. Estimate the likelihood that you will experience poverty at some point in your life. On what are you basing your estimate: personal or family experience or actual statistics?
2. Why are the chances of becoming poor different for people of different races, age groups, and genders? Why are the odds greater for women than for men?

Sources: Rank 2017; Rank and Hirschi 2017; Department of Health and Human Services 2020b.

households cannot meet basic needs, from paying the utility bills to buying dinner (Meyer et al. 2019; Semega et al. 2019).

It is easy for many people, as well as for policymakers, to see poverty as someone else's problem, but consider the probability that you will experience poverty within the next five years. That is the subject of Box 8-3.

One contributor to the United States' high poverty rate has been the large number of workers employed at minimum wage. As Figure 8-4 shows, the federal government raised the minimum wage over the last 70 years, from 75 cents in 1950 to $7.25 in 2009. But in terms of its real value, adjusted for inflation, the minimum wage has failed to keep pace with the cost of living. In fact, its real value today is *lower* than it was at any time from 1950 to 1994. Little wonder, then, that low-income workers can barely scrape by.

The pandemic caused an unprecedented rise in reported unemployment rates—from less than 5 percent to 15–20 percent. Yet the lower rates of white unemployment relative to Black and Hispanic unemployment held constant. We will look more closely at the special challenges faced by low-wage workers and by the poor, in general, in the Chapter 14 policy section, Government and Economic Responses to the Coronavirus Pandemic (Bureau of Labor Statistics 2020f, 2020g).

Sociologists have long had an interest in the impact of substandard work on society, beginning with the writings of Karl Marx, Émile Durkheim, and Max Weber. Their interest increased with the global economic decline that began in 2008, which trapped many people in jobs they did not want or left them unemployed.

In this section, we'll consider just how social scientists define *poverty.* We'll also take a closer look at the people who fall into that category—including the working poor.

Studying Poverty

The efforts of sociologists and other social scientists to better understand poverty are complicated by the difficulty of defining it. This problem is evident even in government programs that conceive of poverty in either absolute or relative terms. **Absolute poverty** refers to a minimum level of subsistence that no family should be expected to live below.

One commonly used measure of absolute poverty is the federal government's *poverty line,* a money income figure that is adjusted annually to reflect the consumption requirements of families based on their size and composition. The poverty line serves as an official definition of which people are poor. In 2020, for example, any family of four (two adults and two children) with a combined income of $26,200 or less fell below the poverty line. This definition determines which individuals and families will be eligible for certain government benefits (Department of Health and Human Services 2020b).

Although by absolute standards, poverty has declined in the United States, it remains higher than in many other industrial nations. As Figure 8-5 shows, a comparatively high proportion of U.S. households are poor, meaning that they are unable to purchase basic consumer goods. If anything, this cross-national comparison understates the extent of poverty in the United States, since U.S. residents are likely to pay more for housing, health care, child care, and education than residents of other countries, where such expenses are often subsidized.

In contrast to absolute poverty, **relative poverty** is a floating standard of deprivation by which people at the bottom of a society, whatever their lifestyles, are judged to be disadvantaged *in comparison with the nation as a whole.* Therefore, even if the poor of 2020 are better off in absolute terms than the poor of the 1930s or 1960s, they are still seen as deserving of special assistance.

Debate has been growing over the accuracy of the federal government's

FIGURE 8-4   U.S. MINIMUM WAGE ADJUSTED FOR INFLATION

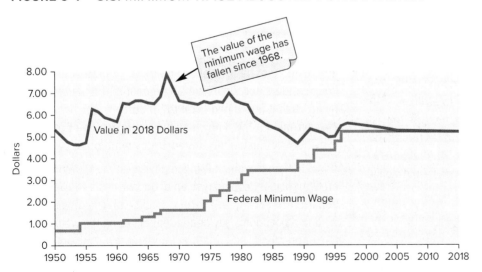

Note: In 2009 the federal minimum wage was raised to $7.25. Some states legislate different standards. As of March 2020, minimums were actually lower in 2 states (Georgia and Wyoming) and higher in 28 states and the District of Columbia.
Source: Author's estimate; Department of Labor 2020a; Kurtz et al. 2019.

FIGURE 8-5   POVERTY IN SELECTED COUNTRIES

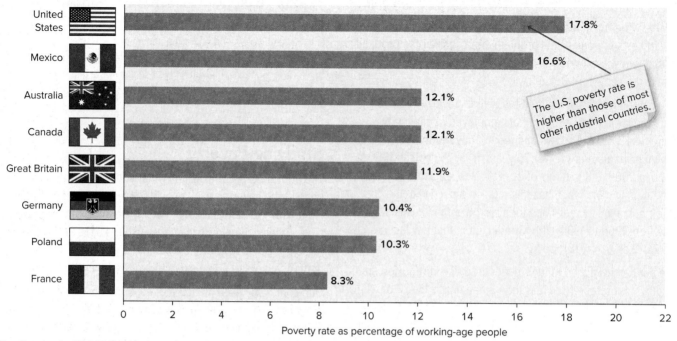

Note: Data are for 2016–2017 or latest year reported in 2020. Poverty threshold is 50 percent of a nation's median household income. Globally poverty rates increased following the coronavirus pandemic affecting data such as these. However the relative relationship between nations has not changed.
Organization for Economic Co-Operation and Development. 2020a. "Poverty Ratio." Accessible at oecd.org. *Flags:* admin_design/Shutterstock

measure of poverty, which has remained largely unchanged since 1963. If noncash benefits such as Medicare, Medicaid, tax credits, food stamps (the Supplemental Nutrition Assistance Program, or SNAP), public housing, and health care and other employer-provided fringe benefits were included, the reported poverty rate would be lower. On the other hand, if out-of-pocket medical expenses and mandatory work expenses for transportation and child care were included, the poverty rate would be higher. Furthermore, although the current poverty measure does consider family size, it does not consider a household's location, whether in a relatively expensive city like New York or in a less expensive rural area. Nor does it consider whether a householder pays rent or a mortgage installment, lives at home or with someone else.

To address some of these shortcomings, in 2010 the federal government launched a second statistic called the Supplemental Poverty Measure (SPM), which is used to estimate economic hardship. The SPM is a relative poverty measure that is based on a broad range of changing household resources and expenses. It was calculated beginning in late 2011, but does not replace the poverty line in determining a household's eligibility for benefits (Pearce 2014).

Who Are the Poor?

Not only does the category of the poor defy any simple definition; it counters the common stereotypes about "poor people." For example, many people in the United States believe that the poor are able to work but will not. Yet about 37 percent of

poor adults age 18–64 do work outside the home—33 percent of them full-time—compared to 53 percent of all adults. Such stereotypes lead to a faulty picture of the poor and mistaken notions about how to reduce poverty (Semega et al. 2019: 50).

Though many of the poor live in urban slums, a majority live outside those poverty-stricken areas. Poverty is no stranger in rural areas, from Appalachia to hard-hit farming regions to Native American reservations. Table 8-4 provides additional statistical information regarding low-income people in the United States.

Feminization of Poverty

Since World War II, an increasing proportion of the poor people of the United States have been women, many of whom are divorced or never-married mothers. In 1959, female householders accounted for 26 percent of the nation's poor; by 2018, that figure had risen to 50 percent (see Table 8-4). This alarming trend, known as the **feminization of poverty,** is evident not just in the United States but around the world.

About half of all women living in poverty in the United States are in transition, coping with an economic crisis caused by the departure, disability, or death of a husband. The other half tend to be economically dependent either on the welfare system or on friends and relatives living nearby. A major factor in the feminization of poverty has been the increase in families with women as single heads of the household. Conflict theorists and other observers trace the higher rates of poverty among women to three distinct factors: the difficulty in finding

TABLE 8-4 WHO ARE THE POOR IN THE UNITED STATES?

Group	Percentage of the Population of the United States	Percentage of the Poor of the United States
Age		
Under 18 years old	22%	31%
18 to 64 years old	61	56
65 years and older	17	13
Race-Ethnicity		
Whites (non-Hispanic)	60	43
Blacks	13	23
Hispanics	19	28
Asians and Pacific Islanders	6	4
Family Composition		
Married couples with both members present	74	39
Female householders	18	50
Male householders	8	11
Nativity		
Native born	86	84
Foreign born (naturalized citizen)	7	6
Foreign born (not citizens)	7	10
People with Disabilities	8	9

Think about It Which factors are most closely related to poverty? Why do you think this is the case?

Note: People with disabilities includes ages 18–64. Poverty levels increased following the coronavirus pandemic affecting data such as these. However the relative relationship between groups has not changed. Note: Family composition data are for primary families.
Source: Shrider, Emily A., Melissa Kollar, Frances Chen, And Jessica Semega. 2021. *Income and Poverty in the United States: 2020.* September 14. Report Number P60-273. Tables B-1, B-2. Accessible at www.census.gov.

affordable child care, sexual harassment, and sex discrimination in the labor market (Burns 2010).

The Underclass

More than 1 in 6 people who live in urban areas are poor. These highly visible urban residents are the focus of most government efforts to alleviate poverty. Yet according to many observers, the plight of the urban poor is growing worse, owing to the devastating interplay of inadequate education and limited employment prospects. Traditional employment opportunities in the industrial sector are largely closed to the unskilled poor. Past and present discrimination heightens these problems for those low-income

Mark Kostich/Getty Images
Even if this single parent works her way up the ladder, supporting her family will still be difficult.

urban residents who are Black or Hispanic (Parker et al. 2018).

Along with other social scientists, sociologist William Julius Wilson (1996, 2012a, 2012b) and his colleagues (2004) have used the term **underclass** to describe the long-term poor who lack training and skills. According to a 2019 analysis of the census data of the fifty largest metropolitan areas, 12 million people living in central cities and another 24 million in suburban areas reside in areas of concentrated low incomes. People of color, especially African Americans, are disproportionately likely to live in economically declining areas. The Hispanic population of economically declining areas has been rapidly increasing, indicating increased segregation and concentration.

Poverty, unfortunately, is not limited to just one part of America. Rural poverty is about 3 percentage points higher than urban poverty. Further, historically high-poverty counties are disproportionately rural and continue to be geographically concentrated in Appalachia and Native American lands, the Southern "Black Belt," the Mississippi Delta, and the Rio Grande Valley.

Looking at concentrations of poverty alone cannot help us consider the association between social inequality and poverty. There are areas with high proportions of people living in poverty as well as those of high affluence. Nationally, 88% of the population of highly affluent neighborhoods are white and non-Hispanic, compared with only 16% of those living in highly concentrated areas of poverty.

Analyses of the poor in general reveal that they are not a static social class. The overall composition of the poor changes continually, because some individuals and families near the top edge of poverty move above the poverty level after a year or two, while others slip below it. Still, hundreds of thousands of people remain in poverty for many years at a time. Black Americans and Latinos are more likely than white people to be persistently poor. Both Latinos and Black Americans are less likely than white people to leave the welfare rolls as a result of welfare reform (Goetz et al. 2019; Institute for Research on Poverty 2020; Institute on Metropolitan Community Opportunity 2019; Jäntti 2009; Sampson 2011).

Explaining Poverty

Why is it that poverty pervades a nation of such vast wealth? In 2020, poverty levels matched those of 50 years earlier. Sociologist Herbert Gans

(1995), who has applied functionalist analysis to the existence of poverty, argues that various segments of society actually *benefit* from the existence of the poor. Gans has identified a number of social, economic, and political functions that the poor perform for society:

- The presence of poor people means that society's dirty work—physically dirty or dangerous, dead-end and underpaid, undignified and menial jobs—will be performed at low cost.

- Poverty creates jobs for occupations and professions that serve the poor. It creates both legal employment (public health experts, welfare caseworkers) and illegal jobs (drug dealers, numbers runners).

- The identification and punishment of the poor as deviants upholds the legitimacy of conventional social norms and mainstream values regarding hard work, thrift, and honesty.

- Within a relatively hierarchical society, the existence of poor people guarantees the higher status of the rich. As psychologist William Ryan (1976) noted, affluent people may justify inequality (and gain a measure of satisfaction) by *blaming the victims* of poverty for their disadvantaged condition.

- Because of their lack of political power, the poor often absorb the costs of social change. Under the policy of deinstitutionalization, mental patients released from long-term hospitals have been transferred primarily to low-income communities and neighborhoods. Similarly, halfway houses for rehabilitated drug abusers, rejected by more affluent communities, often end up in poorer neighborhoods.

In Gans's view, then, poverty and the poor actually satisfy positive functions for many nonpoor groups in the United States.

THINKING CRITICALLY

How do you identify areas of poverty in your community or one nearby? Do you consider residents' achieved or ascribed characteristics?

Life Chances

Max Weber saw class as being closely related to people's **life chances**—that is, their opportunities to provide themselves with material goods, positive living conditions, and favorable life experiences (Gerth and Mills 1958). Life chances are reflected in measures such as housing, education, and health. Occupying a higher social class in a society improves your life chances and brings greater access to social rewards. In contrast, people in the lower social classes are forced to devote a larger proportion of their limited resources to the necessities of life. In some cases, life chances are a matter of life and death. Despite advances in medicine, the longevity gap between the affluent and the poor remains and is widening. A man whose earnings place him in the top tenth of the population can expect to live 14 years longer than one in the bottom tenth (Tavernise 2016).

In times of danger, the affluent and powerful have a better chance of surviving than people of ordinary means. When the supposedly unsinkable British ocean liner *Titanic* hit an iceberg in 1912, it was not carrying enough lifeboats to accommodate all passengers. Plans had been made to evacuate only first- and second-class passengers. About 62 percent of the first-class passengers survived the disaster. Despite a rule that women and children would go first, about a third of those passengers were male. In contrast, only 25 percent of the third-class passengers survived. The first attempt to alert them to the need to abandon ship came well after other passengers had been notified. In an ironic demonstration of continuing social inequality, a luxury travel organization called Bluefish charges passengers $100,000 each to view the underwater remains of the *Titanic* from a deep-sea submersible (Butler 1998; Crouse 1999; Prestwich 2017; Riding 1998).

Class position also affects people's ability to deal with epidemics. The global spread of the coronavirus affected most people, but affluent households were better able to deal with it. Not only did affluent people have more and better health care options; they were also better able to withstand the socioeconomic implications of the epidemic. They could work remotely or telecommute. They could have needed supplies, services, and food brought to them if they chose to or were required to isolate themselves. In contrast, the precarious workers, such as same-day deliverers or warehouse workers, had to continue to work in public, exposed to the virus, or if forced into quarantine, would lose vital income. The affluent are much more likely than low-income workers to have jobs with liberal sick days and are much less likely to lose their jobs because of absence. Their children are equipped with the latest electronics to continue their studies uninterrupted if they choose not to attend classes or if in-person classes are suspended (Warzel 2020).

Wealth, status, and power may not ensure happiness, but they certainly provide additional ways of coping with problems and disappointments. For this reason, the opportunity for advancement—for social mobility—is of special significance to those on the bottom of society. Most people want the rewards and privileges that are granted to high-ranking members of a culture. What can society do to increase their social mobility? One strategy is to offer financial aid to college students from low-income families, on the theory that education lifts people out of poverty. Yet such programs are not having as great an effect as their authors once hoped (Box 8-4).

Social Mobility

In the movie *Maid in Manhattan,* Jennifer Lopez plays the lead in a modern-day Cinderella story, rising from the lowly status of chambermaid in a big-city hotel to a company supervisor and the girlfriend of a well-to-do politician. The ascent of a person from a poor background to a position of prestige, power, or financial reward is an example of social mobility. Formally defined, the term **social mobility** refers to the movement of individuals or groups from one position in a society's stratification system to another. But how significant—how frequent, how dramatic—is mobility in a class society such as the United States?

USE YOUR SOCIOLOGICAL IMAGINATION

Imagine a society in which there are no social classes— no differences in people's wealth, income, and life chances. What would such a society be like? Would it be stable, or would its social structure change over time?

THINKING CRITICALLY

How do people's life chances affect society as a whole?

SOCIOLOGY IN EDUCATION

8-4 Student Debt

Today's young people have been dubbed Millennials, but a more appropriate name for them might be Generation Debt. We have seen that an important aspect of stratification is not just income but wealth, measured by the assets people hold. For an increasing number of students, debt from student loans follows them for years, lowering their assets and affecting their plans not only for the present but the future. Student debt is not a rare occurrence. As of 2019, over 44 million people owed more than $1.6 trillion in federal-backed student loan debt.

Every year, millions of prospective college students and their parents struggle through the intricate and time-consuming process of applying for financial aid. Originally, financial aid programs were intended to level the playing field—to allow qualified students from all walks of life to attend college, regardless of the cost. But have those programs fulfilled their promise?

> *Statistics that show the educational level in the United States rising overall obscure the widening gap between the advantaged and the less advantaged.*

Student debt may well force students to make less than desirable career choices after leaving college. Borrowers with high amounts of debt report levels of satisfaction with their career choices around 11 percentage points lower than those who graduated from college without debt.

Another significant change in the pattern of student indebtedness is that it is higher among students of for-profit schools, which often offer extensive online courses. These colleges account for about 9 percent of student enrollment but 25 percent of borrowers and 46 percent of those who default on their loans.

Despite the spiraling cost of an education, the widespread difficulty in paying for college stems from three trends. First, over the past few decades, colleges and universities have been moving away from making outright grants, such as scholarships, to deserving students, and toward low-interest student loans. Second, much of the assistance schools offer in the form of loans is not based strictly on need. Third, interest rates on federally guaranteed loans have risen steadily, increasing the burden of repayment.

The differential impact of student debt along racial and social lines is apparent. Analysis using data from the Survey of Consumer Finances reveals a system that is divided along class and racial lines. Because of the student debt-finance system, Black and Latino students tend to have higher loan balances. In addition, high numbers of low-income students and students of color drop out without receiving the credentials they worked for.

These trends in financial aid for higher education are closely tied to trends in social inequality. As noted earlier in this chapter, over the past half century, rather than declining, inequality in income and wealth has

sshepard/Getty Images

actually increased. In a variation on the truism that the rich tend to get richer while the poor get poorer, the rich are getting better educations and the poor are getting poorer educations. The significant burden that student debt posed was underscored when during the pandemic the federal government temporarily allowed borrowers to suspend payments and suspend interest mounting further. In 2020 alone, this freed families from $50 billion of payments. Not surprisingly, calls increased to reduce outstanding payments or erase them entirely especially for the less affluent.

LET'S DISCUSS

1. How important do you think student loans are? Without them, would you be able to cover college expenses?
2. What might be the impact of student loan debt on recent college graduates' career paths?

Sources: Dynarski 2019; Frost 2019; Gold 2019.

Open versus Closed Stratification Systems

Sociologists use the terms *open stratification system* and *closed stratification system* to indicate the degree of social mobility in a society. An **open system** implies that the position of each individual is influenced by his or her *achieved* status. Such a system encourages competition among members of society. Despite widening inequality and the continuing debate about inequality, 60 percent of people in 2019 believed that people can get ahead if they are willing to work (Horowitz et al. 2020).

At the other extreme of social mobility is the **closed system**, which allows little or no possibility of individual social mobility. The slavery and caste systems of stratification are examples of closed systems. In such societies, social placement is based on *ascribed* statuses, such as race or family background, which cannot be changed.

Types of Social Mobility

An elementary school teacher who becomes a police officer moves from one social position to another of the same rank. Each occupation has the same prestige ranking: 60 on a scale ranging from a low of 0 to a high of 100 (see Table 8-3). Sociologists call this kind of movement **horizontal mobility.** However, if the teacher were to become a lawyer (prestige ranking of 76), he or she would experience **vertical mobility,** the movement of an individual from one social position to another of a different rank. Vertical mobility can also involve moving *downward* in a society's stratification system, as would be the case if the teacher became a bank teller (ranking of 50). Pitirim Sorokin ([1927] 1959) was the first sociologist to distinguish between horizontal and vertical mobility. Most sociological analysis, however, focuses on vertical mobility.

One way of examining vertical social mobility is to contrast its two types, intergenerational and intragenerational mobility. **Intergenerational mobility** involves changes in the social position of children relative to their parents. Thus, a plumber whose father was a physician provides an example of downward intergenerational mobility. The celebrated movie star Leonardo DiCaprio, who was raised by a single mother in a neighborhood frequented by drug dealers and prostitutes, illustrates upward intergenerational mobility. Because education contributes significantly to

upward mobility, any barrier to the pursuit of advanced degrees can definitely limit intergenerational mobility.

Figure 8-6 shows intergenerational mobility based on income. In 1978–1980, a national survey looked at the family income of 6,000 young people. Two decades later, in 1997–2003, researchers followed up on those young adults and their income. The results showed a strong stickiness in both the bottom and top quintiles, or fifths, of the income distribution. Just over 33 percent of those whose parents were in the bottom quintile and 37 percent of thosewho were in the top quintile remained in the same quintile as adults. Yet the study also showed mobility: almost 66 percent of those in the bottom quintile moved up, and over 60 percent of those at the top experienced downward mobility.

Among men born in the 1960s, this consistent intergenerational mobility formerly resulted largely from economic growth. This has changed. Family incomes are slightly higher than in the last generation, but only because women have moved into the paid labor force to supplement their husbands' earnings. With so few women left to join the labor force, most families will need to increase their wages to raise their incomes further. Most families have become content to try to pay their bills rather than move up the socioeconomic ladder (Currier 2017; Sawhill and Haskins 2009).

FIGURE 8-6   INTERGENERATIONAL INCOME MOBILITY

Over a 25-year period, adult children often end up in the same income bracket as their parents. For example, as the first column shows, only 7 percent of those who begin in the bottom quintile reach the top quintile as adults; their story is one of rags to riches. By comparison, a third of the people who begin in the bottom quintile (33 percent) stay at the bottom, where they began.

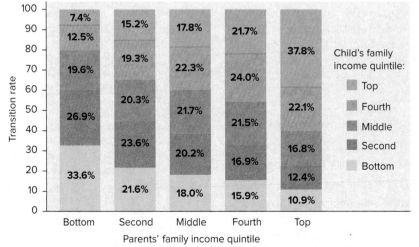

Think about It Given current economic trends, would you expect a similar pattern to hold for your generation?

Source: Mazumder 2008.

THINKING CRITICALLY

Is the United States moving toward a more open or a more closed stratification system? Explain your answer.

What has happened more recently? Let's follow the Millennials, those born between 1980 and 1994. Now in their late twenties or thirties, they are the most recent group to most likely have completed their schooling and become established in their occupations. We can measure their upward social mobility by comparing their current occupations with the occupations of parents when the Millennials were growing up. These comparisons are based on occupation prestige.

The resulting estimates confirm that the opportunity to move up has declined. Millennials might be the first American generation to experience as much downward mobility as upward mobility, although they are still young enough to make up lost ground. Among Americans born in the late 1980s, 44 percent are in jobs with higher socioeconomic status than their parents', and 49 percent are in jobs with *lower* socioeconomic status than their parents' (5 percent matched their parents' status).

In general, sons born after 1940—the Baby Boomers, GenXers, and Millennials—are significantly less likely to surpass their fathers in occupational attainment than were members of previous generations. Fewer janitors' sons are becoming doctors today. For daughters, the situation is a bit different, as those who entered the labor force beginning in the 1980s had job opportunities their forbears did not experience, but as this opening up the job market has leveled off, so have their experiences of upward social mobility (Hout 2019).

Intragenerational mobility involves changes in social position within a person's adult life. A woman who begins work as a teacher's aide and eventually becomes superintendent of the school district experiences upward intragenerational mobility. A man who becomes a taxicab driver after his accounting firm goes bankrupt undergoes downward intragenerational mobility.

Intragenerational mobility is now common, as there is a relatively close association between the social class of children and that of their parents. For example, affluent families in the top 1 percent spend $1.3 million more than do middle-class families on *each* of their children. The additional spending represents both education and enrichment activities, such as tutoring in the fine arts and athletics (Markovits 2019).

Social Mobility in the United States

The belief in upward mobility is an important value in our society. Does that mean that the United States is indeed the land of opportunity? Not unless such ascriptive characteristics as

race, gender, and family background have ceased to be significant in determining one's future prospects. We can see the impact of these factors in the occupational structure.

Occupational Mobility There is a great deal of mobility in the United States, but much of it is minor. That is, people who reach an occupational level above or below that of their parents usually advance or fall back only one or two out of a possible eight occupational levels. Thus, the child of a laborer may become an artisan or a technician, but he or she is less likely to become a manager or professional. The odds against reaching the top are extremely high unless one begins from a relatively privileged position.

The Impact of Education The impact of formal schooling on adult status is even greater than that of family background (although as we have seen, family background influences the likelihood that one will receive higher education). Furthermore, education represents an important means of intergenerational mobility. A person who was born into a poor family but who graduates from college has a one in five chance of entering the top fifth of all income earners as an adult (Isaacs et al. 2008).

The impact of education on mobility has diminished somewhat in the past decade, however. An undergraduate degree—a BA or a BS—serves less as a guarantee of upward mobility now than it did in the past, simply because more and more entrants into the job market hold such a degree. Moreover, intergenerational mobility is declining, since there is no longer such a stark difference between generations. In earlier decades, many high school–educated parents successfully sent their children to college, but today's college students are increasingly likely to have college-educated parents (Greenstone et al. 2013; Sawhill and Morton 2007).

The Impact of Race and Ethnicity Sociologists have long documented the fact that the class system is more rigid for African Americans than it is for members of other racial groups. African American men who have good jobs, for example, are less likely than white men to see their adult children attain the same status. The cumulative disadvantage of discrimination plays a significant role in the disparity between the two groups' experiences. Compared to white households, the relatively modest wealth of African American households means that adult African American children are less likely than adult white children to receive financial support from their parents. Indeed, young African American couples are much more likely than young white couples to be assisting their parents—a sacrifice that hampers their social mobility.

African American rates of upward intergenerational social mobility are lower. Based on national income data beginning in 1968 and following three generations, Black children are more likely to be born into poverty than white children, and they are less likely to escape. In fact, the majority of Black adults raised

Stockbyte/Getty Images

If this lawyer were the daughter of a car mechanic, her rise to the upper-middle class would illustrate intergenerational mobility. If she had begun as a paralegal and worked her way up the occupational ladder, her career would illustrate intragenerational mobility.

Women have traditionally been and still are more likely than men to be employed in precarious work. There is little likelihood of upward social mobility in such jobs, they usually add only modestly to household income, and they provide little protection in terms of health insurance or pension opportunities (Howell and Kalleberg 2019).

Women's employment opportunities are much more limited than men's. Moreover, according to recent research, women whose skills far exceed the jobs offered them are more likely than men to withdraw entirely from the paid labor force. Their withdrawal violates an assumption common to traditional mobility studies: that most people will aspire to upward mobility and seek to make the most of their opportunities.

In contrast to men, women have a rather large range of clerical occupations open to them. But the modest salary ranges and limited prospects for advancement many of these positions provide limit the possibility of upward mobility. Self-employment as shopkeepers, entrepreneurs, independent professionals, and the like—an important road to upward mobility for men—is more difficult for women, who find it harder to secure the necessary financing. Although sons commonly follow in the footsteps of their fathers, women

at the bottom of the stratification system remain stuck there as adults, compared to only a third of whites. In summary, Black Americans are more likely to stay in the bottom and fall from the middle (Raj et al. 2020).

Latino social mobility shows a more mixed picture. Hispanics whose parents were both born outside the United States are substantially better off than their immigrant parents. They have higher incomes; more are college graduates and homeowners; and fewer live in poverty. The immigrants themselves often face work situations that have significantly lower prestige than what they left behind, even if their absolute incomes are higher.

The Latino wealth and asset picture is bleaker and more resembles that of African Americans. The most recent data show that the median wealth of white non-Hispanic households is 42 times that of Hispanic households. This lopsided wealth ratio is the largest since the government first published these data in the 1980s. Even the wealthiest 10 percent of Latino households have only a third as much net worth as the top 5 percent of white households (Nieves and Asante-Muhammad 2018; Rodriguez 2017).

The Impact of Gender Studies of mobility, even more than those of class, have traditionally ignored the significance of gender, but some research findings are now available that explore the relationship between gender and mobility.

Paul Warner/Entertainment/Getty Images

Mary Barra, CEO of General Motors, began her career in 1980 as a plant engineer. In 2014 she reached the top of the corporate ladder. Despite equal opportunity laws, occupational barriers still limit women's climb to the top. As of December 2019, women ran just 33 of the *Fortune* 500 companies; men ran the other 467.

are unlikely to move into their fathers' positions. Consequently, gender remains an important factor in shaping social mobility. Women in the United States (and in other parts of the world) are especially likely to be trapped in poverty, unable to rise out of their low-income status.

On the positive side, though today's women lag behind men in employment, their earnings have increased faster than their mothers' did at a comparable age, so that their incomes are substantially higher. The one glaring exception to this trend is the daughters of low-income parents. Because these women typically care for children—many as single

parents—and sometimes for other relatives as well, their mobility is severely restricted (Beller 2009; Economic Mobility Project 2014).

THINKING CRITICALLY

Which factor—occupation, education, race and ethnicity, or gender—do you expect will have the greatest effect on your own social mobility? Explain.

social policy and Stratification

Executive Compensation

Few topics in the news today have led to such public outrage as the compensation received by top executives in the private sector. In the wake of recent corporate meltdowns, such as those involving several huge mortgage lending and financial investment firms, executive salaries and bonuses that run into the millions of dollars have begun to strike people as inappropriate. Is multimillion-dollar compensation really necessary, much less desirable, to attract talented corporate leaders?

Looking at the Issue

In 2018, the pay of top executives at the 350 largest U.S. corporations averaged $17.2 million per year. Over the last forty years, CEO compensation grew by 1008 percent, while the compensation of a typical worker rose just 12 percent. While wage growth for the majority of Americans has remained stagnant, CEO pay has grown exponentially, fueling widespread inequality (Mishel and Wolfe 2018).

Kirk Anderson, Kirktoons

Although executive pay has always been high in the United States, in recent years it has grown dramatically. The corporate executives who head private companies now earn the highest incomes in the nation. In fact, the gap between their salaries and those of average

workers has widened significantly over time. In 1965, top executives earned only 24 times the average worker's pay. By 2019, CEO-to-worker compensation had reached a ratio of 287-to-1. This was not as large as it had been prior to the Great Recession, but it did show that chief executive officers recovered nicely from the economic decline and never suffered as so many rank-and-file workers did (AFL-CIO 2019).

Applying Sociology

From a functionalist perspective, such generous compensation seems reasonable given the potential for gain that a talented executive brings to a corporation. Today, even a small increase in a multibillion-dollar company's performance can add hundreds of millions of dollars to its bottom line. Not surprisingly, then, competition to attract top-performing executives to a company is fierce. Not all these executives are successful all the time, however; sometimes their leadership reduces profits. Critics point out that many highly paid executives preside over companies that lose money and eliminate many rank-and-file jobs.

Conflict theorists question not only the relatively high levels of executive compensation, but also the process through which executives' pay is determined. The board of directors, which holds the responsibility for determining executives' pay, has an incentive to go along with arrangements that are favorable to top executives. Board members themselves earned an average of about $305,000 in 2018, so they have a natural desire to avoid conflict over high salaries. Furthermore, board members are often CEOs themselves or at least aspire to that role, so they have little reason to keep compensation plans more reasonable. Even in 2020 during the pandemic, most CEOs salaries were shielded from cuts, although a few saw some decline due to dwindling profits (DiNapoli 2020; McLaughlin 2019).

Taking an almost interactionist approach, sociologist Thomas DiPrete and his colleagues have observed that today, corporations must report executives' compensation relative to their peer group's compensation—that is, to the compensation received by leaders of similar businesses of similar size. Although members of such peer groups do not interact in the way that members of a primary group or even a secondary group would, they do form a social network. Thus, public comparisons of executive compensation within particular industries may influence board members' decisions, prompting them to tie executives' compensation more directly to their performance (DiPrete et al. 2010).

Initiating Policy

Although policymakers have long been concerned about executive compensation, until recently hard data have been difficult to obtain. Before 1992, corporations were required to disclose executives' pay, but not in a uniform manner. Many companies disguised the dollar amounts by literally spelling the words out in the midst of long, densely written documents. Today, the law mandates that companies publish "summary compensation tables." In 2006, reporting requirements were expanded to cover retirement packages, including the "golden parachute" clauses that protect executives who bail out of failing companies.

So has there been no policy action in the last generation? In 2015, the Securities and Exchange Commission approved a rule that requires companies to report pay-ratio levels between their chief

executives and a sample of their employees across different positions, beginning in 2018. While many cheered this move toward transparency, some noted that lobbyists have plenty of time to stop the rule's full implementation and accountants could find ways to maneuver around it. Furthermore, this action affects only publicly traded corporations and does not affect private family-owned businesses such as State Farm Insurance, the Albertsons and Publix supermarket chains, and Mars candy (Securities and Exchange Commission 2017).

Take the Issue with You

1. Should corporate executives earn high salaries even when their companies lose money? Explain. How do you think functionalists would defend such a practice?

2. What do you think of the "golden parachute" clauses that allow executives to bail out of failing companies unharmed? What might be the effect of such clauses on executives' performance? On shareholders and on lower-level employees?

3. Relate the increases in executive compensation over the past half century to changes in U.S. social structure during that time. How have these changes affected you and your family?

MASTERING THIS CHAPTER

Summary

Stratification is the structured ranking of entire groups of people that perpetuates unequal economic rewards and **power** in a society. In this chapter we examine four general systems of stratification, the explanations offered by functionalist and conflict theorists for the existence of **social inequality,** and the relationship between stratification and **social mobility.**

1. Some degree of **social inequality** characterizes all cultures.

2. Systems of social **stratification** include **slavery, castes,** the **estate system,** and social classes.

3. Karl Marx saw that differences in access to the means of production created social, economic, and political inequality, as well as two distinct classes, owners and laborers.

4. Max Weber identified three analytically distinct components of stratification: **class, status group,** and **power.**

5. Functionalists argue that stratification is necessary to motivate people to fill society's important positions. Conflict theorists see stratification as a major source of societal tension and conflict. Interactionists stress the importance of social class in determining a person's lifestyle.

6. One consequence of social class in the United States is that both **income** and **wealth** are distributed unevenly.

7. Many of those who live in poverty are full-time workers who struggle to support their families at minimum-wage jobs. The long-term poor— those who lack the training and skills to lift themselves out of poverty—form an **underclass.**

8. Functionalists find that the poor satisfy positive functions for many of the nonpoor in the United States.

9. One's **life chances**—opportunities for obtaining material goods, positive living conditions, and favorable life experiences—are related to one's social class. Occupying a high social position improves a person's life chances.

10. **Social mobility** is more likely to be found in an **open system** that emphasizes **achieved status** than in a **closed system** that emphasizes **ascribed status.** Race, gender, and family background are important factors in social mobility.

11. During the past half century, the gap between executive compensation and the average worker's pay has increased enormously. Although corporations claim that talented leaders enhance their performance, making executive pay packages well worth the money, the federal government is attempting to make executive pay more transparent.

Key Terms

Absolute poverty A minimum level of subsistence that no family should be expected to live below. (199)

Achieved status A social position that a person attains largely through his or her own efforts. (184)

Ascribed status A social position assigned to a person by society without regard for the person's unique talents or characteristics. (184)

Bourgeoisie Karl Marx's term for the capitalist class, comprising the owners of the means of production. (190)

Capitalism An economic system in which the means of production are held largely in private hands and the main incentive for economic activity is the accumulation of profits. (186)

Caste A hereditary rank, usually religiously dictated, that tends to be fixed and immobile. (186)

Class A group of people who have a similar level of wealth and income. (191)

Class consciousness In Karl Marx's view, a subjective awareness held by members of a class regarding their common vested interests and the need for collective political action to bring about social change. (190)

Class system A social ranking based primarily on economic position in which achieved characteristics can influence social mobility. (187)

Closed system A social system in which there is little or no possibility of individual social mobility. (204)

Conspicuous consumption Purchasing goods not to survive but to flaunt one's superior wealth and social standing. (191)

Dominant ideology A set of cultural beliefs and practices that helps to maintain powerful social, economic, and political interests. (193)

Estate system A system of stratification under which peasants were required to work land leased to them by nobles in exchange for military protection and other services. Also known as *feudalism*. (187)

Esteem The reputation that a specific person has earned within an occupation. (195)

False consciousness A term used by Karl Marx to describe an attitude held by members of a class that does not accurately reflect their objective position. (190)

Feminization of poverty A trend in which women constitute an increasing proportion of the poor people of both the United States and the world. (200)

Horizontal mobility The movement of an individual from one social position to another of the same rank. (204)

Income Refers to salaries and wages, interest on savings, stock dividends, and rental income. (184)

Intergenerational mobility Changes in the social position of children relative to their parents. (204)

Intragenerational mobility Changes in social position within a person's adult life. (205)

Life chances Max Weber's term for the opportunities people have to provide themselves with material goods, positive living conditions, and favorable life experiences. (202)

Objective method A technique for measuring social class that assigns individuals to classes on the basis of criteria such as occupation, education, income, and place of residence. (195)

Open system A social system in which the position of each individual is influenced by his or her achieved status. (204)

Power The ability to exercise one's will over others. (191)

Precarious work Employment that is poorly paid, and from the worker's perspective, insecure and unprotected. (189)

Prestige The respect and admiration that an occupation holds in a society. (195)

Proletariat Karl Marx's term for the working class in a capitalist society. (190)

Relative poverty A floating standard of deprivation by which people at the bottom of a society, whatever their lifestyles, are judged to be disadvantaged *in comparison with the nation as a whole*. (199)

Slavery A system of enforced servitude in which some people are owned by other people. (184)

Social inequality A condition in which members of society have differing amounts of wealth, prestige, or power. (183)

Social mobility Movement of individuals or groups from one position in a society's stratification system to another. (203)

Socioeconomic status (SES) A measure of social class that is based on income, education, and occupation. (196)

Status group A term used by Max Weber to refer to people who have the same prestige or lifestyle, independent of their class positions. (191)

Stratification A structured ranking of entire groups of people that perpetuates unequal economic rewards and power in a society. (184)

Underclass The long-term poor who lack training and skills. (201)

Vertical mobility The movement of an individual from one social position to another of a different rank. (204)

Wealth An inclusive term encompassing all of a person's material assets, including land, stocks, and other types of property. (184)

TAKING SOCIOLOGY with you

1. Compare a show, movie, or book about a working class family to one about an upper or upper-middle class family. Note any social inequalities you notice. Share your findings with the class.

2. Over the next week, think about your gut reaction to the conspicuous consumption and leisure of peers on social media. What effect do these displays have on you? Do you find yourself feeling jealous or resentful? Are you passing judgement on the conspicuous consump-

tion? What do you think motivated such displays? Share your experience with your classmates.

3. Listen to a recent TED Talk (https://www.ted.com/) or a podcast about poverty in the United States today. Take notes and summarize the talk or podcast for your classmates.

4. **Writing Sociology.** Find an article or news story about modern-day slavery. Write a report to share with the class.

Self-Quiz

Read each question carefully and then select the best answer.

1. Which of the following describes a condition in which members of a society have different amounts of wealth, prestige, or power?
   a. esteem
   b. mobility
   c. slavery
   d. social inequality

2. In Karl Marx's view, the destruction of the capitalist system will occur only if the working class first develops
   a. bourgeois consciousness.
   b. false consciousness.
   c. class consciousness.
   d. caste consciousness.

3. Which of the following were viewed by Max Weber as analytically distinct components of stratification?
   a. conformity, deviance, and social control
   b. class, status, and power
   c. class, caste, and age
   d. class, prestige, and esteem

4. Which sociological perspective argues that stratification is universal and that social inequality is necessary so that people will be motivated to fill socially important positions?
   a. the functionalist perspective
   b. the conflict perspective
   c. the interactionist perspective
   d. the labeling perspective

5. British sociologist Ralf Dahrendorf viewed social classes as groups of people who share common interests resulting from their authority relationships. Dahrendorf's ideology aligns best with which theoretical perspective?
   a. the functionalist perspective
   b. the conflict perspective
   c. the interactionist perspective
   d. sociocultural evolution

6. The respect or admiration that an occupation holds in a society is referred to as
   a. status.
   b. esteem.
   c. prestige.
   d. ranking.

7. Approximately how many people in the United States live below the poverty line established by the federal government?
   a. 5 percent
   b. 10 percent
   c. 15 percent
   d. 25 percent

8. Which sociologist has applied functionalist analysis to the existence of poverty and argues that various segments of society actually benefit from the existence of the poor?
   a. Émile Durkheim
   b. Max Weber
   c. Karl Marx
   d. Herbert Gans

9. A measure of social class that is based on income, education, and occupation is known as
   a. the objective method.
   b. stratification.
   c. socioeconomic status.
   d. the open system.

10. A plumber whose father was a physician is an example of
    a. downward intergenerational mobility.
    b. upward intergenerational mobility.
    c. downward intragenerational mobility.
    d. upward intragenerational mobility.

11. _____ is the most extreme form of legalized social inequality for individuals or groups.

12. In the _____ system of stratification, or feudalism, peasants were required to work land leased to them by nobles in exchange for military protection and other services.

13. Karl Marx viewed _____ differentiation as the crucial determinant of social, economic, and political inequality.

14. _____ _____ is the term Thorstein Veblen used to describe the extravagant spending patterns of those at the top of the class hierarchy.

15. _____ poverty is the minimum level of subsistence that no family should be expected to live below.

16. _____ poverty is a floating standard of deprivation by which people at the bottom of a society, whatever their lifestyles, are judged to be disadvantaged in comparison with the nation as a whole.

17. Sociologist William Julius Wilson and other social scientists have used the term _____ to describe the long-term poor who lack training and skills.

18. Max Weber used the term _____ _____ to refer to people's opportunities to provide themselves with material goods, positive living conditions, and favorable life experiences.

19. An open class system implies that the position of each individual is influenced by the person's _____ status.

20. _____ mobility involves changes in social position within a person's adult life.

Paralaxis/iStock/Getty Images

The great contrast in living conditions We see Paraisopolis shanty town with high rise apartment buildings in the background in the city of Sao Paulo, Brazil

▶ INSIDE

The Global Divide

Stratification in the World System

Stratification within Nations: A Comparative Perspective

Social Policy and Global Inequality: Rethinking Welfare in Europe and North America

Leonard Zhukovsky/123RF

Could you live on less than $2 a day, including your rent, if you lived away from home?

Although global poverty rates have been cut in half since 2000, more than one in ten people still live in extreme poverty.

❝ While global poverty rates have been cut by more than half since 2000, one in ten people in developing regions still lives on less than US$1.90 a day, the internationally agreed poverty line, and millions of others live on slightly more. Significant progress has been made in Eastern and Southeastern Asia, but up to 42 percent of the population in sub-Saharan Africa continues to live below the poverty line."

While many people think that poverty means only lack of income and the resources people need to earn an income, it means much more: hunger, malnutrition, lack of education, lack of access to basic government services, discrimination, exclusion from opportunities of all kinds, and lack of agency. Approximately 10 percent of the world's population still lives in conditions of extreme poverty. These people must continually struggle to meet their most basic needs, such as food, clean water, and access to education. And poverty affects men and women unequally: for every 100 men age 25 to 34 who live in poverty, there are 122 women. And by 2030, more than 160 million children will still be at risk of extreme poverty.

"Poverty facts and figures:

- 736 million people lived below the international poverty line of US$1.90 a day in 2015.
- In 2018, almost 8 percent of the world's workers and their families lived on less than US$1.90 per person per day.
- Most people living below the poverty line belong to two regions: southern Asia and sub-Saharan Africa.
- High poverty rates are often found in small, fragile, and conflict-affected countries.
- As of 2018, 55 percent of the world's population had no access to at least one social protection cash benefit.

The persistence of poverty, including extreme poverty, remains a major concern in Africa, the least developed countries, small island developing states, some middle-income countries, and countries in situations of conflict." Therefore the UN General Assembly proclaimed the Third United Nations Decade for the Eradication of Poverty (2018–2027). This Third Decade will focus on the development goals related to poverty eradication, including the Sustainable Development Goals. ❞

Source: United Nations 2018.

While global poverty rates have been cut by more than half since 2000, one in ten people in developing regions still lives on less than US$1.90 a day.

The United Nations was conceived in 1941 in the multination Atlantic Charter to defend life, liberty, independence, and religious freedom and to preserve human rights and justice worldwide. Peacekeeping has continued to be its major objective, but as developing nations, many of which were the former colonies of the more developed founding countries, attained leadership roles, the needs of the global poor have become more central to the UN's daily activities. As the U.N. statement, "Global Poverty," makes clear, the organization seeks to improve global social conditions. In 2000 the United Nations launched the Millennium Project, one of whose objectives was to halve extreme poverty by 2015. We will examine these efforts later in the chapter.

What economic and political conditions explain the divide between rich nations and poor? Within developing nations, how are wealth and income distributed, and how much opportunity does the average worker have to move up the social ladder? How do race and gender affect social mobility in these countries? In this chapter we will focus on global inequality, beginning with the global divide. We will consider the impact of colonialism and neocolonialism, globalization, the rise of multinational corporations, and the trend toward modernization.

Selcuk Acar/NurPhoto/Getty Images

UN Secretary-General António Guterres is greeted on his visit to the Central African Republic. Eradicating global poverty has been made a major goal of the international organization.

Then we will focus on stratification within nations, in terms of the distribution of wealth and income as well as social mobility. The chapter closes with a Social Policy section on welfare reform in Europe and North America.

The Global Divide

In some parts of the world, the people who have dedicated their lives to fighting starvation refer to what they call "coping mechanisms"—ways in which the desperately poor attempt to control their hunger. Eritrean women will strap flat stones to their stomachs to lessen their hunger pangs. In Mozambique, people eat the grasshoppers that have destroyed the crops, calling them "flying shrimp." Though dirt eating is considered a pathological condition (called *pica*) among the well-fed, the world's poor eat dirt to add minerals to their diet. And in many countries, mothers have been known to boil stones in water, to convince their hungry children that supper is almost ready. As they hover over the pot, these women hope that their mal-nourished children will fall asleep (McNeil 2004).

Around the world, inequality is a significant determinant of hu-man behavior, opening doors of opportunity to some and clos-ing them to others. Indeed, disparities in life chances are so extreme that in some places, the poorest of the poor may not be aware of them. Western media images may have circled the globe, but in extremely depressed rural areas, those at the bottom of society are not likely to see them.

A few centuries ago, such vast divides in global wealth did not exist. Except for a very few rulers and landowners, everyone in the world was poor. In much of Europe, life was as difficult as it was in Asia or South America. This was true until the Indus-trial Revolution and rising agricultural productivity produced explosive economic growth. The resulting rise in living stan-dards was not evenly distributed across the world.

The global divide between wealthy and poor nations can be seen clearly in the following comparison. Researchers looked at four statistical measures—how long on average a person lives, how likely is a baby to survive her or his first year, and the rates of homicide and incarceration. In every case, the experiences of the poorest of the poor in the United States matched up perfectly with the experiences of those living in the poorest countries. For example, the homicide rate in large cities in the United States with a poverty rate above 25 percent is comparable to the murder rate in Colombia and the Dominican Republic. In contrast, U.S. cities with low pov-erty rates have homicide rates similar to those of other rich countries, such as the Netherlands, Japan, and Sweden. These data show that, although as we will see throughout

Steve Morgan/Photofusion Picture Library/Alamy Stock Photo

Andrew Gombert/EPA-EFE/REX/Shutterstock

What do we stand in line for? People's needs and desires differ dra-matically depending on where they live. Eager customers line up out-side a store in Berlin to purchase newly released iPhones; residents of Ethiopia line up to receive water.

THINKING CRITICALLY

Relate Durkheim's, Tönnies's, and Lenski's theories of social structure (presented in Chapter 5) to the global divide that exists today. Could sociocultural evolution have something to do with the global divide?

this chapter there is a vast divide between rich and poor nations, the typical person in a low-income country is equivalent to the poorest of the poor in the United States (Shaefer et al. 2018).

Stratification in the World System

Although the divide between industrialized and developing nations is sharp, sociologists recognize a continuum of nations, from the richest of the rich to the poorest of the poor. For example, in 2019, the average value of goods and services produced per citizen (or per capita gross national income) in the industrialized countries of the United States, the Netherlands, Switzerland, Ireland, and Norway was more than $62,000. In at least 23 poorer countries, the value was just $2,000 or less. However, most countries fell somewhere between those extremes, as Figure 9-1 shows (World Bank 2019c).

Still, the contrasts are stark. In the wake of the coronavirus pandemic, these distinctions between rich and poor nations will only grow. The World Bank's (2020b) analysis showed that the global economic downturn was more severe and more widespread than any since at least 1870. Poorer countries will suffer most, because beyond the blow to their own economies, investment, aide, and tourism from rich nations will continue to be much lower than before. The developed nations will take care of their own economies and people first.

Three forces discussed here are particularly responsible for the long-term domination of the world marketplace by a few nations: the legacy of colonialism, the advent of multinational corporations, and modernization.

The Legacy of Colonialism

Colonialism occurs when a foreign power maintains political, social, economic, and cultural domination over a people for an extended period. In simple terms, it is rule by outsiders. The long reign of the British Empire over much of North America, parts of Africa, and India was an example of colonial domination. The same can be said of French rule over Algeria, Tunisia, and other parts of North Africa. Relations between the colonial nation and colonized people are similar to those between the dominant capitalist class and the proletariat, as described by Karl Marx.

By the 1980s, colonialism had largely disappeared. Most of the nations that were colonies before World War I had achieved political independence and established their own governments. However, for many of those countries, the transition to genuine self-rule was not yet complete. Colonial domination had established patterns of economic exploitation that continued even after nationhood was achieved—in part because former colonies were unable to develop their own industry and technology. Their dependence on more industrialized nations, including their former colonial masters, for managerial and technical expertise, investment capital, and manufactured goods kept former colonies in a subservient position. Such continuing dependence and foreign domination are referred to as **neocolonialism.**

The economic and political consequences of colonialism and neocolonialism are readily apparent. Drawing on the conflict perspective, sociologist Immanuel Wallerstein (1974, 1979a, 2000, 2012) viewed the global economic system as being divided between nations that control wealth and nations from which resources are taken. Through his **world systems analysis,** Wallerstein described an interdependent global economy resting on unequal economic and political relationships. Critical to his analysis is the understanding that by themselves, nations do not, nor have they ever, constituted whole systems. Instead, they exist within a larger, global social context.

In Wallerstein's view, certain industrialized nations (among them the United States, Japan, and Germany) and their global corporations dominate the *core* of this system (Figure 9-2). At the *semiperiphery* of the system are countries with marginal economic status, such as Israel, Ireland, and South Korea. Wallerstein suggested that the poor developing countries of Asia, Africa, and Latin America are on the *periphery* of the world economic system. The key to Wallerstein's macro-level analysis is the exploitative relationship of *core* nations toward *noncore* nations. Core nations and their corporations control and exploit noncore nations' economies. Unlike other nations, they are relatively independent of outside control (Chase-Dunn and Grimes 1995; G. Williams 2013).

The division between core and periphery nations is significant and remarkably stable. A study by the International Monetary Fund (2000; Alvaredo 2011) found little change over the course of the past 125 years for the more than 24 economies that were studied. The only changes were Japan's movement up into the group of core nations and China's movement down toward the margins of the semiperiphery nations. Yet Immanuel Wallerstein (2012:9) speculated that the world system as we currently understand it may soon undergo unpredictable changes. The world is becoming increasingly urbanized, a trend that is gradually eliminating the large pools of low-cost workers in rural areas. In the future, core nations will have to find other ways to reduce their labor costs. Exhaustion of land and water resources through clear-cutting and pollution is also driving up the costs of production.

Wallerstein's world systems analysis is the most widely used version of **dependency theory.** According to this macro-level theory, even as developing countries make economic advances, they remain weak and subservient to core nations and corporations in an increasingly intertwined global economy. This interdependency allows industrialized nations to continue to exploit developing countries. In a sense, dependency theory applies the conflict perspective on a global scale.

In the view of world systems analysts and dependency theorists, a growing share of the human and natural resources of developing countries is being redistributed to the core industrialized nations. This redistribution happens in part because

MAPPING LIFE WORLDWIDE

FIGURE 9-1   GROSS NATIONAL INCOME PER CAPITA

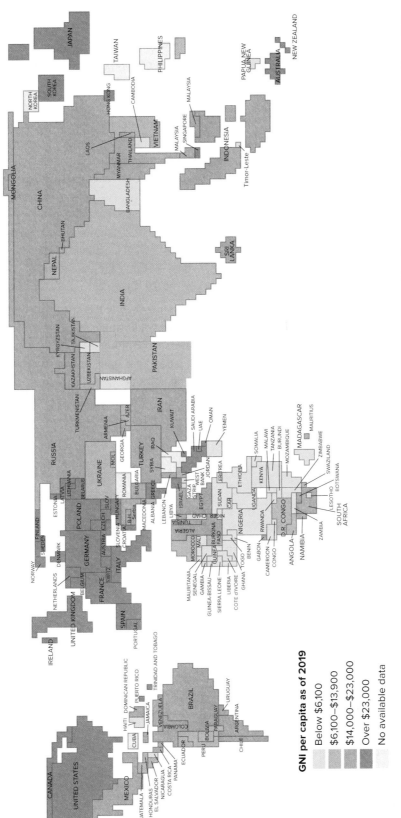

GNI per capita as of 2019

- Below $6,100
- $6,100–$13,900
- $14,000–$23,000
- Over $23,000
- No available data

Note: Country sizes based on 2019 estimates, incomes based on 2019 estimates. Includes only those countries with populations of 3 million or more. Gross national incomes are mid-year. GNI in purchasing power parity compiled by the Population Reference Bureau. Gross national income declined after the coronavirus pandemic, affecting data such as these. However, the relative positions of nations have not changed.

Sources: Weeks 2012; World Bank 2019c.

This stylized map reflects the relative population sizes of the world's nations. The color for each country shows the gross national income ﬂthe total value of goods and services produced by the nation in a given year) per capita.

FIGURE 9-2   WORLD SYSTEMS ANALYSIS

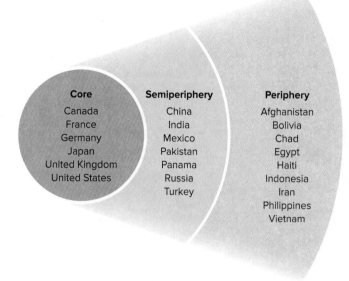

Core	Semiperiphery	Periphery
Canada	China	Afghanistan
France	India	Bolivia
Germany	Mexico	Chad
Japan	Pakistan	Egypt
United Kingdom	Panama	Haiti
United States	Russia	Indonesia
	Turkey	Iran
		Philippines
		Vietnam

Note: Figure shows only a partial listing of countries, selected by the author.

developing countries owe huge sums of money to industrialized nations as a result of foreign aid, loans, and trade deficits. The global debt crisis has intensified the Third World dependency begun under colonialism, neocolonialism, and multinational investment. International financial institutions are pressuring indebted countries to take severe measures to meet their interest payments. The result is that developing nations may be forced to devalue their currencies, freeze workers' wages, increase the privatization of industry, and reduce government services and employment.

Closely related to these problems is **globalization,** the worldwide integration of government policies, cultures, social movements, and financial markets through trade and the exchange of ideas. Because world financial markets transcend governance by conventional nation-states, international

John Wong/EPA/REX/Shutterstock

Chinese workers assemble toys for export to the United States. Globalization impacts both foreign and domestic workers, limiting employment opportunities at home and worsening working conditions abroad.

organizations such as the World Bank and the International Monetary Fund have emerged as major players in the global economy. The function of these institutions, which are heavily funded and influenced by core nations, is to encourage economic trade and development and to ensure the smooth operation of international financial markets. As such, they are seen as promoters of globalization and defenders primarily of the interests of core nations.

Critics call attention to a variety of issues, including violations of workers' rights, the destruction of the environment, the loss of cultural identity, and discrimination against minority groups in periphery nations. The impact of globalization appears to be most problematic for developing countries in Latin America and Africa. In Asia, developing nations seem to do better. Foreign investment there involves the high-tech sector, which produces more sustainable economic growth. Even there, however, globalization definitely has not reduced income disparities, either between nations or within countries (Kerbo 2006).

Further reflecting the disparity between nations is the steady movement of young people to foreign countries to seek educational opportunities. This attempt to improve their future prospects has gone on for generations. While the coronavirus pandemic upended international students' academic programs, there remains a continuing desire to study abroad. Box 9-1 looks more closely at this.

Some observers see globalization and its effects as the natural result of advances in communications technology, particularly the Internet and worldwide transmission of the mass media. Others view it more critically, as a process that allows multinational corporations to expand unchecked, as we will see shortly (Chase-Dunn et al. 2000; Guenther and Kasi 2015).

USE YOUR SOCIOLOGICAL IMAGINATION

You are traveling through a developing country. What evidence do you see of neocolonialism and globalization?

Poverty Worldwide

In developing countries, any deterioration of the economic well-being of those who are least well off threatens their very survival. By U.S. standards, even those who are well-off in the developing world are poor. Those who are poor in developing countries are truly destitute.

Global poverty has declined in recent years, as we will see in the next section when we review efforts overseas by the United Nations. However, large concentrations of impoverished people remain primarily in two types of areas: The global poor

SOCIOLOGY IN EDUCATION

9-1   International Students

One of the most visible aspects of the global nature of our everyday experiences is the students on college campuses who come from foreign countries. Nearly 900,000 foreign or international students attend colleges in the United States, and they represent nearly 6 percent of total enrollment. This number has doubled over the last ten years.

While the number of international students has fluctuated, it has steadily increased, even since 9/11. At the same time, the nation of origin of foreign students has changed over time, as shown in the accompanying figure, generally because of travel restrictions imposed by the United States or the sending nation.

Economically, international students make a major contribution to higher education in the United States, as their costs are paid by their families or home government. Student visas prohibit them from taking jobs while they are here. Beyond the contribution in dollars, the presence of international students affords Americans the opportunity to enrich their own education by interacting with students from a variety of nations.

Once here, international students must overcome numerous problems during their time in the United States. Adapting to the new social environment of college is often challenging for Americans, much more for young adults coming from abroad. Problems commonly encountered by these students in-

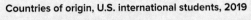

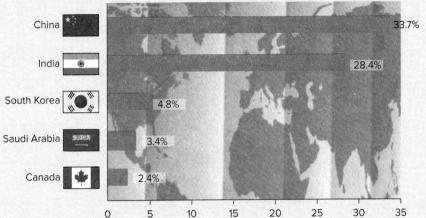

Countries of origin, U.S. international students, 2019

China — 33.7%
India — 28.4%
South Korea — 4.8%
Saudi Arabia — 3.4%
Canada — 2.4%

Source: Institute of International Education 2019; *flags*: admin_design/Shutterstock

clude financial stress, culture shock, discrimination or racism, homesickness, and language difficulties.

Adapting to the new social environment of college is often challenging for Americans, much more for young adults coming from abroad.

International exchange is a two-way street: many American students study abroad, although it is rarely for an entire degree program. At any given time, for every three foreign students here, one American is abroad, most likely at a college in Western Europe.

LET'S DISCUSS

1. Think about any interactions you may have had with international students. How do these interactions differ from those you have with U.S. students?
2. What are the benefits to international students of receiving their education in the United States? Do these benefits differ for students from core versus periphery nations?

Sources: Banjon and Olson 2016, Institute of International Education 2019.

can be found either within very fragile areas, such as sub-Saharan Africa and the West Bank and Gaza Strip adjoining Israel, or in relatively isolated areas of China and India.

Millennium Development Goals

As was noted at the beginning of this chapter, in 2000 the United Nations launched the Millennium Project, whose objective was to halve extreme poverty worldwide by the year 2015.

Peter Probst/Alamy Stock Photo

The United Nations, founded after World War II with 51 member nations, now comprises 193 countries.

The Millennium development goals targeted eight areas: poverty, education, gender equality, child mortality, maternal health, disease, the environment, and global partnership. Each goal was supported by 21 specific targets and more than 60 indicators.

At the time the Millennium Project was launched, only five countries were giving foreign aid at the target rate: Denmark, Luxembourg, Great Britain, Norway, and Sweden. This was before the coronavirus pandemic caused developed nations to refocus economic and social needs in their own societies. Although in dollar terms the U.S. government delivers far more aid to foreign countries and multinational organizations than any other nation, the amount is not impressive considering the nation's tremendous wealth compared to other countries. In terms of the percentage of gross national income, the United States' contribution is among the lowest of the 23 most advanced industrialized countries, on a par with South Korea's (Figure 9-3).

FIGURE 9-3   FOREIGN AID PER CAPITA IN EIGHT COUNTRIES

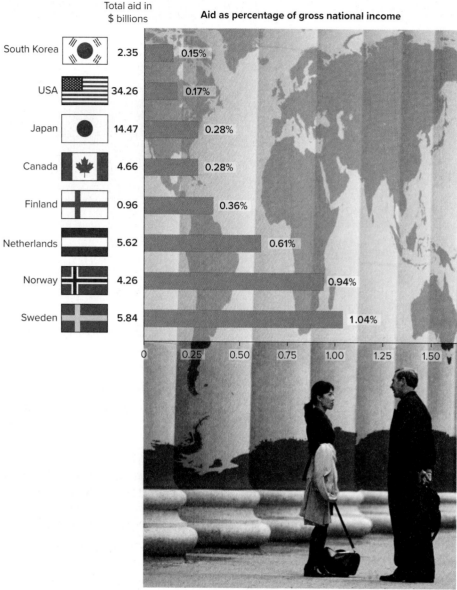

Total aid in $ billions

Aid as percentage of gross national income

Country	Total aid in $ billions	Aid as % of GNI
South Korea	2.35	0.15%
USA	34.26	0.17%
Japan	14.47	0.28%
Canada	4.66	0.28%
Finland	0.96	0.36%
Netherlands	5.62	0.61%
Norway	4.26	0.94%
Sweden	5.84	1.04%

0   0.25   0.50   0.75   1.00   1.25   1.50

Note: Development assistance in 2018.
Source: Organisation for Economic Co-operation and Development 2019.
Flags: admin_design/Shutterstock; *photo:* PhotoDisc Imaging/Getty Images

While many objectives were not achieved, a great deal of attention was given to reducing world poverty. The number of people living on less than $1.25 a day was reduced from 1.9 billion in 1990 to 836 million in 2015, narrowly missing the ambitious target of halving the proportion of people suffering from hunger. Back in 1990, it was assumed that making these advances would take a huge increase in assistance from industrial countries, which, for the most part, did not occur. Rather, selective developing countries benefited from significantly increased commodity prices sustained by rapid industrialization and urbanization of their emerging economies. China was a stellar example of this: that country alone experienced a drop of 470 million people living below $1.25 a day and accounted for almost half of the global decline in poverty. Despite the improvement, hundreds of millions of people remain in poverty or, as our chapter-opening excerpt described, have a spending pattern of $2 a day or below.

The coronavirus pandemic reversed the trend toward reduction in global poverty. The World Bank estimated that not only did few people escape extreme poverty in 2020 but also that an additional 100 million people were pushed back down into extreme poverty.

Beyond the objective to reduce poverty, the Development Goals were expanded to include significantly reducing income inequality *within* countries by 2030. As poverty declined worldwide, income inequality rose. The global organization argues that inequality is not inevitable. Two changes that would greatly ameliorate poverty would be instituting tax policies that benefit the nonaffluent and allowing overseas workers who transfer their wages to family in the homeland to do so with little or no extra cost (United Nations Department of Economic and Social Affairs 2016).

Eradicating poverty in all its forms remains one of the greatest challenges in terms of social inequality. The coronavirus pandemic prompted United Nations Secretary General António Guterres (2020) to declare that "we must tackle the devastating social and economic dimensions of this crisis." Particularly vulnerable, he noted, were developing nations and especially people in conflict settings.

The number of people living in extreme poverty, according to the United Nations, dropped by more than half between 1990 and 2015. The lasting impact of the pandemic on economic growth and social inequality will last a minimum of five years *after* it totally ends globally. In the short term—that is, through 2030—the number of people in extreme poverty is expected to *double* what it was projected to be had the pandemic not occurred.

THINKING CRITICALLY

Do you agree that inequality is not inevitable? Explain your answer.

Multinational Corporations

We have seen that globalization has not necessarily improved the lives of the poor in the developing world. Another trend that does not always serve developing countries well has been the rise of multinational corporations. Worldwide, corporate giants play a key role in neocolonialism. The term **multinational corporation** refers to commercial organizations that are headquartered in one country but do business throughout the world. Such private trade and lending relationships are not new; merchants have conducted business abroad for hundreds of years, trading gems, spices, garments, and other goods. However, today's multinational giants are not merely buying and selling overseas; they are also *producing* goods all over the world (Wallerstein 1974).

Moreover, today's "global factories" (factories throughout the developing world that are run by multinational corporations) may soon have the "global office" sitting alongside them.

Alexander Mazurkevich/Shutterstock

Open displays of social inequality are apparent in every nation. In Mumbai, India, billionaire Mukesh Ambani built this 27-story home for his wife and three children, complete with three helicopter pads and a 160-vehicle garage. To run the building, Ambani employs a staff of 600.

Multinationals based in core countries are beginning to establish reservation services and centers for processing data and insurance claims in periphery nations. As service industries become a more important part of the international marketplace, many companies are concluding that the low costs of overseas operations more than offset the expense of transmitting information around the world.

Do not underestimate the size of these global corporations. As Figure 9-4 shows, the total revenues of multinational businesses are on a par with the total value of goods and services exchanged in *entire nations.* Foreign sales represent an important source of profit for multinational corporations, which are constantly seeking to expand into other countries (in many cases, developing nations). The economy of the United States depends heavily on foreign commerce, much of which is conducted by multinationals. Since 1984 when the United States started to reduce trade restrictions, international trade has grown faster than the economy as a whole. Since 2011, trade accounts for about 15 percent of the total value of all goods and services produced in the United States (Organisation for Economic Co-operation and Development 2020a).

Functionalist and conflict theorists differ on the social and economic effects of multinational corporations, as we will see next.

Functionalist Perspective Functionalists believe that multinational corporations can actually help the developing nations of the world. They bring jobs and industry to areas where subsistence agriculture once served as the only means of survival. Multinationals also promote rapid development through the diffusion of inventions and innovations from industrialized nations. Viewed from a functionalist perspective, the combination of skilled technology and management provided by multinationals and the relatively cheap labor available in developing nations is ideal for a global enterprise. Multinationals can take maximum advantage of technology while reducing costs and boosting profits.

Through their international ties, multinational corporations also make the nations of the world more interdependent. These ties may prevent certain disputes from reaching the point of serious conflict. A country cannot afford to sever diplomatic relations or engage in warfare with a nation that is the headquarters for its main business suppliers or a key outlet for its exports.

Conflict Perspective Conflict theorists challenge this favorable evaluation of the impact of multinational corporations. They emphasize that multinationals exploit local workers to maximize profits. The pool of cheap labor in the developing world prompts multinationals to move factories out of core countries. An added bonus for the multinationals is that the developing world discourages strong trade unions.

FIGURE 9-4   MULTINATIONAL CORPORATIONS COMPARED TO NATIONS

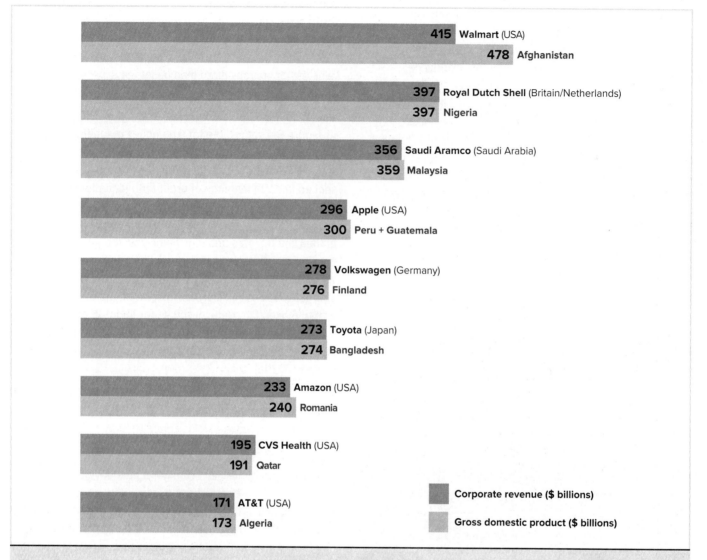

415	Walmart (USA)
478	Afghanistan
397	Royal Dutch Shell (Britain/Netherlands)
397	Nigeria
356	Saudi Aramco (Saudi Arabia)
359	Malaysia
296	Apple (USA)
300	Peru + Guatemala
278	Volkswagen (Germany)
276	Finland
273	Toyota (Japan)
274	Bangladesh
233	Amazon (USA)
240	Romania
195	CVS Health (USA)
191	Qatar
171	AT&T (USA)
173	Algeria

Corporate revenue ($ billions)

Gross domestic product ($ billions)

Think about It What happens to society when corporations grow richer than countries and spill across international borders?

Note: While the cornonavirus pandemic deeply affected the GDP of nations and corporate revenues, the comparisons are still relevant.
Sources: Ranking prepared by author. Revenue from corporate quarterly report statements for 2019. GDP for 2018 (World Bank 2020a).

In industrialized countries, organized labor insists on decent wages and humane working conditions, but governments seeking to attract or keep multinationals may develop a "climate for investment" that includes repressive antilabor laws which restrict union activity and collective bargaining. If labor's demands become too threatening, the multinational firm will simply move its plant elsewhere, leaving a trail of unemployment behind. Nike, for example, moved its factories from the United States to Korea to Indonesia to Vietnam in search of the lowest labor costs. Conflict theorists conclude that on

Photodisc Collection/Getty Images

the whole, multinational corporations have a negative social impact on workers in *both* industrialized and developing nations.

Several sociologists who have surveyed the effects of foreign investment by multinationals conclude that although it may at first contribute to a host nation's wealth, it eventually increases economic inequality within developing nations. This conclusion holds true for both income and land ownership. The upper and middle classes benefit most from economic expansion; the lower classes benefit least. As conflict theorists point out, multinationals invest in limited economic sectors and restricted regions of a nation. Although certain sectors of the host nation's economy expand, such as hotels and expensive restaurants, their very expansion appears to retard growth in agriculture and other economic sectors. Moreover, multinational corporations often buy out or force out local entrepreneurs and companies, thereby increasing economic and cultural dependence (Chase-Dunn and Grimes 1995; Kerbo 2012; Wallerstein 1979b).

USE YOUR SOCIOLOGICAL IMAGINATION

Think of something you bought recently that was made by a multinational corporation. How do you know the maker was a multinational?

Modernization

Globalization and the rise of multinational corporations have affected developing countries not just economically, but culturally. Around the world, millions of people are witnessing a revolutionary transformation of their day-to-day life. Contemporary social scientists use the term **modernization** to describe the far-reaching process through which periphery nations move from traditional or less developed institutions to those characteristic of more developed societies.

Sociologist Wendell Bell (1981), whose definition of modernization we are using, notes that modern societies tend to be urban, literate, and industrial. These societies have sophisticated transportation and media systems. Their families tend to be organized within the nuclear family model rather than the extended-family model. Thus, members of societies that undergo modernization must shift their allegiance from traditional authorities, such as parents and priests, to newer authorities, such as government officials.

Many sociologists are quick to note that terms such as *modernization* and even *development* contain an ethnocentric bias. The unstated assumption behind these terms is that "they" (people living in developing nations) are struggling to become more like "us" (people in core industrialized nations). Viewed from a conflict perspective, these terms perpetuate the dominant ideology of capitalist societies.

The term *modernization* also suggests positive change. Yet change, if it comes, often comes slowly, and when it does it tends to serve the affluent segments of industrialized nations. This truism seems to apply to the spread of the latest electronic technologies to the developing world.

A similar criticism has been made of **modernization theory,** a functionalist approach that proposes that modernization and

development will gradually improve the lives of people in developing nations. According to this theory, even though nations develop at uneven rates, the development of peripheral nations will be assisted by innovations transferred from the industrialized world. Critics of modernization theory, including dependency theorists, counter that any such technology transfer only increases the dominance of core nations over developing nations and facilitates further exploitation.

When we see all the Coca-Cola and Apple signs going up in developing nations, it is easy to assume that globalization and economic change are effecting cultural change. But that is not always the case, researchers note. Distinctive cultural traditions, such as a particular religious orientation or a nationalistic identity, often persist and can soften the impact of modernization on a developing nation. Some contemporary sociologists emphasize that both industrialized and developing countries are "modern." Increasingly, researchers gauge modernization using a series of social indicators—among them degree of urbanization, energy use, literacy, political democracy, and use of birth control. Clearly, some of these are subjective indicators; even in industrialized nations, not everyone would agree that wider use of birth control is an example of progress (Armer and Katsillis 1992; Hedley 1992; Inglehart and Baker 2000).

Current modernization studies generally take a convergence perspective. Using the indicators just noted, researchers focus on how societies are moving closer together, despite traditional differences. From a conflict perspective, the moderniza-

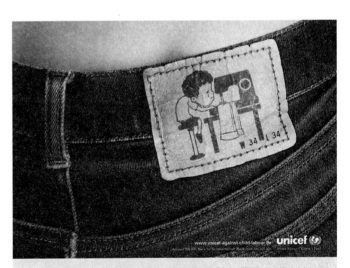

The commercial titled JEANS was done by Springer & Jacoby Werbung advertising agency for AGAINST CHILD LABOUR (a UNICEF campaign) in Germany. Copywriter: Sven Keitel; Art Director: Claudia Todt; Creative Director: Timm Weber/ Bettina Olf.

Where am I wearing? This UNICEF poster reminds affluent Western consumers that the brand-name jeans they wear may be produced by exploited workers in developing countries. In sweatshops throughout the developing world, nonunion garment workers—some of them children—labor long hours for what we would consider extremely low wages—even if for the workers in those semiperiphery countries, wages are relatively high.

TABLE 9-1   SOCIOLOGICAL PERSPECTIVES ON GLOBAL INEQUALITY

Tracking Sociological Perspectives

Approach	Sociological Perspective	Explanation
World systems analysis	Functionalist and conflict	Unequal economic and political relationships maintain sharp divisions between nations.
Dependency theory	Conflict	Industrialized nations exploit developing nations through colonialism and multinational corporations.
Modernization theory	Functionalist	Developing nations move away from traditional cultures and toward the cultures of industrialized nations.

tion of developing nations often perpetuates their dependence on and continued exploitation by industrialized nations. Conflict theorists view such continuing dependence on foreign powers as an example of contemporary neocolonialism.

Table 9-1 summarizes the three major approaches to global inequality.

population. The inequality across the world is replicated within countries, including the United States, which itself hosts the largest number of billionaires. Figure 9-5 compares the distribution of income, as shown in the difference between the wealth held by the highest and lowest quintiles of the population (World Bank 2020a).

THINKING CRITICALLY

Relate modernization theory to dependency theory. Do you agree with critics that modernization will increase the dominance of core nations? Why or why not?

USE YOUR SOCIOLOGICAL IMAGINATION

Imagine that the United States borders a country with a much higher standard of living. In this neighboring country, the salaries of workers with a new college degree start at $200,000 a year. What is life in the United States like?

Stratification within Nations: A Comparative Perspective

At the same time that the gap between rich and poor nations is widening, so too is the gap between rich and poor citizens *within* nations (see Box 9-2). As discussed earlier, stratification in developing nations is closely related to their relatively weak and dependent position in the global economy. Local elites work hand in hand with multinational corporations and prosper from such alliances. At the same time, the economic system creates and perpetuates the exploitation of industrial and agricultural workers. That is why foreign investment in developing countries tends to increase economic inequality.

Distribution of Wealth and Income

Global inequality is staggering. Just as a few corporations have amassed great sums of money, so have a very few individuals. The world's 26 wealthiest individuals have accumulated wealth equal to that of more than half of the world's

FIGURE 9-5   DISTRIBUTION OF INCOME IN NINE NATIONS

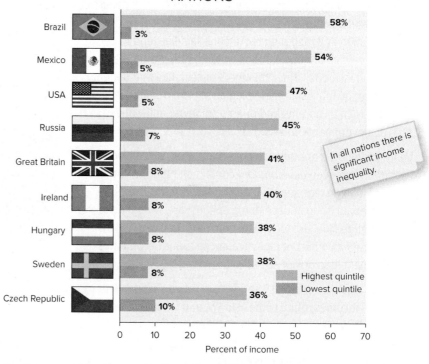

Brazil 58% / 3%
Mexico 54% / 5%
USA 47% / 5%
Russia 45% / 7%
Great Britain 41% / 8%
Ireland 40% / 8%
Hungary 38% / 8%
Sweden 38% / 8%
Czech Republic 36% / 10%

Highest quintile
Lowest quintile

In all nations there is significant income inequality.

Note: Data are considered comparable although based on statistics covering 2015 to 2017. Incomes declined after the coronavirus pandemic, but income disparities either remained unchanged or increased.
Source: World Bank 2020a. *Flags:* admin_design/Shutterstock

SOCIOLOGY IN THE GLOBAL COMMUNITY

9-2 Social Stratification in Japan

Until recently, virtually all Japanese households saw themselves as middle class. From the 1960s, when the post-war recovery was largely complete until very recently, 90 percent self-identified as middle class, compared to 44 percent in national surveys in the United States.

Is this self-image an accurate picture of Japan? Where are the poor? The working class? The upper class?

Sociologists in Japan refer to "the quiet transformation" now occurring, as the Japanese people begin to truly recognize poverty, affluence, and differentiation within the middle class. Why the change in self-image? The immediate post–World War II period was marked by broad and dramatic upward social mobility, which led to a general belief that everyone was doing well economically. The media spoke of "the 100 million general middle class." Culturally, the Japanese lack the practice of **conspicuous consumption**, that is, people flaunting their superior wealth and social standing, that is so prominent in many other nations (see Chapter 8). Mansions, yachts, and private jets are largely absent.

By the 1980s things began to change: upward mobility slowed overall, and the recognition of social inequality began to increase.

While Japan does not have as extreme a social divide as the United States, the country does know inequality. According to the United Nations, the bottom 40 percent of the Japanese population receives only 20 percent of the income. In the United States that figure is even lower, at 15 percent. At the other end of the income distribution, the richest tenth of Japanese account for 25 percent of all income. This compares to 31 percent in the United States.

Besides opening policy debates about the poor and challenges to middle-class households, Japan has begun to publicly recognize the limited opportunities for women as well as the discrimination faced by Japan's

While Japan does not have as extreme a social divide as the United States, the country does know inequality.

MoJoeMoJo/Shutterstock

relatively small population of immigrants and racial minorities.

LET'S DISCUSS

1. What does it mean for a society if its people all think of themselves as belonging to the same social class? What are some of the effects this might have on social interaction?
2. Do you think of the United States as a similarly homogeneous society, or as a highly stratified one? What evidence do you have for your belief?

Sources: Chiavacci 2008; General Social Survey 2019; Koike 2015; Sudo 2019; Tsutsui 2017; World Bank 2019b.

Social Mobility

Mobility in Industrial Nations Studies of intergenerational mobility in industrialized nations have found the following patterns:

*   Substantial similarities exist in the ways that parents' positions in the stratification system are transmitted to their children.
*   As in the United States, mobility opportunities in other nations have been influenced by structural factors, such as labor market changes that lead to the rise or decline of an occupational group within the social hierarchy.
*   Immigration continues to be a significant factor in shaping a society's level of intergenerational mobility.

Cross-cultural studies suggest that intergenerational mobility has been increasing over the past 50 years in most but not all countries. In particular, researchers have noted a common pattern of movement away from agriculture-based occupations. However, they are quick to point out that growth in mobility does not necessarily bring growth in equality. Indeed, despite the evidence of steady upward mobility, their studies show that the gap between the rich and the poor has grown. Over the past 30 years, poverty levels in the 30 largest industrial economies have remained relatively constant (Eurostat 2015; Organisation for Economic Co-operation and Development 2008).

Mobility in Developing Nations Mobility patterns in industrialized countries are usually associated with both intergenerational and intragenerational mobility. However, in developing nations, macro-level social and economic changes often overshadow micro-level movement from one occupation to another. For example, there is typically a substantial wage differential between rural and urban areas, which leads to high levels of migration to the cities. Yet the urban industrial sectors of developing countries generally cannot provide sufficient employment for all those seeking work.

In large developing nations, the most socially significant mobility is the movement out of poverty. This type of mobility is difficult to measure and confirm, however, because economic trends can differ from one area of a country to another. As noted earlier in this chapter, in China, large numbers of people have moved out of poverty. However, income has not grown as rapidly in the rural areas of China as in the cities, or in some regions compared to others. In China, people who live in rural areas are basically shut out of the economic gains enjoyed by residents who live in centers of skilled labor and technology. Similarly, in India during the 1990s and through 2015, poverty declined in urban areas but may have remained static at best in rural areas. Around the world, downward social mobility is also dramatically influenced by catastrophes such as crop failure and warfare.

Despite the continuing struggles of massive numbers of people, the global economic situation is not entirely bleak. Although economists have documented the persistence of poverty around the world despite some gains, they have also noted some growth in the number of people who enjoy a middle-class lifestyle. At the beginning of the 21st century, millions of people entered the middle class in the populous nations of China, India, Russia, Brazil, and Mexico. Entrepreneurship, microfinancing, merchandising, and in some countries, a growing, relatively well-paid government sector have fostered this increase in upward social mobility (Beddoes 2012; India, Government of 2009).

In Box 9-3 we consider how people today see their opportunities for advancement. Is there a difference between the way people view this crucial question in developing countries versus rich countries?

SOCIOLOGY IN THE GLOBAL COMMUNITY

9-3 Getting Ahead Globally

Surveys of public opinion across 27 nations show some consistent views about mobility and getting ahead. A majority of people in all these countries believe that getting a good education and working hard are key to getting ahead. But in these same countries, majorities agree that the gap between the rich and the poor is a problem.

So what are the opportunities for mobility? Generally the poorer the country, the more optimistic people are that their children will grow up to be financially better off than they are themselves. As shown in the accompanying figure, adults in industrial countries are more cautious that their children's lives will improve.

However, despite this optimism about their children's future, in some countries a large proportion of people see more opportunities abroad than at home. For example, 23 percent of Mexicans and 42 percent of Senegalese recommend that young people move abroad for "a good life." Yet even in nations that face massive social challenges, staying at home is heavily favored. For example, 53 percent of parents in the Palestinian Territory and 66 percent in Pakistan recommend that their children stay at home.

When parents counsel young people to go abroad, it is most often to industrial countries, even though they understand the great disparity between rich and poor in those nations. Economic optimism seems to be greatest when the parents' own status is the most marginal. These findings point to the need to frame discussions of social mobility within the context of a particular society.

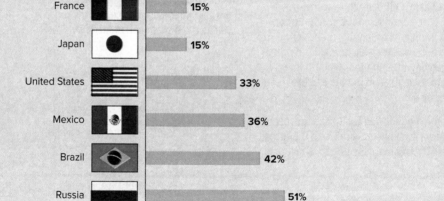

Will Children, When They Grow Up, Be Better Off Than Their Parents?

Country	Percentage answering "Yes"
France	15%
Japan	15%
United States	33%
Mexico	36%
Brazil	42%
Russia	51%
India	66%
Philippines	69%

Note: Selected results from a 27-nation survey conducted May-August 2018.
Source: Author, based on Stokes 2018, p. 6. *Flags:* admin_design/Shutterstock

Generally the poorer the country, the more optimistic people are that their children will grow up to be financially better off than they are themselves.

LET'S DISCUSS

1. Are your relatives optimistic about your economic future? Are you? On what factors do you base your opinion?

2. Why do you think people in poor countries are more optimistic about their children's futures than those in rich ones?

Sources: Banyan 2014; Pew Research Center 2014b.

Gender Differences in Mobility The challenges that women and girls face in developing countries are not limited to any one continent. Karuna Chanana Ahmed, an anthropologist from India who has studied women in developing nations, calls women the most exploited of oppressed people. Beginning at birth women face sex discrimination. They are commonly fed less than male children, are denied educational opportunities, and are often hospitalized only when they are critically ill. Inside or outside the home, women's work is devalued. When economies fail, as they did in Asian countries in the late 1990s, women are the first to be laid off from work (J. Anderson and Moore 1993; Kristof 1998).

Surveys show a significant degree of *female infanticide* (the killing of baby girls) in China and rural areas of India. Only one-third of Pakistan's sexually segregated schools are for women, and one-third of those schools have no buildings. In Kenya and Tanzania, it is illegal for a woman to own a house. In Saudi Arabia, women are prohibited from inheriting as much as their brothers do, walking alone in public, and socializing with men outside their families.

Only recently have researchers begun to investigate the impact of gender on the mobility patterns of developing nations. Many aspects of the development process—especially modernization in rural areas and the rural-to-urban migration just described—

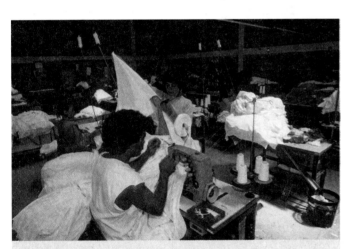

Eco Images/Universal Images Group/Getty Images

In developing countries, people who hope to rise out of poverty often move from the country to the city, where employment prospects are better. The jobs available in industrialized urban areas offer perhaps the best means of upward mobility. These women work in a T-shirt factory in San José, Costa Rica.

may result in the modification or abandonment of traditional cultural practices and even marital systems. The effects on women's social standing and mobility are not necessarily positive. As a country develops and modernizes, women's vital role in food production deteriorates, jeopardizing both their autonomy and their material well-being. Moreover, the movement of families to the cities weakens women's ties to relatives who can provide food, financial assistance, and social support (Lawson 2008; United Nations Secretary General 2014).

In the Philippines, however, women have moved to the forefront of the indigenous peoples' struggle to protect their ancestral land from exploitation by outsiders. Having established their right to its rich minerals and forests, members of indigenous groups had begun to feud among themselves over the way in which the land's resources should be developed. Aided by the United Nations Partners in Development Programme, women volunteers established the Pan-Cordillera Women's Network for Peace and Development, a coalition of women's groups dedicated to resolving local disputes. The women mapped boundaries, prepared development plans, and negotiated more than 2,000 peace pacts among community members. They have also run in elections, campaigned against social problems, and organized residents to work together for the common good (United Nations Development Programme 2000:87; United Nations Secretary General 2014).

Studies of the distribution of wealth and income within various countries, together with cross-cultural research on mobility, consistently reveal stratification based on class, gender, and other factors within a wide range of societies. Clearly, a worldwide view of stratification must include not only the sharp contrast *between* wealthy and impoverished nations but also the layers of hierarchy *within* industrialized nations and developing nations. In the Social Policy section that follows, we will see that even in the relatively wealthy countries of Europe and North America, significant numbers of families require assistance from the government to meet their basic needs.

THINKING CRITICALLY

Contrast social mobility in developing and industrialized nations. Do you think the differences will eventually disappear? Why or why not?

socialpolicy and Global Inequality

Rethinking Welfare in Europe and North America

In Orlando, Florida, Keith Barrett worked as a behind-the-scenes software engineer at Disney World for 10 years. He and his fellow tech workers maintained the computers that handled ticket sales and hotel reservations. Then all 250 of them were suddenly laid off. Disney planned to replace them with guest workers from India and even required them to train the new workers as a condition for receiving severance pay.

After her second child was born, Kirsty Holden requested flexible hours. She had worked at the legal department of a large British government agency for 13 years and was surprised to have her request rejected. She appealed and won, but when she returned to work on a part-time basis, the trouble began. She had no assigned desk, and the whole working environment made her feel unwelcome. Faced with bullying and discrimination, Holden eventually decided to become a freelancer and work for herself. This made her part of a growing trend of self-employed female workers.

Every morning, Fabiana Barbosa de Souza commutes to work in Rio de Janiero, hugs her employer's children, and begins her daily tasks. In Mexico City, Ignacia 'Nachita' Ponciano begins her day in a similar way, but she has a shorter commute—she lives in her employer's home. Nachita says this about her employers: "I've been here my whole life and my son was born here. Yes, I see the family here as my own family." Fabiana and Nachita are just two of over 18 million domestic workers in Latin America. Domestic work is one of the major occupations for women across the region, but over three-quarters of domestic workers work off the books, without any regulation or benefits. In recent years, rules mandating minimum wage and other protections have been introduced in more than a dozen countries, but most workers still merely scrape by (Greenhouse 2019; Keating 2019; Tan 2019).

These are the faces of people living on the edge. In a time of economic stress and growing need, governments in all parts of the world are searching for the right solution to welfare: How much subsidy should they provide? How much responsibility should fall on the shoulders of the poor?

Looking at the Issue

Are "safety nets" and welfare state policies jeopardized by demographic and economic pressures such as aging, globalization, and technological progress? Is social assistance in wealthy countries too generous, or is it too paltry to even begin to meet workers' needs? Claims are repeatedly made on both sides of this issue (Filgueira et al. 2018).

Close examination of the effectiveness of existing economic security programs reveals that aid for children in low-income families has a significant impact. In the decade after policymakers in many nations altered public assistance systems in the mid-1990s, such assistance became much less effective at protecting children from deep poverty—that is, at lifting their incomes above *half* of the poverty line—and children's deep poverty rose. But during the Great Recession that began in 2008, assistance policies for children in poverty and deep poverty grew stronger, bolstered by temporary recovery initiatives, preventing what likely would have been a large surge in deep poverty among children. Then again in 2020, the federal government spent trillions of dollars during the coronavirus pandemic to prop up households and businesses. But where do we go from there (Trisi and Saenz 2020)?

Applying Sociology

Many sociologists tend to view the debate over welfare reform in industrialized nations from a conflict perspective: the "haves" in positions of policymaking listen to the interests of other "haves," while the cries of the "have-nots" are drowned out. Critics of welfare reform believe that the nation's economic problems are unfairly blamed on welfare spending and the poor. From a conflict perspective, this backlash against welfare recipients reflects deep fears and hostility toward the nation's urban, predominantly African American and Hispanic underclass.

Those who are critical of the backlash note that "welfare scapegoating" conveniently ignores the lucrative federal handouts that go to *affluent* individuals and families. For example, while federal housing aid to the poor was cut drastically in the 1980s,

Pascal Saez/Alamy Stock Photo

Even some European countries with strong social safety nets have begun to cut back benefits. These civil servants in Granada, Spain, are protesting salary cutbacks.

tax deductions for mortgage interest and property taxes more than doubled.

Conflict theorists have noted an oft-ignored aspect of the welfare system, administrative sanctions. The law allows administrators to end welfare payments if clients fail to complete job-readiness classes, community work, or job searches. A great deal of discretion is used in applying sanctions. According to one study, Black clients are more likely to be sanctioned than white clients (Schram et al. 2009).

Those who take a conflict perspective also urge policymakers and the general public to look closely at **corporate welfare**—the tax breaks, bailouts, direct payments, and grants that the government gives to corporations—rather than looking closely at the comparatively small allowances being given to mothers and their children. Yet any suggestion to curtail such corporate welfare brings a strong response from special-interest groups that are much more powerful than any coalition on behalf of the poor.

One example of corporate welfare is the huge federal bailouts given to distressed financial institutions in fall 2008 and to bankrupt automobile companies in 2009, then to airline companies and banks in 2020. Although the outlay of hundreds of billions of dollars was vital to the nation's economic recovery, the measure received relatively little scrutiny from Congress. Just a few months later, however, when legislation was proposed to extend the safety net for laid-off workers—unemployment compensation, food stamps, subsidized child care, assistance to the homeless, disability support, and infant nutrition—it met with loud demands for the monitoring of expenditures.

Corporate welfare is not limited to federal actions. In 2017, cities across the United States held their breath to hear who would be lucky enough to secure one of the planned Amazon corporate centers. Dozens of urban and rural areas had offered millions of dollars in incentives to attract the giant corporation and the jobs it promised. But this is only one highly visible example of strapped local communities offering tax incentives to wealthy corporations. Annually, U.S. public schools lose close to $2 billion through corporate tax incentives over which the schools themselves have little or no control. This happens when states and cities give tremendous tax credits to encourage corporate relocation or to subsidize the building of sports arenas (Russ 2018).

Initiating Policy

The government likes to highlight welfare-reform success stories. Though many people who once depended on tax dollars are now working and paying taxes themselves, it is much too soon to see if "workfare" will be successful. The new jobs that were generated by the booming economy of the late 1990s were an unrealistic test of the system. Prospects have faded for the hard-core jobless—people who are difficult to train or are encumbered by drug or alcohol abuse, physical disabilities, or child care needs—since that boom passed.

True, fewer people remain on the rolls since welfare reform was enacted in August 1996. By June 2019 just under 900,000 families were still on the rolls, less than one-fourth of the high of 5.1 million in 1994. But while those families that have left the rolls are modestly better off now, most of their breadwinners continue to hold low-paying, unskilled jobs (Department of Health and Human Services 2020a).

European governments have encountered many of the same citizen demands as in North America: keep our taxes low. Europe's safety net was further weakened by financial crises in Greece and, to a lesser extent, Spain and Portugal, but the greatest strain came from attempts to care for millions of refugees from Africa and Syria. Even Denmark, despite its long history of social welfare programs, is feeling the pinch. Student stipends are being reduced, early retirement plans have been reduced, and the maximum time for receiving unemployment benefits has been cut in half (although it is still a generous *two years*). Yet by any standard, the European safety net is still significantly stronger than that of the United States (Daley 2013; Organisation for Economic Co-operation and Development 2016).

This decline in public assistance has not escaped public attention. Erik O. Wright, 2012 president of the American Sociological Society, has observed that public demonstrations about social inequality are "not a uniquely American event . . . [they are] part of a global wave of protests." Wright senses rising concern that "harsh inequalities" are becoming "increasingly illegitimate. It would appear the present trends in welfare policy are doing little to address these concerns" (E. O. Wright 2011).

Take the Issue with You

1. Do you personally know anyone who has had to depend on public assistance, such as food stamps? If so, what were the circumstances? Would you yourself need government assistance under such circumstances?

2. Do you think the government financial assistance to people and households was adequate during the coronavirus pandemic? Do you think people considered it welfare? Why or why not?

3. Why do you think western and northern European countries have more generous welfare programs than the United States?

MASTERING THIS CHAPTER

Summary

Worldwide, stratification can be seen both in the gap between rich and poor nations and in the inequality within countries. This chapter examines the global divide and stratification in the world economic system; the impact of **globalization, modernization,** and **multinational corporations** on developing countries; and the distribution of wealth and income within various nations.

1. Developing nations account for most of the world's population and most of its births, but they also bear the burden of most of its poverty, disease, and childhood deaths.

2. Former colonized nations are kept in a subservient position, subject to foreign domination, through the process of **neocolonialism.**

3. Drawing on the conflict perspective, sociologist Immanuel Wallerstein's **world systems analysis** views the global economic system as one divided between nations that control wealth (core nations) and those from which resources are taken (periphery nations).

4. According to **dependency theory,** even as developing countries make economic advances, they remain weak and subservient to core nations and corporations in an increasingly integrated global economy.

5. **Globalization,** or the worldwide integration of government policies, cultures, social movements, and financial markets through trade and the exchange of ideas, is a controversial trend that critics blame for contributing to the cultural domination of periphery nations by core nations.

6. Poverty is a worldwide problem that blights the lives of billions of people. In 2000 the United Nations launched the Millennium Project, with the goal of halving extreme poverty worldwide by the year 2015.

7. **Multinational corporations** bring jobs and industry to developing nations, but they also tend to exploit workers in order to maximize profits.

8. Many sociologists are quick to note that terms such as **modernization** and even *development* contain an ethnocentric bias.

9. According to **modernization theory,** the development of periphery countries will be assisted by innovations transferred from the industrialized world.

10. In Europe and North America, countries have been forced to cut back welfare programs after a deep recession drained their treasuries. Even Denmark, known worldwide for its social safety net, has had to cut benefits.

Key Terms

Colonialism The maintenance of political, social, economic, and cultural domination over a people by a foreign power for an extended period. (page 214)

Conspicuous consumption Purchasing goods not to survive but to flaunt one's superior wealth and social standing. (page 223)

Corporate welfare Tax breaks, bailouts, direct payments, and grants that the government gives to corporations. (227)

Dependency theory An approach that contends that industrialized nations continue to exploit developing countries for their own gain. (214)

Globalization The worldwide integration of government policies, cultures, social movements, and financial markets through trade and the exchange of ideas. (216)

Modernization The far-reaching process through which periphery nations move from traditional or less developed institutions to those characteristic of more developed societies. (221)

Modernization theory A functionalist approach that proposes that modernization and development will gradually improve the lives of people in developing nations. (221)

Multinational corporation A commercial organization that is headquartered in one country but does business throughout the world. (219)

Neocolonialism Continuing dependence of former colonies on foreign countries. (214)

World systems analysis The global economy as an interdependent system of economically and politically unequal nations. (214)

Self-Quiz

Read each question carefully and then select the best answer.

1. The maintenance of political, social, economic, and cultural domination over a people by a foreign power for an extended period is referred to as
   a. neocolonialism.
   b. government-imposed stratification.
   c. colonialism.
   d. dependency.

2. In viewing the global economic system as divided between nations that control wealth and those that are controlled and exploited, sociologist Immanuel Wallerstein drew on the
   a. functionalist perspective.
   b. conflict perspective.
   c. interactionist perspective.
   d. dramaturgical approach.

3. Which of the following nations would Immanuel Wallerstein classify as a *core* country within the world economic system?
   a. Germany
   b. South Korea
   c. Ireland
   d. Mexico

4. In reviewing the results of the Millennium Development Goals, which country has made the most dramatic change in reducing poverty over the last 15 years?
   a. India
   b. China
   c. Greece
   d. United States

5. The Millennium Project was launched and overseen by the
   a. Bill and Melinda Gates Foundation.
   b. United Nations.
   c. U.S. Department of State.
   d. International Monetary Fund.

6. Which sociological perspective argues that multinational corporations can actually help the developing nations of the world?
   a. the interactionist perspective
   b. the feminist perspective
   c. the functionalist perspective
   d. the conflict perspective

7. Which of the following terms is used by contemporary social scientists to describe the far-reaching process by which peripheral nations move from traditional or less developed institutions to those characteristic of more developed societies?
   a. dependency
   b. globalization
   c. industrialization
   d. modernization

8. Social mobility in developing nations is most often accomplished by
   a. moving from rural areas to urban centers.
   b. receiving a college degree.
   c. accepting foreign aid.
   d. following in the occupation of one's parents.

9. Global inequality is staggering with the 26 wealthiest ipeople accumulating wealth to what proportion of the world's wealth?
   a. 1 percent
   b. 10 percent or one-tenth
   c. 20 percent
   d. 50 percent or half

10. Karuna Chanana Ahmed, an anthropologist from India who has studied developing nations, calls which group the most exploited of oppressed people?
    a. foreign aid recipients
    b. government bureaucrats
    c. the elderly
    d. women

11. Colonial domination established patterns of economic exploitation leading to former colonies remaining dependent on more industrialized nations. Such continuing dependence and foreign domination are referred to as _____.

12. According to Immanuel Wallerstein's analysis, the United States is at the _____ while neighboring Mexico is on the _____ of the world economic system.

13. Wallerstein's world systems analysis is the most widely used version of _____ theory.

14. In many developing nations, _____ is defined as the minimum income a person needs to survive, typically $1 to $2 a day.

15. _____ factories are factories found throughout the developing world that are run by multinational corporations.

16. As _____ industries become a more important part of the international marketplace, many companies have concluded that the low costs of overseas operations more than offset the expense of transmitting information around the world.

17. Viewed from a(n) _____ perspective, the combination of skilled technology and management provided by multinationals and the relatively cheap labor available in developing nations is ideal for a global enterprise.

18. Modernization theory reflects the _____ perspective.

19. In large developing nations, the most significant form of social mobility is the movement out of _____.

20. Tax breaks, bailouts, direct payments, and grants to businesses are all forms of _____ _____.

10 Racial and Ethnic Inequality

Diego G Diaz/Shutterstock

U.S. society is becoming increasingly diverse as immigrants from around the world bring their skills, languages, and cultures with them to their new home. Pictured here are new citizens participating in a naturalization ceremony at Tom McCall Waterfront Park in Portland, Oregon.

▶ INSIDE

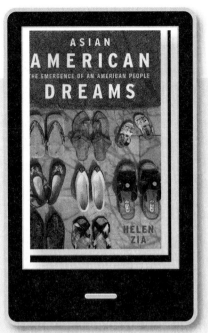

Ira C. Roberts

> What does it mean to be a "real American"?
>
> For Helen Zia, as for many other Americans, the question arises continually.

Chinkee, Chink. Jap, Nip, zero, kamikaze. Dothead, flat face, flat nose, slant eye, slope. Slit, mamasan, dragon lady. Gook, VC, Flip, Hindoo.

By the time I was ten, I'd heard such words so many times I could feel them coming before they parted lips. I knew they were meant in the unkindest way. Still, we didn't talk about these incidents at home; we just accepted them as part of being in America, something to learn to rise above.

The most common taunting didn't even utilize words but a string of unintelligible gobbledygook that kids—and adults—would spew as they pretended to speak Chinese or some other Asian language. It was a mockery of how they imagined my parents talked to me.

Truth was that Mom and Dad rarely spoke to us in Chinese, except to scold or call us to dinner. Worried that we might develop an accent, my father insisted that we speak English at home. This, he explained, would lessen the hardships we might encounter and make us more acceptable as Americans.

I'll never know if my father's language decision was right. On the one hand, I, like most Asian Americans, have been complimented countless times on my spoken English by people who assumed I was a foreigner. "My, you speak such good English," they'd cluck. "No kidding, I ought to," I would think to myself, then wonder: should I thank them for assuming that English isn't my native language? Or should I correct them on the proper usage of "well" and "good"?

More often than feeling grateful for my American accent, I've wished that I could jump into a heated exchange of rapid-fire Chinese, volume high and spit flying. But with a vocabulary limited to "Ni hao?" (How are you?) and "Ting bu dong" (I hear but don't understand), meaningful exchanges are woefully impossible. I find myself smiling and nodding like a dashboard ornament. I'm envious of the many people I know who grew up speaking an Asian language yet converse in English beautifully.

Armed with standard English and my flat New Jersey "a," I still couldn't escape the name-calling. I became all too familiar with other names and faces that supposedly matched mine—Fu Manchu, Suzie Wong, Hop Sing, Madame Butterfly, Charlie Chan, Ming the Merciless—the "Asians" produced for mass consumption. Their faces filled me with shame whenever I saw them on TV or in the movies. They defined my face to the rest of the world: a sinister Fu, Suzie the whore, subservient Hop Sing, pathetic Butterfly, cunning Chan, and warlike Ming. Inscrutable Orientals all, real Americans none. **"**

Source: Zia 2000: 109–110.

> *Truth was that Mom and Dad rarely spoke to us in Chinese, except to scold or call us to dinner. Worried that we might develop an accent, my father insisted that we speak English at home.*

Helen Zia, the successful journalist and community activist who wrote this reminiscence of her childhood, is the daughter of Chinese immigrants to the United States. As her account shows, Zia experienced blatant prejudice against Chinese Americans, even though she spoke flawless English. In fact, new immigrants and their families have faced stereotyping and hostility, whether they were white or non-white, Asian, African, Middle Eastern, or East European. In this multicultural society, those who are different from the dominant social group have never been truly welcome.

What sense are we to make of the issues of race, ethnicity, and immigration in the 21st century? Today, members of racial and ethnic minorities still struggle with the pressure to assimilate. Those who do assimilate still face continued prejudice and discrimination. Like class, race and ethnicity still affect people's place and status in a stratification system, not only in this country, but throughout the world. High incomes, a good command of English, and hard-earned professional credentials do not always override racial and ethnic stereotypes or protect those who fit them from the sting of racism. The recent protest marches underscored both that many people feel that racial equality and justice have not yet been achieved, and that many others fail to recognize when they act in a racist manner.

What is prejudice, and how is it institutionalized in the form of discrimination? In what ways have race and ethnicity affected the experience of immigrants from other countries? What are the fastest-growing minority groups in the United States today? In this chapter we will focus on the meaning of race and ethnicity. We will begin by identifying the basic characteristics of a minority group and distinguishing between racial and ethnic groups. Then we will examine the dynamics of prejudice and discrimination. After considering four sociological perspectives on race and ethnicity, we'll take a look at common patterns of intergroup relations. The following section will describe the major racial and ethnic groups in the United States. Finally, in the Social Policy section we will explore the global refugee crisis of the early 21st century.

Minority, Racial, and Ethnic Groups

Sociologists frequently distinguish between racial and ethnic groups. The term **racial group** describes a group that is set apart from others because of physical differences that have taken on social significance. whites, African Americans, and Asian Americans are all considered racial groups in the United States. While race does turn on physical differences, it is the culture of a particular society that constructs and attaches social significance to those differences, as we will see later. Unlike racial groups, an **ethnic group** is set apart from others primarily because of its national origin or distinctive cultural patterns. In the United States, Puerto Ricans, Jews, and Polish Americans are all categorized as ethnic groups (Table 10-1).

Minority Groups

A numerical minority is any group that makes up less than half of some larger population. The population of the United States includes thousands of numerical minorities, including television actors, green-eyed people, tax lawyers, and descendants of the Pilgrims who arrived on the *Mayflower*. However, these numerical minorities are not considered to be minorities in the sociological sense; in fact, the number of people in a group does not necessarily determine its status as a social minority (or a dominant group). When sociologists define a minority group, they are concerned primarily with the economic and political power, or powerlessness, of that group. A **minority group** is a subordinate group whose members have significantly less control or power over their own lives than the members of a dominant or majority group have over theirs.

Sociologists have identified five basic properties of a minority group: unequal treatment, physical or cultural traits, ascribed status, solidarity, and in-group marriage (Wagley and Harris 1958):

1. Members of a minority group experience unequal treatment compared to members of a dominant group. For example, the management of an apartment complex may refuse to rent to African Americans, Hispanics, or Jews. Social inequality may be created or maintained by prejudice, discrimination, segregation, or even extermination.

2. Members of a minority group share physical or cultural characteristics that distinguish them from the dominant group. Each society arbitrarily decides which characteristics are most important in defining groups.

3. Membership in a minority (or dominant) group is not voluntary; people are born into the group. Thus, race and ethnicity are considered *ascribed* statuses.

4. Minority group members have a strong sense of group solidarity. William Graham Sumner, writing in 1906, noted that people make distinctions between members of their own

TABLE 10-1   RACIAL AND ETHNIC GROUPS IN THE UNITED STATES

Classification	Number in Thousands	Percentage of Total Population
Racial Groups		
Whites (non-Hispanic)	197,034	60.2
Blacks/African Americans	41,617	12.7
Native Americans, Alaskan Natives	2,802	0.9
Asian Pacific Americans	23,569	7.2
Chinese	5,144	1.6
Asian Indians	4,506	1.4
Filipinos	4,090	1.3
Vietnamese	2,163	0.7
Koreans	1,894	0.6
Japanese	1,542	0.5
Pacific Islanders, Native Hawaiians	626	0.2
Other Asian Americans	3,630	1.1
Arab Americans	2,110	0.6
Two or more races	11,280	3.5
Ethnic Groups		
White ancestry		
Germans	41,222	12.6
Irish	30,805	9.4
English	22,807	7.0
Italians	16,412	5.0
Poles	8,887	2.7
Scottish and Scots-Irish	8,145	2.5
French	7,275	2.2
Jews	6,925	2.1
Hispanics (or Latinos)	59,763	18.3
Mexican Americans	36,987	11.3
Puerto Ricans	5,701	1.7
Cubans	2,364	0.7
Salvadorans	2,316	0.7
Dominicans	2,083	0.6
Guatemalans	1,525	0.5
Colombians	1,229	0.4
Other Hispanics	67,567	2.3
TOTAL (all groups)	**327,167**	

Think about It Did any of the numbers or percentages in Table 10-1 surprise you? How do you think the percentages have been changing in recent decades?

Note: Arab American population excluded from white total. All data are for 2018. Percentages do not total 100 percent, and when subcategories are added, they do not match totals in major categories because of overlap between groups (e.g., Polish American Jews or people of mixed ancestry such as Irish and Italian). Only the seven largest white ancestry groups listed.
Sources: American Community Survey 2019a: Tables B02001, B02016, B02018, B03001, B04006; Sheskin and Dashefsky 2018.

group (the *in-group*) and everyone else (the *out-group*). When a group is the object of long-term prejudice and discrimination, the feeling of "us versus them" can and often does become extremely intense.

5. Members of a minority group generally marry others from the same group. A member of a dominant group is often unwilling to marry into a supposedly inferior minority group. In addition, the minority group's sense of solidarity encourages marriage within the group and discourages marriage to outsiders.

Race

Many people think of race as a series of biological classifications. However, research shows that that is not a meaningful way of differentiating people. Genetically, there are no systematic differences between the races that affect people's social behavior and abilities. Instead, sociologists use the term *racial group* to refer to those minorities (and the corresponding dominant groups) who are set apart from others by obvious physical differences. But what is an "obvious" physical difference? Each society labels those differences that people consider important, while ignoring other characteristics that could serve as a basis for social differentiation.

Social Construction of Race Because race is a social construction, the process of defining races typically benefits those who have more power and privilege than others. In the United States, we see differences in both skin color and hair color. Yet people learn informally that differences in skin color have a dramatic social and political meaning, whereas differences in hair color do not.

When observing skin color, many people in the United States tend to lump others rather casually into the traditional categories of "Black," "white," and "Asian." Subtle differences in skin color often go unnoticed. In many nations of Central America and South America, in contrast, people recognize color gradients on a continuum from light to dark skin color. Brazil has approximately 40 color groupings, while in other countries people may be described as "Mestizo Hondurans," "Mulatto Colombians," or "African Panamanians." What we see as "obvious" differences, then, are subject to each society's social definitions.

The largest racial minorities in the United States are African Americans (or Blacks), Native Americans (or American Indians), and Asian Pacific Americans (Japanese Americans, Chinese Americans, Hawaiians, and other Asian Pacific peoples). Figure 10-1 provides information about the population of racial and ethnic groups in the United States over the past five centuries, projected through 2060.

FIGURE 10-1 RACIAL AND ETHNIC GROUPS IN THE UNITED STATES, 1500–2060 (PROJECTED)

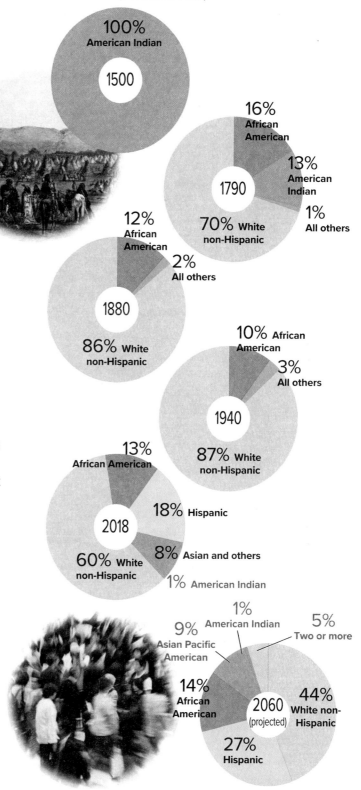

Sources: Author's estimate; Bureau of the Census 2004a; 2018b.
Top photo: Library of Congress Prints and Photographs Division [LC-USZC2-1745]; *bottom photo:* Ken Usami/Photodisc/Getty Images

The racial and ethnic composition of what is today the United States has been undergoing change not just for the past 50 years, but for the past 500. Five centuries ago the land was populated only by indigenous Native Americans.

Given current population patterns, it is clear that the nation's diversity will continue to increase. By 2011, for the first time ever, census data revealed that the majority of all children ages three and under were either Hispanic or non-white. This turning point marked the beginning of a pattern in which the nation's minority population will slowly become the majority. By 2014, the majority of people under age 18 in the United States belonged to racial or ethnic minority groups (Colby and Ortman 2015).

Racial definitions are crystallized through what Michael Omi and Howard Winant (2015) have called **racial formation,** a sociohistorical process in which racial categories are created, inhabited, transformed, and destroyed. In this process, those who have power define groups of people according to a racist social structure. The creation of a reservation system for Native Americans in the late 1800s is one example of racial formation. Federal officials combined what were distinctive tribes into a single racial group, which we refer to today as Native Americans. The extent and frequency with which peoples are subject to racial formation are such that no one escapes it.

Another example of racial formation from the 1800s was known as the "one-drop rule." If a person had even a single drop of "Black blood," that person was defined and viewed as Black, even if he or she *appeared* to be white. Clearly, race had social significance, enough so that white legislators established official standards about who was "Black" and who was "white."

The one-drop rule was a vivid example of the *social construction of race*—the process by which people come to define a group as a race based in part on physical characteristics, but also on historical, cultural, and economic factors. For example, in the 1800s, immigrant groups such as Italian and Irish Americans were not at first seen as being "white," but as foreigners who were not necessarily trustworthy. The social construction of race is an ongoing process that is subject to debate, especially in a diverse society such as the United States, where each year increasing numbers of children are born to parents of different racial backgrounds.

Recognition of Multiple Identities In 1900, in an address to the Anti-Slavery Union in London, scholar W. E. B. DuBois predicted that "the color line" would become the foremost problem of the 20th century. DuBois, born a free Black man in 1868, had witnessed prejudice and discrimination throughout the United States. His comment was prophetic. Today, over a century later, race and ethnicity still carry enormous weight in the United States (DuBois [1900] 1969).

The color line has blurred significantly since 1900, however. Interracial marriage is no longer forbidden by law and custom. Thus, Geetha Lakshmi-narayanan, a native of Ann Arbor, Michigan, is both white and Asian Indian. Often mistaken for a Filipina or Latina, she has grown accustomed to the blunt question "What are you?" (Navarro 2005).

In the late 20th century, with immigration from Latin America rising, the fluid nature of racial formation became evident. Suddenly, people were speaking about the "Latin Americanization" of the United States, or about a biracial, Black/white society being replaced by a triracial one. The 2000 census was the first time the U.S. government officially recognized different social constructions of racial identity—for example, that a person could be Asian American *and* white. Many people did select just one racial category in Census 2000 and in annual census surveys since then. Overall, just over 11 million people, or 3.3 percent of the population, selected two or more racial groups in 2018 (American Community Survey 2019a; Bonilla-Silva 2004).

This statistical finding of millions of multiracial people obscures how individuals are often asked to handle their identity. For example, the enrollment forms for government programs typically include only a few broad racial-ethnic categories. This approach to racial categorization is part of a long history that dictates single-race identities. Still, many individuals, especially young adults, struggle against social pressure to choose a single identity, and instead openly embrace multiple heritages. Public figures, rather than hide their mixed ancestry, now flaunt it. Singer Mariah Carey celebrates her Irish American background, and former President Barack Obama speaks of being born in Hawaii to a Kenyan father and a white mother from Kansas.

USE YOUR SOCIOLOGICAL IMAGINATION

Using a major streaming service, how quickly do you think you could find a television show in which all the characters share your racial or ethnic background? What about a show in which all the characters share a different background from yours—how quickly could you find one?

Ethnicity

An ethnic group, unlike a racial group, is set apart from others because of its national origin or distinctive cultural patterns. Among the ethnic groups in the United States are peoples with a Spanish-speaking background, referred to collectively as *Latinos* or *Hispanics*, such as Puerto Ricans, Mexican Americans, Cuban Americans, and other Latin Americans. Other ethnic groups in this country include Jewish, Irish, Italian, and Norwegian Americans. Although these groupings are convenient, they serve to obscure differences *within* ethnic categories (as in the case of Hispanics), as well as to overlook the mixed ancestry of so many people in the United States.

The distinction between racial and ethnic minorities is not always clear-cut. Some members of racial minorities, such as Asian Americans, may have significant cultural differences from other racial groups. At the same time, certain ethnic minorities, such as Latinos, may have obvious physical differences that set them apart from other ethnic groups in the United States.

Despite categorization problems, sociologists continue to feel that the distinction between racial groups and ethnic groups is socially significant. In most societies, including the United States, socially constructed physical differences tend to be more visible than ethnic differences. Partly as a result of this fact, stratification along racial lines is more resistant to change than stratification along ethnic lines. Over time, members of an ethnic minority can sometimes become indistinguishable from the majority—although the process may take generations and may never include all members of the group. In contrast, members of a racial minority find it much more difficult to blend in with the larger society and gain acceptance from the majority.

THINKING CRITICALLY

Why does the social construction of race defy the traditional notion of race as a biological category?

Prejudice and Discrimination

Looking at the United States in the 21st century, some people wonder aloud if race and ethnicity are still relevant to social stratification. After all, African Americans have served as secretary of state, secretary of defense, chairman of the Joint Chiefs of Staff, and, most notably, president of the United States; the office of attorney general has been held by both an African American and a Hispanic. As historic as these leaders' achievements have been, however, in every case their elevation meant that they entered an overwhelmingly white government department or assembly.

At the same time, college campuses across the United States have been the scene of bias-related incidents. Student-run newspapers and radio stations have ridiculed racial and ethnic minorities; threatening literature has been stuffed under the doors of minority students; graffiti endorsing the views of white supremacist organizations such as the Ku Klux Klan have been scrawled on university walls. In some cases, there have even been violent clashes between groups of white and Black students. In 2018, students staged protests, sit-ins, and hunger strikes over incidents such as prejudiced statements by college leaders, hassling of Black students by campus police, fraternities issuing invitations to "white girls only," and human

feces on bathroom walls in the form of swastikas. What causes such ugly incidents?

Prejudice

Prejudice is a negative attitude toward an entire category of people, often an ethnic or racial minority. If you resent your roommate because he or she is sloppy, you are not necessarily guilty of prejudice. However, if you immediately stereotype your roommate on the basis of such characteristics as race, ethnicity, or religion, that is a form of prejudice. Prejudice tends to perpetuate false definitions of individuals and groups.

Sometimes prejudice results from **ethnocentrism**—the tendency to assume that one's own culture and way of life represent the norm or are superior to all others. Ethnocentric people judge other cultures by the standards of their group, which leads quite easily to prejudice against cultures they view as inferior.

One important and widespread ideology that reinforces prejudice is **racism,** the belief that one race is supreme and all others are innately inferior. When racism prevails in a society, members of subordinate groups generally experience

Paul Bereswil/Sport/Getty Images

Even successful members of minority groups like point guard Jeremy Lin are subjected to ethnic slurs. "Chinks in the Armor" proclaimed a headline on ESPN's website in 2012 after Lin, who had spearheaded a multigame winning streak, had a bad night. The network later apologized for the remark.

RESEARCH TODAY

10-1   Avoiding Interracial Relationships Online

Racial bias is rife in online dating. Black people, for example, are ten times more likely to contact white people on dating sites than white people are to contact Black people. African American women and Asian men are likely to be rated substantially lower than members of other ethnic groups, whereas Asian women and white men are the most likely to be rated highly by other users.

IInformation scientists have looked at online dating platforms that seemingly permit users to maintain their racial biases and discriminate based on race. Dating apps typically allow users to match with people of their same race or to identify racial or ethnic groups from which they do not wish to consider potential partners. Even if members of online dating platforms don't choose to self-segregate, as of 2017 top sites with histories of previously successful matches involving people of the same race began automatically screening for same-race potential dates and filtering out matches of different racial or ethnic backgrounds.

Should dating apps bolster people's existing prejudices, or should they work against

them? The sites themselves certainly seem to learn from these prejudices. A 2018 study examined racial bias on the 25 highest grossing dating apps in the United States. It found that race frequently played a role in how matches were found. Nineteen of the apps requested users to indicate their own race or ethnicity, 11 collected users' preferred ethnicity in a potential partner, and 17 allowed users to filter potential dates by ethnicity.

Operators of dating platforms typically do not see an issue with allowing users to identify their own race and select dates on the basis of race. The administrators' rationale

> *Should dating apps bolster people's existing prejudices, or should they work against them? The sites themselves certainly seem to learn from these prejudices.*

is that they are giving the users what they want, either as expressed consciously by ticking off a race selection box, or unconsciously by having an online history of successful same-race dates.

In the days before the Internet, people met potential dates in bars and clubs, in the workplace, in places of religious worship, and through friends, all of which tended to support racial and ethnic biases. Online dating may break down some of these barriers, but it has also allowed participants to continue many prejudiced ways of thinking.

LET'S DISCUSS

1. Do you think you might use a dating site some day? Would you want it to ask about ethnicity or racial background? Why or why not?
2. What are some other situations in which this kind of bias might affect the choices a person makes?

Sources: Hutson et al. 2018; McMullan 2019; Rockett 2018.

female: Antonio Guillem/Shutterstock; male: vadymvdrobot/123RF

prejudice, discrimination, and exploitation. In 1990, as concern mounted about racist attacks in the United States, Congress passed the Hate Crimes Statistics Act. As a result, hate crimes are now increasingly reported and investigated in much the same way as conventional crimes against property and people.

Prejudice comes from a number of sources, including the open expression of prejudiced views and the idea that taking advantage of some other group may help one's own group to

advance. In Box 10-1, we consider research on how people use online dating sites to avoid potential dates, much less marriage partners, who are of a different racial or ethnic background.

Prejudice is also rooted in racial and ethnic **stereotypes**—unreliable generalizations about all members of a group that do not recognize individual differences within the group. The dominant or majority group creates these stereotypes through the process of racial formation. As the interactionist

William I. Thomas noted, the dominant group's "definition of the situation" is often so powerful, it can mold the individual personality. That is, people respond not only to the objective features of a situation or person, but to the *social meaning* that situation or person carries. Thus, the false images or stereotypes created by the dominant group can have real consequences (Thomas 1923).

Color-Blind Racism

Over the past three generations, nationwide surveys have consistently shown growing support among whites for integration, interracial dating, and the election of minority group members to public office—including the presidency of the United States. How can this trend be explained, given the persistence of residential segregation and the commission of thousands of hate crimes every year? The answer, to some extent, is that prejudice and discriminatory attitudes are no longer expressed as freely as they once were. According to some, they are often couched in terms of equal opportunity.

According to some people, **color-blind racism** is the use of the principle of race neutrality to defend a racially unequal status quo. Proponents of race neutrality claim they believe that everyone should be treated equally. However, some say that the way these proponents apply the principle to government policy is anything but neutral. They say that proponents of this approach oppose affirmative action, public welfare assistance, and, to a large extent, government-funded health insurance, all of which they accuse the proponents of seeing largely as favors to minority groups. Yet, according to these critics, the proponents do not object to practices that privilege whites, such as college admissions criteria that give preference to the relatives of alumni. Nor do they oppose tax breaks for homeowners, most of whom are white, or government financial aid to college students, who are also disproportionately white.

Color-blind racism has also been referred to by critics as "covert racism." These critics claim that although its proponents rarely speak of racism, other indicators of social status, such as social class or citizenship, tend to become proxies for race. Thus, they maintain that many of the proponents can convince themselves that they are not racist—nor do they know anyone who is—and yet remain prejudiced against "welfare mothers" and "immigrants." They claim that such people can conclude, mistakenly, that racial tolerance, or even racial and ethnic equality, has been achieved.

Researchers who have surveyed white attitudes toward African Americans over the past several decades have reached two inescapable conclusions. First, people's attitudes do change. In periods of social upheaval, dramatic attitudinal shifts can occur within a single generation. Second, less racial progress was made in the late 20th and early 21st centuries than in the relatively brief period of the 1950s and 1960s.

Today, economically disadvantaged groups have become so closely associated with urban decay, homelessness, welfare, and crime that those problems are now viewed by some as racial issues, even if they are not labeled as such. The tendency to blame the victims of these social ills complicates their resolution, especially at a time when government's ability to address social problems is limited by recession, antitax initiatives, and concern over terrorism. In short, some people claim the color line is still in place, even if more and more people refuse to acknowledge its existence.

Discriminatory Behavior

Prejudice often leads to **discrimination,** the denial of opportunities and equal rights to individuals and groups because of prejudice or other arbitrary reasons. Say that a white corporate president with a prejudice against Asian Pacific Americans has to fill an executive position. The most qualified candidate for the job is a Vietnamese American. If the president refuses to hire this candidate and instead selects an inferior white candidate, he or she is engaging in an act of racial discrimination.

Prejudiced *attitudes* should not be equated with discriminatory *behavior.* Although the two are generally related, they are not identical; either condition can be present without the other. A prejudiced person does not always act on his or her biases. The white corporate president, for example, might choose—despite his or her stereotypes—to hire the Vietnamese American. That would be prejudice without discrimination. On the other hand, a white corporate president with a completely respectful view of Vietnamese Americans might refuse to hire them for executive posts out of fear that biased clients would take their business elsewhere. In that case, the president's action would constitute discrimination without prejudice.

A field experiment by sociologist Devah Pager, then a doctoral candidate at the University of Wisconsin–Madison, documented racial discrimination in hiring. Pager sent four polite, well-dressed young men out to look for an entry-level job in Milwaukee, Wisconsin. All were 23-year-old college students, but they presented themselves as high school graduates with similar job histories. Two of the men were Black and two were white. One Black applicant and one white applicant claimed to have served 18 months in jail for a felony conviction—possession of cocaine with intent to distribute.

As one might expect, the four men's experiences with 350 potential employers were vastly different. Predictably, the white applicant with a purported prison record received only half as many callbacks as the other white applicant—17 percent compared to 34 percent. But as dramatic as the effect of his criminal record was, the effect of his race was more significant. Despite his prison record, he received slightly more callbacks than the Black applicant *with no criminal record* (17 percent compared to 14 percent). Race, it seems, was more of a concern to potential employers than a criminal background.

The implications of this research are not limited to any one city, such as Milwaukee. Similar studies have confirmed discriminatory handling of job applications in Chicago; New York City; Long Island, New York; San Diego; and Washington, D.C. Over time, the cumulative effect of such differential behavior by employers contributes to significant differences in income. Figure 10-2 vividly illustrates the income inequality between white men and almost everyone else (Pedulla and Pager 2019; Pager et al. 2009).

If race serves as a barrier, why do Asian American men earn more income than white men (see Figure 10-2)? Not all Asian American men earn high incomes; indeed, some Asian American groups, such as Laotians and Vietnamese, have high levels of poverty. Nevertheless, a significant number of Asian Americans have advanced degrees that qualify them for highly paid jobs, and this raises the median income for the group as a whole.

In the 21st century a new marketplace has blossomed in the United States and other industrial countries—the **sharing economy** made up of online economic transactions that place buyers and sellers in direct peer-to-peer contact with no change of ownership of goods and services. One concern about the sharing economy is the emergence of old-fashioned discrimination in this new market. For example, Airbnb, which facilitates online transactions between landlords and tenants, has been found to be a vehicle for discrimination based on race, gender, religion, and sexual identity. A 2016 study found that requests from guests with distinctively African American names are 16 percent less likely to receive accommodations through Airbnb than those with distinctively white names.

Researchers at universities such as MIT, Stanford, and the University of Washington have found that Black users often have to wait longer for rides on

services such as Uber and Lyft. Black users are also far more likely than white users to have rides canceled by Uber drivers. Representatives from both Uber and Lyft said that their companies have strong nondiscrimination guidelines for their drivers. In fact, they counter that, compared to taxi companies, they are more available to people living in underserved areas that taxis have historically neglected. Yet some individual drivers still avoid customers whose online profile suggests they are not white. Clearly as online options continue to multiply and evolve, society will have to remain vigilant against the parallel evolution of new ways to discriminate (Edelman et al. 2017; Glusac 2016).

Discrimination persists even for the most educated and qualified minority group members from the best family backgrounds. Despite their talents and experiences, they sometimes encounter attitudinal or organizational bias that prevents them from reaching their full potential. The term **glass ceiling** refers to an invisible barrier that blocks the promotion of a qualified individual in a work environment because of the individual's gender, race, or ethnicity (R. Schaefer 2021).

FIGURE 10-2   U.S. MEDIAN INCOME BY RACE, ETHNICITY, AND GENDER

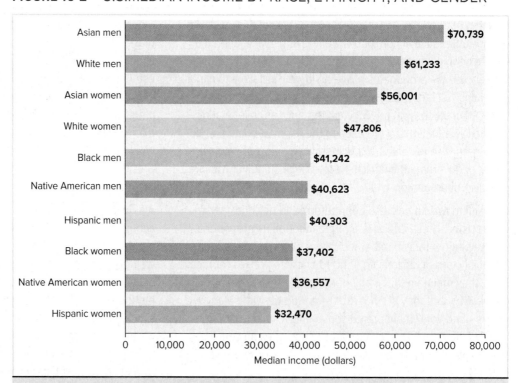

Think about It What are some possible implications of the differences in earning power between members of different groups?

Note: Data released in 2020 for income earned in 2019. Median income is from all sources and is limited to year-round, full-time workers at least 16 years old. Data for white men and women are for non-Hispanics. While the coronavirus pandemic deeply affected people's income, the comparisons are still relevant.
Source: American Community Survey 2020a:Table S2002.

Income gaps remain significant: Hispanic and Native American women must work for nearly two years or more to earn what Asian and white men earn in one year.

USE YOUR SOCIOLOGICAL IMAGINATION

How might online social networking maintain prejudice and discrimination?

The Privileges of the Dominant

One aspect of discrimination that is often overlooked is the privileges that dominant groups enjoy at the expense of others. For instance, we tend to focus more on the difficulty women have getting ahead at work and getting a hand at home than on the ease with which men manage to make their way in the world and avoid household chores. Similarly, we concentrate more on discrimination against racial and ethnic minorities than on the advantages members of the white majority enjoy. Indeed, most white people rarely think about their "whiteness," taking their status for granted.

Sociologists and other social scientists are becoming increasingly interested in what it means to be "white," for white privilege is the proverbial other side of the coin of racial discrimination. In this context, **white privilege** refers to rights or immunities granted to people as a particular benefit or favor simply because they are white. This view of whiteness as a privilege echoes an observation by W. E. B. DuBois that rather than wanting fair working conditions for all laborers, White workers had accepted the "public and psychological wage" of whiteness ([1935] 1962:700; Ferber and Kimmel 2008).

The feminist scholar Peggy McIntosh (1988) became interested in white privilege after noticing that most men would not acknowledge that there were privileges attached to being male—even if they would agree that being female had its disadvantages. Did white people suffer from a similar blind spot regarding their racial privilege? she wondered. Intrigued, McIntosh began to list all the ways in which she benefited from her whiteness. She soon realized that the list of unspoken advantages was long and significant.

McIntosh found that as a white person, she rarely needed to step out of her comfort zone, no matter where she went. If she wished to, she could spend most of her time with people of her race. She could find a good place to live in a pleasant neighborhood, buy the foods she liked to eat from almost any grocery store, and get her hair styled in almost any salon. She could attend a public meeting without feeling that she did not belong, that she was different from everyone else.

McIntosh discovered, too, that her skin color opened doors for her. She could cash checks and use credit cards without suspicion, browse through stores without being shadowed by security guards. She could be seated without difficulty in a restaurant. If she asked to see the manager, she could assume he or she would be of her race. If she needed help from a doctor or a lawyer, she could get it.

McIntosh also realized that her whiteness made the job of parenting easier. She did not need to worry about protecting her children from people who didn't like them. She could be sure that their schoolbooks would show pictures of people who looked like them, and that their history texts would describe white people's achievements. She knew that the television programs they watched would include white characters.

Finally, McIntosh had to admit that others did not constantly evaluate her in racial terms. When she appeared in public, she didn't need to worry that her clothing or behavior might reflect poorly on white people. If she was recognized for an achievement, it was seen as her achievement, not that of an entire race. And no one ever assumed that the personal opinions she voiced should be those of all white people. Because McIntosh blended in with the people around her, she wasn't always onstage.

Recently events have highlighted the many ways in which whites are privileged. For example, a Black graduate student falls asleep in a college dormitory common area. A white student calls the police; when they arrive, they demand more

Hero Images/Getty Images

Race is often not remarked on when white people hold professional positions and jobs with authority and prestige. Is this an indicator of privilege in the workplace?

identification from the Black woman than her college ID. Or employees of a coffee shop summon police to check out two African American men having a business meeting there. The emotional situation is reduced when the third member of the meeting, a white man, arrives. Or police are summoned when three Black women are leaving the Airbnb house they rented. Neighbors become suspicious because the women leave carrying suitcases. Would any of these incidents have occurred if the student or customers were privileged by being white?

In 2020, millions of people spontaneously marched in protest in cities large and small following the videotaped death of George Floyd at the hands of four Minneapolis policemen. The calls for significant police reform were met with counter calls for law and order.

In the wake of the Great Recession that began in the United States in 2007, researchers looked at the differential impact of home loan practices and found evidence of **redlining,** a devastating form of racial bias. African Americans, Latino people, and others fall victim to this pattern of discrimination against people trying to buy homes in minority and racially changing neighborhoods. Redlining was especially rampant in the first half of the 20th century, but evi-

dence of its persistence still appears. Controlling for a variety of personal financial factors and home values, the researchers found that Black residents of Black neighborhoods in Baltimore, Maryland, paid 5 to 11 percent more in monthly payments than comparable white residents of white neighborhoods.

It has not been just scholars who unearthed redlining in the 21st century. The federal government levied a $22 million fine on the Hudson City Savings Bank, the nation's seventh largest, whose executives had purposefully avoided building bank branches in Black and Latino/a neighborhoods where home loans could be offered to local residents. This was not an isolated case: in 2015 alone, fines were also applied to banks in Buffalo, Milwaukee, Providence, Rochester, and St. Louis (Rugh et al. 2015; Swarns 2015).

USE YOUR SOCIOLOGICAL IMAGINATION

How often do you think people are privileged because of their race or ethnicity? How about yourself—how often are you privileged?

TAKING SOCIOLOGY TO WORK

Jennifer Michals, **Program Assistant, Center for Native American and Indigenous Research, Northwestern University**

Jennifer Michals did not start out as a sociology major: Her curiosity about human behavior led her first to psychology. However, after her introduction to C. Wright Mills's concept of the sociological imagination in her first sociology course, she realized that sociology offered the lens she needed to see the connection between the individual and society. She went on to obtain both a B.A. and an M.A. in sociology at DePaul University.

Sociology also provided Michals with the sense of agency and social responsibility she needs in her position, where she develops scholarship and research in Native American and Indigenous Studies as well as works to broaden the college's outreach in Chicago and the upper Midwest. She provides support for students, faculty, and community who are engaged in research about issues such as food sovereignty, land and identity, and cultural and linguistic revival. She is also part of a team that is developing a Native American and Indigenous Studies minor.

Michals has a mixed heritage of Ojibwe, Potawatomi, and Kickapoo and is enrolled as a Citizen of the Nation Potawatomi. Her work involves building relationships with the urban native community, in addition to the surrounding Great Lakes tribes. The Center is committed to community-based research and prioritizing the needs of native communities. Michals's team participated in the Oneida White Corn Harvest where they spent three days at a corn cooperative,

Jennifer Michals

harvesting the corn and braiding the cobs. They learned about native and indigenous food systems, and the efforts being undertaken to revitalize native and indigenous food practices and ecological knowledge.

In her position, she attended the American Indian Science and Engineering Society's annual conference for the first time. She found it incredible to meet so many bright high school and college students engaged in STEM and making an impact in the world.

Michals feels that her sociology background prepared her to be culturally competent: in other words, knowledgeable, aware, and sensitive to native and indigenous peoples. It also made her conscious of the social factors and structural inequalities that exist in society, and this helps her make an impact on issues facing native and indigenous people.

LET'S DISCUSS

1. What are some specific ways that the courses you are now taking can help you prepare for a future career? What other courses might you take to help you build skills for a future career.
2. Do some research on Native American or other minority communities in your region. What specific needs do these communities have that sociology can help address?

Library of Congress Prints and Photographs Division [LC-DIG-fsa-8a26761]

Before passage of the Civil Rights Act (1964), segregation of public accommodations was the norm throughout the South. Whites used the most up-to-date bathrooms, waiting rooms, and even drinking fountains, while Blacks ("Colored") were directed to older facilities in inferior condition. Such separate but unequal arrangements are a blatant example of institutional discrimination.

Institutional Discrimination

Discrimination is practiced not only by individuals in one-to-one encounters but also by institutions in their daily operations. Social scientists are particularly concerned with the ways in which structural factors such as employment, housing, health care, and government operations maintain the social significance of race and ethnicity. **Institutional discrimination** (or systemic discrimination) refers to the denial of opportunities and equal rights to individuals and groups that results from the normal operations of a society. This kind of discrimination consistently affects certain racial and ethnic groups more than others.

The Commission on Civil Rights (1981:9–10) identified various forms of institutional discrimination:

- Rules requiring that only English be spoken at a place of work, even when it is not a business necessity to restrict the use of other languages.
- Preferences shown by law and medical schools in the admission of children of wealthy and influential alumni, nearly all of whom are white.
- Restrictive employment-leave policies, coupled with prohibitions on part-time work, that make it difficult for the heads of single-parent families (most of whom are women) to obtain and keep jobs.

In some cases, even seemingly neutral institutional standards can have discriminatory effects. African American students at a midwestern state university protested a policy under which fraternities and sororities that wished to use campus facilities for a dance were required to pay a $150 security deposit to cover possible damages. They complained that the policy had a discriminatory impact on minority student organizations. Campus police countered that the university's policy applied to all student groups interested in using the facilities. However, since the overwhelmingly white fraternities and sororities at the school had their own houses, which they used for dances, the policy indeed affected only the African American and other minority organizations.

Attempts have been made to eradicate or compensate for institutional discrimination. The 1960s saw the passage of many pioneering civil rights laws, including the landmark 1964 Civil Rights Act which prohibits discrimination in public accommodations and publicly owned facilities on the basis of race, color, creed, national origin, sex, and gender.

The 2020 protests for racial justice called for an end to racism in institutions such as law enforcement. This charge was often rejected as many of the privileged only associate racism with the most explicit forms of bigotry—institutional racism cannot be as easily videotaped as assaults.

For more than 40 years, affirmative action programs have been instituted to overcome past discrimination. **Affirmative action** refers to positive efforts to recruit minority group members or women for jobs, promotions, and educational opportunities. Many people resent these programs, arguing that advancing one group's cause merely shifts the discrimination to another group. By giving priority to African Americans in admissions, for example, schools may overlook more qualified white candidates. In many parts of the country and many sectors of the economy, affirmative action is being rolled back, even though it was never fully implemented.

Another example of institutional discrimination concerns two different types of voting requirements. The first is state laws that bar citizens with past felony convictions from voting. The laws vary from state to state, but some states, including Florida, Iowa, and Virginia, effectively have lifetime bans that are more likely to affect African American voters than members of other groups. In fact, in seven states (Alabama, Florida, Kentucky, Mississippi, Tennessee, Virginia, and Wyoming) these laws effectively prevent at least 15 percent of African Americans from voting. Second are laws that require

IDs to vote, sometimes an officially issued photo ID, ostensibly to prevent voter fraud. However, there is little evidence that people have been impersonating eligible voters at the polls and, typically, these laws disproportionately suppress the vote of Hispanic, Black, and Asian American citizens (Jonsson 2019; Lai and Lee 2016; National Conference of State Legislatures 2020).

Discriminatory practices continue to pervade nearly all areas of life in the United States today. In part, that is because various individuals and groups actually *benefit* from racial and ethnic discrimination in terms of money, status, and influence. Discrimination permits members of the majority to enhance their wealth, power, and prestige at the expense of others. Less qualified people get jobs and promotions simply because they are members of the dominant group. Such individuals and groups will not surrender these advantages easily. We'll turn now to a closer look at this functionalist analysis, as well as the conflict, labeling, and interactionist perspectives on race and ethnicity.

THINKING CRITICALLY

Which would be more socially significant, the elimination of prejudice or the elimination of discrimination? Explain.

Sociological Perspectives on Race and Ethnicity

Relations among racial and ethnic groups lend themselves to analysis from four major sociological perspectives. Viewing race from the macro level, functionalists observe that racial prejudice and discrimination serve positive functions for dominant groups. Conflict theorists see the economic structure as a central factor in the exploitation of minorities. Labeling theorists note the way in which minorities are singled out for differential treatment by law enforcement officers. On the micro level, interactionist researchers stress the manner in which everyday contact between people from different racial and ethnic backgrounds contributes to tolerance or hostility.

Functionalist Perspective

What possible use could racial bigotry have? Functionalist theorists, while agreeing that racial hostility is hardly to be admired, point out that it serves positive functions for those who practice discrimination.

Anthropologist Manning Nash (1962) identified three functions of racially prejudiced beliefs for the dominant group:

1. Racist views provide a moral justification for maintaining an unequal society that routinely deprives a minority group of its rights and privileges. Southern whites justified slavery by believing that Africans were physically and spiritually subhuman and devoid of souls.

2. Racist beliefs discourage the subordinate minority from attempting to question its lowly status, which would be to question the very foundations of society.

3. Racial myths suggest that any major societal change (such as an end to discrimination) would only bring greater poverty to the minority and lower the majority's standard of living. As a result, racial prejudice grows when a society's value system (one underlying a colonial empire or slavery, for example) is threatened.

Although racial prejudice and discrimination may serve the powerful, such unequal treatment can also be dysfunctional for a society, and even for the dominant group. Sociologist Arnold Rose (1951) outlined four dysfunctions that are associated with racism:

moodboard/Brand X Pictures/Getty Images

In U.S. retail stores, Black customers have different experiences from white customers. They are more likely than whites to have their checks or credit cards refused and more likely to be followed by security personnel.

1. A society that practices discrimination fails to use the resources of all individuals. Discrimination limits the search for talent and leadership to the dominant group.

2. Discrimination aggravates social problems such as poverty, delinquency, and crime, and places the financial burden of alleviating those problems on the dominant group.

3. Society must invest a good deal of time and money to defend its barriers to the full participation of all members.

4. Racial prejudice and discrimination often undercut goodwill and friendly diplomatic relations between nations.

Conflict Perspective

Conflict theorists would certainly agree with Arnold Rose that racial prejudice and discrimination have many harmful consequences for society. Sociologists have used **exploitation theory** (or *Marxist class theory*) to explain the basis of racial subordination in the United States. Karl Marx viewed the exploitation of the lower class as a basic part of the capitalist economic system. From a Marxist point of view, racism keeps minorities in low-paying jobs, thereby supplying the capitalist ruling class with a pool of cheap labor. Moreover, by forcing racial minorities to accept low wages, capitalists can restrict the wages of *all* members of the proletariat. Workers from the dominant group who demand higher wages can always be replaced by minorities who have no choice but to accept low-paying jobs (Blauner 1972; Cox 1948; Hunter 2000).

The conflict view of race relations seems persuasive in a number of instances. Japanese Americans were the object of little prejudice until they began to enter jobs that brought them into competition with whites. The movement to keep Chinese immigrants out of the United States became most fervent during the latter half of the 19th century, when Chinese and whites fought over dwindling work opportunities. Both the enslavement of Blacks and the extermination and removal westward of Native Americans were economically motivated.

However, the exploitation theory is too limited to explain prejudice in its many forms. Not all minority groups have been exploited to the same extent. In addition, many groups (such as the Quakers and the Mormons) have been victimized by prejudice for other than economic reasons. Still, as Gordon Allport (1979:210) concludes, the exploitation theory correctly "points a sure finger at one of the factors involved in prejudice, . . . rationalized self-interest of the upper classes."

Labeling Perspective

One practice that fits both the conflict perspective and labeling theory is racial profiling. **Racial profiling** is any arbitrary action initiated by an authority based on race, ethnicity, or national origin rather than on a person's behavior. Generally, racial profiling occurs when law enforcement officers, including customs officials, airport security, and police, assume that people who fit a certain description are likely to be engaged in illegal activities. Beginning in the 1980s with the emergence of the crack cocaine market, skin color became a key characteristic in racial profiling. This practice is often based on very explicit stereotypes. For example, one federal antidrug initiative encouraged officers to look specifically for people with dreadlocks and for Latino men traveling together.

Profiling is actually not new. In 1897 W. E. B. DuBois coined the term **double consciousness** to refer to the division of an individual's identity into two or more social realities. He used the term to describe the experience of being Black in white America. African Americans can be highly educated and hold respectable jobs but still be treated with suspicion (DuBois [1903] 1961).

Already back in the 1990s, increased attention to racial profiling and accompanying force used by law enforcement led to special reports and commissions, but no significant legislation was passed against it. Racial profiling and policing tactics have become a more visible part of the national discussion in recent years. Two developments have been especially important. First is the #BlackLivesMatter (BLM) movement, which emerged to call attention to the shooting deaths of African Americans, especially men, usually by police officers. BLM was organized in 2013 after a neighborhood watch coordinator in Florida shot and killed Trayvon Martin, an unarmed Black 17-year old. The shooter's acquittal was broadly viewed as a miscarriage of justice. Defensively, some counter the phrase "Black lives matter" with "All lives matter" and call attention to the dangerous position in which police officers often find themselves.

Second, cameras on bystanders' smartphones and police body cams have led to a video record of law-enforcement encounters with African American civilians that many interpret as excessive, and sometimes lethal, shows of force. The 2020 death of unarmed George Floyd in Minneapolis led to spontaneous nationwide marches in support of BLM. Not surprisingly, a national survey showed that only 9 percent of African Americans, compared to 42 percent of whites, felt that police around the country treat racial and ethnic groups equally (Pew Research Center 2020).

Profiling also refers to continuing calls, sometimes angry and strident, for greater scrutiny of Muslims, including Muslim Americans, in the wake of terrorist episodes by Islamic extremists. Notably, then–presidential candidate Donald Trump in 2015 called for a ban on all Muslims entering the United States pending thorough background checks. A national survey of all likely voters at the time showed that over one-third supported Trump's proposal. However, this singling out of people on the basis of their religion received strong condemnation from other political leaders. The broad level of support nonetheless

Scott Olson/News/Getty Images

Ethnic and religious minorities believe that profiling to maintain national security unfairly targets them.

underscores the persistent temptation to use profiling, whether racial or religious, as a shortcut to maintaining public safety (McCormick 2015; Marist Poll 2015: Question 7F).

Racial profiling persists despite overwhelming evidence that it is not effective in identifying potential troublemakers. A massive study that examined over 100 million traffic stop-and-search incidents from 31 states between 2011 and 2016 found that Black drivers were stopped more often than others. Controlling for age, gender, time, and location, Blacks and Latinos are twice as likely to be searched than whites—a disparity not justified by the outcome: minorities searched were less likely to have contraband than were white motorists.

A similar pattern emerged in a study on the likelihood of force being used against drivers: force was three times more likely to be used against Latinos and Blacks than for white drivers. A study of New York City police officers that included 4.43 million stops between 2004 and mid-2012 found that Blacks and Latinos accounted for 83 percent of people who were stopped and frisked. A related study found that whites were 50 percent more likely to be carrying weapons (Center for Constitutional Rights 2011; Stanford Open Policing Project 2019).

Interactionist Perspective

A Hispanic woman is transferred from a job on an assembly line to a similar position working next to a white man. At first, the white man is patronizing, assuming that she must be incompetent. She is cold and resentful; even when she needs assistance, she refuses to admit it. After a week, the growing tension between the two leads to a bitter quarrel. Yet over time, each slowly comes to appreciate the other's strengths and talents. A year after they began working together, these two workers become respectful friends. This story is an example of what interactionists call the *contact hypothesis* in action.

The **contact hypothesis** states that in cooperative circumstances, interracial contact between people of equal status will cause them to become less prejudiced and to abandon old stereotypes. People begin to see one another as individuals and discard the broad generalizations characteristic of stereotyping. Note the phrases *equal status* and *cooperative circumstances.* In the story just told, if the two workers had been competing for one vacancy as a supervisor, the racial hostility between them might have worsened (Allport 1979; Fine 2008).

As Latinos and other minorities slowly gain access to better-paying and more responsible jobs, the contact hypothesis may take on even greater significance. The trend in our society is toward increasing contact between individuals from dominant and subordinate groups. That may be one way of eliminating—or at least reducing—racial and ethnic stereotyping and prejudice. Another may be the establishment of interracial coalitions, an idea suggested by sociologist William Julius Wilson (1999). To work, such coalitions would obviously need to be built on an equal role for all members.

Table 10-2 summarizes the four major sociological perspectives on race. No matter what the explanation for racial and ethnic distinctions—functionalist, conflict, labeling, or interactionist—these socially constructed inequalities can have powerful consequences in the form of prejudice and discrimination. In the next section, we will see how inequality based on the ascribed characteristics of race and ethnicity can poison people's interpersonal relations, depriving whole groups of opportunities others take for granted.

THINKING CRITICALLY

Describe an example of labeling that you are personally familiar with. Analyze its significance.

Tracking Sociological Perspectives

TABLE 10-2 SOCIOLOGICAL PERSPECTIVES ON RACE AND ETHNICITY

Perspective	Emphasis
Functionalist	The dominant majority benefits from the subordination of racial minorities.
Conflict	Vested interests perpetuate racial inequality through economic exploitation.
Labeling	People are profiled and stereotyped based on their racial and ethnic identity.
Interactionist	Cooperative interracial contacts can reduce hostility.

Think about It Consider an example of discrimination that you are familiar with. Which theoretical view best explains it?

Spectrum of Intergroup Relations

Racial and ethnic groups can relate to one another in a wide variety of ways, ranging from friendships and intermarriages to hostility, from behaviors that require mutual approval to behaviors imposed by the dominant group.

Genocide

One devastating pattern of intergroup relations is **genocide**—the deliberate, systematic killing of an entire people or nation. This term describes the killing of 1 million Armenians by Turkey beginning in 1915. It is most commonly applied to Nazi Germany's extermination of 6 million European Jews, as well as gays, lesbians, and the Roma ("Gypsies"), during World War II. The term *genocide* is also appropriate in describing the United States' policies toward Native Americans in the 19th century. In 1800, the Native American (or American Indian) population of the United States was about 600,000; by 1850, it had been reduced to 250,000 through warfare with the U.S. cavalry, disease, and forced relocation to inhospitable environments.

The *expulsion* of a people is another means of acting out racial or ethnic prejudice. For example, in 2017, the military of Myanmar (Burma), encouraged by extremist Buddhist monks, carried out genocide against the Rohingya, a Muslim minority. The Rohingya have lived in Myanmar since at least the 8th century, but for years their movement has been restricted, and they have been denied access to education and prohibited from government jobs. Most recently, the government has begun to regard them as illegal immigrants, killing thousands in an effort to push them out of the country.

In a variation of expulsion, called *secession,* failure to resolve an ethnic or racial conflict results in the drawing of formal boundaries between the groups. In 1947, India was partitioned into two separate countries in an attempt to end violent conflict between Hindus and Muslims. The predominantly Muslim areas in the north became the new country of Pakistan; the rest of India became predominantly Hindu.

Hafiz Johari/Shutterstock

Some 600,000 ethnic Rohingya refugees fled their homes in Myanmar after being violently expelled by the military.

Secession, expulsion, and genocide are extreme behaviors, clustered on the negative end of what is called the Spectrum of Intergroup Relations (Figure 10-3). More typical intergroup relations follow four identifiable patterns: (1) segregation, (2) amalgamation, (3) assimilation, and (4) pluralism. Each pattern defines the dominant group's actions and the minority group's responses. Intergroup relations are rarely restricted to only one of the four patterns, although invariably one does tend to dominate. Think of these patterns primarily as ideal types.

Segregation

Separate schools, separate seating on buses and in restaurants, separate washrooms, even separate drinking fountains—these were all part of the lives of African Americans in the South when segregation ruled early in the 20th century. **Segregation** refers to the physical separation of two groups of people in terms of residence, workplace, and social events. Generally, a dominant group imposes this pattern on a minority group. Segregation is rarely complete, however. Intergroup contact inevitably occurs, even in the most segregated societies.

FIGURE 10-3   SPECTRUM OF INTERGROUP RELATIONS

EXPULSION	SEGREGATION	ASSIMILATION
INCREASINGLY UNACCEPTABLE ⇐ ⇦ ⇨ ⇨ MORE TOLERABLE		
EXTERMINATION or genocide SECESSION or partitioning		FUSION or amalgamation or melting pot PLURALISM or multiculturalism

Sources: Prepared by author, Richard T. Schaefer.

From 1948 (when it received its independence) to 1990, the Republic of South Africa severely restricted the movement of Black South Africans and other non-whites by means of a wide-ranging system of segregation known as **apartheid.** Apartheid even included the creation of separate homelands where Black people were expected to live. However, decades of local resistance to apartheid, combined with international pressure, led to marked political changes in the 1990s. In 1994, a prominent Black activist, Nelson Mandela, was elected South Africa's president in the first election in which Blacks (the majority of the nation's population) were allowed to vote. Mandela had spent almost 28 years in South African prisons for his anti-apartheid activities. His election was widely viewed as the final blow to South Africa's oppressive policy of segregation.

In contrast to the enforced segregation in South Africa, the United States exemplifies an unmandated but nevertheless persistent separation of the races. In their book *American Apartheid,* sociologists Douglas Massey and Nancy Denton (1993) described segregation in U.S. cities using 1990 census data. As the book's title suggests, the racial makeup of U.S. neighborhoods resembles the rigid government-imposed segregation that prevailed for so long in South Africa.

Analysis of data shows continuing segregation in the United States. Scholars use a segregation index to measure separation. This index ranges from 0 (complete integration) to 100 (complete segregation), where the value indicates the percentage of the minority group that needs to move for the minority group to be distributed exactly like white people. Thus a segregation index of 60 for Blacks–whites would mean that 60 percent of African Americans would have to move for Blacks to have the same residential pattern as whites. In metropolitan areas such as New York City, St. Louis, Chicago, and Los Angeles, the segregation index is higher than 66 (Frey 2016).

The major change in residential segregation over the last generation has been the trend for suburban communities to become homogeneous—overwhelmingly white or Black or Latino. Representative of this trend is the town of Ferguson, Missouri, a St. Louis suburb whose population changed from 25 percent Black to 65 percent Black in just 20 years. In 2015, Ferguson was rocked by police–civilian encounters and protest following the shooting death of an unarmed Black man, Michael Brown, by a white police officer. The incident drew attention to the overwhelmingly white makeup of the city's police force and government and gave credence to the #BlackLivesMatter social movement. Five years later, Ferguson's newly elected Black mayor said of the protests following the death of George Floyd in Minneapolis that it is crucial that police officers work with communities to make people "feel that they are being served, instead of being hunted" (Holcombe and Padget 2020).

Amalgamation

Amalgamation happens when a majority group and a minority group combine to form a new group. Through intermarriage over several generations, various groups in society combine to form a new group. This pattern can be expressed as A + B + C → D, where A, B, and C represent different groups in a society, and D signifies the end result, a unique cultural-racial group unlike any of the initial groups (W. Newman 1973).

The belief in the United States as a "melting pot" became compelling in the first part of the 20th century, particularly since that image suggested that the nation had an almost divine mission to amalgamate various groups into one people. However, in actuality, many residents were not willing to include Native Americans, Jews, African Americans, Asian Pacific Americans, and Irish Roman Catholics in the melting pot. Therefore, this pattern does not adequately describe dominant–subordinate relations in the United States. There *has* been a significant increase in interracial marriage among whites, Blacks, Asians, and Hispanics in recent years—a trend we will examine in Chapter 12.

Assimilation

In India, many Hindus complain about Indian citizens who copy the traditions and customs of the British. In France, people of Arab and African origin, many of them Muslims, complain they are treated as second-class citizens—a charge that provoked riots from 2006 through 2017. And in the United States, some Italian Americans, Polish Americans, Hispanics, and Jews have changed their ethnic-sounding family names to names that are typically found among white Protestant families.

Barbara Penoyar/Getty Images

Assimilation is the process through which a person forsakes his or her cultural tradition to become part of a different culture. Generally, it is practiced by a minority group member who wants to conform to the standards of the dominant group. Assimilation can be described as a pattern in which A + B + C → A. The majority, A, dominates in such a way that members of minorities B and C imitate it and attempt to become indistinguishable from it (W. Newman 1973).

USE YOUR SOCIOLOGICAL IMAGINATION

A recent comparison study of immigrant groups in the United States, Canada, and Europe found that for the most part, assimilation has progressed further in the United States than in Europe, although more slowly than in Canada. In the United States, the rate of assimilation has generally been constant across groups.

Pluralism

In a pluralistic society, a subordinate group does not have to forsake its lifestyle and traditions to avoid prejudice or discrimination. **Pluralism** is based on mutual respect for one another's cultures among the various groups in a society. This pattern allows a minority group to express its own culture and still participate without prejudice in the larger society. Earlier, we described amalgamation as A + B + C → D, and assimilation as A + B + C → A. Using this same approach, we can conceive of pluralism as A + B + C → A + B + C. All the groups coexist in the same society (W. Newman 1973).

In the United States, pluralism is more of an ideal than a reality. There are distinct instances of pluralism—the ethnic neighborhoods in major cities, such as Koreatown, Little Tokyo, Andersonville (Swedish Americans), and Spanish Harlem—yet there are also limits to cultural freedom. To survive, a society must promote a certain consensus among its members regarding basic ideals, values, and beliefs. Thus, if a Hungarian immigrant to the United States wants to move up the occupational ladder, he or she cannot avoid learning the English language.

Switzerland exemplifies the modern pluralistic state. There, the absence of both a national language and a dominant religious faith leads to a tolerance for cultural diversity. In addition, various political devices safeguard the interests of ethnic groups in a way that has no parallel in the United States. In contrast, Great Britain has had difficulty achieving cultural pluralism in a multiracial society. East Indians, Pakistanis, and Blacks from the Caribbean and Africa experience prejudice and discrimination within the dominant white society there. Some British advocate cutting off all Asian and Black immigration, and a few even call for expulsion of those non-whites currently living in Britain.

THINKING CRITICALLY

Give examples of amalgamation, assimilation, segregation, and pluralism that you have seen at your school or in your community.

Race and Ethnicity in the United States

Few societies have a more diverse population than the United States; the nation is truly a multiracial, multiethnic society. Of course, that has not always been the case. The population of what is now the United States has changed dramatically since the arrival of European settlers in the 1600s, as Figure 10-1 shows. Immigration, colonialism, and in the case of Blacks, slavery, determined the racial and ethnic makeup of our present-day society.

Today, the largest racial minorities in the United States are African Americans, Native Americans, and Asian Pacific Americans. The largest ethnic groups are Latinos, Jews, and the various white ethnic groups. Figure 10-4 shows where the major racial and ethnic minorities are concentrated.

African Americans

"I am an invisible man," wrote Black author Ralph Ellison in his novel *Invisible Man* (1952:3). "I am a man of substance, of flesh and bone, fiber and liquids—and I might even be said to possess a mind. I am invisible, understand, simply because people refuse to see me."

Over six decades later, many African Americans still feel invisible. Despite their large numbers, they have long been treated as second-class citizens. Currently, by the standards of the federal government, more than 1 out of every 5 African Americans—as opposed to 1 out of every 12 white non-Hispanics—is poor (Semega et al. 2019:13).

Contemporary institutional discrimination and individual prejudice against African Americans are rooted in the history of slavery in the United States. Many other subordinate groups had little wealth and income, but as sociologist W. E. B. DuBois ([1909] 1970) and others have noted, enslaved African Americans were in an even more oppressive situation, because by law they could not own property and could not pass on the benefits of their labor to their children. Today, African Americans and sympathetic whites are calling for *slave reparations* to compensate for the injustices of forced servitude. Reparations could include official expressions of apology from governments such as the United States, ambitious programs to improve African Americans' economic status, or even direct payments to descendants of enslaved people. While the economic loss

MAPPING LIFE NATIONWIDE

FIGURE 10-4 MINORITY POPULATION BY COUNTY

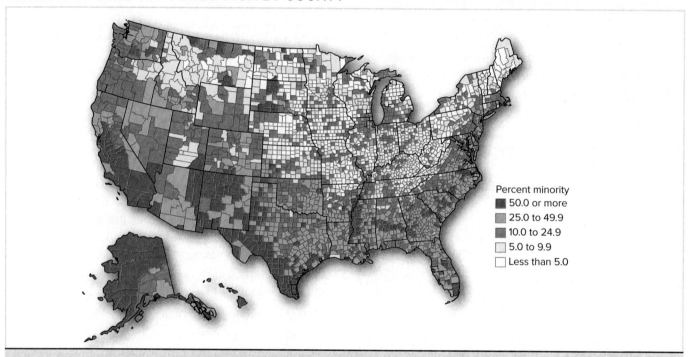

Percent minority
- 50.0 or more
- 25.0 to 49.9
- 10.0 to 24.9
- 5.0 to 9.9
- Less than 5.0

Think about It The United States is a diverse nation. Why, in many parts of the country, can't people see that diversity in their towns?

Source: Jones-Puthoff 2013:Slide 5.

In four states (California, Hawaii, New Mexico, and Texas) and the District of Columbia, as well as in about one out of every nine counties, minorities constitute the numerical majority.

caused by enslavement would easily reach trillions of dollars, the primary reason for discussing reparations tends to focus on the need and appropriateness of an apology (Coates 2014).

The end of the Civil War did not bring genuine freedom and equality for Black Southerners. The Southern states passed Jim Crow laws to enforce official segregation, and the Supreme Court upheld them as constitutional in 1896. In addition, Blacks faced the danger of lynching campaigns, often led by the Ku Klux Klan, during the late 1800s and early 1900s. From a conflict perspective, whites maintained their dominance formally through legalized segregation and informally by means of vigilante terror and violence (Franklin and Higginbotham 2011).

During the 1960s, a vast civil rights movement emerged, with many competing factions and strategies for change. The Southern Christian Leadership Conference (SCLC), founded by Dr. Martin Luther King Jr., used nonviolent civil disobedience to oppose segregation. The Student Nonviolent Coordinating Committee (SNCC) also used nonviolent tactics under the leadership of John Lewis. The National Association for the Advancement of Colored People (NAACP) favored use of the courts to press for equality for African Americans. But many younger Black leaders, most notably Malcolm X, turned toward an ideology of Black power. Proponents of **Black power** rejected the goal of assimilation into white middle-class society. They de-

fended the beauty and dignity of Black and African cultures and supported the creation of political and economic institutions controlled by African Americans (Ture and Hamilton 1992).

Despite numerous courageous actions to achieve Black civil rights, Black and white citizens are still separate, still unequal. From birth to death, Blacks suffer in terms of their life chances. Life remains difficult for millions of poor Blacks, who must attempt to survive in ghetto areas shattered by high unemployment and abandoned housing. Today the median household income of Blacks is still 60 percent that of whites, and the unemployment rate among Blacks is more than twice that of whites. The 2020 coronavirus pandemic only served to exacerbate unemployment differences, as African Americans were disproportionately employed as frontline healthcare workers and in hard-hit sectors such as mass transit, the hospitality industry, and brick and mortar retail outlets.

Some African Americans—especially middle-class men and women—have made economic gains over the past 60 years. For example, data show that the number of African Americans in management increased nationally from 2.4 percent of the total in 1958 to 7.8 percent in 2019. Yet Blacks still represented 7 percent or less of all engineers, web developers, college professors, lawyers, and police officers (Bureau of Labor Statistics 2020b; Riley 2020).

Native Americans

Today, about 2.8 million Native Americans represent a diverse array of cultures distinguishable by language, family organization, religion, and livelihood. The outsiders who came to the United States—European settlers—and their descendants came to know these native peoples' forefathers as "American Indians." By the time the Bureau of Indian Affairs (BIA) was organized as part of the War Department in 1824, Indian–white relations had already included more than two centuries of hostile actions that had led to the virtual elimination of native peoples (see Figure 10-1). During the 19th century, many bloody wars wiped out a significant part of the Indian population. By the end of the century, schools for Indians—operated by the BIA or by church missions—prohibited the practice of Native American cultures. Yet at the same time, such schools did little to make the children effective members of white society.

Today, life remains difficult for members of the 554 tribal groups in the United States, whether they live in cities or on reservations. For example, one Native American teenager in six has attempted suicide—a rate four times higher than the rate for other teenagers. Traditionally, some Native Americans have chosen to assimilate and abandon all vestiges of their tribal cultures to escape certain forms of prejudice. However, since the 1990s, an increasing number of people in the United States were openly claiming a Native American identity. Since 1960, the federal government's count of Native Americans has tripled.

Native Americans have made some progress in redressing their past mistreatment. In 2009, the federal government settled a 13-year-old lawsuit for the recovery of lease payments due on tribal lands used by the government for oil and gas exploration and grazing. Although the $3.4 billion settlement was large, it was long overdue—some of the government's debts dated back to 1887—and from the perspective of tribal leaders, it was too little, too late. The United States is not the only country that has tried to redress the government's past actions toward indigenous peoples (see Box 10-2).

The introduction of gambling on Indian reservations has transformed the lives of some Native Americans. In 1988, Congress passed a law that stipulated that states must negotiate agreements with tribes interested in commercial gaming; they cannot prevent tribes from engaging in gambling operations. The income from gambling operations is not evenly distributed, and it does not necessarily mean that life chances of tribal members are greatly improved. For every success, there are areas where poverty rates have actually increased. In summary, while the advent of gaming has definitely transformed American Indian country, overall economic development still remains a major challenge (Conner and Franklin 2019).

The 2020 BLM protests caused a rethinking of the historical treatment of all people of color in the United States. With this came renewed calls to end the use of mascot names that were

©Peabody Essex Museum, Salem, Massachusetts, USA/Bridgeman Images

Artist David Bradley, a Minnesota Chippewa, shows a Santa Fe Super Chief speeding down a track behind a tribal village that is celebrating a feast day. Tourists watch the dancers, buy fry bread, and frequent a casino (top left of the image). Note the portrayal of inroads on Native American lands: the land development billboard on the right and the bulldozer cutting into a mesa at the top right.

Think about It What message do you think Bradley's painting conveys?

viewed by many to disparage Native Americans. Pressure grew to rename many organizations, from professional sports teams to high school mascots (Davis-Delano et al. 2020).

USE YOUR SOCIOLOGICAL IMAGINATION

You are a Native American whose tribe is about to open a reservation-based casino. Will the casino further the assimilation of your people into mainstream society or encourage pluralism? Explain your reasoning.

Asian Pacific Americans

Asian Pacific Americans are a diverse group, one of the fastest-growing segments of the U.S. population. Among the many groups of Americans of Asian descent are Vietnamese Americans, Chinese Americans, Japanese Americans, and Korean Americans (Figure 10-5).

SOCIOLOGY IN THE GLOBAL COMMUNITY

10-2   The Māori of New Zealand

Virtually all countries with a history of colonization have contemporary populations descended from the original indigenous people. New Zealand in the South Pacific is no exception.

According to current thinking, large-scale movements of Polynesian settlers from several Pacific island groups in the mid-14th century were the origin of today's Māori ("MAOW-ree") people of New Zealand. In a few generations, they developed their own culture, religious practices, and social structure independent of other Polynesian societies. On what is today New Zealand, they lived in tribal groups more or less independent of one another.

However, with the growth of British settlement in the 1700s and the setters' efforts to dominate, the roughly 70,000 native people began a unification movement to better resist further loss of culture and land. Partly in response to this movement to create a unified kingdom, the British launched an invasion in 1863, seizing land on behalf of the Crown. The land was given to colonial soldiers to farm and defend.

The next hundred years were marked by resistance by the Māori people and little acceptance of them by the British, despite their service on behalf of the British in World War I and World War II. Finally, in 1995, the now-independent government of New Zealand gave a full apology, along with some financial compensation, to the Māori people. It also returned portions of Māori land. Nonetheless, tribunals continue to this day

to adjudicate over contested treaties and make agreements toward a "full and final settlement."

Today's Māori population is younger than New Zealand's population as a whole. The Māori currently comprise about 17 percent of New Zealand's population, and that number is slowly growing. Because only 4 percent use the Māori language, efforts to teach it are now under way, with the goal of offering lessons in the language to all students by 2025.

In modern times the Māori people have become increasingly urbanized. In 1936, about 17 percent lived in urban areas, but seventy years later that number had risen to 84 percent. Rural areas still remain significant keepers of the Māori cultural heritage. Regardless, the people face tough economic conditions—20 percent of their children live in poverty, compared to 11 percent of white New Zealanders.

> *Studies show that the openness and sharing nature of the Māori culture often work in the people's favor as they enter the workforce. Also they have begun to take part in entrepreneurial activities.*

There are positive developments. Studies show that the openness and sharing nature of the Māori culture often work in the

Christian J Kober/Alamy Stock Photo

people's favor as they enter the workforce. Also they have begun to take part in entrepreneurial activities. The government has approved some villages to legally grow and sell marijuana as the nation moves toward approving the medicinal use of cannabis. Growing marijuana provides income to economically hard-pressed rural areas while building on the agricultural know-how of the Māori peoples.

LET'S DISCUSS

1. Compare the British treatment of the Maori to that of the U.S. government toward Native Americans. What factors explain the treatment of aboriginal peoples by white settlers? What other examples can you think of?
2. Where would you place today's New Zealand society on the spectrum of intergroup relations? Explain your answer.

Sources: Graham-McLay 2018a, 2018b; Houkamau and Sibley 2019; Reilly et al. 2018; Statistics New Zealand 2019, 2020.

"Asian Americans are a success! They achieve! They succeed! They have no protests, no demands. They just do it!" This is the general image that many people in the United States hold of Asian Pacific Americans as a group. Asian Pacific Americans constitute a **model minority**—a group that, despite past prejudice and discrimination, succeeds economically, socially, and educationally without resorting to political or violent confrontations with whites.

Examining aspects of the educational and economic status of Asian Americans in Box 10-3 allows a more thorough exploration of this view.

Chinese Americans   Unlike enslaved African people and Native Americans, the Chinese were initially encouraged to immigrate to the United States. From 1850 to 1880, thousands of Chinese im-

migrated to this country, lured by job opportunities created by the discovery of gold. However, as employment possibilities decreased and competition for mining jobs grew, the Chinese became the target of a bitter campaign to limit their numbers and restrict their rights. Chinese laborers were exploited, then discarded.

In 1882, Congress enacted the Chinese Exclusion Act, which prevented Chinese immigration and even forbade Chinese in the United States to send for their families. As a result, the Chinese population declined steadily until after World War II. More recently, the descendants of the 19th-century immigrants have been joined by a new influx from Hong Kong and Taiwan. These groups may contrast sharply in their degree of assimilation, desire to live in Chinatowns, and feelings about this country's relations with the People's Republic of China.

FIGURE 10-5   ASIAN PACIFIC AMERICAN POPULATION BY ORIGIN, 2018

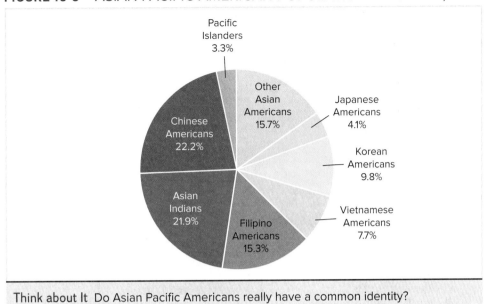

Think about It Do Asian Pacific Americans really have a common identity?

Sources: American Community Survey 2019a: Tables BO2016, BO2018.

Asian Indians are such a diverse population. India, a country of more than 1.3 billion people that is fast becoming the most populous nation in the world, is multiethnic. The Indian government recognizes 18 official languages, each belonging to a people with its own cultural heritage. Some languages can be written in more than one type of script.

Hindus are in the majority, both in India and among immigrants to the United States, but significant religious minorities include Sikhs, Muslims, Jains, and Zoroastrians. Religion among Asian Indians presents a diverse picture. About half (58 percent) are Hindu, 19 percent are Christian, and 10 percent are Muslim. Among initial immigrants, religious orthodoxy often is stronger than it is in India. Many Asian Indians also recognize local practices, with 73 percent of the Hindus in the United States celebrating Christmas.

Although other Indian traditions are maintained, older immigrants see challenges not only from U.S. culture but also from pop culture from India, which is imported through motion pictures and magazines. The situation is very dynamic as the

Currently, about 5.1 million Chinese Americans live in the United States. Some Chinese Americans have entered lucrative occupations, yet many immigrants struggle to survive under living and working conditions associated with the poorest of America's recent immigrants. While the Chinatowns of many large cities are often associated with Chinese Americans living in the United States, the vast majority neither lives nor works in Chinatowns. Most have escaped the poverty and overcrowded housing of these areas or have never experienced them at all.

Nonetheless, Chinatown remains important for many of those who now live outside its borders, although less so than in the past. For many Chinese, movement out of Chinatown is a sign of success. Indeed, a 2019 study showed that Chinese Americans enjoy higher wages when engaged in the same businesses far from Chinatowns. Upon moving out, however, they may encounter discriminatory real-estate practices and white parents' fears about their children playing with Chinese American youths (Liang et al. 2018).

Asian Indians After Chinese Americans, the second-largest Asian Pacific American group, immigrants from India and their descendants, numbers over 4.5 million. It is difficult to generalize about Asian Indian Americans because

Everett Collection/Alamy Stock Photo

Rarely does an Indian American star in, much much less write, her own television show, but Mindy Kaling of *The Mindy Project* (2012-2018) does both. While the Asian American community largely applauded this pathbreaker, some criticized the show because her character dated a white guy. In response, Kaling asked why no one writes about white leads on shows who don't date outside their race. For example, on *Seinfeld* Jerry Seinfeld's character dated over 100 women—all white.

RESEARCH TODAY

10-3   Is There a Model Minority?

Some observers point to Asian Americans as a **model minority**—as an affirmation of the ideal that anyone can get ahead in the United States.

Asian Americans, as a group, do have impressive school-enrollment rates in comparison with the total population. In 2018, 56 percent of Asian Americans 25 years of age or older held bachelor's degrees, compared with 39 percent of the white non-Hispanic population. These rates vary among Asian American groups: Asian Indians, Filipino Americans, Korean Americans, Chinese Americans, and Japanese Americans have higher levels of educational achievement than other Asian American groups. Yet other groups, such as Vietnamese Americans, the Hmong, and Pacific Islanders, including Native Hawaiians, have much lower levels of education than white Americans.

How does this positive stereotype play out in real life? The idea that all Asian American students are academic stars or whiz kids can be burdensome: Asian Americans who do only modestly well in school may face criticism from their parents or teachers for their failure to conform to the whiz kid image. Some Asian American youths receive little support for their interest in vocational pursuits or athletics and may disengage from school altogether when faced with these expectations. As two sociologists observed after doing research at Cupertino, California, schools, an "Asian fail" means receiving a B or B+ on a school assignment, while a "white fail" means an F.

Despite the widespread belief that they constitute a model minority, Asian Pacific Americans are also victims of both prejudice and violence. At issue is what has been termed the "perpetual foreigner" view. After the terrorist attacks of September 11, 2001, and especially with the 2020 Coronavirus epidemic, anti-Asian feelings emerged.

Overall the family income of Asian Pacific Americans approaches parity with that of

Paul Burns/DigitalVision/Getty Images

Despite the widespread belief that they constitute a model minority, Asian Pacific Americans are also victims of both prejudice and violence.

whites because of their greater achievement in formal schooling. If we look at specific educational levels, however, whites earn more than their Asian counterparts of the same age. With each additional year of schooling, Asian Pacific Americans' annual average earnings increase by at least $2,300, whereas whites' earnings increase by almost $3,000. As a group, Asian Pacific Americans have significantly more formal schooling than whites, but they have lower household family income. We should note that some Asian Pacific Americans' education was obtained overseas and, therefore, may be devalued by U.S. employers. Yet, in the end, educational attainment does not pay off as much for Asian Americans as it does for white non-Hispanics.

According to research, the model minority myth seems to be embraced by people who subscribe to color-blind racism—the use of race-neutral principles to defend the racially

unequal status quo. Individuals who view Asian Pacific Americans as uniformly successful are also likely to see discrimination as absent in both school and work; for them, inequality is essentially a thing of the past. The holders of the model minority notion often endorse anti-Asian American sentiments such as seeing them as perpetual foreigners.

Even being regarded as a model minority does not prevent Asian Americans from being scapegoated. During the coronavirus pandemic of 2020, Chinese Americans specifically, and other Asian Americans as well, faced a surge of verbal and physical assaults. Some attackers chose to use the term "Chinese virus" to refer to the cause of the pandemic, thus scapegoating Asians.

As viewed from the conflict perspective, the model minority myth is yet another instance of blaming the victim: If Asian Pacific Americans have succeeded, then Blacks and Latinos must be responsible for their own low status, thus absolving society of any responsibility.

LET'S DISCUSS

1. Explain why being thought of as a member of a model minority may have negative consequences for a person of Asian Pacific American descent.
2. Explain the model minority myth in terms of conflict theory.

Sources: Bureau of the Census 2019b: Table 1; Chou and Feagin 2014; Nguyen, Carter, and Carter 2019; Parks and Yoo 2016; Tavernise and Oppel 2020.

Asian Indian population navigates the 21st century in the United States (Desilver 2014).

Filipino Americans Filipinos are the third-largest Asian American group in the United States, with 4 million people. For geographic reasons, social scientists consider them to be of Asian

extraction, but physically and culturally this group also reflects centuries of Spanish and U.S. colonial rule, as well as the more recent U.S. military occupation.

Filipinos began immigrating to the United States as American nationals when the U.S. government gained possession of the Philippine Islands at the end of the Spanish–American War

(1899). When the Philippines gained their independence in 1948, Filipinos lost their unrestricted immigration rights, although farmworkers were welcome to work in Hawai'i's pineapple groves. Aside from this exception, immigration was restricted to 50 to 100 Filipinos a year until 1965, when the Immigration Act lifted the strict quotas.

Today, a significant percentage of Filipino immigrants are well-educated professionals who work in the field of health care. Although they are a valuable human resource in the United States, their immigration has long drained the medical establishment in the Philippines. When the U.S. Immigration and Naturalization Service stopped giving preference to physicians, Filipino doctors began entering the country as nurses—a dramatic illustration of the incredible income differences between the two countries. Like other immigrant groups, Filipino Americans save much of their income and send a significant amount of money, called **remittances,** back to their extended families.

For several reasons, Filipino Americans have not coalesced in a single formal social organization, despite their numbers. Their strong loyalty to the family (*sa pamilya*) and to the church—particularly Roman Catholicism—reduces their need for a separate organization. Moreover, their diversity complicates the task of uniting the Filipino American community, which reflects the same regional, religious, and linguistic distinctions that divide their homeland. Thus, the many groups that Filipino Americans have organized tend to be club-like or fraternal in nature. Because those groups do not represent the general population of Filipino Americans, they remain largely invisible to Anglos. Although Filipinos remain interested in events in their homeland, they also seek to become involved in broader, non-Filipino organizations and to avoid exclusive activities (McNamara and Batalova 2015; Padilla 2008).

Vietnamese Americans   Vietnamese Americans came to the United States primarily during and after the Vietnam War—especially after U.S. withdrawal from the conflict in 1975. Refugees from the communist government in Vietnam, assisted by local agencies, settled throughout the United States, tens of thousands of them in small towns. Over time, however, Vietnamese Americans have gravitated toward the larger urban areas, establishing Vietnamese restaurants and grocery stores in their ethnic enclaves there.

In 1995, the United States resumed normal diplomatic relations with Vietnam. Gradually, the *Viet Kieu,* or Vietnamese living abroad, began to return to their old country to visit, but usually not to take up permanent residence. Shuttling between two nations, Viet Kieu leave their cultural mark on both countries. Today, almost 50 years after the end of the Vietnam War, sharp differences of opinion remain among Vietnamese Americans, especially the older ones, concerning the war and the present government of Vietnam (Harris 2015; Rkasnuam and Batalova 2014).

Korean Americans   At over 1.8 million, the population of Korean Americans now exceeds that of Japanese Americans. Yet Korean Americans are often overshadowed by other groups from Asia.

Today's Korean American community is the result of three waves of immigration. The initial wave arrived between 1903 and 1910, when Korean laborers migrated to Hawai'i. The second wave followed the end of the Korean War in 1953; most of those immigrants were wives of U.S. servicemen and war orphans. The third wave, continuing to the present, has reflected the admissions priorities set up in the 1965 Immigration Act. These well-educated immigrants arrive in the United States with professional skills. Yet because of language difficulties and discrimination, many must settle at least initially for positions of lower responsibility than those they held in Korea and must suffer through a period of disenchantment. Stress, loneliness, and family strife may accompany the pain of adjustment.

In the early 1990s, the apparent friction between Korean Americans and another subordinate racial group, African Americans, attracted nationwide attention. Conflict between the two groups was dramatized in Spike Lee's 1989 movie *Do the Right Thing.* The situation stemmed from Korean Americans' position as the latest immigrant group to cater to the needs of inner-city populations abandoned by those who have moved up the economic ladder. This type of friction is not new; generations of Jewish, Italian, and Arab merchants have encountered similar hostility from what to outsiders seems an unlikely source—another oppressed minority (K. Kim 1999; Zong and Batalova 2017).

Japanese Americans   Approximately 1.5 million Japanese Americans live in the United States. As a people, they are relatively recent arrivals. In 1880, only 148 Japanese lived in the United States, but by 1920 there were more than 110,000. Japanese immigrants—called the *Issei* (pronounced ee-say), or first generation—were usually males seeking employment opportunities. Many whites saw them (along with Chinese immigrants) as a "yellow peril" and subjected them to prejudice and discrimination.

In 1941, the attack on Hawai'i's Pearl Harbor by Japan had severe repercussions for Japanese Americans. The federal government decreed that all Japanese Americans on the West Coast must leave their homes and report to "evacuation camps." In effect, Japanese Americans became scapegoats for the anger that other people in the United States felt concerning Japan's role in World War II. By August 1943, in an unprecedented application of guilt by virtue of ancestry, 113,000 Japanese Americans had been forced into hastily built camps. In striking contrast, only a few German Americans and Italian Americans were sent to evacuation camps (Hosokawa 1969).

In 1983, a federal commission recommended government payments to all surviving Japanese Americans who had been held in detention camps. The commission reported that the detention was motivated by "race prejudice, war hysteria, and a failure of political leadership." It added that "no documented acts of espionage, sabotage, or fifth-column activity were shown to have been committed" by Japanese Americans. In 1988, President Ronald Reagan signed the Civil Liberties Act, which required the federal government to issue individual apologies for all violations of Japanese Americans' constitutional rights, and established a $1.25 billion trust fund to pay reparations to the approximately 77,500 surviving Japanese Americans who had been interned (Department of Justice 2000).

Arab Americans

Arab Americans are immigrants, and their descendants, from the 22 nations of the Arab world. As defined by the League of

George Rose/Getty Images

In Chicago, a young Muslim woman sports an "I Love New York" T-shirt. Across the United States, racial and ethnic diversity has increased dramatically.

Arab States, these are the nations of North Africa and what is popularly known as the Middle East, including Lebanon, Syria, Palestine, Morocco, Iraq, Saudi Arabia, and Somalia. Not all residents of those countries are Arab; for example, the Kurds, who live in northern Iraq, are not Arab. And some Arab Americans may have immigrated to the United States from non-Arab countries such as Great Britain or France, where their families have lived for generations.

The Arabic language is the single most unifying force among Arabs, although not all Arabs, and certainly not all Arab Americans, can read and speak Arabic. Moreover, the language has evolved over the centuries so that people in different parts of the Arab world speak different dialects. Still, the fact that the Koran (or Qur'an) was originally written in Arabic gives the language special importance to Muslims, just as the Torah's compilation in Hebrew gives that language special significance to Jews.

Estimates of the size of the Arab American community differ widely. Over 2 million people of Arab ancestry reside in the United States. Among those who identify themselves as Arab Americans, the most common country of origin is Lebanon, followed by Syria, Egypt, and Palestine. In 2000, these four countries of origin accounted for two-thirds of all Arab Americans. Their rising numbers have led to the development of Arab retail centers in several cities, including Dearborn and Detroit, Michigan; Los Angeles; Chicago; New York City; and Washington, D.C.

As a group, Arab Americans are extremely diverse. Many families have lived in the United States for several generations; others are foreign born. Their points of origin range from the

FIGURE 10-6   ARAB AMERICAN RELIGIOUS AFFILIATIONS, 2010

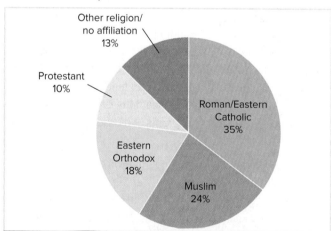

Think about It Are you surprised that most Arab Americans are Christian?

Note: Roman/Eastern Catholic includes Roman Catholic, Maronite, and Melkite (Greek Catholic); Eastern Orthodox includes Antiochian, Syrian, Greek, and Coptic; Muslim includes Sunni, Shi'a, and Druze.
Sources: Arab American Institute 2010, based on 2002 Zogby International Survey.

metropolis of Cairo, Egypt, to the rural villages of Morocco. Despite the stereotype, most Arab Americans are *not* Muslim (Figure 10-6). Nor can Arab Americans be characterized as having a specific family type, gender role, or occupational pattern.

In spite of this great diversity, profiling of potential terrorists at airports has put Arab and Muslim Americans under special surveillance. For years, a number of airlines and law enforcement authorities have used appearance and ethnic-sounding names to identify and take aside Arab Americans and search their belongings. After the terrorist attacks of September 2001 and more recent attacks in Europe and North America, criticism of this practice declined as concern for the public's safety mounted (Shams 2018).

Latinos

Together, the various groups included under the general category *Latinos* or *Hispanics* represent the largest minority in the United States. There are more than 57 million Hispanics in this country, including 36 million Mexican Americans, more than 5 million Puerto Ricans, and smaller numbers of Cuban Americans and people of Central and South American origin (Figure 10-7). The last group represents the fastest-growing and most diverse segment of the Hispanic community.

The rise of the Hispanic population of the United States—fueled by comparatively high birthrates and immigration levels—has Latinos beginning to flex their muscles as voters. In the 2016 presidential election, the Latino population

FIGURE 10-7 HISPANIC POPULATION BY ORIGIN, 2018

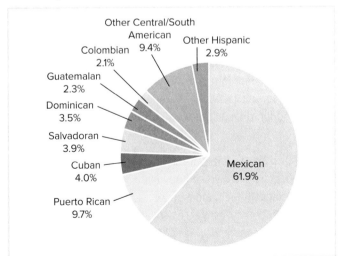

Think about It Do Hispanic Americans really have a common identity?

Note: "Other Hispanic" includes Spanish Americans and Latinos identified as mixed ancestry as well as other Central and South Americans not otherwise indicated by specific country. All nationalities with more than one million in population are specified.
Sources: American Community Survey 2019a:Table BO3001.

accounted for more than 9 percent of eligible voters. As Hispanics age and immigrants become citizens, their presence in the voting booth will be felt even more strongly; see also Box 14-1.

The various Latino groups share a heritage of Spanish language and culture, which can cause serious problems in their assimilation. An intelligent student whose first language is Spanish may be presumed slow or even unruly by English-speaking schoolchildren, and frequently by English-speaking teachers as well. The labeling of Latino children as underachievers, as learning disabled, or as emotionally disturbed can act as a self-fulfilling prophecy for some children. Bilingual education aims at easing the educational difficulties experienced by Hispanic children and others whose first language is not English.

The educational difficulties of Latino students certainly contribute to Hispanics' generally low economic status. In 2019, about 20 percent of all Hispanic households earned less than $25,000, compared with 15 percent of white non-Hispanic households; the poverty rate was 15.7 percent for Hispanics, compared to 7.3 percent for white non-Hispanics. Although Latinos are not as affluent as white non-Hispanics, a middle class is beginning to emerge (Semega et al. 2019: Tables A-2, 6-1).

Mexican Americans The largest Latino population is Mexican Americans, who can be further subdivided into those descended from residents of the territories annexed after the Mexican–American War of 1848 and those who have immigrated from Mexico to the United States. The opportunity for Mexican migrants to earn in one hour in the United States what it would take an entire day to earn in Mexico has pushed millions of legal and unauthorized immigrants north.

Many people view Mexican Americans as primarily an immigrant group. Since at least 2000, however, the number of Mexican Americans who were born in the United States has far exceeded those who immigrated here. Overall, Mexican Americans accounted for half of the nation's population growth

Kevin Sullivan/Digital First Media/Orange County Register/Getty Images

between 2010 and 2017, but the rate of growth has slowed more recently. Two-thirds of them were born here; the other third are new arrivals (Flores 2017).

Puerto Ricans The second-largest segment of Latinos in the United States is Puerto Ricans. Since 1917, residents of Puerto Rico have held the status of American citizens; many have migrated to New York and other eastern cities. Unfortunately, Puerto Ricans have experienced serious poverty both in the United States and on the island. Those who live in the continental United States earn barely half the family income of whites. As a result, many have returned to the island to take advantage of cheaper living conditions and supportive extended families. However, in recent years the economic situation of Puerto Rico has deteriorated to the point that beginning in 2010, the numbers of Puerto Ricans leaving for the mainland U.S. have been increasing (L. Alvarez 2015).

In 2017, the devastation caused by the Category 4 Hurricane Maria underscored the ongoing economic problems facing the island of Puerto Rico. Compared to the mainland states

Steven Petteway, Collection of the Supreme Court of the United States

Sonia Sotomayor was born in the Bronx, New York, of Puerto Rican parents. In 2009 she became the first Hispanic, and one of only four women, ever to be appointed to the U.S. Supreme Court. Of the other 108 justices, two have been African American men and 106 have been white men.

ravaged by hurricanes during the same season, Puerto Rico took much longer to resume telecommunications and electricity, provide basic medical services, restore bridges and roads, and reopen public entities like schools. Then the island was hit by a series of earthquakes in January 2020 that caused few fatalities yet heavily destroyed power plants and once again plunged the population into darkness. Most of the island was facing another long period without dependable electrical power. Ambitious economic restructuring plans were poised to take effect in 2020, just as the coronavirus pandemic hit the mainland economy. As a result the plans were put off indefinitely (Scurria 2020).

Cuban Americans Cuban immigration to the United States dates back as far as 1831, but it began in earnest following Fidel Castro's assumption of power in the Cuban revolution (1959). At the time it was seen as a refugee crisis, much like those described in the policy section at the end of this chapter. The first wave of 200,000 Cubans included many professionals with relatively high levels of schooling; these men and women were largely welcomed as refugees from communist tyranny. However, more recent waves of immigrants have aroused growing concern, partly because they were less likely to be skilled professionals. Throughout these waves of immigration, Cuban Americans have been encouraged to locate around the United States. Nevertheless, many continue to settle in (or return to) metropolitan Miami, Florida, with its warm climate and proximity to Cuba.

The Cuban experience in the United States has been mixed. Cuban Americans in Miami have expressed concern over what they view as the indifference of the city's Roman Catholic hierarchy. Like other Hispanics, Cuban Americans are underrepresented in leadership positions within the church. Beginning in 2013 renewed U.S.–Cuban diplomatic relations led to discussion of easing the movement of both Cuban Americans and Cubans. This policy ended in January 2017, forcing Cubans who wanted to immigrate to the United States to navigate the maze of programs faced by migrants from any other nation, with the added difficulty that visa offices are virtually nonexistent in Cuba.

Central and South Americans Immigrants from Central and South America are a diverse population that has not been closely studied. Indeed, most government statistics treat members of this group collectively as "other," rarely differentiating among them by nationality. Yet people from Chile and Costa Rica have little in common other than their hemisphere of origin and the Spanish language—if that. The fact is, not all Central and South Americans speak Spanish. Immigrants from Brazil, for example, speak Portuguese; immigrants from French Guyana speak French; and immigrants from Suriname speak Dutch.

Racially, many of the nations of Central and South America follow a complex classification system that recognizes a multitude of color gradients. Experience with this multiracial system does not prepare immigrants to the United States for the stark Black–white racial divide that characterizes U.S. society. Beyond their diversity in color and language, immigrants from Central and South America are differentiated by social class distinctions, religious differences, urban or rural upbringings, and dialects. Some of them may come from indigenous populations, especially in Guatemala and Belize. If so, their social identity would be separate from any national allegiance.

In short, social relations among Central and South Americans defy generalization. The same can be said about their relations with other Latinos and with non-Hispanics. Central and South Americans do not form, nor should they be expected to form, a cohesive group. Nor do they easily form coalitions with Cuban Americans, Mexican Americans, or Puerto Ricans.

Jewish Americans

Jews constitute about 2 percent of the population of the United States. They play a prominent role in the worldwide Jewish community, because the United States has the world's largest concentration of Jews. Like the Japanese, many Jewish immigrants came to this country and became white-collar professionals in spite of prejudice and discrimination.

We are considering Jews as an ethnic group, but Jewishness is not only a scholarly question but also a policy issue. Israel's Law of Return extends Israeli citizenship to all Jews (typically anyone who has one Jewish grandparent), including converts to Judaism, but many people there feel it should not apply to converts. Many Jews, in the United States, Israel, and worldwide, are not observant of the faith. Yet overwhelmingly Jews share a cultural and historical tradition.

Anti-Semitism—anti-Jewish prejudice—has often been vicious in the United States, although rarely so widespread and never so formalized as in Europe. In many cases, Jews have been used as scapegoats for other people's failures. Not surprisingly, Jews have not achieved equality in the United States. Despite high levels of education and professional training, they are still conspicuously absent from the top management of large corporations (except for the few firms founded by Jews). Nonetheless, a national survey in 2009 showed that one out of four people in the United States blamed "the Jews" for the financial crisis. In addition, private social clubs and fraternal groups frequently continue to limit membership to Gentiles (non-Jews), a practice upheld by the Supreme Court in the 1964 case *Bell v. Maryland* (Malhotra and Margalit 2009).

The Anti-Defamation League (ADL) of B'nai B'rith publishes an annual survey of reported anti-Semitic incidents. Although the number has fluctuated over the 40 years the ADL has been recording such incidents, there were nearly 1,900 such incidents in 2018. Recently, reports of anti-Semitic incidents have escalated dramatically. Significantly more anti-Semitic incidents have been reported at schools as well as in public places (parks and streets), businesses, colleges, or Jewish institutions. A chilling development is the growing use of social media as a vehicle for anti-Semitism, either delivering such messages or allowing people to reach websites that spread intolerance. The rise of social media has allowed the instantaneous transmission of anti-Semitic messages, informing followers of hate groups where to meet or strike. According to a 2018 study, a staggering 4.2 million anti-Semitic tweets were found in English in just one year—an average of over 81,000 a week (Anti-Defamation League 2018, 2019).

As is true for other minorities discussed in this chapter, Jewish Americans face the choice of maintaining ties to their long religious and cultural heritage or becoming as indistinguishable as possible from Gentiles. Many Jews have tended to assimilate, as is evident from the rise in marriages between Jews and Christians. Before 1970, 83 percent of Jews married another Jew, but since 2000 that percentage has dropped to 42 percent or less. This means

Gordon Chibroski/Portland Press Herald/Getty Images

Although Hebrew schools today continue to teach the Hebrew language and prayers, the emphasis more and more is on traditional Jewish values of social justice and engaging the larger community. These teens from a New York Jewish travel-community service group are writing a wish for world peace on a painting that was inspired by a Hebrew song.

today that American Jews are more likely to marry a Gentile than a Jew (Pew Religion and Public Life 2013).

White Ethnics

A significant segment of the population of the United States is made up of white ethnics whose ancestors arrived from Europe within the last century and a half. The nation's white ethnic population includes about 45 million people who claim at least partial German ancestry, 32 million Irish Americans, 17 million Italian Americans, and 9 million Polish Americans, as well as immigrants from other European nations. Some of these people continue to live in close-knit ethnic neighborhoods, whereas others have largely assimilated and left the "old ways" behind.

David L. Moore–OR/Alamy Stock Photo

White Americans often express their ethnicity with special celebrations, such as this Scandinavian Festival parade in Junction City, Oregon. Participants proudly display the flag of Denmark.

Many white ethnics today identify only sporadically with their heritage. **Symbolic ethnicity** refers to an emphasis on concerns such as ethnic food or political issues rather than on deeper ties to one's ethnic heritage. It is reflected in an Irish American family making a trip to a Celtic heritage festival, Italian Americans celebrating a ceremonial event such as St. Joseph's Day, or Danish Americans joining for a Julefest. Such practices are another example of the social construction of race and ethnicity. Except in cases in which new immigration reinforces old traditions, symbolic ethnicity tends to decline with each passing generation (Bielberg 2017; Gans 1979).

Although a white ethnic identity may be a point of pride to those who share it, it is not necessarily celebrated at the expense of disadvantaged minorities. It is all too easy to assume that race relations are a zero-sum game in which one group gains at the expense of the others. Rather, the histories of several white ethnic groups, such as the Irish and the Italians, show that once-marginalized people can rise to positions of prestige and influence (Alba 2009).

That is not to say that white ethnics and racial minorities have not been antagonistic toward one another because of economic competition—an interpretation that agrees with the conflict approach to sociology. As Blacks, Latinos, and Native Americans emerge from the lower class, they must compete with working-class whites for jobs, housing, and educational opportunities. In times of high unemployment or inflation, any such competition can easily generate intense intergroup conflict.

In many respects, the story of white ethnics raises the same basic issues as that of other subordinate people in the United

States. How ethnic can people be—how much can they deviate from an essentially white, Anglo-Saxon, Protestant norm—before society punishes them for their willingness to be different? Our society does seem to reward people for assimilating, yet as we have seen, assimilation is no easy process. In the years to come, more and more people will face the challenge of fitting in, not only in the United States but around the world, as the flow of immigrants from one country to another continues to increase.

THINKING CRITICALLY

Mexican American culture seems alive in many Mexican American communities. Native Americans routinely display their tribal identities. Why do white ethnic identities seem more elusive?

Immigration and Continuing Diversity

A significant segment of the population of the United States is made up of white ethnics whose ancestors arrived from Europe within the last 150 years. The United States has long had policies to determine who has preference to enter the country. Often, clear racial and ethnic biases are built into these policies. In the 1920s, U.S. policy gave preference to people from western Europe, while making it difficult for residents of southern and eastern Europe, Asia, and Africa to enter the country.

FIGURE 10-8   LEGAL MIGRATION TO THE UNITED STATES, 1820–2020

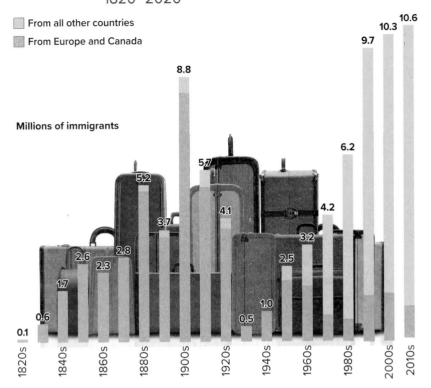

☐ From all other countries
☐ From Europe and Canada

Millions of immigrants

10.6
10.3
9.7
8.8
6.2
5.7
5.2
4.2
4.1
3.7
3.2
2.8
2.6
2.5
2.3
1.7
1.0
0.6
0.5
0.1

1820s 1840s 1860s 1880s 1900s 1920s 1940s 1960s 1980s 2000s 2010s

Sources: Office of Immigration Statistics 2018; author's estimates. pixhook/Getty Images

For the past five decades, the majority of immigrants to the United States have come from outside Europe and Canada.

Since the 1960s, policies in the United States have encouraged the immigration of people who have relatives here as well as of those who have needed skills. This change has significantly altered the pattern of sending nations. Previously, Europeans dominated, but for the last 40 years, immigrants have come primarily from Latin America and Asia (see Figure 10-8). This means that in the future, an ever-growing proportion of the United States will be Asian or Hispanic. To a large degree, fear and resentment of this growing racial and ethnic diversity is a key factor in opposition to immigration. Many people are very concerned that the new arrivals do not reflect how they define the nation's cultural and racial heritage.

Feeling pressure for immigration control, Congress passed the Immigration Reform and Control Act in 1986. The act marked a historic change in the nation's immigration policy. For the first time, hiring unauthorized workers was outlawed, and employers who violated the law were subject to fines and even prison sentences. Just as significant a change was the extension of amnesty and legal status to many unauthorized immigrants already living in the United States.

The act has had mixed results. Substantial numbers of immigrants who gain unauthorized entry continue to enter the country each year. An estimated 10.5 million are present at any given time, a marked increase since 1990, when their

number was around 3.5 million, but lower than the maximum of over 12.2 million reached in 2007. Over 66 percent of unauthorized immigrants have been in the United States at least 10 years and over a third live with U.S.-born children. The presence of unauthorized immigrants has led to a wide array of policy suggestions, from mass deportations and the creation of a wall along the 2,000-mile Mexico–US border to a pathway to full citizenship for those here illegally, after meeting certain criteria and paying hefty fees (Krogstad et al. 2017; Passel 2019)

Despite people's fears, immigration performs many valuable functions. For the receiving society, it alleviates labor shortages such as those that exist in the fields of health care and technology in the United States. For the sending nation, migration can relieve economies unable to support large numbers of people. However, migration may rob a nation of a large proportion of its professional class. Often overlooked are the large amounts of money immigrants send back to their home nations. The World Bank estimates that globally immigrants from developing nations send about $600 billion per year back to their home countries (Ratha et al. 2019).

Immigration can be dysfunctional as well. Although studies generally show that it has a positive impact on the receiving nation's economy, areas that receive high concentrations of immigrants may have difficulty meeting short-term social service needs. Furthermore, when migrants with skills of educational potential leave developing countries, their absence can be dysfunctional for those nations. No amount of money sent back home can make up for the loss of valuable human resources.

In contrast, conflict theorists have noted how much of the debate over immigration is phrased in economic terms. The debate intensifies when the arrivals are of different racial and ethnic backgrounds from the host population. Fear and dislike of "new" ethnic groups divide countries throughout the world, as we will see in the Social Policy section, which focuses on the worldwide challenge of growing numbers of refugees.

THINKING CRITICALLY

On balance, do the functions of immigration to the United States outweigh the dysfunctions? Explain your answer.

socialpolicy and Racial and Ethnic Inequality

Global Refugee Crisis

In October 2015, Christian Fabel, mayor of the German town of Sumte, received an official-sounding e-mail saying that his village needed to take in immediately 1,000 refugees from the Middle East, Africa, and Afghanistan. His wife thought it was a joke, since Sumte had a population of only 102. It was genuine, however. This is only one illustration of the long-standing global refugee crisis (Higgins 2015).

The Office of the United Nations High Commissioner for Refugees (UNHCR) was established on December 14, 1950, and began work in Geneva, Switzerland, on January 1, 1951. Initially, it was given a three-year mandate to help solve the plight of about 1 million European refugees remaining in the aftermath of World War II. After three years the agency was supposed to disband, the refugee problem resolved once and for all. Seventy years later, however, UNHCR is still here, and the plight of the world's uprooted people remains as serious as ever.

Looking at the Issue

As of mid-2019, more than 70 million people worldwide were forcibly displaced as a result of conflict and persecution. This number represents twice the population of Canada. Several additional million people remain displaced because of natural disasters, although updated statistics are not available. About half of the uprooted are refugees who fled their home countries, while the other half are people who remain displaced by conflict within their own homelands—so-called "internally displaced" people (UNHCR 2019).

Refugees are people who live outside their country of citizenship for fear of political or religious persecution. Unlike refugees, immigrants are people who choose to move not because of a direct threat of persecution or death but most often to improve their lives by finding work, going to school, reuniting with family, or some other reasons. Unlike refugees, who cannot safely return home, migrants face no such impediment. If they choose to return home, they will continue to receive the protection of their government.

The United States, insulated by distance from wars and famines throughout much of the world, has been able to be selective about which and how many refugees to welcome. The United States resettles between 56,000 and 85,000 refugees annually and hosted over 1 million refugees between 1990 and 2014. Table 10-3 lists the major sources of refugees to the United States.

According to the United Nations treaty on refugees, which our government ratified in 1968, countries are obliged to refrain from forcibly returning people to territories where their lives or liberty might be endangered. However, it is not always clear whether a person is fleeing for his or her personal safety or to escape poverty. Although people in the latter category may be of humanitarian interest, they do not meet the official definition of refugees and are subject to deportation.

Refugees are people who are granted the right to enter a country while still residing abroad. **Asylees** are foreigners who have already entered a nation and seek protection because of persecution or a

TABLE 10-3   TOP SOURCES OF REFUGEES, 2016 AND 2019

2016		2018	
1. Dem. Rep. of Congo	16,370	1. Dem. Rep. of Congo	12,958
2. Syria	12,587	2. Burma (Myanmar)	9,932
3. Burma (Myanmar)	12,347	3. Ukraine	4,451
4. Iraq	9,880	4. Eritrea	1,757
5. Somalia	9,020	5. Afghanistan	1,198
Total of all countries	84,988		29,916
Ceiling	85,000		35,000

Sources: Mossaad 2019. Tables 1 and 3. Office of Immigration Statistics 2020: Table 14.

well-founded fear of persecution. This persecution may be based on the individual's race, religion, nationality, membership in a particular social group, or political opinion.

Because asylees, by definition, are already here, they are either granted legal entry or returned to their home country. In recent years, sudden and prolonged conflicts in Africa, Asia, and the Middle East have increased by millions the numbers of people who flee their countries without first securing permission before entering neighboring countries. This became especially poignant in 2015, as millions of Syrians, Afghans, and others entered member countries of the European Union, particularly Greece and Hungary.

Applying Sociology

In many countries where refugees seek to settle, the economy is in desperate need of workers. Consequently, refugees could ultimately, even if not in the short run, function to provide a needed economic boost. The 2015 surge of refugees into Europe from Syria, Afghanistan, Iraq, and other war-ravaged countries presents a striking contrast to the relatively older population of western Europe. The hundreds of thousands of predominantly young people are trying to enter a region where the population is older than in almost any other place on earth. Researchers contend that the influx of youthful refugees could be a long-term benefit to an aging Europe, renewing the supply of younger workers who are needed to support the continent's large numbers of retirees (Desilver 2015).

Conflict theorists point out that framing the issue as a "refugee crisis" may inadvertently stigmatize the refugees as the ones responsible for the problem, thus "blaming the victim" (Ryan 1976). The refugees are overwhelmingly the result, not the cause, of civil unrest, warfare, persecution, and poverty. Indeed sometimes affluent industrial countries play a role in creating the social conditions leading to the involuntary mass migrations.

Ed Fischer/CartoonStock

Recently, industrial nations, including the United States, have increased restrictions on accepting refugees.

Initiating Policy

Decisions to open or close a nation's borders are difficult to make. Many countries have sought to develop long-term strategies to head off refugees. These may take the form of providing international assistance to make the social conditions better in the home country or creating livable refugee camps near the origin of the exodus to facilitate movement back when the situations improve. A 2015 summit meeting in Malta with European and African leaders sought to develop a consensus about what could be done to improve life in much of Africa and head off the tens of thousands of young Africans who try to cross a treacherous desert and sea in hope of reaching brighter prospects in Europe (Sengupta 2015).

Deciding where to locate refugees within a country can be critical to both the migrants' successful transition and the host country's willingness to continue to accept refugees in the future. In the 1970s, when the United States accepted Vietnamese refugees at the end of the war there, religious organizations played a critical role in receiving immigrants. As a result, Vietnamese refugees were dispersed throughout the country. Ultimately many resettled in large cities near fellow refugees, but the initial dispersal helped remove concerns that any one area was receiving "too many."

More recently, Chicago and the Dallas–Fort Worth metropolitan areas have received large numbers of Syrian refugees. Nongovernmental agencies assisting with refugee settlement have made a concerted effort to place refugees in more affordable medium-sized cities, and as a result, Boise, Idaho, has accepted more refugees than Los Angeles and New York City combined and Worcester, Massachusetts, has taken in more than Boston. Through 2019, the United States had accepted about 18,000 refugees, a fraction of the nearly 5 million registered with the United Nations (Mossaad 2019; Park 2015).

People in potential receiving countries remain hostile to refugees, especially those from Middle Eastern countries. A series of terrorist attacks in France in 2015 changed Europe's migrant focus from one of compassion to one of concerns about security. The murder of over 130 civilians in Paris left many wondering, there and elsewhere, whether potential terrorists might be hiding among future refugees and ayslees. Hate speech quickly spread across social media.

The challenge facing refugees grew even greater with the coronavirus pandemic of 2020. Conditions in overcrowded temporary refugee camps greatly exacerbated the effects of the virus. In addition, many nations, including the United States, blocked entry even for initial screening until the pandemic passed (Ahmed et al. 2020; S. Smith 2017).

Unfortunately, but predictably, natural disasters, public health challenges, and foreign military campaigns will bring new refugee issues. Measured responses are needed, as are innovative ways to reduce the creation of refugees in the first place.

Take the Issue with You

1. Did you or your family come to the United States as refugees or asylees? Explain the circumstances.

2. Is it fair to say that affluent countries play a role in creating a refugee crisis? Explain your answer.

3. Do you work or take classes with recent refugees to the United States? Are they well accepted into your community? What kinds of prejudice and discrimination do they face?

MASTERING THIS CHAPTER

Summary

The social dimensions of race and ethnicity are important factors in shaping people's lives, both in the United States and in other countries. In this chapter, we examine the meaning of race and ethnicity and study the major **racial** and **ethnic** groups of the United States.

1. A **racial group** is set apart from others by physical differences; an **ethnic group** is set apart primarily by national origin or cultural patterns.

2. When sociologists define a **minority group**, they are concerned primarily with the economic and political power, or powerlessness, of the group.

3. **Prejudice** often but not always leads to **discrimination**. Sometimes, through **color-blind racism**, prejudiced people try to use the principle of racial neutrality to defend a racially unequal status quo.

4. **Institutional discrimination** results from the normal operations of a society.

5. Functionalists point out that discrimination is both functional and dysfunctional for a society. Conflict theorists explain racial subordination through **exploitation theory**. Interactionists pose the **contact hypothesis** as a means of reducing prejudice and discrimination.

6. **Racial profiling** is any arbitrary action initiated by an authority based on race, ethnicity, or national origin rather than on a person's behavior. Based on false stereotypes of certain racial and ethnic groups, the practice is not an effective way to fight crime.

7. Four patterns describe typical intergroup relations in North America and elsewhere: **segregation, amalgamation, assimilation**, and **pluralism**. Pluralism remains more of an ideal than a reality.

8. Contemporary prejudice and discrimination against African Americans are rooted in the history of slavery in the United States.

9. Asian Pacific Americans are the product of the fastest-growing immigration and represent a vast array of cultures.

10. The various groups included under the general term *Latinos* (or *Hispanics*) represent the largest ethnic minority in the United States.

11. Worldwide, immigration is at an all-time high, fueling controversy not only in the United States but in the European Union as well. The sources of immigration to the United States have changed throughout the country's history, but the social issues they ignite remain constant.

12. Conflict and economic turmoil in the developing world have created a continuing immigration crisis in Europe and the United States, as receiving countries struggle to absorb large numbers of **refugees** and **asylees**.

Key Terms

Affirmative action Positive efforts to recruit minority group members or women for jobs, promotions, and educational opportunities. (page 241)

Amalgamation The process through which a majority group and a minority group combine to form a new group. (246)

Anti-Semitism Anti-Jewish prejudice. (257)

Apartheid A former policy of the South African government, designed to maintain the separation of Blacks and other non-whites from the dominant whites. (246)

Assimilation The process through which a person forsakes his or her cultural tradition to become part of a different culture. (247)

Asylees Foreigners who have already entered a receiving country because of persecution of a well-founded fear of persecution. (260)

Black power A political philosophy, promoted by many younger Blacks in the 1960s, that supported the creation of Black-controlled political and economic institutions. (248)

Color-blind racism The use of the principle of race neutrality to defend a racially unequal status quo. (237)

Contact hypothesis An interactionist perspective which states that in cooperative circumstances, interracial contact between people of equal status will reduce prejudice. (244)

Discrimination The denial of opportunities and equal rights to individuals and groups because of prejudice or other arbitrary reasons. (237)

Double consciousness W. E. B. Du Bois's term to refer to the division of an individual's identity into two or more social realities. (243)

Ethnic group A group that is set apart from others primarily because of its national origin or distinctive cultural patterns. (232)

Ethnocentrism The tendency to assume that one's own culture and way of life represent the norm or are superior to all others. (235)

Exploitation theory A Marxist theory that views racial subordination in the United States as a manifestation of the class system inherent in capitalism. (243)

Genocide The deliberate, systematic killing of an entire people or nation. (245)

Glass ceiling An invisible barrier that blocks the promotion of a qualified individual in a work environment because of the individual's gender, race, or ethnicity. (238)

Institutional discrimination or systemic discrimination The denial of opportunities and equal rights to individuals and groups that results from the normal operations of a society. (241)

Minority group A subordinate group whose members have significantly less control or power over their own lives than the members of a dominant or majority group have over theirs. (232)

Model minority A group that, despite past prejudice and discrimination, succeeds economically, socially, and educationally without resorting to political or violent confrontations with whites (250)

Pluralism Mutual respect for one another's cultures among the various groups in a society, which allows minorities to express their cultures without experiencing prejudice. (247)

Prejudice A negative attitude toward an entire category of people, often an ethnic or racial minority. (235)

Racial formation A sociohistorical process in which racial categories are created, inhabited, transformed, and destroyed. (234)

Racial group A group that is set apart from others because of physical differences that have taken on social significance. (232)

Racial profiling Any arbitrary action initiated by an authority based on race, ethnicity, or national origin rather than on a person's behavior. (243)

Racism The belief that one race is supreme and all others are innately inferior. (235)

Redlining The pattern of discrimination against people who try to buy homes in minority and racially changing neighborhoods. (240)

Refugees People living outside their country of citizenship for fear of political or religious persecution. (260)

Remittances The monies that immigrants return to their families of origin. Also called migradollars. (253)

Segregation The physical separation of two groups of people in terms of residence, workplace, and social events; often imposed on a minority group by a dominant group. (245)

Sharing economy Connecting owners of underused assets with others willing to pay to use them. (238)

Stereotype An unreliable generalization about all members of a group that does not recognize individual differences within the group. (236)

Symbolic ethnicity An ethnic identity that emphasizes concerns such as ethnic food or political issues rather than deeper ties to one's ethnic heritage. (258)

White privilege Rights or immunities granted to people as a particular benefit or favor simply because they are white. (239)

1. Watch a show or movie or read a book featuring a character or family that is from a minority group or a community made up mostly of minorities. Make note of the following—treatment, cultural traits, solidarity, and in-group marriage. Alternatively, you could choose a show, movie, or book featuring a white character, family, or community and make note of examples of the privileges they enjoy (probably without even realizing it). Share your findings with the class.

2. Talk with an older relative about your family's past. Did your ancestors experience prejudice or discrimination because of their race or ethnicity, and if so, in what way? Do they feel that attitudes towards their race or ethnicity have changed? Do they feel further change is needed? Share your findings with the class.

3. Do some research about how identifying terms for Hispanics in the United States have changed over time and which terms are currently preferred and by whom. Discuss your findings with the class.

4. **Writing Sociology.** Go to *The Conversation's* website (https://theconversation.com/us) or another reputable site covering current events and read about a topic from this chapter, e.g., Black Lives Matter, slavery reparations, or antisemitism. Summarize the story and share your summary with the class.

Self-Quiz

Read each question carefully and then select the best answer.

1. Sociologists have identified five basic properties of a minority group. Which of the following is *not* one of those properties?
   a. unequal treatment
   b. physical traits
   c. ascribed status
   d. generally marry within one's own group

2. The largest racial minority group in the United States is
   a. Asian Pacific Americans.
   b. African Americans.
   c. Native Americans.
   d. Jewish Americans.

3. Racism is a form of which of the following?
   a. achieved status
   b. discrimination
   c. prejudice
   d. both b and c

4. Suppose that a white employer refuses to hire a qualified Vietnamese American but hires an inferior white applicant. This decision is an act of
   a. prejudice.
   b. ethnocentrism.
   c. discrimination.
   d. stigmatization.

5. Suppose that a workplace requires that only English be spoken, even when it is not a business necessity to restrict the use of other languages. This requirement would be an example of
   a. prejudice.
   b. scapegoating.
   c. a self-fulfilling prophecy.
   d. institutional discrimination.

6. Working together as computer programmers for an electronics firm, a Hispanic woman and a Jewish man overcome their initial prejudices and come to appreciate each other's strengths and talents. This scenario is an example of
   a. the contact hypothesis.
   b. a self-fulfilling prophecy.
   c. amalgamation.
   d. reverse discrimination.

7. Intermarriage over several generations, resulting in various groups combining to form a new group, would be an example of
   a. amalgamation.
   b. assimilation.
   c. segregation.
   d. pluralism.

8. Alphonso D'Abruzzo changed his name to Alan Alda. His action is an example of
   a. amalgamation.
   b. assimilation.
   c. segregation.
   d. pluralism.

9. During World War II, members of which of the following groups were victimized as scapegoats in the United States?
   a. African Americans
   b. Korean Americans
   c. Japanese Americans
   d. Latinos

10. Advocates of *Marxist class theory* argue that the basis for racial subordination in the United States lies within the capitalist economic system. Another representation of this point of view is reflected in which of the following theories?
    a. exploitation
    b. functionalist
    c. interactionist
    d. contact

11. Sociologists consider race and ethnicity to be _____ statuses, since people are born into racial and ethnic groups.

12. The one-drop rule was a vivid example of the social _____ of race—the process by which people come to define a group as a race based in part on physical characteristics, but also on historical, cultural, and economic factors.

13. _____ are unreliable generalizations about all members of a group that do not recognize individual differences within the group.

14. Sociologists use the term _____ to refer to a negative attitude toward an entire category of people, often an ethnic or racial minority.

15. When white Americans can use credit cards without suspicion and browse through stores without being shadowed by security guards, they are enjoying _____.

16. _____ refers to positive efforts to recruit minority group members or women for jobs, promotions, and educational opportunities.

17. After the Civil War, the Southern states passed "_____" laws to enforce official segregation, and the Supreme Court upheld them as constitutional in 1896.

18. In the 1960s, proponents of _____ rejected the goal of assimilation into white, middle-class society. They defended the beauty and dignity of Black and African cultures and supported the creation of Black-controlled political and economic institutions.

19. _____ _____ refers to an emphasis on concerns such as ethnic food or political ties rather than deeper ties to one's ethnic heritage.

20. Collectively, Mexican Americans and Puerto Ricans are a part of a larger ethnic group called _____.

_____

Stratification by Gender and Sexuality

Jupiterimages/Getty Images

Gender stratification exists in all societies. Around the world, most occupations are dominated by either men or women.

▶ INSIDE

Social Construction of Gender

Labeling and Human Sexuality

Sociological Perspectives on Gender

Women: The Oppressed Majority

The Workforce of the United States

Emergence of a Collective Consciousness

Social Policy and Gender Stratification: Workplace Sexual Harassment

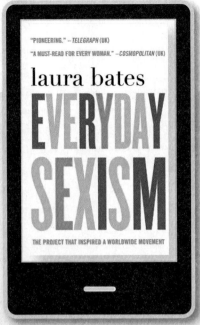

Ira C. Roberts

> What constitutes sexism or sexual harassment?
>
> In her book *Everyday Sexism*, Laura Bates showed that a series of continual "tiny pinpricks" are just as effective at subjugating women as are more overt actions.

" The funny thing is that when [my revelation] came, in March 2012, it wasn't something dramatic or extreme, or even particularly out of the ordinary. It was just another week of little pinpricks: the man who appeared as I sat outside a café, seized my hand, and refused to let go; the guy who followed me off the bus and lewdly propositioned me all the way to my front door. I started for the first time really thinking about how many of these little incidents I was putting up with from day to day.

I recalled the boss who'd sent me strange e-mails about his sexual fantasies and mysteriously terminated my freelance contract with no explanation almost immediately after learning I had a boyfriend. The senior colleague who, on my first day working as an admin temp—age just seventeen—propositioned me via the company's internal e-mail system. The answer was that these events were normal. They hadn't seemed exceptional enough for me to object to them because they weren't out of the ordinary. Because this kind of thing was just part of life—or, rather, part of being a woman.

And I started to wonder how many other women had had similar experiences and, like me, had just accepted them and rationalized them and got on with it without stopping to protest or ask why.

So I started asking around—among friends and family, at parties, even in the supermarket. Over the course of a few weeks, I asked every woman I met whether she'd ever encountered this sort of problem. I honestly thought that if I asked twenty or thirty women, one or two would remember something significant from the past.

What actually happened took me completely by surprise. Every single woman I spoke to had a story. And they weren't just random one-time events but reams and reams of tiny pinpricks—just like my own experiences. Yet put them together and the picture created by this mosaic of miniatures was strikingly clear. This inequality, this pattern of casual intrusion whereby women could be leered at, touched, harassed, and abused without a second thought, was sexism: implicit, explicit, commonplace, and deep-rooted, pretty much everywhere you'd care to look.

The more stories I heard, the more I tried to talk about the problem. And yet time and time again I found myself coming up against the same response: Women are equal now, more or less. You're making a fuss about nothing. You're overreacting.

You really need to learn to take a compliment.

Gradually, as I became more aware of the sheer scale of the problem, people didn't want to acknowledge it, or talk about it—in fact, they often simply refused, point-blank, to believe it still existed. And it wasn't just men who took this view; it was women, too—telling me I was getting worked up about nothing, or being oversensitive, or simply looking for problems where there weren't any. "

Source: Bates 2014: 1–3.

Every single woman I spoke to had a story. And they weren't just random one-time events but reams and reams of tiny pinpricks—just like my own experiences.

British writer Laura Bates launched a website in 2012 seeking examples of everyday sexism. Within three years she had 100,000 entries from people around the world. The circumstances take place in the workplace, in schools at all levels, at parties, on the street, at athletic events, and on social media. While most postings are women describing their being victimized, there are men who also come forward about their being subjected to inappropriate treatment just because they are men. As Bates (2014:325) says of her Everyday Sexism Project, "This is not a men-versus-women issue. It's about people versus prejudice" (Everyday Sexism Project 2020; Sanghani 2015).

How is treatment of women and men regarded today? Are women in the United States still oppressed because of their gender? Have men's and women's positions in society changed? How do gender roles differ from one culture to another? In this chapter we will study these and other questions by looking first at how various cultures, including our own, assign women and men to particular social roles. We'll consider the complexity of human sexual behavior, both gay and straight, as well as other sexual identities. Then we will address the sociological explanations for gender stratification. We will see that around the world, women constitute an oppressed majority of the population. We'll learn that women have developed a collective consciousness of their oppression and the way in which their gender combines with other factors to create social inequality. Finally, we will close the chapter with a Social Policy section on workplace sexual harassment.

Social Construction of Gender

How many airline passengers do you think are startled on hearing a female captain's voice from the cockpit? What do we make of a father who announces that he will be late for work because his son has a routine medical checkup? Consciously or unconsciously, we are likely to assume that flying a commercial plane is a *man's* job and that most parental duties are, in fact, a *woman's*. Gender is such a routine part of our everyday activities that we typically take notice only when someone deviates from conventional behavior and expectations.

Although a few people begin life with an unclear sexual identity, the overwhelming majority begin with a definite sex and quickly receive societal messages about how a person of that sex should behave. In fact, virtually all societies have established social distinctions between females and males that do not inevitably result from biological differences between the sexes (such as women's reproductive capabilities).

In studying gender, sociologists are interested in the gender-role socialization that leads females and males to behave differently. In Chapter 4, **gender roles** were defined as expectations regarding the proper behavior, attitudes, and activities of males and females. The application of dominant gender roles leads to many forms of differentiation between women and men. Both sexes are capable of learning to cook and sew, yet most Western societies determine that women should perform those tasks. Both men and women are capable of learning to weld and to fly airplanes, but those functions are generally assigned to men.

As we will see throughout this chapter, however, social behavior does not mirror the mutual exclusivity suggested by these gender roles. Nor are gender roles independent: in real life, the way men behave influences women's behavior, and the way women behave affects men's behavior. Thus, most people do not display strictly "masculine" or "feminine" qualities all the time. Indeed, such standards can be ambiguous. For instance, though men are supposed to be unemotional, they are allowed to become emotional when their favorite athletic team wins or loses a critical game. Yet our society still focuses on "masculine" and "feminine" qualities as if men and women must be evaluated in those terms. Despite recent inroads by women into male-dominated occupations, our construction of gender continues to define significantly different expectations for females and males.

Gender roles are evident not only in our work and behavior but also in how we react to others. We are constantly "doing gender" without realizing it. If the father mentioned earlier sits in the doctor's office with his son in the middle of a workday, he will probably receive approving glances from the receptionist and from other patients. "Isn't he a wonderful father?" runs through their minds. But if the boy's mother leaves *her* job and sits with the son in the doctor's office, she will not receive such silent applause.

We socially construct our behavior so as to create or exaggerate male–female differences. For example, men and women come in a variety of heights, sizes, and ages. Yet traditional norms regarding marriage and even casual dating tell us that in heterosexual couples, the man should be older, taller, and wiser than the woman. As we will see throughout this chapter, such social norms help to reinforce and legitimize patterns of male dominance.

Gender Roles in the United States

Gender-Role Socialization Male babies get blue blankets; females get pink ones. Boys are expected to play with trucks, blocks, and toy soldiers; girls receive dolls and kitchen goods. Boys must be masculine—active, aggressive, tough, daring, and dominant—but girls must be feminine—soft, emotional, sweet, and submissive. These traditional gender-role patterns have been influential in the socialization of children in the United States.

An important element in traditional views of proper "masculine" and "feminine" behavior is **homophobia,** fear of and prejudice against homosexuality.

Gideon Mendel/Corbis/Getty Images

Gender roles discourage men from entering certain low-paying female-dominated occupations, such as child care. Only 7 percent of day-care workers are male (Bureau of Labor Statistics 2020b).

TABLE 11-1   COMPARISON OF PRIMARY AND SECONDARY GROUPS

Norm Violations by Women	Norm Violations by Men
Send men flowers	Wear fingernail polish
Spit in public	Do needlepoint in public
Use men's bathroom	Throw housewares party
Buy jock strap	Cry in public
Buy/chew tobacco	Have pedicure
Talk knowledgeably about cars	Apply to babysit
Open doors for men	Shave body hair

Think about It Do you agree that these behaviors test the boundaries of conventional gender behavior? How have those standards changed since the experiment was completed in 2000?

Sources: Adapted by author from Kunkel 2016 and Nielsen et al. 2000:287.

In an experiment testing gender-role stereotypes, sociology students were asked to behave in ways that might be regarded as violations of gender norms, and to keep notes on how others reacted. This is a sample of their choices of behavior over a seven-year period.

Homophobia contributes significantly to rigid gender-role socialization, since many people stereotypically associate male homosexuality with femininity and lesbianism with masculinity. Consequently, men and women who deviate from traditional expectations about gender roles are often presumed to be gay. Despite the advances made by the LGBTQ movement, the continuing stigma attached to homosexuality in our culture places pressure on all males (whether gay or not) to exhibit only narrow masculine behavior and on all females (whether lesbian or not) to exhibit only narrow feminine behavior.

It is *adults,* of course, who play a critical role in guiding children into those gender roles deemed appropriate in a society. Parents are normally the first and most crucial agents of socialization. But other adults, older siblings, the mass media, and religious and educational institutions also exert an important influence on gender-role socialization, in the United States and elsewhere.

It is not hard to test how rigid gender-role socialization can be. Just try transgressing some gender norm—say, by smoking a cigar in public if you are female, or by carrying a purse if you are male. That was exactly the assignment given to sociology students at the University of Colorado and Luther College in Iowa. Profes sors asked students to behave in ways that they thought violated the norms of how a man or woman should act. The students had no trouble coming up with gender-norm transgressions (Table 11-1), and they kept careful notes on others' reactions to their behavior, ranging from amusement to disgust.

Women's Gender Roles How does a girl develop a feminine self-image, while a boy develops one that is masculine? In part,

dpa picture alliance archive/Alamy Stock Photo

Women's roles have undergone major rethinking in the United States. In 2004 Army reservist Tammy Duckworth, who was elected to Congress in 2012 and to the Senate in 2016, was co-piloting a Black Hawk helicopter in Iraq when a rocket-propelled grenade hit the aircraft and severely wounded her; she lost both legs. At the time, although women in uniform often served in dangerous roles, they were officially banned from combat operations.

they do so by identifying with females and males in their families and neighborhoods and in the media. If a young girl regularly sees female television characters of all ages and body types, she is likely to grow up with a normal body image. And it will not hurt if the women she knows—her mother, sister, parents' friends, and neighbors—are comfortable with their body types, rather than constantly obsessed with their weight. In contrast, if this young girl sees only wafer-thin actresses and models on television, her self-image will be quite different. Even if she grows up to become a well-educated professional, she may secretly regret falling short of the media stereotype—a thin, sexy young woman in a bathing suit.

Television is far from alone in stereotyping women. Studies of children's books published in the United States in the 1940s, 1950s, and 1960s found that females were significantly underrepresented in central roles and illustrations. Virtually all female characters were portrayed as helpless, passive, incompetent, and in need of a strong male caretaker. Studies of picture books published from the 1970s through the present have found some improvement, but males still dominate the central roles. While males are portrayed as a variety of

Liderina/Shutterstock

Recent national surveys show that both men and women prefer working outside of the home rather than engaging in full-time child care.

characters, females tend to be shown mostly in traditional roles, such as mother, grandmother, or volunteer, even if they also hold nontraditional roles, such as working professional.

Traditional gender roles have restricted females more severely than males. This chapter shows how women have been confined to subordinate roles in the political and economic institutions of the United States. Yet it is also true that gender roles have restricted males. A valuable area of research is to explore the ways in which women and men are represented in new media, including those created and distributed by users (Collins 2011; Etaugh 2003).

Men's Gender Roles Stay-at-home fathers? Until recent decades such an idea was unthinkable. Yet in a 2019 nationwide survey, 26 percent of employed men with children at home said that they preferred to stay at home and take care of the house and family. That lifestyle preference is more common among women, however; 36 percent of employed women said they preferred to stay at home with children. But while people's conceptions of gender roles are obviously changing, the fact is that men who stay at home to care for their children are still an unusual phenomenon. In 2019, among married couples with children under 18, both parents worked in 67 percent of all households, the mother stayed at home in 27 percent, and the father stayed at home in just 6 percent (American Community Survey 2019a: Table B23007; Brenan 2019b).

While attitudes toward parenting may be changing, studies show little change in the traditional male gender role. Men's roles are socially constructed in much the same way as women's are. Family, peers, and the media all influence how a boy

or man comes to view his appropriate role in society. The male gender role, besides being antifeminine (no "sissy stuff"), includes proving one's masculinity at work and sports—often by using force in dealing with others—as well as initiating and controlling all sexual relations (Coontz 2012).

Males who do not conform to the socially constructed gender role face constant criticism and even humiliation, both from children when they are boys and from adults as men. It can be agonizing to be treated as a "chicken" or a "sissy" as a youth—particularly if such remarks come from one's father or brothers. And grown men who pursue nontraditional occupations, such as preschool teaching or nursing, must constantly deal with others' misgivings and strange looks. In one study, interviewers found that such men frequently had to alter their behavior to minimize others' negative reactions. One 35-year-old nurse reported that he had to claim he was "a carpenter or something like that" when he "went clubbing," because women weren't interested in getting to know a male nurse. The subjects made similar accommodations in casual exchanges with other men (Cross and Bagilhole 2002:215).

At the same time, boys who successfully adapt to cultural standards of masculinity may grow up to be inexpressive men who cannot share their feelings with others. They remain forceful and tough, but as a result they are also closed and isolated. In fact, a small but growing body of scholarship suggests that for men as well as women, traditional gender roles may be disadvantageous. In many communities across the nation, girls seem to outdo boys in high school, grabbing a disproportionate share of the leadership positions, from valedictorian to class president to yearbook editor—everything, in short, except captain of the boys' athletic teams. Their advantage continues after high school. In the 1980s, girls in the United States became more likely than boys to go to college. Since then, women have consistently accounted for 54 to 57 percent of first-year students at community colleges and four-year colleges. This trend is projected to continue through at least 2028 (National Center for Education Statistics 2019d).

USE YOUR SOCIOLOGICAL IMAGINATION

What evidence can you see of women's changing roles over the past few generations?

STR/EPA/Newscom

Being harassed or groped on public transit is a problem for women all over the world. In Tokyo, separate subway cars are reserved for women to protect them from sex offenses.

Around the world, anthropologists have documented highly diverse constructions of gender that do not always conform to our ideals of masculinity and femininity. Beginning with the path-breaking work of Margaret Mead ([1935] 2001) and continuing through contemporary fieldwork, these scholars have shown that gender roles can vary greatly from one physical environment, economy, and political system to the next.

In any society, gender stratification requires not only individual socialization into traditional gender roles within the family, but also the promotion and support of those traditional roles by other social institutions, such as religion and education. Moreover, even with all major institutions socializing the young into conventional gender roles, every society has women and men who resist and successfully oppose the stereotypes: strong women who become leaders or professionals, gentle men who care for children, and so forth. It seems clear that differences between the sexes are not dictated by biology. Indeed, the maintenance of traditional gender roles requires constant social controls—and those controls are not always effective.

Aside from these disadvantages, many men find that traditional masculinity does not serve them well in the job market. The growth of a service economy over the past two generations has created a demand for skills, attitudes, and behaviors that are the antithesis of traditional masculinity. Increasingly, this sector is the place where low-skilled men must look for jobs. As a British study showed, many out-of-work men are reluctant to engage in the kind of sensitive, deferential behavior required by service sector jobs (Nixon 2009).

In the past 50 years, inspired in good part by the contemporary feminist movement (examined later in the chapter), increasing numbers of men in the United States have criticized the restrictive aspects of the traditional male gender role. Some men have taken strong public positions in support of women's struggle for full equality and have even organized voluntary associations for the purpose. However, their actions have been countered by other men who feel they are unfairly penalized by laws related to alimony, child support and custody, sexual harassment, family violence, and affirmative action (Kimmel 2008; National Organization for Men Against Sexism 2020).

The construction of gender is different in different cultures, but it also undergoes change in the same culture over time. However, questioning gender roles is not without controversy even in a liberal, industrial country like Sweden, as we see in Box 11-1. "Gender neutral" can become the basic everyday curriculum (UN Women 2016).

THINKING CRITICALLY

Compare the social construction of gender with the social construction of race.

Cross-Cultural Perspective

To what extent do actual biological differences between the sexes contribute to the cultural differences associated with gender? This question brings us back to the debate over "nature versus nurture." In assessing the alleged and real differences between men and women, it is useful to examine cross-cultural data.

Labeling and Human Sexuality

Gender roles are a very important part of how we interact in everyday life, but they do not actually define who we are or how we see ourselves. The relationship between gender roles and our self-identity is complex. As we have seen, gender roles involve cultural expectations that we learn through social interaction with other members of society.

SOCIOLOGY IN THE GLOBAL COMMUNITY

11-1 No Gender, Please: It's Preschool!

Few schools receive as much global attention as did Egalia, a small, co-educational, state-supported preschool that opened in Stockholm, Sweden, in 2010. Egalia follows a curriculum that omits gender designations. Some of the school's practices are not unusual in today's educational environment: both boys and girls are encouraged to use cooking utensils, build with blocks, and play with dolls and trucks. Blue and pink designations are absent. But in addition, at Egalia staff members avoid using words like "him" or "her" (*han* or *hon* in Swedish). They use the gender-neutral personal pronoun, *hen*, instead, to create a more egalitarian and inclusive atmosphere. In 2015, the Swedish national encyclopedia accepted *hen* as a gender-neutral personal pronoun.

From the color and placement of toys to the choice of books, every detail has been carefully planned to make sure the children don't fall into conventional gender stereotypes. "Society expects girls to be girlie, nice and pretty and boys to be manly, rough and outgoing," says Jenny Johnsson, a 31-year-old teacher. "Egalia gives them a fantastic opportunity to be whoever they want to be."

Some parents worry things have gone too far. An obsession with obliterating gender roles, they say, could make the children confused and ill-prepared to face the world outside kindergarten. Since 1998 Swedish preschools have been mandated by law to counteract traditional gender roles and gender patterns. However, preschools often reproduce rather than counteract these gender roles and patterns. Many Swedes

georgi1969/iStock/Getty Images Plus/Getty Images

From the color and placement of toys to the choice of books, every detail has been carefully planned to make sure the children don't fall into conventional gender stereotypes.

think that preschools are not working hard enough to counteract traditional gender roles and patterns. The government mandate is purposefully vague, so that unless a school has a very committed staff, as at Egalia, traditional gender roles emerge.

Egalia works to create conditions for children to grow up free from expectations based on their gender. Consequently, criticism abounds. At the beginning, anonymous threats to employees and break-ins were widely covered in the media. Some dismissed the school as an elite project that failed to address the real needs of society.

Praise was easy to find too. The preschool maintains a waiting list. Internationally Egalia has been showcased as a model for all preschools and its gender approach has been considered a resource for educating preschool employees.

Some scholars had speculated that while the gender-neutral curriculum may please the parents, it will have no lasting impact on the children. Yet initial research shows a tremendous increase in everyday use of gender-neutral pronouns in Swedish conversations. *Hen* is now so common that its use is no longer a distraction. While there is only so much a three-letter word can do, it does appear to cause people to rethink the construction of gender.

It would be interesting to study the long-term impact of an Egalia-like education. Perhaps it will help eliminate gender differences, or perhaps the influence of the mass media and experiences outside the school will undercut the mission of such programs.

LET'S DISCUSS

1. Think back to your early educational experiences (day care, preschool, and kindergarten). Did they reinforce or help eliminate societal gender-role stereotypes?
2. To what extent do you think preschool or education in general can change gender-role stereotypes?

Sources: Acar Erdol 2019; Asklöv 2019; Noack 2015; Scott 2017; Soffel 2011.

Gender and Human Sexuality

Related but different are gender identity and sexual identity. **Gender identity** refers to how people see themselves: as male or female or something else. This identity can be different from one's biological sex at birth, although most people develop a gender identity that conforms to that biological identity.

Sexual identity, also referred to as sexual orientation, is the self-awareness of being romantically or sexually attracted to a defined group of people. Typically, people become aware of

Stefanie Keenan/Daily Front Row/Entertainment/Getty Images

Lady Gaga's hit single "Born This Way" was written as an anthem to diversity and acceptance of all people, including gays and lesbians. Famously, she sang a duet of her hit "Fashion" with drag performer RuPaul and appeared on his TV show, *RuPaul's Drag Race*.

their gender identity at a very young age, but a strong sexual identity may not emerge until well into adolescence.

Society's recognition that gender is not necessarily fixed at birth as either male or female and that individuals are not automatically heterosexual has emerged only in the last generation, perhaps, and even in the last 10 years. Today, online sites routinely include or solicit descriptions of almost any kind of human sexuality. Increasing numbers of jurisdictions around the world accept same-sex marriage on equal footing with traditional heterosexual marriage. Beginning in 2014, Facebook offered, instead of the original two choices of self-designation (male or female), 50 designations that users could choose for gender identity.

Despite this recognition in social media of a broadening of sexual identities, society is only just beginning to avoid stigmatizing people who do not conform to the either/or male–female paradigm. Until recently, these individuals have occupied a lower position in the social stratification hierarchy.

Labeling and Identity

We have seen how society singles out certain groups of people by labeling them in positive or negative ways—as "good kids" or "delinquents," for example. Labeling theorists have also studied how labels are used to sanction certain sexual behaviors as "deviant."

The definition of deviant sexual behavior has varied significantly over time and in different cultures. Until 1973, the American Psychiatric Association considered homosexuality a "sociopathic personality disorder," which in effect meant that homosexuals should seek therapy. Two years later, however, the association removed homosexuality from its list of mental illnesses. Today, the organization publicly proclaims that "being gay is just as healthy as being straight." To use Goffman's term, mental health professionals have removed the *stigma* from this form of sexual expression. As a result, in the United States and many other countries, consensual sex between same-sex adults is no longer a crime (American Psychological Association 2008; OutRight Action International 2020).

Despite the change in health professionals' attitudes, however, the social stigma of homosexuality lingers. As a result, many people prefer the more positive terms *gay* and *lesbian*. Others, in defiance of the stigma, have proudly adopted the pejorative term *queer* in a deliberate reaction to the ridicule they have borne because of their sexual identity. Still others maintain that constructing one's sexual identity as either homosexual or heterosexual is too limiting. Indeed, such labels ignore those who are *bisexual*, or sexually attracted to both sexes.

Placing gays and lesbians on equal footing in the stratification system with heterosexuals is just one part of reducing stratification by sex. We are only just beginning to address the disadvantages involved in other sexual identities, such as transgender.

Many people find the male and female categories either too restrictive or inaccurate descriptions of how they identify. In the United States and many other societies, we are moving

Brandon Thibodeaux/The New York Times/Redux Pictures

Many people assume that individuals who defy the traditional labels of male-female are either relatively young or the subject of tabloid media. For most transgender people this is not the case. Phyllis Frye has served as a judge in the Houston municipal courts since 2010 after a lifetime of personal and professional struggle. She transitioned from male to female in the 1970s.

toward a gender spectrum where, while many people identify themselves as either male or female, many others see themselves as somewhere between these two traditional fixed categories. One such a group is *transgendered persons,* or those whose current gender identity does not match their physical identity at birth. Some transgendered people see themselves as both male and female. Others, called *transexuals,* may take hormones or undergo surgery in an effort to draw physically closer to their chosen gender identity. Transgendered people are sometimes confused with *transvestites,* or cross-dressers who wear the clothing of the opposite sex. Transvestites are typically men, either gay or heterosexual, who choose to wear women's clothing.

The use of these terms even in a positive or nonjudgmental way is problematic, since they still imply that human sexuality can be confined in neat, mutually exclusive categories. Moreover, the destigmatization of these labels tends to reflect the influence of the socially privileged—that is, the affluent—who have the resources to overcome the stigma. In contrast, the traditional Native American concept of the *two spirit,* a personality that blends the masculine and the feminine, has been largely ridiculed or ignored (Hines 2018).

What does constitute sexual deviance, then? The broadening of sexual identities beyond the traditional heterosexual categories means that people may more openly express who they are sexually as well as engage in consensual relationships that in the past were considered wrong or even criminal. The answer to the question of what is deviance seems to change with each generation.

Transgender people have recently experienced public expressions of acceptance, but stigmatization continues. In both the private and public sectors, efforts have been made to allow transgender people to use the bathrooms that correspond with their gender identity, yet some legislators have sought to require people to use bathrooms that match the sex on their original birth certificates, regardless of how they identify themselves. The willingness of state governments to allow people to indicate that they are neither male nor female on their officially issued driver's licenses is an implicit recognition of gender fluidity. As of 2020 at least 18 states and District of Columbia offered such an option, which can affect a person's ability to vote without difficulty (Fielding 2020).

THINKING CRITICALLY

What are some consequences for society as a whole of recognizing that sexual identity exists along a continuum?

Reliable information about people's desire to discriminate on the basis of sexual identity or sexual orientation is difficult to obtain and consequently is almost totally lacking. Consequently, scholars must use innovative research methods to attempt to measure differential treatment between members of the LGBTQ community and heterosexuals. In Box 11-2, we consider some of this recent research.

Sociological Perspectives on Gender

Cross-cultural studies indicate that societies dominated by men are much more common than those in which women play the decisive role. Sociologists have turned to all the major theoretical perspectives to understand how and why these social distinctions are established. Each approach focuses on culture rather than biology as the primary determinant of gender differences. Yet in other respects, advocates of these sociological perspectives disagree widely.

Functionalist Perspective

Functionalists maintain that gender differentiation has contributed to overall social stability. Sociologists Talcott Parsons and Robert Bales (1955) argued that to function most effectively, the family requires adults who specialize in particular roles. They viewed the traditional gender roles as arising out of the need to establish a division of labor between marital partners.

Parsons and Bales contended that women take the expressive, emotionally supportive role and men the instrumental, practical role, with the two complementing each other. **Expressiveness** denotes concern for the maintenance of harmony and the internal emotional affairs of the family. **Instrumentality** refers to an emphasis on tasks, a focus on more distant goals, and a concern for the external relationship between one's family and other social institutions. According to this theory, women's interest in expressive goals frees men for instrumental tasks, and vice versa. Women become anchored in the family as wives, mothers, and household managers; men become anchored in the occupational world outside the home. Of course, Parsons and Bales offered this framework in the 1950s, when many more women were full-time homemakers than is true today. These theorists did not explicitly endorse traditional gender roles, but they implied that dividing tasks between spouses was functional for the family as a unit.

Given the typical socialization of women and men in the United States, the functionalist view is initially persuasive. However, it would lead us to expect girls and women who have no interest in children to nevertheless become babysitters and mothers. Similarly, males who love spending time with children might be programmed into careers in the business world. Such differentiation might harm the individual who does not fit into prescribed roles, as well as deprive society of

RESEARCH TODAY

11-2   Measuring Discrimination Based on Sexual Identity

How do we measure discrimination based on sexual identity when people who are victimized are reluctant to come forward for fear of attracting further hostility? *Audit studies* are a type of experiment used in the social sciences to create matched cases and test for discrimination. As described in Chapter 10, Devah Pager conducted an audit study to document the willingness of employers to interview a hypothetical white man with jail time versus a Black man with no jail time.

Two audit studies have measured discrimination experienced by gay men, lesbians, transgender individuals, and bisexuals. The first involved gay male job seekers. Researchers send a pair of résumés in response to job postings in seven states. In one version of the résumé, the applicant had an important leadership position in a gay organization while in high school, whereas the other applicant had a similar position but in the "Progressive and Socialist Alliance." The results were:

- 7.5 percent of gay males received a call-back, whereas
- 11.5 percent of non-gay males received a callback.

What about applicants for jobs at organizations that specifically prohibit discrimination based on sexual orientation? The results were quite similar:

- 8.7 percent of gay males received a call-back, whereas

- 11.6 percent of non-gay males received a callback.

As anyone who has submitted a job application knows, few people receive callbacks. But as the above data show, the gay applicant was much less likely to receive a callback than was the straight applicant.

> *Job seekers who could be identified as not conforming to society's heterosexual norm of society were at a distinct disadvantage.*

In a second study, researchers sent résumés to employers in four states. The applicants were allegedly recent female college graduates. In this case, once again, half of the women showed past leadership in a LGBTQ student organization to signal identity as being a queer woman—that is, a lesbian, bisexual, or transgender individual. In this case, the results showed:

- 12 pwercent of the queer females received a callback, whereas
- 17 percent of the non-queer females received a callback.

Once again, job seekers who could be identified as not conforming to society's heterosexual norm were at a distinct disadvantage.

There are limitations to these studies, as researchers note. However, based on studies of racial and ethnic discrimination in employment practices, LGBTQ individuals are at a disadvantage. In 2020, the Supreme Court ruled in *Bostock* v. *Clayton* and related cases that the Civil Rights Act of 1964 protects gay and transgender rights. This ruling should improve opportunities for LGBTQ job seekers.

LET'S DISCUSS

1. What other types of discrimination could audit studies help to illuminate? Describe a proposed experiment.
2. How do you think the incidence of anti-gay discrimination will change over time? What social forces will be responsible for the change?

Sources: Mallory and Sears 2020; Mishel 2016; Pager 2007; Tilcsik 2011; Tilscik et al. 2015.

---

the contributions of many talented people who feel confined by gender stereotyping. Moreover, the functionalist approach does not convincingly explain why men should be assigned categorically to the instrumental role and women to the expressive role.

Conflict Perspective

Viewed from a conflict perspective, the functionalist approach masks the underlying power relations between men and women. Parsons and Bales never explicitly presented the expressive and instrumental roles as being of unequal value to society, yet their inequality is quite evident. Although social institutions may pay lip service to women's expressive skills, men's instrumental skills are more highly rewarded, in terms of both money and prestige. Consequently, according to feminists and conflict theorists, any division of labor by gender into

instrumental and expressive tasks is far from neutral in its impact on women.

Conflict theorists contend that the relationship between females and males has traditionally been one of unequal power, with men in a dominant position over women. Men may originally have become powerful in preindustrial times because their size, physical strength, and freedom from childbearing duties allowed them to dominate women physically. In contemporary societies, such considerations are not so important, yet cultural beliefs about the sexes are long established, as anthropologist Margaret Mead and feminist sociologist Helen Mayer Hacker (1951, 1974) both stressed. Such beliefs support a social structure that places males in controlling positions.

Conflict theorists, then, see gender differences as a reflection of the subjugation of one group (women) by another group (men). If we use an analogy to Marx's analysis of class conflict,

DreamPictures/Shannon Faulk/Blend Images LLC

Conflict theorists emphasize that men's work is uniformly valued, whereas women's work (whether unpaid labor in the home or wage labor) is devalued. This woman is working on an assembly line.

we can say that males are like the bourgeoisie, or capitalists; they control most of the society's wealth, prestige, and power. Females are like the proletariat, or workers; they can acquire valuable resources only by following the dictates of their bosses. Men's work is uniformly valued; women's work (whether unpaid labor in the home or wage labor) is devalued.

THINKING CRITICALLY

Which aspects of the functionalist and conflict perspectives on gender make the most sense to you? Explain.

Feminist Perspective

A significant component of the conflict approach to gender stratification draws on feminist theory. Although use of the term *feminist theory* is comparatively recent, the critique of women's position in society and culture goes back to some of the earliest works that have influenced sociology. Among the most important are Mary Wollstonecraft's *A Vindication of the Rights of Woman* (originally published in 1792), John Stuart Mill's *The Subjection of Women* (originally published in 1869), and Friedrich Engels's *The Origin of the Family, Private Property, and the State* (originally published in 1884).

Engels, a close associate of Karl Marx, argued that women's subjugation coincided with the rise of private property during industrialization. Only when people moved beyond an agrarian economy could males enjoy the luxury of leisure and withhold rewards and privileges from women. Drawing on the work of

Marx and Engels, many contemporary feminist theorists view women's subordination as part of the overall exploitation and injustice that they see as inherent in capitalist societies. Some radical feminist theorists, however, view the oppression of women as inevitable in *all* male-dominated societies, whether they are labeled capitalist, socialist, or communist (Brown 2012).

Feminist sociologists would find little to disagree with in the conflict theorists' perspective, but are more likely to embrace a political agenda. Rather than be caught up in discussing progress toward gender equality over the last generation, they would draw attention to the need for greater progress. Feminists would also argue that until the 1970s, the very discussion of women and society, however well meant, was distorted by the exclusion of women from academic thought, including sociology. We have noted the many accomplishments of Jane Addams and Ida Wells-Barnett, but they generally worked outside the discipline, focusing on what we would now call applied sociology and social work. At the time, their efforts, while valued as humanitarian, were seen as unrelated to the research and conclusions being reached in academic circles, which of course were male academic circles (Ferguson 2017).

Intersections with Race, Class, and Other Social Factors

Contemporary feminists recognize the differential treatment of some women not only because of their gender but also because of the intersection of their race, ethnicity, and socioeconomic status. Simply put, whites dominate these poor, non-white women because they are non-white; men dominate them because they are women; and the affluent dominate them because they are poor. **Intersectionality** refers to the overlapping and interdependent system of advantage and disadvantage that positions people in society (Crenshaw 1989).

Awareness of intersectionality grew as female scholars noted that the emphasis on race could conceal other related processes of domination. For example, many women experience social inequality not only because of their gender but also because of their race and ethnicity. These citizens face two separate but intersecting subordinate statuses. A disproportionate share of this low-status group also is poor. African American feminist Patricia Hill Collins (2000, 2019:232–234) views intersectionality as creating a **matrix of domination** (Figure 11-1). Whites dominate non-whites, men dominate women, and the affluent dominate the poor—race, class, and gender are interconnected.

Gender, race, and social class are not the only systems of oppression, but they profoundly affect women and people of color

FIGURE 11-1   INTERSECTIONALITY: THE MATRIX OF DOMINATION

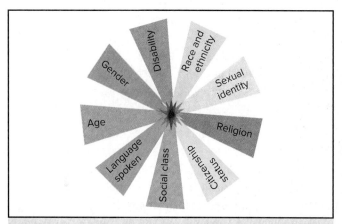

Think about It What are the implications of the matrix of domination for an immigrant woman from Central America? For an immigrant man from Syria?

Source: Developed by author

Intersectionality illustrates how several social factors—including gender, social class, language spoken, and race and ethnicity—intersect and overlap to create a matrix of domination with a cumulative impact on a person's social standing.

in the United States. Other forms of categorization and stigmatization can also be included in this matrix. If we turn to a global stage, we can add citizenship status and being perceived as a "colonial subject" even long after colonialism has ended.

Critics argue that intersectionality overemphasizes "identity politics," or the formation of alliances based on allegedly shared social groupings. Yet intersectionality is not so much about the identities themselves as it is about how society uses and abuses these identities to exclude some people and privilege others. Addressing exclusion and acknowledging privilege is not easy, and as we have seen, it requires profound social change (Crenshaw 2015; Ferguson 2017).

Gender, race, and social class are not the only sources of oppression in the United States, though they profoundly affect women and people of color. Other forms of categorization and stigmatization that might be included in the matrix are sexual orientation, religion, disability, and age. If we apply the matrix to the world as a whole, we might add citizenship status or perceived colonial or neocolonial status to the list (Romero 2018).

Though feminists have addressed themselves to the needs of minority women, these women are oppressed much more by their race and ethnicity than by their gender. The question for Latinas (Hispanic women), African American women, Asian American women, and Native American women

Inti St Clair/Digital Vision/Getty Images

appears to be whether they should unite with their brothers against racism or challenge them for their sexism. Those who stress the importance of intersectionality emphasize the need for action across both color and social class lines. Social organizing and community activism go hand and hand with intersectionality studies. As Karl Marx stated a century and half ago, it is not enough to describe the inequality; one must work for social justice (Collins 2015, Crenshaw 1991).

The discussion of gender roles among African Americans has always provoked controversy. Advocates of Black nationalism contend that feminism only distracts women from participating fully in the African American struggle. The existence of feminist groups among Blacks, in their view, simply divides the Black community, thereby serving the dominant white majority. In contrast, Black feminists such as bell hooks (1994) argue that little is to be gained by accepting the gender-role divisions of the dominant society, which place women in a separate, subservient position. Though the media commonly portray Black women in a negative light—as illiterates, welfare queens, or prostitutes—Black feminists emphasize that it is not solely whites and the white-dominated media who focus on such negative images. Black men (most recently, Black male rap artists) have also portrayed Black women in a negative way (Threadcraft 2008; Wilkins 2012).

Historically, Native Americans stand out as an exception to the patriarchal tradition in North America. At the time of the European settlers' arrival, Native American gender roles varied greatly from tribe to tribe. Southern tribes, for reasons unclear to today's scholars, were usually matriarchal and traced their descent through the mother. European missionaries, who sought to make the native peoples more like Europeans, set out to transform this arrangement, which was not entirely universal. Like members of other groups, some Native American women have resisted gender stereotypes (Lajimodiere 2013; Rose 2015).

Because sociologists have usually considered Latinas as part of either the Hispanic or feminist movements, they have ignored their distinctive experience. In the past, Latinas have been excluded from decision making in the two social institutions that most affect their daily lives: the family and the church. Particularly in the lower class, the Hispanic family suffers from the pervasive tradition of male domination. And the Catholic Church relegates women to supportive roles, while reserving the leadership positions for men (Bray 2012; M. Ortega 2015).

Prior to this chapter, much of our discussion has focused on the social effects of race and ethnicity, coupled with poverty, low incomes, and meager wealth. The matrix of domination highlights the confluence

of these factors with gender discrimination, which we must include to fully understand the plight of women of color.

Interactionist Perspective

While functionalists and conflict theorists who study gender
stratification typically focus on macro-level social forces and
institutions, interactionist researchers tend to examine gender
stratification on the micro level of everyday behavior. The key
to this approach is the way gender is socially constructed in
everyday interactions. We "do gender" by reinforcing traditionally masculine and feminine actions. For example, a man
"does masculinity" by opening a door for his girlfriend; she
"does femininity" by consenting to his assistance. Obviously,
the social construction of gender goes beyond these relatively
trivial rituals. Interactionists recognize, too, that people can
challenge traditional gender roles. A female golfer who uses
the men's tees and a man who actively arranges a birthday
luncheon at work are redoing gender (Deutsch 2007; West
and Zimmerman 1987, 2009).

Interactionists recognize that social interaction need not be
positive or productive; therefore, the prevalence and causes of
domestic violence are a subject of research. The social distancing and self-isolation that took place during the 2020 response
to the coronavirus pandemic increased the likelihood that
abusers and potential victims would have to remain together
under stressful conditions. This was further complicated by the
presence of children, who otherwise would be at school, and
the decline of the workplace or third space, which in normal
circumstances serves as a social escape (Dastagir 2020).

Table 11-2 summarizes the major sociological perspectives on
gender.

Women: The Oppressed Majority

Many people, both male and female, find it difficult to conceive
of women as a subordinate and oppressed group. Yet take a
look at the political structure of the United States: women remain noticeably underrepresented. At the beginning of 2022,

Tracking Sociological Perspectives

TABLE 11-2 SOCIOLOGICAL PERSPECTIVES ON
GENDER

Theoretical Perspective	Emphasis
Functionalist	Gender differentiation contributes to social stability
Conflict	Gender inequality is rooted in the female–male power relationship
Feminist	Women's subjugation is integral to society and social structure
Interactionist	"Doing gender" is reflected in every day behavior; domestic violence

for example, only 9 of the nation's 50 states had a female gov-
ernor (Alabama, Iowa, Kansas, Maine, Michigan, New Mexico,
New York, Oklahoma, Oregon, and South Dakota).

Women have made slow but steady progress in certain political arenas. In 1981, out of 535 members of Congress, there
were only 21 women: 19 in the House of Representatives and
2 in the Senate. In contrast, the Congress that held office as of
mid-2022 had 145 women: 121 in the House and 24 in the
Senate.

In October 1981, Sandra Day O'Connor was sworn in as the
nation's first female Supreme Court justice; since then as of
early 2022, four additional women have sat on the Court:
Ruth Bader Ginsburg, Elena Kagan, Sonia Sotomayor, and
Amy Coney Barrett. Still, among the first 46 U.S. presiden-
cies, no woman ever served as president of the United
States. The same goes for chief justice of the Supreme Court.
Notably Kamala Harris became vice president in 2022. This
may have smoothed the way for a woman president, since
a 2019 national survey showed that 94 percent of the electorate would vote for a woman if nominated by their party
(McCarthy 2019).

Sexism and Sex Discrimination

Just as African Americans are victimized by racism, women in
our society are victimized by sexism. **Sexism** is the ideology
that one sex is superior to the other. The term is generally
used to refer to male prejudice and discrimination against
women. In Chapter 10, we noted that Blacks can suffer from
both individual acts of racism and institutional discrimination.
Institutional discrimination (or systemic discrimination) was
defined as the denial of opportunities and equal rights to individuals and groups that results from the normal operations of
a society. In the same sense, women suffer from both individual acts of sexism (such as sexist remarks and acts of violence)
and institutional sexism.

It is not simply that particular men in the United States are biased in their treatment of women. All the major institutions of our society—including the government, armed forces, large corporations, the media, universities, and the medical establishment—are controlled by men. These institutions, in their normal, day-to-day operations, often discriminate against women and perpetuate sexism. For example, if the central office of a nationwide bank sets a policy that single women are a bad risk for loans—regardless of their incomes and investments—that bank will discriminate against women in state after state. It will do so even at branches where loan officers hold no personal biases toward women, but are merely "following orders."

Our society is run by male-dominated institutions, yet with the power that flows to men come responsibility and stress. Men have higher reported rates of certain types of mental illness than women, and a greater likelihood of death due to heart attack or stroke. The pressure on men to succeed, and then to remain on top in the competitive world of work, can be especially intense. That is not to suggest that gender stratification is as damaging to men as it is to women. But it is clear that the power and privilege men enjoy are no guarantee of personal well-being.

The Status of Women Worldwide

According to a detailed overview of the status of the world's women, issued by the World Bank in 2015, a renewed gender strategy is needed to raise the bar on gender equality. Both public and private sectors need to reduce the differential constraints for poor women and men in economic spheres. In many parts of the world, women still lag far behind men in their earnings and in their ability to speak out politically (World Economic Forum 2020).

The critique applies to all nations. The World Economic Forum, which hosts the annual Davos conference, has for fourteen years calculated a Global Gender Gap Index using data on women's progress in 153 nations in health, education, economy, and politics. Table 11-3 shows the nations showing the least and greatest gaps between men and women. Ranks of some other countries include Canada at 19th, Mexico 25th, United States 53rd, and Japan 121st. Relatively speaking,

TABLE 11-3   THE GLOBAL GENDER GAP

Top Ten Nations with Smallest Gap	Bottom Ten Nations with Greatest Gap
1. Iceland	144. Oman
2. Norway	145. Lebanon
3. Finland	146. Saudi Arabia
4. Sweden	147. Chad
5. Nicaragua	148. Iran
6. New Zealand	149. Congo
7. Ireland	150. Syria
8. Spain	151. Pakistan
9. Rwanda	152. Iraq
10. Germany	153. Yemen

Think about It Do any of these rankings surprise you? Why?

Source: World Economic Forum 2020.

women in the United States do well in education but less well in health and politics.

Regardless of culture, however, women everywhere suffer from second-class status. It is estimated that women grow half the world's food, but they rarely own land. They constitute one-third of the world's paid labor force, but are generally found in the lowest-paying jobs. Single-parent households headed by women, which appear to be on the rise in many nations, are typically found in the poorest sections of the population. The feminization of poverty has become a global phenomenon. As in the United States, women around the world are underrepresented politically.

Despite these challenges, women are not responding passively. They are mobilizing, individually and collectively. Given the significant underrepresentation of women in government offices and national legislatures, however, the task is difficult.

Not surprisingly, there is a link between the wealth of industrialized nations and the poverty of women in developing countries. Viewed from a conflict perspective or through the lens of Immanuel Wallerstein's world systems analysis, the economies of developing nations are controlled and exploited by industrialized countries and multinational corporations based in those countries. Much of the exploited labor in developing nations, especially in the nonindustrial sector, is performed by women. Women workers typically toil long hours for low pay, but contribute significantly to their families' incomes (UN Women 2015).

In industrialized countries, women's unequal status can be seen in the division of housework, as well as in the jobs they hold and the pay they earn. We profile the gender divide in Japan in Box 11-3.

SOCIOLOGY IN THE GLOBAL COMMUNITY

11-3   Gender Inequality in Japan

Gender inequality is not difficult to document in Japan. While Japan has the world's highest literacy rate and high school enrollment rate for women, half of Japanese women still quit their jobs when they have their first child. Women hold only 15 percent of managerial positions, compared to 41 percent in the United States.

It is also not hard to understand the contemporary inequality. Until the period after World War II, Japanese women could not vote and they had little say about where to live, compared to their husbands. Even after Japanese women were granted the right to vote, the assumption persisted that they would leave the labor force upon getting married to care for the home and prepare for the inevitable arrival of children.

In 1985, Japan's parliament—at the time, 97 percent men—passed an Equal Employment bill that encouraged employers to end sex discrimination in hiring, assignment, and promotion policies. Feminist organizations were dissatisfied with the law, because it lacked strong sanctions against companies that did not comply. In a landmark ruling issued in late 1996, a Japanese court for the first time held an employer liable for denying promotions due to sex discrimination.

Has the court's decision made a difference? Women's labor-force participation has increased, but primarily only in part-time positions, where women account for 70 percent of such workers. Women in full-time positions have moved up the occupational hierarchy a bit, but mainly by delaying marriage or by not marrying at all. Once married, college-educated Japanese women still often

leave the labor force except perhaps for part-time employment. Working mothers can expect to do about 90 percent of the household chores.

Continuing labor shortages are forcing Japan as a whole to look to women. In 2019, the Japanese Prime Minister launched a "Womenomics" campaign to promote diversity and

Jgalione/E+/Getty Images

Once married, college-educated Japanese women still often leave the labor force except perhaps for part-time employment. Working mothers can expect to do about 90 percent of the household chores.

promote female mangers, and public opinion has finally changed. In 1987, 43 percent of Japanese adults agreed that married women should stay home, but by 2000 the proportion had dropped to 25 percent. On the political front, Japanese women remain vastly underrepresented. In a 2020 study of women in government around the world, Japan, where only 9.9 percent of the national legislators are women, ranked 166th of 190 countries (in comparison, the United States ranked 79th).

Given the situation, even if it is improving a bit, women in Japan have increasingly begun to start their own businesses. This is a tactic similar to that used by minorities in the United States, who, when blocked at the usual entry points to economic success, create their own. While start-up money is important, aspiring Japanese businesswomen are finding training and mentoring by female entrepreneurs to be invaluable.

LET'S DISCUSS

1. Consider life in a society in which women are greatly underrepresented in business and government. What are the advantages and disadvantages to women? to men?
2. What is the relationship between women's underrepresentation in business and in government?

Sources: Abe 2011; Economist 2017a; International Labor Organization 2020; Inter-Parliamentary Union 2020; Mun 2010; Rich 2019; Saito 2018.

THINKING CRITICALLY

Describe an institution you are part of from a functionalist, conflict, and interactionist perspective.

The Workforce of the United States

Forty years ago, the U.S. Commission on Civil Rights concluded that the passage in the Declaration of Independence proclaiming that "all men are created equal" has been taken

too literally for too long—especially with respect to women's opportunities for employment. In this section we will see how gender bias has limited women's opportunities for employment outside the home, at the same time that it forces them to carry a disproportionate burden inside the home (Commission on Civil Rights 1976).

Labor Force Participation

Women's participation in the paid labor force in the United States has steadily increased over the past 50 years. As Figure 11-2 shows, most women with children are in the labor force today, including women with children under age 3.

FIGURE 11-2   WOMEN'S PARTICIPATION IN THE LABOR FORCE, 1975–2018

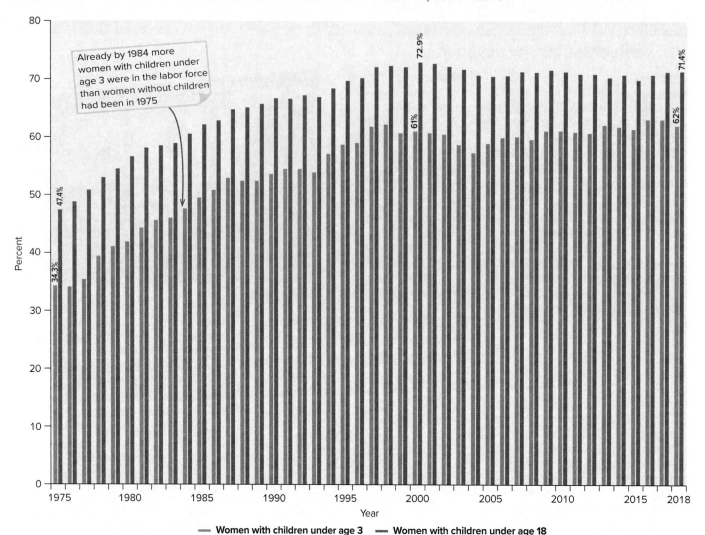

Source: Bureau of Labor Statistics 2019e: Table 7.

Still, women entering the job market find their options restricted in important ways. Women are *underrepresented* in occupations historically defined as "men's jobs," which often carry much greater financial rewards and prestige than women's jobs (Table 11-4).

Women from all groups and men from minority groups sometimes encounter attitudinal or organizational bias that prevents them from reaching their full potential. As we saw in Chapter 10, the term **glass ceiling** refers to an invisible barrier that blocks the promotion of a qualified individual in a work environment because of the individual's gender, race, or ethnicity. Furthermore, women and minority men confront not only a glass ceiling that limits their upward mobility, but glass walls that reduce their ability to move horizontally into fast-track jobs that lead directly up to the highest rungs on the corporate ladder.

When women do gain entry to corporate boards of directors, the response in the financial world is not entirely positive.

Despite objective tests that show strong financial performance under gender-diverse leadership, some investors tend to balk. Small investors often sell their shares when women become corporate leaders, apparently falling for the stereotype that associates males with success. This sell pattern is not characteristic of larger investors, who have long argued that gender-diverse leadership is good for business (Green 2019).

This type of inequality is not unique to the United States. Worldwide, women hold less than 17 percent of corporate board positions. In recognition of the underrepresentation of women on boards of directors, the Norwegian legislature established minimum quotas for the number of female board members of publicly traded companies. In response, about three-quarters of public Norwegian companies chose to become private rather than comply with the law. Despite that backlash, many countries, including Australia, Canada, France, India, Israel, and Spain, followed with their own quota laws (Shankland 2015; Thorne and Konigsburg 2020).

TABLE 11-4   U.S. WOMEN IN SELECTED OCCUPATIONS: WOMEN AS A PERCENTAGE OF ALL WORKERS IN THE OCCUPATION

Underrepresented		Overrepresented	
Firefighters	5%	College teachers	51%
Airline pilots	5%	High school teachers	60%
Police officers	15%	Flight attendants	65%
Clergy	16%	Waitstaff	68%
Civil engineers	17%	Librarians	80%
Computer programmers	20%	Elementary school teachers	80%
Chefs and head cooks	23%	Social workers	84%
Architects	32%	Registered nurses	87%
Computer systems analysts	38%	School psychologists	90%
Dentists	39%	Child-care workers	95%
Lawyers	39%	Dental hygienists	95%
Physicians	40%		

Note: Women constitute 47 percent of the labor force age 16 and over.
Source: Bureau of Labor Statistics 2022a. Household Data Annual Averages.

Compensation

He works. She works. Both are surgeons—a high-status occupation with considerable financial rewards. He makes $246,000. She makes $172,000.

These median annual earnings for physicians in the United States, released by the Census Bureau, are typical of the results of the bureau's detailed study of occupations and income. Take judges. He earns $126,000, she earns $80,200. Statisticians at the bureau looked at the median annual earnings for no fewer than 821 occupations ranging from dishwasher to chief executive. After adjusting for workers' ages, education, and work experience, they came to an unmistakable conclusion: across the board, there is a substantial gender gap in the median earnings of full-time workers. Even when men and women work in the same workplace, pay inequities remain.

Men do not always earn more than women for doing the same work. Researchers at the Census Bureau found two occupations out of 821 in which women typically earn about 1 percent more income than men: hazardous materials recovery and telecommunications line installation. These two occupations employed less than 1 out of every 1,000 workers the bureau studied. Forecasting analyses show no convincing evidence that the wage gap is narrowing.

What accounts for these yawning wage gaps between men and women in the same occupation? Scholars at the Census Bureau studied the following characteristics of men and women in the same occupation:

- Age and degree of formal education
- Marital status and the presence of children at home
- Specialization within the occupation (for example, family practice versus surgical practice)
- Years of work experience
- Hours worked per year

Taking all these factors into consideration reduced the pay gap between men and women by only 3 cents. Women still earned 83 cents for every dollar earned by men. In sum, the disparity in pay between men and women cannot be explained by pointing to women's career choices (Bureau of Labor Statistics 2020c; Kronberg 2020; Weinberg 2007; Women's Bureau 2018).

Legally, sex discrimination in wage payments is difficult to prove. Witness the case of former Goodyear worker Lilly Ledbetter, who learned 19 years after she was hired that she was being paid less than men doing the same job. Ledbetter sued and was awarded damages, only to have the Supreme Court overturn the decision on the grounds that she made her claim more than six months after the first discriminatory paycheck was issued. Congress relaxed this restriction in 2009 (Pear 2009).

What happens to men who enter traditionally women's occupations? Research shows that the glass ceiling that women face does not appear to hamper them. Instead, men who enter traditionally female occupations are more likely than women to rise to the top. Male elementary school teachers become principals; male nurses become supervisors. The term **glass escalator** refers to this advantage men experience in occupations dominated by women. Whereas women who enter traditionally male occupations may be seen as tokens, men who move out of sex-typical jobs are likely to be advantaged.

THINKING CRITICALLY

If wage disparities between women and men cannot be explained by women's career choices, what do you think does explain them?

THINKING CRITICALLY

Would you argue that women have come either very far or not far enough in their labor force participation? Explain.

Social Consequences of Women's Employment

Today, many women face the challenge of trying to juggle work and family. Their situation has many social consequences. For one thing, it puts pressure on child care facilities, public financing of day care, and even the fast-food industry, which provides many of the meals women used to prepare themselves. For another, it raises questions about what responsibility male wage earners have in the household.

Who does the housework when women become productive wage earners? Compared with their male partners, women who work outside the home are twice as likely have overall responsibility for running the household, three times more likely to oversee children's schedules, and eight times more likely to take time off to care for a sick child. In addition, they are three times as likely to serve as volunteers in school or community activities.

Sociologist Arlie Hochschild (1990, 2016) has used the phrase **second shift** to describe the double burden—work outside the home followed by child care and housework—that many women face and few men share equitably. Unfortunately, today's workplace is becoming a 24/7 virtual office thanks to the advent of mobile information technologies. As these devices take over what little personal time employees have left, the physical toll on women becomes even more burdensome. In Box 11-4 we consider what research shows about the division of household labor.

The greater amounts of time women put into caring for their children, and to a lesser degree into housework, take a special toll on women who are pursuing careers. In a survey published in the *Harvard Business Review,* about 40 percent of women indicated that they had voluntarily left work for months or years, compared to only 24 percent of men. As Figure 11-3 shows, women were much more likely than men to take time off for family reasons. Even women in the most prestigious professions have difficulty balancing home and work responsibilities. In the Social Policy section of Chapter 12 we will consider family leave. The absence of such a benefit has different impacts on women than on men.

Emergence of a Collective Consciousness

Feminism is an ideology that favors equal rights for women. The feminist movement of the United States was born in upstate New York, in a town called Seneca Falls, in the summer of 1848. On July 19, the first women's rights convention began, attended by Elizabeth Cady Stanton, Lucretia Mott, and other pioneers in the struggle for women's rights. This first wave of *feminists,* as they are currently known, battled ridicule and scorn as they fought for legal and political equality for women. They were not afraid to risk controversy on behalf of their cause; in 1872, Susan B. Anthony was arrested for attempting to vote in that year's presidential election.

Ultimately, the early feminists won many victories, among them the passage and ratification of the Nineteenth Amendment to the Constitution, which granted women the right to vote in national elections beginning in 1920. But suffrage did not lead to other reforms in women's social and economic position, and in the early and middle 20th century the women's movement became a much less powerful force for social change.

The second wave of feminism in the United States emerged in the 1960s and came into full force in the 1970s. In part, the movement was inspired by three pioneering books arguing for women's rights: Simone de Beauvoir's *The Second Sex,* Betty Friedan's *The Feminine Mystique,* and Kate Millett's *Sexual Politics.* In addition, the general political activism of the 1960s led women—many of whom were working for Black civil rights or against the war in Vietnam—to reexamine their own powerlessness. The sexism often found within even allegedly progressive and radical political circles convinced many women that they needed to establish a movement for women's liberation (Stansell 2011).

As more and more women became aware of sexist attitudes and practices, including attitudes they themselves had accepted through socialization into traditional gender roles, they began to challenge male dominance. A sense of sisterhood, much like the class consciousness that Marx hoped would emerge in the proletariat, became evident. Individual women

RESEARCH TODAY

11-4 Who Does the Housework?

The American Time Use Survey (ATUS) interviewed up to 400,000 households over a ten-year period, measuring the amount of time people spent doing various activities, such as paid work, child care, volunteering, and socializing. These data offer insight into how working parents balance the demands of child care, work, leisure, and other activities in their lives. The accompanying figure shows the relative amounts of time men and women with children spend weekly engaged in a variety of tasks. The differences are significant. While men spend more time on lawn care, women spend two or three times the time men do on child care, food preparation, and housework.

These data come from very detailed interviews. Primary child care activities, for example, include time spent providing physical care; playing with children; reading with children; assisting with homework; attending children's events; taking care of children's health care needs; and dropping off, picking up, and waiting for children. Time spent in child care is not exaggerated, as a child's presence during the activity is not enough in itself to be classified as child care. For example, "watching television with my child" was viewed as a leisure activity, not child care.

Time-use studies conducted in other industrial nations show similar differences along gender lines. Significantly an even more detailed time-use study from Great Britain

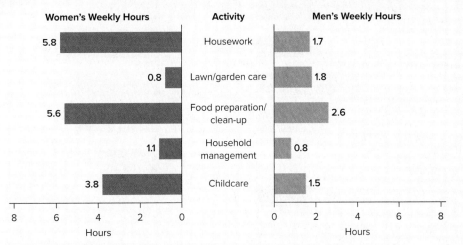

The majority of women with children are in the labor force today, including women with children under age 3

Note: Data from American Time Use Survey based on primary or main activities in households where both spouses work full-time and a child under age 18 lives in the home.
Source: Developed by author based on data in Bureau of Labor Statistics 2019d: Table A-7.

> *While men spend more time on lawn care, women spend two or three times the time men do on child care, food preparation, and housework.*

looked at these disparities over time and found that the gender differences are greatest at the critical time when men and women are trying to establish themselves in their careers.

LET'S DISCUSS

1. Ask an adult you know to keep careful track of how much time they spend each day on work, leisure, child care, and housework. Compare your records with your classmates'. Do you see differences based on gender?
2. If gender differences are greatest when children are young and parents are in their late twenties and early thirties, what differences would you expect to emerge in the later careers of women and men?

Sources: Bureau of Labor Statistics 2019d; Gershuny and Sullivan 2018.

---

identified their interests with those of the collectivity *women.* No longer were women happy in submissive, subordinate roles ("false consciousness" in Marxist terms).

By the 1980s, however, the movement's influence was beginning to wane. In 1998, in a provocative cover illustration, the editors of *Time* magazine asked "Is Feminism Dead?" Young women, they wrote, seemed to take women's improved status for granted, to see their mothers' struggles for equal rights as irrelevant to their own lives. Fewer women, they noted, were identifying themselves as feminists.

How do today's women perceive the movement? In 2016, 17 percent of women and 10 percent of men considered themselves "strong feminist"; just 2 percent of women and 5 percent of men accepted the label of "anti-feminist." Women under 35 were just as likely to identify as feminist as those

over 50, which contradicts the notion that younger women are not in tune with the feminist tradition (Cai and Clement 2016).

Is feminism dead? Many feminists resent that question, because it seems to imply that all their concerns have been resolved. Today's feminists argue that they have moved beyond early criticism that the movement was too obsessed with the concerns of white middle-class women, that it marginalized African American feminists and others. Indeed, current polling shows that African Americans and Latinas are more likely than others to call themselves feminists. Recognizing the legal and economic victories they have achieved over the last 50 years, feminists are now working to improve women's lives in nonindustrial countries, where they focus on eliminating malnutrition, starvation, extreme poverty, and violence (Swanson 2013).

FIGURE 11-3 WHY LEAVE WORK?

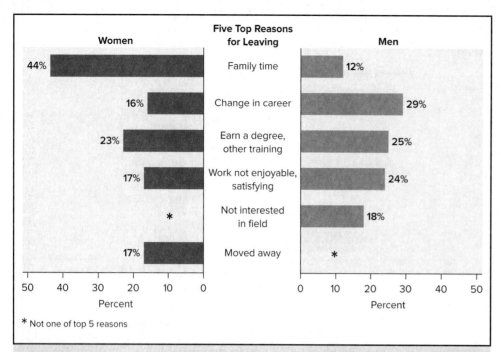

Five Top Reasons for Leaving

Women	Reason	Men
44%	Family time	12%
16%	Change in career	29%
23%	Earn a degree, other training	25%
17%	Work not enjoyable, satisfying	24%
*	Not interested in field	18%
17%	Moved away	*

* Not one of top 5 reasons

Think about It Relate the information in Figure 11-3 to the time use survey data described in Box 11-4 above.

Note: Based on a representative Harris Interactive survey of "highly qualified" workers, defined as those with a graduate degree, a professional degree, or a high honors undergraduate degree.
Source: Hewlett and Luce 2005.

Contemporary women's activism is directed toward a number of issues: reproductive freedom, pay equity, domestic violence, sex trafficking, and workplace harassment, as discussed in this chapter's Social Policy section. Whether it will coalesce remains to be seen, but there are increasing calls to pass an Equal Rights Amendment. The proposed amendment to the Constitution came close to receiving the necessary ratification by two-thirds of the states in the 1970s. At the time, proponents argued that the amendment would provide women the kind of equality they still lacked, despite a patchwork of laws designed to ensure it. Congress had placed a time limit for states to ratify the amendment of 1982, but nonetheless supporters continued to work for approval in the remaining states. In 2020, Virginia became the required 38th state to ratify the amendment, so efforts began to have Congress revoke the 1982 deadline. Although the outcome and legality remain unclear, the persistence of women to work collectively for social change remains certain (Groppe 2020).

In the Social Policy section, we discuss a continuing problem that feminism brought out into the open but has not seemed able to cure: sexual harassment.

THINKING CRITICALLY

What is the most important issue for feminism to address today? Why? Compare your response with that of your classmates or friends.

social policy and Gender Stratification

Workplace Sexual Harassment

On her very first day at work as an engineer at Uber in 2015, Susan Fowler's manager texted her that he was "looking for a woman to have sex with" (Fowler 2020). Regarding such communication as inappropriate, Fowler sought assistance from the human resource department. The person she contacted acknowledged that the behavior was sexual harassment, but since the manager was such "a high performer," it was "probably just an innocent mistake on his part." She was advised to change departments rather than risk future bad evaluations if she did not cooperate with his demands.

When Fowler's situation became public in her 2,900 word blog post, 20 Uber executives were fired, including one of the company's co-founders. Similar sexual harassment firings and lawsuits hit major figures at other tech companies, movie studios, television news networks, business corporations, and branches of government.

In response, the proportion of people who saw sexual harassment as a "major problem" increased from 50 percent in 1958 to 69 percent in 2017 but fell back somewhat to 62 percent in 2019. Surveys have consistently shown a sharp gender divide. In 2019, 70 percent of women saw sexual harassment as a major problem, compared to 53 percent of men (Brenan 2019a).

Looking at the Issue

Under evolving legal standards, sexual harassment is recognized as any unwanted and unwelcome sexual advances that interfere with a person's ability to perform and enjoy the benefits of a job. In recent years, sexual harassment firings and lawsuits have hit politicians and major figures at tech companies, movie studios, television news networks, and other corporations.

The most obvious example of sexual harassment is the boss who tells an employee, "Put out or get out!" However, the unwelcome advances that constitute sexual harassment may take the form of subtle pressures regarding sexual activity, inappropriate touching, attempted kissing, or sexual assault. *Sexual assault* typically refers to a violent act subject to criminal prosecution.

Based on the 1986 unanimous decision in *Meritor Savings Bank v. Vinson*, the Supreme Court declared that sexual harassment by a supervisor violates the federal law against sex discrimination in the workplace as outlined in the 1964 Civil Rights Act. The law applies equally to male and female victims, and the harasser can be a nonemployee such as a customer or client. In addition, workplace sexual harassment does not necessarily have to involve economic injury. Each month, about $40 million in damages are paid as a result of successful sexual harassment suits under federal law.

Regardless, a 2013 Supreme Court ruling, *Vance v. Ball State University*, makes it difficult to win a judgment against an employer unless the perpetrator is a supervisor with the ability to hire and fire. Also, a request for a federal remedy under this law must be filed within 180 days of the incident. Companies may also enact their own harsher sanctions. Although legal remedies are available, the challenge is to stop the behavior and to deal with it appropriately when it does occur.

The rise of the #MeToo movement on social media in 2017 created a vehicle to bring concerns over sexual harassment to the public's attention. African American activist Tanya Burke actually launched the #MeToo hashtag on the platform MySpace in 2006 as a way to bring victims together online. Ironically she and others are today concerned that the movement fails to sufficiently consider the challenges faced by minority women (Harris 2019).

Mike Flanagan/CartoonStock

Despite all the news and workplace training, many people do not understand what is meant by sexual harassment.

Applying Sociology

Functionalists acknowledge that the persistence of gender roles in a given culture may make it more likely for men to take advantage of women sexually. A sociological study of female Iraqi war veterans documented the ways in which the women try to avoid being sexualized by male soldiers. Two techniques they used were to come across as much less feminine, even masculine in behavior, or to try to convey a sisterly role with the men in their unit. Obviously male soldiers did not have to manage their behavior in the same way (Crowley and Sandhoff 2017).

Interactionists have noted that while "sexual harassment" has become a useful label for a broad range of unacceptable workplace behavior, it remains vicious behavior and its commonplace use in conversation should not ignore that fact. Further, interactionists have observed that online activity can work in two different ways: as a vehicle for harassment as well as a tool victims can use to mobilize support and make contact with other victims. The emergence of the #MeToo movement has made it easier for people to share their experiences of sexual harassment.

Conflict theorists and feminists see sexual harassment as a product of unequal power—men wielding their authority over women, and bosses over employees. Disgraced Hollywood producer Harvey Weinstein was viewed as so valuable to his studio that his 2015 employment contract explicitly stated that the studio would pay any settlements for his sexual misconduct.

While recent public attention and national focus may lead companies to put good policies in place, the conflict view points to the continual entry of low-skilled workers vulnerable to inappropriate demands from their supervisors.

Sociological research documents that workplace sexual harassment has lifetime impacts on women. Experiences with being the victim of harassment causes financial stress by precipitating job changes and can significantly repress a woman's desired upward mobility (McLaughlin et al. 2017).

Initiating Policy

As we already noted, the federal government considers sexual harassment a form of discrimination that violates the Civil Rights Act of 1964. This ruling applies to all levels of government and to private employers with 15 or more employees. It applies equally to male and female victims, and the harasser can even be a nonemployee such as a customer or client. Unlawful workplace sexual harassment does not necessarily have to involve economic injury.

Each month about $40 million in benefits is paid to victims of successful sexual harassment lawsuits, despite restrictions such as the *Vance v. Ball State University* ruling. Other legal jurisdictions have stiffer definitions and companies also may enact their own harsher sanctions. So while legal remedies may seem available, they are not used often enough. The challenge is to stop the behavior and to deal with it appropriately when it does occur (Equal Employment Opportunity Commission 2018).

Strengthening the federal protections against workplace sexual harassment is unlikely, as Congress is having difficulty dealing with its own staff's claims of sexual harassment. Even in the wake of the #MeToo movement, Congress did not act until 2018 to end the provision that allows the government to pay the legal expenses of members of congress who are charged with sexual assault or harassment.

In the wake of recent accusations of public figures, human resource managers in both the private and public sectors have begun to reexamine anti-harassment programs. Perhaps less time should be spent on trying to clarify the distinction between sexual harassment and an innocent compliment, for example. Instead of restricting programming to a slide presentation, perhaps employers should seek to empower workers with techniques for both avoiding and responding to instances of sexual harassment.

Also, employers must encourage the reporting of such incidents and develop a fair review process for complaints. According to a 2016 study of the Equal Employment Opportunity Commission, three out of four individuals who experience harassment never talk to a supervisor, manager, or union representative about the harassing conduct. The main reasons for their silence are fears that no one will believe the claim, that no action will be taken, or that they will suffer social or professional reprisal (Feldblum and Lipnic 2018).

The handling of sexual harassment complaints came into sharp focus in recent years as it became apparent that many supervisors were aware of the incidents and even in many cases persuaded victims not to report them. Employers, whether in government or the private sector, should do more to encourage the reporting of such incidents and to develop a fair review process to deal with all complaints.

Take the Issue with You

1. Have you ever experienced sexual harassment? Have you ever, perhaps unwittingly, been a harasser? How common do you think such incidents are?

2. Why is sexual harassment hard to define? Why is it hard to eliminate from the workplace and other settings?

3. What policy changes in a workplace might help either prevent sexual harassment or assist victims in seeking redress? Explain your reasoning.

MASTERING THIS CHAPTER

Summary

Gender is an ascribed status that provides a basis for social differentiation. This chapter examines the social construction of gender, theories of stratification by gender, women as an oppressed majority group, women in the workforce of the United States, and the emergence of a collective consciousness.

1. In the United States, the social construction of gender continues to define significantly different expectations for females and males.

2. **Gender roles** show up in our work and behavior and in how we react to others. Throughout history, these roles have restricted women much more than they have men.

3. Anthropological research points to the importance of cultural conditioning in defining the social roles of males and females.

4. Stratification exists by sexual as well as by gender identity. Not only gays but also transgender people suffer from stigma.

5. Functionalists maintain that sex differentiation contributes to overall social stability, but conflict theorists charge that the relationship between females and males is one of unequal power, with men dominating women. This dominance shows up in people's everyday interactions.

6. Many women experience **intersectionality,** or differential treatment, not only because of their gender but because of their race, ethnicity, and social class as well. Patricia Hill Collins has termed this convergence of social forces the **matrix of domination.**

7. As one example of their micro-level approach to the study of gender stratification, interactionists have analyzed men's verbal dominance over women through conversational interruptions.

8. Women around the world live and work with pervasive **sexism** and **institutional discrimination.**

9. In the United States today, almost as many women as men participate in the paid labor force, but women are underrepresented in managerial positions and underpaid compared to men in the same jobs.

10. As women have taken on more and more hours of paid employment outside the home, they have been only partially successful in getting their husbands to take on more homemaking duties, including child care.

11. Many women agree with the positions of the feminist movement but reject the label *feminist.*

12. Sexual harassment is both difficult to define and to eliminate, despite decades of court rulings and workplace training.

Key Terms

Expressiveness Concern for the maintenance of harmony and the internal emotional affairs of the family. (273)

Feminism An ideology that favors equal rights for women. (282)

Gender identity How people see themselves, as male or female, or something else. (271)

Gender role Expectations regarding the proper behavior, attitudes, and activities of males and females. (267)

Glass ceiling An invisible barrier that blocks the promotion of a qualified individual in a work environment because of the individual's gender, race, or ethnicity. (280)

Glass escalator The advantage men experience in occupations dominated by women. (281)

Homophobia Fear of and prejudice against homosexuality. (267)

Institutional discrimination or systemic discrimination The denial of opportunities and equal rights to individuals and groups that results from the normal operations of a society. (277)

Instrumentality An emphasis on tasks, a focus on more distant goals, and a concern for the external relationship between one's family and other social institutions. (273)

Intersectionality The overlapping and interdependent system of advantage and disadvantage that positions people in society on the basis of race, class, gender, and other characteristics. (275)

Matrix of domination The cumulative impact of oppression because of race and ethnicity, gender, and social class, as well as religion, sexual orientation, disability, age, and citizenship status. (275)

Second shift The double burden—work outside the home followed by child care and housework—that many women face and few men share equitably. (282)

Sexism The ideology that one sex is superior to the other. (277)

Sexual identity The self-awareness of being romantically or sexually attracted to a defined group of people. Also referred to as *sexual orientation*. (271)

TAKING SOCIOLOGY with you

1. Analyze songs for ways gender is socially constructed. Try doing this also with songs of genres you normally don't listen to and with songs from different time periods in the past. Take notes over the next several days and discuss your findings with the class.

2. Interview an older relative or acquaintance about changes they have or have not seen, wish they'd seen, and didn't like seeing with regards to gender norms. Take notes and share your findings with the class.

3. Create a list of possible gender norm transgressions. Observe people in public to identify examples of these behaviors and take notes on how others respond to these behaviors. Compare your findings with other students in your class.

4. **Writing Sociology.** Go to the Geena Davis Institute of Gender in Media website (https://seejane.org/) or another reputable site focusing on gender representation. Choose a topic to research regarding the inequality of representation of gender in the media and summarize it. Share your summary with the class. If you so choose, see if you can get your summary published in the school newspaper to raise awareness of the issue.

Self-Quiz

Read each question carefully and then select the best answer.

1. Both males and females are physically capable of learning to cook and sew, yet most Western societies determine that women should perform these tasks. This illustrates the operation of
   a. gender roles.
   b. sociobiology.
   c. homophobia.
   d. comparable worth.

2. An important element in traditional views of proper "masculine" and "feminine" behavior is fear of homosexuality. This fear, along with accompanying prejudice, is referred to as
   a. lesbianism.
   b. femme fatalism.
   c. homophobia.
   d. claustrophobia.

3. The most crucial agents of socialization in teaching gender roles in the United States are
   a. peers.
   b. teachers.
   c. media personalities.
   d. parents.

4. Research by anthropologist Margaret Mead has shown that
   a. biology is the most important factor in determining the social roles of males and females.
   b. cultural conditioning is the most important factor in determining the social roles of males and females.
   c. biology and cultural conditioning have an equal impact in determining the social roles of males and females.
   d. biology and cultural conditioning have a negligible impact in determining the social roles of males and females.

5. Which sociological perspective would acknowledge that it is not possible to change gender roles drastically without dramatic revisions in a culture's social structure?
   a. functionalist perspective
   b. dramaturgical perspective
   c. interactionist perspective
   d. social control

6. The term *sexism* is most commonly used to refer to
   a. female prejudice and discrimination against men.
   b. male prejudice and discrimination against women.
   c. female discrimination against men and male discrimination against women equally.
   d. discrimination between members of the same sex.

7. Which of these statements is true?
   a. More boys than girls take AP exams.
   b. Women in the United States are more likely than men to attend college.
   c. Women in the United States are less likely than men to obtain doctoral degrees.
   d. all of the above

8. Which sociological perspective distinguishes between instrumental and expressive roles?
   a. functionalist perspective
   b. conflict perspective
   c. interactionist perspective
   d. labeling theory

9. Contemporary feminists recognize the differential treatment of some women not only because of their gender, but also because of their
   a. race.
   b. ethnicity.
   c. socioeconomic status.
   d. all of the above

10. The sense of sisterhood that became evident during the rise of the contemporary feminist movement resembled the Marxist concept of
    a. alienation.
    b. dialectics.
    c. class consciousness.
    d. false consciousness.

11. Talcott Parsons and Robert Bales contend that women take the _____, emotionally supportive role in the family and that men take the _____, practical role, with the two complementing each other.

12. A significant component of the _____ approach to gender stratification draws on feminist theory.

13. It is not simply that particular men in the United States are biased in their treatment of women. All the major institutions of our society—including the government, the armed forces, large corporations, the media, universities, and the medical establishment—are controlled by men. This situation is symptomatic of institutional _____.

14. Women from all groups and men from minority groups sometimes encounter attitudinal or organizational bias that prevents them from reaching their full potential. This is known as the _____ _____.

15. Sociologist Arlie Hochschild has used the phrase _____ to describe the double burden that many women face and few men share equitably: work outside the home followed by child care and housework.

16. Within the general framework of their theory, _____ sociologists maintain that gender differentiation has contributed to overall social stability.

17. Through the rise of contemporary _____, women are developing a greater sense of group solidarity.

18. _____ contributes significantly to rigid gender-role socialization, since many people stereotypically associate male homosexuality with femininity and lesbianism with masculinity.

19. The term _____ _____ _____ was coined by feminist theorist Patricia Hill Collins to describe the convergence of social forces that contributes to the subordinate status of poor, non-white women.

20. The author of the pioneering argument for women's rights, *The Feminine Mystique*, was _____.

Answers

1 (a); 2 (c); 3 (d); 4 (b); 5 (d); 6 (b); 7 (b); 8 (a); 9 (d); 10 (c); 11 expressive, instrumental; 12 conflict; 13 discrimination; 14 glass ceiling; 15 second shift; 16 functionalist; 17 feminism; 18 Homophobia; 19 matrix of domination; 20 Betty Friedan

The Family and Household Diversity

Ariel Skelley/Getty Images

A family gathers outside for dinner as a part of a multigenerational reunion. Despite marital strains and geographic separation, countless families come together every year to reaffirm the importance of this social institution.

▶ INSIDE

Do you know adult children in their 20s and 30s who continue to live at home or have returned to their parents' home?

Some people call these families "accordion families" because they expand and contract as the adult children come and go.

66 William Rollo and his wife arrived in Newton [Massachusetts] in 1989 after having lived in Seattle, Philadelphia, and Summit, New Jersey. Their eldest son, John, grew up in Newton and did well enough in high school to attend the liberal arts college Williams, one of the nation's most selective. Even so, he beat it home after graduating and has lived with his parents for several years while preparing to apply to graduate school. 'A lot of my friends are living at home to save money,' he explains.

Tight finances are not all that is driving John's living arrangements. The young man had choices and decided he could opt for more of the ones he wanted if he sheltered under his parents' roof. John is saving money from his job in an arts foundation for a three-week trip to Africa, where he hopes to work on a mobile health-care project in a rural region. It's a strategic choice designed to increase his chances to be accepted into Harvard University's competitive graduate program in public health.

John needs to build up his credentials if he wants to enter a school like that. To get from here to there, he needs more experience working with patients in clinics or out in the field. It takes big bucks to travel to exotic locations, and a master's degree will cost him dearly, too. In order to make good on his aspirations, John needs his parents to cover him for the short run. On his own, John could pay the rent on an apartment, especially if he had roommates. What he can't

afford is to pay for both privacy *and* travel, to support himself *and* save for his hoped-for future. Autonomy turns out to be the lesser priority, so he has returned to the bedroom he had before he left for college, and there he stays.

If John had no goals, no sense of direction, William would not be at ease with this 'boomerang arrangement.' Hiding in the basement playing video games would not do. Happily, that is not on John's agenda. William is glad to help his son realize his ambitions. What really matters is that the work *means* something. It will help to remake the world, something William has not felt he could contribute to very directly in his work. Having a son who can reach a bit higher—if not financially, then morally—is an ambition worth paying for.

And it will cost this family, big time. William and Janet have invested nearly two hundred thousand dollars in John's education already. They will need to do more if John is going to become a public health specialist. They are easily looking at another fifty thousand dollars, even if John attends a local graduate program and continues to live with them. Fortunately, there are excellent options—some of the nation's finest—close by. Whatever it costs, they reason, the sacrifice is worth it. 99

On his own, John could pay the rent on an apartment, especially if he had roommates. What he can't afford is to pay for both privacy and travel, to support himself and save for his hoped-for future.

Source: Newman 2012:xv–xvii.

In this excerpt from *The Accordion Family: Boomerang Kids, Anxious Parents, and the Private Toll of Global Competition,* sociologist Katherine S. Newman describes one of the major trends in family life today. In the United States as well as in many other countries, parenthood is being extended as single adult children remain at home, or return home after college or a brief foray into the job market. The coronavirus pandemic pushed millions of Americans, especially young adults, to move in with family members. By the summer of 2020, 52 percent of 18- to 29-year-olds were living at home.

Some of those adult children were still pursuing an education, but in many cases financial difficulties underlay their living arrangements. For younger job seekers, employment is often short term or low paying—not secure enough to support a separate household. And with many marriages ending in divorce—most commonly in the first seven years—divorced sons

and daughters often return to their parents, sometimes with their own children in tow (Friedman 2019; Smock and Schwartz 2020).

Whether we refer to such combined households as "accordion families," as Newman does, or to the returning adult children as "boomerang kids," this trend is an example of the increasing complexity of family life. The family of today is not what it was a century ago, or even a generation ago. New roles, new gender distinctions, and new child-rearing patterns have all combined to create new forms of family life. Today, for example, more and more women are taking the breadwinner's role, whether married or as a single parent. Blended families—the result of divorce and remarriage—are almost the norm. And many people are seeking intimate relationships without being married, whether in gay partnerships or in cohabiting arrangements (Cherlin 2021).

The word *family* is inadequate to describe some of these arrangements, including cohabiting partners, same-sex marriages, and single-parent households. In 2011, the nation crossed a major threshold: the majority of births to women under age 30 occurred outside of marriage (Cherlin 2011; Wildsmith et al. 2011).

This chapter addresses family and household diversity in the United States as well as other parts of the world. As we will see, family patterns differ from one culture to another and even within the same culture. Despite the differences, however, the family is universal—found in every culture. A **family** can be defined as a set of people related by blood, marriage, or some other agreed-on relationship, or adoption, who share the primary responsibility for reproduction and caring for members of society.

What are families in different parts of the world like? How do people select their mates? When a marriage fails, how does the divorce affect the children? What are the alternatives to the nuclear family, and how prevalent are they? In this chapter we will look at the family and intimate relationships from the functionalist, conflict, interactionist, and feminist points of view. We'll examine variations in marital patterns and family life, including child rearing, paying particular attention to the increasing numbers of people in dual-income and single-parent families. We'll consider the similarities and differences between gay and straight relationships. We'll examine divorce in the United States and consider diverse lifestyles such as cohabitation and marriage without children. Finally, in the Social Policy section we'll confront the issue of family leave, comparing policies in the United States with those in other parts of the world.

Global View of the Family

Among Tibetans, a woman may be married simultaneously to more than one man, usually brothers. This system allows sons to share the limited amount of good land. Among the Betsileo of Madagascar, a man has multiple wives, each one living in a different village where he cultivates rice. Wherever he has the best rice field, that wife is considered his first or senior wife. Among the Yanomami of Brazil and Venezuela, it is considered proper to have sexual relations with your opposite-sex cousins if they are the children of your mother's brother or your father's sister. But if your opposite-sex cousins are the children of your mother's sister or your father's brother, the same practice is considered to be incest (Haviland et al. 2017; Kottak and Lukas 2019).

As these examples illustrate, there are many variations in the family from culture to culture. Yet the family as a social institution exists in all cultures. Moreover, certain general principles concerning its composition, kinship patterns, and authority patterns are universal.

Composition: What Is the Family?

If we were to take our information on what a family is from what we see on television, we might come up with some strange scenarios. The media do not always present a realistic view of the family. Moreover, many people still think of the family in very narrow terms—as a married couple and their unmarried children living together. However, this is but one type of family, what sociologists refer to as a **nuclear family.** The term *nuclear family* is well chosen, since this type of family serves as the nucleus, or core, on which larger family groups are built.

Most people in the United States see the married heterosexual couple with their own children as the preferred family

FIGURE 12-1   LIVING ARRANGEMENTS OF ADULTS AGE 18 AND OVER, 1967 AND 2019

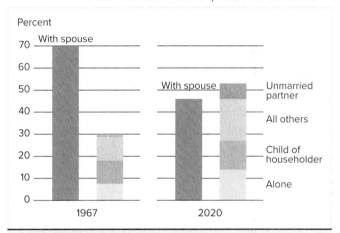

Think about It How do you predict this graph will change over the next 20 years?

Note: "All others" includes adults who are single parents, or who live with a parent, roommate, sibling, foster child, or grandchild.
Sources: Bureau of the Census 2017d: Figure AD-3a; American Community Survey 2020a: Table 12007.

arrangement. Yet less than a quarter of the nation's family households fit this model. The proportion of households in the United States that is composed of married heterosexual couples with children at home has decreased steadily over the past 50 years and is expected to continue shrinking (see Figure 12-1). At the same time, the number of single-parent households has increased (American Community Survey 2019a).

A family in which relatives—such as grandparents, aunts, or uncles—live in the same home as parents and their children is known as an **extended family.** Although not common, such living arrangements do exist in the United States. The structure of the extended family offers certain advantages over that of the nuclear family. Crises such as death, divorce, and illness put less strain on family members, since more people can provide assistance and emotional support. In addition, the extended family constitutes a larger economic unit than the nuclear family. If the family is engaged in a common enterprise—a farm or a small business—the additional family members may represent the difference between prosperity and failure.

In considering these different family types, we have limited ourselves to the form of marriage that is characteristic of the United States—monogamy. The term **monogamy** describes a form of marriage in which an individual has only one partner. Until recently, the societal expectation was that the couple would be a man and a woman. Now same-sex marriage is commonplace in many parts of the United States. Regardless, observers, noting the high rate of divorce in the United States, have suggested that "serial monogamy" is a more accurate description of the form marriage takes in this country. In **serial monogamy,** a person may have several spouses in a lifetime, but only one spouse at a time.

Some cultures allow an individual to have several husbands or wives simultaneously. This form of marriage is known as **polygamy.** In fact, most societies throughout the world, past and present, have preferred polygamy to monogamy. According to a mid-20th century analysis of 565 societies, polygamy was preferred in more than 80 percent. While polygamy declined steadily through most of the 20th century, in at least 32 countries, 5 percent of all women are in polygamous marriages (Barber 2009; Murdock 1957).

There are two basic types of polygamy. According to Murdock, the most common—endorsed by the majority of cultures he sampled—is *polygyny*. **Polygyny** refers to the marriage of a man to more than one woman at the same time. The wives are often sisters, who are expected to hold similar values and have already had experience sharing a household. In polygynous societies, relatively few men actually have multiple spouses. Most individuals live in monogamous families; having multiple wives is viewed as a mark of status.

The other principal variation of polygamy is **polyandry,** in which a woman may have more than one husband at the same time. Polyandry, however, is exceedingly rare today, though it is accepted in some extremely poor societies. Like many other societies, polyandrous cultures devalue the social worth of women.

By the end of the 20th century, polygamy had been relegated to the margins of U.S. society, and to discussion of other cultures. Recently, however, it has resurfaced.

Most households in the United States do not consist of two parents living with their unmarried children.

As the concept of marriage is redefined to include same-sex marriage, Mormon fundamentalists and Muslims who practice polygamy have asked why it should not also embrace polygamy. Indeed, in his dissent to the Supreme Court's *Obergefell* decision, which recognized the right to same-sex marriage (discussed in detail later in the chapter), Chief Justice John Roberts raised that very possibility. However, no court has indicated even a tolerance of plural marriage (Baude 2015).

Kinship Patterns: To Whom Are We Related?

Many of us can trace our roots by looking at a family tree or by listening to elderly family members talk about their lives—and about the lives of ancestors who died long before we were

Burke/Triolo Productions/Brand X/Corbis

born. Yet a person's lineage is more than simply a personal history; it also reflects societal patterns that govern descent. In every culture, children encounter relatives to whom they are expected to show an emotional attachment. The state of being related to others is called **kinship.** Kinship is culturally learned, however, and is not totally determined by biological or marital ties. For example, adoption creates a kinship tie that is legally acknowledged and socially accepted.

The family and the kin group are not necessarily one and the same. Whereas the family is a household unit, kin do not always live together or function as a collective body on a daily basis. Kin groups include aunts, uncles, cousins, in-laws, and so forth. In a society such as the United States, the kinship group may come together only rarely, for a wedding or funeral. However, kinship ties frequently create obligations and responsibilities. We may feel compelled to assist our kin, and we may feel free to call on them for many types of aid, including loans and babysitting.

How do we identify kinship groups? The principle of descent assigns people to kinship groups according to their relationship to a mother or father. There are three primary ways of determining descent. The United States follows the system of **bilateral descent,** which means that both sides of a person's

family are regarded as equally important. For example, no higher value is given to the brothers of one's father than to the brothers of one's mother.

Most societies—according to George Murdock, 64 percent—give preference to one side of the family or the other in tracing descent. In **patrilineal** (from the Latin *pater,* "father") **descent**, only the father's relatives are significant in terms of property, inheritance, and emotional ties. Conversely, in societies that favor **matrilineal** (from the Latin *mater,* "mother") **descent**, only the mother's relatives are significant.

New forms of reproductive technology will necessitate a new way of looking at kinship. Today, a combination of biological and social processes can "create" a family member, requiring that more distinctions be made about who is related to whom.

Authority Patterns: Who Rules?

Imagine that you have recently married and must begin to make decisions about the future of your new family. You and your spouse face many questions. Where will you live? How will you furnish your home? Who will do the cooking, the shopping, the cleaning? Whose friends will be invited to dinner? Each time a decision must be made, an issue is raised: Who has the power to make the decision? In simple terms, who rules the family? Conflict theorists examine these questions in the context of traditional gender stratification, under which men have held a dominant position over women.

Societies vary in the way power is distributed within the family. A society that expects males to dominate in all family decision making is termed a **patriarchy.** In patriarchal societies, such as Iran, the eldest male often wields the greatest power, although wives are expected to be treated with respect and kindness. An Iranian woman's status is typically defined by her relationship to a male relative, usually as a wife or daughter. In many patriarchal societies, women find it more difficult to obtain a divorce than a man does. In contrast, in a **matriarchy,** women have greater authority than men. Matriarchies, which are very uncommon, emerged among Native American tribal societies and in nations in which men were absent for long periods because of warfare or food-gathering expeditions (Farr 1999).

In a third type of authority pattern, the **egalitarian family,** spouses are regarded as equals. That does not mean, however, that all decisions are shared in such families. Wives may hold authority in some spheres, husbands in others. Many sociologists believe the egalitarian family has begun to replace the patriarchal family as the social norm in the United States.

Family form may take seemingly endless varieties. For example, consider a group of families ruled for more than a generation by a patriarch who determined every aspect of daily life, including sexual expression.

USE YOUR SOCIOLOGICAL IMAGINATION

In your family, which relatives do you have a significant relationship with? Which do you hardly ever see? Explain the reasons for the difference in relationships.

ImagesBazaar/Alamy Stock Photo

Although spouses in an egalitarian family may not share all their decisions, they regard themselves as equals. This pattern of authority is becoming more common in the United States.

Sociological Perspectives on the Family

Do we really need the family? Over a century ago, Friedrich Engels ([1884] 1959), a colleague of Karl Marx, described the family as the ultimate source of social inequality because of its role in the transfer of power, property, and privilege. More recently, conflict theorists have argued that the family contributes to societal injustice, denies women opportunities that are extended to men, and limits freedom in sexual expression and mate selection. In contrast, the functionalist view focuses on the ways in which the family gratifies the needs of its members and contributes to social stability. The interactionist view considers the intimate, face-to-face relationships that occur in the family. And the feminist approach examines the role of the wife and mother, especially in the absence of an adult male.

Functionalist Perspective

The family performs six paramount functions, first outlined over 80 years ago by sociologist William F. Ogburn (Ogburn and Tibbits 1934):

1. **Reproduction.** For a society to maintain itself, it must replace dying members. In this sense, the family contributes to human survival through its function of reproduction.

2. **Protection.** In all cultures, the family assumes the ultimate responsibility for the protection and upbringing of children.

3. **Socialization.** Parents and other kin monitor a child's behavior and transmit the norms, values, and language of their culture to the child.

4. **Regulation of sexual behavior.** Sexual norms are subject to change both over time (for instance, in the customs for dating) and across cultures (compare strict Saudi Arabia to the more permissive Denmark). However, whatever the time period or cultural values of a society, standards of sexual behavior are most clearly defined within the family circle.

5. **Affection and companionship.** Ideally, the family provides members with warm and intimate relationships, helping them to feel satisfied and secure. Of course, a family member may find such rewards outside the family—from peers, in school, at work—and may even perceive the home as an unpleasant or abusive setting. Nevertheless, we expect our relatives to understand us, to care for us, and to be there for us when we need them.

6. **Provision of social status.** We inherit a social position because of the family background and reputation of our parents and siblings. The family presents the newborn child with an ascribed status based on race and ethnicity that helps to determine his or her place within society's stratification system. Moreover, family resources affect children's ability to pursue certain opportunities, such as higher education.

Traditionally, the family has fulfilled a number of other functions, such as providing religious training, education, and recreational outlets. But Ogburn argued that other social institutions have gradually assumed many of those functions. Education once took place at the family fireside; now it is the responsibility of professionals working in schools and colleges. Even the family's traditional recreational function has often been transferred to outside groups such as soccer leagues, athletic clubs, and Twitter (Cherlin 2020).

Conflict Perspective

Conflict theorists view the family not as a contributor to social stability, but as a reflection of the inequality in wealth and power that is found within the larger society. Feminist and conflict theorists note that the family has traditionally legitimized and perpetuated male dominance. Throughout most of human history—and in a wide range of societies—husbands have exercised overwhelming power and authority within the family. Not until the first wave of contemporary feminism in the United States, in the mid-1800s, was there a substantial challenge to the historic status of wives and children as the legal property of husbands.

While the egalitarian family has become a more common pattern in the United States in recent decades—owing in good part to the activism of feminists beginning in the late 1960s and early 1970s—male dominance over the family has hardly disappeared. The number of fathers who are at home with their children for any reason has nearly doubled since 1989. It reached its highest point in 2010, just after the official end of the Great Recession. Since that time, the number has fallen slightly. Side by side with this trend is a continuing rapid increase in the number of fathers who do not live with the family, leaving all caretaking to the mother or other caregivers. Sociologists have found that while married men are increasing their involvement in child care, their wives still perform a disproportionate amount of it. Furthermore, for every stay-at-home dad there are five stay-at-home moms.

Unfortunately, many husbands (and some wives) reinforce their power and control over spouses and children through acts of domestic violence. During the coronavirus pandemic, domestic violence hotlines experienced 20-30 percent increases in call volume, as already tense couple relationships were further stressed by isolation, unemployment, and anxiety over the virus (Al-Harshani 2020; Bureau of Census 2019h: Table CH-1; Hardesty and Ogolsky 2020).

Conflict theorists also view the family as an economic unit that contributes to societal injustice. The family is the basis for transferring power, property, and privilege from one generation to the next. Although the United States is widely viewed as a land of opportunity, social mobility is restricted in important ways. Children inherit the privileged or less-than-privileged social and economic status of their parents (and in some cases, of earlier generations). The social class of parents significantly influences children's socialization experiences and the degree of protection they receive. Thus, the socioeconomic status of a child's family will have a marked influence on his or her nutrition, health care, housing, educational opportunities, and in many respects, life chances as an adult. For this reason, conflict theorists argue that the family helps to maintain inequality.

Interactionist Perspective

Interactionists focus on the micro level of family and other intimate relationships. They are interested in how individuals interact with one another, whether they are cohabiting partners or longtime married couples. For example, in a study of both Black and white two-parent households, researchers found that when fathers are more involved with their children (reading to them, helping them with homework, or restricting their television viewing), the children have fewer behavior problems, get along better with others, and are more responsible.

Interactionists are increasingly studying the nature of the relationships between stepparents and stepchildren. The persistent divorce rate and the likelihood of a third of those divorced remarrying mean that these relationships have become a significant part of parenting, particularly from the vantage point of the children. Research documents the wide variation in the social roles that stepparents play. Some become parentlike figures, while others are more like friends or honorary aunts and uncles. Stepparents who do not live with their stepchildren regularly may have more distant relationships (Cherlin 2021; Smock and Schwartz 2020).

Dating, long of interest to interactionists, has increasingly gone online and the research has continued as shown in Box 12-1.

Feminist Perspective

Because "women's work" has traditionally focused on family life, feminist sociologists have taken a strong interest in the family as a social institution. Research on gender roles in child care and household chores has been extensive. Sociologists have looked particularly closely at how women's work outside the home impacts their child care and housework—duties Arlie Hochschild (1990, 2016) has referred to as the "second shift." Today, researchers recognize that for many women, the second shift includes the care of aging parents as well.

Feminist theorists have urged social scientists and social agencies to rethink the notion that families in which no adult male is present are automatically a cause for concern, or even dysfunctional. They have also contributed to research on single women, single-parent households, and lesbian couples. In the case of single mothers, researchers have focused on the resiliency of many such households, despite economic stress. According to Velma McBride Murray and her colleagues (2001) at the University of Georgia, such studies show that among African Americans, single mothers draw heavily on kinfolk for material resources, parenting advice, and social support. Considering feminist research on the family as a whole, one researcher concluded that the family is the "source of women's strength" (Few-Demo and Allen 2020).

Finally, feminists who take the interactionist perspective stress the need to investigate neglected topics in family studies. For instance, in a growing number of dual-income households, the wife earns a higher income than the husband. When wives earn more than their husbands do, research matching labor surveys and tax records has uncovered a puzzling thing. In such families, husbands say they earn more than they do, and wives underreport their income. Social norms and accepted gender norms drive expectations and behavior, including how we report information about ourselves to others (Murray-Close and Heggeness 2018).

Table 12-1 summarizes the four major theoretical perspectives on the family.

Tracking Sociological Perspectives

TABLE 12-1 SOCIOLOGICAL PERSPECTIVES ON THE FAMILY

Theoretical Perspective	Emphasis
Functionalist	The family as a contributor to social stability Roles of family members
Conflict	The family as a perpetuator of inequality Transmission of poverty or wealth across generations
Interactionist	Relationships among family members
Feminist	The family as a perpetuator of gender roles Female-headed households

OUR WIRED WORLD

12-1   Love Is in the Air and on the Web

According to a 2020 national survey, 3 in 10 people, or 52 percent of individuals who have never married, have used an online dating site or mobile dating app. Among online daters overall, 12 percent report marrying or entering a committed relationship with someone they met through an online dating site. As a source of romantic partners, the Internet is second only to friends—ahead of family, workplace, and neighborhood.

Significantly, online networking is especially important to mate-seekers under 50. It is especially important to gays and lesbians: 21 percent of those who seek a same-sex relationship do so successfully online, compared to 11 percent of those seeking a heterosexual relationship. Sociologists have observed that members of groups with a thin or limited market for romantic partners are more likely to go online.

There are significant gender differences with Internet dating sites. Women are more likely to complain that men do not offer a detailed enough profile, especially when it comes to religion or hobbies. They are also more likely to complain about continued contact with dates with whom they indicated they were no longer interested.

As we might suspect, **impression management**—the altering of the presentation of the self in order to

> *According to a 2020 national survey, 3 in 10 people, or 52 percent of individuals who have never married, have used an online dating site or mobile dating app.*

create distinctive appearances and satisfy particular audiences—is common in online dating. That is, prospective mates make a conscious attempt to present themselves in a favorable light.

Compared to real-world dating, online dating services offer users more opportunity to manage their self-presentations, based on the way they answer questions about themselves. Do you want to come across as serious, athletic, or fun-loving? Then compose your answers accordingly. And why stop there? Although not much research has been done on the topic, studies show that the majority of those who participate in online dating think that others often lie about their age, marital status, and appearance. In response, some people have gone online to check public records and search for discrepancies in the way others answer questions.

So prolific have online dating sites become that they have bred new occupations. There

are now people who specialize in taking photographs designed for these sites, in editing people's profiles before they place them online, and even in advising clients on how to best to respond to online inquiries they receive from potential matches.

Online dating and mate selection, then, is not the same as meeting people face-to-face. Through an online dating service, a person can now meet and date complete strangers. Studies show that online daters are more apprehensive about meeting online prospects in person than they are about meeting people they don't know in the real world.

During the coronavirus pandemic, people actively moved their messaging online, particularly in cities that mandated shelter-in-place orders. Regardless of the circumstances, online platforms make finding partners easier when schedules, distance, or other barriers intrude.

LET'S DISCUSS

1. Do you think you might someday use an online dating site to meet someone? Why or why not?
2. Which method of locating other singles do you think would be more useful, going to an online dating site or using an app to locate singles near you? Explain.

Sources: Jacobs 2016; M. Rosenfeld and Thomas 2012; Vogels 2020a; 2020b; Zarrabi 2020

THINKING CRITICALLY

How would functionalist, conflict, interactionist, and feminist theorists explain a polygamous family structure?

Marriage and Family

Currently, over 94 percent of all men and women in the United States marry at least once during their lifetimes. Historically, the most consistent aspect of family life in this country has been the high rate of marriage. In fact, despite the high rate of divorce, there are some indications of a miniboom in marriages of late (American Community Survey 2019a: Table S1201).

In this part of the chapter, we will examine various aspects of love, marriage, and parenthood in the United States and

contrast them with cross-cultural examples. Though we're used to thinking of romance and mate selection as strictly a matter of individual preference, sociological analysis tells us that social institutions and distinctive cultural norms and values also play an important role.

Courtship and Mate Selection

One unmistakable trend in mate selection is that the process appears to be taking longer today than in the past. A variety of factors, including concerns about financial security and personal independence, have contributed to this delay in marriage. Back in 1950, men were typically age 23 and women 20 when they were first married. In 2019, the average age was almost 30 for men and 28 years for women. Most people are now well into their 20s or even 30s before they marry, both in the United States and in most other countries (Figure 12-2).

FIGURE 12-2 MEDIAN AGE AT FIRST MARRIAGE

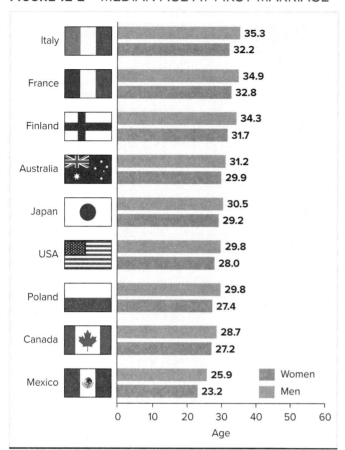

Country	Women	Men
Italy	35.3	32.2
France	34.9	32.8
Finland	34.3	31.7
Australia	31.2	29.9
Japan	30.5	29.2
USA	29.8	28.0
Poland	29.8	27.4
Canada	28.7	27.2
Mexico	25.9	23.2

Think about It Why do people marry earlier in Mexico than in Finland?

Note: Data for marriages 2017–2019.

Toni Anne Barson/Getty Images

John Legend and Chrissey Teigen married in 2013. He is African American; her mother is Thai and her father is Norwegian American. Such unions are becoming increasingly common and accepted. They are also blurring the definitions of race. What race will the children of these couples be considered to be? Why do you think so?

Aspects of Mate Selection Many societies have explicit or unstated rules that define potential mates as acceptable or unacceptable. These norms can be distinguished in terms of endogamy and exogamy. **Endogamy** (from the Greek *endon,* "within") specifies the groups within which a spouse must be found and prohibits marriage with others. For example, in the United States, many people are expected to marry within their racial, ethnic, or religious group, and are strongly discouraged or even prohibited from marrying outside the group. Endogamy is intended to reinforce the cohesiveness of the group by suggesting to the young that they should marry someone "of their own kind."

Even in the United States, interracial and interethnic marriages are still the exception. According to a census report released in 2018, the percentage of married-couple households that are interracial or interethnic is only just over 10 percent. The most common among the 5.8 million couples are the 2.3 million couples in which one partner is Hispanic and the other is non-Hispanic. Black-White couples account for another 473,000 (Rico et al. 2018).

In contrast, **exogamy** (from the Greek *exo,* "outside") requires mate selection outside certain groups, usually one's family or certain kinfolk. The **incest taboo,** a social norm common to

virtually all societies, prohibits sexual relationships between certain culturally specified relatives. For those of us in the United States, this taboo means that we must marry outside the nuclear family. We cannot marry our siblings, and in most states we cannot marry our first cousins.

Another factor that influences the selection of a marriage partner is **homogamy,** the conscious or unconscious tendency to select a mate with personal characteristics similar to one's own. The "like marries like" rule can be seen in couples with similar personalities and cultural interests. However, mate selection is unpredictable. Though some people may follow the homogamous pattern, others observe the "opposites attract" rule: one person is dependent and submissive—almost childishly so—while the other is dominant and controlling.

The Love Relationship Today's generation of college students seems more likely to hook up or cruise in large packs than to engage in the romantic dating relationships of their parents' and grandparents' generations. Still, at some point in their adult lives, the great majority of today's students will meet someone they love and enter into a long-term relationship that focuses on creating a family.

SOCIOLOGY IN THE GLOBAL COMMUNITY

12-2   Arranged and Hybrid Marriage

In some cultures, the proverbial question is not "Does he or she love me?" but rather "Whom do my parents want me to marry?" An **arranged marriage** occurs when other people (often the parents) choose a person's marital partner. Typically, in arranged marriages, the two people do not even know each other, much less have any mutual romantic interest.

The idea of arranged marriages seems strange to most young people who grow up in U.S. culture, which romanticizes finding the right partner. In an arranged marriage, the bride and groom start off on neutral ground, with no romantic expectations of each other. Understanding develops between them as the relationship matures. The partners are assumed to be compatible because they come from very similar social, economic, and cultural backgrounds.

Historically, arranged marriages were not unusual; even today they are common in many parts of Asia and Africa and also among some religious groups in the United States, such as the ultra-Orthodox Jewish community. In cultures where arranged marriage is common, young people are socialized to expect and look forward to such unions. But change is occurring, and in-

The idea of arranged marriages seems strange to most young people who grow up in U.S. culture, which romanticizes finding the right partner.

creasingly such couples are pursuing hybrid marriage. In a **hybrid marriage** the son or daughter may identify the prospective spouse, but the marriage is contingent on the parents' approval of that choice.

Arranged	Hybid	Romantic
Couple has no choice		Couple has complete autonomy

Are arranged marriages in the United States successful? Several studies (based on small samples) that attempt to answer this question have come to widely different conclusions. Some studies have found that arranged marriages result in higher marital satisfaction, while others find lower marital satisfaction or no difference from love-based marriages.

Many young people do still embrace their parents' tradition. As one first-year female Princeton student of Asian Indian ancestry put it, "In a lot of ways, it's easier. I don't have pressure to look for a boyfriend." Young people like her will look to their parents and other relatives to help them find a mate, thus entering into a hybrid marriage, or accept a match with a partner who has been selected in their parents' home country, thus entering into an arranged marriage.

LET'S DISCUSS

1. Describe some of the differences between cultures that practice arranged marriage versus cultures that practice romantic marriage. How do their views of the importance of the individual versus the family differ?

2. Imagine that your parents and/or a matchmaker are going to arrange a marriage for you. What kind of mate will they select? Will your chances of having a successful marriage be better or worse than if you selected your own mate?

Sources: Allendorf 2019; Chakravorty, Kapur, and Singh 2017; Herschthal 2004; Regan, Lakhanpal, and Anguiano 2012.

Parents in the United States tend to value love highly as a rationale for marriage, so they encourage their children to develop intimate relationships based on love and affection. Songs, films, books, magazines, television shows, and even cartoons and comic books reinforce the theme of love. At the same time, our society expects parents and peers to help a person confine his or her search for a mate to "socially acceptable" members of the opposite sex.

Though most people in the United States take the importance of falling in love for granted, the coupling of love and marriage is by no means a cultural universal. Many of the world's cultures give priority in mate selection to factors other than romantic feelings. In societies with *arranged marriages* engineered by parents or religious authorities, economic considerations play a significant role. The newly married couple is expected to develop a feeling of love *after* the legal union is formalized, if at all (J. Lee 2013).

In Box 12-2, we consider one cultural practice of Asian Indians and other immigrant groups that is not a part of American mainstream culture: arranged marriages.

Variations in Family Life and Intimate Relationships

Within the United States, social class, race, and ethnicity create variations in family life. Studying these variations will give us a more sophisticated understanding of contemporary family styles in our country.

Social Class Differences   Various studies have documented the differences in family organization among social classes in the United States. In the upper class, the emphasis is on lineage and maintenance of family position. If you are in the upper class, you are not simply a member of a nuclear family, but rather a member of a larger family tradition (think of the Rockefellers or the Kennedys). As a result, upper-class families are quite concerned about what they see as proper training for children.

Lower-class families do not often have the luxury of worrying about the "family name"; they must first struggle to pay their bills and survive the crises often associated with a life of poverty. Such families are more likely to have only one parent at home, which creates special challenges in child care and financial management. Children from lower-class families typically assume adult responsibilities—including marriage and parenthood—at an earlier age than children from affluent homes. In part, that is because they may lack the money needed to remain in school.

Social class differences in family life remain significant, especially among those with children. Compared to lower-class families, middle-class families tend to schedule more of their children's time, or even to overstructure it. In addition, low-income households face many different types of concentrated disadvantage, especially job insecurity and precarious work, if the adults are employed at all (Cooper and Pugh 2020).

A marriage model has emerged that shows some distinct social class differences. Among the college-educated, both spouses are delaying marriage, which typically means that both have solid earnings and relatively stable job futures. Not surprisingly, divorce rates are relatively low among college-educated people, especially among those who married during the first decade of the 21st century, when compared to non-college-educated couples (Adamy and Overberg 2020).

Finally, in her book *The Accordion Family* (see the chapter-opening excerpt), Katherine S. Newman (2012) noted that the accordion or boomerang family differs by social class. An upper-middle-class family like the one described in the opening excerpt can afford to provide space to an adult child who is working toward an advanced degree. Less privileged families tend to hang on to their adult children for the labor or income they can contribute to the family's welfare.

Many racial and ethnic groups appear to have distinctive family characteristics. However, racial and class factors are often closely related. In examining family life among racial and ethnic minorities, keep in mind that certain patterns may result from class as well as cultural factors.

Racial and Ethnic Differences The subordinate status of racial and ethnic minorities in the United States profoundly affects their family lives. For example, the lower incomes of African Americans, Native Americans, most Hispanic groups, and selected Asian American groups make creating and maintaining successful marital unions a difficult task. The economic restructuring of the past 60 years, described by sociologist William Julius Wilson (1996, 2009) and others, has especially affected people living in inner cities and desolate rural areas, such as reservations. Furthermore, the immigration policy of the United

Blend Images/Getty Images

States has complicated the successful relocation of intact families from Asia and Latin America.

The African American family suffers from many negative and inaccurate stereotypes. It is true that in a significantly higher proportion of Black than white families, no father is present in the home (Figure 12-3). Yet Black single mothers often belong to stable, functioning kin networks, which mitigate the pressures of sexism and racism. Members of these networks—predominantly female kin such as mothers, grandmothers, and aunts—ease financial strains by sharing goods and services. In addition to these strong kinship bonds, Black family life has emphasized deep religious commitment and high aspirations for achievement (DuBois [1909] 1970; Umaña-Taylor and Hill 2020).

Like African Americans, Native Americans draw on family ties to cushion many of the hardships they face. On the Navajo reservation, for example, teenage parenthood is not regarded as the crisis that it is elsewhere in the United States. The Navajo trace their descent matrilineally. Traditionally, couples reside with the wife's family after marriage, allowing the grandparents to help with the child rearing. While the Navajo do not approve of teenage parenthood, the deep emotional commitment of their extended families provides a warm home environment for children, even when no father is present or involved (Dalla and Gamble 2001; John 2012).

Sociologists also have taken note of differences in family patterns among other racial and ethnic groups. For example, Mexican American men have been described as exhibiting a sense of virility, personal worth, and pride in their maleness that is called **machismo.** Mexican Americans are also described as being more familistic than many other subcultures. **Familism (or *familismo*)** refers to pride in the extended family, expressed through the maintenance of close ties and strong obligations to kinfolk outside the immediate family. Traditionally, Mexican Americans have placed proximity to their extended families above other needs and desires.

FIGURE 12-3   RISE OF SINGLE-PARENT FAMILIES IN THE UNITED STATES, 1970–2019

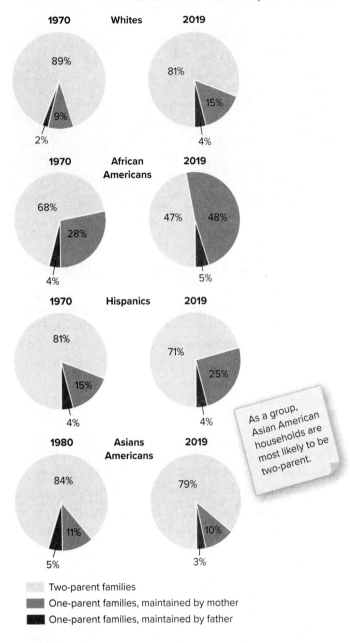

Two-parent families
One-parent families, maintained by mother
One-parent families, maintained by father

As a group, Asian American households are most likely to be two-parent.

Note: Families are groups with children under 18. Early data for Asian Americans are for 1980. White data are for non-Hispanic whites. Not included are unrelated people living together with no children present. All data exclude children who live with neither parent.
Sources: Bureau of the Census 2008a:56; 2019f: Table C3.

Although familism is often seen as a positive cultural attribute, it may also have negative consequences. Sociologists who have studied the relatively low college application rates of Hispanic students have found they have a strong desire to stay at home. Even the children of college-educated parents express this preference, which diminishes the likelihood of their getting a four-year degree and dramatically reduces the possibility that they will apply to a selective college.

These family patterns are changing, however, in response to changes in Latinos' social class standing, educational

achievements, and occupations. Like other Americans, career-oriented Latinos in search of a mate but short on spare time are turning to Internet sites. As Latinos and other groups assimilate into the dominant culture of the United States, their family lives take on both the positive and negative characteristics associated with white households (Hossain et al. 2015).

Child-Rearing Patterns

The Nayars of southern India acknowledge the biological role of fathers, but the mother's eldest brother is responsible for her children. In contrast, uncles play only a peripheral role in child care in the United States. Caring for children is a universal function of the family, yet the ways in which different societies assign this function to family members can vary significantly. Even within the United States, child-rearing patterns are varied. A trend that began in the 20th century and has only accelerated into the 21st century is a dramatic rearrangement of children's living situation, which began in the 1950s. Today fewer than one in five children lives in a household with a father present and working, a mother present, and no other step or custodial children present (P. Cohen 2014).

We'll take a look here at parenthood and grandparenthood, adoption, dual-income families, single-parent families, and stepfamilies.

Parenthood and Grandparenthood   The socialization of children is essential to the maintenance of any culture. Consequently, parenthood is one of the most important (and most demanding) social roles in the United States. Sociologist Alice Rossi (1968, 1984) has identified four factors that complicate the transition to parenthood and the role of socialization. First, there is little anticipatory socialization for the social role of caregiver. The normal school curriculum gives scant attention to the subjects most relevant to successful family life, such as child care and home maintenance. Second, only limited learning occurs during the period of pregnancy itself. Third, the transition to parenthood is quite abrupt. Unlike adolescence, it is not prolonged; unlike the transition to work, the duties of caregiving cannot be taken on gradually. Finally, in Rossi's view, our society lacks clear and helpful guidelines for successful parenthood. There is little consensus on how parents can produce happy and well-adjusted offspring—or even on what it means to be well adjusted. For these reasons, socialization for parenthood involves difficult challenges for most men and women in the United States.

Greater life expectancy has increased the likelihood of grandparents playing a role in the lives of both their adult children and their grandkids. About 10 percent of all children live with a grandparent. In over 15 percent of these households, no parent is present, so a grandparent truly is raising the child. The presence of grandparents in the household is more common among African American, Latino, and immigrant families. In Figure 12-4 we see that often the grandparent is providing a

Lori Waselchuck/New York Times/Redux Pictures

When nine-year-old Blake Brunson shows up for a basketball game, so do his *eight* grandparents—the result of his parents' remarriages. Blended families can be very supportive to children, but what message do they send to them on the permanency of marriage?

financial role in the household as well as a social one (Carr and Utz 2020).

Adoption   In a legal sense, **adoption** is the transfer of the legal rights, responsibilities, and privileges of parenthood to a new legal parent or parents. In many cases, these rights are transferred from a biological parent or parents (often called birth parents) to an adoptive parent or parents. Every year, about 125,000 children are adopted (Adoption Network 2020).

Viewed from a functionalist perspective, government has a strong interest in encouraging adoption. Policymakers, in fact, have both a humanitarian and a financial stake in the process. In theory, adoption offers a stable family environment for chil-

FIGURE 12-4   GRANDPARENTS WHO SUPPORT GRANDCHILDREN, 2018

Grandparents Still Work to Support Grandchildren

About 1.3 Million Grandparents in the Labor Force Are Responsible for Most of the Basic Care of Coresident Grandchildren Under Age 18

	Grandparents in labor force	Responsible for care of coresident grandchildren	Grandparents not in labor force
60 years old and over	396,993		683,257
30 to 59 years old	941,399		395,165

Note: Coresident refers to grandparents and grandchildren living in the same household.
Source: Bureau of the Census 2019g. *Hand:* Jamie Grill/Getty Images

dren who otherwise might not receive satisfactory care. Moreover, government data show that unwed mothers who keep their babies tend to be of lower socioeconomic status and often require public assistance to support their children. The government can lower its social welfare expenses, then, if children are transferred to economically self-sufficient families. From an interactionist perspective, however, adoption may require a child to adjust to a very different family environment and parental approach to child rearing.

There are two legal methods of adopting an unrelated person: the adoption may be arranged through a licensed agency, or in some states it may be arranged through a private agreement sanctioned by the courts. Adopted children may come from the United States or from abroad. In 2018, 4,058 children entered the United States as the adopted children of U.S. citizens (Bureau of Consular Affairs 2020).

Having a new child is a major adjustment for everyone in the family; adopting a child is an even bigger adjustment. If the adopted child comes from another culture and is racially or ethnically different from the adopting family, the challenge is that much greater.

The 2010 earthquake in Haiti drew attention to the foreign perspective on international adoptions, which is not always positive. When well-meaning people from the United States arrived in Haiti to rescue alleged orphans and arrange for their adoption in other countries, government officials objected. Some of the children, it turned out, were not orphans; their parents were simply too poor to care for them. For the governments of overstressed developing nations, adoption can be both a solution and a problem.

Adoption is controversial not only abroad but at home as well. In some cases, those who adopt children are not married. In 1995, an important court decision in New York held that a couple does not need to be married to adopt a child. Under this ruling, unmarried heterosexual couples, lesbian couples, and gay couples can all adopt children in New York. Within a year of the 2015 *Obergefell* Supreme Court decision ending bans on same-sex marriages, courts ruled against prohibitions of gay and lesbian couples adopting children. We will revisit the topic of adoption by gay and lesbian couples in Box 12-3.

Dual-Income Families   The idea of a family consisting of a wage-earning husband and a wife who stays at home has largely given way to the dual-income household. Among couples with children under 18, 93 percent of the men and 72 percent of the women were in the labor force in 2018 (Bureau of Labor Statistics 2019e).

The practice of married people living apart has risen 44 percent since 2000 to 3.96 million, 2018 census data show. The data include couples who live apart for all reasons *except* marital discord, including incarceration or living in a nursing home,

Cheryl Gerber/The New York Times/Redux

Miles Harvey reads to his children via Skype. Harvey, who is happily married, lives 900 miles from his family in Chicago. He accepted a job in New Orleans for economic reasons.

but a sizable number do this for work. The share of adult married couples who live apart is highest among adults in their 20s and 30s, when careers are typically being built, and falls as couples approach retirement.

THINKING CRITICALLY

What stresses does living apart place on family life? What economic or social factors make it acceptable?

Why has there been such a rise in the number of dual-income couples? A major factor is economic need, coupled with a desire by both men *and* women to pursue their careers. As a result, these couples spend more on travel and housing. Typically, one spouse rents an apartment in the city where he or she works, while the other holds down the home front, whether in an owned or rented property. Couples living apart are nothing new: for generations men have worked at transient jobs as soldiers, truck drivers, or traveling salesmen. Now, however, the woman's job is often the one that creates the separation. The existence of such household arrangements reflects an acceptance of the egalitarian family type (Sklar 2020).

Single-Parent Families In recent decades, the stigma attached to unwed mothers and other single parents has significantly diminished. **Single-parent families,** in which only one parent is present to care for the children, can hardly be viewed as a rarity in the United States. In 2019, a single parent headed about 19 percent of non-Hispanic white families with children

under 18, 29 percent of Hispanic families with children, and 53 percent of African American families with children (see Figure 12-3).

The lives of single parents and their children are not inevitably more difficult than life in a traditional nuclear family. It is as inaccurate to assume that a single-parent family is necessarily deprived as it is to assume that a two-parent family is always secure and happy. Nevertheless, life in a single-parent family can be extremely stressful, in both economic and emotional terms. A family headed by a single mother faces especially difficult problems when the mother is a teenager.

Why might low-income teenage women wish to have children and face the obvious financial difficulties of motherhood? Viewed from an interactionist perspective, these women tend to have low self-esteem and limited options; a child may provide a sense of motivation and purpose for a teenager whose economic worth in our society is limited at best. Given the barriers that many young women face because of their gender, race, ethnicity, and class, many teenagers may believe they have little to lose and much to gain by having a child.

According to a widely held stereotype, "unwed mothers" and "babies having babies" in the United States are predominantly African American. However, this view is not entirely accurate. African Americans account for a disproportionate share of births to unmarried women and teenagers, but the majority of all babies born to unmarried teenage mothers are born to white adolescents. Moreover, since 1980, birthrates among Black teenagers have generally declined (Hamilton 2020).

Stepfamilies Approximately 45 percent of all people in the United States will marry, divorce, and then remarry. The rising rates of divorce and remarriage have led to a noticeable increase in stepfamily relationships.

The exact nature of blended families has social significance for adults and children alike. Certainly resocialization is required when an adult becomes a stepparent or a child becomes a

USE YOUR SOCIOLOGICAL IMAGINATION

What personal experience do you have with child rearing by grandparents, dual-income families, or single-parent families? Describe what you observed using sociological concepts.

stepchild and stepsibling. Moreover, an important distinction must be made between first-time stepfamilies and households where there have been repeated divorces, breakups, or changes in custodial arrangements.

In evaluating the rise of stepfamilies, some observers have assumed that children would benefit from remarriage because they would be gaining a second custodial parent, and would potentially enjoy greater economic security. However, after reviewing many studies of stepfamilies, sociologist Andrew J. Cherlin (2021) concluded that children whose parents have remarried do not have higher levels of well-being than children in divorced single-parent families.

Stepparents can play valuable and unique roles in their stepchildren's lives, but their involvement does not guarantee an improvement in family life. In fact, standards may decline. Studies suggest that children raised in families with stepmothers are likely to have less health care, education, and money spent on their food than children raised by biological mothers. The measures are also negative for children raised by stepfathers, but only half as negative as in the case of stepmothers. These results don't mean that stepmothers are "evil"—it may be that the stepmother holds back out of concern for seeming too intrusive, or relies mistakenly on the biological father to carry out parental duties (Jensen and Howard 2015; Raley and Sweeney 2020).

Divorce

In the United States, the pattern of family life includes commitments both to marriage and to self-expression and personal growth. Needless to say, the tension between those competing commitments can undermine a marriage, working against the establishment of a lasting relationship. This approach to family life is distinctive to the United States. In some nations, such as Italy, the culture strongly supports marriage and

discourages divorce. In others, such as Sweden, people treat marriage the same way as cohabitation, and both arrangements are just as lasting (Cherlin 2021).

Statistical Trends in Divorce

Just how common is divorce? Surprisingly, this is not a simple question; divorce statistics are difficult to interpret. The media frequently report that one out of every two marriages ends in divorce, but that figure is misleading. It is based on a comparison of all divorces that occur in a single year (regardless of when the couples were married) with the number of new marriages in the same year.

Marriage is showing signs of longevity. About 70 percent of marriages that began in the 1990s were still together as of late 2014. Those who married in the first decade of the 21st century are showing even more of a tendency to stay together. Given current trends, two-thirds of marriages will never end in divorce (C. Miller 2014).

In many countries, divorce began to increase in the late 1960s but then leveled off; since the late 1980s, it has declined by 30 percent. (Figure 12-5 shows the pattern in the United States.) This trend is due to two factors: first, couples wait longer to marry, and second, married people tend to be better educated and have higher incomes than those who do not marry (Cohen 2020).

Getting divorced obviously does not sour people on marriage: about 40 percent of all marriages are remarriages. Women are less likely than men to remarry because many retain custody of their children after a divorce, which complicates a new adult relationship (Raley and Sweeney 2020).

Some people regard the nation's high rate of remarriage as an endorsement of the institution of marriage, but it does lead to the new challenges of a kin network composed of both current and prior marital relationships. Such networks can be particularly complex if children are involved or if an ex-spouse remarries.

FIGURE 12-5 TRENDS IN MARRIAGE AND DIVORCE IN THE UNITED STATES, 1920–2017

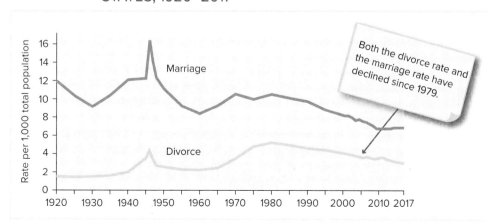

Sources: Bureau of the Census 1975:64; Centers for Disease Control and Prevention 2012b, 2017.

As with other aspects of daily life, social media are adapting to changes in marriage. In 2016 Facebook introduced a Compassion Team that helps users erase ex-spouses and ex-partners from their online presence and to remove feeds from other sites that may only serve to make a difficult time more difficult (Green 2016).

Factors Associated with Divorce

Perhaps the most important factor in the increase in divorce over the past hundred years has been the greater social *acceptance* of divorce. It is no longer considered necessary to endure an unhappy marriage. More important, various religious denominations have relaxed their negative attitudes toward divorce, so that most religious leaders no longer treat it as a sin.

The growing acceptance of divorce is a worldwide phenomenon. The majority of people in a cross-national study see divorce as morally acceptable or do not even view it as a moral issue. Out of 40 nations, in just 12 do at least 40 percent of respondents find divorce unacceptable; those nations are in Latin America, Africa, and Asia. Globally, gambling and alcohol are much more likely to raise moral indignation than divorce (Poushter 2014; Wang and Schofer 2018).

In the United States, several factors have contributed to the growing social acceptance of divorce:

- Most states have adopted more liberal divorce laws in the past four decades. No-fault divorce laws, which allow a couple to end their marriage without fault on either side (by specifying adultery, for instance), accounted for an initial surge in the divorce rate after they were introduced in the 1970s, but appear to have had little effect beyond that.

- Divorce has become a more practical option in newly formed families, since families tend to have fewer children now than in the past.

- A general increase in family incomes, coupled with the availability of free legal aid to some poor people, has meant that more couples can afford costly divorce proceedings.

- As society provides greater opportunities for women, more and more wives are becoming less dependent on their husbands, both economically and emotionally. They may feel more able to leave a marriage if it seems hopeless.

Impact of Divorce on Children

Divorce is traumatic for all involved, but it has special meaning for the more than 1 million children whose parents divorce each year. Of course, for some of these children, divorce signals the welcome end to a very dysfunctional relationship. Perhaps that is why a national study that tracked 6,332 children both before and after their parents' divorce found that their behavior did not suffer from the marital breakups. Other studies have shown greater unhappiness among children who live amid parental conflict than among children whose parents are divorced.

Still, it would be simplistic to assume that children are automatically better off following the breakup of their parents' marriage. The interests of the parents do not necessarily serve children well. Custodial arrangements can take a long time to work out and are not necessarily followed. Recent data show that only about 53 percent of court-ordered child support to custodial mothers is paid. Overwhelmingly, where only one parent has custody of children, that parent is the mother. The proportion of children who live with custodial mothers with incomes below the poverty level is 32 percent. Only about half as many custodial fathers live in poverty (H. Kim 2011; Grall 2020).

Lesbian and Gay Relationships

The lifestyles of lesbians and gay men are varied. Some live in long-term, monogamous relationships; others live alone or with roommates. The possibility of living openly in a long-term relationship, like any opposite sex couple, emerged dramatically with the 2015 Supreme Court *Obergefell* decision. In *Obergefell v. Hodges* the Court heard the case of Jim Obergefell, who had married his terminally ill partner in 2011 in a state where same-sex marriage was legal. However, because the couple's home state of Ohio did not recognize same-sex marriage, his name could not be listed on his deceased spouse's death certificate. The Court, in a surprising 5-4 vote, chose to go beyond ruling on the specifics of the case and declared that the Constitution guarantees the right to same-sex marriage. Within two years of the decision, over 60 percent of cohabiting same-sex couples had become legally married.

THINKING CRITICALLY

In a society that maximizes the welfare of all family members, how easy should it be for couples to divorce? How easy should it be to get married?

With marriage legalized, states and social agencies now began to deal with another new social reality: same-sex divorce. In the short run, the issue is exceedingly complicated, because in the years before the Supreme Court decision, many gay couples traveled to jurisdictions where same-sex marriage was legal to be married and then returned to live in their home states where it was not (for example, Massachusetts began recognizing such unions back in 2004). Couples who seek divorce usually must either return to the place where they were married and reestablish legal residence or try to work through the still-undefined process in their home state. It will be many years before it is possible to identify the divorce and remarriage patterns of same-sex couples (Masci et al. 2019; Rosenfeld 2017).

In addition to marriage equality, the last few years have seen dramatic changes in legal discrimination against lesbian, gay, bisexual, and transgender, and queer (LGBTQ) people. Although significant barriers remain, especially in family law and in publicly expressed prejudicial attitudes, progress has been made in other areas. Increasingly, businesses are seeing the benefit of hiring LGBTQ people. In 2012 the CIA began active recruitment in the LGBTQ community—a sharp departure from the past, when the CIA and other federal agencies routinely denied security clearances to gay men and women. As a result, even before the *Obergefell* decision, 92 percent of lesbian, gay, bisexual, and transgender adults felt that society had become more accepting in the previous decade (G. Allen 2012; Suh 2014).

LumiNola/Getty Images

USE YOUR SOCIOLOGICAL IMAGINATION

What is the significance of legalizing same-sex marriage for the couple's relatives? For the wider society?

The acceptance of LGBTQ relationships has been slow and unequal, especially when it comes to couples seeking to adopt children, as we see in Box 12-3.

With marriage legally broadened, all the topics discussed in this chapter, from divorce to child rearing, have expanded dramatically to encompass marriage with two women and two men. Do such households differ from each other? Do they differ from opposite-sex partnerships? Even before *Obergefell*, queer theorists argued that gays and lesbians are often understudied by researchers (although that is beginning to change). In particular, queer theorists point to the relative lack of high-quality research on LGBTQ households and their relationship to the larger society, not to mention non-LGBTQ relatives. As the campaign for same-sex marriage gains momentum, some scholars see a need to focus on gay men and lesbians who do not fit the new "gay norm," who reject the desire to create a nuclear family household. Continuing to focus on the margins of society, queer theorists argue for more attention to people of color, the working class, the poor, and immigrants in the LGBTQ community (Reczek 2020; Tornello et al. 2015).

Diverse Lifestyles

Marriage is no longer the presumed route from adolescence to adulthood. Instead, it is treated as just one of several paths to maturity. As a result, the marriage ceremony has lost much of its social significance as a rite of passage. The nation's marriage rate has declined since 1960 because people are postponing marriage until later in life, and because more couples, including same-sex couples, are deciding to form partnerships without marriage (Cohen 2020).

Cohabitation

Cohabitation has become so common that among adults ages 18 to 44, 59 percent have lived with an unmarried partner at some point in their lives, while only 50 percent have ever been married. Some observers have described this trend as "retreat from marriage." In a national survey released in 2019, most Americans said that cohabitation was acceptable, but many still saw societal benefits in marriage.

Couples who are cohabiting or married give similar reasons for their relationships, such as love and companionship. Not surprisingly, married couples are more likely to see children in their future, while those who are cohabiting are more likely to indicate they do so for financial reasons or because of "convenience."

Cohabiting women are more likely than cohabiting men to say that love and wanting to have children someday were major reasons why they moved in with their partner. For example, 80 percent of cohabiting women cite love as a major factor, compared with 63 percent of cohabiting men. No such gender differences are evident when married adults respond to the same question (Cherlin 2020; Horowitz et al. 2019; Sassler and Lichter 2020).

RESEARCH TODAY

12-3   Challenges to LGBTQ Adoption

Traditionally in the United States adoption and foster care were only open to married opposite-sex couples. Gradually procedures were broadened so that most agencies worked with single parents. Placements to LGBTQ individuals or couples have begun only relatively recently, as in the past many states prohibited such placements. Even in those states where LGBTQ adoption was legal, many agencies would work only with heterosexual individuals and couples.

Obergefell put same-sex couples on equal footing with opposite-sex couples with family service agencies. However, other rulings had allowed religious agencies to deny services to couples and individuals whose lifestyles conflicted with their beliefs. This meant that many private agencies continued to limit child placements only to opposite-sex married couples.

The issue is a vital one to LGBTQ parents, who are much more exposed to the adoption and foster care system than are straight parents. Of the estimated 114,000 same-sex couples raising children in the United States, one in five are raising adopted or foster children. This is a significantly higher proportion than the 3 percent of heterosexual couples doing so.

In 2012 President Barack Obama issued an administrative order that included sexual orientation and gender identity as protected classes and thus ended religious groups from denying placements with LGBTQ individuals or couples. As of 2020, there were about 428,000 children in foster care across the United States. Each year, some 50,000 children are adopted through the U.S. child welfare system, but about 20,000 others "age out" before being placed with an adoptive family. Therefore, many family-service professionals welcomed broadening the potential pool of adoptive parents.

> *Of the estimated 114,000 same-sex couples raising children in the United States, one in five are raising adopted or foster children.*

In 2019, the Trump administration proposed a new rule that would allow foster care and adoption agencies to deny their services to LGBTQ families on faith-based grounds. The change was proposed, on the basis of

freedom of religion, to permit religious agencies to act according to their beliefs, which might include disapproval of LGBTQ lifestyles. The proposals noted that some faith-based agencies had stopped doing any adoption and foster care placements rather than open them to the LGBTQ community.

One can anticipate legal challenges to continue regarding faith-based family services for some time, whatever the federal policy may be.

LET'S DISCUSS

1. Should agencies be allowed to deny adoption placements to LGBTQ couples or individuals on the basis of religious beliefs? Why or why not?
2. From a child's point of view, compare the experience of adoption by a same-sex family to that of adoption by an opposite-sex family. What might be the advantages and disadvantages of each? What might be the challenges?

Sources: Adoption Network 2020; Goldberg and Conron 2018; Taylor 2019.

People tend to associate cohabitation with younger, childless couples. Although that stereotype may have been accurate a generation or more ago, it is not now. Since 1970, the number of unmarried couples with children has increased 12-fold.

Periodically, legislators attempt to bolster the desirability of a lifelong commitment to marriage. In 2002, President George W. Bush backed funding for an initiative to promote marriage among those who receive public assistance. Under the Healthy Marriage and Responsible Fatherhood Initiative, the federal government created a resource center that promoted marriage-related programs. As of 2020, the initiative funded 36 organizations across the country and in one territory to provide comprehensive healthy relationship and marriage education services, as well as job and career advancement activities to promote economic stability and overall improved family well-being (Office of Family Assistance 2019).

Remaining Single

Back in 1950, there were about 4 million Americans living alone, and a little less than 10 pecent of all households were

one-person households. At that time, living alone was most common in the Western states, such as Alaska, Montana, and Nevada, because that was where single migrant men went.

As of 2019, there were more than 36 million people living alone, or over 28 percent of all American households. This is an enormous change. Today single people are most likely to be found in big cities all across the country. In most cities, between 35 and 45 percent of the population is single. In Manhattan, the center of New York City, about half of all households contain only one person.

Being single has emerged both as a deliberate choice and also because marriage is no longer something that young adults seek automatically as a step toward adulthood. With each passing generation, marriage is less likely to be seen as a critical step to be taken. The likelihood of being married by age 32 has decreased with each passing generation:

- 26% of Millennials (born 1981–1996)
- 36% of Gen Xers (born 1965–1980)

- 48% of Baby Boomers (born 1946–1964
- 65% of Silent Generation (born 1928–1945)

Most unmarried Millennials (69%) say that they would like to marry, but compared to their predecessors, a higher proportion will remain single or be single for extended periods of their lives (Bureau of the Census 2019h; Gemmill 2019; Klinenberg 2012).

A 2020 government report showed the lowest rate of new marriages since data collection was begun in 1867. The trend toward maintaining a single lifestyle for a longer period is related to the growing economic independence of young people. This trend is especially significant for women. Freed from financial needs, women don't necessarily need to marry to enjoy a satisfying life. Divorce, late marriage, and longevity also figure into this trend (Curtin and Sutton 2020).

There are many reasons why a person may choose not to marry. Some singles do not want to limit their sexual intimacy to one lifetime partner. Some men and women do not want to become highly dependent on any one person—and do not want anyone depending heavily on them. In a society that values individuality and self-fulfillment, the single lifestyle can offer certain freedoms that married couples may not enjoy. Even divorced parents may not feel the need to remarry. Andrew J. Cherlin (2009) contends that a single parent who connects with other adults, such as grandparents, to form a solid, supportive relationship for child rearing should not feel compelled to re-partner.

Over the last 50 years, childlessness has become an important social phenomenon. Since the mid-1970s, when data were first made available, the share of women who never gave birth to a biological child doubled: from 10 percent in 1976 to about 20 percent by 2019. Research indicates that a little more than one-half (56 percent) of eventually childless women anticipated childlessness before turning age 30. Other women came to expect childlessness later in the life course (Bureau of the Census 2019e).

Marriage without Children

There has been a modest increase in childlessness in the United States and other industrial countries. According to available data, about 16 to 22 percent of women will now complete their childbearing years without having borne any children, compared to 9 to 10 percent in 1980 (*Economist* 2017c).

USE YOUR SOCIOLOGICAL IMAGINATION

What would happen to our society if many more married couples suddenly decided not to have children? How would society change if cohabitation and/or singlehood became the norm?

Childlessness within marriage has generally been viewed as a problem that can be solved through such means as adoption and artificial insemination. More and more couples today, however, choose not to have children and regard themselves as child-free rather than childless. They do not believe that having children automatically follows from marriage, nor do they feel that reproduction is the duty of all married couples. Childless couples have formed support groups (with names like No Kidding) and set up websites.

Economic considerations have contributed to this shift in attitudes; having children has become quite expensive. According to a government estimate made for 2015, the average middle-class family will spend $284,570 to feed, clothe, and shelter a child from birth to age 18. If the child attends college, that amount could double, depending on the college chosen. In 1960, parents spent only 2 percent of their income on child care and education; now they spend 16 percent, reflecting the rising dependence on nonfamily child care. Aware of the financial pressures, some couples are weighing the advantages of a child-free marriage (Lino et al. 2017).

Childless couples are beginning to question current practices in the workplace. While applauding employers' efforts to provide child care and flexible work schedules, some nevertheless express concern about tolerance of employees who leave early to take children to doctors, ball games, or after-school classes. As more dual-career couples enter the paid labor force and struggle to balance career and familial responsibilities, conflicts with employees who have no children may increase (Blackstone 2014).

Family leave is an issue important to almost all the families we have considered in this chapter. All working parents, whether they are single, gay, or straight, struggle to find ways to care for children and for elderly and sick family members. The Social Policy section that follows considers family leave issues in the United States and throughout the world.

Amos Morgan/Photodisc/Getty Images

socialpolicy and the Family

Family Leave Worldwide

Kim Knoblauch gave birth to her first baby in the United States. The only "maternity leave" pay she received was one month's accrued vacation and sick time, and when she was ready to return to work, her job no longer existed. Because she worked for a small company, the federal requirement that her job be protected for 12 weeks did not apply.

Four years later, her husband's job had taken Knoblauch and her family to Germany, where she had a very different experience. The family was entitled to Germany's full range of maternity and postpartum benefits.

The day after baby Eva came home from the hospital, a midwife came to Knoblauch's home to weigh her, check the cord stump, and help with breast-feeding. In addition, the family was entitled to *Kindergeld*, a government allowance that helps cover the costs of child rearing. Because she had two children, Knoblauch collected about $180 per month (Expatica 2020).

Protecting parents in the workplace has a long history worldwide. Historically policies were enacted allowing pregnant women to work, prohibiting child labor, and providing family health and life insurance. In recent generations, countries have created programs that require employers to allow new mothers to take leaves of absence. At first, most laws provided only for unpaid leave. Later paid leave was required, and finally, the benefits were extended to new fathers.

Looking at the Issue

Paid parental leave for mothers and fathers with newborns or newly adopted children is common in industrial countries. When Australia enacted its family leave law in 2010, this left the United States as the only industrialized nation that did not mandate paid family leave. The United States does not even require employers to grant unpaid leave, which would guarantee the new parents a job when they returned to work.

In the United States family leave is left to employers' discretion, including decisions about paid versus unpaid leave or even whether an employee can use accrued sick leave. This is not typical at all. Of the 185 countries surveyed by the International Labor Organization, only two provided no cash benefits for women during maternity leave—the United States and Papua New Guinea. Figure 12-6 compares policies in selected countries.

Applying Sociology

As noted earlier in the chapter, functionalists identify a series of paramount functions that societies provide, including socialization of children, which is particularly critical for newborns ornewly adopted children. To functionalists family leave is particularly important as a means of facilitating the parent–child interaction that is crucial to socialization.

Interactionists look at family leave policy as having direct impact on everyday relations both at work and home. In the workplace the issue is how supervisors, peers, and subordinates adjust to the

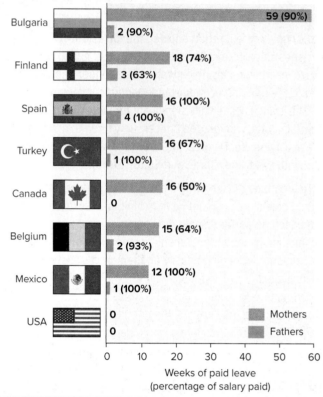

FIGURE 12-6   PAID PARENTAL LEAVE

- Bulgaria: 59 (90%) Mothers / 2 (90%) Fathers
- Finland: 18 (74%) Mothers / 3 (63%) Fathers
- Spain: 16 (100%) Mothers / 4 (100%) Fathers
- Turkey: 16 (67%) Mothers / 1 (100%) Fathers
- Canada: 16 (50%) Mothers / 0 Fathers
- Belgium: 15 (64%) Mothers / 2 (93%) Fathers
- Mexico: 12 (100%) Mothers / 1 (100%) Fathers
- USA: 0 Mothers / 0 Fathers

Weeks of paid leave
(percentage of salary paid)

Think about It What effects on parents and the entire family would you expect to find as a result in differences in family leave policy?

Note: Data for 2018 compiled in 2020. The economic costs of the coronavirus pandemic have pressured some governments to reduce parental leave benefits, and the United States still does not require any such benefits.
Source: Organisation for Economic Co-operation and Development, 2020b.
Flags: admin_design/Shutterstock

absence of the worker. At home, the focus would be on how family leave policies affect the household. For example, research suggests that when mothers are granted family leave, infants are more likely to be breast-fed, which lowers illness and hospitalization rates for infants and benefits women's health. Beyond these health advantages, paid maternity leave yields economic gains in terms of reduced health care costs, reduced recruitment and retraining costs, and improved long-term earnings for women (Heymann with McNeill 2013).

Conflict theorists note the inherent class bias in family leave policy. In the United States, employees who receive paid leave are a relatively small number of relatively affluent workers. The much larger group of workers in retail and service jobs are left out. Existing or proposed leave policies are often based on a worker's current job history, which favors higher-level employees. Most paid leave programs in the United States are limited to long-term, full-time employees, who are greatly advantaged over the many people, particularly women, who piece together several jobs or work part-time. Unless family leave is heavily supported by government, this portion of the workforce will be unable to participate.

To seek an effective solution, one is reminded of Karl Marx and Friedrich Engel's ([1847] 1955) refrain about workers of all countries uniting. Dividing family leave policies between full-time professionals and the rest of the labor force will only contribute to inequality among workers (Tucker 1978:473, 500).

Moreover, even when family leave plans exist, companies seem to stigmatize the use of these policies beyond the very limited assistance given to new mothers, especially in the United States. Feminist scholars contend that this results from a flexibility stigma. **Flexibility stigma** is the devaluation of workers who seek or are presumed to need flexible work arrangements. Research shows that women often face a tough and unfair choice: they can either be stigmatized for taking advantage of leave options or remain in precarious, low-paying jobs (Jacobs and Padavic 2015).

Gary John Norman/Getty Images

In contrast to the United States, many developed nations guarantee paid parental leave. As pictured here, Croatia provides mothers with 100 percent of their pay for 30 weeks; fathers receive 42 percent of their pay for 26 weeks.

Initiating Policy

The FMLA (Family and Medical Leave Act) enacted in 1993 entitles eligible employees of covered employers to take unpaid, job-protected leave for specified family and medical reasons with continuation of group health insurance coverage for up to 12 weeks. Advocates have sought unsuccessfully to expand these provisions. One such proposal is the FAMILY Act (Family and Medical Insurance Leave Act), which would provide paid leave of up to 66 percent of regular wages, with a maximum amount of $1,000 per week.

Opponents question the cost of the program to the employer or the government, while supporters point to studies showing that such a policy would promote family stability, confer long-term health benefits, and lower public assistance rates. FAMILY or another proposal, the Healthy Families Act, has been introduced to Congress regularly; as of early 2018, Congress held hearings on the bill. On a positive note, the Trump administration included in its 2018 budget a provision for a national paid-leave plan for parents after birth or adoption. In 2020 President Donald Trump became the first Republican president to propose a national parental leave policy. No legislative action was introduced, so a national mandate awaits another administration and Congress (Miller 2020).

In 2020, Congress addressed the heightened parenting needs during the pandemic through the Families First Coronavirus Response Act (FFCRA), which provided funding for 12 weeks of emergency leave (10 weeks paid) to care for a child whose school or place of care is unavailable. But the United States still lacks a permanent and comprehensive paid family and medical leave policy. Even with these temporary provisions, only 20 percent of private-sector workers had access to paid family leave in 2020 to care for a child or a sick family member. Black and Hispanic workers were much less likely than white, non-Hispanic workers to have access to paid family leave.

While parental leave enjoys wide support worldwide, including in the United States, existing programs are being scrutinized in the wake of the pandemic as cash-strapped governments and businesses look to recover economically. It remains to be seen whether changes in parental leave policies are short term or lead to a longer-term rethinking of this social policy.

As the federal government struggles to develop a mandated policy, selected private corporations continue to introduce path-breaking family-friendly policies. Notably in 2015 Facebook announced that 12,000 global employees would receive four months of paid parental and maternity leave. About the same time, co-founder Mark Zuckerberg announced that he would take two months of parental leave when his wife, Priscilla Chan, gave birth to their first child (Zorthian 2015).

There is reason to be optimistic, as parental leave enjoys wide support worldwide, as well as in the United States. But as with most policy issues, the devil lies in the details. How much coverage should be included, for how long, and who should pay for it—employers or taxpayers? How any paid parental leave policy can be achieved in the United States remains to be seen.

Take the Issue with You

1. Do you know of a family that has been in a situation where a paid family leave policy would have greatly benefited them? Describe the circumstances. What benefits, if any, were available?

2. Research the family leave policies of your employer or the employer of someone you know. How could they be improved? Which employees are they designed to benefit?

3. Do you agree that family leave benefits should be mandatory? What kind of program would you design? Who do you think should pay for it?

MASTERING THIS CHAPTER

Summary

The **family,** in its many varying forms, is present in all human cultures. This chapter examines the state of marriage, the family, and other intimate relationships in the United States and considers alternatives to the traditional **nuclear family.**

1. **Families** vary from culture to culture and even within the same culture.

2. The structure of the **extended family** can offer certain advantages over that of the **nuclear family.**

3. Societies determine **kinship** by descent from both parents (**bilateral descent**), from the father only (**patrilineal descent**), or from the mother only (**matrilineal descent**).

4. Sociologists do not agree on whether the **egalitarian family** has replaced the patriarchal family as the social norm in the United States.

5. William F. Ogburn outlined six basic functions of the family: reproduction, protection, socialization, regulation of sexual behavior, companionship, and the provision of social status.

6. Conflict theorists argue that male dominance of the family contributes to societal injustice and denies women opportunities that are extended to men.

7. Interactionists focus on how individuals interact in the family and in other intimate relationships.

8. Feminists stress the need to broaden research on the family. Like conflict theorists, they see the family's role in socializing children as the primary source of sexism.

9. People select mates in a variety of ways. Some marriages are arranged; in other societies, people choose their own mates. Some societies require mates to be chosen within a certain group (**endogamy**) or outside certain groups (**exogamy**). And consciously or unconsciously, many people look for a mate with similar personal characteristics (**homogamy**).

10. In the United States, family life varies with social class, race, and ethnicity.

11. Currently, in the majority of all married couples in the United States, both husband and wife work outside the home.

12. **Single-parent families** account for an increasing proportion of U.S. families.

13. Among the factors that contribute to the rising divorce rate in the United States are greater social acceptance of divorce and the liberalization of divorce laws in many states.

14. More and more people are living together without marrying, a practice known as **cohabitation.** People are also staying single longer, and some married couples are deciding not to have children.

15. The Supreme Court's *Obergefell* decision legalized same-sex marriage in all 50 states in 2015. As a result, gays and lesbians enjoy legal marriage equality, but many legal challenges remain.

16. Unlike many countries all over the world, the United States has no laws that mandate family leave, paid or unpaid, or any other social benefits to families with children.

Key Terms

Adoption In a legal sense, the transfer of the legal rights, responsibilities, and privileges of parenthood to a new legal parent or parents. (page 301)

Arranged marriage A marriage in which others (often the parents) choose a person's marital partner. (298)

Bilateral descent A kinship system in which both sides of a person's family are regarded as equally important. (293)

Cohabitation The practice of living together as a male–female couple without marrying. (305)

Egalitarian family An authority pattern in which spouses are regarded as equals. (293)

Endogamy The restriction of mate selection to people within the same group. (296)

Exogamy The requirement that people select a mate outside certain groups. (297)

Extended family A family in which relatives—such as grandparents, aunts, or uncles—live in the same home as parents and their children. (291)

Familism (*Familismo*) Pride in the extended family, expressed through the maintenance of close ties and strong obligations to kinfolk outside the immediate family. (299)

Family A set of people related by blood, marriage or some other agreed-on relationship, or adoption, who share the primary responsibility for reproduction and caring for members of society. (291)

Flexibility stigma The devaluation of workers who seek or who are presumed to need flexible work arrangements. (309)

Homogamy The conscious or unconscious tendency to select a mate with personal characteristics similar to one's own. (297)

Hybrid marriage a marriage in which the son or daughter may identify the prospective spouse, but the marriage is contingent on the parents approving that choice. (298)

Impression management A term used by Erving Goffman to refer to the altering of the presentation of the self in order to create distinctive appearances and satisfy particular audiences. (296)

Incest taboo The prohibition of sexual relationships between certain culturally specified relatives. (297)

Kinship The state of being related to others. (293)

Machismo A sense of virility, personal worth, and pride in one's maleness. (299)

Matriarchy A society in which women dominate in family decision making. (293)

Matrilineal descent A kinship system in which only the mother's relatives are significant. (293)

Monogamy A form of marriage in which an individual has only one partner. (292)

Nuclear family A married couple and their unmarried children living together. (291)

Patriarchy A society in which men dominate in family decision making. (293)

Patrilineal descent A kinship system in which only the father's relatives are significant. (293)

Polyandry A form of polygamy in which a woman may have more than one husband at the same time. (292)

Polygamy A form of marriage in which an individual may have several husbands or wives simultaneously. (292)

Polygyny A form of polygamy in which a man may have more than one wife at the same time. (292)

Serial monogamy A form of marriage in which a person may have several spouses in his or her lifetime, but only one spouse at a time. (292)

Single-parent family A family in which only one parent is present to care for the children. (302)

TAKING SOCIOLOGY with you

1. Over the next week, watch a few different streaming TV series that feature a family with children living at home. Tally the different household types that are central to each show and make a graph. Does it reflect reality? (Remember that fewer than one in five children live in a household with a working father present, a mother present, and no other step- or custodial children present.) Share your findings with the class.

2. Interview a grandparent or other older member of your family about how current households within your wider family network differ from the various households in the family when they were younger. What is their view on the reasons for these differences? Compare your interview with those of your classmates.

3. Tally the number of songs you hear over the next week, noting how many of them are about love. What percentage of the total number of songs you heard were about love? What does this tell you? Do you see any problems with this? Discuss your findings with the class.

4. **Writing Sociology.** Look for recent news stories about paid family leave in the United States. Has anything changed from family leave in the past? Does it look like further change is forthcoming? Write a report about your findings and share it with the class.

Self-Quiz

Read each question carefully and then select the best answer.

1. Alice, age seven, lives in a private home with her parents, her grandmother, and her aunt. Alice's family is an example of a(n)
   a. nuclear family.
   b. dysfunctional family.
   c. extended family.
   d. polygynous family.

2. In which form of marriage may a person have several spouses in his or her lifetime, but only one spouse at a time?
   a. serial monogamy
   b. monogamy
   c. polygamy
   d. polyandry

3. The marriage of a woman to more than one man at the same time is referred to as
   a. polygyny.
   b. monogamy.
   c. serial monogamy.
   d. polyandry.

4. Which system of descent is followed in the United States?
   a. matrilineal
   b. patrilineal
   c. bilateral
   d. unilateral

5. According to the functionalist perspective, which of the following is *not* one of the paramount functions performed by the family?
   a. mediation
   b. reproduction
   c. regulation of sexual behavior
   d. affection and companionship

6. Which norm requires mate selection outside certain groups, usually one's own family or certain kinfolk?
   a. exogamy
   b. endogamy
   c. matriarchy
   d. patriarchy

7. According to the discussion of social class differences in family life and intimate relationships, which of the following statements is true?
   a. Social class differences in family life are more striking than they once were.
   b. The upper class emphasizes lineage and maintenance of family position.
   c. Among the poor, women usually have no role in the economic support of the family.
   d. In examining family life among racial and ethnic minorities, most patterns result from cultural, but *not* class, factors.

8. One recent development in family life in the United States has been the extension of parenthood as adult children continue to live at home or return home after college. The reason for this is
   a. the rising divorce rate.
   b. high rents.
   c. financial difficulties.
   d. all of the above

9. In the United States, the *majority* of all babies born to unmarried teenage mothers are born to whom?
   a. African American adolescents
   b. White adolescents
   c. Latina adolescents
   d. Asian American adolescents

10. Which of the following factors is associated with the high divorce rate in the United States?
    a. the liberalization of divorce laws
    b. the fact that contemporary families have fewer children than earlier families did
    c. earning ability of husbands and wives
    d. all of the above

11. The principle of _____ assigns people to kinship groups according to their relationship to an individual's mother or father.

12. _____ emerged among Native American tribal societies, and in nations in which men were absent for long periods because of warfare or food-gathering expeditions.

13. In the view of many sociologists, the _____ family has begun to replace the patriarchal family as the social norm in the
United States.

14. As _____ theorists point out, the social class of couples and their children significantly influences the socialization experiences to which the children are exposed and the protection they receive.

15. _____ focus on the micro level of family and other intimate relationships; for example, they are interested in whether people are cohabiting partners or are longtime married couples.

16. The rule of _____ specifies the groups within which a spouse must be found and prohibits marriage with others.

17. Social class differences in family life are less striking today than they once were; however, in the past, _____ _____ -class families were found to be more authoritarian in rearing children and more inclined to use physical punishment.

18. Caring for children is a(n) _____ function of the family, yet the ways in which different societies assign this function to family members can vary significantly.

19. Viewed from the _____ perspective, the government has a strong interest in encouraging adoption.

20. The rising rates of divorce and remarriage have led to a noticeable increase in _____ relationships.

_____

Answers

1 (c); 2 (a); 3 (d); 4 (c); 5 (a); 6 (a); 7 (b); 8 (d); 9 (b); 10 (d); 11 descent; 12 Matriarchies; 13 egalitarian; 14 conflict; 15 Interactionists; 16 endogamy; 17 lower; 18 universal; 19 functionalist; 20 stepfamily

312

Education and Religion

Andrew Cribb/Alamy Stock Photo

Prospective students and their parents tour the campus of Yale University. From informal learning in the family to formal study at institutions of higher learning, education is a cultural universal.

▶ INSIDE

Sociological Perspectives on Education

Schools as Formal Organizations

Durkheim and the Sociological Approach to Religion

World Religions

Sociological Perspectives on Religion

Components of Religion

Religious Organization

Social Policy and Education: Religion in the Schools

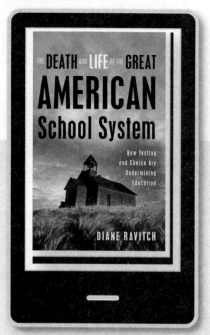

©Ira C. Roberts/Chad
Enterprises Corporation

> What makes a teacher great? What qualities make teaching and learning both effective and memorable?
>
> After a long career, Diane Ravitch lost faith in the educational reforms she had once championed as a way to rescue failing schools. Searching for a better answer, she looked back on her own experience in high school, to her favorite English teacher.

66 My favorite teacher was Mrs. Ruby Ratliff. She is the teacher I remember best, the one who influenced me most, who taught me to love literature and to write with careful attention to grammar and syntax. More than fifty years ago, she was my homeroom teacher at San Jacinto High School in Houston, and I was lucky enough to get into her English class as a senior..

Mrs. Ratliff did nothing for our self-esteem. She challenged us to meet her exacting standards. I think she imagined herself bringing enlightenment to the barbarians (that was us). When you wrote something for her class, which happened with frequency, you paid close attention to proper English. Accuracy mattered. She had a red pen and she used it freely. Still, she was always sure to make a comment that encouraged us to do a better job. Clearly she had multiple goals for her students, beyond teaching literature and grammar. She was also teaching about character and personal responsibility. These are not the sorts of things that appear on any standardized test.

If Mrs. Ratliff were planning to teach these days, I expect that her education professors and supervisors would warn her to get rid of that red pen, to abandon her insistence on accuracy, and to stop being so judgmental. And they would surely demand that she replace those dated poems and essays with young adult literature that teaches adolescents about the lives of other adolescents just like themselves.

I think of Mrs. Ratliff when I hear the latest proposals to improve the teaching force. Almost every day, I come across a statement by a journalist, superintendent, or economist who says we could solve all our problems in American education if we could just recruit a sufficient number of "great" teachers. I believe Mrs. Ratliff was a great teacher, but I don't think she would have been considered "great" if she had been judged by the kind of hard data that is used now. The policy experts who insist that teachers should be judged by their students' scores on standardized tests would have been frustrated by Mrs. Ratliff. Her classes never produced hard data. They didn't even produce test scores. How would the experts have measured what we learned? We never took a multiple-choice test. We wrote essays and took written tests, in which we had to explain our answers, not check a box or fill in a bubble. If she had been evaluated by the grades she gave, she would have been in deep trouble, because she did not award many A grades. An observer might have concluded that she was a very ineffective teacher who had no measurable gains to show for her work. 99

Source: Ravitch 2010: 169, 179, 171.

Clearly she had multiple goals for her students, beyond teaching literature and grammar. She was also teaching about character and personal responsibility. These are not the sorts of things that appear on any standardized test.

In her book *The Death and Life of the Great American School System,* education historian Diane Ravitch laments society's failure to improve the quality of education in the United States. In recalling her favorite teacher, Ravitch questions what she sees as the current tendency to reduce the art of teaching to test cramming and relying solely on standardized tests as measures of students' performance. She is really asking the same questions that sociologists ask about education: what are its goals, and what is it supposed to accomplish, for individuals and for society as a whole?

Education is a cultural universal. As such it is an important aspect of socialization, the lifelong process of learning the attitudes, values, and behavior considered appropriate to members of a particular culture. Socialization can occur in the classroom or at home, through interactions with parents, teachers, friends, and even strangers. Exposure to books, films, television, and other forms of communication also promotes socialization. When learning is explicit and formalized—when some people consciously teach, while others adopt the role of a learner—the process of socialization is called **education.** But students learn far more about their society at school than what is included in the curriculum.

Over 100 years ago, sociologist Émile Durkheim ([1912] 2001) defined **religion** as a "unified system of beliefs and practices relative to sacred things." Like education, religion plays a major role in people's lives, and religious practices of some sort are evident in every society. That makes religion a cultural universal, along with other common practices or beliefs found in every culture, such as dancing, food preparation, the family, and personal names. At present, an estimated 4 billion people belong to the world's many religious faiths.

When religion's influence on other social institutions in a society diminishes, the process of **secularization** is said to be under way. During this process, religion will survive in the private sphere of individual and family life (as in the case of many Native American families); it may even thrive on a personal level. At the same time, other social institutions—such as the economy, politics, and education—maintain their own sets of norms, independent of religious guidance. Even so, religion is enormously resilient. Although specific faiths or organizations may change, their transformation does not signal the demise of religious faith. Rather, it contributes to the diversity of religious expression and organization.

What social purposes do religion and education serve? Do public schools offer everyone a way up the socioeconomic ladder, or do they reinforce divisions among social classes? Does religion help to hold society together or foster social change? We will begin this chapter with a discussion of the four sociological perspectives on education: functionalist, conflict, feminist, and interactionist. We'll look at schools as formal organizations—as bureaucracies and subcultures of teachers and students. We'll also examine homeschooling, a movement away from institutionalized education and its much-publicized failures.

Next we'll turn to a discussion of the sociological perspective on religion, followed by an overview of the world's major religions. We'll explore religion's role in social integration, social support, social change, and social control. Then we'll examine three important components of religious behavior—belief, ritual, and experience—as well as the basic forms of religious organization, including new religious movements. Finally, in the Social Policy section we'll return to the topic of religious belief in a discussion of the controversial issue of religion in the schools.

Sociological Perspectives on Education

Besides being a major industry in the United States, education is the social institution that formally socializes members of our society. In the past few decades, increasing proportions of people have obtained high school diplomas, college degrees, and advanced professional degrees. Figure 13-1 shows the proportion of the college-educated population in selected countries.

Functionalist Perspective

Like other social institutions, education has both manifest (open, stated) and latent (hidden) functions. The most basic *manifest* function of education is the transmission of knowledge. Schools teach students how to read, speak foreign languages, and repair automobiles. Another important manifest function is the bestowal of status. Because many believe this function is performed inequitably, we will consider it later, in the section on the conflict view of education.

FIGURE 13-1   ANTICIPATED HIGHER EDUCATION GRADUATION RATES (BA/BS), SELECTED COUNTRIES

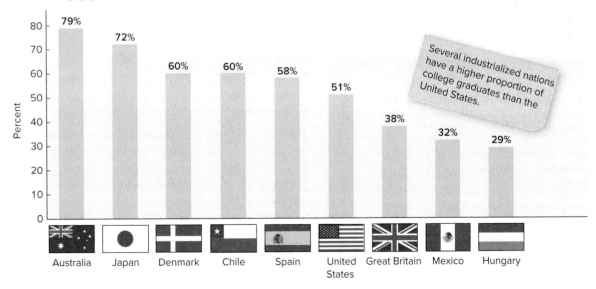

Several industrialized nations have a higher proportion of college graduates than the United States.

Note: For adults ages 25 to 64 for 2015–2017. The percentages are estimates of the eventual proportion of the entire adult population that will attain at least a college degree, given current students' rate of degree completion.
Sources: Organisation for Economic Co-operation and Development. 2020c. Flags: admin_design/Shutterstock

Throughout the world, education has become a vast and complex social institution that prepares citizens for the roles demanded by other social institutions, such as the family, government, and the economy. The functionalist, conflict, feminist, and interactionist perspectives offer distinctive views of education as a social institution.

In addition to these manifest functions, schools perform a number of *latent* functions: transmitting culture, promoting social and political integration, maintaining social control, and serving as an agent of change.

Transmitting Culture   As a social institution, education performs a rather conservative function—transmitting the dominant culture. Schooling exposes each generation of young people to the existing beliefs, norms, and values of their culture. In our society, we learn respect for social control and reverence for established institutions, such as religion, the family, and the presidency. Of course, this statement is true of many other cultures as well. While schoolchildren in the United States are hearing about the accomplishments of George Washington and Abraham Lincoln, British children are hearing about the distinctive contributions of Queen Elizabeth I and Winston Churchill.

Kim Karpeles/Alamy Stock Photo

Schools transmit culture in traditional ways, such as through social studies lessons, as well as in some more innovative ways. Here a mural on a school in Pilsen, a Latino neighborhood in Chicago, underscores pride in the Latino heritage of the students and their families.

All governments shape culture through education, but some do so more forcefully than others. Beginning in 2010, the South Korean government required publishers to submit textbooks for approval; once approved, teachers could choose from any of the books that had been deemed satisfactory. Since then, educators and scholars have protested the intrusion. In response, a more democratically inclined government ended the policy in 2017, giving schools free choice of books to be read by schoolchildren (Sang-Hun 2017).

Promoting Social and Political Integration   Many institutions require students in their first year or two of college to live on campus, to foster a sense of community among diverse groups. Education serves the latent function of promoting social and political integration by transforming a population composed of diverse racial, ethnic, and religious groups into a society whose members share—to some extent—a common identity. Historically, schools in the United States have played an important role in socializing the children of immigrants into the norms, values, and beliefs of the dominant culture. From a functionalist perspective, the common identity and social integration fostered by education contribute to societal stability and consensus (J. Collins 2009; Touraine 1974).

In the past, the integrative function of education was most obvious in its emphasis on promoting a common language. Immigrant children were expected to learn English. In some instances, they were even forbidden to speak their native language on school grounds. More recently, bilingualism has been defended both for its educational value and as a means of encouraging cultural diversity. However, critics argue that bilingualism undermines the social and political integration that education has traditionally promoted.

Maintaining Social Control   In performing the manifest function of transmitting knowledge, schools go far beyond teaching skills like reading, writing, and mathematics. Like other social institutions, such as the family and religion, education prepares young people to lead productive and orderly lives as adults by introducing them to the norms, values, and sanctions of the larger society.

Through the exercise of social control, schools teach students various skills and values essential to their future positions in the labor force. They learn punctuality, discipline, scheduling, and responsible work habits, as well as how to negotiate the complexities of a bureaucratic organization. As a social institution, education reflects the interests of both the family and another social institution, the economy. Students are trained for what is ahead, whether it be the assembly line or a physician's office. In effect, then, schools serve as a transitional agent of social control, bridging the gap between parents and employers in the life cycle of most individuals (Bowles and Gintis [1976] 2011; Foley 2011).

Schools direct and even restrict students' aspirations in a manner that reflects societal values and prejudices. School administrators may allocate ample funds for athletic programs but give much less support to music, art, and dance. Teachers and guidance counselors may encourage male students to pursue careers in the sciences but steer female students into careers as early childhood teachers. Such socialization into traditional gender roles can be viewed as a form of social control.

THINKING CRITICALLY

How do the functions of integration and social control reinforce each other? How do they work against each other?

Serving as an Agent of Change So far, we have focused on the conservative functions of education—on its role in transmitting the existing culture, promoting social and political integration, and maintaining social control. Yet education can also stimulate or bring about desired social change. Sex education classes were introduced to public schools in response to the soaring pregnancy rate among teenagers. Affirmative action in admissions—giving priority to females or minorities—has been endorsed as a means of countering racial and sexual discrimination. And Project Head Start, an early childhood program that serves nearly one million children annually, has sought to compensate for the disadvantages in school readiness experienced by children from low-income families.

These educational programs can transform and have transformed people's lives. For example, continued formal education has had a positive effect on the income people earn; median earnings rise significantly with each step up the educational ladder. Consider the significance of those increased earnings when they stretch over an entire lifetime. Obviously, racial, ethnic, and gender differences in income are also significant. Yet as significant as those inequalities are, the best indicator of a person's lifetime earnings is still the number of years of formal schooling that the person has received (see Figure 13-2) (Julian and Kominski 2011; Wessel and Banchero 2012).

Numerous sociological studies have revealed that additional years of formal schooling are also associated with openness to new ideas and liberal social and political viewpoints. Sociologist Robin Williams points out that better-educated people tend to have greater access to factual information, to hold more diverse opinions, and to possess the ability to make subtle distinctions in analysis. Formal education stresses both the importance of qualifying statements (in place of broad generalizations) and the need at least to question (rather than simply accept) established truths and practices. The scientific method, which relies on *testing* hypotheses, reflects the questioning spirit that characterizes modern education (R. Williams et al. 1964).

Conflict Perspective

The functionalist perspective portrays contemporary education as a basically benign institution. For example, it argues that

FIGURE 13-2 ANNUAL EARNINGS BY DEGREE LEVEL, 2018

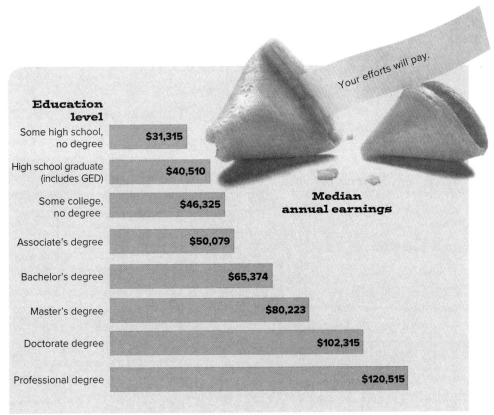

Education level	Median annual earnings
Some high school, no degree	$31,315
High school graduate (includes GED)	$40,510
Some college, no degree	$46,325
Associate's degree	$50,079
Bachelor's degree	$65,374
Master's degree	$80,223
Doctorate degree	$102,315
Professional degree	$120,515

Note: Total money earnings for full-time, year-round workers are 25 and over.
Sources: U.S. Census Bureau 2018b: Table PINC-03.1.3.2.1; Fortune cookies: Don Farrall/Photodisc/Getty Images

schools rationally sort and select students for future high-status positions, thereby meeting society's need for talented and expert personnel. In contrast, the conflict perspective views education as an instrument of elite domination. Conflict theorists point out the sharp inequalities that exist in the educational opportunities available to different racial and ethnic groups. In 2019, the nation marked the 65th anniversary of the Supreme Court's landmark decision *Brown v. Board of Education,* which declared unconstitutional the segregation of public schools.

Yet today, our schools are still characterized by racial isolation. For example, white students account for half of the nation's public school enrollment, yet the typical white student attends a school where 70 percent of his or her peers are white. Despite the dramatic suburbanization of African American and Hispanic families in recent decades, across the nation, 92 percent of Latino students and 91 percent of Black students still attend majority non-white schools—schools whose students are overwhelmingly minority (Frankenberg et al. 2019).

Conflict theorists also argue that the educational system socializes students into values dictated by the powerful, that schools stifle individualism and creativity in the name of maintaining order, and that the level of change they promote is relatively insignificant. From a conflict perspective, the inhibiting effects of education are particularly apparent in the "hidden curriculum" and the differential way in which status is bestowed.

The Hidden Curriculum Schools are highly bureaucratic organizations, as we will see later. To maintain order, many teachers rely on rules and regulations. Unfortunately, the need for control and discipline can take precedence over the learning process. Teachers may focus on obedience to the rules as an end in itself, in which case students and teachers alike become victims of what Philip Jackson (1968) has called the *hidden curriculum.*

The term **hidden curriculum** refers to standards of behavior that are deemed proper by society and are taught subtly in schools. According to this curriculum, children must not speak until the teacher calls on them and must regulate their activities according to the clock or bells. In addition, they are expected to concentrate on their own work rather than to assist other students who learn more slowly. A hidden curriculum is evident in schools around the world. For example, Japanese schools offer guidance sessions that seek to improve the classroom experience and develop healthy living skills. In

© Brand X Pictures/PunchStock

effect, these sessions instill values and encourage behaviors that are useful in the Japanese business world, such as self-discipline and openness to group problem solving and decision making (Okano and Tsuchiya 1999).

In a classroom that is overly focused on obedience, value is placed on pleasing the teacher and remaining quiet rather than on creative thought and academic learning. Habitual obedience to authority may result in the type of distressing behavior documented by Stanley Milgram in his classic obedience studies.

Another example of hidden curriculum, although some would argue it is not very hidden, is the marginalization in sex and relationships education in schools of anything other than heterosexual relationships. Queer theorists and others contend that young people do not receive unbiased information or, indeed, any information about lesbian, gay, and transgender lifestyles. While this is no longer the case in some school districts, others have chosen to abandon sex and relationship education altogether rather than be more inclusive in the curriculum (B. Smith 2015).

USE YOUR SOCIOLOGICAL IMAGINATION

In what ways does the high school you attend convey the hidden curriculum of education?

Credentialism Seventy years ago, a high school diploma was the minimum requirement for entry into the paid labor force of the United States. Today, a college diploma is virtually the bare minimum. This change reflects the process of **credentialism**—a term used to describe an increase in the lowest level of education needed to enter a field.

In recent decades, the number of occupations that are viewed as professions has risen. Credentialism is one symptom of this trend. Employers and occupational associations typically contend that such changes are a logical response to the increasing complexity of many jobs. However, research shows that in many cases, employers place overeducated applicants ahead in labor queues—as the job competition model predicts. Max Weber anticipated this possibility as early as 1916, concluding that the "universal clamor for the creation of educational certificates in all fields makes for the formation of a privileged stratum in businesses and in offices" (Di Stasio 2017; Gerth and Mills 1958: 240–241).

Bestowal of Status Sociologists have long recognized that schooling is central to social stratification. Both functionalist and conflict theorists agree that education performs the important function of bestowing status. According to Kingsley Davis and Wilbert E. Moore (1945), society must distribute its members among a variety of social positions. Education can contribute to this process by sorting people into appropriate levels and courses of study that will prepare them for positions in the labor force.

As noted earlier, an increasing proportion of people in the United States are obtaining high school diplomas, college degrees, and advanced professional degrees. From a functionalist perspective, this widening bestowal of status is beneficial not only to particular recipients but to society as a whole.

Conflict theorists are far more critical of the *differential* way in which education bestows status. They stress that schools sort pupils according to their social class backgrounds. Although the educational system helps certain poor children to move into middle-class professional positions, it denies most disadvantaged children the same educational opportunities afforded to children of the affluent. In this way, schools tend to reinforce social inequality. Higher education in particular acts more like a sieve that sorts people out of the educated classes

sozaijiten/Datacraft/Getty Images

In Tokyo, parents escort their daughter to an admissions interview at a highly competitive private school. Some Japanese families enroll children as young as 2 years of age in cram schools. Like parents in the United States, Japanese parents know that higher education bestows status.

than a social ladder that helps all with ambition to rise (Domina et al. 2019).

The status that comes with advanced training is not cheap and has been getting progressively more expensive for several decades. Over the past 50 years, average tuition and fees at community colleges have risen at a relatively modest pace that matches the inflation rate (Figure 13-3). The increases have been greater at four-year institutions. At the same time as tuition has been increasing, financial aid has become more difficult to obtain (see Box 8-4).

FIGURE 13-3 COSTS OF TUITION, ROOM, AND BOARD, 1963–2018

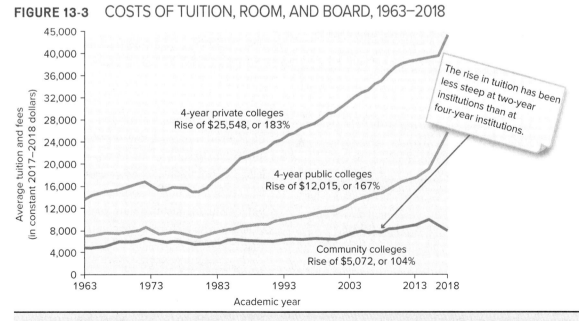

Think about It What additional costs are involved in going to college besides tuition, room, and board?

Note: Community college data exclude private colleges. Private 4-year college data exclude for-profit colleges.
Sources: National Center for Education Statistics 2019a.

Even a single school can reinforce class differences by putting students in tracks. The term **tracking** refers to the practice of placing students in specific curriculum groups on the basis of their test scores and other criteria. Tracking begins very early, often in reading groups during first grade. The practice can reinforce the disadvantages that children from less affluent families may face if they haven't been exposed to reading materials, computers, and other forms of educational stimulation during their early childhood years. To ignore this connection between tracking and students' race and social class is to fundamentally misunderstand how schools perpetuate the existing social structure.

Children placed in academic tracks (with the expectation that they will attend college) typically receive text-based instruction that demands written and verbal displays of knowledge. In contrast, students in nonacademic tracks receive watered-down, slower-paced instruction that aims them toward the world of work after high school. Studies of tracking show that children placed in lower tracks tend to come from low-income or one-parent households or from minority groups. The most damaging aspect of tracking is that it can become a caste system: Once students are placed into low-ability groups, they remain there and are seldom promoted to high-ability groups later on (Domina et al. 2019).

Conflict theorists hold that the educational inequalities produced by tracking are designed to meet the needs of modern capitalist societies. Samuel Bowles and Herbert Gintis ([1976] 2011) have argued that capitalism requires a skilled, disciplined labor force, and that the educational system of the United States is structured with that objective in mind. Citing numerous studies, they offer support for what they call the **correspondence principle.** According to this approach, schools promote the values expected of individuals in each social class and perpetuate social class divisions from one generation to the next. Thus, working-class children, assumed to be destined for subordinate positions, are likely to be placed in high school vocational and general tracks, which emphasize close supervision and compliance with authority. In contrast, young people from more affluent families are likely to be directed to college preparatory tracks, which stress leadership and decision making—the skills they are expected to need as adults (Golann 2015; McLanahan and Percheski 2008).

Sam Edwards/age fotostock

THINKING CRITICALLY

What are the functions and dysfunctions of tracking in schools? In what ways might tracking have a positive impact on the self-concepts of various students? In what ways might it have a negative impact?

Feminist Perspective

The educational system of the United States, like many other social institutions, has long been characterized by discriminatory treatment of women. In 1833, Oberlin College became the first institution of higher learning to admit female students—some 200 years after the first men's college was established. But Oberlin believed that women should aspire to become wives and mothers, not lawyers and intellectuals. In addition to attending classes, female students washed men's clothing, cared for their rooms, and served them at meals. In the 1840s, Lucy Stone, then an Oberlin undergraduate and later one of the nation's most outspoken feminist leaders, refused to write a commencement address because it would have been read to the audience by a male student.

Sexism in education has showed up in many ways—in textbooks with negative stereotypes of women, counselors' pressure on female students to prepare for "women's work," and unequal funding for women's and men's athletic programs. But perhaps nowhere has educational discrimination been more evident than in the employment of teachers. The positions of university professor and college administrator, which hold relatively high status in the United States, have been generally filled by men. Public school teachers, who earn much lower salaries, have been largely female.

Women have made great strides in one area: the proportion of women who continue their schooling. As recently as 1969, twice as many men as women received college degrees; today, women outnumber men at college commencements. Moreover, women's access to graduate education and to medical, dental, and law schools has increased dramatically in the past few decades as a result of the Education Act of 1972. Box 13-1 examines the far-reaching effects of Title IX, the part of the act that concerns discrimination against women in education.

Much has been made of the superior academic achievement of girls and women. Today, researchers are beginning to examine the reasons for their comparatively strong performance in school—or to put it another way, for men's lackluster performance. Some studies suggest that men's aggressiveness, together with the fact that they do better in the workplace than women, even with less schooling, predisposes them to undervalue higher education. While the "absence of men" on many college campuses has captured headlines, it has also created a false crisis in public discourse. Few students realize their potential exclusively through formal education; other factors, such as ambition and personal talent, contribute to their success. And many students, including low-income and immigrant children, face much greater challenges than the so-called gender gap in education (Sutherland 2015).

SOCIOLOGY IN EDUCATION

13-1 The Debate over Title IX

Few federal policies have had such a visible effect on education as Title IX, which mandates gender equity in education in federally funded schools. Congressional amendments to the Education Act of 1972 have brought significant changes for both men and women at all levels of schooling. Title IX eliminated sex-segregated classes, prohibited sex discrimination in admissions and financial aid, and mandated that girls receive more opportunities to play sports, in proportion to their enrollment and interest.

Under this landmark legislation, to receive federal funds, a school or college must pass one of three tests. First, the numbers of male and female athletes must be proportional to the numbers of men and women enrolled at the school. Second, lacking that, the school must show a continuing history of expanding opportunities for female athletes. Or third, the school must demonstrate that the level of female participation in sports meets female students' level of interest or ability.

Today, Title IX is still one of the more controversial attempts ever made by the federal government to promote equality for all citizens. Its consequences for the funding of college athletics programs are hotly debated, while its real and lasting effects on college admissions and employment are often forgotten. Critics charge that men's teams have suffered from proportional funding of women's teams and athletic

scholarships, since schools with tight athletic budgets can expand women's sports only at the expense of men's sports. Yet from 1972, when Title IX was passed, to 2017, the number of female athletes participating in high school sports jumped from 244,000 to over 3.4 million.

From the women's point of view, however, the increased funding for women's sports has benefited men in some ways. In terms of coaching and administration, men have increasingly replaced women as directors of women's sports and as coaches on the sidelines.

Critics charge that men's teams have suffered from proportional funding of women's teams and athletic scholarships.

Sociologists caution that the social effects of sports on college campuses are not all positive. Michael A. Messner, professor of sociology at the University of Southern California, reports that teenage girls who play sports simply for fun have more positive body images than girls who don't play sports. But those who are "highly involved" in sports are more likely than other girls to take steroids and to become risk takers. He remains skeptical of a system that propels a lucky few college athletes to stardom each year while

CS Productions/Jupiterimages/ Brand X/Alamy Stock Photo

leaving the majority, many of them African Americans, without a career or an education. Certainly that was not the kind of equal opportunity legislators envisioned when they wrote Title IX.

LET'S DISCUSS

1. Has Title IX had an effect on you personally? If so, explain. On balance, do you think the increase in women's participation in sports has been good for society as a whole?
2. How might Title IX affect the way students and the public view gender roles?

Sources: G. Anderson 2019; Messner 2002, 2018; National Federation of State High School Associations 2019.

Interactionist Perspective

High school students know who they are—the kids who qualify for a free lunch. So stigmatized are they that in some schools, these students will buy a bit of food in the cash line or simply go without eating to avoid being labeled a "poor kid." School officials in San Francisco are so concerned about their plight that they moved to cashless cafeterias, in which everyone, rich or poor, uses a debit card (Pogash 2008).

The labeling approach suggests that if we treat people in particular ways, they may fulfill our expectations. Children who are labeled as "troublemakers" may come to view themselves as delinquents. Similarly, a dominant group's stereotyping of racial minorities may limit their opportunities to break away from expected roles.

Can the labeling process operate in the classroom? Because interactionist researchers focus on micro-level classroom dynamics, they have been particularly interested in this question. Sociologist Howard S. Becker (1952) studied public schools in low-income and affluent areas of Chicago. He noticed that administrators expected less of students from poor neighborhoods, and wondered if teachers accepted their view. A decade later, in *Pygmalion in the Classroom,* psychologist Robert Rosenthal and school principal Lenore Jacobson documented what they referred to as a **teacher-expectancy effect**—the impact that a teacher's expectations about a student's performance may have on the student's actual achievements. This effect is especially evident in the lower grades (through Grade 3).

Studies in the United States have revealed that teachers wait longer for an answer from a student they believe to be a high

Tracking Sociological Perspectives

TABLE 13-1   SOCIOLOGICAL PERSPECTIVES ON EDUCATION

Theoretical Perspective	Emphasis
Functionalist	Transmission of the dominant culture
	Integration of society
	Promotion of social norms, values, and sanctions
	Promotion of desirable social change
Conflict	Domination by the elite through unequal access to schooling
	Hidden curriculum
	Credentialism
	Bestowal of status
Interactionist	Teacher-expectancy effect
Feminist	Treatment of female students
	Role of women's education in economic development

Think about It Which of the emphases listed in the table have you witnessed in the schools you have attended?

achiever and are more likely to give such children a second chance. In one experiment, teachers' expectations were even shown to have an impact on students' athletic achievements. Teachers obtained better athletic performance—as measured in the number of sit-ups or push-ups performed—from those students of whom they *expected* higher numbers. Despite the controversial nature of these findings, researchers continue to document the existence of the teacher-expectancy effect. Interactionists emphasize that ability alone may be less predictive of academic success than one might think (Rosenthal and Jacobson 1968, 1992; Trang and Hansen 2020).

Table 13-1 summarizes the four major theoretical perspectives on education.

Schools as Formal Organizations

Nineteenth-century educators would be amazed at the scale of schools in the United States in the 21st century. The nation has about 15 million high school students today, compared to 11 million in 1990 (ProQuest 2019: Table 249).

In many respects, today's schools, when viewed as an example of a formal organization, are similar to factories, hospitals, and business firms. Like those organizations, schools do not operate autonomously; they are influenced by the market of potential students. This statement is especially true of private schools, but could have broader impact if acceptance of voucher plans and other school choice programs increases. The parallels between schools and other types of formal organizations will become more apparent as we examine the bureaucratic nature of schools, teaching as an occupation, and the student subculture.

Bureaucratization of Schools

It simply is not possible for a single teacher to transmit culture and skills to children of varying ages who will enter many diverse occupations. The growing number of students being served by school systems and the greater degree of specialization required within a technologically complex society have combined to bureaucratize schools.

Max Weber noted five basic characteristics of bureaucracy, all of which are evident in the vast majority of schools, whether at the elementary, secondary, or even college level:

1. **Division of labor.** Specialized experts teach particular age levels and specific subjects. Public elementary and secondary schools now employ instructors whose sole responsibility is to work with children with learning disabilities or physical impairments.

2. **Hierarchy of authority.** Each employee of a school system is responsible to a higher authority. Teachers must report to principals and assistant principals and may also be supervised by department heads. Principals are answerable to a superintendent of schools, and the superintendent is hired and fired by a board of education.

3. **Written rules and regulations.** Teachers and administrators must conform to numerous rules and regulations in the performance of their duties. This bureaucratic trait can become dysfunctional; the time invested in completing required forms could instead be spent in preparing lessons or conferring with students.

4. **Impersonality.** As class sizes have swelled at schools and universities, it has become more difficult for teachers to give personal attention to each student. In fact, bureaucratic norms may actually encourage teachers to treat all students in the same way, despite the fact that students have distinctive personalities and learning needs.

5. **Employment based on technical qualifications.** At least in theory, the hiring of instructors is based on professional competence and expertise. Promotions are normally dictated by written personnel policies; people who excel may be granted lifelong job security through tenure.

Functionalists take a generally positive view of the bureaucratization of education. Teachers can master the skills needed to work with a specialized clientele, since they no longer are expected to cover a broad range of instruction. The chain of command within schools is clear. Students are presumably treated in an unbiased fashion because of uniformly applied rules. Finally, security of position protects teachers from

GaudiLab/Shutterstock

Despite efforts to establish positive relationships among students and between teachers and students, many young people view their schools as impersonal institutions.

unjustified dismissal. In general, then, functionalists stress that the bureaucratization of education increases the likelihood that students, teachers, and administrators will be dealt with fairly—that is, on the basis of rational and equitable criteria.

In contrast, conflict theorists argue that the trend toward more centralized education has harmful consequences for disadvantaged people. The standardization of educational curricula, including textbooks, will generally reflect the values, interests, and lifestyles of the most powerful groups in our society, and may ignore those of racial and ethnic minorities. In addition, the disadvantaged, more so than the affluent, will find it difficult to sort through complex educational bureaucracies and to organize effective lobbying groups. Therefore, in the view of conflict theorists, low-income and minority parents will have even less influence over citywide and statewide educational administrators than they have over local school officials (Bowles and Gintis [1976] 2011; Katz 1971).

Sometimes schools can seem overwhelmingly bureaucratic, with the effect of stifling rather than nourishing intellectual curiosity in students. This concern has led many parents and policymakers to push for school choice programs—allowing parents to choose the school that suits their children's needs, and forcing schools to compete for their "customers."

In the United States, another significant countertrend to the bureaucratization of schools is the availability of education over the Internet, which was significantly increased during the coronavirus pandemic of 2020. Increasingly, colleges and universities are reaching out via the web, offering entire courses and even majors to students in the comfort of their homes. Online curricula provide flexibility for working students and

---

 ## TAKING SOCIOLOGY TO WORK

Diane Belcher Gray, **Assistant Director of Volunteer Services, New River Community College**

Not until Diane Belcher Gray enrolled at New River Community College in Dublin, Virginia, did she realize that social work had always been part of her daily life. To this mother of two teenagers, helping people in need was something she just did, without even thinking about it.

Today, as assistant director of Volunteer Services at New River, Belcher Gray assists Partners for Success, a mentoring program that matches struggling students with people in the community who have the time and energy to help them. With the director, she recruits and trains a "talent bank" of mentors, matches the mentors with student partners, and develops support programs for students experiencing problems with child care, transportation, and other necessities. The program's goal is to develop confident and successful learners who can take charge of their own studies.

Before she moved to Volunteer Services, Belcher Gray was an administrative assistant in Workforce Development at New River, where she helped youths who lack direction and workers laid off from local factories to develop more marketable skills. In that job, she facilitated new students' transition to college, helping them to register and apply for financial aid and connecting them with professors in their fields of interest. Belcher Gray also worked directly with the administration to develop a special fast-track program for laid-off workers.

Courtesy of Diane Belcher Gray

As in all human services jobs, people skills, particularly sensitivity and compassion, are of paramount importance in Belcher Gray's work. An understanding of the social and economic forces that affect the larger society is also essential. Belcher Gray credits her sociology courses with helping her to "engage where needed." "Sociology exposed me to other people's situations and the role of society in creating them," she explains. "It helped me look beyond the individual level to understand societal impacts and solutions."

Asked to advise current sociology majors, Belcher Gray says, "Drink it up, try and take it all in, relate it to the real world. Take notice of current cultural and economic conditions, understanding that when you attempt to 'fix' one part of society you must also be aware of how that will affect other parts of society."

LET'S DISCUSS

1. Have you, like Diane Belcher Gray, realized through education that something you were doing without thinking about it has helped to prepare you for employment? Explain.
2. Do some research on Dublin, Virginia, and the surrounding area. What kind of economy does this community have? Relate the layoffs the community has been experiencing to larger societal forces.

others who may have difficulty attending conventional classes because of distance or disability. Research on this type of learning is just beginning, so the question of whether teacher–student contact can thrive online remains to be settled. Computer-mediated instruction may also have an impact on instructors' status as employees, which we will discuss next, as well as on alternative forms of education like homeschooling.

USE YOUR SOCIOLOGICAL IMAGINATION

How would you make your school less bureaucratic? What would it be like?

Teachers: Employees and Instructors

Whether they serve as instructors of preschoolers or of graduate students, teachers are employees of formal organizations with bureaucratic structures. There is an inherent conflict in serving as a professional in a bureaucracy. The organization follows the principles of hierarchy and expects adherence to its rules, but professionalism demands the individual responsibility of the practitioner. This conflict is very real for teachers, who experience all the positive and negative consequences of working in bureaucracies.

A teacher undergoes many stresses every day. While teachers' academic assignments have become more specialized, the demands on their time remain diverse and contradictory. Conflicts arise from serving as an instructor, a disciplinarian, and an employee of a school district at the same time. In too many schools, discipline means dealing with violence. Burnout is one result of these stresses: in any given year about one in

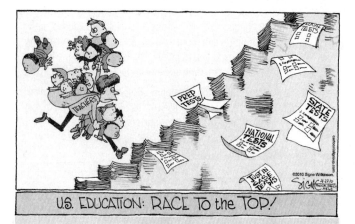

U.S. EDUCATION: RACE TO THE TOP!

Signe Wilkinson Editorial Cartoon used with the permission of Signe Wilkinson, the Washington Post Writers Group and the Cartoonist Group. All rights reserved.

From preschool through high school, teachers face a variety of challenges, including preparing students for standardized tests.

four middle school teachers leaves teaching (Ladd and Sorensen 2019).

Given these difficulties, does teaching remain an attractive profession in the United States? In 2019, 3 percent of male first-year college students and 5 percent of female students indicated that they were interested in becoming either elementary or high school teachers. These figures are dramatically lower than the 11 percent of first-year male students and 37 percent of first-year female students who held those occupational aspirations in 1966 (Pryor et al. 2007:76, 122; Stolzenberg et al. 2019).

Undoubtedly, economic considerations enter into students' feelings about the attractiveness of teaching. In 2018, the average salary for all public elementary and secondary school teachers in the United States was reported at $60,477, placing teachers somewhere near the average of all the nation's wage earners. In most other industrialized countries, teachers' salaries are higher in relation to the general standard of living. Of course, teachers' salaries vary considerably from state to state (Figure 13-4), and even more from one school district to another. Nevertheless, the economic reward for teaching is minuscule compared to some career options: the CEO of a major corporation makes more money in a day than the average teacher makes in a year.

The status of any job reflects several factors, including the level of education required, financial compensation, and the respect given the occupation by society. The teaching profession (see Table 8-3) is feeling pressure in all three of these areas. First, the level of formal schooling required for teaching remains high, and the public has begun to call for new competency examinations. Second, the statistics just cited demonstrate that teachers' salaries are significantly lower than those of many professionals and skilled workers. Third, the overall prestige of the teaching profession has declined in the past decade. Many teachers have become disappointed and frustrated and have left the educational world for careers in other professions (Banchero 2014).

Student Subcultures

An important latent function of education relates directly to student life: schools provide for students' social and recreational needs. Education helps toddlers and young children to develop interpersonal skills that are essential during adolescence and adulthood. In their high school and college years, students may meet future husbands and wives and establish lifelong friendships. It is important to remember that these informal aspects of schools, community colleges, and universities do not exist independently of schools' explicit educational functions. Furthermore, informal social systems can be as important as the academic system in determining students' positive and negative outcomes (Crosnoe 2011).

MAPPING LIFE NATIONWIDE

FIGURE 13-4   AVERAGE SALARY FOR TEACHERS

- ■ Over $60,000
- ■ $54,000–59,999
- ■ $52,000–53,999
- ■ $49,000–51,000
- ■ Under $49,000

Think about It What factors might account for the wide disparities in average salaries in different states?

Note: Data released in 2019 for 2017–2018
Sources: National Education Association 2019.

The national average salary was $60,477. State averages ranged from $44,926 in Mississippi to $84,227 in New York.

When people observe high schools, community colleges, or universities from the outside, students appear to constitute a cohesive, uniform group. However, the student subculture is actually quite complex and diverse. From middle school through college, athletics offers a ready vehicle for the development of a subculture. Interestingly, even though student athletes may come from diverse backgrounds and have very different academic abilities and interests, the common identity with a sport, whether tennis or ultimate frisbee, can offer a sense of identity (Arrington 2019).

Amid the close-knit and often rigidly segregated cliques that emerge in schools, lesbian, gay, bisexual, and transgender (LGBTQ) students are particularly vulnerable. Peer group pressure to conform is intense at this age. Although coming to terms with one's sexuality is difficult for all adolescents, it can be downright dangerous for those whose sexual identity does not conform to societal expectations.

Teachers and administrators are becoming more sensitized to these issues. Perhaps more important, some schools are creating gay–straight alliances (GSAs), school-sponsored support groups that bring gay teens together with sympathetic straight peers. Begun in Los Angeles in 1984, these programs

numbered nearly 3,000 nationwide in 2005; most were founded after the murder of Matthew Shepard, a gay college student, in 1998. In some districts parents have objected to these organizations, but the same court rulings that protect the right of Bible groups to meet on school grounds also protect GSAs. In 2003, the gay–straight movement reached a milestone when the New York City public schools moved an in-school program for gays, bisexuals, and transgendered students to a separate school. The Harvey Milk High School was named in memory of San Francisco's first openly gay city supervisor, who was assassinated in 1978 (Gay, Lesbian and Straight Education Network 2020).

We can find a similar diversity of student groups at the college level. Sociologists have identified four distinctive subcultures among college students:

1. The *collegiate* subculture focuses on having fun and socializing. These students define what constitutes a "reasonable" amount of academic work (and what amount of work is "excessive" and leads to being labeled a "grind"). Members of the collegiate subculture have little commitment to academic pursuits. Athletes often fit into this subculture.

2. The *academic* subculture identifies with the intellectual concerns of the faculty and values knowledge for its own sake.

3. The *vocational* subculture is interested primarily in career prospects and views college as a means of obtaining degrees that are essential for advancement.

4. Finally, the *nonconformist* subculture is hostile to the college environment and seeks ideas that may or may not relate to academic studies. This group may find outlets through campus publications or issue-oriented groups.

Each college student is eventually exposed to these competing subcultures and must determine which (if any) seems most in line with his or her feelings and interests (Clark and Trow 1966; Horowitz 1987; Sperber 2000).

FIGURE 13-5   COLLEGE CAMPUSES BY RACE AND ETHNICITY: THEN, NOW, AND IN THE FUTURE

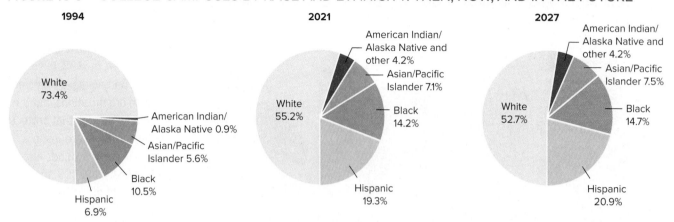

1994

White 73.4%
American Indian/Alaska Native 0.9%
Asian/Pacific Islander 5.6%
Black 10.5%
Hispanic 6.9%

2021

American Indian/Alaska Native and other 4.2%
Asian/Pacific Islander 7.1%
White 55.2%
Black 14.2%
Hispanic 19.3%

2027

American Indian/Alaska Native and other 4.2%
Asian/Pacific Islander 7.5%
White 52.7%
Black 14.7%
Hispanic 20.9%

Note: Percentages do not add to 100 due to rounding error. Nonresident aliens whose race/ethnicity is unknown are excluded.
Sources: Hussar and Bailey 2019.

As in high school, one could expect LGBTQ students to form their own clique or group according to more specific sexual identities. The 2016 survey of all entering college students found, for example, that 43 percent of transgender students self-evaluate themselves as having below average social confidence, compared to only 20 percent of all first-year students. Yet transgender students are more likely to have high levels of civil engagement, to seek out valuable information, and to ask questions in classes (Eagan et al. 2017:14–16).

We have noted the growing ethnic and racial diversity in the nation, and this trend is especially true of higher education. As Figure 13-5 shows, college campuses are becoming increasingly diverse: in 1994, 27 percent of students were non-white or Hispanic; in 2027, that percentage is projected to rise to 47 percent.

Sociologist Joe R. Feagin has studied a distinctive collegiate subculture: Black students at predominantly white universities. These students must function academically and socially within universities where there are few Black faculty members or administrators, where harassment of Blacks by campus police is common, and where curricula place little emphasis on Black contributions. Feagin (1989:11) suggests that "for minority students life at a predominantly white college or university means long-term encounters with pervasive whiteness." In Feagin's view, Black students at such institutions experience both blatant and subtle racial discrimination, which has a cumulative impact that can seriously damage the students' confidence (see also Chun and Feagin 2019).

USE YOUR SOCIOLOGICAL IMAGINATION

What distinctive subcultures can you identify at your school?

Homeschooling

When most people think of school, they think of bricks and mortar and the teachers, administrators, and other employees who staff school buildings. But for an increasing number of students in the United States, home is the classroom and the teacher is a parent. About 1.7 million students are typically being educated at home, according to a 2019 government report. For these students, the issues of bureaucratization and social structure are less significant than they are for public school students.

In the 1800s, after the establishment of public schools, families that taught their children at home lived in isolated environments or held strict religious views that were at odds with the secular environment of public schools. But today homeschooling attracts a broader range of families—only about half provide religious instruction as a part of homeschooling. Poor academic quality, peer pressure, and school violence motivate many parents to teach their children at home. In addition, some immigrants choose homeschooling as a way to ease

Ariel Skelley/Blend Images LLC

Student subcultures are more diverse today than in the past. Many adults are returning to college to obtain further education, advance their careers, or change their line of work.

their children's transition to a new society (National Center for Education Statistics 2019b).

While supporters of homeschooling believe children can do just as well or better in homeschools as in public schools, critics counter that because homeschooled children are isolated from the larger community, they lose an important chance to improve their socialization skills. But proponents of homeschooling claim their children benefit from contact with others besides their own age group. They also see homeschools as a good alternative for children who suffer from attention-deficit/hyperactivity disorder (ADHD) and learning disorders (LDs). Such children often do better in smaller classes, which present fewer distractions to disturb their concentration.

Quality control is an issue in homeschooling. While homeschooling is legal in all 50 states, 11 states require no notification that a child will be homeschooled and only 5 states have extensive regulations. Who are the people who are running homeschools? In general, they tend to have higher-than-average educational levels—45 percent have college degrees or higher degrees. This would lead one to expect positive educational outcomes for the children, but research comparing learning outcomes for homeschooled versus non-homeschooled children is difficult to conduct (Home School Legal Defense Association 2020; National Center for Education Statistics 2019b).

With the coronavirus pandemic, tens of millions of households shifted into homeschooling, presenting challenges to teachers, school districts, and parents, many of whom were also working from home. As with all aspects of the institution of education, the expansion of learning at home exposed social inequality: the poor had greater difficulty in accessing online learning platforms, and at the same time, their households were disproportionately hurt financially by business shutdowns (Casey 2020).

THINKING CRITICALLY

Select two functions of education and suggest how they could be fulfilled through homeschooling.

Durkheim and the Sociological Approach to Religion

How do sociologists study religion? The same way we study other social institutions such as education or politics. If a group believes that it is being directed by a "vision from God," sociologists do not attempt to prove or disprove the revelation. Instead, they assess the effects of the religious experience on the group. What sociologists are interested in is the social impact of religion on individuals and institutions.

Émile Durkheim was perhaps the first sociologist to recognize the critical importance of religion in human societies. He saw its appeal for the individual, but more important, he stressed the *social* impact of religion. In Durkheim's view, religion is a collective act that includes many forms of behavior in which people interact with others. As in his work on suicide, Durkheim was not so much interested in the personalities of religious believers as he was in understanding religious behavior within a social context.

As we saw earlier in the chapter, Durkheim defined religion as a "unified system of beliefs and practices relative to sacred things." In his view, religion involves a set of beliefs and practices that are uniquely the property of religion, as opposed to other social institutions and ways of thinking. Durkheim ([1912] 2001) argued that religious faiths distinguish between certain transcending events and the everyday world. He referred to those realms as the *sacred* and the *profane.*

The **sacred** encompasses elements beyond everyday life that inspire awe, respect, and even fear. People become part of the sacred realm only by completing some ritual, such as prayer or sacrifice. Because believers have faith in the sacred, they accept what they cannot understand. In contrast, the **profane** includes the ordinary and commonplace. This concept can be confusing, however, because the same object can be either sacred or profane, depending on how it is viewed. A normal dining room table is profane, but it becomes sacred to some Christians if it bears the elements of a communion. A candelabra becomes sacred to Jews if it is a menorah. For Confucians and Taoists, incense sticks are not mere decorative items, but highly valued offerings to the gods in religious ceremonies that mark the new and full moons.

Following the direction established by Durkheim a century ago, contemporary sociologists view religion in two different ways. First, they study the norms and values of religious faiths by examining their substantive beliefs. For example, it is possible to compare the degree to which Christian faiths interpret the Bible literally, or Muslim groups follow the Qur'an (or Koran), the sacred book of Islam. At the same time, sociologists examine religion in terms of the social functions it fulfills, such as providing social support or reinforcing social norms. By exploring both the beliefs and the functions of religion, we can better understand its impact on the individual, on groups, and on society as a whole.

THINKING CRITICALLY

Compare the sociological approach to religion to the way a historian or religious thinker might approach the topic.

World Religions

Worldwide, tremendous diversity exists in religious beliefs and practices. Overall, about 84 percent of the world's population adheres to some religion; thus, only about 15 percent is nonreligious. This level of adherence changes over time and also varies by country and age group. However, in general and especially in industrial nations, people are tending to move away from both organized religion and, more basically, any firm belief in God (see Box 13-2).

Christianity is the largest single faith in the world; the second largest is Islam (Table 13-2). Although global news events often suggest an inherent conflict between Christians and Muslims, the two faiths are similar in many ways. Both are monotheistic (based on a single deity); both include a belief in prophets, an afterlife, and a judgment day. In fact, Islam recognizes Jesus as a prophet, though not as the son of God. Both faiths impose a moral code on believers, which varies from fairly rigid proscriptions for fundamentalists to relatively relaxed guidelines for liberals.

Over the next 40 years, as shown in Figure 13-6, Christians will remain the largest religious group, but Islam will grow faster than any other major world religious group. The growth of Islam is primarily due to the young age of its followers: fertility rates among Muslims are high. But another factor leading to growth is conversion, particularly in Africa. Over the same period of time, Christianity can expect to see level growth or some decline due to two similar factors: low fertility, plus the trend of people in North American and Europe to become unaffiliated with any major religion.

The followers of Islam, called *Muslims,* believe that Islam's holy scriptures were received from Allah (God) by the prophet Mohammad nearly 1,400 years ago. They see Mohammad as the last in a long line of prophets, preceded by Adam, Abraham, Moses, and Jesus. Islam is more communal in its expression than Christianity, particularly the more individualistic Protestant denominations. Consequently, in countries that are predominantly Muslim, the separation of religion and the state is not considered necessary or even desirable. In fact, Muslim governments often reinforce Islamic practices through their laws. Muslims do vary sharply in their interpretation of several traditions, some of which—such as the wearing of veils by women—are more cultural than religious in origin.

Like Christianity and Islam, Judaism is monotheistic. Jews believe that God's true nature is revealed in the Torah, which Christians know as the first five books of the Old Testament. According to these scriptures, God formed a covenant, or pact, with Abraham and Sarah, the ancestors of the tribes of Israel. Even today, observant Jews believe, this covenant holds them accountable to God's will. If they follow both the letter and spirit of the Torah, a long-awaited Messiah will one day bring

RESEARCH TODAY

13-2   The Growth of "None of the Above"

The questionnaire before you asks simply "Which of the following religions best describes your faith?" More and more people check "none of the above."

National surveys reveal an increasing proportion of people, especially in industrialized countries, who identify themselves as having no religion. These people have come to be called the nones. From the 1940s through the 1960s, no more than 3 percent of the adult population indicated they had no religious affiliation. Belonging to a specific religious group, literally being "a member," was an automatic expectation, like belonging to a household or workplace. Indeed, the census even asked people their religious affiliation until 1957, but has never done so since then.

Then in the 21st century, the proportion increased to over 10 percent. National surveys done between 2016 and 2020 show somewhere between 21 and 35 percent identifying

In 2019, 31 percent of incoming U.S. college students had no religious preference (or were agnostic or atheist), compared to 17 percent of their mothers.

as nones, depending upon on how the survey question is worded. In 2019, 31 percent of incoming U.S. college students had no religious preference (or were agnostic or atheist), compared to 17 percent of their mothers.

The growth of the "none of the above" category does not mean that the respondents do not have God in their lives. Only about a third of nones say that they do not believe in God.

Why the decline in organized religion? Religion is just one of many social institutions—

including law enforcement, financial organizations, and Congress—that have lost public trust in an age of the failure of authority figures. For example, scandals in the Roman Catholic Church have accelerated organized religion's rapid loss of moral stature. People may believe in some divine spirit but still find it difficult to accept any formal religious organization. An additional factor is the continuing growth in the number of interfaith marriages. Not joining a formal religion means that a couple need not choose between the two spouses' faiths..

LET'S DISCUSS

1. Why might a person who believes in God not adhere to any organized religion?
2. What specific social changes might account for the increasing number of nones?

Sources: Alper 2019; Blumberg 2016; Gallup 2020c; Stolzenberg et al. 2019; Thompson 2019.

TABLE 13-2   MAJOR WORLD RELIGIONS

Summing Up

Faith	Current Following, in Millions (and Percentage of World Population)	Primary Location of Followers Today	Founder (and Approximate Birth Date)	Important Texts (and Holy Sites)
Buddhism	499 (6.9%)	Southeast Asia, Mongolia, Tibet	Gautama Siddhartha (563 b.c.)	Triptaka (areas in Nepal)
Christianity	2,276 (31.2%)	Europe, North America, South America	Jesus (6 b.c.)	Bible (Jerusalem, Rome)
Hinduism	1,099 (15.1%)	India, Indian communities overseas	No specific founder (1500 b.c.)	Sruti and Smrti texts (seven sacred cities, including Vavansi)
Islam	1,753 (24.1%)	Middle East, Central Asia, North Africa, Indonesia	Mohammad (a.d. 570)	Qur'an, or Koran (Mecca, Medina, Jerusalem)
Judaism	14 (0.2%)	Israel, United States, France, Russia	Abraham (2000 b.c.)	Torah, Talmud (Jerusalem)

Sources: Pew Research Center 2017b; Swatos 1998. Data as of 2017

FIGURE 13-6   PROJECTED CHANGE IN GLOBAL RELIGIOUS AFFILIATION 2015–2060

Percent of global population, 2015–2060

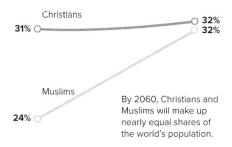

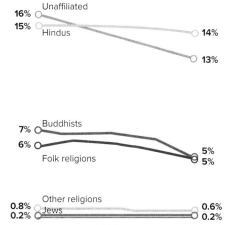

Think about It What other social factors besides population growth might cause the number of followers of a religion to shrink or grow?

Note: Folk religions include African traditional religions, Chinese folk religions, Native American religions, and Australian aboriginal religions. Other religions include Baha'i faith, Taoism, Jainism, Shintoism, Sikhism, Tenrikyo, Wicca, Zoroastrianism, and many others.
Sources: Pew Research Center. The Changing Global Religious Landscape. April 5, 2017.

paradise to earth. Although Judaism has a relatively small following compared to other major faiths, it forms the historical foundation for both Christianity and Islam. That is why Jews revere many of the same sacred Middle Eastern sites as Christians and Muslims.

Two other major faiths developed in a different part of the world, India. The earliest, Hinduism, originated around 1500 b.c. Hinduism differs from Judaism, Christianity, and Islam in that it embraces a number of gods and minor gods, although most worshippers are devoted primarily to a single deity, such as Shiva or Vishnu. Hinduism is also distinguished by a belief in reincarnation, or the perpetual rebirth of the soul after death. Unlike Judaism, Christianity, and Islam, which are based largely on sacred texts, Hindu beliefs have been preserved mostly through oral tradition.

A second religion, Buddhism, developed in the sixth century b.c. as a reaction against Hinduism. This faith is founded on the teachings of Siddhartha (later called Buddha, or "the enlightened one"). Through meditation, followers of Buddhism strive to overcome selfish cravings for physical or material pleasures, with the goal of reaching a state of enlightenment, or nirvana. Buddhists created the first monastic orders, which are thought to be the models for monastic orders in other religions, including Christianity. Though Buddhism emerged in India, its followers were eventually driven out of that country by the Hindus. It is now found primarily in other parts of Asia. (Contemporary adherents of Buddhism in India are relatively recent converts.)

Although the differences among religions are striking, they are exceeded by variations within faiths. Consider the variations within Christianity, from relatively liberal denominations such as Presbyterians or the United Church of Christ to the more conservative members of the Church of Jesus Christ of Latter-day Saints (the Mormons) and Greek Orthodox Catholics. Similar variations exist within Islam, Judaism, and other world religions (C. Adams 2015; Swatos 1998).

Sociological Perspectives on Religion

Since religion is a cultural universal, it is not surprising that it plays a basic role in human societies. In sociological terms, it performs both manifest and latent functions. Among its *manifest* (open and stated) functions, religion defines the spiritual world and gives meaning to the divine. It provides an explanation for events that seem difficult to understand, such as what lies beyond the grave. The *latent* functions of religion are unintended, covert, or hidden. Even though the manifest function of a church service is to offer a forum for religious worship, it might at the same time fulfill a latent social function as a meeting ground for unmarried members.

Functionalists and conflict theorists both evaluate religion's impact on human societies. We'll consider a functionalist view of religion's role in integrating society, providing social

Think about It What religious practices were you taught as a child? What was their function?

Jonathan Nackstrand/AFP/Getty Images

Most of the world's religions seek to give children an appreciation of their faith, an example of an integrative function. Jewish youths who spin the dreidel, a four-sided top, during the Hanukkah holiday are recalling a tradition born before Christianity, when the children of Greek Jews who studied the Torah secretly in caves played with the tops to pass the time.

support, and promoting social change, and then look at religion from the conflict and feminist perspectives, as a means of social control. Note that for the most part, religion's impact is best understood from a macro-level viewpoint that is oriented toward the larger society. Its social support function is an exception: it is best understood on the micro, or individual, level.

The Integrative Function of Religion

Émile Durkheim viewed religion as an integrative force in human society—a perspective that is reflected in functionalist thought today. Durkheim sought to answer a perplexing question: "How can human societies be held together when they are generally composed of individuals and social groups with diverse interests and aspirations?" In his view, religious bonds often transcend these personal and divisive forces. Durkheim acknowledged that religion is not the only integrative force; nationalism or patriotism may serve the same end.

How does religion provide this "societal glue"? Religion, whether it be Buddhism, Islam, Christianity, or Judaism, gives meaning and purpose to people's lives. It offers certain ultimate values and ends to hold in common. Although they are subjective and not always fully accepted, these values and ends help society to function as an integrated social system. For example, funerals, weddings, bar and bat mitzvahs, and confirmations serve to integrate people into larger communities by providing shared beliefs and values about the ultimate questions of life.

The integrative power of religion can be seen, too, in the role that churches, synagogues, and mosques have traditionally played and continue to play for immigrant groups in the United States. For example, Roman Catholic immigrants may settle near a parish church that offers services in their native language, such as Polish or Spanish. Similarly, Korean immigrants may join a Presbyterian church that has many Korean American members and follows religious practices like those of churches in Korea. Like other religious organizations, these Roman Catholic and Presbyterian churches help to integrate immigrants into their new homeland.

In recent years, the most talked about immigrant religious group has been Muslims. Throughout the world, including the United States, Muslims are divided into a variety of sects, including Sunni and Shia (or Shiite). However, inside and outside these sects, people express their Islamic faith in many different ways. To speak of Muslims as being either Sunni or Shia would be like speaking of Christians as either Roman Catholic or Baptist.

Depending on the circumstances, Islam in the United States can be integrative by faith, ethnicity, or both. The great majority of Muslims in the United States are Sunni Muslims—literally, those who follow the *Sunnah,* or way of the Prophet. Compared to other Muslims, Sunnis tend to be more moderate in

A major function of religion is to provide necessary services for people who are destitute or in distress. Here volunteers serve breakfast at a soup kitchen in Detroit, Michigan. During the coronavirus pandemic such outreach efforts continued, but not as face-to-face activities, as faith-based groups sought to deliver take-out meals and other supplies.

Through its emphasis on the divine and the supernatural, religion allows us to "do something" about the calamities we face. During the coronavirus pandemic, religious institutions, even though they were forced to curtail face-to-face interaction, sought to offer comfort to their own followers as well as those of other sacred traditions.

Religion and Social Change

The Weberian Thesis When someone seems driven to work and succeed, we often attribute the Protestant work ethic to that person. The term comes from the writings of Max Weber, who carefully examined the connection between religious allegiance and capitalist development. Weber's findings appeared in his pioneering work *The Protestant Ethic and the Spirit of Capitalism* ([1904] 2011).

Weber noted that in European nations with both Protestant and Catholic citizens, an overwhelming number of business leaders, owners of capital, and skilled workers were Protestant. In his view, this fact was no mere coincidence. Weber pointed out that the followers of John Calvin (1509–1564), a leader of the Protestant Reformation, emphasized a disciplined work ethic, this-worldly concerns, and a rational orientation to life that have become known as the **Protestant ethic.** One by-product of the Protestant ethic was a drive to accumulate savings that could be used for future investment. This "spirit of capitalism," to use Weber's phrase, contrasted with the moderate work hours, leisurely work habits, and lack of ambition that Weber saw as typical of the times.

Few books on the sociology of religion have aroused as much commentary and criticism as Weber's work. It has been hailed as one of the most important theoretical works in the field and an excellent example of macro-level analysis. Like Durkheim, Weber demonstrated that religion is not solely a matter of intimate personal beliefs. He stressed that the collective nature of religion has consequences for society as a whole. Indeed, a recent analysis of historical economic data shows that the Protestant ethic was an important factor in the growth of capitalism from 1500 through 1870 (Sanderson et al. 2011).

Weber provided a convincing description of the origins of European capitalism. However, this economic system has now been adopted by non-Calvinists in many parts of the world. Studies done in the United States today show little or no difference in achievement orientation between Roman Catholics and Protestants. Apparently, the "spirit of capitalism" has

their religious orthodoxy. The Shia, who come primarily from Iraq and Iran, are the second-largest group. Shia Muslims are more attentive to guidance from accepted Shia scholars than are Sunnis. In sufficient numbers, these two Muslim groups will choose to worship separately, even if they must cross ethnic or linguistic lines to do so. Whatever group Muslims belong to, however, there has been a remarkable increase in the number of Islamic places of worship in the United States. Between 2000 and 2010, the number of mosques rose 74 percent (Bagby 2012; Selod 2008a).

In some instances, religious loyalties are *dysfunctional;* that is, they contribute to tension and even conflict between groups or nations. During the Second World War, the German Nazis attempted to exterminate the Jewish people; approximately 6 million European Jews were killed. In modern times, nations such as Lebanon (Muslims versus Christians), Israel (Jews versus Muslims, as well as Orthodox versus secular Jews), Northern Ireland (Roman Catholics versus Protestants), India (Hindus versus Muslims, and more recently, Sikhs), and Myanmar (Buddhists versus Rohinga Muslims) have been torn by clashes that are in large part based on religion.

Religion and Social Support

Most of us find it difficult to accept the stressful events of life—the death of a loved one, serious injury, bankruptcy, divorce, and so forth—especially when something "senseless" happens. How can family and friends come to terms with the death of a high school student, not even 20 years old?

Robertharding/Alamy Stock Photo

A Protestant congregation worships at Sunday service. Although Weber traced the "spirit of capitalism" to Protestant teachings, in the United States today Protestants and Catholics share the same work ethic.

emerged as a generalized cultural trait rather than a specific religious tenet (Greeley 1989).

Conflict theorists caution that Weber's theory—even if it is accepted—should not be regarded as an analysis of mature capitalism, as reflected in the rise of multinational corporations. Marxists would disagree with Weber not on the origins of capitalism, but on its future. Unlike Marx, Weber believed that capitalism could endure indefinitely as an economic system. He added, however, that the decline of religion as an overriding force in society opened the way for workers to express their discontent more vocally (R. Collins 1980).

Liberation Theology Sometimes the clergy can be found in the forefront of social change. Many religious activists, especially in the Roman Catholic Church in Latin America, support **liberation theology**—the use of a church in a political effort to eliminate poverty, discrimination, and other forms of injustice from a secular society. Advocates of this religious movement sometimes sympathize with Marxism. Many believe that radical change, rather than economic development in itself, is the only acceptable solution to the desperation of the masses in impoverished developing countries. Activists associated with liberation theology believe that organized religion has a moral responsibility to take a strong public stand against the oppression of the poor, racial and ethnic minorities, and women (T. Cooper 2015).

The term *liberation theology* dates back to the publication in 1973 of the English translation of *A Theology of Liberation*. The book was written by a Peruvian priest, Gustavo Gutiérrez, who

lived in a slum area of Lima during the early 1960s. After years of exposure to the vast poverty around him, Gutiérrez concluded that "in order to serve the poor, one had to move into political action." Eventually, politically committed Latin American theologians came under the influence of social scientists who viewed the domination of capitalism and multinational corporations as central to the hemisphere's problems. One result was a new approach to theology that built on the cultural and religious traditions of Latin America rather than on models developed in Europe and the United States (Calles Barger 2019; Gutiérrez 1990).

During the 1980s, the Vatican issued statements on liberation theology, praising the movement's concern for the poor and for justice, but also condemning its tendency to rely too heavily on Marxist theory. Attitudes have changed, however: Pope Francis has joked that he has now celebrated mass with some of the most strident liberation theologists (Wooden 2019).

USE YOUR SOCIOLOGICAL IMAGINATION

The social support that religious groups provide is suddenly withdrawn from your community. How will your life or the lives of others change? What will happen if religious groups stop pushing for social change?

Religion and Social Control: A Conflict Perspective

Liberation theology is a relatively recent phenomenon that marks a break with the traditional role of churches. It was this traditional role that Karl Marx ([1844] 1964) opposed. In his view, religion *impeded* social change by encouraging oppressed people to focus on otherworldly concerns rather than on their immediate poverty or exploitation. Marx described religion as an opiate that was particularly harmful to oppressed peoples. He felt that religion often drugged the masses into submission by offering a consolation for their harsh lives on earth: the hope of salvation in an ideal afterlife. For example, during the period of slavery in the United States, white masters forbade Blacks to practice native African religions, while encouraging them to adopt Christianity, which taught them that obedience would lead to salvation and eternal happiness in the hereafter. Viewed from a

ZUMA Press/Alamy Stock Photo

While women comprise an increasing proportion of Christian clergy in the United States, most congregations are still likely to see a man at the front of their church on any given Sunday.

Feminist Perspective

Drawing on the feminist approach, researchers and theorists have stressed the fundamental role women play in religious socialization. Most people develop their allegiance to a particular faith in their childhood, with their mothers playing a critical role in the process. Significantly, nonworshipping mothers tend to influence their children to be highly skeptical of organized religion.

However, women generally take a subordinate role in religious governance. Indeed, most faiths have a long tradition of exclusively male spiritual leadership. Furthermore, because most religions are patriarchal, they tend to reinforce men's dominance in secular as well as spiritual matters. Women do play a vital role as volunteers, staff, and religious educators, but even today, religious decision making and leadership typically fall to the men. Exceptions to this rule, such as the Shakers and Christian Scientists, as well as Hinduism and Wicca, with their goddess heritages, are rare (R. Schaefer and Zellner 2015).

In the United States, women are much more likely than men to be affiliated with religion, to pray, to believe in God, to claim that religion is important in their lives, and to attend weekly worship services. Yet organized religion typically does not give them leadership roles. Nationally, women compose 21 percent

conflict perspective, Christianity may have pacified certain slaves and blunted the rage that often fuels rebellion.

Religion does play an important role in propping up the existing social structure. The values of religion, as already noted, tend to reinforce other social institutions and the social order as a whole. From Marx's perspective, however, religion's promotion of social stability only helps to perpetuate patterns of social inequality. According to Marx, the dominant religion reinforces the interests of those in power.

For example, contemporary Christianity reinforces traditional patterns of behavior that call for the subordination of the less powerful. The role of women in the church is an example of this uneven distribution of power. Assumptions about gender roles leave women in a subservient position both within Christian churches and at home. In fact, women find it as difficult to achieve leadership positions in many churches as they do in large corporations. A "stained glass ceiling" tends to stunt clergywomen's career development, even in the most liberal denominations.

Like Marx, conflict theorists argue that to whatever extent religion actually does influence social behavior, it reinforces existing patterns of dominance and inequality. From a Marxist perspective, religion keeps people from seeing their lives and societal conditions in political terms—for example, by obscuring the overriding significance of conflicting economic interests. Marxists suggest that by inducing a "false consciousness" among the disadvantaged, religion lessens the possibility of collective political action that could end capitalist oppression and transform society.

Tracking Sociological Perspectives

TABLE 13-3 SOCIOLOGICAL PERSPECTIVES ON RELIGION

Theoretical Perspective	Emphasis
Functionalist	Religion as a source of social integration and unification; Religion as a source of social support for individuals
Conflict	Religion as a potential obstacle to structural social change; Religion as a potential source of structural social change (through liberation theology)
Feminist	Religion as an instrument of women's subordination, except for their role in religious socialization
Interactionist	Individual religious expression through belief, ritual, and experience

of U.S. clergy, though they account for 34 percent of students enrolled in theological institutions. Women clerics typically have shorter careers than men, often in related fields that do not involve congregational leadership, such as counseling. In faiths that restrict leadership positions to men, women serve unofficially (Association of Theological Schools 2017: Table 2-12A; Bureau of Labor Statistics 2020b).

Table 13-3 summarizes the four major sociological perspectives on religion.

Components of Religion

All religions have certain elements in common, yet those elements are expressed in the distinctive manner of each faith. These patterns of religious behavior, like other patterns of social behavior, are of great interest to sociologists—especially interactionists—because they underscore the relationship between religion and society.

Religious beliefs, religious rituals, and religious experience all help to define what is sacred and to differentiate the sacred from the profane. Let's examine these three components of religion, as seen through the eyes of interactionists.

Belief

Some people believe in life after death, in supreme beings with unlimited powers, or in supernatural forces. **Religious beliefs** are statements to which members of a particular religion adhere. These views can vary dramatically from religion to religion.

In the late 1960s, something rather remarkable took place in the expression of religious beliefs in the United States. Denominations that held to relatively liberal interpretations of religious scripture (such as the Presbyterians, Methodists, and Lutherans) declined in membership, while those that held to more conservative interpretations grew in numbers. Furthermore, in most faiths, those members who held strict views of scripture became more outspoken, questioning those who remained open to a variety of newer interpretations.

This trend toward *fundamentalism* ran counter to the secularization that was evident in the wider society. **Fundamentalism** may be defined as an emphasis on doctrinal conformity and the literal interpretation of sacred texts. The phrase "religious fundamentalism" was first applied to Protestant believers in the United States who took a literal interpretation of the Bible, but fundamentalism is found worldwide among all major religious groups, including Roman Catholicism, Islam, and Judaism. Even in relatively new faiths, some adherents contend that too much has changed. For followers of many religions, fundamentalists can be as challenging to accommodate as secularists.

The Adam and Eve account of creation found in Genesis, the first book of the Old Testament, is an example of a religious belief. **Creationism,** the literal interpretation of the Biblical account of the creation of humanity and the universe, is used by fundamentalists to argue that evolution should not be presented as an established scientific fact. The political and legal implications of this belief are considered in the Social Policy section of this chapter.

In recent decades, the importance of religion in people's daily life has varied widely among countries. Figure 13-7 shows

Ahmad Faizal Yahya/Flickr/Getty Images

Pilgrims on hajj to the Grand Mosque in Mecca, Saudi Arabia. Islam requires all Muslims who are able to undertake this religious ritual at least once in a lifetime.

FIGURE 13-7   RELIGION IS VERY IMPORTANT IN MY LIFE

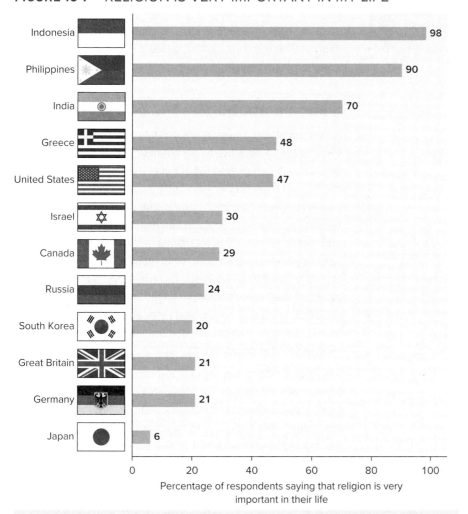

Percentage of respondents saying that religion is very important in their life

Country	Percentage
Indonesia	98
Philippines	90
India	70
Greece	48
United States	47
Israel	30
Canada	29
Russia	24
South Korea	20
Great Britain	21
Germany	21
Japan	6

Think about It Are you surprised by the variation in the importance of how people feel about religion from one nation to another? Why or why not?

Note: Data are from 2018.
Sources: Poushter, Jacob, and Janell Fetterolf. A Changing World: Global Views on Diversity, Gender Equality, Family Life and the Importance of Religion. April 22, 2019. Accessible at www.pewresearch.org.
Flags: admin_design/Shutterstock

the percentage of people who answered "Yes" to the question, "Is religion very important in your life?" in a number of different countries.

Ritual

Religious rituals are practices required or expected of members of a faith. Rituals usually honor the divine power (or powers) worshipped by believers; they also remind adherents of their religious duties and responsibilities. Rituals and beliefs can be interdependent; rituals generally affirm beliefs, as in a public or private statement confessing a sin. Like any social institution, religion develops distinctive norms to structure people's behavior. Moreover, sanctions are attached to religious rituals, whether rewards (bar mitzvah gifts) or penalties (expulsion from a religious institution for violation of norms).

During the coronavirus pandemic, person-to-person contact, a cornerstone of most religious rituals, underwent dramatic change. A digital pulpit emerged, as leaders of all faiths took to the Internet to reach their followers. Even annual rituals such as Passover seders, breaking fast during Ramadan, and Easter sunrise services moved online.

For Muslims, a very important ritual is the *hajj,* a pilgrimage to the Grand Mosque in Mecca, Saudi Arabia. Every Muslim who is physically and financially able is expected to make this trip at least once. Each year 3 million pilgrims go to Mecca during the one-week period indicated by the Islamic lunar calendar. Muslims from all over the world make the *hajj,* including those in the United States, where many tours are arranged to facilitate the trip.

Experience

In the sociological study of religion, the term **religious experience** refers to the feeling or perception of being in direct contact with the ultimate reality, such as a divine being, or of being overcome with religious emotion. A religious experience may be rather slight, such as the feeling of exaltation a person receives from hearing a choir sing Handel's "Hallelujah Chorus." But many religious experiences are more profound, such as a Muslim's experience on a *hajj.* In his autobiography, the late African American activist Malcolm X ([1964] 1999:338) wrote of his *hajj* and how deeply moved he was by the way that Muslims in Mecca came together across race and color lines. For Malcolm X, the color blindness of the Muslim world "proved to me the power of the One God."

Another profound religious experience, for many Christians, is being *born again*—that is, at a turning point in one's life, making a personal commitment to Jesus. According to a 2018 national survey, 41 percent of people in the United States claim they have had a born-again Christian experience at some time in their lives. The collective nature of religion, as emphasized by Durkheim, is evident in the way the beliefs and rituals of a particular faith can create an atmosphere either friendly or indifferent to this type of religious experience (Newport 2018).

TABLE 13-4   COMPONENTS OF RELIGION

Summing Up		
Element	Definition	Examples
Belief	Statement to which members of a particular religion adhere	Creation account Sacred characters or people
Ritual	Practice required or expected of members of a faith	Worship Prayer Singing or chanting
Experience	Feeling or perception of being in direct contact with the ultimate reality (such as a divine being) or of being overcome with religious emotion	Born-again experience Communion with Holy Spirit

THINKING CRITICALLY

Which component of religion is easiest to measure? Which is hardest to measure? Explain.

Table 13-4 summarizes the three components of religion.

Religious Organization

The collective nature of religion has led to many forms of religious association. In modern societies, religion has become increasingly formalized. Specific structures such as churches, synagogues, and mosques have been constructed for religious worship; individuals have been trained for occupational roles within various fields. These developments make it possible to distinguish clearly between the sacred and secular parts of one's life—a distinction that could not be made easily in earlier times, when religion was largely a family activity carried out in the home.

Sociologists find it useful to distinguish between four basic forms of organization: the ecclesia, the denomination, the sect, and the new religious movement, or cult. We can see differences among these four forms of organization in their size, power, degree of commitment that is expected from members, and historical ties to other faiths.

Ecclesiae

An **ecclesia** (plural, *ecclesiae*) is a religious organization that claims to include most or all members of a society and is recognized as the national or official religion. There are 43 countries that have official state religions. Since virtually everyone belongs to the faith, membership is by birth rather than conscious decision. Examples of ecclesiae include Islam in Saudi Arabia and Buddhism in Thailand (Masci 2017).

Generally, ecclesiae are conservative, in that they do not challenge the leaders of a secular government. In a society with an ecclesia, the political and religious institutions often act in harmony and reinforce each other's power in their relative spheres of influence. In the modern world, ecclesiae are declining in power.

Denominations

A **denomination** is a large, organized religion that is not officially linked to the state or government. Like an ecclesia, it tends to have an explicit set of beliefs, a defined system of authority, and a generally respected position in society. Denominations claim as members large segments of a population. Generally, children accept the denomination of their parents and give little thought to membership in other faiths. Denominations also resemble ecclesiae in that they make few demands on members. However, there is a critical difference between these two forms of religious organization. Although the denomination is considered respectable and is not viewed as a challenge to the secular government, it lacks the official recognition and power held by an ecclesia.

The United States is home to a large number of denominations. In good measure, this diversity is a result of our nation's immigrant heritage. Many settlers brought with them the religious commitments native to their homelands. Some Christian denominations in the United States, such as the Roman Catholics, Episcopalians, and Lutherans, are the outgrowth of ecclesiae established in Europe. New Christian denominations also emerged, including the Church of Jesus Christ of Latter-day Saints and Christian Scientists. Within the past generation, immigrants have increased the number of Muslims, Hindus, and Buddhists living in the United States.

Sects

A **sect** is a relatively small religious group that has broken away from some other religious organization to renew what it considers the original vision of the faith. Many sects, such as that led by Martin Luther during the Reformation, claim to be the "true church," because they seek to cleanse the established faith of what they regard as extraneous beliefs and rituals. Max Weber ([1916] 1958:114) termed the sect a "believer's church," because affiliation is based on conscious acceptance of a specific religious dogma.

Sects are fundamentally at odds with society and do not seek to become established national religions. Unlike ecclesiae and denominations, they require intensive commitments and demonstrations of belief by members. Partly owing to their outsider status, sects frequently exhibit a higher degree of religious fervor and loyalty than more established religious groups. Recruitment focuses mainly on adults, and acceptance comes through conversion.

Sects are often short-lived. Those that survive may become less antagonistic to society over time and begin to resemble denominations. In a few instances, sects have endured over several generations while remaining fairly separate from society. Sociologist J. Milton Yinger (1970:226–273) uses the term **established sect** to describe a religious group that is the outgrowth of a sect, yet remains isolated from society. Hutterites, Jehovah's Witnesses, Seventh-day Adventists, and Amish are contemporary examples of established sects in the United States (Schaefer and Zellner 2015).

USE YOUR SOCIOLOGICAL IMAGINATION

Choose a religious tradition other than your own. How would your religious beliefs, rituals, and experience differ if you had been raised in that tradition?

New Religious Movements or Cults

In 1997, 38 members of the Heaven's Gate cult were found dead in southern California after a mass suicide timed to occur with the appearance of the Hale-Bopp comet. They believed the comet hid a spaceship on which they could catch a ride once they had broken free of their "bodily containers."

Partly as a result of the notoriety generated by such groups, the popular media have stigmatized the word *cult,* associating it with the occult and the use of intense and forceful conversion techniques. The stereotyping of cults as uniformly bizarre and unethical has led sociologists to abandon the term and refer instead to a *new religious movement (NRM).* While some NRMs exhibit strange behavior, many do not. They attract new members just like any other religion, and often follow teachings similar to those of established Christian denominations, though with less ritual.

Sects are difficult to distinguish from cults. A **new religious movement (NRM)** or **cult** is generally a small, secretive religious group that represents either a new religion or a major innovation of an existing faith. NRMs are similar to sects in that they tend to be small and are often viewed as less respectable than more established faiths. Unlike sects, however, NRMs normally do not result from schisms or breaks with established ecclesiae or denominations. Some cults, such as those focused on UFO sightings, may be totally unrelated to existing faiths. Even when a cult does accept certain fundamental tenets of a dominant faith—such as a belief in Jesus as divine or in Mohammad as a messenger of God—it will offer new revelations or insights to justify its claim to being a more advanced religion (Stark and Bainbridge 1979, 1985).

Like sects, NRMs may be transformed over time into other types of religious organization. An example is the Christian Science Church, which began as a new religious movement under the leadership of Mary Baker Eddy. Today, this church exhibits the characteristics of a denomination. In fact, most major religions, including Christianity, began as cults. NRMs may be in the early stages of developing into a denomination or new religion, or they may just as easily fade away through the loss of members or weak leadership (R. Schaefer and Zellner 2008, 2015).

Comparing Forms of Religious Organization

How can we determine whether a particular religious group falls into the sociological category of ecclesia, denomination, sect, or NRM? As we have seen, these types of religious organization have somewhat different relationships to society. Ecclesiae are recognized as national churches; denominations, although not officially approved by the state, are generally widely respected. In contrast, sects and NRMs are much more likely to be at odds with the larger culture.

TABLE 13-5 CHARACTERISTICS OF ECCLESIAE, DENOMINATIONS, SECTS, AND NEW RELIGIOUS MOVEMENTS

Summing Up

Characteristic	Ecclesia	Denomination	Sect	New Religious Movement (or Cult)
Size	Very large	Large	Small	Small
Wealth	Extensive	Extensive	Limited	Variable
Religious services	Formal, little participation	Formal, little participation	Informal, emotional	Variable
Doctrines	Specific, but interpretation may be tolerated	Specific, but interpretation may be tolerated	Specific, purity of doctrine emphasized	Innovative, pathbreaking
Clergy	Well-trained, full-time	Well-trained, full-time	Trained to some degree	Unspecialized
Membership	By virtue of being a member of society	By acceptance of doctrine	By acceptance of doctrine	By an emotional commitment
Relationship to the state	Recognized, closely aligned	Tolerated	Not encouraged	Ignored or challenged

Sources: Adapted from Vernon 1962; see also Chalfant et al. 1994.

RESEARCH TODAY

13-3 Wicca: Religion or Quasi-Religion?

For two years President Trump called the investigation into Russian influence in the 2016 election a "witch hunt." The meaning to listeners was clear: since there are no witches, a witch hunt is an investigation into something that does not exist. Yet today thousands of people, both men and women, do view themselves as Witches; they practice a little-known religion called Wicca (which should not be confused with Satanism—there is no place in the Craft for devil worship).

Wicca (Anglo-Saxon for witch and wizard) is a modern form of Witchcraft, practiced for the last hundred years. The Englishman Gerald Gardner, born in 1884, drew on past rituals to found the Craft. Gardner stressed the importance of worshipping skyclad, or "clothed by the sky"—that is, naked. Being skyclad, he believed, helped a person to gain insight.

Not all Wiccans follow in Gardner's tradition. Today, Wiccan ritual takes on a dizzying variety of forms, ranging from the elementary to the highly detailed and sophisticated. A Wiccan circle or meeting can include a single heartfelt prayer or a highly complex and time-consuming ritual. Like members of more accepted religions, Wiccans observe several rituals associated with the life cycle. Parents name their children at a Wiccaning, which includes a dedication to the Goddess and the God. Contemporary Wiccans also celebrate a wedding-like ceremony called a handfasting, which is typically performed by a High Priest and/or Priestess.

Just as Wiccans' worship varies, so does their organization. Some Witches practice alone, as a solitaire; others practice in a group of similarly minded Witches, called a coven. A coven may include just 3 or 4 Witches, male and/or female, or as many as 30; members tend to come and go just as they do in a church, temple, or mosque. In a mixed coven, the assembly is often

Scott Olson/Getty Images

governed by a High Priest or Priestess, or by both.

> *Revealing one's membership in any nontraditional group is always difficult, but perhaps especially so for Wiccans, who refer to the experience as "coming out of the broom closet."*

Revealing one's membership in any nontraditional group is always difficult, but perhaps especially so for Wiccans, who refer to the experience as "coming out of the broom closet." Many Wiccans are young, and so must come out to their parents. Parental reactions range from cutting off contact with the Witch to wanting to learn more about

the Craft. Many parents treat the religion as a "phase" in their child's spiritual journey.

Most scholars treat Wicca as a **quasi-religion,** a category that includes organizations that may see themselves as religious, but are seen by others as "sort of religious." National surveys that allow respondents to self-identify showed 8,000 Wiccans in 1990; 134,000 in 2001; and 342,000 in 2008, the latest year for which reliable national data are available. These estimates suggest either an increase in willingness to identify as Wiccan or an absolute growth in the faithful— probably both.

LET'S DISCUSS

1. Do you know anyone who practices Wicca? If so, describe the person's practices.
2. Do you think that Wicca should be considered a religion? Why or why not?

*Sources:*Bosker 2020; Holson 2019; Kosmin and Keysar 2009; Schaefer and Zellner 2015

Still, ecclesiae, denominations, and sects are best viewed as types along a continuum rather than as mutually exclusive categories. Table 13-5 summarizes some of the primary characteristics of the ideal types. Since the United States has no ecclesiae, sociologists studying this country's religions have focused on the denomination and the sect. These religious forms have been pictured on either end of a continuum, with

denominations accommodating to the secular world and sects protesting against established religions. Although NRMs also are included in the table, they lie outside the continuum, because they generally define themselves in terms of a new view of life rather than in terms of existing religious faiths. In fact, one of the most controversial NRMs, Wicca, may not fully qualify as a religion (Box 13-3).

Sociologists look at religion from an organizational perspective, which tends to stress the stability of religious adherence, but there are other ways to view religion. From an individual perspective, religion and spirituality are remarkably fluid. People often change their places of worship or move from one denomination to another. In many countries, including the United States, churches, temples, and mosques operate in a highly competitive market.

One sign of this fluidity is the rapid rise of still another form of religious organization, the electronic church. Facilitated by cable television and satellite transmission, *televangelists* (as they are called) direct their messages to more people—especially in the United States—than are served by all but the largest denominations. While some televangelists are affiliated with religious denominations, most give viewers the impression that they are dissociated from established faiths.

As we move well into the 21st century, scholars debate the impact of the Internet on religion. Some argue that the growth in Internet usage helps to explain the increase in the number of unaffiliated adults, as more people find websites that question long-held beliefs or simply spend large amounts of time online, leaving less time for group activities. On the other hand, religious groups worldwide are rapidly adapting to new media, though not without unevenness and ineptitude at times. Facebook, blogs, texting, and streaming are still less prevalent among organized religions than in the corporate world, but new media are nevertheless transforming the ways in which religious faiths socially interact with people and enhance their sense of religious community (Downey 2014; Thumma 2012).

An ongoing controversy in the United States is the relationship between education and religion. The degree to which religion can be present in public education is the subject of the Social Policy section of this chapter.

THINKING CRITICALLY

In sociological terms, what attracts people to new religious movements?

socialpolicy and Education

Religion in the Schools

Should public schools be allowed to sponsor organized prayer in the classroom? How about Bible reading, or just a collective moment of silence? Can athletes at public schools offer up a group prayer in a team huddle? Should students be able to initiate voluntary prayers at school events? Each of these situations involves the question of whether there is a role for prayer in the schools and whether strict separation of church and state should be maintained.

Another controversy concerns the teaching of theories about the origin of humans and the universe. Mainstream scientific thinking holds that humans evolved over billions of years from one-celled organisms, and that the universe came into being 15 billion years ago as a result of a huge cosmic explosion (the big bang theory). These theories are challenged by people who hold to the biblical account of the creation of humans and the universe some 10,000 years ago—a viewpoint known as **creationism**.

Looking at the Issue

The issues just described go to the heart of the First Amendment's provisions regarding religious freedom. On the one hand, the government must protect the right to practice one's religion; on the other, it cannot take any measures that would seem to establish one religion over another (separation of church and state). In the key case of *Engle v. Vitale*, the Supreme Court ruled in 1962 that the use of nondenominational prayer in New York schools was "wholly inconsistent" with the First Amendment's prohibition against government establishment of religion. In finding that organized school prayer violated the Constitution—even when no student was required to participate—the Court argued, in effect, that promoting

Huw Aaron/www.CartoonStock.com

People on both sides of the debate between evolution and creationism invoke the name of Albert Einstein. Evolutionists emphasize the need for verifiable scientific data, like that which confirmed Einstein's groundbreaking scientific theories. Advocates of intelligent design quote the Nobel Prize–winning physicist's assertion that religion and science should coexist.

religious observance was not a legitimate function of government or education. Subsequent Court decisions have allowed voluntary school prayer by students, but forbid school officials to sponsor any prayer or religious observance at school events (Yokotsuka 2019).

Despite these rulings, many public schools still regularly lead their students in prayer recitations or Bible readings. Public schools and even states have mandated a moment of silence at the start of the school day, in what critics contend is a transparent attempt to get around *Engle v. Vitale* and similar legal precedents. Although legislators clearly intended to set aside time for prayer or religious thoughts when they created these "moments," to date the courts have recognized such policies as constitutional, and the federal government treats them as secular rather than sacred as long as teachers and other school employees may neither require, encourage, nor discourage students from praying during such time periods (Center for Faith and Opportunity Initiatives 2020).

As with school prayer, the teaching of creationism has significant support among the general public. Unlike Europeans, many people in the United States seem highly skeptical of evolutionary theory, which is taught as a matter of course in science classes. In 2019, a national survey showed that 40 percent of adults believe that God created humans in their present form (Brenan 2019c).

In 1987, the Supreme Court ruled that states could not compel the teaching of creationism in public schools if the primary purpose was to promote a religious viewpoint. In response, those who believe in the divine origin of life have recently advanced a concept called **intelligent design (ID)**, the idea that life is so complex that it could only have been created by divine design. Though this concept is not based explicitly on the biblical account of creation, fundamentalists feel comfortable with it. Supporters of intelligent design consider it a more accurate account of the origin of life than Darwinism and hold that at the very least, ID should be taught as an alternative to the theory of evolution.

In 2005, in *Kitzmiller v. Dove Area School District,* a federal judge ended a Pennsylvania school district's plans to require teachers to present the concept in class. In essence, the judge found ID to be "a religious belief," a subtler but similar approach to creationism in that both find God's fingerprints in nature. The issue continues to be hotly debated and is expected to be the subject of future court cases (Khazan 2019).

Applying Sociology

Supporters of school prayer and of creationism feel that strict Court rulings have forced too great a separation between what

Émile Durkheim called the *sacred* and the *profane*. They insist that the use of nondenominational prayer can in no way lead to the establishment of an ecclesia in the United States. Moreover, they believe that school prayer—and the teaching of creationism—can provide the spiritual guidance and socialization that many children today do not receive from parents or regular church attendance. Many communities also believe that schools should transmit the dominant culture of the United States by encouraging prayer.

Opponents of school prayer and creationism argue that a religious majority in a community might impose viewpoints specific to its faith at the expense of religious minorities. These critics question whether school prayer can remain truly voluntary. Drawing on the interactionist perspective and small group research, they suggest that children will face enormous social pressure to conform to the beliefs and practices of the majority..

Initiating Policy

Public school education is fundamentally a local issue, so most initiatives and lobbying have taken place at the local or state level. Federal courts have taken a hard line on religion in the public schools. Religion–school debates show no sign of ending. The activism of religious fundamentalists in the public school system raises the question, "Whose ideas and values deserve a hearing in classrooms?" Critics see this campaign as one step toward sectarian religious control of public education. They worry that at some point in the future, teachers may not be able to use books or make statements that conflict with fundamentalist interpretations of the Bible. For advocates of a liberal education and of intellectual (and religious) diversity, this is a genuinely frightening prospect.

Take the Issue with You

1. Was there organized prayer in any school you attended? Was creationism part of the curriculum?

2. Do you think that promoting religious observance is a legitimate function of education?

3. How might a conflict theorist view the issue of organized school prayer? Do you have any experience with educational reform, either as a student yourself or as a parent? If so, describe the changes that you witnessed. Were they successful in improving educational outcomes?

MASTERING THIS CHAPTER

Summary

Education and **religion** are cultural universals found throughout the world in various forms. This chapter examines the sociological views of education and analyzes schools as an example of formal organizations. It also examines the major world religions, the functions and dimensions of religion, and the four basic types of religious organization.

1. The transmission of knowledge and bestowal of status are manifest functions of **education**. Among the latent functions are transmitting culture, promoting social and political integration, maintaining social control, and serving as an agent of social change.

2. In the view of conflict theorists, education serves as an instrument of elite domination by creating standards for entry into occupations, bestowing status unequally, and subordinating the role of women.

3. Teacher expectations about a student's performance can sometimes have an impact on the student's actual achievements.

4. Today, most schools in the United States are organized in a bureaucratic fashion. Weber's five basic characteristics of bureaucracy are all evident in schools.

5. Homeschooling has become a viable alternative to traditional public and private schools. An estimated 1.7 million or more American children are now educated at home.

6. Émile Durkheim stressed the social impact of **religion** in attempting to understand individual religious behavior within the context of the larger society.

7. Eighty-nine percent of the world's population adheres to some form of religion. Tremendous diversity exists in religious beliefs and practices, which may be heavily influenced by culture.

8. Religion helps to integrate a diverse society and provides social support in time of need.

9. Max Weber saw a connection between religious allegiance and capitalistic behavior, which he termed the **Protestant ethic.**

10. In **liberation theology,** the teachings of Christianity become the basis for political efforts to alleviate poverty and social injustice.

11. From a Marxist point of view, religion serves to reinforce the social control of those in power. It discourages collective political action, which could end capitalist oppression and transform society.

12. Religious behavior is expressed through **religious beliefs, rituals, and experience.**

13. Sociologists have identified four basic types of religious organization: the **ecclesia,** the **denomination,** the **sect,** and the **new religious movement (NRM),** or **cult**.

14. Today, the question of how much religion, if any, should be permitted in U.S. public schools is a matter of intense debate.

Key Terms

Correspondence principle A term used by Bowles and Gintis to refer to the tendency of schools to promote the values expected of individuals in each social class and to perpetuate social-class divisions from one generation to the next. (320)

Creationism The literal interpretation of the Biblical account of the creation of humanity and the universe. (334)

Credentialism An increase in the lowest level of education needed to enter a field. (318)

Denomination A large, organized religion that is not officially linked to the state or government. (336)

Ecclesia A religious organization that claims to include most or all members of a society and is recognized as the national or official religion. (336)

Education A formal process of learning in which some people consciously teach, while others adopt the social role of learner. (314)

Established sect J. Milton Yinger's term for a religious group that is the outgrowth of a sect, yet remains isolated from society. (337)

Fundamentalism An emphasis on doctrinal conformity and the literal interpretation of sacred texts. (334)

Hidden curriculum Standards of behavior that are deemed proper by society and are taught subtly in schools. (318)

Intelligent design (ID) The idea that life is so complex that it could only have been created by divine design. (340)

Liberation theology Use of a church, primarily Roman Catholic, in a political effort to eliminate poverty, discrimination, and other forms of injustice from a secular society. (332)

New religious movement (NRM) or cult A small, secretive religious group that represents either a new religion or a major innovation of an existing faith. (337)

Profane The ordinary and commonplace elements of life, as distinguished from the sacred. (327)

Protestant ethic Max Weber's term for the disciplined work ethic, thisworldly concerns, and rational orientation to life emphasized by John Calvin and his followers. (331)

Quasi-religion A scholarly category that includes organizations that may see themselves as religious but may be seen by others as "sort of religious." (338)

Religion According to Émile Durkheim, a unified system of beliefs and practices relative to sacred things. (314)

Religious belief A statement to which members of a particular religion adhere. (334)

Religious experience The feeling or perception of being in direct contact with the ultimate reality, such as a divine being, or of being overcome with religious emotion. (335)

Religious ritual A practice required or expected of members of a faith. (335)

Sacred Elements beyond everyday life that inspire awe, respect, and even fear. (327)

Sect A relatively small religious group that has broken away from some other religious organization to renew what it considers the original vision of the faith. (336)

Secularization The process through which religion's influence on other social institutions diminishes. (315)

Teacher-expectancy effect The impact that a teacher's expectations about a student's performance may have on the student's actual achievements. (321)

Tracking The practice of placing students in specific curriculum groups on the basis of their test scores and other criteria. (320)

1. Watch a documentary about a cult or new religious movement. What are their recruitment practices? What made recruits want to join? How did the recruits' family members feel? Were certain members of the cult or movement banished? Did anyone voluntarily leave? Was it difficult to leave? Take notes and share your findings with the class.

2. Watch a movie or read a book about a teacher or volunteer making a difference at a school with disadvantaged and under-served students. How was this person able to make a difference? What impact did this person have on the students? Tell your classmates about the movie or book.

3. Debate the fairness of tenure. One group of students will take a pro stance and another group will take a con stance. Prepare for the debate by doing research and coming up with talking points with your team.

4. **Writing Sociology.** Look up the latest news on voucher plans or school choice programs. Write a report about your findings, including your own personal opinions about such programs, and share it with the class.

Self-Quiz

Read each question carefully and then select the best answer.

1. In the United States, we expect that cab drivers will know how to get around a city. This expectation is an example of which of the following?
   a. Max Weber
   b. Karl Marx
   c. Émile Durkheim
   d. Talcott Parsons

2. An evangelical church offers services in the native language of an immigrant community. This practice is an example of
   a. the integrative function of religion.
   b. the charismatic function of religion.
   c. the social control function of religion.
   d. none of the above

3. The use of a church, primarily Roman Catholic, in a political effort to eliminate poverty, discrimination, and other forms of injustice evident in a secular society is referred to as
   a. quasi-religion.
   b. ritualism.
   c. religious experience.
   d. liberation theology.

4. The Adam and Eve account of creation found in Genesis, the first book of the Old Testament, is an example of a religious
   a. ritual.
   b. experience.
   c. custom.
   d. belief.

5. Which of the following is *not* an example of an ecclesia?
   a. the Lutheran Church in Sweden
   b. Islam in Saudi Arabia
   c. Buddhism in Thailand
   d. the Episcopal Church in the United States

6. John Calvin, a leader of the Protestant Reformation, emphasized
   a. a disciplined work ethic.
   b. this-worldly concerns.
   c. a rational orientation to life.
   d. all of the above

7. Most recent research on ability grouping raises questions about its
   a. effectiveness, especially for lower-achieving students.
   b. failure to improve the prospects of higher-achieving students.
   c. ability to improve the prospects of lower- and higher-achieving students.
   d. both a and b

8. Seventy years ago, a high school diploma was the minimum requirement for entry into the paid labor force of the United States. Today, a college diploma is virtually the bare minimum. This change reflects the process of
   a. tracking.
   b. credentialism.
   c. the hidden curriculum.
   d. the correspondence principle.

9. Samuel Bowles and Herbert Gintis have argued that capitalism requires a skilled, disciplined labor force and that the educational system of the United States is structured with that objective in mind. Citing numerous studies, they offer support for what they call
   a. tracking.
   b. credentialism.
   c. the correspondence principle.
   d. the teacher-expectancy effect.

10. The teacher-expectancy effect is most closely associated with
    a. the functionalist perspective.
    b. the conflict perspective.
    c. the interactionist perspective.
    d. anomie theory.

11. The _____ encompasses elements beyond everyday life that inspire awe, respect, and even fear, as compared to the _____ , which includes the ordinary and the commonplace.

12. Wicca is an example of a(n) _____ .

13. _____ is the largest single faith in the world; the second largest is _____
_____ .

14. Because they are _____ , most religions tend to reinforce men's dominance in secular as well as spiritual matters.

15. The single largest denomination in the United States is _____ _____
_____ .

16. Unlike ecclesiae and denominations, _____ require intensive commitments and demonstrations of belief by members.

17. In the past, the integrative function of education was most obvious through its emphasis on promoting a common _____
_____ .

18. Schools perform a variety of _____ functions, such as transmitting culture, promoting social and po-litical integration, and maintaining social control.

19. Sociologist _____ _____ points out that better-edu-cated people tend to have greater access to information, to hold more diverse opinions, and to possess the ability to make subtle distinctions in anal-ysis.

20. The fact that religion helped many people and communities endure the coronavirus pandemic is an example of the _____
_____ _____ function of religion.

_____

14 Government and the Economy

Paul M. Driftmier/Shutterstock

During the coronavirus pandemic, some citizens protested over government shutdown orders and face covering mandates that they considered to be excessive.

▶ INSIDE

344

Ira C. Roberts/Chad Enterprises Corporation

How much power do you think you have over the U.S. economy? Over the economic policies of the U.S. government?

According to sociologist G. William Domhoff, unless you belong to the corporate elite, you have no real power.

❝ How can the owners and managers of highly competitive corporations develop the policy unity to shape government policies? And how can large corporations have such great power in a democratic country? The step-by-step argument and evidence presented in previous chapters provide the foundation for a theory that can explain these paradoxes—a *class-domination* theory of power in the United States.

Domination means that the commands of a group or class are carried out with relatively little resistance, which is possible because that group or class has been able to establish the organizations, rules, and customs through which everyday life is conducted. Domination, in other words, is the institutionalized outcome of great distributive power ("power over"). The corporate rich are a dominant class in terms of this definition because the cumulative effect of their various distributive powers leads to a situation in which most Americans generally accept (or acquiesce in) their policies. Even when there are highly vocal complaints, the routinized ways of acting in the United States follow from the rules and regulations needed by the corporate community to continue to grow and make profits.

The overall distributive power of the dominant class is first of all based in its structural power, which falls to it by virtue of being owners and high-level executives in corporations that sell goods and services for a profit in a market economy that is fashioned in good part to benefit the sellers of goods and services, not employees or consumers. The power to invest or not invest and to hire and fire employees leads to a political context in which most elected officials try to do as much as they can to create a favorable investment climate in order to avoid being voted out of office in the event of an economic downturn. This structural power is augmented by the ability to create new policies through the policy-planning network, which it was possible for the corporate rich to develop gradually over many decades because their common economic interests and social cohesion give them enough unity to sustain such an endeavor.

Our final sample of participants (10 prisoners and 11 guards) were selected from over 75 volunteers recruited through ads in the city and campus newspapers. . . . Half were randomly assigned to role-play being guards, the others to be prisoners. Thus, there were no measurable differences between the guards and the prisoners at the start of this experiment.

But even these powers might not have been enough to generate a system of extreme class domination if the bargains and compromises embodied in the Constitution had not led unexpectedly to a two-party system in which one party was controlled by the Northern rich and the other by the Southern rich. This in turn reinforced a personality-oriented candidate-selection process that is heavily dependent on large campaign donations—now and in the nineteenth century as well. The system of party primaries is the one adaptation to this constrictive two-party system that has provided some openings for insurgent liberals and trade unionists on one side and social conservatives and libertarians on the other.

Structural power, policies generated in the policy-planning network, and control of the two parties resulted in a polity in which there is little or no organized public opinion on specific legislative issues that is independent of the limits, doubts, and obfuscations generated by the opinion-shaping network. In addition, the fragmented and constrained system of government crafted by the Founding Fathers led to a relatively small federal government that is easily entered and influenced by wealthy and well-organized private citizens, whether through Congress, the separate departments of the executive branch, or a myriad of regulatory agencies.

Despite their lack of power, many Americans feel a sense of empowerment because they have religious freedom, freedom of expression, the right to vote, and the hope that they can make more money or rise in the class structure if they try hard enough. Those with educational credentials and/or secure employment experience a degree of dignity and respect that allows them to hold their heads high and maintain their sense of self-regard, because elite arrogance and condescension toward average people is rarely expressed publicly. Then, too, liberals and leftists retain hope because they had success in helping to expand individual rights and freedom—for people of color, for women, and for gays and lesbians.

But individual rights and freedoms do not necessarily add up to distributive power. In the same time period between 1965 and 2000 in which individual rights and freedoms expanded, corporate power also became greater because industrial unions were decimated, the civil rights movement dissipated, and the liberal-labor alliance splintered as part of the resistance to the integration of job sites, neighborhoods, and schools. Thus, class domination actually increased in recent decades in spite of increases in individual freedom. It is therefore possible to have class domination in a society based on individualistic liberal values, as many decisions by the Supreme Court also demonstrate. ❞

Source: Domhoff 2014a: 192–194.

Despite their lack of power, many Americans feel a sense of empowerment because they have religious freedom, freedom of expression, the right to vote, and the hope that they can make more money or rise in the class structure if they try hard enough.

In this excerpt from his book *Who Rules America? The Triumph of the Corporate Rich,* G. William Domhoff explains how large corporations increased their power in recent decades. The general public seems to share Domhoff's assertion about who rules America: in December 2019, 68 percent felt that big corporations have too much power and should be strongly regulated to better serve the public interest (Halpin et al. 2019; see also Domhoff 2020a, 2020b).

The unequal distribution of power in the United States, where a small group of corporate elites wields more power than the entire citizenry, is compounded by inequality of income and wealth. The same is true of the world as a whole. A 2019 report from OXFAM, a human-rights organization, provided some startling data:

- Billionaires now have more wealth than ever before. Between 2017 and 2019, a new billionaire was created every two days

- The wealth of the world's billionaires increased by $900 billion in 2019 alone, or $2.5 billion each day. Meanwhile, the wealth of the poorest half of the world's population, 3.8 billion people, fell by 11 percent.

- If the world's richest people were to pay just 0.5 percent more tax on their wealth, that would raise more money than it would cost to educate all 262 million children who do not go to school worldwide *and* provide health care that would save the lives of an estimated 3.3 million people (OXFAM 2019).

The inequality both within the United States and between the United States and other nations—between the big industrial powers and the developing world—underscores the importance of understanding our economic and political institutions. To many observers, the massive concentration of economic resources in the hands of just a few threatens our founding fathers' vision of an inclusive political and economic system. Instead of moving forward together, Americans seem increasingly split by inequality in economic and political power—a trend that will inevitably heighten social tensions.

This chapter will present a combined analysis of the economy and government. It is hard to imagine two social institutions more intertwined. Besides serving as the largest employer in the nation, government at all levels regulates commerce and entry into many occupations. At the same time, the economy generates the revenue to support government services.

We'll begin the chapter with a macro-level analysis of two ideal types of *economic system,* capitalism and socialism. The term **economic system** refers to the social institution through which goods and services are produced, distributed, and consumed. As with social institutions such as the family, religion, and government, the economic system shapes other

Stockbyte/Getty Images

The unequal distribution of power and wealth is especially visible outside the wealthy industrial nations. A young boy scavenges for items that might be of use to his family on Smokey Mountain, a massive landfill in Manila, Philippines. Thousands pick through the rubbish despite landslides that take the lives of scavengers. About half of Manila's 11 million people live in slums.

aspects of the social order and is in turn influenced by them. Throughout this textbook, you have been reminded of the economy's impact on social behavior—for example, on individual and group behavior in factories and offices. You have studied the work of Karl Marx and Friedrich Engels, who emphasized that a society's economic system can promote social inequality. And you have learned that foreign investment in developing countries can intensify inequality among residents.

Next, we consider the **political system,** by which we mean the social institution that is founded on a recognized set of procedures for implementing and achieving society's goals. In the United States, the political system holds the ultimate responsibility for addressing social policy issues such as child care, the AIDS crisis, and welfare reform. We'll examine some general theories of power and authority, with the four major types of government in which that power and authority is exerted. We'll see how politics works, with particular attention to citizens' participation and the changing role of women. We'll look at two models of power in the United States, the elite and the pluralist models. Then we'll consider war, peace, and terrorism.

In the following section we'll return to the economy to look at ways in which economies around the world are changing in response to globalization. Finally, in the Social Policy section we'll explore the government's response to the coronavirus pandemic.

Economic Systems

The sociocultural evolution approach developed by Gerhard Lenski categorizes preindustrial society according to the way in which the economy is organized. The principal types of pre-industrial society, as you recall, are hunting-and-gathering so-cieties, horticultural societies, and agrarian societies.

The *Industrial Revolution*—which took place largely in England during the period 1760 to 1830—brought about changes in the social organization of the workplace. People left their home-steads and began working in central locations such as facto-ries. As the Industrial Revolution proceeded, a new form of social structure emerged: the **industrial society,** a society that depends on mechanization to produce its goods and services.

The scope of these large economies is massive, as Figure 14-1 shows. Over the last three centuries, industrialization has greatly increased the wealth of nations. Since 1990 China, which only began to mechanize its rural areas in the last half of the 20th century, has grown from eleventh-largest economy in the world to second largest.

Two basic types of economic system distinguish contemporary industrial societies: capitalism and socialism. As described in the following sections, capitalism and socialism are ideal types of economic system. No nation precisely fits either model. In-stead, each nation's economy represents a mixture of capital-ism and socialism, although one type or the other is generally more useful in describing a society's economic structure.

Capitalism

In preindustrial societies, land was the source of virtually all wealth. The Industrial Revolution changed all that. It required that certain individuals and institutions be willing to take sub-stantial risks to finance new inventions, machinery, and busi-ness enterprises. Eventually, bankers, industrialists, and other holders of large sums of money replaced landowners as the most powerful economic force. These people invested their funds in the hope of realiz-ing even greater profits, and thereby became owners of property and business firms.

The transition to private ownership of business was accompanied by the emer-gence of the capitalist eco-nomic system. **Capitalism** is an economic system in which the means of produc-tion are held largely in pri-vate hands and the main incentive for economic activ-ity is the accumulation of profits. In practice, capitalist systems vary in the degree to which the government regulates private ownership and economic activity (D. Rosenberg 1991).

Immediately following the Industrial Revolution, the prevailing form of capitalism was what is termed **laissez-faire** ("let them do"). Under the principle of laissez-faire, as expounded and endorsed by British economist Adam Smith (1723–1790), people could compete freely, with minimal government inter-vention in the economy.

FIGURE 14-1   WORLD'S LARGEST ECONOMIES

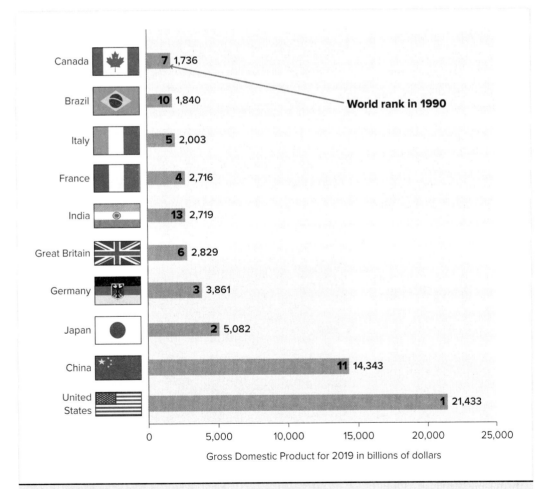

Gross Domestic Product for 2019 in billions of dollars

Think about It Note the changes in rank since 1990. What further changes would you expect to see in the next 30 years?

Note: While the coronavirus pandemic has led to reductions in national GDPs, the comparisons are still relevant.
Source: World Bank 2021a. *Flags:* admin_design/Shutterstock

Business retained the right to regulate itself and operated essentially without fear of government interference (Smelser 1963).

Two centuries later, capitalism has taken on a somewhat different form. Private ownership and maximization of profits still remain the most significant characteristics of capitalist economic systems. However, in contrast to the era of laissez-faire, capitalism today features government regulation of economic relations. Without regulations, business firms can mislead consumers, endanger workers' safety, and even defraud the companies' investors—all in the pursuit of greater profits. That is why the government of a capitalist nation often monitors prices, sets safety and environmental standards for industries, protects the rights of consumers, and regulates collective bargaining between labor unions and management. Yet under capitalism as an ideal type, government rarely takes over ownership of an entire industry.

Contemporary capitalism also differs from laissez-faire in another important respect: capitalism tolerates monopolistic practices. A **monopoly** exists when a single business firm controls the market. Domination of an industry allows the firm to effectively control a commodity by dictating pricing, quality standards, and availability. Buyers have little choice but to yield to the firm's decisions; there is no other place to purchase the product or service. Monopolistic practices violate the ideal of free competition cherished by Adam Smith and other supporters of laissez-faire capitalism.

Some capitalistic nations, such as the United States, outlaw monopolies through antitrust legislation. Such laws prevent any business from taking over so much of an industry that it controls the market. The U.S. federal government allows monopolies to exist only in certain exceptional cases, such as the utility and transportation industries. Even then, regulatory agencies scrutinize these officially approved monopolies to protect the public. The protracted legal battles between the Justice Department and Microsoft, owner of the dominant operating system for personal computers, illustrates the uneasy relationship between government and private monopolies in capitalistic countries.

Conflict theorists point out that although *pure* monopolies are not a basic element of the economy of the United States, competition is still much more restricted than one might expect in what is called a *free enterprise system*. In numerous industries, a few companies largely dominate the field and keep new enterprises from entering the marketplace.

During the severe economic downturn that began in 2008, the United States moved even farther away from the laissez-faire ideal. To keep major financial institutions from going under, the federal government invested hundreds of billions of dollars in distressed banking, investment, and insurance companies. Then in 2009, the government bailed out the failing

Mark Steinmetz/McGraw-Hill

For more than a century, the board game of Monopoly has entertained millions of people around the world. In the game, players strive to dominate the fictitious economy, gleefully bankrupting other players. Ironically, Monopoly was developed to demonstrate the weaknesses of capitalist economies, such as excessive rents and the tendency for money to accumulate in the hands of a few.

automobile industry. This massive bailout paled in comparison to federal measures taken to support the economic shutdown during the 2020 coronavirus pandemic. While wage workers and small businesses received assistance, the federal government's first step was to reassure the energy, airline, and cruise industries that they would be taken care of during the crisis.

Tom Stoddart/Hulton Archive/Getty Images

Workers mine for coltan with sweat and shovels. The sudden increase in demand for the metal by U.S. computer manufacturers caused incursions into the Congo by neighboring countries hungry for capital to finance a war. Too often, globalization can have unintended consequences for a nation's economy and social welfare.

As we have seen in earlier chapters, globalization and the rise of multinational corporations have spread the capitalistic pursuit of profits around the world. Especially in developing countries, governments are not always prepared to deal with the sudden influx of foreign capital and its effects on their economies. One particularly striking example of how unfettered capitalism can harm developing nations is found in the Democratic Republic of Congo. The Congo has significant deposits of the metal columbite-tantalite—coltan, for short—which is used in the production of electronic circuit boards. Until the market for cell phones, pagers, and laptop computers heated up, U.S. manufacturers got most of their coltan from Australia. But at the height of consumer demand, they turned to miners in the Congo to increase their supply.

Predictably, the escalating price of the metal—as much as $600 a kilogram at one point, or more than three times the average Congolese worker's yearly wages—attracted undesirable attention. Soon the neighboring countries of Rwanda, Uganda, and Burundi, at war with one another and desperate for resources to finance the conflict, were raiding the Congo's national parks, slashing and burning to expose the coltan beneath the forest floor. Indirectly, the sudden increase in the demand for coltan was financing war and the rape of the environment. Beginning in 2017, most major manufacturers pledged to buy only from legitimate suppliers. Yet much of the coltan that makes it way into the supply chain is still collected by children under the harshest of working conditions (Tsango 2020).

Socialism

Socialist theory was refined in the writings of Karl Marx and Friedrich Engels. These European radicals were disturbed by the exploitation of the working class that emerged during the Industrial Revolution. In their view, capitalism forced large numbers of people to exchange their labor for low wages. The owners of an industry profit from the labor of workers primarily because they pay workers less than the value of the goods produced.

As an ideal type, a socialist economic system attempts to eliminate such economic exploitation. Under **socialism,** the means of production and distribution in a society are collectively rather than privately owned. The basic objective of the economic system is to meet people's needs rather than to maximize profits. Socialists reject the laissez-faire philosophy that free competition benefits the general public. Instead, they believe that the central government, acting as the representative of the people, should make basic economic decisions. Therefore, government ownership of all major industries—including steel production, automobile manufacturing, and agriculture—is a primary feature of socialism as an ideal type.

In practice, socialist economic systems vary in the extent to which they tolerate private ownership. For example, in Great Britain, a nation with some aspects of both a socialist and a capitalist economy, passenger airline service was once concentrated in the government-owned corporation British Airways. Even before the airline was privatized in 1987, however, private airlines were allowed to compete with it.

Socialist nations differ from capitalist nations in their commitment to social service programs. For example, the U.S. government provides health care and health insurance to the elderly and poor through the Medicare and Medicaid programs. But socialist countries typically offer government-financed medical care to *all* citizens. In theory, the wealth of the people as a collectivity is used to provide health care, housing, education, and other key services to each individual and family.

Marx believed that socialist societies would eventually "wither away" and evolve into *communist* societies. As an ideal type, **communism** refers to an economic system under which all property is communally owned and no social distinctions are made on the basis of people's ability to produce. In recent decades, Russia, the People's Republic of China, Vietnam, Cuba, and nations in Eastern Europe were popularly thought of as examples of communist economic systems. However, this usage represents an incorrect application of a term with sensitive political connotations. All nations known as communist in the 21st century actually fell far short of the ideal type (Walder and Nguyen 2008).

By the early 1990s, Communist parties were no longer ruling the nations of Eastern Europe. By 2020 Moscow had 70 billionaires, while world-leading New York City's had 116. In the same year traditionally communist China had 67 billionaires in its capital of Beijing (*Forbes* 2020).

As we have seen, capitalism and socialism are ideal types of economic system. In reality, the economy of each industrial society—including the United States, the European Union, and Japan—includes elements of both capitalism and socialism (Table 14-1). Whatever the differences—whether a society more closely fits the ideal type of capitalism or socialism—all industrial societies rely chiefly on mechanization in the production of goods and services.

The Informal Economy

In many countries, one aspect of the economy defies description as either capitalist or socialist. In the **informal economy,** transfers of money, goods, or services take place but are not

TABLE 14-1 CHARACTERISTICS OF THE THREE MAJOR ECONOMIC SYSTEMS

Economic System	Characteristics	Contemporary Examples
Capitalism	Private ownership of the means of production Accumulation of profits the main incentive	Canada Mexico United States
Socialism	Collective ownership of the means of production Meeting people's needs the basic objective	Russia Venezuela
Communism	Communal ownership of all property No social distinctions made on basis of people's ability to produce	Cuba North Korea

Note: Countries listed in the right-hand column are typical of one of the three economic systems, but not perfectly so. In practice, the economies of most countries include a mix of elements from the three major systems.

reported to the government. Examples of the informal economy include trading services with someone—say, a haircut for a computer lesson; selling goods on the street; and engaging in illegal transactions, such as gambling or drug deals. The informal economy also includes off-the-books work in landscaping, child care, and housecleaning. Participants in this type of economy avoid taxes and government regulations.

In the United States, the informal economy accounts for about 8 percent of total economic activity. In other industrialized nations it varies, from between 20 and 30 percent of the labor force in industrial nations of Europe and North America to 85 percent in developing nations of Asia and Africa (Bjelland and Montello 2020:323; Loayza 2016).

Functionalists contend that bureaucratic regulations sometimes contribute to the rise of an informal, or underground, economy. In the developing world, governments often set up burdensome business regulations that overworked bureaucrats must administer. When requests for licenses and permits pile up, delaying business projects, legitimate entrepreneurs find they need to go underground to get anything done. Despite its apparent efficiency, this type of informal economy is dysfunctional for a country's overall political and economic well-being. Since informal firms typically operate in remote locations to avoid detection, they cannot easily expand when they become profitable. And given the limited protection for their property and contractual rights, participants in the informal economy are less likely than others to save and invest their income.

Whatever the functions an informal economy may serve, it is in some respects dysfunctional for workers. Working conditions in these illegal businesses are often unsafe or dangerous, and the jobs rarely provide any benefits to those who become ill or cannot continue to work. Perhaps more significant, the longer a worker remains in the informal economy, the less likely that person is to make the transition to the formal economy. No matter how efficient or productive a worker, employers expect to see experience in the formal economy on a job application. Experience as a successful street vendor or self-employed cleaning person does not carry much weight with interviewers (Venkatesh 2006; WIEGO 2016).

Power and Authority

In any society, someone or some group—whether it be a tribal chief, a dictator, or a parliament—makes important decisions about how to use resources and how to allocate goods. One cultural universal, then, is the exercise of power and authority. Inevitably, the struggle for power and authority involves **politics,** which political scientist Harold Lasswell (1936) tersely defined as "who gets what, when, and how." In their study of politics and government, sociologists are concerned with social interactions among individuals and groups and their impact on the larger political and economic order.

Power

Power lies at the heart of a political system. According to Max Weber, **power** is the ability to exercise one's will over others. To put it another way, whoever can overcome the resistance of others and control their behavior is exercising power. Power relations can involve large organizations, small groups, or even people in an intimate association.

Because Weber developed his conceptualization of power in the early 1900s, he focused primarily on the nation-state and its sphere of influence. Today scholars recognize that the trend toward globalization has brought new opportunities, and with them new concentrations of power. Power is now exercised on a global as well as a national stage, as countries and multinational corporations vie to control access to resources and manage the distribution of capital (R. Schaefer 2008b).

There are three basic sources of power within any political system: force, influence, and authority. **Force** is the actual or threatened use of coercion to impose one's will on others. When leaders imprison or even execute political dissidents, they are applying force; so, too, are terrorists when they seize or bomb an embassy or assassinate a political leader.

Influence, on the other hand, refers to the exercise of power through a process of persuasion. A citizen may change his or her view of a Supreme Court nominee because of a newspaper editorial, the expert testimony of a law school dean before the Senate Judiciary Committee, or a stirring speech by a political activist at a rally. Recently this persuasive power, as we noted in Chapter 1, has taken on meaning through **influencers**—social media users who have established credibility in a specific industry, have access to a huge audience, and can persuade others to act based on their recommendations. Sociologists would consider these people, as well as that law school dean testifying before Congress, as exerting influence. Now let's take a look at the third source of power, *authority.*

Types of Authority

The term **authority** refers to institutionalized power that is recognized by the people over whom it is exercised. Sociologists commonly use the term in connection with those who hold legitimate power through elected or publicly acknowledged positions. A person's authority is often limited. Thus, a referee has the authority to decide whether a penalty should be called during a football game, but has no authority over the price of tickets to the game.

Max Weber ([1913–1922] 1947) developed a classification system for authority that has become one of the most useful and frequently cited contributions of early sociology. He identified three ideal types of authority: traditional, rational-legal, and charismatic. Weber did not insist that only one type applies to a given society or organization. All can be present, but their relative importance will vary. Sociologists have found Weber's typology valuable in understanding different manifestations of legitimate power within a society.

Traditional Authority Until the middle of the past century, Japan was ruled by a revered emperor whose absolute power was passed down from generation to generation. In a political system based on **traditional authority,** legitimate power is conferred by custom and accepted practice. A king or queen is accepted as ruler of a nation simply by virtue of inheriting the crown; a tribal chief rules because that is the accepted practice. The ruler may be loved or hated, competent or destructive; in terms of legitimacy, that does not matter. For the traditional

leader, authority rests in custom, not in personal characteristics, technical competence, or even written law. People accept the ruler's authority because that is how things have always been done. Traditional authority is absolute when the ruler has the ability to determine laws and policies.

Rational-Legal Authority The U.S. Constitution gives Congress and our president the authority to make and enforce laws and policies. Power made legitimate by law is known as **rational-legal authority.** Leaders derive their rational-legal authority from the written rules and regulations of political systems, such as a constitution. Generally, in societies based on rational-legal authority, leaders are thought to have specific areas of competence and authority but are not thought to be endowed with divine inspiration, as in certain societies with traditional forms of authority.

Charismatic Authority Joan of Arc was a simple peasant girl in medieval France, yet she was able to rally the French people and lead them into major battles against English invaders. How was this possible? As Weber observed, power can be legitimized by the *charisma* of an individual. The term **charismatic authority** refers to power made legitimate by a leader's exceptional personal or emotional appeal to his or her followers.

Charisma lets a person lead or inspire without relying on set rules or traditions. In fact, charismatic authority is derived more from the beliefs of followers than from the actual qualities of leaders. So long as people perceive a charismatic leader such as Jesus, Joan of Arc, Gandhi, Malcolm X, or Martin Luther King Jr. as having qualities that set him or her apart from ordinary citizens, that leader's authority will remain secure and often unquestioned.

RichardBakerFarnborough/Alamy Stock Photo

English billionaire Richard Branson is known for his charismatic leadership style. Founder of Virgin Group, which comprises more than 400 companies, he is currently overseeing Virgin Orbit, a rocket that is to take paying customers into orbit around the Earth.

Observing charismatic authority from an interactionist perspective, sociologist Carl Couch (1996) points out that the growth of electronic media has facilitated the development of charismatic authority. During the 1930s and 1940s, the heads of state of the United States, Great Britain, and Germany all used radio to issue direct appeals to citizens. Now, television and the Internet allow leaders to "visit" people's homes and communicate with them.

As we noted earlier, Weber used traditional, rational-legal, and charismatic authority as ideal types. In reality, particular leaders and political systems combine elements of two or more of these forms. Presidents John F. Kennedy, Ronald Reagan, Barack Obama, and Donald Trump wielded power largely through the rational-legal basis of their authority. At the same time, they were unusually charismatic leaders who commanded the personal loyalty of large numbers of citizens. We will revisit this issue of government authority, as it emerged during the coronavirus pandemic, in the Social Policy section.

THINKING CRITICALLY

At your school, what are some examples of the three types of authority?

Types of Government

Each society establishes a political system through which it is governed. In modern industrialized nations, these formal systems of government make a significant number of critical political decisions. We will survey five basic types of government here: monarchy, oligarchy, dictatorship, totalitarianism, and democracy.

Monarchy

A **monarchy** is a form of government headed by a single member of a royal family, usually a king, queen, or some other hereditary ruler. In earlier times, many monarchs claimed that God had granted them a divine right to rule. Typically, they governed on the basis of traditional forms of authority, sometimes accompanied by the use of force. By the beginning of the 21st century, however, monarchs held genuine governmental power in only a few nations, such as Monaco. Most monarchs now have little practical power; they serve primarily ceremonial purposes.

Oligarchy

An **oligarchy** is a form of government in which a few individuals rule. A rather old method of governing that flourished in ancient Greece and Egypt, oligarchy now often takes the form of military rule. In developing nations in Africa, Asia, and Latin America,

small factions of military officers will forcibly seize power, either from legally elected regimes or from other military cliques.

Strictly speaking, the term *oligarchy* is reserved for governments that are run by a few selected individuals. However, the People's Republic of China can be classified as an oligarchy if we stretch the meaning of the term. In China, power rests in the hands of a large but exclusive ruling *group*, the Communist Party. In a similar vein, drawing on conflict theory, one might argue that many industrialized nations of the West should be considered oligarchies (rather than democracies), since only a powerful few—leaders of big business, government, and the military—actually rule. Later in this chapter, we will examine the *elite model* of the U.S. political system in greater detail.

Dictatorship and Totalitarianism

A **dictatorship** is a government in which one person has nearly total power to make and enforce laws. Dictators rule primarily through the use of coercion, which often includes torture and executions. Typically, they *seize* power rather than being freely elected (as in a democracy) or inheriting power (as in a monarchy). Some dictators are quite charismatic and manage to achieve a certain popularity, though their supporters' enthusiasm is almost certainly tinged with fear. Other dictators are bitterly hated by the people over whom they rule.

Frequently, dictators develop such overwhelming control over people's lives that their governments are called *totalitarian*. (Monarchies and oligarchies may also achieve this type of dominance.) **Totalitarianism** involves virtually complete government control and surveillance over all aspects of a society's social and political life. Germany during Hitler's reign, the Soviet Union in the 1930s, and North Korea today are classified as totalitarian states.

Democracy

In a literal sense, **democracy** means government by the people. The word *democracy* originated in two Greek roots—*demos*, meaning "the populace" or "the common people," and *kratia*, meaning "rule." Of course, in large, populous nations such as the United States, government by the people is impractical at the national level. Americans cannot vote on every important issue that comes before Congress. Consequently, popular rule is generally maintained through **representative democracy**, a form of government in which certain individuals are selected to speak for the people.

THINKING CRITICALLY

Contrast the use of power, as defined by Max Weber, in a dictatorship and in a democracy.

ChFoinatoPress/Getty Images

North Korea has a totalitarian government whose leaders attempt to control all aspects of people's lives. Masses of people paid homage to Kim Jong-un as a great leader at the 2015 celebration of the 70th anniversary of the Worker's Party of Korea.

The United States is commonly classified as a representative democracy, since the elected members of Congress and state legislatures make our laws. However, critics have questioned whether our democracy really is representative. Even today, the poor, many racial and ethnic groups, the working class, the LGBTQ community, and people with disabilities have questioned whether their views are truly included in the political debate.

Do Congress and the state legislatures genuinely represent the masses, including minorities? Are the people of the United States legitimately self-governing, or has our government become a forum for powerful elites? We will explore these issues in the remainder of the chapter.

Political Behavior in the United States

Citizens of the United States take for granted many aspects of their political system. They are accustomed to living in a nation with a Bill of Rights, two major political parties, elections by secret ballot, an elected president, state and local governments distinct from the national government, and so forth. Yet each society has its own ways of governing itself and making decisions. U.S. residents expect Democratic and Republican candidates to compete for public office; residents of Cuba and the People's Republic of China are accustomed to one-party rule by the Communist Party. In this section, we will examine several aspects of political behavior within the United States.

Participation and Apathy

In theory, a representative democracy will function most effectively and fairly if an informed and active electorate communicates its views to government leaders. Unfortunately, that is hardly the case in the United States. Virtually all citizens are

familiar with the basics of the political process, and many identify to some extent with a political party. By the summer of 2020, 50 percent of eligible voters leaned toward the Democrats and 38 percent leaned toward the Republicans.

Yet such numbers do not reflect two trends of the last 20 years. First, those who do identify with a major party are becoming increasingly polarized from one another. Republicans and Democrats are less likely to share similar views on social issues of the day. Second, more people than ever before do not fully identify with a party, but most indicate that they are at least leaning toward the Republicans and Democrats (Jones 2020).

By the 1980s, it had become clear that many people in the United States were beginning to be turned off by political parties, politicians, and big government. The most dramatic indication of this growing alienation came from voting statistics. Today, voters of all ages and races appear to be less enthusiastic than ever about elections, even presidential contests. For example, in the presidential election of 1896, almost 80 percent of eligible voters in the United States went to the polls. After that voter turnout steadily declined to end up below 60 percent. Yet the 2020 presidential election, with focus on the heated Trump-Biden race, turnout did increase to about 67 percent (Figure 14-2).

In the end, political participation makes government accountable to the voters. If participation declines, government operates with less of a sense of accountability to society. This issue is most serious for the least powerful individuals and groups in the United States. Historically, voter turnout has been particularly low among members of racial and ethnic minorities. However, in surveys following recent presidential elections, almost the same or a higher proportion of African Americans than whites reported that they actually voted.

Many more potential voters fail to register to vote. The poor—whose focus understandably is on survival—are traditionally underrepresented among voters as well. The low turnout found among these groups is explained at least in part by their common feeling of powerlessness. Yet these low statistics encourage political power brokers to continue to ignore the interests of the less affluent and the nation's minorities.

The segment of the voting population that has shown the most apathy is the

Frank Micelotta/Getty Images

FIGURE 14-2   VOTER TURNOUT WORLDWIDE

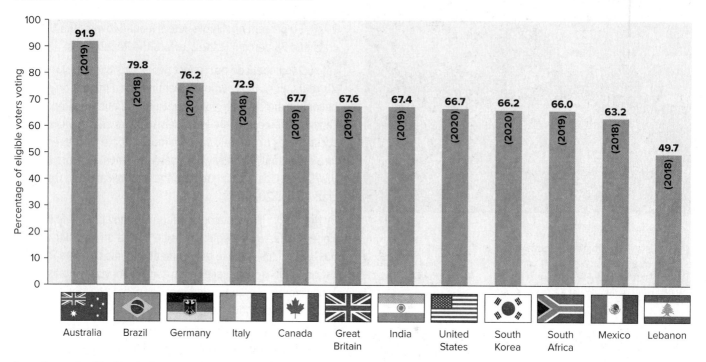

Source: International Institute for Democracy and Electoral Assistance 2020. *Flags:* admin_design/Shutterstock

young. Even the 2012 and 2016 presidential elections, held against the background of Obama's bid for a second term and the newsworthy Trump–Clinton race, did not pique the interest of voters ages 18 to 24. Fifty-one percent or fewer of them voted, compared to over 70 percent of those age 65 and older.

What lies behind voter apathy among the young? The popular explanation is that people—especially young people—are alienated from the political system, turned off by the shallowness and negativity of candidates and campaigns. However, because young people do vote as they age, other explanations seem more plausible, such as the difficulty of registering or absentee voting. Young people do not see voting as a duty but often see it as the candidates' responsibility to persuade them to vote (*Economist* 2017d; File 2017).

USE YOUR SOCIOLOGICAL IMAGINATION

Your school or workplace suddenly ceases to exhibit one of the five characteristics of bureaucracy. Which characteristic is it, and what are the consequences?

Race and Gender in Politics

Because politics is synonymous with power and authority, we should not be surprised that political strength is lacking in marginalized groups, such as women and racial and ethnic minorities. Nationally, women did not get the vote until 1920. Most Chinese Americans were turned away from the polls until

1926. And African Americans were disenfranchised until 1965, when national voting rights legislation was passed. Predictably, it has taken these groups some time to develop their political power and begin to exercise it effectively.

Progress toward the inclusion of minority groups in government has been slow. Following the 2020 midterm election,

Bill Pugliano/Stringer/Getty Images

Michigan Congresswoman Rashida Tlaib, first elected in 2018, grew up as the eldest of fourteen children of immigrant Palestinian parents. Eventually, she became a civil rights lawyer and, as of 2020, she is one of three Muslims and eight Arab Americans in Congress.

RESEARCH TODAY

14-1 The Latino Political Voice

Until the late twentieth century, Latinos' political activity remained outside conventional electoral activities. Instead, it focused primarily on grassroots organizing over specific issues such as migrant workers' rights. But as numbers of Hispanics who were eligible to vote began to grow, they recognized their political clout over local elections and even congressional seats.

A growing Hispanic population has not necessarily meant a growing presence in the voting booth. The Latino population includes many individuals who are under the legal age to vote as well as many who are not citizens. Current estimates indicate that only about half of Hispanics are eligible to vote, compared to 74 percent of non-Hispanics.

Yet the growing Latino presence has led Hispanic communities to anticipate that they will have greater political representation in the future. As shown in the figure, Latino participation has grown greatly over the past 30 years and is expected to double as a proportion of the electorate by 2030.

> *Both major political parties have begun to recognize that Latinos are a force in the election process, even in presidential elections.*

Both major political parties have begun to recognize that Latinos are a force in the election process, even in presidential elections. The numbers of Latinos in key swing or battleground states, such as Colorado, Florida, Michigan, Missouri, Nevada, New Mexico, Ohio, and Virginia, are now sufficient to affect which party captures the state's electoral votes.

Presidential candidates and nominees for other offices make an effort to reach out to the Hispanic community by visiting neighborhoods and issuing statements and campaign literature in Spanish. Like African Americans, many Latinos resent that political movers and shakers seem to rediscover that they exist once every four years. Latino community leaders derisively label candidates' fascination with Latino concerns around election time as either *fiesta politics* or *Hispandering*. Between major elections, only modest efforts have been made to court Hispanic interests, except by Latino elected officials; however, this may change as Latino presence at the ballot box is felt.

Democrats—who typically capture over 60, sometimes 70, percent of the Latino vote—have clearly garnered the allegiance of Hispanics voters with their more positive stance on immigration reform and backing of renewed diplomatic relations with Cuba. Yet some Hispanic voters, especially younger men, are showing sympathy to Republican candidates pointedly because they prefer a stronger stance on immigration policy, as well as taking conservative positions on social issues such as gun control and abortion.

Neither Republicans or Democrats can afford to dismiss the Latino vote, or take it for granted. The Hispanic community's rapid growth, increasing proportions of voter registration, and growing electoral participation guarantee future efforts by politicians to gain their support.

LET'S DISCUSS

1. In what ways are Latinos, as a voting group, similar to other ethnic and racial groups? In what ways are they different?
2. Read the news for a few days to determine two specific ways in which Latino issues are important to current politics, either on a national or local level.

Sources: Brennan Center 2015; Cohn 2014; Krogstad et al. 2020; Taylor et al. 2012.

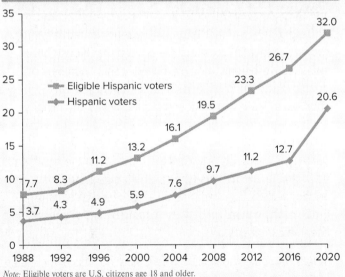

LATINO PARTICIPATION IN PRESIDENTIAL ELECTIONS, 1988–2020 (IN MILLIONS)

Eligible Hispanic voters: 1988: 7.7; 1992: 8.3; 1996: 11.2; 2000: 13.2; 2004: 16.1; 2008: 19.5; 2012: 23.3; 2016: 26.7; 2020: 32.0

Hispanic voters: 1988: 3.7; 1992: 4.3; 1996: 4.9; 2000: 5.9; 2004: 7.6; 2008: 9.7; 2012: 11.2; 2016: 12.7; 2020: 20.6

Note: Eligible voters are U.S. citizens age 18 and older.
Source: González 2020; Lopez et al. 2016; Noe-Bustamente et al. 2020.

27 percent of members of Congress were women and 23 percent were members of racial and ethnic minorities. While these represented record numbers, it meant that white non-Hispanic men constituted two out of three of the nation's top-elected representatives.

Today, with record-high numbers of Blacks and Latinos holding elective office, many critics decry the fact that politicians seem to recognize minority racial and ethnic groups only at election time. In Box 14-1, we consider the growing political voice of Hispanic Americans.

Female politicians may be enjoying more electoral success now than in the past, but there is some evidence that the media cover them differently from male politicians. A content analysis of newspaper coverage of recent gubernatorial races

FIGURE 14-3 WOMEN IN NATIONAL LEGISLATURES, SELECTED COUNTRIES

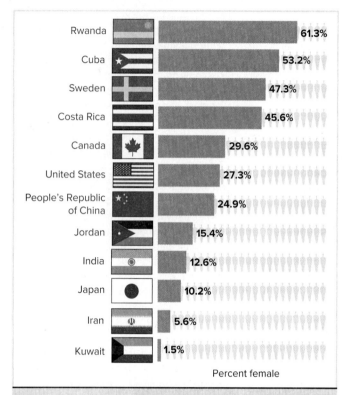

Country	Percent female
Rwanda	61.3%
Cuba	53.2%
Sweden	47.3%
Costa Rica	45.6%
Canada	29.6%
United States	27.3%
People's Republic of China	24.9%
Jordan	15.4%
India	12.6%
Japan	10.2%
Iran	5.6%
Kuwait	1.5%

Percent female

Think about It Why do you think being elected to Congress is so difficult for women?

Note: Data are for lower legislative houses only, as of January 1, 2021; data on upper houses, such as the U.S. Senate, are not included.
Source: Inter-Parliamentary Union 2021. Flags: admin_design/Shutterstock

showed that reporters wrote more often about a female candidate's personal life, appearance, or personality than a male candidate's, and less often about her political positions and voting record. Furthermore, when political issues were raised in newspaper articles, reporters were more likely to illustrate them with statements made by male candidates than by female candidates (Devitt 1999; Dittmar et al. 2018).

Figure 14-3 shows the representation of women in selected national legislatures. While the proportion of women in national legislatures has increased in the United States and many other nations, in all but one country women still do not account for half the members of the national legislature. The African Republic of Rwanda, the exception, ranks the highest, with 61.3 percent of its legislative seats held by women. Overall, the United States ranked 68th among 193 nations in the proportion of women serving as national legislators as of January 2021.

To remedy this situation, many countries have adopted quotas for female representatives. In some, the government sets aside a certain percentage of seats for women, usually from 14 to 30 percent. In others, political parties have decided that 20 to 40 percent of their candidates should be women. Currently 86 countries and some territories have some kind of female quota system (International Institute for Democracy and Electoral Assistance 2018b).

THINKING CRITICALLY

In the United States, which plays a more significant role in political behavior, gender or race? Explain.

Models of Power Structure in the United States

Who really holds power in the United States? Do "we the people" genuinely run the country through our elected representatives? Or is it true that behind the scenes, a small elite controls both the government and the economic system? It is difficult to determine the location of power in a society as complex as the United States. In exploring this critical question, social scientists have developed two basic views of our nation's power structure: the power elite and the pluralist models.

Power Elite Models

Karl Marx believed that 19th-century representative democracy was essentially a sham. He argued that industrialized societies were dominated by relatively small numbers of people who owned factories and controlled natural resources. In Marx's view, government officials and military leaders were essentially servants of this capitalist class and followed their wishes. Therefore, any key decisions made by politicians inevitably reflected the interests of the dominant bourgeoisie. Like others who share an **elite model** of power relations, Marx believed that society is ruled by a small group of individuals who share a common set of political and economic interests.

Mills's Model Sociologist C. Wright Mills took this model a step further in his pioneering work *The Power Elite* ([1956] 2000b). Mills described a small group of military, industrial, and government leaders who controlled the fate of the United States—the **power elite.** Power rested in the hands of a few, both inside and outside government.

A pyramid illustrates the power structure of the United States in Mills's model (Figure 14-4a). At the top are the corporate rich, leaders of the executive branch of government, and heads of the military (whom Mills called the "warlords"). Directly below are local opinion leaders, members of the

FIGURE 14-4   POWER ELITE MODELS

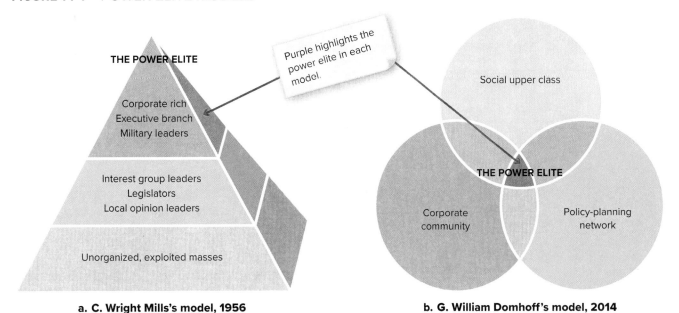

Purple highlights the power elite in each model.

a. C. Wright Mills's model, 1956

b. G. William Domhoff's model, 2014

Sources: (a): Author based on Mills [1956] 2000b. (b): Domhoff 2014a. ©2014 by The McGraw-Hill Companies, Inc. All rights reserved. Used with permission.

legislative branch of government, and leaders of special-interest groups. Mills contended that these individuals and groups would basically follow the wishes of the dominant power elite. At the bottom of the pyramid are the unorganized, exploited masses.

The power elite model is in many respects similar to the work of Karl Marx. The most striking difference is that Mills believed that the economically powerful coordinate their maneuvers with the military and political establishments to serve their common interests. He rejected Marx's belief that by itself, the economic structure of capitalism could create a ruling class. Still, the powerless masses at the bottom of Mills's power elite model certainly bring to mind Marx's portrait of the oppressed workers of the world, who have "nothing to lose but their chains."

A fundamental element in Mills's thesis is that the power elite not only includes relatively few members but also operates as a self-conscious, cohesive unit. Although not necessarily diabolical or ruthless, the elite comprises similar types of people who interact regularly with one another and have essentially the same political and economic interests. Mills's power elite is not a conspiracy, but rather a community of interest and sentiment among a small number of influential people (A. Hacker 1964).

The effort to curb the power of those who influence political campaign financing received a blow in the Supreme Court's 2010 decision in *Citizens United v. the Federal Election Commission,* which ended restrictions on the amount of campaign contributions by organizations, corporations, lobbyists, and individuals wishing to create their own campaign materials or to launch media advertising spots.

In this era of globalization and networking, it is reasonable to also talk of a *global elite.* This is often regarded as consisting of individuals who run multinational investment and giant corporations. In addition there is a relatively small number of people, perhaps fewer than 200, who sit on boards, serve as officers of international organizations, and network with each other on a fairly regular basis. However, there is also evidence that despite some coordination, there remains significant conflict among the elite (Inoue 2019).

Domhoff's Model   Over the past three decades, sociologist G. William Domhoff (2014a, 2014b, 2018), author of the chapter-opening excerpt, has agreed with Mills that a powerful elite runs the United States. He finds that it is still largely older, white, male, and upper class. However, Domhoff stresses the role played both by elites of the corporate community and by leaders of organizations in the policy-planning network, such as chambers of commerce and labor unions. Many of the people in both groups are also members of the social upper class. And he notes the presence of a small number of women and minority men in key positions—groups that were excluded from Mills's top echelon and are still underrepresented today.

Though the three groups in Domhoff's power elite model overlap, as Figure 14-4b shows, they do not necessarily agree on specific policies. Domhoff notes that in the electoral arena, two coalitions have exercised influence. A *corporate-conservative coalition* has played a large role in both political parties, generating support for particular candidates through direct-mail appeals. A *liberal-labor coalition* is based in unions, local environmental organizations, a segment of the minority group community, liberal churches, and the university and arts communities (Zweigenhaft and Domhoff 2006).

2020 Images/Alamy Stock Photo

Then president Donald Trump meets with corporate leaders of energy companies at the White House in 2020. Is this an example of good governance and private-public sector cooperation, or of members of a power elite going about their business?

Pluralist Model

Several social scientists insist that power in the United States is shared more widely than the elite models indicate. In their view, a pluralist model more accurately describes the nation's political system. According to the **pluralist model,** many competing groups within the community have access to government, so that no single group is dominant.

The pluralist model suggests that a variety of groups play a significant role in decision making. Typically, pluralists make use of intensive case studies or community studies based on observation research. One of the most famous—an investigation of decision making in New Haven, Connecticut—was reported by Robert Dahl (1961). Dahl found that although the number of people involved in any important decision was rather small, community power was nonetheless diffuse. Few political actors exercised decision-making power on all issues. One individual or group might be influential in a battle over urban renewal, but have little impact on educational policy.

The pluralist model, however, has not escaped serious questioning. Domhoff (1978, 2014a) reexamined Dahl's study of decision making in New Haven and argued that Dahl and other pluralists had failed to trace how local elites who were prominent in decision making belonged to a larger national ruling class. In addition, studies of community power, such as Dahl's work in New Haven, can examine decision making only on issues that become part of the political agenda. They fail to address the potential power of elites to keep certain matters entirely out of the realm of government debate.

The most significant criticism of the pluralist model is that, as originally proposed, it failed to note that it is largely a pluralism of white Americans from which racial and ethnic minorities are largely absent. Yes, there are important Black, Latino, and Asian decision makers, but their influence is overwhelmingly felt in policy areas where members of racial and ethnic minorities dominate, such as voting rights or immigration reform. Even in those areas whites continue to play significant roles, while minorities are rarely important actors in political spheres composed primarily of whites (Berry and Junn 2015; Pinderhughes 1987).

Historically, pluralists have stressed ways in which large numbers of people can participate in or influence governmental decision making. New communications technologies are increasing the opportunity to be heard, not just in countries such as the United States, but in developing countries the world over. One common point of the elite and pluralist perspectives stands out, however: in political systems, power is unequally distributed. All citizens may be equal in theory, yet those who are high in the nation's power structure are "more equal." Social upheaval, such as the Arab Spring uprisings of 2010–2012, creates broad political participation, but ultimately long-term decision making remains in the hands of relatively few (Freedman 2014; Ishak 2013).

Regardless of the form of government, social media and people's ability to access it has transformed political life, as Box 14-2 illustrates.

Perhaps the ultimate test of power, no matter what a nation's power structure, is the decision to go to war. Because the rank and file of any army is generally drawn from the lower classes—the least powerful groups in society—such a decision has life-and-death consequences for people far removed from the center of power. In the long run, if the general population is not convinced that war is necessary, military action is unlikely to succeed. Thus, war is a risky way in which to address conflict between nations. In the following section we will contrast war and peace as ways of addressing societal conflict, and more recently, the threat of terrorism.

THINKING CRITICALLY

Which is a better model of the power structure in the United States, the power elite model or the pluralist model? Justify your answer.

OUR WIRED WORLD

14-2 Politicking Online

Until recently, citizens could exercise their political rights by voting, supporting candidates for office with their time or money, and writing an occasional letter to the local newspaper. Public rallies or protests, though not for everyone, were another way to display support for a particular politician or social issue. Then came the Internet and social media, and the possibilities for politicking broadened dramatically.

The social media and online landscape has changed dramatically over the past decade, both in the United States and globally. Today, social media is the major force in people's political and civic engagement. Even individuals who are not engaged with politics learn from others what is happening on the different social media platforms. Social media has emerged as the go-to platform for finding news and engaging politically. This development is not lost on those seeking elective office. Given the lower cost of online advertising, candidates are making wider use of online advertising.

Although online politicking is more common among younger people, the differences between age groups are not great. For example, 43 percent of those under age 30 seek out digital political material, compared to 22 percent of those age 50 to 64.

Early analysis of Twitter use by politicians in Europe suggests that social media may be mostly "preaching to the converted," but given the low cost of such outreach, producing any new votes, confirming supporters in their choice, and making them more likely to vote would be significant political outcomes.

Earlier in this chapter we noted the poor voting turnout of young people. Online politicking would seem to be an obvious way to increase their engagement in election politics. However, 18- to 21-year-olds are not typically included in the voter databases available to campaigns, so to receive campaign information, the young voter must contact the campaign. This will most likely become less of an issue as political campaigns become more sophisticated in locating potential voters.

> Today, social media is the major force in people's political and civic engagement. Even individuals who are not engaged with politics learn from others what is happening on the different social media platforms.

Given the tendency of the Internet and social media to encourage political activity, governments have tried to suppress them. Nations frequently clamp down on online activity that opposes the central government or asserts human rights, such as the right to freedom of expression or to minority or religious views. In addition, in recent years—a time of the Brexit decision in Great Britain, the 2016 presidential election, a variety of other political contests, and the origins of the coronavirus pandemic—digital disruption

and misinformation from China, Russia, and North Korea, among other nations, has been a growing concern. The challenge of dealing with these disruptions comes just as people are relying more on digital sources for their information about important political decisions.

Like citizens, governments also use the Internet to reach well beyond national borders. In what has been described as "public diplomacy," the U.S. State Department has taken to using Twitter abroad. In 2012, within minutes of violent attacks on U.S. embassies and consulates in the Middle East, the U.S. embassy in Cairo tweeted an emergency number to American citizens, and thanked fellow tweeters for their condolences on the murder of the ambassador to Libya.

Twitter became a useful media platform for presidential candidate Donald Trump, and he continued to use it after he became president. About one out of six news stories about the president mentions his tweets, although not always in a favorable light.

LET'S DISCUSS

1. Do you use the Internet or social media for political purposes? If so, do those in your social network affect your political views or participation?

2. What might be some drawbacks of online political activity?

Sources: Anderson and Rainie 2020; Auxier et al. 2019; Fowler et al. 2019; Greico and Gottfried 2017; Vergeer 2015.

War and Peace

Conflict is a central aspect of social relations. Too often it becomes ongoing and violent, engulfing innocent bystanders as well as intentional participants. Sociologists Theodore Caplow and Louis Hicks (2002:3) have defined **war** as conflict between organizations that possess trained combat forces equipped with deadly weapons. This meaning is broader than the legal definition, which typically requires a formal declaration of hostilities.

War

Sociologists approach war in three different ways. Those who take a *global view* study how and why two or more nations

become engaged in military conflict. Those who take a *nation-state view* stress the interaction of internal political, socioeconomic, and cultural forces. And those who take a *micro view* focus on the social impact of war on individuals and the groups they belong to (Kiser 1992; Wimmer 2014).

From the nation-state perspective, there is little to be said for the supposed socioeconomic benefits of war. Although armed conflicts increase government expenditures on troops and weapons, which tend to stimulate the economy, they also divert workers from civilian health and medical services. Thus, they have a negative effect on civilians' life chances, causing higher levels of civilian mortality. It is exceedingly difficult for a society to engage in armed conflict while maintaining citizens' well-being at home (Carlton-Ford 2010).

MAPPING LIFE WORLDWIDE

FIGURE 14-5 GLOBAL PEACE INDEX

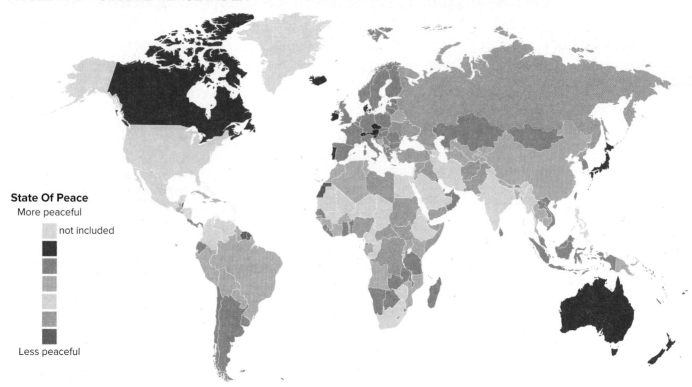

State Of Peace
More peaceful

not included

Less peaceful

Source: International Institute for Democracy and Electoral Assistance 2020. *Flags:* admin_design/Shutterstock

Although the decision to go to war is made by government leaders, public opinion plays a significant role in its execution. By 1971, the number of U.S. soldiers killed in Vietnam had surpassed 50,000, and antiwar sentiment was strong. Surveys done at that time showed the public was split roughly equally on the question of whether war was an appropriate way to settle differences between nations.

A major change in the composition of the U.S. military is the growing presence of women. Women now account for 16 percent of enlisted personnel and 18 percent of the officer corps, serving not just as support personnel but as a part of all combat units. The first casualty of the war in Iraq, in fact, was Private First Class Lori Piestewa, a member of the Hopi tribe and a descendant of Mexican settlers in the Southwest.

From a micro view, war can bring out the worst as well as the best in people. In 2004, graphic images of the abuse of Iraqi prisoners by U.S. soldiers at Iraq's Abu Ghraib prison shocked the world. For social scientists, the deterioration of the guards' behavior brought to mind Philip Zimbardo's mock prison experiment, done in 1971. Although the results of the experiment, highlighted in Chapter 5, have been applied primarily to civilian correctional facilities, Zimbardo's study was actually funded by the Office of Naval Research. In July 2004, the U.S. military began using a documentary film about the experiment to train military interrogators to avoid mistreatment of prisoners (Zarembo 2004a; Zimbardo 2004).

A new technology introduced to the modern battlefield has been the use of militarized drones—unmanned aviation systems. They are deployed to gather intelligence as well as to carry and drop bombs. An escalating number of nations have used drones as weapons, including the United States, China, Israel, and Nigeria. As with previous new technologies used in warfare, the use of drones raises a host of issues—potential for collateral damage; stress on the drone pilots, who are typically far removed from the both the aircraft and target area; the inability to fight back, and relative ease of deployment, given the lack of death toll in the nation using the technology (Etzioni 2013; Chamayou 2015).

Peace

Sociologists have considered **peace** both as the absence of war and as a proactive effort to develop cooperative relations among nations. While we will focus here on international relations, we should note that the vast majority of armed conflicts occur *within* rather than between states. Often, outside powers become involved in these internal conflicts, either as supporters of particular factions or in an attempt to broker a peace accord. The countries where such conflicts occur would not be considered core nations in world systems analysis (Institute for Economics and Peace 2015a; Kriesberg 1992; D. Smith 1999).

Another way of picturing the relative peacefulness of nations around the world is the Global Peace Index (Figure 14-5). This

TAKING SOCIOLOGY TO WORK

Joseph W. Drummond, **Management Analyst, U.S. Army Space and Missile Defense Command**

When Joseph Drummond entered Morehouse College, he was planning to major in political science. But after taking an introductory sociology course, he felt that sociology gave him a clearer picture of the complexity and interconnectedness of society. "The career track that I had in mind was to enter the field of sociology as a researcher/policy maker," he explains. However, he soon ran into "a disconnect between academia and policymaking," and an apparent lack of representation of sociologists at the policymaking level.

Courtesy of Joseph W. Drummond

Drummond credits one of his sociology professors for steering him toward quantitative courses. "If you ever plan on having a job," the professor suggested, "make sure you have a lot of classes with quantitative analysis—for example, statistics and data analysis. These classes tell whatever company you want to work for that you have practical skills." Later, when Drummond asked his current employer why he had gotten the job he now holds, he was told that his data analysis and social statistics courses had made him competitive.

Today, Drummond works at the U.S. Army's Space and Missile Defense Command (SMDC), near Huntsville, Alabama. He began there as an intern, after responding to an e-mail from Morehouse College's career office. Drummond is now a junior analyst with a team that formulates and develops doctrine, organization, and material requirements for Army units assigned to space and missile defense. In a typical workweek, he reviews military force structure—units, battalions, and so on—and helps to implement directives from Department of the Army headquarters. "A lot of what we do is attempting to translate very high-level guidance to something that's practical," he explains.

Drummond values the support and professional development he has received from the Army, including classes on program management, data analysis, national security, and force management. An Army-sponsored Technology and Government in Your Future event emphasized the need for interns to pursue graduate studies in math and science to land the best jobs. Drummond says the real-world experience he got as an intern at SMDC not only brought classroom theory to life; it also made him more attractive to future employers.

Asked how he uses sociology in his work, Drummond replies that his academic training has helped him to look critically at problems and to think about the second- and third-order effects of a decision. Seeing society from a macro-level view is also invaluable to him. "When U.S. leadership began to realize that a 'hearts and minds' campaign means that we need to understand the social-historical context of the people whose country we're occupying, that changed the way that we did business and also impacted the way U.S. military force structure was managed," he explains. "A lot of people had problems making the connection." Finally, sociology has taught Drummond not to take things at face value. "Most problems/issues that we come across very seldom have easy fixes," he notes. "Sociology taught me that thorough analysis means leaving no stone unturned."

LET'S DISCUSS

1. Have you ever considered a career in national defense? Do you know anyone with a college degree who works in the field?
2. Why do you think quantitative analysis is such an important skill to employers? How might you use it in your career?

index is based on 23 indicators, including organized internal conflict, violent crime, political instability, weapons exports, and a nation's level of military expenditures compared to its neighbors'.

Currently, Iceland and New Zealand are at the top of the index (very peaceful); Syria and Afghanistan are at the bottom (great civil unrest). The United States ranks 128th on this list of 163 nations, between Saudi Arabia and South Africa. The map shows that the world contains large areas with very high levels of peace—North America and Europe for example. Yet many people live in the least peaceful countries.

Sociologists and other social scientists who draw on sociological theory and research have tried to identify conditions that deter war. One of their findings is that international trade may act as a deterrent to armed conflict. As countries exchange goods, people, and then cultures, they become more integrated and less likely to threaten each other's security. Viewed from this perspective, not just trade but immigration and foreign exchange programs have a beneficial effect on international relations.

Another means of fostering peace is the activity of international charities and activist groups called nongovernmental organizations (NGOs). The Red Cross and Red Crescent and Doctors Without Borders donate their services wherever they are needed, without regard to nationality. In the past decade or more, these global organizations have been expanding in number, size, and scope. By sharing news of local conditions and clarifying local issues, they often prevent conflicts from escalating into violence and war. Some NGOs have initiated cease-fires, reached settlements, and even ended warfare between former adversaries.

Finally, many analysts stress that nations cannot maintain their security by threatening violence. Peace, they contend, can best be maintained by developing strong mutual security agreements between potential adversaries (Etzioni 1965; Shostak 2002).

Since 9/11, the United States has begun to recognize that its security can be threatened not just by nation-states, but by political groups that operate outside the bounds of legitimate authority. Indeed, terrorism is now considered the foremost threat to U.S. security.

USE YOUR SOCIOLOGICAL IMAGINATION

Do you hear much discussion of how to promote worldwide peace, or do the conversations you hear focus more on ending a particular conflict? Which approach would more likely result in a positive outcome? Why?

Terrorism

Acts of terror, whether perpetrated by a few or by many people, can be a powerful political force. Formally defined, **terrorism** is the use or threat of violence against random or symbolic targets in pursuit of political aims. For terrorists, the end justifies the means. They believe that the status quo is oppressive and that desperate measures are essential to end the suffering of the deprived. Convinced that working through the formal political process will not effect the desired political change, terrorists insist that illegal actions—often directed against innocent people—are needed. Ultimately, they hope to intimidate society and thereby bring about a new political order.

People sometimes remark that we have become numbed to the violence we witness, both personally and through the media. An analysis from 1970 through 2018 of the direct and indirect impact of about 170,000 incidents of terrorism in 163 nations in terms of lives lost, injuries, property damage, and emotional toll of the after-effects has been used to produce the Global Terrorism Index (Figure 14-6).

At the time the analysis was made, the United States ranked 22nd, just below Kenya and just ahead of Nigeria, in danger of terrorism. The top three countries experiencing terrorism are Afghanistan, Iran, and Nigeria. These three nations account for three-quarters of the world's fatalities due to terrorism. Among the nations in the least danger of terrorism are countries as varied as Cuba and Singapore.

An essential aspect of contemporary terrorism involves use of the media. Terrorists may wish to keep secret their individual identities, but they want their political messages and goals to receive as much publicity as possible. Drawing on Erving Goffman's dramaturgical approach, sociologist Alfred McClung Lee (1983) has likened terrorism to the theater, where certain scenes are played out in predictable fashion. Whether through calls to the media, anonymous manifestos, or other means, terrorists typically admit responsibility for and defend their violent acts.

Sociologists and others have studied the role of labeling in how behavior comes to be regarded as "terrorism." Social media allows groups labeled "terrorist," such as Boko Haram, ISIS, the Taliban, and Al-Qaeda, to define their activities as justified and the actions of nation-states against them as unlawful and evil. As labeling theory shows, the label used depends on one's point of view. What constitutes terrorism has increasingly been expanded to refer to domestic terrorism: actions taken by a nation's citizens without necessarily any inspiration from outside. Only recently have white supremacist groups been tagged as terrorism (Watts 2019).

Since September 11, 2001, governments worldwide have renewed their efforts to fight terrorism. Although the public generally regards increased surveillance and social control as a necessary evil, these measures have nonetheless raised governance issues. For example, some citizens in the United States and elsewhere have questioned whether measures such as the USA Patriot Act of 2001 threaten civil liberties. Citizens have also complained about the heightened anxiety created by the vague alerts issued by the federal government from time to time. Worldwide, immigration and the processing of refugees have slowed to a crawl, separating families and preventing employers from filling job openings. As these efforts to combat political violence illustrate, the term *terrorism* is an apt one (R. Howard and Sawyer 2003; A. Lee 1983; R. Miller 1988).

Increasingly, governments are becoming concerned about another form of political violence, the potential for malicious cyberattacks. In an age in which computer viruses can spread worldwide through the Internet, this kind of attack could render a nation's computer systems useless, or even shut down its power plants. A few years ago, such a scenario would have been considered pulp fiction, but it is now the subject of contingency planning throughout the world. Furthermore, nation-states have now begun to employ hacking techniques previously used only by criminal groups. Recently Russia has targeted key elections in the United States and Europe, and North Korea carries out ransomware attacks (Gidwani 2017).

THINKING CRITICALLY

What is the greatest threat to world peace, and how would you counter it?

Changing Economies

As advocates of the power elite model point out, the trend in capitalist societies has been toward concentration of ownership by giant corporations, especially multinational ones. In the following sections we will examine five outgrowths of this trend in the United States: the changing face of the workforce, deindustrialization, the sharing economy, the temporary workforce, and offshoring. As these trends show, any change in the economy has social and political implications.

MAPPING LIFE WORLDWIDE

FIGURE 14-6 GLOBAL TERRORISM INDEX

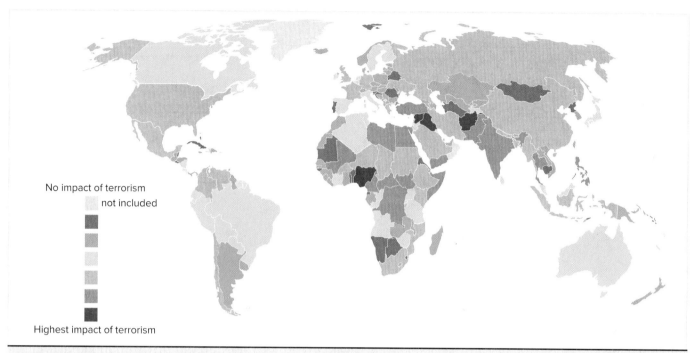

No impact of terrorism
   not included

Highest impact of terrorism

Think about It Do any of the rankings in either Figure 14-5 or Figure 14-6 surprise you?

Source: Institute for Economics and Peace 2019b.

The Global Terrorism Index measures the impact of terrorism in 163 countries. To account for the lasting effects of terrorism, each country is given a score that represents a five-year weighted average.

The Changing Face of the Workforce

The workforce in the United States is constantly changing. During World War II, when men were mobilized to fight abroad, women entered the workforce in large numbers. And with the rise of the civil rights movement in the 1960s, minorities found numerous job opportunities opening to them. Box 14-3 takes a closer look at the active recruitment of women and minorities into the workplace, known as *affirmative action.*

Although predictions are not always reliable, sociologists and labor specialists foresee a workforce increasingly composed of women and racial and ethnic minorities. In 1950, over 86 percent of men were in the labor force, compared to 34 percent of women. By 2025, it is projected that 66 percent of men will be in the labor force, compared to 55 percent of the women (Toossi 2016).

The dynamics of minority workers are even more dramatic, as shown in Figure 14-7. From 1996 to 2028, the proportion of the labor force composed of white non-Hispanic workers is expected to drop from about 75 percent to 58 percent.

More and more, then, the workforce reflects the diversity of the population, as ethnic minorities enter the labor force and immigrants and their children move from marginal jobs or employment in the informal economy to positions of greater visibility

and responsibility. The impact of this changing labor force is not merely statistical. A more diverse workforce means that relationships between workers are more likely to cross gender, racial, and ethnic lines. Interactionists note that people will soon find themselves supervising and being supervised by people very different from themselves.

Deindustrialization

What happens when a company decides it is more profitable to move its operations out of a long-established community to another part of the country, or out of the country altogether? People lose jobs; stores lose customers; the local government's tax base declines and it cuts services. This devastating process has occurred again and again.

The term **deindustrialization** refers to the systematic, widespread withdrawal of investment in basic aspects of productivity, such as factories and plants. Giant corporations that deindustrialize are not necessarily refusing to invest in new economic opportunities. Rather, the targets and locations of investment change, and the need for labor decreases as advances in technology continue to automate production. First, companies may move their plants from the nation's central cities to the suburbs. The next step may be relocation from suburban areas of the Northeast and Midwest to the South, where

RESEARCH TODAY

14-3   Affirmative Action

2003 Mike Keefe. The Denver Post. Used by permission of Cagle Cartoons, Inc.

The Supreme Court's many decisions on the constitutionality of affirmative action programs have made it difficult for organizations to encourage diversity without transgressing the law.

The term *affirmative action* first appeared in an executive order issued by President John F. Kennedy in 1961. That order called for contractors to "take affirmative action to ensure that applicants are employed, and that employees are treated during employment, without regard to their race, creed, color, or national origin." In 1967, the order was amended by President Lyndon Johnson to prohibit discrimination on the basis of sex as well, but affirmative action remained a vague concept. Currently, **affirmative action** refers to positive efforts to recruit minority group members or women for jobs, promotions, and educational opportunities.

Sociologists—especially conflict and feminist theorists—view affirmative action as a legislative attempt to reduce the inequality embedded in the social structure by increasing opportunities for groups who were deprived in the past, such as women and African

Americans. Despite the clear disparity in earnings between white males and other groups, however, many people doubt that everything done in the name of affirmative action is desirable. Critics warn against hiring and admissions quotas, complaining that they constitute a kind of "reverse discrimination" against white males.

Affirmative action became a prominent issue in state and national political campaigns in 1996, when California's voters approved by a 54 to 46 percent margin the California Civil Rights Initiative. Better known as Proposition 209, this measure amended the state constitution to *prohibit* any program that gives preference to women and minorities in college admissions, hiring, promotion, or government contracts. In other words, it aimed to abolish affirmative action programs. The courts have since upheld the measure. However, beginning in 2017, the Trump administration and

> *Critics warn against hiring and admissions quotas, complaining that they constitute a kind of "reverse discrimination" against white males.*

the Justice Department's Civil Rights Division used their resources to back claims of college-admission discrimination against white applicants.

Colleges and universities have responded with new policies designed to broaden opportunities for traditionally underrepresented minority students. However, opponents of affirmative action continue to argue in court that such actions unconstitutionally disadvantage white applicants. And colleges continue to reexamine their policies in light of the latest legal rulings.

Increasingly, critics of affirmative action are calling for color-blind policies that would end affirmative action. Presumably, such policies would allow all applicants to be judged fairly. However, opponents warn against the danger of **color-blind racism**—the use of the principle of race neutrality to defend a racially unequal status quo. Will "color-blind" policies put an end to institutional practices that now favor whites, they ask?

LET'S DISCUSS

1. Is affirmative action part of the admissions policy at your local college or university? If so, do you think the policy has helped to level the playing field? Might it have excluded some qualified white applicants?
2. Take a poll of your classmates. What percentage of the class supports affirmative action in hiring and college admissions? How does that group break down in terms of gender, race, and ethnicity?

Sources: Diamond and Rose 2018; Hunt 2015; MacCoun 1989; Sunwolf and Seibold 1998.

---

labor laws place more restrictions on unions. Finally, a corporation may simply relocate *outside* the United States to a country with a lower rate of prevailing wages. General Motors, for example, decided to build a multi-billion-dollar plant in China rather than in Kansas City or even in Mexico (Lynn 2003).

Although deindustrialization often involves relocation, in some instances it takes the form of corporate restructuring, as companies seek to reduce costs in the face of growing worldwide competition. When such restructuring occurs, the impact on the bureaucratic hierarchy of formal organizations

can be significant. A large corporation may choose to sell off or entirely abandon less productive divisions and to eliminate layers of management viewed as unnecessary. Wages and salaries may be frozen and benefits cut—all in the name of restructuring. Increasing reliance on automation, especially new technology, also is making deep impacts on the workforce. The use of digital technology in nearly every business sector will be explored in greater detail in Chapter 16.

The term **downsizing** was introduced in 1987 to refer to reductions taken in a company's workforce as part of

FIGURE 14-7   INCREASING DIVERSITY IN THE U.S. LABOR FORCE

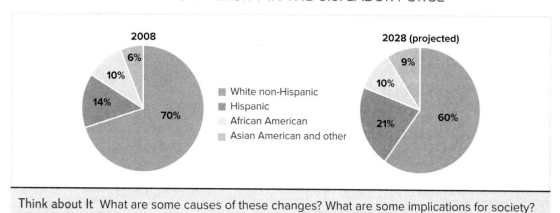

Think about It What are some causes of these changes? What are some implications for society?

*Source:*Bureau of Labor Statistics 2019f.

deindustrialization. Viewed from a conflict perspective, the unprecedented attention given to downsizing in the mid-1990s reflected the continuing importance of social class in the United States. Conflict theorists note that job loss has long been a feature of deindustrialization among blue-collar workers. But when large numbers of middle-class managers and other white-collar employees with substantial incomes began to be laid off, suddenly the media began expressing great concern over downsizing.

Deindustrialization has long been a focus of social scientists and economists, but the 2016 presidential election brought it into focus as a political issue. Candidate Donald Trump made deindustrialization a major issue by focusing on what he presented as existing unfavorable U.S. trade policies and lack of incentives for new business. Many political analysts of the 2016 election outcome assign Trump's victory to his success in capturing previously Democratic strongholds in Iowa, Michigan, and Wisconsin, where the decline in manufacturing opportunities has been especially striking (Pacewicz 2016).

The social costs of deindustrialization and downsizing cannot be overemphasized. Plant closings lead to substantial unemployment in a community, which has a devastating impact on both the micro and macro levels. On the micro level, the unemployed person and his or her family must adjust to a loss of spending power. Painting or re-siding the house, buying health insurance or saving for retirement, even thinking about having another child must be put aside. Both marital happiness and family cohesion may suffer as a result. Although many dismissed workers eventually re-enter the paid labor force, they must often accept less desirable positions with lower salaries and fewer benefits. Unemployment and underemployment are tied to many of the social problems discussed throughout this textbook, among them the need for child care and the controversy over welfare.

THINKING CRITICALLY

What evidence of deindustrialization or downsizing do you see, specifically, in your community? What broad economic shifts brought about those changes?

The Sharing Economy

Why pay a high retail price for a product or service, in a store or online, when you can buy or rent it more cheaply from a stranger? This is the principle behind a range of online services that enable people to share cars (such as Uber and Lyft), accommodations (Airbnb), pet care, bicycles, household appliances, and other items. **Sharing economy** refers to connecting owners of underused assets with others willing to pay to use them.

Critics argue that the sharing economy is just an extension of the temporary workforce and that most of sharing economy entrepreneurs would prefer to work for a firm with better wages, legal protection, guaranteed minimum weekly hours, and fringe benefits (see Chapter 10). They argue that it is not a coincidence that many peer-to-peer rental firms were founded between 2008 and 2010, in the midst of the Great Recession, when conventional employment opportunities tanked. Others argue that the sharing economy serves to commodify services that might otherwise have been given away for free such as offering rides or places to sleep to friends or acquaintances.

Consumers of the sharing economy are attracted to the notion that they may be saving money, and workers like the income and flexible work. However, established businesses question the quality of the services rendered. For example, taxi companies and hotel chains question the nature of their competition

Blue Room/Alamy Stock Photo

spvvk/123RF

Gutted factories like this one in Boston, Massachusetts, contrast with the glamorous corporate campus of Google Corporation in Mountain View, California. Deindustrialization and the rise of high technology have shifted the U.S. labor market, displacing many workers in the process.

in this emerging online marketplace. In addition, governments are beginning to regulate such services, especially when the taxes that competing businesses would pay for their income are not being paid in the sharing economy (DuPuis and Rainwater 2014; *The Week* 2014; White 2015).

The Temporary Workforce

Over the last four decades, U.S. employers have been relying more and more on the part-time workforce. The recent economic downturn and the slow recovery that followed only accelerated the trend, which began in 1970. In March 2020, about 25 million of the 156 million people employed in the United States were working part-time, mostly because of non-economic reasons—slack work, unfavorable business conditions, or inability to find full-time work. Many of them worked at more than one job (Bureau of Labor Statistics 2020d).

This pattern of expanding part-time work is slowly reshaping the U.S. workforce. Traditionally, businesses employed workers through good times and bad, protecting them from economic ups and downs. In numerous industries, however, that is no longer the case. As was described in Chapter 8, millions of Americans have been reduced to doing **precarious work**—employment that is poorly paid, and from the worker's perspective, insecure and unprotected. People who engage in precarious work often cannot support a household, and they are vulnerable to falling into poverty. These workers typically do not enjoy benefits like health insurance, paid sick leave, or even unemployment compensation.

Certainly some workers seek out part-time jobs, welcoming the flexibility they offer. For example, students taking college classes may prefer part-time work. For most workers, however, part-time employment is not a first choice. In response to the trend away from traditional full-time jobs, more and more workers are adopting a "free agent mentality," actively seeking work wherever and whenever they can find it instead of expecting to be hired full-time.

Offshoring

U.S. firms have been outsourcing certain types of work for generations. For example, moderate-sized businesses such as furniture stores and commercial laundries have long relied on outside trucking firms to make deliveries to their customers. The trend toward **offshoring** carries this practice one step further, by transferring other types of work to foreign contractors. Now, even large companies are turning to overseas firms, many of them located in developing countries. Offshoring has become the latest tactic in the time-worn business strategy of raising profits by reducing costs.

Significantly, the transfer of work from one country to another is no longer limited to manufacturing. Office and professional jobs are being exported, too, thanks to advanced telecommunications. Table 14-2 lists those occupations most likely to be offshored.

In 2012, complaints about working conditions in Apple's factories in China called attention to the fact that the company's financial success had been built on outsourced labor. At one

TABLE 14-2 OCCUPATIONS MOST VULNERABLE TO OFFSHORING

Rank	Occupation
1	Computer programming
2	Data entry
3	Electrical and electronics drafting
4	Mechanical drafting
5	Computer and information science, research
6	Actuarial science
7	Mathematics
8	Statistics
9	Mathematical science (all other)
10	Film and video editing

Sources: Bureau of Labor Statistics data cited in Hira 2008; Moncarz et al. 2008.

time, Apple manufactured its computers in the United States. Today the company still employs about 43,000 full-time workers in the United States, and another 20,000 full-time workers abroad. However, Apple contracts on a short-term basis with an additional 700,000 workers who both engineer and build its products overseas. As complaints grew about Apple's offshoring, economists released estimates that in the next four years, another 375,000 well-paid jobs in information technology, human resources, and finance and merchandising would be lost to overseas competition (China Labor Watch 2015; P. Davidson 2012; Duhigg and Bradsher 2012).

Offshoring is not completely inevitable. In a recent countertrend called *reshoring*, widely reported in the media, some U.S. companies have been bringing manufacturing jobs and service centers back to the United States. Donald Trump, both as candidate and as President, made such efforts a major policy position. His success was limited, which became particularly evident during the coronavirus pandemic, when

Americans realized that much of the personal protective equipment used by health care workers and first responders was produced in China. Most experts agree that while reshoring is occurring on a case-by-case basis, it has not offset continued offshoring of jobs (Tankersley 2020).

Because offshoring, like outsourcing in general, tends to improve the efficiency of business operations, it can be viewed as functional to society. Offshoring also increases economic interdependence in the production of goods and services, both in enterprises located just across town and in those located around the globe. Still, conflict theorists charge that this aspect of globalization furthers social inequality. Although moving high-tech work to developing countries does help to lower a company's costs, the impact on technical and service workers at home is clearly devastating. Certainly middle-class workers are alarmed by the trend. Because offshoring increases efficiency, economists oppose efforts to block the practice and instead recommend assistance to displaced workers.

There is a downside to offshoring for foreigners, as well. Although outsourcing is a significant source of employment for the upper-middle class in developing countries, hundreds of millions of other foreign workers have seen little to no positive impact from the trend. Thus the long-term impact of offshoring on developing nations is difficult to predict.

In the Social Policy section, we examine government's response to the coronavirus epidemic of 2020.

USE YOUR SOCIOLOGICAL IMAGINATION

Do you know anyone whose job has been transferred to a foreign country? If so, was the person able to find a comparable job in the same town, or did he or she have to relocate? How long was the person unemployed?

social policy and Government and the Economy

The Response to the Coronavirus Pandemic

On January 19, 2020, a 35-year-old man arrived at an urgent care clinic in Snohomish County, Washington, with a 4-day history of cough and fever. The next day, January 20, the Centers for Disease Control confirmed on its website that this person tested positive for the novel coronavirus, Covid-19. Eleven days later the case description was posted on the website of the *New England Journal of Medicine* (Holshue et al. 2020).

At the time, the general public largely ignored this occurrence. Indeed, subsequent research showed that many cases occurred earlier but went undetected. However, the coronavirus pandemic was to

emerge as a life-altering event throughout the world. "Social isolation," "shelter in place," and "PPE" became household terms. Colleges and universities sent students home; millions of people were laid off from the jobs, while millions more worked remotely. Dining out, entertainment venues, and tourism shut down globally. Religous services were canceled or moved online. Consumers could not find essentials items like toilet paper and hand sanitizer. By the end of the first year of the pandemic, there were over 100 million reported cases and over 2 million reported deaths worldwide; approximately one quarter occurred in the United States.

Lindsey Horton/Centers for Disease Control and Prevention

A public health worker in the West African country of Guinea demonstrates proper hand-washing technique during the 2014 Ebola outbreak. Such government messages became worldwide during the 2020 coronavirus pandemic.

Looking at the Issue

With varying degrees of success and transparency, governments around the world used their power to take steps to protect their citizens from becoming victims of the coronavirus. A common step was to issue guidelines about proper behavior: to stay at home, to maintain a safe distance from others while outdoors or in public places, or use face coverings when venturing outside. On a massive scale, efforts to contain the virus emerged as a study of **obedience,** or compliance with higher authorities in a hierarchical structure, as we discussed in Chapter 5.

Authorities did not necessarily agree on the proper steps to contain the virus, with each other across nations and even within the same country. For example, in the United States, governors varied on whether face-to-face religious services and burial ceremonies involving large numbers of people in close proximity could be continued.

Social control measures also varied widely. Some societies, such as Sweden, gave their citizens great latitude, while others, such as Hungary, took advantage of the situation to give the government massive control over citizens' activity and continued that control after the pandemic had long passed.

An important element of social control was the use of tracking and surveillance mechanisms. Traditionally, to contain contagious diseases, public health officials interview patients to determine with whom they may have had contact. Those contacts are then put in quarantine to suppress the spread of the infection. However, the success of this method is limited, both by individuals' recollections and by their willingness to name their contacts. In 2020, location-tracking technology allowed governments to determine patients' contacts with greater exactitude. For example, the government of Taiwan created "electronic fences," monitoring phone signals to alert police if those in home quarantine moved away from their address or turned off their phones. Authorities then contacted the patient, sometimes in person, within 15 minutes. Many applauded such

surveillance tools as a reasonable health care step while others decried them as an invasion of privacy (Hinshaw and Panyui 2020; Lee 2020).

Applying Sociology

To interactionists, the societal response to the pandemic was dramatic, but it nevertheless reinforced long-held observations. Households who sheltered in place during this time of uncertainty reached out to seek comfort from others. However, contact was through the phone or social media. As self-quarantine continued, people started to reach out to people with whom they had not been in contact for some time. Negative reactions occurred as well: the pandemic led to expressions of hostility or public shaming toward those who failed to take the coronavirus seriously and continued to publicly congregate despite government urgings to do otherwise (Etzioni 2020).

From the conflict perspective, the pandemic exacerbated persistent social inequality. Not only were the poor less likely to receive the necessary life-saving health care or paid sick leave, but often they lived in the most densely populated areas and worked at jobs that could not be done online, making them more likely to be exposed to the virus. At the other extreme, some of the wealthiest moved swiftly to shield their personal fortunes as the world economy began to deteriorate (Elignon et al. 2020).

In a different social context, conflict theorists considered how racial minorities were being stigmatized. Asian Americans in general, and specifically Chinese Americans, were scapegoated as being responsible for the virus, which had originated in Wuhan, China. Also the widely practiced use of homemade face coverings took on special significance for many groups, particularly Black men. In several states Black men wearing masks were summarily handcuffed, including a Miami physician who was standing on his front lawn wearing protective gear, having just returned from the hospital (De La Garza 2020; Tavernise and Oppel 2020).

Feminist theorists pointed out how the pandemic affected women more severely than men: women were more likely to be engaged in

Jerry King/CartoonStock

Individuals and businesses alike faced a bewildering number of bureaucratic hurdles when they applied for funding under the many hastily drawn up government assistance programs implemented during the coronavirus pandemic.

precarious work as well as to have fundamental rights to health care curbed. During the pandemic hospitals postponed elective surgeries to make space available for COVID-19 patients; seven states seized this opportunity to ban all abortions except in life-threatening circumstances. This took place despite physicians' groups such as the American College of Obstetricians and Gynecologists' objections (Turret et al. 2020).

Initiating Policy

It would be difficult to imagine an occasion when governments were so eager to intervene in their economies. Even nations engulfed in war would transform the nature of government-economy relationship, but not in a matter of a month or two. Such transformation has never been common, yet within a month after the crisis began, industrial nations had launched new spending programs equivalent to up to one-fifth of their annual gross domestic products, the sum total of all goods and services produced in an entire year (*Economist* 2020a).

In the United States, the Coronavirus Aid, Relief, and Economic Security Act (CARES Act) provided $2 trillion in COVID-19 relief. A portion of this went to the Paycheck Protection Program, which allowed small businesses to cover payroll expenses when demand was down or employees must shelter at home. Another portion of the CARES Act provided direct cash relief to anyone who earned less than $99,000 in 2019.

Despite the large amounts of money expended, the government response to the pandemic crisis revealed holes in the government safety net designed to serve those most in need as well as an economy that struggled to adjust in a timely fashion. Also the need to maintain social distance meant that agency offices were closed. Therefore would-be recipients of government aid had to apply online—an option closed to the truly disadvantaged (DeParle 2020).

Some see reason for optimism in the post-pandemic world. Some moves made quickly, such as providing paid sick leave to low-wage workers or reexamining dangerous working conditions, may persist. Sociologist Sherry Turkle (2020) sees electronic devices becoming a new source of inspiration: during the crisis, people turned to the Internet to obtain social contact, to seek inspirational messages, and to enjoy artistic performances. Online learning at all levels, from preschool through college and adult education, online religious services, and telemedicine all expanded or were instituted as emergency stopgaps. Eventually, these new platforms may bring needed services to a broader population if the barriers of accessing new technology can be overcome (Pawel 2020).

Taking Sociology with You

1. How were you affected by the pandemic? Which sociological theories best explain your experiences?

2. Using sociological concepts, explain why politicians were so quick to respond to the coronavirus pandemic with new social programs.

3. What obstacles might prevent poor people, either in the United States or elsewhere, from improving their lives through new online services once the crisis is over? Might the government have a role to play in removing those obstacles?

MASTERING THIS CHAPTER

Summary

Every society must have an **economic system** for producing, distributing, and consuming goods and services. It must also have a **political system** to allocate those valued resources. This chapter examines the three major economic systems; the sources of **power** and **authority** in political systems; the four major types of government; political behavior, including voter apathy and women's representation in government; two basic models of the power structure in the United States; **war, peace,** and **terrorism;** changing economies; and the political and economic response to the coronavirus pandemic.

1. With the Industrial Revolution, a new form of social structure emerged: the **industrial society.**

2. Systems of **capitalism** vary in the degree to which the government regulates private ownership and economic activity, but all emphasize the profit motive.

3. The basic objective of **socialism** is to eliminate economic exploitation and meet people's needs.

4. Marx believed that **communism** would evolve naturally out of socialism.

5. In developing nations, the **informal economy** represents a significant part of total economic activity. Yet because this sector depends largely on women's work, it is undervalued.

6. There are three basic sources of **power** within any political system: **force, influence,** and **authority.**

7. Max Weber identified three ideal types of authority: **traditional, rational-legal,** and **charismatic.**

8. There are four basic types of government: **monarchy, oligarchy, dictatorship,** and **democracy.**

9. Although political participation makes government accountable to citizens, voters display a great deal of apathy, both in the United States and in other countries.

10. Women are still underrepresented in politics, but are becoming more successful at winning election to public office.

11. Advocates of the **elite model** of the U.S. power structure see the nation as being ruled by a small group of individuals who share common political and economic interests: a **power elite.** Advocates of a **pluralist model** believe that power is shared more widely among conflicting groups.

12. **War** may be defined as conflict between organizations that possess trained combat forces equipped with deadly weapons, including militarized drones—a definition that includes conflict created by **terrorism. Peace** is the absence of war, or more broadly, a proactive effort to develop cooperative relations among nations.

13. **Affirmative action** is intended to remedy the effects of discrimination against minority groups and women in education and the workplace. The concept is controversial, however, because some people see it as reverse discrimination against majority groups.

14. The world's economies are changing, both in the United States and abroad. In the United States, workers are coping with **deindustrialization, offshoring,** the **sharing economy,** and temporary work, much of which can be considered **precarious**.

15. The coronavirus pandemic showed in the most dramatic fashion the intersection of the economy and government as well as the importance of government programs to people's livelihoods and safety.

Key Terms

Authority Institutionalized power that is recognized by the people over whom it is exercised. (351)

Capitalism An economic system in which the means of production are held largely in private hands and the main incentive for economic activity is the accumulation of profits. (347)

Charismatic authority Max Weber's term for power made legitimate by a leader's exceptional personal or emotional appeal to his or her followers. (351)

Color-blind racism The use of the principle of race neutrality to defend a racially unequal status quo. (364)

Communism As an ideal type, an economic system under which all property is communally owned and no social distinctions are made on the basis of people's ability to produce. (349)

Deindustrialization The systematic, widespread withdrawal of investment in basic aspects of productivity, such as factories and plants. (363)

Democracy In a literal sense, government by the people. (352)

Dictatorship A government in which one person has nearly total power to make and enforce laws. (352)

Downsizing Reductions taken in a company's workforce as part of deindustrialization. (364)

Economic system The social institution through which goods and services are produced, distributed, and consumed. (346)

Elite model A view of society as being ruled by a small group of individuals who share a common set of political and economic interests. (356)

Force The actual or threatened use of coercion to impose one's will on others. (351)

Industrial society A society that depends on mechanization to produce its goods and services. (347)

Influence The exercise of power through a process of persuasion. (351)

Influencer A social media user who has established credibility in a specific industry, such as fashion or electronics or toys. (351)

Informal economy Transfers of money, goods, or services that are not reported to the government. (349)

Laissez-faire A form of capitalism under which people compete freely, with minimal government intervention in the economy. (347)

Monarchy A form of government headed by a single member of a royal family, usually a king, queen, or some other hereditary ruler. (352)

Monopoly Control of a market by a single business firm. (348)

Obedience Compliance with higher authorities in a hierarchical structure. (368)

Offshoring The transfer of work to foreign contractors. (366)

Oligarchy A form of government in which a few individuals rule. (352)

Peace The absence of war, or more broadly, a proactive effort to develop cooperative relations among nations. (360)

Pluralist model A view of society in which many competing groups within the community have access to government, so that no single group is dominant. (358)

Political system The social institution that is founded on a recognized set of procedures for implementing and achieving society's goals. (346)

Politics In Harold Lasswell's words, "who gets what, when, and how." (350)

Power The ability to exercise one's will over others. (350)

Power elite A term used by C. Wright Mills to refer to a small group of military, industrial, and government leaders who control the fate of the United States. (356)

Precarious work Employment that is poorly paid, and, from the worker's perspective, insecure and unprotected. (366)

Rational-legal authority Power made legitimate by law. (351)

Representative democracy A form of government in which certain individuals are selected to speak for the people. (352)

Sharing economy Connecting owners of underused assets with others willing to pay to use them. (365)

Socialism An economic system under which the means of production and distribution are collectively owned. (349)

Terrorism The use or threat of violence against random or symbolic targets in pursuit of political aims. (362)

Totalitarianism Virtually complete government control and surveillance over all aspects of a society's social and political life. (352)

Traditional authority Legitimate power conferred by custom and accepted practice. (351)

War Conflict between organizations that possess trained combat forces equipped with deadly weapons. (359)

TAKING SOCIOLOGY with you

1. In TV shows, streaming series, and/or on social media, look for examples of informal economic activity. Why do you suppose the activity is being conducted informally? Take notes over the next several days. Discuss your findings with the class.

2. In TV shows, streaming series, and/or or on social media, look for examples of the three basic sources of power (force, influence, and authority). How is the power exercised and by whom? Take notes over the next several days and compare your findings with the class.

3. Within your immediate and extended family, ask members if they would mind disclosing if they are or are not registered to vote and why. Of those who are registered, did they all vote in the most recent election? Why or why not? Share your findings with the class

4. **Writing Sociology.** Find an article about problems that resulted from the practice of offshoring during the coronavirus pandemic. What was the impact? Summarize the article and share it with the class.

Self-Quiz

Read each question carefully and then select the best answer.

1. Which two basic types of economic system distinguish contemporary industrial societies?
   a. capitalism and communism
   b. capitalism and socialism
   c. socialism and communism
   d. capitalism and dictatorship

2. According to the discussion of capitalism in the text, which of the following statements is true?
   a. The means of production are held largely in private hands.
   b. The main incentive for economic activity is the accumulation of profits.
   c. The degree to which the government regulates private ownership and economic activity will vary.
   d. all of the above

3. G. William Domhoff's model is an example of a(n)
   a. elite theory of power.
   b. pluralist theory of power.
   c. functionalist theory of power.
   d. interactionist theory of power.

4. In terms of voter turnout, the United States typically ranks
   a. highest among all countries.
   b. highest among industrialized nations.
   c. lowest among industrialized nations.
   d. lowest among all countries.

5. What are the three basic sources of power within any political system?
   a. force, influence, and authority
   b. force, influence, and democracy
   c. force, legitimacy, and charisma
   d. influence, charisma, and bureaucracy

6. Which of the following is *not* part of the classification system of authority developed by Max Weber?
   a. traditional authority
   b. pluralist authority
   c. legal-rational authority
   d. charismatic authority

7. According to C. Wright Mills, power rests in the hands of the
   a. people.
   b. representative democracy.
   c. aristocracy.
   d. power elite.

8. The systematic, widespread withdrawal of investment in basic aspects of productivity such as factories and plants is called
   a. deindustrialization.
   b. socialism.
   c. postindustrialization.
   d. gentrification.

9. Sociologists and labor specialists foresee a workforce increasingly composed of
   a. women.
   b. racial minorities.
   c. ethnic minorities.
   d. all of the above

10. The positive efforts to recruit minority group members or women for jobs, promotions, and educational opportunities are referred to as
    a. equal rights
    b. affirmative action
    c. work programs
    d. equal action

11. The principle of _____ _____, as expounded and endorsed by the British economist Adam Smith, was the prevailing form of capitalism immediately following the Industrial Revolution.

12. Under _____ , the means of production and distribution in a society are collectively rather than privately owned, and the basic objective of the economic system is to meet people's needs rather than to maximize profits.

13. _____ is an economic system under which all property is communally owned and no social distinctions are made based on people's ability to produce.

14. _____ theorists point out that while pure monopolies are not a basic element of the economy of the United States, competition is much more restricted than one might expect in what is called a free enterprise system.

15. Some capitalist nations, such as the United States, outlaw _____ through antitrust legislation.

16. The elite model of political power implies that the United States has a(n) _____ as its form of government.

17. Sexism has been the most serious barrier to women interested in holding public office. To remedy this situation, many countries have adopted _____ for female representatives.

18. _____ is the exercise of power through a process of persuasion.

19. The United States is commonly classified as a(n) _____ _____, because the elected members of Congress and state legislatures make our laws.

20. Advocates of the _____ model suggest that competing groups within the community have access to government, so that no single group is dominant.

15 Health, Population, and the Environment

Hiroshi Watanabe/Getty Images

Health and the environment are clearly affected by population. Bogotá, the sprawling mountaintop capital of Colombia, is usually choked with traffic so bad that officials ban cars for entire days. The quarantine resulting from the coronavirus pandemic gave a new, fresh, healthy look to the view.

▶ INSIDE

How critical is the need to address climate change? Is it the most important issue that young people should address?

Greta Thunberg thinks it is.

picture alliance/Getty Images

❝My message is that we'll be watching you.

This is all wrong. I shouldn't be up here. I should be back in school on the other side of the ocean. Yet you all come to us young people for hope. How dare you!"

Thunberg received the immediate attention of those assembled as she opened her speech at United Nations headquarters in New York in 2019. The ninth grader from Stockholm, Sweden, also got the attention of the world, as she expressed her frustration with governments' slow progress at reducing carbon emissions. Carbon emissions come from burning fossil fuels—coal, petroleum, and natural gas—and accumulate in the atmosphere.

She, and world's environmental scientists, view it as essential to significantly reduce carbon emissions within the next decade to have any chance at reducing the warming of the global climate that has been documented over the last century. While she delivered her message in a strident fashion, she is not fear mongering: she is explaining the science of climate change.

She firmly believes that policymakers and political leaders are not acting as if they care about the planet's future. Further, she criticized politicians for presenting solutions or plans as if they were anywhere close to what was needed to leave future generations with a healthy planet. The real changes that need to be made are too uncomfortable to be a part of public statements or seriously advanced government policies.

Her speech and continuing public presence first inspired protests by high school students and then spread to college campuses. She declared that making these changes now is necessary if she and other young people will be able to tell their grandchildren that they did everything they could.

She spoke the simple truths, knowing that her message will mean viewing economic growth differently and setting aside any business-as-usual model of the environment.

"And change is coming, whether you like it or not.

"Thank you. ❞

Source: Thunberg 2019.

I shouldn't be up here. I should be back in school on the other side of the ocean. Yet you all come to us young people for hope. How dare you!

Swedish climate activist Greta Thunberg, age 16, challenged global government leaders at the 2019 United Nations Climate Action Summit to move beyond "business as usual." She first came to world attention in 2018 when she started the "Fridays for the Future" movement by skipping school and sitting in front of Sweden's Parliament holding a sign reading "SKOL-STREJK FÖR KLIMATET" ("SCHOOL STRIKES FOR CLIMATE").

In May 2019 she published a newspaper essay in which she proposed that young people should follow the lead of the students of Marjory Stoneman Douglas High School in Florida who had recently organized to protest gun violence in the United States. Few were impressed by this suggestion, but Thunberg, unfunded and with few initial followers, continued to demonstrate in front of Parliament.

Her effort gained supporters and spread across Europe and then the world as students joined her climate strikes. Many saw her as symbolizing the frustration and agony they feel over a future that they perceive to be in jeopardy. We will return to Thunberg and other activist efforts later in this chapter (Alter et al. 2019).

Thunberg's movement points to the main questions we address in this chapter: What defines a healthy environment? How is the environment connected to our health as a society? How do health and health care vary from one social class to another and from one nation to another? In this chapter, we present a sociological overview of health, illness, health care, and medicine as a social institution. We begin by examining how functionalists, conflict theorists, interactionists, and labeling theorists look at health-related issues. Then we study the distribution of diseases in a society by social class, race and ethnicity, gender, and age.

We'll look too at the evolution of the U.S. health care system. Sociologists are interested in the roles people play in the health care system and the organizations that deal with issues of health and sickness. Therefore, we will analyze the interactions among physicians, nurses, and patients; alternatives to traditional health care; the role of government in providing health care services to the needy; and the issues people with mental illness face.

The study of population is closely linked to both health and environment. In our coverage of population, we focus on patterns of birth, death, and fertility in societies at different stages of evolution. This overview of population trends leads to a discussion of migration, a major factor in population change.

Later in the chapter, we examine the environmental problems facing the world in the 21st century. We'll draw on the functionalist and conflict perspectives to better understand environmental issues. We'll see that it is important not to over-simplify the relationships among health, population, and the environment. Finally, in the Social Policy section we explore the recent developments in environmentalism.

Sociological Perspectives on Health and Illness

How can we define health? Imagine a continuum with health on one end and death on the other. In the preamble to its 1946 constitution, the World Health Organization defined **health** as a "state of complete physical, mental, and social well-being, and not merely the absence of disease and infirmity" (Leavell and Clark 1965:14). In this definition, the "healthy" end of the continuum represents an ideal rather than a precise condition.

Along the continuum, individuals define themselves as healthy or sick on the basis of criteria established by themselves and relatives, friends, co-workers, and medical practitioners. Health and illness, in other words, are socially constructed. They are rooted in culture and are defined by claims makers—people who describe themselves as healthy or ill—as well as by a broad range of interested parties, including health care providers, pharmaceutical firms, and even food providers (Conrad and Barker 2010).

Because health is socially constructed, we can consider how it varies in different situations or cultures. Why is it that you may consider yourself sick or well when others do not agree? Who controls definitions of health and illness in our society, and for what ends? What are the consequences of viewing yourself (or of being viewed) as ill or disabled? By drawing on four socio-logical perspectives—functionalism, conflict theory, interac-tionism, and labeling theory—we can gain greater insight into the social context that shapes definitions of health and the treatment of illness.

Functionalist Perspective

Illness entails breaks in our social interactions, both at work and at home. From a functionalist perspective, being sick must therefore be controlled, so that not too many people are re-leased from their societal responsibilities at any one time. Functionalists contend that an overly broad definition of illness would disrupt the workings of a society.

Sickness requires that one take on a social role, if only tempo-rarily. The **sick role** refers to societal expectations about the attitudes and behavior of a person viewed as being ill. Sociolo-gist Talcott Parsons (1951, 1975), well known for his contribu-tions to functionalist theory, outlined the behavior required of people who are considered sick. They are exempted from their normal, day-to-day responsibilities and generally do not suffer blame for their condition. Yet they are obligated to try to get well, which includes seeking competent professional care. This obligation arises from the common view that illness is dysfunctional, because it can undermine social stability. At-tempting to get well is particularly important in the world's de-veloping countries. Modern automated industrial societies can absorb a greater degree of illness or disability than horticul-tural or agrarian societies, in which the availability of workers is far more critical (Conrad and Leiter 2019).

According to Parsons's theory, physicians function as *gate-keepers* for the sick role. They verify a patient's condition ei-ther as "illness" or as "recovered." The ill person becomes dependent on the physician, because the latter can control valued rewards (not only treatment of illness, but also excused absences from work and school). Parsons suggests that the physician–patient relationship is somewhat like that between parent and child. Like a parent, the physician helps the patient to enter society as a full and functioning adult.

The concept of the sick role is not without criticism. First, pa-tients' judgments regarding their own state of health may be related to their gender, age, social class, and ethnic group. For example, younger people may fail to detect warning signs of a

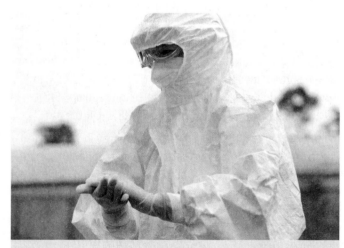

Eugeneonline/Getty Images

The coronavirus pandemic forced more and more health workers to wear personal protective equipment (PPE) like this, when it was available. Many social changes have occurred, from small to large scale, such as a major rethinking among employers of the previous practice of discouraging workers to call in sick and stay home when not feeling well.

dangerous illness, while elderly people may focus too much on the slightest physical malady. Second, the sick role may be more applicable to people who are experiencing short-term illnesses than to those with recurring, long-term illnesses. Finally, even simple factors, such as whether a person is employed, seem to affect one's willingness to assume the sick role—as does the impact of socialization into a particular occupation or activity. For example, beginning in childhood, athletes learn to define certain ailments as "sports injuries" and therefore do not regard themselves as "sick." Nonetheless, sociologists continue to rely on Parsons's model for functionalist analysis of the relationship between illness and societal expectations of the sick (Frank 2015).

USE YOUR SOCIOLOGICAL IMAGINATION

Describe some situations you have witnessed that illustrate different definitions of the "sick role."

Conflict Perspective

Conflict theorists observe that the medical profession has assumed a preeminence that extends well beyond whether to excuse a student from school or an employee from work. Sociologist Eliot Freidson (1970:5) has likened the position of medicine to that of former state religions—it has an officially approved monopoly of the right to define health and illness and to treat illness. Conflict theorists use the term *medicalization of society* to refer to the growing role of medicine as a major institution of social control.

The Medicalization of Society

Social control involves techniques and strategies for regulating behavior in order to enforce the distinctive norms and values of a culture. Typically, we think of informal social control as occurring within families and peer groups, and formal social control as being carried out by authorized agents such as police officers, judges, school administrators, and employers. Viewed from a conflict perspective, however, medicine is not simply a "healing profession"; it is a regulating mechanism.

How does medicine manifest its social control? First, medicine has greatly expanded its domain of expertise in recent decades. Physicians now examine a wide range of issues, among them sexuality, old age, anxiety, obesity, child development, alcoholism, and drug addiction. We tolerate this expansion of the boundaries of medicine because we hope that these experts can bring new "miracle cures" to complex human problems, as they have to the control of certain infectious diseases.

In defining these new conditions, physicians determine and control the course of treatment, and even affect patients' views of themselves. Once a problem is viewed using this **medical model,** it becomes more difficult for common people to join the discussion and exert influence on decision making. It also becomes more difficult to view these issues as being shaped by social, cultural, or psychological factors, rather than simply by physical or medical factors (Caplan 1989; Conrad and Bergey 2015; Zola 1972, 1983).

Second, medicine serves as an agent of social control by retaining absolute jurisdiction over many health care procedures. It has even attempted to guard its jurisdiction by placing health care professionals such as chiropractors and nurse-midwives outside the realm of acceptable medicine. Despite the fact that midwives first brought professionalism to child delivery, they have been portrayed as having invaded the "legitimate" field of obstetrics. Nurse-midwives have sought licensing as a way to achieve professional respectability, but physicians continue to exert power to ensure that midwifery remains a subordinate occupation. During the coronavirus pandemic, many states lifted these barriers to facilitate

Hill Street Studios/Getty Images

The growing concern about obesity among the young has focused attention on their eating habits and their need for exercise. Concern about obesity is a sign of the medicalization of society.

in-home deliveries by women who were unable or unwilling to deliver their babies in hospitals that were overwhelmed by patients inflicted with COVID-19 (Simpson 2020).

Inequities in Health Care   The medicalization of society is but one concern of conflict theorists as they assess the workings of health care institutions. As we have seen throughout this textbook, in analyzing any issue, conflict theorists seek to determine who benefits, who suffers, and who dominates at the expense of others. Viewed from a conflict perspective, glaring inequities exist in health care delivery in the United States. For example, poor areas tend to be underserved because medical services concentrate where people are wealthy.

Similarly, from a global perspective, obvious inequities exist in health care delivery. Today, the United States has about 26 physicians per 10,000 people, while collectively all the African nations have fewer than 2 per 10,000. This situation is only worsened by the **brain drain**—the immigration to the United States and other industrialized nations of skilled workers, professionals, and technicians who are desperately needed in their home countries. As part of this brain drain, physicians, nurses, and other health care professionals have come to the United States from developing countries such as India, Pakistan, and various African states (World Bank 2019b).

Conflict theorists view their emigration out of the Third World as yet another way in which the world's core industrialized nations enhance their quality of life at the expense of developing countries. One way the developing countries suffer is in lower life expectancy. In Africa and much of Latin America and Asia, life expectancy is far lower than in industrialized nations.

Conflict theorists emphasize that inequities in health care have clear life-and-death consequences. From a conflict perspective, the dramatic differences in *infant mortality rates* around the world (Figure 15-1) reflect, at least in part, unequal distribution of health care resources based on the wealth or poverty of various nations. The **infant mortality rate** is the number of deaths of infants under 1 year old per 1,000 live births in a given year. This measure is an important indicator of a society's level of health care; it reflects prenatal nutrition, delivery procedures, and infant screening measures. Still, despite the wealth of the United States, at least 54 nations have *lower* infant mortality rates. Conflict theorists point out that unlike the United States, these countries offer some form of government-supported health care for all citizens, which typically leads to greater availability and use of prenatal care.

USE YOUR SOCIOLOGICAL IMAGINATION

From a sociological point of view, what might be the greatest challenge to reducing inequities in health care?

Interactionist Perspective

From an interactionist point of view, patients are not passive; often, they actively seek the services of a health care practitioner. In examining health, illness, and medicine as a social institution, then, interactionists engage in micro-level study of the roles played by health care professionals and patients. Interactionists are particularly interested in how physicians learn to play their occupational role. For example, in one of his earliest works, sociologist Howard Becker took the perspective that

FIGURE 15-1   INFANT MORTALITY RATES IN SELECTED COUNTRIES

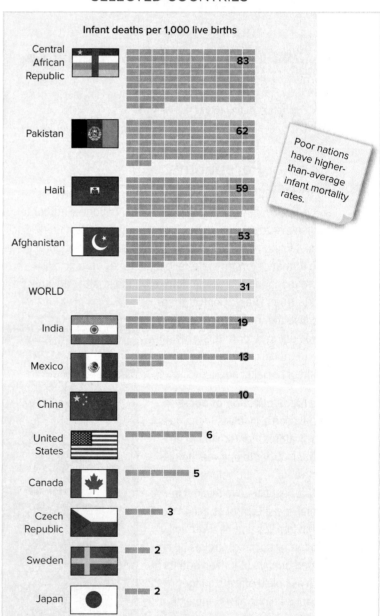

Poor nations have higher-than-average infant mortality rates.

Think about It   Why do you think the United States has a relatively high infant mortality rate for a rich country?

Sources Population Reference Bureau, 2020. Accessible at www.prf.org.
Flags: admin_design/Shutterstock

ERproductions Ltd./Getty Images

With the use of electronic medical records and telemedicine, medical professionals increasingly turn their attention away from the patient and toward the screen.

medical education socialized students into the role of a doctor as much as it transferred medical knowledge to them (H. Becker et al. 1961).

Recently interactionists have turned their attention to the impact of the ever-present computer screen on doctor–patient interaction. Today more than three-quarters of physicians scan the screen for past visits and test results and enter their observations for the current visit while interacting with a patient. As a result, face-to-face interaction has been reduced by one-third. So concerned has the medical profession become about this trend that, drawing on social interaction studies, doctors are now told to review the electronic medical record before seeing the patient and to share the computer screen so the patient can become more involved in the visit (Duke et al. 2013; Reddy 2015).

Labeling Perspective

Labeling theory helps us to understand why certain people are *viewed* as deviants, "bad kids," or criminals, whereas others whose behavior is similar are not. Labeling theorists also suggest that the designation "healthy" or "ill" generally involves social definition by others. Just as police officers, judges, and other regulators of social control have the power to define certain people as criminals, health care professionals (especially physicians) have the power to define certain people as sick. Moreover, like labels that suggest nonconformity

or criminality, labels that are associated with illness commonly reshape how others treat us and how we see ourselves.

A historical example illustrates perhaps the ultimate extreme in labeling social behavior as a sickness. As enslavement of Africans in the United States came under increasing attack in the 19th century, medical authorities provided new rationalizations for the oppressive practice. Noted physicians published articles stating that the skin color of Africans deviated from "healthy" white skin coloring because Africans suffered from congenital leprosy. Moreover, the continuing efforts of enslaved Africans to escape from their white masters were classified as an example of the "disease" of drapetomania (or "crazy runaways"). The prestigious *New Orleans Medical and Surgical Journal* suggested that the remedy for this "disease" was to treat slaves kindly, as one might treat children. Apparently, these medical authorities would not entertain the view that it was healthy and sane to flee slavery or join in a slave revolt (T. Szasz 2010).

A new concern about how illness can be stigmatized grows out of the dependence on electronic health records. As more and more medical records are digitized to facilitate access by medical professionals, concerns have increased over how a person's medical history may be viewed or misinterpreted if the records are improperly shared. There are a host of medical labels, from cancer survivor to diabetic, that could result in discrimination, despite laws prohibiting such practices (Stablen et al. 2015).

Similarly, labeling theorists suggest that behaviors viewed today as mental illnesses may not really be illnesses. Instead, the individual's problems arise from living in society, not from physical maladies. From this perspective, a variety of life experiences treated as illnesses today may not be illnesses at all. Premenstrual syndrome, post-traumatic stress disorders, and hyperactivity are examples of medically recognized disorders that labeling theorists would consider questionable.

Probably the most noteworthy medical example of labeling is the case of homosexuality. For years, psychiatrists classified being gay or lesbian not as a lifestyle but as a mental disorder subject to treatment. This official sanction became an early target of the growing gay and lesbian rights movement in the United States. In 1974, members of the American Psychiatric Association finally voted to drop homosexuality from the standard manual on mental disorders.

Table 15-1 summarizes four major sociological perspectives on health and illness. Although they may seem quite different, two common themes unite them. First, any person's

TABLE 15-1   SOCIOLOGICAL PERSPECTIVES ON HEALTH AND ILLNESS

Tracking Sociological Perspectives

	Functionalist	Conflict	Interactionist	Labeling
Major emphasis	Control of the number of people who are considered sick	Overmedicalization Gross inequities in health care	Doctor–patient relationship Interaction of medical staff	Definition of illness and health
Controlling factors	Physician as gatekeeper	Medical profession Social inequities	Medical profession	Medical profession
Proponents	Talcott Parsons	Thomas Szasz Irving Zola	Howard Becker	Thomas Szasz

health or illness is more than an organic condition, since it is subject to the interpretation of others. The impact of culture, family and friends, and the medical profession means that health and illness are not purely biological occurrences, but sociological occurrences as well. Second, since members of a society (especially industrial societies) share the same health care delivery system, health is a group and societal concern. Although health may be defined as the complete well-being of an individual, it is also the result of one's social environment, as the next section will show (Cockerham 2017).

THINKING CRITICALLY

Describe an occasion on which people you know disagreed about a socially applied medical label. What was the label, and why did people disagree?

Social Epidemiology and Health

Social epidemiology is the study of the distribution of disease, impairment, and general health status across a population. Initially, epidemiologists concentrated on the scientific study of epidemics, focusing on how they started and spread. Contemporary social epidemiology is much broader in scope, concerned not only with epidemics but also with nonepidemic diseases, injuries, drug addiction and alcoholism, suicide, and mental illness. Epidemiologists have taken on the new role of tracking bioterrorism. In 2001, they mobilized to trace the anthrax outbreak and prepare for any terrorist use of smallpox or other lethal microbes. Epidemiologists draw on the work of a wide variety of scientists and researchers, among them physicians, sociologists, public health officials, biologists, veterinarians, demographers, anthropologists, psychologists, and meteorologists.

Epidemiologists have found that worldwide, an estimated 38 million people were infected with HIV at the end of 2019. Although the spread of AIDS is stabilizing, with fewer new cases reported, the disease is not evenly distributed. Those areas that are least equipped to deal with it—the developing nations

of sub-Saharan Africa—face the greatest challenge. Unfortunately, there is no vaccine to prevent HIV, as there is for smallpox or polio (Figure 15-2).

When disease data are presented as rates, or as the number of reports per 100,000 people, they are called **morbidity rates.** (The term **mortality rate** refers to the rate of *death* in a given population.) Sociologists find morbidity rates useful because they may reveal that a specific disease occurs more frequently in one segment of a population. As we shall see, social class, race, ethnicity, gender, gender identity, and age can all affect a population's morbidity rates.

Social Class

Social class is clearly associated with differences in morbidity and mortality rates. Studies in the United States and other countries have consistently shown that people in the lower classes have higher rates of mortality, morbidity, and long-term disability than others.

FIGURE 15-2   AIDS BY THE NUMBERS WORLDWIDE

	New infections (children)	New HIV infections (millions)	AIDS related deaths (millions)	People accessing treatment (millions)
2001	550 000	3.4		
2004	550 000	3.0	2.3	
2007	480 000	2.7	2.2	2.9
2010	360 000	2.5	1.9	6.6
2013	250 000	2.1	1.3	13.0
2016	160 000	1.8	1.0	20.9
2018	160 000	1.7	0.8	23.3

Think about It What factors might be responsible for the changes shown in the figure?

Sources: UNAIDS 2013, 2019.

Why is class linked to health? Crowded living conditions, substandard housing, poor diet, and stress all contribute to the ill health of many low-income people in the United States. In certain instances, poor education may lead to a lack of awareness of measures necessary to maintain good health. Financial strains are certainly a major factor in the health problems of less affluent people.

What is particularly troubling about social class differences is that they appear to be cumulative. Little or no health care in childhood or young adulthood is likely to mean more illness later in life. The longer that low income presents a barrier to adequate health care, the more chronic and difficult to treat illness becomes.

Another reason for the link between social class and health is that the poor—many of whom belong to racial and ethnic minorities—are less able than others to afford quality medical care. The affluent are more likely than others to have health insurance, either because they can afford it or because they have jobs that provide it. Pharmacists report that people purchase only those medications they "need the most," or buy in small quantities, such as four pills at a time.

Several changes in health insurance requirements went into effect with the 2010 Patient Protection and Affordable Care Act (Obamacare), but provisions took effect over several years, and over time, both state and federal actions have changed the law's impact. Prior to the coronavirus pandemic, the proportion of the population that was uninsured had dropped, reaching a low of 8.5 percent in 2018 (see Figure 15-3). However, income levels still make a difference in the ability to purchase insurance. Households that earn less than $25,000 per year are more than four times as likely to be uninsured as those that earn over $150,000. The job loss during the pandemic, led to an estimated 2.9 million more people uninsured (Banthin et al. 2020; Berchick, Barnett, and Upton 2019).

Finally, in the view of Karl Marx and contemporary conflict theorists, capitalist societies such as the United States care more about maximizing profits than they do about the health and safety of industrial workers. As a result, government agencies do not take forceful action to regulate conditions in the workplace, and workers suffer many preventable job-related injuries and illnesses. As we will see later in this chapter, research also shows that the lower classes are more vulnerable to environmental pollution than are the affluent, not only where they work but where they live.

USE YOUR SOCIOLOGICAL IMAGINATION

In what ways do the costs of health care affect the way you receive medical services?

Race and Ethnicity

The health profiles of many racial and ethnic minorities reflect the social inequality evident in the United States. The poor economic and environmental conditions of groups such as African Americans, Hispanics, and Native Americans are manifested in high morbidity and mortality rates for those groups. It is true that some diseases, such as sickle-cell anemia among Blacks, have a clear genetic basis. But in most instances, environmental factors contribute to the differential rates of disease and death.

As noted earlier, infant mortality is regarded as a primary indicator of health care. There is a significant gap in the United States between the infant mortality rates of African Americans and whites. Generally, the rate of infant death is more than twice as high among Blacks (Office of Minority Health 2019).

National studies have shown that the medical establishment is not exempt from racism. Discrimination and prejudice are often overlooked by the media, which tend to focus on the most overt forms of racism, such as hate crimes. Studies show that minorities receive inferior medical care even when they are insured. Despite having access to care, Blacks, Latinos, and Native Americans are treated unequally as a result of racial prejudice and differences in the quality of various health care plans. Furthermore, national clinical studies have shown that even allowing for differences in income and insurance coverage, racial and ethnic minorities are less likely than other groups to receive both standard health care and life-saving treatment for conditions such as HIV infection (Centers for Disease Control and Prevention 2016; National Academies of Sciences, Engineering, and Medicine 2017a).

Drawing on the conflict perspective, sociologist Howard Waitzkin (1986) suggests that racial tensions also contribute to the medical problems of Blacks. In his view, the stress that results from racial prejudice and discrimination helps to explain the higher rates of heart disease found among African Americans compared to whites. Hypertension, which affects over 41 percent of Blacks but fewer than 29 percent of non-Hispanic whites, is believed to be a critical factor in high mortality rates from heart disease, kidney disease, and stroke found among African Americans (Gillespie and Hurvitz 2013; Office of Minority Health 2019).

Some Mexican Americans and many other Latinos adhere to cultural beliefs that make them less likely than others to use the established medical system. They may interpret their illnesses according to **curanderismo**, or traditional folk medicine—a form of holistic health care and healing. *Curanderismo* is a tradition of the Southwestern United States common among Hispanics and Latin America. Today this tradition is increasingly recognized and integrated with existing health care systems. Colleges offer courses on the subject for health and social work students (University of New Mexico 2020).

MAPPING LIFE NATIONWIDE

FIGURE 15-3   PERCENTAGE WITHOUT HEALTH INSURANCE

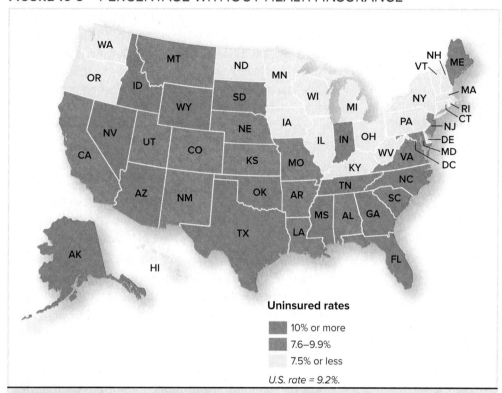

Uninsured rates

- 10% or more
- 7.6–9.9%
- 7.5% or less

U.S. rate = 9.2%.

Think about It Do you know of families who don't have health insurance? If so, how has the lack of insurance affected decisions about their health care?

Note: In 2019, people without private or government health insurance, not covered by Medicaid, Medicare, or military health care. The economic upheaval created by the coronavirus pandemic increased the level of uninsurance, but the relative differences between states is largely unchanged.
Source: Keisler-Starkey and Bunch 2020: Table A-3.

Disparities along the racial and ethnic divide were also apparent during the recent coronavirus pandemic, as research has shown in the Box 15-1, "The Color of COVID-19."

Gender

A large body of research indicates that compared with men, women experience a higher occurrence of many illnesses, although they tend to live longer. There are some variations—for example, men are more likely to have parasitic diseases, whereas women are more likely to become diabetic—but as a group, women appear to be in poorer health than men.

The apparent inconsistency between the ill health of women and their greater longevity deserves an explanation, and researchers have advanced a theory. Women's lower rate of cigarette smoking (reducing their risk of heart disease, lung cancer, and emphysema), lower consumption of alcohol (reducing the risk of auto accidents and cirrhosis of the liver), and lower rate of employment in dangerous occupations explain about one-third of their greater longevity than men. Moreover, some clinical studies suggest that the differences in morbidity may actually be less pronounced than the data show. Researchers argue that women are much more likely than men to

seek treatment, to be diagnosed as having a disease, and thus to have their illnesses reflected in the data examined by epidemiologists.

From a conflict perspective, women have been particularly vulnerable to the medicalization of society, with everything from birth to beauty being treated in an increasingly medical context. Such medicalization may contribute to women's higher morbidity rates compared to those of men. Ironically, even though women have been especially affected by medicalization, medical researchers have often excluded them from clinical studies. Female physicians and researchers charge that sexism lies at the heart of such research practices, and insist that there is a desperate need for studies of female subjects (Centers for Disease Control and Prevention 2016; Kapoor et al. 2019).

THINKING CRITICALLY

Which is a more important factor in the adequate delivery of health care, race or gender? Explain.

Age

Health is the overriding concern of the elderly. Most older people in the United States report having at least one chronic illness, but only some of those conditions are potentially life threatening or require medical care. At the same time, health problems can affect the quality of life of older people in important ways. Almost half of older people in the United States are troubled by arthritis, and many have visual or hearing impairments that can interfere with the performance of everyday tasks.

Older people are also especially vulnerable to certain mental health problems. Alzheimer's disease, the leading cause of dementia in the United States, afflicts an estimated 5.9 million people and, along with other forms of dementia, is present in one-third of seniors at the time of their death. While some

RESEARCH TODAY

15-1 The Color of COVID-19

Analysis of the morbidity and mortality from COVID-19 showed that everyone was vulnerable: young and old, men and women, people from every geographic region and economic stratum. Yet as with most other unexpected and calamitous events, people who belonged to racial and ethnic minorities were most vulnerable.

African Americans and Latinos are more likely to experience comorbidity with COVID-19. **Comorbidity** refers to the presence of more than one disorder in the same person. So when African Americans and Latinos came down with COVID-19, they were also more likely than whites to have hypertension, diabetes, high cholesterol, coronary artery disease, or atrial fibrillation, a heart condition.

Clinically, America's racial and ethnic minorities were ill equipped to survive the pandemic if they caught the disease. They were also more likely to be exposed to contagion: Black Americans and Latinos are more likely than whites to work in service sector jobs, less likely to own a car, and less likely to own their homes. They are therefore more likely to be in close physical contact

with other people because of the ways they travel, the kinds of work they do, and the conditions in which they live. All of these social factors contribute to their vulnerability to an epidemic.

Clinically, America's racial and ethnic minorities were ill equipped to survive the pandemic if they caught the disease. They were also more likely to be exposed to contagion.

Even in very rural areas, minorities were more susceptible than whites. People who live on the Navajo reservation experienced very high COVID-19 morbidity and mortality as they had to deal with an infectious disease in a remote area with a scarcity of running water. Applying for federal assistance or health care equipment is much more difficult for a tribal nation than for a city or state.

Once ill, members of racial and ethnic minority communities are more likely to be functioning without a primary physician or adequate health insurance. They are more likely to work at jobs that do not provide sick leave. As the pandemic grew more intense, people were assured that their health care costs for COVID-19 would be covered, but this assurance would not carry much weight in minority communities, which are accustomed to functioning outside the established health care delivery system.

LET'S DISCUSS

1. To what degree do the comorbidity issues that minority communities experience hold for other conditions besides COVID-19? To what degree do the social factors affect the general health of minority communities?
2. What other factors might make rural dwellers, regardless of race or ethnicity, more or less vulnerable to the pandemic?

Sources: Boule 2020; Romero 2020; Yancy 2020.

---

individuals with Alzheimer's exhibit only mild symptoms, the risk of severe problems resulting from the disease rises substantially with age (Alzheimer's Association 2019).

Not surprisingly, older people in the United States are much more likely to use health services than younger people. This means that older people spend much more: by the time one reaches age 65, average annual healthcare costs are $11,300 per person in the United States. This is nearly triple the annual average for people in their 20s and 30s. The disproportionate use of the U.S. health care system by older people is a critical factor in all discussions about the cost of health care and possible reforms of the health care system (Registered Nursing 2020).

Gender Identity

As society begins to recognize the existence of diversity in gender identities, scholars are studying the significance of gender identity for health care delivery. Virtually all of today's medical professionals and service providers received training that was oriented to heterosexual individuals and households, with little recognition that people seeking health care may be lesbian and gay. Only in the last few years has awareness embraced bisexual and transgender identities.

As conflict theorists point out, historically LGBTQ people and their families have encountered intolerance similar to that faced by racial and ethnic minorities in the social institution of health care. The 2015 legalization of same-sex marriage reduced the stigma accorded to people whose gender identity does not conform to the traditional norm of male–female couples. Queer theorists call for research that does not assume the heterosexual norm and considers the health care needs of people with a variety of gender identities.

Research to date is limited to small studies dealing with wellness issues. For example, one study of 18 children of transgender parents found that having a transgender parent did not affect any of the children's developmental goals. Another suggests that LGBTQ individuals have lower levels of self-reported health, compared with straight individuals. This may result from lower utilization of health services, either because of prior unfavorable experiences or because of lack of health insurance. Until recently, same-sex couples have not had access to their partners' health insurance benefits.

One obvious area of future study, given the stress that LGBTQ people face throughout their lives, is the delivery of mental health services. While it is wrong to assume that all or even most LGBTQ individuals have mental health problems, clearly research is needed in this area, especially as society changes its views toward different gender identities (Johns et al. 2019; Lewis et al. 2019).

In sum, to achieve greater access and reduce health disparities, federal health officials must overcome inequities that are rooted not just in age, but also in social class, race and ethnicity, gender, and gender identity.

Health Care in the United States

As the entire nation is well aware, the costs of health care have skyrocketed (Figure 15-4). By 2000, the amount spent on health care already equaled that spent on education, defense, prisons, farm subsidies, food stamps, and foreign aid combined. By the year 2028, total expenditures for health care in the United States are expected to exceed $6.1 trillion. The implementation of the 2010 Affordable Care Act, discussed later, has slowed the growth of health care costs. Given the complex, often inefficient health care delivery system in the United States, it is to be seen whether this dampening of growth will continue (Buntin and Graves 2020).

The health care system of the United States has moved far beyond the days when general practitioners living in a neighborhood or community typically made house calls and charged modest fees for their services. How did health care become a big business involving nationwide hospital chains and marketing campaigns? How have these changes reshaped the interactions between doctors, nurses, and patients? We will address these questions in this section.

A Historical View

Today, state licensing and medical degrees confer authority on medical professionals that is maintained from one generation to the next. However, health care in the United States has not always followed this model. The "popular health movement" of the 1830s and 1840s emphasized preventive care and what is termed "self-help." Strong criticism was voiced of "doctoring" as a paid occupation. New medical philosophies or sects established medical schools and challenged the authority and methods of traditional doctors. By the 1840s, most states had repealed medical licensing laws.

In response, through the leadership of the American Medical Association (AMA), founded in 1848, "regular" doctors attacked lay practitioners, sectarian doctors, and female physicians. Once they had institutionalized their authority through standardized programs of education and licensing, they conferred it only on those who completed their programs. The authority of the physician no longer depended on lay attitudes or on the person occupying the sick role; it was built into the structure of the medical profession and the health care

FIGURE 15-4 TOTAL HEALTH CARE EXPENDITURES IN THE UNITED STATES, 1960–2028 (PROJECTED)

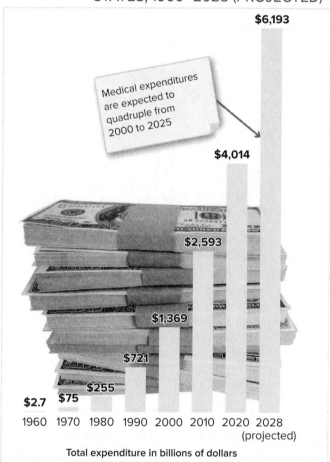

Medical expenditures are expected to quadruple from 2000 to 2025

$6,193
$4,014
$2,593
$1,369
$721
$255
$75
$2.7

1960   1970   1980   1990   2000   2010   2020   2028 (projected)

Total expenditure in billions of dollars

Think about It What social changes in the United States might account for the rise in health care costs from $75 billion in 1970 to over $5.2 trillion in 2025?

Sources: Centers for Medicare and Medicaid Services 2020a.
Photo:: Comstock Images/Alamy Stock Photo

system. By the 1920s, physicians controlled hospital technology, the division of labor of health personnel, and indirectly, other professional practices such as nursing and pharmacy (R. Coser 1984).

Patients have traditionally relied on medical personnel to inform them of health care issues, but increasingly they are turning to the media for health care information. Recognizing this change, pharmaceutical firms advertise their prescription drugs directly to potential customers through television and magazines. The Internet is another growing source for patient information. Medical professionals are understandably suspicious of these new sources of information.

Physicians and Patients

Traditionally, physicians have held a position of dominance in their dealings with patients. The functionalist and interactionist perspectives offer a framework for understanding the professional socialization of physicians as it relates to patient care. Functionalists suggest that established physicians and medical school professors serve as mentors or role models who transmit knowledge, skills, and values to the passive learner—the medical student. Interactionists emphasize that students are molded by the medical school environment as they interact with their classmates.

Both approaches argue that the typical training of physicians in the United States leads to rather dehumanizing physician–patient encounters. Dr. Lori Alvord, a Navajo surgeon, has observed that the physician–patient relationship is "central to the development of trust. It is a time when patients have voluntarily given control over their bodies to others, and this can be frightening. The experiences the patient has at the time of surgery are also important, and I try to make sure that our surgical environment, to the extent possible, is a positive experience" (Alvord 2009).

Despite many efforts to introduce a humanistic approach to patient care into the medical school curriculum, patient overload and cost-cutting by hospitals have tended to undercut positive relations. Moreover, widespread publicity about malpractice suits and high medical costs has further strained the physician–patient relationship. Interactionists have closely examined compliance and negotiation between physician and patient. They concur with Talcott Parsons's view that the relationship is generally asymmetrical, with doctors holding a position of dominance and controlling rewards.

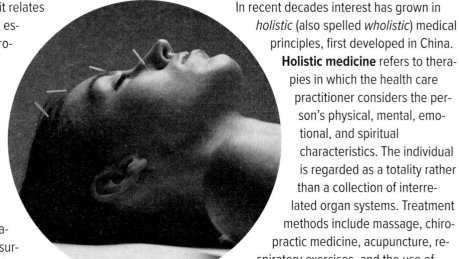

Anthony Saint James/Photodisc/Getty Images

USE YOUR SOCIOLOGICAL IMAGINATION

If you were a patient, would you put yourself entirely in the physician's hands, or would you do some research on your own? If you were a doctor, would you want your patient checking medical information on the Internet? Explain your positions.

Alternatives to Traditional Health Care

In traditional forms of health care, people rely on physicians and hospitals for the treatment of illness. More and more adults are using additional techniques to be healthy. If a nonmainstream practice is used together with conventional medicine, it is considered *complementary*. If a nonmainstream practice is used in place of conventional medicine, it's considered *alternative*. These techniques are increasingly seen as part of preventive health practices and are sometimes even covered by health insurance.

In recent decades interest has grown in *holistic* (also spelled *wholistic*) medical principles, first developed in China. **Holistic medicine** refers to therapies in which the health care practitioner considers the person's physical, mental, emotional, and spiritual characteristics. The individual is regarded as a totality rather than a collection of interrelated organ systems. Treatment methods include massage, chiropractic medicine, acupuncture, respiratory exercises, and the use of herbs as remedies. Nutrition, exercise, and visualization may also be used to treat ailments that are generally treated through medication or hospitalization.

Practitioners of holistic medicine do not necessarily function totally outside the traditional health care system. Some have medical degrees and rely on X-rays and EKG machines for diagnostic assistance. Others who staff holistic clinics, often referred to as *wellness clinics,* reject the use of medical technology. The recent resurgence of holistic medicine comes amid widespread recognition of the value of nutrition and the dangers of overreliance on prescription drugs (especially those used to reduce stress, such as Valium).

The medical establishment—professional organizations, research hospitals, and medical schools—has generally served as a stern protector of traditionally accepted health care techniques. However, a major breakthrough occurred in 1992 when the federal government began to accept grant requests into alternative medicine. A government-sponsored national survey found that one in four adults in the United States had used some form of "complementary and alternative medicine" during the previous month or year. Examples included acupuncture, folk medicine, meditation, yoga, homeopathic treatments, megavitamin therapy, and chiropractic treatment. When prayer was included as an alternative or complementary form of medicine, the proportion of adults who used alternative medicine rose to over 62 percent (Black et al. 2015; National Center for Complementary and Integrative Health 2020).

On the international level, the World Health Organization (WHO) monitors the use of alternative medicine around the world. According to WHO, government funding of research into alternative medicine is not common. Other than the United States, only eleven other nations, including China and India, sponsor such research. WHO's goal internationally is to encourage the development of universal training programs and ethical standards for practitioners of alternative medicine.

Over 80 percent of the world's population depends on herbal medicines and products for healthy living (World Health Organization 2019).

The Role of Government

Not until the 20th century did health care receive federal aid. The first significant involvement was the 1946 Hill-Burton Act, which provided subsidies for building and improving hospitals, especially in rural areas. A far more important change came with the enactment in 1965 of two wide-ranging government assistance programs: Medicare, which is essentially a compulsory health insurance plan for the elderly, and Medicaid, which is a noncontributory federal and state insurance plan for the poor. These programs greatly expanded federal involvement in health care financing for needy men, women, and children.

Given the high rates of illness and disability among elderly people, Medicare has had a huge impact on the health care system. Initially, Medicare simply reimbursed health care providers such as physicians and hospitals for the billed costs of their services. However, in 1983, as the overall costs of Medicare increased dramatically, the federal government introduced a price-control system. Under this system, private hospitals often transfer patients whose treatment may be unprofitable to public facilities. In fact, many private hospitals conduct "wallet biopsies"—that is, investigate the financial status of potential patients. Those judged undesirable are then refused admission or dumped. Although a federal law passed in 1987 made it illegal for any hospital receiving Medicare funds to dump patients, the practice continues (Venkatesh et al. 2019).

The 2010 Affordable Care Act improved health insurance coverage for people of all ages, especially young adults, who were allowed to remain longer on their parents' policies. President Obama's administration had pushed for the act in response to several problems, including high out-of-pocket costs for the uninsured and the inability of people with preexisting conditions to get insurance. In 2012 and again in 2015 the Supreme Court upheld the federal government's authority to implement the law's provisions.

Opponents of the program, which they dubbed "Obamacare," made legislative changes to the law and have continued to seek legal challenges. Critics complain that the act is too expensive for taxpayers, and unnecessarily—perhaps even

John Bazemore/AP Images

Tensions ran high as the Supreme Court heard arguments on the constitutionality of controversial new federal health care legislation. These citizens are indicating their opposition to the 2010 Affordable Care Act. Objections like these led Congress to change the law to give more control to states and individuals rather than try to establish national standards for health insurance coverage.

unconstitutionally—dictates citizens' health care decisions. However, some of the program's provisions, such as the mandate that insurance companies can no longer deny coverage for preexisting conditions, and the requirement that insurers must cover dependent children through age 26, are extremely popular. This has made it difficult for critics to agree on a replacement or even on modifications.

What Is Mental Illness?

Like other illnesses, mental disorders affect not just individuals and their families, but society as a whole. In industrial economies, mental disorders are a significant cause of disability.

Thus, as a British medical journal declared in connection with the Global Mental Health Summit, there can be "no health without mental health" (Prince et al. 2007).

Sadly, the words *mental illness* and *insanity* evoke dramatic and often inaccurate images of emotional problems. Though the media routinely emphasize the most violent behavior of those with emotional disturbances, mental health and mental illness can more appropriately be viewed as a continuum of human behavior. Using this definition, we can consider a person to have a mental disorder "if he or she is so disturbed that coping with routine, everyday life is difficult or impossible." The term **mental illness** should be reserved for a disorder of the brain that disrupts a person's thinking, feeling, and ability to interact with others (J. Coleman and Cressey 1980:315; McLean 2017).

Traditionally, people in the United States have maintained a negative and suspicious view of those with mental disorders. Holding the status of "mental patient" or even "former mental patient" can have unfortunate and undeserved consequences. Voting rights are denied in some instances, acceptance for jury duty is problematic, and past emotional problems are an issue in divorce and custody cases. Moreover, content analysis of network television programs and films shows that mentally ill characters are uniformly portrayed in a demeaning and derogatory fashion; many are labeled as "criminally insane," "wackos," or "psychos." From an interactionist perspective, a key social institution is shaping social behavior by manipulating symbols and intensifying people's fears about the mentally ill (Diefenbach and West 2007).

In 2012, a tragic mass shooting at an elementary school in Newtown, Connecticut, led to renewed scrutiny of the role of mental illness in incidents of gun violence. The shooter was said to have had a mental illness, for which he apparently went untreated. As a result, some people argued that to curb gun violence, legislators should focus on mental health rather than on gun control. Unfortunately, such public debates tend to perpetuate the false assumption that people with mental illness are dangerous, furthering the *stigma* associated with their illness. The term **stigma,** coined by the interactionist Erving Goffman (1963), describes the labels society uses to devalue members of certain social groups.

A review of the available survey data shows that over time, the general public has become more sophisticated about mental illness, and perhaps a bit more open to disclosure, recognition, and response to mental health problems. Yet since 1950, people have become much more likely to associate "violence" with "mental illness," despite overwhelming evidence to the contrary. In fact, the vast majority of people with psychiatric disorders *do not* commit violent acts. Only 3–4 percent of

Doug Schneider/Alamy Stock Photo

For generations, many thousands of people with mental illness were effectively removed from society and placed in residential facilities. The now abandoned Harlem Valley Psychiatric Center in Dover, New York, which operated from 1924 to 1993, included 80 buildings; at its peak it housed 5,000 patients.

violent crime in the United States can be attributed to mental illness, while people with those illnesses are actually 10 times more likely to be victims of violent crime than the general population (Gass and Mendoza 2017).

Just as availability of physical health care differs across class and race lines, so does availability of mental health care. The health insurance available to the less advantaged is less likely to offer reimbursement for mental health services. Practitioners of such services are often unfamiliar with the lifestyle and culture of those from low income backgrounds and members of racial and ethnic minorities. As a result, members of these communities are less likely to receive care than are members of more privileged communities. Many Latinos and members of other immigrant communities face the added challenge of finding practitioners who can effectively communicate in their native language. As one Long Beach, California, Mexican-American dealing with a variety of frustrations said, "The therapist just couldn't understand my cultural background because it wasn't her own" (Weber 2019).

THINKING CRITICALLY

What factors perpetuate the social stigma associated with mental illness? How could that stigma be eliminated?

Theoretical Models of Mental Disorders

In studying mental illness, we can draw on both the medical model and a more sociological approach derived from labeling theory. Each model rests on distinctive assumptions regarding treatment of people with mental disorders.

According to the medical model, mental illness is rooted in biological causes that can be treated through medical intervention. Problems in brain structure or in the biochemical balance in the brain, sometimes due to injury and sometimes due to genetic inheritance, are thought to be at the bottom of these disorders. The U.S. Surgeon General (1999) released an exhaustive report on mental health in which he declared that the accumulated weight of scientific evidence leaves no doubt about the physical origins of mental illness.

That is not to say that social factors do not contribute to mental illness. Just as culture affects the occurrence of illness and its treatment, so too it can affect mental illness. In fact, the very definition of mental illness differs from one culture to the next. Mainstream U.S. culture, for instance, considers hallucinations highly abnormal. However, many traditional cultures view them as evidence of divine favor and confer a special status on those who experience them. As we have noted throughout this textbook, a given behavior may be viewed as normal in one society, disapproved of but tolerated in a second, and labeled as sick and heavily sanctioned in a third.

A major focus of the controversy over the medical model is the *Diagnostic and Statistical Manual of Mental Disorders (DSM)*, which came out in its fifth edition in 2013 (*DSM-5*). The *DSM*, which was introduced in 1952 by the American Psychiatric Association (APA), is intended to establish standard criteria for diagnosing mental disorders. Over time, however, the classification of various conditions has changed, seeming to undercut the notion that mental disorders are fixed medical conditions. A 1987 revision, for example, dropped the diagnosis "sexual orientation disturbance," ending the treatment of homosexuality as a curable disorder. In *DSM-5,* binge eating and some forms of hoarding have been added to the list of disorders, and bereavement has been removed as a symptom of depression.

Importantly, the *DSM* is more than an academic volume. The categories it sets forth become the basis for insurance coverage, special educational and behavioral services, and medical prescriptions, and may qualify those with a diagnosis for disability benefits. Although supporters of the *DSM* acknowledge its limitations, they stress the need for practitioners to reach a consensus on the definition and treatment of mental disorders (American Psychiatric Association 2013; Satel 2013; Scheid 2013).

In contrast to the medical model, labeling theory suggests that some behaviors that are viewed as mental illnesses may not really be illnesses. For example, the U.S. Surgeon General's report (1999:5) notes that "bereavement symptoms" of less than two months' duration do not qualify as a mental disorder, but beyond that they may be redefined. Sociologists would see this approach to bereavement as labeling by those with

the power to affix labels rather than as an acknowledgment of a biological condition.

Psychiatrist Thomas Szasz (pronounced Sahz), in his book *The Myth of Mental Illness* (2010), advanced the view that numerous personality disorders are not diseases, but simply patterns of conduct labeled as disorders by significant others. The response to Szasz's challenging thesis was sharp: the commissioner of the New York State Department of Hygiene demanded his dismissal from his university position because Szasz did not "believe" in mental illness. But many sociologists embraced his model as a logical extension of examining individual behavior in a social context.

In sum, the medical model is persuasive because it pinpoints the causes of mental illness and offers treatment for disorders. Yet proponents of the labeling perspective maintain that mental illness is a distinctively social process, whatever other processes are involved. From a sociological perspective, the ideal approach to mental illness integrates the insights of labeling theory with those of the medical approach (Horwitz 2002; Scheid 2013).

Patterns of Care

For most of human history, those who suffered from mental disorders were deemed the responsibility of their families. Yet mental illness has been a matter of governmental concern much longer than physical illness has. That is because severe emotional disorders threaten stable social relationships and entail prolonged incapacitation. As early as the 1600s, European cities began to confine the insane in public facilities along with the poor and criminals. Prisoners, indignant at being forced to live with "lunatics," resisted this approach. The isolation of people with mental illness from others in the same facility and from the larger society soon made physicians the central and ultimate authority over their welfare.

A major policy development in caring for those with mental disorders came with the passage of the Community Mental Health Centers Act (1963). The CMHC program, as it is known, not only increased the federal government's involvement in the treatment of people with mental illness. It also established community-based mental health centers to treat clients on an *outpatient* basis, thereby allowing them to continue working and living at home. The program showed that outpatient treatment could be more effective than the institutionalized programs of state and county mental hospitals.

A troubling trend as state facilities for the mentally ill were closed was an increase in the number of people with mental illness who wind up in jail. About 1 in 7 state and federal prisoners and 1 in 4 people in jail have been diagnosed with serious mental disorders (Bronson and Berzofsky 2017).

The Mental Health Parity and Addiction Equity Act of 2008, which took effect in 2010, required insurers to extend comparable

Pool/Getty Images

Seeking assistance for better mental health is never easy. During the coronavirus pandemic, when people were expected to shelter in place, clients used teleconferences with trained and certified therapists to receive assistance.

benefits for mental and physical health care beginning in 2014. Despite initial concerns that this provision would greatly increase the costs of health care, initial studies indicate that this has not been the case. In fact, the Affordable Care Act took steps to further reduce the disparity between insurance coverage for mental and physical health. However, this is only a positive outcome if one has a good insurance plan, as limited coverage and costly deductibles reduce the value of insurance coverage for both physical and mental illnesses (National Alliance on Mental Illness 2018, 2020).

Population

The study of population issues engages the attention of both natural and social scientists. The biologist explores the nature of reproduction and casts light on factors that affect **fertility,** the level of reproduction in a society. The medical pathologist examines and analyzes trends in the causes of death. Geographers, historians, and psychologists also have distinctive contributions to make to our understanding of population. Sociologists, more than these other researchers, focus on the *social* factors that influence population rates and trends.

In their study of population issues, sociologists are aware that the norms, values, and social patterns of a society profoundly affect various elements of population, such as fertility, *mortality* (the death rate), and migration. Fertility is influenced by people's age of entry into sexual

unions and by their use of contraception—both of which, in turn, reflect the social and religious values that guide a particular culture. Mortality is shaped by a nation's level of nutrition, acceptance of immunization, and provisions for sanitation, as well as its general commitment to health care and health education. Migration from one country to another can depend on marital and kinship ties, the relative degree of racial and religious tolerance in various societies, and people's evaluation of their employment opportunities.

Demography: The Study of Population

Demography is the scientific study of population. It draws on several components of population, including size, composition, and territorial distribution, to understand the social consequences of population change. Demographers study geographic variations and historical trends in their effort to develop population forecasts. They also analyze the structure of a population—the age, gender, race, and ethnicity of its members. A key figure in this analysis was Thomas Malthus.

Malthus's Thesis and Marx's Response The Reverend Thomas Robert Malthus (1766–1834), who was educated at Cambridge University, spent his life teaching history and political economy. He strongly criticized two major institutions of his

Gianni Muratore/Alamy Stock Photo

An immigration officer checks the passports of passengers arriving at Palermo Airport, on the Italian island of Sicily. Population growth is a dynamic process that is affected not just by birthrate and death rate, but by the migration of people from one place or country to another.

time—the church and slavery—yet his most significant legacy to contemporary scholars is his still-controversial *Essays on the Principle of Population,* published in 1798.

Essentially, Malthus held that the world's population was growing more rapidly than the available food supply. He argued that food supply increases in arithmetic progression (1, 2, 3, 4, and so on), whereas population expands by geometric progression (1, 2, 4, 8, and so on). According to his analysis, the gap between food supply and population will continue to grow over time. Even though the food supply will increase, it will not increase nearly enough to meet the needs of an expanding world population.

Malthus advocated population control to close the gap between rising population and the food supply, yet he explicitly denounced artificial means of birth control because they were not sanctioned by religion. For Malthus, one appropriate way to control population was to postpone marriage. He argued that couples must take responsibility for the number of children they choose to bear; without such restraint, the world would face widespread hunger, poverty, and misery (Mayhew 2014).

Karl Marx strongly criticized Malthus's views on population. He could not accept the Malthusian notion that rising world population, rather than capitalism, was the cause of social ills. In Marx's opinion, there was no special relationship between world population and the supply of resources (including food). If society were well ordered, increases in population would lead to greater wealth, not to hunger and misery.

Of course, Marx did not believe that capitalism operated under these ideal conditions. He maintained that capitalism devoted resources to the financing of buildings and tools rather than to the equitable distribution of food, housing, and other necessities of life. Marx's work is important to the study of population because he linked overpopulation to the unequal distribution of resources. His concern with the writings of Malthus also testifies to the importance of population in political and economic affairs.

The insights of Malthus and Marx regarding population issues have come together in what is termed the *neo-Malthusian view,* best exemplified by the work of Paul Ehrlich (1968; Ehrlich and Ehrlich 1990), author of *The Population Bomb.* Neo-Malthusians agree with Malthus that population growth is outstretching the world's natural resources. However, in contrast to the British theorist, they insist that birth control measures are needed to regulate population increases. Showing a Marxist bent, neo-Malthusians condemn the developed nations, which despite their low birthrates consume a disproportionately large share of world resources. While rather pessimistic about the future, these theorists stress that birth control and sensible use of resources are essential responses to rising world population (J. Tierney 1990; Weeks 2016).

Studying Population Today The relative balance of births and deaths is no less important today than it was during the lifetime of Malthus and Marx. The suffering that Malthus spoke of is certainly a reality for many people of the world. Malnutrition accounts for 45 percent of the 6 million annual children deaths in developing countries. Warfare and large-scale migration intensify problems of population and food supply. For example, recent strife in Syria, Afghanistan, the Congo, and Iraq has caused maldistribution of food supplies, leading to regional health concerns. Combating world hunger may require reducing human births, dramatically increasing the world's food supply, or perhaps both. The study of population-related issues, then, seems to be essential (World Health Organization 2018).

In the United States and most other countries, the census is the primary mechanism for collecting population information. A **census** is an enumeration, or counting, of a population. The Constitution of the United States requires that a census be held every 10 years to determine congressional representation. This periodic investigation is supplemented by **vital statistics,** or records of births, deaths, marriages, and divorces that are gathered through a registration system maintained by governmental units. In addition, other government surveys provide up-to-date information on commercial developments, educational trends, industrial expansion, agricultural practices, and the status of groups such as children, the elderly, racial minorities, and single parents.

In administering a nationwide census and conducting other types of research, demographers employ many

Cartoon by Manny Francisco 2008. Used by permission of Cagle Cartoons, Inc.

In this cartoon, Manny Francisco, based in the heavily populated Philippine Islands, takes a grim Malthusian view of world hunger.

skills and techniques, including questionnaires, interviews, and sampling. The precision of population projections depends on the accuracy of a series of estimates demographers must make. First, they must determine past population trends and establish a current base population. Next, birthrates and death rates must be determined, along with estimates of future fluctuations. In projecting a nation's population trends for the future, demographers must consider migration as well, since a significant number of individuals may enter and leave a country.

Elements of Demography Demographers communicate population facts with a language derived from the basic elements of human life—birth and death. The **birthrate** (or more specifically, the *crude birthrate*) is the number of live births per 1,000 population in a given year. In 2019, for example, there were 12.4 live births per 1,000 people in the United States. The birthrate provides information on the reproductive patterns of a society.

One way demographers can project future growth in a society is to make use of the **total fertility rate (TFR).** The TFR is the average number of children born alive to any woman, assuming that she conforms to current fertility rates. The TFR reported for the United States in 2020 was 1.87 live births per woman, compared to more than 7 births per woman in a developing country such as Niger.

Mortality, like fertility, is measured in several different ways. The **death rate** (also known as the *crude death rate*) is the number of deaths per 1,000 population in a given year. In 2017, the United States had a death rate of 8.0 per 1,000 population. The infant mortality rate serves as an important indicator of a society's level of health care; it reflects prenatal nutrition, delivery procedures, and infant screening measures. The infant mortality rate also functions as a useful indicator of future population growth, since those infants who survive to adulthood will contribute to further population increases.

A general measure of health used by demographers is **life expectancy,** the median number of years a person can be expected to live under current mortality conditions. Usually the figure is reported as life expectancy *at birth*. At present, Japan reports a life expectancy at birth of 86 years—higher than the United States' figure of 79 years. In contrast, life expectancy at birth is as low as 53 in Zambia (ProQuest 2019).

The **growth rate** of a society is the difference between births and deaths, plus the difference between *immigrants* (those who enter a country to establish permanent residence) and *emigrants* (those who leave a country permanently) per 1,000 population. For the world as a whole, the growth rate is simply the difference between births and deaths per 1,000 population, since worldwide immigration and emigration must of necessity be equal (Figure 15-5).

FIGURE 15-5 POPULATION GROWTH RATE IN SELECTED COUNTRIES

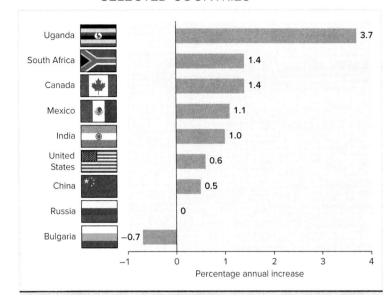

Think about It What sociological factors might cause a country to have a negative population growth rate?

Note:: Most recent data (2018).
Sources: World Bank Databank 2019. World Bank, 2019a. Accessible at www.databank.worldbank.org. *Flags:* admin_design/Shutterstock

World Population Patterns

One important aspect of demographic work involves a study of the history of population. But how is that possible? After all, official national censuses were relatively rare before 1850. Researchers interested in early population must turn to archaeological remains, burial sites, baptismal and tax records, and oral history sources. In the next section we will see what such detective work has told us about changes in population over time.

Demographic Transition On October 30, 2011, Danica May Camacho was born in a hospital in Manila, Philippines. She was designated by the United Nations to symbolically represent the 7 billionth person on earth. Until modern times, relatively few humans lived in the world. One estimate places the global population of a million years ago at only 125,000 people. As Table 15-2 indicates, in the past 200 years the world's population has exploded (Coleman 2011).

The phenomenal growth of population in recent times can be accounted for by changing patterns in births and deaths. Beginning in the late 1700s—and continuing until the mid-1900s—death rates in northern and western Europe gradually decreased. People were beginning to live longer because of advances in food production, sanitation, nutrition, and public health care. But while death rates fell, birthrates remained high; as a result, this period of European history brought unprecedented population growth. By the late 1800s, however, the birthrates of many European countries had begun to decline, and the rate of population growth had also decreased.

TABLE 15-2 ESTIMATED TIME FOR EACH SUCCESSIVE INCREASE OF 1 BILLION PEOPLE IN WORLD POPULATION

Population Level	Time Taken to Reach New Population Level	Year of Attainment
First billion	Human history before 1800	1804
Second billion	123 years	1927
Third billion	32 years	1959
Fourth billion	15 years	1974
Fifth billion	13 years	1987
Sixth billion	12 years	1999
Seventh billion	12 years	2011
Eighth billion	15 years	2026
Ninth billion	16 years	2042

Sources: Bureau of the Census 2013; Kunzig 2011:40.

The changes in birthrates and death rates that occurred in 19th-century Europe serve as an example of demographic transition. Demographers use the term **demographic transition** to describe changes in birthrates and death rates that occur during a nation's development, resulting in new patterns of vital statistics. In many nations today, we are seeing a demographic transition from high birthrates and death rates to low birthrates and death rates. As Figure 15-6 shows, this process typically takes place in three stages:

1. Pretransition stage: high birthrates and death rates with little population growth.

2. Transition stage: declining death rates—primarily the result of reductions in infant deaths—along with high to medium fertility, resulting in significant population growth.

3. Posttransition stage: low birthrates and death rates with little population growth.

The demographic transition should be regarded not as a law of population growth, but rather as a generalization of the population history of industrial nations. This concept helps us understand world population problems better. About two-thirds of the world's nations have yet to pass fully through the second stage of the demographic transition. Even if such nations make dramatic advances in fertility control, their populations will nevertheless increase greatly because of the large base of people already at prime childbearing age.

The pattern of demographic transition varies from nation to nation. One particularly useful distinction is the contrast between the rapid transition now occurring in developing nations—which include about two-thirds of the world's population—and that which occurred over the course of almost a century in more industrialized countries. In developing nations, the demographic transition

FIGURE 15-6   DEMOGRAPHIC TRANSITION

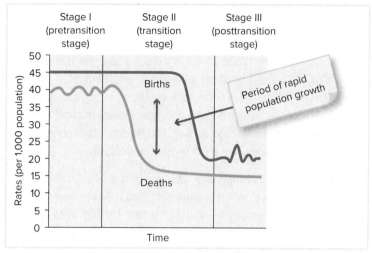

Richard T. Schaefer

Demographers use the concept of demographic transition to describe changes in birthrates and death rates that occur during a nation's development. This graph shows the pattern that takes place in developing nations. In the first stage, both birthrates and death rates are high, so there is little population growth. In the second stage, the birthrate remains high while the death rate declines sharply, leading to rapid population growth. By the last stage, which many developing countries have yet to enter, the birthrate declines as well, reducing population growth.

has involved a rapid decline in death rates, with adjustments in birthrates in some nations but not in others.

Specifically, after World War II, the death rates of developing nations began a sharp decline. This revolution in "death control" was triggered by antibiotics, immunization, insecticides (such as DDT, used to strike at malaria-bearing mosquitoes), and largely successful campaigns against such fatal diseases as smallpox. Substantial medical and public health technology was imported almost overnight from more developed nations. As a result, the drop in death rates that had taken a century in Europe was telescoped into two decades in many developing countries.

Birthrates had little time to adjust. Cultural beliefs about the proper size of families could not change as quickly as the falling death rates. For centuries, couples had given birth to as many as eight or more children, knowing that perhaps only two or three would survive to adulthood. Families were more willing to accept technological advances that prolonged life than to abandon fertility patterns that reflected time-honored tradition and religious training. The result was an astronomical population explosion that was well under way by the middle 1900s. By the middle 1970s, however, demographers observed a slight decline in the growth rate of some developing nations, as family-planning efforts began to take hold (Haub 2013; R. Lee and Reher 2011).

The Population Explosion   Often, rapid population growth is referred to in emotional terms as the "population bomb" or the "population explosion." Such striking language is not surprising, given the staggering increases in world population recorded during the 20th century (Table 15-2).

SOCIOLOGY IN THE GLOBAL COMMUNITY

15-2 Population Policy in China

In a residential district in Shanghai, a member of the local family-planning committee knocks on the door of a childless couple. Why, she inquires, have they not started a family? Such a question would have been unthinkable in 1979, when family-planning officials, in an attempt to avoid a looming population explosion, began resorting to sterilization to enforce the government rule of one child per family.

Then in 2015, the Communist Party dramatically announced it was replacing the one-child policy with a two-child allowance. This was seen as a way to confront two challenges: stagnating economic growth and an aging population, with a growing proportion of elderly people with fewer and fewer younger adults to look after them.

The legacy of nearly two generations of one child per family will not disappear soon. For example, in an effort to ensure that their one child would be a male capable of perpetuating the family line, many couples chose to abort female fetuses or quietly allowed female infants to die of neglect. As a result, in 2015, among children age 1 to 4, the sex ratio was about 116 males to 100 females—well above the normal ratio at birth of 105 to 100.

As a result of the high sex ratio, Chinese officials worry about a future with too few women. In about 20 years, they expect, almost one-fifth of young men will be unable to find brides. In an attempt to reverse the situation, the government is paying the parents of daughters to speak with other parents and persuade them to raise girls.

> *No other country in the world faces the prospect of caring for such a large population of seniors with so little social support.*

Another legacy of the one-child policy is a shortage of caretakers for the elderly. Coupled with improvements in longevity, the generation-long decline in births has greatly increased the ratio of dependent elders to able-bodied children. The migration of young adults within China has further compromised the care of the elderly. To compound the crisis, barely one in four of China's elders receives any pension at all. No other country in the world faces the prospect of caring for such a large population of seniors with so little social support.

While the two-child policy received a lot of attention in China and globally, it remains to be seen if people will adjust their family plans, given the mixed economic outlook most households face. Unlike countries such as the United States, Australia, and Canada, China can count only on internal population growth. It does not receive immigrants who can supply a young and dynamic workforce.

LET'S DISCUSS

1. Does any government, no matter how overpopulated a country is, have a right to sterilize women who do not voluntarily limit the size of their families? Why or why not?
2. What do you think has been the most dramatic consequence of the one-child policy?

Sources: Burkitt 2015; Erlanger 2015; Qi and Wang 2018; Zhang 2020.

Beginning in the 1960s, governments in certain developing nations sponsored or supported campaigns to encourage family planning. In China, the government's strict one-child policy actually produced a negative growth rate in some urban areas (Box 15-2).

Yet even if family-planning efforts are successful in reducing fertility rates, the momentum toward a growing world population is well established. Developing nations face the prospect of continued population growth, since a substantial proportion of their population is approaching the childbearing years (see the population pyramid for Syria at the top of Figure 15-7).

A **population pyramid** is a special type of bar chart that shows the distribution of a population by gender and age; it is generally used to illustrate the population structure of a society. As Figure 15-7 shows, a substantial portion of the population of Afghanistan consists of children under age 15, whose childbearing years are still to come. Thus, the built-in momentum for population growth is much greater in Afghanistan (and in many other developing countries in other parts of the world) than in the United States and especially in many European nations (see the population pyramid for Italy in the middle of Figure 15-7).

Consider the population data for India, which in 2000 surpassed 1 billion residents. Sometime around 2026, India's population will exceed China's. The substantial momentum for growth that is built into India's age structure means that the nation will face a staggering increase in population in the coming decades, even if its birthrate declines sharply (United Nations Department of Economic and Social Affairs 2019).

Population growth is not a problem in all nations. Today, a handful of countries are even adopting policies that encourage growth. One such country is Japan, where the total fertility rate has fallen sharply. Nevertheless, a global perspective underscores the serious consequences that could result from continued population growth overall.

USE YOUR SOCIOLOGICAL IMAGINATION

You are living in a country that is so heavily populated that basic resources such as food, water, and living space are running short. What will you do? How will you respond to the crisis if you are a government social planner? A politician? An ordinary citizen?

FIGURE 15-7   POPULATION STRUCTURE OF SYRIA, ITALY, AND THE UNITED STATES, 2021

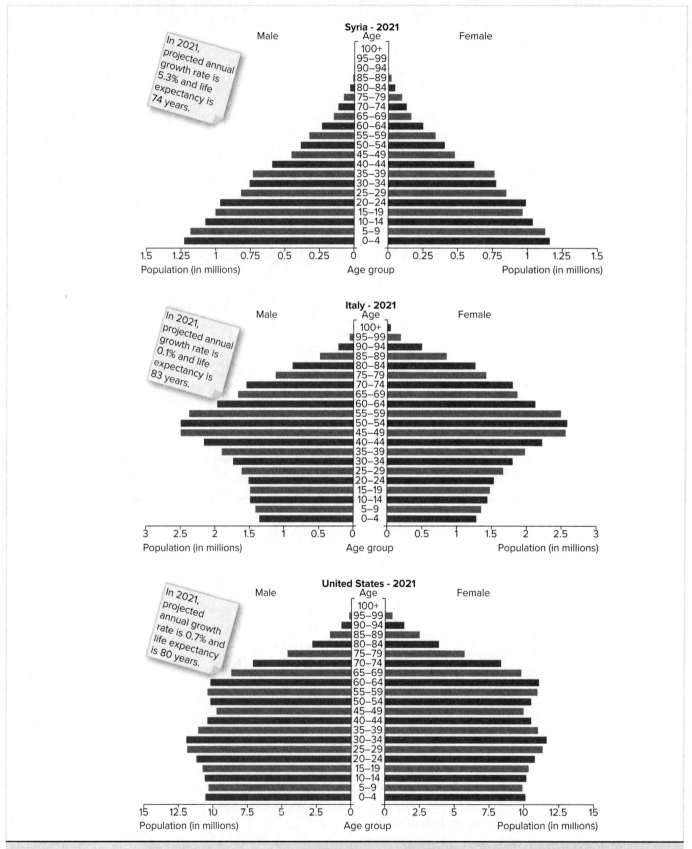

Think about It Describe the relationship between a country's fertility rate and the age of its population as shown in the graphs. How can the total population of each of these countries be expected to change over the next 50 years?

Sources: Bureau of the Census. 2020a. Accessible www.census.gov.

Fertility Patterns in the United States

Over the past six decades, the United States and other industrial nations have passed through two different patterns of population growth—the first marked by high fertility and rapid growth (stage II in the theory of demographic transition), and the second marked by declining fertility and little growth (stage III). Sociologists are keenly aware of the social impact of these fertility patterns.

The Baby Boom The most recent period of high fertility in the United States has often been referred to as the baby boom. During World War II, large numbers of military personnel were separated from their spouses. When they returned, the annual number of births began to rise dramatically. Still, the baby boom was not a return to the large families common in the 1800s. In fact, there was only a slight increase in the proportion of couples having three or more children. Instead, the boom was the result of a striking decrease in the number of childless marriages and one-child families. Although a peak was reached in 1957, the nation maintained a relatively high birthrate of over 20 live births per 1,000 population until 1964. By 2020 the birthrate had fallen to under 12 live births per 1,000 population (Centers for Disease Control and Prevention 2020a).

It would be a mistake to attribute the baby boom solely to the return home of large numbers of soldiers. High wages and general prosperity during the postwar period encouraged many married couples to purchase homes and have children. In addition, several sociologists—as well as feminist author Betty Friedan (1963)—have noted the strong societal pressure on women during the 1950s to marry and become mothers and homemakers (Bouvier 1980).

Stable Population Growth Although the total fertility rate of the United States has remained low over the past three decades, the nation continues to grow in size because of two factors: the momentum built into our age structure by the postwar population boom and continued high rates of immigration. First, because of the upsurge of births beginning in the 1950s, there are now many more people in their childbearing years than in older age groups (in which most deaths occur). This growth of the childbearing population represents a "demographic echo" of the baby boom generation. Consequently, the number of people born each year in the United States continues to exceed the number who die.

Second, the nation allows immigrants to enter each year. Looking ahead, immigration is the main driver of population growth. Projections show that immigrants, legal and illegal, together with their children and grandchildren, will account for 88 percent of population growth between 2015 and 2065. To put it another way, if all immigration had stopped on January 1, 2020, and previous immigrants had no more children, the United States would have 114 million fewer people by 2065 (Johnson 2020; Lopez et al. 2015).

Many countries other than the United States will not experience population growth but rather are expected to reach **zero population growth (ZPG).** ZPG is the state of a population in which the number of births plus immigrants equals the number of deaths plus emigrants. In the recent past, although some nations have achieved ZPG, it has been relatively short-lived. Yet today, projections of population change between 2019 and 2060 indicate that 55 countries, including 30 in Europe, are showing a *decline* in population (United Nations Department of Community and Social Affairs 2019).

What would a society with stable population growth be like? In demographic terms, it would be quite different from the United States of around 2019. There would be relatively equal numbers of people in each age group, and the median age of the population might perhaps be as high as 45 (compared to 37.2 in 2010). As a result, the population pyramid of the United States (as shown in Figure 15-7) would look more like a rectangle.

There would also be a much larger proportion of older people, especially age 75 and over. These citizens would place a greater demand on the nation's social service programs and health care institutions. In the United States today, the drop in births that began with the Great Recession of 2008, coupled with a slowdown in immigration, has created concerns about the growing gap between the working-age population that funds social programs and the senior citizens who rely on those programs (Last 2013).

On a more positive note, the economy would be less volatile under ZPG, since the number of entrants into the paid labor force would remain stable. ZPG would also lead to changes in family life. With fertility rates declining, women would devote fewer years to child rearing and to the social roles of motherhood; the proportion of married women entering the labor force would continue to rise.

THINKING CRITICALLY

Compare the social issues experienced by a country undergoing rapid population growth with those of a country undergoing population decline.

Migration

Along with births and deaths, migration is one of the three factors that affect population growth or decline. The term **migration** refers to the relatively permanent movement of people, with the purpose of changing their place of residence. Migration usually describes movement over a sizable distance, rather than from one side of a city to another.

As a social phenomenon, migration is fairly complex; it results from a variety of factors. The most important tend to be

radekprocyk/123RF

Refugees at this camp in Turkey are fleeing the violent conflict in Syria which began in 2011. Catastrophic conflicts such as war and terrorism often trigger massive international migrations.

economic—financial failure in the "old country" and a perception of greater economic opportunity and prosperity in the new homeland. Other factors that contribute to migration include racial and religious bigotry, dislike for prevailing political regimes, and a desire to reunite one's family. All these forces combine to *push* some individuals out of their homelands and *pull* them to areas they believe to be more attractive.

International Migration

International migration—changes of residence across national boundaries—has been a significant force in redistributing the world's population during certain periods of history. For example, the composition of the United States has been significantly altered by immigrants who came here beginning in the 19th century and continuing through the present. Their entry was encouraged or restricted by various immigration policies at different times.

In the past decade, immigration has become a controversial issue throughout much of Europe. Western Europe in particular has become a desirable destination for individuals and families from former colonies or former communist-bloc countries who are fleeing the poverty, persecution, and warfare of their native lands. The number of immigrants and, most recently, refugees from Myanmar, Syria, Iraq, and Afghanistan has been increasing at a time of widespread unemployment and housing shortages, provoking a striking rise in anti-foreign (and often openly racist) sentiment in Germany, France, the Netherlands, and other countries.

As of mid-2019, more than 70 million people worldwide were forcibly displaced as a result of conflict and persecution. About half of the uprooted were refugees who fled their home countries, while the other half were people who remain displaced by conflict within their own homelands—so-called "internally displaced" people (United Nations High Commissioner for Refugees 2020).

Internal Migration

Migratory movements within societies can vary in important ways. In traditional societies, migration often represents a way of life, as people move to accommodate the changing availability of fertile soil and wild game. In industrial societies, people may relocate because of job transfers or because they believe that a particular region offers better employment opportunities or a more desirable climate.

Although nations typically have laws and policies governing movement across their borders, the same is not true of internal movement. Generally, the residents of a country are legally free to move from one locality to another. Of course, that is not the case in all nations; historically, the Republic of South Africa restricted the movement of Blacks and other non-whites through the system of segregation known as *apartheid*.

USE YOUR SOCIOLOGICAL IMAGINATION

What would happen if present patterns of migration, both internal and international, reversed themselves? How would your hometown change? What would be the effect on the nation's economy? Would your own life change?

Sociological Perspectives on the Environment

We have seen that the environment people live in has a noticeable effect on their health. Those who live in stressful, overcrowded places suffer more from disease than those who do not. Likewise, people have a noticeable effect on their environment. Around the world, increases in population, together with the economic development that accompanies them, have had serious environmental consequences. We can see signs of despoliation almost everywhere: our air, our water, and our land are being polluted, whether we live in St. Louis, Mexico City, or Lagos, Nigeria.

Though environmental problems may be easy to identify, devising socially and politically acceptable solutions to them is much more difficult. In this section we will see what sociologists have to say about the trade-off between economic growth and development and its effects on the environment. In the section that follows, we will look more closely at specific environmental issues.

Human Ecology

Human ecology is the study of the interrelationships between people and their environment. As the environmentalist Barry Commoner (1971:39) put it, "Everything is connected to everything else." Human ecologists focus on how the physical environment shapes people's lives and on how people influence the surrounding environment.

There is no shortage of illustrations of the interconnectedness of people and their environment. For example, scientific research has linked pollutants in the physical environment to people's health and behavior. The increasing occurrence of asthma, lead poisoning, and cancer have all been tied to human alterations to the environment. Similarly, the rise in melanoma (skin cancer) diagnoses has been linked to global warming. Ecological changes in our food and diet have been related to early obesity and diabetes. And finally, global population growth has had a huge impact on the environment (see Table 15-2 in the Population section of this chapter).

With its view that "everything is connected to everything else," human ecology stresses the trade-offs inherent in every decision that alters the environment. In facing the environmental challenges of the 21st century, government policymakers and environmentalists must determine how they can fulfill humans' pressing needs for food, clothing, and shelter while preserving the environment.

Conflict Perspective on the Environment

World systems analysis shows how a growing share of the human and natural resources of developing countries is being redistributed to the core industrialized nations. This process only intensifies the destruction of natural resources in poorer regions of the world. From a conflict perspective, less affluent nations are being forced to exploit their mineral deposits, forests, and fisheries in order to meet their debt obligations. The poor turn to the only means of survival available to them: they plow mountain slopes, burn plots in tropical forests, and overgraze grasslands (Pellow and Brehm 2013).

Brazil exemplifies this interplay between economic troubles and environmental destruction. Each year more than 5.7 million acres of forest are cleared for crops and livestock. The elimination of the rain forest affects worldwide weather patterns, heightening the gradual warming of the earth. These socioeconomic patterns, with their harmful environmental consequences, are evident not only in Latin America but in many regions of Africa and Asia.

Conflict theorists are well aware of the environmental implications of land use policies in the Third World, but they contend that focusing on the developing countries is ethnocentric. First, throughout most of history, developed countries have been the major source of greenhouse gas emissions. Only recently have developing nations begun to emit greenhouse gases in the same quantities as developed nations (Environmental Protection Agency 2012). (Greenhouse gas emissions will be discussed in more detail later.)

Second, the industrialized nations of North America and Europe account for only 12 percent of the world's population but are responsible for 60 percent of worldwide consumption. Who, these theorists ask, is more to blame for environmental deterioration: the poverty-stricken and "food-hungry" populations of the world or the "energy-hungry" industrialized nations? The money that residents of developed countries spend on ocean cruises each year could provide clean drinking water for everyone on the planet. Ice cream expenditures in Europe alone could be used to immunize every child in the world. Thus, conflict theorists charge, the most serious threat to the environment comes from the global consumer class (Pellow and Brehm 2013).

Allan Schnaiberg (1994) further refined this analysis by shifting the focus from affluent consumers to the capitalist system as the cause of environmental troubles. In his view, a capitalist

helovi/E+/Getty Images

Many households recycle or adjust the thermostat to save energy, but few go as far as the dwellers of the Earthship pictured here. This dwelling, part of a community in Taos, New Mexico, utilizes passive solar heat and is made of both natural and recycled materials, such as tires. The goal is minimal reliance on public utilities and fossil fuels.

system creates a "treadmill of production" because of its inherent need to build ever-expanding profits. This treadmill necessitates the creation of increasing demand for products, the purchase of natural resources at minimal cost, and the manufacturing of products as quickly and cheaply as possible—no matter what the long-term environmental consequences. Indeed, over a century ago, Max Weber predicted that rampant industrialism would continue until "the last ton of fossil fuel has burnt to ashes" ([1904] 2011:157).

Ecological Modernization

Critics of the human ecological and conflict models argue that they are too rooted in the past. People who take these approaches, they charge, have become bogged down in addressing existing practices. Instead, proponents of **ecological modernization** focus on the alignment of environmentally favorable practices with economic self-interest through constant adaptation and restructuring (Gould and Lewis 2015).

Ecological modernization can occur on both the macro and micro levels. On a macro level, adaptation and restructuring can mean reintegrating industrial waste back into the production process. On a micro level, it can mean reshaping individual lifestyles, including the consumption patterns described at the start of this chapter. In a sense, those who practice ecological modernization seek to refute the oft-expressed notion that being environmentally conscious means "going back to nature" or "living off the grid." Even modest changes in production and consumption patterns, they believe, can increase environmental sustainability (Adua et al. 2016).

Environmental Justice

Consider Flint, Michigan, a city whose population is two-thirds Black and Hispanic. This city of over 100,000 was experiencing

Detroit Free Press/ZUMA Wire/Alamy Stock Photo

Bankrupt Flint, Michigan, a predominantly Black and Hispanic city, was forced to acquire a cheaper water supply that ended up polluting the drinking water with dangerous levels of lead.

hard times due to the closing of automobile factories. The city budget was stretched beyond its limits, and the government was taken over by the state of Michigan. Seeking to save money, in 2014 the city government chose to obtain its tap water from the Flint River, which was cheaper than buying treated water from Detroit, as it had for 50 years.

Very soon the new water source was found to cause the city's aging pipes to leach lead at unsafe levels into the water supply. This had many serious health effects on the city's people; the most severe was possible permanent injury to brain development in young children. Eventually the state of Michigan addressed the problem, first by distributing bottled water and later by addressing the underlying problem, but much irreparable damage was done. Ironically, at about the same time the state had approved a tax subsidy for a private beverage company to access a pure water aquifer in the northern part of the state to bottle water for commercial use throughout the Midwest (Michigan Civil Rights Commission 2017).

The conflict perspective sees the case of Flint as one in which pollution disproportionately harms minority groups. They view such examples as instances of where environmental justice comes into play. **Environmental justice** is a legal strategy based on claims that racial minorities are subjected disproportionately to environmental hazards. Some observers have heralded environmental justice as the "new civil rights of the 21st century" (Kokmen 2008:42). Since the start of the environmental justice movement, activists and scholars have discovered other environmental disparities that break along racial and social class lines. In general, poor people and people of color are much more likely than others to be victimized by the everyday consequences of our built environment, including the air pollution from expressways and incinerators.

Flint, Michigan, is not the only place where minority groups face toxic conditions. A national study found that the racial and ethnic composition of a community predicts drinking water quality in that community: members of minority groups are much more likely to drink low-quality water than are whites. Nationwide, people who live near toxic sites are much more likely to be African American. While income is an important factor, because poor people, regardless of race, face environmental hazards in their neighborhoods, when the researchers controlled for income differences, a significant racial gap remained. Black families are more likely to live near toxic sites than are white families with similar incomes. Also, over time whites are more likely to be able to move away from toxic communities than are their Black neighbors (Pais et al. 2014; Switzer and Teadoro 2018).

The environmental justice movement has become globalized, for several reasons. Studies show that economic inequality between nations has been increased by the unchecked growth of industrial nations, which has also harmed the environments

SOCIOLOGY IN THE GLOBAL COMMUNITY

15-3 Environmental Refugees

Three years after the Indian Ocean swallowed his home on the Bangladeshi coast, farmer Ajmad Miyah despairs of ever settling down again. He has no land or possessions, and he survives by working in other people's fields in exchange for food. "I've accepted that this is reality," the 36-year-old Miyah said. "My house will always be temporary now, like me on this Earth."

Miyah's circumstances are becoming increasingly common. Between 2008 and 2017, an average of more than 21 million people were displaced each year by weather-related events, the equivalent of 41 people every minute.

As with so many other aspects of life, the environment and population are tightly linked. Famine, typhoons, rising sea levels, expanding deserts, chronic water shortages, and earthquakes, among other environmental events, lead to migration. **Environmental refugees** are people forced to leave their communities because of natural disasters, or the effects of climate change and global warming. A particularly deadly aspect of this forced movement is that overwhelmingly the migrants are vulnerable poor people who move to developing countries that are unprepared to receive them.

Some scholars have argued that global development inequalities, as described by world systems analysis, are one of the root causes of vulnerability to environmental changes and hazards. For example, human displacement from large development projects, such as dams, irrigation systems, and land reforms, has huge social impacts.

> *The International Red Cross estimates that there are more environmental refugees fleeing natural disasters than political refugees fleeing war.*

Movement created by environmental changes is not new. Migration has been a frequent response to climate variability and change in the past. Examples include migration from environmental hardships, such as the drying of the Great Plains in the 1930s (the Dust Bowl, as it was called), and from environmental calamities, such as Hurricane Katrina in 2005. But these environmental refugees largely remained within their own countries. Increasingly, environmental refugees must cross international borders to find a place of safety.

The International Red Cross estimates that there are more environmental refugees fleeing natural disasters than political refugees fleeing war. In 10 countries affected by both conflict- and disaster-induced displacement, natural hazards displaced five times more people than armed conflict.

In 2018, extreme weather events such as severe drought in Afghanistan, tropical cyclone Gita in Samoa, and flooding in the Philippines resulted in acute humanitarian needs. According to the Internal Displacement Monitoring Centre, there were 18.8 million new disaster-related internal displacements recorded the year before. Future prospects for reducing the flow of environmental refugees are not promising.

LET'S DISCUSS

1. What environmental disasters are most likely to confront your community?
2. What does it mean to say that a person's home is temporary? What would make a person feel that way?

Sources: Environmental Justice Foundation 2015, 2017; Hunter et al. 2015; National Geographic 2015; UNHCR 2020.

---

of less developed nations. This harm occurs in many ways, but the primary one is increased temperatures, which are devastating to crop production, human health, and labor production (Diffenbaugh and Burke 2019).

An important aspect of the globalization of the environmental justice movement has been drawing attention to the growing number of environmental refugees, as described in Box 15-3.

THINKING CRITICALLY

How are the physical and human environments connected in your neighborhood or community?

Environmental Issues

Around the world, people are recognizing the need to address challenges to the environment. We will discuss the enormous challenge of global warming in this section, along with three broad areas of environmental concern. Two of them, air and

water pollution, are thought to be contributors to global warming.

Air Pollution

Worldwide, air pollution causes 4.2 million premature deaths each year. It is estimated that 91 percent of these deaths occur in developing countries. This mortality is due to exposure to very small particles that cause or exacerbate cardiovascular and respiratory disease. Unfortunately, in many regions around the world, residents have come to accept smog and polluted air as normal. Air pollution is caused primarily by emissions from automobiles and secondarily by emissions from electric power plants and heavy industries.

Although people are capable of changing their behavior, they are unwilling to make drastic permanent changes. During the coronavirus pandemic, the cessation of much human activity, especially travel, resulted in a marked, though temporary, improvement in air quality, but it did not solve the ongoing problem. Outdoor air pollution continues to be a major environmental health problem affecting everyone in low-, middle-, and high-income countries alike.

The United States is a major source of air pollution. According to the latest reports, in 2016–2018, more American cities had days of high pollution compared to 2015–2017, and many cities measured increased levels of pollution year-round. Nearly five in ten people, or over 150 million Americans, live in counties with unhealthy pollution. However as a whole, the nation's air quality ranks 12th best among 98 nations with available data in the world (American Lung Association 2020; IQAIR 2020; World Health Organization 2018).

Water Pollution

Throughout the United States, dumping of waste materials by industries and local governments has polluted streams, rivers, and lakes. Consequently, many bodies of water have become unsafe for drinking, fishing, and swimming. Around the world, pollution of the oceans is an issue of growing concern. Such pollution results regularly from waste dumping and is made worse by fuel leaks from shipping and occasional oil spills. When the oil tanker Exxon *Valdez* ran aground in Prince William Sound, Alaska, in 1989, its cargo of more than 11 million gallons of crude oil spilled into the sound and washed onto the shore, contaminating 1,285 miles of shoreline. All together, about 11,000 people joined in a massive cleanup effort that cost over $2 billion. Globally, oil tanker spills occur regularly. The oil spilled from BP's Deepwater Horizon oil platform in 2010 is estimated at *sixteen times* or more that of the Exxon *Valdez* (ITOPF 2006; Shapley 2010).

While the Exxon *Valdez* disaster was a very specific source of water pollution, about 80 percent of water pollution actually comes from the land. One of the biggest sources is runoff from many small sources, like septic tanks, cars, trucks, and boats, plus larger sources, such as farms and ranches. Millions of motor vehicle engines drop small amounts of oil each day onto roads and parking lots, and much of this makes its way to the water. In addition, some water pollution actually starts as air pollution, as particles settle into waterways and oceans. Clearly environmental concerns are interrelated (National Oceanic and Atmospheric Administration 2018).

THINKING CRITICALLY

Which issue is more significant in your local community, air or water pollution? Why?

Climate Change

Climate change is an observable alteration of the global atmosphere that affects natural weather patterns over several

Steve Allen/Brand X Picture/Alamy Stock Photo

decades or longer. Periods of climate change occurred well before humans walked the earth. Recently, climate change has included rapid *global warming.*

The term **global warming** refers to the significant rise in the earth's surface temperatures that occurs when industrial gases like carbon dioxide (CO_2) turn the planet's atmosphere into a virtual greenhouse. These *greenhouse gases,* which also include methane, nitrous oxide, and ozone, trap heat in the lower atmosphere. Even one additional degree of warmth in the globe's average surface temperature can increase the likelihood of wildfires, shrinkage of rivers and lakes, expansion of deserts, and torrential downpours, including typhoons and hurricanes. Greenhouse emissions are highest in highly industrialized nations such as Germany, Russia, and Japan. However, these nations have made efforts to reduce the emission of CO_2. In developing nations such as China and India, CO_2 emissions have greatly increased, even when population growth is taken into consideration.

"The End of Snow?" asked a newspaper headline during the 2014 Winter Olympics. Although snow will not disappear from the earth, climatologists predict that finding suitable sites for the snow-dependent international competition will become increasingly difficult. Of the 19 cities that have hosted the Winter Olympics in the past, as few as 10 might be cold enough to do so in 2050, and just 6 in 2100. For people digging out from the record snowfalls of 2014–2015, that prediction might have seemed laughable, but the global trend is toward reduced snowfall. Decline in the snowpack is now jeopardizing half of all ski resorts in the northeastern United States; if it continues, they may not be viable 30 years from now. Similar trends are threatening ski resorts in the western United States. More important, snowpack is not just for skiers; the spring runoff from

RECYCLING

Fran/www.CartoonStock.com

While many people try to do their bit by recycling, the bigger concern is reducing overall carbon emissions. Here efforts have fallen behind even the modest objectives that the major industrial nations have established for themselves.

melting snow is critical to maintaining water supplies (Fox 2014).

Although scientific concern over global warming has heated up, climate change remains low on policymakers' list of concerns. The problem seems abstract, and in many countries, officials think that the real impact of any action they may take depends on decisive action by other nations. The current major global initiative is the 2015 Paris Agreement. The agreement pledges 196 nations to respond to climate change by cutting emissions to keep the global temperature within 2 degrees Celsius (3.6 degrees Fahrenheit) of preindustrial levels.

Under the Paris Agreement each nation is allowed to set its own targets and timetables. Some countries, such as Canada and Norway, are reducing emissions at home while expanding fossil-fuel sales abroad, which is counterproductive from a global perspective. Reflecting concern that the Paris Agreement would hamper the nation's economy, President Trump declared that the United States would officially withdraw the United States from the agreement in 2020 (Heath 2020; Sengupta 2019)

We can view global warming from the point of view of world systems analysis. Historically, core nations have been the major emitters of greenhouse gases. Today, however, manufacturing has moved to semiperiphery and periphery nations, where greenhouse gas emissions are escalating. Ironically, many of the forces that are now calling for a reduction in the human activity that contributes to global warming are located in core nations, which have contributed disproportionately to

the problem. We want our hamburgers, but we decry the destruction of the rain forests to create grazing land for cattle. We want inexpensive clothes and toys, but we condemn developing countries for depending on coal-fired power plants.

What are the causes of this global environmental crisis? Some observers, such as Paul Ehrlich and Anne Ehrlich, see the pressure of world population growth as the central factor in environmental deterioration. They argue that population control is essential in preventing widespread starvation and environmental decay.

Barry Commoner, a biologist, counters that the primary cause of environmental ills is the increasing use of technological innovations that are destructive to the environment—among them plastics, detergents, synthetic fibers, pesticides, herbicides, and chemical fertilizers. Conflict theorists see the despoliation of the environment through the lens of world systems analysis. And interactionists stress efforts by informed individuals and groups to reduce their carbon footprint—that is, their daily or even lifetime production of greenhouse gases—through careful selection of the goods they

Andrew Woodley/Alamy Stock Photo

Vacation in an unspoiled paradise! Increasingly, people from developed countries are turning to ecotourism as an environmentally friendly way to see the world. The new trend bridges the interests of environmentalists and businesspeople, especially in developing countries. These birdwatchers, accompanied by a local guide, are vacationing in Uganda.

consume (Carbon Trust 2015; Commoner 1990, 2007; Ehrlich and Ellison 2002).

The Social Policy section that follows discusses environmentalism, a widespread social movement that emerged in the 1970s as people throughout the world began to see how all the environmental problems we have discussed in this section interacted.

THINKING CRITICALLY

Why is it harder for societies to address the problem of climate change than an immediate threat such as a pandemic?

socialpolicy and the Environment

Environmentalism

April 22, 2020, marked the fiftieth anniversary celebration of Earth Day, but it was unlike any previous commemoration. Gone were volunteer efforts to clean up parks and beaches, as people worldwide sheltered in place due to the coronavirus pandemic. The continuing absence of much of the world's customary human traffic led to the best air quality indexes seen in a generation from Los Angeles to Delhi to Beijing. Porpoises swam playfully in the once-filthy canals of Venice, Italy. Sea turtles migrated across empty beaches for their annual nesting rituals. Ironically, this pause in human activity seemed to show people the world's environmental problems.

Looking at the Issue

Sociologist Manuel Castells (2010a:72) has declared environmentalism "the most comprehensive, influential movement of our time." Several social trends helped to mobilize the environmental movement. First, the activist subculture of the 1960s and early 1970s encouraged people, especially young people, to engage in direct action regarding social issues. Second, the dissemination of scientific knowledge about serious environmental problems like oil spills and air pollution alarmed many Americans. And third, the growing popularity of outdoor recreation increased the number of people who were concerned about the environment. In this climate of broad-based interest in environmental issues, many organizations that had once focused narrowly on the conservation of natural resources evolved into full-fledged environmental groups (Dunlap and Mertig 1991).

Today, Earth Day has been enshrined on the calendars of city councils, zoos, and museums worldwide. Environmental issues have also moved up the agenda of mainstream political parties. Increasingly, efforts to publicize environmental concerns and create support for action have moved to the Internet. Although times have changed, two beliefs continue to galvanize environmentalists: the environment is in dire need of protection, and the government must take strong action in response. Although environmentalists recognize that they must "think locally" and monitor their own carbon footprints, they also see preservation of the environment as a global challenge.

The general public has a mixed reaction to environmental issues. On the one hand, many people question the scientific arguments behind the theory of climate change. On the other, many recognize that there is a trade-off between economic growth and preserving the environment (Figure 15-8).

Today's college students show less interest in the environment than students of past decades. In 2018, 35.8 percent of first-year college students in the United States wanted to clean up the environment—down from 45.9 percent in 1972. U.S. high school students' interest in the issue does not compare favorably with that of teens in other major countries. In a 30-nation comparative study, 15-year-olds in the United States tied those in another country for 22nd place in their knowledge of environmental issues (Organisation for Economic Co-operation and Development 2009b; Stolzenberg et al. 2019).

While surveys show modest proportions of young adults embracing environmental issues, Greta Thunberg was able to reach large numbers of youth with her earnest speech. As a result, many corporations made new environmental commitments, and talk of a Green Deal for earth modeled after the New Deal that helped ease the country out of the Depression seemed to gain new traction. Yet the upending of the world economy during the pandemic made many of these commitments problematic. According to Thunberg, the coronavirus pandemic emphasized the importance of listening to experts during a time of crisis, and the same idea should be applied to climate change. She acknowledged that the scientific community was necessarily redirected toward an immediate threat, but she took comfort in the knowledge that science has the answers for us today and in the future (Alter et al. 2019; Piccolo 2020).

Applying Sociology

Sociologists would be quick to stress that environmentalism is not a single movement. Today's activities often have grown out of conservation and preservation movements. Another long-term theme has been animal rights, which has addressed cruelty to pets and domesticated animals historically but now also questions the use of animals for purposes of testing or entertainment. The *ecofeminist* movement, which emerged in the 1980s, focuses on the typically male-dominated decision-making processes that have endangered our environment and the need to empower women to make these decisions. As climate change has become globally recognized as a major problem, U.S.-based organizations have become networked with like-minded activists throughout the world (Swer 2019).

Even those who support environmentalists' goals are troubled by the fact that nationwide, the most powerful environmental organizations are predominantly white, male-dominated, and affluent. One study notes that while women are overrepresented in the environmental

FIGURE 15-8 THE ENVIRONMENT VERSUS ECONOMIC GROWTH

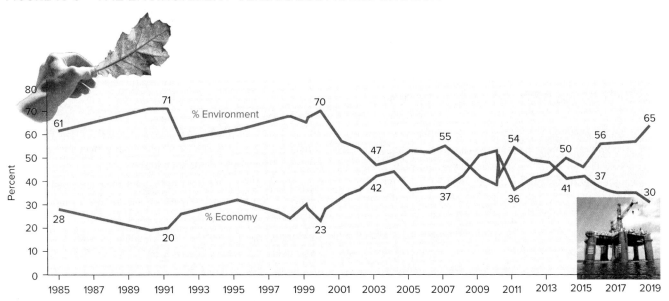

Note: Question asked: With which of these statements do you most agree: protection of the environment should be given priority, even at the risk of curbing economic growth, OR economic growth should be given priority, even if the environment suffers to some extent?

Sources: Saad, Lydia. "Preference for Environment Over Economy Largest Since 2000." April 4, 2019. Accessible at www.gallup.com. Photos: (leaf): Dynamic Graphics Group/Getty Images (*drilling platform*): Malcolm Fife/age fotostock

movement (particularly in grassroots environmental groups), men continue to hold most of the high-profile upper-management positions in mainstream national organizations. The perceived middle-class orientation of the movement is especially relevant given the class, racial, and ethnic factors associated with environmental hazards. As we saw earlier in the context of environmental justice, low-income communities and areas with significant minority populations are more likely than affluent white communities to be located near waste sites.

Viewed from a conflict perspective, the disproportionate exposure of the poor and minorities to environmental pollutants can act as a disincentive for others to take action. As sociologist Andrew Szasz (2007) noted in his book *Shopping Our Way to Safety*, more affluent households can try to avoid exposing themselves and their children to health hazards by drinking bottled spring water, installing water and air filters in their homes, and buying organic food. Unfortunately, these individual actions have the unintended consequence of weakening collective environmental efforts.

Another concern, from the conflict perspective, is the fact that many environmental movements either do not include the poor and minorities or do not address their concerns. Although environmental justice issues have been well publicized, environmentalists do not always consider the implications of their demands for excluded groups (Rudel et al. 2011).

Danita Delimont/Alamy Stock Photo

Some observers note that the overwhelming whiteness of the U.S. environmental movement has led it to de-emphasize issues of concern to low-income people, including the issue of environmental justice.

Initiating Policy

Currently, public opinion in the United States favors environmental progress over energy production. The Great Recession had the side-effect of reducing consumption, and as a result, energy use. The nations of the world convened in Paris in 2015 to map out a short-term and long-term strategy to combat global warming. But as has been noted, not a single fossil-fuel-burning power plant will be closed down in the immediate future as a result of the many declarations arising from that meeting.

Environmentalists are torn between two imperfect choices: applauding the steps forward (which Greenpeace did after the 2015 Paris Agreement), or criticizing governments for not doing more and urging followers to work locally (as Friends of the Earth International did) (Bond 2015).

The one certainty moving forward is that environmentalism is not a static, unchanging social phenomenon. One can anticipate that all groups' efforts will be informed by new scientific studies, but it is uncertain whether efforts to improve the environment will primarily center on global concerns such as climate change or on local issues.

It is likely that environmentalists, recognizing that green issues are intertwined with issues of economic growth and fairness, will seek to form coalitions with grassroots political and economic activists. Coalitions between environmentalists, business, and labor would sustain development while also addressing environmental issues.

For example, such coalitions might work toward the creation of energy-efficient products and the promotion of ecotourism that financially rewards preservation of natural resources. This multipronged approach is familiar to sociologists, whose study of society shows again and again that society is shaped by and reshapes the environment around it (Gould and Lewis 2015).

Take the Issue with You

1. In your community, how would you act locally to preserve the environment? Describe your community's environmental problems and explain how you would seek to solve them.

2. How do you see the trade-off between the economy and the environment? Which is more important? Is it possible to improve both at the same time? Explain.

3. Thinking globally about the environment, list what you consider the most pressing priorities. How important are world hunger and economic justice compared to global warming, clean air and water, and economic development? Are some of your priorities related? In what way?

MASTERING THIS CHAPTER

Summary

Both culture and the environment have a significant effect on our **health** and well-being. The concept of health is shaped by social definitions of behavior. This chapter considers sociological perspectives on health and the environment; the distribution of disease in a society; the evolution of the U.S. health care system; the closely connected issues of population and migration; and the environmental issues facing our planet.

1. According to Talcott Parsons's functionalist perspective, physicians function as gatekeepers for the **sick role,** either verifying a person's condition as "illness" or designating the person as "recovered."

2. Conflict theorists use the term *medicalization of society* to refer to medicine's growing role as a major institution of social control.

3. Labeling theorists suggest that the designation of a person as "healthy" or "ill" generally involves social definition by others. These definitions affect how others see us and how we view ourselves.

4. Contemporary **social epidemiology** is concerned not only with epidemics but also with nonepidemic diseases, injuries, drug addiction and alcoholism, suicide, and mental illness.

5. Studies have consistently shown that people in the lower classes have higher rates of **mortality** and disability than others.

6. Racial and ethnic minorities have higher rates of **morbidity** and mortality than whites. Women tend to be in poorer health than men but to live longer. Older people are especially vulnerable to mental health problems, such as Alzheimer's disease.

7. The preeminent role of physicians in the U.S. health care system has given them a position of dominance in their dealings with patients.

8. Many people use alternative health care techniques, such as **holistic medicine** and self-help groups.

9. Mental disorders may be viewed from two different perspectives, the **medical model** and the sociological model, which is based on **labeling theory.** In the United States, society has traditionally taken a negative, suspicious attitude toward people with mental disorders.

10. Thomas Malthus suggested that the world's population was growing more rapidly than the available food supply and that food shortages would increase over time. Karl Marx saw capitalism, not rising population, as the real cause of social ills.

11. Roughly two-thirds of the world's nations have not yet passed through the second stage of **demographic transition.** Their populations will continue to grow rapidly, whereas some developed nations' population growth has stabilized or even declined.

12. The most important factors in **migration** tend to be economic, although war and ecological catastrophe are major spurs to movement of people.

13. **Human ecology** is an area of study that stresses the interrelationships between people and their environment.

14. Conflict theorists charge that the most serious threat to the environment comes from Western industrialized nations.

15. **Environmental justice** addresses the disproportionate subjection of minorities to environmental hazards.

16. Three broad areas of environmental concern include air pollution, water pollution, and global warming. Though globalization can contribute to environmental woes, it can also have beneficial effects.

17. Environmentalism is a social movement that is dominated by affluent white people from industrialized countries. Increasingly, however, people of all races, ethnicities, social classes, and nationalities are becoming concerned about global warming and the threat it poses to our planet's health.

Key Terms

Birthrate The number of live births per 1,000 population in a given year. Also known as the *crude birthrate*. (page 389)

Brain drain The immigration to the United States and other industrialized nations of skilled workers, professionals, and technicians who are desperately needed in their home countries. (376)

Census An enumeration, or counting, of a population. (388)

Climate change An observable alteration of the global atmosphere that affects natural weather patterns over several decades or longer. (398)

Comorbidity The presence of more than one disorder in the same person. (381)

Curanderismo Latino/a folk medicine, a form of holistic health care and healing. (379)

Death rate The number of deaths per 1,000 population in a given year. Also known as the *crude death rate*. (389)

Demographic transition A term used to describe the change from high birthrates and death rates to low birthrates and death rates. (389)

Demography The scientific study of population. (387)

Ecological modernization The alignment of environmentally favorable practices with economic self-interest through constant adaptation and restructuring. (396)

Environmental justice A legal strategy based on claims that racial minorities are subjected disproportionately to environmental hazards. (396)

Environmental refugee A person who has been displaced by rising seas, destructive storms, expanding deserts, water shortages, or high levels of toxic pollutants. (397)

Fertility The level of reproduction in a society. (387)

Global warming A significant rise in the earth's surface temperatures that occurs when industrial gases like carbon dioxide turn the planet's atmosphere into a virtual greenhouse. (398)

Growth rate The difference between births and deaths, plus the difference between immigrants and emigrants, per 1,000 population. (389)

Health As defined by the World Health Organization, a state of complete physical, mental, and social well-being, and not merely the absence of disease and infirmity. (374)

Holistic medicine Therapies in which the health care practitioner considers the person's physical, mental, emotional, and spiritual characteristics. (383)

Human ecology An area of study that is concerned with the interrelationships between people and their environment. (394)

Infant mortality rate The number of deaths of infants under 1 year old per 1,000 live births in a given year. (376)

Labeling theory An approach to deviance that attempts to explain why certain people are viewed as deviants while others engaged in the same behavior are not. (377)

Life expectancy The median number of years a person can be expected to live under current mortality conditions. (389)

Medical model An approach in which medical experts define illness or disease, determine and control the course of treatment, and even affect patients' views of themselves. (375)

Mental illness A disorder of the brain that disrupts a person's thinking, feeling, and ability to interact with others. (385)

Migration The relatively permanent movement of people, with the purpose of changing their place of residence. (393)

Morbidity rate The rate of disease in a given population. (378)

Mortality rate The rate of death in a given population. (378)

Population pyramid A special type of bar chart that shows the distribution of a population by gender and age. (391)

Sick role Societal expectations about the attitudes and behavior of a person viewed as being ill. (374)

Social epidemiology The study of the distribution of disease, impairment, and general health status across a population. (378)

Stigma A label used to devalue members of certain social groups. (385)

Total fertility rate (TFR) The average number of children born alive to any woman, assuming that she conforms to current fertility rates. (389)

Vital statistics Records of births, deaths, marriages, and divorces gathered through a registration system maintained by governmental units. (388)

Zero population growth (ZPG) The state of a population in which the number of births plus immigrants equals the number of deaths plus emigrants. (393)

TAKING SOCIOLOGY with you

1. Research one or more Generation Z climate activists and take notes on what they're doing, including how and why. Share your findings with the class. Discuss if and to what degree the age and efforts of these activists motivate you to become more active.

2. Monitor your own activities over the next week. Is there anything you could be doing differently to have less of a negative impact on the environment? Discuss with the class.

3. Learn more about complementary non-pharmacological interventions such as therapy dogs currently being integrated into hospitals, nursing homes, and hospice care facilities. Take notes on their use and effectiveness and share your findings with the class.

4. Writing Sociology. Go to the United States Department of Labor's Occupational Safety and Health Administration (OSHA) website and choose a topic of interest, such as chemical hazards and toxic waste (https://www.osha.gov/topics/text-index). Write a report about what OSHA does to ensure the safety and health of workers with regards to that topic. Share your report with the class.

Self-Quiz

Read each question carefully and then select the best answer.

1. Which sociologist developed the concept of the sick role?
   a. Émile Durkheim
   b. Talcott Parsons
   c. C. Wright Mills
   d. Erving Goffman

2. Regarding health care inequities, the conflict perspective would note that
   a. physicians serve as gatekeepers for the sick role, either verifying a patient's condition as "illness" or designating the patient as "recovered."
   b. patients play an active role in health care by failing to follow a physician's advice.
   c. emigration out of the Third World by physicians is yet another way that the world's core industrialized nations enhance their quality of life at the expense of developing countries.
   d. the designation "healthy" or "ill" generally involves social definition by others.

3. Which one of the following nations has the lowest infant mortality rate?
   a. the United States
   b. Mozambique
   c. Canada
   d. Japan

4. Compared with whites, Blacks have higher death rates from
   a. heart disease.
   b. diabetes.
   c. cancer.
   d. all of the above.

5. Which theorist contends that capitalist societies, such as the United States, care more about maximizing profits than they do about the health and safety of industrial workers?
   a. Robert Merton
   b. Talcott Parsons
   c. Erving Goffman
   d. Karl Marx

6. Which program is essentially a compulsory health insurance plan for the elderly?
   a. Medicare
   b. Medicaid
   c. Blue Cross
   d. Healthpac

7. Which of the following is a criticism of the sick role?
   a. Patients' judgments regarding their own state of health may be related to their gender, age, social class, and ethnic group.
   b. The sick role may be more applicable to people experiencing short-term illnesses than to those with recurring long-term illnesses.
   c. Even such simple factors as whether a person is employed or not seem to affect the person's willingness to assume the sick role.
   d. all of the above

8. The final stage of the demographic transition is marked by
   a. high birthrates and high death rates.
   b. high birthrates and low death rates.
   c. low birthrates and high death rates.
   d. low birthrates and low death rates.

9. Which of the following approaches stresses the alignment of environmentally favorable practices with economic self-interest?
   a. conflict theory
   b. demographic transition
   c. ecological modernization
   d. environmental justice

10. Conflict theorists would contend that blaming developing countries for the world's environmental deterioration contains an element of
    a. ethnocentrism.
    b. culture shock.
    c. separatism.
    d. goal displacement.

11. A(n) _____ studies the effects of social class, race and ethnicity, gender, and age on the distribution of disease, impairment, and general health across a population.

12. From a(n) _____ perspective, "being sick" must be controlled so as to ensure that not too many people are released from their societal responsibilities at any one time.

13. The immigration to the United States and other industrialized nations of skilled workers, professionals, and technicians who are desperately needed by their home countries is known as the _____ _____.

14. Traditionally, the relationship between doctors and nurses has paralleled _____ dominance of the larger society.

15. Sociologists find it useful to consider _____ rates because they reveal that a specific disease occurs more frequently among one segment of a population compared with another.

16. _____ , or the scientific study of populations, draws on several components, including size, composition, and territorial distribution.

17. _____ _____ are records of births, deaths, marriages, and divorces that are gathered through a registration system maintained by governmental units.

18. The biologist _____ _____ blames environmental degradation primarily on technological innovations such as plastics and pesticides.

19. Regarding environmental problems, three broad areas of concern stand out: _____ pollution, _____ _____ pollution, and _____ _____.

20. _____ _____ is a legal strategy based on claims that racial minorities are subjected disproportionately to environmental hazards.

_____

Answers

1 (b); 2 (c); 3 (d); 4 (d); 5 (d); 6 (a); 7 (d); 8 (d); 9 (d); 10 (c); 11 social epidemiologist; 12 functionalist; 13 brain drain; 14 male; 15 morbidity; 16 Demography; 17 Vital statistics; 18 Barry/Commoner; 19 air; water; global warming 20 Environmental justice.

16 Social Change in the Global Community

NurPhoto/Getty Images

The people of Hong Kong protested the introduction of an extradition bill in 2019 that would have allowed authorities to extradite residents of Hong Kong to China. The so-called pro-democracy marches were met with violent resistance by the authorities, but ultimately the bill was suspended for now.

▶ INSIDE

How do electronic media affect the ways you communicate with others, on a personal level as well as throughout the wider social world?

Sociologist Victoria Carty believes that social media have had a revolutionary effect on social movements in recent years.

❝ Digital natives, millennials, Gen Y, Gen 2.0: however you label them, the generation born roughly between 1980 and 2000 has been immersed in revolutionary digital technologies since birth. For those of you who fit into this age cohort, life was experienced very differently in the 1990s, and these technological novelties have had vast repercussions at the individual and societal level. The way people communicate has fundamentally changed with the advent of new information communication technologies (ICTs), from e-mail to Snapchat. Not only can messages, photos, and videos be sent instantly, they have the potential to be spread far and wide throughout social networks—and the ramifications have been felt in all areas of society.

On a personal level, new technology has resulted in a radical shift in the way individuals view themselves and their social ties. Students of previous generations, for example, interacted in a much more limited though intimate way. Friendships and ways of communicating consisted of conversations in the cafeteria at lunch, bonding through sports or other extracurricular activities, sitting next to someone in class and passing secret notes (on paper!), or having neighborhood playmates. The main vehicle of communication was physically going to friends' houses to see whether they were free to play or using the telephone—the one or two stationary phones inside the house that the whole family shared. In sum, communication was initiated, shared, and sustained among people who knew each other personally, and it took effort on the part of the receiver and sender of information. This has changed in many ways as communication now, for

many people, takes place to a great extent through digital venues, especially among youth.

Unsurprisingly, the rise of digital technology and social media also deeply affects contentious politics as well as the organization of and participation in social movements. Over the past several years, there has been an explosion of protest activity among young people around the globe as they embrace a new vision of the future and demand radical changes in the existing economic and political systems. *Time* magazine, in fact, named the protester as its Person of the Year in 2011. . . .

In essence, the media ecology can either accelerate—or, conversely, impede—serious political discussion and debate, and ultimately facilitate displays of collective behavior. With new digital technology at their disposal, social movement actors have access to innovative media outlets that help nurture a new political terrain within which they can discuss grievances, disseminate information, and collectively make demands.

There are, of course, many factors to consider when examining recent forms of collective behavior—namely, the austere economic conditions around the globe, political disenfranchisement, and a lack of accountability among political elites. People are challenging political authorities, entrenched dictators, and political and economic systems once taken for granted. On a more micro and individual level, and particularly as it pertains to youth, individuals aided by digital technology are mobilizing to confront skyrocketing debt and current policies regarding immigration through contentious politics. ❞

Source: Carty 2015.

Unsurprisingly, the rise of digital technology and social media also deeply affects contentious politics as well as the organization of and participation in social movements.

In *Social Movements and New Technology*, sociologist Victoria Carty reflects on the recent explosion in electronic media and the impact it is having on social movements worldwide. She herself had been involved in protests regarding U.S. involvement in the civil turmoil in Central America and later the 1990 Gulf War (Operation Desert Shield), but at the time, before the rise of social media, she understandably felt far removed from what was really going on. Even finding out where meetings or activities were being held was difficult—one had to rely on word of mouth. But as she describes, the ready availability of

social media changed all that and caused protest movements themselves to evolve in new and unexpected ways.

Social change often follows the introduction of new electronic social media. **Social change** is defined as significant alteration over time in behavior patterns and culture (W. Moore 1967). But what constitutes a "significant" alteration? Certainly the dramatic rise in formal education in the last century represents a change that has had profound social consequences. Other social changes that have had long-term and important consequences include the emergence of slavery as a system of

FIGURE 16-1 DECLINING DRIVE-INS, 1954–2019

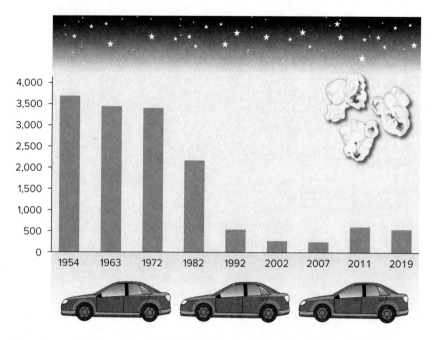

Source: Bureau of the Census 2017a, United Drive-In Theater Owners Association 2019.(photo): ESB Professional/Shutterstock

FIGURE 16-2 WALKING TO WORK, 1980–2018

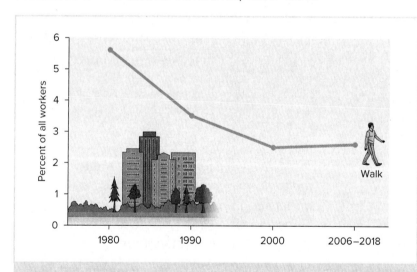

Think about It What factors might account for these two social changes? Are the changes in walking patterns and the numbers of drive-in movies connected?

Source: Aevez 2019: Table 1; McKenzie 2014.

stratification, the Industrial Revolution, and the increased participation of women in the paid labor forces of the United States and Europe.

Consider two changes to which you probably have not given much thought. First is the decline of drive-in movie theaters in the United States (Figure 16-1). You may have never been to a drive-in, but half a century ago they were a major entertainment destination. Now we go to a multiplex or stream movies ratherthan go to a drive-in. Interestingly, in the aftermath of the coronavirus pandemic, some of the remaining drive-ins were the first theaters to re-open and thus were the first to run new Hollywood releases. Social distancing was maintained by using only every other car spot as well as by delivering food to the patrons rather than letting them congregate in the dining area (Karmi 2020).

A second example of social change is walking to work (Figure 16-2). Who does that anymore in the United States? Not many. In certain urban areas it is a bit more common—12 percent in Seattle, 13 percent in Washington, D.C., and San Francisco, and 15 percent in Boston, but almost anywhere else, it just does not happen (Aevaz 2019: Table 2).

How does social change happen? Is the process unpredictable, or can we make certain generalizations about it? How has globalization contributed to social change? In this chapter we examine the process of social change, with special emphasis on the impact of globalization. We begin with *social movements*—collective efforts to bring about deliberate social change. We will see that recent advances in communications technology have allowed some social movements to circle the world.

Next, we examine three theories of social change: the evolutionary, functionalist, and conflict perspectives. Then we discuss vested interests, which often attempt to block changes they see as threatening. And we recognize the influence of globalization in spreading social change around the world, noting the rapid social change that has occurred over a matter of decades in the Middle Eastern city-state of Dubai. Finally, we turn to the unanticipated social change that occurs when innovations such as new technologies sweep through society. The chapter closes with a Social Policy section on a controversial aspect of global social change, the creation of *transnationals*—immigrants with an allegiance to more than one nation.

Social Movements

Although such factors as the physical environment, population, technology, and social inequality serve as sources of change, it is the *collective* effort of individuals organized into social movements that ultimately leads to change. Sociologists use the term **social movement** to refer to an organized collective activity to bring about or resist fundamental change in an existing group or society (Benford 1992). Herbert Blumer (1955:19) recognized the special importance of social movements when he defined them as "collective enterprises to establish a new order of life."

In many nations, including the United States, social movements have had a dramatic impact on the course of history and the evolution of the social structure. Consider the actions of abolitionists, suffragists, civil rights workers, activists opposed to the war in Vietnam, and Occupy Wall Street and #BlackLivesMatter protesters. Members of each social movement stepped outside traditional channels for bringing about social change, yet each had a noticeable influence on public policy. Decades ago, equally dramatic collective efforts helped to topple communist regimes in Eastern Europe in a largely peaceful manner, in nations that many observers had thought were "immune" to such social change.

Though social movements imply the existence of conflict, we can also analyze their activities from a functionalist perspective. Even when they are unsuccessful, social movements contribute to the formation of public opinion. Initially, people thought the ideas of Margaret Sanger and other early advocates of birth control were radical, yet contraceptives are now widely available in the United States.

Because social movements know no borders, even nationalistic movements are deeply influenced by global events. Increasingly, social movements are taking on an international dimension from the start. Global enterprises, in particular, lend themselves to targeting through global mobilization, whether they are corporations like McDonald's or governmental bodies like the World Trade Organization. Global activism is not new, however; it began with the writing of Karl Marx, who sought to mobilize oppressed peoples in other industrialized countries. Today, activist networking is facilitated by the Internet. Participation in global activism is much more widespread now than in the past, and passions are quicker to ignite.

How and why do social movements emerge? Obviously, people are often discontented with the way things are. What causes them to organize at a particular moment in a collective effort to effect change? Sociologists rely on two explanations for why people mobilize: the relative deprivation and resource mobilization approaches.

Relative Deprivation Approach

Those members of a society who feel most frustrated and disgruntled by social and economic conditions are not necessarily the worst off in an objective sense. Social scientists have long recognized that what is more significant is the way in which people *perceive* their situation. As Karl Marx pointed out, although the misery of the workers was important to their perception of their oppressed state, so was their position *in relation to* the capitalist ruling class (Marx and Engels [1847] 1955).

The term **relative deprivation** is defined as the conscious feeling of a negative discrepancy between legitimate expectations and present actualities. In other words, things aren't as good as you hoped they would be. Such a state may be characterized by scarcity rather than a complete lack of necessities (as we saw in the distinction between absolute and relative poverty in Chapter 8). A relatively deprived person is dissatisfied because he or she feels downtrodden relative to some appropriate reference group. Thus, blue-collar workers who live in two-family houses on small plots of land—though hardly at the bottom of the economic ladder—may nevertheless feel

NurPhoto/Getty Images

Some people do not think that public employees such as police, sanitation workers, or teachers should demonstrate for better working conditions. However, as many school districts went years without significant pay raises yet increased class size, teachers "went to the street." Here we see teachers in Chicago protesting a variety of issues.

deprived in comparison to corporate managers and professionals who live in lavish homes in exclusive suburbs.

In addition to the feeling of relative deprivation, two other elements must be present before discontent will be channeled into a social movement. People must feel that they have a *right* to their goals, that they deserve better than what they have. At the same time, the disadvantaged group must perceive that its goals cannot be attained through conventional means. This belief may or may not be correct. Whichever is the case, the group will not mobilize into a social movement unless there is a shared perception that members can end their relative deprivation only through collective action.

USE YOUR SOCIOLOGICAL IMAGINATION

Why might well-off people feel deprived?

Critics of this approach have noted that people don't need to feel deprived to be moved to act. In addition, this approach fails to explain why certain feelings of deprivation are transformed into social movements, whereas in similar situations, no collective effort is made to reshape society. Consequently, in recent years, sociologists have paid increasing attention to the forces needed to bring about the emergence of social movements (G. Martin 2015).

Resource Mobilization Approach

It takes more than desire to start a social movement. It helps to have money, political influence, access to the media, and personnel. The term **resource mobilization** refers to the ways in which a social movement utilizes such resources. Indeed, the success of a movement for change will depend in good part on what resources it has and how effectively it mobilizes them. In other words, recruiting adherents and marshaling resources is critical to the growth and success of social movements.

Leadership is a central factor in the mobilization of the discontented into social movements. Often, a movement will be led by a charismatic figure, such as Dr. Martin Luther King Jr. As Max Weber described it in 1904, *charisma* is that quality of an individual that sets him or her apart from ordinary people. Of course, charisma can fade abruptly, which helps to account for the fragility of certain social movements.

Why do certain individuals join a social movement while others who are in similar situations do not? Some of them are recruited to join. Karl Marx recognized the importance of

recruitment when he called on workers to become *aware* of their oppressed status and to develop a class consciousness. Like theorists of the resource mobilization approach, Marx held that a social movement (specifically, the revolt of the proletariat) would require leaders to sharpen the awareness of the oppressed. They would need to help workers to overcome feelings of **false consciousness,** or attitudes that did not reflect workers' objective position, in order to organize a revolutionary movement. Similarly, one of the challenges faced by women's liberation activists of the late 1960s and early 1970s was to convince women that they were being deprived of their rights and of socially valued resources (D. Miller 2014; Peoples 2019).

Gender and Social Movements

Sociologists point out that gender and sexual identities are important elements in understanding social movements. Our society has traditionally been dominated by male leaders and policymakers, and day-to-day life tends to assume that relationships are heterosexual. Further, traditional examination of the sociopolitical system tends to focus on such male-dominated corridors of power as legislatures and corporate boardrooms, to the neglect of more female-dominated domains such as households, community-based groups, and faith-based networks. While the feminist approach is changing that bias, many scholars still consider social movements only through a framing that entirely overlooks same-sex relationships.

Scholars of social movements now realize that gender can affect even the way we view organized efforts to bring about or resist change. For example, an emphasis on using rationality and cold logic to achieve goals helps to obscure the importance of passion and emotion in successful social movements. It would be difficult to find any movement—from labor battles to voting rights to animal rights—in which passion was not part of the consensus-building force. Yet calls for a more serious study of the role of emotion are frequently seen as applying only to the women's movement, because emotion is traditionally thought of as being feminine. Thus the feminist perspective informs all social protest activities, not those that seem to be women centered (Hurwitz and Taylor 2012; Taylor et al. 2020).

USE YOUR SOCIOLOGICAL IMAGINATION

Try to imagine a society without any social movements. Under what conditions could such a society exist? Would you want to live in it?

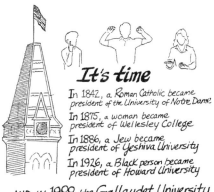

It's time

In 1842, a Roman Catholic became president of the University of Notre Dame.

In 1875, a woman became president of Wellesley College

In 1886, a Jew became president of Yeshiva University

In 1926, a Black person became president of Howard University

AND IN 1988, the Gallaudet University presidency belongs to a DEAF person.

To show OUR solidarity behind OUR mandate for a deaf president of OUR university, you are invited to participate in a historic RALLY!

Gallaudet Univ. ⟹ TUESDAY, MARCH 1ST
Football Field ⟹ 12:30–3:00 pm
BE THERE: signs, pickets, symbols and all

Illustration reprinted by permission of the publisher from John B. Christiansen and Sharon N. Barnartt, Deaf President Now! The 1988 Revolution at Gallaudet University. Gallaudet University Press, 1995, p. 22. (*photo*): Susan Biddle/The Washington Post/Getty Images

Gallaudet University in Washington, D.C., is the only four-year liberal arts college for deaf students in the United States. A leaflet was distributed in 1988 as part of a successful effort by students, faculty, and alumni to force the appointment of the university's first deaf president. In 2007, after that president's retirement, students protested once again over the election process. Ultimately an experienced college administrator who was born deaf was appointed. The mobilization of resources, including leaflets, is one key to the success of a social movement.

New Social Movements

Beginning in the late 1960s, European social scientists observed a change in both the composition and the targets of emerging social movements. Previously, traditional social movements had focused on economic issues, often led by labor unions or by people who shared the same occupation. However, many social movements that have become active in recent decades—including the contemporary women's movement, the peace movement, and the environmental movement—do not have the social-class roots typical of the labor protests in the United States, Europe, and Bangladesh over the past century (Tilly 1993, 2004).

The term **new social movement** refers to an organized collective activity that addresses values and social identities, as well as improvements in the quality of life. These movements may be involved in developing collective identities. Many have complex agendas that go beyond a single issue, and even cross national boundaries. Educated, middle-class people are significantly represented in some of these new social movements, such as the women's movement and the movement for lesbian and gay rights. Box 16-1 describes the women's movements in South Korea, India, and Bangladesh.

New social movements generally do not view government as their ally in the struggle for a better society. While they typically do not seek to overthrow the government, they may criticize, protest, or harass public officials. Researchers have found that members of new social movements show little inclination to accept established authority, even scientific or technical authority. This characteristic is especially evident in the environmental and anti–nuclear power movements, whose activists present their own experts to counter those of government or big business).

The environmental movement is one of many new movements with a worldwide focus (see the Social Policy section in Chapter 15). In their efforts to reduce air and water pollution, curtail global warming, and protect endangered animal species, environmental activists have realized that strong regulatory measures within a single country are not sufficient. Similarly, labor union leaders and human rights advocates cannot adequately address exploitative sweatshop conditions in a developing country if multinational corporations can simply move their factories to another country, where workers earn even less. Whereas traditional views of social movements tended to emphasize resource mobilization on a local level, new social movement theory offers a broader, global perspective on social and political activism.

THINKING CRITICALLY

What aspects of traditional gender roles explain the roles that women and men typically play in social movements?

SOCIOLOGY IN THE GLOBAL COMMUNITY

16-1   Women's Social Movements in South Korea, India, and Bangladesh

Women have long played a significant role in social movements. Scholars have taken two different approaches to studying these movements: a macro-level or national approach, and a more local approach to new social movements.

The macro-level approach has proved useful in studying the women's movement in South Korea. In 1987, a nationwide movement that included a variety of women's organizations toppled the country's longtime authoritarian ruler. In the democratic environment that followed his overthrow, women joined together in the Korean Women's Association United (KWAU) to seek a voice on issues involving families, the environment, education, and sexuality, including sexual harassment and assault.

Eventually, the women's movement in South Korea became an institutionalized collaborator with the central government, even receiving government grants. Progress on women's issues has not been steady, however, as some administrations have been less friendly than others to the KWAU. To gain traction, the KWAU reached out to the United Nations in its efforts to further women's social equality, and to other international bodies, such as those seeking to curb human trafficking. One of the more visible activities of the KWAU has been to organize the annual Women's Day activities. In recent years these have sparked a campaign and demonstrations on behalf of living wages and more employment opportunities for women.

In India, the women's social movement tends to be locally based, often in farming communities, where about 60 percent of the nation's 1.4 billion people live. As in other parts of the developing world, rural families in India are quite poor. For decades, villagers have been moving to the cities in hopes of earning a better income, only to be exploited in sweatshops and multinational factories. In the mid-1980s, 5,000 striking

Ahn Young-joon/AP Images

The driving force behind the annual Women's Day in South Korea has been the Korean Women's Association United (KWAU). The protest sign reads, "Preserve a living wage."

From workers' rights to the voting booth, from education to freedom from sexual violence, women's issues are an increasingly common feature of politics throughout the world.

textile workers returned to their rural villages to mobilize support for their movement. As the strike wore on, some of those women remained in the villages and sought work on government drought-relief projects. However, there weren't enough jobs for the villagers, much less for the striking textile workers.

This experience inspired a new social movement in rural India. With unemployment threatening an expanded population in rural villages, activists formed what came to be called the *Shoshit, Shetkari, Kashtakari, Kamgar, Mukti Sangharsh* (SSKKMS), which means "exploited peasants, toilers, workers liberation struggle." The movement's initial goal was to provide drought relief for farmers, but the deeper goal was to empower rural residents.

Also on the local level, Bangladeshi women, with the assistance of a charitable organization, began to share their positive

experiences of developing fishponds on small parcels of land. The harvested fish added needed protein to their diet and also became a market product to sell. The successes and challenges of this program ultimately were shared with agricultural development programs nationwide as well as in Mozambique, Burkina Faso, and Uganda.

In most respects, women in Bangladesh occupy a more inferior social position than do women in India or other south Asian nations. Researchers have found that for women who move from rural to urban areas, virtually all indicators of women's empowerment move in a positive direction. In other words, migrating to the city improves women's lives. Once in the city, the women, while they did not organize themselves into a movement, nonetheless shared their experiences and tips on how to acquire land and set aside savings. In addition, they made their own decisions on how to spend the money they earned, rather than yielding to their husbands. They also made decisions regarding the expenditure of loan money, personal and children's health care, having consensual sex with their partners, buying heavy goods for family, movement outside of the home, and using social media.

LET'S DISCUSS

1. What do you think might explain the differences between women's social movements and issues in South Korea and in India?
2. What would happen if "powerless" people in the United States formed a social movement of their own? Would it succeed? Why or why not?

Sources: Hur 2011; Korean Women's Association United 2016; Mitra 2013; Sengupta 2009; Singh 2019; Sony et al. 2020; Subramaniam 2006.

Table 16-1 summarizes the sociological approaches that have contributed to social movement theory. Each has added to our understanding of the development of social movements.

Communications and the Globalization of Social Movements

Today, through social media, activists can reach a large number of people around the world almost instantaneously, with relatively little effort and expense. As the chapter-opening excerpt shows, social networking allows organizers of social movements to enlist like-minded people without face-to-face contact, or even simultaneous interaction.

Ways of communicating have undergone dramatic change in the last ten years, and social movements are an important driver of that change. Hashtags arise to allow people to protest or to show their support for causes, but the almost universal desire for advancement and equality sometimes turns them into tools for marketing consumer goods. The need for real-time information about government action and inaction has propelled Twitter feeds into a legitimate news site. Social media have empowered feminists, immigration protesters (both for and against), LGBTQ protesters (also for and against), and environmentalists (Costanza-Chock 2014, 2019).

Sociologists have begun to refer to such electronic enhancement of established social movements as **computer-mediated communication (CMC).** Computer-mediated communication may be defined as communicative interaction through two or more networked devices, such as a computer or cell phone. The term applies to a variety of text-based or video interactions, including e-mails and text messages, some of which may be supported by social media. This kind of electronic communication strengthens a group's solidarity, allowing fledgling social movements to grow and develop faster than they might otherwise. Thus the face-to-face contact that once was critical to a social movement is no longer necessary. As Box 16-2 suggests, however, the legitimacy of such online movements is a matter of opinion (Castells 2010b).

TABLE 16-1 CONTRIBUTIONS TO SOCIAL MOVEMENT THEORY

Summing Up

Approach	Emphasis
Relative deprivation	Social movements are especially likely to arise when expectations are frustrated.
Resource mobilization	The success of social movements depends on which resources are available and how effectively they are used.
New social movement	Social movements arise when people are motivated by value issues and social identity questions.

Nicholas Kamm/AFP/Getty Images

During the coronavirus pandemic many people were reluctant to accept government orders to remain at home or limit outdoor and face-to-face retail business activity.

The new global communication technology allows us to collect every single bit of data about a person including medical information. This could be critical in stemming a communicable disease such as COVID-19. It would allow contact tracing by identifying everyone patients had been in contact with during the incubation period for an infection. Such tracing would allow for sustainable and effective quarantine of contacts to prevent additional transmission. Whether people will willingly allow themselves to be monitored for public health is unclear. Interestingly, initial surveys show that only 30 percent of people in usually obedient Singapore were willing to turn the government app on (Messier 2020).

USE YOUR SOCIOLOGICAL IMAGINATION

Have you ever learned about a social movement outside the United States through social media?

Theories of Social Change

We have defined *social change* as significant alteration over time in behavior patterns and culture. Social change can occur so slowly as to be almost undetectable to those it affects, but it can also happen with breathtaking rapidity. As Figure 16-3 shows, it is anticipated that occupational groups like health care, services, and computer-related fields will grow well above the projected growth of 5 percent for all jobs.

Explaining social change is clearly a challenge in the diverse and complex world we inhabit today.

OUR WIRED WORLD

16-2 Organizing for Controversy via Computer-Mediated Communication

Social movements are not just visible on the street but also online. Manuel Castells observed that since communication is central to social transformations, and because communication has itself undergone transformation, so will the mobilization of social movements. Hashtags such as HandsUpDon'tShoot, MeToo, TimesUp, and BlackLivesMatter, to name just a few, serve as online rallying points for specific causes. What gives this form of communication such power?

Unlike more traditional forms of communication, social media can be used almost anywhere by almost anyone with a cause, from street protesters to people trying to launch a petition from home. The widespread use of computer-mediated communication in antigovernment social movements is not lost on those in authority, who monitor and sometimes seek to control citizens' access to networked communications. Around

Photodisc/Getty Images

On the street or on the Internet, social movements may be seen either as promoting desirable social change or as supporting negative behaviors that many people find objectionable.

the world, government leaders worry about people using the Internet and social media to incite terrorist acts.

Just as disturbing to many people are sites that promote what they see as destructive or self-destructive behavior, such as websites that encourage self-injury or anorexia and bulimia (disorders characterized by little or no eating or by overeating and purging). Social media groups for those who engage in these life-threatening behaviors are flourishing. Screen displays urge participants to "go public" by sending in for a beaded bracelet that supports their behavior.

To counteract these sites, members of the medical community have established websites to promote recovery and safe behavior. Their actions illustrate the double-edged nature of free expression. On the street or on the Internet, social movements may be seen either as promoting desirable social change or as supporting negative behaviors that many people find objectionable.

Online activism does not necessarily broaden participation. It is very difficult for people who are poor, those with limited education, or those who live in areas with poor Internet access to participate, must less initiate, online protests. Furthermore, many online viewers are more likely to be impressed by sophisticated websites than by the digital equivalent of a hand painted placard.

LET'S DISCUSS

1. Have you ever been involved in a social or political movement whose legitimacy some people considered questionable? If so, what was the movement, and what were the objections to it? Did you consider the objections to be legitimate?
2. Can any social movement ever be totally free from controversy? Would you want to live in a society in which controversy is not tolerated?

Sources: Castells 2014; Cloud 2019; Dougherty and Elron 2020; Ilten and McInverney 2019; Schradie 2018.

Nevertheless, theorists from several disciplines have sought to analyze social change. In some instances, they have examined historical events to arrive at a better understanding of contemporary changes. We will review three theoretical approaches to change—evolutionary, functionalist, and conflict—and then take a look at resistance to social change.

Evolutionary Theory

The pioneering work of Charles Darwin (1809–1882) in biological evolution contributed to 19th-century theories of social change. Darwin's approach stresses a continuing progression

of successive life-forms. For example, human beings came at a later stage of evolution than reptiles and represent a more complex form of life. Social theorists seeking an analogy to this biological model originated **evolutionary theory,** in which society is viewed as moving in a definite direction. Early evolutionary theorists generally agreed that society was progressing inevitably toward a higher state. As might be expected, they concluded in ethnocentric fashion that their behavior and culture were more advanced than those of earlier civilizations.

Auguste Comte (1798–1857), a founder of sociology, was an evolutionary theorist of change. He saw human societies as

FIGURE 16-3   THE CHANGING U.S. ECONOMY, 1997–2028 (PROJECTED)

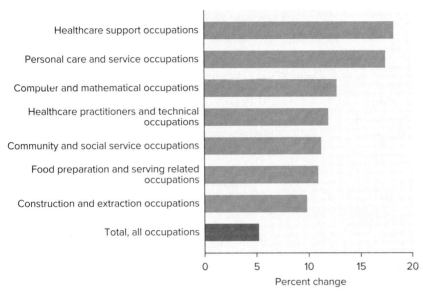

Healthcare support occupations

Personal care and service occupations

Computer and mathematical occupations

Healthcare practitioners and technical occupations

Community and social service occupations

Food preparation and serving related occupations

Construction and extraction occupations

Total, all occupations

Percent change

Source: Dubina et al. 2019: Table 12.

moving forward in their thinking, from mythology to the scientific method. Similarly, Emile Durkheim ([1893] 1933) maintained that society progressed from simple to more complex forms of social organization.

Today, evolutionary theory influences sociologists in a variety of ways. For example, it has encouraged sociobiologists to investigate the behavioral links between humans and other animals. It has also influenced human ecology, the study of the interaction between communities and their environment (Maryanski et al. 2015).

Functionalist Perspective

Because functionalist sociologists focus on what *maintains* a system, not on what changes it, they might seem to offer little to the study of social change. Yet as the work of sociologist Talcott Parsons demonstrates, functionalists have made a distinctive contribution to this area of sociological investigation.

Parsons (1902–1979), a leading proponent of the functionalist perspective, viewed society as being in a natural state of equilibrium. By "equilibrium," he meant that society tends toward a state of stability or balance. Parsons would view even prolonged labor strikes or civilian riots as temporary disruptions in the status quo rather than as significant alterations in social structure. Therefore, according to his **equilibrium model,** as changes occur in one part of society, adjustments must be made in other parts. If not, society's equilibrium will be threatened and strains will occur.

Reflecting the evolutionary approach, Parsons (1966) maintained that four processes of social change are inevitable. *Differentiation* refers to the increasing complexity of social

organization. The transition from medicine man to physician, nurse, and pharmacist is an illustration of differentiation in the field of health. This process is accompanied by *adaptive upgrading,* in which social institutions become more specialized in their purposes. The division of physicians into obstetricians, internists, surgeons, and so forth is an example of adaptive upgrading.

The next process Parsons identified is the *inclusion* of groups that were previously excluded because of their gender, race, ethnicity, or social class. Medical schools have practiced inclusion by admitting increasing numbers of women and African Americans. Finally, Parsons contends that societies experience *value generalization,* the development of new values that tolerate and legitimate a greater range of activities. The acceptance of preventive and alternative medicine is an example of value generalization: society has broadened its view of health care. All four processes identified by Parsons stress consensus—societal agreement on the nature of social organization and values (S. Best 2015).

Although Parsons's approach explicitly incorporates the evolutionary notion of continuing progress, the dominant theme in his model is stability. Society may change, but it remains stable through new forms of integration. For example, in place of the kinship ties that provided social cohesion in the past,

Think about It Which theory of social change does this best exemplify?

Fayez Nureldine/AFP/Getty Images

Social change manifests itself in very different ways from culture to culture. Beginning in 2018, women in Saudi Arabia were allowed to enter stadiums to watch soccer for the first time, although they were restricted to segregated "family sections" and separate stadium entrances.

people develop laws, judicial processes, and new values and belief systems.

Conflict Perspective

The functionalist perspective minimizes the importance of change. It emphasizes the persistence of social life and sees change as a means of maintaining society's equilibrium (or balance). In contrast, conflict theorists contend that social institutions and practices persist because powerful groups have the ability to maintain the status quo. Change has crucial significance, since it is needed to correct social injustices and inequalities.

Karl Marx accepted the evolutionary argument that societies develop along a particular path. However, unlike Comte and Spencer, he did not view each successive stage as an inevitable improvement over the previous one. History, according to Marx, proceeds through a series of stages, each of which exploits a class of people. Ancient society exploited slaves; the estate system of feudalism exploited serfs; modern capitalist society exploits the working class. Ultimately, through a socialist revolution led by the proletariat, human society will move toward the final stage of development: a classless communist society, or "community of free individuals," as Marx described it in 1867 in *Das Kapital* (see Bottomore and Rubel 1956:250).

THINKING CRITICALLY

Think back over the events of the past few days. Identify two occasions on which different people defined the same social reality differently.

As we have seen, Marx had an important influence on the development of sociology. His thinking offered insights into such institutions as the economy, the family, religion, and government. The Marxist view of social change is appealing because it does not restrict people to a passive role in responding to inevitable cycles or changes in material culture. Rather, Marxist theory offers a tool for those who wish to seize control of the historical process and gain their freedom from injustice. In contrast to functionalists' emphasis on stability, Marx argues that conflict is a normal and desirable aspect of social change. In fact, change must be encouraged as a means of eliminating social inequality.

One conflict theorist, Ralf Dahrendorf (1958), has noted that the contrast between the functionalist perspective's emphasis on stability and the conflict perspective's focus on change reflects the contradictory nature of society. Human societies are stable and long-lasting, yet they also experience serious conflict. Dahrendorf found that the functionalist and conflict

TABLE 16-2   SOCIOLOGICAL PERSPECTIVES ON SOCIAL CHANGE

Tracking Sociological Perspectives	
Evolutionary	Social change moves society in a definite direction, frequently from simple to more complex.
Functionalist	Social change must contribute to society's stability. Modest adjustments must be made to accommodate social change.
Conflict	Social change can correct social injustices and inequalities.

perspectives were ultimately compatible, despite their many points of disagreement. Indeed, Parsons spoke of new functions that result from social change, and Marx recognized the need for change so that societies could function more equitably.

Table 16-2 summarizes the differences between the three major perspectives on social change.

Resistance to Social Change

Efforts to promote social change are likely to meet with resistance. In the midst of rapid scientific and technological innovations, many people are frightened by the demands of an ever-changing society. Moreover, certain individuals and groups have a stake in maintaining the existing state of affairs.

Social economist Thorstein Veblen (1857–1929) coined the term **vested interests** to refer to those people or groups who will suffer in the event of social change. For example, efforts to regulate, restrict, or ban a product or service typically encounter stiff opposition from those who provide those goods and services. Recent history has witnessed major lobbying efforts to resist regulation by such industries as tobacco, alcohol, and firearms. More recently, policymakers and health professionals have advocated increased restriction if not an outright ban of tanning salons, to prevent unnecessary exposure to ultraviolet light, a proven cause of skin cancer. In 2003 Brazil became the first country to ban tanning beds for people under 18; in 2009 the ban was extended to cover all use for solely aesthetic purposes. Not surprisingly, a variety of organizations have sprung up in the United States to fight against similar restrictions and to discredit research that shows tanning devices to be carcinogenic to humans.

On a more micro level, studies show that individuals, even those who have in the past shown a willingness to embrace social change, tend to resist change if the status quo is treating them well (Ford 2018:133).

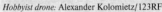
Hobbyist drone: Alexander Kolomietz/123RF   *Military drone:* U.S. Air Force

The increasing use of drones has led to a variety of concerns. For example, hobbyist drones, shown on the left, might interfere with commercial air traffic or invade people's privacy. Military drones raise ethical concerns related to the use of unmanned aircraft in combat and surveillance.

Economic and Cultural Factors

Economic factors play an important role in resistance to social change. For example, it can be expensive for manufacturers to meet high standards for the safety of products and workers, and for the protection of the environment. Conflict theorists argue that in a capitalist economic system, many firms are not willing to pay the price of meeting strict safety and environmental standards. They may resist social change by cutting corners or by pressuring the government to ease regulations.

Communities, too, protect their vested interests, often in the name of "protecting property values." The abbreviation *NIMBY* stands for "not in my backyard," a cry often heard when people protest landfills, prisons, nuclear power facilities, and even bike trails and group homes for people with developmental disabilities. The targeted community may not challenge the need for the facility, but may simply insist that it be located elsewhere. The "not in my backyard" attitude has become so common that it is almost impossible for policymakers to find acceptable locations for facilities such as hazardous-waste dumps (Jasper 2014).

On the world stage, what amounts to a "not on planet Earth" campaign has emerged. Members of this movement stress many issues, from profiteering to nuclear proliferation, from labor rights to the eradication of poverty and disease. Essentially an antiglobalization movement, it manifests itself at international meetings of trade ministers and heads of state.

Like economic factors, cultural factors frequently shape resistance to change. William F. Ogburn (1922) distinguished between material and nonmaterial aspects of culture. *Material culture* includes inventions, artifacts, and technology; *nonmaterial culture* encompasses ideas, norms, communications,

and social organization. Ogburn pointed out that one cannot devise methods for controlling and using new technology before the introduction of a technique. Thus, nonmaterial culture typically must respond to changes in material culture. Ogburn introduced the term **culture lag** to refer to the period of maladjustment when the nonmaterial culture is still struggling to adapt to new material conditions. Aerial drones are a recent example of culture lag in action. At least 50 countries use such unmanned aircraft for military surveillance or launching air-to-ground missiles or bombs. The civilian population has embraced drones for work purposes, such as surveying agricultural land, and for recreation. Yet society has only begun to deal with the nonmaterial aspects of this technology, whether it be the moral issues of unmanned warfare or the need to restrict drones from interfering with aircraft or invading people's privacy.

USE YOUR SOCIOLOGICAL IMAGINATION

What kind of social change do you find the hardest to accept? The easiest?

Resistance to Technology

Technology is cultural information about the ways in which the material resources of the environment may be used to satisfy human needs and desires. Technological innovations are examples of changes in material culture that often provoke resistance. The Industrial Revolution, which took place largely in England during the period 1760 to 1830, was a scientific revolution focused on the application of nonanimal sources of power to labor tasks. As this revolution proceeded, societies came to rely on new inventions that facilitated agricultural and industrial production and on new sources of energy, such as steam. In some industries, the introduction of power-driven machinery reduced the need for factory workers and made it easier for factory owners to cut wages.

Strong resistance to the Industrial Revolution emerged in some countries. In England, beginning in 1811, masked craft workers took extreme measures: they mounted nighttime raids on factories and destroyed some of the new machinery. The government hunted these rebels, known as **Luddites,** and ultimately banished or hung them. In a similar effort in France, angry workers threw their *sabots* (wooden shoes) into factory machinery to destroy it, giving rise to the term *sabotage.* While the resistance of the Luddites and the French workers was short-lived and unsuccessful, they have come to symbolize resistance to technology.

Are we now in the midst of a second industrial revolution, with a contemporary group of Luddites engaged in resisting? Many sociologists believe that we are living in a *postindustrial society.* It is difficult to pinpoint exactly when this era began. Generally, it is viewed as having begun in the 1950s, when for the first time the majority of workers in industrial societies became involved in services rather than in the actual manufacture of goods.

Just as the Luddites resisted the Industrial Revolution, people today resist continual technological change. The term *neo-Luddites* refers to those who are wary of technological innovations and who question the incessant expansion of information technology. Neo-Luddites object to the increasing destruction of the natural and agrarian world and the "throw-it-away" mentality of contemporary capitalism, with its resulting pollution of the environment. On top of that, people who regularly use all sorts of technology now sigh "I'm not good with technology" when faced with the latest new device or software rollout.

A slang term, *urban amish,* refers specifically to those who resist technological devices that have become part of our daily lives, such as smartphones and tablets. Such people insist that whatever the presumed benefits of industrial and postindustrial technology, such technology has distinctive social costs and may present a danger to both the future of the human species and our planet (Coron and Gilbert 2020; Urban Dictionary 2020).

Other people will resist a new technology simply because they find it difficult to use or because they suspect that it will complicate their lives. Both these objections are especially true of new information and media technologies. Whether it is hoverboards or Fitbits, many consumers are leery of these so-called must-have items.

Global Social Change

The recent past has been a truly dramatic time in history to consider global social change. Maureen Hallinan (1997), in her presidential address to the American Sociological Association, asked those present to consider just a few of the recent events: the collapse of communism; terrorism in various parts of the world, including the United States; major regime changes and severe economic disruptions in Africa, the Middle East, and Eastern Europe; the spread of AIDS; and the computer revolution. Just a few months after her remarks came the first verification of the cloning of a complex animal, Dolly the sheep. Since then, scientists have made significant strides in treating AIDS, new pandemic diseases such as COVID-19 have emerged, scholars debate the promise and threat of artificial intelligence, and scientists are building the world's largest library of human genetic information.

USE YOUR SOCIOLOGICAL IMAGINATION

What social factors might make a person or group more or less likely to embrace social change?

Anticipating Change

In this era of massive social, political, and economic change, global in scale, is it possible to predict change? Some technological changes seem obvious, but the collapse of communist governments in the former Soviet Union and Eastern Europe in the early 1990s took people by surprise. Yet prior to the Soviet collapse, sociologist Randall Collins (1986, 1995), a conflict theorist, had observed a crucial sequence of events that most observers had missed.

In seminars as far back as 1980, and in a book published in 1986, Collins had argued that Soviet expansionism had resulted in an overextension of resources, including disproportionate spending on military forces. Such an overextension will strain a regime's stability. Moreover, geopolitical theory suggests that nations in the middle of a geographic region, such as the Soviet Union, tend to fragment into smaller units over time. Collins predicted that the coincidence of social crises on several frontiers would precipitate the collapse of the Soviet Union. And that is just what happened.

During the coronavirus pandemic, many observers questioned the accuracy of health reports from countries such as North Korea and China as well as the failure to count cruise ship casualties in national totals. Sociologist Kelly Austin (2020) anticipated this gamesmanship with public health data in her examination of malaria data over a five-year period in Uganda.

left: Howard Boylan/Getty Images; right: David Cannon/Getty Images

Since 1990, the area surrounding the Emirates Golf Club in Dubai changed dramatically.

The government reported drops in the number of cases of the deadly infectious disease in certain areas, but local townspeople reported increases. Drawing upon world-systems analysis, Austin found that all nations are under intense pressure to conform to certain standards, which encourages governments, such as Uganda's, to perhaps not dig deeply enough into the official data they receive. While it may help the government's reputation to report incorrect data, it is dysfunctional to the well-being of disadvantaged people worldwide.

In her presidential address, Maureen Hallinan (1997) cautioned that we need to move beyond the restrictive models of social change—the linear view of evolutionary theory and the assumptions about equilibrium in the functionalist perspective. Hallinan noted that upheavals and major shifts do occur, and that sociologists must learn to predict their occurrence, as Collins did with the Soviet Union. Imagine, for example, the dramatic nonlinear social change that accompanies the transformation of a small, undeveloped principality into a major financial and communications hub called Dubai.

Social Change in Dubai

The story of Dubai, a Middle Eastern principality the size of Rhode Island, is a tale of two cities. When the Maktoum family took control of Dubai (pronounced Doo-Bye) in 1883, it was a pearl-fishing village on the Persian Gulf. But in 1966, the discovery of oil changed everything. When the state's oil reserves proved too limited to fund significant economic and social change, Dubai reinvented itself as a free-trade oasis. By 2000 it had become a tax-free information-technology hub. In less than a single generation—barely a decade—Dubai had transformed itself into what *Forbes* magazine calls the richest city in the world. This is a place that in the late 1950s had no electricity and no paved roads.

Wide-eyed journalists have described Dubai's air-conditioned indoor ski run, open year-round in a country where the daytime temperature averages 83 degrees. Then there is the

162-story Burj Khalifa, which opened in 2010; at more than a half-mile high, it is by far the world's tallest building. At one point, so much of the city was under construction that 10 percent of the world's construction cranes were located there.

A constitutional monarchy, Dubai is no democratic utopia—there are no contested elections, and there is little public opposition to the government. Socially, however, Dubai is relatively progressive for an Arab state. Women are encouraged to work, and there is little separation of the sexes, as is common in neighboring states. Alcohol is freely available, speech is relatively free, and the media are largely uncensored.

The citizens of Dubai share its affluence: they receive cheap electricity, free land and water, free health care and education (including graduate study abroad), as well as an average subsidy of $55,000 per year. They pay no income or property taxes. Ironically, the government handouts that citizens enjoy mean that most have little interest in competitive work, so high-skilled positions tend to go to foreigners. The social consequences of Dubai's wealth have been less than benign, however. Environmentally, the cost of its lavish lifestyle is exorbitant. In 2020, the country opened the largest coal-fired power plant in the region.

Another significant social problem, hidden from the investment bankers and tourists who visit Dubai, is the treatment of immigrant laborers. About 95 percent of people living in Dubai are temporary workers, primarily from Asia but also from Nigeria and Yemen. A million of them—seven times the number of Dubai nationals—come from India alone. These migrant laborers sold everything they owned to come to Dubai and take jobs stacking bricks, watering lawns, and cleaning floors. The pay is good, considering the lack of cash-paying jobs in their home countries, but it is very low by Western standards.

Female domestic workers are excluded from even the weak regulations that protect migrant laborers in construction. They often face significant abuse and exploitation with little opportunity to report any grievances.

Dubai's aspirations to further upward social change were hit deeply by the 2008 global recession, plummeting oil prices, and then the coronavirus pandemic, which affected the tourism and petroleum industries upon which the city of over 2 million people depends. Yet compared to much of the Arab world, Dubai remains known for a measured tolerance for outside cultural influences and an intolerance for corruption (Begum 2017; Gorney 2014; Krane 2009, 2010, 2020; Mouawad 2014; Pile 2017).

THINKING CRITICALLY

Could some of the problems Dubai faces have been anticipated?

Technology and the Future

Technological advances—the airplane, the automobile, the television, the atomic bomb, and more recently, the computer, digital media, and the smartphone—have brought striking changes to our cultures, our patterns of socialization, our social institutions, and our day-to-day social interactions. Technological innovations are, in fact, emerging and being accepted with remarkable speed (see the chapter-opening excerpt).

Computer Technology

The past decade witnessed an explosion of computer technology in the United States and around the world. Its effects were particularly noteworthy with regard to the Internet, the world's largest computer network. In 2020 the Internet reached 4.6 billion users, compared to just 50 million in 1996. Box 16-3 sketches the worldwide access to and use of the Internet.

The Internet evolved from a computer system built in 1962 by the U.S. Defense Department to enable scholars and military researchers to continue their government work even if part of the nation's communications system were destroyed by a nuclear attack. Until a generation ago, it was difficult to gain access to the Internet without holding a position at a university or a government research laboratory. Today, however, virtually anyone can reach the Internet with a cell phone or a computer. People buy and sell cars, trade stocks, auction off items, research new medical remedies, vote, and track down long-lost friends online—to mention just a few of the thousands of possibilities.

Unfortunately, not everyone can get onto the information highway, especially not the less affluent. Moreover, this pattern of inequality is global. The core nations that Immanuel Wallerstein described in his world systems analysis have a virtual monopoly on information technology; the peripheral nations of Asia, Africa, and Latin America depend on the core nations both for technology and for the information it provides. For example, North America, Europe, and a few industrialized nations in other regions possess almost all the world's *Internet hosts*—computers that are connected directly to the worldwide network.

Regardless of social class position, we have all been affected by advances in robotics developed and operated through computer technology. Digitization is transforming entire industries. The coronavirus pandemic led to the development of disinfecting robots first used in China and then worldwide. Falling prices of computing, combined with increased adaptability, have brought about an astronomical rise in the sale of robots in the industrial workplace (see Figure 16-4).

The unsettling aspect of this technological innovation is the possibility that such advances could eliminate people's jobs. This concern is not new; throughout the 20th century, first machines and then sophisticated robots took the place of human workers. Today, with software becoming steadily more sophisticated and affordable, the pace of technological innovation is increasing.

Artificial Intelligence

In 1968, Philip Dick wrote a novel called *Do Androids Dream of Electric Sheep?* that described a post-apocalyptic Earth with humans living in off-world colonies, attended by robotic

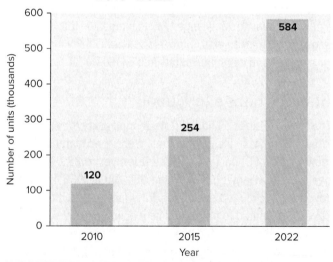

FIGURE 16-4 ESTIMATED ANNUAL GLOBAL SALE OF INDUSTRIAL ROBOTS, 2010–2022

Source: International Federation of Robotics 2019: 13, 16.

Increasingly, routine jobs are done robotically. In addition to industrial robots typically used in manufacturing and delivery, service robots work in every area from surgery to window washing. The growth in use of autonomous operating devices has led to the observation that jobs are increasingly divided into two categories, lousy and lovely, with fewer and fewer ordinary jobs in between.

OUR WIRED WORLD

16-3 The Internet's Global Profile

The old notion of an Internet accessed primarily in the United States and dominated by English-only content is passé. In fact, usage patterns are changing so fast, generalizing about global use of the Internet requires careful research and phrasing.

For example, Figure A, Internet Users by World Region, shows an Internet that is dominated by users in Asia and Europe, two relatively populous continents. However, Figure B, Internet Penetration by World Region, shows a dramatically different picture,

one in which the *proportion* of people in each region who access the Internet is highest in North America. That is, numerically, most Internet users live in Asia and Europe, but the likelihood of a person

The old notion of an Internet accessed primarily in the United States and dominated by English-only content is passé.

being an Internet user is greatest in North America. Figure B shows dramatically low Internet use in Africa, where less than 40 percent of residents access the global network.

Though English is still the primary language of Internet users, as Figure C shows, use of the Chinese language has become much more common. Interestingly, 94 percent of all Japanese speakers and German speakers use the Internet, compared to 60 percent of all Chinese speakers, though

FIGURE A INTERNET USERS BY WORLD REGION

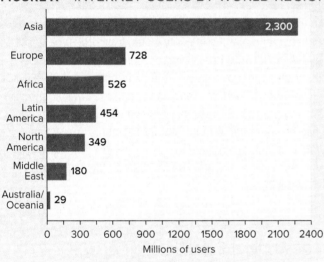

FIGURE B INTERNET PENETRATION BY WORLD REGION

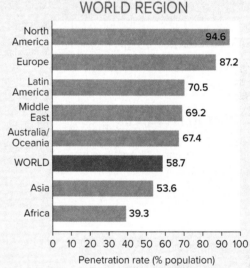

FIGURE C INTERNET'S TOP 10 LANGUAGES

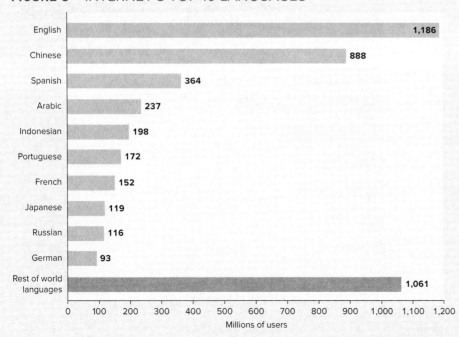

in absolute terms, speakers of Japanese and of German are a significantly smaller group.

LET'S DISCUSS

1. Of the three figures shown here, which do you think presents the most sociologically significant statistics? Explain.
2. Why do you think the use of Chinese on the Internet has increased so dramatically in just a decade? What kind of information would you expect to find in Chinese? Who would use it?

Note: Data as of March 2020 (Figures A and B) and April 2019 (Figure C).
Source: Internet World Stats 2020.

science photo/Shutterstock

The future of technology is difficult to predict. For example, 3D printers are now widely available, although still expensive, and are used increasingly to transmit both designs and objects.

servants. Subsequently made into the motion picture *Blade Runner*, this depiction of a very dreary and frightening world was set in the year 2022.

THINKING CRITICALLY

Do you sometimes see your future more in the electronic world than in the people and places around you?

images, its impact is increasingly widespread in our everyday lives. Sociologists view the adoption of AI as an example of **diffusion**—the process by which a cultural item spreads from group to group or society to society. We benefit from AI in ride-sharing apps like Uber and Lyft, autopilots on aircraft, spam filters, plagiarism checkers, mobile check deposits, online shopping, and fraud protection.

As COVID-19 spread around the globe, there was a surge in the use of cutting-edge technologies, especially AI, to track and control the pandemic. While many people worry that AI threatens human society with loss of individual control and of privacy, to public health officials and world governments the ever-expanding capabilities of AI quickly became a key element in defense against disease. AI platforms fed mountains of pharmaceutical data and research studies quickly determined that certain medications could potentially be used to treat COVID-19 patients.

Surprisingly, global surveys in 2018–2019 of human resource workers found that the majority would trust orders generated by AI. Almost two-thirds of workers said they would trust orders from a robot over those from their manager, and half have already turned to a robot instead of their manager for advice. At American Express, deciding which product offer is most relevant to different customer segments is now handled by AI, eliminating the need for managers and employees to even discuss these tasks (Adams 2020; Kobielus 2020; Schawbel 2019).

Robots and forms of artificial intelligence are another example of the way in which advances in material culture occur more quickly than changes in nonmaterial culture. **Artificial intelligence,** or AI, refers to the ability of machines, rather than humans, to address problems and perform tasks in a manner that achieves some measure of success. In the past, AI has been associated with defeating humans at chess or *Jeopardy!* but increasingly it is used to perform real-world tasks, from recognizing images to operating automotive vehicles to medical decision making.

While for the general public AI may be most visible in virtual games and computer-generated

FIGURE 16-5   THE IMPACT OF ARTIFICIAL INTELLIGENCE ON SELECT OCCUPATIONS

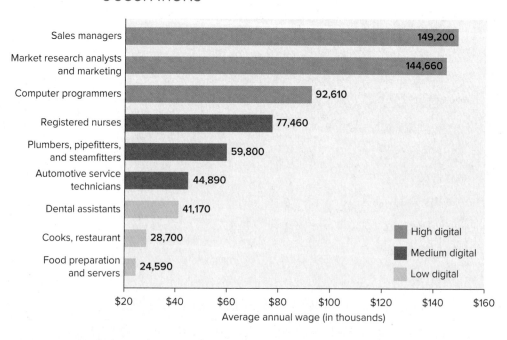

Source: The Brookings Institution in Muro et al 2019; Bureau of Labor Statistics 2020e.

What is the implication for workers' livelihood? The use of AI in the workplace can prompt anxiety among workers. Researchers on behalf of the Brookings Institution made a detailed analysis of changes in potential earnings that AI poses for 740 occupations, covering 96 percent of all job titles. Figure 16-5 shows how the impact of AI varies widely across occupations and affects many high-paying occupations.

In the following sections, we examine various aspects of our technological future and consider their impact on social change, including the social strain they will cause. We focus in particular on recent developments in computer technology, electronic censorship, biotechnology, and artificial intelligence.

Another observation about AI reflects the conflict theorists' orientation: whatever positive advances AI brings, they will not be experienced by the world's entire population. Developing nations will lag behind industrial nations, and within affluent countries, the useful applications of AI will be concentrated among those at the top of the stratification hierarchy (Sharma 2017).

THINKING CRITICALLY

Which aspect of AI do you find most promising? Most unsettling? Explain.

Privacy and Censorship in a Global Village

Today, new robots, cars with automatic parking capability, and smartphones are bringing about sweeping social change. While much of that change is beneficial, there are some negative effects. Recent advances in computer technology have made it increasingly easy for business firms, government agencies, and even criminals to retrieve and store information about everything from our buying habits to our web-surfing patterns. In public places, at work, and on the Internet, surveillance devices now track our every move, be it a keystroke or an ATM withdrawal. The ever-present cell phone enables the most pervasive and sophisticated attacks on people's privacy and anonymity.

From a sociological point of view, the complex issues of privacy and censorship can be considered illustrations of culture lag. As usual, the material culture (technology) is changing faster than the nonmaterial culture (norms for controlling the use of technology). Too often, the result is an anything-goes approach to the use of new technologies.

Legislation regarding the surveillance of electronic communications has not always upheld citizens' right to privacy. In 1986, the federal government passed the Electronic

Communications Privacy Act, which outlawed the surveillance of telephone calls except with the permission of both the U.S. attorney general and a federal judge. Telegrams, faxes, and e-mail did not receive the same degree of protection, however. Then in 2001, one month after the terrorist attacks of September 11, Congress passed the Patriot Act, which relaxed existing legal checks on surveillance by law enforcement officers. As a result, federal agencies are now freer to gather electronic data, including credit card receipts and banking records. In 2005, Americans learned that the National Security Agency was covertly monitoring phone calls with the cooperation of major U.S. telecommunications companies. Since then, federal courts have ruled that wiretapping without warrants is legal (ACLU 2015b).

As enterprises both anticipate and confront lawsuits over privacy violations and other impacts of AI-driven applications, corporate legal officers are telling their businesses to make the building, use, and supervision of apps as transparent as possible. By the end of 2020, chief legal officers in most enterprises required that their data science teams automatically log every step in development and even write plain-language explanations for the public, policymakers, and courts.

Sociologists' views on the use and abuse of new technologies differ depending on their theoretical perspective. Functionalists take a generally positive view of the Internet, pointing to

USE YOUR SOCIOLOGICAL IMAGINATION

Do you hold strong views regarding the privacy of your electronic communications? When using a smartphone or similar device, do you ever suspect you are being watched or your actions monitored?

Andre Kudyusov/Photodisc/Alamy Stock Photo

its manifest function of facilitating communication. From their perspective, the Internet performs the latent function of empowering those with few resources—from hate groups to special-interest organizations—to communicate with the masses. Conflict theorists, in contrast, stress the danger that the most powerful groups in a society will use technology to violate the privacy of the less powerful. Indeed, officials in the People's Republic of China censor online discussion groups and web postings that criticize the government. The same abuses can occur in the United States, civil liberties advocates remind us, if citizens are not vigilant in protecting their right to privacy (Kobielus 2020; Magnier 2004).

If anything, people seem to be less vigilant today about maintaining their privacy than they were before the information age. Young people who have grown up browsing the Internet seem to accept the existence of the cookies and spyware they pick up while surfing. Many see no risk in providing personal information about themselves to the strangers they meet online. Predictably a 2019 national survey showed that one-third of those under 30 see benefits in the government and companies collecting data about them online, while only one-fifth of those over fifty years agree (Auxier et al. 2019; Turkle 2004).

Biotechnology and the Gene Pool

Another field in which technological advances have spurred global social change is biotechnology. Sex selection of fetuses, genetically engineered organisms, cloning of sheep, cows, and some small animals—these have been among the significant yet controversial scientific advances in the field of biotechnology. George Ritzer's (2018) concept of McDonaldization applies to the entire area of biotechnology. Just as the fast-food concept has permeated society, no phase of life now seems exempt from therapeutic or medical intervention. In fact, sociologists view many aspects of biotechnology as an extension of the recent trend toward the medicalization of society. Through genetic manipulation, the medical profession is expanding its turf still further (Clarke et al. 2003; Human Genome Project 2018).

One notable success of biotechnology—an unintended consequence of modern warfare—has been progress in the treatment of traumatic injuries. In response to the massive numbers of soldiers who survived serious injury in Iraq and Afghanistan, military doctors and therapists have come up with electronically controlled prosthetic devices. Their innovations include artificial limbs that respond to thought-generated nerve impulses, allowing amputees to move legs, arms, and even individual fingers. These applications of computer science to the rehabilitation of the injured will no doubt be extended to civilians.

One startling biotechnological advance is the possibility of altering human behavior or physical traits through genetic engineering. This sometimes takes the form of *genome editing,* in which scientists change the genome sequence by adding, replacing, or removing elements in the DNA. Fish and plant genes have already been mixed to create frost-resistant potato and tomato crops. More recently, human genes have been implanted in pigs to provide humanlike kidneys for organ transplant. William F. Ogburn probably could not have anticipated such scientific developments when he wrote of culture lag over 90 years earlier. However, advances like these or even the successful cloning of sheep illustrate again how quickly material culture can change, and how nonmaterial culture moves more slowly in absorbing such changes (National Academies of Sciences, Engineering, and Medicine 2017b).

Although today's biotechnology holds itself out as totally beneficial to human beings, it is in constant need of monitoring. Biotechnological advances have raised many difficult ethical and political questions, among them the desirability of tinkering with the gene pool, which could alter our environment in unexpected and unwanted ways. In particular, controversy has been growing concerning genetically modified (GM) food, an

Trevor Snapp/Bloomberg/Getty Images

A Ugandan farmer checks the price of coffee beans on his cell phone.

issue that arose in Europe but has since spread to other parts of the world, including the United States. The idea behind the technology is to increase food production and make agriculture more economical. But critics use the term *Frankenfood* (as in "Frankenstein") to refer to everything from breakfast cereals made from genetically engineered grains to fresh GM tomatoes. Members of the antibiotech movement object to tampering with nature, and are concerned about the possible health effects of GM food. Supporters of genetically modified food include not just biotech companies, but those who see the technology as a way to help feed the burgeoning populations of Africa and Asia (Shuttleworth 2015).

In contrast, less expensive and less controversial technologies can further agriculture where they are needed more, in the developing world. Consider cell phones. Unlike most new technologies, the majority of the world's cell phones are used in *less* developed countries. Relatively cheap and not as dependent as computers on expensive communications infrastructure, cell phones are common in the world's poorest areas. In Uganda, farmers use them to check weather forecasts and commodity prices. In South Africa, laborers use them to look for work. African farmers are using an iCow app that enables them to track each cow's individual gestation so they will never miss the valuable opportunity to expand their herd. Researchers at the London Business School have found that in developing countries, a 10 percent increase in cell phone use is correlated with a 0.6 percent rise in GDP (Bures 2011; Schneider 2015).

The Social Policy section that follows considers *transnationals,* immigrants who travel back and forth between the developing and developed worlds, forging human rather than technological links.

social policy and Globalization

Transnationals

Around the world, new communications technologies—cell phones, the Internet—have hastened the process of globalization. Yet without human capital, these innovations would not have spurred the huge increase in global trade and development that occurred over the last several decades. Who are the people behind the trend toward globalization? Often, they are people who see a business opportunity abroad and strike out on their own to take advantage of it. In the process, many of them become migrants.

To facilitate trade and investment with other countries, migrants often exploit their social connections and their familiarity with their home language and culture. In Southeast Asia, for example, Chinese migrants dominate the trade with China; in Africa, Indian migrants dominate. Some migrants invest directly in their home countries to get the manufactured goods they sell abroad. Opportunities abound, and those with capital and good business skills can become quite wealthy.

Between 2010 and 2019, the share of the working-age population willing to permanently migrate abroad increased in every region of the world; the total increase was 51 million. The fastest increase was in Africa and Western Asia. The slowest increase was in North America—that is, Canada, Mexico, and the United States (see Figure 16-6).

The millions of migrant laborers who leave home in search of a better life also play a role in the global economy, filling jobs where there are shortages in the labor market. Although they do not become wealthy working as landscapers or short-order cooks, they consider themselves better off than they were in the old country. Unfortunately, citizens of the host countries often react negatively to the migrants' arrival, worrying that they will take jobs away from the native-born.

Looking at the Issue

About 272 million people, or 3.5 percent of the world's population, were international migrants in 2019. That is more than double the number in 1970. The rest of the world's population were "stayers"—that is, people who continued to live in the countries where they were born. Of the migrants, about 150 million were migrant workers (United Nations Department of Economic and Social Affairs 2019a).

Figure 16-7 shows the wide difference in countries' reliance on workers from abroad. While transnationals play an important role in virtually every nation, in some countries the impact is dramatic.

Globalization has changed the immigrant experience as well as the labor market. In generations past, immigrants read foreign language newspapers to keep in touch with events in their home countries. Today, the Internet gives them immediate access to their countries and kinfolk. In this global framework, immigrants are less likely than they were in the past to think of themselves as residents of just one country. **Transnationals** are immigrants who sustain multiple social relationships that link their societies of origin with their societies of settlement.

Applying Sociology

As with other issues, sociologists differ in their opinion of transnationals, depending on their theoretical perspective. Functionalists see the free flow of immigrants, even when it is legally restricted, as one way for economies to maximize their use of human labor. Given the law of supply and demand, they note, countries with too few workers will inevitably attract laborers, while those with too many will become unattractive to residents.

FIGURE 16-6   ORIGINS AND DESTINATIONS OF TRANSNATIONALS, 2019

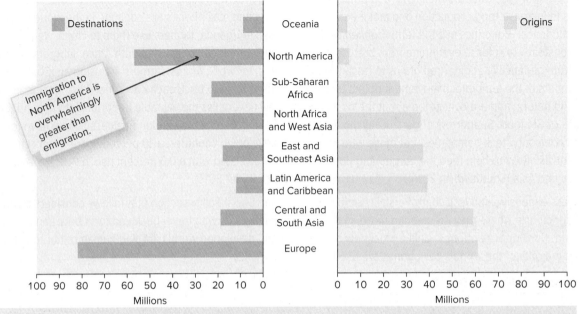

Immigration to North America is overwhelmingly greater than emigration.

Think about It What factors explain transnationals' points of origin and choices of destinations?

Source: United Nations Department of Economic and Social Affairs 2019a: Figure 2.

FIGURE 16-7   MIGRANTS AS A PERCENTAGE OF TOTAL POPULATION IN SELECTED COUNTRIES, 2019

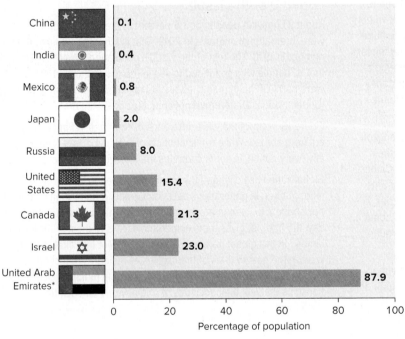

Country	Percentage
China	0.1
India	0.4
Mexico	0.8
Japan	2.0
Russia	8.0
United States	15.4
Canada	21.3
Israel	23.0
United Arab Emirates*	87.9

*Includes Dubai.

Source: United Nations Population Division 2020. *Flags:* admin_design/Shutterstock

Functionalists also embrace the assimilationist view of immigration, which emphasizes how people forsake their cultural tradition to become a part of their new society. The recognition that many transnationals sustain multiple relationships, including homeland connections, amends the assimilationist view, which ignores this aspect of

immigrants' daily lives in their new homes (Waldinger 2015).

Interactionists are interested in the day-to-day relationships transnationals have with the people around them, from those of their country of origin to those of the host country and fellow workers from other countries. These scholars are studying transnationals' involvement in local ethnic organizations, to see whether their membership facilitates or retards their integration into the host society. They have discovered that members of global social networks provide one another with mutual support and trust.

Transnationals also participate in social movements. Many transnationals immigrate either to a country with greater political freedom (for example, an Iranian immigrant to Great Britain) or from a more tolerant society to one with better work opportunities (for example, a Filipino worker in Dubai). In these situations, transnational migrants often monitor social movements that interest them via computer. They may also facilitate the growth of a social movement from a distance, by providing information, money, or both (Aunio and Staggenborg 2011).

Another question of interest to interactionists is how transnationals see themselves—how they see their own identities as well as those of their children. In effect, transnationals negotiate their identities, depending on which social network they belong to at the moment. Some sociologists note that while being a transnational can be exhilarating, it can also isolate a person, even in a city of millions. Others worry that transnationals may become "world citizens" who are so cosmopolitan that they will lose touch with their national identities (Gorman and Senquin 2018).

Feminist theorists call attention to the way that migration has historically occurred in waves: first men moved to seek better opportunities, while women stayed behind until their husbands could afford to send for them. Women's responsibilities were to care for the household and maintain connections to the larger kinship network. In today's world of global social media, women play a critical role in maintaining communications and the flow of information across borders. Physical proximity is no longer a prerequisite for family maintenance (Herrera 2013).

Feminists and conflict theorists are concerned about the degree to which female transnationals are subjected to sexual exploitation. All too often women and girls who cross national boundaries to find employment are forced to perform dehumanizing work (Wilson et al. 2015).

Another macro-level concern of conflict theorists is that transnational routes between host and recipient nations can become routinized in a way that regularizes forms of dependent and global inequality. Sending nations provide workers of optimal working ages, while the recipient country employs them at minimal wages for as long as they remain economically useful. Often they are housed in substandard, overcrowded dormitory-type conditions, which were exposed for their inadequacies as the coronavirus pandemic spread through them in Singapore and other countries (Beech 2020).

Initiating Policy

Although connecting to two societies can be an enriching experience, transnationals face continuing adjustment problems in their new home countries. As we saw with Dubai, immigrant laborers often face difficult living and working conditions. Some sending countries, such as Indonesia and the Philippines, have created national agencies to ensure the protection of their workers abroad. Their objective is ambitious, given that funding for the agencies is limited, and diplomatic and legal challenges complicate their task (United Nations Development Programme 2009:102–104).

Another unresolved transnational issue is voter eligibility. Not all nations allow dual citizenship; even those countries that do may not allow absent nationals to vote. The United States and Great Britain are

rather liberal in this regard, permitting dual citizenship and allowing émigrés to continue to vote. Mexico, in contrast, has been reluctant to allow citizens who have emigrated to vote. Mexican politicians worry that the large number of Mexicans who live abroad (especially those in the United States) might vote differently from local voters, causing different outcomes (P. Levitt and Jaworsky 2007; Sellers 2004).

Finally, the controversial issue of unauthorized immigration has yet to be settled, perhaps because of culture lag. That is, both public attitudes and government policies (nonmaterial culture) have not kept pace with, much less adjusted to, the increasing ease of migration around the globe (material culture). Though globalization has created a global labor market—one that many countries depend on, legal or illegal—the general public's attitude toward unauthorized immigration remains hostile, especially in the United States.

Antagonism is by no means limited to transnationals who are in a nation illegally. A 2018 international survey found that more than 30 percent of the people in the United States, France, Poland, Greece, Spain, and Italy, and over 60 percent in South Africa, Greece, and Hungary, view immigrants as a burden to their country and are resistant to the social change that immigration brings (Gonzalez-Barrera and Connor 2019).

Take the Issue with You

1. Suppose you live in an impoverished developing country and have the opportunity to earn a much higher income by emigrating to the United States. Will you do it, even if it means entering the country illegally and working long hours doing menial labor? If so, how will you justify your decision to those who condemn unauthorized immigration?

2. The U.S. economy depends on the cheap labor that immigrants provide. Should immigrants receive the same social services that U.S. citizens receive? What about their children who are born in the United States (and therefore are U.S. citizens)? Explain your reasoning.

3. Globalization has increased international trade and development at the same time that it has strained nations' social service systems, as migrant workers flow toward countries offering the most extensive social protection. On balance, do you think its overall effect has been beneficial or harmful? What might be done to alleviate the harmful effects of globalization?

MASTERING THIS CHAPTER

Summary

Social change is significant alteration over time in behavior patterns and culture, including norms and values. Sometimes social change is promoted by **social movements,** but more often it is the unintended effect of technological progress. This chapter examines social movements, communications and the globalization of social change, sociological theories of social change, resistance to change, global social change, and the potential effects of **technology** on the future.

1. **Social movements** are more structured than other forms of collective behavior and persist over longer periods.

2. A group will not mobilize into a social movement without a shared perception that its **relative deprivation** can be ended only through collective action.

3. The success of a social movement depends in good part on effective **resource mobilization.**

4. **New social movements** tend to focus on more than just economic issues, and often cross national boundaries.

5. Advances in communications technology—especially the Internet—have had a major impact on social movements.

6. Early advocates of the **evolutionary theory** of social change believed that society was progressing inevitably toward a higher state.

7. Talcott Parsons, a leading advocate of the functionalist perspective, viewed society as being in a natural state of equilibrium or balance.

8. Conflict theorists see change as having crucial significance, since it is needed to correct social injustices and inequalities.

9. Because people with a disproportionate share of society's wealth, status, and power are likely to suffer from social change, they have a stake in maintaining the status quo. Such people, whom Veblen called **vested interests,** will resist change.

10. The period of maladjustment when a nonmaterial culture is still struggling to adapt to new material conditions is known as **culture lag.**

11. We are living in a time of sweeping social, political, and economic change—change that occurs not just on a local or national basis, but on a global scale.

12. Computer technology has made it increasingly easy for any individual, business firm, or government agency to retrieve more and more of our personal information.

13. Although **artificial intelligence,** or AI, is quickly taking over many tasks once performed only by humans, its benefits will not be shared equally throughout the world's population.

14. Advances in biotechnology have raised difficult ethical questions about genetic engineering.

15. Globalization has increased the international migration of laborers, producing a new kind of immigrant. **Transnationals** are immigrants who sustain multiple social relationships that link their societies of origin with their societies of settlement.

Key Terms

Artificial intelligence The ability of machines, rather than humans, to address problems and perform tasks in a manner that achieves some measure of success. (page 422)

Computer-mediated communication (CMC) Communicative interaction through two or more networked devices, such as a computer or cell phone. The term applies to a variety of text-based or video interactions, including e-mails, chat rooms, and text messages, some of which may be supported by social media. (413)

Culture lag A period of maladjustment when the nonmaterial culture is still struggling to adapt to new material conditions. (417)

Diffusion The process by which a cultural item spreads from group to group or society to society. (422)

Equilibrium model Talcott Parsons's functionalist view that society tends toward a state of stability or balance. (415)

Evolutionary theory A theory of social change that holds that society is moving in a definite direction. (414)

False consciousness A term used by Karl Marx to describe an attitude held by members of a class that does not accurately reflect their objective position. (410)

Luddites Rebellious craft workers in 19th-century England who destroyed new factory machinery as part of their resistance to the Industrial Revolution. (418)

New social movement An organized collective activity that addresses values and social identities, as well as improvements in the quality of life. (411)

Relative deprivation The conscious feeling of a negative discrepancy between legitimate expectations and present actualities. (409)

Resource mobilization The ways in which a social movement utilizes such resources as money, political influence, access to the media, and personnel. (410)

Social change Significant alteration over time in behavior patterns and culture, including norms and values. (407)

Social movement An organized collective activity to bring about or resist fundamental change in an existing group or society. (409)

Technology Cultural information about the ways in which the material resources of the environment may be used to satisfy human needs and desires. (417)

Transnational An immigrant who sustains multiple social relationships that link his or her society of origin with the society of settlement. (425)

Vested interests Veblen's term for those people or groups who will suffer in the event of social change, and who have a stake in maintaining the status quo. (416)

1. Try turning off all your electronic devices—phone, laptop, and so on—for a specific period, say a day. Afterward, analyze the experiment from a sociological perspective. What functions did you lose while you were without the devices? Did you gain anything from the experience? Share your experience with the class.

2. Discuss with the class how you see social change and social movements affecting your life over the next 10–20 years. Draw upon the concepts described in the sections of this chapter on social movements and theories of social change.

3. Choose a new technology that interests you and analyze it from a sociological point of view. What do you think this technology might contribute to society? What might be some negative effects of the technology? Take notes and share your conclusions with the class.

4. **Writing Sociology.** Choose a social movement that you are interested in and do some research on it. Which sociological theory fits this movement better—relative deprivation or resource mobilization? What has been the role of communication in the movement? Write a report and share it with the class.

Self-Quiz

Read each question carefully and then select the best answer.

1. You are a student and do not own a car. All your close friends have vehicles of their own. You feel downtrodden and dissatisfied. You are experiencing
   a. relative deprivation.
   b. resource mobilization.
   c. false consciousness.
   d. depression.

2. It takes more than desire to start a social movement; it helps to have money, political influence, access to the media, and workers. The ways in which a social movement uses such things are referred to collectively as
   a. relative deprivation.
   b. false consciousness.
   c. resource mobilization.
   d. economic independence.

3. Karl Marx held that leaders of social movements must help workers overcome feelings of
   a. class consciousness.
   b. false consciousness.
   c. socialist consciousness.
   d. surplus value.

4. Organized collective activities that promote autonomy and self-determination, as well as improvements in the quality of life, are referred to as
   a. new social movements.
   b. social revolutions.
   c. resource mobilizations.
   d. crazes.

5. The text cites which of the following as a recognized definition of social change?
   a. tumultuous, revolutionary alternatives that lead to changes in leadership
   b. a significant alteration over time in behavior patterns and culture
   c. regular alteration in a consistent social frame of reference
   d. subtle alterations in any social system

6. Nineteenth-century theories of social change reflect the pioneering work in biological evolution done by
   a. Albert Einstein.
   b. Harriet Martineau.
   c. James Audubon.
   d. Charles Darwin.

7. According to Talcott Parsons's equilibrium model, during which process do social institutions become more specialized in their purposes?
   a. differentiation
   b. adaptive upgrading
   c. inclusion
   d. value generalization

8. Which of the following statements regarding Karl Marx is *not* true?
   a. Marx accepted the evolutionary argument that societies develop along a particular path.
   b. Marx believed that history proceeds through a series of stages, each of which exploits a class of people.
   c. Marx accepted Parsons's equilibrium model, which states that as changes occur in one part of society, there must be adjustments in other parts if stability is to be maintained.
   d. Marx argued that conflict is a normal and desirable aspect of social change.

9. Which of the following terms did William F. Ogburn use to refer to the period of maladjustment during which the nonmaterial culture is still struggling to adapt to new material conditions?
   a. economic shift
   b. political turmoil
   c. social change
   d. culture lag

10. Which sociological perspective sees transnationals as a way for economies to maximize their use of human labor?
    a. functionalist
    b. conflict
    c. interactionist
    d. feminist

11. _____ _____ are organized collective activities to bring about or resist fundamental change in an existing group or society.

12. A person suffering from relative deprivation is dissatisfied because he or she feels downtrodden relative to some appropriate _____ group.

13. Early evolutionary theorists concluded in a(n) _____ fashion that their own behavior and culture were more advanced than those of earlier civilizations.

14. Talcott Parsons used the term _____ to refer to the increasing complexity of social organization.

15. Social economist Thorstein Veblen coined the term _____ to refer to those people or groups who will suffer in the event of social change.

16. The term _____ refers to those who are wary of technological innovations, and who question the incessant expansion of industrialization, the increasing destruction of the natural and agrarian world, and the "throw-it-away" mentality of contemporary capitalism.

17. In 2001, one month after the terrorist attacks of September 11, Congress passed the _____ Act, which relaxed existing legal checks on surveillance by law enforcement officers. Federal agencies are now free to gather data electronically, including credit card receipts and banking records.

18. Conflict theorists are concerned that new technological advances in _____ will not be evenly experienced by the world population—that developing nations will lag far behind industrial nations.

19. In developing countries, _____ _____ are a less expensive way of furthering agriculture than is biotechnology.

20. The _____ perspective would stress the danger that the most powerful groups in a society will use technology to violate the privacy of the less powerful.

_____

Answers

1 (a); 2 (c); 3 (b); 4 (a); 5 (b); 6 (d); 7 (b); 8 (c); 9 (d); 10 (a); 11 Social movements; 12 reference; 13 ethnocentric; 14 differentiation; 15 vested interests; 16 neo-Luddites; 17 Patriot; 18 artificial intelligence or AI; 19 cell phones; 20 conflict

glossary

Absolute poverty A minimum level of subsistence that no family should be expected to live below.

Achieved status A social position that a person attains largely through his or her own efforts.

Adoption In a legal sense, the transfer of the legal rights, responsibilities, and privileges of parenthood to a new legal parent or parents.

Affirmative action Positive efforts to recruit minority group members or women for jobs, promotions, and educational opportunities.

Agrarian society The most technologically advanced form of preindustrial society. Members engage primarily in the production of food, but increase their crop yields through technological innovations such as the plow.

Alienation A condition of estrangement or dissociation from the surrounding society.

Amalgamation The process through which a majority group and a minority group combine to form a new group.

Anomie Durkheim's term for the loss of direction felt in a society when social control of individual behavior has become ineffective.

Anomie theory of deviance Robert Merton's theory of deviance as an adaptation of socially prescribed goals or of the means governing their attainment, or both.

Anti-Semitism Anti-Jewish prejudice.

Anticipatory socialization Processes of socialization in which a person rehearses for future positions, occupations, and social relationships.

Apartheid A former policy of the South African government, designed to maintain the separation of Blacks and other non-whites from the dominant whites.

Applied sociology The use of the discipline of sociology with the specific intent of yielding practical applications for human behavior and organizations.

Argot Specialized language used by members of a group or subculture.

Arranged marriage A marriage in which others (often the parents) choose a person's marital partner.

Artificial intelligence The ability of machines, rather than humans, to address problems and perform tasks in a manner that achieves some measure of success.

Ascribed status A social position assigned to a person by society without regard for the person's unique talents or characteristics.

Assimilation The process through which a person forsakes his or her cultural tradition to become part of a different culture.

Asylees Foreigners who have already entered a host country and now seek protection because of persecution or a well-founded fear of persecution.

Authority Institutionalized power that is recognized by the people over whom it is exercised.

Basic sociology Sociological inquiry conducted with the objective of gaining a more profound knowledge of the fundamental aspects of social phenomena. Also known as *pure sociology*.

Bilateral descent A kinship system in which both sides of a person's family are regarded as equally important.

Bilingualism The use of two languages in a particular setting, such as the workplace or schoolroom, treating each language as equally legitimate.

Birthrate The number of live births per 1,000 population in a given year. Also known as the *crude birthrate*.

Black power A political philosophy, promoted by many younger Blacks in the 1960s, that supported the creation of Black-controlled political and economic institutions.

Bourgeoisie Karl Marx's term for the capitalist class, comprising the owners of the means of production.

Brain drain The immigration to the United States and other industrialized nations of skilled workers, professionals, and technicians who are desperately needed in their home countries.

Bureaucracy A component of formal organization that uses rules and hierarchical ranking to achieve efficiency.

Bureaucratization The process by which a group, organization, or social movement becomes increasingly bureaucratic.

Capitalism An economic system in which the means of production are held largely in private hands and the main incentive for economic activity is the accumulation of profits.

Caste A hereditary rank, usually religiously dictated, that tends to be fixed and immobile.

Causal logic The relationship between a condition or variable and a particular consequence, with one leading to the other.

Census An enumeration, or counting, of a population.

Charismatic authority Max Weber's term for power made legitimate by a leader's exceptional personal or emotional appeal to his or her followers.

Class A group of people who have a similar level of wealth and income.

Class consciousness In Karl Marx's view, a subjective awareness held by members of a class regarding their common vested interests and the need for collective political action to bring about social change.

Class system A social ranking based primarily on economic position in which achieved characteristics can influence social mobility.

Classical theory An approach to the study of formal organizations that views workers as being motivated almost entirely by economic rewards.

Climate change An observable alteration of the global atmosphere that affects natural weather patterns over several decades or longer.

Clinical sociology The use of the discipline of sociology with the specific intent of altering social relationships or restructuring social institutions.

Closed system A social system in which there is little or no possibility of individual social mobility.

Coalition A temporary or permanent alliance geared toward a common goal.

Code of ethics The standards of acceptable behavior developed by and for members of a profession.

Cognitive theory of development Jean Piaget's theory that children's thought progresses through four stages of development.

Cohabitation The practice of living together as a male–female couple without marrying.

Colonialism The maintenance of political, social, economic, and cultural domination over a people by a foreign power for an extended period.

Color-blind racism The use of the principle of race neutrality to defend a racially unequal status quo.

Communism As an ideal type, an economic system under which all property is communally owned and no social distinctions are made on the basis of people's ability to produce.

Comorbidity The presence of more than one disorder in the same person

Computer-mediated communication (CMC) Communicative interaction through two or more networked devices, such as a computer or cell phone. The term applies to a variety of text-based or video interactions, including e-mails, chat rooms, and text messages, some of which may be supported by social media.

Conflict perspective A sociological approach that assumes that social behavior is best understood in terms of tension between groups over power or the allocation of resources, including housing, money, access to services, and political representation.

Conformity Going along with peers—individuals of our own status who have no special right to direct our behavior.

Conspicuous consumption Purchasing goods not to survive but to flaunt one's superior wealth and social standing.

Contact hypothesis An interactionist perspective which states that in cooperative circumstances, interracial contact between people of equal status will reduce prejudice.

Content analysis The systematic coding and objective recording of data, guided by some rationale.

Control group The subjects in an experiment who are not introduced to the independent variable by the researcher.

Control theory A view of conformity and deviance that suggests that our connection to members of society leads us to systematically conform to society's norms.

Control variable A factor that is held constant to test the relative impact of an independent variable.

Corporate welfare Tax breaks, bailouts, direct payments, and grants that the government gives to corporations.

Correlation A relationship between two variables in which a change in one coincides with a change in the other.

Correspondence principle A term used by Bowles and Gintis to refer to the tendency of schools to promote the values expected of individuals in each social class and to perpetuate social-class divisions from one generation to the next.

Counterculture A subculture that deliberately opposes certain aspects of the larger culture.

Creationism The literal interpretation of the Biblical account of the creation of humanity and the universe.

Credentialism An increase in the lowest level of education needed to enter a field.

Crime A violation of criminal law for which some governmental authority applies formal penalties.

Cross-tabulation A table or matrix that shows the relationship between two or more variables.

Cultural capital Noneconomic goods, such as family background and education, which are reflected in a knowledge of language and the arts.

Cultural relativism The viewing of people's behavior from the perspective of their own culture.

Cultural transmission A school of criminology that argues that criminal behavior is learned through social interactions.

Cultural universal A common practice or belief found in every culture.

Culture The totality of learned, socially transmitted customs, knowledge, material objects, and behavior.

Culture lag A period of maladjustment when the nonmaterial culture is still struggling to adapt to new material conditions.

Culture shock The feeling of surprise and disorientation that people experience when they encounter cultural practices that are different from their own.

Curanderismo Latino/a folk medicine, a form of holistic health care and healing.

Cybercrime Illegal activity primarily conducted through the use of computer hardware or software.

Death rate The number of deaths per 1,000 population in a given year. Also known as the *crude death rate.*

Degradation ceremony An aspect of the socialization process within some total institutions, in which people are subjected to humiliating rituals.

Deindustrialization The systematic, widespread withdrawal of investment in basic aspects of productivity, such as factories and plants.

Democracy In a literal sense, government by the people.

Demographic transition A term used to describe the change from high birthrates and death rates to low birthrates and death rates.

Demography The scientific study of population.

Denomination A large, organized religion that is not officially linked to the state or government.

Dependency theory An approach that contends that industrialized nations continue to exploit developing countries for their own gain.

Dependent variable The variable in a causal relationship that is subject to the influence of another variable.

Deviance Behavior that violates the standards of conduct or expectations of a group or society.

Dictatorship A government in which one person has nearly total power to make and enforce laws.

Differential association A theory of deviance proposed by Edwin Sutherland that holds that violation of rules results from exposure to attitudes favorable to criminal acts.

Differential justice Differences in the way social control is exercised over different groups.

Diffusion The process by which a cultural item spreads from group to group or society to society.

Digital divide The relative lack of access to the latest technologies among low-income groups, racial and ethnic minorities, rural residents, and the citizens of developing countries.

Discovery The process of making known or sharing the existence of an aspect of reality.

Discrimination The denial of opportunities and equal rights to individuals and groups because of prejudice or other arbitrary reasons.

Dominant ideology A set of cultural beliefs and practices that helps to maintain powerful social, economic, and political interests.

Double consciousness The division of an individual's identity into two or more social realities.

Downsizing Reductions taken in a company's workforce as part of deindustrialization.

Dramaturgical approach A view of social interaction, popularized by Erving Goffman, in which people are seen as theatrical performers.

Dysfunction An element or process of a society that may disrupt the social system or reduce its stability.

Ecclesia A religious organization that claims to include most or all members of a society and is recognized as the national or official religion.

Ecological modernization The alignment of environmentally favorable practices with economic self-interest through constant adaptation and restructuring.

Economic system The social institution through which goods and services are produced, distributed, and consumed.

Education A formal process of learning in which some people consciously teach, while others adopt the social role of learner.

Egalitarian family An authority pattern in which spouses are regarded as equals.

Elite model A view of society as being ruled by a small group of individuals who share a common set of political and economic interests.

Endogamy The restriction of mate selection to people within the same group.

Environmental justice A legal strategy based on claims that racial minorities are subjected disproportionately to environmental hazards.

Environmental refugee A person who has been displaced by rising seas, destructive storms, expanding deserts, water shortages, or high levels of toxic pollutants.

Equilibrium model Talcott Parsons's functionalist view that society tends toward a state of stability or balance.

Established sect J. Milton Yinger's term for a religious group that is the outgrowth of a sect, yet remains isolated from society.

Estate system A system of stratification under which peasants were required to work land leased to them by nobles in exchange for military protection and other services. Also known as *feudalism*.

Esteem The reputation that a specific person has earned within an occupation.

Ethnic group A group that is set apart from others primarily because of its national origin or distinctive cultural patterns.

Ethnocentrism The tendency to assume that one's own culture and way of life represent the norm or are superior to all others.

Ethnography The study of an entire social setting through extended systematic fieldwork.

Evolutionary theory A theory of social change that holds that society is moving in a definite direction.

Exogamy The requirement that people select a mate outside certain groups.

Experiment An artificially created situation that allows a researcher to manipulate variables.

Experimental group The subjects in an experiment who are exposed to an independent variable introduced by a researcher.

Exploitation theory A Marxist theory that views racial subordination in the United States as a manifestation of the class system inherent in capitalism.

Expressiveness Concern for the maintenance of harmony and the internal emotional affairs of the family.

Extended family A family in which relatives—such as grandparents, aunts, or uncles—live in the same home as parents and their children.

F

Face-work A term used by Erving Goffman to refer to the efforts people make to maintain the proper image and avoid public embarrassment.

False consciousness A term used by Karl Marx to describe an attitude held by members of a class that does not accurately reflect their objective position.

Familism (Familismo) Pride in the extended family, expressed through the maintenance of close ties and strong obligations to kinfolk outside the immediate family.

Family A set of people related by blood, marriage or some other agreed-on relationship, or adoption, who share the primary responsibility for reproduction and caring for members of society.

Feminism An ideology that favors equal rights for women.

Feminist perspective A sociological approach that views inequity in gender as central to all behavior and organization.

Feminization of poverty A trend in which women constitute an increasing proportion of the poor people of both the United States and the world.

Fertility The level of reproduction in a society.

Flexibility stigma The devaluation of workers who seek or who are presumed to need flexible work arrangements.

Folkway A norm governing everyday behavior whose violation raises comparatively little concern.

Force The actual or threatened use of coercion to impose one's will on others.

Formal norm A norm that has been written down and that specifies strict punishments for violators.

Formal organization A group designed for a special purpose and structured for maximum efficiency.

Formal social control Social control that is carried out by authorized agents, such as police officers, judges, school administrators, and employers.

Functionalist perspective A sociological approach that emphasizes the way in which the parts of a society are structured to maintain its stability.

Fundamentalism An emphasis on doctrinal conformity and the literal interpretation of sacred texts.

G

Gatekeeping The process by which a relatively small number of people in the media industry control what material eventually reaches the audience.

Gemeinschaft A term used by Ferdinand Tönnies to describe a close-knit community, often found in rural areas, in which strong personal bonds unite members.

Gender identity How people see themselves, as male or female, or something else.

Gender role Expectations regarding the proper behavior, attitudes, and activities of males and females.

Generalized other A term used by George Herbert Mead to refer to the attitudes, viewpoints, and expectations of society as a whole that a child takes into account in his or her behavior.

Genocide The deliberate, systematic killing of an entire people or nation.

Gesellschaft A term used by Ferdinand Tönnies to describe a community, often urban, that is large and impersonal, with little commitment to the group or consensus on values.

Glass ceiling An invisible barrier that blocks the promotion of a qualified individual in a work environment because of the individual's gender, race, or ethnicity.

Glass escalator The advantage men experience in occupations dominated by women.

Global sociology A level of sociological analysis that makes comparisons between entire nations, using entire societies as units of analysis.

Global warming A significant rise in the earth's surface temperatures that occurs when industrial gases like carbon dioxide turn the planet's atmosphere into a virtual greenhouse.

Globalization The worldwide integration of government policies, cultures, social movements, and financial markets through trade and the exchange of ideas.

Goal displacement Overzealous conformity to official regulations of a bureaucracy.

Group Any number of people with similar norms, values, and expectations who interact with one another on a regular basis.

Growth rate The difference between births and deaths, plus the difference between immigrants and emigrants, per 1,000 population.

H

Hate crime A criminal offense committed because of the offender's bias against a race, religion, ethnic group, national origin, or sexual orientation. Also referred to as bias crime.

Hawthorne effect The unintended influence that observers of experiments can have on their subjects.

Health As defined by the World Health Organization, a state of complete physical, mental, and social well-being, and not merely the absence of disease and infirmity.

Hidden curriculum Standards of behavior that are deemed proper by society and are taught subtly in schools.

Holistic medicine Therapies in which the health care practitioner considers the person's physical, mental, emotional, and spiritual characteristics.

Homogamy The conscious or unconscious tendency to select a mate with personal characteristics similar to one's own.

Homophobia Fear of and prejudice against homosexuality.

Horizontal mobility The movement of an individual from one social position to another of the same rank.

Horticultural society A preindustrial society in which people plant seeds and crops rather than merely subsist on available foods.

Human ecology An area of study that is concerned with the interrelationships between people and their environment.

Human relations approach An approach to the study of formal organizations that emphasizes the role of people, communication, and participation in a bureaucracy and tends to focus on the informal structure of the organization.

Hunting-and-gathering society A preindustrial society in which people rely on whatever foods and fibers are readily available in order to survive.

Hybrid marriage A marriage in which the son or daughter may identify the prospective spouse, but the marriage is contingent on the parents approving that choice.

Hyper-local media Reporting that is highly local and typically Internet-based.

Hyperconsumerism The practice of buying more than we need or want, and often more than we can afford; a preoccupation of postmodern consumers.

Hypothesis A speculative statement about the relationship between two or more variables.

Ideal type A construct or model for evaluating specific cases.

Impression management A term used by Erving Goffman to refer to the altering of the presentation of the self in order to create distinctive appearances and satisfy particular audiences.

In-group Any group or category to which people feel they belong.

Incest taboo The prohibition of sexual relationships between certain culturally specified relatives.

Income Refers to salaries and wages, interest on savings, stock dividends, and rental income.

Independent variable The variable in a causal relationship that causes or influences a change in another variable.

Index crimes The eight types of crime tabulated each year by the FBI in the *Uniform Crime Reports*: murder, rape, robbery, assault, burglary, theft, motor vehicle theft, and arson.

Industrial society A society that depends on mechanization to produce its goods and services.

Infant mortality rate The number of deaths of infants under 1 year old per 1,000 live births in a given year.

Influence The exercise of power through a process of persuasion.

Influencer A social media user who has established credibility in a specific industry, such as fashion or electronics or toys.

Informal economy Transfers of money, goods, or services that are not reported to the government.

Informal norm A norm that is generally understood but not precisely recorded.

Informal social control Social control that is carried out casually by ordinary people through such means as laughter, smiles, and ridicule.

Innovation The process of introducing a new idea or object to a culture through discovery or invention.

Institutional discrimination The denial of opportunities and equal rights to individuals and groups that results from the normal operations of a society.

Instrumentality An emphasis on tasks, a focus on more distant goals, and a concern for the external relationship between one's family and other social institutions.

Intelligent design (ID) The idea that life is so complex that it could only have been created by divine design.

Interactionist perspective A sociological approach that generalizes about everyday forms of social interaction in order to explain society as a whole.

Intergenerational mobility Changes in the social position of children relative to their parents.

Intersectionality The overlapping and interdependent system of advantage and disadvantage that positions people in society on the basis of race, class, gender, and other characteristics.

Interview A face-to-face, phone, or online questioning of a respondent to obtain desired information.

Intragenerational mobility Changes in social position within a person's adult life.

Invention The combination of existing cultural items into a form that did not exist before.

Iron law of oligarchy A principle of organizational life developed by Robert Michels, under which even a democratic organization will eventually develop into a bureaucracy ruled by a few individuals.

Kinship The state of being related to others.

Labeling theory An approach to deviance that attempts to explain why certain people are viewed as deviants while others engaged in the same behavior are not.

Labor union Organized workers who share either the same skill or the same employer.

Language An abstract system of word meanings and symbols for all aspects of culture; includes gestures and other nonverbal communication.

Latent function An unconscious or unintended function that may reflect hidden purposes.

Law Governmental social control.

Liberation theology Use of a church, primarily Roman Catholic, in a political effort to eliminate poverty, discrimination, and other forms of injustice from a secular society.

Life chances Max Weber's term for the opportunities people have to provide themselves with material goods, positive living conditions, and favorable life experiences.

Life course approach A research orientation in which sociologists and other social scientists look closely at the social factors that influence people throughout their lives, from birth to death.

Life expectancy The median number of years a person can be expected to live under current mortality conditions.

Looking-glass self A concept used by Charles Horton Cooley that emphasizes the self as the product of our social interactions.

Luddites Rebellious craft workers in 19th-century England who destroyed new factory machinery as part of their resistance to the Industrial Revolution.

Machismo A sense of virility, personal worth, and pride in one's maleness.

Macrosociology Sociological investigation that concentrates on large-scale phenomena or entire civilizations.

Manifest function An open, stated, and conscious function.

Mass media Print and electronic means of communication that carry messages to widespread audiences.

Master status A status that dominates others and thereby determines a person's general position in society.

Material culture The physical or technological aspects of our daily lives.

Matriarchy A society in which women dominate in family decision making.

Matrilineal descent A kinship system in which only the mother's relatives are significant.

Matrix of domination The cumulative impact of oppression because of race and ethnicity, gender, and social class, as well as religion, sexual orientation, disability, age, and citizenship status.

McDonaldization The process by which the principles of bureaucratization have increasingly shaped organizations worldwide.

Mean A number calculated by adding a series of values and then dividing by the number of values.

Mechanical solidarity A collective consciousness that emphasizes group solidarity, characteristic of societies with minimal division of labor.

Median The midpoint or number that divides a series of values into two groups of equal numbers of values.

Medical model An approach in which medical experts define illness or disease, determine and control the course of treatment, and even affect patients' views of themselves.

Mental illness A disorder of the brain that disrupts a person's thinking, feeling, and ability to interact with others.

Mesosociology An intermediate level of sociological analysis that focuses on formal organizations and social movements.

Microsociology Sociological investigation that stresses the study of small groups, often through experimental means.

Midlife crisis A stressful period of self-evaluation that begins at about age 40.

Migration The relatively permanent movement of people, with the purpose of changing their place of residence.

Minority group A subordinate group whose members have significantly less control or power over their own lives than the members of a dominant or majority group have over theirs.

Mode The single most common value in a series of scores.

Model minority A group that, despite past prejudice and discrimination, succeeds economically, socially, and educationally without resorting to political or violent confrontations with whites.

Modernization The far-reaching process through which periphery nations move from traditional or less developed institutions to those characteristic of more developed societies.

Modernization theory A functionalist approach that proposes that modernization and development will gradually improve the lives of people in developing nations.

Monarchy A form of government headed by a single member of a royal family, usually a king, queen, or some other hereditary ruler.

Monogamy A form of marriage in which an individual has only one partner.

Monopoly Control of a market by a single business firm.

Morbidity rate The rate of disease in a given population.

Mores Norms deemed highly necessary to the welfare of a society.

Mortality rate The rate of death in a given population.

Multinational corporation A commercial organization that is headquartered in one country but does business throughout the world.

Narcotizing dysfunction The phenomenon in which the media provide such massive amounts of coverage that the audience becomes numb and fails to act on the information, regardless of how compelling the issue.

Natural science The study of the physical features of nature and the ways in which they interact and change.

Naturally occurring retirement community (NORC) An area that has gradually become an informal center for senior citizens.

Neocolonialism Continuing dependence of former colonies on foreign countries.

New religious movement (NRM) or cult A small, secretive religious group that represents either a new religion or a major innovation of an existing faith.

New social movement An organized collective activity that addresses values and social identities, as well as improvements in the quality of life.

Nonmaterial culture Ways of using material objects, as well as customs, beliefs, philosophies, governments, and patterns of communication.

Nonverbal communication The sending of messages through the use of gestures, facial expressions, and postures.

Norm An established standard of behavior maintained by a society.

Nuclear family A married couple and their unmarried children living together.

Obedience Compliance with higher authorities in a hierarchical structure.

Objective method A technique for measuring social class that assigns individuals to classes on the basis of criteria such as occupation, education, income, and place of residence.

Observation A research technique in which an investigator collects information through direct participation, by closely watching a group or community.

Offshoring The transfer of work to foreign contractors.

Oligarchy A form of government in which a few individuals rule.

Open system A social system in which the position of each individual is influenced by his or her achieved status.

Operational definition An explanation of an abstract concept that is specific enough to allow a researcher to assess the concept.

Opinion leader Someone who influences the opinions and decisions of others through day-to-day personal contact and communication.

Organic solidarity A collective consciousness that rests on mutual interdependence, characteristic of societies with a complex division of labor.

Organized crime The work of a group that regulates relations between criminal enterprises involved in illegal activities, including prostitution, gambling, and the smuggling and sale of illegal drugs.

Out-group A group or category to which people feel they do not belong.

Patriarchy A society in which men dominate in family decision making.

Patrilineal descent A kinship system in which only the father's relatives are significant.

Peace The absence of war, or more broadly, a proactive effort to develop cooperative relations among nations.

Percentage A portion of 100.

Peter principle A principle of organizational life, originated by Laurence J. Peter, according to which every employee within a hierarchy tends to rise to his or her level of incompetence.

Pluralism Mutual respect for one another's cultures among the various groups in a society, which allows minorities to express their cultures without experiencing prejudice.

Pluralist model A view of society in which many competing groups within the community have access to government, so that no single group is dominant.

Political system The social institution that is founded on a recognized set of procedures for implementing and achieving society's goals.

Politics In Harold Lasswell's words, "who gets what, when, and how."

Polyandry A form of polygamy in which a woman may have more than one husband at the same time.

Polygamy A form of marriage in which an individual may have several husbands or wives simultaneously.

Polygyny A form of polygamy in which a man may have more than one wife at the same time.

Population pyramid A special type of bar chart that shows the distribution of a population by gender and age.

Postindustrial society A society whose economic system is engaged primarily in the processing and control of information.

Postmodern society A technologically sophisticated society that is preoccupied with consumer goods and media images.

Power The ability to exercise one's will over others.

Power elite A term used by C. Wright Mills to refer to a small group of military, industrial, and government leaders who control the fate of the United States.

Precarious work Employment that is poorly paid, and from the worker's perspective, insecure and unprotected.

Prejudice A negative attitude toward an entire category of people, often an ethnic or racial minority.

Prestige The respect and admiration that an occupation holds in a society.

Primary group A small group characterized by intimate, face-to-face association and cooperation.

Profane The ordinary and commonplace elements of life, as distinguished from the sacred.

Professional criminal A person who pursues crime as a day-to-day occupation, developing skilled techniques and enjoying a certain degree of status among other criminals.

Proletariat Karl Marx's term for the working class in a capitalist society.

Protestant ethic Max Weber's term for the disciplined work ethic, this-worldly concerns, and rational orientation to life emphasized by John Calvin and his followers.

Qualitative research Research that relies on what is seen in field or naturalistic settings more than on statistical data.

Quantitative research Research that collects and reports data primarily in numerical form.

Quasi-religion A scholarly category that includes organizations that may see themselves as religious but may be seen by others as "sort of religious."

Queer theory The study of society from the perspective of a broad spectrum of sexual identities, including heterosexuality, homosexuality, and bisexuality.

Questionnaire A printed or written form used to obtain information from a respondent.

R

Racial formation A sociohistorical process in which racial categories are created, inhabited, transformed, and destroyed.

Racial group A group that is set apart from others because of physical differences that have taken on social significance.

Racial profiling Any arbitrary action initiated by an authority based on race, ethnicity, or national origin rather than on a person's behavior.

Racism The belief that one race is supreme and all others are innately inferior.

Random sample A sample for which every member of an entire population has the same chance of being selected.

Rational-legal authority Power made legitimate by law.

Redlining The pattern of discrimination against people trying to buy homes in minority and racially changing neighborhoods.

Reference group Any group that individuals use as a standard for evaluating themselves and their own behavior.

Refugees People living outside their country of citizenship for fear of political or religious persecution.

Relative deprivation The conscious feeling of a negative discrepancy between legitimate expectations and present actualities.

Relative poverty A floating standard of deprivation by which people at the bottom of a society, whatever their lifestyles, are judged to be disadvantaged *in comparison with the nation as a whole.*

Reliability The extent to which a measure produces consistent results.

Religion According to Émile Durkheim, a unified system of beliefs and practices relative to sacred things.

Religious belief A statement to which members of a particular religion adhere.

Religious experience The feeling or perception of being in direct contact with the ultimate reality, such as a divine being, or of being overcome with religious emotion.

Religious ritual A practice required or expected of members of a faith.

Remittances The monies that immigrants return to their families of origin. Also called *migradollars.*

Representative democracy A form of government in which certain individuals are selected to speak for the people.

Research design A detailed plan or method for obtaining data scientifically.

Resocialization The process of discarding former behavior patterns and accepting new ones as part of a transition in one's life.

Resource mobilization The ways in which a social movement utilizes such resources as money, political influence, access to the media, and personnel.

Rite of passage A ritual marking the symbolic transition from one social position to another.

Role conflict The situation that occurs when incompatible expectations arise from two or more social positions held by the same person.

Role exit The process of disengagement from a role that is central to one's self-identity in order to establish a new role and identity.

Role strain The difficulty that arises when the same social position imposes conflicting demands and expectations.

Role taking The process of mentally assuming the perspective of another and responding from that imagined viewpoint.

S

Sacred Elements beyond everyday life that inspire awe, respect, and even fear.

Sample A selection from a larger population that is statistically representative of that population.

Sanction A penalty or reward for conduct concerning a social norm.

Sandwich generation The generation of adults who simultaneously try to meet the competing needs of their parents and their children.

Science The body of knowledge obtained by methods based on systematic observation.

Scientific management approach Another name for the classical theory of formal organizations.

Scientific method A systematic, organized series of steps that ensures maximum objectivity and consistency in researching a problem.

Second shift The double burden—work outside the home followed by child care and housework—that many women face and few men share equitably.

Secondary analysis A variety of research techniques that make use of previously collected and publicly accessible information and data.

Secondary group A formal, impersonal group in which there is little social intimacy or mutual understanding.

Sect A relatively small religious group that has broken away from some other religious organization to renew what it considers the original vision of the faith.

Secularization The process through which religion's influence on other social institutions diminishes.

Segregation The physical separation of two groups of people in terms of residence, workplace, and social events; often imposed on a minority group by a dominant group.

Self According to George Herbert Mead, a distinct identity that sets us apart from others.

Serial monogamy A form of marriage in which a person may have several spouses in his or her lifetime, but only one spouse at a time.

Sexism The ideology that one sex is superior to the other.

Sexual identity The self-awareness of being romantically or sexually attracted to a defined group of people. Also referred to as *sexual orientation.*

Sharing economy Connecting owners of underused assets with others willing to pay to use them.

Sick role Societal expectations about the attitudes and behavior of a person viewed as being ill.

Significant other A term used by George Herbert Mead to refer to an individual who is most important in the development of the self, such as a parent, friend, or teacher.

Single-parent family A family in which only one parent is present to care for the children.

Slavery A system of enforced servitude in which some people are owned by other people.

Social capital The collective benefit of social networks, which are built on reciprocal trust.

Social change Significant alteration over time in behavior patterns and culture, including norms and values.

Social constructionist perspective An approach to deviance that emphasizes the role of culture in the creation of the deviant identity.

Social control The techniques and strategies for preventing deviant human behavior in any society.

Social disorganization theory The theory that crime and deviance are caused by the absence or breakdown of communal relationships and social institutions.

Social epidemiology The study of the distribution of disease, impairment, and general health status across a population.

Social inequality A condition in which members of society have differing amounts of wealth, prestige, or power.

Social institution An organized pattern of beliefs and behavior centered on basic social needs.

Social interaction The ways in which people respond to one another.

Social media Websites and online applications that enable people to create and share content or to participate in social networking.

Social mobility Movement of individuals or groups from one position in a society's stratification system to another.

Social movement An organized collective activity to bring about or resist fundamental change in an existing group or society.

Social network A series of social relationships that link a person directly to others, and through them indirectly to still more people.

Social role A set of expectations for people who occupy a given social position or status.

Social science The study of the social features of humans and the ways in which they interact and change.

Social structure The way in which a society is organized into predictable relationships.

Socialism An economic system under which the means of production and distribution are collectively owned.

Socialization The lifelong process in which people learn the attitudes, values, and behaviors appropriate for members of a particular culture.

Societal-reaction approach Another name for labeling theory.

Society A fairly large number of people who live in the same territory, are relatively independent of people outside their area, and participate in a common culture.

Sociobiology The systematic study of how biology affects human social behavior.

Sociocultural evolution Long-term social trends resulting from the interplay of continuity, innovation, and selection.

Socioeconomic status (SES) A measure of social class that is based on income, education, and occupation.

Sociological imagination An awareness of the relationship between an individual and the wider society, both today and in the past.

Sociology The scientific study of social behavior and human groups.

Status A term used by sociologists to refer to any of the full range of socially defined positions within a large group or society.

Status group A term used by Max Weber to refer to people who have the same prestige or lifestyle, independent of their class positions.

Stereotype An unreliable generalization about all members of a group that does not recognize individual differences within the group.

Stigma A label used to devalue members of certain social groups.

Stratification A structured ranking of entire groups of people that perpetuates unequal economic rewards and power in a society.

Subculture A segment of society that shares a distinctive pattern of customs, rules, and traditions that differs from the pattern of the larger society.

Survey A study, generally in the form of an interview or questionnaire, that provides researchers with information about how people think and act.

Symbol A gesture, object, or word that forms the basis of human communication.

Symbolic ethnicity An ethnic identity that emphasizes concerns such as ethnic food or political issues rather than deeper ties to one's ethnic heritage.

Teacher-expectancy effect The impact that a teacher's expectations about a student's performance may have on the student's actual achievements.

Technology Cultural information about the ways in which the material resources of the environment may be used to satisfy human needs and desires.

Terrorism The use or threat of violence against random or symbolic targets in pursuit of political aims.

Theory In sociology, a set of statements that seeks to explain problems, actions, or behavior.

Third place A social setting in addition to the "first place" of home and the "second place" of work where people routinely gather.

Total fertility rate (TFR) The average number of children born alive to any woman, assuming that she conforms to current fertility rates.

Total institution A term coined by Erving Goffman to refer to an institution that regulates all aspects of a person's life under a single authority, such as a prison, the military, a mental hospital, or a convent.

Totalitarianism Virtually complete government control and surveillance over all aspects of a society's social and political life.

Tracking The practice of placing students in specific curriculum groups on the basis of their test scores and other criteria.

Traditional authority Legitimate power conferred by custom and accepted practice.

Trained incapacity The tendency of workers in a bureaucracy to become so specialized that they develop blind spots and fail to notice obvious problems.

Transnational An immigrant who sustains multiple social relationships that link his or her society of origin with the society of settlement.

Transnational crime Crime that occurs across multiple national borders.

Underclass The long-term poor who lack training and skills.

Validity The degree to which a measure or scale truly reflects the phenomenon under study.

Value A collective conception of what is considered good, desirable, and proper—or bad, undesirable, and improper—in a culture.

Value neutrality Max Weber's term for objectivity of sociologists in the interpretation of data.

Variable A measurable trait or characteristic that is subject to change under different conditions.

Verstehen The German word for "understanding" or "insight"; used by Max Weber to stress the need for sociologists to take into account the subjective meanings people attach to their actions.

Vertical mobility The movement of an individual from one social position to another of a different rank.

Vested interests Veblen's term for those people or groups who will suffer in the event of social change, and who have a stake in maintaining the status quo.

Victimization survey A questionnaire or an interview given to a sample of the population to determine whether people have been victims of crime.

Victimless crime A term used by sociologists to describe the willing exchange among adults of widely desired but illegal goods and services.

Visual sociology The use of photographs, film, and video to study society.

Vital statistics Records of births, deaths, marriages, and divorces gathered through a registration system maintained by governmental units.

War Conflict between organizations that possess trained combat forces equipped with deadly weapons.

Wealth An inclusive term encompassing all of a person's material assets, including land, stocks, and other types of property.

White privilege Rights or immunities granted to people as a particular benefit or favor simply because they are White.

White-collar crime Illegal acts committed by affluent, "respectable" individuals in the course of business activities.

World systems analysis The global economy as an interdependent system of economically and politically unequal nations.

Zero population growth (ZPG) The state of a population in which the number of births plus immigrants equals the number of deaths plus emigrants.

references

A

Abe, Yukiko. 2011. "The Equal Employment Opportunity Law and Labor Force Behavior of Women in Japan." *Journal of the Japanese and International Economies* 25 (March): 39–55.

Aberle, David F., A. K. Cohen, A. K. Davis, M. J. Leng, Jr., and F. N. Sutton. 1950. "The Functional Prerequisites of a Society." *Ethics* 60 (January):100–111.

Acar Erdol, Tuba. 2019. "Practicing Gender Pedagogy: The Case of Egalia." *Egitimde Nitel Arastirmalar Dergisi: Journal of Qualitative Research in Education* 7(4): 1365–1385.

ACLU. 2015b. "NSA Surveillance." Accessible at www.aclu.org.

Acosta, R. Vivian, and Linda Jean Carpenter. 2001. "Women in Intercollegiate Sport: A Longitudinal Study: 1977–1998." Pp. 302–308 in *Sport in Contemporary Society: An Anthology,* 6th ed., edited by D. Stanley Eitzen. New York: Worth.

Adams, Charles Joseph. 2015. "Classification of Religions." *Britannica Online*. May 1. Accessible at www.britannica.com.

Adams, R. Dallon. 2020. "Artificial Intelligence Is Predicting Coronavirus Outbreaks Before They Start." April 30. Accessible at www. techrepublic.com.

Adams, Tyrene L., and Stephen A. Smith. 2008. *Electronic Tribes: The Virtual Worlds of Geeks, Gamas, Shamans, and Scammers.* Austin: University of Texas Press.

Adamy, Janet, and Paul Overberg. 2020. "Affluent Americans Still Say 'I Do'; More in the Middle Class Don't." *Wall Street Journal*, March 8. Accessible at www.wsj.com.

Addams, Jane. 1910. *Twenty Years at Hull-House.* New York: Macmillan.

———. 1930. *The Second Twenty Years at Hull-House.* New York: Macmillan.

Adler, Patricia A., and Peter Adler. 2011. *The Tender Cut: Inside the Hidden World of Self-Injury.* New York: New York University Press.

———, ———, and John M. Johnson. 1992. "Street Corner Society Revisited." *Journal of Contemporary Ethnography* 21 (April):3–10.

Adoption Network. 2020. "U.S. Adoption Statistics." March 27. Accessible at www. adoptionnetwork.com.

Adorno, Theodor. [1971] 1991. *The Culture Industry.* London: Routledge.

Adua, Lazarus, Richard York, and Beth-Anne Schuelke-Leech. 2016. "The Human Dimensions of Climate Change: A Micro-level Assessment of Views from the Ecological Modernization, Political Economy and Human Ecology Perspectives." *Social Science Research* 56 (March): 26–43.

Aevaz, Romic. 2019. "2018 ACS Survey: While Most Americans' Commuting Trends Are Unchanged, Teleworking Continues to Grow, and Driving Alone Dips in Some Major Cities." October 18. Accessible at www.enotrans.org.

AFL-CIO. 2019. "Executive Paywatch." Accessible at ww.aflcio.org.

Ahmed, Azam, Miriam Jordon, and Kirk Semple. 2020. "With Border Closed, Disaster Is Looming." *New York Times*, March 23, p. A7.

Al-Arshani, Sarah. 2020. 9 large metro police departments reported 'double-digit percentage jumps' in domestic violence 911 calls as more people shelter at home. *Business Insider* (April 6). Accessible at www.businessinsider.com.

Alba, Richard D. 2009. *Blurring the Color Line: The New Chance for a More Integrated America.* Cambridge, MA: Harvard University Press.

Albas, Cheryl, and Daniel Albas. 1996. "An Invitation to the Ethnographic Study of University Examination Behavior: Concepts, Methodology and Implications." *Canadian Journal of Higher Education* 26 (3):1–26.

Albas, Daniel, and Cheryl Albas. 1988. "Aces and Bombers: The Post-Exam Impression Management Strategies of Students." *Symbolic Interaction* 11 (Fall):289–302.

Albrecht, Gary L. 2004. "Disability: Sociological Perspectives." Pp. 3710–3713 in *International Encyclopedia of the Social and Behavioral Sciences,* edited by Neil J. Smelser and Paul B. Baltes. New York: Elsevier.

Allen, Bem P. 1978. *Social Behavior: Fact and Falsehood.* Chicago: Nelson-Hall.

Allen, Greg. 2012. "Mission Diversify: CIA Begins LGBT Recruiting." December 2. Accessible at www.wbur.org.

Allendorf, Keera. 2019. "Parents' Valuation of Approving a Child's Spouse in a Context of Marital Change." *Journal of Family Issues* 40 (15): 2097–2122.

Allport, Gordon W. 1979. *The Nature of Prejudice.* 25th anniversary ed. Reading, MA: Addison-Wesley.

Alper, Becka. 2019. "Why America's 'Nones' Don't Identify with a Religion." August 8. Accessible at www.pewresearch.org.

Alter, Charlotte, Suyin Haynes, and Justin Worland. 2019. "The Conscience." *Time* (December 23): 51–65.

Altia News. 2017. "Social Media in Afghanistan-Internews." Accessible at https://internews.org.

Alvaredo, Facundo. 2011. "Inequality over the Past Century." *Finance & Development* 48 (3):29.

Alvarez, Lizette. 2015. "Puerto Ricans Seeking New Lives Put Stamp on Central Florida." *New York Times,* August 25, pp. A1, A14.

Alvord, Lori. 2009. "Dispatches from the Cutting Edge of Healing: Surgery and Spirit." July 3. Accessible at www.religiondispatches.com.

Alzheimer's Association. 2019. *Quick Facts.* Accessible at www.alz.org.

American Academy of Pediatrics. 2016. "Media and Young Minds." Policy Statement issued November 20. Accessible at www.aappublicrelations.org.

———. 2020. "Media and Children." Accessible at www.aap.org.

American Bar Association. 1997. *Section of the Individual Rights and Responsibilities: Section of Litigation (Capital Punishment).* Chicago: Division for Policy Administration, ABA.

American Civil Liberties Union. 2020. "Debtors' Prisons." Accessible at aclu.org.

American Community Survey. 2016. *2015 American Community Survey 1-Year Estimates.* Accessible at www.census.gov.

———. 2018b. "2013–2017 5-Year Estimates." Accessible at www.census.gov.

———. 2019a. "2018 American Community Survey 1-Year Estimates." Accessible at www. census.gov.

———. 2019a. "American Community Survey 1-Year Estimates." Tables R1502, 1902. Accessible at www.census.gov

American Lung Association. 2020. *State of the Air 2020.* Washington, DC: American Lung Association.

American Psychiatric Association. 2013. *Diagnostic and Statistical Manual of Mental Disorders,* Fifth Edition (DSM-5™). Arlington, VA: American Psychiatric Publishing.

American Psychological Association. 2008. "Being Gay Is Just as Healthy as Being Straight." Accessed February 25 at www.apa.org.

American Society of Plastic Surgeons. 2019. "Plastic Surgery Procedural Statistics." February 15. Accessible at www.plasticsurgery.org.

American Sociological Association. 2013. *21st Century Careers with an Undergraduate Degree in Sociology.* Washington, DC: ASA.

———. 2018. *Code of Ethics.* June. Accessible at www.asanet.org.

———. 2020a. *Current Sections.* May 22. Accessible at www.asanet.org.

———. 2020b. *2019 Guide to Graduate Departments of Sociology.* Washington, DC: American Sociological Association.

Amish America. 2019. "The Ugly Reality Behind Amish 'Reality' TV." Posted on August 16, 2019 in *Amish Controversies.* Accessible at www. amishamerica.com.

Amnesty International. 2015. "Death Sentences and Executions 2014." February 11, 2016. Accessible at amnestyusa.org.

———. 2019. *Death Sentences and Executions 2018.* Accessible at www.amnesty.org.

Anatale, Alex, Atsushi Yamanaka, and Didier Nkurikiyimfura. 2013. "The Metamorphosis to a Knowledge-Based Society: Rwanda." Chapter 2.2 in *The Global Information Technology Report 2013: Growth and Jobs in a Hyperconnected World,* edited by Beñat Bilbao-Osorio, Soumitra Dutta, and Bruno Lanvin. April 10. Geneva, Switzerland: World Economic Forum. Accessible at www.weforum.org/reports/global-information-technology-report-2013.

Anderson, Elijah. 1990. *Streetwise: Race, Class, and Change in an Urban Community.* Chicago: University of Chicago Press.

Anderson, Greta. 2019. "More Title IX Lawsuits by Accusers and Accused." *Inside Higher Ed* (October 3). Accessible at www.insidehighered.com.

Anderson, Gretchen. 2009. *Love, Actually: A National Survey of Adults 18+ on Love, Relationships, and Romance.* Washington, DC: AARP.

Anderson, Janna, and Lee Rainie. 2020. "Many Tech Experts Say Digital Disruption Will Hurt Democracy." February 21. Accessible at www.pewresearch.org.

Anderson, John Ward, and Molly Moore. 1993. "The Burden of Womanhood." *Washington Post National Weekly Edition* 10 (March 22–28):6–7.

Anderson, Monica, and Jingjing Jiang. 2018a. *Teens' Social Media & Technology 2018.* May 31. Accessible at www.pewresearch.org.

———, and ———. 2018b. *Teens' Social Media Habits and Experiences.* November 28. Accessible at www.pewresearch.org.

Anti-Defamation League. 2018. "Groundbreaking ADL Analysis Estimates 4.2 Million Anti-Semitic Tweets in One-Year Period." May 7. Accessible at www.adl.org.

———. 2019. *Audit of Anti-Semitic Incidents: Year in Review 2018.* Accessible at www.adl.org.

———. 2020. "Hate Crime Laws: Protected Categories." January 29. Accessible at https://www.adl.org/grapicacy-adi-hate-crime-map.

Arab American Institute. 2010. "Demographics." Accessed March 7, www.aaiusa.org/arab-americans/22/demographics.

Argetsinger, Amy, and Jonathan Krim. 2002. "Stopping the Music." *Washington Post National Weekly Edition* 20 (December 2):20.

Armed Campuses. 2015. "Guns on Campus: Laws for Public Colleges and Universities." Accessed October 25 at http://armedcampuses.org.

Armer, J. Michael, and John Katsillis. 1992. "Modernization Theory." Pp. 1299–1304, vol. 4, in *Encyclopedia of Sociology,* edited by Edgar F. Borgatta and Marie L. Borgatta. New York: Macmillan.

Arrington, Jovanah. 2019. "There's No I in 'Team': Student Athlete Identity at an NCAA Division II University." Master's thesis. Accessible at https://digitalcommons.humboldt.edu/etd/331.

Asklöv, Elin. 2019. "Swedish 'Hen' Is Here to Stay: The Success of a Made-Up Gender-Neutral Pronoun." *Babel Magazine* (March 22). Accessible at www.babbel.com.

Association of Theological Schools. 2020. *ATS 2019–2020 Annual Data Tables.* Accessible at www.ats.edu.

Atchley, Robert C. 1976. *The Sociology of Retirement.* New York: Wiley.

Aunio, Anna-Lisa, and Suzanne Staggenborg. 2011. "Transnational Linkages and Movement Communities." *Sociology Compass* 5 (5):364–375.

Austin, Chammie. 2009. *Impression Management.* Accessed January 11, 2012, www.education.com/reference/article/impression-management.

Austin, Kelly F. 2020. "Opposing Observations and the Political-Economy of Malaria Vulnerability: A Community-Based Study in Bududa, Uganda." *Journal of World-Systems Research* 26 (1). Accessible at www.jwsr.pitt.edu.

Auxier, Brooke, Monica Anderson, and Madhu Kummar. 2019. "10 Tech-related Trends That Shaped the Decade." *Factank* (December 30). Accessible at www.pewresearch.org.

———, Lee Rainie, Monica Anderson, Andrew Perrin, Madhu Kumar, and Erica Turner. 2019. "Americans and Privacy: Concerned, Confused and Feeling Lack of Control Over their Personal Information." November 15. Accessible at www.pewresearch.org.

Azumi, Koya, and Jerald Hage. 1972. *Organizational Systems.* Lexington, MA: Heath.

B

Bacon Lovers' Talk. 2009. "Bacon Lovers' Talk." Accessed February 4 at www.bacontalk.com/.

Bagby, Ihsam. 2012. *The American Mosque 2011.* Washington, DC: Council on American-Islamic Relations.

Baker, Therese L. 1999. *Doing Social Research.* 3rd ed. New York: McGraw-Hill.

Bakshy, Eytan, Solomon Messing, and Lada A. Adamie. 2016. "Exposure to Ideologically Diverse News and Opinion on Facebook." *Science* 348 (June 5):1130–1132.

Banchero, Stephanie. 2014. "Young Teachers Stick Around." *Wall Street Journal,* April 8, p. A3.

Banjon, Delphine N., and Myrna R. Olson. 2016. "Issues and Trends of International Students in the United States." *International Journal of Education* 4(1).

Banthin, Jessica, Michael Simpson, Mathew Buettgens, Linda J. Blumberg, and Robin Wang. 2020. Changes in Health Insurance Coverage Due to the COVID-19 Recession: Preliminary Estimates Using Microsimulation. June. Robert Wood Johnson Foundation and Urban Institute. Accessible at www.urban.org.

Banyan, By. 2014. "The Optimistic Continent." *The Economist* (October 9). Accessible at www.economist.com.

Baran, Stanley J. 2015. *Introduction to Mass Communications: Media, Literacy, and Culture.* 8th ed. Updated Edition. New York: McGraw-Hill.

———. 2017. *Introduction to Mass Communication: Media Literacy and Culture.* 9th ed. New York: McGraw-Hill.

———, and Dennis K. Davis. 2015. *Mass Communication Theory: Foundations, Ferment, and Future.* 7th ed. Belmont, CA: Cengage.

Barber, Nigel. 2009. "The Wide World of Polygamy: We Hate It, Others Love It." *Psychology Today* (February 19). Accessible at www.psychologytoday.com.

Barbière, Cécile. 2014. "French Fear 'Cultural Dumping' from Netflix's EU Expansion." July 31. Accessible at www.euractiv.com.

Bartlett, Thomas. 2009. "How the International Essay Mill Has Changed Cheating." *Chronicle of Higher Education* (March 20): A1, A22–A25.

———. 2011. "A Database Named Desire: 2 Scientists Examine Online Searches for Sex." *Chronicle of Higher Education* 57 (August 12):A12.

Bates, Laura. 2014. *Everyday Sexism: The Project That Inspired a Worldwide Movement.* New York: Thomas Dunne Books.

Baude, William. 2015. "Is Polygamy Next?" *New York Times,* July 21, p. A27.

Baudrillard, Jean. [1970] 1998. *The Consumers Society.* London: Sage.

BBC News. 2005. "Indonesian Village Report: January 12, 2005." Accessed January 19 at www.theworld.org.

Bearman, Peter S., James Moody, and Katherine Stovel. 2004. "Chains of Affection: The Structure of Adolescent Romantic and Sexual Networks." *American Journal of Sociology* 110 (July):44–91.

Beaubien, Jason, and Rebecca Davis. 2015. "A Teen Who Fled Syria Had High Hopes of Life in Lebanon." October 25. Accessible at npr.org.

Becker, Anne E. 2007. "Facets of Acculturation and Their Diverse Relations to Body Shape Concerns in Fiji." *International Journal of Eating Disorders* 40 (1):42–50.

Becker, Howard S. 1952. "Social Class Variations in the Teacher-Pupil Relationship." *Journal of Educational Sociology* 25 (April):451–465.

———. [1953] 2015. *Becoming a Marijuana User.* Chicago: University of Chicago Press.

———. 1963. *The Outsiders: Studies in the Sociology of Deviance.* New York: Free Press.

——— (ed.). 1964. *The Other Side: Perspectives on Deviance.* New York: Free Press.

———. 1974. "Photography and Sociology." *Studies in the Anthropology of Visual Communication* 1: 3–26. Accessible at lucy.ukc.ac.uk/becker.html. Reproduced in *Doing Things Together: Selected Papers.* 1986. Evanston: Northwestern University Press.

———, Blanche Greer, Everett C. Hughes, and Anselm Strauss. 1961. *Boys in White: Student Culture in Medical School.* Chicago: University of Chicago Press.

Beckwith, Cary. 2019. "Who Belongs? How Status Influences the Experience of *Gemeinschaft.*" *Social Psychology Quarterly* 82 (1):31–50.

Beddoes, Zanny Milton. 2012. "For Richer, for Poorer." *The Economist* (October 13): Special Report.

Beech, Hannah. 2020. "After Initial Successes, Infections Are Surging in Migrant Dormitories." *New York Times,* April 21, p. A5.

Begum, Rothna. 2017. "Gulf States' Slow March Toward Domestic Workers' Rights." June 16. Accessible at www.hrw.org.

Bekker, Jessie. 2019. "Nevada's High Suicide Rate a Mystery." May 16. *Las Vegas Review-Journal.* Accessible at reviewjournal.com.

Bell, Daniel. 1953. "Crime as an American Way of Life." *Antioch Review* 13 (Summer):131–154.

———. [1973] 1999. *The Coming of Post-Industrial Society: A Venture in Social Forecasting.* With new foreword. New York: Basic Books.

Bell, Wendell. 1981. "Modernization." Pp. 186–187 in *Encyclopedia of Sociology.* Guilford, CT: DPG Publishing.

Bellair, Paul. 2017. "Social Disorganization Theory." July. *Oxford Research Encyclopedia.* Accessible at www.oxfordre.com.

Beller, Emily. 2009. "Bringing Intergenerational Social Mobility Research into the Twenty-First Century: Why Mothers Matter." *America Sociological Review* 74 (August):507–528.

Bellman, Eric, and Adith Malhotra. 2017. "Digital Divide Leaves India's Women Behind." *Wall Street Journal,* October 14, pp. B1, B2.

Benford, Robert D. 1992. "Social Movements." Pp. 1880–1887, vol. 4, in *Encyclopedia of Sociology,* edited by Edgar F. Borgatta and Marie Borgatta. New York: Macmillan.

Bennett, John T. 2015. *The Sequester, the Pentagon, and the Little Campaign That Could.* Washington, DC: New America.

Berchick, Edward R., Jessica C. Barnett, and Rachel D. Upton. 2019. *Health Insurance in the United States: 2018-Tables.* September 10. Report Number P60-267. Accessible at www.census.gov.

Berger, Peter, and Thomas Luckmann. 1966. *The Social Construction of Reality.* New York: Doubleday.

Berry, Justin A., and Jane Junn. 2015. "Silent Citizenship among Asian Americans and Latinos: Opting Out or Left Out?" *Citizenship Studies* 19 (5):570-590.

Best, Joel. 2004. *Deviance: Career of a Concept.* Belmont, CA: Wadsworth Thomson.

Best, Shaun. 2015. *Talcott Parsons: Despair and Modernity.* Farnham, UK: Ashgate.

Bialik, Carol. 2010. "Seven Careers in a Lifetime? Think Twice, Researchers Say." *Wall Street Journal,* September 4, p. A6.

Bialystok, Ellen. 2018. "Bilingual Education for Young Children: Review of the Effects and Consequences." *International Journal of Bilingual Education and Bilingualism* 21 (6):666-679.

Bielberg, Larry. 2017. "10 Global Christmas Traditions in the U.S." *USA Today,* December 3, p. 6D.

Bielby, Denise D., and C. Lee Harrington. 2008. *Global TV: Exporting Television and Culture in the World Market.* New York: New York University Press.

Billitteri, Thomas, J. 2009. "Middle-Class Squeeze." *CQ Researcher* 19 (March 6):201-224.

Bjelland, Mark D., and Daniel R. Montello. 2020. *Human Geography: Landscapes of Human Activities.* 13th ed. New York: McGraw-Hill.

Black, Donald. 1995. "The Epistemology of Pure Sociology." *Law and Social Inquiry* 20 (Summer):829-870.

Black, Lindsey, Tainya Clarke, Patricia Barnes, Barbara Stussman, and Richard L. Hanin. 2015. "Use of Complementary Health Approaches among Children Aged 4-17 Years in the United States: National Health Interview Survey, 2007-2012." *National Health Statistics Reports* (No. 78). Hyattsville, MD: National Center for Health Statistics. Accessible at www.nccih.nih.gov.

Blackstone, Amy. 2014. "Doing Family Without Having Kids." *Sociology Compass* 6 (1): 52-62.

Blais, Allison, and Lynn Rasic. 2011. *A Place of Remembrance: Official Book of the National September 11 Memorial.* Washington, DC: National Geographic.

Blauner, Robert. 1972. *Racial Oppression in America.* New York: Harper and Row.

Blumberg, Antonia. 2016. "American Religion Has Never Looked Quite Like It Does Today." April 15. Accessible at www.huffingtonpost.com.

Blumberg, Stephen J., and Julian V. Luke. 2007. "Coverage Bias in Traditional Telephone Surveys of Low-Income and Young Adults." *Public Opinion Quarterly* 71 (5):734-749.

———. 2018. "Wireless Substitution: Early Release of Estimates from the National Health Interview Survey, July-December 2017." June 2018. Accessible at www.cdc.gov.

Blumer, Herbert. 1955. "Collective Behavior." Pp. 165-198 in *Principles of Sociology,* 2nd ed., edited by Alfred McClung Lee. New York: Barnes and Noble.

———. 1969. *Symbolic Interactionism: Perspective and Method.* Englewood Cliffs, NJ: Prentice Hall.

Board of Governors of the Federal Reserve Bank. 2019. *Distributional Financial Accounts: Overview of Third Quarter 2019.* December 23. Accessible at www.federalreserve.gov.

Bond, Patrick. 2015. "Can Climate Activists' 'Movement Below' Transcend Negotiators' 'Paralysis Above'?" *Journal of World-Systems Research* 21(No. 2). Accessible at www.jwsr.otg.

Bonilla-Silva, Eduardo. 2004. "From Bi-Racial to Tri-Racial: Towards a New System of Racial Stratification in the USA." *Ethics and Racial Studies* 27 (November):931-950.

———. 2014. *Racism without Racists.* 4th ed. New York: Rowman and Littlefield.

———. 2019. "Racists, Class Anxieties, Hegemonic Racism, and Democracy in Trump's Americas." *Social Currents* 6(1):14-31.

Bosker, Bianca. 2020. "The Witching Hour." *The Atlantic* (March): 14-16.

Bothwell, Jonathan. 2017. "Myths of the 1 Percent: What Puts Some People at the Top." *Wall Street Journal,* November 24, p. B2.

Bottomore, Tom, and Maximilien Rubel, eds. 1956. *Karl Marx: Selected Writings in Sociology and Social Philosophy.* New York: McGraw-Hill.

Boule, Jamelle. 2020. "Why Coronavirus Is Killing African-Americans More than Others: Higher Rates of Infection and Death Among Minorities Demonstrate the Racial Character of Inequality in America." *New York Times,* April 14. Accessible at www.nytimes.org.

Bourdieu, Pierre, and Jean-Claude Passerson. 1990. *Reproduction in Education, Society and Culture.* 2nd ed. London: Sage. Originally published as *La reproduction.*

Bouvier, Leon F. 1980. "America's Baby Boom Generation: The Fateful Bulge." *Population Bulletin* 35 (April).

Bowles, Samuel, and Herbert Gintis. [1976] 2011. *Schooling in Capitalist America: Educational Reform and the Contradictions of Economic Life.* With a new introduction by the authors. Chicago: Haymarket Books.

Brannigan, Augustine. 1992. "Postmodernism." Pp. 1522-1525 in *Encyclopedia of Sociology,* vol. 3, edited by Edgar F. Borgatta and Marie L. Borgatta. New York: Macmillan.

Bray, Karen. 2012. "What's in a Name? Tracing the Development of Latina Theologies of Their Own." *Theological and Philosophical Studies* (March). Accessible at www.drew.edu.

Brenan, Megan. 2019a. "U.S. Men Less Concerned than in 2017 about Sexual Harassment." March 18. Accessible at www.gallup.com.

———. 2019b. "Record-High 56% of U.S. Prefer Working to Homemaking." Accessible at www.gallup.com.

———. 2019c. "40% of Americans Believe in Creationism." July 26. Accessible at www.gallup.com.

Brennan Center. 2015. "Voting Rights and Elections." Accessed November 12 at www.brennan-center.org.

Bronson, Jennifer, and Marcus Berzofsky. 2017. "Indicators of Mental Health Problems Reported by Prisoners and Jail Inmates, 2011-12." June. Accessible at www.bjs.gov.

Brooks, David. 2011. "Huntington's Clash Revisited." *New York Times,* March 3: Op-Ed at http://nytimes.com.

Brown, David. 2009. "Doing a Number on Surveys." *Washington Post National Weekly Edition* 26 (January 19):37.

Brown, David K. 2001. "The Social Sources of Educational Credentialism: Status Cultures, Labor Markets, and Organizations." *Sociology of Education* 74 (Extra issue):19-34.

Brown, Heather. 2012. *Marx on Gender and the Family.* Leiden, Netherlands: Brill.

Bruni, Frank. 2016. "How Facebook Warps Our Worlds." *New York Times,* May 22, News in Review, p. 3.

Bryman, Alan. 1995. *Disney and His Worlds.* London: Routledge.

Buchholz, Katharina. "This Chart Shows the Age That People Get Married Across the World." September 3. Accessible at www.weforum.com.

Buntin, Melinda Beeuwckes, and John A Graves. 2020. "How the ACA Dented the Cost Curve." *Health Affairs* 39 (3). Accessible at www.healthaffairs.org.

Burawoy, Michael. 2005. "For Public Sociology." *American Sociological Review* 70 (February):4-28.

Bureau of the Census. 1975. *Historical Statistics of the United States, Colonial Times to 1970.* Washington, DC: U.S. Government Printing Office.

———. 2004a. *Statistical Abstract of the United States, 2004-2005.* Washington, DC: U.S. Government Printing Office.

———. 2005b. "American Fact Finder: Places with United States." Accessible at http://factfinder.census.gov.

———. 2008a. *Statistical Abstract of the United States, 2008.* Washington, DC: U.S. Government Printing Office.

———. 2013. "Labor Force Statistics from the Current Population Survey. Table 11. Employed Persons by Detailed Occupation, Sex, Race, and Hispanic or Latino Ethnicity." February 6. Accessible at www.census.gov.

———. 2015b. "How Do We Know? Child Care, an Important Part of Life." May 12. Accessible at www.census.gov.

———. 2017a. "Halloween: October 31, 2017." September 7. CB17-FF.18. Accessible at www.census.gov.

———. 2017d. *Current Population Surveys, Annual Social and Economic Supplement. 1967-2017.* Accessible at www.census.gov.

———. 2018b. "Projected Race and Hispanic Origin: Main Projections Series for the United States. 2017-2060." March. Accessible at www.census.gov.

———. 2019a. "Table MS-2. Estimated Median Age at First Marriage: 1890 to Present." Accessible at ww.census.gov.

———. 2019b. "Educational Attainment in the United States: 2018." February 21. Accessible at www.census.gov.

———. 2019d. "Personal Income." *Current Population Survey (CPS): Annual Social and Economic (ASEC) Supplement.* Accessible at www.census.gov.

———. 2019e. "Fertility of Women in the United States: 2018." Accessible at www.census.gov.

———. 2019f. "Historical Living Arrangements of Children." October 16. Accessible at www.census.gov.

———. 2019g. "National Grandparents Day: September 8, 2019". Accessible at www.census.gov.

———. 2019h. "America's Families and Living Arrangements: 2019." Accessible at www.census.gov.

———. 2020a. *International Database.* Accessible at www.census.gov.

Bureau of Consular Affairs. 2020. "Adoption Statistics." Accessible at www.state.gov.

Bureau of Labor Statistics. 2018b. "Contingent and Alternative Employment Arrangements Summary." June 7. Accessible at www.bls.gov.

———. 2019a. *Occupational Outlook Handbook: Post-secondary Teachers.* Accessible at www.bls.gov.

———. 2019c. "Occupational Employment and Wages, May 2018. Childcare Workers." Modified March 29, 2019. Accessible at www.bls.gov.

———. 2019d. *American Time Use Survey.* June 19. Accessible at http://www.bls.gov/atus/.

———. 2019e. *Women in the Labor Force: A Databook.* December. Accessible at www.bls.gov.

———. 2019f. "Hispanic Share of the Labor Force Projected to Be 20.9 Percent by 2028." *The Economics Daily* (October 2). Accessible at ww.bls.gov.

———. 2019i. "Number of Jobs, Labor Market Experience, and Earnings Growth: Results from a National Longitudinal Survey." August 22. Accessible at www.bls.gov.

———. 2020a. "Union Affiliation of Employed Wage and Salary Workers by State." Table 5. Last modified January 19. Accessible at www.bls.gov.

———. 2020b. "Employed Persons by Detailed Occupation, Sex, Race, and Hispanic or Latino Identity." Table 11. Accessible at www.bls.gov.

———. 2020c. "Usual Weekly Earnings of Wage and Salary Workers Fourth Quarter 2019." January 17. Accessible at www.bls.gov.

———. 2020d. "Household Data Seasonally Adjusted. A-6. Employed and Unemployed Full- and Part-Time Workers by Sex and Age, Seasonally Adjusted." Accessible at www.bls.gov.

———. 2020e. *Occupational Employment Statistics. May 2019 National Occupational Employment and Wage Estimates United States.* Last day modified March 20. Accessible at www.bls.gov.

———. 2020f. Employment status of the civilian population by race, sex, and age. May 11. Accessible at www.bls.gov

———. 2020g. Unemployment Rate- Hispanic or Latino. May 22. Accessible at www.bls.gov.

Bures, Frank. 2011. "Can You Hear Us Now?" *Utne Reader* (March–April):8–9, 11.

Burger King. 2009. "Whopper Sacrifice." Accessed February 4 at www.whoppersacrifice.com/.

Burger, Andrew. 2015. "Report, April 6." Accessible at www.telecompetitor.com.

Burger, Jerry M. 2009. "Replicating Milgram: Would People Still Obey Today?" *American Psychologist* 64 (January):1–11.

———. 2014. "Situational Features in Milgram's Experiment That Kept His Participants Shocking." *Journal of Social Issues* 70 (3):489–500.

Burkitt, Laurie. 2015. "China's Leaders Scrap One-Child Policy." *Wall Street Journal,* October 30, p. A7.

Burns, Melinda. 2010. "Workfare and the Low-Wage Woman." *Miller-McClune* (November–December): 76–81.

Butler, Daniel Allen. 1998. *"Unsinkable": The Full Story.* Mechanicsburg, PA: Stackpole Books.

Butler, Stuart M., and Carmen Diaz. 2016. "'Third Places' as Community Builders." September 14. Accessible at www.brookings.edu.

C

Cai, Weiyl, and Scott Clement. 2016. "What Americans Think about Feminism Today." *Washington Post,* January 27. Accessible at www.washingtonpost.com.

Calles Barger, Lillian. 2019. *The World Come of Age: An Intellectual History of Liberation Theology.* New York: Oxford University Press.

Campbell, Frances, Gabriella Conti, James J. Heckman, Seong Hyeok Moon, Rodrigo Pinto Elizabeth Pungello, and Yi Pan. 2014. "Early Childhood Investments Substantially Boost Adult Health." *Science* (March 28). Accessible at http://science.sciencemag.org/.

Caplan, Ronald L. 1989. "The Commodification of American Health Care." *Social Science and Medicine* 28 (11):1139–1148.

Caplow, Theodore, and Louis Hicks. 2002. *Systems of War and Peace.* 2nd ed. Lanham, MD: University Press of America.

Carbon Trust. 2015. "About the Carbon Trust." Accessed December 17 at www.carbontrust.co.uk/about-carbon-trust/pages/default.aspx.

Carey, Benedict. 2017. "How Fiction Becomes Fact on Social Media." *New York Times,* October 24, pp. D1, D4.

———. 2017. "Katrina and Its Hard-Learned Lessons." *New York Times,* September 12, pp. D1, D6.

Carlton-Ford, Steve. 2010. "Major Armed Conflicts, Militarization, and Life Chances." *Armed Forces and Society* 36 (October):864–899.

Carnes, Jerry. 2019. "Why Is Clarkston So Diverse?" May 29. Accessible at www.11alive.com.

Carr, Deborah, and Rebecca L. Utz. 2020. "Families in Later Life: A Decade in Review." *Journal of Marriage and Family* 82 (February): 346–363.

Carty, Victoria. 2015. *Social Movements and New Technology.* Boulder, CO: Westview Press.

Casey, Nicholas. 2020. "For Classmates, Zoom Exposes a Class Divide." *New York Times,* April 5, p. 11.

Castells, Manuel. 2010a. *The Rise of the Network Society.* 2nd ed. With a new preface. Malden, MA: Wiley-Blackwell.

———. 2010b. *The Power of Identity.* 2nd ed. With a new preface. Malden, MA: Wiley-Blackwell.

———. 2014. "Forward." In Sasha Costanza-Chock, *Out of the Shadows, Into the Streets! Transmedia Organizing and the Immigrant Rights Movement.* Cambridge, MA: The MIT Press.

CBS News. 1979. Transcript of *Sixty Minutes* segment, "I Was Only Following Orders." March 31, pp. 2–8.

Center on Budget and Policy Priorities. 2019. *The Earned Income Tax Credit.* December 10. Accessible at www.cbpp.org.

———. 2014. "Northeast Florida Center for Community Initiatives (CCI)." Accessed January 20, 2016, at www.unf.edu.

Center for Constitutional Rights. 2011. "Stop-and-Frisks of New Yorkers in 2010 Hit All-Time High at 600,601; 87 percent of Those Stopped Black and Latino." March 2. Accessible at www.ccrjustice.org.

Center for Faith and Opportunity Initiatives. 2020. "Guidance on Constitutionally Protected Prayer and Religious Expression in Public Elementary and Secondary Schools." January 16. Accessible at www.ed.gov.

Centers for Disease Control and Prevention. 2012b. "National Marriage and Divorce Rate Trends." Accessed February 24 at www.cdc.gov/nchs/nvss/marriage_divorce_tables.htm.

———. 2016. "Strategies for Reducing Health Disparities—Selected CDC-Sponsored Interventions, United States, 2016." *Morbidity and Mortality Weekly Report* 65 (1).

———. 2017. "Marriage and Divorce." January 20. Accessible at www.cdc.gov.

———. 2020a. *NCHS: Births and General Fertility Rates.* January 27. Accessible at www.cdec.gov.

———. 2020b. Firearm Violence Prevention. May 22. Accessible at ww.census.gov.

Centers for Medicare and Medicaid Services. 2020a. "CMS Office of the Actuary Releases 2018-2027 Projections of National Health Expenditures." February 20. Accessible at www.cms.gov.

Chakravorty, Sanjoy, Deuesh Kapur, and Niruikar Singh. 2017. *The Other One Percent: Indians in America.* New York: Oxford University Press.

Chalfant, H. Paul, Robert E. Beckley, and C. Eddie Palmer. 1994. *Religion in Contemporary Society.* 3rd ed. Itasca, IL: F. E. Peacock.

Chamayou, Grégoire. 2015. *A Theory of the Drone.* Trans. by Janet Lloyd. New York: The New Press.

Chambliss, William. 1973. "The Saints and the Roughnecks." *Society* 11 (November–December): 24–31.

———, and Aida Y. Hass. 2012. *Criminology.* New York: McGraw-Hill.

Chase-Dunn, Christopher, and Peter Grimes. 1995. "World-Systems Analysis." Pp. 387–417 in *Annual Review of Sociology, 1995,* edited by John Hagan. Palo Alto, CA: Annual Reviews.

———, Yukio Kawano, and Benjamin D. Brewer. 2000. "Trade Globalization Since 1795: Waves of Integration in the World System." *American Sociological Review* 65 (February):77–95.

Cheng, Shu-Ju Ada. 2003. "Rethinking the Globalization of Domestic Service." *Gender and Society* 17 (2):166–186.

Cherlin, Andrew J. 2003. "Should the Government Promote Marriage?" *Contexts* 2 (Fall):22–29.

———. 2009. *The Marriage-Go-Round: The State of Marriage and the Family in America Today.* New York: Knopf.

———. 2011. "The Increasing Complexity of Family Life in the United States." September 8. Accessible at www.prb.org/Articles/2011/us-complex-family-life.aspx?p=1.

———. 2020. "Degrees of Change: An Assessment of the Deinstitutionalization of Marriage Thesis." *Journal of Marriage and Family* 82 (February): 62–80.

———. 2021. *Public and Private Families: An Introduction.* New York: McGraw-Hill.

Chesney-Lind, Meda. 2017. Linking Criminal Theory and Social Practice. Pp. 99–107 in Sharon Dolovich and Alexandra Natapoff (eds.) *The New Criminal Justice Thinking. New York.* New York University Press.

Chetty, Raj, Nathaniel Hendron, Maggie J. Jones, and Sonya R. Porter. Race and Economic Opportunity in the United States: An Intergenerational Perspective. National Bureau of Economic Research 2020. Accessible at www.equality-of-opportunity.org.

Chiavacci, David. 2008. "From Class Struggle to General Middle-Class Society to Divided Society: Societal Models of Inequality in Postwar Japan." *Social Science Japan Journal* 11 (1):5–27.

Child Care Aware. 2020. "The U.S. and the High Price of Child Care: 2019." Accessible at www.childcareaware.org.

China Labor Watch. 2015. "Analyzing Labor Conditions of Pegatron and Foxconn: Apple's Low-Cost Reality." February 11. Accessible at www.chinalaborwatch.com.

Chou, Rosalind S., and Joe R. Feagin. 2014. *The Myth of the Model Minority: Asian Americans Facing Racism.* Second Edition. Boulder: Paradigm Publishers.

Chun, Edna, and Joe R. Feagin. 2019. *Rethinking Diversity Frameworks in Higher Education.* New York: Routledge/CRC Press.

Chung, Esther K., Leny Mathew, Amy C. Rothkopf, Irma T. Elo, James C. Cayne, and Jennifer F. Culhane. 2009. "Parenting Attitudes and Infant Spanking: The Influence of Childhood Experiences." *Pediatrics* 124 (August):278-286.

Clark, Burton, and Martin Trow. 1966. "The Organizational Context." Pp. 17-70 in *The Study of College Peer Groups,* edited by Theodore M. Newcomb and Everett K. Wilson. Chicago: Aldine.

Clarke, Adele E., Janet K. Shim, Laura Maro, Jennifer Ruth Fusket, and Jennifer R. Fishman. 2003. "Bio Medicalization: Technoscientific Transformations of Health, Illness, and U.S. Biomedicine." *American Sociological Review* 68 (April):161-194.

Client Partners. 2020. "Client Friend." Accessible at www.clientpartners.planet.bindcloud.jp.

Cloud, Dana L., ed. 2019. "Progressive Social Movements and the Internet." In *The Oxford Encyclopedia of Communication and Critical Cultural Studies.* Cambridge: Oxford University Press.

Coates, Ta-Nehisi. 2014. "The Case for Reparations." *The Atlantic* (June).

Cockerham, William C. 2017. *Medical Sociology.* 14th ed. New York: Routledge.

Coffman, Katherine B., Lucas C. Coffman, and Keith M. Marzilli Ericson. 2013. "The Size of the LGBT Population and the Magnitude of Anti-Gay Sentiment Are Substantially Underestimated." NBER Working Paper No. 19508. Accessible at www.nber.org/papers/w19508.

Cohen, Cathy J., Matthew D. Luttig, and Jon C. Rogowski. 2017. *Millennials Speak Out About the Direction of the Country.* May. Accessible at www.genforwardsurvey.com.

Cohen, Patricia. 2011. "Genetic Basis for Crime: A New Look." *New York Times,* June 11.

———. 2012. "At 9/11 Museum, Talking Through an Identity Crisis." *New York Times,* June 3, pp. 1, 14, 21.

Cohen, Philip. 2014. "Family Diversity Is the New Normal for America's Children." Council on Contemporary Families. November 4. Accessible at https://contemporaryfamilies.org/the-new-normal/.

——— 2020. "The Coming Divorce Decline." *Socius: Sociological Research for a Dynamic World* 5(6).

Cohn, Nate. 2014. "Why Hispanics Don't Have a Larger Political Voice." *New York Times,* June 17, p. A3.

Colby, Sandra L., and Jennifer M. Ortman. 2015. "Projections of the Size and Composition of U.S. Population: 2014 to 2060." *Current Population Reports* P25-1153. March. Washington, DC: U.S. Government Printing Office. Accessible at www.census.gov.

Coleman, James William, and Donald R. Cressey. 1980. *Social Problems.* New York: Harper and Row.

Colin, Chris. 2016. "The Incredibly True Story of Renting a Friend in Tokyo." *Afar* (March/April 2016). Accessible at www.afar.com.

Collins, James. 2009. "Social Reproduction in Classrooms and Schools." *Annual Review of Anthropology* 38:33-48.

Collins, Patricia Hill. 2000. *Black Feminist Thought: Knowledge, Consciousness, and the Politics of Empowerment.* Revised 10th anniv. 2nd ed. New York: Routledge.

———. 2015. "Intersectionality's Definitional Dilemmas." *Annual Review of Sociology* 41:1-20.

———. 2019. *Intersectionality as Critical Social Theory.* Durham, NC: Duke University Press.

Collins, Randall. 1975. *Conflict Sociology: Toward an Explanatory Sociology.* New York: Academic Press.

———. 1980. "Weber's Last Theory of Capitalism: A Systematization." *American Sociological Review* 45 (December):925-942.

———. 1986. *Weberian Sociological Theory.* New York: Cambridge University Press.

———. 1995. "Prediction in Macrosociology: The Case of the Soviet Collapse." *American Journal of Sociology* 100 (May):1552-1593.

Collins, Rebecca L. 2011. "Content Analysis of Gender Roles in Media: Where Are We Now and Where Should We Go?" *Sex Roles* 64 (February): 290-298.

Collins, Terry. 2019. "Facial Recognition Is Facing Lawsuits." *USA Today,* November 19, pp. 1B, 2B.

Colucci, Jim. 2008. "All the World's a Screen." *Watch!* (June):50-53.

Commission on Civil Rights. 1976. *Fulfilling the Letter and Spirit of the Law: Desegregation of the Nation's Public Schools.* Washington, DC: U.S. Government Printing Office.

———. 1981. *Affirmative Action in the 1980s: Dismantling the Process of Discrimination.* Washington, DC: U.S. Government Printing Office.

Commoner, Barry. 1971. *The Closing Circle.* New York: Knopf.

———. 1990. *Making Peace with the Planet.* New York: Pantheon.

———. 2007. "At 90, an Environmentalist from the 70's Still Has Hope." *New York Times,* June 19, p. D2.

Concave Brand Tracking. 2017. "Spider-Man Product Placement Top 5." July 12. Accessible at www.concavebt.com.

Conger, Kate, Richard Fausset, and Serge F. Kovaleski. 2019. "Tech-Savvy City Bans a Crime-Fighting Tool: Facial Recognition." *New York Times,* May 15, pp. A1, A12.

Connelly, Roxanne, Vernon Gayle, and Paul S. Lambert. 2017. "A Review of Occupation-Based Social Classifications for Social Survey Research." *Methodological Innovations* (April 19).

Conner, Thaddieus, and Aimee L. Franklin. 2019. "20 Years of Indian Gaming: Reassessing and Still Winning." *Social Science Quarterly* (May): 793-807.

Connor, John M., and Robert H. Lande. 2019. "Does Crime Pay? Penalties and Profits." *Antitrust Magazine* 33 (Spring). Accessible at www.antitrustmagazine.org.

Conrad, Peter, and Kristin K. Barker. 2010. "The Social Construction of Illness: Key Insights and Policy Implications." *Journal of Health and Social Behavior* 51 (5):567-579.

———, and Meredith Bergey. 2015. "Medicalization: Sociological and Anthropological Perspectives." Pp. 105-109 in James O. Wright (ed.), *International Encyclopedia of the Social & Behavioral Sciences* (Second Edition). Amsterdam: Elsevier.

———, and Valerie Leiter. 2019. *The Sociology of Health and Illness: Critical Perspectives.* 10th ed. Thousand Oaks, CA: Sage.

Cooky, Cheryl, Michael Messner, and Michele Mustro. 2015. "It's Dude Time! A Quarter Century of Excluding Women's Sports in Televised News and Highlight Shows." *Communication and Sport* 3 (September):261-287.

Cooley, Charles Horton. [1865-1929]1956. *The Two Major Works of Charles H. Cooley: Social Organization & Human Nature and the Social Order.* New York: Free Press.

Coontz, Stephanie. 2012. "The Myth of Male Decline." *New York Times,* September 30 (Section SR), pp. 1, 8.

Cooper, K., S. Day, A. Green, and H. Ward. 2007. "Maids, Migrants and Occupational Health in the London Sex Industry." *Anthropology and Medicine* 14 (April):41-53.

Cooper, Marianne, and Allison J. Pugh. 2020. "Families Across the Income Spectrum: A Decade in Review." *Journal of Marriage and Family* 82 (February): 272-299.

Cooper, Thia. 2015. "Liberation Theology in Latin America: Dead or Alive?" In *The Changing World Religion Map,* pp. 1955-1969. Springer Netherlands.

Coritore, Matthew, Amir Goldberg, and Sameer B. Strivastava. 2020. "The New Analytics of Culture." *Harvard Business Review* (January-February):76-83.

Cornet, Liza J. M., and Jean-Louis Van Gelder. 2020. "Virtual Reality: A Use for Criminal Justice Practice." *Psychology, Crime & Law* 26 (7):631-647.

Coron, Clotilde, and Patrick Gibert. 2020. *Technological Change.* New York: John Wiley & Sons.

Coser, Lewis A. 1977. *Masters of Sociological Thought: Ideas in Historical and Social Context.* 2nd ed. New York: Harcourt Brace Jovanovich.

Coser, Rose Laub. 1984. "American Medicine's Ambiguous Progress." *Contemporary Sociology* 13 (January):9-13.

Costanza-Chock, Sasha. 2014. *Out of the Shadows, Into the Streets! Transmedia Organizing and the Immigrant Rights Movement.* Cambridge, MA: The MIT Press.

———. 2019. "Interview: Technology Isn't the Driver of Social Movements, It's the Other Way Around." December 17. Interview by Anna Bonet Martínez and Bart Grugeon Plana (Universitat Oberta de Cataluny). Accessible at www.uoc.edu.

Couch, Carl J. 1996. *Information Technologies and Social Orders.* Edited with an introduction by David R. Maines and Shing-Ling Chien. New York: Aldine de Gruyter.

Counter Extremism Project. 2017. "Anwar al-Awlaki. Part III: Anwar al-Awlaki Online." August. Accessible at www.counterextremism.com.

Cox, Oliver C. 1948. *Caste, Class, and Race: A Study in Social Dynamics.* Detroit: Wayne State University Press.

Crenshaw, Kimberlé. 1989. *Demarginalizing the Intersection of Race and Sex: A Black Feminist Critique of Antidiscrimination Doctrine, Feminist Theory, and Antiracist Politics.* Chicago: University of Chicago Legal Foundation.

———. 1991. "Mapping the Margins: Intersectionality, Identity Politics, and Violence against Women of Color." *Stanford Law Review* 43 (July):1241-1299.

———. 2015. "Why Intersectionality Can't Wait." *The Washington Post,* December 24. Accessible at www.washingtonpost.com.

Crosnoe, Robert. 2011. *Fitting In, Standing Out: Navigating the Social Challenges of High School to Get an Education.* New York: Cambridge University Press.

Cross, Simon, and Barbara Bagilhole. 2002. "Girls' Jobs for the Boys? Men, Masculinity and Non-Traditional Occupations." *Gender, Work, and Organization* 9 (April):204-226.

Croteau, David, and William Horton, and Stefania Milan. 2012. *Media/Society: Industries, Images, and Audiences.* 4th ed. Thousand Oaks, CA: Sage.

Crouse, Kelly. 1999. "Sociology of the Titanic." *Teaching Sociology Listserv.* May 24.

Crowley, Kacy, and Michelle Sandhoff. 2017. "Just a Girl in the Army: U.S. Iraq War Veterans Negotiating Femininity in a Culture of Masculinity." *Armed Forces and Society* 43 (2):221-237.

Cuff, E. C., W. W. Sharrock, and D. W. Francis, eds. 1990. *Perspectives in Sociology.* 3rd ed. Boston: Unwin Hyman.

Currie, Elliot. 1985. *Confronting Crime: An American Challenge.* New York: Pantheon.

———. 1998. *Crime and Punishment in America.* New York: Metropolis Books.

Currier, Erin. 2017. *The State of the American Dream*: Episode 1. January 31. Podcast from the Pew Charitable Trusts. Accessible at www.pewtrusts.org.

Curtin, Sally C, and Paul D. Sutton. 2020. Marriage Rates in the United States, 1900-2018. *Health E-Stats.* April. Accessible at www.cdc.gov.

D

Dahl, Robert A. 1961. *Who Governs?* New Haven, CT: Yale University Press.

Dahrendorf, Ralf. 1958. "Toward a Theory of Social Conflict." *Journal of Conflict Resolution* 2 (June): 170-183.

———. 1959. *Class and Class Conflict in Industrial Society.* Stanford, CA: Stanford University Press.

Daley, Suzanne. 2013. "Danes Rethink a Welfare State Ample to a Fault." *New York Times,* April 12, pp. 1, 13.

Dalla, Rochelle L., and Wendy C. Gamble. 2001. "Teenage Mothering and the Navajo Reservation: An Examination of Intergovernmental Perceptions and Beliefs." *American Indian Culture and Research Journal* 25 (1):1-19.

Dastagir, Alia E. 2020. "Home Isolation Is Fertile Ground for Domestic Abuse." *USA Today,* March 19, pp. 1D, 2D.

Davidson, Paul. 2012. "More U.S. Service Jobs Go Overseas." *USA Today,* December 7, p. B1.

Davies, Christie. 1989. "Goffman's Concept of the Total Institution: Criticisms and Revisions." *Human Studies* 12 (June):77-95.

Davis, Kingsley. 1947. "A Final Note on a Case of Extreme Isolation." *American Journal of Sociology* 52 (March):432-437.

———, and Wilbert E. Moore. 1945. "Some Principles of Stratification." *American Sociological Review* 10 (April):242-249.

Davis-Delano, Laurel R., Joseph P. Gone, and Stephanie A. Fryberg. 2020. The psychosocial effects of Native American mascots: a comprehensive review of empirical research findings. *Race Ethnicity and Education* 23(5):613-633.

Death Penalty Information Center. 2016. "Facts about the Death Penalty." February 3, 2016. Accessible at www.deathpenaltyinformationcenter.org.

———. 2018. "Behind the Curtain: Secrecy and the Death Penalty in the United States." November 20. Accessible at www.deathpenaltyinfo.org.

———. 2020a. "Facts about the Death Penalty." January 16. Accessible at www.deathpenaltyinfo.org.

———. 2020b. "Description of Innocence Cases." Accessible at www.deathpenaltyinfo.org.

Deegan, Mary Jo, ed. 1991. *Women in Sociology: A Bio-Biographical Sourcebook.* Westport, CT: Greenwood.

———. 2003. "Textbooks, the History of Sociology, and the Sociological Stock of Knowledge." *Sociological Theory* 21 (November):298-305.

Deerwester, Jayne. 2019. "Hurricane Dorian vs. the Bahamas: How These Popular Destinations Fared against the Storm." *USA Today* (September 3). Accessible at usatoday.com.

De La Garza, Alejandro. 2020. "'It Conjures Up Every Facial Stereotype.' For Black Men, Homemade Masks May Be a Risk All Their Own." Time (April 17). Accessible at www.time.com.

Department of Health and Human Services. 2020. "U.S. Federal Poverty Guidelines Used to Determine Financial Eligibility for Certain Federal Programs." January 17. Accessible at www.hhs.gov.

———. 2020a. "TANF: Total Number of Families." Accessible at www.acf.hhs.gov.

Department of Justice. 2000. *The Civil Liberties Act of 1988: Redress for Japanese Americans.* Accessed June 29 at www.usdoj.gov/crt/ora/main.html.

———. 2008. "Hate Crime Statistics, 2007." Accessible at www.fbi.gov/ucr/ucr.htm.

———. 2017. "Crime in the United States, 2016." Accessible at www.fbi.gov.

Department of Labor. 2020a. "Minimum Wage." Accessible at www.dol.gov.

Department of State. 2019. *2019 Trafficking in Persons Report.* Accessible at www.state.gov.

Desilver, Drew. 2014. "5 Facts about Indian Americans." September 30. Accessible at www.pewresearch.org.

———. 2015. "Refugee Surge Brings Youth to an Aging Europe." October 8. Accessible at pewresearch.org.

Desmond, Mathew. 2019. "In Order to Understand the Brutality of American Capitalism, You Have to Start on the Plantation." *New York Times Magazine* (August 14). Accessible at www.nytimes.com.

Dettling, Lisa J., Joanne W. Hsu, Lindsay Jacobs, Kevin B. Moore, and Jeffrey P. Thompson. 2017. "Recent Trends in Wealth-Holding by Race and Ethnicity: Evidence from the Survey of Consumer Finances." *FEDS Notes* (September 27). Accessible at www.federalreserve.gov.

Deutsch, Francine M. 2007. "Undoing Gender." *Gender and Society* 21 (February):106-127.

Devitt, James. 1999. *Framing Gender on the Campaign Trail: Women's Executive Leadership and the Press.* New York: Women's Leadership Conference.

Diamond, Shari Seidman, and Mary R. Rose. 2018. "The Contemporary American Jury." *Annual Review of Law and Social Science* 14:239-258.

Diefenbach, Donald L., and Mark D. West. 2007. "Television and Attitudes toward Mental Health Issues: Cultivation Analysis and the Third Person Effect." *Journal of Community Psychology* 35 (2):181-195.

Diffenbaugh, Noah S., and Marshall Burke. 2019. "Global Warming Has Increased Global Inequality." *PNAS* 116 (May 14): 9808-9813.

DiNapoli, Jessica. 2020. U.S. firms shield CEO pay as pandemic hits workers, investors. May 28, 2020. Accessible at www.reuters.com.

Dinovitzer, Ronit, Nancy Reichman, and Joyce Sterling. 2009. "The Differential Valuation of Women's Work: A New Look at the Gender Gap in Lawyers' Incomes." *Social Forces* 88 (2): 819-864.

DiPrete, Thomas A., Gregory M. Eirich, and Matthew Pittinsky. 2010. "Compensation Benchmarking, Leapfrogs, and the Surge in Executive Pay." *American Journal of Sociology* 115 (May):1671-1712.

Di Stasio, Valentina. 2017. "Who Is Ahead in the Labor Queue? Institutions' and Employers' Perspective on Overeducation, Undereducation, and Horizontal Mismatches." *Sociology of Education* 90 (2): 109-126.

Dittmar, Kelly, Kira Sanbonmatsu, and Susan J. Carroll. 2018. *A Seat at the Table: Congresswomen's Perspectives on Why Their Presence Matters.* New York: Oxford

Dodds, Klaus. 2000. *Geopolitics in a Changing World.* Harlow, UK: Pearson Education.

Domhoff, G. William. 1978. *Who Really Rules? New Haven and Community Power Reexamined.* New Brunswick, NJ: Transaction.

———. 2014a. *Who Rules America? The Triumph of the Corporate Rich.* 7th ed. New York: McGraw-Hill.

———. 2014b. "Is the Corporate Elite Fractured, or Is There Continuing Corporate Dominance? Two Contrasting Views." *Class, Race and Corporate Power* 3 (1): Article 1.

———. 2018. *Who Rules America?* Accessible at www.whorulesamerica.net.

———. 2020a. *Who Rules America?* Accessible at www.whorulesamerica.net.

———. 2020b. "Who Declares COVID-19 a Pandemic? Insight into Power Elite in USA." *Scholars' Circle Interview.* April 15. Accessible at www.armoudian.com.

Domina, Thomas, Andrew McEachin, Paul Hanselman, Priyanka Agarwal, NaYooung Hwang, and Ryan W. Lewis. 2019. "Beyond Tracking and Detracking: The Dimensions of Organizational Differentiation in Schools." *Sociology of Education* 92 (3): 293-322.

Doress, Irwin, and Jack Nusan Porter. 1977. *Kids in Cults: Why They Join, Why They Stay, Why They Leave.* Brookline, MA: Reconciliation Associates.

Dougherty, Conor, and John Elron. 2020. "How to Protest When You're Ordered Not to Gather." *New York Times,* April 30, p. B3.

Downey, Allen B. 2014. "Religious Affiliation, Education and Internet Use." March 21. arXiv:1403.5534. Accessible at www.arxiv.org.

Dubina, Kevin S., Teresa L. Morisi, Michael Riely, and Andrea B. Wagoner. 2019. "Projections and Overview, 2018–28." *Monthly Labor Review* (October). Accessible at www.bls.gov.

DuBois, W. E. B. [1899] 1995. *The Philadelphia Negro: A Social Study.* Philadelphia: University of Pennsylvania Press.

———. [1900] 1969. "To the Nations of the World." Pp. 19–23 in *An ABC of Color,* edited by W. E. B. DuBois. New York: International Publishers.

———. [1903] 1961. *The Souls of Black Folks. Essays and Sketches.* New York: Fawcett.

———. [1903] 2003. *The Negro Church.* Walnut Creek, CA: AltaMira Press.

———. [1909] 1970. *The Negro American Family.* Atlanta University. Reprinted 1970. Cambridge, MA: MIT Press.

———. [1935] 1962. *Black Reconstruction in America 1860–1880.* New York: Athenaeum.

———. [1940] 1968. *Dusk of Dawn.* New York: Harcourt Brace. Reprint. New York: Schocken Books.

———. 2018. "More Americans Say Pornography Is Morally Acceptable." June 5. Accessible at www.gallup.com.

Duhigg, Charles, and Keith Bradsher. 2012. "How U.S. Lost Out on iPhone Work." *New York Times,* January 22, p. A1.

Duke P., R. M. Frankel, and S. Reis. 2013. "How to Integrate the Electronic Health Record and Patient-Centered Communication into the Medical Visit: A Skills-Based Approach." *Teaching and Learning in Medicine* 25 (4):358–365.

Dunlap, Riley E. and Robert J. Brulle. 2019. "Sociology and Climate Changes." *Global Dialogue* 9(2). Accessible at www.isa-sociology.org.

———, and Angela G. Mertig. 1991. "The Evolution of the U.S. Environmental Movement from 1970 to 1990: An Overview." *Society of National Resources* 4 (July–September):209–218.

DuPuis, Nicole, and Brooks Rainwater. 2014. *The Sharing Economy: An Analysis of Current Sentiment Surrounding Homesharing and Ridesharing.* Washington, DC: National League of Cities. Accessible at www.nlc.org.

Durex. 2013. *The Face of Global Sex 2013. First Sex Using a Condom and Its Impact on Future Sexual Behavior.* Slough, Berkshire, United Kingdom: Durex.

Durkheim, Émile. [1893] 1933. *Division of Labor in Society.* Translated by George Simpson. Reprint. New York: Free Press.

———. [1895] 1964. *The Rules of Sociological Method.* Translated by Sarah A. Solovay and John H. Mueller. Reprint. New York: Free Press.

———. [1897] 1951. *Suicide.* Translated by John A. Spaulding and George Simpson. Reprint. New York: Free Press.

———. [1912] 2001. *The Elementary Forms of Religious Life.* A new translation by Carol Cosman. New York: Oxford University Press.

Dynarski, Susan. 2019. "Student Debt." *Pathways: State of the Union Inequality Report.* Pp. 11–13. Accessible at www.inequality.stanford.edu.

E

Eagan, Kevin, Ellen Bara Stolzenberg, Hilary B. Zimmerman, Melissa Whang Sayson, and Cecila Rios-Aguilar. 2017. *The American Freshman: National Norms Fall 2016.* Los Angeles: Higher Education Research Institute, UCLA.

Ebaugh, Helen Rose Fuchs. 1988. *Becoming an Ex: The Process of Role Exit.* Chicago: University of Chicago Press.

Eckholm, Erik. 2015. "ISIS Incitement on Internet Raises Second Thoughts About First Amendment." *New York Times,* December 28, p. A10.

Economic Mobility Project. 2014. *Women's Work: The Economic Mobility of Women across a Generation.* April. Washington, DC: Pew Charitable Trusts.

The Economist. 2017a. "Women Are Working More, But Few Are Getting Ahead." (November 18): 32–33.

———. 2017c. "The Rise of Childlessness." (July 29): 51–52.

———. 2017d. "Not Turning Out." February 4: 51–52.

———. 2019b. "The Generation Game." (January 5):1–16.

———. 2019c. "Remembrance of Posts Past." (February 2):21–22.

———. 2019d. "Seek and You Shall Find." (June 8):81.

———. 2019e. "Net Loss." (November 9):53–54.

———. 2020a. "Everything's Under Control." (March 28): 7.

Edelman, Benjamin, Michael Luca, and Dan Svirsky. 2017. "Racial Discrimination in the Sharing Economy: Evidence from a Field Experiment." *American Economic Journal: Applied Economics.* (April):1–22.

Edgell, Stephen, Hedi Gottfied, and Edward Granter (eds.). 2017. *The SAGE Handbook of the Sociology of Work and Employment.* London: Sage.

Edmonson, Kate. 2019a. "ICE Used Facial Recognition to Mine State Driver's License Databases." *New York Times,* July 7. Accessible at www.nytimes.com.

———. 2019b. "Just What Does A.I. Think of You?" *New York Times,* September 24, p. C3.

Edney, Anna. 2019. "Teens Say They Don't Vape, They 'Juul.' That Makes the Activity Hard to Track." *Los Angeles Times.* April 29. Accessible at www.latimes.com.

Edwards, Nelta. 2010. "Using Nail Polish to Teach about Gender and Homophobia." *Teaching Sociology* 38 (4):362–372.

Ehrenreich, Barbara. 2001. *Nickel and Dimed: On (Not) Getting By in America.* New York: Metropolitan.

Ehrlich, Paul R. 1968. *The Population Bomb.* New York: Ballantine.

———, and Anne H. Ehrlich. 1990. *The Population Explosion.* New York: Simon and Schuster.

———. and Katherine Ellison. 2002. "A Looming Threat We Won't Face." *Los Angeles Times,* January 20, p. M6.

Eitzen, D. Stanley. 2009. *Fair and Foul: Beyond the Myths and Paradoxes of Sport.* 4th ed. Lanham, MD: Rowman & Littlefield.

Elignon, John, Audra D. S. Burch, Dionne Searcey, and Richard A. Oppel Jr. 2020. "Black Americans Bear the Brunt as Deaths Climb." *New York Times,* April 8, pp. A1, A17.

Ellison, Ralph. 1952. *Invisible Man.* New York: Random House.

Ellwood, Mark. 2019. "Why Cruise Lines Are Putting So Much Money into Private Islands." July 11. Accessible at www.cntraveler.com.

Engels, Friedrich [1884] 1959. "The Origin of the Family, Private Property, and the State." Pp. 392–394, excerpted in *Marx and Engels: Basic Writings on Politics and Philosophy,* edited by Lewis Feuer. Garden City, NY: Anchor Books.

Environmental Justice Foundation. 2015. "Climate Justice: Protecting Climate Refugees." Accessed December 17 at www.ejfoundation.org.

———. 2017. *Beyond Borders: Our Changing Climate– Its Role in Conflict and Displacement.* London: EJF. Accessible at www.ejfoundation.org.

Environmental Protection Agency. 2012. Global Greenhouse Gas Data, Figure 3, Total Greenhouse Gas Emissions by Region, from Global Anthropogenic Emissions of Non-CO2 Greenhouse Gases 1990-2020, EPA Report 430-R-06-003. June 2006. www.epa.gov/climatechange/emissions/globalghg.html.

Equal Employment Opportunity Commission. 2018. "Charges Alleging Sexual Harassment and Facts About Sexual Harassment." Accessible at www.eeoc.gov.

Erikson, Emily, and Nicholas Occhiuto. 2017. "Social Networks and Macrosocial Change." *Annual Reviews of Sociology* 43 (1):229–248.

Erikson, Kai. 1966. *Wayward Puritans: A Study in the Sociology of Deviance.* New York: Wiley.

Erlanger, Steven. 2015. "As China Seeks More Births, Higher Limit May Not Be the Answer." *New York Times,* November 10, p. A9.

Etaugh, Claire. 2003. "Witches, Mothers and Others: Females in Children's Books." *Hilltopics* (Winter):10–13.

Etzioni, Amitai. 1964. *Modern Organization.* Englewood Cliffs, NJ: Prentice Hall.

———. 1965. *Political Unification.* New York: Holt, Rinehart and Winston.

———. 2013. "The Great Drone Debate." *Military Review* (March–April):2–12.

———. 2020. "The Sociology of Surviving the Coronavirus." *The National Interest* (March 16). Accessible at https://nationalinterest.org.

Eurostat. 2015. "People at Risk of Poverty or Social Exclusion." *European Union.* October 25. Accessible at www.ec.euroipa.eu.

———. 2020. "Mean Age at First Marriage by Sex." September 3. Accessible at www.ec.europa.eu.

Everyday Sexism Project. 2020. "Catalogue Instances of Sexism." Accessible at www.everydaysexism.com.Ewing, Maura. 2015. "Punished for Being Poor." *Pacific Standard Magazine* (September–October):16–17.

Expatica. 2020. "German Social Security, Registration, Contributions, and Benefits." March 23. Accessible at www.expatica.com.

F

Farley, Melissa, and Victor Malarek. 2008. "The Myth of the Victimless Crime." *New York Times,* March 12, p. A27.

Farr, Grant M. 1999. *Modern Iran.* New York: McGraw-Hill.

Feagin, Joe R. 1989. *Minority Group Issues in Higher Education: Learning from Qualitative Research.* Norman: Center for Research on Minority Education, University of Oklahoma.

Federal Bureau of Investigation. 2019. "2018 Hate Crime Statistics." Accessible at www.fbi.gov.

————. 2020. *Crime in the United States, 2018.* Accessible at www.fbi.gov.

Feldblum, Chai R., and Victoria A. Lipnic (Co-chairs). 2018. *Select Task Force on the Study of Harassment in the Workplace.* June. Accessible at www.eeoc.gov.

Feldman, Lindsey Raisa. 2018. "Forging Selfhood: Social Categorisation and Identity in Arizona's Prison Wildfire Programme." *Howard Journal of Crime and Justice* 57(1):1-16.

Ferber, Abby L., and Michael S. Kimmel. 2008. "The Gendered Face of Terrorism." *Sociology Compass* 2:870-887.

Ferguson, Kathy E. 2017. "Feminist Theory Today." *Annual Review of Political Science* 20:269-286.

Few-Demo, April L., and Katherine R. Allen. 2020. "Gender, Feminist, and Intersectional Perspectives on Families: A Decade in Review." *Journal of Marriage and Family* 82 (February): 326-345.

Fielding, Sarah. 2020. "The system is unfair": US trans and non-binary people hit by voting barriers. June 16. Accessible at www.theguardian.org.

Fiji TV. 2020. Home page. Accessible at www.fijitv.com.fj.

File, Thom. 2017. "Voting in America: A Look at the 2016 Presidential Election." May 10. Accessible at www.census.gov.

Filgueira, Fernando, Orsetta Causa, Marc Fleurbaey, and Gianluca Grimalda. 2018. *Rethinking the Welfare State in the Global Economy.* June 14. Accessible www.g20-insights.org.

Fine, Gary C. 1987. *With the Boys: Little League Baseball and Preadolescent Culture.* Chicago: University of Chicago Press.

————. 2008. "Robbers Cave." Pp. 1163-1164, vol. 3, in *Encyclopedia of Race, Ethnicity, and Society,* edited by Richard T. Schaefer. Thousand Oaks, CA: Sage.

Finlay, Jessica. 2020. "Michigan Minds COVID-19 and Social Infrastructure." Institute for Social Research, University of Michigan. March 30. Accessible at www.isr.umich.edu.

Fiss, Peer C., and Paul M. Hirsch. 2005. "The Discourse of Globalization: Framing of an Emerging Concept." *American Sociological Review* (February):29-52.

Fjellman, Stephen M. 1992. *Vinyl Leaves: Walt Disney World and America.* Boulder, CO: Westview Press.

Flacks, Richard. 1971. *Youth and Social Change.* Chicago: Markham.

Fletcher, Connie. 1995. "On the Line: Women Cops Speak Out." *Chicago Tribune Magazine,* February 19, pp. 14-19.

Flores, Antonio. 2017. "How the U.S. Hispanic Population Is Changing." September 18. Accessible at www.pewresearch.org.

Flores, Glenn, M. Abreu, C. P. Barone, R. Bachur, and H. Lin. 2012. "Errors of Medical Interpretation and Their Potential Clinical Consequences: A Comparison of Professional versus Ad Hoc versus No Interpreters." *Annals of Emergency Medicine* 60 (5):545-553.

Foladare, Irving S. 1969. "A Clarification of 'Ascribed Status' and 'Achieved Status.'" *The Sociological Quarterly* 10 (Winter, No. 1):53-61.

Foley, Douglas. 2011. "The Rise of Class Culture in Theory in Educational Anthropology." Chapter 6 in Bradley Lester and Mica Pollock (eds.), *A Companion to the Anthropology of Education.* New York: Wiley.

Fonseca, Felicia. 2008. "Dine College on Quest to Rename Navajo Cancer Terms." *News from Indian Country* 22 (January 7):11.

Forbes. 2020. "Forbes World's Billionaires List: The Richest in 2020." March 18. Accessible at www.forbes.com.

Ford, Kristie A. (ed.). 2018. *Facilitating Change Through Intergroup Dialogue: Social Justice Advocacy in Practice.* New York: Routledge.

Foucault, Michel. 1978. *The History of Sexuality. Vol. 1, An Introduction.* New York: Vintage.

Fowler, Erika Franklin, Michael M. Franz, Gregory John Martin, Zachary F. Peskowitz, and Travis N. Ridout. 2019. "Political Advertising Online and Offline." August 31. Paper presented at the American Political Science Association.

Fowler, Susan. 2020. *Whistleblower: My Journey to Silicon Valley and Fight for Justice at Uber.* New York: Viking.

Fox, Porter. 2014. "The End of Snow?" *New York Times,* February 9 (Section SR), pp. 1, 6.

Francis, Theo. 2017. "Why You Work for a Giant Company." *Wall Street Journal,* April 7, p. A10.

Frank, Arthur W. 2015. "From Sick Role to Narrative Subject: An Analytic Memoir." *Health* (London). November 18. Pii: 1363459315615395. [Epub ahead of Print].

Franke, Richard Herbert, and James D. Kaul. 1978. "The Hawthorne Experiments: First Statistical Interpretation." *American Sociological Review* 43 (October):623-643.

Frankenberg, Erica, Jongyeon Ee, Jennifer B. Ayscue, and Gary Orfield. 2019. "Harming Our Common Future: America's Segregated Schools 65 Years after *Brown.*" May 10. Accessible at www.civilrightsproject.ucla.edu.

Franklin, John Hope, and Evelyn Brooks Higginbotham. 2011. *From Slavery to Freedom.* 9th ed. New York: McGraw-Hill.

Freedman, Des. 2014. *The Contradictions of Media Power.* London: Bloomsbury.

Freedom House. 2019. *Freedom of the Net 2019: The Crisis of Social Media.* November. Accessible at www.freedomhouse.org.

Freese, Jeremy. 2008. "Genetics and the Social Science Explanation of Individual Outcomes." *American Journal of Sociology* 114 (Suppl.):51-535.

Freidson, Eliot. 1970. *Profession of Medicine.* New York: Dodd, Mead.

Freudenburg, William R. 2005. "Seeing Science, Courting Conclusions: Reexamining the Intersection of Science, Corporate Cash, and the Law." *Sociological Forum* 20 (March):3-33.

Frey, William H. 2016. *Analysis of 2000 Census and 2011-2015 American Community Survey* (Released December 8, 2016). Table 2: Segregation Measured by Dissimilarity Index: Metropolitan Areas over One Million Population, 2000 and 2011-2015. Accessible at https://www.brookings.edu.

Friedan, Betty. 1963. *The Feminine Mystique.* New York: Dell.

Friedman, Zack. 2019. "50% of Nation's Millennials Heading Back Home with Their Parents after College." *Forbes* (June 6). Accessible at www.forbes.com.

Frost, Riordan. 2019. *Piling Ever Higher: The Continued Growth of Student Loans.* Cambridge MA: Joint Center for Housing Studies of Harvard University.

G

Galbraith, John Kenneth. 1977. *The Age of Uncertainty.* Boston, MA: Houghton Mifflin.

Gallup. 2019. "Taxes: Gallup Historical Trends." Accessible at www.gallup.com.

————. 2020a. "Death Penalty." Accessible at www.gallup.com.

————. 2020b. "Crime." Accessible at www.gallup.com.

————. 2020c. "Religion." March 30. Accessible at www.gallup.com.

Gans, Herbert J. 1979. "Symbolic Ethnicity: The Future of Ethnic Groups and Cultures in America." *Ethnic and Racial Studies* 2 (January): 1-20.

————. 1995. *The War against the Poor: The Underclass and Antipoverty Policy.* New York: Basic Books.

Garfinkel, Harold. 1956. "Conditions of Successful Degradation Ceremonies." *American Journal of Sociology* 61 (March):420-424.

Gasparro, Annie, and Julie Jargon. 2012. "McDonald's to Go Vegetarian India." *Wall Street Journal,* September 5, p. B7.

Gass, Henry, and Jessica Mendoza. 2017. "On Gun Violence, Blaming Mental Illness May Only Deepen Stigma." *Christian Science Monitor* (November 22):10-11.

Gates, Gary J. 2012. "LGBT VOTE 2012." Los Angeles: The Williams Institute. Accessible at www.law.ucla.edu/williamsinstitute.

Gaudin, Sharon. 2009. "Facebook Has Whopper of a Problem with Burger King Campaign." *Computerworld,* January 15.

Gay, Lesbian and Straight Education Network. 2020. "Our Work." Accessible at www.glsen.org.

Gecas, Viktor. 2004. "Socialization, Sociology of." Pp. 14525-14530 in *International Encyclopedia of the Social and Behavioral Sciences,* edited by Neil J. Smelser and Paul B. Baltes. Cambridge, MA: Elsevier.

Gemmill, Alison. 2019. "From Some to None? Fertility Expectation Dynamics of Permanently Childless Women." *Demography* 56 (1): 129-149.

General Social Survey. 2019. "GSS Data Explorer: Subjective Social Class 2018." Accessible at www.gssdataexplorer.norc.org.

GenForward. 2016. *GenForward Pre-Election 2016 Toplines.* November. Accessible at www.genforwardsurvey.com.

Gershuny, Jonathan, and Oriel Sullivan. 2019. *What We Really Do All Day: Insights from the Centre for Time Research.* London: Pelican Books.

Gerth, H. H., and C. Wright Mills. 1958. *From Max Weber: Essays in Sociology.* New York: Galaxy.

Ghaziani, Amin, and Matt Brim (eds.). 2019. *Imagining Queer Methods.* New York: New York University Press.

Giddings, Paul J. 2008. *Ida: A Sword among Lions.* New York: Amistad.

Gidwani, Toni. 2017. "The Future of Cyber Attacks." December 28. Accessible at www.securitytoday.com.

Gillespie, C., and K. Hurvitz. 2013. "Prevalence of Hypertension and Controlled Hypertension—United States, 2007-2010." *Morbidity and Mortality Weekly Report (MMWR)* 62(3):144-148.

Gilmore, Karen. 2019. "Is Emerging Adulthood a New Developmental Phase?" *Journal of the American Psychoanalytic Association* 67 (August):625-653.

Giordano, Peggy C. 2003. "Relationships in Adolescence." Pp. 257–281 in *Annual Review of Sociology,* 2003, edited by Karen S. Cook and John Hagan. Palo Alto, CA: Annual Reviews.

Gitlin, Todd. 2002. *Media Unlimited: How the Torrent of Images and Sounds Overwhelms Our Lives.* New York: Henry Holt.

Glusac, Elaine. 2016. "My House Is Your House. Or Is It?" *New York Times,* June 26, Sect. TR, p. 8.

Goel, Vindu, and Sheera Frenkel. 2019. "In India Election, False Posts and Hate Speech Flummox Facebook." *New York Times,* April 1, pp. A1, A10.

Goering, Laurie. 2008b. "Outsourced to India: Stress." *Chicago Tribune,* April 20, pp. 1, 18.

Goetz, Edward G., Anthony Damiano, and Rashad A. Williams. 2019. "Racially Concentrated Areas of Affluence: A Preliminary Investigation." *Cityscape: A Journal of Policy Development and Research* 21 (1): 99–123.

Goffman, Erving. 1952. "On Cooling the Mark Out: Some Aspects of Adaptation to Failure." *Psychiatry* 15 (4):451–463.

———. 1959. *The Presentation of Self in Everyday Life.* New York: Doubleday.

———. 1961. *Asylums: Essays on the Social Situation of Mental Patients and Other Inmates.* Garden City, NY: Doubleday.

———. 1963. *Stigma: Notes on Management of Spoiled Identity.* Englewood Cliffs, NJ: Prentice Hall.

Golann Joanne W. 2015. "The Paradox of Success at a No-Excuses School." *Sociology of Education* 88 (April, no. 2):103–119.

Gold, Howard R. 2019. "Who Is at Fault for Student-loan Defaults?" *Chicago Booth Review* (May 13).

Goldberg, Emma. 2020. Medical Care Lost in Translation. *New York Times* (April 21): D8.

Goldberg, Shoshana K., and Keith J. Conron. 2018. "How Many Same-Sex Couples in the U.S Are Raising Children?" July. The Williams Institute of the UCLA School of Law. Accessible at www.williamsinstitute.law.ucla.edu.

Golden, Fran. 2016. "Cruise Ship Turns Away from Haiti amid Protests." *USA Today,* January 20. Accessible at www.usatoday.com.

Goldenberg, Claude, and Kristin Wagner. 2015. "Bilingual Education: Reviving an American Tradition." *American Educator* (Fall). Accessible at www.aft.org.

Goldstein, Dana, and Julie Bosman. 2020. "Future of Day Care Centers Is Uncertain as Parents Weigh Risks of Contagion." *New York Times* (May 29). Accessible at www.nytimes.com.

Gonzalez-Barrera, Ana, and Philip Connor. 2019. "Around the World, More Say Immigrants Are a Stength Than a Burden." March 14. Accessible at www.pewresearch.org.

Gorman, Brandon, and Charles Senquin. 2018. "World Citizens on the Periphery: Threat and Identification with Global Society." *American Journal of Sociology* 124 (November): 705–61.

Gorney, Cynthia. 2014. "Far from Home." *National Geographic* (February):7–95.

Gould, Kenneth A., and Tammy L. Lewis (eds.). 2015. *Twenty Lessons in Environmental Sociology.* 2nd ed. New York: Oxford University Press.

Gould, Larry A. 2002. "Indigenous People Policing Indigenous People: The Potential Psychological and Cultural Costs." *Social Science Journal* 39:171–188.

Graells-Garrido, Eduardo, Mounia Lalmas, and Ricardo Baeza-Yates. 2016. "Data Portraits and Intermediary Topics: Encouraging Exploration of Politically Diverse Profiles." July. *Proceedings of the 21st International Conference on Intelligent User Interfaces.* Pp. 228–240. London: Yahoo Labs.

Graham-McLay, Charlotte. 2018a. "After Years of Stigma, New Zealand Embraces Māori Language." *New York Times,* September 17, p. A4.

———. 2018b. "A Fading Māori Town Is Pinning All Its Hopes on a Marijuana Boom." *New York Times,* November 18, p. A6.

Grall, Timothy. 2020. "Custodial Mothers and Fathers and Their Child Support: 2015." Revised January. *Current Population Reports* P60-262. Accessible at ww.census.gov.

Gramlich, John, and Katherine Schaeffer. 2019. "7 Facts about Guns in the U.S." October 22. Accessible at www.pewresearch.org.

Gramsci, Antonio. 1929. *Selections from the Prison Notebooks.* Edited and translated by Quintin Hoare and Geoffrey Nowell Smith. London: Lawrence and Wishort.

Grattet, Ryken. 2011. "Societal Reactions to Deviance." *Annual Review of Sociology* 37:185–204.

Greeley, Andrew M. 1989. "Protestant and Catholic: Is the Analogical Imagination Extinct?" *American Sociological Review* 54 (August): 485–502.

Green, Jeff. 2019. Investors penalize companies for adding women to their boards. November 25. Accessible at www.bloombetrg.com.

Green, Penelope, 2016. "Tech Support." *New York Times,* March 13, Sunday Styles, pp. 1, 14.

Greenhouse, Steven. 2019. *Beaten Down, Worked Up: The Past, Present, and Future of American Labor.* New York: Penguin/Random House.

Greenstone, Michael, Adam Looney, Jeremy Patashnik, and Muxin Yu. 2013. "Thirteen Economic Facts about Social Mobility and the Role of Education." June. Accessible at www.brookings.edu.

Gregor, Alison. 2013. "A NORC, Up Close and Personal." *New York Times,* May 5, p. 8.

Greico, Elizabeth, and Jeffrey Gottfried. 2017. "In Trump's First 200 Days, News Stories Citing His Tweets Were More Likely to Be Negative." October 18. Accessible at www.pewreserch.org.

Grind, Kirsten, Sam Schechner, Robert McMillan, and John West. 2019. "How Google Shapes Its Search Results—and Why." *Wall Street Journal,* November 16, pp. B1, B6–B10.

Grollman, Eric Anthony. 2018. "Sexual Orientation Differences in Whites' Racial Attitudes." *Sociological Forum* 33 (1):186–210.

Groppe, Maureen. 2020. "House Use Breathes Life into Equal Rights Amendment." *USA Today,* February 14, p. 3A.

Grygiel, Jennifer. 2016. "Teaching Lesson. 2016 AEJMC Best Practices in Ethics in an Emerging Media Environment Teaching Competition." September 9. Accessible at www.jennifergrygiel.com.

Guenther, Julia, and Eswarappa Kasi. 2015. "Globalization and People at the Margins: Experiences from the Global South." *Journal of Developing Societies* 31 (1):1–7.

Guo, Guang, Michael E. Roettger, and Tianji Cai. 2008. "The Integration of Genetic Propensities into Social-Control Models of Delinquency and Violence among Male Youths." *American Sociological Review* 73 (August):543–568.

Guterres, António. 2020. "The Recovery from the COVID-19 Crisis Must Lead to a Different Economy." March 31. Accessible at www.un.org.

Gutiérrez, Gustavo. 1990. "Theology and the Social Sciences." Pp. 214–225 in *Liberation Theology at the Crossroads: Democracy or Revolution?* edited by Paul E. Sigmund. New York: Oxford University Press.

Guttman A. 2019. "Global Instagram Influencer Market Size from 2017 to 2020 (in billion U.S. dollars)." Accessible at www.statista.com.

H

Hacker, Andrew. 1964. "Power to Do What?" Pp. 134–146 in *The New Sociology,* edited by Irving Louis Horowitz. New York: Oxford University Press.

Hacker, Helen Mayer. 1951. "Women as a Minority Group." *Social Forces* 30 (October):60–69.

———. 1974. "Women as a Minority Group, Twenty Years Later." Pp. 124–134 in *Who Discriminates against Women?* edited by Florence Denmark. Beverly Hills, CA: Sage.

Hall, Judith A., Terrence G. Horgan, and Nora A. Murphy. 2019. "Nonverbal Communication." *Annual Review of Psychology* 70:271–294.

Hallinan, Maureen T. 1997. "The Sociological Study of Social Change." *American Sociological Review* 62 (February):1–11.

Halpin, John, Karl Agne, and Nisha Jain. 2019. "America Decides." December 5. Accessible at www.americanprogress.org.

Hamilton, Brady E. 2020. State Teen Birth Rates by Race and Hispanic Origin: United States, 2017–2018. *National Vital Statistics Reports* 89 (6).

Hardesty, Jennifer L., and Brian G. Ogolsky. 2020. "A Sociological Perspective on Intimate Partner Violence Research: A Decade in Review." *Journal of Marriage and Family* 82 (February): 454–477.

Harlow, Harry F. 1971. *Learning to Love.* New York: Ballantine.

Harper, Douglas. 1988. "Visual Sociology: Expanding Sociological Vision." *American Sociologist* (Spring):54–70.

Harrell, Erika. 2015. *Victims of Identity Theft, 2014.* September 27. Washington, DC: U.S. Government Printing Office.

Harrington, Michael. 1980. "The New Class and the Left." Pp. 123–138 in *The New Class,* edited by B. Bruce Briggs. Brunswick, NJ: Transaction.

Harris, Aisha. 2019. "#MeToo Moves Forward." *New York Times,* October 16, p. C1.

Harris, Scott. 2015. "Returning to Homeland, Vietnamese Americans Make Their Mark." *Los Angeles Times,* August 30. Accessible at www.latimes.com.

Haub, Carl. 2013. "Were the Population Alarmists Right or Wrong?" Washington, DC: Population Reference Bureau. Accessed April 24 at http://demographicsrevealed.org/2013/03/26/were-the-population-alarmists-right-or-wrong/.

Haviland, William A., Harald E. L. Prins, Dana Walrath, and Bunny McBride. 2015. *Cultural Anthropology—The Human Challenge.* 14th ed. Boston, MA: Cengage.

———, ———, Bunny McBride, and Dana Walrath. 2017. *Cultural Anthropology—The Human Challenge.* 15th ed. Boston, MA: Cengage.

Hawdon, James, and John Ryan. 2011. "Social Relations That Generate and Sustain Solidarity after a Mass Tragedy." *Social Forces* 89 (4):1383-1384.

Hayden, H. Thomas. 2004. "What Happened at Abu Ghraib." Accessed August 7 at www.military.com.

Heath, Ryan. 2020. "U.N. Chief Says There's a Bigger Threat than Coronavirus." *Politico* (April 21). Accessible at www.politico.com.

Hecht, Jaime. 2016. "Preparing for a 21st Century Job Hunt with a BA in Sociology." *Footnotes* (March-April):4, 18.

Heckert, Druann, and Amy Best. 1997. "Ugly Duckling to Swan: Labeling Theory and the Stigmatization of Red Hair." *Symbolic Interaction* 20 (4):365-384.

Hedley, R. Alan. 1992. "Industrialization in Less Developed Countries." Pp. 914-920, vol. 2, in *Encyclopedia of Sociology,* edited by Edgar F. Borgatta and Marie L. Borgatta. New York: Macmillan.

Hellmich, Nanci. 2001. "TV's Reality: No Vast American Waistlines." *USA Today,* October 8, p. D7.

Herman, Max Arthur. 2005. *Fighting in the Streets: Ethnic Succession and Urban Unrest in Twentieth-Century America.* New York: Peter Lang.

Herrera, Giaconda. 2013. "Gender and International Migration: Contributions and Cross-Fertilizations." *Annual Review of Sociology* 39:471-489.

Herrman, John. 2018. "The Cambridge Analytica Scandal Revealed How Much We All Trusted Facebook—and Clarified What the Company Is Really Capable Of." *New York Times Magazine* (April 15):12-15.

Herschthal, Eric. 2004. "Indian Students Discuss Pros, Cons of Arranged Marriages." *Daily Princetonian,* October 20.

Hess, Amanda. 2017. "Having Built a Bubble, Sites Sell a Way Out." *New York Times,* March 5, pp. A12, A21.

Hewlett, Sylvia Ann, and Carolyn Buck Luce. 2005. "Off-Ramps and On-Ramps: Keeping Talented Women on the Road to Success." *Harvard Business Review* (March):43-53.

Heymann, Jody, with Kristen McNeill. 2013. *Children's Chances: How Countries Can Move from Surviving to Thriving.* Cambridge, MA: Harvard University Press.

Hibben, Kristen Cibelli, Beth-Ellen Pennell, and Lesli Scott. 2017. Minimizing Interviewer Effects. May 12, OECD Seminar on Managing the Quality of Data Collection in Largescale Assessments. Accessible at www.oecd.org

Higgins, Andrew. 2015. "German Village of 102 Braces for 750 Asylum Seekers." *New York Times,* October 31, pp. 1, 10.

Hill, Katherine. 2020. "How to Home School During Coronavirus." *New York Times,* March 23. Accessible at www.nytimes.com.

Hill, Michael R., and Susan Hoecker-Drysdale, eds. 2001. *Harriet Martineau: Theoretical and Methodological Perspectives.* New York: Routledge.

Hinduja, Sameer, and Justin W. Patchin. 2015. " Cyberbulying Legislation and Case Law." Updated January. Accessible at www.cyberbullying.org.

Hines, Alice. 2018. "The Ultimate List of Cool Happenings." *New York Times,* July 19, p. D6.

Hinshaw, Drew, and Szabolcs Panyi. 2020. "Orban Allowed to Rule by Decree." *Wall Street Journal,* March 31, p. A9.

Hira, Ron. 2008. "An Overview of the Offshoring of U.S. Jobs." Pp. 14-15 in Marlene A. Lee and Mark Mather, "U.S. Labor Force Trends." *Population Bulletin* 63 (June).

Hirschi, Travis. 1969. *Causes of Delinquency.* Berkeley: University of California Press.

Hirst, Paul, and Grahame Thompson. 1996. *Globalization in Question: The International Economy and the Possibilities of Governance.* Cambridge, UK: Polity Press.

Hitlin, Steven, and Jane Allyn Piliavin. 2004. "Values: Reviving a Dormant Concept." Pp. 359-393 in *Annual Review of Sociology, 2004,* edited by Karen S. Cook and John Hagan. Palo Alto, CA: Annual Reviews.

Hochschild, Arlie Russell. 1990. "The Second Shift: Employed Women Are Putting in Another Day of Work at Home." *Utne Reader* 38 (March-April): 66-73.

———. 2016. "The Right vs. the Family." *Dissent* 63 (1): 42-47.

Holcombe, Madeline, & Sharif Paget. 2020. Ferguson's first black elected mayor says videos of police abuse help to get rid of bad officers. June 4. Accessible at www.cnn.com

Holden, Constance. 1980. "Identical Twins Reared Apart." *Science* 207 (March 21):1323-1328.

———. 1987. "The Genetics of Personality." *Science* 257 (August 7):598-601.

Holmes, Paul. 2019. "Provoke19: How March for Our Lives Went from Moment to Movement." October 24. Accessible at www.holmesreport.com.

Holshue, Michael et al. 2020. "First Case of 2019 Novel Coronavirus in the United States." January 31. Accessible at www.NEJM.org; republished *New England Journal of Medicine* 382 (March 5): 929-936.

Holson, Laura M. 2019. "As Cries of Witch Hunt Flood the Air, a Witch Contemplates the Irony." *New York Times,* October 13, p. 21.

Homans, George C. 1979. "Nature versus Nurture: A False Dichotomy." *Contemporary Sociology* 8 (May):345-348.

Home School Legal Defense Association. 2020. "Homeschool Laws in Your State." Accessible at www.hslda.org.

hooks, bell. 1994. *Feminist Theory: From Margin to Center.* 2nd ed. Boston: South End Press.

Hootsuite & We Are Social. 2019. "Digital 2019 Global Digital Overview." Accessible at https://datareportal.com/reports/digital-2019-global-digital-overview.

Horkheimer, Max, and Theodore Adorno. [1944] 2002. *Dialectic of Enlightenment.* Palo Alto, CA: Stanford University Press.

Horner, James. 2015. "Speak Out: Should Students and Faculty Be Allowed to Carry Guns on College Campuses?" *Annenberg Classroom.* Accessed October 23 at annenbergclassroom.org.

Horowitz, Helen Lefkowitz. 1987. *Campus Life.* Chicago: University of Chicago Press.

Horowitz, Juliana Menasce, Ruth Igielnik, and Rakesh Kochhar. 2020. "Most Americans Say There Is Too Much Economic Inequality in the U.S., but Fewer Than Half Call It a Top Priority." January 9. Accessible at www.pewresearch.org.

Horowitz, Juliana, Nikki Graf, and Gretchen Livingston. 2019. "Marriage and Cohabitation in the U.S." November 6. Accessible at www.pewresearch.org.

Horwitz, Allan V. 2002. *Creating Mental Illness.* Chicago: University of Chicago Press.

Hosokawa, William K. 1969. *Nisei: The Quiet Americans.* New York: Morrow.

Hossain, Ziarat, Soyoung Lee, and Ashley Martin-Cuellar. 2015. "Latino Mothers' and Fathers' Caregiving with Their School-Age Children." *Hispanic Journal of Behavioral Sciences* (May, No. 2):186-203.

Houkamau, Carla A., and Chris G. Sibley. 2019. "The Role of Culture and Identity for Economic Values: A Qualitative Study of Māori Attributes." *Journal of the Royal Society of New Zealand* 49 (supplement):118-131.

Hout, Michael. 2019. "Social Mobility." *Pathways: The Poverty and Inequality Report 2019,* pp. 29-32. Accessible at www.inequality.stanford.edu.

Howard, Russell D., and Reid L. Sawyer. 2003. *Terrorism and Counterterrorism: Understanding the New Security Environment.* Guilford, CT: McGraw-Hill/Dushkin.

Howell, David R., and Arne L. Kalleberg. 2019. "Declining Job Quality in the United States: Explanations and Evidence." *RSF: The Russell Sage Foundation Journal of the Social Sciences* 5 (4):1-53.

Huang, Gary. 1988. "Daily Addressing Ritual: A Cross-Cultural Study." Presented at the annual meeting of the American Sociological Association, Atlanta.

Hughes, Everett. 1945. "Dilemmas and Contradictions of Status." *American Journal of Sociology* 50 (March):353-359.

Human Genome Project. 2018. "All about Us." Last modified February 11, 2015. Archived and accessed January 15, 2018, at www.genome.gov.

Hunt, Jennifer S. 2015. "Race, Ethnicity, and Culture in Jury Decision Making." *Annual Review of Law and Social Science* 11:269-288.

Hunter, Herbert M., ed. 2000. *The Sociology of Oliver C. Cox: New Perspectives: Research in Race and Ethnic Relations,* vol. 2. Stamford, CT: JAI Press.

Hunter, Lori M., Jessie K. Luna, and Rachel M. Norton. 2015. "Environmental Dimensions of Migration." *Annual Review of Sociology* 41: 377-397.

Huntington, Samuel P. 1993. "The Clash of Civilizations?" *Foreign Affairs* 72 (Summer):22-49.

Hur, Song-Woo. 2011. "Mapping South Korean Women's Movements During and After Democratization: Shifting Identities." *East Asian Social Movements,* edited by J. Broadbent and V. Brockman.

Hurn, Christopher J. 1985. *The Limits and Possibilities of Schooling,* 2nd ed. Boston: Allyn and Bacon.

Hurwitz, Heather McKee, and Verta Taylor. 2012. "Women's Cultures and Social Movements in Global Context." *Sociology Compass* 6 (October): 808-822.

Hussar, William J., and Tabitha M. Bailey. 2019. *Projections of Education Statistics to 2027.* Washington, DC: National Center for Education Statistics, 2019.

Hutson, Jevan, Jessie G. Taft, Solon Barocas, and Karen Levy. 2018. "Debiasing Desire: Addressing Bias and Discrimination on Intimate Platforms."

Proceedings of the ACM Humanities Interaction 2 (no. CSCW): article 73.

Hutson, Matthew. 2014. "Espousing Equality, but Embracing a Hierarchy." *New York Times,* June 22, sect. BU, p. 3.

Igo, Sarah E. 2007. *The Average American: Surveys, Citizens, and the Making of a Mass Public.* Cambridge, MA: Harvard University Press.

Ilten, Carla, and Paul-Brian McInerney. 2019. " Social Movements and Digital Technology." Pp. 198–220 in Janet Vertesi and David Ribes (eds.). *digitalISTS: A Field Guide for Science & Technology.* Princeton, NJ: Rutgers University Press.

India, Government of. 2009. *India: Urban Poverty Report 2009.* February 3. New Delhi: Ministry of Housing and Urban Poverty Alleviation. Accessible at www.in.undp.org.

Inglehart, Ronald, and Wayne E. Baker. 2000. "Modernization, Cultural Change, and the Persistence of Traditional Values." *American Sociological Review* 65 (February):19–51.

Ingram, Noble. 2019. "Internet Access and the 'Homework Gap.'" *Christian Science Monitor Weekly* (January 14):21.

Inoue, Hiroko. 2019. "Book Review: Giants: The Global Power Elite." *Journal of World-Systems Research* 25 (2): 518–522.

Institute for Economics and Peace. 2015a. *Global Peace Index 2015.* Accessible at www.economicsandpeace.org.

———. 2019a. *Global Peace Index 2019.* Sydney: Institute for Economics and Peace. Accessible at www.economicsandpeace.org.

———. 2019b. *Global Terrorism Index 2019.* Sydney: Institute for Economics and Peace. Accessible at www.economicsandpeace.org.

Institute of International Education. 2019. "Places of Origin 2019." Accessible at www.iie.org.

Institute for Research on Poverty. 2020. "Many Rural Americans Are Still 'Left Behind.'" January. *Fast Focus Research/Policy Brief* No. 44-2020. Accessible at https://www.irp.wisc.edu.

Institute on Metropolitan Community Opportunity. 2019. *American Neighborhood Change in the 21st Century.* April. Minneapolis: University of Minnesota Law School.

Inter-Parliamentary Union. 2020. "Percentage of Women in Parliaments." March 1. Accessible at www.data.ipu.org.

Interbrand. 2019. "Best Global Brands 2019: Rankings." Accessible at www.interbrand.com.

International Center for Academic Integrity. 2015. "Statistics." Accessed February 11, 2016, at www.academicintegrity.org.

———. 2018. "Statistics." Accessible at www.academicintegrity.org.

International Federation of Robotics. 2019. *Executive Summary WR 2019 Industrial Robots.* Frankfurt Germany: IFR. Accessible at www.ifr.org.

International Institute for Democracy and Electoral Assistance. 2013. *Atlas of Electoral Gender Quotas.* Accessible at www.idea.int.

———. 2014. "Voter Turnout Database–Custom Query." Accessed January 26 at www.idea.int/vt/viewdata.cfm#.

———. 2015. *Databases and Networks.* Accessed December 7 at www.idea.int.

———. 2018a. *Voter Turnout Database.* Accessible at www.idea.int.

_____. 2018b. *Atlas of Electoral Gender Quotas.* Accessible at www.idea.int.

International Institute for Democracy and Electoral Assistance. 2020. *Voter Turnout Database.* Accessible at www.idea.int.

International Labour Organization. 2015. "New ILO Figures Show 150 Million Migrants in the Global Workforce." December 16. Accessible at www.ilo.org.

_____. 2017. "Trade Union Density." Accessible at www.ilo.org.

_____. 2017a. *World Employment Social Outlook. Trends 2017.* Geneva, Switzerland: International Labour Organization. January 12. Accessible at www.ilo.org.

_____. 2019. "ILOSTAT: Statistics on Union Membership." Accessible at https://ilostat.ilo.org.

_____. 2020. "ILOSTAT: SDG Indicator 5.5.2–Female Share of Employment in Managerial Positions." Accessible at www.ilo.org.

International Monetary Fund. 2000. *World Economic Outlook: Asset Prices and the Business Cycle.* Washington, DC: International Monetary Fund.

International Survey Social Programme. 2014. "ISSP 2012- Family and Changing Gender Roles IV Variable Report." October 29. Cologne Germany: GESIS Leibniz Institute for Social Sciences.

International Survey Study Programme. 2019. *ISSP 2017-Social Networks and Social Resources, Variable Report.* August 19. Cologne Germany: GESIS. Accessible at www.gesis.org.

International Telecommunication Union. 2012. "Global Technology Development Figures." October 11. Accessed November 14, 2013, at www.itu.int/net/pressoffice/press_releases/2012/70.aspx#.UoUJgKW50pE.

International Trade Union Confederation. 2009. "Davos: World Unions Call for Action against Corporate Grand Theft." Accessed January 31 at www.ituc-csi.org/spip.php?article2736.

———. 2014. *ITUC Global Poll 2014.* Accessible at www.ituc-csi.org.

———. 2017. *ITUC 2017 Global Poll.* Accessible at www.ituc-csi.org.

International Visual Sociology Association. 2016. "About IVSA." Accessible at www.visualsociology.org.

———. 2018. "About IVSA." Accessible at www.visualsociology.org.

———. 2020. "What Does Visual Sociology Mean to You?" Accessible at www.visualsociology.org.

Internet Crime Complaint Center. 2012. *The 2011 Internet Crime Report.* Washington, DC: The National White Collar Crime Center. Accessible at www.ic3.gov/media/annualreport/2011_IC3Report.pdf.

———. 2015. *The 2014 Internet Crime Report.* Washington, DC: The National White Collar Crime Center. Accessible at www.ic53.gov.

Internet World Stats. 2014. "Usage and Population Statistics" and "Internet World Users by Language." Updated on March 28. Accessed March 29 at www.internetworldstats.com.

———. 2015. "Usage and Population Statistics" and "Internet World Users by Language." Updated on March 29. Accessed March 29 at www.internetworldstats.com.

———. 2017. "Usage and Population Statistics." Accessible at www.internetworldstats.com.

———. 2018. "Internet Usage Statistics. The Internet Big Picture." Accessed January 2 at www.internetworldstats.com.

_____.2020. "Usage and Population Statistics." Updated as of April 20. Accessed at www.internetworldstats.com.

IQAIR. 2020. *2020 World Air Quality Report.* Accessible at www.iqair.com.

Ironside, Virginia. 2011. "Romania's Orphanages: Locking the Past Away." *The Independent (UK)* (November 29). Accessed September 25, 2012, at www.independent.co.uk/life-style/health-and-families/features/romanias-orphanages-locking-the-past-away-6269173.html.

Isaacs, Julia B. 2007b. *Economic Mobility of Men and Women.* Washington, DC: Economic Mobility Project.

———, Isabel V. Sawhill, and Ron Haskins. 2008. *Getting Ahead or Losing Ground: Economic Mobility in America.* Washington, DC: Pew Charitable Trusts.

Ishak, Adam. 2013. "The New Media in Post-Revolution Egypt." January 21. Accessible at Roskilde University at http://rudar.ruc.dk/handle/1800/9886.

ITOPF. 2006. "Statistics: International Tanker Owners Pollution Federation Limited." Accessed May 2 at www.itopf.com/stats.html.

Jackson, Mathew O. 2019. *The Human Network: How We're Connected and Why It Matters.* London: Atlantic Books.

Jackson, Philip W. 1968. *Life in Classrooms.* New York: Holt.

Jacobs, Andres. 2010. "As China's Economy Grows, Pollution Worsens Despite New Efforts to Control It." *New York Times,* July 29, p. A4.

Jacobs, Anna W., and Irene Padavic. 2015. "Hours, Scheduling and Flexibility for Women in the US Low-Wage Labour Force." *Gender, Work and Organization* 22 (No. 1, January).

Jacobs, Emma. 2016. "Online Dating Sites Breed New Careers." *Financial Times,* July 8, p. 10.

Jacobs, Tom. 2009. "Hot Men of the Links." *Miller-McCune* (May–June):79.

Jacobsen, Linda A., Mark Mather, and Genevieve Dupuis. 2012. "Household Change in the United States." *Population Bulletin* 67 (September).

Jaffee, Daniel. 2012. "Weak Coffee: Certification and Co-Optation in the Fair Trade Movement." *Social Problems* 59 (1):94–116.

Jain, Saranga, and Kathleen Kurz. 2007. *New Insights on Preventing Child Marriage: A Global Analysis of Factors and Programs.* Washington, DC: International Center for Research on Women.

James, Selma. 2012. *Sex, Race and Class: The Perspective of Winning: A Selection of Writings 1952-2011.* Oakland, CA: PM Press.

Jan, Tracy. 2017. "PayPal Escalates the Tech Industry's War on White Supremacy." *Washington Post,* August 17. Accessible at www.washingtonpost.com.

Janta, Barbara. 2014. *Caring for Children in Europe.* Brussels: RAND Europe.

Jäntti, Markus. 2009. "Mobility in the United States in Comparative Perspectives." *Focus* 26 (Fall).

Japan Aisaika Organization. 2020. "Aisaika Organization Prospectus." Accessible at www.aisaika.org

Jarosz, Beth, and Mark Mather. 2017. "Losing Ground: Young Women's Well-Being Across Generations in the United States." *Population Bulletin* 21 (June).

Jasper, James M. 1997. *The Art of Moral Protest: Culture, Biography, and Creativity in Social Movements.* Chicago: University of Chicago Press.

———. 2013. "The End of 'Online Dating.'" *USA Today,* February 14, pp. 1A, 2A.

———. 2014. *Protest: A Cultural Introduction to Social Movements.* Cambridge, UK: Polity Books.

Jenkins, Henry. 2006. *Convergence Culture: Where Old and New Media Collide.* New York: New York University Press.

Jennings, Rebecca. 2014. "A Bridge Across the Technology Divide." *Monash University Communications* (June):32–35.

Jensen, Gary F. 2005. "Social Organization Theory." In *Encyclopedia of Criminology,* edited by Richard A. Wright and J. Mitchell Miller. Chicago: Fitzrog Dearborn.

Jensen, Todd, and Matthew O. Howard. 2015. "Perceived Stepparent–Child Relationship Quality: A Systematic Review of Stepchildren's Perspectives." *Marriage and Family Review* 51 (2):99–153.

Jervis, Rick. 2008. "New Orleans Homicides up 30% over 2006 Level." *USA Today,* January 3, p. 3A.

Jesella, Kara. 2008. "Blogging's Glass Ceiling." *New York Times,* July 27, Style section, pp. 1, 2.

Joas, Hans, and Wolfgang Knöbl. 2009. *Social Theory: Twenty Introductory Lectures.* Cambridge, UK: Cambridge University Press.

John, Robert. 2012. "The Native American Family." Pp. 361–410 in *Ethnic Families in America: Patterns and Variations.* 5th ed., edited by Roosevelt Wright Jr., Charles H. Mindel, Thanh Van Tran, and Robert W. Halsenstein. Upper Saddle River, NJ: Pearson.

Johns, Michelle M., V. Paul Poteat, Stacey S. Horn, and Joseph Kosci. 2019. "Strengthening Our Schools to Promote Resilience and Health Among LGBTQ Youth: Emerging Evidence and Research Priorities from the State of LGBTQ Youth Health and Wellbeing Symposium." *LGBT Health* 6 (4): 146–155.

Johnson, Benton. 1975. *Functionalism in Modern Sociology: Understanding Talcott Parsons.* Morristown, NJ: General Learning.

Johnson, Bobbie. 2010. "Privacy No Longer a Social Norm, Says Facebook Founder." January 10. Accessed December 2, 2013, at www.theguardian.com/technology/2010/jan/11/facebook-privacy.

Johnson, David R., and Liang Zhang. 2020. "Intrastate and Interstate Influences on the Introduction and Enactment of Campus Carry Legislation, 2004–2016." *Educational Researcher.* First published online January at https://doi.org/10.3102/0013189X20902121.

Johnson, Ian. 2012. "A Promise to Tackle China's Problems, but Few Hints of a Shift in Path." *New York Times,* November 16, p. A19.

Johnson, Sandra. 2020. "A Changing Nation: Population Projections Under Alternative Immigration Scenarios." *Current Population Reports P25-1146.* February. Accessible at www.census.gov.

Jones, Jeffrey M. 2013. "Americans Still Divided on Energy-Environment Trade-Off." April 10. Accessible at www.gallup.com/poll/161729/americans-divided-energy-environment-trade-off.aspx.

———. 2017. "Americans Hold Record Liberal Views on Most Value Issues." May 11. Accessible at www.gallup.com.

———. 2020. "U.S. Party Preferences Have Swung Sharply Toward Democrats. July 16. Accessible at www.gallup.com.

Jones-Puthoff, Alexa. 2013. *Is the U.S. Population Getting Older and More Diverse?* June 14. Accessible at www.census.gov/newsroom/cspan/pop_diverse/.

Jonsson, Patrik. 2019. "Florida Voters Gave Ex-felons Right to Vote. Then Lawmakers Stepped In." *The Christian Science Monitor Weekly* (June 2), pp. 10–11.

Juhász, Levente, and Henry Hochmair. 2017. "Where to Catch'em All–A Geographical Analysis of Pokémon Go Locations." *Geo-spatial Information Science* 20:241–251.

Julian, Tiffany, and Robert Kominski. 2011. *Education and Synthetic Work-Life Earnings Estimates.* ACS-14. Washington, DC: U.S. Government Printing Office.

Juniper Research. 2015. *Cybercrime and the Internet of Threats.* Basingstoke, UK: Juniper Research.

K

Kalleberg, Arne L. 2009. "Precarious Work, Insecure Workers: Employment Relations in Transition." *American Sociological Review* 74 (February):1–22.

———. 2012. "The Social Contract in an Era of Precarious Work." *Pathways* (Fall):3–6.

———, and Steven P. Vallas. 2018. "Probing Precarious Work: Theory, Research, and Politics." *Research in The Sociology of Work* 31: 1–30.

Kambayashi, Takehiko. 2008. "Japanese Men Shout the Oft-Unsaid 'I Love You.'" *Christian Science Monitor,* February 13.

Kaneda, Toshiko, and Genevieve Dupuis. 2017. *2017 World Population Data Sheet.* Washington, DC: Population Reference Bureau. Accessible at www.prb.orbg.

Kapoor, Mudità, Deepak Agrawal, Shamika Ravi, Ambuj Roy, S. V. Subramaniand, and Randeep Guleria. 2019. "Missing Women Patients: Gender Discrimination in Access to Healthcare." August 8. Accessible at www.brookings.edu.

Karabell, Zachary. 2020. Globalization? Don't Count On it. *Wall Street Journal* (March 21): C1, C2.

Karmel, Tom. 2015. "Skills Deepening or Credentialism? Education Qualifications and Occupational Outcomes, 1996–2011." *Australian Journal of Labour Economics* 18 (April, no. 1).

Karmi, Faith. 2020. "At These Movie Theatres, the Shows Have Gone On Despite the Coronavirus Pandemic." April 24. Accessible at www.cnn.com.

Katovich, Michael A. 1987. Correspondence. June 1.

Katz, Michael. 1971. *Class, Bureaucracy, and the Schools: The Illusion of Educational Change in America.* New York: Praeger.

Keane, Helen, Megan Weier, Doug Fraser, and Coral Gartner. 2017. "'Anytime, Anywhere': Vaping as Social Practice." *Critical Public Health* 27 (4):465-476.

Keating, Sarah. 2019. "Is 'Flexibility Stigma' Driving Women Out of the Offices?" September 13. Accessible at www.bbc.com.

Kennicott, Philip. 2011. "Review: 9/11 Memorial in New York." *Washington Post.* Accessed August 26 at www.washingtonpost.com.

Kenny, Charles. 2009. "Revolution in a Box." *Foreign Policy* (November):68–74.

Kerbo, Harold R. 2006. *World Poverty: The Roots of Global Inequality and the World System.* New York: McGraw-Hill.

———. 2012. *Social Stratification and Inequality.* 8th ed. New York: McGraw-Hill.

Kesmodel, David, and Danny Yadron. 2010. "E-Cigarettes Spark New Smoking War." *Wall Street Journal,* August 25, pp. A1, A12.

Kessler Institute. 2017. "Survey Shows Cheating and Academic Dishonesty Prevalent in Colleges and Universities." February 6. Accessible at www.prnewswire.com.

Khazan, Olga, 2019. "I Was Never Taught Where Humans Came From." *The Atlantic* (September 19). Accessible at www.theatlantic.com.

Kidder, Jeffrey L. 2012. "Parkour, the Affective Appropriation of Urban Space, and the Real/Virtual Dialectic." *City and Community* 11 (September): 229–253.

Killewald, Alexandra, Fabian T. Pfeffier, and Jared N. Schachner. 2017. "Wealth Inequality and Accumulation." *Annual Review of Sociology* 43:379-404.

Kim, Hyun Sik. 2011. "Consequences of Parental Divorce for Child Development." *American Sociological Review* 76 (3):487-511.

Kim, Kwang Chung. 1999. *Koreans in the Hood: Conflict with African Americans.* Baltimore, MD: Johns Hopkins University Press.

Kimmel, Michael S. 2008. *The Gendered Society.* 3rd ed. New York: State University of New York at Stony Brook.

Kinsey, Alfred C., Wardell B. Pomeroy, and Clyde E. Martin. 1948. *Sexual Behavior in the Human Male.* Philadelphia: Saunders.

———, ———, and Paul H. Gebhard. 1953. *Sexual Behavior in the Human Female.* Philadelphia: Saunders.

Kiser, Edgar. 1992. "War." Pp. 2243-2247 in *Encyclopedia of Sociology,* edited by Edgar F. Borgatta and Marie L. Borgatta. New York: Macmillan.

Kitchener, Richard F. 1991. "Jean Piaget: The Unknown Sociologist." *British Journal of Sociology* 42 (September):421-442.

Klein, Lloyd. 1994. "We're Going to Disney World: Consumers Credit and the Consumption of Social Experience." *Free Inquiry in Creative Sociology* 22 (November):117-124.

Klein, Naomi. 1999. *No Logo: Money, Marketing, and the Growing Anti-Corporate Movement.* New York: Picador (St. Martin's Press).

Klinenberg, Erik. 2012. *Going Solo: The Extraordinary Rise and Surprising Appeal of Living Alone.* New York: Penguin Books.

Knowles, Ryan T., and Antonio J. Castro. 2019. "The implications of ideology on teachers' beliefs regarding civic education." *Teaching and Teacher Education* (January): 226–239.

Knudsen, Morten. 2010. "Surprised by Method–Functional Method and System Theory." *Forum: Qualitative Social Research* 11 (September): article 12.

Kobielus, James. 2020. "Artificial Intelligence Predictions for 2020." March 16. First

Koike, Yuriko. 2015. "Why Inequality Is Different in Japan." March 2. Accessible at www.weforun.org.

Kokmen, Leyla. 2008. "Environmental Justice for All." *Utne Reader* (March–April):42–46.

Kopf, Dan. 2020. "The Ages That People Get Married Around the World." February 13. Accessible at www.qz.com.

Korean Women's Association United. 2016. "About KAWU." Accessible at www.women21.or.kr.

Kosmin, Barry A., and Ariela Keysar. 2009. *American Religious Identification Survey.* Hartford, CT: Trinity College.

Kottak, Conrad, and Scott Lukas. 2019. *Anthropology: Appreciating Human Diversity.* 18th ed. New York: McGraw-Hill.

Krane, Jim. 2009. *Dubai: The Story of the World's City.* London: Atlantic Books.

———. 2010. "To Spend or Not to Spend." Interviewed on Al Jazeera television, March 26. Accessed April 20 at http://english.aljazeera.net/programmes/countingthecost/2010/03/201032510494187263.html.

———. 2020. "Great. But Not Nearly Enough of Offset Carbon Emitted." April 29. Accessible at https://twitter.com/jimkrane?lang+en.

Kratz, Corinne A., and Iman Karp. 1993. "Wonder and Worth: Disney Museums in World Showcase." *Museum Anthropology* 17 (3):32–42.

Kraybill, Donald. 2019. *The Amish of Lancaster County.* 2nd Edition. Lanham, MD: Rowman and Littlefield.

Kriesberg, Louis. 1992. "Peace." Pp. 1432–1436 in *Encyclopedia of Sociology,* edited by Edgar F. Borgatta and Marie L. Borgatta. New York: Macmillan.

Krishnamurthy, Mathangi. 2018. *1-800-Worlds: The Making of the Indian Call Centre Economy.* New Delhi: Oxford University Press.

Kristof, Nicholas D. 1998. "As Asian Economies Shrink, Women Are Squeezed Out." *New York Times,* June 11, pp. A1, A12.

Krogstad, Jens Manuel, Ana Gonzalez-Barrera, and Christine Tamir. 2020. "Latino Democratic Voters Place High Importance on 2020 Presidential Election." January 17. Accessible at www.pewresearch.org.

Krogstad, Jens Manuel, Jeffrey S. Passel, and D'Vera Cohn. 2017. "5 Facts About Illegal Immigration in the U.S." April 27. Accessible at www.pewresearch.org.

Kronberg, Anne-Kathrin. 2020. "Workplace Gender Pay Gaps: Does Gender Matter Less the Longer Employees Stay?" *Work and Occupations* 47 (1): 3–43.

Kunkel, Charlotte A. 2016. "From Protest to Praxis or Being Real in the Classroom." In *Teaching Gender and Sex in Contemporary America,* Kristin Haltinnern and Ryanne Pilgeram (eds.). New York: Springer.

Kunzig, Robert. 2011. "Seven Billion." *National Geographic* (January):40–69.

Kurtz, Annalyn, Tal Yellin, and Will Hoop. 2019. "The U.S. Minimum Wage through the Years." April 19. Accessible at cnn.com.

Ladd, Helen F., and Lucy Sorensen. 2019. "Teacher Turnover and the Disruption of Teacher Staffing." April 29. Accessible at www.brookings.edu.

Ladner, Joyce. 1973. *The Death of White Sociology.* New York: Random Books.

Lai, K. K. Rebecca, and Jasmine C. Lee. 2016. "10 Percent of Florida Adults Are Ineligible to Vote. Why?" *New York Times,* October 7, p. A13.

Lajimodiere, Denise K. 2013. "American Indian Females and Stereotypes: Warriors, Leaders, Healers, Feminists; Not Drudges, Princesses, Prostitutes.*" Multicultural Perspectives* 15 (Issue 2).

Lakhani, Chiraq M., Braden T. Tierney, Arjun K. Manrai, Jian Yang, Peter M. Visscher, and Chirag J. Patel. 2019. "Repurposing Large Health Insurance Claims Data to Estimate Genetic and Environmental Contributions in 560 Phenotypes." *Nature Genetics* 5:327–334.

Landtman, Gunnar. [1938] 1968. *The Origin of Inequality of the Social Class.* New York: Greenwood (original edition 1938, Chicago: University of Chicago Press).

Lasswell, Harold D. 1936. *Politics: Who Gets What, When, How.* New York: McGraw-Hill.

Last, Jonathan. 2013. *What to Expect When No One's Expecting: America's Coming Demographic Disaster.* New York: Encounter Books.

Laumann, Edward O., John H. Gagnon, and Robert T. Michael. 1994a. "A Political History of the National Sex Survey of Adults." *Family Planning Perspectives* 26 (February):34–38.

———, ———, ———, and Stuart Michaels. 1994b. *The Social Organization of Sexuality: Sexual Practices in the United States.* Chicago: University of Chicago Press.

Lavrakas, Paul J., Charles D. Shuttles, Charlotte Steel, and Howard Fienberg. 2007. "The State of Surveying Cell Phone Numbers in the United States: 2007 and Beyond."*Public Opinion Quarterly* 71 (5):840–854.

Lawson, Sandra. 2008. *Girls Count.* New York: Goldman Sachs.

Lazarsfeld, Paul, Bernard Beretson, and H. Gaudet. 1948. *The People's Choice.* New York: Columbia University Press.

———, and Robert K. Merton. 1948. "Mass Communication, Popular Taste, and Organized Social Action." Pp. 95–118 in *The Communication of Ideas,* edited by Lymon Bryson. New York: Harper and Brothers.

Leap, Braden. 2020. "A New Type of (White) Provider: Shifting Masculinities in Mainstream Country Music from the 1980s to the 2010s." *Rural Sociology* 85 (1):165–189..

Leavell, Hugh R., and E. Gurney Clark. 1965. *Preventive Medicine for the Doctor in His Community: An Epidemiologic Approach.* 3rd ed. New York: McGraw-Hill.

Lee, Alfred McClung. 1983. *Terrorism in Northern Ireland.* New York: Rowman & Littlefield.

Lee, Ji Hyun. 2013. "Modern Lessons from Arranged Marriages." *New York Times,* January 18. Accessible at www.nytimes.com/2013/01/20/fashion/weddings/parental-involvement-can-help-in-choosing-marriage-partners-experts-say.html?pagewanted=all.

Lee, Ronald D., and David S. Reher. 2011. "Introduction: The Landscape of Demographic Transition and Its Aftermath." *Population and Development Review* 37 (Supplement):1–7.

Lee, Yimou. 2020. "Taiwan's New 'Electronic Fence' for Quarantines Leads Wave of Virus Monitoring." March 20. Accessible at www.reuters.com.

Lemert, Charles. ed. 2013. *Social Theory: The Multicultural, Global, and Classical Readings.* 5th ed. Philadelphia: Westview.

Lengermann, Patricia Madoo, and Jill Niebrugge-Brantley. 1998. *The Women Founders: Sociology and Social Theory, 1830–1930.* Boston, MA: McGraw-Hill.

Lenski, Gerhard. 1966. *Power and Privilege: A Theory of Social Stratification.* New York: McGraw-Hill.

Levin, Kevin M. 2019. *Searching for Black Confederates: The Civil War's Most Persistent Myth.* Chapel Hill: University of North Carolina Press.

Levinson, Daniel J. 1978. *The Seasons of a Man's Life.* With Charlotte N. Darrow et al. New York: Knopf.

———. 1996. *The Seasons of a Woman's Life.* With Judy D. Levinson. New York: Knopf.

Levitt, Peggy, and B. Nadya Jaworsky. 2007. "Transnational Migration Studies: Past Developments and Future Trends." *Annual Review of Sociology* 33:129–156.

Levitt, Steven D., and Stephen J. Dubner. 2006. *Freakonomics: A Rogue Economist Explores the Hidden Side of Everything.* Revised and expanded edition. New York: Morrow.

———, and Sudhir Venkatesh. 2000. "An Economic Analysis of a Drug-Selling Gang's Finances." *Quarterly Journal of Economics* (August): 775–789.

Lewis, Rebecca C. 2020. "What to Know about the State's New Bail Reform Law." January 14. Accessible at www.cityandstateny.com.

Lewis, Robin J., Sarah J. Ehlke, Alexander T. Shappie, Abby L. Braitman, and Kristin E. Heron. 2019. "Health Disparities among Exclusively Lesbian, Mostly Lesbian, and Bisexual Young Women." *LGBT Health* 6 (8): 400–408.

Li, Angran, and Daniel Hamlin. 2019. "Is Daily Parental Help with Homework Helpful? Reanalyzing National Data Using a Propensity Score-Based Approach." *Sociology of Education* 92 (4): 367–385.

Liang, Zai, Jiejin Li, Glenn Deane, Zhen Li, and Bo Zhou. 2018. "From Chinatown to Every Town: New Patterns of Employment for Low-Skilled Chinese Immigrants in the United States." *Social Forces* 97 (December): 893–920.

The Liman Program, Yale Law School Association of State Correctional Administrators. 2015. *Time-in Cell: The ASCA-Liman 2014 National Survey of Administrative Segregation in Prison.* Available at law.yale.edu.

Lin, Liza, and Timothy Martin. 2020. "Virus Surveillance Clashes with Privacy." *Wall Street Journal,* April 16, pp. A1, A9.

Linn, Susan, and Alvin F. Poussaint. 1999. "Watching Television: What Are Children Learning about Race and Ethnicity?" *Child Care Information Exchange* 128 (July):50–52.

Lino, Mark, Kevin Kuczynski, Nestor Rodriguez, and Tusa Rebecca Schap. 2017. *Expenditures on Children by Families, 2015.* Miscellaneous Publication No. 1528-2015. U.S. Department of Agriculture, Center for Nutrition Policy and Promotion.

Linton, Ralph. 1936. *The Study of Man.* New York: Appleton-Century Crofts.

Liptak, Adam. 2008. "From One Footnote, a Debate over the Tangles of Law, Science and Money." *New York Times,* November 25, p. A13.

Liska, Allen E., and Steven F. Messner. 1999. *Perspectives on Crime and Deviance.* 3rd ed. Upper Saddle River, NJ: Prentice Hall.

Livingston, Gretchen. 2018. "More than One in Ten U.S. Parents Are Also Caring for an Adult." November 29. Pew Research Center. Accessible at pewresearch.org.

Livingstone, Sonia. 2004. "The Challenge of Changing Audiences." *European Journal of Communication* 19 (March):75–86.

Loayza, Norman V. 2016. "Informality in the Process of Development and Growth." July 20. Accessible at www.worldbank.org.

Lofland, Lyn H. 1975. "The 'Thereness' of Women: A Selective Review of Urban Sociology." Pp. 144–170 in *Another Voice,* edited by M. Millman and R. M. Kanter. New York: Anchor/Doubleday.

Lopez, Mark Hugo, Ana Gonzalez-Barrera, Jens Manuel Krogstad, and Gustavo López. 2016. "Democrats Maintain Edge as Party 'More Concerned' for Latinos, but Views Similar to 2012." October 11. Accessible at www.pewresearch.org.

———, Jeffrey Passel, and Molly Rohal. 2015. "Modern Immigration Wave Brings 59 Million to U.S., Driving Population Growth and Change Through 2065." September 28. Accessible at www.pewresearch.org.

Luhnow, David. 2014. "Most Violent Region in the World: Latin America." *Wall Street Journal,* April 12, p. A9.

Lukacs, Georg. 1923. *History and Class Consciousness.* London: Merlin.

Lynch, James P. 2012. *Corrections in the United States.* May 4. Accessible at www.bjs.gov.

Lynn, Barry C. 2003. "Trading with a Low-Wage Tiger." *American Prospect* 14 (February):10–12.

MacCoun, Robert J. 1989. "Experimental Research on Jury Decision-Making," *Science* 244 (June 2): 1046–1050.

Machalek, Richard, and Michael W. Martin. 2010. "Evolution, Biology and Society: A Conversation for the 21st-Century Sociology Classroom." *Teaching Sociology* 38 (1):35–45.

Mack, Mick G. 2003. "Does Exercise Status Influence the Impressions Formed by College Students?" *College Student Journal* 37 (December).

Mack, Raymond W., and Calvin P. Bradford. 1979. *Transforming America: Patterns of Social Change.* 2nd ed. New York: Random House.

Magga, Ole Henrik. 2006. "Diversity in Sami Terminology for Reindeer, Snow, and Ice." *International Social Science Journal* 58 (March):25–34.

Magnier, Mark. 2004. "China Clamps Down on Web News Discussion." *Los Angeles Times,* February 26, p. A4.

Maher, Kris. 2019. "Unions Lose Members after Ruling." *Wall Street Journal,* November 22, p. A3.

Malcolm X, with Alex Haley. [1964] 1999. *The Autobiography of Malcolm X.* Revised with Epilogue by Alex Haley and Afterword by Ossie Davis. New York: One World, Ballantine Books.

Males, Mike, and Meda Chesney-Lind. 2010. "The Myth of Mean Girls." *New York Times,* April 2, p. A21.

Malhotra, Neil, and Yotam Margalit. 2009. "State of the Nation: Anti-Semitism and the Economic Crisis." *Boston Review* (May–June). Accessible at http://bostonreview.net/BR34.3/malhotra_margalit.php.

Mallory, Christy, and Brad Sears. 2020. "LGBT Discrimination, Policy, and Law in the US." Accessible at www.williams.law.ucla.edu.

Mancini, Tiziana, Federica Sibilla, Dimitris Argiropoulos, Michele Rossi, and Marina Everri. 2019. "The Opportunities and Risks of Mobile Phones for Refugees' Experience: A Scoping Review." PLoS ONE 14(12): e0225684. https://doi. org/10.1371/journal.pone.0225684.

Mandel, Hadas. 2016. "The Role of Occupational Attributes in Gender Earnings Inequality, 1970–2010. *Social Science Research* 55 (January):122–138.

Mani, Deepti. 2018. "Education in South Korea." *World Education News + Reviews.* October 16. Accessible at https://wenr.wes.org/2018/10/education-in-south-korea.

Marist Poll. 2015. "PBS NewsHour/Marist Poll: Summary of National Findings." September. Accessible at www.pbs-newshour-marist-poll-sep2015.pdf.

Marketing Charts. 2018. "Super Bowl 2018 Data [Updated]." Accessible at www.marketingcharts.com.

Markovits, Daniel. 2019. *The Meritocracy Report.* New York: Penguin Press.

Martin, Dominique, Jean-Luc Metzger, and Philippe Pierre. 2006. "The Sociology of Globalization: Theoretical and Methodological Reflections." *International Sociology* 21 (July):499–521.

Martin, Greg. 2015. *Understanding Social Movements.* New York: Palgrave.

Martin, Isaac, and Monica Prasad. 2014. "Taxes and Fiscal Sociology." *Annual Review of Sociology* 40:331–345.

Martin, Karin A. 2009. "Normalizing Heterosexuality: Mothers' Assumptions, Talk, and Strategies with Young Children." *American Sociological Review* 74 (April):190–207.

Martin, Marvin. 1996. "Sociology Adapting to Changes." *Chicago Tribune,* July 21, sec. 18, p. 20.

Martin, Susan E. 1994. "Outsider within the Station House: The Impact of Race and Gender on Black Women Politics." *Social Problems* 41 (August):383–400.

Martineau, Harriet. [1837] 1962. *Society in America.* Edited, abridged, with an introductory essay by Seymour Martin Lipset. Reprint. Garden City, NY: Doubleday.

———. [1838] 1989. *How to Observe Morals and Manners.* Philadelphia: Leal and Blanchard. Sesquentennial edition, edited by M. R. Hill, Transaction Books.

Martinez-Carter, Karina. 2013. "How the Elderly Are Treated Around the World." *The Week* (July 23). Accessible at www.theweek.com.

Marx, Karl. [1844] 1964. "Contribution to the Critique of Hegel's Philosophy of Right." In *On Religion, Karl Marx and Friedrich Engels.* New York: Schocken Books.

———, and Friedrich Engels. [1847] 1955. *Selected Work in Two Volumes.* Reprint. Moscow: Foreign Languages Publishing House.

Maryanski, Alexandra, Richard Machalek, and Jonathan H. Turner. 2015. *Handbook on Evolution and Society: Toward an Evolutionary Social Science.* New York: Palgrave.

Masci, David. 2017. "Key Facts About Government-Favored Religion Around the World." *Factank* (October 3). Accessible at www.pewresearch.org.

Masci, David, Anna Brown, and Jocelyn Kiley. 2019. "5 Facts about Same-Sex Marriage." *Factank* (June 24). Accessible at www.pewresearch.org.

Massey, Douglas S. and Nancy A. Denton. 1993. *American Apartheid: Segregation and the Making of the Underclass.* Cambridge, MA: Harvard University Press.

Mayhew, Robert J. 2014. *Malthus: The Life and Legacies of an Untimely Prophet.* Cambridge, MA: Harvard University Press.

Mazumder, Bhashkar. 2008. *Upward Intergenerational Economic Mobility in the United States.* Washington, DC: Economic Mobility Project.

McCall, Leslie. 2008. "What Does Class Inequality Among Women Look Like? A Comparison with Men and Families, 1970–2000." In Annette Lareau and Dalton Conley (eds.), *Social Class, How Does It Work?* pp. 293–325. New York: Russell Sage Foundation.

McCarthy, Justin. 2018. "Two in Three Americans Now Support Legalizing Marijuana." October 22. Accessible at www.news.gallup.com.

———. 2019. "Less than Half in U.S. Would Vote for a Socialist for President." May 9. Accessible at www.gallup.com.

McClellan, Jennifer. 2019. "One-Third of Middle- and High-Schoolers Were Bullied Last Year, Study Shows." *USA Today*, September 24. Accessible at www.usatoday.com.

McCormick, John. 2015. "Bloomberg Politics Poll." December 9. Accessible at www.bloomberg.com.

McGeeney, Kyley. 2016. "Pew Research Center Will Call 75% Cellphones for Surveys in 2016." January 5. Accessible at www.pewresearch.org.

McIntosh, Peggy. 1988. "White Privilege and Male Privilege: A Personal Account of Coming to See Correspondence through Work and Women's Studies." Working Paper No. 189, Wellesley College Center for Research on Women, Wellesley, MA.

McKenzie, Brian. 2014. "Modes Less Traveled—Bicycling and Walking to Work in the United States: 2008–2012." May. *American Community Survey Reports ACS-25.* Accessible at www.census.gov.

McKinley, Jesse, and Jeffery C. Mays. 2020. "After Anti-Semitic Incidents, New Bail Law in NY Comes Under Attack." *New York Times* (January 8). Accessible at www.nytimes.com.

McLanahan, Sara, and Christine Percheski. 2008. "Family Structure and the Reproduction of Inequalities." *Annual Review of Sociology* 38: 257–276.

McLane, Daisann. 2013. "Getting Off on the Wrong Foot." *National Geographic Traveler* (January):28.

McLaughlin, Heather, Christopher Uggen, and Amy Blackstone. 2017. "The Economic and Career Effects of Sexual Harassment on Working Women." *Gender & Society* 37 (June): 333–358.

McLaughlin, Tim. 2019. "U.S. Company Directors Compensated More Than Ever, But Now Risk Backlash." November 8. Accessible at www.reuters.com.

McLean, Brendan, 2017. "What Does It Mean to Have Mental Illness?" March 1. Accessible at www.nami.org.

McLuhan, Marshall. 1964. *Understanding Media: The Extensions of Man.* New York: New American Library.

———. 1967. *The Medium Is the Message: An Inventory of Effects.* New York: Bantam Books.

McMullan, Thomas. 2019. "Are the Algorithms That Power Dating Apps Racially Biased?" *Wired* (February 17). Accessible at www.wired.com.

McNamara, Keith, and Jeanne Batalova. 2015. "Filipino Immigrants in the United States." July 21. Accessible at www.migrationpolicy.org.

———. 2004. "When Real Food Isn't an Option." *New York Times*, September 3, pp. A1, A5.

Mead, George Herbert. [1934] 2015. *Mind, Self, and Society: The Definitive Edition.* Chicago: University of Chicago Press.

———. 1964a. In *On Social Psychology*, edited by Anselm Strauss. Chicago: University of Chicago Press.

———. 1964b. "The Genesis of the Self and Social Control." Pp. 267–293 in *Selected Writings: George Herbert Mead*, edited by Andrew J. Reck. Indianapolis: Bobbs-Merrill.

Mead, Margaret. [1935] 2001. *Sex and Temperament in Three Primitive Societies.* New York: Perennial, HarperCollins.

Mehl, Matthias R., Simine Vazire, Nairán Ramírez-Esparza, Richard B. Slatcher, and James W. Pennebaker. 2007. "Are Women Really More Talkative Than Men?" *Science* 317 (July 6):82.

Mendez, Jennifer Bickman. 1998. "Of Mops and Maids: Contradictions and Continuities in Bureaucratized Domestic Work." *Social Problems* 45 (February):114–135.

Merton, Robert. 1948. "The Bearing of Empirical Research upon the Development of Social Theory." *American Sociological Review* 13 (October): 505–515.

———. 1968. *Social Theory and Social Structure.* New York: Free Press.

———, and Alice S. Kitt. 1950. "Contributions to the Theory of Reference Group Behavior." Pp. 40–105 in *Continuities in Social Research: Studies in the Scope and Methods of the American Soldier*, edited by Robert K. Merton and Paul L. Lazarsfeld. New York: Free Press.

Messier, Helen. 2020. *The Future of Medicine.* In John Schroeter, ed. *After Shock.* Abundant World Institute.

Messner, Michael A. 2002. "Gender Equity in College Sports: 6 Views." *Chronicle of Higher Education* 49 (December 6): B9–B10.

———. 2018. *No Slam Dunk: Gender, Sport and the Unevenness of Social Change (Critical Issues in Sport and Society).* New Brunswick NJ: Rutgers University Press.

Meston, Cindy M., and David M. Buss. 2007. "Why Humanoids Have Sex." *Archives of Sexual Behavior* 36 (August).

Meyer, Bruce D., Derek Wu, Victoria Mooers, and Carla Medali. 2019. "The Use and Misuse of Income Data and Extreme Poverty in the United States." September. Accessible at www.census.gov.

Michels, Robert. 1915. *Political Parties.* Glencoe, IL: Free Press (reprinted 1949).

Michigan Civil Rights Commission. 2017. *The Flint Water Crisis: Systemic Racism Through the Lens of Flint.* February 17. Lansing MI: Michigan Department of Civil Rights.

Milgram, Stanley. 1963. "Behavioral Study of Obedience." *Journal of Abnormal and Social Psychology* 67 (October):371–378.

———. 1975. *Obedience to Authority: An Experimental View.* New York: Harper and Row.

Miller, Claire C. 2014. "The Divorce Surge Is Over, but the Myth Lives On." *New York Times*, December 2, p. A3.

Miller, Claire Cain. 2020. "Trump Called for Paid Family Leave. Here's Why Few Democrats Clapped." *New York Times*, February 5. Accessible at www.nytimes.com.

Miller, Conrad. 2017. "The Persistent Effect of Temporary Affirmative Action." *American Economic Journal: Applied Economics* 9(3):152–190.

Miller, David L. 2014. *Introduction to Collective Behavior and Collective Action.* 3rd ed. Long Grove, IL: Waveland Press.

———, and JoAnne DeRoven Darlington. 2002. "Fearing for the Safety of Others: Disasters and the Small World Problem." Paper presented at Midwest Sociological Society, Milwaukee, WI.

Miller, Reuben. 1988. "The Literature of Terrorism." *Terrorism* 11 (1):63–87.

Millman, Oliver, and Fiona Harvey. 2019. "US Is Hotbed of Climate Change Denial Major Global Survey Finds." May 8. Accessible at www.theguardian.com.

Mills, C. Wright. [1956] 2000b. *The Power Elite.* New edition. Afterword by Alan Wolfe. New York: Oxford University Press.

———. [1959] 2000a. *The Sociological Imagination.* 40th anniversary edition. New Afterword by Todd Gitlin. New York: Oxford University Press.

Milner, Adrienne. 2020. "Colorblind Racism." *Sociology of Race and Ethnicity* 6 (1):130–135.

Miner, Horace. 1956. "Body Ritual among the Nacirema." *American Anthropologist* 58 (June): 503–507.

Minton, Todd D., and Daniela Golinelli. 2014. *Jail Inmates at Midyear 2013–Statistical Tables.* Washington, DC: U.S. Department of Justice, Office of Justice Programs, Bureau of Justice Statistics.

Mishel, E. 2016. "Discrimination Against Queer Women in the U.S. Workforce: A Résumé Audit Study." *Socius: Sociological Research for a Dynamic World* 2:1–13.

Mishel, Lawrence, and Julia Wolfe. 2018. "CEO Compensation Grew by 940% since 1979." August 14. Accessible at www.epi.org.

Mitra, Aditi. 2013. *Voices of Privilege and Sacrifice from Women Volunteers in India.* Lexington, MA: Lexington Books.

Monaghan, Peter. 1993. "Sociologist Jailed Because He 'Wouldn't Snitch' Ponders the Way Research Ought to Be Done." *Chronicle of Higher Education* 40 (September 1):A8, A9.

Monahan, Torin. 2011. "Surveillance as Cultural Practice." *The Sociological Quarterly* 52: 495–508.

Moncarz, Roger J., Michael G. Wolf, and Benjamin Wright. 2008. "Service-Providing Occupations, Offshoring, and the Labor Market." *Monthly Labor Review* (December):71–86.

Montgomery, Marilyn J., and Gwendolyn T. Sorell. 1997. "Differences in Love Attitudes across Family Life Stages." *Family Relations* 46:55–61.

Moore, Malcolm. 2012. "China's New Leader X, Jinping Warns Communist Party Forces 'Severe Challenges.'" *Telegraph (London)* (November 15). Accessed at www.telegrapj.co.ul.

Moore, Wilbert E. 1967. *Order and Change: Essays in Comparative Sociology.* New York: Wiley.

Morath, Eric. 2016. "Soaring Child-Care Costs Squeeze Families." *Wall Street Journal*, July 2, p. A3.

Morgan, Rachel E., and Barbara A. Oudekerk. 2019. *Criminal Victimization, 2018.* Accessible at www.bjs.gov.

Morgan, Steve. 2017. "Cybersecurity Ventures Predicts Cybercrime Damages Will Cost the World $6 Trillion Annually by 2021." October 16. Accessible at www.cyberrtsecurityventures.com.

Morris, Aldon. 2015. *The Scholar Denied: W. E. B. DuBois and the Birth of Modern Sociology.* Oakland: University of California Press.

Morris, R. C. 2017. "Mitigating the Effects of Parental Incarceration through Social Intervention: A Longitudinal and Comparative Analysis of the Efficacy of Big Brothers Big Sisters." *Journal of Applied Social Science* 11 (1):25–47.

Moskos, Peter. 2008. *Cop in the Hood: My Year Policing Baltimore's Eastern District.* Princeton, NJ: Princeton University Press.

Mossaad, Nadwa. 2019. *Refugees and Asylees: 2018.* October. Accessible at www.dhs.gov.

Mouawad, Jad. 2014. "Once a Humble Refueling Stop, Dubai Is Crossroad to the World." *New York Times*, June 19, pp. A1, A4.

Mueller, G. O. 2001. "Transnational Crime: Definitions and Concepts." Pp. 13–21 in *Combating Transnational Crime: Concepts, Activities, and Responses*, edited by P. Williams and D. Vlassis. London: Franklin Cass.

Mulhere, Kaitlin. 2015. "Momentum for Campus Carry." *Inside Higher Education*, March 30. Accessible at www.insidehighered.com.

Mun, Eunmi. 2010. "Sex Typing of Jobs in Hiring: Evidence from Japan." *Social Forces* 88 (5): 1999–2026.

Murdock, George P. 1945. "The Common Denominator of Cultures." Pp. 123–142 in *The Science of Man in the World Crisis*, edited by Ralph Linton. New York: Columbia University Press.

———. 1949. *Social Structure.* New York: Macmillan.

———. 1957. "World Ethnographic Sample." *American Anthropologist* 59 (August):664–687.

Muro, Mark, Jacob Winter, and Robert Maxim. 2019. "What Jobs Are Affected by AI?" November. Accessible at www.brookings.edu.

Murphy, Dean E. 1997. "A Victim of Sweden's Pursuit of Perfection." *Los Angeles Times*, September 2, pp. A1, A8.

Murray, Velma McBride, Amanda Willert, and Diane P. Stephens. 2001. "The Half-Full Glass: Resilient African American Single Mothers and Their Children." *Family Focus* (June): F4–F5.

Murray-Close, Marta, and Misty L. Heggeness. 2018. "Manning Up and Womaning Down: How Husbands and Wives Report Their Earnings When She Earns More." Working Paper SEHSD-WP2018-20. Accessible at www.census.gov.

N

Nash, Manning. 1962. "Race and the Ideology of Race." *Current Anthropology* 3 (June):285–288.

National Academies of Sciences, Engineering, and Medicine. 2017a. *Communities in Action: Pathways to Health Equity.* Washington, DC: The National Academies Press.

———. 2017b. *Human Genome Editing.* Washington, DC: The National Academies Press.

National Advisory Commission on Criminal Justice. 1976. *Organized Crime.* Washington, DC: U.S. Government Printing Office.

National Alliance for Caregiving. 2015. *Caregiving in the U.S.* June. Accessible at www.caregiving.org.

National Alliance on Mental Illness. 2018. "What Is Mental Health Parity?" Accessible at www.nami.org.

———. 2020. "Mental Health Parity at Risk." Accessible at www.nami.org.

National Center for Complementary and Integrative Health. 2020. "Complementary, Alternative, or Integrative Health: What's in a Name?" Accessible at www.nccih.nih.com.

National Center for Education Statistics. 2019a. *Digest of Education Statistics 2019.* Accessible at www.nces.edu.

———. 2019b. "Homeschooling in the United States: Results from the 2012 and 2016 Parent and Family Involvement Survey." Accessible at www.nces.gov.

———. 2019c. "Fast Facts: Child Care." Accessible at nces.ed.gov.

———. 2019d. "Undergraduate Enrollment." Updated May 2019. Accessible at www.nces.gov.

National Conference of State Legislatures. 2020. "Voter Identification Requirements/Voter ID Laws." January 16. Accessible at www.ncsl.org.

National Education Association. 2019. *Rankings and Estimates: Rankings of the States 2018 and Estimates of School Statistics 2019.* April. Accessible at www.nea.org.

National Federation of State High School Sports Associations. 2019. *Annual Report 2018-2019.* Accessible at nfhs.org.

———. 2015. "Climate Refugees." Accessed December 17 at www. education.nationalgeographic.org/encyclopedia/climate-refugee/.

National Institute on Aging. 1999. *Early Retirement in the United States.* Washington, DC: U.S. Government Printing Office.

National Oceanic and Atmospheric Administration. 2018. "What Is the Biggest Source of Pollution in the Ocean?" June 25. Accessible at www.noaa.gov.

National Organization for Men Against Sexism. 2020. "What is NOMAS?" Accessible at www.nomas.org.

———. 2019. *Definite Postgraduate Commitments of Doctorate Recipients by Sex and Major Field of Study 2017.* Accessible at www.nsf.gov.

Navarro, Mireya. 2005. "When You Contain Multitudes." *New York Times,* April 24, pp. 1, 2.

Needham, Paul. 2011. "9/11 Memorial Review: At Ground Zero, Staying Above Ground Matters." September 9. Accessible at www.huffingtonpost.com.

Nielsen, Joyce McCarl, Glenda Walden, and Charlotte A. Kunkel. 2000."Gendered Heteronormativity: Empirical Illustrations in Everyday Life." *Sociological Quarterly* 41 (2):283-296.

Neuman, Lawrence W. 2009. *Understanding Research.* Boston, MA: Allyn and Bacon.

Neves, Barbara Barbosa. 2013. "Social Capital and Internet Use: The Irrelevant, the Bad, and the Good." *Sociology Compass* 7/8:599-611.

New York Times. 2019. "Editorial: We Have a White Nationalist Terrorist Problem." August 4. Accessible at www.nytimes.com.

Newman, Katherine S. 2012. *The Accordion Family: Boomerang Kids, Anxious Parents, and the Private Toll of Global Competition.* Boston, MA: Beacon Press.

Newman, William M. 1973. *American Pluralism: A Study of Minority Groups and Social Theory.* New York: Harper and Row.

Newport, Frank. 2017a. "Majority Say Wealthy Americans, Corporations Taxed Too Little." April 18. Accessible at www.gallup.com.

———. 2017b. "American Public Opinion: ACA and Tax Reform." September 29. Accessible at www.gallup.com.

———. 2018. "5 Things to Know About Evangelicals in America." May 13. Accessible at www.gallup.com.

———. 2019. "Americans' Long-standing Interest in Taxing the Rich." February 22. Accessible at www.gallup.com.

Newsday. 1997. "Japan Sterilized 16,000 Women." September 18, p. A19.

Nguyen, Jenny, Scott Carter, and Shannon K. Carter. 2019. "From Yellow Peril to Model Minority: Perceived Threat by Asian Americans in Employment." *Social Science Quarterly* 100 (3): 565-577.

NICHD. 2007. "Children Who Complete Intensive Early Childhood Program Show Gains in Adulthood: Greater College Attendance, Lower Crime and Depression." Accessed January 7, 2008, at www.nichd.nih.gov/news.releases/early_interventions_082107.cfm.

Nieves, Emanuel, and Dedrick Asante-Muhammad. 2018. *Running in Place: Why the Racial Wealth Divide Keeps Black and Latino Families from Achieving Economic Security.* Washington: Prosperity Now. Accessible at www.prosperitynow.org.

Niles, Meredith T., Benjamin F. Emery, Andrew J. Reagan, Peter Sheridan Dodds, and Christopher M. Danforth. 2019. "Social Media Usage Patterns during Natural Hazards." February 13. Accessible at https://doi.org/10.1371/journal.pone.0210484.

Nixon, Darren. 2009. "'I Can't Put a Smiley Face On': Working-Class Masculinity, Emotional Labor and Service Work in the 'New Economy.'" *Gender, Work and Organization* 16 (3): 300-322.

Noack, Rick. 2015. "Sweden Is about to Add a Gender-Neutral Pronoun to Its Official Dictionary." April 1. Accessible at washingtonpost.com.

Noe-Bustamente, Luis, Abby Budman, and Mark Hugo Lopez. 2020. "Where Latinos Have the Most Eligible Voters in the 2020 Election." *Factank* (January 31). Accessible at www.pewresearch.org.

Nolan, Patrick D. 2004. "Ecological-Evolutionary Theory: A Reanalysis and Reassessment of Lenski's Theory for the 21st Century." *Sociological Theory* 22 (June):328-337.

———. and ———. 2015. *Human Societies: An Introduction to Macrosociology.* 12th ed. New York: Oxford University Press.

NORC. 2019. *General Social Survey 2016.* Accessible GSS at www.gssdataexplorer.org.

NORML. 2020. "State Information." As of January 2020. Accessible at www.norml.org.

Nowrasteh, Alex. 2019. "Crime Along the Mexican Border Is Lower than in the Rest of the Country." *Cato At Liberty.* January 8, 2019. Accessible at www.cato.org.

O

Office for the Aging. 2020. "Naturally Occurring Retirement Community (NORC)." New York State Office for the Aging. Accessible at https://aging.ny.gov/naturally-occurring-retiement-comunity-norc.

Office of Family Assistance. 2019. "Responsible Fatherhood." April 30. Accessible at www.acf.hhs.gov.

Office of Immigration Statistics. 2018. *2017 Yearbook of Immigration Statistics.* Accessible at www.dhs.gov

Office of Minority Health. 2019. "Infant Mortality and African Americans." November 8.

Ogas, Ogi, and Sai Gaddam. 2011. *A Billion Wicked Thoughts: What the World's Largest Experiment Reveals about Human Desire.* New York: Dutton.

Ogburn, William F. 1922. *Social Change with Respect to Culture and Original Nature.* New York: Huebsch (reprinted 1966, New York: Dell).

———, and Clark Tibbits. 1934. "The Family and Its Functions." Pp. 661-708 in *Recent Social Trends in the United States,* edited by Research Committee on Social Trends. New York: McGraw-Hill.

Okano, Kaori, and Motonori Tsuchiya. 1999. *Education in Contemporary Japan: Inequality and Diversity.* Cambridge, UK: Cambridge University Press.

Omi, Michael, and Howard Winant. 2015. *Racial Formation in the United States.* 3rd ed. New York: Routledge.

Organisation for Economic Co-operation and Development. 2008. "Growing Unequal? Income Distribution and Poverty in OECD Countries." Geneva, Switzerland: OECD.

———. 2009b. "Green at Fifteen? How 15-Year-Olds Perform in Environmental Sciences and Geosciences in PISA 2006." PISA, OECD Publishing. Accessible at www.oecd.org.

———. 2016. "Social Spending Stays at Historically High Levels in Many OECD Countries." October. Accessible at www.oecd.org.

———. 2019. "Development Aid Drops in 2018, Especially for Neediest Countries." April 10. Accessible at www.oecd.org.

———. 2020. "Trade in Goods and Services (indicator)." Accessible at ww.oecd.org.

———. 2020a. "Poverty Ratio." Accessible at oecd.org.

———. 2020b. "OECD Family Database PF2.1: Parental Leave Systems." Accessible at www.oecd.org.

———. 2020c. Tertiary Graduation Rate. Accessible at www.oecd.org.

Ormond, James. 2005. "The McDonaldization of Football." Accessed January 23, 2006, at http://courses.essex.ac.uk/sc/sc111.

Ortega, Mariana. 2015. "Latina Feminism, Experience and the Self." *Philosophy Compass* 10 (April):244-254.

OutRight Action International. 2020. Home page. Accessible at www.outrightinternational.org.

Oxfam. 2019. "Public Good or Private Wealth?" December. Accessible at www.oxfam.org.

———. 2020. *Time to Care: Unpaid and Underpaid Care Work and the Global Inequality Crisis.* Crowley, England: Oxfam House.

P

Pace, Richard. 1993. "First-Time Televiewing in Amazonia: Television Acculturation in Gurupa, Brazil." *Ethnology* 32:187-205.

———. 1998. *The Struggle for Amazon Town.* Boulder, CO: Lynne Rienner.

Pacewicz, Josh. 2016. "Here's the Real Reason Rust Belt Cities and Towns Voted for Trump." *Washington Post,* December 20.

Padilla, Efren N. 2008. "Filipino Americans." Pp. 493–497 in vol. 1, *Encyclopedia of Race, Ethnicity, and Society,* edited by Richard T. Schaefer. Thousand Oaks, CA: Sage.

Page, Charles H. 1946. "Bureaucracy's Other Face." *Social Forces* 25 (October):89–94.

Pager, Devah. 2007. *Marked: Race, Crime, and Funding Work in an Era of Mass Incarceration.* Chicago: University of Chicago Press.

———, Bruce Western, and Bart Bonikowski. 2009. "Discrimination in a Low-Wage Labor Market: A Field Experiment." *American Sociological Review* 74 (October):777–799.

Pais, Jeremy, Kyle Crowder, and Liam Downey. 2014. "Unequal Trajectories: Racial and Class Differences in Residential Exposure to Industrial Hazard." *Social Forces* 92 (March):1189–1215.

Pariser, Ei. 2011a. *The Filter Bubble. What the Internet Is Hiding from You.* New York: Penguin Press.

———. 2011b. "In Our Own Little Internet Bubbles." *Guardian Weekly,* June 24, p. 32.

Park, Haeyoun. 2015. "A Trickle of Syrian Refugees Settles Across the United States." *New York Times,* November 3, p. A18.

Park, Robert E. 1922. *The Immigrant Press and Its Control.* New York: Harper.

Parker, Kim, Juliana Horowitz, Anna Brown, Richard Fry, D'Vera Cohn, and Ruth Igielnik. 2018. "What Unites and Divides Urban, Suburban and Rural Communities." May 22. Accessible www.pewresearch.org.

Parkin, Stephen, and Ross Coomber. 2009. "Value in the Visual: On Public Injecting, Visual Methods and Their Potential for Informing Policy (and Change)." *Methodological Innovations Online* 4 (2):21–36.

Parks, Sarah J., and Hyung Choi Yoo. 2016. "Does Endorsement of the Model Minority Myth Relate to Anti-Asian Sentiments Among White College Students? The Role of a Color-Blind Racial Attitude." *Asian American Journal of Psychology* 7 (4): 287–294.

Parsons, Talcott. 1951. *The Social System.* New York: Free Press.

———. 1966. *Societies: Evolutionary and Comparative Perspectives.* Englewood Cliffs, NJ: Prentice Hall.

———. 1975. "The Sick Role and the Role of the Physician Reconsidered." *Milbank Medical Fund Quarterly Health and Society* 53 (Summer): 257–278.

———, and Robert Bales. 1955. *Family: Socialization and Interaction Process.* Glencoe, IL: Free Press.

Passache, Franz. 2017. "Remaining Vigilant on Hate, Violence and Intolerance." Accessible August 27 on linkedin.com and originally published on PayPal Stories August 15.

Passel, Jeffrey, 2019. "Measuring Illegal Immigration: How Pew Research Center Counts Unauthorized Immigrants in the U.S." July 12. Accessible at www.pewresearch.org.

Passero, Kathy. 2002. "Global Travel Expert Roger Axtell Explains Why." *Biography* (July):70–73, 97–98.

Patterson, Orlando. 2020. "All Things Unequal." *New York Times Book Review* (February 23): 1, 20.

Pavlik, John V. 2013. "Trends in New Media Research: A Critical Review of Recent Scholarship." *Sociology Compass* 7 (1):1–12.

Pawel, Miriam. 2020. "How Much Is the Coronavirus Shaping the Future?" *New York Times,* March 20, p. A23.

Pear, Robert. 2009. "Congress Relaxes Rules on Suits over Pay Inequity." *New York Times,* January 28, p. A14.

Pearce, Diana M. 2014. "Competing Poverty Measures: An Analysis." *Footnotes* (January):5, 7.

Pedulla, David S., and Devah Pager. 2019. "Race and Networks in the Job Search Process." *American Sociological Review* 84 (6):983–1002.

Pellow, David N., and Hollie Nyseth Brehm. 2013. "An Environmental Sociology for the Twenty-First Century." *Annual Review of Sociology* 39:229–250.

Peoples, Clayton D. 2019. "Classical and Contemporary Conventional Theories of Social Movements." Pp. 17–34 in Berch Berberoglu B., ed., *The Palgrave Handbook of Social Movements, Revolution, and Social Transformation.* London: Palgrave Macmillan Handbooks.

Perrin, Andrew and Monica Anderson. 2019. "Share of U.S. Adults Using Social Media, Including Facebook, Is Mostly Unchanged Since 2018." September 21. Accessible at www.pewresearch.com.

Peter, Laurence J., and Raymond Hull. 1969. *The Peter Principle.* New York: Morrow.

Petrie, Michelle, and James E. Coverdill. 2010. "Who Lives and Dies on Death Row? Race, Ethnicity, and Post-Sentence Outcomes in Texas." *Social Problems* 57 (4):630–652.

Petrowski, Nicole, Claudia Cappa, and Peter Gross. 2017. "Estimating the number of children in formal alternative care: Challenges and results." *Child Abuse & Neglect* 70 (August): 388–398.

Pew Religion and Public Life. 2013. *A Portrait of Jewish Americans: Findings from a Pew Research Center Survey of U.S. Jews.* October 1. Accessible at www.pewresearch.org.

Pew Research Center. 2014b. "Emerging and Developing Economies Much More Optimistic Than Rich Countries about the Future." October 9. Accessible at www.pewresearch.org.

———. 2015d. "The American Middle Class Is Losing Ground." December 9. Accessible at www.pewresearchcenter.org.

———. 2017b. *The Changing Global Religious Landscape.* April 5. Accessible at www.pewresearch.org.

———. 2020. "Majority of public favors giving civilians the power to sue police officers for misconduct." July 9. Accessible at www.pewresearchcenter.org.

Philips, Dave. 2017. "Lessons from Hurricane Katrina Helped in Houston." *New York Times,* September 8, p. A9.

Phillips, Susan A. 1999. *Wallbangin': Graffiti and Gangs in L.A.* Chicago: University of Chicago Press.

Piaget, Jean. 1954. *Construction of Reality in the Child.* Translated by Margaret Cook. New York: Basic Books.

Piccolo, Alexa. 2020. "Environmental Education: Knowledge Is Power!" February 21. Accessible at www.oecd.org.

Pile, Tim. 2017. "The Good, Bad, and Ugly Sides to Dubai." *South China Morning Post,* January 5. Accessible at www.scmp.com.

Pincus, Fred L. 2008. "Reverse Discrimination." Pp. 1159–1161, vol. 3, in *Encyclopedia of Race, Ethnicity, and Society,* edited by Richard T. Schaefer. Thousand Oaks, CA: Sage.

Pinderhughes, Dianne. 1987. *Race and Ethnicity in Chicago Politics: A Reexamination of Pluralist Theory.* Urbana: University of Illinois Press.

Piturro, Marlene. 2012. "NORCs: Some of the Best Retirement Communities Occur Naturally." May 30. Accessed November 14, 2013, at www.nextavenue.org/article/2012-05/norcs-some-best-retirement-communities-occur-naturally.

Poder, Thomas C. 2011. "What Is Really Social Capital? A Critical Review." *American Sociologist* 42:341–367.

Pogash, Carol. 2008. "Poor Students in High School Suffer Stigma from Lunch Aid." *New York Times,* March 1, pp. A1, A14.

Polderman, Tinca J. C., Beben Benyamin, Christiaan A. de Leeuw, Patrick F. Sullivan, Arjen van Bochoven, Peter M. Visscher, and Danielle Posthuma. 2015. "Meta-analysis of the Heritability of Human Traits Based on Fifty Years of Twin Studies." *Nature Genetics* (47):702–709.

Pomrenze, Yin. and Darran Simon. 2018. Black men arrested at Philadelphia Starbucks reach agreements. May 2. Accessible at www.cnn.com.

Population Reference Bureau. 2019. "The 2019 American Community Survey Includes Changes to Several Questions." January 16. Accessible at www.prb.org.

———. 2020. "Indicators: Infant Mortality Rate." Accessible 9 at www.prb.org.

Portulans Institute. 2019. "Networked Readiness Index 2016." Accessible at portulansinstitute.org.

Poushter, Jacob. 2014. "What's Morally Acceptable? It Depends on Where in the World You Live." April 15. Accessible at www.pewresearch.org.

———, and Janell Fetterolf. 2019. *A Changing World: Global Views on Diversity, Gender Equality, Family Life and the Importance of Religion.* April 22. Accessible at www.pewresearch.org.

———, and Christine Huang. 2019. "Climate Change Still Seen as the Top Global Threat, but Cyberattacks a Rising Concern." February 19. Accessible at www.pewresearch.org.

Powell, Jerome H. 2019. "Renewing the Promise of the Middle Class." May 9. Accessible at www.federalreserve.gov > newsevents > speech > powell20190509a.

Prestwich, Emma. 2017. "Titanic Dives to Start Again in 2018, for the Cool Price of US$100,000." *Huffington Post.* March 22. Accessible at www.huffingtonpost.ca.

Prince, Martin, Vikram Patel, Shekhar Saxena, Mario Maj, Johanna Maselko, Michael Phillips, and Atif Rahman. 2007. "No Health without Mental Health." *The Lancet* 370 (September 8):859–877.

ProQuest. 2019. *ProQuest Statistical Abstract of the United States 2020.* Issued December 2019. Lanham MD: Rowman & Littlefield.

Pryor, John H., Kevin Egan, Laura Palucki Blake, Sylvia Hurtado, Jennifer Berdan, Matthew H. Case, and Linda DeAngelo. 2013. *The American Freshman: National Norms for Fall 2012.* Los Angeles: Higher Education Research Institute, UCLA.

———, Sylvia Hurtado, Victor B. Saenz, José Luis Santos, and William S. Korn. 2007. *The American Freshman: Forty Year Trends.* Los Angeles: Higher Education Research Institute, UCLA.

Putnam, Robert D. 2015. *Our Kids: The American Dream in Crisis.* New York: Simon and Schuster.

Q

Qi, Liyan, and Fanfan Wang. 2018. "Limit to China's Economic Rise: Not Enough Babies." *The Wall Street Journal*, April 30, pp. A1, A10.

Quadagno, Jill. 2018. *Aging and the Life Course: An Introduction to Social Gerontology.* 7th Ed. New York: McGraw-Hill.

Quinney, Richard. 1970. *The Social Reality of Crime.* Boston, MA: Little, Brown.

———. 1974. *Criminal Justice in America.* Boston, MA: Little, Brown.

———. 1979. *Criminology.* 2nd ed. Boston, MA: Little, Brown.

———. 1980. *Class, State and Crime.* 2nd ed. New York: Longman.

R

Raley, R. Kelly, and Megan M. Sweeney. 2020. "Divorce, Partnering, and Stepfamilies: A Decade in Review." *Journal of Marriage and Family* 82 (February): 981–999.

Ramstad, Evan. 2011. "Studying Too Much Is a New No-No in Upwardly Mobile South Korea." *Wall Street Journal,* October 6, p. A1.

Rank, Mark. 2017. "Changing the World, One Website at a Time." *Contexts* (Summer):74–75.

———, and Thomas A. Hirschi. 2017. "Confronting Poverty: Tools for Understanding American Inequality." Accessible at www. confrontingpoverty.org.

Ratha, Dilip, Supriyo De, Eung Ju Kim, Sonia Plaza, Ganesh Seshan, and Nadege Desiree. 2019. "Data Release: Remittances to Low- and Middle-Income Countries on Track to Reach $551 Billion in 2019 and $597 Billion by 2021." October 16. Accessible at www. worldbank.org.

Ratnesar, Romesh. 2011. "The Menace Within." *Stanford Magazine* (July/August). Accessible at www.stanfordalumni.org.

Ravenelle, Alexandra. 2017. "A Return to Gemeinschaft: Digital Impression Management and the Sharing Economy." Pp. 27–45 in Jessie Daniels, Karen Gregory, and Tessie McMillan Cottom, eds., *Digital Sociologies.* Princeton, NJ: Princeton University Press.

Ravitch, Diane. 2010. *The Death and Life of the Great American School System: How Testing and Choice Are Undermining Education.* New York: Basic Books.

Reczek, Corine. 2020. "Sexual- and Gender-Minority Families: A 2010 to 2020 Decade in Review." *Journal of Marriage and Family* 82 (February): 300–325.

Reddy, Sumathi. 2015. "Screen Time for Doctors." *Wall Street Journal,* December 15, pp. D1, D3.

Regan, Pamela C., Saloni Lakhanpal, and Carlos Anguiano. 2012. "Relationship Outcomes in Indian-American Love-Based and Arranged Marriages." *Psychological Reports* 110 (3): 915–924.

Registered Nursing. 2020. "Here's How Much Your Healthcare Costs Will Rise as You Age." Accessible at www.registerednursing.org.

Reilly, Michael, Suzanne Duncan, Gianna Leoni, Lachy Patterson, Lyn Corter, Matiu Rātima, and Poia Rewi (eds.). 2018. *Te Koparapara: An Introduction to the Māori World.* Auckland, NZ: University of Auckland Press.

Reinharz, Shulamit. 1992. *Feminist Methods in Social Research.* New York: Oxford University Press.

Reitzes, Donald C., and Elizabeth J. Mutran. 2006. "Lingering Identities in Retirement." *Sociological Quarterly* 47:333–359.

Rich, Motoko. 2019. "Japan Wants Women in the Office. Housework Gets in the Way." *New York Times,* February 3, pp. 1, 10.

Rico, Brittany, Rose M. Kreider, and Lydi Anderson. 2018. "Growth in Interracial and Interethnic Married-Couple Households." Accessible at www.census.gov.

Riding, Alan. 1998. "Why 'Titanic' Conquered the World." *New York Times,* April 26, sec. 2, pp. 1, 28, 29.

Riley, Jason L. 2020. "Minorities Bear the Lockdown's Economic Brunt." *Wall Street Journal,* March 25, p. A19.

Ripley, Amanda. 2011. "Teacher, Leave Those Kids Alone." *Time,* December 5, pp. 46–49.

Ritzer, George. 2018. *The McDonaldization of Society: Into the Digital Age.* Ninth edition. Newbury Park CA: Sage Publishing.

———, and Paul Dean. 2019. *Globalization: The Essentials.* 2nd ed. New York: Wiley-Blackwell.

Rkasnuam, Hataipreuk, and Jeanne Batalova. 2014. "Vietnamese Immigrants in the United States." August 25. Accessible at www.migrationpolicy. org.

Robb, Michael. B., Willow Bay, and Tina Vennegaard. 2017. *The New Normal: Parents, Teens, and Digital Devices in Japan.* San Francisco, CA: Common Sense. Accessible at www. commonsensemedia.org.

———, ———, and ———. 2018. *The New Normal: Parents, Teens, and Digital Devices in the United Kingdom.* San Francisco, CA: Common Sense. Accessible at www.commonsensemedia.org.

Rockett, Darcel. 2018. "Filtering Potential Partners by Ethnicity." *Chicago Tribune,* October 28, sect. NRW, p. 25.

Rodriguez, Eric. 2017. "Addressing the Wealth Gap for Hispanic Families." *Federal Reserve Bank of St. Louis Review* 99 (1):53–58.

Romero, Mary. 2018. *Introducing Intersectionality.* London: Polity.

Romero, Simon. 2020. "Navajos Race to Shield Reservation After a Sharp Rise in Deaths." *New York Times,* April 10, p. A13.

Roose, Kevin. 2017. "Forget Washington. Facebook's Problems Abroad Are Far More Disturbing." *New York Times,* October 29. Accessible at www.nytimes.com.

———. 2019. "Don't Scoff at Influencers. They're Taking Over the World." *New York Times,* July 16, pp. B1, B9.

Rose, Arnold. 1951. *The Roots of Prejudice.* Paris: UNESCO.

Rose, Christina. 2015. "8 Reasons Why Feminism Matters in Indian Country." March 4. Accessible at indiancountrytodaynetwork.com.

Rose, Peter I., Myron Glazer, and Penina Migdal Glazer. 1979. "In Controlled Environments: Four Cases of Intense Resocialization." Pp. 320–338 in *Socialization and the Life Cycle,* edited by Peter I. Rose. New York: St. Martin's Press.

Rosen, Eva, and Sudhir Alladi Venkatesh. 2008. "A Perversion of Choice: Sex Work Offers Just Enough in Chicago's Urban Ghetto." *Journal of Contemporary Ethnography* (August):417–441.

Rosenberg, H. Douglas. 1991. "Capitalism." Pp. 33–34 in *Encyclopedic Dictionary of Sociology,* 4th ed., edited by Dushkin Publishing Group. Guilford, CT: Dushkin.

Rosenfeld, Jake, and Meredith Klegkamp. 2012. "Organized Labor and Racial Wage Inequality in the United States." *American Journal of Sociology* 117 (March):1460–1502.

Rosenfeld, Michael J. 2017. "Moving a Mountain: The Extraordinary Trajectory of Same-Sex Marriage Approval in the United States." *Socius: Sociological Research for a Dynamic World* 3:1–22.

———, and Reuben J. Thomas. 2012. "Searching for a Mate: The Rise of the Internet as a Social Intermediary." *American Sociological Review* 77 (4):523–547.

Rosenthal, Robert, and Lenore Jacobson. 1968. *Pygmalion in the Classroom.* New York: Holt.

———. and ———. 1992. *Pygmalion in the Classroom: Teacher Expectations and Pupils' Intellectual Development.* Newly expanded edition. Bancyfelin, UK: Crown House.

Roosevelt, Margot. 2020. Coronavirus energies the labor movement. Can it last? *Los Angeles Times* (May 2). Accessible at www.oatimes.com.

Rossi, H. Peter. 1987. "No Good Applied Social Research Goes Unpunished." *Society* 25 (November–December):73–79.

Rossi, S. Alice 1968. "Transition to Parenthood." *Journal of Marriage and Family* 30 (February): 26–39.

———. 1984. "Gender and Parenthood." *American Sociological Review* 49 (February):1–19.

Rossides, W. Daniel. 1997. *Social Stratification: The Interplay of Class, Race, and Gender.* 2nd ed. Upper Saddle River, NJ: Prentice Hall.

Roszak, Theodore. 1969. *The Making of a Counterculture.* Garden City, NY: Doubleday.

Rourke, Matt. 2019. "Sexual Harassment in City's Police Force." *The Philadelphia Tribune* (August 27). Accessible at www.phillytrib.com.

Rubin, J. Alissa. 2003. "Pat-Down on the Way to Prayer." *Los Angeles Times,* November 25, pp. A1, A5.

Rudel, Thomas K., J. Timmons Roberts, and Jo Ann Carmin. 2011. "Political Economy of the Environment." *Annual Review of Sociology* 37:221–238.

Rueb, Emily S. 2015. "The Battle of the Birdmen." *New York Times,* August 2, pp. 20–21.

Rugh, Jacob S., Len Albright, and Douglas S. Massey. 2015. "Race, Space, and Cumulative Disadvantage: A Case Study of the Subprime Lending Collapse." *Social Problems* 62:186–218.

Russ, Hilary. 2018. "Corporate Tax Breaks Cost U.S Schools Billions of Lost Revenue: Report." December 4. Accessible at www.reuters.com.

Ryan, Camille. 2013. *Language Use in the United States.* ACS-22. Washington, DC: U.S. Government Printing Office.

Ryan, William. 1976. *Blaming the Victim.* Rev. ed. New York: Random House.

Saad, Lydia. 2012a. "U.S. Acceptance of Gay/Lesbian Relations Is the New Normal: For Third Year, Majority Says Gay/Lesbian Relations Are Morally Acceptable." Accessible at www.gallup.com.

———— 2019. "Preference for Environment Over Economy Largest Since 2000." April 4. Accessible at www.gallup.com.

Saguy, Abigail, and Rene Almeling. 2008. "Fat in the Fire? Science, the News Media, and the 'Obesity Epidemic.'" *Sociological Forum* 23 (March):53–83.

Said, W. Edward. 2001. "The Clash of Ignorance." *Nation,* October 22.

Saito, Mari. 2018. "Japan Inc. Rethinks Women's Work." *New York Times,* March 9, pp. B1, B6.

Salem, Richard, and Stanislaus Grabarek. 1986. "Sociology B.A.s in a Corporate Setting: How Can They Get There and of What Value Are They?" *Teaching Sociology* 14 (October): 273–275.

Sampson, Robert. 2011. *Great American City: Chicago and the Enduring Neighborhood Effect.* Chicago: University of Chicago Press.

————, and W. Byron Graves. 1989. "Community Structure and Crime: Testing Social-Disorganization Theory." *American Journal of Sociology* 94 (January):774–802.

Samuelson, Paul A., and William D. Nordhaus. 2010. *Economics.* 19th ed. New York: McGraw-Hill.

Sandberg, Sheryl. 2015. *Lean In: Women, Work, and the Will to Lead.* New York: Knopf.

Sanderson, Stephen K., Seth A. Abrutyn, and Kristopher R. Proctor. 2011. "Testing the Protestant Ethic Thesis with Quantitative Historical Data: A Research Note." *Social Forces* 89 (March): 905–912.

Sanghani, Radhika. 2015. "A Day in the Life of the Everyday Sexism Hashtag." *The Daily Telegraph,* April 16.

Sang-Hun, Choe. 2017. "South Korea's New Leader Abolishes State-Issued History Textbooks." *New York Times,* May 12.

Sassler, Sharon, and Daniel T. Lichter. 2020. "Cohabitation and Marriage: Complexity and Diversity in Union-Formation Patterns." *Journal of Marriage and Family* 82 (February): 35–61.

Satel, Sally. 2013. "Why the Fuss over the D.S.M.-5?"*New York Times*, May 12, Week in the News, p. 5.

Sawhill, Isabel, and Ron Haskins. 2009. "If You Can Make It Here . . ." *Washington Post National Weekly Edition,* November 9, p. 27.

————, and John E. Morton. 2007. *Economic Mobility: Is the American Dream Alive and Well?* Washington, DC: Economic Mobility Project, Pew Charitable Trusts.

Sawyer, Wendy. 2020. How to find and interpret crime data during the coronavirus pandemic: 5 tips. April 24. Accessible at www.prisonpolicy.org

Scarce, Rik. 2005. *Contempt of Court: A Scholar's Struggle for Free Speech Behind Bars.* Walnut Creek, CA: AltaMira Press.

Schaefer, Eric. 1999. *Bold! Daring! Shocking! True! A History of Exploitation Films, 1919-1959.* Durham NC: Duke University Press.

Schaefer, Richard. T. 2008b. "'Power' and 'Power Elite.'" In *Encyclopedia of Social Problems,* edited by Vincent Parrillo. Thousand Oaks, CA: Sage.

————. 2021. *Racial and Ethnic Groups.* 15th Edition Updated. New York: Pearson.

————, and William W. Zellner. 2008. *Extraordinary Groups.* 8th ed. New York: Worth.

————, and ————. 2015. *Extraordinary Groups.* 9th ed. Long Grove, IL: Waveland Press.

Schaeffer, Katherine. 2019. "Share of Americans Who Favor Stricter Gun Laws Has Increased Since 2017." October 16. Accessible at www.pewresearch.org.

Schawbel, Dan. 2019. "How Artificial Intelligence Is Redefining the Role of Manager." November 15. Accessible at www.weforum.org.

Scheadler, Travis, and Audrey Wagstaff. 2018. "Exposure to Women's Sports: Changing Attitudes Toward Female Athletes." *The Sport Journal.* Accessible at www.thesportsjournal.com.

Scheid, L. Teresa. 2013. "A Decade of Critique: Notable Books in the Sociology of Mental Health." *Contemporary Sociology* 42 (2):177–183.

Schmalleger, Frank. 2020. *Criminology.* 5th ed. New York: Pearson.

Schnaiberg, Allan. 1994. *Environment and Society: The Enduring Conflict.* New York: St. Martin's Press.

Schneider, Suzannah. 2015. "Five Ways Cell Phones Are Changing Agriculture in Africa." January 25. Accessible at www.foodtank.com.

Schrad, Mark Lawrence. 2014. "Ukraine and ISIS Are Not Justifications of a 'Clash of Civilizations.'" *Washington Post,* September 22, Op-Ed at washingtonpost.com.

Schradie, Jen. 2018. "The Digital Activism Gap: How Class and Costs Shape Online Collective Action." *Social Problems* 65: 51–74.

Schram, Sanford F., Ruhard C. Fording, Joe Soss, and Linda Houser. 2009. "Deciding to Discipline: Race, Choice and Punishment at the Frontlines of Welfare Reform." *American Sociological Review* 74 (June):398–422.

Schreiber, Noam, and Stephanie Strom. 2015. "Labor Board Ruling Eases Way for Fast-Food Unions' Efforts." *New York Times,* August 24, pp. A1, A3.

Schur, M. Edwin. 1965. *Crimes without Victims: Deviant Behavior and Public Policy.* Englewood Cliffs, NJ: Prentice Hall.

————. 1968. *Law and Society: A Sociological View.* New York: Random House.

————. 1985. "'Crimes without Victims': A 20-Year Reassessment." Paper presented at the annual meeting of the Society for the Study of Social Problems.

Schwartz, H. Shalom, and Anat Bardi. 2001. "Value Hierarchies across Cultures: Taking a Similarities Perspective." *Journal of Cross-Cultural Perspective* 32 (May):268–290.

Scott, Gregory. 2001. "Broken Windows behind Bars: Eradicating Prison Gangs through Ecological Hardening and Symbolic Cleansing." *Corrections Management Quarterly* 5 (Winter):23–36.

Scott, Katy. 2017. "These 3 Schools Want to Wipe Away Gender Stereotypes from an Early Age." September 26. Accessible at www.cnn.com.

Scott, Susie. 2016. *Negotiating Identity: Symbolic Interactionist Approaches to Social Identity.* New York: Wiley.

Scoville, David. 2010. "Disneyland Deconstructed: Postmodernism Revealed." April 16. Accessible at http://davidscoville.blogspot.com/2010/04/Disneyland-deconstructed-postmodernism.html.

Scurria, Andrew. 2020. "Puerto Rico Debt Overhaul Is on Hold." *Wall Street Journal,* March 23, p. A3.

Seamster, Louise. 2019. "Black Debt, White Debt." *Contexts* 18 (Winter): 30–35.

Securities and Exchange Commission. 2017. "Commission Guidance in Pay Ratio Disclosure." September 21. Accessible at www.sec.gov.

Sedgwick, Eve Kosofsky. 1990. *Epistemology of the Closet.* Berkeley: University of California Press.

Sefiha, Ophir. 2012. "Bad Sports: Explaining Sport Related Deviance." *Sociology Compass* 6:949–961.

Segal, L. Nancy. 2012. *Born Together–Reared Apart. O Brother, Who Art Thou.* Cambridge, MA: Harvard University Press.

Sege, Robert D., and Benjamin S. Siegel. 2018. "Effective Discipline to Raise Healthy Children." *Pediatrics* 142 (December):1–10.

Sellers, Frances Stead. 2004. "Voter Globalization." *Washington Post National Weekly Edition,* November 29, p. 22.

Selod, Saher Farooq. 2008a. "Muslim Americans." Pp. 920–923, vol. 2, in *Encyclopedia of Race, Ethnicity, and Society,* edited by Richard T. Schaefer. Thousand Oaks, CA: Sage.

Semega, Jessica L.,, Melissa Kollar, John Creamer, and Abinash Mohanty. 2019. *Income and Poverty in the United States: 2018.* Current Population Reports P60-266. Accessible at www.census.gov.

————, Kyla R. Fontenot, and Melissa A. Kollar. 2019. *Income and Poverty in the United States: 2018.* Washington, DC: U.S. Government Printing Office.

Sengupta, Somini. 2009. "An Empire for Poor Working Women, Guided by a Gandhian Approach." *New York Times,* March 7, p. A6.

————. 2015. "Europe Tries Incentives and Persuasion to Keep Migrants at Home." *New York Times.* September 12, p. A12.

————. 2019. "U.N. Report Says Rise in Emissions Is Still Alarming." *New York Times,* November 27, pp. A1, A10.

Sernau, Scott. 2001. *Worlds Apart: Social Inequalities in a New Century.* Thousand Oaks, CA: Pine Forge Press.

Sesame Street. 2018. "Little Children, Big Challenges: Incarceration." Accessible at www.sesamestreet.org.

Shaban, Hamza. 2019. "Twitter Reveals Its Daily Active User Numbers for the First Time." *Washington Post,* February 7. Accessible at www.washingtonpost.com.

Shachtman, Tom. 2006. *Rumspringa: To Be or Not to Be Amish.* New York: North Point Press.

Shaefer, H. Luke, Pinghui Wu, and Kathryn Edin. 2018. "Can Poverty in America Be Compared to Conditions in the World's Poorest Countries?" *American Journal of Medical Research* 4 (1):84–92.

Shahbaz, Adrian, and Allie Funk. 2019. "Freedom on the Net 2019 Key Finding: Governments Harness Big Data for Social Media Surveillance." Accessible at www.freedomhouse.org.

Shams, Tahseen. 2018. "Visibility as Resistance by Muslim Americans in a Surveillance and Security Atmosphere." *Sociology Forum* 33 (March): 73–94.

Shane, Scott. 2015. "Calls to Erase Digital Legacy of a Militant." *New York Times,* December 19, pp. A1, A3.

———, and Mike Isaac. 2017. "Facebook to Turn Over Russian-Linked Ads to Congress." *New York Times,* September 21. Accessible at www.nytimes.com.

Shankland, Stephen. 2015. "Like It or Not, Europe's Quota System Puts Women on Boards." *CNET.* May 7. Accessible at www.cnet.com.

Shannon, Joel. 2020. Poll: Most Americans want significant police reform. *USA Today* (June 29): 1A, 4A.

Shapiro, P. Joseph. 1993. *No Pity: People with Disabilities Forging a New Civil Rights Movement.* New York: Times Books.

Shapley, Dan. 2010. "4 Dirty Secrets of the Exxon Valdez Oil Spill." Accessed May 3 at www.thedailygreen.com.

Sharma, Ruchir. 2017. "No, That Robot Will Not Steal Your Job." *New York Times,* October 8, section SR, p. 3.

Sharp, M. Ansel, Charles A. Register, and Paul W. Grimes. 2013. *Economics of Social Issues.* 20th ed. New York: McGraw-Hill.

Shaw, R. Clifford, and Henry D. McKay. 1942. *Juvenile Delinquency and Urban Areas.* Chicago: University of Chicago Press.

Shear, Michael D. 2016. "Obama Bans Federal Solitary Confinement for Youths." *New York Times,* January 26, p. A18.

Sheehan, Charles. 2005. "Poor Seniors Take On Plans of Condo Giant." *Chicago Tribune,* March 22, pp. 1, 9.

Sherman, Arloc. 2007. *Income Inequality Hits Record Levels, New CBO Data Show.* Washington, DC: Center on Budget and Policy Priorities.

Sheskin, Ira, and Arnold Dashefsky. 2018. "Jewish Population in the United States." In *American Jewish Year Book 2017.* Philadelphia: The Jewish Publication Society of America. Accessible at www.jewishvirtuallibrary.com.

Shostak, B. Arthur. 2002. "Clinical Sociology and the Art of Peace Promotion: Earning a World without War." Pp. 325–345 in *Using Sociology: An Introduction from the Applied and Clinical Perspectives,* edited by Roger A. Straus. Lanham, MD: Rowman & Littlefield.

Shuttleworth, Jay. 2015. "Teaching the Social Issues of a Sustainable Food Supply." *The Social Studies* 106 (4):159–169.

Silva, M. Jennifer. 2012. "Constructing Adulthood in an Age of Uncertainty." *American Sociological Review* 77 (4):505–522.

Silva-Bonilla, Ruth. 1985. *¡Ay !Ay! amor: No me quieras tanto . (El marco social; de la violencia contra la mjuer en, a vida con yugal).* Rio Padras: Puerto Rico Campus, University of Puerto Rico.

Silver, Ira. 1996. "Role Transitions, Objects, and Identity." *Symbolic Interaction* 10 (1):1–20.

Simmons, Alicia D., and Lawrence D. Bobo. 2015. "Can Non-Full-Probability Internet Surveys Yield Useful Data? A Comparison with Full-Probability Fact-to-Face Surveys in the Domain of Race and Social Inequality Attitudes." *Sociological Methodology:*1–31.

Simpson, April. 2020. "Fearing Coronavirus, Many Rural Black Women Avoid Hospitals to Give Birth at Home." *Stateline Article* (April 17). Accessible at www.pewresearch.org.

Simpson, Sally S. 2013. "White-Collar Crime: A Review of Recent Developments and Promising Directions for Future Research." *Annual Review of Sociology* 39:309–331.

———. 2019. "Reimagining Sutherland 80 Years after White-collar Crime." 2019. *Criminology* 57 (January):189–207.

Singh, Meena Ritu. 2019. "Women Empowerment in Bangladesh: A Political Scenario." *ACADEMICIA: An International Multidisciplinary Research Journal* 9 (8). Accessible at www.scirp.org.

Sklar, Judith. 2020. "When Living Apart Keeps You Together." February 12. Accessible at www.curbed.com.

Slater, Mel, Angus Antley, Adam Davison, David Swapp, Cristoph Guger, Chris Baker, Nancy Pistrang, and Marla V. Sanchez-Vives. 2006. "A Virtual Reprise of the Stanley Milgram Obedience Experiments." *PLoS ONE* 1(1): e39. doi:10.1371/journal.pone.0000039.

Slug-Lines.com. 2020. "What's New." Accessible at www.slug-lines.com.

Smear, Michael D., Maggie Haberman, Nicholas Confessore, Karen Yourish, Larry Buchanan, and Keith Collins. 2019. "The Twitter Presidency." *New York Times,* November 3, Section F.

Smelser, Neil. 1963. *The Sociology of Economic Life.* Englewood Cliffs, NJ: Prentice Hall.

———. 1997. *Problematics of Sociology.* Berkeley: University of California Press.

Smith, Bethany. 2015. "The Existence of a Hidden Curriculum in Sex and Relationships Education in Secondary Schools." *Transformations* 1 (1): 42–55.

Smith, Dan. 1999. *The State of the World Atlas.* 6th ed. London: Penguin.

Smith, Samantha. 2017. "Young People Less Likely to View Iraqi, Syrian Refugees as Major Threat to U.S." February 3. Accessible at www.pewresearch.org.

Smith, Stacy L., Marc Choueiti, Katherine Pieper, Ariana Case, and Angel Choi. 2018. *Inequality in 1,100 Popular Films: Examining Portrayals of Gender, Race/Ethnicity, LGBT, & Disability from 2007 to 2017.* July 2018. USC Annenberg Inclusion Initiative. Accessible at www.annenberg.usc.edu.

Smith, Tom W. 2003. *Coming of Age in 21st Century America: Public Attitudes toward the Importance and Timing of Transition to Adulthood.* Chicago: National Opinion Research Center.

———, Michael Davern, Jeremy Freese, and Michael Hout. 2017. *General Social Surveys, 1972-2016: Cumulative Codebook.* Principal Investigator, Tom W. Smith; Co-Principal Investigators, Peter V. Marsden and Michael Hout. Chicago: NORC.

———, ———, ———, and Stephan L. Morgan. 2019. *General Social Surveys, 1972-2018.* Chicago: NORC.

Smock, Pamela J., and Christine R. Schwartz. 2020. "The Demography of Families: A Review of Patterns and Change." *Journal of Marriage and Family* 82 (February): 9–34.

Soffel, Jenny. 2011. "Gender Bias Fought at Egalia Preschool in Stockholm, Sweden." June 26. Accessible at www.huffingtonpost.com.

Sony, Sonya Farhana, Bokul Hossain, and Siddiqur Rahman. 2020. "Internal Migration and Women Empowerment: A Study on Female Garments Workers in Dhaka City of Bangladesh." *Advances in Applied Sociology* 10:74–91.

Sorokin, A. Pitirim. [1927] 1959. *Social and Cultural Mobility.* New York: Free Press.

Southern Poverty Law Center. 2019a. "Active Hate Groups in the United States 2018." *Intelligence Report* (Spring):43–55. Accessible at www.splcenter.org.

———. 2019b. "Active Hate Groups in the United States 2018." *Intelligence Report* (Spring):56–61. Accessible at www.splcenter.org.

———. 2020. "The Year in Hate and Extremism." March 18. Accessible at www.splcenter.org.

Spalter-Roth, Roberta, Nicole Van Vooren, and Mary S. Senter. 2013. "Using the Bachelor's and Beyond Project to Help Launch Students in Careers." Accessed November 1 at www.asanet.org/documents/research/docs/B%26BLaunchingCareers.pptx.

Spectrum Group. 2019. *Market Insights Report 2019.* March 12. Accessible at www.spectrum.com.

Spencer, Chelsea, Allen Mallory, Michelle Toews, Sandra Stith, and Leila Wood. 2017. "Why Sexual Assault Survivors Do Not Report to Universities: A Feminist Analysis." *Family Relations* (February):166–179.

Sperber, Murray. 2000. *Beer and Circus: How Big-Time College Sports Is Crippling Undergraduate Education.* New York: Henry Holt.

Sprague, Joey. 2005. *Feminist Methodologies for Critical Research: Bridging Differences.* Lanham, MD: AltaMira Press.

St. John, Warren. 2009. *Outcasts United.* New York: Spiegel & Grau Trade Paperbacks.

Stablen, Timothy, Joseph Lorenzo Hall, Chauna Pervis, and Denise L. Anthony. 2015. "Negotiating Stigma in Health Care: Disclosure and the Role of Electronic Health Records." *Health Sociology Review* 24 (Issue 3).

Stanford Open Policing Project. 2019. "Findings: The Results of Our Nationwide Analysis of Traffic Stops and Searches." February 15. Accessible at https://openpolicing.stanford.edu.

Stansell, Christine. 2011. *The Feminist Promise: 1792 to the Present.* New York: The Modern Library.

Stark, Rodney, and William Sims Bainbridge. 1979. "Of Churches, Sects, and Cults: Preliminary Concepts for a Theory of Religious Movements." *Journal for the Scientific Study of Religion* 18 (June):117–131.

———, and ———. 1985. *The Future of Religion.* Berkeley: University of California Press.

Statista. 2017. 2018. "Most Popular Television Shows Based on Audience Demand in France in May 2017 (in Million Average Demand Expressions)." Accessible at www.statista.com.

Statistics New Zealand. 2019. "New Zealand as a Village of 100 People: Our Population." September 22. Accessible at www.stats.govt.nz.

———. 2020. "Child Poverty Statistics: Year Ended June 2019." February 24. Accessible at www.stats.govt.nz.

Stern, Scott M. 2019. "The Making of a White Supremacist Myth." *The New Republic* (October 28). Accessible at www.newrepublic.com.

Stevick, A. Richard. 2007. *Growing Up Amish: The Teenage Years.* Baltimore, MD: Johns Hopkins University Press.

Stokes, Bruce. 2018. "A Decade After the Financial Crisis, Economic Confidence Rebounds in Many Countries." September 18. Accessible at www.pewcenter.org.

Stolzenberg, Ellen Bara, Kevin Eagan, Melissa C. Aragon, Natacha M. Cesar-Davis, Sidronio

Jasacobo, Victoria Couch, and Cecilia Rios-Aguilar. 2019. *The American Freshman: National Norms Fall 2017.* Expanded Version. Los Angeles: Higher Education Research Institute, UCLA.

Stryker, Roy Emerson, and Nancy Wood. [1935–1943] 1973. *In This Proud Land.* Greenwich: New York Graphic Society.

Subramaniam, Mangala. 2006. *The Power of Women's Organization: Gender, Caste, and Class in India.* Lanham, MD: Lexington Books.

Subramanian, Ram, Ruth Delaney, Stephen Roberts, Nancy Fishman, and Peggy McGarry. 2015. *Incarceration's Front Door: The Misuse of Jails in America.* New York: The Vera Institute.

Suchar, Charles S. 1997. "Grounding Visual Sociology Research in Shooting Scripts." *Qualitative Sociology* 20 (1):33–55.

Sudo, Naoki. 2019. "Why Do the Japanese Still See Themselves as Middle Class? The Impact of Socio-Structural Changes on Status Identification." *Social Science Japan Journal* 22 (Winter): 25–44.

Suh, Michael. 2014. "2013 Survey of LGBT Adults." September 18. Accessible at www.pewsocialtrends.org.

Suitor, J. Jill, Staci A. Minyard, and Rebecca S. Carter. 2001. "'Did You See What I Saw?' Gender Differences in Perceptions of Avenues to Prestige among Adolescents." *Sociological Inquiry* 71 (Fall):437–454.

Sumner, William G. 1906. *Folkways.* New York: Ginn.

Sunstein, Cass. 2002. *Republic.com.* Rutgers, NJ: Princeton University Press.

Sunwolf, and David R. Seibold. 1998. "Jurors' Intuitive Rules for Deliberation: A Structurational Approach to Communication in Jury Decision Making." *Communication Monographs* 65 (December):282–307.

Sutherland, Anna. 2015. "What's Behind the Reversal of the Gender Gap in Higher Education?" October 12. Accessible at www.family-studies.org.

Sutherland, H. Edwin. 1937. *The Professional Thief.* Chicago: University of Chicago Press.

———. 1940. "White-Collar Criminality." *American Sociological Review* 5 (February):1–11.

———. 1949. *White Collar Crime.* New York: Dryden.

———. 1983. *White Collar Crime: The Uncut Version.* New Haven, CT: Yale University Press.

———, Donald R. Cressey, and David F. Luckenbill. 1992. *Principles of Criminology.* 11th ed. New York: Rowman & Littlefield.

Sutton, Jeanette, C. Ben Gibson, Nolan Edward Phillips, Emma S. Spiro, Cedar League, Britta Johnson, Sean M, Fitzhugh, and Carter T. Butts. 2015. "A Cross-Hazard Analysis of Terse Message Retransmission on Twitter." *Proceedings of the National Academy of Sciences* 111 (48): 14793–14798.

Swanson, Emily. 2013. "Poll: Few Identify as Feminists, but Most Believe in Equality of Sexes." *Huffington Post,* April 15. Accessible at www.huffingtonpost.com.

Swarns, Rachel L. 2015. "Biased Lending Evolves, and Blacks Face Trouble Getting Mortgages." *New York Times,* October 30. Accessible at nytimes.com.

Swatos, H. William, Jr., ed. 1998. *Encyclopedia of Religion and Society.* Lanham, MD: AltaMira.

Sweet, Kimberly. 2001. "Sex Sells a Second Time." *Chicago Journal* 93 (April):12–13.

Swer, Gregory M. 2019. "The Seeds of Violence: Ecofeminism, Technology, and Ecofeminist Philosophy of Technology." Pp. 247–263 in Loh J., Coeckelbergh M., eds., *Feminist Philosophy of Technology.* Stuttgart: Springer.

Swidler, Ann. 1986. "Culture in Action: Symbols and Strategies." *American Sociological Review* 51 (April):273–286.

Switzer, David, and Manuel P. Teodoro. 2018. "Class, Race, Ethnicity, and Justice in Safe Drinking Water Compliance." *Social Science Quarterly* 99 (2): 524-535.

Szasz, Andrew. 2007. *Shopping Our Way to Safety: How We Changed from Protecting the Environment to Protecting Ourselves.* Minneapolis: University of Minnesota Press.

Szasz, Thomas. 2010. *The Myth of Mental Illness: Foundations of a Theory of Personal Conduct.* 50th Anniversary Edition. New York: Harper Perennial.

Tabuchi, Hiroko. 2013. "Desperate Hunt for Day Care." *New York Times,* February 27, pp. A4, A9.

Tan, Gerald. 2019. "Domestic Workers in Latin America Struggle to Escape Poverty." October 17. Accessible at www.america.cgtn.com.

Tankersley, Jim. 2020. "Trump's Push to Bring Back Jobs to U.S. Shows Limited Results." *New York Times,* August 13. Accessible at www.nytimes.com.

Tavernise, Sabrina. 2016. "Life Spans of the Rich Leave the Poor Behind." *New York Times,* February 13, pp. A1, A11.

———, and Richard A. Oppel, Jr. 2020. "Spit On, Yelled At, Attacked: Chinese-Americans Fear for Safety." *New York Times,* March 24, pp. A1, A11.

Taylor, David G., and David Strutton. 2016. "Does Facebook Usage Lead to Conspicuous Consumption? The Role of Envy, Narcissism and Self-Promotion." *Journal of Research in Interactive Marketing* 10 (3):231–248.

Taylor, Derrick Bryson. 2019. "Adoption Groups Could Turn Away L.G.B.T. Families under Proposed Rule." *New York Times,* November 2. Accessible at www.nytimes.com.

———. 2020. "For Black Men, Fear That Masks Will Invite Racial Profiling." *New York Times,* April 14. Accessible at www.nytimes.com.

Taylor, Paul, Ana Gonzalez-Barrera, Jeffrey S. Passel, and Mark Hugo Lopez. 2012. "An Awakened Giant: The Hispanic Electorate Is Likely to Double by 2030." November 14. Accessible at www.pewhispanic.org.

Taylor, Verta, Nancy Whittier, and Leila J. Rupp, eds. 2020. *Feminist Frontiers.* 19th ed. Lanham MD: Rowman & Littlefield.

Tett, Gillian. 2015. *The Silo Effect: The Peril of Expertise and the Promise of Breaking Down Barriers.* New York: Simon & Schuster.

Themed Entertainment Association. 2019. *Theme Index and Museum Index 2018, Global Attractions Attendance Report.* Burbank CA: TEA.

Thomas, Melvin, Cedric Herring, Hayward Derrick Horton, Mose Semyonov, Loren Henderson, and Patrick L. Mason. 2020. "Race and the Accumulation of Wealth: Racial Differences in Net Worth over the Life Course, 1989–2009." *Social Problems* 67: 20–39.

Thomas, R. Murray. 2003. "New Frontiers in Cheating." In *Encyclopaedia Britannica 2003 Book of the Year.* Chicago: Encyclopaedia Britannica.

Thomas, William I. 1923. *The Unadjusted Girl.* Boston: Little, Brown.

Thompson, Derek. 2019. "Three Decades Ago, America Lost Its Religion. Why?" *The Atlantic* (September 26). Accessible at www.theatlantic.com.

Thompson, Tony. 2005. "Romanians Are Being Paid to Play Computer Games for Westerners." *Guardian Weekly,* March 25, p. 17.

Thomson, Lizzie. 2020. Psychologicalists tell us why we can't stop staring at ourselves on every Zoom chat. April 10. Accessible at www.metro.co.uk.

Thorne, Sharon, and Dan Konigsburg. 2020. "Gender Parity in the Boardroom Won't Happen on Its Own." *Harvard Business Review* (February 12). Accessible at www.hbr.org.

Thornthwaite, Louise, Nikola Balnave, and Alison Barnes. 2018. "Unions and Social Media: Prospects for Gender Inclusion." *Gender, Work, and Organization* 25: (4)::410-417).

Threadcraft, Shatema. 2008. "Welfare Queen." In *Encyclopedia of Race, Ethnicity and Society,* edited by Richard T. Schaefer. Thousand Oaks, CA: Sage.

Thumma, Scott. 2012. *Virtually Religious: Technology and Internet Use in American Congregations.* Hartford Institute. Accessible at www.hartfordinstitute.org/research/religion_web_articles.html.

Thunberg, Greta. 2019. "Greta Thunberg's Full Speech at the United Nations Climate Action Summit." September 23. Accessible at www.nbcnews.com.

Tierney, John. 1990. "Betting the Planet." *New York Times Magazine* (December 2):52–53, 80–81, 76, 78, 71, and 74.

Tiffany, Kaitlyn. 2019. "The Hired Guns of Instagram." June 19. Accessible at www.vox.com.

Tilcsik, András. 2011. "Pride and Prejudice: Employment Discrimination against Openly Gay Men in the United States." *American Journal of Sociology* September 117(2):586–626.

———, Michel Anteby, and Carly Knight. 2015. "Concealable Stigma and Occupational Segregation: Toward a Theory of Gay and Lesbian Occupations." *Administrative Science Quarterly* 60(3): 446-481.

Tilly, Charles. 1993. *Popular Contention in Great Britain 1758-1834.* Cambridge, MA: Harvard University Press.

———. 2004. *Social Movements, 1768-2004.* Boulder, CO: Paradigm.

Tokle, R., and W. Pedersen. 2019. "'Cloud Chasers' and 'Substitutes': E-Cigarettes, Vaping Subcultures and Vaper Identities." *Sociology of Health and Illness* 41(5):917-932.

Tönnies, Ferdinand. [1887] 1988. *Community and Society.* Rutgers, NJ: Transaction.

Tonry, Michael (ed.). 2014. "Why Crime Rates Fall and Why They Don't." Special Issue of *Crime and Justice* 43 (No. 1).

Toossi, Mitra. 2012. "Labor Force Projections to 2020: A More Slowly Growing Labor Force." *Monthly Labor Review* (January):43–64.

———. 2016. "A Look at the Future of the U.S. Labor Force to 2060." September. Accessible at www.bls.gov.

———, and Elka Torpey. 2017. "Older Workers: Labor Force Trends and Career Options." May. Accessible at www.bls.gov.

Toppo, Greg. 2011. "The Search for a New Way to Test Schoolkids." *USA Today,* March 18, p. A4.

Tornello, Samantha L., Bettina N. Sonnenberg, and Charlotte J. Patterson. 2015. "Division of Labor Among Gay Fathers: Associations with Parent, Couple, and Child Adjustment." *Psychology of Sexual Orientation and Gender Diversity* 2 (4): 365-375.

Touraine, Alain. 1974. *The Academic System in American Society.* New York: McGraw-Hill.

Trang, Kim T., and David M. Hansen. 2020. "The Roles of Teacher Expectations and School Composition on Teacher-Child Relationship Quality." *Journal of Teacher Education* (Forthcoming).

Transactional Records Access Clearinghouse. 2016. "White Collar Crime Convictions Continue to Decline." April 7. Accessible at www.trac.syr.edu.

Trimble, Lindsey B., and Julie A. Kmec. 2011. "The Role of Social Networks in Getting a Job." *Sociology Compass* 5 (2):165-178.

Trisi, Danilo, and Matt Saenz. 2020. "Policy Brief: Deep Poverty Among Children Rose in TANF's First Decade, Then Fell as Other Programs Strengthened." February 27. Accessible at www.ccbp.org.

Tsango, Esdras. 2020. "Children in the Democratic Republic of Congo Mine for Coltan and Face Abuse to Supply Smartphone Industry." February 29. Accessible at www.abc.net.au.

Tsutsui, Kiyoteru. 2017. "Human Rights and Minority Activism in Japan: Transformation of Movement Actorhead and Local-Global Feedback Loop." 2017. *American Journal of Sociology* 122 (January):1050-1103.

Ture, Kwame, and Charles Hamilton. 1992. *Black Power: The Politics of Liberation.* With new Afterword by authors. New York: Vintage Books.

Turkle, Sherry. 2004. "How Computers Change the Way We Think." *Chronicle of Higher Education* 50 (January 30):B26-B28.

———. 2011. *Alone Together: Why We Expect More from Technology and Less from Each Other.* New York: Basic Books.

———. 2017. *Alone Together: Why We Expect More from Technology and Less from Each Other.* Revised and Expanded Edition. New York: Basic Books.

———. 2020. "A Healthier Digital Lifestyle." *Politico* (March 20). Accessible at www.politico.com.

Turret, Erica, Sara Tannerbaum, and Keith Blake Schultz. 2020. "COVID-19 Does Not Change the Right to Abortion." *Health Affairs* (April 17). Accessible at www.healthaffairs.org.

U

Umaña-Taylor, Adriana J., and Nancy E. Hill. 2020. "Ethnic-Racial Socialization in the Family: A Decade's Advance on Precursors and Outcomes." *Journal of Marriage and Family* 82 (February): 244-271.

UN Women. 2015. *Progress of the World's Women 2015-2016. Transforming Economics. Realizing Rights.* Accessible at www.unwomen.org.

———. 2016. "Coverage: UN Women Executive Director in Afghanistan." July 26. Accessible at www.unwomen.org.

UNAIDS. 2013. *AIDS by the Numbers.* November 20. Accessible at www.unaids.org/en/media/unaids/contentassets/images/infographics/2013/20131120aidsbythenumbers01/20131120_aidsbythenumbers_en.pdf.

———. 2019. *UNAIDS/AIDS by the Numbers.* Accessible at www.unaids.org.

UNHCR.. 2018. "Lifesaving Assistance Is Needed." January 2. Accessible at www.unchr.org.

———. 2019. "Figures at a Glance." June 18. Accessible at www.unhcr.org.

———. 2020. "Climate Changes and Disaster Replacement." United Nations High Commissioner for Refugees. Accessible at www.unhch.org.

UNICEF. 2018. *Child Marriages.* Updated March 2018. Accessible at ww.unicef.org.

United Drive-In Theatre Owners Association. 2020. "Statistics." October 2019. Accessible at www.uditoa.org.

United Nations. 2018. "Global Poverty." December 8. Accessible at www.un.org.

United Nations Department of Economic and Social Affairs. 2016. "Policy Integration and the 2030 Agenda: Policy Tools and Approaches to Tackle Inequality." *Policy Brief* (March). Accessible at www.un.org.

———. 2019. *World Population Prospects 2019.* Accessible at www.un.org.

———. 2019a. "International Migrants Numbered 272 Million in 2019, Continuing an Upward Trend in All Major World Regions." *Population Facts* No. 2019/4. Accessible at www.un.org.

United Nations Development Programme. 2000. *Poverty Report 2000: Overcoming Human Poverty.* Washington, DC: UNDP.

———. 2009. *Overcoming Barriers: Human Mobility and Development.* New York: Palgrave Macmillan.

United Nations High Commissioner for Refugees. 2020. "Climate Changes and Disaster Replacement." United Nations High Commissioner for Refugees. Accessible at www.unhcr.org.

United Nations Office on Drugs and Crime. 2015b. *Crime and Criminal Justice Statistics.* Accessed October 26 at unodc.org.

———. 2018. "Transnational Organized Crime." Accessible at www.unodc.org,

United Nations Population Division. 2020. *International Migrant Stock 2019: Country Profiles.* Accessible at www.un.org.

United Nations Secretary General. 2014. *The World Survey on the Role of Women in Development.* New York: United Nations. Accessible at unwomen.org.

University of Michigan. 2003. *Information on Admissions Lawsuits.* Accessed August 8 at www.umich.edu/urel/admissions.

University of New Mexico. 2020. "UNM Curanderismo Class." Accessible at www.unm.gov.

Urban Dictionary. 2020. "Urban Amish." Accessible at www.urbandictionary.com.

U.S. English. 2020. "Making English the Official Language." Accessed January 2 at www.usenglish.org.

U.S. Surgeon General. 1999. *Surgeon General's Report on Mental Health.* Washington, DC: U.S. Government Printing Office.

USAHello. 2020. "What Is FindHello." Accessible at www.usahello.org.

V

van den Berghe, Pierre L. 1978. *Race and Racism: A Comparative Perspective.* 2nd ed. New York: Wiley.

Van den Scott, Lisa Jo K. 2018. "Visual Methods in Ethnography." *Journal of Contemporary Ethnography* 47 (6):719-728.

Van Gennep, Arnold. [1909] 1960. *The Rites of Passage.* Translated by Monika B. Vizedom and Gabrielle L. Caffee. Chicago: University of Chicago Press.

Vasilogambros, Matt. 2018. "Hundreds of New State Gun Laws Expand Access." *Tribune News Service in The Hutchinson* (Kansas City). March 4.

Vaughan, R. M. 2007. "Cairo's Man Show." *Utne Reader* (March-April):94-95.

Veblen, Thorstein. [1899] 1964. *Theory of the Leisure Class.* New York: Macmillan. New York: Penguin.

———. 1914. *The Instinct of Workmanship and the State of the Industrial Arts.* New York: Macmillan.

Venkatesh, Arjun K. et al. 2019. "Association between Insurance Stats and Access to Hospital Care in Emergency Department Disposition." *Journal of American Medical Association Internal Medicine* 179 (5): 686-693.

Venkatesh, Sudhir Alladi. 2006. *Off the Books: The Underground Economy of the Urban Poor.* Cambridge, MA: Harvard University Press.

———. 2008. *Gang Leader for a Day: A Rogue Sociologist Takes to the Streets.* New York: Penguin Press.

Vergeer, Maurice. 2015. "Twitter and Political Campaigning." *Sociology Compass* 99:745-760.

Vernon, Glenn. 1962. *Sociology and Religion.* New York: McGraw-Hill.

Vogels, Emily A. 2020a. "10 Facts about Americans and Online Dating." *Factank* (February 8). Accessible at www.pewresearch.org.

———. 2020b. "About Half of Never-Minded Americans Have Used an Online Dating Site or App." *Factank* (March 24). Accessible at www.pewresearch.org.

W

Wachter-Boettcher, Sara. 2017. *Technically Wrong: Sexist Apps, Biased Algorithms, and Other Threats of Toxic Tech.* New York: Norton.

Wagley, Charles, and Marvin Harris. 1958. *Minorities in the New World: Six Case Studies.* New York: Columbia University Press.

Waitzkin, Howard. 1986. *The Second Sickness: Contradictions of Capitalist Health Care.* Chicago: University of Chicago Press.

———, and Giang Hoang Nguyen. 2008. "Ownership, Organization, and Income Inequality: Market Transition in Rural Vietnam." *American Sociological Review* 73 (April):251-269.

Waldinger, Roger. 2015. *The Cross-Border Connection: Immigrants, Emigrants, and Their Homelands.* Cambridge, MA: Harvard University Press.

Walk Free Foundation. 2019. "2019 Global Estimates." Accessible at www.alliance87.org.

Wallender, Andrew. 2020. "Nonprofit workers turn uncertainty." *Daily Labor Report* (May 11). Accessible at www.bloomberglaw.com.

Wallerstein, Immanuel. 1974. *The Modern World System.* New York: Academic Press.

———. 1979a. *Capitalist World Economy.* Cambridge, UK: Cambridge University Press.

———. 1979b. *The End of the World as We Know It: Social Science for the Twenty-First Century.* Minneapolis: University of Minnesota Press.

———. 2000. *The Essential Wallerstein.* New York: New Press.

———. 2012. "Reflections on an Intellectual Adventure." *Contemporary Sociology* 41 (1):6–12.

Wang, Cheng-Tong Lir, and Evan Schofer. 2018. "Coming Out of Penumbras: World Culture and Cross-National Variation in Divorce Rates." *Social Forces* 97 (2): 675–704.

Warzel, Charlie. 2020. "Quarantine as Class Warfare." *New York Times,* March 7, p. A24.

Watts, Clint. 2019. "Our New Terrorism Problem." *Wall Street Journal,* August 10, pp. C1–C2.

Weber, Jared. 2019. "Spanish-speaking Therapists Needed." *USA Today,* August 1, pp. 1A, 3A.

Weber, Max. [1904] 1949. *Methodology of the Social Sciences.* Translated by Edward A. Shils and Henry A. Finch. Glencoe, IL: Free Press.

———. [1904] 2011. *The Protestant Ethic and the Spirit Capitalism.* The Revised 1920 Edition. Translation by Stephen Kalberg. New York: Oxford University Press.

———. [1913–1922] 1947. *The Theory of Social and Economic Organization.* Translated by A. Henderson and T. Parsons. New York: Free Press.

———. [1916] 1958. *The Religion of India: The Sociology of Hinduism and Buddhism.* New York: Free Press.

The Week. 2014. "A New Way of Doing Business." September 4:11.

Weeks, John R. 2012. *Population: An Introduction to Concepts and Issues.* 11th ed. Belmont, CA: Cengage.

———. 2016. *Population: An Introduction to Concepts and Issues.* 12th ed. Boston, MA: Cengage.

Wei, Junhow. 2016. "'I'm the Next American Idol': Cooling Out, Accounts, and Perseverance at Reality Talent Show Auditions." *Symbolic Interaction* 39 (1):3–25.

Weinberg, Daniel H. 2004. "Evidence from Census 2000 About Earnings by Detailed Occupation for Men and Women." CENSR-15. Washington, DC: U.S. Government Printing Office.

———. 2007. "Earnings by Gender: Evidence from Census 2000." *Monthly Labor Review* (July–August):26–34.

Weintraub, Ellen L. 2019. "Don't Abolish Political Ads on Social Media. Stop Microtargeting." *The Washington Post,* November 1. Accessible at www.thewashingtonpost.com.

Weiss-Meyer, Amy. 2017. "Apps for Refugees." *The Atlantic* (May):24–25.

Wells-Barnett, Ida B. 1970. *Crusade for Justice: The Autobiography of Ida B. Wells.* Edited by Alfreda M. Duster. Chicago: University of Chicago Press.

Wesolowski, Amy, Nathan Eagle, Andrew J. Tatem, David L. Smith, Abdisalam M. Noor, Robert W. Snow, and Caroline O. Buckee. 2012. "Quantifying the Impact of Human Mobility on Malaria." *Science* (October 12):267–270.

———, and Stephanie Banchero. 2012. "Education Slowdown Threatens U.S." *Wall Street Journal,* April 26, p. A1.

West, Candace, and Don H. Zimmerman. 1987. "Doing Gender." *Gender and Society* 1 (June): 125–151.

———. and ———. 2009. "Accounting for Doing Gender." *Gender & Society* 23:112–122.

Westergaard-Nielsen, Niels. 2008. *Low-Wage Work in Denmark.* New York: Russell Sage Foundation.

White, Gillian. 2015. "In the Sharing Economy, No One's an Employee." June 15. Accessible at www.theatlantic.com.

Whyte, John. 2010. "Media Portrayal of People Who Are Obese." *AMA Journal of Ethics* 12 (April):320–323.

Whyte, Willam Foote. [1943] 1993. *Street Corner Society: Social Structure of an Italian Slum.* 4th ed. Chicago: University of Chicago Press.

WIEGO. 2016. "About the Informal Economy: Women in Informal Employment: Globalizing and Organizing." Accessed February 26 at www.wiego.org.

Wildsmith, Elizabeth, Nicole R. Steward-Streng, and Jennifer Manlove. 2011. "Childbearing Outside of Marriage: Estimates and Trends in the United States." *Child Trends Research Brief* #2011-29. Accessible at www.childtrends.org.

Wilford, John Noble. 1997. "New Clues Show Where People Made the Great Leap to Agriculture." *New York Times,* November 18, pp. B9, B12.

Wilkerson, Isabel. 2020. Caste The Origins of Our Discontents. New York: Random House.

Wilkins, Amy C. 2012. "Becoming Black Women: Intimate Stories and Intersectional Identities." *Social Psychological Quarterly* 75 (2):173–196.

Williams, Audra. 2015. "Stop Shaming Syrian Refuges for Using Their Cellphones." *The Daily Dot,* September 11. Accessible at www.dailydot.com/opinion/syria-refugees-cell-phone-use/.

Williams, Gregory P. 2013. "Special Contribution: Interview with Immanuel Wallerstein, Retrospective on the Origins of World-Systems Analysis." *Journal of World-Systems Research* 19 (1):202–210.

Williams, Robin M., Jr. 1970. *American Society.* 3rd ed. New York: Knopf.

———. with John P. Dean and Edward A. Suchman. 1964. *Strangers Next Door: Ethnic Relations in American Communities.* Englewood Cliffs, NJ: Prentice Hall.

Wilson, Bincy, Filomena M. Critelli, and Barbra A. Ritter. 2015. "Transnational Responses to Commercial Sexual Exploitation: A Comprehensive Review of Interventions." *Women's Studies International Forum* 48 (January–February):71–80.

Wilson, Edward O. 1975. *Sociobiology: The New Synthesis.* Cambridge, MA: Harvard University Press.

———. 1978. *On Human Nature.* Cambridge, MA: Harvard University Press.

———. 2000. *Sociobiology: The New Synthesis.* Cambridge, MA: Belknap Press, Harvard University Press.

Wilson, William Julius. 1996. *When Work Disappears: The World of the New Urban Poor.* New York: Knopf.

———. 1999. *The Bridge over the Racial Divide: Rising Inequality and Coalition Politics.* Berkeley: University of California Press.

———. 2009. *More Than Just Race: Being Black and Poor in the Inner City.* New York: Norton.

———. 2012a. *The Declining Significance of Race: Blacks and Changing American Institutions.* 3rd ed. Chicago: University of Chicago Press.

———. 2012b. *The Truly Disadvantaged: The Inner City, the Underclass and Public Policy.* 2nd ed. Chicago: University of Chicago Press.

———, J. M. Quane, and B. H. Rankin. 2004. "Underclass." In *International Encyclopedia of Social and Behavioral Sciences.* New York: Elsevier.

Wimmer, Andreas. 2014. "War." *Annual Review of Sociology* 40:173–197.

Winickoff, Jonathan P., Joan Friebely, Susanne E. Tanski, Cheryl Sherrod, George E. Matt, Melbourne F. Hovell, and Robert C. McMillen. 2009. "Beliefs about the Health Effects of 'Thirdhand' Smoke and Home Smoking Bans." *Pediatrics* 123 (January):74–79.

Wirth, Louis. 1931. "Clinical Sociology." *American Journal of Sociology* 37 (July):49–60.

Wolf, Naomi. 1992. *The Beauty Myth: How Images of Beauty Are Used against Women.* New York: Anchor Books.

Wolff, Edward N. 2017. *A Century of Wealth in America.* Cambridge, MA: Belknap/Harvard.

Women's Bureau. 2018. "Earnings." Accessible at www.dol.org.

Wooden, Cindy. 2019. "Pope Reflects in Changed Attitudes Toward Liberation Theology." *Crux: Taking the Catholic Pulse* (February 14). Accessible at www.cruxnow.com.

World Bank. 2019a. *World Bank Databank 2019.* Accessible at www.databank.worldbank.org.

———. 2019b. *World Development Indicators database: Country.* Updated July 15. Accessed at www.data.worldbank.org.

———. 2019c. *World Development Indicators database: Size of the Economy.* Updated August 27. Accessible at data.worldbank.org.

———. 2020. "The World Bank Data." Accessible at www.worldbankgroup.org.

World Economic Forum. 2020. *Global Gender Gap Report 2020.* Geneva, Switzerland. Accessible www.weforum.org.

World Health Organization. 2018. "Ambient (Outdoor) Air Pollution." Accessible at www.who.int.

———. 2019. *WHO Global Report on Traditional and Complementary Medicine.* Geneva, Switzerland: World Health Organization. Accessible at www.who.int.

———. 2020. "Coronavirus Disease (COVID-19) Pandemic." Accessible at www.who.int.

World Population Review. 2020. "Crime Rate by Country 2020." Accessible at www.worldpopulationreview.com.

Wortham, Robert A. 2008. "DuBois, William Edward Burghardt." Pp. 423–427, vol. 1, in *Encyclopedia of Race, Ethnicity, and Society,* edited by Richard T. Schaefer. Thousand Oaks CA: Sage.

Wright, Charles R. 1986. *Mass Communication: A Sociological Perspective.* 3rd ed. New York: Random House.

Wright, Earl, II. 2012. "Why, Where, and How to Infuse the Atlanta Sociological Laboratory into the Sociology Curriculum." *Teaching Sociology* 40 (43):257–270.

———. 2020. *Jim Crow Sociology: The Black and Southern Roots of American Sociology.* Cincinnati, OH: University of Cincinnati Press.

Wright, Eric R., William P. Gronfein, and Timothy J. Owens. 2000. "Deinstitutionalization, Social Rejection, and the Self-Esteem of Former Mental Patients." *Journal of Health and Social Behavior* (March).

Wright, Erik O. 2011. "The Classical Marxist Theory of the History of Capitalism's Future." October 3. Accessed January 20, 2012, at www.ssc.wisc.edu/~wright/621-2011/lecture%208%20 2011%20-%20Classical%20Theory%20of%20 Capitalisms%20future.pdf.

———. 2015. *Understanding Class.* London: Verso.

Y

Yam, Kai Chi. 2017. "When Joking with Your Employees Leads to Bad Behavior." *Harvard Business Review* (March 17). Accessible at www.hbr.org.

Yancy, Clyde W. 2020. "COVID-19 and African Americans." *Journal of the American Medical Association* 323(19):1891–1892.

Yinger, J. Milton. 1970. *The Scientific Study of Religion.* New York: Macmillan.

Yokotsuka, Shino. 2019. "Embracing Religious Freedom? A Battle Over Public School Prayer in the USA and Japan." *Oxford Journal of Law and Religion* 8 (October): 590–614.

Young, Kevin, ed. 2004. *Sporting Bodies, Damaged Selves.* New York: Elsevier.

Yourish, Karen, and Larry Buchanan. 2013. "State Gun Laws Enacted in Year Since Newtown." *New York Times,* December 11, p. A20.

Yusef, Kideste, Randy B. Nelson, and Felecia Dix-Richardson. 2019. "Florida's Historically Black Colleges and Universities Address Racial Disparities within the Criminal Justice System Using Results-Based Accountability." *Race and Justice* 9 (1):22–45.

Z

Zarembo, Alan. 2004a. "A Theater of Inquiry and Evil." *Los Angeles Times,* July 15, pp. A1, A24, A25.

Zarrabi, Roxy. 2020. "6 Potential Advantages of Dating During a Pandemic." *Psychology Today* (March 30). Accessible at www.psychologytoday.com.

Zellner, William M. 1995. *Counter Cultures: A Sociological Analysis.* New York: St. Martin's Press.

Zernike, Kate. 2002. "With Student Cheating on the Rise, More Colleges Are Turning to Honor Codes." *New York Times,* November 2, p. A10.

Zhang, Linda. 2020. "China's Declining Birth Rates and Changes in CCP Population Policies." *China Brief* 20 (4). Accessible at www.jamestown.org.

Zia, Helen. 2000. *Asian American Dreams: The Emergence of an American People.* New York: Farrar, Straus & Giroux.

Zimbardo, Philip G. 1972. "Pathology of Imprisonment." Society 9 (April):4, 6, 8.

———. 2004. "Power Turns Good Soldiers into 'Bad Apples.'" *Boston Globe,* May 9. Also accessible at www.prisonexp.org.

———. 2007a. "Revisiting the Stanford Prison Experiment: A Lesson in the Power of the Situation." *Chronicle of Higher Education* 53 (March 20): B6, B7.

———. 2015. "Philip Zimbardo Thinks We All Can Be Evil." Interview by Jon Ronson. *New York Times Magazine* (July 19): 58.

———. 2018. "Philip Zimbardo's Response to Recent Criticisms of the Stanford Prison Experiment." June 23. Accessible at www.prisonexp.org.

———, Craig Haney, W. Curtis Banks, and David Jaffe. 1974. "The Psychology of Imprisonment: Privation, Power, and Pathology." In *Doing unto Others: Joining, Molding, Conforming, Helping, and Loving,* edited by Zick Rubin. Englewood Cliffs, NJ: Prentice Hall.

———, ———, ———, and ———. 1974. "The Psychology of Imprisonment: Privation, Power, and Pathology." Pp. 61–73 in Zick Rubin, ed., *Doing unto Others: The Patterns of Social Behavior.* Englewood Cliffs, NJ: Prentice-Hall.

———, Robert L. Johnson, and Vivian McCann Hamilton. 2009. *Psychology: Core Concepts.* 6th ed. Upper Saddle River, NJ: Pearson.

Zirin, Dave. 2008. "Calling Sports Sociology off the Bench." *Contexts* (Summer):28–31.

Zittrain, Jonathan. 2008. *The Future of the Internet and How to Stop It.* New Haven, CT: Yale University Press.

Zola, Irving K. 1972. "Medicine as an Institution of Social Control." *Sociological Review* 20 (November):487–504.

———. 1983. *Socio-Medical Inquiries.* Philadelphia: Temple University Press.

Zong, Jie, and Jeanne Batalova. 2017. "Korean Immigrants in the United States." February 8. Accessible at www.migrationpolicy.org.

Zorthian, Julia. 2015. "Facebook Expanding Worldwide Parental Leave to Four Months." *Time,* November 29. Accessible at www.time.com.

Zweigenhaft, Richard L., and G. William Domhoff. 2006. *Diversity in the Power Elite: How It Happened, Why It Matters.* 2nd ed. New York: Rowman & Littlefield.

name index

subject index

careers in, 138
censorship of, 148–150, 148f
defined, 131
handling misinformation on, 148
natural disasters, response to, 112
politicking on, 360
social movements and, 407, 413
social networks and, 142–144, 142f
teens controlling access to, 90
usage of, 140f, 414
use by terrorists, 362
social media consulting, 138
social mobility, 203–207, 208
in developing nations, 223–224, 224
education and, 202
gender and, 206–207, 206, 224
impact of education on, 205–206
in industrialized nations, 223
migration for, 224
occupational mobility, 205
in open v. closed systems, 203
roles of race and ethnicity in, 205–206
types of, 203–205, 204f
social movements, 408–413, 409, 413t, 427, 428
bureaucratization of, 119
communications technologies and, 407, 413, 413, 414, 427
ecofeminist movement, 400
environmentalism, 401, 410
gender and, 410
new social movements, 410–413, 413t
relative deprivation approach, 409, 413t
resource mobilization approach, 409–410, 410, 413t
role of communications in, 413, 413, 414
transnationals in, 427
women's, 412, 412
Social Movements and New Technology (Carty), 407
social networks, 12, 111, 126, 142–144
communal bonds and, 168
of corporate executives, 207
on executive compensation, 207, 207–208
in formal organizations, 119
online marketing through, 142f, 143
social policy, 22–23
bilingualism, 72–73, 72f, 74
censorship, 148–150
child care, 96, 96–97
coronavirus pandemic, response to, 367–369, 368
death penalty in United States/ worldwide, 177–179, 177f, 178
environmentalism, 400–402, 401f
family leave, 308–309, 308f, 309
global refugee crisis, 260–261, 260t
labor unions, 124–126, 125f
religion in schools, 338–340, 339
on sexual harassment, 286
studying human sexuality, 46f
transnationals, 425–427, 426f, 428
welfare, 226–227, 226

on workplace sexual harassment, 284–286, 285
social reality, 102–103
social reformers, 11–12
social roles, 105–106, 126
role conflict, 105–106
role exit, 106–107, 107
role strain, 106
social sciences, 3–6, 5t, 25
social service programs, 349
social status, 294
social stratification, in Japan, 223, 223
social structure, 101, 103–114, 126
Gemeinschaft and *Gesellschaft,* 120, 121t, 127
global perspective on, 120–124
groups. See groups
mechanical and organic solidarity, 120, 126
social institutions. See social institutions
social networks. See social networks
social policy: labor unions, 124–126, 125f
social roles, 106–107, 126
sociocultural evolution approach, 120–124, 121t
statuses. See status
social support, religion as, 331
social welfare, 227, 228
social work, 22–23
societal-reaction approach. See labeling theory
Society for the Study of Social Problems, 12
society(ies), 55, 73. See also specific stages of society
analysis of, 12
contradictory nature of, 416
extinction of, 113
growth rate of, 388
law and, 161, 162f
McDonaldization of, 69, 118
medicalization of, 375, 375, 381, 394
Society in America (Martineau), 8
sociobiology, 56, 415
sociocultural evolution, 120–124, 121t, 127
industrial societies, 122
postindustrial and postmodern societies, 122–124
preindustrial societies, 120, 121
socioeconomic status (SES), 196
of child's family, 294
in matrix of domination, 275–276, 276f
Sociological Abstracts, 48–49
sociological imagination, 3, 20–23, 25
sociological research, 28–52
on affirmative action, 362, 364
on Amish subculture, 86
attitudes toward marijuana, 47–48, 47f
content analysis, 40
cross-cultural, 103–104, 223
on disability as master status, 104–105
ethics of, 41–43
feminist. See feminist perspective
on human sexuality, 46–47, 46f–47f

on Latino political activity, 355, 355f
Milgram experiment, 158
mock prison experiment, 358
on popularity among college students, 88
on poverty, 199–200, 200f
on prison population issues, 44, 44–46
on racial discrimination in hiring, 236–238
report writing, 48–49
on rewards of crime, 165
role of technology in, 44–46
scientific method in, 30–34, 30f, 50
on sexual identity and discrimination, 272
of small-group bureaucracies, 118
on social norms in workplace, 114
on Twitter, 112
voluntary termination of employment, gender and, 282
on white attitudes toward Blacks, 237, 237
on white privilege, 238–240
sociology, 1–23, 25
careers in. See careers in sociology
common sense and, 6
development of, 7–13
fields within, 19–23
fiscal, 194
major theoretical perspectives, 13–16, 17t
nature of, 3–6
race, gender and religion, 21–22
social sciences and, 3–6, 5t, 25
sociological imagination and, 3
sociological theory, 6–7
visual sociology, 9, 39, 138
software piracy, 156
solitary confinement, 161
Somalia, 57f, 143, 215f
Souls of Black Folk (DuBois), 9f
South Africa, Republic of, 215f
apartheid in, 246, 394
government efforts to reduce income inequality in, 64f
population growth rate in, 389f
voter turnout, 354f
South Americans, 254f, 256–257
Southern Christian Leadership Conference (SCLC), 248
South Korea, 215f
educational system in, 316
foreign aid per capita in, 218f
global brands of, 135f
importance of religion in, 335f
Internet penetration in, 146f
mass media in, 138
voter turnout, 354f
women's social movements in, 412, 412
South Sudan, 57f
Soviet Union, 352, 418
Spain, 64f, 135f, 215f, 226, 227, 308f, 315f
Spanish-American War (1899), 252
Spanish language, 256, 420f

Spectrum of Intergroup Relations, 245, 246f
Spencer, Herbert, 8
SPM (Supplemental Poverty Measure), 200
sports, 55, 156
bureaucratization of, 118
coverage of female athletes, 141–142
theoretical perspectives on, 18, 18
Title IX and, 320, 321
SSKKMS *(Shoshit, Shetkari, Kashtakari, Kamgar, Mukti Sangharsh),* 412
stability
social change and, 415
of U.S. population growth, 392f, 393
stability phase of retirement, 94
Stanford University, 101
"Star-Spangled Banner", 74
Star Wars (game), 141
State Department, U.S., 359
statistics
on crime. See crime statistics
in measuring social class, 196
in sociological research, 46, 46f
on trends in divorce, 303, 303f
vital, 388
status, 103–104, 126
achieved. See achieved statuses
ascribed. See ascribed statuses
bestowed by education, 319–320, 319f
conferred by mass media, 133, 133t
employment and, 104
in interpersonal conversations, 277
master status, 104
occupational, of teaching, 324
provided by family, 294
socioeconomic status (SES), 196, 275–276, 276f, 294
of women, 278
status group, 191, 208
stay-at-home dads, 268–269
stepfamilies, 294, 302–303
stepparents, 303
stereotypes (stereotyping), 137, 262
female television characters, 267
of males and success, 278
in mass media, 137, 141
negative, 161, 320
of poor people, 200
prejudice rooted in, 237
racial profiling and, 243
of women, 141, 320
stigma (stigmatization), 403
body image and, 156
deviance and, 156, 179
flexibility, 309, 310
in high schools, 320–321
of homosexuals in media, 137
of illness, 377
lacking, for white-collar crime, 171
of mental illness, 385
of sexual identities, 271
Stohr, Oskar, 80
stratification, 182–210
artificial intelligence technology and, 423

Applications of *Sociology*'s Major Theoretical Approaches

Sociology provides comprehensive coverage of the major sociological perspectives. This summary table includes a sample of the topics in the text that have been explored using the major approaches. The numbers in parentheses indicate the pertinent chapters.

FUNCTIONALIST PERSPECTIVE

Defined and explained (1)
Adoption (12)
AIDS and social networks (15)
Anomie theory of deviance (7)
Bilingualism (3)
Bureaucratization of schools (13)
Charter schools (13)
Cow worship in India (1)
Culture (3, 13)
Davis and Moore's view of stratification (8)
Debtors' prisons (7)
Disengagement theory of aging (11)
Dominant ideology (3)
Durkheim's view of deviance (7)
Dysfunctions of racism (10)
Education (13)
Ethnocentrism (3)
Executive compensation (8)
Family (12)
Family leave policies (12)
Formal organizations (6)
Functions of dying (11)
Functions of racism (10)
Gans's functions of poverty (8)
Gay marriage (12)
Global refugee crisis (10)
Human rights (9)
Gender stratification (11)
Government response to coronavirus pandemic (14)
Health and illness (15)
Human ecology (15)
Human rights (9)
In-groups and out-groups (5)
Integrative function of religion (13)
Media and social norms (6)
Media and socialization (6)
Media and status conferral (6)
Media promotion of consumption (6)
Merton's theory of deviance (7)
Modernization theory (9)
Multinational corporations (9)
Narcotizing effect of the media (6)
Offshoring (14)
Population policy (15)
Race and ethnicity (10)
Religion (13)
Sick role (15)
Social change (13, 16)

Social control (7, 13)
Social institutions (5)
Socialization in schools (4, 13)
Sports (1)
Subcultures (3)
Transnationals (16)
Urban ecology (15)
Workplace sexual harassment (11)

CONFLICT PERSPECTIVE

Defined and explained (1)
Abortion (11)
Access to health care (15)
Affirmative action (14)
Age stratification (11)
AIDS crisis (15)
Bilingualism (3)
Bureaucratization of schools (13)
Capitalism (13, 14)
Censorship (6)
Charter schools (13)
Class differentiation (8)
Coronavirus pandemic (14)
Corporate welfare (9)
Correspondence principle (13)
Credentialism (13)
Culture (3)
Day care funding (4)
Deviance (7)
Disability as a master status (5)
Domestic violence (12)
Dominant ideology (3, 6, 8)
Downsizing (14)
Education (13)
Elite model of the U.S. power structure (14)
Environmental issues (16)
Executive compensation (8)
Exploitation theory of discrimination (10)
Family (12)
Family leave policies (12)
Gay marriage (12)
Gender stratification (11)
Gender equity in education (13)
Global refugee crisis (10)
Government response to coronavirus pandemic (14)
Gun control (7)
Health care inequities (15)
Hidden curriculum (13)
Human rights (9)
Iron Law of Oligarchy (5)
Labor unions (5)
Marx's view of stratification (8)
Media gatekeeping (6)
Media stereotypes (6)
Media violence (6)
Medicalization of society (15)
Model minority (10)
Multinational corporations (9)
New urban sociology (15)
Offshoring (14)

Population policy (15)
Poverty (8)
Privacy and technology (16)
Race and ethnicity (10)
Racial profiling (10)
Racism and health (15)
Religion and social control (13)
Sex education (13)
Social change (16)
Social control (7)
Social institutions (5)
Socialization in schools (4)
Sports (1)
Subcultures (3)
Tracking (13)
Transnationals (16)
Victimless crimes (7)
Welfare programs (9)
White-collar crime (7)
World systems analysis (9, 15)
Workplace sexual harassment (11)

INTERACTIONIST PERSPECTIVE

Defined and explained (1)
Activity theory of aging (11)
Adoption (12)
Affirmative action (14)
AIDS and its impact (15)
Censorship (6)
Charismatic authority (14)
Conspicuous consumption (8)
Contact hypothesis (10)
Coronavirus pandemic (14)
Culture (3)
Cultural transmission of deviance (7)
Differential association (7)
Doctor–patient interaction (15)
Domestic violence (11)
Dramaturgical approach (4, 14)
Electronic communication (6)
Executive compensation (8)
Family (12)
Family leave policies (12)
Family styles (12)
Gay marriage (12)
Gender stratification (11)
Gun control (7)
Health and illness (15)
Human relations approach (5)
Interracial and interethnic friendships (10)
Labor unions (5)
Looking-glass self (4)
Media and social capital (6)
Media interaction (3)
Media violence (6)
Obedience (7)
Presentation of the self (4)
Race and ethnicity (10)
Racial profiling (10)

School prayer (13)
Social disorganization theory (7)
Social institutions (5)
Sports (1)
Stepparent-stepchild relationships (12)
Tattoo symbols of 9/11 (1)
Teacher-expectancy effect (13)
Teenage pregnancy (12)
The "Third Place" (1)
Transnationals (16)
Workplace sexual harassment (11)

FEMINIST PERSPECTIVE

Coronavirus pandemic (14)
Culture (3)
Defined and explained (1)
Cell phone access (6)
Day care funding (4)
Deviance (7)
Domestic violence (12)
Dominant ideology (3)
Education (13)
Ethnographic research (2)
Family (12)
Family leave policies (12)
Gender identity (15)
Gender stratification (11)
Government response to coronavirus pandemic (14)
Intersectionality (11)
Language (3)
LGBQT student subcultures (13)
Media stereotypes (6)
Media violence (6)
Population policy (15)
Pornography (6)
Rape (7)
Religion (13)
Research methodology (2)
Social mobility (9)
Social movements (16)
Sports (1)
Transnationals (16)
Victimless crimes (7)
Wage inequality (5)
Women in film (2)
Workplace sexual harassment (11)

LABELING THEORY

Defined and explained (7)
AIDS and labeling (15)
Disabilities and labeling (5)
Gender identity (11)
Health and illness (15)
Latino students (10)
Racial profiling (10)
Societal reaction approach (7)
Teacher-expectancy effect (13)
Terrorism (15)

Coverage of Race and Ethnicity, Gender, and Social Class

Sociology provides comprehensive coverage of race and ethnicity, gender, and social class and of the intersection of those variables. This summary table includes a sample of the related topics in the text. The dots that precede the entries indicate the type of coverage:

- ● RACE AND ETHNICITY
- ● GENDER
- ● SOCIAL CLASS

CHAPTER 1
- Atlanta Sociological Laboratory
- Class conflict
- Community health care
- Elijah Anderson
- Gender and talkativeness
- Inequality and climate change
- Ida Wells-Barnett
- W. E. B. DuBois
- Social inequality

CHAPTER 2
- Gender and movies
- Gender and scouting
- Gender and self-injury
- Gender stereotyping in children's coloring books
- Racial attitudes in the LGBTQ community
- Televised sports coverage

CHAPTER 3
- Culture and food
- Culture and values
- Ethnicity and language
- Ethnicity and nonverbal communication
- Ethnocentrism in education
- Gender and language
- How millennials view race
- Indian call center subculture
- Linguistic diversity in the U.S.
- Views on government's role in reducing income inequality

CHAPTER 4
- Double consciousness
- Gender roles
- Race and socialization
- Rites of passage
- Socialization of Amish children

CHAPTER 5
- Cultural differences in social interaction
- Ethnicity and role strain
- Gender and formal organizations
- Gender and social institutions
- Gender and wage inequality
- Marx and alienation
- Race and social institutions
- Race as a master status
- Race/ethnicity and jury deliberations
- Social class and social institutions

CHAPTER 6
- Coverage of women's sports
- Digital divide
- Ethnic stereotypes
- Forced choices online
- Gender and online gaming
- Gender stereotypes
- Pornography
- Race and audience perceptions
- Race and Internet use
- Removal of Confederate battle flag
- Social media use during Arab Spring
- Underrepresentation of Latinos in media

CHAPTER 7
- Differential justice
- Ethnicity and deviance
- Gender and deviance
- Hate crimes
- Race and the death penalty
- Race in Milgram's obedience experiment
- Racial profiling
- Social class and deviant identity
- White-collar crime

CHAPTER 8
- Entire chapter
- Caste system in India
- Class warfare in the U.S.
- Ethnicity and wealth
- Feminization of poverty
- Gender and income
- Gender and social class
- Gender and social mobility
- Human trafficking
- Precarious work
- Income inequality
- Race and poverty
- Race and social mobility
- Race and wealth
- Residential segregation
- Risk of becoming poor
- Shrinking middle class
- Social class and financial aid
- Student debt
- Unpaid work
- Voter ID requirements

CHAPTER 9
- Ethnicity, wealth, and poverty
- Gender and social mobility
- Millennium Development Goals
- Multinational corporations
- Social class in Japan

CHAPTER 10
- Entire chapter
- Affirmative action
- Asian Indians
- Black Lives Matter

- Central and South Americans
- Economic status of racial/ethnic groups
- Ethnic inequality
- Global immigration
- Immigration and diversity
- Institutional discrimination
- Model minority stereotype
- Multiple racial/ethnic identities
- Race relations as a zero-sum game
- Racial bias in online dating
- Racial profiling
- Redlining
- Status of Māori of New Zealand
- white privilege

CHAPTER 11
- Entire chapter
- Abortion rights
- Afghani women
- Bias against female board members
- Bias in hiring based on sexual orientation
- Cross-cultural perspective on gender
- Fluidity of gender identity
- Gender and human sexuality
- Gender and preschool
- Gender inequality in housework
- Global Gender Gap Index
- Matrix of domination
- Sex discrimination
- Women in combat
- Women in Japan
- Workplace sexual harassment

CHAPTER 12
- Accordion family
- Arranged and hybrid marriage
- Gay marriage
- Households in which women earn more than their husbands
- Internet dating
- LGBTQ adoption
- Male dominance of family
- Navajo family
- Parental leave
- Racial/ethnic differences in family life
- Single fathers
- Single-parent families by racial/ethnic group
- Social class differences in family life
- Stay-at-home fathers

CHAPTER 13
- Bias in awarding scholarships
- Black students at white universities

- *Brown v. Board of Education* legacy
- College enrollment among racial minorities and women
- Educational inequality
- Gender equity in education
- Gender gap in education
- Hidden curriculum
- Hurricane Maria and Puerto Rico
- Islam in the United States
- Racial isolation in public schools
- Religion and economic progress
- Religion and social change
- Schooling of girls in developing nations

CHAPTER 14
- Affirmative action
- Gender quotas
- Global elite
- Informal economy
- Latino political participation
- Power elite
- Race and gender in politics
- Racial/ethnic composition of labor force
- Women in politics
- Women in uniform

CHAPTER 15
- Cultural beliefs of immigrants
- Ecofeminism
- Environmental justice
- Environmental refugees
- Gender and health
- Midwives
- Navajo medicine
- Racial/ethnic population and hazardous waste sites
- Racial/ethnic disparities during coronavirus pandemic
- Racial/ethnic and class disparities in mental health care
- Racism and health
- Social class and health
- Women as physicians and surgeons

CHAPTER 16
- False consciousness
- Gender and social movements
- Marx and social change
- Relative deprivation
- Social class and social movements
- Transnationals
- United States: A changing nation
- Vested interests
- Women and new social movements in South Korea, India, and Bangladesh